Spon's
Architects'
and Builders'
Price Book

Spon's Architects' and Builders' Price Book

Edited by

DAVIS LANGDON & EVEREST

Chartered Quantity Surveyors

2000

One hundred and twenty fifth edition

London and New York

First edition 1873
One hundred and twenty fifth edition 2000
published by E & FN Spon
11 New Fetter Lane, London EC4P 4EE

Simultaneously published in the USA and Canada
by E & FN Spon
29 West 35th Street, New York, NY 10001

E & FN Spon is an imprint of the Taylor & Francis Group

Printed and bound in Great Britain by
TJ International Ltd, Padstow, Cornwall

Publisher's note
This book has been produced from camera-ready copy supplied by the authors.

British Library Cataloguing in Publication Data
A catalogue record for this book is available from the British Library

Library of Congress Cataloging in Publication Data
A catalogue record for this book has been requested

ISBN 0-419-25420-X

Preface to the Millennium Edition

We approach the Millennium with a reasonable optimism tinged with caution. Fears towards the end of 1998 of a slump in UK economic recovery have been overtaken by the optimism of spring and rejuvenated housing demands. After an apparent 'glitch' in DETR new orders figures for the first quarter of 1999, latest indications are that these preliminary figures were not as severe as originally suggested and that overall new workload is being maintained at 1998 levels (at 1995 constant prices). Forecasts for the growth of new construction work in 1999 and 2000 range from 1% to 1.5%.

It would appear that we have arrived on a plateau which nevertheless could offer the construction industry a 'bumpy ride' during the forthcoming year. Heavy infrastructure works are expected to continue falling away; railway contracts will include large tranches of electrical and communications work; public housing is likely to fall further; industrial work has been affected by a reduction of input investment from Asian countries and a number of millennium and lottery funded/leisure projects will be nearing completion. Countering these negative indicators, the private housing market still appears buoyant (and is likely to continue so whilst interest rates are low), there is still a high demand for suitable office space and the Government has promised to raise output in the education and health sectors by encouraging more use of PFI/PPP initiatives.

The authors are conscious of the annual cycle of optimism and pessimism which pervades the construction industry and a longer 7 to 10 year cycle (the last one commencing in 1992) which often runs a parallel with the UK economic cycles. If further international monetary problems do not beset the UK economy again this year then, although investment in certain sectors is falling, it is hoped that construction activity may continue apace without experiencing too severe a fall in demand.

At the time of going to press, our previous forecast suggested that tender prices may rise from 2.5% to 6% up to the Millennium. However, in the second quarter of 1999 an unexpected increase in certain trade prices was experienced. Taking account of this and the 7% to 8% increase in "all-in" hourly rates in June 1999, we have set a new index of 350 for the 2000 edition of Spon's A & B, an increase of 7.7% over the previous edition.

Readers of Spon's A&B are reminded that Spon's is the only price book in which key rates are checked against current tender prices. Therefore although "officially quoted" materials and labour prices have increased by 37% from fourth quarter 1989, the high point of the late 80's boom, to the second quarter 1999, tender prices, which reflect actual prices paid for construction projects, have fallen by 5% over the same period. Compared with the previous edition, the gap continues to narrow. Only Spon's A&B accurately reflects this real movement in tender prices.

1999 sees the third and final year of a three year wage agreement original signed on 23 July 1997. From 28 June 1999, NJCBI Labourers received a 7.6% increase in their basic weekly wage to £177.45 and Craft Operatives a further 10% to £235.95. These labour rates have been taken into account in the preparation of this year's book along with materials prices as at June/July 1999.

The EEC's Working Time Directive came into effect in the UK as from 1 October 1998. Initially this caused some implementation problems in the construction industry. Although a new Building and Civil Engineering stamp scheme to provide operatives with holiday pay, based on average wages including bonuses, has been proposed, by mid June 1999 not all unions had agreed to the scheme. Notwithstanding this, it was hoped that an 'approved' scheme will be in place and come into effect in August 1999. The other change in legislation is the introduction of the Construction Industry Scheme (formerly the Construction Industry Tax Deduction Scheme) from 1 August 1999. The Inland Revenue estimates that about half of the 400,000 holders of the earlier 714C certificate will not qualify for the new CIS5 and CIS6 certificates, and, therefore, will have to pay tax at source. The onus for collecting this could not only fall on 'traditional' contractors, but also on certain clients, such as property investors, housing associations, retailers, etc., who directly employ small sub-contract/self-employed labour.

In this Millennium edition, we have introduced two new sections. The introduction in July 1999 of new contaminated land provisions contained within part IIa of the Environmental Protection Act 1990, will encourage the recycling of brownfield land, pages ix - xii therefore examines the costs associated with the remediation of such land. We have also added a new Approximate Estimating section in the form of Building Prices Per Functional Units, see pages 677 - 681, which can be used to give cost advice during the very early stages of those building projects such as hospitals, hotels, schools, etc. where there exists a close relationship between its cost and the number of functional units it accommodates. Other changes this year include the amendment of Measured Work terminology in accordance with the revised Standard Method of Measurement 7th Edition, issued in May 1998, in addition to the usual new items introduced into both the Measured Work (Part III) and the Approximate Estimates (Part IV) sections.

Readers are reminded of the services available in Spon's Price Book Update, where details of significant changes to the published information are given. The printed update is circulated free of charge every three months, until the publication of next year's Price Book.

The reader's attention is drawn to the fact that since 1989 all non-domestic building work, refurbishment and alterations, have been subject to VAT, currently at 17.5%.

Prices included within this edition do not include VAT, which must be added if appropriate.

The book is divided into five parts as follows:

Part I: Fees and Daywork

This section contains Fees for Professional Services, Daywork and Prime Cost.

Part II: Rates of Wages

This section includes authorised wage agreements applicable to the Building and associated Industries.

Part III: Prices for Measured Work

This section contains Prices for Measured Work - Major Works, and Prices for Measured Work - Minor Works (on coloured paper).

Part IV: Approximate Estimating

This section contains the Building Cost and Tender Price Index, information on regional price variations, prices per square metre for various types of buildings, approximate estimates, cost limits and allowances for "public sector" building work and a procedure for valuing property for insurance purposes.

Part V: Tables and Memoranda

This section contains general formulae, weights and quantities of materials, other design criteria and useful memoranda associated with each trade, and a list of useful Trade Associations.

While every effort is made to ensure the accuracy of the information given in this publication, neither the Editors nor Publishers in any way accept liability for loss of any kind resulting from the use made by any person of such information.

DAVIS LANGDON & EVEREST
Chartered Quantity Surveyors
Princes House
39 Kingsway
London
WC2B 6TP

The Landfill Tax

The Tax

The Landfill tax came into operation on 1 October 1996. It is levied on operators of licensed landfill sites at the following rates:

    £2 per tonne - Inactive or inert wastes.
                       Included are soil, stones, brick, plain and reinforced concrete, plaster and glass.

    £10 per tonne - All other taxable wastes.
                       Included are timber, paint and other organic wastes generally found in demolition work, builders skips etc.

From 1 April 1999 the rate of for "all other taxable wastes" was increased from £7 to £10 per tonne, whilst the rate for "inactive of inert wastes" remained at £2 per tonne.

It is intended to raise the standard rate of landfill tax for "all other taxable wastes" in future years by an additional £1 per tonne each year. These increases will take place at least until 2004 when the standard rate will become £15 per tonne.

Mixtures containing wastes not classified as inactive or inert will not qualify for the lower rate of tax unless the amount of non-qualifying material is small and there is no potential for pollution. Water can be ignored and the weight discounted.

Calculating the Weight of Waste

There are two options:

* If licensed sites have a weighbridge, tax will be levied on the actual weight of waste.

* If licensed sites do not have a weighbridge, tax will be levied on the permitted weight of the lorry based on an alternative method of calculation based on volume to weight factors for various categories of waste.

Likely Effect on Prices

The tax will be paid by Landfill site operators only. They will have to increase their prices to recoup the additional costs. This additional cost should be taken into account when using rates from this book.

As an example, Spon's A & B rates for mechanical disposal could be affected as follows:

*	Inactive waste	Spon's A & B rate 1999	£9.50 per m³
		Tax, 2 t per m³ (unbulked) @ £2.00	£4.00 per m³
		Revised Spons rate (page 117)	£13.50 per m³

Likely Effect on Prices - cont'd

*   Active waste   Active waste will normally be disposed of by skip and will probably be mixed
                              inactive waste. The tax levied will depend on the weight of the materials in the
                              skip which can vary significantly.

Exemptions

The following disposals will be exempt from Landfill Tax:

*   dredgings which arise from the maintenance of inland waterways and harbours.
*   naturally occurring materials arising from mining or quarrying operations.
*   waste resulting from the cleaning up of historically contaminated land, although to obtain an exemption
     it is necessary to first obtain a contaminated land certificate from Customs and Excise.
*   waste removed from one site to be used on another or to be recycled or incinerated.

An additional exemption will be introduced from the 1st October 1999 for inert waste used to restore landfill
sites and to fill working and old quarries with a planning condition or obligation in existence to fill the void.

For further information contact the Landfill Tax Helpdesk, Telephone: 0645 128484.

Land Remediation

Statutory framework

July 1999 will see the introduction of new contaminated land provisions, contained in part IIa of the Environmental Protection Act 1990. A primary objective of the measures is to encourage the recycling of brownfield land.

Under the Act action to remediate land is required only where there are unacceptable actual or potential risks to health or the environment. Sites that have been polluted from previous land use may not need remediating until the land use is changed. In addition, it may be necessary to take action only where there are appropriate, cost-effective remediation processes that take the use of the site into account.

Local authorities are not required to make public any records of sites that have been investigated for contamination. The risks involved in the purchase of potentially contaminated sites is high, particularly considering that a transaction can result in the transfer of liability for historic contamination from the vendor to the purchaser.

The contaminated land provisions of the Environmental Protection Act 1990 are only one element of a series of statutory measures dealing with pollution and land remediation that are to be introduced this year. Others include:

* groundwater regulations, including pollution prevention measures

* an integrated prevention and control regime for pollution

* selections of the Water Resources Act 1991, which deals with works notices for site controls, restoration and clean up.

The contaminated land measures incorporate statutory guidance on the inspection, definition, remediation, apportionment of liabilities and recovery of costs of remediation. The measures are to be applied in accordance with the following criteria:

* the standard of remediation should relate to the present use

* the costs of remediation should be reasonable in relation to the seriousness of the potential harm

* the proposals should be practical in relation to the availability of remediation technology, impact of site constraints and the effectiveness of the proposed clean-up method.

Liability for the costs of remediation rests with either the party that "caused or knowingly permitted" contamination, or with the current owners or occupiers of the land.

Apportionment of liability, where shared, is determined by the local authority. Although owners or occupiers become liable only if the polluter cannot be identified, the liability for contamination is commonly passed on when land is sold.

The ability to forecast the extent and cost of remedial measures is essential for both parties, so that they can be accurately reflected in the price of the land. If neither the polluter nor owner can be found, the clean-up is funded from public resources.

Land remediation techniques

There are two principal approaches to remediation - dealing with the contamination in situ or off site. The selection of the approach will be influenced by factors such as: initial and long term cost, timeframe for remediation, types of contamination present, depth and distribution of contamination, the existing and planned topography, adjacent land uses, patterns of surface drainage, the location of existing on-site services, depth of excavation necessary for foundations and below-ground services, environmental impact and safety, prospects for future changes in land use and long-term monitoring and maintenance of in situ treatment.

In situ techniques

A range of in situ techniques is available for dealing with contaminants, including:

*   Dilution - the reduction of the concentrations of contaminants to below trigger levels by on-site mixing with cleaner material.

*   Clean cover - a layer of clean soil is used to segregate contamination from receptor. This technique is best suited to sites with widely dispersed contamination. Costs will vary according to the need for barrier layers to prevent migration of the contaminant.

*   On-site encapsulation - the physical containment of contaminants using barriers such as slurry trench cut-off walls. The cost of on-site encapsulation varies in relation to the type and extent of barriers required, the costs of which range from £35/m² to more than £100/m².

There are also in situ techniques for treating more specific contaminants, including:

*   Bio-remediation - for removal of oily, organic contaminants through natural digestion by micro-organisms. The process is slow, taking from one to three years, and is particularly effective for the long-term improvement of a site, prior to a change of use.

*   Soil washing - involving the separation of a contaminated soil fraction or oily residue through a washing process. The dewatered contaminant still requires disposal to landfill. In order to be cost effective, 70 - 90% of soil mass needs to be recovered.

*   Vacuum extraction - involving the extraction of liquid and gas contaminants from soil by vacuum.

*   Thermal treatment - the incineration of contaminated soils on site. The uncontaminated soil residue can be recycled. By-products of incineration can create air pollution and exhaust air treatment may be necessary.

*   Stabilisation - cement or lime, is used to physically or chemically bound oily or metal contaminants to prevent leaching or migration. Stabilisation can be used in both in situ and off-site locations.

Off-site techniques

Removal is the most common and cost-effective approach to remediation in the UK, providing a broad spectrum solution by dealing with all contaminants. Removal is suited to sites where sources of contamination can be easily identified.

If used in combination with material-handling techniques such as soil washing, the volume of material disposed at landfill sites can be significantly reduced. The disadvantages of the technique include the fact that the contamination is not destroyed, there are risks of pollution during excavation and transfer; road haulage may also cause a local nuisance.

Cost drivers

Cost drivers relate to the selected remediation technique, site conditions and the size and location of a project.

The wide variation of indicative costs of land remediation techniques shown below is largely because of differing site conditions.

Indicative costs of land remediation techniques (excluding landfill tax)		
Remediation technique	Unit	Rate (£/unit)
Removal	disposed material (m³)	40 - 140
Clean cover	surface area of site (m²)	20 - 40
On-site encapsulation	encapsulated material (m³)	20 - 75
Bio-remediation	treated material (tonne)	30 - 80
Soil washing	treated material (tonne)	40 - 80
Soil flushing	treated material (tonne)	60 - 100
Vacuum extraction	treated material (tonne)	50 - 100
Thermal treatment	treated material (tonne)	750 - 1200

Factors that need to be considered include:

*   waste classification of the material

*   underground obstructions, pockets of contamination and live services

*   ground water flows and the requirement for barriers to prevent the migration of contaminants

*   health and safety requirements and environmental protection measures

*   location, ownership and land use of adjoining sites

*   distance from landfill tips, capacity of the tip to accept contaminated materials, and transport restrictions

Other project related variables include size, access to disposal sites and tipping charges; the interaction of these factors can have a substantial impact on overall unit rates.

The table below sets out the costs of remediation using *dig-and-dump* methods for different sizes of project. Variation in site establishment and disposal cost accounts for 60 - 70% of the range in cost.

Cost drivers - cont'd

Variation in the costs of land remediation by removal			
Item	Disposal Volume (less than 3000 m³) (£/m³)	Disposal Volume (3000 - 10 000 m³) (£/m³)	Disposal Volume (more than 10 000 m³) (£/m³)
General items and site organisation costs	40 - 60	20 - 35	5 -15
Site investigation and testing	3 - 10	2 - 5	1 - 3
Excavation and backfill	12 - 20	9 - 18	6 - 12
Disposal costs (including tipping charges but not landfill tax)	15 - 30	20 - 35	25 - 45
Haulage	10 - 20	9 - 12	8 - 15
Total (£/m³)	80 - 140	60 - 105	45 - 90
Allowance for site abnormals	*0 - 5 +*	*0 - 15 +*	*0 - 10 +*

The strict health and safety requirements of remediation can push up the overall costs of site organisation to as much as 50% of the overall project cost. A high proportion of these costs are fixed and, as a result, the unit costs of site organisation increase disproportionally on smaller projects.

Haulage costs are largely determined by the distances to a licensed tip. Current average haulage rates, based on a return journey range from £1.10 to £1.40 a mile. Short journeys to tips, which involve proportionally longer standing times, typically incur higher mileage rates.

A further source of cost variation relates to tipping charges. The table below summarises typical tipping charges for 1999, exclusive of landfill tax:

Typical 1999 tipping charges (excluding landfill tax)	
Waste classification	Charges (£/tonne)
Non-hazardous wastes	5 - 10
Hazardous wastes	10 - 20
Special waste	12 - 25
Contaminated liquid	12 - 35
Contaminated sludge	35 - 45

Tipping charges fluctuate in relation to the grades of material a tip can accept at any point in time. This fluctuation is a further source of cost risk.

Over the past two years, prices at licensed tips have varied by as much as 50%. In addition, a special waste regulation charge of £15 per load, equivalent to 80 p a tonne, is also payable.

Landfill tax, currently charged at £10 a tonne for active waste, is also payable, although exemptions are currently available for the disposal of historically contaminated material (refer also to *"Landfill Tax"* on page vii).

Contents

PART III - PRICES FOR MEASURED WORK - cont'd

Prices for Measured Work - Minor Works

PART IV - APPROXIMATE ESTIMATING

PART V - TABLES AND MEMORANDA

Acknowledgements

The Editors wish to record their appreciation of the assistance given by many individuals and organisations in the compilation of this edition.

Material suppliers and sub-contractors who have contributed this year include:

Abbey Building Supplies Company
213 Stourbridge Road
Halesowen
West Midlands
B63 3QY
Building Fixings and Fastenings
Tel: 0121 550 7674
Fax: 0121 585 5031

Ace Minimix
British Rail Goods Yard
York Way
Kings Cross
London
N1 0AU
Ready mixed concrete
Tel: 0171 837 7011
Fax: 0171 278 5333

Aco Technologies Ltd
Hitchin Road
Shefford
Bedfordshire
SG17 5TE
Drainage Channels
Tel: 01462 816 666
Fax: 01462 815 895

Akzo Nobel Decorative Coatings Ltd
PO Box 37
Crown House
Hollins Road
Darwen
Lancashire
BB3 0BG
Paints, Varnishes etc.
Tel: 01254 704 951
Fax: 01245 774 414

Akzo Nobel Woodcare
Meadow Lane
St Ives
Cambridgeshire
PE17 4UY
"Sadolin" Stains and Preservatives
Tel: 01480 496 868
Fax: 01480 496 801

Albion Concrete Products Ltd
Pipe House Wharf
Morfa Road
Swansea
West Glamorgan
SA1 1TD
Precast Concrete Pipes and Manhole Rings, etc.
Tel: 01792 655 968
Fax: 01792 644 461

Alexander Adams Ltd
Hylton Bridge Farm
West Boldon
Tyne and Wear
NE36 0BB
Raised Access Floors and Accessories
Tel: 0191 519 0707
Fax: 0191 519 2121

Alfred McAlpine Slate Ltd
Penrhyn Quarry
Bethesda
near Bangor
Gwynedd
LL57 4YG
Natural Welsh Slates
Tel: 01248 600 656
Fax: 01248 601 171

Altro Floors
Works Road
Letchworth
Hertfordshire
SG6 1NW
"Altro" Sheet and Tile Flooring and Stair Nosings
Tel: 01454 412 992
Fax: 01454 415 931

Alumasc Building Products Ltd
Station Road
Burton Latimer
Kettering
Northamptonshire
NN15 5JP
Aluminium Rainwater Goods
Tel: 01536 383 838
Fax: 01536 383 830

Aluminium RW Supplies Ltd
Ryan House
Unit 6
Dumballs Road
Cardiff
South Glamorgan
CF1 6JE
Aluminium Rainwater Goods
Tel: 01222 390 576
Fax: 01222 238 410

AN Wallis & Company Ltd
Greasley Street
Bulwell
Nottingham
NG6 8NJ
Lightning Conductors
Tel: 0115 927 1721
Fax: 0115 977 0069

Ancon CCL Ltd
President Way
President Park
Sheffield
South Yorkshire
S4 7UR
Steel Reinforcement for Concrete
Tel: 0114 275 5224
Fax: 0114 276 8543

Architectural Aluminium Company Ltd
Ty Verlon Industrial Estate
Cardiff Road
Cadoxton
Barry
South Glamorgan
CF6 7NW
"Kawneer" Curtain Walling
Tel: 01446 738 151
Fax: 01446 721 887

Ardex UK Ltd
Homefield Road
Haverhill
Suffolk
CB9 8QP
Building Concrete Admixtures
Tel: 01440 714 939
Fax: 01440 703 424

Armstrong World Industries Ltd
Building Products Operation
38 Market Square
Uxbridge
Middlesex
UB8 1NG
Tiles and Sheet Flooring
Tel: 0800 371 849
Fax: 01895 274 287

Ash Resources
West Burton
Retford
Nottinghamshire
DN22 9BL
Lytag
Tel: 01427 881 234
Fax: 01427 881 000

Associated Asphalt
PO Box 60
Henley-on-Thames
Oxfordshire
RG9 4EZ
Bitumen Macadam Surfacing
Tel: 01491 575 921
Fax: 01491 579 713

Balcas Kildare Ltd
Naas
County Kildare
Ireland
Medium Density Fibreboard Profiles
Tel: 00 353 45 877 671
Fax: 00 353 45 877 073

BDC Concrete Products Ltd
Corporation Road
Newport
Gwent
South Wales
NP9 0WT
"Pedesta" Paving
Tel: 01633 244 181
Fax: 01633 216 655

Beacon Hill Brick Company Ltd
Wareham Road
Corfe Mullen
Wimborne
Dorset
BH21 3RX
Facing Bricks
Tel: 01202 697 633
Fax: 01202 605 141

Binns Fencing Ltd
Harvest Works
Cranborne Road
Potters Bar
Hertfordshire
EN6 3JF
Fencing
Tel: 01707 855 555
Fax: 01707 857 565

Bison Concrete Products Ltd
Amington House
Silica Road
Tamworth
Staffordshire
B77 4AZ
Precast Concrete Flooring Systems
Tel: 01827 641 41
Fax: 01827 690 09

Blue Circle Cement
Blue Circle House
The Shore
Northfleet
Gravesend
Kent
DA11 9AN
Cement, Lime and Flintag
Tel: 01474 564 344
Fax: 01474 537 404

Bolton Brady Ltd
Blenheim Place
Unit H/A
Dunston Industrial Estate
Dunston
Tyne and Wear
NE11 9HF
Roller Shutters
Tel: 0191 460 5201
Fax: 0191 460 1877

Bonar Floors Ltd
High Holburn Road
Ripley
Derbyshire
DE5 3NT
Entrance Matting and Aluminium Matwell Frames
Tel: 01773 744 121
Fax: 01773 744 142

Bourne Steel Ltd
St Clements House
St Clements Road
Poole
Dorset
BH12 4GP
Structural Steelwork
Tel: 01202 746 666
Fax: 01202 732 002

BRC Building Products Ltd
Carver Road
Astonfields Industrial Estate
Staffordshire
ST16 3BP
Brick Reinforcement
Tel: 01785 222 288
Fax: 01785 240 029

British Gypsum Ltd
Head Office
East Leake
Loughborough
Leicestershire
LE12 6HX
Plasterboard and Plaster Products
Tel: 0115 945 1000
Fax   0115 945 1901

British Sisalkraft Ltd
Commissioners Road
Strood
Rochester
Kent
ME2 4ED
Roof Finish Underlays and Insulation
Tel: 01634 290 505
Fax: 01634 291 029

British Steel plc, British Steel Strip Products
PO Box 10
Newport
Gwent
NP9 OXN
Metal panels, claddings and sheets
Tel: 01633 290 022
Fax: 01639 872 493

British Steel plc, Tubes & Pipes
Corby Works
PO Box 101
Weldon Road
Corby
Northamptonshire
NN17 5UA
Steel and aluminium frames
Tel: 01536 402 121
Fax: 01536 404 111

British Steel Distribution, P & S Services
Spitalgate Industrial Estate
Grantham
Lincolnshire
NG31 7UP
Floor and roof beams
Tel: 01476 566 830
Fax: 01476 562 459

Builders Iron & Zincwork Ltd
Millmarsh Lane
Brimsdown
Enfield
Middlesex
EN3 7QA
Roof Trims and Accessories
Tel: 0181 443 3300
Fax: 0181 804 6672

Burlington Slate Ltd
Cavendish House
Kirkby-in-Furness
Cumbria
LA17 7UN
"Westmoreland" Slating
Tel: 01229 889 681
Fax: 01229 889 466

Callenders Construction Products
Harvey Road
Burnt Mills Industrial Estate
Basildon
Essex
SS13 1EJ
Flooring, Roofing and Damp Proofing Products
Tel: 01268 591 155
Fax: 01268 591 165

Camas Building Materials
Hulland Ward
Ashbourne
Derbyshire
DE6 3ET
Reconstructed Stone Walling and Roofing
Tel: 01335 372 222
Fax: 01335 370 074

Cape Calsil
Iver Lane
Uxbridge
Middlesex
UB8 2JQ
Boarding and TRADA Firecheck Panelling
Tel: 01895 463 000
Fax: 01895 259 262

Caradon Catnic Ltd
Pontygwindy Estate
Caerphilly
Mid Glamorgan
CF8 2WJ
Steel Lintels and "Garador" Products
Tel: 01222 337 900
Fax: 01222 863 178

Caradon Garador Ltd
Bunford Lane
Yeovil
Somerset
BA20 2YA
Garage Doors
Tel: 01935 443 700
Fax: 01935 443 744

Caradon Terrain Ltd
Larkfield Road Estate
Aylesford
Maidstone
Kent
ME20 7PJ
Above and Below Ground Drainage Goods
Tel: 01622 717 811
Fax: 01622 716 920

Cavity Trays Ltd
Administration Centre
Lufton Trading Estate
Yeovil
Somerset
BA21 5HU
Cavity Trays, Closers and Associated Products
Tel: 01935 474 769
Fax: 01935 428 223

CB Watson Stonemasonry Ltd
The Stoneyard
Off Atlantic Way
No 2 Dock
Barry
South Glamorgan
CF63 3RA
Stonework
Tel: 01446 732 965
Fax: 01446 736 679

CCS Scotseal Ltd
Unit 3
Lyon Road
Linwood Industrial Estate
Paisley
Scotland
PA3 3BQ
External insulation of external walls
Tel: 01505 324 262
Fax: 01505 323 618

CEP Ceilings Ltd
Verulam Road
Common Road Industrial Estate
Stafford
Staffordshire
ST16 3EA
Ceiling Tiles
Tel: 01785 251 309
Fax: 01785 463 185

CF Anderson & Son Ltd
228 London Road
Marks Tey
Colchester
Essex
C06 1HD
Wrought Softwood Boarding and Panel Products
Tel: 01206 211 666
Fax: 01206 212 450

Cordek Ltd
Gillmans Industrial Estate
Natts Lane
Billinghurst
West Sussex
RH14 9EY
Trough Moulds
Tel: 01403 783 383
Fax: 01403 783 521

Cox Building Products Ltd
Icknield Way
Tring
Hertfordshire
HP23 4RF
Rooflights
Tel: 01442 824 222
Fax: 01442 823 351

Crittal Windows
Springwood Drive
Braintree
Essex
CM7 2YN
Aluminium and Steel Windows
Tel: 01376 324 106
Fax: 01376 349 662

Daniel Platt Ltd
Brownhills Tileries
Tunstall
Stoke-on-Trent
Staffordshire
ST6 4NY
Quarry & Ceramic Floor Tiles
Tel: 01782 577 187
Fax: 01782 577 877

Decra Roof Systems (UK) Ltd
Unit 7
Church Road Industrial Estate
Lowfield Heath
Crawley
West Sussex
RH11 0YA
"Decra Stratos" Roofing System and Accessories
Tel: 01293 545 058
Fax: 01293 562 709

Dennis Ruabon Ltd
Hafod Tileries
Ruabon
Wrexham
Clywdd
LL14 6ET
Quarry Floor Tiles
Tel: 01978 843 484
Fax: 01978 843 276

Derbyshire Engineering Services Ltd
Bingswood Trading Estate
Whaley Bridge
High Peak
SK23 7LY
Structural steelwork
Tel: 01663 734 139
Fax: 01663 732 983

Dow Construction Products
2 Heathrow Boulevard
284 Bath Road
West Drayton
Middlesex
UB7 0DQ
Insulation Products
Tel: 0181 917 5050
Fax: 0181 917 5413

Drainage Systems
Brickhouse Lane
West Bromwich
West Midlands
B70 0DX
Manholes and Inspection Chambers
Tel: 0121 521 2900
Fax: 0121 522 2197

Dufaylite Developments Ltd
Cromwell Road
St Neots
Huntingdon
Cambridgeshire
PE19 1QW
"Dufaylite Clayboard"
Tel: 01480 215 000
Fax: 01480 405 526

Durabella Ltd
Unit 5
Eastways Industrial Estate
Withan
Essex
CM8 3YQ
"Westbourne" flooring
Tel: 01376 535 000
Fax: 01376 517 217

Envirodoor Markus Ltd
Great Gutter Lane (East)
Willerby
Hull
North Humberside
HU10 6BS
Sliding and Folding Doors
Tel: 01482 659 375
Fax: 01482 655 131

Eternit (UK) Ltd
Meldreth
Royston
Hertfordshire
SG8 5RL
Sheeting, Boards and Tiles
Tel: 01763 264 686
Fax: 01763 262 338

Eurobrick Systems Ltd
Unit 6
Bonville Business Centre
Dixon Road
Brislington
Bristol
BS4 5QW
Insulated Brick Cladding System
Tel: 0117 971 7117
Fax: 0117 971 7217

Eurocom Enterprise Ltd
75 Tithe Barn Drive
Bray
Maidenhead
Berkshire
SL6 2DD
Terne Coated Stainless Steel Roofing
Tel: 01628 687 022
Fax: 01628 687 023

Euroroof Ltd
Denton Drive
Northwich
Cheshire
CW9 7LU
"Anticon" Sarking Membrane
Tel: 01606 482 22
Fax: 01606 499 40

Evode Ltd
Common Road
Stafford
Staffordshire
ST16 3EH
"Evo-Stik" and "Flashband" Products
Tel: 01785 257 236
Fax: 01785 241 615

Expamet Building Products
PO Box 52
Longhill Industrial Estate (North)
Hartlepool
Cleveland
TS25 1PR
Expanded Metal Building Products
Tel: 01429 866 611
Fax: 01429 866 633

Forbo-Nairn Ltd
PO Box 1
Den Road
Kirkcaldy
Fife
KY1 2SB
Tiles and Sheet Flooring
Tel: 01592 643 777
Fax: 01592 643 999

Forticrete Ltd
East Cranmore
Near Shepton Mallet
Somerset
BA4 4SQ
Concrete and Stone Faced Blocks
Tel: 01749 880 441
Fax: 01749 880 551

Forticrete Ltd
Thornley Station Industrial Estate
Salters Lane
Shotton Colliery
County Durham
DH6 2QA
"Astra" Glazed Blocks
Tel: 01429 838 001
Fax: 01429 836 206

Forticrete Roofing Products
Heath Road
Leighton Buzzard
Bedfordshire
LU7 8ER
"Hardrow" Slating
Tel: 01525 851 100
Fax: 01525 850 432

Fosroc Ltd
Coleshill Road
Tamworth
Staffordshire
B78 3TL
Admixtures, Expansion Joint Fillers etc
Tel: 01827 262 222
Fax: 01827 262 444

Geoffrey Pike Ltd
Garnet Close
Greycaines Industrial Estate
Watford
Hertfordshire
WD2 4JL
Marble and Granite Wall and Floor Coverings
Tel: 01923 224 884
Fax: 01923 238 124

Gerflor Ltd
Rothwell Road
Warwick
Warwickshire
CV34 5PY
Sheet and Tile Flooring
Tel: 01926 401 500
Fax: 01926 401 647

Gil Airvac International Ltd
PO Box 3025
Artex Avenue
Rustington
West Sussex
BN16 3TB
Aluminium Louvres
Tel: 01903 782 060
Fax: 01903 859 213

Glamorgan Aluminium Company Ltd
Ipswich Road
Cardiff
CF3 7UR
"Kawneer" Curtain Walling
Tel: 01222 497 808
Fax: 01222 471 796

Glenigan Cost Information Services
41 - 47 Seabourne Road
Bournemouth
Dorset
BH5 2HU
**The Heavyside Building Materials
Price Guide**
Tel: 01202 432 121
Fax: 01202 421 807

Glynwed Foundries
PO Box 3
Sinclair Works
Ketley
Telford
TF1 4AD
Manhole and Duct Covers
Tel: 01952 641 414
Fax: 01952 243 760

GRAB Industrial Flooring Ltd
Park Road
South Wigston
Leicester
LE18 4QD
Resin Based Flooring
Tel: 0116 277 0024
Fax: 0116 277 4038

Grace Servicised
Expansion Jointing and Waterproofing Division
Ajax Avenue
Slough
Berkshire
SL1 4BH
Expansion Joint Fillers and Waterbars
Tel: 01753 692 929
Fax: 01753 691 623

Granwood Flooring Ltd
PO Box 60
Alfreton
Derbyshire
DE55 4ZX
Sports Flooring
Tel: 01773 606 060
Fax: 01773 540 043

Halfen Ltd
Humphrys Road
Woodside Estate
Dunstable
Bedfordshire
LU5 4TP
Building Fixings and Fastenings
Tel: 01582 470 300
Fax: 01582 470 304

Hanson Brick Ltd
Stewartby
Bedford
MK43 9LZ
"London Brand" Facing Bricks
Tel: 01990 258 258
Fax: 01234 762 040

Hanson Bath & Portland Stone
Bumpers Lane
Wakeham
Portland
Dorset
DT5 1HY
Natural Stone
Tel: 01305 820 207
Fax: 01305 860 275

Hanson Conbloc Ltd
PO Box 14
Appleford Road
Sutton Courtenay
Abingdon
Oxfordshire
OX14 4UB
Building Block Products
Tel: 01235 848 877
Fax: 01235 848 767

Hanson Southern
Garston Road
Frome
Somerset
BA11 1RS
Cotswold Stone
Tel: 01373 453 333
Fax: 01373 452 964

Harcros Timber & Building Supplies Ltd
Harcros House
1 Central Road
Worcester Park
Surrey
KT4 8DN
Structural Timber
Tel: 0181 337 6666
Fax: 0181 255 2280

Harvey Fabrication Ltd
Hancock Road
London
E3 3DA
Galvanised Tank & Water Cylinders
Tel: 0181 981 7811
Fax: 0181 981 7815

HCC Protective Coatings Ltd
Freshwater Road
Dagenham
Essex
RM8 1RU
Paints and Primers
Tel: 0181 590 6030
Fax: 0181 599 3527

Hepworth Building Products Ltd
Hazelhead
Crow Edge
Sheffield
South Yorkshire
S36 4HG
Clay Drainage Goods
Tel: 01226 763 561
Fax: 01226 764 827

Herberts Ltd
Freshwater Road
Dagenham
Essex
RM8 1RU
Heavy Duty Coatings
Tel: 0181 590 6030
Fax: 0181 599 3527

Hillaldam Coburn Ltd
Unit 6
Wyvern Estate
Beverly Way
New Malden
Surrey
KT3 4PH
Sliding and Folding Door Gear
Tel: 0181 336 1515
Fax: 0181 336 1414

Hilti (Great Britain) Ltd
Trafford Wharf Road
Trafford Park
Manchester
M17 1BY
Fixings
Tel: 0161 886 1000
Fax: 0161 872 1240

Hinton, Perry & Davenhill Ltd
Dreadnought Works
Pensnett
Brierley Hill
Staffordshire
DY5 4TH
Overlap Roof Tiling
Tel: 01384 774 05
Fax: 01384 745 53

HSS Hire Shops
Group Office
25 Willow Lane
Mitcham
Surrey
CR4 4TS
Paint Guns
Tel: 0181 260 3100
Fax: 0181 687 5005

Hudevad Britain
Hudevad House
130-132 Terrace Road
Walton-on-Thames
Surrey
KT12 2EA
Hot Water Radiators and Fittings
Tel: 01932 247 835
Fax: 01932 247 694

Hunter Plastics Ltd
Nathan Way
London
SE28 0AE
Plastic Rainwater Goods
Tel: 0181 855 9851
Fax: 0181 317 7764

Huntley & Sparks Ltd
Building Products Division
Sterling House
Crewkerne
Somerset
TA18 8LL
"Rigifix" Column Guards
Tel: 01460 722 22
Fax: 01460 764 02

Ibstock Building Products Ltd
Ibstock
Leicestershire
LE67 6HS
Facing Bricks
Tel: 01530 261 999
Fax: 01530 261 888

IG Ltd
Avondale Road
Cwmbran
Gwent
NP44 1XY
"Weatherbeater" Doors & Frames
Tel: 01633 486 486
Fax: 01633 486 465

IMI Yorkshire Copper Tube Ltd
East Lancashire Road
Kirkby
Liverpool
L33 7TU
Copper Piping
Tel: 0151 546 2700
Fax: 0151 549 2139

IMI Yorkshire Fittings Ltd
PO Box 166
Haigh Park Road
Leeds
LS1 1RD
"Yorkshire" & "Kuterlite" Fittings
Tel: 0113 270 1104
Fax: 0113 271 5275

Industrial Textiles & Plastics Ltd
Providence Hill
Husthwaite
York
North Yorkshire
YO6 3SN
Roof Finish Underlays and Insulation
Tel: 01347 868 767
Fax: 01347 868 737

Interface Europe Ltd
Ashlyns Hall
Chestham Road
Berkhamstead
Buckinghamshire
HP4 2ST
Non-woven Carpet Tiling
Tel: 01442 285 000
Fax: 01442 876 053

James Halstead Ltd
PO Box 3
Radcliffe New Road
Whitefield
Manchester
M45 7NR
"Polyflor" Contract Flooring
Tel: 0161 767 1111
Fax: 0161 767 1128

James Latham (Western)
Badminton Road
Yate
Bristol
Avon
BS17 5JX
Softwood, Hardwood and Panel Products
Tel: 01454 315 421
Fax: 01454 323 488

Jandor-Hansen
Clausen House
Perivale Industrial Park
Horsenden Lane South
Perivale
Middlesex
UB6 7QE
Industrial Doors
Tel: 0181 998 4321
Fax: 0181 991 1374

Jewson Ltd
Sutherland House
Matlock
Foleshill
Coventry
West Midlands
CV1 4JQ
Standard Joinery Products
Tel: 01203 669 100
Fax: 01203 637 582

John Brash & Co Ltd
The Old Shipyard
Gainsborough
Lincolnshire
DN21 1NG
Cedar Shingling
Tel: 01427 613 858
Fax: 01427 810 218

John Newton & Co Ltd
12 Verney Road
London
SE16 3DH
Waterproofing Lathing
Tel: 0171 237 1217
Fax: 0171 252 2769

Jonathan James Ltd
15 - 17 New Road
Rainham
Essex
RM13 8DJ
Plastering and Screeding
Tel: 01708 556 921
Fax: 01708 520 751

Junckers Ltd
Wheaton Court Commercial Centre
Wheaton Road
Whitham
Essex
CM8 3UJ
Hardwood Flooring
Tel: 01376 517 512
Fax: 01376 514 401

Kelsey Roofing Industries Ltd
Kelsey House
Millfield Road
Horbury
Wakefield
West Yorkshire
WF4 5EB
Sheet Roof Claddings
Tel: 01924 263 033
Fax: 01924 263 113

Keymer Handmade Clay Tiles
Nye Road
Burgess Hill
West Sussex
RH15 0LZ
Roof Tiling
Tel: 01444 232 931
Fax: 01444 871 852

Kitsons Insulation Products Ltd
Unit A389
Western Avenue
Team Valley Trading Estate
Gateshead
Tyne and Wear
NE11 0SZ
Pipe Insulation Products
Tel: 0191 482 1261
Fax: 0191 491 0700

Klargester Environmental Engineering Ltd
College Road
Aston Clinton
Aylesbury
Buckinghamshire
HP22 5EW
Petrol Interceptors and Septic Tanks
Tel: 01296 633 000
Fax: 01296 633 001

Kriscut Concrete Drilling & Sawing Ltd
15 Dawley Road
Hayes
Middlesex
UB3 1LT
Diamond Drilling
Tel: 0181 561 8378
Fax: 0181 573 9776

Kvaerner Cementation Foundations Ltd
Maple Cross House
Denham Way
Maple Cross
Rickmansworth
Hertfordshire
WD3 2SW
Piling
Tel: 01923 423 100
Fax: 01923 777 834

Lafarge Redland Precast Ltd
Six Hills
Melton Mowbray
Leicestershire
LE14 3PD
Precast Concrete Paving Units
Tel: 01509 882 121
Fax: 01509 882 050

Lamatherm Products Ltd
Forge Factory Estate
Maesteg
Mid Glamorgan
CF34 0AU
Under Floor Cavity Barriers
Tel: 01656 730 833
Fax: 01656 730 115

Langley Waterproofing Systems Ltd
Bishop Crewe House
North Street
Daventry
Northamptonshire
NN1 5PN
Roof Tiling
Tel: 01327 704 778
Fax: 01327 704 845

Leaderflush Doors + Shapland
PO Box 5404
Nottingham
Nottinghamshire
NG16 4BU
Internal Doors
Tel: 0870 240 0666
Fax: 0870 240 0777

Light Alloy Ltd
Dales Road
Ipswich
Suffolk
IP1 4R J
"Zig Zag" Loft Ladders
Tel: 01473 740 445
Fax: 01473 240 002

Llewellyn Timber Engineering
Bleak Hall
Milton Keynes
Buckinghamshire
MK6 1LA
Roof Trusses
Tel: 01908 679 222
Fax: 01908 678 631

Luxaflex Blinds (Hunter Douglas Ltd)
Swanscombe Business Centre
17 London Road
Swanscombe
Kent
DA10 0LH
Roller and Vertical Blinds
Tel: 01322 624 580
Fax: 01322 624 558

Luxcrete Ltd
Premier House
Disraeli Road
Park Royal
Harlesden
London
NW10 7BT
Pavement and Roof Lighting
Tel: 0181 965 7292
Fax: 0181 961 6337

Maccaferri (Ltd)
47 George Street
Perth
Scotland
PH1 5LA
Gabions
Tel: 01738 621 317
Fax: 01738 442 283

Manthorpe Building Products Ltd
Manthorpe House
Brittain Drive
Codnor Gate Industrial Estate
Ripley
Derbyshire
DE5 3ND
Cavity Closers
Tel: 01773 743 555
Fax: 01773 748 736

Marflex International Ltd
Unit 40
Vale Business Park
Llandow Industrial Estate
Cowbridge
South Glamorgan
CF71 7PB
Flue Linings and Blocks
Tel: 01446 775 551
Fax: 01446 772 468

Marley Building Materials Ltd
Station Road
Coleshill
Birmingham
B46 1HP
Roof Tiles, Pavings and "Thermalite" Blocks
Tel: 01675 462 081
Fax: 01675 468 485

Marley Extrusions Ltd
Dickley Lane
Lenham
Maidstone
Kent
ME17 2DE
Drainage Goods
Tel: 01622 858 888
Fax: 01622 858 725

Marley Floors Ltd
Dickley Lane
Lenham
Maidstone
Kent
ME17 2DE
Sheet and Tile Flooring
Tel: 01622 854 000
Fax: 01622 854 219

Marshalls Mono Ltd
Brier Lodge
Southowram
Halifax
West Yorkshire
HX3 9SY
Concrete Block Paving
Tel: 01422 306 000
Fax: 01422 330 185

MDT Ducting Ltd
PO Box 618
Sutton Coldfield
West Midlands
B73 5SL
Trunking Systems and Conduits
Tel: 0121 384 6200
Fax: 0121 377 8938

Metsec Plc
Broadwell Road
Oldbury
Warley
West Midlands
B69 4HE
Lattice Beams
Tel: 0121 552 1541
Fax: 0121 544 5520

Moelven Laminated Timber Structures Ltd
Unit 10
Vicarage Farm
Winchester Road
Fair Oak
Eastleigh
Hampshire
SO50 7HD
"Glulam" Laminated Timber Beams
Tel: 01703 695 566
Fax: 01703 695 577

MPG Contracts Ltd
Construction House
579 High Road
London
N17 6SB
Granolithic Paving
Tel: 0181 885 3733
Fax: 0181 801 3115

Mustang Metal Products
Unit 6
Worcester Trading Estate
Blackpole
Worcester
Worcestershire
WR3 8HR
Rainwater Goods
Tel: 01905 455 151
Fax: 01905 755 055

Myson Radiators
Eastern Avenue
Team Valley Trading Estate
Gateshead
Tyne and Wear
NE11 0PG
Hot Water Radiators and Fittings
Tel: 0191 491 7500
Fax: 0191 491 7568

Natural Stone Products
Stone Middleton
Hope Valley
Derbyshire
S32 4TR
Granite and Cobble setts; "Yorkstone" Pavings
Tel: 01433 639 999
Fax: 01433 639 170

NT Laidlaw
Pennine House
Carrs Road
Cheadle
Cheshire
SK8 2BW
Ironmongery
Tel: 0161 491 4343
Fax: 0161 491 4355

Nullifire Ltd
Torrington Avenue
Coventry
West Midlands
CV4 9TJ
Joint Fillers
Tel: 01203 855 000
Fax: 01203 469 547

Owen-Corning Building Products (UK) Ltd
PO Box 10
Stafford Road
St Helens
Merseyside
WA10 3NS
Building Insulation Products
Tel: 0800 627 465
Fax: 01744 612 007

Parkwood Mellowes Ltd
Ridgacre Road
West Bromwich
West Midlands
B71 1BB
Patent Glazing
Tel: 0121 525 4444
Fax: 0121 553 4019

Pendock Ltd
Halesfield 19
Telford
Shropshire
TF7 4QT
Skirting Trunking and Casing Profiles
Tel: 01952 580 590
Fax: 01952 587 805

Phi Group Ltd
Harcourt House
13 Royal Crescent
Cheltenham
Gloucestershire
GL50 3DA
Crib Walling
Tel: 01242 510 199
Fax: 01242 222 569

Pilkington Cardiff
Dumballs Road
Cardiff
CF1 6UN
Glazing
Tel: 01222 399 899
Fax: 01222 372 004

Pilkington Tiles Ltd
PO Box 4
Rake Lane
Clifton Junction
Swinton
Manchester
M27 8LP
Glazed Wall/Floor Tiles
Tel: 0161 727 1133
Fax: 0161 727 1122

Precision Metal Forming Ltd
Swindon Road
Cheltenham
Gloucestershire
GL51 9LS
BSC Sheeting
Tel: 01242 527 511
Fax: 01242 518 929

Premdor
Groundwell Industrial Estate
Swindon
Wiltshire
SN2 5AZ
Hardwood Joinery
Tel: 01793 708 231
Fax: 01793 708 290

Promat Fire Protection Ltd
Whaddon Road
Meldreth
Near Royston
Hertfordshire
SG8 5RL
Fireproofing Materials
Tel: 01763 262 310
Fax: 01763 262 342

Quelfire
PO Box 35
Caspian Road
off Atlantic Street
Altrincham
Cheshire
WA14 5QA
Fire Protection Compound
Tel: 0161 928 7308
Fax: 0161 941 2635

Quiligotti Contracts Ltd
PO Box 4
Clifton Junction
Manchester
M27 8LB
Terrazzo Products
Tel: 0161 727 1130
Fax: 0161 727 1170

Redland Roof Systems Ltd
Regent House
Station Approach
Dorking
Surrey
RH4 1TG
Roof Tiling
Tel: 01306 872 000
Fax: 01306 872 111

Rentokil Ltd
Industrial Products
Felcourt
East Grinstead
West Sussex
RH19 2JY
Flame Retardant Products
Tel: 01342 833 022
Fax: 01342 326 229

Rex Bousfield Ltd
Holland Road
Hurst Green
Oxted
Surrey
RH8 9BD
Fire Retardant Chipboarding
Tel: 01883 717 033
Fax: 01883 717 890

RG Shackell and Son
37 Ball Road
Llanrumney
Cardiff
South Glamorgan
Wax and French Polishing
Tel: 01222 798 130
Fax: 01222 798 130

Richard Lees Steel Decking Ltd
Moor Farm Road West
The Airfield
Ashbourne
Derbyshire
DE6 1HD
Structural Steel Deck Flooring
Tel: 01335 300 999
Fax: 01335 300 888

RMC Aggregates (Northern) Ltd
RMC House
8-9 Blezard Business Park
Brenkley Way
Seaton Burn
Newcastle-upon-Tyne
Tyne & Wear
NE13 6DR
Aggregates
Tel: 0191 217 0299
Fax: 0191 217 0298

RMC Concrete Products Ltd
London Road
Wick
Bristol
BS30 5SJ
Paving Blocks
Tel: 0117 937 3371
Fax: 0117 937 3002

RMC Panel Products Ltd
Waldorf Way
Denby Dale Road
Wakefield
West Yorkshire
WF2 8DH
Plasterboard Angle Support System
Tel: 01924 362 081
Fax: 01924 290 126

Rockwool Ltd
Pencoed
Bridgend
Mid Glamorgan
CF35 6NY
Cavity Wall Batts
Tel: 01656 862 621
Fax: 01656 862 302

RSA Waterheating Ltd
Somerton Works
Newport
Gwent
NP9 0XV
Water Heaters and Boilers
Tel: 01633 277 711
Fax: 01633 276 004

Ruberoid Building Products Ltd
Business Development Manager
Tewin Road
Welwyn Garden City
Hertfordshire
AL7 1BP
Roofing Felts, DPC's
Tel: 01707 373 750
Fax: 01707 375 060

Rugby Joinery
Watch House Lane
Doncaster
South Yorkshire
DN5 9LR
Standard Joinery Products
Tel: 01302 394 000
Fax: 01302 787 383

Ryton's Building Products Ltd
Design House
Orion Way
Kettering Business Park
Kettering
Northamptonshire
NN15 6NL
Roof Ventilation Products
Tel: 01536 511 874
Fax: 01536 310 455

Sandtoft Roof Tiles Ltd
Heckmondwike Tileries
Spen Vale Street
Off Station Lane
Heckmondwike
West Yorkshire
WF16 0PU
Clay Roof Tiling
Tel: 01924 413 950
Fax: 01924 413 953

Sealmaster Ltd
Brewery Road
Pampisford
Cambridge
Cambridgeshire
CB2 4HG
Intumescent Strips and Glazing Compound
Tel: 01223 832 851
Fax: 01223 837 215

Sealocrete Pla Ltd
Greenfield Lane
Rochdale
Lancashire
OL11 2LD
Building Aids, Repair and Maintenance Materials
Tel: 01706 352 255
Fax: 01706 860 880

Sheffield Insulation Ltd
Sanderson Street
off Scotswood Road
Newcastle upon Tyne
Tyne and Wear
NE4 7LW
Cavity Wall Insulation
Tel: 0191 2735 843
Fax: 0191 2739 213

Simpson Strong-Tie
Winchester Road
Cardinal Point
Tamworth
Staffordshire
B78 3HG
Expanded Metal Arch Formers,
Wall Ties etc
Tel: 01827 255 600
Fax: 01827 255 616

Sinclair Foundry Products
Sinclair Works
PO Box 3
Ketley
Telford
Shropshire
TF1 4AD
Cast Iron Disposal Goods
Tel: 01952 641 414
Fax: 01952 243 760

Stanton Plc
Lows Lane
Stanton-by-Dale
Ilkeston
Derbyshire
DE7 4QU
Ductile Iron Pipes and Fittings
Tel: 0115 930 5000
Fax: 0115 930 0737

Steel Foundations Ltd
Stevin House
Springwell Road
Gateshead
Tyne and Wear
NE9 7SP
Piling Services
Tel: 0191 417 3545
Fax: 0191 416 2894

Stressline Ltd
Station Road
Stoney Stanton
Leicester
LE9 4LX
Concrete Lintels
Tel: 01455 272 457
Fax: 01455 274 564

Swish Products Ltd
Building Products Division
Lichfield Road Industrial Estate
Tamworth
Staffordshire
B79 7TF
Claddings, Fascias, Bargeboards and Soffits
Tel: 01827 317 200
Fax: 01827 317 201

Tarmac Topblock Ltd
Wergs Hall
Wergs Hall Road
Wolverhampton
WV8 2HZ
Concrete Blocks
Tel: 01902 754 131
Fax: 01902 743 171

Tarmac Topmix Ltd
Wergs Hall
Wergs Hall Road
Wolverhampton
WV8 2HZ
Ready mixed Concrete
Tel: 01902 353 522
Fax: 01902 743 171

Terminix Peter Cox Ltd
Heritage House
234 High Street
Sutton
Surrey
SM1 1NX
Chemical and Damp-Proofing Products
Tel: 0181 661 6600
Fax: 0181 642 0677

The Colour Centre
Portland Street
Newport
Gwent
NP9 2DP
Paints, Varnishes and Stains
Tel: 01633 212 481
Fax: 01633 254 801

The Rawlplug Company Ltd
Skibo Drive
Thornliebank Industrial Estate
Glasgow
Scotland
G46 8JR
"Kemfix" Chemical Anchors
Tel: 0141 638 7961
Fax: 0141 273 2333

The Velux Company Ltd
Woodside Way
Glenrothes East
Fife
KY7 4ND
"Velux" Roof Windows & Flashings
Tel: 01592 772 211
Fax: 01592 771 839

The Welconstruct Company
Woodgate Business Park
Kettles Wood Drive
Birmingham
B32 3GH
Lockers and ShelvingSystems
Tel: 0121 421 9000
Fax: 0121 421 9888

Tilcon Ltd
PO Box 5
Fell Bank
Birtley
Chester-le-Street
DH3 2ST
Mortars
Tel: 0191 492 4000
Fax: 0191 410 8489

Tremco Ltd
86 - 88 Bestobell Road
Slough
Berkshire
SL1 4SZ
Damp Proofing
Tel: 01753 691 696
Fax: 01753 822 640

Uponor Ltd
PO Box 1
Hillcote Plant
Blackwell
Near Alfreton
Derbyshire
DE55 5JD
MDPE Piping and Fittings
Tel: 01773 811 112
Fax: 01773 812 343

USG (UK) Ltd
1 Swan Road
South West Industrial Estate
Peterlee
Co Durham
SR8 2HS
Ceiling Grid Systems, Panels and Tiles
Tel: 0191 586 1121
Fax: 0191 586 0097

Vandex (UK) Ltd
PO Box 88
Leatherhead
Surrey
KT22 7YF
"Vandex Super" & "Premix"
Tel: 01372 363 040
Fax: 01372 363 373

Vencel Resil Ltd
Arndale House
18-20 Spital Street
Dartford
Kent
DA1 2HT
"Jablite" Products
Tel: 01322 626 600
Fax: 01322 626 610

Vigers Hardwood Flooring Systems Ltd
Esgors Farm
Thornwood Common
Epping
Essex
CM16 6LY
Hardwood Flooring Systems
Tel: 01992 572 653
Fax: 01992 572 663

Visqueen Agri
Yarm Road
Stockton-on-Tees
Cleveland
TS18 3GE
Roof Finish Underlays and Insulation
Tel: 01642 672 288
Fax: 01642 664 325

Walter Llewellyn & Sons Ltd
19 North Street
Portslade
Brighton
Sussex
BN41 1ED
Purpose Made Joinery
Tel: 01273 439 494
Fax: 01273 430 741

Wavin Building Products Ltd
Parsonage Way
Chippenham
Wiltshire
SN15 5PN
uPVC Drainage Goods
Tel: 01249 654 121
Fax: 01249 443 286

Wellfill Insulation Ltd
284 High Road
North Weald
Essex
CM16 6EG
Cavity Wall Insulation
Tel: 01992 522 026
Fax: 01992 523 376

Wicanders
Amorim House
Star Road
Partridge Green
Horsham
West Sussex
RH13 8RA
Floor Coverings
Tel: 01403 710 001
Fax: 01403 710 003

William Blyth Ltd
Hoe Hill
Barton-on-Humber
Lincolnshire
DN18 5ET
Roof Tiles
Tel: 01652 632 175
Fax: 01652 660 966

Yeoman Aggregates Ltd
Stone Terminal
Horn Lane
Acton
London
W3 9EH
Hardcore, Gravels etc
Tel: 0181 896 6800
Fax: 0181 896 6811

DAVIS LANGDON & EVEREST

Authors of Spon's Price Books

Davis Langdon & Everest is an independent practice of Chartered Quantity Surveyors, with some 750 staff in 20 UK offices and, through Davis Langdon & Seah International, some 2,200 staff in 85 offices worldwide.

DLE manages client requirements, controls risk, manages cost and maximises value for money, throughout the course of construction projects, always aiming to be - and to deliver - the best.

TYPICAL PROJECT STAGES, DLE INTEGRATED SERVICES AND THEIR EFFECT:

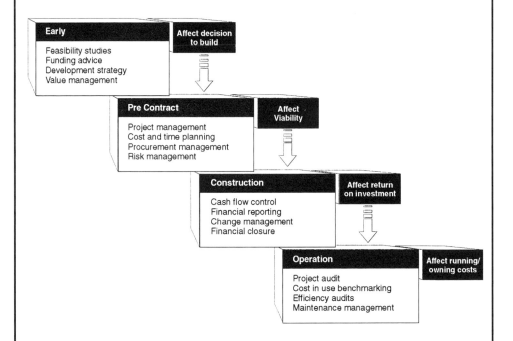

EUROPE → *ASIA* → *AUSTRALIA* → *AFRICA* → *AMERICA*
GLOBAL REACH → *LOCAL DELIVERY*

How to Use this Book

First-time users of *Spon's Architects' and Builders' Price Book* and others who may not be familiar with the way in which prices are compiled may find it helpful to read this section before starting to calculate the costs of building work. The level of information on a scheme and availability of detailed specifications will determine which section of the book and which level of prices users should refer to.

For preliminary estimates/indicative costs before drawings are prepared, refer to the average overall *Building Prices per Functional Units* (see Part IV) and multiply this by the proposed number of units to be contained within the building (ie. number of bedrooms etc.) or *Building Prices per Square Metre* rates (see Part IV) and multiply this by the gross internal floor area of the building (the sum of all floor areas measured within external walls) to arrive at an overall preliminary cost. These rates include Preliminaries (the Contractors' costs) but make no allowance for the cost of External Works or VAT.

For budget estimates where preliminary drawings are available, one should be able to measure approximate quantities for all the major components of a building and multiply these by individual rates contained in the *Approximate Estimating* section (see Part IV). This should produce a more accurate estimate of cost than using overall prices per square metre. Labour and other incidental associated items, although normally measured separately within Bills of Quantities, are deemed included within approximate estimate rates.

For more detailed estimates or documents such as Bills of Quantities (Quantities of supplied and fixed components in a building, measured from drawings), either use rates from *Prices for Measured Work - Major Works* or *Prices for Measured Work - Minor Works*, depending upon the overall value of the contract. All such prices used may need adjustment for size, site constraints, local conditions location and time, etc., and users are referred to page 674 for an example of how to adjust an estimate for some of these factors. Items within the Measured Works sections are made up of many components: the cost of the material or product; any additional materials needed to carry out the work; the labour involved in unloading and fixing, etc. These components are usually broken down into:

Prime Cost

Commonly known as the "PC", Prime Cost is the actual price of the material such as bricks, blocks, tiles or paint, as sold by suppliers. Prime Cost is given "per square metre", "per 100 bags" or "each" according to the way the supplier sells the product. Unless otherwise stated, prices in *Spon's Architects' and Builders' Price Book* (hereafter referred to as *Spon's A & B*), are deemed to be "delivered to site", (in which case transport costs will be included) and also take account of trade and quantity discounts. Part loads generally cost more than whole loads but, unless otherwise stated, Prime Cost figures are based on average prices for full loads delivered to a hypothetical site in Acton, London W3. Actual prices for "live" tenders will depend on the distance from the supplier, the accessibility of the site, whether the whole quantity ordered is to be supplied in one delivery or at specified dates and market conditions prevailing at the time. Prime Cost figures for commonly-used alternative materials are supplied in tabular form at the beginning of some work sections although these are quoted at "list" prices, readers should deduct their appropriate discount before substituting them as alternatives in rate build ups.

Labour

This figure covers the cost of the operation and is calculated on the gang wage rate (skilled or unskilled) and the time needed for the job. A full explanation and build-up is provided on page 93. Particular shortages have been noted in the Bricklaying, Carpentry, Joinery and Shuttering trades. In response to these pressures and corresponding hikes in daily rates/measured prices, basic labour rates for Bricklayers, Carpenters and Joiners have been enhanced by using the plus 15% and plus 25% bonus payment figures for these trades as outlined on page 94. Extras such as highly skilled craft work, difficult access, intermittent working and the need for additional labourers to back up the craftsman (e.g. for handling heavy concrete blocks etc.) all add to the cost. Large regular or continuous areas of work are cheaper to install than smaller intricate areas, since less labour time is wasted moving from one area to another.

Materials

Material prices include the cost of any ancillary materials, nails, screws, waste, etc., which may be needed in association with the main material product/s. If the material being priced varies from a standard measured rate, then identify the difference between the original PC price and the material price and add this to your alternative material price before adding to the labour cost to produce a new overall Total rate. Alternative material prices, where given, are quoted before discount whereas PC values of materials are after deduction of appropriate trade and quantity discounts, therefore straight substitution of alternative material prices for PC values will result in the actual rate for those alternative materials.

Example:

	PC £	Labour hours	Labour £	Material £	Unit	Total Rate £
100 mm Thermalite block (see page 169)	6.53	0.50	7.11	7.53	m²	**14.64**
100 mm Toplite standard block (£6.77 see page 169 - less 20% discount)	5.42					

Sundries £7.53 - 6.53 = 1.00 + 5.42 = £6.42

100 mm Toplite block	5.42	0.50	7.11	6.42	m²	**13.53**

Plant

Plant covers the use of machinery ranging from JCBs to shovels and static plant including running costs such as fuel, water supply (which is metered on a construction site), electricity and rubbish disposal. Some items of plant are included within the "Groundwork" section; other items are included within the Preliminaries section.

Overheads and profit

The general overheads of the Contractor's business, the head office overheads and any profit sought on capital and turnover employed, is usually covered under a general item of overheads and profit which is applied either to all measured rates as a percentage, or alternatively added to the tender summary or included within Preliminaries (site specific overhead costs). At the present time, we are not including any allowance for overheads and profit on measured rates, preferring to leave the level of this, if appropriate, to users.

Preliminaries

Site specific overheads on a contract, such as insurance, site huts, security, temporary roads and the statutory health and welfare of the labour force, are not directly assignable to individual items so they are generally added as a percentage or calculated allowance after all building component items have been costed and summed. Preliminaries will vary from contract to contract according to the type of construction, difficulties of the site, labour shortage, inclement weather or involvement with other contractors, etc. The overall Preliminary addition for a scheme should be adjusted to allow for these factors.

Preliminary costs have risen slightly since publication of the last edition, but we have retained these, as the last edition at 11 to 13%. We have continued to formally exclude any allowance for overheads and profit in either the Major or Minor Works Sections, but acknowledge that the rates currently presented may include some allowance for these items in line with market rates.

The first five of these six items combine to form the **Price for Measured Work.** It will be appreciated that a variation in any one item in any group will affect the final Measured Work price. Any cost variation must be weighed against the total cost of the contract, and a small variation in Prime Cost where the items are ordered in thousands may have more effect on the total cost than a large variation on a few items, while a change in design which introduces the need to use, e.g. earth-moving equipment, which must be brought to the site for that one task, will cause a dramatic rise in the contract cost. Similarly, a small saving on multiple items will provide a useful reserve to cover unforeseen extras.

Fees and Daywork

This part of the book contains the following sections:

Keep your figures up to date, free of charge
Now available on the web at www.efnspon.com

This section, and most of the other information in this Price Book, is brought up to date every three months with the Price Book Updates, until the next annual edition.

The Updates are available free to all Price Book purchasers.

To ensure you receive your free copies, either complete the reply card from the centre of the book and return it to us or register via the website www.efnspon.com

The updates will also be available to download from the website.

Fees for Professional Services

Extracts from the scales of fees for architects, quantity surveyors and consulting engineers are given together with extracts from the Town and Country Planning Regulations 1993. From the 1st April 1999 local authorities were given the power to set their own charges for building control functions carried out in respect of the Building Regulations 1991, the charges for the London Borough of Ealing have therefore been given as guidance. These extracts are reproduced by kind permission of the bodies concerned, in the case of Building Regulation Charges, by kind permission of the London Borough of Ealing. Attention is drawn to the fact that the full scales are not reproduced here and that the extracts are given for guidance only. The full authority scales should be studied before concluding any agreement and the reader should ensure that the fees quoted here are still current at the time of reference.

ARCHITECTS' FEES

Standard Form of Agreement for the Appointment of an Architect (SFA/99), pages 4 and 5
Conditions of Engagement for the Appointment of an Architect (CE/99), page 4 (brief notes only)
Small Works (SW/99), page 4 (brief notes only)
Employer's Requirements (DB1/99), page 4 (brief notes only)
Contractor's Proposals (DB2/99), page 4 (brief notes only)
Form of Appointment as Planning Supervisor (PS/99), page 4 (brief notes only)
Form of Appointment as Sub-Consultant (SC/99), page 4 (brief notes only)
Form of Appointment as Project Manager (PM/99), page 4 (brief notes only)

QUANTITY SURVEYORS' FEES

Scale 36,   inclusive scale of professional charges, page 9
Scale 37,   itemised scale of professional charges, page 13
Scale 40,   professional charges for housing schemes for Local Authorities, page 30
Scale 44,   professional charges for improvements to existing housing and environmental improvement works, page 35
Scale 45,   professional charges for housing schemes financed by the Housing Corporation, page 37
Scale 46,   professional charges for the assessment of damage to buildings from fire etc., page 42
Scale 47,   professional charges for the assessment of replacement costs for insurance purposes, page 44

CONSULTING ENGINEERS' FEES

Introduction to revised Agreements, page 45
Summary of conditions of engagement, page 47
Graphical Illustration of fee scales, page 49

PLANNING REGULATION FEES

Part I: General provisions, page 52
Part II: Scale of Fees, page 56

THE BUILDING (LOCAL AUTHORITY CHARGES) REGULATIONS 1998

Charge Schedules, page 59
Charges for erection of one or more small new domestic buildings and connected work, page 61
Charges for erection of certain small domestic buildings, garages, carports and extensions, page 62
Charges for building work other than to which tables 1 and 2 apply, page 63

ARCHITECTS' FEES

RIBA Forms of Appointment 1999
♦ include forms to cover all aspects of an Architect's practice;
♦ identify the traditional roles of an Architect;
♦ reflect or take into account recent legislation such as the Housing Grants, Construction and Regeneration Act 1996, the Arbitration Act 1996 (*applies to England and Wales only*), the Unfair Terms in Consumer Contracts Regulations 1994, Latham issues etc;
♦ update the Outline Plan of Work Stage titles and descriptions;
♦ are sufficiently flexible for use with English or Scottish Law [1]; the building projects of any size (except small works); other professional services [2]; different project procedures.

> [1] The Royal Incorporation of Architects in Scotland will publish appropriate replacement pages for use where the law of Scotland applies to the Agreement.
> [2] Excluding acting as adjudicator, arbitrator, expert witness, conciliator, party wall surveyor etc.

All forms require the Architect to agree with the Client the amount of professional indemnity insurance cover for the project.

Standard Form of Agreement for the Appointment of an Architect (SFA/99)
The core document from which all other forms are derived. Suitable for use where an Architect is to provide professional services for a fully designed building project in a wide range of size or complexity and/or to provide other professional services. Used with Articles of Agreement. Includes optional Services Supplement.

Conditions for Engagement for the Appointment of an Architect (CE/99)
Suitable for use where an Architect is to provide services for a fully designed building project and/or to provide other professional services where a Letter of Appointment is preferred in lieu of Articles of Agreement. Includes optional (modified) Services Supplement and draft Model letter.

Small Works (SW/99)
Suitable for the provision of professional services where the cost of construction is not expected to exceed £150,000 and use of the JCT Agreement for Minor Works is appropriate. The appointment is made by a specially drafted Letter of Appointment, the Conditions and an optional Schedule of Services for Small Works.

Employer's Requirements (DB1/99)
A supplement to amend SFA/99 and CE/99 where an Architect is appointed by the Employer Client to prepare Employer's Requirements for a Design and Build contract. Includes replacement Services Supplement and notes on completion for initial appointment, where a change to Design and Build occurs later or where "consultant switch" is contemplated.

Contractor's Proposals (DB2/99)
A supplement to amend SFA/99 where an Architect is appointed by the Contractor Client to prepare Contractor's Proposals under a Design and Build contract. Includes replacement Services Supplement and notes on completion for initial appointment and for "consultant switch".

Form of Appointment as Planning Supervisor (PS/99)
Used with Articles of Agreement. Provides for the Planning Supervisor to prepare the Health and Safety File and the pre-tender Health and Safety Plan.

Form of Appointment as Sub-Consultant (SC/99)
Suitable for use where a Consultant wishes (another Consultant (Sub-Consultant) or Specialist) to perform a part of his responsibility but not for use where the intention is for the Client to appoint Consultants or Specialists directly. Used with Articles of Agreement. Includes draft form of Warranty to the Client.

Form of Appointment as Project Manager (PM/99)
Suitable for a wide range of projects where the Client wishes to appoint a Project Manager to provide a management service and/or other professional service. Used with Articles of Agreement. Does not duplicate or conflict with the Architect's services under other RIBA forms.

ARCHITECTS' FEES

Guides

Matters connected with using and completing the forms are covered in "The Architect's Contract: A guide to RIBA Forms of Appointment 1999 and other Architect's appointments". The guidance covers the Standard Form (SFA/99) including a worked example; the options for calculating fees ie. percentages, calculated or fixed lump sums, time charges and other methods; the other forms in the suite; the Design and Build amendments including advice on 'consultant switch' and 'novation' agreements; and topics for other appointments connected with dispute resolution, etc. Notes on appointments for Historic Buildings and Community Architecture projects are also included.

A series of guides "Engaging an Architect", addressed directly to clients, is also published on topics associated with the appointment of an Architect. These guides include graphs showing indicative percentage fees for the architect's normal services in stages C-L under SFA/99, CE/99 or SW/99 for works to new and existing buildings. Indicative hourly rates are also shown. Tables 2, 3 and 4 on page 8 show by interpolation of the graphs the indicative fees for different classes of building adjusted to reflect current tender price indices. Table 1 gives the classification of buildings. Indicative fees do not include expenses, disbursements or VAT fees.

The appointing documents and guides are published by:
RIBA Publications, Construction House, 56-64 Leonard Street, London. EC2A 4LT.
Telephone: 0171 251 0791   Fax: 0171 608 2375

The Standard Form of Agreement for the Appointment of an Architect (SFA/99)
SFA/99 is the core document, which is used as the basis for all the documents in the RIBA 1999 suite. It should be suitable for any Project to be procured in the 'traditional' manner. Supplements are available for use with Design and Build procurement. It is used with Articles of Agreement and formal attestation underhand or as a deed.

There are some changes from SFA/92 in presentation, in some of the responsibilities and liabilities of the parties, to some definitions and clauses and their arrangement for greater clarity or flexibility, for compliance with the Construction Act; and to ensure that each role of the Architect is separately identified.

It comprises:

♦ the formal declaration of intent - Recitals and Articles;

♦ Appendix to the Conditions;

♦ Schedule 1 - Project Description;

♦ Schedule 2 - Services indicating the roles the Architect is to perform, which Work Stages apply and any other services required. A table of 'Other activities' identifies items not included in 'Normal Services';

♦ Schedule 3 - Fess and Expenses;

♦ Schedule 4 - Other appointments;

♦ the Conditions governing performance of the contract and obligations of the parties;

♦ a Services Supplement describing the Architect's roles and activities' which can be edited to suit the requirements of the Project or removed if it is not suitable for the Project, and if appropriate, another inserted in its place; and

♦ notes on completion.

ARCHITECTS' FEES

Table 1   Classification by building type

Type	Class 1	Class 2
Industrial	Storage sheds	Speculative factories and warehouses Assembly and machine workshops Transport garages
Agricultural	Barns and sheds	Stables
Commercial	Speculative shops Surface parks	Multi-storey and underground car parks
Community		Community halls
Residential		Dormitory hostels
Education		
Recreation		
Medical/Social services		

ARCHITECTS' FEES

Class 3	Class 4	Class 5
Purpose-built factories and warehouses		
Animal breeding units		
Supermarkets Banks Purpose-built shops Office developments Retail warehouses Garages/showrooms	Department stores Shopping centres Food processing units Breweries Telecommunications and computer buildings Restaurants Public houses	High risk research and production buildings Research and development laboratories Radio, TV and recording studios
Community centres Branch libraries Ambulances and fire stations Bus stations Railway stations Airports Police stations Prisons Postal buildings Broadcasting	Civic centres Churches and crematoria Specialist libraries Museums and art galleries Magistrates/County Courts	Theatres Opera houses Concert halls Cinemas Crown Courts
Estates housing and flats Barracks Sheltered housing Housing for single people Student housing	Parsonages/manses Apartment blocks Hotels Housing for the handicapped Housing for the frail elderly	Houses and flats for individual clients
Primary/nursery/first schools	Other schools, including middle and secondary University complexes	University laboratories
Sports halls Squash courts	Swimming pools Leisure complexes	Leisure pools Specialised complexes
Clinics	Health centres General hospitals Nursing homes Surgeries	Teaching hospitals Hospital laboratories Dental surgeries

Fees for Professional Services

Table 2   Indicative percentage fees for new works

Construction Cost £	Class 1 %	Class 2 %	Class 3 %	Class 4 %	Class 5 %
50,000	7.90	8.70	-	-	-
75,000	7.25	7.80	8.40	-	-
100,000	7.10	7.60	8.20	8.90	9.60
250,000	6.20	6.70	7.20	7.80	8.40
500,000	5.75	6.25	6.75	7.25	7.90
1,000,000	5.40	5.90	6.20	6.80	7.50
2,500,000	5.15	5.60	6.10	6.60	7.10
5,000,000	-	-	5.97	6.50	7.00
over 10,000,000	-	-	5.95	6.45	6.97

Table 3   Indicative percentage fees for works to existing buildings

Construction Cost £	Class 1 %	Class 2 %	Class 3 %	Class 4 %	Class 5 %
50,000	11.60	12.60	-	-	-
75,000	10.70	11.60	12.40	-	-
100,000	10.40	11.30	12.20	13.15	14.10
250,000	9.30	10.10	10.85	11.75	12.55
500,000	8.70	9.45	10.20	11.05	11.80
1,000,000	8.25	9.00	9.70	10.55	11.30
2,500,000	-	-	9.25	10.00	10.75
5,000,000	-	-	9.10	9.85	10.55
over 10,000,000	-	-	9.00	9.75	10.45

Table 4   Indicative hourly rates

Type of work	General	Complex	Specialist
Partner/Director or equivalent	£95	£140	£180
Senior Architect	£75	£105	£140
Architect	£55	£75	£95

QUANTITY SURVEYORS' FEES

Author's Note:

The Royal Institution of Chartered Surveyors formally abolished the standard Quantity Surveyors' fee scales with effect from 31 December 1998. A guidance booklet to assist practitioners in compiling fee proposals is due to be published, although this has not materialised at the time of going to press. The last standard Quantity Surveyors' fee scales have therefore been reproduced here in order to assist the reader until the guidance booklet is published.

SCALE 36 INCLUSIVE OF PROFESSIONAL CHARGES FOR QUANTITY SURVEYING SERVICES FOR BUILDING WORKS ISSUED BY THE ROYAL INSTITUTION OF CHARTERED SURVEYORS.
The scale is recommended and not mandatory.

EFFECTIVE FROM JULY 1988

1.0. GENERALLY

1.1 This scale is for the use when an inclusive scale of professional charges is considered to appropriate by mutual agreement between the employer and the quantity surveyor.

1.2. This scale does not apply to civil engineering works, housing schemes financed by local authorities and the Housing Corporation and housing improvement work for which separate scales of fees have been published.

1.3. The fees cover quantity surveying services as may be required in connection with a building project irrespective of the type of contract from initial appointment to final certification of the contractor's account such as:

(a) Budget estimating; cost planning and advice on tendering procedures and contract arrangements.

(b) Preparing tendering documents for main contract and specialist sub-contracts; examining tenders received and reporting thereon or negotiating tenders and pricing with a selected contractor and/or sub-contractors.

(c) Preparing recommendations for interim payments on account to the contractor; preparing periodic assessments of anticipated final cost and reporting thereon; measuring work and adjusting variations in accordance with the terms of the contract and preparing final account, pricing same and agreeing totals with the contractor.

(d) Providing a reasonable number of copies of bills of quantities and other documents; normal travelling and other expenses. Additional copies of documents, abnormal travelling and other expenses (e.g. in remote areas or overseas) and the provision of checkers on site shall be charged in addition by prior arrangement with the employer.

1.4. If any of the materials used in the works are supplied by the employer or charged at a preferential rate, then the actual or estimated market value thereof shall be included in the amounts upon which fees are to be calculated.

1.5. If the quantity surveyor incurs additional costs due to exceptional delays in building operations or any other cause beyond the control of the quantity surveyor then the fees may be adjusted by agreement between the employer and the quantity surveyor to cover the reimbursement of these additional costs.

1.6. The fees and charges are in all cases exclusive of value added tax which will be applied in accordance with legislation.

1.7. Copyright in bills of quantities and other documents prepared by the quantity surveyor is reserved to the quantity surveyor.

QUANTITY SURVEYORS' FEES

2.0. INCLUSIVE SCALE

2.1.   The fees for the services outlined in para.1.3, subject to the provision of para. 2.2, shall
be as follows:

(a)   **Category A:** Relatively complex works and/or works with little or no repetition.

Examples:
Ambulance and fire stations; banks; cinemas; clubs; computer buildings; council
offices; crematoria; fitting out of existing buildings; homes for the elderly; hospitals and
nursing homes; laboratories; law courts; libraries; "one off" houses; petrol stations;
places of religious worship; police stations; public houses, licensed premises;
restaurants; sheltered housing; sports pavilions; theatres; town halls; universities,
polytechnics and colleges of further education (other than halls of residence and
hostels); and the like.

Value of work	£	Category A fee £	£
Up to	150 000	380 + 6.0% (Minimum fee £3 380)	
150 000 -	300 000	9 380 + 5.0% on balance over	150 000
300 000 -	600 000	16 880 + 4.3% on balance over	300 000
600 000 - 1 500 000		29 780 + 3.4% on balance over	600 000
1 500 000 - 3 000 000		60 380 + 3.0% on balance over	1 500 000
3 000 000 - 6 000 000		105 380 + 2.8% on balance over	3 000 000
Over	6 000 000	189 380 + 2.4% on balance over	6 000 000

(b)   **Category B:** Less complex works and/or works with some element of repetition.

Examples:
Adult education facilities; canteens; church halls; community centres; departmental
stores; enclosed sports stadia and swimming baths; halls of residence; hostels; motels;
offices other than those included in Categories A and C; railway stations; recreation
and leisure centres; residential hotels; schools; self-contained flats and maisonettes;
shops and shopping centres; supermarkets and hypermarkets; telephone exchanges;
and the like.

Value of work	£	Category B fee £	£
Up to	150 000	360 + 5.8% (Minimum fee £3 260)	
150 000 -	300 000	9 060 + 4.7% on balance over	150 000
300 000 -	600 000	16 110 + 3.9% on balance over	300 000
600 000 - 1 500 000		27 810 + 2.8% on balance over	600 000
1 500 000 - 3 000 000		53 010 + 2.6% on balance over	1 500 000
3 000 000 - 6 000 000		92 010 + 2.4% on balance over	3 000 000
Over	6 000 000	164 010 + 2.0% on balance over	6 000 000

(c)   **Category C:** Simple works and/or works with a substantial element of repetition.

Examples:
Factories; garages; multi-storey car parks; open-air sports stadia; structural shell
offices not fitted out; warehouses; workshops; and the like.

QUANTITY SURVEYORS' FEES

Value of work £		Category C fee	£
Up to	150 000	300 + 4.9% (Minimum fee £2 750)	
150 000 -	300 000	7 650 + 4.1% on balance over	150 000
300 000 -	600 000	13 800 + 3.3% on balance over	300 000
600 000 -	1 500 000	23 700 + 2.5% on balance over	600 000
1 500 000 -	3 000 000	46 200 + 2.2% on balance over	1 500 000
3 000 000 -	6 000 000	79 200 + 2.0% on balance over	3 000 000
Over	6 000 000	139 200 + 1.6% on balance over	6 000 000

(d) Fees shall be calculated upon the total of the final account for the whole of the work including all nominated sub-contractors' and nominated supplier's accounts. When work normally included in a building contract is the subject of a separate contract for which the quantity surveyor has not been paid fees under any other clause hereof, the value of such work shall be included in the amount upon which fees are charged.

(e) When a contract comprises buildings which fall into more than one category, the fee shall be calculated as follows:

(i) The amount upon which fees are chargeable shall be allocated to the categories of work applicable and the amounts so allocated expressed as percentages of the total amount upon which fees are chargeable.

(ii) Fees shall then be calculated for each category on the total amount upon which fees are chargeable.

(iii) The fee chargeable shall then be calculated by applying the percentages of work in each category to the appropriate total fee and adding the resultant amounts.

(iv) A consolidated percentage fee applicable to the total value of the work may be charged by prior agreement between the employer and the quantity surveyor. Such a percentage shall be based on this scale and on the estimated cost of the various categories of work and calculated in accordance with the principles stated above.

(f) When a project is subject to a number of contracts then, for the purpose of calculating fees, the values of such contracts shall not be aggregated but each contract shall be taken separately and the scale of charges (paras. 2.1 (a) to (e)) applied as appropriate.

2.2. Air conditioning, heating, ventilating and electrical services

(a) When the services outlined in para. 1.3 are provided by the quantity surveyor for the air conditioning, heating, ventilating and electrical services there shall be a fee for these services in addition to the fee calculated in accordance with para. 2.1 as follows:

Value of work £		Additional fee	£
Up to	120 000	5.0%	
120 000 -	240 000	6 000 + 4.7% on balance over	120 000
240 000 -	480 000	11 640 + 4.0% on balance over	240 000
480 000 -	750 000	21 240 + 3.6% on balance over	480 000
750 000 -	1 000 000	30 960 + 3.0% on balance over	750 000
1 000 000 -	4 000 000	38 460 + 2.7% on balance over	1 000 000
Over	4 000 000	119 200 + 2.4% on balance over	4 000 000

(b) The value of such services, whether the subject of separate tenders or not, shall be aggregated and the total value of work so obtained used for the purpose of calculating the additional fee chargeable in accordance with para. (a). (Except that when more than one firm of consulting engineers is engaged on the design of these services, the separate values for which each such firm is responsible shall be aggregated and the additional fees charged shall be calculated independently on each such total value so obtained.)

QUANTITY SURVEYORS' FEES

    (c)   Fees shall be calculated upon the basis of the account for the whole of the air conditioning, heating, ventilating and electrical services for which bills of quantities and final accounts have been prepared by the quantity surveyor.

2.3   Works of alteration
On works of alteration or repair, or on those sections of the work which are mainly works of alteration or repair, there shall be a fee of 1.0% in addition to the fee calculated in accordance with paras. 2.1 and 2.2.

2.4.   Works of redecoration and associated minor repairs
On works of redecoration and associated minor repairs, there shall be a fee of 1.5% in addition to the fee calculated in accordance with paras. 2.1 and 2.2.

2.5.   Generally
If the works are substantially varied at any stage or if the quantity surveyor is involved in an excessive amount of abortive work, then the fees shall be adjusted by agreement between the employer and the quantity surveyor.

3.0.   ADDITIONAL SERVICES

3.1.   For additional services not normally necessary, such as those arising as a result of the termination of a contract before completion, liquidation, fire damage to the buildings, services in connection with arbitration, litigation and investigation of the validity of contractors' claims, services in connection with taxation matters, and all similar services where the employer specifically instructs the quantity surveyor, the charges shall be in accordance with para. 4.0 below.

4.0.   TIME CHARGES

4.1. (a)   For consultancy and other services performed by a principal, a fee by arrangement according to the circumstances including the professional status and qualifications of the quantity surveyor.
     (b)   When a principal does work which would normally be done by a member of staff, the charge shall be calculated as para. 4.2 below.

4.2. (a)   For services by a member of staff, the charges for which are to be based on the time involved, such charges shall be calculated on the hourly cost of the individual involved plus 145%.
     (b)   A member of staff shall include a principal doing work normally done by an employee (as para. 4.1 (b) above), technical and supporting staff, but shall exclude secretarial staff or staff engaged upon general administration.
     (c)   For the purpose of para. 4.2 (b) above, a principal's time shall be taken at the rate applicable to a senior assistant in the firm.
     (d)   The supervisory duties of a principal shall be deemed to be included in the addition of 145% as para. 4.2 (a) above and shall not be charged separately.
     (e)   The hourly cost to the employer shall be calculated by taking the sum of the annual cost of the member of staff of:

       (i)   Salary and bonus but excluding expenses;
      (ii)   Employer's contributions payable under any Pension and Life Assurance Schemes;
     (iii)   Employer's contributions made under the National Insurance Acts, the Redundancy Payments Act and any other payments made in respect of the employee by virtue of any statutory requirements; and
     (iv)   Any other payments or benefits made or granted by the employer in pursuance of the terms of employment of the member of staff;

and dividing by 1,650.

QUANTITY SURVEYORS' FEES

5.0. INSTALMENT PAYMENTS

5.1 In the absence of agreement to the contrary, fees shall be paid by instalments as follows:

(a) Upon acceptance by the employer of a tender for the works, one half of the fee calculated on the amount of the accepted tender.

(b) The balance by instalments at intervals to be agreed between the date of the first certificate and one month after final certification of the contractor's account.

5.2. (a) In the event of no tender being accepted, one half of the fee shall be paid within three months of completion of the tender documents. The fee shall be calculated upon the basis of the lowest original bona fide tender received. In the event of no tender being received, the fee shall be calculated upon a reasonable valuation of the works based upon the tender documents.

(b) In the event of the project being abandoned at any stage other than those covered by the foregoing, the proportion of fee payable shall be by agreement between the employer and the quantity surveyor.

NOTE: In the foregoing context "bona fide tender" shall be deemed to mean a tender submitted in good faith without major errors of computation and not subsequently withdrawn by the tenderer.

SCALE 37 ITEMISED SCALE OF PROFESSIONAL CHARGES FOR QUANTITY SURVEYING SERVICES FOR BUILDING WORK ISSUED BY THE ROYAL INSTITUTION OF CHARTERED SURVEYORS.

The scale is recommended and not mandatory.

EFFECTIVE FROM JULY 1988

1.0. GENERALLY

1.1. The fees are in all cases exclusive of travelling and other expenses (for which the actual disbursement is recoverable unless there is some prior arrangement for such charges) and of the cost of reproduction of bills of quantities and other documents, which are chargeable in addition at net cost.

1.2. The fees are in all cases exclusive of services in connection with the allocation of the cost of the works for purposes of calculating value added tax for which there shall be an additional fee based on the time involved (see paras. 19.1 and 19.2).

1.3. If any of the materials used in the works are supplied by the employer or charged at a preferential rate, then the actual or estimated market value thereof shall be included in the amounts upon which fees are to be calculated.

1.4. The fees are in all cases exclusive of preparing a specification of the materials to be used and the works to be done, but the fees for preparing bills of quantities and similar documents do include for incorporating preamble clauses describing the materials and workmanship (from instructions given by the architect and/or consulting engineer)

1.5. If the quantity surveyor incurs additional costs due to exceptional delays in building operations or any other cause beyond the control of the quantity surveyor then the fees may be adjusted by agreement between the employer and the quantity surveyor to cover the reimbursement of these additional costs.

1.6. The fees and charges are in all cases exclusive of value added tax which will be applied in accordance with legislation.

QUANTITY SURVEYORS' FEES

1.7. Copyright in bills of quantities and other documents prepared by the quantity surveyor is reserved to the quantity surveyor.

CONTRACTS BASED ON BILLS OF QUANTITIES: PRE-CONTRACT SERVICES

2.0. BILLS OF QUANTITIES

2.1. Basic scale

For preparing bills of quantities and examining tenders received and reporting thereon.

(a) **Category A:** Relatively complex works and/or works with little or no repetition.

Examples:
Ambulance and fire stations; banks; cinemas; clubs; computer buildings; council offices; crematoria; fitting out of existing buildings; homes for the elderly; hospitals and nursing homes; laboratories; law courts; libraries; "one off" houses; petrol stations; places of religious worship; police stations; public houses; licensed premises; restaurants; sheltered housing; sports pavilions; theatres; town halls; universities, polytechnics and colleges of further education (other than halls of residence and hostels); and the like.

Value of work	£	Category A fee	£	£
Up to	150 000	230 + 3.0% (Minimum fee £1730)		
150 000 -	300 000	4 730 + 2.3% on balance over	150 000	
300 000 -	600 000	8 180 + 1.8% on balance over	300 000	
600 000 -	1 500 000	13 580 + 1.5% on balance over	600 000	
1 500 000 -	3 000 000	27 080 + 1.2% on balance over	1 500 000	
3 000 000 -	6 000 000	45 080 + 1.1% on balance over	3 000 000	
Over	6 000 000	78 080 + 1.0% on balance over	6 000 000	

(b) **Category B:** Less complex works and/or works with some element of repetition.

Examples:
Adult education facilities; canteens; church halls; community centres; departmental stores; enclosed sports stadia and swimming baths; halls of residence; hostels; motels; offices other than those included in Categories A and C; railway stations; recreation and leisure centres; residential hotels; schools; self-contained flats and maisonettes; shops and shopping centres; supermarkets and hypermarkets; telephone exchanges; and the like.

Value of work		Category B fee	£	£
Up to	150 000	210 + 2.8% (Minimum fee £1 680)		
150 000 -	300 000	4 410 + 2.0% on balance over	150 000	
300 000 -	600 000	7 410 + 1.5% on balance over	300 000	
600 000 -	1 500 000	11 910 + 1.1% on balance over	600 000	
1 500 000 -	3 000 000	21 810 + 1.0% on balance over	1 500 000	
3 000 000 -	6 000 000	36 810 + 0.9% on balance over	3 000 000	
Over	6 000 000	63 810 + 0.8% on balance over	6 000 000	

(c) **Category C:** Simple works and/or works with a substantial element of repetition

Examples:
Factories; garages; multi-storey car parks; open-air sports stadia; structural shell offices not fitted out; warehouses; workshops and the like.

QUANTITY SURVEYORS' FEES

Value of work	£	Category C fee	£
		£	
Up to	150 000	180 + 2.5% (Minimum fee £1 430)	
150 000 -	300 000	3 930 + 1.8% on balance over	150 000
300 000 -	600 000	6 630 + 1.2% on balance over	300 000
600 000 -	1 500 000	10 230 + 0.9% on balance over	600 000
1 500 000 -	3 000 000	18 330 + 0.8% on balance over	1 500 000
3 000 000 -	6 000 000	30 330 + 0.7% on balance over	3 000 000
Over	6 000 000	51 330 + 0.6% on balance over	6 000 000

(d)   The scales of fees for preparing bills of quantities (paras. 2.1 (a) to (c)) are overall scales based upon the inclusion of all provisional and prime cost items, subject to the provision of para. 2.1 (g). When work normally included in a building contract is the subject of a separate contract for which the quantity surveyor has not been paid fees under any other clause hereof, the value of such work shall be included in the amount upon which fees are charged.

(e)   Fees shall be calculated upon the accepted tender for the whole of he work subject to the provisions of para. 2.6. In the event of no tender being accepted, fees shall be calculated upon the basis of the lowest original bona fide tender received. In the event of no such tender being received, the fees shall be calculated upon a reasonable valuation of the works based upon the original bills of quantities.

NOTE: In the foregoing context "bona fide tender" shall be deemed to mean a tender submitted in good faith without major errors of computation and not subsequently withdrawn by the tenderer.

(f)   In calculating the amount upon which fees are charged the total of any credits and the totals of any alternative bills shall be aggregated and added to the amount described above. The value of any omission or addition forming part of an alternative bill shall not be added unless measurement or abstraction from the original dimension sheets was necessary.

(g)   Where the value of the air conditioning, heating, ventilating and electrical services included in the tender documents together exceeds 25% of the amount calculated as described in paras. 2.1 (d) and (e), then, subject to the provisions of para. 2.2, no fee is chargeable on the amount by which the value of these services exceeds the said 25%. In this context the term "value" excludes general contractor's profit, attendance, builder's work in connection with the services, preliminaries and any similar additions.

(h)   When a contract comprises buildings which fall into more than one category, the fee shall be calculated as follows:

(i)   The amount upon which fees are chargeable shall be allocated to the categories of work applicable and the amounts so allocated expressed as percentages of the total amount upon which fees are chargeable.

(ii)   Fees shall then be calculated for each category on the total amount upon which fees are chargeable.

(iii)   The fee chargeable shall then be calculated by applying the percentages of work in each category to the appropriate total fee and adding the resultant amounts.

(j)   When a project is the subject of a number of contracts then, for the purpose of calculating fees, the values of such contracts shall not be aggregated but each contract shall be taken separately and the scale of charges (paras. 2.1 (a) to (h)) applied as appropriate.

(k)   Where the quantity surveyor is specifically instructed to provide cost planning services the fee calculated in accordance with paras. 2.1 (a) to (j) shall be increased by a sum calculated in accordance with the following table and based upon the same value of work as that upon which the aforementioned fee has been calculated:

QUANTITY SURVEYORS' FEES

Categories A & B: (as defined in paras. 2.1 (a) and (b)).

Value of work £	Fee	£
	£	
Up to 600 000	0.70%	
600 000 - 3 000 000	4 200 + 0.40% on balance over	600 000
3 000 000 - 6 000 000	13 800 + 0.35% on balance over	3 000 000
Over 6 000 000	24 300 + 0.30% on balance over	6 000 000

Category C: (as defined in paras. 2.1 (c))

Value of work £	Fee	£
	£	
Up to 600 000	0.50%	
600 000 - 3 000 000	3 000 + 0.30% on balance over	600 000
3 000 000 - 6 000 000	10 200 + 0.25% on balance over	3 000 000
Over 6 000 000	17 700 + 0.20% on balance over	6 000 000

2.2.   Air conditioning, heating, ventilating and electrical services

(a)   Where bills of quantities are prepared by the quantity surveyor for the air conditioning, heating, ventilating and electrical services there shall be a fee for these services (which shall include examining tenders received and reporting thereon), in addition to the fee calculated in accordance with para. 2.1, as follows:

Value of work £	Additional fee	£
	£	
Up to 120 000	2.50%	
120 000 - 240 000	3 000 + 2.25% on balance over	120 000
240 000 - 480 000	5 700 + 2.00% on balance over	240 000
480 000 - 750 000	10 500 + 1.75% on balance over	480 000
750 000 - 1 000 000	15 225 + 1.25% on balance over	750 000
Over 1 000 000	18 350 + 1.15% on balance over	1 000 000

(b)   The values of such services, whether the subject of separate tenders or not, shall be aggregated and the total value of work so obtained used for the purpose of calculating the additional fee chargeable in accordance with para. (a). (Except that when more than one firm of consulting engineers is engaged on the design of these services, the separate values for which each such firm is responsible shall be aggregated and the additional fees charged shall be calculated independently on each such total value so obtained.)

(c)   Fees shall be calculated upon the accepted tender for the whole of the air conditioning, heating, ventilating and electrical services for which bills of quantities have been prepared by the quantity surveyor. In the event of no tender being accepted, fees shall be calculated upon the basis of the lowest original bona fide tender received. In the event of no such tender being received, the fees shall be calculated upon a reasonable valuation of the services based upon the original bills of quantities.

NOTE   In the foregoing context "bona fide tender"' shall be deemed to mean a tender submitted in good faith without major errors of computation and not subsequently withdrawn by the tenderer.

(d)   When cost planning services are provided by the quantity surveyor for air conditioning, heating, ventilating and electrical services (or for any part of such services) there shall be an additional fee based on the time involved (see paras. 19.1 and 19.2). Alternatively the fee may be on a lump sum or percentage basis agreed between the employer and the quantity surveyor.

QUANTITY SURVEYORS' FEES

      NOTE   The incorporation of figures for air conditioning, heating, ventilating and electrical services provided by the consulting engineer is deemed to be included in the quantity surveyor's services under para. 2.1.

2.3.   Works of alteration
On works of alteration or repair, or on those sections of the works which are mainly works of alteration or repair, there shall be a fee of 1.0% in addition to the fee calculated in accordance with paras. 2.1 and 2.2.

2.4.   Works of redecoration and associated minor repairs,
On works of redecoration and associated minor repairs, there shall be a fee of 1.5% in addition to the fee calculated in accordance with paras. 2.1 and 2.2.

2.5.   Bills of quantities prepared in special forms
Fees calculated in accordance with paras. 2.1, 2.2, 2.3 and 2.4 include for the preparation of bills of quantities on a normal trade basis. If the employer requires additional information to be provided in the bills of quantities or the bills to be prepared in an elemental, operational or similar form, then the fee may be adjusted by agreement between the employer and the quantity surveyor.

2.6.   Reduction of tenders

(a)   When cost planning services have been provided by the quantity surveyor and a tender, when received, is reduced before acceptance, and if the reductions are not necessitated by amended instructions of the employer or by the inclusion in the bills of quantities of items which the quantity surveyor has indicated could not be contained within the approved estimate, then in such a case no charge shall be made by the quantity surveyor for the preparation of bills of reductions and the fee for the preparation of the bills of quantities shall be based on the amount of the reduced tender.

(b)   When cost planning services have not been provided by the quantity surveyor and if a tender, when received, is reduced before acceptance, fees are to be calculated upon the amount of the unreduced tender. When the preparation of bills of reductions is required, a fee is chargeable for preparing such bills of reductions as follows:

(i)   2.0% upon the gross amount of all omissions requiring measurement or abstraction from original dimensional sheets.
(ii)   3.0% upon the gross amount of all additions requiring measurement.
(iii)   0.5% upon the gross amount of all remaining additions.

NOTE: The above scale for the preparation of bills of reductions applies to work in all categories.

2.7   Generally
If the works are substantially varied at any stage or if the quantity surveyor is involved in an excessive amount of abortive work, then the fees shall be adjusted by agreement between the employer and the quantity surveyor.

3.0.   NEGOTIATING TENDERS

3.1. (a)   For negotiating and agreeing prices with a contractor:

Value of work	£	Fee	£
Up to	150 000	0.5%	
150 000 -	600 000	750 + 0.3% on balance over	150 000
600 000 -	1 200 000	2 100 + 0.2% on balance over	600 000
Over	1 200 000	3 300 + 0.1% on balance over	1 200 000

QUANTITY SURVEYORS' FEES

    (b)   The fee shall be calculated on the total value of the works as defined in paras. 2.1 (d), (e), (f), (g) and (j).

    (c)   For negotiating and agreeing prices with a contractor for air conditioning, heating, ventilating and electrical services there shall be an additional fee as para. 3.1 (a) calculated on the total value of such services as defined in para. 2.2 (b).

4.0. CONSULTATIVE SERVICES AND PRICING BILLS OF QUANTITIES

4.1.   Consultative services

Where the quantity surveyor is appointed to prepare approximate estimates, feasibility studies or submissions for the approval of financial grants or similar services, then the fee shall be based on the time involved (see paras. 19.1 and 19.2) or alternatively, on a lump sum or percentage basis agreed between the employer and the quantity surveyor.

4.2.   Pricing bills of quantities

    (a)   For pricing bills of quantities, if instructed, to provide an estimate comparable with tenders, the fee shall be one-third (33.33%) of the fee for negotiating and agreeing prices with a contractor, calculated in accordance with paras. 3.1 (a) and (b).

    (b)   For pricing bills of quantities, if instructed, to provide an estimate comparable with tenders for air conditioning, heating, ventilating and electrical services the fee shall be one-third (33.33%) of the fee calculated in accordance with para. 3.1. (c).

CONTRACTS BASED ON BILLS OF QUANTITIES: POST-CONTRACT SERVICES

Alternative scales (I and II) for post-contract services are set out below to be used at the quantity surveyor's discretion by prior agreement with the employer.

5.0. ALTERNATIVE I: OVERALL SCALE OF CHARGES FOR POST-CONTRACT SERVICES

5.1.   If the quantity surveyor appointed to carry out the post-contract services did not prepare the bills of quantities then the fees in paras. 5.2 and 5.3 shall be increased to cover the additional services undertaken by the quantity surveyor.

5.2.   Basic scale

For taking particulars and reporting valuations for interim certificates for payments on account to the contractor, preparing periodic assessments of anticipated final cost and reporting thereon, measuring and making up bills of variations including pricing and agreeing totals with the contractor, and adjusting fluctuations in the cost of labour and materials if required by the contract.

    (a)   **Category A:** Relatively complex works and/or works with little or no repetition.

    Examples:
Ambulance and fire stations; banks; cinemas; clubs; computer buildings; council offices; crematoria; fitting out existing buildings; homes for the elderly; hospitals and nursing homes; laboratories; law courts; libraries; "one-off" houses; petrol stations; places of religious worship; police stations; public houses; licensed premises; restaurants; sheltered housing; sports pavilions; theatres; town halls; universities, polytechnics and colleges of further education (other than halls of residence and hostels); and the like.

QUANTITY SURVEYORS' FEES

Value of work £		Category A fee £	£
Up to	150 000	150 + 2.0% (Minimum fee £1 150)	
150 000 -	300 000	3 150 + 1.7% on balance over	150 000
300 000 -	600 000	5 700 + 1.6% on balance over	300 000
600 000 -	1 500 000	10 500 + 1.3% on balance over	600 000
1 500 000 -	3 000 000	22 200 + 1.2% on balance over	1 500 000
3 000 000 -	6 000 000	40 200 + 1.1% on balance over	3 000 000
Over	6 000 000	73 200 + 1.0% on balance over	6 000 000

(b)   **Category B**: Less complex works and/or works with some element of repetition.

Examples:
Adult education facilities; canteens; church halls; community centres; departmental stores; enclosed sports stadia and swimming baths; halls of residence; hostels; motels; offices other than those included in Categories A and C; railway stations; recreation and leisure centres; residential hotels; schools; self-contained flats and maisonettes; shops and shopping centres; supermarkets and hypermarkets; telephone exchanges; and the like.

Value of work £		Category B fee £	£
Up to	150 000	150 + 2.0% (Minimum fee £1 150)	
150 000 -	300 000	3 150 + 1.7% on balance over	150 000
300 000 -	600 000	5 700 + 1.5% on balance over	300 000
600 000 -	1 500 000	10 200 + 1.1% on balance over	600 000
1 500 000 -	3 000 000	20 100 + 1.0% on balance over	1 500 000
3 000 000 -	6 000 000	35 100 + 0.9% on balance over	3 000 000
Over	6 000 000	62 100 + 0.8% on balance over	6 000 000

(c)   **Category C**: Simple works and/or works with a substantial element of repetition.

Examples:
Factories; garages; multi-storey car parks; open-air sports stadia; structural shell offices not fitted out; warehouses; workshops; and the like.

Value of work £		Category C fee £	£
Up to	150 000	120 + 1.6% (Minimum fee £920)	
150 000 -	300 000	2 520 + 1.5% on balance over	150 000
300 000 -	600 000	4 770 + 1.4% on balance over	300 000
600 000 -	1 500 000	8 970 + 1.1% on balance over	600 000
1 500 000 -	3 000 000	18 870 + 0.9% on balance over	1 500 000
3 000 000 -	6 000 000	32 370 + 0.8% on balance over	3 000 000
Over	6 000 000	56 370 + 0.7% on balance over	6 000 000

(d)   The scales of fees for post-contract services (paras. 5.2 (a) to (c)) are overall scales based upon the inclusion of all nominated sub-contractors' and nominated suppliers' accounts, subject to the provision of para. 5.2 (g). When work normally included in a building contract is the subject of a separate contract for which the quantity surveyor has not been paid fees under any other clause hereof, the value of such work shall be included in the amount on which fees are charged.

(e)   Fees shall be calculated upon the basis of the account for the whole of the work, subject to the provisions of para. 5.3.

(f)   In calculating the amount on which fees are charged the total of any credits is to be added to the amount described above.

QUANTITY SURVEYORS' FEES

(g)   Where the value of air conditioning, heating, ventilating and electrical services included in the tender documents together exceeds 25% of the amount calculated as described in paras. 5.2. (d) and (e) above, then, subject to provisions of para. 5.3, no fee is chargeable on the amount by which the value of these services exceeds the said 25%. In this context the term "value" excludes general contractors' profit, attendance, builders work in connection with the services, preliminaries and other similar additions.

(h)   When a contract comprises buildings which fall into more than one category, the fee shall be calculated as follows:

  (i)   The amount upon which fees are chargeable shall be allocated to the categories of work applicable and the amounts so allocated expressed as percentages of the total amount upon which fees are chargeable.
  (ii)   Fees shall then be calculated for each category on the total amount upon which fees are chargeable.
  (iii) The fee chargeable shall then be calculated by applying the percentages of work in each category to the appropriate total fee and adding the resultant amounts.

(j)   When a project is the subject of a number of contracts then, for the purposes of calculating fees, the values of such contracts shall not be aggregated but each contract shall be taken separately and the scale of charges (paras. 5.2 (a) to (h)), applied as appropriate.

(k)   When the quantity surveyor is required to prepare valuations of materials or goods off site, an additional fee shall be charged based on the time involved (see paras. 19.1 and 19.2).

(l)   The basic scale for post-contract services includes for a simple routine of periodically estimating final costs. When the employer specifically requests a cost monitoring service which involves the quantity surveyor in additional or abortive measurement an additional fee shall be charged based on the time involved (see paras. 19.1 and 19.2), or alternatively on a lump sum or percentage basis agreed between the employer and the quantity surveyor.

(m)   The above overall scales of charges for post-contract services assume normal conditions when the bills of quantities are based on drawings accurately depicting the building work the employer requires. If the works are materially varied to the extent that substantial remeasurement is necessary then the fee for post contract services shall be adjusted by agreement between the employer and the quantity surveyor.

5.3. Air conditioning, heating, ventilating and electrical services

(a)   Where final accounts are prepared by the quantity surveyor for the air conditioning, heating, ventilating and electrical services there shall be a fee for these services, in addition to the fee calculated in accordance with para. 5.2, as follows:

Value of work	£	Additional fee	£
	£	£	
Up to	120 000	2.00%	
120 000 -	240 000	2 400 + 1.60% on balance over	120 000
240 000 -	1 000 000	4 320 + 1.25% on balance over	240 000
1 000 000 -	4 000 000	13 820 + 1.00% on balance over	1 000 000
Over	4 000 000	43 820 + 0.90% on balance over	4 000 000

(b)   The values of such services, whether the subject of separate tenders or not, shall be aggregated and the total value of work so obtained used for the purpose of calculating the additional fee chargeable in accordance with para. (a). (Except that when more than one firm of consulting engineers is engaged on the design of these services the separate values for which each such firm is responsible shall be aggregated and the additional fee charged shall be calculated independently on each such total value so obtained.)

QUANTITY SURVEYORS' FEES

(c) The scope of the services to be provided by the quantity surveyor under para. (a) above shall be deemed to be equivalent to those described for the basic scale for post-contract services.

(d) When the quantity surveyor is required to prepare periodic valuations of materials or goods off site, an additional fee shall be charged based on the time involved (see paras. 19.1 and 19.2).

(e) The basic scale for post-contract services includes for a simple routine of periodically estimating final costs. When the employer specifically requests a cost monitoring service which involves the quantity surveyor in additional or abortive measurement an additional fee shall be based on the time involved (see paras. 19.1 and 19.2), or alternatively on a lump sum or percentage basis agreed between the employer and the quantity surveyor.

(f) Fees shall be calculated upon the basis of the account for the whole of the air conditioning, heating, ventilating and electrical services for which final accounts have been prepared by the quantity surveyor.

6.0. ALTERNATIVE II: SCALE OF CHARGES FOR SEPARATE STAGES OF POST-CONTRACT SERVICES

6.1. If the quantity surveyor appointed to carry out the post-contract services did not prepare the bills of quantities then the fees in paras. 6.2 and 6.3 shall be increased to cover the additional services undertaken by the quantity surveyor.

NOTE: The scales of fees in paras. 6.2 and 6.3 apply to work in all categories (including air conditioning, heating, ventilating and electrical services).

6.2. Valuations for interim certificates

(a) For taking particulars and reporting valuations for interim certificates for payments on account to the contractor.

Total of valuations £	Fee	£
Up to 300 000	0.5%	
300 000 - 1 000 000	1 500 + 0.4% on balance over	300 000
1 000 000 - 6 000 000	4 300 + 0.3% on balance over	1 000 000
Over 6 000 000	19 300 + 0.2% on balance over	6 000 000

NOTES:

1. Subject to note 2 below, the fees are to be calculated on the total of all interim valuations (i.e. the amount of the final account less only the net amount of the final valuation).

2. When consulting engineers are engaged in supervising the installation of air conditioning, heating, ventilating and electrical services and their duties include reporting valuations for inclusion in interim certificates for payments on account in respect of such services, then valuations so reported shall be excluded from any total amount of valuations used for calculating fees.

(b) When the quantity surveyor is required to prepare valuations of materials or goods off site, an additional fee shall be charged based on the time involved (see paras. 19.1 and 19.2).

6.3. Preparing accounts of variation upon contracts
For measuring and making up bills of variations including pricing and agreeing totals with the contractor:

(a) An initial lump sum of £600 shall be payable on each contract.

QUANTITY SURVEYORS' FEES

(b) 2.0% upon the gross amount of omissions requiring measurement or abstraction from the original dimension sheets.

(c) 3.0% upon the gross amount of additions requiring measurement and upon dayworks.

(d) 0.5% upon the gross amount of remaining additions which shall be deemed to include all nominated sub-contractors' and nominated suppliers' accounts which do not involve measurement or checking of quantities but only checking against lump sum estimates.

(e) 3.0% upon the aggregate of the amounts of the increases and/or decreases in the cost of labour and materials in accordance with any fluctuations clause in the conditions of contract, except where a price adjustment formula applies.

(f) On contracts where fluctuations are calculated by the use of a price adjustment formula method the following scale shall be applied to the account for the whole of the work:

Value of work	£	Fee	
		£	£
Up to	300 000	300 + 0.5%	
300 000 -	1 000 000	1 800 + 0.3% on balance over	300 000
Over	1 000 000	3 900 + 0.1% on balance over	1 000 000

(g) When consulting engineers are engaged in supervising the installation of air conditioning, heating, ventilating and electrical services and their duties include for the adjustment of accounts and pricing and agreeing totals with the sub-contractors for inclusion in the measured account, then any totals so agreed shall be excluded from any amounts used for calculating fees.

6.4. Cost monitoring services

The fee for providing all approximate estimates of final cost and/or a cost monitoring service shall be based on the time involved (see paras. 19.1 and 19.2), or alternatively on a lump sum or percentage basis agreed between the employer and the quantity surveyor.

7.0. BILLS OF APPROXIMATE QUANTITIES, INTERIM CERTIFICATES AND FINAL ACCOUNTS

7.1. Basic scale

For preparing bills of approximate quantities suitable for obtaining competitive tenders which will provide a schedule of prices and a reasonably close forecast of the cost of the works, but subject to complete remeasurement, examining tenders and reporting thereon, taking particulars and reporting valuations for interim certificates for payments on account to the contractor, preparing periodic assessments of anticipated final cost and reporting thereon, measuring and preparing final account, including pricing and agreeing totals with the contractor and adjusting fluctuations in the cost of labour and materials if required by the contract:

(a) **Category A:** Relatively complex works and/or works with little or no repetition.

Examples:
Ambulance and fire stations; banks; cinemas; clubs; computer buildings; council offices; crematoria; fitting out existing buildings; homes for the elderly; hospitals and nursing homes; laboratories; law courts; libraries; "one-off" houses; petrol stations; places of religious worship; police stations; public houses; licensed premises; restaurants; sheltered housing; sports pavilions; theatres; town halls; universities, polytechnics and colleges of further education (other than halls of residence and hostels); and the like.

QUANTITY SURVEYORS' FEES

Value of work	£	Category A fee	£
Up to	150 000	380 + 5.0% (Minimum fee £2 880)	
150 000 -	300 000	7 880 + 4.0% on balance over	150 000
300 000 -	600 000	13 880 + 3.4% on balance over	300 000
600 000 -	1 500 000	24 080 + 2.8% on balance over	600 000
1 500 000 -	3 000 000	49 280 + 2.4% on balance over	1 500 000
3 000 000 -	6 000 000	85 280 + 2.2% on balance over	3 000 000
Over	6 000 000	151 280 + 2.0% on balance over	6 000 000

(b)   **Category B**: Less complex works and/or works with some element of repetition

Examples:
Adult education facilities; canteens; church halls; community centres; departmental stores; enclosed sports stadia and swimming baths; halls of residence; hostels; motels; offices other than those included in Categories A and C; railway stations; recreation and leisure centres; residential hotels; schools; self-contained flats and maisonettes; shops and shopping centres; supermarkets and hypermarkets; telephone exchanges; and the like.

Value of work	£	Category B fee	£
Up to	150 000	360 + 4.8% (Minimum fee £2 760)	
150 000 -	300 000	7 560 + 3.7% on balance over	150 000
300 000 -	600 000	13 110 + 3.0% on balance over	300 000
600 000 -	1 500 000	22 110 + 2.2% on balance over	600 000
1 500 000 -	3 000 000	41 910 + 2.0% on balance over	1 500 000
3 000 000 -	6 000 000	71 910 + 1.8% on balance over	3 000 000
Over	6 000 000	125 910 + 1.6% on balance over	6 000 000

(c)   **Category C**: Simple works and/or works with a substantial element of repetition.
Examples:
Factories; garages; multi-storey car parks; open air sports stadia; structural shell offices not fitted out; warehouses; workshops; and the like.

Value of work	£	Category C fee	£
Up to	150 000	300 + 4.1% (Minimum fee £2 350)	
150 000 -	300 000	6 450 + 3.3% on balance over	150 000
300 000 -	600 000	11 400 + 2.6% on balance over	300 000
600 000 -	1 500 000	19 200 + 2.0% on balance over	600 000
1 500 000 -	3 000 000	37 200 + 1.7% on balance over	1 500 000
3 000 000 -	6 000 000	62 700 + 1.5% on balance over	3 000 000
Over	6 000 000	107 700 + 1.3% on balance over	6 000 000

(d)   The scales of fees for pre-contract and post-contract services (paras. 7.1 (a) to (c)) are overall scales based upon the inclusion of all nominated sub-contractors' and nominated suppliers' accounts, subject to the provision of para. 7.1. (g). When work normally included in a building contract is the subject of a separate contract for which the quantity surveyor has not been paid fees under any other clause hereof, the value of such work shall be included in the amount on which fees are charged.

(e)   Fees shall be calculated upon the basis of the account for the whole of the work, subject to the provisions of para. 7.2.

(f)   In calculating the amount on which fees are charged the total of any credits is to be added to the amount described above.

QUANTITY SURVEYORS' FEES

(g)　Where the value of air conditioning, heating, ventilating and electrical services included in tender documents together exceeds 25% of the amount calculated as described in paras. 7.1. (d) and (e), then, subject to the provisions of para. 7.2 no fee is chargeable on the amount by which the value of these services exceeds the said 25%. In this context the term "value" excludes general contractors' profit, attendance, builders' work in connection with the services, preliminaries and any other similar additions.

(h)　When a contract comprises buildings which fall into more than one category, the fee shall be calculated as follows.

(i)　The amount upon which fees are chargeable shall be allocated to the categories of work applicable and the amount so allocated expressed as percentages of the total amount upon which fees are chargeable.

(ii)　Fees shall then be calculated for each category on the total amount upon which fees are chargeable.

(iii)　The fee chargeable shall then be calculated by applying the percentages of work in each category to the appropriate total fee adding the resultant amounts.

(j)　When a project is the subject of a number of contracts then, for the purpose of calculating fees, the values of such contracts shall not be aggregated but each contract shall be taken separately and the scale of charges (paras. 7.1(a) to (h)) applied as appropriate.

(k)　Where the quantity surveyor is specifically instructed to provide cost planning services, the fee calculated in accordance with paras. 7.1 (a) to (j) shall be increased by a sum calculated in accordance with the following table and based upon the same value of work as that upon which the aforementioned fee has been calculated:

Categories A & B: (as defined in paras. 7.1 (a) and (b))

Value of work £	Fee	£
	£	
Up to 600 000	0.70%	
600 000 - 3 000 000	4 200 + 0.40% on balance over	600 000
3 000 000 - 6 000 000	13 800 + 0.35% on balance over	3 000 000
Over 6 000 000	24 300 + 0.30% on balance over	6 000 000

Category C: (as defined in para. 7.1 (c))

Value of work £	Fee	£
	£	
Up to 600 000	0.50%	
600 000 - 3 000 000	3 000 + 0.30% on balance over	600 000
3 000 000 - 6 000 000	10 200 + 0.25% on balance over	3 000 000
Over 6 000 000	17 700 + 0.20% on balance over	6 000 000

(l)　When the quantity surveyor is required to prepare valuations of materials or goods off site, an additional fee shall be charged based on the time involved (see paras. 19.1 and 19.2).

(m)　The basic scale for post-contract services includes for a simple routine of periodically estimating final costs. When the employer specifically requests a cost monitoring service which involves the quantity surveyor in additional or abortive measurement an additional fee shall be charged based on the time involved (see paras. 19.1 and 19.2), or alternatively on a lump sum or percentage basis agreed between the employer and the quantity surveyor.

QUANTITY SURVEYORS' FEES

7.2. Air conditioning, heating, ventilating and electrical services

(a) Where bills of approximate quantities and final accounts are prepared by the quantity surveyor for the air conditioning, heating, ventilating and electrical services there shall be a fee for these services in addition to the fee calculated in accordance with para. 7.1 as follows:

Value of work £	Category A fee	
	£	£
Up to 120 000	4.50%	
120 000 - 240 000	5 400 + 1.85% on balance over	120 000
240 000 - 480 000	10 020 + 3.25% on balance over	240 000
480 000 - 750 000	17 820 + 3.00% on balance over	480 000
750 000 - 1 000 000	25 920 + 2.50% on balance over	750 000
1 000 000 - 4 000 000	32 170 + 2.15% on balance over	1 000 000
Over 4 000 000	96 670 + 2.05% on balance over	4 000 000

(b) The value of such services, whether the subject of separate tenders or not, shall be aggregated and the value of work so obtained used for the purpose of calculating the additional fee chargeable in accordance with para. (a). (Except that when more than one firm of consulting engineers is engaged on the design of these services, the separate values for which each such firm is responsible shall be aggregated and the additional fees charged shall be calculated independently on each such total value so obtained.)

(c) The scope of the services to be provided by the quantity surveyor under para. (a) above shall be deemed to be equivalent to those described for the basic scale for pre-contract and post-contract services.

(d) When the quantity surveyor is required to prepare valuations of materials or goods off site, an additional fee shall be charged based on the time involved (see paras. 19.1 and 19.2).

(e) The basic scale for post-contract services includes for a simple routine of periodically estimating final costs. When the employer specifically requests a cost monitoring service, which involves the quantity surveyor in additional or abortive measurement, an additional fee shall be charged based on the time involved (see paras. 19.1 and 19.2), or alternatively on a lump sum or percentage basis agreed between the employer and the quantity surveyor.

(f) Fees shall be calculated upon the basis of the account for the whole of the air conditioning, heating, ventilating and electrical services for which final accounts have been prepared by the quantity surveyor.

(g) When cost planning services are provided by the quantity surveyor for air conditioning, heating, ventilating and electrical services (or for any part of such services) there shall be an additional fee based on the time involved (see paras. 19.1 and 19.2) or alternatively on a lump sum or percentage basis agreed between the employer and quantity surveyor.

NOTE: The incorporation of figures for air conditioning, heating, ventilating and electrical services provided by the consulting engineer is deemed to be included in the quantity surveyor's services under para 7.1.

7.3. Works of alteration
On works of alteration or repair, or on those sections of the work which are mainly works of alteration or repair, there shall be a fee of 1.0% in addition to the fee calculated in accordance with paras. 7.1 and 7.2

7.4. Works of redecoration and associated minor repairs
On works of redecoration and associated minor repairs, there shall be a fee of 1.5% in addition to the fee calculated in accordance with paras. 7.1 and 7.2.

QUANTITY SURVEYORS' FEES

7.5.   Bills of quantities and/or final accounts prepared in special forms
Fees calculated in accordance with paras. 7.1, 7.2, 7.3 and 7.4 include for the preparation of bills of quantities and/or final accounts on a normal trade basis. If the employer requires additional information to be provided in the bills of quantities and/or final accounts or the bills and/or final accounts to be prepared in an elemental, operational or similar form, then the fee may be adjusted by agreement between the employer and the quantity surveyor.

7.6.   Reduction of tenders

(a)   When cost planning services have been provided by the quantity surveyor and a tender, when received, is reduced before acceptance and if the reductions are not necessitated by amended instructions of the employer or by the inclusion in the bills of approximate quantities of items which the quantity surveyor has indicated could not be contained within the approved estimate, then in such a case no charge shall be made by the quantity surveyor for the preparation of bills of reductions and the fee for the preparation of bills of approximate quantities shall be based on the amount of the reduced tender.

(b)   When cost planning services have not been provided by the quantity surveyor and if a tender, when received, is reduced before acceptance, fees are to be calculated upon the amount of the unreduced tender. When the preparation of bills of reductions is required, a fee is chargeable for preparing such bills of reductions as follows:

(i)   2.0% upon the gross amount of all omissions requiring measurement or abstraction from original dimension sheets.
(ii)   3.0% upon the gross amount of all additions requiring measurement.
(iii)   0.5% upon the gross amount of all remaining additions.

NOTE: The above scale for the preparation of bills of reductions applies to work in all categories.

7.7.   Generally
If the works are substantially varied at any stage or if the quantity surveyor is involved in an excessive amount of abortive work, then the fees shall be adjusted by agreement between the employer and the quantity surveyor.

8.0. NEGOTIATING TENDERS

8.1   (a)   For negotiating and agreeing prices with a contractor:

Value of work	£	Fee	£
Up to	150 000	0.5%	
150 000 -	600 000	750 + 0.3% on balance over	150 000
600 000 -	1 200 000	2 100 + 0.2% on balance over	600 000
Over	1 200 000	3 300 + 0.1% on balance over	1 200 000

(b)   The fee shall be calculated on the total value of the works as defined in paras. 7.1 (d), (e), (f), (g) and (j).
(c)   For negotiating and agreeing prices with a contractor for air conditioning, heating, ventilating and electrical services there shall be an additional fee as para. 8.1 (a) calculated on the total value of such services as defined in para. 7.2 (b).

QUANTITY SURVEYORS' FEES

9.0. CONSULTATIVE SERVICES AND PRICING BILLS OF APPROXIMATE QUANTITIES

9.1. Consultative services
Where the quantity surveyor is appointed to prepare approximate estimates, feasibility studies or submissions for the approval of financial grants or similar services, then the fee shall be based on the time involved (see paras. 19.1 and 19.2) or alternatively, on a lump sum or percentage basis agreed between the employer and the quantity surveyor.

9.2. Pricing bills of approximate quantities
For pricing bills of approximate quantities, if instructed, to provide an estimate comparable with tenders, the fees shall be the same as for the corresponding services in paras. 4.2 (a) and (b).

10.0. INSTALMENT PAYMENTS

10.1. For the purpose of instalment payments the fee for preparation of bills of approximate quantities only shall be the equivalent of forty per cent (40%) of the fees calculated in accordance with the appropriate sections of paras. 7.1 to 7.5, and the fee for providing cost planning services shall be in accordance with the appropriate sections of para. 7.1 (k); both fees shall be based on the total value of the bills of approximate quantities ascertained in accordance with the provisions of para. 2.1 (e).

10.2. In the absence of agreement to the contrary, fees shall be paid by instalments as follows:

(a) Upon acceptance by the employer of a tender for the works the above defined fees for the preparation of bills of approximate quantities and for providing cost planning services.
(b) In the event of no tender being accepted, the aforementioned fees shall be paid within three months of completion of the bills of approximate quantities.
(c) The balance by instalments at intervals to be agreed between the date of the first certificate and one month after certification of the contractor's account.

10.3. In the event of the project being abandoned at any stage other than those covered by the foregoing, the proportion of fee payable shall be by agreement between the employer and the quantity surveyor.

11.0. SCHEDULES OF PRICES

11.1. The fee for preparing, pricing and agreeing schedules of prices shall be based on the time involved (see paras. 19.1 and 19.2). Alternatively, the fee may be on a lump sum or percentage basis agreed between the employer and the quantity surveyor.

12.0. COST PLANNING AND APPROXIMATE ESTIMATES

12.1. The fee for providing cost planning services or for preparing approximate estimates shall be based on the time involved (see paras. 19.1 and 19.2). Alternatively, the fee may be on a lump sum or percentage basis agreed between the employer and the quantity surveyor.

CONTRACTS BASED ON SCHEDULES OF PRICES: POST-CONTRACT SERVICES

QUANTITY SURVEYORS' FEES

13.0. FINAL ACCOUNTS

13.1. Basic Scale

    (a)   For taking particulars and reporting valuations for interim certificates for payments on account to the contractor, preparing periodic assessments of anticipated final cost and reporting thereon, measuring and preparing final account including pricing and agreeing totals with the contractor, and adjusting fluctuations in the cost of labour and materials if required by the contract, the fee shall be equivalent to sixty per cent (60%) of the fee calculated in accordance with paras. 7.1 (a) to (j).

    (b)   When the quantity surveyor is required to prepare valuations of materials or goods off site, an additional fee shall be charged on the basis of the time involved (see paras. 19.1 and 19.2).

    (c)   The basic scale for post-contract services includes for a simple routine of periodically estimating final costs. When the employer specifically requests a cost monitoring service which involves the quantity surveyor in additional or abortive measurement an additional fee shall be charged based on the time involved (see paras. 19.1 and 19.2), or alternatively on a lump sum or percentage basis agreed between the employer and the quantity surveyor.

13.2. Air conditioning, heating, ventilating and electrical services
Where final accounts are prepared by the quantity surveyor for the air conditioning, heating, ventilating and electrical services there shall be a fee for these services, in addition to the fee calculated in accordance with para. 13.1, equivalent to sixty per cent (60%) of the fee calculated in accordance with paras. 7.2 (a) to (f).

13.3. Works of alterations
On works of alteration or repair, or on those sections of the work which are mainly works of alteration or repair, there shall be a fee of 1.0% in addition to the fee calculated in accordance with paras. 13.1 and 13.2.

13.4. Works of redecoration and associated minor repairs
On works of redecoration and associated minor repairs, there shall be a fee of 1.5% in addition to the fee calculated in accordance with paras. 13.1 and 13.2.

13.5. Final accounts prepared in special forms
Fees calculated in accordance with paras. 13.1,13.2,13.3 and 13.4 include for the preparation of final accounts on a normal trade basis. If the employer requires additional information to be provided in the final accounts or the accounts to be prepared in an elemental, operational or similar form, then the fee may be adjusted by agreement between the employer and the quantity surveyor.

PRIME COST CONTRACTS: PRE-CONTRACT AND POST-CONTRACT SERVICES

14.0. COST PLANNING

14.1. The fee for providing a cost planning service shall be based on the time involved (see paras. 19.1 and 19.2). Alternatively, the fee may be on a lump sum or percentage basis agreed between the employer and the quantity surveyor.

QUANTITY SURVEYORS' FEES

15.0. ESTIMATES OF COST

15.1. (a)   For preparing an approximate estimate, calculated by measurement, of the cost of work, and, if required under the terms of the contract, negotiating, adjusting and agreeing the estimate:

Value of work	£	Fee	£
		£	
Up to	30 000	1.25%	
30 000 -	150 000	375 + 1.00% on balance over	30 000
150 000 -	600 000	1 575 + 0.75% on balance over	150 000
Over	600 000	4 950 + 0.50% on balance over	600 000

(b)   The fee shall be calculated upon the total of the approved estimates.

16.0. FINAL ACCOUNTS

16.1. (a)   For checking prime costs, reporting for interim certificates for payments on account to the contractor and preparing final accounts:

Value of work	£	Fee	£
		£	
Up to	30 000	2.50%	
150 000 -	150 000	750 + 2.00% on balance over	30 000
150 000 -	600 000	3 150 + 1.50% on balance over	150 000
Over	600 000	9 900 + 1.25% on balance over	600 000

(b)   The fee shall be calculated upon the total of the final account with the addition of the value of credits received for old materials removed and less the value of any work charged for in accordance with para. 16.1 (c).

(c)   On the value of any work to be paid for on a measured basis, the fee shall be 3%.

(d)   When the quantity surveyor is required to prepare valuations of materials or goods off site, an additional fee shall be charged based on the time involved (see paras. 19.1 and 19.2).

(e)   The above charges do not include the provision of checkers on the site. If the quantity surveyor is required to provide such checkers an additional charge shall be made by arrangement.

17.0. COST REPORTING AND MONITORING SERVICES

17.1.   The fee for providing cost reporting and/or monitoring services (e.g. preparing periodic assessments of anticipated final costs and reporting thereon) shall be based on the time involved (see paras. 19.1 and 19.2) or alternatively, on a lump sum or percentage basis agreed between the employer and the quantity surveyor.

18.0. ADDITIONAL SERVICES

18.1.   For additional services not normally necessary, such as those arising as a result of the termination of a contract before completion, liquidation, fire damage to the buildings, services in connection with arbitration, litigation and investigation of the validity of contractors' claims, services in connection with taxation matters and all similar services where the employer specifically instructs the quantity surveyor, the charges shall be in accordance with paras. 19.1 and 19.2.

QUANTITY SURVEYORS' FEES

19.0. TIME CHARGES

19.1. (a) For consultancy and other services performed by a principal, a fee by arrangement according to the circumstances including the professional status and qualifications of the quantity surveyor.

(b) When a principal does work which would normally be done by a member of staff, the charge shall be calculated as para. 19.2 below.

19.2. (a) For services by a member of staff, the charges for which are to be based on the time involved, such charges shall be calculated on the hourly cost of the individual involved plus 145%.

(b) A member of staff shall include a principal doing work normally done by an employee (as para. 19.1 (b) above), technical and supporting staff, but shall exclude secretarial staff or staff engaged upon general administration.

(c) For the purpose of para. 19.2 (b) above, a principal's time shall be taken at the rate applicable to a senior assistant in the firm.

(d) The supervisory duties of a principal shall be deemed to be included in the addition of 145% as para. 19.2 (a) above and shall not be charged separately.

(e) The hourly cost to the employer shall be calculated by taking the sum of the annual cost of the member of staff of:

(i) Salary and bonus but excluding expenses;

(ii) Employer's contributions payable under any Pension and Life Assurance Schemes;

(iii) Employer's contributions made under the National Insurance Acts, the Redundancy Payments Act and any other payments made in respect of the employee by virtue of any statutory requirements; and

(iv) Any other payments or benefits made or granted by the employer in pursuance of the terms of employment of the member of staff;

and dividing by 1,650.

19.3. The foregoing Time Charges under paras. 19.1 and 19.2 are intended for use where other paras. of the Scale (not related to Time Charges) form a significant proportion of the overall fee. In all other cases an increased time charge may be agreed.

20.0. INSTALMENT PAYMENTS

20.1. In the absence of agreement to the contrary, payments to the quantity surveyor shall be made by instalments by arrangement between the employer and the quantity surveyor.

SCALE 40 PROFESSIONAL CHARGES FOR QUANTITY SURVEYING SERVICES IN CONNECTION WITH HOUSING SCHEMES FOR LOCAL AUTHORITIES
The scale is recommended and not mandatory.

EFFECTIVE FROM FEBRUARY 1983

1.0 GENERALLY

1.1 The scale is applicable to housing schemes of self-contained dwellings regardless of type (e.g. houses, maisonettes, bungalows or flats) and irrespective of the amount of repetition of identical types or blocks within an individual housing scheme and shall also apply to all external works forming part of the contract for the housing scheme. This scale does not apply to improvement to existing dwellings.

QUANTITY SURVEYORS' FEES

1.2   The fees set out below cover the following quantity surveying services as may be required:

    (a)   Preparing bills of quantities or other tender documents; checking tenders received or negotiating tenders and pricing with a selected contractor; reporting thereon.

    (b)   Preparing recommendations for interim payments on account to the contractor; measuring work and adjusting variations in accordance with the terms of the contract and preparing the final account; pricing same and agreeing totals with the contractor; adjusting fluctuations in the cost of labour and materials if required by the contract.

    (c)   Preparing periodic financial statements showing the anticipated final cost by means of a simple routine of estimating final costs and reporting thereon, but excluding cost monitoring (see para. 1.4).

1.3   Where the quantity surveyor is appointed to prepare approximate estimates to establish and substantiate the economic viability of the scheme and to obtain the necessary approvals and consents, or to enable the scheme to be designed and constructed within approved cost criteria an additional fee shall be charged based on the time involved (see para. 7.0) or, alternatively, on a lump sum or percentage basis agreed between the employer and the quantity surveyor. (Cost planning services, see para. 3.0).

1.4   When the employer specifically requests a post-contract cost monitoring service which involves the quantity surveyor in additional or abortive work an additional fee shall be charged based on the time involved (see para. 7.0) or, alternatively, on a lump sum or percentage basis agreed between the employer and the quantity surveyor.

1.5   The fees are in all cases exclusive of travelling and other expenses (for which the actual disbursement is recoverable unless there is some prior arrangement for such charges) and of the cost of reproduction of bills of quantities and other documents, which are chargeable in addition at net cost.

1.6   The fees are in all cases exclusive of services in connection with the allocation of the cost of the works for purposes of calculating value added tax for which there shall be an additional fee based on the time involved (see para. 7.0).

1.7   When work normally included in a building contract is the subject of a separate contract for which the quantity surveyor has not been paid fees under any other clause thereof, the value of such work shall be included in the amount upon which fees are charged.

1.8   If any of the materials used in the works are supplied by the employer or charged at a preferential rate, then the estimated or actual value thereof shall be included in the amount upon which fees are to be calculated.

1.9   The fees are in all cases exclusive of preparing a specification of the materials to be used and the works to be done, but the fees for preparing bills of quantities and similar documents do include for incorporating preamble clauses describing the materials and workmanship (from information given by the architect and/or consulting engineer).

1.10   If the quantity surveyor incurs additional costs due to exceptional delays in building operations or any other cause beyond the control of the quantity surveyor, then the fees shall be adjusted by agreement between the employer and the quantity surveyor to cover the reimbursement of these additional costs.

1.11   When a project is the subject of a number of contracts then for the purposes of calculating fees, the values of such contracts shall not be aggregated but each contract shall be taken separately and the scale of charges applied as appropriate.

1.12   The fees and charges are in all cases exclusive of value added tax which will be applied in accordance with legislation.

QUANTITY SURVEYORS' FEES

1.13 Copyright in bills of quantities and other documents prepared by the quantity surveyor is reserved to the quantity surveyor.

2.0 BASIC SCALE

2.1 The basic fee for the services outlined in para. 1.2 shall be as follows:-

Value of work		Fee	
		£	£
Up to	75 000	250 + 4.6%	
75 000 -	150 000	3 700 + 3.6% on balance over	75 000
150 000 -	750 000	6 400 + 2.3% on balance over	150 000
750 000 -	1 500 000	20 200 + 1.7% on balance over	750 000
Over	1 500 000	32 950 + 1.5% on balance over	1 500 000

2.2 Fees shall be calculated upon the total of the final account for the whole of the work including all nominated sub-contractors' and nominated suppliers' accounts.

2.3 For services in connection with accommodation designed for the elderly or the disabled or other special category occupants for whom special facilities are required an addition of 10% shall be made to the fee calculated in accordance with para. 2.1.

2.4 When additional fees under para. 2.3 are chargeable on a part or parts of a scheme, the value of basic fee to which the additional percentages shall be applied shall be determined by the proportion that the values of the various types of accommodation bear to the total of those values.

2.5 When the quantity surveyor is required to prepare an interim valuation of materials or goods off site, an additional fee shall be charged based on the time involved (see para. 7.0).

2.6 If the works are substantially varied at any stage and if the quantity surveyor is involved in an excessive amount of abortive work, then the fee shall be adjusted by agreement between the employer and the quantity surveyor.

2.7 The fees payable under paras. 2.1 and 2.3 include for the preparation of bills of quantities or other tender documents on a normal trade basis. If the employer requires additional information to be provided in bills of quantities, or bills of quantities to be prepared in an elemental, operational or similar form, then the fee may be adjusted by agreement between the employer and the quantity surveyor.

3.0 COST PLANNING

3.1 When the quantity surveyor is specifically instructed to provide cost planning services, the fee calculated in accordance with paras. 2.1 and 2.3 shall be increased by a sum calculated in accordance with the following table and based upon the amount of the accepted tender.

Value of work	£	Fee	
		£	£
Up to	150 000	0.45%	
150 000 -	750 000	675 + 0.35% on balance over	150 000
Over	750 000	2 775 + 0.25% on balance over	750 000

3.2 Cost planning is defined as the process of ascertaining a cost limit, where necessary, within the guidelines set by any appropriate Authority, and thereafter checking the cost of the project within that limit throughout the design process. It includes the preparation of a cost plan (based upon elemental analysis or other suitable criterion) checking and revising it where required and effecting the necessary liaison with other consultants employed.

QUANTITY SURVEYORS' FEES

3.3 (a) When cost planning services have been provided by the quantity surveyor and bills of reductions are required, then no charge shall be made by the quantity surveyor for the bills of reductions unless the reductions are necessitated by amended instructions of the employer or by the inclusion in the bills of quantities of items which the quantity surveyor has indicated could not be contained within the approved estimate.

(b) When cost planning services have not been provided by the quantity surveyor and bills of reductions are required, a fee is chargeable for preparing such bills of reductions as follows:

(i) 2.0% upon the gross amount of all omissions requiring measurement or abstraction from original dimension sheets.
(ii) 3.0% upon the gross amount of all additions requiring measurement.
(iii) 0.5% upon the gross amount of all remaining additions.

4.0 HEATING, VENTILATING AND ELECTRICAL SERVICES

(a) When bills of quantities and the final account are prepared by the quantity surveyor for the heating, ventilating and electrical services, there shall be a fee for these services in addition to the fee calculated in accordance with paras. 2.1 and 2.3 as follows:

Value of work £		Fee £		£
Up to	60 000	4.50%		
60 000 -	120 000	2 700 + 3.85%	on balance over	60 000
120 000 -	240 000	5 010 + 3.25%	on balance over	120 000
240 000 -	375 000	8 910 + 3.00%	on balance over	240 000
375 000 -	500 000	12 960 + 2.50%	on balance over	375 000
Over	500 000	16 085 + 2.15%	on balance over	500 000

(b) The value of such services, whether the subject of separate tenders or not shall be aggregated and the total value of work so obtained used for the purpose of calculating the additional fee chargeable in accordance with para. (a). (Except that when more than one firm of consulting engineers is engaged on the design of these services, the separate values for which each such firm is responsible shall be aggregated and the additional fees charged shall be calculated independently on each such total value so obtained).

(c) The scope of the services to be provided by the quantity surveyor under para. (a) above shall be deemed to be equivalent to those outlined in para. 1.2.

(d) Fee shall be calculated upon the basis of the account for the whole of the heating, ventilating and electrical services for which final accounts have been prepared by the quantity surveyor.

5.0 INSTALMENT PAYMENTS

5.1 In the absence of agreement to the contrary, fees shall be paid by instalments as follows:

(a) Upon receipt by the employer of a tender for the works sixty per cent (60%) of the fees calculated in accordance with paras. 2.0 and 4.0 in the amount of the accepted tender plus the appropriate recoverable expenses and the full amount of the fee for cost planning services if such services have been instructed by the employer.

(b) The balance of fees and expenses by instalments at intervals to be agreed between the date of the first certificate and one month after final certification of the contractor's account.

5.2 In the event of no tender being accepted, sixty per cent (60%) of the fees, plus the appropriate recoverable expenses, and the full amount of the fee for cost planning services if such services have been instructed by the employer, shall be paid within three months of the completion of the tender documents. The fee shall be calculated on the amount of the lowest original bona fide tender received. In the event of no tender being received, the fee shall be calculated on a reasonable valuation of the work based upon the tender documents.

QUANTITY SURVEYORS' FEES

NOTE: In the foregoing context "bona fide tender" shall be deemed to mean a tender submitted in good faith without major errors of computation and not subsequently withdrawn by the tenderer.

5.3   In the event of the project being abandoned at any stage other than those covered by the foregoing, the proportion of fee payable shall be by agreement between the employer and the quantity surveyor.

5.4   When the quantity surveyor is appointed to carry out post-contract services only and has not prepared the bills of quantities then the fees shall be agreed between the employer and the quantity surveyor as a proportion of the scale set out in paras. 2.0 and 4.0 with an allowance for the necessary familiarisation and any additional services undertaken by the quantity surveyor. The percentages stated in paras. 5.1 and 5.2 are not intended to be used as a means of calculating the fees payable for post-contract services only.

6.0   ADDITIONAL SERVICES

6.1   For additional services not normally necessary such as those arising as a result of the termination of a contract before completion, liquidation, fire damage to the buildings, services in connection with arbitration, litigation and investigation of the validity of contractors' claims, services in connection with taxation matters, and all similar services where the employer specifically instructs the quantity surveyor, the charge shall be in accordance with para. 7.0.

7.0   TIME CHARGES

7.1   (a)   For consultancy and other services performed by a principal, a fee by arrangement according to the circumstances, including the professional status and qualifications of the quantity surveyor.
       (b)   When a principal does work which would normally be done by a member of staff, the charge shall be calculated as para. 7.2.

7.2   (a)   For services by a member of staff, the charges for which are to be based on the time involved, such hourly charges shall be calculated on the basis of annual salary (including bonus and any other payments or benefits previously agreed with the employer) multiplied by a factor of 2.5, plus reimbursement of payroll costs, all divided by 1600. Payroll costs shall include inter alia employer's contributions payable under any Pension and Life Assurance Schemes, employer's contributions made under the National Insurance Acts, the Redundancy Payments Act and any other payments made in respect of the employee by virtue of any statutory requirements. In this connection it would not be unreasonable in individual cases to take account of the cost of providing a car as part of the "salary" of staff engaged on time charge work when considering whether the salaries paid to staff engaged on such work are reasonable.
       (b)   A member of staff shall include a principal doing work normally done by an employee (as para. 7.1 (b) above), technical and supporting staff, but shall exclude secretarial staff or staff engaged upon general administration.
       (c)   For the purpose of para. 7.2 (b) above a principal's time shall be taken at the rate applicable to a senior assistant in the firm.
       (d)   The supervisory duties of a principal shall be deemed to be included in the multiplication factor as para. 7.2 (a) above and shall not be charged separately.

7.3   The foregoing Time Charges under paras. 7.1 and 7.2 are intended for use where other paras. of the scale (not related to Time Charges) form a significant proportion of the overall fee. In all other cases an increased Time Charge may be agreed.

QUANTITY SURVEYORS' FEES

SCALE 44 PROFESSIONAL CHARGES FOR QUANTITY SURVEYING SERVICES IN CONNECTION WITH IMPROVEMENTS TO EXISTING HOUSING AND ENVIRONMENTAL IMPROVEMENT WORKS
The scale is recommended and not mandatory.

EFFECTIVE FROM FEBRUARY 1973

1. This scale of charges is applicable to all works of improvement to existing housing for local authorities, development corporations, housing associations and the like and to environmental improvement works associated therewith or of a similar nature.

2. The fees set out below cover such quantity surveying services as may be required in connection with an improvement project irrespective of the type of contract or contract documentation from initial appointment to final certification of the contractor's account such as:

    (a) Preliminary cost exercises and advice on tendering procedures and contract arrangements.
    (b) Providing cost advice to assist the design and construction of the project within approved cost limits.
    (c) Preliminary inspection of a typical dwelling of each type.
    (d) Preparation of tender documents; checking tenders received and reporting thereon or negotiating tenders and agreeing prices with a selected contractor.
    (e) Making recommendations for and, where necessary, preparing bills of reductions except in cases where the reductions are necessitated by amended instructions of the employer or by the inclusion in the bills of quantities of items which the quantity surveyor has indicated could not be contained within the approved estimate.
    (f) Analysing tenders and preparing details for submission to a Ministry or Government Department and attending upon the employer in any negotiations with such Ministry or Government Department.
    (g) Recording the extent of work required to every dwelling before work commences.
    (h) Preparing recommendations for interim payments on account to the contractor; preparing periodic assessments of the anticipated final cost of the works and reporting thereon
    (j) Measurement of work and adjustment of variations and fluctuations in the cost of labour and materials in accordance with the terms of the contract and preparing final account, pricing same and agreeing totals with the contractor.

3. The services listed in para. 2 do not include the carrying out of structural surveys.

4. The fees set out below have been calculated on the basis of experience that all of the services described above will not normally be required and in consequence these scales shall not be abated if, by agreement, any of the services are not required to be provided by the quantity surveyor.

QUANTITY SURVEYORS' FEES

IMPROVEMENT WORKS TO HOUSING

5.   The fee for quantity surveying services in connection with improvement works to existing housing
      and external works in connection therewith shall be calculated from a sliding scale based upon the
      total number of houses or flats in a project divided by the total number of types substantially the
      same in design and plan as follows:

Total number of houses or flats divided by total number of types substantially the same in design and plan	Fee
not exceeding 1	see note below
exceeding 1 but not exceeding 2	7.0%
exceeding 2 but not exceeding 3	5.0%
exceeding 3 but not exceeding 4	4.5%
exceeding 4 but not exceeding 20	4.0%
exceeding 20 but not exceeding 50	3.6%
exceeding 50 but not exceeding 100	3.2%
exceeding 100	3.0%

      and to the result of the computation shall be added 12.5%

NOTE: For schemes of only one house or flat per type an appropriate fee is to be agreed between
          the employer and the quantity surveyor on a percentage, lump sum or time basis.

ENVIRONMENTAL IMPROVEMENT WORKS

6.   The fee for quantity surveying services in connection with environmental improvement works
      associated with improvements to existing housing or environmental improvement works of a similar
      nature shall be as follows:

Value of work £		Fee £		£
Up to	50 000	4.5%		
50 000 -	200 000	2 250 + 3.0%	on balance over	50 000
200 000 -	500 000	6 750 + 2.1%	on balance over	200 000
Over	500 000	13 050 + 2.0%	on balance over	500 000

      and to the result of that computation shall be added 12.5%

GENERALLY

7.   When tender documents prepared by a quantity surveyor for an earlier scheme are re-used without
      amendment by the quantity surveyor for a subsequent scheme or part thereof for the same
      employer, the percentage fee in respect of such subsequent scheme or the part covered by such
      reused documents shall be reduced by 20%.

8.   The foregoing fees shall be calculated upon the separate totals of the final account for improvement
      works to housing and environmental Government works respectively including all nominated
      sub-contractors' and nominated suppliers' accounts and (subject to para. 5 above) regardless of the
      amount of repetition within the scheme. When environmental improvement works are the subject
      of a number of contracts then for the purpose of calculating fees, the values of such contracts shall
      not be aggregated but each contract shall be taken separately and the scale of charges in para. 6
      above applied as appropriate.

9.   In cases where any of the materials used in the works are supplied by the employer, the estimated
      or actual value thereof is to be included in the total on which the fee is calculated.

QUANTITY SURVEYORS' FEES

10. In the absence of agreement to the contrary, fees shall be paid by instalments as follows:

   (a) Upon acceptance by the employer of a tender for the works, one half of the fee calculated on the amount of the accepted tender.
   (b) The balance by instalments at intervals to be agreed between the date of the first certificate and one month after final certification of the contractor's account.

11. (a) In the event of no tender being accepted, one half of the fee shall be paid within three months of completion of the tender documents. The fee shall be calculated on the amount of the lowest original bona fide tender received. If no such tender has been received, the fee shall be calculated upon a reasonable valuation of the work based upon the tender documents.
   (b) In the event of the project being abandoned at any stage other than those covered by the foregoing, the proportion of fee payable shall be by agreement between the employer and the quantity surveyor.

12. If the works are substantially varied at any stage or if the quantity surveyor is involved in an excessive amount of abortive work, then the fee shall be adjusted by agreement between the employer and the quantity surveyor.

13. When the quantity surveyor is required to perform additional services in connection with the allocation of the costs of the works for purposes of calculating value added tax there shall be an additional fee based on the time involved.

14. For additional services not normally necessary such as those arising as a result of the termination of the contract before completion, liquidation, fire damage to the buildings, services in connection with arbitration, litigation and claims on which the employer specifically instructs the surveyor to investigate and report, there shall be an additional fee to be agreed between the employer and the quantity surveyor.

15. Copyright in the bills of quantities and other documents prepared by the quantity surveyor is reserved to the quantity surveyor.

16. The foregoing fees are in all cases exclusive of travelling expenses and lithography or other charges for copies of documents, the net amount of such expenses and charges to be paid for in addition. Subsistence expenses, if any, to be charged by arrangement with the employer.

17. The foregoing fees and charges are in all cases exclusive of value added tax which shall be applied in accordance with legislation current at the time the account is rendered.

SCALE 45 PROFESSIONAL CHARGES FOR QUANTITY SURVEYING SERVICES IN CONNECTION WITH HOUSING SCHEMES FINANCED BY THE HOUSING CORPORATION

EFFECTIVE FROM JANUARY 1982 - reprinted 1989

1. (a) This scale of charges has been agreed between The Royal Institution of Chartered Surveyors and the Housing Corporation and shall apply to housing schemes of self-contained dwellings financed by the Housing Corporation regardless of type (e.g. houses, maisonettes, bungalows or flats) and irrespective of the amount of repetition of identical types or blocks within an individual housing scheme.
   (b) This scale does not apply to services in connection with improvements to existing dwellings.

2. The fees set out below cover the following quantity surveying services as may be required in connection with the particular project:

   (a) Preparing such estimates of cost as are required by the employer to establish and substantiate the economic viability of the scheme and to obtain the necessary approvals and consents from the Housing Corporation but excluding cost planning services (see para. 10)
   (b) Providing pre-contract cost advice (e.g. approximate estimates on a floor area or similar basis) to enable the scheme to be designed and constructed within the approved cost criteria but excluding cost planning services (see para. 10).

QUANTITY SURVEYORS' FEES

(c) Preparing bills of quantities or other tender documents; checking tenders received or negotiating tenders and pricing with a selected contractor; reporting thereon.

(d) Preparing an elemental analysis of the accepted tender (RICS/BCIS Detailed Form of Cost Analysis excluding the specification notes or equivalent).

(e) Preparing recommendations for interim payments on account to the contractor; measuring the work and adjusting variations in accordance with the terms of the contract and preparing the final account, pricing same and agreeing totals with the contractor; adjusting fluctuations in the cost of labour and materials if required by the contract.

(f) Preparing periodic post-contract assessments of the anticipated final cost by means of a simple routine of periodically estimating final costs and reporting thereon, but excluding a cost monitoring service specifically required by the employer.

3. The fees set out below are exclusive of travelling and of other expenses (for which the actual disbursement is recoverable unless there is some special prior arrangement for such charges) and the cost of reproduction of bills of quantities and other documents, which are chargeable in addition at net cost.

4. Copyright in the bills of quantities and other documents prepared by the quantity surveyor is reserved to the quantity surveyor.

5. (a) The basic fee for the services outlined in para. 2 (regardless of the extent of services described in para. 2) shall be as follows:

Value of work		Fee	
		£	£
Up to	75 000	210 + 3.8%	
75 000 -	150 000	3 060 + 3.0% on balance over	75 000
150 000 -	750 000	5 310 + 2.0% on balance over	150 000
750 000 -	1 500 000	17 310 + 1.5% on balance over	750 000
Over	1 500 000	28 560 + 1.3% on balance over	1 500 000

(b) (i) For services in connection with Categories 1 and 2 Accommodation designed for Old People in accordance with the standards described in Ministry of Housing and Local Government Circulars 82/69 and 27/70 (Welsh Office Circulars 84/69 & 30/70), there shall be a fee in addition to that in accordance with para. 5 (a), calculated as follows:

Category 1   An addition of five per cent (5%) to the basic fee calculated in accordance with para. 5 (a)

Category 2   An addition of twelve and a half per cent (12.5%) to the basic fee calculated in accordance with para. 5 (a).

(ii) For services in connection with Accommodation designed for the Elderly in Scotland in accordance with the standards described in Scottish Housing Handbook Part 5, Housing for the Elderly, the fee shall be calculated as follows:

Mainstream and Amenity Housing	Basic fee in accordance with para. 5 (a)
Basic Sheltered Housing (i.e. Amenity Housing plus Warden's accommodation and alarm system)	An addition of five per cent (5%) to the basic fee calculated in accordance with para. 5 (a)
Sheltered Housing, including optional facilities	An addition of twelve and a half per cent (12.5%) of the basic fee calculated in accordance with para. 5 (a)

QUANTITY SURVEYORS' FEES

    (c)   (i)   For services in connection with Accommodation designed for Disabled People in accordance with the standards described in Department of Environment Circular 92/75 (Welsh Office Circular 163/75), there shall be an addition of fifteen per cent (15%) to the fee calculated in accordance with paragraph 5 (a).

           (ii)   For services in connection with Accommodation designed for the Disabled in Scotland in accordance with the standards described in Scottish Housing Handbook Part 6, Housing for the Disabled, there shall be an addition of fifteen per cent (15%) to the fee calculated in accordance with para. 5 (a).

    (d)   For services in connection with Accommodation designed for Disabled Old People, the fee shall be calculated in accordance with para. 5 (c).

    (e)   For services in connection with Subsidised Fair Rent New Build Housing, there shall be a fee, in addition to that in accordance with paras. 5 (a) to (d), calculated as follows:

Value of work £	Category A fee £	£
Up to 75 000	20 + 0.40%	
75 000 - 150 000	320 + 0.20% on balance over	75 000
150 000 - 500 000	470 + 0.07% on balance over	150 000
Over 500 000	715	

6.   (a)   Where additional fees under paras. 5 (b) to (d) are chargeable on a part or parts of a scheme, the value of basic fee to which the additional percentages shall be applied shall be determined by the proportion that the values of the various types of accommodation bear to the total of those values.

    (b)   Fees shall be calculated upon the total of the final account for the whole of the work including all nominated sub-contractors' and nominated suppliers' accounts.

    (c)   If any of the materials used in the works are supplied free of charge to the contractor, the estimated or actual value thereof shall be included in the amount upon which fees are to be calculated.

    (d)   When a project is the subject of a number of contracts then, for the purpose of calculating fees, the values of such contracts shall not be aggregated but each contract shall be taken separately and the scale of charges applied as appropriate.

7.   If bills of quantities and final accounts are prepared by the quantity surveyor for the heating, ventilating or electrical services, there shall be an additional fee by agreement between the employer and the quantity surveyor subject to the approval of the Housing Corporation.

8.   In the absence of agreement to the contrary, fees shall be paid by instalments as follows:

    (a)   Upon receipt by the employer of a tender for the works, or when the employer certifies to the Housing Corporation that the tender documents have been completed, a sum on account representing ninety per cent (90%) of the anticipated sum under para. 8 (b) below.

    (b)   Upon acceptance by the employer of a tender for the works, sixty per cent (60%) of the fee calculated on the amount of the accepted tender, plus the appropriate recoverable expenses.

    (c)   The balance of fees and expenses by instalments at intervals to be agreed between the date of the first certificate and one month after final certification of the contractor's account.

9.   (a)   In the event of no tender being accepted, sixty per cent (60%) of the fee and the appropriate recoverable expenses shall be paid within six months of completion of the tender documents. The fee shall be calculated on the amount of the lowest original bona fide tender received. In the event of no tender being received, the fee shall be calculated upon a reasonable valuation of the work based upon the tender documents.

    NOTE: In the foregoing context "bona fide tender" shall be deemed to mean a tender submitted in good faith without major errors of computation and not subsequently withdrawn by the tenderer.

QUANTITY SURVEYORS' FEES

(b)   In the event of part of the project being postponed or abandoned after the preparation of the bills of quantities or other tender documents, sixty per cent (60%) of the fee on this part shall be paid within three months of the date of postponement or abandonment.

(c)   In the event of the project being postponed or abandoned at any stage other than those covered by the foregoing, the proportion of fee payable shall be by agreement between the employer and the quantity surveyor.

10.   (a)   Where with the approval of the Housing Corporation the employer instructs the quantity surveyor to carry out cost planning services there shall be a fee additional to that charged under para. 5 as follows:

Value of work	£	Category A fee	
		£	£
Up to	150 000	0.45%	
150 000 -	750 000	675 + 0.35% on balance over	150 000
Over	750 000	2 775 + 0.25% on balance over	750 000

(b)   Cost planning is defined as the process of ascertaining a cost limit where necessary, within guidelines set by any appropriate Authority, and thereafter checking the cost of the project within that limit throughout the design process. It includes the preparation of a cost plan (based upon elemental analysis or other suitable criterion) checking and revising it where required and effecting the necessary liaison with the other consultants employed.

11.   If the quantity surveyor incurs additional costs due to exceptional delays in building operations or any other cause beyond the control of the quantity surveyor, then the fees shall be adjusted by agreement between the employer and the quantity surveyor to cover the reimbursement of these additional costs.

12.   When the quantity surveyor is required to prepare an interim valuation of materials or goods off site, an additional fee shall be charged based on the time involved (see paras. 15 and 16) in respect of each such valuation.

13.   If the Works are materially varied to the extent that substantial remeasurement is necessary, then the fee may be adjusted by agreement between the employer and the quantity surveyor.

14.   For additional services not normally necessary, such as those arising as a result of the termination of a contract before completion, fire damage to the buildings, cost monitoring (see para. 2 (f)), services in connection with arbitration, litigation and investigation of the validity of contractors' claims, services in connection with taxation matters and similar all services where the employer specifically instructs the quantity surveyor, the charges shall be in accordance with paras. 15 & 16.

15.   (a)   For consultancy and other services performed by a principal, a fee by arrangement according to the circumstances, including the professional status and qualifications of the quantity surveyor.

(b)   When a principal does work which would normally be done by a member of staff, the charge shall be calculated as para. 16.

16.   (a)   For services by a member of staff, the charges for which are to be based on the time involved, such hourly charges shall be calculated on the basis of annual salary (including bonus and any other payments or benefits previously agreed with the employer) multiplied by a factor of 2.5, plus reimbursement of payroll costs, all divided by 1600. Payroll costs shall include inter alia employer's contributions payable under any Pension and Life Assurance Schemes, employer's contributions made under the National Insurance Acts, the Redundancy Payments Act and any other payments made in respect of the employee by virtue of any statutory requirements in this connection it would not be unreasonable in individual cases to take account of the cost of providing a car as part of the "salary" of staff engaged on time charge work when considering whether the salaries paid to staff engaged on such work are reasonable.

QUANTITY SURVEYORS' FEES

(b)   A member of staff shall include a principal doing work normally done by an employee (as para. 15 (b) above), technical and supporting staff, but shall exclude secretarial staff or staff engaged upon general administration.

(c)   For the purpose of para. 16 (b) above a principal's time shall be taken at the rate applicable to a senior assistant in the firm.

(d)   The supervisory duties of a principal shall be deemed to be included in the multiplication factor as para. 16 (a) above and shall not be charged separately.

17.   The foregoing Time Charges under paras. 15 and 16 are intended for use where other paras. of the scale (not related to Time Charges) form a significant proportion of the overall fee. In all other cases an increased time charge may be agreed.

18.   (a)   In the event of the employment of the contractor being determined due to bankruptcy or liquidation, the fee for the services outlined in para. 2, and for the additional services required, shall be recalculated to the aggregate of the following:

    (i)   Fifty per cent (50%) of the fee in accordance with paragraphs 5 and 6 calculated upon the total of the Notional Final Account in accordance with the terms of the original contracts.

    (ii)   Fifty per cent (50%) of the fee in accordance with paragraphs 5 and 6 calculated upon the aggregate of the total value (which may differ from the total of interim valuations) of work up to the date of determination in accordance with the terms of the original contract plus the total of the final account for the completion contract;

    (iii)   A charge based upon time involved (in accordance with paragraphs 15 and 16) in respect of dealing with those matters specifically generated by the liquidation (other than normal post-contract services related to the completion contract), which may include (inter alia):

> Site inspection and (where required) security (initial and until the replacement contractor takes possession);
> Taking instructions from and/or advising the employer;
> Representing the employer at meeting(s) of creditors;
> Making arrangements for the continued employment of sub-contractors and similar related matters;
> Preparing bills of quantities or other appropriate documents for the completion contract, obtaining tenders, checking and reporting thereon;
> The additional cost (over and above the preparation of the final account for the completion contract) of pre-paring the Notional Final Account; pricing the same;
> Negotiations with the liquidator (trustee or receiver).

(b)   In calculating fees under para. 18 (a) (iii) above, regard shall be taken of any services carried out by the quantity surveyor for which a fee will ultimately be chargeable under para. 18 (a) (i) and (ii) above in respect of which a suitable abatement shall be made from the fee charged (e.g. measurement of variations for purposes of the completion contract where such would contribute towards the preparation of the contract final account).

(c)   Any interim instalments of fees paid under para. 8 in respect of services outlined in para. 2 shall be deducted from the overall fee computed as outlined herein.

(d)   In the absence of agreement to the contrary fees and expenses in respect of those services outlined in para. 18 (a) (iii) above up to acceptance of a completion tender shall be paid upon such acceptance; the balance of fees and expenses shall be paid in accordance with para. 8 (c).

(e)   For the purpose of this Scale the term "Notional Final Account" shall be deemed to mean an account indicating that which would have been payable to the original contractor had he completed the whole of the works and before deduction of interim payments to him.

19.   The fees and charges are in all cases exclusive of Value Added Tax which will be applied in accordance with legislation.

QUANTITY SURVEYORS' FEES

EXPLANATORY NOTE:

(Source: Chartered Quantity Surveyor, August 1986)

For rehabilitation projects the basic fee set out in paragraph 5 (a) of the scale will apply with the addition of a further 1% fee calculated upon the total of the final account for rehabilitation works including all nominated sub-contractors' and nominated suppliers' accounts.

In the case of special housing categories (e.g., elderly people) the additional percentage should be applied before the application of the additional percentage set out in paragraph 5 (b). The provisions of paragraph 6 (a) of the scale will also apply.

There is no longer any distinction between "hostel" and "cluster dwellings" which now have a single category of shared housing.

For shared housing new build projects other than those specified below the fee should be calculated in accordance with paragraph 5 (a) plus an enhancement of 10%.

For shared housing rehabilitation projects other than those specified below the fee should be calculated in accordance with paragraph 5 (a) of the scale plus 1% plus an enhancement of 10%.

For shared housing projects comprising wheelchair accommodation (as described in the Housing Corporation's Design and Contract Criteria) or frail elderly accommodation (as described in Housing Corporation circular HCO1/85) the fee should be calculated in accordance with paragraph 5 (a), (plus 1% for rehabilitation schemes where applicable) plus an enhancement of 15%.

The additional percentage set out in paragraph 5 (b) does not apply to shared housing projects, but the provisions of paragraph 6 (a) are applicable.

SCALE 46   PROFESSIONAL CHARGES FOR QUANTITY SURVEYING SERVICES IN CONNECTION WITH LOSS ASSESSMENT OF DAMAGE TO BUILDINGS FROM FIRE, ETC ISSUED BY THE ROYAL INSTITUTION OF CHARTERED SURVEYORS.
The scale is recommended and not mandatory.

EFFECTIVE FROM JULY 1988

1.   This scale of professional charges is for use in assessing loss resulting from damage to buildings by fire etc., under the "building" section of an insurance policy and is applicable to all categories of buildings.

2.   The fees set out below cover the following quantity surveying services as may be required in connection with the particular loss assessment:

(a)   Examining the insurance policy.
(b)   Visiting the building and taking all necessary site notes.
(c)   Measuring at site and/or from drawings and preparing itemised statement of claim and pricing same.
(d)   Negotiating and agreeing claim with the loss adjuster.

3.   The fees set out below are exclusive of the following:

(a)   Travelling and other expenses (for which the actual disbursement is recoverable unless there is some special prior arrangement for such charge.)
(b)   Cost of reproduction of all documents, which are chargeable in addition at net cost.

4.   Copyright in all documents prepared by the quantity surveyor is reserved.

QUANTITY SURVEYORS' FEES

5.   (a)   The fees for the services outlined in paragraph 2 shall be as follows:

Agreed Amount of Damage £	Fee	£
	£	
Up to 60 000	see note 5(c) below	
60 000 - 180 000	2.5%	
180 000 - 360 000	4 500 + 2.3% on balance over	180 000
360 000 - 720 000	8 640 + 2.0% on balance over	360 000
Over 720 000	15 840 + 1.5% on balance over	720 000

and to the result of that computation shall be added 12.5%

(b)   The sum on which the fees above shall be calculated shall be arrived at after having given effect to the following:

(i)   The sum shall be based on the amount of damage, including such amounts in respect of architects', surveyors and other consultants' fees for reinstatement, as admitted by the loss adjuster.

(ii)   When a policy is subject to an average clause, the sum shall be the agreed amount before the adjustment for "average".

(iii)   When, in order to apply the average clause, the reinstatement value of the whole subject is calculated and negotiated an additional fee shall be charged commensurate with the work involved.

(c)   Subject to 5 (b) above, when the amount of the sum on which fees shall be calculated is under £60,000 the fee shall be based on time involved as defined in Scale 37 (July 1988) para. 19 or on a lump sum or percentage basis agreed between the building owner and the quantity surveyor.

6.   The foregoing scale of charges is exclusive of any services in connection with litigation and arbitration.

7.   The fees and charges are in all cases exclusive of value added tax which shall be applied in accordance with legislation.

QUANTITY SURVEYORS' FEES

SCALE 47 PROFESSIONAL CHARGES FOR THE ASSESSMENT OF REPLACEMENT COSTS BUILDINGS FOR INSURANCE, CURRENT COST ACCOUNTING AND OTHER PURPOSES ISSUED BY THE ROYAL INSTITUTION OF CHARTERED SURVEYORS
The scale is recommended and not mandatory.

EFFECTIVE FROM JULY 1988

1.0 GENERALLY

1.1. The fees are in all cases exclusive of travelling and other expenses (for which the actual disbursement is recoverable unless there is some prior arrangement for such charges).

1.2. The fees and charges are in all cases exclusive of value added tax which will be applied in accordance with legislation.

2.0 ASSESSMENT OF REPLACEMENT COSTS OF BUILDINGS FOR INSURANCE PURPOSES

2.1. Assessing the current replacement cost of buildings where adequate drawings for the purpose are available.

Assessed current costs £		Fee		
		£		£
Up to	700 000		0.2%	
140 000 -	700 000	280 +	0.075% on balance over	140 000
700 000 -	4 200 000	700 +	0.025% on balance over	700 000
Over	4 200 000	1 575 +	0.01% on balance over	4 200 000

2.2. Fees to be calculated on the assessed cost, i.e. base value, for replacement purposes including allowances for demolition and the clearance but excluding inflation allowances and professional fees.

2.3. Where drawings adequate for the assessment of costs are not available or where other circumstances require that measurements of the whole or part of the buildings are taken, an additional fee shall be charged based on the time involved or alternatively on a lump sum basis agreed between the employer and the surveyor.

2.4 when the assessment is for buildings of different character or on more than one site, the costs shall not be aggregated for the purpose of calculating fees.

2.5 For current cost accounting purposes this scale refers only to the assessment of replacement cost of buildings.

2.6 The scale is appropriate for initial assessments but for annual review or a regular reassessment the fee should be by arrangement having regard to the scale and to the amount of work involved and the time taken.

2.7. The fees are exclusive of services in connection with negotiations with brokers, accountants or insurance companies for which there shall be an additional fee based upon the time involved.

CONSULTING ENGINEERS' FEES

INTRODUCTION

A scale of professional charges for consulting engineering services in connection with civil engineering works is published by the Association of Consulting Engineers (ACE)

Copies of the document can be obtained direct from:

> The Association of Consulting Engineers
> Alliance House
> 12 Caxton Street
> London SW1H OQL
> Tel: 0171 222 6557
> Fax: 0171 222 0750

Comparisons

Instead of the previous arrangement of having different agreements designed for each major discipline of engineering, these new agreements have been developed primarily to suit the different roles that Consulting Engineers may be required to perform, with variants of some of them for different disciplines. The agreements have been standardised as far as possible whilst retaining essential differences. Greater attention is required than with previous agreements to ensure the documents are completed properly. This is because of the perceived need to allow for a wider choice of arrangements, particularly of methods of payment.

The agreements are not intended to be used as unsigned reference material with the details of an engagement being covered in an exchange of letters, although much of their content could be used as a basis for drafting such correspondence.

Forms of Agreement

The initial agreements are for use where a Consulting Engineer is engaged as follows:

- ♦ as a Lead Consultant
- ♦ directly by the Client, but not as Lead Consultant
- ♦ to provide Design Services for a Design and Construct Contractor
- ♦ to provide Report and Advisory Services
- ♦ as a Project Manager
- ♦ as Planning Supervisor in accordance with the Construction (Design and Management) Regulations 1994

Each of Agreements A, B and C are published in two variants

- ♦ Variant 1 Civil and Structural Engineering
- ♦ Variant 2 The Engineering of Electrical and Mechanical Services in Buildings

Each agreement comprises the following:

- ♦ Memorandum of Agreement
- ♦ Conditions of Engagement
- ♦ Schedule of Services

CONSULTING ENGINEERS' FEES

Memorandum of Agreement

There is a different memorandum for each agreement, reflecting in each instance the particular relationships between the parties. It is essential that the memorandum be fully completed. Spaces are provided for entry of important and specific details relevant to each commission such as nominated individuals, limits of liability, requirements for professional indemnity insurance, the frequency of site visits and meetings, and requirements for collateral warranties. All the memoranda are arranged for execution under hand; some also have provision for execution as deeds.

Conditions of Engagement

These have been standardised as far as possible and thus contain much that is common between the agreements, but parts differ and are peculiar to individual agreements to reflect the responsibilities applying. The conditions can normally stand as drafted but clauses may be deleted and others be added should the circumstances so require for a particular commission.

Schedule of Services

This section, which has significant differences between the agreements and variants, describes the services to be performed. These services include both standard *Normal Services*, the majority of which will usually be required, and standard *Additional Services* of which only some will be required. Standard Normal Services may be deleted if not required or not relevant to a particular commission; further Services, both Normal and Additional may be added in spaces provided. It may be agreed in advance, when known that certain of the Additional Services will clearly be required, that these will be treated and paid for as Normal Services for a particular commission.

Remuneration / Fees and Disbursements

The agreements no longer contain information on renumeration because of the forthcoming Competition Act. A guidance booklet for clients is to published in order to assist them in assessing the consulting engineers' fees and disbursements, although this has not materialised at the time of going to press. The graphs showing the relationships of costs with appropriate levels of fees have been withdrawn from the latest agreements, however they have been reproduced on pages ??? to ??? in order to give guidance to readers until the official guidance booklet is published.

Collateral Warranties

The Association is convinced that collateral warranties are generally unnecessary and should only be used in exceptional circumstances. The interests of clients, employers and others are better protected by taking out project or BUILD type latent defects insurance. nevertheless, in response to observations raised when the pilot editions excluded any mention of warranties, references and arrangements have been included in the Memorandum and elsewhere by which Consulting Engineers may agree to enter into collateral warranty agreements; these should however only be given when the format and requirements thereof have been properly defined and recorded in advance of undertaking the commission.

Requirements for the provision of collateral warranties will be justified even less with commissions under Agreement D than with those under the other ACE agreements. Occasional calls may be made for them, such as when a client intends to dispose of property and needs evidence of a duty of care being owed to specific third parties, but these will be few and far between.

CONSULTING ENGINEERS' FEES

Need for formal documentation

The Association of Consulting Engineers recommends that formal written documentation should be executed to record the details of each commission awarded to a Consulting Engineer. These Conditions are published as model forms of agreement suitable for the purpose. However, even if these particular Conditions are not used, it is strongly recommended that, whenever a Consulting Engineer is appointed, there should be at least an exchange of letters defining the duties to be performed and the terms of payment.

Appointments outside the United Kingdom

These conditions of Engagement are designed for use within the UK. For work overseas it is impracticable to give definite recommendations; circumstances differ too widely between countries. There are added complications in documentation relating to local legislation, import customs, conditions of payment, insurance, freight, etc. Furthermore, it is often necessary to arrange for visits to be made by principals and senior staff whose absence abroad during such periods represents a serious reduction of their earning power. The additional duties, responsibilities and non-recoverable costs involved, and the extra work on general co-ordination, should be reflected in the levels of fees. Special arrangements are also necessary to cover travelling and other out-of-pocket expenses in excess of those normally incurred on similar work in the UK, including such matters as local cost-of-living allowances and the cost of providing home-leave facilities for expatriate staff.

CONDITIONS OF ENGAGEMENT

Obligations

The following is a brief summary of the conditions of engagement. It is recommended that reference should be made to the full document of the Association of Consulting Engineers Conditions of Engagement, 1995 before making an engagement. Amendments have been made to the "Payments" and "Adjudication" provisions of the document by virtue of the Housing Grants, Construction and Regeneration Act 1996 (Part II) which came into force on 1st May 1998. The amendments apply to those contracts where the Engineer is engaged in relation to all "construction operations", excluding those contracts with residential occupiers. The amendments basically give statutory power to the payment and adjudication clauses previously contained within the document.

Obligations of the Consulting Engineer

The responsibilities of the Consultant Engineer for the works are as set out in the actual agreement. The various standard clauses in the Conditions relate to such matters as: differentiating between Normal and Additional services; the duty to exercise skill and care; the need for Client's written consent to the assignment or transfer of any benefit or obligation of the agreement; the rendering of advice if requested on the appointment of other consultants and specialist sub- consultants; any recommendations for design of any part of the Works by Contractors or Sub-contractors (with the proviso that the Consulting Engineer is not responsible for detailed design of contractors or for defects or omissions in such design); the designation of a Project Leader; the need for timeliness in requests to the Client for information, etc.; freezing the design once it has been given Client approval; and the specific exclusion of any duty to advise on the actual or possible presence of pollution or contamination or its consequences.

Obligations of the Client

The Consultant Engineer shall be supplied with all necessary data and information in good time. The Client shall designate a Representative authorised to make decisions on his behalf and ensure that all decisions, instructions, and approvals are given in time so as not to delay or disrupt the Consultant Engineer.

CONSULTING ENGINEERS' FEES

Site Staff

The Consulting Engineer may employ site staff he feels are required to perform the task, subject to the prior written agreement of the Client. The Client shall bear the cost of local office accommodation, equipment and running costs.

Commencement, Determination, Postponement, Disruption and Delay

The Consulting Engineer's appointment commences at the date of the execution of the Memorandum of Agreement or such earlier date when the Consulting Engineer first commenced the performance of the Services, subject to the right of the Client to determine or postpone all or any of the Services at any time by Notice. The Client or the Consulting Engineer may determine the appointment in the event of a breach of the Agreement by the other party after two weeks notice. In addition, the Consulting Engineer may determine his appointment after two weeks notice in the event of the Client failing to make proper payment. The Consulting Engineer may suspend the performance of all or any of the Services for up to twenty-six weeks if he is prevented or significantly impeded from performance by circumstances outside his control. The appointment may be determined by either party in the event of insolvency subject to the issue of notice of determination.

Payments

The Client shall pay fees for the performance of the agreed service(s) together with all fees and charges to the local or other authorities for seeking and obtaining statutory permissions, for all site staff on a time basis, together with additional payments for any variation or the disruption of the Consulting Engineer's work due to the Client varying the task list or brief, or delay caused by the Client, others or unforeseeable events. If any part of any invoice submitted by the Consulting Engineer is contested, payment shall be made in full of all that is not contested. Payments shall be made within 28 days of the date of the Consulting Engineer's invoice; interest shall be added to all amounts remaining unpaid thereafter.

Ownership of Documents and Copyright

The Consulting Engineer retains the copyright in all drawings, reports, specifications, calculations, etc. prepared in connection with the Task; with the agreement of the Consulting Engineer and subject to certain conditions, the Client may have a licence to copy and use such intellectual property solely for his own purpose on the Task in hand, subject to reservations. The Consulting Engineer must obtain the client's permission before he publishes any articles, photographs or other illustrations relating to the Task, nor shall he disclose to any person any information provided by the Client as private and confidential unless so authorised by the Client.

Liability, Insurance and Warranties

The liability of the Consulting Engineer is defined, together with the duty of the Client to indemnify the Consulting Engineer against all claims, etc. in excess of the agreed liability limit. The Consulting Engineer shall maintain Professional Indemnity Insurance for an agreed amount and period at commercially reasonable rates, together with Public Liability Insurance and shall produce the broker's certificates for inspection to show that the required cover is being maintained as and when requested by the Client. The Consulting Engineer shall enter into and provide collateral warranties for the benefit of other parties if so agreed.

Disputes and Differences

Provision is made for mediation to solve disputes, subject to a time limit of six weeks of the appointment of the mediator at which point it should be referred to an independent adjudicator. Further action could be taken by referring the dispute to an arbitrator.

CURRENT OUTPUT PRICE INDEX

The current Output Price Index for second quarter 1999 is **371** (1975 = 100).

CONSULTING ENGINEERS' FEES

GRAPH SHOWING RELATIONSHIP OF PERCENTAGE FEE WITH COST

AGREEMENT A(1), LEAD CONSULTANT, CIVIL/STRUCTURAL

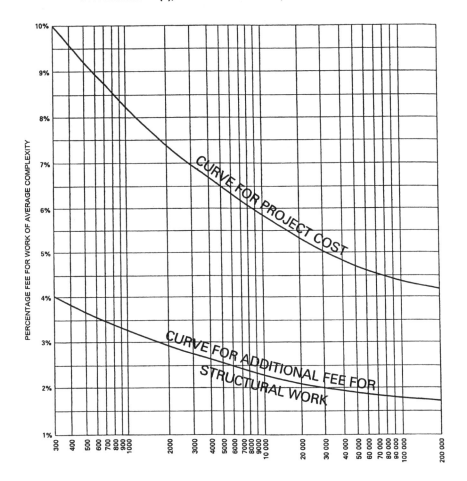

PROJECT/WORKS COST IN £ DIVIDED BY OUTPUT PRICE INDEX (1975=100)

Note: When Project Cost divided by Output Price Index is below 300, time charges should be used. When the figure for structural work is below 300, the additional fee for this work should be negotiated at around 4% of its cost.

CONSULTING ENGINEERS' FEES

GRAPH SHOWING RELATIONSHIP OF PERCENTAGE FEE WITH COST

AGREEMENT B(1), DIRECTLY ENGAGED CONSULTANT, NOT IN THE LEAD
CIVIL/STRUCTURAL

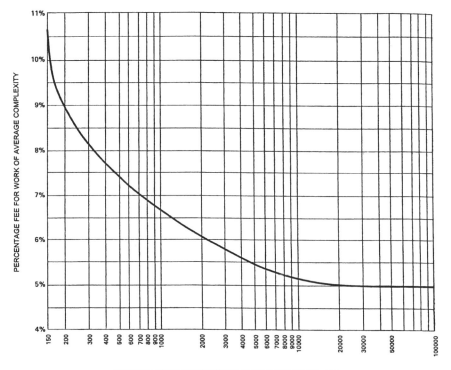

WORKS COST IN £ DIVIDED BY OUTPUT PRICE INDEX (1975=100)

Note: When Works Cost divided by Output Price Index is below 150, time charges should be used.

CONSULTING ENGINEERS' FEES

GRAPH SHOWING RELATIONSHIP OF PERCENTAGE FEE WITH COST

AGREEMENT C(1), DESIGN FOR CONTRACTOR, CIVIL/STRUCTURAL

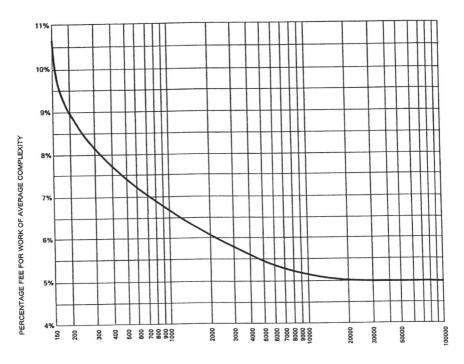

WORKS COST IN £ DIVIDED BY OUTPUT PRICE INDEX (1975 = 100)

Note: When Works Cost divided by Output Price Index is below 150, time charges should be used.

THE TOWN AND COUNTRY PLANNING (FEES FOR APPLICATIONS AND DEEMED APPLICATIONS) (AMENDMENT) REGULATIONS 1997
Operative from 1st October 1997

The following extracts from the Town and Country Planning Fees Regulations, available from HMSO, relate only to those applications which meet the "deemed to qualify clauses" laid down in regulations 1 to 12 of S.I. No. 1989/193, updated by 1 to 5 of S.I. 1991/2735, 1992/1817, 1992/3052 and 1993/3170.
Further advice on the interpretation of these regulations can be found in the 1990 Town and Country Planning Acts and S.I. 1989/193 and 1990/2473.

SCHEDULE 1

PART I: GENERAL PROVISIONS

1.   (1)   Subject to paragraphs 3 to 11, the fee payable under regulation 3 or regulation 10 shall be calculated in accordance with the table set out in Part II of this Schedule and paragraphs 2 and 12 to 16.

      (2)   In the case of an application for approval of reserved matters, references in this Schedule to the category of development to which an application relates shall be construed as references to the category of development authorised by the relevant outline planning permission.

2.   Where an application or deemed application is made or deemed to be made by or on behalf of a parish council or by or on behalf of a community council, the fee payable shall be one-half of the amount as would otherwise be payable.

3.   (1)   Where an application or deemed application is made or deemed to be made by or on behalf of a club, society or other organisation(including any persons administering a trust) which is not established or conducted for profit and whose objects are the provision of facilities for sport or recreation, and the conditions specified in subparagraph (2) are satisfied, the fee payable shall be £190).

      (2)   The conditions referred to in subparagraph (1) are:

         (a)   that the application or deemed application relates to:

            (i)   the making of a material change in the use of land to use as a playing field; or

            (ii)   the carrying out of operations (other than the erection of a building containing floor space) for purposes ancillary to the use of land as a playing field, and to no other development: and

         (b)   that the local planning authority with whom the application is lodged, or (in the case of a deemed application) the Secretary of State, is satisfied that the development is to be carried out on land which is, or is intended to be, occupied by the club, society or organisation and used wholly or mainly for the carrying out of its objects.

4.   (1)   Where an application for planning permission or an application for approval of reserved matters is made not more than 28 days after the lodging with the local planning authority of an application for planning permission or, as the case may be, an application for approval of reserved matters:

         (a)   made by or on behalf of the same applicant;

         (b)   relating to the same site; and

         (c)   relating to the same development or, in the case of an application for approval of reserved matters, relating to the same reserved matters in respect of the same building or buildings authorised by the same outline planning permission, and a fee of the full amount payable in respect of the category or categories of development to which the applications relate has been paid in respect of the earlier application, the fee payable in respect of the later application shall, subject to sub-paragraph (2) be one-quarter of the amount paid in respect of the earlier application.

      (2)   Sub-paragraph (1) apply only in respect of one application made by or on behalf of the same applicant in relation to the same development or in relation to the same reserved matters (as the case may be).

THE TOWN AND COUNTRY PLANNING (FEES FOR APPLICATIONS
AND DEEMED APPLICATIONS) (AMENDMENT) REGULATIONS 1997

5. (1) This paragraph applies where:
    (a) an application is made for approval of one or more reserved matters ("the current application"); and
    (b) the applicant has previously applied for such approval under the same outline planning permission and paid fees in relation to one or more such applications; and
    (c) no application has been made under that permission other than by or on behalf of the applicant.
  (2) Where the amount paid as mentioned in sub-paragraph (1) (b) is not less than the amount which would be payable if the applicant were by his current application seeking approval of all the matters reserved by the outline permission (and in relation to the whole of the development authorised by the permission), the fee payable in respect of the current application shall be £190.
  (3) Where:
    (a) a fee has been paid as mentioned in sub-paragraph (1) (b) at a rate lower than that prevailing at the date of the current application; and
    (b) sub-paragraph (2) would apply if that fee had been paid at the rate applying at that date, the fee in respect of the current application shall be the amount specified in sub-paragraph (2).

6. Where an application is made pursuant to section 31A of the 1971 Act the fee payable in respect of the application shall be £95.

7A Where an application relates to development to which section 73A(b) of the Town and Country Planning Act 1990 applies, the fee payable in respect of the application shall be:
    (a) where the application relates to development carried out within planning permission, the fee that would be payable if the application were for planning permission to carry out that development;
    (b) £95 in any case

7B. Where an application is made for the renewal of planning permission and:
    (a) a planning permission has previously been granted for development which has not yet begun, and
    (b) a limit as to the time by which the development must be begun was imposed under section 91 (limit of duration of planning permission) or section 92 (outline planning permission) of the Town and Country Planning Act 1990 which has not yet expired, the fee payable in respect of the application shall be £95.

8. (1) This paragraph applies where applications are made for planning permission or for the approval of reserved matters in respect of the development of land lying in the areas of:
    (a) two or more local planning authorities in a metropolitan county or in Greater London; or
    (b) two or more district planning authorities in a non-metropolitan county; or
    (c) one or more such local planning authorities and one or more such district planning authorities.
  (2) A fee shall be payable only to the local planning authority or district planning authority in whose area the largest part of the relevant land is situated: and the amount payable shall be:
    (a) where the applications relate wholly or partly to a county matter within the meaning of paragraph 32 of Schedule 16 to the Local Government Act 1972, and all the land is situated in a single non-metropolitan county, the amount which would have been payable if application had fallen to be made to one authority in relation to the whole development;
    (b) in any other case, one and a half times the amount which would have been payable if application had fallen to be made to a single authority or the sum of the amounts which would have been payable but for this paragraph, whichever is the lesser.

THE TOWN AND COUNTRY PLANNING (FEES FOR APPLICATIONS
AND DEEMED APPLICATIONS) (AMENDMENT) REGULATIONS 1997

9.   (1)   This paragraph applies where application for planning permission is deemed to have been
              made by virtue of section 88B (3) of the 1971 Act in respect of such land as is mentioned in
              paragraph 8 (1).
       (2)   The fee payable to the Secretary of State shall be the amount which would be payable by
              virtue of paragraph 8 (2) if application for the like permission had been made to the relevant
              local or district planning authority on the date on which notice of appeal was given in
              accordance with section 88 (3) of the 1971 Act.
10.   (1)   Where:
              (a)   application for planning permission is made in respect of two or more alternative
                     proposals for the development of the same land; or
              (b)   application for approval of reserved matters is made, in respect of two or more
                     alternative proposals for the carrying out of the development authorised by an outline
                     planning permission, and application is made in respect of all of the alternative
                     proposals on the same date and by or on behalf of the same applicant, a single fee
                     shall be payable in respect of all such alternative proposals, calculated as provided in
                     sub-paragraph (2).
       (2)   Calculations shall be made, in accordance with this Schedule, of the fee appropriate to each
              of the alternative proposals and the single fee payable in respect of all the alternative
              proposals shall be the sum of:
              (a)   an amount equal to the highest of the amounts calculated in respect of each of the
                     alternative proposals; and
              (b)   an amount calculated by adding together the amounts appropriate to all of the
                     alternative proposals, other than the amount referred to in subparagraph (a), and
                     dividing that total by the figure of 2.
11.   In the case of an application for planning permission which is deemed to have been made by virtue
       of section 95 (6) of the 1971 Act, the fee payable shall be the sum of £190.
12.   Where, in respect of any category of development specified in the table set out in Part II of this
       Schedule, the fee is to be calculated by reference to the site area:
       (a)   that area shall be taken as consisting of the area of land to which the application relates or,
              in the case of an application for planning permission which is deemed to have been made by
              virtue of section 88B (3) of the 1971 Act, the area of land to which the relevant enforcement
              notice relates; and
       (b)   where the area referred to in sub-paragraph (a) above is not an exact multiple of the unit of
              measurement specified in respect of the relevant category of development, the fraction of a
              unit remaining after division of the total area by the unit of measurement shall be treated as
              a complete unit.
13.   (1)   In relation to development within any of the categories 2 to 4 specified in the table in Part II
              of this Schedule, the area of gross floor space to be created by the development shall be
              ascertained by external measurement of the floor space, whether or not it is to be bounded
              (wholly or partly) by external walls of a building.
       (2)   In relation to development within category 2 specified in the said table, where the area of
              gross floor space to be created by the development exceeds 75 sq metres and is not an exact
              multiple of 75 sq metres, the area remaining after division of the total number of square
              metres of gross floor space by the figure of 75 shall be treated as being 75 sq metres.
       (3)   In relation to development within category 3 specified in the said table, where the area of
              gross floor space exceeds 540 sq metres and the amount of the excess is not an exact
              multiple of 75 sq metres, the area remaining after division of the number of square metres of
              that excess area of gross floor space by the figure of 75 shall be treated as being 75 sq
              metres.

THE TOWN AND COUNTRY PLANNING (FEES FOR APPLICATIONS
AND DEEMED APPLICATIONS) (AMENDMENT) REGULATIONS 1997

14. (1) Where an application (other than an outline application) or a deemed application relates to development which is in part within category 1 in the table set out in Part II of this Schedule and in part within category 2, 3, or 4, the following sub-paragraphs shall apply for the purpose of calculating the fee payable in respect of the application or deemed application.

(2) An assessment shall be made of the total amount of gross floor space which is to be created by that part of the development which is within category 2, 3 or 4 ("the non-residential floor space"), and the sum payable in respect of the non-residential floor space to be created by the development shall be added to the sum payable in respect of that part of the development which is within category 1, and subject to sub-paragraph (4), the sum so calculated shall be the fee payable in respect of the application or deemed application.

(3) For the purpose of calculating the fee under sub-paragraph (2)-
   (a) Where any of the buildings is to contain floor space which it is proposed to use for the purposes of providing common access or common services or facilities for persons occupying or using that building for residential purposes and for persons occupying or using it for non-residential purposes ("common floor space"), the amount of non-residential floor space shall be assessed, in relation to that building, as including such proportion of the common floor space as the amount of non-residential floor space in the building bears to the total amount of gross floor space in the building to be created by the development;
   (b) where the development falls within more than one of categories 2, 3 and 4 an amount shall be calculated in accordance with each such category and the highest amount so calculated shall be taken as the sum payable in respect of all of the non-residential floor space.

(4) Where an application or deemed application to which this paragraph applies relates to development which is also within one or more than one of the categories 5 to 13 in the table set out in Part II of this Schedule, an amount shall be calculated in accordance with each such category and if any of the amounts so calculated exceeds the amount calculated in accordance with sub-paragraph (2) that higher amount shall be the fee payable in respect of all of the development to which the application or deemed application relates.

15. (1) Subject to paragraph 14, and sub-paragraph (2), where an application or deemed application relates to development which is within more than one of the categories specified in the table set out in Part II of this Schedule:
   (a) an amount shall be calculated in accordance with each such category; and
   (b) the highest amount so calculated shall be the fee payable in respect of the application or deemed application.

(2) Where an application is for outline planning permission and relates to development which is within more than one of the categories specified in the said table, the fee payable in respect of the application shall be £190 for each 0.1 hectares of the site area, subject to a maximum of £4,750.

16. In the case of an application for planning permission which is deemed to have been made by virtue of section 88B (3) of the 1971 Act, references in this Schedule to the development to which an application relates shall be construed as references to the use of land or the operations (as the case may be) to which the relevant enforcement notice relates; references to the amount of floor space or the number of dwelling houses to be created by the development shall be construed as references to the amount of floor space or the number of dwelling houses to which that enforcement notice relates; and references to the purposes for which it is proposed that floor space be used shall be construed as references to the purposes for which floor space was stated to be used in the enforcement notice.

THE TOWN AND COUNTRY PLANNING (FEES FOR APPLICATIONS
AND DEEMED APPLICATIONS) (AMENDMENT) REGULATIONS 1997

PART II: SCALE OF FEES

Category of development   Fee Payable

I. Operations

1. The erection of dwelling houses (other than development within category 6 below).

    (a) Where the application is for outline planning permission £190 for each 0.1 hectare of the site area, subject to a maximum of £4,750;

    (b) in other cases, £190 for each dwelling house to be created by the development, subject to a maximum of £9,500.

2. The erection of buildings (other than buildings coming within categories 1,3, 4, 5 or 7.)

    (a) Where the application is for outline planning permission £190 for each 0.1 hectare of the the site area, subject to a maximum of £4,750;

    (b) in other cases:

        (i) where no floor space is to be created by the development, £95;

        (ii) where the area of gross floor space to be created by the development does not exceed 40 sq metres, £95;

        (iii) where the area of gross floor space to be created by the development exceeds 40 sq metres but does not exceed 75 sq metres, £190; and

        (iv) where the area of gross floor space to be created by the development exceeds 75 sq metres, £190 for each 75 sq metres, subject to a maximum of £9,500.

3. The erection, on land used for the purposes of agriculture, of buildings to be used for agricultural purposes (other than buildings coming within category 4).

    (a) Where the application is for outline planning permission £190 for each hectare of the site area subject to a maximum of £4,750;

    (b) in other cases:

        (i) where the area of gross floor space to be created by the development does not exceed 465 sq metres, £35;

        (ii) where the area of gross floor space to be created by the development exceeds 465 sq metres but does not exceed 540 sq metres, £190; and

        (iii) where the area of gross floor space to be created by development exceeds 540 sq metres, £190 for the first 540 sq metres and £190 for each 75 sq metres in excess of that figure, subject to a maximum of £9,500.

4. The erection of glasshouses on land used for the purposes of agriculture.

    (a) Where the area of gross floor space to be created by the development does not exceed 465 sq metres, £35;

    (b) where the area of gross floor space to be created by the development exceeds 465 sq metres, £1,085.

5. The erection, alteration or replacement of plant or machinery.

£190 for each 0.1 hectare of the site area, subject to a maximum of £9,500.

THE TOWN AND COUNTRY PLANNING (FEES FOR APPLICATIONS
AND DEEMED APPLICATIONS) (AMENDMENT) REGULATIONS 1997

Category of development	Fee Payable
6. The enlargement, improvement or other alteration of existing dwelling houses	(a) Where the application relates to one dwelling house, £95; (b) where the application relates to 2 or more dwelling houses, £190.
7. (a) The carrying out of operations (including the erection of a building within the curtilage of an existing dwelling house, for purposes ancillary to the enjoyment of the dwelling house as such, or the erection or construction of gates, fences, walls or other means of enclosure along a boundary of the curtilage of an existing dwelling house; or (b) the construction of car parks, service roads and other means of access on land used for the purposes of a single undertaking, where the development is required for a purpose incidental to the existing use of the land.	£95
8. The carrying out of any operations connected with exploratory drilling for oil or natural gas.	£190 for each 0.1 hectare of the site area, subject to a maximum of £14,250.
9. The carrying out of any operations not coming within any of the above categories.	£95 for each 0.1 hectare of the site area, subject to a maximum of: (a) in the case of operations for the winning and working of minerals, £14,250; (b) in other cases, £950.

II. Uses of Land

10. The change of use of a building to use as one or more separate dwelling houses.	(a) Where the change is from a previous use as a single dwelling house to use as a two or more single dwelling houses, £190 for each additional dwelling house to be created by the development, subject to a maximum of £9,500. (b) in other cases, £190 for each dwelling house to be created by the development, subject to a maximum of £9,500.
11. (a) The use of land for the disposal of refuse or waste materials or for the deposit of material remaining after minerals have been extracted from land; or (b) the use of land for the storage of minerals in the open.	£95 for each 0.1 hectare of the site area, subject to a maximum of £14,250.
12. The making of a material change in the use of a building or land (other than a material change of use coming within any of the above categories).	£190.

THE TOWN AND COUNTRY PLANNING (FEES FOR APPLICATIONS
AND DEEMED APPLICATIONS) (AMENDMENT) REGULATIONS 1997

SCHEDULE 2

SCALE OF FEES IN RESPECT OF APPLICATIONS FOR CONSENT TO DISPLAY ADVERTISEMENTS

Category of advertisement	Fee payable
1. Advertisements displayed on business premises, on the forecourt of business premises or on other land within the curtilage of business premises, wholly with reference to all or any of the following matters: (a) the nature of the business or other activity carried out on the premises; (b) the goods sold or the services provided on the premises; or (c) the name and qualifications of the person carrying on such business or activity or supplying such goods or services.	£50
2. Advertisements for the purpose of directing members of the public to, or otherwise drawing attention to the existence of, business premises which are in the same locality as the site on which the advertisement is to be displayed but which are not visible from that site.	£50
3. All other advertisements.	£190.

THE BUILDING (LOCAL AUTHORITY CHARGES) REGULATIONS 1998

Author's Note:

On the 31st July 1998 the Minister for Construction, announced his intention of improving the flexibility with which local authorities responsible for building control in England and Wales could respond to competition from the private sector by devolving to individual authorities the setting of charges for building control functions carried out in respect of the Building Regulations 1991.

The Building (Local Authority Charges) Regulations 1998 (the Charges Regulations) require each local authority to prepare a Scheme within which they are to fix their charges. They came into effect on the 1st April 1999. In a number of major cities, uniform levels of fees have been adopted. In some local authorities charges have fallen a third in comparison to those prescribed within the 1991 Regulations. A number of authorities have adopted the Local Government Association (LGA) Model Fee Scheme 2000, which is for local authority distribution only.

Consultation should be made to each local authority for their Charges, however as guidance we have kindly been given permission by the London Borough of Ealing to publish the Charges for their district, which includes Acton W3.

CHARGE SCHEDULES - LONDON BOROUGH OF EALING

With effect from 1st April 1999, there are three main charge Schedule Tables:

Table 1,   For erection of one or more small new domestic buildings and connected work, ie houses and flats up to 3 storeys in height with an internal floor area not exceeding 300 m²;

Table 2,   For erection of certain small domestic building, and extensions, ie detached garages and carports not exceeding 40 m² and not exempt, and extensions including all new loft conversions up to a total of 60 m² at the same time;

Table 3,   For building work other than where Tables 1 and 2 apply. Charges relate to estimated cost of the works.

TYPES OF CHARGES

There are four application types and five types of charge:

1) **Building Notice** applications where the full **Charge** must be paid at time of notification (column 10 in Tables 1, 2 and 3). This is mainly used for small domestic alterations. Where structural work is involved calculations need to be provided. Upon satisfactory completion of works on site a Completion Certificate may be issued;

2) **Full Plan** applications where the **Plan Charge** (column 4 in Tables 1, 2 and 3) must be paid in deposit of plans. A subsequent re-submission, further to a Rejection of Plans, will NOT attract an additional fee for essentially the same work. If the inspection charge is not paid upon the deposit of plans, an invoice will be raised after the first inspection on site as this is when **Inspection Charge** (column 7 in Tables 1, 2 and 3) becomes payable. Where work is to be done to Shops, Factories, Offices, Railway Premises, Hotels and Boarding Houses, and Non-domestic Workplaces a Full Plan Application should be made. It is also appropriate for Domestic Loft Conversions and other Extensions and Erections of Domestic Buildings. It is important to start work before 3 years have expired or the Plan Approval may be withdrawn. Upon satisfactory completion of the works on site a Completion Certificate may be issued;

3) **Regularisation** applications where the full **Charge of 1.2 times the Building Notice Charge** must be paid at time of notification (ie 1.2 times column 8 in Tables 1, 2 and 3). VAT is not chargeable. This is where work started after November 1985 but was not notified to Building Control. It is usually necessary to open up works to show what has been done. A letter may be sent outlining what needs to be done to comply with the Building Regulations. Upon satisfactory completion of works on site a Regularisation Certificate may be issued; and

THE BUILDING (LOCAL AUTHORITY CHARGES) REGULATIONS 1998

TYPES OF CHARGES - cont'd

4)   **Reversion** applications where the full **Charge equal to the Building Notice Charge** must be paid at time of notification (column 8 in Tables 1, 2 and 3). VAT is chargeable. This is where an Approved Inspector has supervised Building Regulations but the work has reverted to Building Control. It is usually necessary to open up works to show what has been done. A letter may be sent outlining what needs to be done to comply with the Building Regulations. Upon satisfactory completion of works on site a Reversion Certificate may be issued.

Unless a required fee is included with an application form, it cannot be accepted as a valid application. Work may not legally start on site until the fee is received. If Cheque(s) are Dishonoured the application also cannot be accepted as valid.

EXEMPTIONS

No fees are charged, **where** we are satisfied **work** is **solely** for the purpose of providing means of access **for disabled persons** or within a building, or for providing facilities designed to secure greater health, safety, welfare or convenience and is carried out in relation to a building to which members of the public are admitted or is a dwelling occupied by a disabled person.

THE BUILDING (LOCAL AUTHORITY CHARGES) REGULATIONS 1998

TABLE 1

CHARGES FOR ERECTION OF ONE OR MORE SMALL NEW DOMESTIC BUILDINGS AND CONNECTED WORK

NOTES

Dwellings in excess of 300 m² in floor area (excluding garage or carport) are to be calculated on estimated cost in accordance with Table 3).

Building in excess of 3 storeys (including any basements) to be calculated on estimated cost in accordance with Table 3.

The charges in this Table includes for works of drainage in connection with erection of a building(s), even where those drainage works are commenced in advance of the plans for the building being deposited.

The charges include for an integral garage and where a garage or carport shares at least one wall of the domestic building. Detached garages are not included in this Table (see Notes Table 2).

Where a Plan or Inspection Charge exceeds £4000.00 (columns 2 and 5) the Council may agree payment in instalments.

Where all dwellings on a site or an estate are substantially the same, it may be possible to offer a discount of 30% reduction on PLAN Charge OR equivalent reduction on the BUILDING NOTICE Charge.

Number of Dwelling	PLAN CHARGE			INSPECTION CHARGE			BUILDING NOTICE		
	CHARGE £	VAT £	TOTAL £	CHARGE £	VAT £	TOTAL £	CHARGE £	VAT £	TOTAL £
(1)	(2)	(3)	(4)	(5)	(6)	(7)	(8)	(9)	(10)
1	140.00	24.50	164.50	160.00	28.00	188.00	300.00	52.50	352.50
2	205.00	35.88	240.88	300.00	52.50	352.50	505.00	88.38	593.38
3	270.00	47.25	317.25	435.00	76.13	511.13	705.00	123.38	828.38
4	335.00	58.63	393.63	575.00	100.63	675.63	910.00	159.25	1,069.25
5	405.00	70.86	475.86	710.00	124.25	834.25	1,115.00	195.13	1,310.13
6	475.00	83.13	558.13	785.00	137.38	922.38	1,260.00	220.50	1,480.50
7	495.00	86.63	581.63	945.00	165.38	1,110.38	1,440.00	252.00	1,692.00
8	515.00	90.13	605.13	1,105.00	193.38	1,298.38	1,620.00	283.50	1,903.50
9	535.00	93.63	628.63	1,265.00	221.38	1,486.38	1,800.00	315.00	2,115.00
10	540.00	94.50	634.50	1,440.00	252.00	1,692.00	1,980.00	346.50	2,326.50
11	545.00	95.38	640.38	1,580.00	276.50	1,856.50	2,125.00	371.88	2,496.88
12	550.00	96.25	646.25	1,720.00	301.00	2,021.00	2,270.00	397.25	2,667.25
13	555.00	97.13	652.13	1,860.00	325.50	2,185.50	2,415.00	422.63	2,837.63
14	560.00	98.00	658.00	2,000.00	350.00	2,350.00	2,560.00	448.00	3,008.00
15	565.00	98.88	663.88	2,140.00	374.50	2,514.50	2,705.00	473.38	3,178.38
16	570.00	99.75	669.75	2,280.00	399.00	2,679.00	2,850.00	498.75	3,348.75
17	575.00	100.63	675.63	2,420.00	423.50	2,843.50	2,995.00	524.13	3,519.13
18	580.00	101.50	681.50	2,560.00	448.00	3,008.00	3,140.00	549.50	3,689.50
19	585.00	102.38	687.38	2,700.00	472.50	3,172.50	3,285.00	574.88	3,859.88
20	590.00	103.25	693.25	2,840.00	497.00	3,337.00	3,430.00	600.25	4,030.25
21	600.00	105.00	705.00	2,940.00	514.50	3,454.50	3,540.00	619.50	4,159.50
22	610.00	106.75	716.75	3,040.00	532.00	3,572.00	3,650.00	638.75	4,288.75
23	620.00	108.50	728.50	3,140.00	549.50	3,689.50	3,760.00	658.00	4,418.00
24	630.00	110.25	740.25	3,240.00	567.00	3,807.00	3,870.00	677.25	4,547.25
25	640.00	112.00	752.00	3,340.00	584.50	3,924.50	3,980.00	696.50	4,676.50
26	650.00	113.75	763.75	3,440.00	602.00	4,042.00	4,090.00	715.75	4,805.75
27	660.00	115.50	775.50	3,540.00	619.50	4,159.50	4,200.00	735.00	4,935.00
28	670.00	117.25	787.25	3,640.00	637.00	4,277.00	4,310.00	754.25	5,064.25
29	680.00	119.00	799.00	3,740.00	654.50	4,394.50	4,420.00	773.50	5,193.50
30	690.00	120.75	810.75	3,840.00	672.00	4,512.00	4,530.00	792.75	5,322.75
31	700.00	122.50	822.50	3,940.00	689.50	4,629.50	4,640.00	812.00	5,452.00
31 AND OVER	For each dwelling in excess of 31 add £5 + VAT (= £5.88 inclusive of VAT)			For each dwelling in excess of 31 add £75 + VAT (= £81.13 inclusive of VAT)			For each dwelling in excess of 31 add £80 + VAT (= £94.00 inclusive of VAT)		

THE BUILDING (LOCAL AUTHORITY CHARGES) REGULATIONS 1998

TABLE 2

CHARGES FOR ERECTION OF CERTAIN SMALL DOMESTIC BUILDINGS, GARAGES, CARPORTS AND EXTENSIONS

NOTES

Detached garages and carports having an internal floor area not exceeding 30 m² are 'exempt buildings', providing that in the case of a garage it is sited at least 1.0 m away from the boundary or is constructed substantially of non-combustible materials.

A carport extension having an internal floor area not exceeding 30 m² would be exempt if it is fully open on at least 2 sides.

Detached garages in excess of 40 m² and extensions in excess of 60 m² in floor area use Table 3.

A new Dormer Windows which does not increase the usable floor area would be an alteration so use Table 3.

If the **total floor area** of all extensions being done at the sam time **exceeds 60 m² use Table 3**.

Loft conversions with new internal useable floor area in roof space are to be treated as an extension in this Table 2.

Extensions more than three storeys high (including any basement) **should use Table 3**.

Chargeable installations of Cavity Fill Insulation, and Unvented Hot Water Systems should use Table 3 (see Table 3 notes).

Extensions to a building that is **NOT wholly domestic** should use **Table 3**.

The **drainage work** necessary in the extensions done under this Table **does NOT attract an additional charge**.

Where on an estate erection of garages or extensions are substantially the same, it may be possible to offer a discount of 30% reduction on PLAN Charge OR a 7½% reduction on the BUILDING NOTICE Charge.

Type of Work	PLAN CHARGE			INSPECTION CHARGE			BUILDING NOTICE		
	CHARGE £	VAT £	TOTAL £	CHARGE £	VAT £	TOTAL £	CHARGE £	VAT £	TOTAL £
(1)	(2)	(3)	(4)	(5)	(6)	(7)	(8)	(9)	(10)
1 Erection of a **detached** building which consists of a **garage or carport** or both having a floor area not exceeding 40m² in total and intended to be used in common with an existing building, and which is not an exempt building.	25.00	4.37	29.37	75.00	13.13	88.13	100.00	17.5	117.50
2 **Any extension of a dwelling** the total floor area of which **does not exceed 10m²,** including means of access and work in connection with that extension.	200.00	35.00	235.00	No inspection charge (included in plan charge)			200.00	35.00	235.00
3 **Any extension of a dwelling** the total floor area of which **exceeds 10m², but does not exceed 40m²,** including means of access and work in connection with that extension.	75.00	13.12	88.12	225.00	39.38	264.38	300.00	52.50	352.50
4 **Any extension of a dwelling** the total floor area of which **exceeds 40m², but does not exceed 60m²,** including means of access and work in connection with that extension.	100.00	17.50	117.50	300.00	52.50	352.50	400.00	70.00	470.00

THE BUILDING (LOCAL AUTHORITY CHARGES) REGULATIONS 1998

TABLE 3

CHARGES FOR BUILDING WORK OTHER THAN TO WHICH TABLES 1 AND 2 APPLY. CHARGES RELATE TO ESTIMATED COST.

NOTES

If some building work is covered by Table 2 and some by Table 3, both fees are payable.

Estimated cost of work should not include any professional fees (e.g. Architect, Quantity Surveyor, etc) nor any VAT.

Installation of cavity fill insulation in accordance with Part D of Schedule 1 to the Principle Regulations where installation is not certified to an approved standard or is not installed by an approved installer, or is part of a larger project this Table Building Notice Charge is payable (columns 8, 9, 10).

Installation of an unvented hot water system in accordance with Part G3 of Schedule 1 to the Principle Regulations where the installation is not part of a larger project and where the authority carry out an inspection, this Table Building Notice Charge is payable (columns 8, 9, 10).

Where a Plan or Inspection Charge exceeds £4,000.00 (columns 2 or 5) the Council may agree payment in instalments.

If application is for erection of work substantially the same type under current regulations, it may be possible to offer a discount of PLAN Charge by 30% OR BUILDING NOTICE Charge by 7½%.

Use Table 1 for Dwellings up to 300 m² in floor area and up to and including 3 storeys high.

ESTIMATED COST OF WORKS £		PLAN CHARGE			INSPECTION CHARGE			BUILDING NOTICE		
		CHARGE £	VAT £	TOTAL £	CHARGE £	VAT £	TOTAL £	CHARGE £	VAT £	TOTAL £
(1)		(2)	(3)	(4)	(5)	(6)	(7)	(8)	(9)	(10)
0 - 2,000		100.00	17.50	117.50	No inspection charge			100.00	17.50	117.50
2,001 - 5,000		165.00	28.87	193.87	(included in plan charge)			165.00	28.87	193.87
5,001 - 6,000		43.50	7.61	51.11	130.50	22.84	153.34	174.00	30.45	204.45
6,001 - 7,000		45.75	8.00	53.75	137.25	24.02	161.27	183.00	32.02	215.02
7,001 - 8,000		48.00	8.40	56.40	144.00	25.20	169.20	192.00	33.60	225.60
8,001 - 9,000		50.25	8.79	59.04	150.75	26.38	177.13	201.00	35.18	236.18
9,001 - 10,000		52.50	9.19	61.69	157.50	27.56	185.06	210.00	36.75	246.75
10,001 - 11,000		54.75	9.58	64.33	164.25	28.74	192.99	219.00	38.32	257.32
11,001 - 12,000		57.00	9.98	66.98	171.00	29.92	200.92	228.00	39.90	267.90
12,001 - 13,000		59.25	10.37	69.62	177.75	31.10	208.86	237.00	41.48	278.48
13,001 - 14,000		61.50	10.76	72.26	184.50	32.29	216.79	246.00	43.05	289.05
14,001 - 15,000		63.75	11.15	74.90	191.25	33.47	224.72	255.00	44.62	299.62
15,001 - 16,000		66.00	11.55	77.55	198.00	34.65	232.65	264.00	46.20	310.20
16,001 - 17,000		68.25	11.95	80.20	204.75	35.83	240.58	273.00	47.78	320.78
17,001 - 18,000		70.50	12.34	82.83	211.50	37.02	248.52	282.00	49.35	331.35
18,001 - 19,000		72.75	12.73	85.48	218.25	38.19	256.44	291.00	50.92	341.92
19,001 - 20,000		75.00	13.13	88.13	225.00	39.38	264.38	300.00	52.50	352.50
20,001 to 100,000	Basic	75.00	13.13	88.13	225.00	39.98	264.38	300.00	52.50	352.50
	+ for each £1,000 or part thereof by which cost exceeds £20,000	2.00	0.35	2.35	6.00	1.05	7.05	8.00	1.40	9.40
100,001 to 1,000,000	Basic	235.00	41.13	276.13	705.00	123.38	828.38	940.00	164.50	1,104.50
	+ for each £1,000 or part thereof by which cost exceeds £100,000	0.90	0.16	1.06	2.60	0.45	3.05	3.50	0.61	4.11
1,000,001 to 10,000,000	Basic	1,020.00	178.50	1,198.50	3,070.00	537.25	3,607.25	4,090.00	715.75	4,805.75
	+ for each £1,000 or part thereof by which cost exceeds £1 m	0.90	0.16	1.06	2.60	0.45	3.05	3.50	0.61	4.11
10,000,001 and Over	Basic	7,210.00	1,261.75	8,471.75	21,630.00	3,785.25	25,415.25	28,840.00	5047.00	33,887.00
	+ for each £1,000 or part thereof by which cost exceeds £10 m	0.50	0.09	0.59	1.50	0.26	1.76	2.00	0.35	2.35

Green Building Handbook: Volume 2

A guide to building products and their impact on the environment

Edited by Tom Woolley, Queens University of Belfast, UK and Sam Kimmins, Ethical Consumer Research Association, UK

From reviews of the Green Building Handbook: 'The Publisher is to be congratulated on this book' - **Building**

This new handbook provides a detailed reference for environmentally concerned purchasers of building products, and complements the first Green Building Handbook. Following the format of the original, this book discusses current issues in green building before moving on to consider eight building component types: Fencing Products, Flat Roofing Membranes, Glazing Products, Electrical Wiring, Adhesives, Straw Bale Building, Interior Decoration and Indoor Air Quality and Ventilation. Invaluable for the specifier, this companion handbook will be useful to all those interested in finding greener ways of designing and making buildings.

Contents: **Part One**. 1.Introduction: a discursive essay highlighting important trends in green building and explaining the rationale and methodology behind the handbook. **Part Two**. How to use the handbook. Key to product table headings. 2. Fencing products. 3. Flat roofing membranes. 4. Glazing products. 5. Electrical wiring. 6. Adhesives. 7. Straw bale building. 8. Interior decoration. 9. Indoor air quality and ventilation. Further reading. Useful information on relevant organizations. Index.

December 1999: 297x210: 152pp
Illus drawings and b+w photographs
Pb: 0-419-25380-7: £29.95

To Order: **Tel:** +44 (0) 8700 768853, or +44 (0) 1264 343071
Fax: +44 (0) 1264 343005, or **Post:** E & FN Spon Customer Services, ITPS Andover, Hants, SP10 5BE, UK

All orders must be pre-paid and will be sent free in the UK. Europe please add: £2.95 for the first book, thereafter £1.25 per book. ROW please add: Airmail £6.50 for the first book, thereafter £2.50 per book. Please add £12.50 delivery charge for items over £100.00.

Daywork And Prime Cost

When work is carried out which cannot be valued in any other way it is customary to assess the value on a cost basis with an allowance to cover overheads and profit. The basis of costing is a matter for agreement between the parties concerned, but definitions of prime cost for the building industry have been prepared and published jointly by the Royal Institution of Chartered Surveyors and the National Federation of Building Trades Employers (now the Building Employers Confederation) for the convenience of those who wish to use them. These documents are reproduced on the following pages by kind permission of the publishers.

The daywork schedule published by the Civil Engineering Contractors Association is included in the A&B's companion title, *"Spons Civil Engineering and Highway Works Price Book"*.

For larger Prime Cost contracts the reader is referred to the form of contract issued by the Royal Institute of British Architects.

BUILDING INDUSTRY

DEFINITION OF PRIME COST OF DAYWORK CARRIED OUT UNDER A BUILDING CONTRACT (DECEMBER 1975 EDITION)

This definition of Prime Cost is published by the Royal Institution of Chartered Surveyors and the National Federation of Building Trades Employers, for convenience and for use by people who choose to use it. Members of the National Federation of Building Trades Employers are not in any way debarred from defining Prime Cost and rendering their accounts for work carried out on that basis in any way they choose. Building owners are advised to reach agreement with contractors on the Definition of Prime Cost to be used prior to issuing instructions.

SECTION 1 - APPLICATION

1.1. This definition provides a basis for the valuation of daywork executed under such building contracts as provide for its use (e.g. contracts embodying the Standard Forms issued by the Joint Contracts Tribunal).

1.2. It is not applicable in any other circumstances, such as jobbing or other work carried out as a separate or main contract, nor in the case of daywork executed during the Defects Liability Period of contracts embodying the above mentioned Standard Forms.

SECTION 2 - COMPOSITION OF TOTAL CHARGES

2.1. The prime cost of daywork comprises the sum of the following costs:
    (a) Labour as defined in Section 3.
    (b) Material and goods as defined in Section 4.
    (c) Plant as defined in Section 5.

2.2. Incidental costs, overheads and profit as defined in Section 6, as provided in the building contract and expressed therein as percentage adjustments are applicable to each of 2.1 (a)-(c).

BUILDING INDUSTRY

SECTION 3 - LABOUR

3.1.   The standard wage rates, emoluments and expenses referred to below and the standard working hours referred to in 3.2 are those laid down for the time being in the rules or decisions of the National Joint Council for the Building Industry and the terms of the Building and Civil Engineering Annual and Public Holiday Agreements applicable to the works, or the rules or decisions or agreements of such body, other than the National Joint Council for the Building Industry, as may be applicable relating to the class of labour concerned at the time when and in the area where the daywork is executed.

3.2.   Hourly base rates for labour are computed by dividing the annual prime cost of labour, based upon standard working hours and as defined in 3.4 (a)-(l), by the number of standard working hours per annum.

3.3.   The hourly rates computed in accordance with 3.2 shall be applied in respect of the time spent by operatives directly engaged on daywork, including those operating mechanical plant and transport and erecting and dismantling other plant (unless otherwise expressly provided in the building contract).

3.4.   The annual prime cost of labour comprises the following:

(a)   Guaranteed minimum weekly earnings (e.g. Standard Basic Rate of Wages, Joint Board Supplement and Guaranteed Minimum Bonus Payment in the case of NJCBI rules).
(b)   All other guaranteed minimum payments (unless included in Section 6).
(c)   Differentials or extra payments in respect of skill, responsibility, discomfort, inconvenience or risk (excluding those in respect of supervisory responsibility - see 3.5).
(d)   Payments in respect of public holidays.
(e)   Any amounts which may become payable by the Contractor to or in respect of operatives arising from the operation of the rules referred to in 3.1 which are not provided for in 3.4 (a)-(d) or in Section 6.
(f)   Employer's National Insurance contributions applicable to 3.4 (a)-(e).
(g)   Employer's contributions to annual holiday credits.
(h)   Employer's contributions to death benefit scheme.
(i)   Any contribution, levy or tax imposed by statute, payable by the contractor in his capacity as an employer.

3.5.   **Note:** Differentials or extra payments in respect of supervisory responsibility are excluded from the annual prime cost (see Section 6). The time of principals, foremen, gangers, leading hands and similar categories, when working manually, is admissible under this Section at the appropriate rates for the trades concerned.

SECTION 4 - MATERIALS AND GOODS

4.1.   The prime cost of materials and goods obtained from stockists or manufacturers is the invoice cost after deduction of all trade discounts but including cash discounts not exceeding 5 per cent and includes the cost of delivery to site.

4.2.   The prime cost of materials and goods supplied from the Contractor's stock is based upon the current market prices plus any appropriate handling charges.

4.3.   Any Value Added Tax which is treated, or is capable of being treated, as input tax (as defined in the Finance Act, 1972) by the Contractor is excluded.

BUILDING INDUSTRY

SECTION 5 - PLANT

5.1. The rates for plant shall be as provided in the building contract.

5.2. The costs included in this Section comprise the following:

(a) Use of mechanical plant and transport for the time employed on daywork.
(b) Use of non-mechanical plant (excluding non-mechanical hand tools) for the time employed on daywork.

5.3. **Note:** The use of non-mechanical hand tools and of erected scaffolding, staging, trestles or the like is excluded (see Section 6).

SECTION 6 - INCIDENTAL COSTS, OVERHEADS AND PROFIT

6.1. The percentage adjustments provided in the building contract, which are applicable to each of the totals of Sections 3, 4 and 5, comprise the following:

(a) Head Office charges.
(b) Site staff, including site supervision.
(c) The additional cost of overtime (other than that referred to in 6.2).
(d) Time lost due to inclement weather.
(e) The additional cost of bonuses and all other incentive payments in excess of any guaranteed minimum included in 3.4. (a).
(f) Apprentices study time.
(g) Subsistence and periodic allowances.
(h) Fares and travelling allowances.
(i) Sick pay or insurance in respect thereof.
(j) Third-party and employers' liability insurance.
(k) Liability in respect of redundancy payments to employees.
(l) Employers' National Insurance contributions not included in Section 3.4.
(m) Tool allowances.
(n) Use, repair and sharpening of non-mechanical hand tools.
(o) Use of erected scaffolding, staging, trestles or the like.
(p) Use of tarpaulins, protective clothing, artificial lighting, safety and welfare facilities, storage and the like that may be available on the site.
(q) Any variation to basic rates required by the Contractor in cases where the building contract provides for the use of a specified schedule of basic plant charges (to the extent that no other provision is made for such variation).
(r) All other liabilities and obligations whatsoever not specifically referred to in this Section nor chargeable under any other Section.
(s) Profit.

6.2. **Note:** The additional cost of overtime, where specifically ordered by the Architect/Supervising Officer shall only be chargeable in the terms of prior written agreement between the parties to the building contract.

BUILDING INDUSTRY

Example of calculation of typical standard hourly base rate (as defined in Section 3) for NJCBI building craftsman and labourer in Grade A areas at 1st July, 1975.

	Rate £	Craftsman £	Rate £	Labourer £
Guaranteed minimum weekly earnings				
Standard Basic Rate	49 wks 37.00	1813.00	31.40	1538.60
Joint Board Supplement	49 wks 5.00	245.00	4.20	205.80
Guaranteed Minimum Bonus	49 wks 4.00	196.00	3.60	176.40
		2254.00		1920.00
Employer's National Insurance Contribution at 8.5%		191.59		163.27
		2445.59		2084.07
Employer's Contribution to :				
CITB annual levy		15.00		3.00
Annual holiday credits	49 wks 2.80	137.20	2.80	137.20
Public holidays (included in guaranteed minimum weekly earnings above)				
Death benefit scheme	49 wks 0.10	4.90	0.10	4.90
Annual labour cost as defined in section 3	£	**2602.69**	£	**2229.17**

Hourly rate of labour as defined in section 3, Clause 3.2 $\dfrac{2602.69}{1904} = £\,1.37$ $\dfrac{2229.17}{1904} = £\,1.17$

Note:

1.   Standard working hours per annum calculated as follows:

52 weeks @ 39 hours		2080
Less		
3 weeks holiday @ 40 hours	120	
7 days public holidays @ 8 hours	56	-176
		1904

2.   It should be noted that all labour costs incurred by the Contractor in his capacity as an employer other than those contained in the hourly rate, are to be taken into account under section 6.

3.   The above example is for the convenience of users only and does not form part of the Definition; all basic costs are subject to re-examination according to the time when and in the area where the daywork is executed.

BUILDING INDUSTRY

For the convenience of readers the example which appears on the previous page has been updated by the Editors for London and Liverpool rates as at 28 June, 1999.

		Rate £	Craftsman £	Rate £	Labourer £
Guaranteed minimum weekly earnings					
Standard Basic Rate	47.8 wks	235.95	11278.41	177.45	8482.11
Guaranteed minimum bonus	47.8 wks	0.00	0.00	0.00	0.00
			11278.41		8482.11
Employer's National Insurance Contribution			891.94		550.79
Employer's Contribution to :					
CITB annual levy at 0.38% of payroll			42.86		32.23
Annual holiday credits and					
Retirement and death benefit scheme	47 wks	20.95	984.65	20.95	984.65
Annual labour cost as defined in section 3			**£ 13197.86**		**£ 10049.79**

Hourly rate of labour as defined in section 3, Clause 3.02
$$\frac{13197.86}{1801.8} = £\,7.32 \qquad \frac{10049.79}{1801.8} = £\,5.58$$

Note:

1. Standard basic rate effective from 28 June 1999.

2. Standard working hours per annum calculated as follows

52 weeks @ 39 hours		2028.0
Less		
4.2 weeks holiday @ 39 hours	163.8	
8 days public holidays @ 7.8 hours	62.4	-226.2
		1801.8

3. All labour costs incurred by the Contractor in his capacity as an employer other than those contained in the hourly rate, are to be taken into account under Section 6.

4. The above examples are for guidance only and do not form part of the Definition; all the basic costs are subject to re-examination.

5. The rates for annual holiday credits and retirement and death benefits are those which came into force in August 1999 and reflects the discount (35p) offered for credit purchase.

6. National Insurance payments are at "not-contracted out" rates applicable from 6th April 1999.

7. In basic rate & GMB 47.8 wks = 46.2 working + 1.6 public holidays.

BUILDING INDUSTRY

DEFINITION OF PRIME COST OF BUILDING WORKS OF A JOBBING OR MAINTENANCE CHARACTER (1980 EDITION)

This Definition of Prime Cost is published by the Royal Institution of Chartered Surveyors and the National Federation of Building Trades Employers for convenience and for use by people who choose to use it. Members of the National Federation of Building Trades Employers are not in any way debarred from defining Prime Cost and rendering their accounts for work carried out on that basis in any way they choose. Building owners are advised to reach agreement with contractors on the Definition of Prime Cost to be used prior to issuing instructions.

SECTION 1 - APPLICATION

1.1.   This definition provides a basis for the valuation of work of a jobbing or maintenance character executed under such building contracts as provide for its use.

1.2.   It is not applicable in any other circumstances, such as daywork executed under or incidental to a building contract.

SECTION 2 - COMPOSITION OF TOTAL CHARGES

2.1.   The prime cost of jobbing work comprises the sum of the following costs:

(a)   Labour as defined in Section 3.
(b)   Materials and goods as defined in Section 4.
(c)   Plant, consumable stores and services as defined in Section 5.
(d)   Sub-contracts as defined in Section 6.

2.2.   Incidental costs, overhead and profit as defined in Section 7 and expressed as percentage adjustments are applicable to each of 2.1 (a)-(d).

SECTION 3 - LABOUR

3.1.   Labour costs comprise all payments made to or in respect of all persons directly engaged upon the work, whether on or off the site, except those included in Section 7.

3.2.   Such payments are based upon the standard wage rates, emoluments and expenses as laid down for the time being in the rules or decisions of the National Joint Council for the Building Industry and the terms of the Building and Civil Engineering Annual and Public Holiday Agreements applying to the works, or the rules of decisions or agreements of such other body as may relate to the class of labour concerned, at the time when and in the area where the work is executed, together with the Contractor's statutory obligations, including:

(a)   Guaranteed minimum weekly earnings (e.g. Standard Basic Rate of Wages and Guaranteed Minimum Bonus Payment in the case of NJCBI rules).
(b)   All other guaranteed minimum payments (unless included in Section 7).
(c)   Payments in respect of incentive schemes or productivity agreements applicable to the works.
(d)   Payments in respect of overtime normally worked; or necessitated by the particular circumstances of the work; or as otherwise agreed between the parties.
(e)   Differential or extra payments in respect of skill, responsibility, discomfort, inconvenience or risk.
(f)   Tool allowance.
(g)   Subsistence and periodic allowances.
(h)   Fares, travelling and lodging allowances.
(j)   Employer's contributions to annual holiday credits.
(k)   Employer's contributions to death benefit schemes.
(l)   Any amounts which may become payable by the Contractor to or in respect of operatives arising from the operation of the rules referred to in 3.2 which are not provided for in 3.2 (a)-(k) or in Section 7.

BUILDING INDUSTRY

(m) Employer's National Insurance contributions and any contribution, levy or tax imposed by statute, payable by the Contractor in his capacity as employer.

Note:

Any payments normally made by the Contractor which are of a similar character to those described in 3.2 (a)-(c) but which are not within the terms of the rules and decisions referred to above are applicable subject to the prior agreement of the parties, as an alternative to 3.2 (a)-(c).

3.3. The wages or salaries of supervisory staff, timekeepers, storekeepers, and the like, employed on or regularly visiting site, where the standard wage rates, etc., are not applicable, are those normally paid by the Contractor together with any incidental payments of a similar character to 3.2 © - (k).

3.4. Where principals are working manually their time is chargeable, in respect of the trades practised, in accordance with 3.2.

SECTION 4 - MATERIALS AND GOODS

4.1. The prime cost of materials and goods obtained by the Contractor from stockists or manufacturers is the invoice cost after deduction of all trade discounts but including cash discounts not exceeding 5 per cent, and includes the cost of delivery to site.

4.2. The prime cost of materials and goods supplied from the Contractor's stock is based upon the current market prices plus any appropriate handling charges.

4.3. The prime cost under 4.1 and 4.2 also includes any costs of:

(a) non-returnable crates or other packaging.
(b) returning crates and other packaging less any credit obtainable.

4.4. Any Value Added Tax which is treated, or is capable of being treated, as input tax (as defined in the Finance Act, 1972 or any re-enactment thereof) by the Contractor is excluded.

SECTION 5 - PLANT, CONSUMABLE STORES AND SERVICES

5.1. The prime cost of plant and consumable stores as listed below is the cost at hire rates agreed between the parties or in the absence of prior agreement at rates not exceeding those normally applied in the locality at the time when the works are carried out, or on a use and waste basis where applicable:

(a) Machinery in workshops.
(b) Mechanical plant and power-operated tools.
(c) Scaffolding and scaffold boards.
(d) Non-mechanical plant excluding hand tools.
(e) Transport including collection and disposal of rubbish.
(f) Tarpaulins and dust sheets.
(g) Temporary roadways, shoring, planking and strutting, hoarding, centering, formwork, temporary fans, partitions or the like.
(h) Fuel and consumable stores for plant and power-operated tools unless included in 5.1 (a), (b), (d) or (e) above.
(j) Fuel and equipment for drying out the works and fuel for testing mechanical services.

BUILDING INDUSTRY

5.2.   The prime cost also includes the net cost incurred by the Contractor of the following services, excluding any such cost included under Sections 3, 4 or 7:

(a)   Charges for temporary water supply including the use of temporary plumbing and storage.
(b)   Charges for temporary electricity or other power and lighting including the use of temporary installations.
(c)   Charges arising from work carried out by local authorities or public undertakings.
(d)   Fees, royalties and similar charges.
(e)   Testing of materials.
(f)   The use of temporary buildings including rates and telephone and including heating and lighting not charged under (b) above.
(g)   The use of canteens, sanitary accommodation, protective clothing and other provision for the welfare of persons engaged in the work in accordance with the current Working Rule Agreement and any Act of Parliament, statutory instrument, rule, order, regulation or bye-law.
(h)   The provision of safety measures necessary to comply with any Act of Parliament.
(j)   Premiums or charges for any performance bonds or insurances which are required by the Building Owner and which are not referred to elsewhere in this Definition.

SECTION 6 - SUB-CONTRACTS

6.1.   The prime cost of work executed by sub-contractors, whether nominated by the Building Owner or appointed by the Contractor, is the amount which is due from the Contractor to the sub-contractors in accordance with the terms of the sub-contracts after deduction of all discounts except any cash discount offered by any sub-contractor to the Contractor not exceeding 2.5%.

SECTION 7 - INCIDENTAL COSTS, OVERHEADS AND PROFIT

7.1.   The percentage adjustments provided in the building contract, which are applicable to each of the totals of Sections 3-6, provide for the following:

(a)   Head Office charges.
(b)   Off-site staff including supervisory and other administrative staff in the Contractor's workshops and yard.
(c)   Payments in respect of public holidays.
(d)   Payments in respect of apprentices' study time.
(e)   Sick pay or insurance in respect thereof.
(f)   Third party employer's liability insurance.
(g)   Liability in respect of redundancy payments made to employees.
(h)   Use, repair and sharpening of non-mechanical hand tools.
(j)   Any variations to basic rates required by the Contractor in cases where the building contract provides for the use of a specified schedule of basic plant charges (to the extent that no other provision is made for such variation).
(k)   All other liabilities and obligations whatsoever not specifically referred to in this Section nor chargeable under any other section.
(l)   Profit.

BUILDING INDUSTRY

SPECIMEN ACCOUNT FORMAT

If this Definition of Prime Cost is followed the Contractor's account could be in the following format:

£

Labour (as defined in Section 3)
    Add ____ % (see Section 7)

Materials and goods (as defined in Section
    Add ____ % (see Section 7)

Plant, consumable stores and services
(as defined in Section 5)
    Add ____ % (see Section 7)

Sub-contracts (as defined in Section 6)
    Add ____ % (see Section 7)   _____

£ _____

VAT to be added if applicable.

SCHEDULE OF BASIC PLANT CHARGES (JANUARY 1990 ISSUE)

This Schedule is published by the Royal Institution of Chartered Surveyors and is for use in connection with Dayworks under a Building Contract.

EXPLANATORY NOTES

1.   The rates in the Schedule are intended to apply solely to daywork carried out under and incidental to a Building Contract. They are NOT intended to apply to:
    (i)   Jobbing or any other work carried out as a main or separate contract; or
    (ii)   Work carried out after the date of commencement of the Defects Liability Period.

2.   The rates in the Schedule are basic and may be subject to an overall adjustment to be quoted by the Contractor prior to the placing of the Contract.

3.   The rates apply to plant and machinery already on site, whether hired or owned by the contractor.

4.   The rates, unless otherwise stated, include the cost of fuel and power of every description, lubricating oils, grease, maintenance, sharpening of tools, replacement of spare parts, all consumable stores and for licences and insurances applicable to items of plant. They do not include the costs of drivers and attendants (unless otherwise stated).

5.   The rates should be applied to the time during which the plant is actually engaged in daywork.

6.   Whether or not plant is chargeable on daywork depends on the daywork agreement in use and the inclusion of an item of plant in this schedule does not necessarily indicate that item is chargeable.

7.   Rates for plant not included in the Schedule or which is not on site and is specifically hired for daywork shall be settled at prices which are reasonably related to the rates in the Schedule having regard to any overall adjustment quoted by the Contractor in the Conditions of Contract.

BUILDING INDUSTRY

MECHANICAL PLANT AND TOOLS

Item of plant	Description/Capacity		Unit	Rate per hour £
BAR-BENDING AND SHEARING MACHINES				
	Power driven - up to			
Bar bending machine	2.00 in (51 mm) diameter rods		each	2.01
Bar shearing machine	1.50 in (38 mm) diameter rods		each	2.00
	2.00 in (51 mm) diameter rods		each	2.00
Bar cropper machine	2,00 in (51 mm) diameter rods		each	1.51
BLOCK AND STONE SPLITTER	Hydraulic		each	0.83
BRICK SAWS				
Brick saw (use of abrasive disc to be charged net and credited)	Power driven (bench type clipper or similar or portable)		each	1.83
COMPRESSORS				
Portable compressor (machine only)	**ft³/min**	**m³/min**		
Nominal delivery of free air per minute at 100 lb/in² (7 kg/cm²) pressure.	80/85	2.41	each	1.30
	125 - 140	3.50 - 3.92	each	1.58
	160 - 175	4.50 - 4.95	each	2.37
	250	7.08	each	3.25
	380	10.75	each	4.80
	600 - 630	16.98 - 17.84	each	6.00
LORRY MOUNTED COMPRESSORS				
(machine plus lorry only)				
Nominal delivery of free air per minute at 100 PSI (7 kg/cm²)	101 - 150	2.86 - 4.24	each	4.12
TRACTOR MOUNTED COMPRESSORS (Machine plus rubber tyred tractors only)	101 - 120	2.86 - 3.40	each	3.63
COMPRESSED AIR EQUIPMENT (with and including up to 50 ft (15.24 m) of air hose)				
Breakers (with six steels)	Light		each	0.47
	Medium (65 lbs)		each	0.47
	Heavy (85 lbs)		each	0.47
Light pneumatic pick (with six steels)			each	0.37
Pneumatic clay spade (one blade)			each	0.22
Chipping hammer (plus six steels)			each	0.65
Hand-held rock drill with rod (bits to be paid for at net cost and credited)	7 kg (15 lbs) class (light)		each	0.33
	16 kg (35 lbs) class (medium)		each	0.37
	20 kg (45 lbs) class (medium)		each	0.37
	25 kg (55 lbs) class (heavy)		each	0.39
Rotary drill (bits to be paid for at net cost and credited)	Up to 0.75 in (19 mm)		each	0.37
	1.25 in (32 mm)		each	0.73
Sander/Grinder			each	0.39
Scabbler (heads extra)	Single head		each	0.48
	Triple head		each	0.65

BUILDING INDUSTRY

Item of plant	Description/Capacity	Unit	Rate per hour £
COMPRESSOR EQUIPMENT ACCESSORIES			
Additional hoses	Per 50 ft (15 m) length	each	0.09
Muffler, tool silencer		each	0.08
CONCRETE BREAKER			
Concrete breaker, portable hydraulic complete with power pack		each	1.33
CONCRETE/MORTAR MIXERS			
Concrete mixer	Diesel, electric or petrol		
	ft³ **m³**		
Open drum without hopper	3/2 0.09/0.06	each	0.40
	4/3 0.12/0.09	each	0.44
	5/3.5 0.15/0.10	each	0.54
Open drum with hopper	7/5 0.20/0.15	each	0.67
Closed drum	8/6.5 0.25/0.18	each	0.90
Reversing drum with hopper weigher and	10/7 0.28/0.20	each	2.44
feed shovel	21/14 0.60/0.40	each	4.17
CONCRETE PUMP			
Lorry mounted concrete pump (metreage charge to be added net)		each	13.70
CONCRETE EQUIPMENT			
Vibrator, poker type	Petrol, diesel or electric up to 3 in diameter	each	0.87
	Air, excluding compressor and hose up to 3 in diameter	each	0.65
	Extra heads	each	0.50
Vibrator, tamper	With tamping board	each	0.87
	Double beam screeder	each	1.19
Power float	29 in - 36 in	each	1.13
CONVEYOR BELTS	Power operated up to 25 ft (7.62 m) long 16 in (400 mm) wide	each	3.15

BUILDING INDUSTRY

Item of plant	Description/Capacity		Unit	Rate per hour £
CRANES				
	Maximum capacity up to			
Mobile rubber tyred	15 cwt (762 kg)		each	5.15
Lorry mounted, telescopic jib, 2 wheel	6 tons (tonnes)		each	10.47
(All rates inclusive of driver)	7 tons (tonnes)		each	1.22
	8 tons (tonnes)		each	13.67
	10 tons (tonnes)		each	14.99
	12 tons (tonnes)		each	16.91
	15 tons (tonnes)		each	19.21
	18 tons (tonnes)		each	20.34
	20 tons (tonnes)		each	22.04
	25 tons (tonnes)		each	24.86
Lorry mounted, telescopic jib, 4 wheel	10 tons (tonnes)		each	15.30
(All rates inclusive of driver)	12 tons (tonnes)		each	17.26
	15 tons (tonnes)		each	19.59
	20 tons (tonnes)		each	22.48
	25 tons (tonnes)		each	25.36
	30 tons (tonnes)		each	28.82
	45 tons (tonnes)		each	31.12
	50 tons (tonnes)		each	33.64
Track-mounted tower crane (electric) (Capacity = max lift in tons x max radius at which can be lifted) (All rates inclusive of driver)	**Capacity (metre/tonnes)**	**Height under hook above ground (m)**		
	up to 10	17	each	7.40
	15	17	each	7.95
	20	18	each	8.50
	25	20	each	10.70
	30	22	each	12.76
	40	22	each	16.75
	50	22	each	21.70
	60	22	each	22.52
	70	22	each	23.07
	80	22	each	23.99
	110	22	each	24.49
	125	30	each	27.20
	150	30	each	29.95
Static tower	To be charged at a percentage of the above rates		each	90% of the above
CRANE EQUIPMENT				
Tipping bucket	Circular			
	0.19 m³	0.25 yd³	each	0.25
	0.57 m³	0.75 yd³	each	0.28
Skip, muck	Up to			
	0.38 m³	0.50 yd³	each	0.25
	0.57 m³	0.75 yd³	each	0.25
	0.76 m³	1.00 yd³	each	0.30
Skip, concrete	Up to			
	0.38 m³	0.50 yd³	each	0.44
	0.57 m³	0.75 yd³	each	0.53
	0.76 m³	1.00 yd³	each	0.76
	1.15 m³	1.50 yd³	each	0.61
Skip, concrete lay down or roll over	0.38 m³	0.50 yd³	each	0.44

BUILDING INDUSTRY

Item of plant	Description/Capacity		Unit	Rate per hour £
DEHUMIDIFIERS				
	litres	**gallons**		
110/240v Water extraction per 24 hours	68	15	each	0.84
	90	20	each	0.97
DIAMOND DRILLING AND CHASING				
Chasing machine drilling	6 in (152 mm)		each	1.35
(Diamond core)	Mini rig up to 35 mm		each	3.16
	3 - 8 in (76 - 203 mm) electric 110v		each	3.33
	3 - 8 in (76 - 203 mm) air		each	4.23
DUMPERS				
Dumper (site use only excluding Tax, Insurance and cost of DERV etc., when operating on highway)	**Makers capacity**			
2 wheel drive	**cwt**	**kg**		
Gravity tip	15	762	each	1.04
Hydraulic tip	20	1016	each	1.25
Hydraulic tip	23	1168	each	1.31
4 wheel drive				
Gravity tip	15	762	each	1.42
Hydraulic tip	25	1270	each	1.61
Hydraulic tip	30	1524	each	1.83
Hydraulic tip	35	1778	each	2.08
Hydraulic tip	40	2032	each	2.33
Hydraulic tip	50	2540	each	2.96
Hydraulic tip	60	3048	each	3.68
Hydraulic tip	80	4064	each	4.72
Hydraulic tip	100	5080	each	6.38
Hydraulic tip	120	6096	each	7.54
ELECTRIC HAND TOOLS				
Breakers	Heavy:	Kango 1800	each	0.87
		Kango 2500	each	0.90
	Medium:	Hilti TP800	each	0.73
Rotary hammers	Heavy:	Kango 950	each	0.55
	Medium:	Kango 627/637	each	0.47
	Light:	Hilti TE12/TE17	each	0.39
Pipe drilling tackle	Ordinary type		set	0.51
	Under pressure type		set	0.83
EXCAVATORS				
Hydraulic full circle slew	Crawler mounted, backactor			
	5/8 yd³	0.50 m³	each	5.01
	3/4 yd³	0.60 m³	each	5.92
	7/8 yd³	0.70 m³	each	8.24
	1 yd³	0.80 m³	each	13.25
Wheeled tractor type	Hydraulic excavator, JCB 3C or similar		each	9.23

BUILDING INDUSTRY

Item of plant	Description/Capacity				Unit	Rate per hour £
MINI EXCAVATORS						
Kubota mini excavators	360° tracked - 1.00 tonne				each	5.38
	360° tracked - 3.50 tonnes				each	7.23
FORKLIFTS	**Payload**		**Max. lift**			
2 wheel drive "Rough terrain"	20 cwt	1016 kg	21 ft 4 in	6.50 m	each	4.38
	20 cwt	1016 kg	26 ft 0 in	7.92 m	each	4.38
	30 cwt	1524 kg	20 ft 0 in	6.09 m	each	4.50
	36 cwt	1829 kg	18 ft 0 in	5.48 m	each	4.50
	50 cwt	2540 kg	12 ft 0 in	3.66 m	each	4.73
4 wheel drive "Rough terrain"	30 cwt	1524 kg	20 ft 0 in	6.09 m	each	5.60
	40 cwt	2032 kg	20 ft 0 in	6.09 m	each	5.78
	50 cwt	2540 kg	12 ft 0 in	3.66 m	each	7.79
HAMMERS						
Cartridge (excluding cartridges and studs)	Hammer DX450				each	0.40
	Hammer DX600				each	0.48
	Hammer spit TS				each	0.48
HEATERS, SPACE	**Btu/hr**					
Paraffin/electric	50 000 - 75 000				each	0.73
	80 000 - 100 000				each	0.77
	150 000				each	0.88
	320 000				each	1.20
HOISTS	**cwt**		**kg**			
Scaffold	Up to 5		254		each	0.90
Mobile (goods only)	Up to 10		508		each	1.43
Static (goods only)	10 to 15		508 - 762		each	1.67
Rack and pinion (goods only)	16		813		each	2.75
	20		1016		each	3.00
	25		1270		each	3.30
Rack and pinion (goods and passenger)	8 person, 1433 lbs		650		each	4.50
	12 person, 2205 lbs		1000		each	4.95
LORRIES	**Plated gross vehicle weight (ton/tonnes)**					
Fixed body	Up to 5.50				each	9.60
	Up to 7.50				each	10.20
Tipper	Up to 16.00				each	11.73
	Up to 24.00				each	14.98
	Up to 30.00				each	17.73
PIPE WORK EQUIPMENT						
Pipe bender	Power driven, 50-150 mm diameter				each	0.75
	Hydraulic, 2 in capacity				each	0.96
Pipe cutter	Hydraulic				each	1.02
Pipe defrosting equipment	Electrical				set	1.83

BUILDING INDUSTRY

Item of plant	Description/Capacity		Unit	Rate per hour £
PIPEWORK EQUIPMENT - cont'd				
Pipe testing equipment	Compressed air		set	1.04
	Hydraulic		set	0.68
Pipe threading equipment	Up to 4 in		set	1.65

PUMPS

Including 20 ft (6 m) length of
suction/delivery hose, couplings, valves
and strainers

Diaphragm:				
"Simplite" 2 in (50 mm)	Petrol or electric		each	0.79
"Wickham" 3 in (76mm)	Diesel		each	1.22
Submersible:				
2 in (50 mm)	Electric		each	0.85
Induced flow:				
"Spate" 3 in (76 mm)	Diesel		each	1.42
"Spate" 4 in (102 mm)	Diesel		each	1.88
Centrifugal, self priming:				
"Univac" 2 in (50 mm)	Diesel		each	1.87
"Univac" 4 in (102 mm)	Diesel		each	2.40
"Univac" 6 in (152 mm)	Diesel		each	3.69

	diameter			
PUMPING EQUIPMENT	**in**	**mm**		
Pump hoses (per 20 ft (6 m) flexible	2	51	each	0.15
flexible suction/delivery including coupling	3	76	each	0.17
valve and strainer	4	102	each	0.19
	6	152	each	0.32

RAMMERS AND COMPACTORS

	lb	**kg**		
Power rammer, Pegson or similar			each	0.88
Soil compactor, plate type				
12 x 13 in (305 x 330 mm)	172	78	each	0.78
20 x 18 in (508 x 457 mm)	264	120	each	0.93

ROLLERS	**cwt**	**kg**		
Vibrating rollers	7.25-8.25	368 - 420	each	1.00
Single roller	10.50	533	each	1.53
Twin roller	13.75	698	each	1.75
	16.75	851	each	2.01
Twin roller with seat and steering wheel	21.00	1067	each	2.75
	27.50	1397	each	2.88
	ton/tonne			
Pavement rollers dead weight	3 - 4		each	2.89
	4 - 6		each	3.75
	6 - 10		each	4.40

BUILDING INDUSTRY

Item of plant	Description/Capacity		Unit	Rate per hour £
SAWS, MECHANICAL	in	m		
Chain saw	21	0.53	each	0.78
	30	0.76	each	1.12
Bench saw	Up to 20	0.51	each	0.80
	Up to 24	0.61	each	1.20
SCREED PUMP	Maximum delivery			
Working volume 7ft³ (200 litres)	Vertical 300 ft (91 m)			
	Horizontal 600 ft (182 m)		each	8.33
Screed pump hose	50/65 mm diameter 13.30 m long		each	1.83
SCREWING MACHINES	13 - 50 mm diameter		each	0.43
	25 - 100 mm diameter		each	0.87
TRACTORS	yd³	m³		
	Up to			
Shovel, tractor (crawler),	0.75	0.57	each	4.70
any type of bucket	1.00	0.76	each	5.70
	1.25	0.96	each	6.62
	1.50	1.15	each	8.15
	1.75	1.34	each	8.98
	2.00	1.53	each	10.69
	2.75 - 3.50	2.10	each	17.27
Shovel, tractor (wheeled)	0.50	0.38	each	3.36
	0.75	0.57	each	4.14
	1.00	0.76	each	5.02
	2.50	1.91	each	7.30
Tractor (crawler) with dozer	Makers rated flywheel horsepower			
	75		each	9.31
	140		each	12.52
Tractor-wheeled (rubber tyred)	Light 48hp		each	4.23
Agricultural type	Heavy 65hp		each	4.68
TRAFFIC LIGHTS	Mains/generator 2-way		set	2.23
	Mains/generator 3-way		set	4.40
	Mains/generator 4-way		set	5.45
	Trailer mounted 2-way		set	2.21
WELDING AND CUTTING AND BURNING SETS				
Welding and cutting set (including oxygen and acetylene, excluding underwater equipment and thermic boring)			each	4.33
Welding set, diesel (excluding electrodes)	300 amp single operator		each	1.84
	480 amp double operator		each	1.89
	600 amp double operator		each	2.35

BUILDING INDUSTRY

Item of plant	Description/Capacity	Unit	Rate per hour £
NON-MECHANICAL PLANT			
BAR BENDING AND SHEARING MACHINES			
Bar bending machine, manual	Up to 1 in (25 mm) diameter rods	each	0.26
Shearing machine, manual	Up to 0.625 in (16 mm) diameter rods	each	0.15
BROTHER OR SLING CHAINS	not exceeding 2 ton/tonne	set	0.28
	2 to 5 ton/tonne	set	0.40
	5 to 10 ton/tonne	set	0.48
DRAIN TESTING EQUIPMENT		set	0.42
LIFTING AND JACKING GEAR	**ton/tonne**		
Pipe winch - including shear legs	0.50	set	0.35
Pipe winch - including gantry	2.00	set	0.72
	3.00	set	0.84
Chain blocks up to 20ft (6.10m) lift	1.00	each	0.35
	2.00	each	0.44
	3.00	each	0.51
	4.00	each	0.66
Pull lift (Tirfor type)	0.75	each	0.35
	1.50	each	0.47
	3.00	each	0.61
PIPE BENDERS	13 - 75 mm diameter	each	0.32
	50 - 100 mm diameter		0.52
PLUMBER'S FURNACE	Calor gas or similar	each	1.20
ROAD WORKS EQUIPMENT			
Barrier trestles or similar		10nr	0.50
Crossing plates (steel sheets)		each	0.32
Danger lamp, including oil		each	0.03
Warning sign		each	0.07
Road cone		10nr	0.11
Flasher unit (battery to be charged at cost)		each	0.06
Flashing bollard (battery to be charged at cost)		each	0.10
RUBBISH CHUTES			
Length of sections 154 cm giving working length of 130 cm			
Standard section		each	0.15
Branch section		each	0.20
Hopper		each	0.16
Fixing frame		each	0.20
Winch Type A	20 m for erection	each	0.29
Winch Type B	40 m for erection	each	0.67

BUILDING INDUSTRY

Item of plant	Description/Capacity	Unit	Rate per hour £
SCAFFOLDING			
Boards		100ft	0.06
Castor wheels	Steel or rubber tyred	100nr	0.87
Fall ropes	Up to 200 ft (61 m)	each	0.44
Fittings (including couplers and base plates)	Steel or alloy	100nr	0.07
Ladders, pole	20 rung	each	0.11
	30 rung	each	0.15
	40 rung	each	0.26

Ladders, extension	Extended length		
	ft	**m**		

	ft	m	Unit	Rate
	20	6.10	each	0.31
	26	7.92	each	0.43
	35	10.67	each	0.64
Putlogs	Steel or alloy	100nr	0.06
Splithead	small	10nr	0.12
	medium	10nr	0.15
	large	10nr	0.16
Staging, lightweight		100ft	1.00
Tube	Steel	100ft	0.02
	Alloy	100ft	0.04
Wheeled tower including castors and boards			
7 ft x 7 ft (2.13 x 2.13 m)	Working platform up to 20 ft (6 m) high	each	0.58
10 ft x 10 ft (3.05 x 3.05 m)		each	0.59
TARPAULINS		10m^2	0.04
TRENCH STRUTS AND SHEETS			
Adjustable steel trench strut	All sizes from 1 ft to 5ft 6 in (0.305 to 1.80 m) extended	10nr	0.06
Steel trench sheet	5 - 14 ft (1.52 - 4.27 m) lengths	100ft	0.16

Rates of Wages

BUILDING INDUSTRY - ENGLAND, WALES AND SCOTLAND

The Building and Civil Engineering Joint Negotiating Committee agreed a three year agreement on pay and conditions for building and civil engineering operatives, it became effective from June 1997 and commenced on 18 August 1997.

1999

With effect from 28 June 1999 a new Working Rule Agreement became effective covering the building and civil engineering industry.

The Working Rule Agreement includes a pay structure with a general operative and additional skilled rates of pay as well as craft rate. Plus rates and additional payments will be consolidated into basic pay to provide the following rates (for a normal 39 hour week):

	£
General operative	177.45
Skill Rate 4	191.10
Skill Rate 3	202.80
Skill Rate 2	216.45
Skill Rate 1	224.64
Craft Rate	235.95

Drivers of excavators with a rated bucket capacity over 7.65 cu metres, and mobile cranes over 120 tonnes capacity will receive an additional payment.

Holidays with Pay and Benefits Schemes

The value of Holiday Stamp Credits will be increased on and from 2 August 1999 by 50 p to £21.30 for adults and £14.75 for those aged under 18.

BUILDING INDUSTRY - ENGLAND, WALES AND SCOTLAND - cont'd

Period of Settlement

The Employers shall not be required to consider any application for a change in the operatives' pay and conditions which would have effect before the last Monday in June 2000.

The composition of the Building and Civil Engineering Joint Negotiating Committee

The parties to the Building and Civil Engineering Joint Negotiating Committee are:

Employers:	Building Employers Confederation
	Civil Engineering Contractors Association
	Major Contractors Group
	National Federation of Roofing Contractors
Trade Unions:	Union of Construction Allied Trade and Technicians
	Transport and General Workers' Union
	General Municipal Boilermakers Union

Young Labourers

Effective from 8 September 1997 - Currently under negotiation

The rates of wages for young labourers shall be the following proportions of the labourers' rates:

At 16 years of age 50%
At 17 years of age 75%
At 18 years of age 100%

Apprentices/Trainees aged under 19 years

Six-month period	Rate per week £
First	76.05
Second	102.96
Third	125.58
Thereafter until skills test is passed*	150.54
On passing skills test and until completion of training period	170.04

*   The NJCBI has agreed to the introduction of skills testing under the National Joint Training Scheme. The first practical skills tests commenced in May 1986.

BUILDING INDUSTRY - ENGLAND, WALES AND SCOTLAND - cont'd

Apprentices/Trainees aged 19 years or over

Six-month period	Rate per week £
First and second	146.25
Third and fourth	154.83
Fifth and sixth	163.41

Ace Minimix

British Rail Goods Yard
York Way
Kings Cross
London N1 0AU
Telephone: (0171) 837 7011
Fax: (0171) 278 5333

Rates of Wages

BUILDING AND ALLIED TRADES JOINT INDUSTRIAL COUNCIL

Authorised rates of wages in the building industry in England and Wales agreed by the Building and Allied Trades Joint Industrial Council.

Effective from 14 June 1999

Subject to the conditions prescribed in the Working Rule Agreement the standard weekly rates of wages shall be as follows:

	£
Craft operative	235.95
Adult general operative	195.00

ROAD HAULAGE WORKERS EMPLOYED IN THE BUILDING INDUSTRY

Authorised rates of pay for road haulage workers in the building industry recommended by the Builders Employers Confederation.

Effective from 28 June 1999

Employers	Operatives
The Building Employers Confederation,	The Transport and General Workers Union,
82 New Cavendish Street,	Transport House,
London	Smith Square,
W1M 8AD	Westminster,
Telephone: 0171 580 5588	London SW1P 3JB
	Telephone: 0171 828 7788

Lorry Drivers

Lorry Drivers employed whole time as such shall be paid the craft basic rate irrespective of the gross weight of the vehicle driven. Lorry drivers required to hold a HGV Class C Licence will receive 5 p above the Craft rate and those required to hold a Class C and E Licence will receive 11 p above the Craft rate.

NOTE: This clause does not apply in Scotland.

	£
Craft Operative	235.95

PLUMBING AND MECHANICAL ENGINEERING SERVICES INDUSTRY

Authorised rates of wages agreed by the Joint Industry Board for the Plumbing and Mechanical Engineering Services Industry in England and Wales

Effective from 4 May 1998 and 24 August 1998

The Joint Industry Board for Plumbing and Mechanical Engineering Services in England and Wales,
Brook House,
Brook Street,
St Neots,
Huntingdon,
Cambridgeshire
PE19 2HW
Telephone: 01480 476925

	Rate per hour 04/05/1998 £	Rate per hour 24/08/1998 £
Operatives		
Technical plumber and Service technician (Gas)	7.12	7.48
Advanced plumber and Service engineer (Gas)	6.37	6.70
Trained plumber and Service fitter (Gas)	5.69	5.98
Apprentice Plumbers and Apprentice Service fitters		
1st year of training	2.32	2.62
2nd year of training	2.97	3.12
3rd year of training	3.35	3.52
3rd year of training with NVQ Level 2	4.08	4.28
4th year of training	4.12	4.33
4th year of training with NVQ Level 2	4.69	4.93
4th year of training with NVQ Level 3	5.18	5.44
Adult Trainees		
1st 6 months of employment	4.47	4.69
2nd 6 months of employment	4.77	5.01
3rd 6 months of employment	4.98	5.23

Profiled Sheet Roofing and Cladding

A Guide to Good Practice

National Federation of Roofing Contractors

Edited by Nick Selves, J. Shanahan and Colin Sproul

This new edition of the NFRC's handbook, is intended as an accessible and practical guide to the application, design and installation of profiled sheeting for roof and wall cladding. It distills the knowledge of many of the leading experts in this area of construction with hands-on site experience.

Profiled Sheet Roofing and Cladding sets out principles whereby all necessary components can be successfully integrated to provide an external envelope meeting all the required performance standards. The special requirements of insulated structures are also considered. It contains up-to-date advice and information on the exceptional performance and developments which have occurred since the earlier second edition was published in 1991.

Contents: Chapter 1. Common Requirements for Light Weight Profiled Cladding. **Chapter 2.** Profiled Metal Roof and Wall Cladding. **Chapter 3**. Built-up Metal Roofing Systems **Chapter 4**. Composite Panels. **Chapter 5**. Fibre-Cement Sheeting. **Chapter 6**. Rooflights. **Chapter 7.** Fasteners and Fixings. **Chapter 8**. Sealants and Profile Fillers. **Chapter 9**. Rainwater Goods. **Chapter** 10. Construction, Safety and Maintenance.

May 1999: 297x210: 128pp
51 line drawings
Pb: 0-419-23940-5: £29.99

To Order: Tel: +44 (0) 8700 768853, or +44 (0) 1264 343071
Fax: +44 (0) 1264 343005, or **Post:** E & FN Spon Customer Services,
ITPS Andover, Hants, SP10 5BE, UK

All orders must be pre-paid and will be sent free in the UK. Europe please add: £2.95 for the first book, thereafter £1.25 per book. ROW please add: Airmail £6.50 for the first book, thereafter £2.50 per book. Please add £12.50 delivery charge for items over £100.00.

PART III

Prices for Measured Work

This part of the book contains the following sections:

Aluminium Design and Construction

John Dwight, Consultant, UK

*Clear and thorough examination of the subject
*Highly illustrated with drawings, photographs and tables

Aluminium Design and Construction address the metal's history and usage, wrought products, alloy selection and fabrication. The book also provides comprehensive rules for making structural calculations, together with the reasoning behind them. Extended coverage is given to key areas including: buckling failure, deflection, weld strength deflection, fatigue and adhesive bonding. The book also covers the design of extruded sections and local softening at welds.

Aluminium Design and Construction provides a clear and thorough examination of the subject. The text is highly illustrated with over 200 drawings, photographs and tables. This book is invaluable reading for structural designers, fabricators, architects and construction professionals.

Contents: Preface. Acknowledgements. About Aluminium. Manufacture. Fabrication. Aluminium Alloys and their sections. Limit State Design and Limiting Stresses. Heat-affected Zone Softening at Welds. Plate Elements in Compression. Beams. Tension and Compression Members. Calculation of Section Properties. Joints. Fatigue. References. Index.

December 1998 234x156 320pp
160 line, 20 halftone
Hb: 0-419-15710-7: £70.00

To Order: Tel: +44 (0) 8700 768853, or +44 (0) 1264 343071
Fax: +44 (0) 1264 343005, or **Post:** E & FN Spon Customer Services, ITPS Andover, Hants, SP10 5BE, UK

All orders must be pre-paid and will be sent free in the UK. Europe please add: £2.95 for the first book, thereafter £1.25 per book. ROW please add: Airmail £6.50 for the first book, thereafter £2.50 per book. Please add £12.50 delivery charge for items over £100.00.

Prices for Measured Works
- Major Works

INTRODUCTION

The rates contained in "Prices for Measured Work - Major Works" are intended to apply to a project in the outer London area costing about £1,300,000 (excluding Preliminaries) and assume that reasonable quantities of all types of work are required. Similarly it has been necessary to assume that the size of the project warrants the sub-letting of all types of work normally sub-let. Adjustments should be made to standard rates for time, location, local conditions, site constraints and any other factors likely to affect costs of a specific scheme.

The distinction between builders' work and work normally sub-let is stressed because prices for work which can be sub-let may well be quite inadequate for the contractor who is called upon to carry out relatively small quantities of such work himself.

As explained in more detail later the prices are generally based on wage rates which came into force on 28 June 1999, material costs as stated, and include no allowance for overheads or profit. They do not allow for preliminary items which are dealt with under a separate heading (see page 97) or for any Value Added Tax.

The format of this section is so arranged that, in the case of work normally undertaken by the Main Contractor, the constituent parts of the total rate are shown enabling the reader to make such adjustments as may be required in particular circumstances. Similar details have also been given for work normally sub-let although it has not been possible to provide this in all instances.

As explained in the Preface, there is a facility available to readers which enables a comparison to be made between the level of prices in this section and current tenders by means of a tender index. The tender index for this Major Works section of Spon's is 350 (as shown on the front cover) which is 3.25% above our forecast tender price index of 339 for the outer London region for the fourth quarter of 1999.

To adjust prices for other regions/times, the reader is recommended to refer to the explanations and examples on how to apply these tender indices, given on pages 671 - 675.

There follow explanations and definitions of the basis of costs in the "Prices for Measured Work" section under the following headings:

- ◆ Overhead charges and profit
- ◆ Labour hours and Labour £ column
- ◆ Material £ column
- ◆ Material/Plant £ columns
- ◆ Total rate £ column

OVERHEAD CHARGES AND PROFIT

For the reasons outlined in the preface to this years' edition, all rates exclude overheads and profit, to reflect our view of the current state of the market at time of going to press.

LABOUR HOURS AND LABOUR £ COLUMNS

"Labour rates" are based upon typical gang costs divided by the number of primary working operatives for the trade concerned, and for general building work include an allowance for trade supervision (see below). "Labour hours" multiplied by "Labour rate" with the appropriate addition for overhead charges and profit (currently zero) gives "Labour £". In some instances, due to variations in gangs used, "Labour rate" figures have not been indicated, but can be calculated by dividing "Labour £" by "Labour hours".

Building craft operatives and labourers

From 28 June 1999 guaranteed minimum weekly earnings in the London area for craft operatives and labourers are £235.95 and £177.45 respectively; to these rates have been added allowances for the items below in accordance with the recommended procedure of the Institute of Building in its "Code of Estimating Practice". The resultant hourly rates on which the "Prices for Measured Work" have generally been based are £7.96 and £6.05 for craft operatives and labourers, respectively.

- Lost time
- Construction Industry Training Board Levy
- Holidays with pay
- Accidental injury, retirement and death benefits scheme
- Sick pay
- National Insurance
- Severance pay and sundry costs
- Employer's liability and third party insurance

NOTE: For travelling allowances and site supervision see "Preliminaries" section.

The table which follows illustrates how the "all-in" hourly rates referred to on page 92 have been calculated. Productive time has been based on a total of 1864 hours worked per year.

		Craft Operatives		Labourers	
		£	£	£	£
Wages at standard basic rate					
productive time	47.8 wks	235.95	11,278.41	177.45	8,482.11
Lost time allowance	0.90 wks	235.95	213.30	177.45	160.41
Non-productive overtime	1.74 wks	235.95	410.55	177.45	308.76
			11,902.26		8,951.29
Extra payments under National Working Rules					
Sick Pay	1 wk		-		-
CITB Allowance (0.38% of payroll)	1 year		46.66		35.09
Public Holiday pay	1.60 wks	235.95	377.52	177.45	283.92
Employer's contribution to annual holiday pay, accidental injury, retirement and death cover scheme	47.0 wks	20.95	984.65	20.95	984.65
National Insurance	47.8 wks	21.22	1,014.32	13.45	642.91
			14,325.41		10,897.86
Severance pay and sundry costs	Plus	1.5%	214.88	1.5%	163.47
			14,540.29		11,061.33
Employer's Liability and Third Party Insurance	Plus	2.0%	290.81	2.0%	221.23
Total cost per annum			**£14,831.10**		**£11,282.56**
Total cost per hour			**£7.96**		**£6.05**

NOTES:

1.   Absence due to sickness has been assumed to be for periods not exceeding 3 days for which no payment is due.

2.   The annual holiday credit stamp contributions are those which came into force on 2 August 1999. The stamp price reflects the discount (35p) offered for credit purchase rather than the discount (70p) available for cash purchase.

3.   All N.I. payments are at not-contracted out rates applicable from 6 April 1999.

The "labour rates" used in the Measured Work sections have been based on the following gang calculations which generally include an allowance for supervision by a foreman or ganger. Alternative labour rates are given showing the effect of various degrees of bonus.

Gang	Total Gang rate £/hour		Productive unit rate £/hour	Alternative labour rates £/hour		
				+5%	+15%	+25%
Groundwork Gang						
1 Ganger	1 x 6.50 =	6.50				
6 Labourers	6 x 6.00 =	36.30				
		42.80	÷ 6.5 = 6.58	6.89	7.50	8.11
Concreting gang						
1 Ganger	1 x 6.90 =	6.90				
4 Labourers	4 x 6.45 =	25.80				
		32.70	÷ 4.5 = 7.27	7.58	8.21	8.84
Steelfixing Gang						
1 Foreman	1 x 8.40 =	8.40				
4 Steelfixers	4 x 7.96 =	31.84				
		40.24	÷ 4.5 = 8.94	9.36	10.19	11.03
Formwork Gang						
1 Foreman	1 x 8.40 =	8.40				
10 Carpenters	10 x 7.96 =	79.60				
1 Labourers	1 x 6.05 =	6.05				
		94.05	÷ 10.5 = 8.96	9.37	10.21	11.05
Bricklaying/Lightweight Blockwork Gang						
1 Foreman	1 x 8.40 =	8.40				
6 Bricklayers	6 x 7.96 =	47.76				
4 Labourers	4 x 6.05 =	24.20				
		80.36	÷ 6.5 = 12.36	12.94	14.09	15.24
Dense Blockwork Gang						
1 Foreman	1 x 8.40 =	8.40				
6 Bricklayers	6 x 7.96 =	47.76				
6 Labourers	6 x 6.05 =	36.30				
		92.46	÷ 6.5 = 14.22	14.88	16.21	17.54
Carpentry/Joinery Gang						
1 Foreman	1 x 8.40 =	8.40				
5 Carpenters	5 x 7.96 =	39.80				
1 Labourer	1 x 6.05 =	6.05				
		54.25	÷ 5.5 = 9.86	10.32	11.24	12.17
Craft Operative (Painter, Wall and Floor Tiler, Slater)	1 x 7.96 =	7.96	÷ 1 = 7.96	8.33	9.07	9.82
1 and 1 Gang						
1 Craft Operative	1 x 7.96 =	7.96				
1 Labourer	1 x 6.45 =	6.45				
		14.41	÷ 1 = 14.41	15.06	16.36	17.67
2 and 1 Gang						
2 Craft Operatives	2 x 7.96 =	15.92				
1 Labourer	1 x 6.45 =	6.45				
		22.37	÷ 2 = 11.19	11.70	12.72	13.75
Small Labouring Gang (making good)						
1 Ganger	1 x 6.90 =	6.90				
4 Labourers	4 x 6.45 =	25.80				
		32.70	÷ 4.5 = 7.27	7.58	8.21	8.84
Drain Laying Gang/Clayware						
2 Labourers	2 x 6.45 =	12.90	÷ 2 = 6.45	6.73	7.29	7.85

Sub-Contractor's operatives
Similar labour rates are shown in respect of sub-let trades where applicable.

Plumbing operatives
From 24 August 1998 the hourly earnings for technical and trained plumbers are £7.48 and £5.98, respectively; to these rates have been added allowances similar to those added for building operatives (see below). The resultant average hourly rate on which the "Prices for Measured Work" have been based is £9.28.

The items referred to above for which allowance has been made are:

Tool allowance
Plumbers' welding supplement
Holidays with pay
Pension and welfare stamp
National Insurance "contracted out" contributions
Severance pay and sundry costs
Employer's liability and third party insurance

No allowance has been made for supervision as we have assumed the use of a team of technical or trained plumbers who are able to undertake such relatively straightforward plumbing works, e.g. on housing schemes, without further supervision.

The table which follows shows how the average hourly rate referred to above has been calculated. Productive time has been based on a total of 1831 hours worked per year.

			Technical Plumber		Trained Plumber	
			£	£	£	£
Wages at standard basic rate						
productive time	1831	hrs	7.48	13,692.89	5.98	10,946.99
Non-productive overtime	34	hrs	7.48	253.57	5.98	202.72
Plumber's welding supplement (gas and arc)	1831	hrs	0.46	842.08		0.00
Tool Allowance	45.2	wks	2.24	101.25	2.24	101.25
Public Holiday Pay	60	hrs	7.48	448.80	5.98	358.80
				15,338.59		11,609.76
Employer's contribution to						
holiday credit/welfare stamps	52	wks	25.00	1,300.00	20.46	1,063.92
pension (6.5% of earnings)	47.8	wks	20.86	997.11	15.79	754.76
National Insurance	47.8	wks	21.89	1,046.34	14.71	703.14
				18,682.04		14,131.58
Severance pay and sundry costs	Plus		1.5%	280.23	1.5%	211.97
				18,962.27		14,343.55
Employer's Liability and Third Party Insurance	Plus		2.0%	379.25	2.0%	286.87
Total cost per annum				**£ 19,341.52**		**£14,630.42**
Total cost per hour				**£10.57**		**£7.99**
Average all-in rate per hour					**£9.28**	

MATERIAL £ COLUMN

Many items have reference to a "PC" value. This indicates the prime cost of the principal material delivered to site in the outer London area assuming maximum discounts for large quantities. When obtaining material prices from other sources, it is important to identify any discounts that may apply. Some manufacturers only offer 5 to 10% discount for the largest of orders; or "firm" orders (as distinct from quotations). For some materials, discounts of 30% to 40% may be obtainable, depending on value of order, preferential position of the purchaser or state of the market.

The "Material £" column indicates the total materials cost including delivery, waste, sundry materials and an allowance (currently zero) for overhead charges and profit for the unit of work concerned. Alternative material prices are given at the beginning of many sections, by means of which alternative "Total rate £" prices may be calculated. All material prices quoted are exclusive of Value Added Tax.

MATERIAL PLANT £ COLUMN

Plant costs have been based on current weekly hire charges and estimated weekly cost of oil, grease, ropes (where necessary), site servicing and cartage charges. The total amount is divided by 30 (assuming 25% idle time) to arrive at a cost per working hour of plant. To this hourly rate is added one hour fuel consumption and one hour for an operator where indicated; the rate to be calculated in accordance with the principles set out earlier in this section, i.e. with an allowance for plus rates, etc.

For convenience the all-in rates per hour used in the calculations of "Prices for Measured Work" are shown below and where included in Material/Plant £ column.

Plant	Labour	"All-in" rate per hour £
Excavator (4 wheeled - 0.76 m³ shovel, 0.24 m³ bucket)	Driver	18.70
Excavator (JCB 3C - 0.24 m³ bucket)	Driver	14.45
Excavator (JCB 3C off centre - 0.24 m³ bucket)	Driver	17.00
Excavator (Hitachi EX120 - 0.53 m³ bucket)	Driver	19.55
Dumper (2.30 m³)	Driver	13.60
Two tool portable compressor (125 cfm)		
per breaking tool		1.85
per punner foot and stem rammer		1.45
Roller		
Bomag BW75S - pedestrian double drum		2.65
Bomag BW120AD - tandem		6.10
5/3.50 cement mixer		1.00
Kango heavy duty breaker		0.80
Power float		1.70
Light percussion drill		0.40

* Operation of compressor by tool operator

TOTAL RATE £ COLUMN

"Total rate £" column is the sum of "Labour £" and "Material £" columns. This column excludes any allowance for "Preliminaries" which must be taken into account if one is concerned with the total cost of work.

The example of "Preliminaries" in the following section indicates that in the absence of detailed calculations currently 11% should be added to all prices for measured work to arrive at total cost.

A PRELIMINARIES

The number of items priced in the "Preliminaries" section of Bills of Quantities and the manner in which they are priced vary considerably between Contractors. Some Contractors, by modifying their percentage factor for overheads and profit, attempt to cover the costs of "Preliminary" items in their "Prices for Measured Work". However, the cost of "Preliminaries" will vary widely according to job size and complexity, site location, accessibility, degree of mechanisation practicable, position of the Contractor's head office and relationships with local labour/domestic Sub-Contractors. It is therefore usually far safer to price "Preliminary" items separately on their merits according to the job.

In amending the Preliminaries/General Conditions section for SMM7, the Joint Committee stressed that the preliminaries section of a bill should contain two types of cost significant item:

1. Items which are not specific to work sections but which have an identifiable cost which is useful to consider separately in tendering e.g. contractual requirements for insurances, site facilities for the employer's representative and payments to the local authority.
2. Items for fixed and time-related costs which derive from the contractor's expected method of carrying out the work, e.g. bringing plant to and from site, providing temporary works and supervision.

A fixed charge is for work the cost of which is to be considered as independent of duration. A time related charge is for work the cost of which is to be considered as dependent on duration. The fixed and time-related subdivision given for a number of preliminaries items will enable tenderers to price the elements separately should they so desire. Tenderers also have the facility at their discretion to extend the list of fixed and time-related cost items to suit their particular methods of construction.

The opportunity for Tenderers to price fixed and time-related items in A30-A37, A40-A44 and A51-A52 have been noted against the following appropriate items although we have not always provided guidance as costs can only be assessed in the light of circumstances of a particular job.

Works of a temporary nature are deemed to include rates, fees and charges related thereto in Sections A36, A41, A42, and A44, all of which will probably be dealt with as fixed charges.

In addition to the cost significant items required by the method, other preliminaries items which are important from other points of view, e.g. quality control requirements, administrative procedures, may need to be included to complete the Preliminaries/General conditions as a comprehensive statement of the employer's requirements.

Typical clause descriptions from a "Preliminaries/General Conditions" section are given below together with details of those items that are usually priced in detail in tenders.

An example in pricing "Preliminaries" follows, and this assumes the form of contract used is the Standard Form of Building Contract 1980 Edition and the value, excluding "Preliminaries", is £1 300 000. The contract is estimated to take 80 weeks to complete and the value is built up as follows:

	£
Labour value	465 000
Material value	395 000
Provisional sums and all Sub-Contractors	440 000
	£ 1 300 000

At the end of the section the examples are summarised to give a total value of "Preliminaries" for the project.

A PRELIMINARIES

A PRELIMINARIES/GENERAL CONDITIONS

Preliminary particulars

A10   Project particulars - Not priced

A11   Drawings - Not priced

A12   The Site/Existing buildings - Generally not priced

The reference to existing buildings relates only to those buildings which could have an influence on cost. This could arise from their close proximity making access difficult, their heights relative to the possible use of tower cranes or the fragility of, for example, an historic building necessitating special care.

A13   Description of the work - Generally not priced

A20   The Contract/Sub-contract
(The Standard Form of Building Contract 1980 Edition is assumed)

Clause no
1.   **Interpretation, definitions, etc.** - Not priced
2.   **Contractor's obligations** - Not priced
3.   **Contract Sum - adjustment - Interim certificates** - Not priced
4.   **Architect's Instructions** - Not priced
5.   **Contract documents - other documents - issue of certificates**
      The contract conditions may require a master programme to be prepared. This will normally form part of head office overheads and therefore is not priced separately here.
6.   **Statutory obligations, notices, fees and charges** - Not priced. Unless the Contractor is specifically instructed to allow for these items.
7.   **Level and setting out of the works** - Not priced
8.   **Materials, goods and workmanship to conform to description, testing and inspection** - Not priced
9.   **Royalties and patent rights** - Not priced

NOTE: The term "Not priced" or "Generally not priced" where used throughout this section means either that the cost implication is negligible or that it is usually included elsewhere in the tender.

10.   **Person-in-charge**
      Under this heading are usually priced any staff that will be required on site. The staff required will vary considerably according to the size, layout and complexity of the scheme, from one foreman-in-charge to a site agent, general foreman, assistants, checkers and storemen, etc. The costs included for such people should include not only their wages, but their total cost to the site including statutory payments, pension, expenses, holiday relief, overtime, etc. Part of the foreman's time, together with that of an assistant, will be spent on setting out the site. Allow, say, £2.15 per day for levels, staff, pegs and strings, plus the assistant's time if not part of the general management team. Most sites usually include for one operative to clean up generally and do odd jobs around the site.
      Cost of other staff, such as buyers, and quantity surveyors, are usually part of head office overhead costs, but alternatively, may now be covered under A40 Management and staff.

A PRELIMINARIES

A20   The Contract/Sub-contract - cont'd

A typical build-up of a foreman's costs might be:

	£
Annual salary	17,600.00
Expenses	1,500.00
Bonus - say	1,800.00
Employer's National Insurance contribution (10.4% on £19 400.00) say	2,018.00
Training levy @ 0.25% say	49.00
Pension scheme (say 6% of salary and bonus) say	1,164.00
Sundries, including Employer's Liability and Third Party (say 3.5% of salary and bonus) say	679.00
	£ 24,810.00
Divide by 47 to allow for holidays: per week	527.87
Say	£ 530.00

Corresponding costs for other site staff should be calculated in a similar manner, e.g.

Site administration	£
General foreman 80 weeks @ £530	42,400.00
Holiday relief 4 weeks @ £530	2,120.00
Assistant foreman 60 weeks @ £265	15,900.00
Storeman/checker 60 weeks @ £195	11,700.00
	£ 72,120.00

11.   **Access for Architect to the Works** - Not priced
12.   **Clerk of Works** - Not priced
13.   **Variations and provisional sums** - Not priced
14.   **Contract Sum** -Not priced
15.   **Value Added Tax - supplemental provisions**
      Major changes to the VAT status of supplies of goods and services by Contractors came into effect on 1 April 1989. It is clear that on and from that date the majority of work supplied under contracts on JCT Forms will be chargeable on the Contractor at the standard rate of tax. In April 1989, the JCT issued Amendment 8 and a guidance note dealing with the amendment to VAT provisions. This involves a revision to clause 15 and the Supplemental Provisions (the VAT agreement). Although the standard rating of most supplies should reduce the amount of VAT analysing previously undertaken by contractors, he should still allow for any incidental costs and expenses which may be incurred.
16.   **Materials and goods unfixed or off-site** - Not priced
17.   **Practical completion and Defects Liability**
      Inevitably some defects will arise after practical completion and an allowance will often be made to cover this. An allowance of say 0.25 to 0.5% should be sufficient, e.g. Example

Defects after completion

Based on 0.25% of the contract sum

£1,300,000 x 0.25%   £ 3,250.00

18.   **Partial possession by Employer** - Not priced
19.   **Assignment and Sub-Contracts** - Not priced

A PRELIMINARIES

A20   The Contract/Sub-contract - cont'd.

19A **Fair wages** - Not priced
20. **Injury to persons and property and Employers indemnity**
     (See Clause no 21)
21. **Insurance against injury to persons and property**
     The Contractor's Employer's Liability and Public Liability policies (which would both be involved under this heading) are often in the region of 0.5 to 0.6% on the value of his own contract work (excluding provisional sums and work by Sub-Contractors whose prices should allow for these insurances). However, this allowance can be included in the all-in hourly rate used in the calculation of "Prices for Measured Work" (see page 93).
     Under Clause 21.2 no requirement is made upon the Contractor to insure as stated by the clause unless a provisional sum is allowed in the Contract Bills.
22. **Insurance of the works against Clause 22 Perils**
     If, at the Contractor's risk, the insurance cover must be sufficient to include the full cost of reinstatement, all increases in cost, professional fees and any consequential costs such as demolition. The average provision for fire risk is 0.10% of the value of the work after adding for increased costs and professional fees.

Contractor's Liability - Insurance of works against fire, etc.	£
Contract value (including "Preliminaries"), say	1,475,000.00
Estimated increased costs during contract period, say 6%	88,500.00
	1,563,500.00
Estimated increased costs incurred during period of reinstatement, say 3%	46,900.00
	1,610,400.00
Professional fees @ 16%	257,700.00
	1,868,100.00
Allow 0.1%	1,868.00

NOTE: Insurance premiums are liable to considerable variation, depending on the Contractor, the nature of the work and the market in which the insurance is placed.

23. **Date of possession, completion and postponement** - Not priced
24. **Damages for non-completion** - Not priced
25. **Extension of time** - Not priced
26. **Loss and expense caused by matters materially affecting regular progress of the works** - Not priced
27. **Determination by Employer** - Not priced
28. **Determination by Contractor** -Not priced
29. **Works by Employer or persons employed or engaged by Employer** - Not priced
30. **Certificates and payments** - Not priced
31. **Finance (No.2) Act 1975 - Statutory tax deduction scheme** - Not priced
32. **Outbreak of hostilities** -Not priced
33. **War damage** - Not priced
34. **Antiquities** - Not priced
35. **Nominated Sub-Contractors** - Not priced here. An amount should be added to the relevant PC sums, if required, for profit and a further sum for special attendance.
36. **Nominated Suppliers -** Not priced here. An amount should be added to the relevant PC sums, if required, for profit.

A PRELIMINARIES

A20   The Contract/Sub-contract - cont'd.

37.   **Choice of fluctuation provisions - entry in Appendix**
The amount which the Contractor may recover under the fluctuations clauses (Clause nos 38, 39 and 40) will vary depending on whether the Contract is "firm", i.e. Clause no 38 is included, or "fluctuating", whether the traditional method of assessment is used, i.e. Clause no 39 or the formula method, i.e. Clause no 40. An allowance should be made for any shortfall in reimbursement under fluctuating contracts.

38.   **Contribution Levy and Tax Fluctuations** (see Clause no 37)

39.   **Labour and Materials Cost and Tax Fluctuations** (see Clause no 37)

40.   **Use of Price Adjustment Formulae** (see Clause no 37)
Details should include special conditions or amendments to standard conditions, the Appendix insertions and the Employer's insurance responsibilities. Additional obligations may include the provision of a performance bond. If the Contractor is required to provide sureties for the fulfilment of the work the usual method of providing this is by a bond provided by one or more insurance companies. The cost of a performance bond depends largely on the financial standing of the applying Contractor. Figures tend to range from 0.25 to 0.50% of the contract sum.

A30-A37 EMPLOYERS' REQUIREMENTS

These include the following items but costs can only be assessed in the light of circumstances on a particular job. Details should be given for each item and the opportunity for the Tenderer to separately price items related to fixed charges and time related charges.

A30   Tendering/Sub-letting/Supply

A31   Provision, content and use of documents

A32   Management of the works

A33   Quality standards/control

A34   Security/Safety/Protection

This includes noise and pollution control, maintaining adjoining buildings, public and private roads, live services, security and the protection of work in all sections.

(i)   Control of noise, pollution and other obligations
The Local Authority, Landlord or Management Company may impose restrictions on the timing of certain operations, particularly noisy of dust-producing operations, which may necessitate the carrying out of these works outside normal working hours or using special tools and equipment. The situation is most likely to occur in built-up areas such as city centres, shopping malls etc., where the site is likely to be in close proximity to offices, commercial or residential property.

(ii)   Maintenance of public and private roads
Some additional value or allowance may be required against this item to insure/protect against damage to entrance gates, kerbs or bridges caused by extraordinary traffic in the execution of the works.

A35   Specific limitations on method/sequence/timing

This includes design constraints, method and sequence of work, access, possession and use of the site, use or disposal of materials found, start of work, working hours, employment of labour and sectional possession or partial possession etc.

A PRELIMINARIES

A36   Facilities/Temporary work/Services

This includes offices, sanitary accommodation, temporary fences, hoardings, screens and roofs, name boards, technical and surveying equipment, temperature and humidity, telephone/facsimile installation and rental/maintenance, special lighting and other general requirements, etc.   The attainment and maintenance of suitable levels necessary for satisfactory completion of the work including the installation of joinery, suspended ceilings, lift machinery, etc. is the responsibility of the contractor.

The following is an example how to price a mobile office for a Clerk of Works

			£
(a)	Fixed charge		
	Haulage to and from site - say		150.00
(b)	Time related charge		
	Hire charge - 15m^2 x 76 weeks @ £2.00/m^2		2,280.00
	Lighting, heating and attendance on office,		
	say 76 weeks @ £25.00		1,900.00
	Rates on temporary building based on £14.00/m^2 per annum		310.00
			4,490.00
(c)	Combined charge		4,640.00

The installation of telephones or facsimiles for the use of the Employer, and all related charges therewith, shall be given as a provisional sum.

A37   Operation/Maintenance of the finished building

A40-A44 CONTRACTORS GENERAL COST ITEMS

For items A41-A44 it shall be clearly indicated whether such items are to be "Provided by the Contractor" or "Made available (in any part) by the Employer".

A40 Management and staff (Provided by the Contractor)

NOTE: The cost of site administrative staff has previously been included against Clause 10 of the Conditions of Contract, where Readers will find an example of management and staff costs.

When required allow for the provision of a watchman or inspection by a security organization. Other general administrative staff costs, e.g. Engineering, Programming and production and Quantity Surveying could be priced as either fixed or time related charges, under this section. For the purpose of this example allow, say, 1% of measured work value for other administrative staff costs.

(a)   Time related charge

Based on 1% of £1,300,000 - say   £ 13,000.00

A PRELIMINARIES

A41 Site accommodation (Provided by the Contractor or made available by the Employer)

This includes all temporary offices laboratories, cabins, stores, compounds, canteens, sanitary facilities and the like for the Contractor's and his domestic sub-contractors' use (temporary office for a Clerk of Works is covered under obligations and restrictions imposed by the Employer).
Typical costs for jack-type offices are as follows, based upon a twelve months minimum hire period they exclude furniture which could add a further £14.00 - £16.00 per week.

Size	Rate per week £
12 ft x 9 ft (10.03 m²)	21.00 (£2.09/m²)
16 ft x 9 ft (13.37 m²)	24.00 (£1.80/m²)
24 ft x 9 ft (20.06 m²)	32.00 (£1.60/m²)
32 ft x 12 ft (35.67 m²)	50.00 (£1.40/m²)

Typical rates for security units are as follows:

Size	Rate per week £
12 ft x 8 ft (8.92 m²)	21.00 (£2.35/m²)
16 ft x 8 ft (11.89 m²)	25.00 (£2.10/m²)
24 ft x 8 ft (17.84 m²)	34.00 (£1.91/m²)
32 ft x 8 ft (23.78 m²)	43.00 (£1.81/m²)

The following example is for one Foreman's office and two security units.

		£
(a)	Fixed charge	
	Haulage to and from site - Foreman's Office, say	150.00
	Haulage to and from site - Storage sheds, say	300.00
		450.00
(b)	Time related charge	
	Hire charge - Foreman's office 15 m² x 76 weeks @ £1.80/m²	2,052.00
	Hire charge - Storage sheds 40 m² x 70 weeks @ £1.80/m²	5,040.00
	Lighting, heating and attendance on office,	
	say 76 weeks @ £25.00	1,900.00
	Rates on temporary building based on £14.00/m² per annum	1,440.00
		10,432.00
(c)	Combined charge	10,884.00

A PRELIMINARIES

A42 Services and facilities (Provided by the Contractor or made available by the Employer)

This generally includes the provision of all of the Contractor's own services, power, lighting, fuels, water, telephone and administration, safety, health and welfare, storage of materials, rubbish disposal, cleaning, drying out, protection of work in all sections, security, maintaining public and private roads, small plant and tools and general attendance on nominated sub-contractors. However, this section does not cover fuel for testing and commissioning permanent installations which would be measured under Sections Y51 and Y81. Examples of build-ups/allowances for some of the major items are provided below:

(i)   Lighting and power for the works
The Contractor is usually responsible for providing all temporary lighting and power for the works and all charges involved. On large sites this could be expensive and involve sub-stations and the like, but on smaller sites it is often limited to general lighting (depending upon time of year) and power for power operated tools for which a small diesel generator and some transformers usually proves adequate.

Typical costs are:

Low voltage diesel generator   £90.00 - £100.00 per week
2.20 to 10 kVA transformer   £10.00 - £50.00 per week

A typical allowance, including charges, installation and fitting costs could be 1% of contract value.

Example
Lighting and power for the works
Combined charge
The fixed charge would normally represent a proportion of the following allowance applicable to connection and supply charges. The residue would be allocated to time related charges.

Dependant on the nature of the work, time of year and
incidence of power operated tools
                                                         _____
based on 1% of £1,300,000 - say   £ 13,000.00
                                                         _____

(ii)   Water for the works

Charges should properly be ascertained from the local Water Authority. If these are not readily available, an allowance of 0.33% of the value of the contract is probably adequate, providing water can be obtained directly from the mains. Failing this, each case must be dealt with on its merits. In all cases an allowance should also be made for temporary plumbing including site storage of water if required.

Useful rates for temporary plumbing include:

Piping   £5.15 per metre
Connection   £150.00
Standpipe   £55.00
Plus an allowance for barrels and hoses.

A PRELIMINARIES

A42 Services and facilities - cont'd

Example

Water for the works
Combined charge
The fixed charge would normally represent a proportion of the following allowance applicable to connection and supply charges. The residue would be allocated to time related charges.

	£
0.33% of £1,300,000	4,290.00
Temporary plumbing, say	400.00
	£ 4,690.00

(iii)   Temporary telephones for the use of the Contractor

Against this item should be included the cost of installation, rental and an assessment of the cost of calls made during the contract.

Installation costs	£99.00
Rental	£28.67 Initial Monthly Payment
	£14.33 Monthly Payment Thereafter
Cost of calls	For sites with one telephone allow about
	£22.00 per week.

Example
Temporary telephones   £

(a)   Fixed charge
       Connection charges
       line with socket outlet   99.00
       external ringing device   10.00
                                                        109.00

(b)   Time related charge
       line rental - 6 quarters - 1 Month   @ £28.67   28.67
                                  17 Months @ £14.33   243.61
       external ringing device rental - 6 quarters @ £2.50   15.00
       call charges - 76 weeks @ £22.00   1,672.00
                                                            1,959.28

(c)   Combined charges, say   £ 2,070.00

(iv)   Safety, health and welfare of workpeople
The Contractor is required to comply with the Code of Welfare Conditions for the Building Industry which sets out welfare requirements for the following:

1.   Shelter from inclement weather
2.   Accommodation for clothing
3.   Accommodation and provision for meals
4.   Provision of drinking water
5.   Sanitary conveniences
6.   Washing facilities
7.   First aid
8.   Site conditions

A PRELIMINARIES

A42 Services and facilities - cont'd

A variety of self-contained mobile or jack-type units are available for hire and a selection of rates is given below:

	£	
Kitchen with cooker, fridge, sink unit, water heater and basin		
32 ft x 10 ft jack-type	75.00	per week
Mess room with water heater, wash basin and seating		
16 ft x 7 ft 6 in mobile	40.00	per week
16 ft x 9 ft jack-type	38.00	per week
Welfare unit with drying rack, lockers, tables, seating, cooker,		
heater, sink and basin		
22 ft x 7 ft 6 in mobile	55.00	per week
Toilets (mains type)		
One pan unit	15.00	per week
Two pan unit mobile	40.00	per week
Four pan unit jack-type	50.00	per week

Allowance must be made in addition for transport costs to and from site, setting up costs, connection to mains, fuel supplies and attendance

Site first aid kit   £ 3.65 per week

A general provision to comply with the above code is often 0.50 to 0.75% of the measured work value. The costs of safety supervisors (required for firms employing more than 20 people) are usually part of head office overhead costs.

Example
Safety, health and welfare
Combined charge
The fixed charge would normally represent a proportion of the following allowance, with the majority allocated to time related charges.

Based on 0.66% of £1,300,000 - say   £ 8,580.00

(v)   Removing rubbish, protective casings and coverings and cleaning the works on completion. This includes removing surplus materials and final cleaning of the site prior to handover. Allow for sufficient "bins" for the site throughout the contract duration and for some operatives time at the end of the contract for final clearing and cleaning ready for handover.

Cost of "bins" - approx. £25.00 each
A general allowance of 0.20% of measured work value is probably sufficient.

Example
Removing rubbish, etc., and cleaning
Combined charge
The fixed charge would normally represent an allowance for final clearing of the works on completion with the residue for cleaning throughout the contract period

Based on 0.2% of £1,300,000 - say   £ 2,600.00

A PRELIMINARIES

A42 Services and facilities - cont'd

(vi) Drying the works
Use or otherwise of an installed heating system will probably determine the value to be placed against this item. Dependant upon the time of year, say allow 0.1% to 0.2% of the contract value to cover this item.

Example
Drying of the works
Combined charge
Generally this cost is likely to be related to a fixed charge only

Based on 0.1% of £1,300,000 - say   £ 1,300.00

(vii) Protecting the works from inclement weather
In areas likely to suffer particularly inclement weather, some nominal allowance should be included for tarpaulins, polythene sheeting, battening, etc., and the effect of any delays in concreting or brickwork by such weather.

(viii) Small plant and tools
Small plant and hand tools are usually assessed as between 0.5% and 1.5% of total labour value.
Combined charge

Based on 1% of labour cost of £465,000 - say   £ 4,650.00

(ix) General attendance on nominated sub-contractors
In the past this item was located after each PC sum. Under SMM7 it is intended that two composite items (one for fixed charges and the other for time related charges) should be provided in the preliminaries bill for general attendance on all nominated sub-contractors.

A43 Mechanical plant

This includes for cranes, hoists, personnel transport, transport, earthmoving plant, concrete plant, piling plant, paving and surfacing plant, etc. SMM6 required that items for protection or for plant be given in each section, whereas SMM7 provides for these items to be covered under A34, A42 and A43, as appropriate.

(i) Plant
Quite often, the Contractors own plant and plant employed by sub-contractors are included in measured rates, (e.g. for earthmoving, concrete or piling plant) and the Editors have adopted this method of pricing where they believe it to be appropriate. As for other items of plant e.g. cranes, hoists, these tend to be used by a variety of trades. An example of such an item might be:

A PRELIMINARIES

A43   Mechanical Plant - cont'd

Example
Tower crane - static 30 m radius - 4/5 tonne max. load

		£
(a)	Fixed charge	
	Haulage of crane to and from site, erection, testing,	
	commissioning & dismantling - say	5,000.00
(b)	Time related charge	
	Hire of crane, say 30 weeks @ 600.00	18,000.00
	electricity fuel and oil - say	5,000.00
	operator 30 weeks x 40 hours @ £10.00	12,000.00
		35,000.00
(c)	Combined charge, say	£ 40,000.00

For the purpose of this example in pricing of Preliminaries, the Editors have assumed that the costs of the above tower crane are included in with "Measured Rates" items and have not therefore carried this total to the Sample Summary.

(ii)   Personnel transport
The labour rates per hour on which "Prices for Measured Work" have been based do not cover travel and lodging allowances which must be assessed according to the appropriate working rule agreement.

Example
Personnel transport

Assuming all labour can be found within the London region, the labour value of £465 000 represents approximately 2050 man weeks. Assume each man receives an allowance of £1.54 per day or £7.70 per week of five days.

Combined/time related charge

2050 man weeks @ £7.70   £ 15,785.00

A44   Temporary works (Provided by the Contractor or made available by the Employer)

This includes for temporary roads, temporary walkways, access scaffolding, support scaffolding and propping, hoardings, fans, fencing etc., hardstanding and traffic regulations etc. The Contractor should include maintaining any temporary works in connection with the items, adapting, clearing away and making good, and all notices and fees to Local Authorities and public undertakings. On fluctuating contracts, i.e. where Clause 39 or 40 is incorporated there Is no allowance for fluctuations in respect of plant and temporary works and in such instances allowances must be made for any increases likely to occur over the contract period.

Examples of build-ups/allowances for some items are provided below:

(i)   Temporary roads, hardstandings, crossings and similar items
Quite often consolidated bases of eventual site roads are used throughout a contract to facilitate movement of materials around the site. However, during the initial setting up of a site, with drainage works outstanding, this is not always possible and occasionally temporary roadways have to be formed and ground levels later reinstated.

A PRELIMINARIES

A44   Temporary works - cont'd

Typical costs are:

Removal of topsoil and provision of a 225 mm thick stone/hardcore base blinded with ashes as a temporary roadway 3.50 m wide and subsequent reinstatement:

on level ground	£22.00 per metre
on sloping ground (including 1m of cut or fill)	£27.50 per metre

Removal of topsoil and provision of 225 mm thick stone/hardcore base blinded with ashes as a temporary hardstanding   £6.45 per m²

Provision of "Aluminium Trakway"; Eve Trakway or equal and approved; portable road system laid directly onto existing surface or onto compacted removable granular base to protect existing surface (Note: most systems are based on a weekly hire charge and laid and removed by the supplier):

Heavy Duty Trakpanel (3.00 m x 2.50 m)	£3.93 per m²/per week
Delivery charge for Trakpanel	£1.83 per m²
Outrigger mats for use in conjunction with Heavy Duty Trakpanel - per set of 4 mats	£80.00 per set/per week
Single Trak Roadway (3.90 m x 1.22 m)	£2.53 per m²/per week
LD20 Eveolution - Light Duty Trakway (roll out system - minimum delivery 75 m)	£4.60 per m²/per first week £1.50 per m²/per week thereafter
Terraplas Walkways (turf protection system) - per section (1.00 m x 1.00 m)	£5.00 per m²/per week

NOTE: Any allowance for special hardcore hardstandings for piling Sub-Contractors is usually priced against the "special attendance" clause after the relevant Prime Cost sum.

(ii)   Scaffolding
The General Contractor's standing scaffolding is usually undertaken by specialist Sub-Contractors who will submit quotations based on the specific requirements of the works. It is not possible to give rates here for the various types of scaffolding that may be required but for the purposes of this section it is assumed that the cost of supplying, erecting, maintaining and subsequently dismantling the scaffolding required would amount to £10,000.00 inclusive of overheads and profit.

(iii)   Temporary fencing, hoarding, screens, fans, planked footways, guardrails, gantries, and similar items.
This item must be considered in some detail as it is dependant on site perimeter, phasing of the work, work within existing buildings, etc.

Useful rates include:

A PRELIMINARIES

A44   Temporary works - cont'd

(iii)   Temporary fencing, hoarding, screens, fans, planked footways, guardrails, gantries, and similar items - cont'd

Hoarding 2.30 m high of 18 mm thick plywood with 50 mm x 100 mm sawn softwood studding, rails and posts, including later dismantling

undecorated	£55.00/m (£23.90/m^2)
decorated one side	£61.50/m (£26.75/m^2)
Pair of gates for hoarding	extra £225.00 per pair
Cleft Chestnut fencing 1.20 m high including dismantling	£6.75/m
Morarflex "T-Plus" scaffold sheeting	£3.25/m^2

Example
Temporary hoarding
Combined fixed charge

	£
Decorated plywood hoarding 100m @ £61.50	6,150.00
extra for one pair of gates	225.00
	£ 6,375.00

(iv)   Traffic regulations
Waiting and unloading restrictions can occasionally add considerably to costs, resulting in forced overtime or additional weekend working. Any such restrictions must be carefully assessed for the job in hand.

A50   Work/Materials by the Employer

A description shall be given of works by others directly engaged by the Employer and any attendance that is required shall be priced in the same way as works by nominated sub-contractors.

A51   Nominated sub-contractors

This section governs how nominated sub-contractors should be covered in the bills of quantities for main contracts. Bills of quantities used for inviting tenders from potential nominated sub-contractors should be drawn up in accordance with SMM7 as a whole as if the work was main contractor's work. This means, for example, that bills issued to potential nominated sub-contractors should include preliminaries and be accompanied by the drawings.

As much information as possible should be given in respect of nominated sub-contractors' work in order that tenderers can make due allowance when assessing the overall programme and establishing the contract period if not already laid down. A simple list of the component elements of the work might not be sufficient, but a list describing in addition the extent and possible value of each element would be more helpful. The location of the main plant, e.g. whether in the basement or on the roof, would clearly have a bearing on tenderers' programmes. It would be good practice to seek programme information when obtaining estimates from sub-contractors so that this can be incorporated in the bills of quantities for the benefit of tenderers.

A percentage should be added for the main contractor's profit together with items for fixed and time related charges for special attendances required by nominated sub-contractors. Special attendances to include scaffolding (additional to the Contractor's standing scaffolding), access roads, hardstandings, positioning (including unloading, distributing, hoisting or placing in position items of significant weight or size), storage, power, temperature and humidity etc.

A52   Nominated suppliers

Goods and materials which are required to be obtained from a nominated supplier shall be given as a prime cost sum to which should be added, if required, a percentage for profit.

A PRELIMINARIES

A53   Work by statutory authorities

Works which are to be carried out by a Local Authority or statutory undertakings shall be given as provisional sums.

A54   Provisional work

One of the more significant revisions in SMM7 is the requirement to identify provisional sums as being for either defined or undefined work.
The new rules require that each sum for defined work should be accompanied in the bills of quantities by a description of the work sufficiently detailed for the tenderer to make allowance for its effect in the pricing of relevant preliminaries. The information should also enable the length of time required for execution of the work to be estimated and its position in the sequence of construction to be determined and incorporated into the programme. Where Provisional Sums are given for undefined work the Contractor will be deemed not to have made any allowance in programming, planning and pricing preliminaries.
Any provision for Contingencies shall be given as a provisional sum for undefined work.

A55   Dayworks

To include provisional sums for:

Labour
Materials and goods
Plant

SAMPLE SUMMARY

Item		£
A20.10	Site administration	72,120.00
A20.17	Defects after completion	3,250.00
A20.22	Insurance of the works against fire, etc.	1,868.00
A36	Clerk of Work's Office	4,640.00
A40	Additional management and staff	13,000.00
A41	Contractor's accommodation	10,884.00
A42(i)	Lighting and power for the works	13,000.00
A42(ii)	Water for the works	4,690.00
A42(iii)	Temporary telephones	1,850.00
A42(iv)	Safety, health and welfare	8,580.00
A42(v)	Removing rubbish, etc., and cleaning	2,600.00
A42(vi)	Drying the works	1,300.00
A42(viii)	Small plant and tools	4,650.00
A43(ii)	Personnel transport	15,785.00
A44(ii)	Scaffolding	10,000.00
A44(iii)	Temporary hoarding	6,375.00
	TOTAL £	174,592.00

It is emphasized that the above is an example only of the way in which Preliminaries may be priced and it is essential that for any particular contract or project the items set out in Preliminaries should be assessed on their respective values.

Preliminaries as a percentage of a total contract will vary considerably according to each scheme and each Contractors' estimating practice. The value of the Preliminaries items in the above example represents approximately a 13% addition to the value of measured work. Current trends are for Preliminaries to vary from 11 to 13% on tenders. For the purposes of an estimate based on the "Prices for Measured Works - Major Works" section in the current edition of Spons the authors recommend that a 11% addition for preliminaries be applied.

D GROUNDWORK Excluding overheads and profit	PC £	Labour hours	Labour £	Material/ Plant £	Unit	Total rate £
D GROUNDWORK						
D20 EXCAVATING AND FILLING						
NOTE: Prices are applicable to excavating in firm soil. Multiplying factors for other soils are as follows:						
Mechanical **Hand**						
Clay x 2.00 x 1.20						
Compact gravel x 3.00 x 1.50						
Soft chalk x 4.00 x 2.00						
Hard rock x 5.00 x 6.00						
Running sand or silt x 6.00 x 2.00						
Site preparation						
Removing trees						
girth 600 mm - 1.50 m	-	20.00	131.60	-	nr	**131.60**
girth 1.50 - 3.00 m	-	35.00	230.30	-	nr	**230.30**
girth exceeding 3.00 m	-	50.00	329.00	-	nr	**329.00**
Removing tree stumps						
girth 600 mm - 1.50 m	-	1.00	6.58	31.36	nr	**37.94**
girth 1.50 - 3.00 m	-	1.00	6.58	45.76	nr	**52.34**
girth exceeding 3.00 m	-	1.00	6.58	62.72	nr	**69.30**
Clearing site vegetation						
bushes, scrub, undergrowth, hedges and trees						
and tree stumps not exceeding 600 mm girth	-	0.04	0.26	-	m²	**0.26**
Lifting turf for preservation						
stacking	-	0.35	2.30	-	m²	**2.30**
Excavating; by machine						
Topsoil for preservation						
average depth 150 mm	-	0.03	0.20	0.98	m²	**1.18**
add or deduct for each 25 mm variation in						
average depth	-	0.01	0.07	0.24	m²	**0.31**
To reduce levels						
maximum depth not exceeding 0.25 m	-	0.06	0.39	1.22	m³	**1.61**
maximum depth not exceeding 1.00 m	-	0.04	0.26	0.85	m³	**1.11**
maximum depth not exceeding 2.00 m	-	0.06	0.39	1.22	m³	**1.61**
maximum depth not exceeding 4.00 m	-	0.08	0.53	1.54	m³	**2.07**
Basements and the like; commencing level exceeding						
0.25 m below existing ground level						
maximum depth not exceeding 1.00 m	-	0.08	0.53	1.02	m³	**1.55**
maximum depth not exceeding 2.00 m	-	0.06	0.39	0.77	m³	**1.16**
maximum depth not exceeding 4.00 m	-	0.08	0.53	1.02	m³	**1.55**
maximum depth not exceeding 6.00 m	-	0.10	0.66	1.28	m³	**1.94**
maximum depth not exceeding 8.00 m	-	0.13	0.86	1.53	m³	**2.39**
Pits						
maximum depth not exceeding 0.25 m	-	0.34	2.24	4.08	m³	**6.32**
maximum depth not exceeding 1.00 m	-	0.29	1.91	3.57	m³	**5.48**
maximum depth not exceeding 2.00 m	-	0.34	2.24	4.08	m³	**6.32**
maximum depth not exceeding 4.00 m	-	0.36	2.37	4.59	m³	**6.96**
maximum depth not exceeding 6.00 m	-	0.39	2.57	4.85	m³	**7.42**
Extra over pit excavating for commencing level						
exceeding 0.25 m below existing ground level						
1.00 m below	-	0.04	0.26	0.51	m³	**0.77**
2.00 m below	-	0.06	0.39	0.77	m³	**1.16**
3.00 m below	-	0.07	0.46	1.02	m³	**1.48**
4.00 m below	-	0.10	0.66	1.28	m³	**1.94**

D GROUNDWORK Excluding overheads and profit	PC £	Labour hours	Labour £	Material/ Plant £	Unit	Total rate £
Trenches, width not exceeding 0.30 m						
maximum depth not exceeding 0.25 m	-	0.28	1.84	3.32	m³	**5.16**
maximum depth not exceeding 1.00 m	-	0.24	1.58	2.81	m³	**4.39**
maximum depth not exceeding 2.00 m	-	0.28	1.84	3.32	m³	**5.16**
maximum depth not exceeding 4.00 m	-	0.34	2.24	4.08	m³	**6.32**
maximum depth not exceeding 6.00 m	-	0.39	2.57	4.85	m³	**7.42**
Trenches, width exceeding 0.30 m						
maximum depth not exceeding 0.25 m	-	0.25	1.65	3.06	m³	**4.71**
maximum depth not exceeding 1.00 m	-	0.21	1.38	2.55	m³	**3.93**
maximum depth not exceeding 2.00 m	-	0.25	1.65	3.06	m³	**4.71**
maximum depth not exceeding 4.00 m	-	0.29	1.91	3.57	m³	**5.48**
maximum depth not exceeding 6.00 m	-	0.36	2.37	4.59	m³	**6.96**
Extra over trench excavating for commencing level exceeding 0.25 m below existing ground level						
1.00 m below	-	0.04	0.26	0.51	m³	**0.77**
2.00 m below	-	0.06	0.39	0.77	m³	**1.16**
3.00 m below	-	0.07	0.46	1.02	m³	**1.48**
4.00 m below	-	0.10	0.66	1.28	m³	**1.94**
For pile caps and ground beams between piles						
maximum depth not exceeding 0.25 m	-	0.42	2.76	5.36	m³	**8.12**
maximum depth not exceeding 1.00 m	-	0.38	2.50	4.85	m³	**7.35**
maximum depth not exceeding 2.00 m	-	0.42	2.76	5.36	m³	**8.12**
To bench sloping ground to receive filling						
maximum depth not exceeding 0.25 m	-	0.10	0.66	1.28	m³	**1.94**
maximum depth not exceeding 1.00 m	-	0.07	0.46	1.53	m³	**1.99**
maximum depth not exceeding 2.00 m	-	0.10	0.66	1.28	m³	**1.94**
Extra over any types of excavating irrespective of depth						
excavating below ground water level	-	0.14	0.92	1.79	m³	**2.71**
next existing services	-	2.75	18.09	1.02	m³	**19.11**
around existing services crossing excavation	-	6.30	41.45	2.81	m³	**44.26**
Extra over any types of excavating irrespective of depth for breaking out existing materials						
rock	-	3.20	21.06	12.08	m³	**33.14**
concrete	-	2.75	18.09	8.71	m³	**26.80**
reinforced concrete	-	3.90	25.66	12.96	m³	**38.62**
brickwork, blockwork or stonework	-	2.00	13.16	6.60	m³	**19.76**
Extra over any types of excavating irrespective of depth for breaking out existing hard pavings, 75 mm thick						
coated macadam or asphalt	-	0.21	1.38	0.47	m²	**1.85**
Extra over any types of excavating irrespective of depth for breaking out existing hard pavings, 150 mm thick						
concrete	-	0.42	2.76	1.42	m²	**4.18**
reinforced concrete	-	0.63	4.15	1.84	m²	**5.99**
coated macadam or asphalt and hardcore	-	0.28	1.84	0.51	m²	**2.35**
Working space allowance to excavations						
reduce levels, basements and the like	-	0.08	0.53	1.02	m²	**1.55**
pits	-	0.21	1.38	2.81	m²	**4.19**
trenches	-	0.20	1.32	2.55	m²	**3.87**
pile caps and ground beams between piles	-	0.22	1.45	2.81	m²	**4.26**
Extra over excavating for working space for backfilling with special materials						
hardcore	-	0.14	0.92	13.08	m²	**14.00**
sand	-	0.14	0.92	20.08	m²	**21.00**
40 mm - 20 mm gravel	-	0.14	0.92	20.50	m²	**21.42**
plain in situ ready mixed designated concrete C7.5 - 40 mm aggregate	-	1.00	7.27	35.57	m²	**42.84**

D GROUNDWORK Excluding overheads and profit	PC £	Labour hours	Labour £	Material/ Plant £	Unit	Total rate £
D20 EXCAVATING AND FILLING - cont'd						
Excavating; by hand						
Topsoil for preservation						
average depth 150 mm	-	0.25	1.65	-	m²	**1.65**
add or deduct for each 25 mm variation in						
average depth	-	0.04	0.26	-	m²	**0.26**
To reduce levels						
maximum depth not exceeding 0.25 m	-	1.56	10.26	-	m³	**10.26**
maximum depth not exceeding 1.00 m	-	1.76	11.58	-	m³	**11.58**
maximum depth not exceeding 2.00 m	-	1.95	12.83	-	m³	**12.83**
maximum depth not exceeding 4.00 m	-	2.15	14.15	-	m³	**14.15**
Basements and the like; commencing level exceeding						
0.25 m below existing ground level						
maximum depth not exceeding 1.00 m	-	2.05	13.49	-	m³	**13.49**
maximum depth not exceeding 2.00 m	-	2.20	14.48	-	m³	**14.48**
maximum depth not exceeding 4.00 m	-	2.95	19.41	-	m³	**19.41**
maximum depth not exceeding 6.00 m	-	3.60	23.69	-	m³	**23.69**
maximum depth not exceeding 8.00 m	-	4.35	28.62	-	m³	**28.62**
Pits						
maximum depth not exceeding 0.25 m	-	2.30	15.13	-	m³	**15.13**
maximum depth not exceeding 1.00 m	-	2.50	16.45	-	m³	**16.45**
maximum depth not exceeding 2.00 m	-	3.00	19.74	-	m³	**19.74**
maximum depth not exceeding 4.00 m	-	3.80	25.00	-	m³	**25.00**
maximum depth not exceeding 6.00 m	-	4.70	30.93	-	m³	**30.93**
Extra over pit excavating for commencing level						
exceeding 0.25 m below existing ground level						
1.00 m below	-	0.45	2.96	-	m³	**2.96**
2.00 m below	-	0.95	6.25	-	m³	**6.25**
3.00 m below	-	1.40	9.21	-	m³	**9.21**
4.00 m below	-	1.85	12.17	-	m³	**12.17**
Trenches, width not exceeding 0.30 m						
maximum depth not exceeding 0.25 m	-	2.00	13.16	-	m³	**13.16**
maximum depth not exceeding 1.00 m	-	2.30	15.13	-	m³	**15.13**
maximum depth not exceeding 2.00 m	-	2.70	17.77	-	m³	**17.77**
maximum depth not exceeding 4.00 m	-	3.30	21.71	-	m³	**21.71**
maximum depth not exceeding 6.00 m	-	4.25	27.96	-	m³	**27.96**
Trenches, width exceeding 0.30 m						
maximum depth not exceeding 0.25 m	-	1.95	12.83	-	m³	**12.83**
maximum depth not exceeding 1.00 m	-	2.05	13.49	-	m³	**13.49**
maximum depth not exceeding 2.00 m	-	2.40	15.79	-	m³	**15.79**
maximum depth not exceeding 4.00 m	-	3.05	20.07	-	m³	**20.07**
maximum depth not exceeding 6.00 m	-	3.90	25.66	-	m³	**25.66**
Extra over trench excavating for commencing level						
exceeding 0.25 m below existing ground level						
1.00 m below	-	0.45	2.96	-	m³	**2.96**
2.00 m below	-	0.95	6.25	-	m³	**6.25**
3.00 m below	-	1.40	9.21	-	m³	**9.21**
4.00 m below	-	1.85	12.17	-	m³	**12.17**
For pile caps and ground beams between piles						
maximum depth not exceeding 0.25 m	-	3.00	19.74	-	m³	**19.74**
maximum depth not exceeding 1.00 m	-	3.20	21.06	-	m³	**21.06**
maximum depth not exceeding 2.00 m	-	3.80	25.00	-	m³	**25.00**
To bench sloping ground to receive filling						
maximum depth not exceeding 0.25 m	-	1.40	9.21	-	m³	**9.21**
maximum depth not exceeding 1.00 m	-	1.60	10.53	-	m³	**10.53**
maximum depth not exceeding 2.00 m	-	1.80	11.84	-	m³	**11.84**
Extra over any types of excavating irrespective of						
depth						
excavating below ground water level	-	0.35	2.30	-	m³	**2.30**
next existing services	-	1.00	6.58	-	m³	**6.58**
around existing services crossing excavation	-	2.00	13.16	-	m³	**13.16**

D GROUNDWORK Excluding overheads and profit	PC £	Labour hours	Labour £	Material/ Plant £	Unit	Total rate £
Extra over any types of excavating irrespective of depth for breaking out existing materials						
rock	-	5.00	32.90	5.30	m^3	38.20
concrete	-	4.50	29.61	4.42	m^3	34.03
reinforced concrete	-	6.00	39.48	6.18	m^3	45.66
brickwork, blockwork or stonework	-	3.00	19.74	2.65	m^3	22.39
Extra over any types of excavating irrespective of depth for breaking out existing hard pavings, 60 mm thick						
precast concrete paving slabs	-	0.30	1.97	-	m^2	1.97
Extra over any types of excavating irrespective of depth for breaking out existing hard pavings, 75 mm thick						
coated macadam or asphalt	-	0.40	2.63	0.35	m^2	2.98
Extra over any types of excavating irrespective of depth for breaking out existing hard pavings, 150 mm thick						
concrete	-	0.70	4.61	0.62	m^2	5.23
reinforced concrete	-	0.90	5.92	0.88	m^2	6.80
coated macadam or asphalt and hardcore	-	0.50	3.29	0.44	m^2	3.73
Working space allowance to excavations						
reduce levels, basements and the like	-	2.30	15.13	-	m^2	15.13
pits	-	2.40	15.79	-	m^2	15.79
trenches	-	2.10	13.82	-	m^2	13.82
pile caps and ground beams between piles	-	2.50	16.45	-	m^2	16.45
Extra over excavation for working space for backfilling with special materials						
hardcore	-	0.80	5.26	11.37	m^2	16.63
sand	-	0.80	5.26	18.37	m^2	23.63
40 mm - 20 mm gravel	-	0.80	5.26	18.79	m^2	24.05
plain in situ ready mixed designated concrete; C7.5 - 40 mm aggregate	-	1.10	8.00	33.86	m^2	41.86
Earthwork support (average "risk" prices)						
Maximum depth not exceeding 1.00 m						
distance between opposing faces not exceeding 2.00 m	-	0.11	0.72	0.32	m^2	1.04
distance between opposing faces 2.00 - 4.00 m	-	0.12	0.79	0.37	m^2	1.16
distance between opposing faces exceeding 4.00 m	-	0.13	0.86	0.47	m^2	1.33
Maximum depth not exceeding 2.00 m						
distance between opposing faces not exceeding 2.00 m	-	0.13	0.86	0.37	m^2	1.23
distance between opposing faces 2.00 - 4.00 m	-	0.14	0.92	0.47	m^2	1.39
distance between opposing faces exceeding 4.00 m	-	0.15	0.99	0.59	m^2	1.58
Maximum depth not exceeding 4.00 m						
distance between opposing faces not exceeding 2.00 m	-	0.17	1.12	0.47	m^2	1.59
distance between opposing faces 2.00 - 4.00 m	-	0.17	1.12	0.59	m^2	1.71
distance between opposing faces exceeding 4.00 m	-	0.19	1.25	0.75	m^2	2.00
Maximum depth not exceeding 6.00 m						
distance between opposing faces not exceeding 2.00 m	-	0.19	1.25	0.56	m^2	1.81
distance between opposing faces 2.00 - 4.00 m	-	0.21	1.38	0.75	m^2	2.13
distance between opposing faces exceeding 4.00 m	-	0.24	1.58	0.94	m^2	2.52
Maximum depth not exceeding 8.00 m						
distance between opposing faces not exceeding 2.00 m	-	0.25	1.65	0.75	m^2	2.40
distance between opposing faces 2.00 - 4.00 m	-	0.30	1.97	0.94	m^2	2.91
distance between opposing faces exceeding 4.00 m	-	0.36	2.37	1.12	m^2	3.49

D GROUNDWORK Excluding overheads and profit	PC £	Labour hours	Labour £	Material/ Plant £	Unit	Total rate £
D20 EXCAVATING AND FILLING - cont'd						
Earthwork support (open boarded)						
Maximum depth not exceeding 1.00 m						
distance between opposing faces not						
exceeding 2.00 m	-	0.30	1.97	0.66	m²	**2.63**
distance between opposing faces 2.00 - 4.00 m	-	0.34	2.24	0.75	m²	**2.99**
distance between opposing faces exceeding						
4.00 m	-	0.38	2.50	0.94	m²	**3.44**
Maximum depth not exceeding 2.00 m						
distance between opposing faces not						
exceeding 2.00 m	-	0.38	2.50	0.75	m²	**3.25**
distance between opposing faces 2.00 - 4.00 m	-	0.42	2.76	0.90	m²	**3.66**
distance between opposing faces exceeding						
4.00 m	-	0.48	3.16	1.12	m²	**4.28**
Maximum depth not exceeding 4.00 m						
distance between opposing faces not						
exceeding 2.00 m	-	0.48	3.16	0.85	m²	**4.01**
distance between opposing faces 2.00 - 4.00 m	-	0.54	3.55	1.04	m²	**4.59**
distance between opposing faces exceeding						
4.00 m	-	0.60	3.95	1.31	m²	**5.26**
Maximum depth not exceeding 6.00 m						
distance between opposing faces not						
exceeding 2.00 m	-	0.60	3.95	0.94	m²	**4.89**
distance between opposing faces 2.00 - 4.00 m	-	0.66	4.34	1.18	m²	**5.52**
distance between opposing faces exceeding						
4.00 m	-	0.76	5.00	1.50	m²	**6.50**
Maximum depth not exceeding 8.00 m						
distance between opposing faces not						
exceeding 2.00 m	-	0.80	5.26	1.22	m²	**6.48**
distance between opposing faces 2.00 - 4.00 m	-	0.90	5.92	1.41	m²	**7.33**
distance between opposing faces exceeding						
4.00 m	-	1.05	6.91	1.87	m²	**8.78**
Earthwork support (close boarded)						
Maximum depth not exceeding 1.00 m						
distance between opposing faces not						
exceeding 2.00 m	-	0.80	5.26	1.31	m²	**6.57**
distance between opposing faces 2.00 - 4.00 m	-	0.88	5.79	1.50	m²	**7.29**
distance between opposing faces exceeding						
4.00 m	-	0.97	6.38	1.87	m²	**8.25**
Maximum depth not exceeding 2.00 m						
distance between opposing faces not						
exceeding 2.00 m	-	1.00	6.58	1.50	m²	**8.08**
distance between opposing faces 2.00 - 4.00 m	-	1.10	7.24	1.79	m²	**9.03**
distance between opposing faces exceeding						
4.00 m	-	1.20	7.90	2.24	m²	**10.14**
Maximum depth not exceeding 4.00 m						
distance between opposing faces not						
exceeding 2.00 m	-	1.25	8.22	1.68	m²	**9.90**
distance between opposing faces 2.00 - 4.00 m	-	1.40	9.21	2.09	m²	**11.30**
distance between opposing faces exceeding						
4.00 m	-	1.55	10.20	2.62	m²	**12.82**
Maximum depth not exceeding 6.00 m						
distance between opposing faces not						
exceeding 2.00 m	-	1.56	10.26	1.87	m²	**12.13**
distance between opposing faces 2.00 - 4.00 m	-	1.70	11.19	2.35	m²	**13.54**
distance between opposing faces exceeding						
4.00 m	-	1.90	12.50	2.99	m²	**15.49**

D GROUNDWORK Excluding overheads and profit	PC £	Labour hours	Labour £	Material/ Plant £	Unit	Total rate £
Maximum depth not exceeding 8.00 m						
distance between opposing faces not						
exceeding 2.00 m	-	1.90	12.50	2.43	m²	**14.93**
distance between opposing faces 2.00 - 4.00 m	-	2.10	13.82	2.81	m²	**16.63**
distance between opposing faces exceeding						
4.00 m	-	2.40	15.79	3.37	m²	**19.16**
Extra over earthwork support for						
Curved	-	0.03	0.20	0.32	m²	**0.52**
Below ground water level	-	0.30	1.97	0.29	m²	**2.26**
Unstable ground	-	0.50	3.29	0.56	m²	**3.85**
Next to roadways	-	0.40	2.63	0.47	m²	**3.10**
Left in	-	0.65	4.28	13.09	m²	**17.37**
Earthwork support (average "risk" prices -						
inside existing buildings)						
Maximum depth not exceeding 1.00 m						
distance between opposing faces not						
exceeding 2.00 m	-	0.19	1.25	0.47	m²	**1.72**
distance between opposing faces 2.00 - 4.00 m	-	0.21	1.38	0.54	m²	**1.92**
distance between opposing faces exceeding						
4.00 m	-	0.24	1.58	0.66	m²	**2.24**
Maximum depth not exceeding 2.00 m						
distance between opposing faces not						
exceeding 2.00 m	-	0.24	1.58	0.54	m²	**2.12**
distance between opposing faces 2.00 - 4.00 m	-	0.26	1.71	0.71	m²	**2.42**
distance between opposing faces exceeding						
4.00 m	-	0.35	2.30	0.79	m²	**3.09**
Maximum depth not exceeding 4.00 m						
distance between opposing faces not						
exceeding 2.00 m	-	0.30	1.97	0.71	m²	**2.68**
distance between opposing faces 2.00 - 4.00 m	-	0.34	2.24	0.85	m²	**3.09**
distance between opposing faces exceeding						
4.00 m	-	0.37	2.43	0.99	m²	**3.42**
Maximum depth not exceeding 6.00 m						
distance between opposing faces not						
exceeding 2.00 m	-	0.37	2.43	0.80	m²	**3.23**
distance between opposing faces 2.00 - 4.00 m	-	0.41	2.70	0.99	m²	**3.69**
distance between opposing faces exceeding						
4.00 m	-	0.47	3.09	1.18	m²	**4.27**
Disposal; by machine						
Excavated material						
off site; to tip not exceeding 13 km (using						
lorries); including Landfill Tax based on inactive						
waste	-	-	-	13.50	m³	**13.50**
on site; depositing in spoil heaps; average 25						
m distance	-	-	-	0.73	m³	**0.73**
on site; spreading; average 25 m distance	-	0.22	1.45	0.49	m³	**1.94**
on site; depositing in spoil heaps; average 50						
m distance	-	-	-	1.22	m³	**1.22**
on site; spreading; average 50 m distance	-	0.22	1.45	0.98	m³	**2.43**
on site; depositing in spoil heaps; average 100						
m distance	-	-	-	2.20	m³	**2.20**
on site; spreading; average 100 m distance	-	0.22	1.45	1.46	m³	**2.91**
on site; depositing in spoil heaps; average 200						
m distance	-	-	-	2.75	m³	**2.75**
on site; spreading; average 200 m distance	-	0.22	1.45	1.95	m³	**3.40**

D GROUNDWORK Excluding overheads and profit	PC £	Labour hours	Labour £	Material/ Plant £	Unit	Total rate £
D20 EXCAVATING AND FILLING - cont'd						
Disposal; by hand						
Excavated material						
off site; to tip not exceeding 13 km (using						
lorries); including Landfill Tax based on inactive						
waste	-	0.80	5.26	21.75	m³	27.01
on site; depositing in spoil heaps; average 25						
m distance	-	1.10	7.24	-	m³	7.24
on site; spreading; average 25 m distance	-	1.45	9.54	-	m³	9.54
on site; depositing in spoil heaps; average 50						
m distance	-	1.45	9.54	-	m³	9.54
on site; spreading; average 50 m distance	-	1.75	11.52	-	m³	11.52
on site; depositing in spoil heaps; average 100						
m distance	-	2.10	13.82	-	m³	13.82
on site; spreading; average 100 m distance	-	2.40	15.79	-	m³	15.79
on site; depositing in spoil heaps; average 200						
m distance	-	3.10	20.40	-	m³	20.40
on site; spreading; average 200 m distance	-	3.40	22.37	-	m³	22.37
Filling to excavations; by machine						
Average thickness not exceeding 0.25 m						
arising from the excavations	-	0.18	1.18	1.95	m³	3.13
obtained off site; hardcore	7.52	0.20	1.32	20.06	m³	21.38
obtained off site; granular fill type one	10.76	0.20	1.32	29.10	m³	30.42
obtained off site; granular fill type two	10.36	0.20	1.32	28.16	m³	29.48
Average thickness exceeding 0.25 m						
arising from the excavations	-	0.15	0.99	1.46	m³	2.45
obtained off site; hardcore	7.52	0.17	1.12	16.98	m³	18.10
obtained off site; granular fill type one	10.76	0.17	1.12	28.37	m³	29.49
obtained off site; granular fill type two	10.36	0.17	1.12	27.43	m³	28.55
Filling to make up levels; by machine						
Average thickness not exceeding 0.25 m						
arising from the excavations	-	0.26	1.71	2.12	m³	3.83
obtained off site; imported topsoil	9.00	0.26	1.71	11.61	m³	13.32
obtained off site; hardcore	7.52	0.30	1.97	20.08	m³	22.05
obtained off site; granular fill type one	10.76	0.30	1.97	29.13	m³	31.10
obtained off site; granular fill type two	10.36	0.30	1.97	28.19	m³	30.16
obtained off site; sand	10.76	0.30	1.97	29.13	m³	31.10
Average thickness exceeding 0.25 m						
arising from the excavations	-	0.22	1.45	1.53	m³	2.98
obtained off site; imported topsoil	9.00	0.22	1.45	11.01	m³	12.46
obtained off site; hardcore	7.52	0.26	1.71	16.91	m³	18.62
obtained off site; granular fill type one	10.76	0.26	1.71	28.30	m³	30.01
obtained off site; granular fill type two	10.36	0.26	1.71	27.35	m³	29.06
obtained off site; sand	10.76	0.26	1.71	28.30	m³	30.01
Filling to excavations; by hand						
Average thickness not exceeding 0.25 m						
arising from the excavations	-	1.25	8.22	-	m³	8.22
obtained off site; hardcore	7.52	1.35	8.88	18.11	m³	26.99
obtained off site; granular fill type one	10.76	1.60	10.53	25.45	m³	35.98
obtained off site; granular fill type two	10.36	1.60	10.53	24.50	m³	35.03
obtained off site; sand	10.76	1.60	10.53	25.45	m³	35.98

D GROUNDWORK Excluding overheads and profit	PC £	Labour hours	Labour £	Material/ Plant £	Unit	Total rate £
Average thickness exceeding 0.25 m						
arising from the excavations	-	1.00	6.58	-	m³	6.58
obtained off site; hardcore	7.52	1.10	7.24	15.52	m³	22.76
obtained off site; granular fill type one	10.76	1.30	8.55	25.45	m³	34.00
obtained off site; granular fill type two	10.36	1.30	8.55	24.51	m³	33.06
obtained off site; sand	10.76	1.30	8.55	25.45	m³	34.00
Filling to make up levels; by hand						
Average thickness not exceeding 0.25 m						
arising from the excavations	-	1.35	8.88	3.38	m³	12.26
obtained off site; imported soil	9.00	1.35	8.88	12.39	m³	21.27
obtained off site; hardcore	7.52	1.50	9.87	21.87	m³	31.74
obtained off site; granular fill type one	10.76	1.66	10.92	29.61	m³	40.53
obtained off site; granular fill type two	10.36	1.66	10.92	28.66	m³	39.58
obtained off site; sand	10.76	1.66	10.92	29.61	m³	40.53
Average thickness exceeding 0.25 m						
arising from the excavations	-	1.10	7.24	2.76	m³	10.00
arising from on site spoil heaps; average 25 m						
distance; multiple handling	-	2.40	15.79	6.01	m³	21.80
obtained off site; imported soil	9.00	1.10	7.24	11.75	m³	18.99
obtained off site; hardcore	7.52	1.45	9.54	19.16	m³	28.70
obtained off site; granular fill type one	10.76	1.55	10.20	29.33	m³	39.53
obtained off site; granular fill type two	10.36	1.55	10.20	28.38	m³	38.58
obtained off site; sand	10.76	1.55	10.20	29.33	m³	39.53
Surface packing to filling						
To vertical or battered faces	-	0.18	1.18	0.17	m²	1.35
Surface treatments						
Compacting						
filling; blinding with sand	-	0.05	0.33	1.40	m²	1.73
bottoms of excavations	-	0.05	0.33	0.03	m²	0.36
Trimming						
sloping surfaces	-	0.18	1.18	-	m²	1.18
sloping surfaces; in rock	-	1.00	6.45	1.24	m²	7.69
Filter membrane; one layer; laid on earth to receive granular material						
"Terram 500" filter membrane or other equal and approved; one layer; laid on earth	-	0.05	0.33	0.41	m²	0.74
"Terram 700" filter membrane or other equal and approved; one layer; laid on earth	-	0.05	0.33	0.43	m²	0.76
"Terram 1000" filter membrane or other equal and approved; one layer; laid on earth	-	0.05	0.33	0.46	m²	0.79
"Terram 2000" filter membrane or other equal and approved; one layer; laid on earth	-	0.05	0.33	0.96	m²	1.29

D30 CAST IN PLACE PILING

NOTE: The following approximate prices, for the quantities of piling quoted, are for work on clear open sites with reasonable access. They are based on 500 mm nominal diameter piles, normal concrete mix 20.00 N/mm² reinforced for loading up to 40,000 kg depending upon ground conditions and include up to 0.16 m of projecting reinforcement at top of pile. The prices do not allow for removal of spoil.

(*   indicates work normally carried out by the Main Contractor)

D GROUNDWORK Excluding overheads and profit	PC £	Labour hours	Labour £	Material/ Plant £	Unit	Total rate £
D30 CAST IN PLACE PILING - cont'd						
Tripod bored cast-in-place concrete piles						
Provision of all plant; including bringing to and						
removing from site; maintenance, erection and						
dismantling at each pile position for 100 nr						
piles	-	-	-	-	item	6650.00
Bored piles						
500 mm diameter piles; reinforced; 10 m long	-	-	-	-	nr	650.00
add for additional pile length up to 15 m	-	-	-	-	m	65.00
deduct for reduction in pile length	-	-	-	-	m	21.00
Cutting off tops of piles*	-	1.30	14.55	-	m	14.55
Blind bored piles						
500 mm diameter	-	-	-	-	m	44.00
Delays						
rig standing time	-	-	-	-	hour	79.50
Extra over piling						
breaking through obstructions	-	-	-	-	hour	100.50
Pile tests						
working to 600 kN/t; using tension piles as reaction;						
first pile	-	-	-	-	nr	3975.00
working to 600 kN/t; using tension piles as reaction;						
subsequent piles	-	-	-	-	nr	3725.00
Rotary bored cast-in-place concrete piles						
Provision of all plant; including bringing to and						
removing from site; maintenance, erection and						
dismantling at each pile position for 100 nr						
piles	-	-	-	-	item	7950.00
Bored piles						
500 mm diameter piles; reinforced; 10 m long	-	-	-	-	nr	325.00
add for additional pile length up to 15 m	-	-	-	-	m	32.00
deduct for reduction in pile length	-	-	-	-	m	15.50
Cutting off tops of piles*	-	1.30	14.55	-	m	14.55
Blind bored piles						
500 mm diameter	-	-	-	-	m	16.50
Delays						
rig standing time	-	-	-	-	hour	134.00
Extra over piling						
breaking through obstructions	-	-	-	-	hour	160.00
Pile tests						
working to 600 kN/t; using tension piles as reaction;						
first pile	-	-	-	-	nr	3725.00
working to 600 kN/t; using tension piles as reaction;						
subsequent piles	-	-	-	-	nr	3175.00
D32 STEEL PILING						
"Frodingham" steel sheeting piling or other equal						
and approved; grade 43A; pitched and driven						
Provision of all plant; including bringing to and						
removing from site; maintenance, erection and						
dismantling; assuming one rig for 1500 m² of						
piling	-	-	-	-	item	3100.00
Driven shell piles						
mild steel; type 1N; 99.10 kg/m²	-	-	-	-	m²	70.00
mild steel; type 2N; 112.30 kg/m²	-	-	-	-	m²	80.00
mild steel; type 3N; 137.10 kg/m²	-	-	-	-	m²	90.00
mild steel; type 4N; 170.80 kg/m²	-	-	-	-	m²	110.00
mild steel; type 5N; 236.90 kg/m²	-	-	-	-	m²	145.00
Burning off tops of piles	-	-	-	-	m	9.00

D GROUNDWORK Excluding overheads and profit	PC £	Labour hours	Labour £	Material/ Plant £	Unit	Total rate £
"Frodingham" steel sheet piling or other equal and approved; extract only Provision of all plant; including bringing to and removing from site; maintenance, erection and dismantling; assuming one rig as before	-	-	-	-	nr	2800.00
Driven shell piles; extract only						
mild steel; type 1N; 99.10 kg/m^2	-	-	-	-	m^2	13.15
mild steel; type 2N; 112.30 kg/m^2	-	-	-	-	m^2	13.15
mild steel; type 3N; 137.10 kg/m^2	-	-	-	-	m^2	13.15
mild steel; type 4N; 170.80 kg/m^2	-	-	-	-	m^2	13.15
mild steel; type 5N; 236.90 kg/m^2	-	-	-	-	m^2	14.15
D40 EMBEDDED RETAINING WALLING						
Diaphragm walls; contiguous panel construction; panel lengths not exceeding 5 m Provision of all plant; including bringing to and removing from site; maintenance, erection and dismantling; assuming one rig for 1000 m^2 of walling	-	-	-	-	item	63500.00
Excavation and disposal for diaphragm wall; excavated material removed from site; Bentonite slurry supplied and disposed of						
600 mm thick walls	-	-	-	-	m^3	195.00
1000 mm thick walls	-	-	-	-	m^3	130.00
Ready mixed reinforced in situ concrete; normal portland cement; C30 - 10 mm aggregate in walls	-	-	-	-	m^3	88.00
Reinforcement bar; BS 4449 cold rolled deformed square high yield steel bars; straight or bent						
25 mm - 40 mm diameter	-	-	-	-	t	580.00
20 mm diameter	-	-	-	-	t	580.00
16 mm diameter	-	-	-	-	t	580.00
Formwork 75 mm thick to form chases	-	-	-	-	m^2	48.00
Construct twin guide walls in reinforced concrete; together with reinforcement and formwork along the axis of the diaphragm wall	-	-	-	-	m	200.00
Delays						
rig standing	-	-	-	-	hour	350.00
D41 CRIB WALLS/GABIONS/REINFORCED EARTH						
Crib walls Precast concrete crib units; "Anda-crib Mini" doweless system or other equal and approved; Phi-O-Group; dry joints; machine filled with crushed rock (excavating and foundations not included)						
125 mm thick	-	-	-	-	m^2	104.50
Precast concrete crib units; "Anda-crib Maxi" doweless system or other wqual and approved; Phi-O-Group; dry joints; machine filled with crushed rock (excavating and foundations not included)						
125 mm thick	-	-	-	-	m^2	133.00
Precast concrete crib units; "Anda-crib Super Maxi" doweless system or other equal and approved; Phi-O-Group; dry joints; machine filled with crushed rock (excavating and foundations not included)						
125 mm thick	-	-	-	-	m^2	152.00

D GROUNDWORK Excluding overheads and profit	PC £	Labour hours	Labour £	Material/ Plant £	Unit	Total rate £
D41 CRIB WALLS/GABIONS/REINFORCED EARTH - cont'd						
Gabion baskets						
Wire mesh gabion baskets; Maccaferri Ltd or other						
equal and approved; galvanised mesh 80 mm x						
100 mm; filling with broken stones 125 mm - 200 mm size						
2.00 x 1.00 x 0.50 m	-	1.58	17.67	59.92	nr	**77.59**
2.00 x 1.00 x 1.00 m	-	1.50	16.79	107.04	nr	**123.83**
3.00 x 1.00 x 0.50 m	-	2.10	23.50	78.33	nr	**101.83**
3.00 x 1.00 x 1.00 m	-	4.20	47.00	144.96	nr	**191.96**
"Reno" mattress gabion baskets or other equal and						
approved; Maccaferri Ltd; filling with broken stones						
125 mm - 200 mm size						
6.00 x 2.00 x 0.17 m	-	0.50	5.59	138.83	nr	**144.42**
6.00 x 2.00 x 0.23 m	-	0.67	7.46	168.00	nr	**175.46**
6.00 x 2.00 x 0.30 m	-	0.75	8.39	198.75	nr	**207.14**
D50 UNDERPINNING						
Excavating; by machine						
Preliminary trenches						
maximum depth not exceeding 1.00 m	-	0.25	1.65	5.55	m³	**7.20**
maximum depth not exceeding 2.00 m	-	0.30	1.97	6.66	m³	**8.63**
maximum depth not exceeding 4.00 m	-	0.35	2.30	7.77	m³	**10.07**
Extra over preliminary trench excavating for						
breaking out existing hard pavings, 150 mm						
thick						
concrete	-	0.70	4.61	0.62	m²	**5.23**
Excavating; by hand						
Preliminary trenches						
maximum depth not exceeding 1.00 m		2.90	19.08		m³	**19.08**
maximum depth not exceeding 2.00 m	-	3.30	21.71	-	m³	**21.71**
maximum depth not exceeding 4.00 m	-	4.25	27.96	-	m³	**27.96**
Extra over preliminary trench excavating for						
breaking out existing hard pavings; 150 mm						
thick						
concrete	-	0.30	1.97	1.55	m²	**3.52**
Underpinning pits; commencing from 1.00 m						
below existing ground level						
maximum depth not exceeding 0.25 m	-	4.40	28.95	-	m³	**28.95**
maximum depth not exceeding 1.00 m	-	4.80	31.58	-	m³	**31.58**
maximum depth not exceeding 2.00 m	-	5.75	37.84	-	m³	**37.84**
Underpinning pits; commencing from 2.00 m						
below existing ground level						
maximum depth not exceeding 0.25 m	-	5.40	35.53	-	m³	**35.53**
maximum depth not exceeding 1.00 m	-	5.80	38.16	-	m³	**38.16**
maximum depth not exceeding 2.00 m	-	6.75	44.41	-	m³	**44.41**
Underpinning pits; commencing from 4.00 m						
below existing ground level						
maximum depth not exceeding 0.25 m	-	6.40	42.11	-	m³	**42.11**
maximum depth not exceeding 1.00 m	-	6.80	44.74	-	m³	**44.74**
maximum depth not exceeding 2.00 m	-	7.75	50.99	-	m³	**50.99**
Extra over any types of excavating irrespective of						
depth						
excavating below ground water level	-	0.35	2.30	-	m³	**2.30**

D GROUNDWORK Excluding overheads and profit	PC £	Labour hours	Labour £	Material/ Plant £	Unit	Total rate £
Earthwork support to preliminary trenches (open boarded - in 3.00 m lengths)						
Maximum depth not exceeding 1.00 m						
distance between opposing faces not						
exceeding 2.00 m	-	0.40	2.63	1.22	m²	**3.85**
Maximum depth not exceeding 2.00 m						
distance between opposing faces not						
exceeding 2.00 m	-	0.50	3.29	1.50	m²	**4.79**
Maximum depth not exceeding 4.00 m						
distance between opposing faces not						
exceeding 2.00 m	-	0.64	4.21	1.87	m²	**6.08**
Earthwork support to underpinning pits (open boarded - in 3.00 m lengths)						
Maximum depth not exceeding 1.00 m						
distance between opposing faces not						
exceeding 2.00 m	-	0.44	2.90	1.31	m²	**4.21**
Maximum depth not exceeding 2.00 m						
distance between opposing faces not						
exceeding 2.00 m	-	0.55	3.62	1.68	m²	**5.30**
Maximum depth not exceeding 4.00 m						
distance between opposing faces not						
exceeding 2.00 m	-	0.70	4.61	2.06	m²	**6.67**
Earthwork support to preliminary trenches (closed boarded - in 3.00 m lengths)						
Maximum depth not exceeding 1.00 m						
1.00 m deep	-	1.00	6.58	2.06	m²	**8.64**
Maximum depth not exceeding 2.00 m						
distance between opposing faces not						
exceeding 2.00 m	-	1.25	8.22	2.62	m²	**10.84**
Maximum depth not exceeding 4.00 m						
distance between opposing faces not						
exceeding 2.00 m	-	1.55	10.20	3.18	m²	**13.38**
Earthwork support to underpinning pits (closed boarded - in 3.00 m lengths)						
Maximum depth not exceeding 1.00 m						
distance between opposing faces not						
exceeding 2.00 m	-	1.10	7.24	2.24	m²	**9.48**
Maximum depth not exceeding 2.00 m						
distance between opposing faces not						
exceeding 2.00 m	-	1.38	9.08	2.81	m²	**11.89**
Maximum depth not exceeding 4.00 m						
distance between opposing faces not						
exceeding 2.00 m	-	1.70	11.19	3.55	m²	**14.74**
Extra over earthwork support for						
Left in	-	0.75	4.93	13.09	m²	**18.02**
Cutting away existing projecting foundations						
Concrete						
maximum width 150 mm; maximum depth 150 mm	-	0.16	1.05	0.12	m	**1.17**
maximum width 150 mm; maximum depth 225 mm	-	0.24	1.58	0.18	m	**1.76**
maximum width 150 mm; maximum depth 300 mm	-	0.32	2.11	0.24	m	**2.35**
maximum width 300 mm; maximum depth 300 mm	-	0.63	4.15	0.47	m	**4.62**
Masonry						
maximum width one brick thick; maximum depth one course high	-	0.05	0.33	0.04	m	**0.37**
maximum width one brick thick; maximum depth two courses high	-	0.14	0.92	0.10	m	**1.02**

D GROUNDWORK Excluding overheads and profit	PC £	Labour hours	Labour £	Material/ Plant £	Unit	Total rate £
D50 UNDERPINNING - cont'd						
Cutting away existing projecting foundations - cont'd						
Masonry - cont'd						
maximum width one brick thick; maximum depth						
three courses high	-	0.27	1.78	0.20	m	1.98
maximum width one brick thick; maximum depth						
four courses high	-	0.45	2.96	0.34	m	3.30
Preparing the underside of the existing work to						
receive the pinning up of the new work						
Width of existing work						
380 mm	-	0.60	3.95	-	m	3.95
600 mm	-	0.80	5.26	-	m	5.26
900 mm	-	1.00	6.58	-	m	6.58
1200 mm	-	1.20	7.90	-	m	7.90
Disposal; by hand						
Excavated material						
off site; to tip not exceeding 13 km (using lorries);						
including Landfill Tax based on inactive waste	-	0.80	5.26	27.19	m³	32.45
Filling to excavations; by hand						
Average thickness exceeding 0.25 m						
arising from the excavations	-	1.00	6.58	-	m³	6.58
Surface treatments						
Compacting						
bottoms of excavations	-	0.05	0.33	0.03	m²	0.36
Plain in situ ready mixed designated concrete C10 -						
40 mm aggregate; poured against faces of excavation						
Underpinning						
thickness not exceeding 150 mm	-	3.70	26.90	62.08	m³	88.98
thickness 150 - 450 rnm	-	3.10	22.54	62.08	m³	84.62
thickness exceeding 450 mm	-	2.70	19.63	62.08	m³	81.71
Plain in situ ready mixed designated concrete; C20						
- 20 mm aggregate; poured against faces of excavation						
Underpinning						
thickness not exceeding 150 mm	-	3.70	26.90	64.94	m³	91.84
thickness 150 - 450 mm	-	3.10	22.54	64.94	m³	87.48
thickness exceeding 450 mm	-	2.70	19.63	64.94	m³	84.57
Extra for working around reinforcement	-	0.30	2.18	-	m³	2.18
Sawn formwork; sides of foundations in						
underpinning						
Plain vertical						
height exceeding 1.00 m	-	1.60	17.92	4.67	m²	22.59
height not exceeding 250 mm	-	0.55	6.16	1.34	m²	7.50
height 250 - 500 mm	-	0.85	9.52	2.50	m²	12.02
height 500 mm - 1.00 m	-	1.30	14.56	4.67	m²	19.23
Reinforcement bar; BS 4449; hot rolled plain						
round mild steel bars						
20 mm diameter nominal size						
bent	256.00	29.00	254.25	287.28	t	541.53
16 mm diameter nominal size						
bent	256.00	31.00	272.13	289.59	t	561.72
12 mm diameter nominal size						
bent	259.00	33.00	290.01	295.04	t	585.05

D GROUNDWORK Excluding overheads and profit	PC £	Labour hours	Labour £	Material/ Plant £	Unit	Total rate £
10 mm diameter nominal size						
bent	263.00	35.00	307.89	303.18	t	**611.07**
8 mm diameter nominal size						
bent	271.00	37.00	324.10	313.89	t	**637.99**
Reinforcement bar; BS 4461; cold worked						
deformed square high yield steel bars						
20 mm diameter nominal size						
bent	256.00	29.00	254.25	287.28	t	**541.53**
16 mm diameter nominal size						
bent	256.00	31.00	272.13	289.59	t	**561.72**
12 mm diameter nominal size						
bent	259.00	33.00	290.01	295.04	t	**585.05**
10 mm diameter nominal size						
bent	263.00	35.00	307.89	303.18	t	**611.07**
8 mm diameter nominal size						
bent	271.00	37.00	324.10	313.89	t	**637.99**
Common bricks; PC £167.20/1000; in cement mortar						
(1:3)						
Walls in underpinning						
one brick thick	-	2.40	34.10	24.66	m²	**58.76**
one and a half brick thick	-	3.30	46.89	36.70	m²	**83.59**
two brick thick	-	4.10	58.26	51.18	m²	**109.44**
Class A engineering bricks; PC £330.00/1000;						
in cement mortar (1:3)						
Walls in underpinning						
one brick thick	-	2.40	34.10	45.46	m²	**79.56**
one and a half brick thick	-	3.30	46.89	67.89	m²	**114.78**
two brick thick	-	4.10	58.26	92.77	m²	**151.03**
Class B engineering bricks; PC £220.00/1000;						
in cement mortar (1:3)						
Walls in underpinning						
one brick thick	-	2.40	34.10	31.37	m²	**65.47**
one and a half brick thick	-	3.30	46.89	46.76	m²	**93.65**
two brick thick	-	4.10	58.26	64.59	m²	**122.85**
Add or deduct for variation of £10.00/1000 in PC						
of bricks						
one brick thick	-	-	-	1.29	m²	**1.29**
one and a half brick thick	-	-	-	1.94	m²	**1.94**
two brick thick	-	-	-	2.58	m²	**2.58**
"Pluvex" (hessian based) damp proof course or						
other equal and approved; 200 mm laps; in						
cement mortar (1:3)						
Horizontal						
width exceeding 225 mm	6.15	0.25	3.55	7.11	m²	**10.66**
width not exceeding 225 mm	6.15	0.50	7.11	7.27	m²	**14.38**
"Hyload" (pitch polymer) damp proof course						
or other equal and approved; 150 mm laps; in						
cement mortar (1:3)						
Horizontal						
width exceeding 225 mm	5.27	0.25	3.55	6.09	m²	**9.64**
width not exceeding 225 mm	5.27	0.50	7.11	6.23	m²	**13.34**

D GROUNDWORK Excluding overheads and profit	PC £	Labour hours	Labour £	Material/ Plant £	Unit	Total rate £
D50 UNDERPINNING - cont'd						
"Ledkore" grade A (bitumen based lead **cored) damp proof course or other equal and** **approved; 200 mm laps; in cement mortar (1:3)**						
Horizontal						
width exceeding 225 mm	11.47	0.33	4.69	13.25	m²	**17.94**
width not exceeding 225 mm	11.47	0.66	9.38	13.56	m²	**22.94**
Two courses of slates in cement mortar (1:3)						
Horizontal						
width exceeding 225 mm	-	1.50	21.32	20.68	m²	**42.00**
width not exceeding 225 mm	-	2.50	35.52	21.15	m²	**56.67**
Wedging and pinning						
To underside of existing construction with						
slates in cement mortar (1:3)						
width of wall - half brick thick	-	1.10	15.63	4.90	m	**20.53**
width of wall - one brick thick	-	1.30	18.47	9.81	m	**28.28**
width of wall - one and a half brick thick	-	1.50	21.32	14.71	m	**36.03**

E IN SITU CONCRETE/LARGE PRECAST CONCRETE
Excluding overheads and profit

E05 IN SITU CONCRETE CONSTRUCTION GENERALLY

MIXED CONCRETE PRICES (£/m³)

Designed mixes

Definition: "Mix for which the purchaser is responsible for specifying the required performances and the producer is responsible for selecting the mix proportions to produce the required performance".

NOTE: The following prices are for designed mix concrete ready for placing excluding any allowance for waste, discount or overheads and profit. Prices are based upon delivery to site within a 5 mile (8 km) radius of concrete mixing plant, using full loads.

| | | Aggregate | | |
| | | 10 mm | 20 mm | 40 mm |
Designed mix	Unit	£	£	£
Grade C7.5; cement to BS12	m³	59.68	57.66	57.01
Grade C7.5; sulphate resisting cement	m³	62.66	60.54	59.86
Grade C10; cement to BS12	m³	60.69	58.64	57.50
Grade C10; sulphate resisting cement	m³	65.79	61.57	60.38
Grade C15; cement to BS12	m³	61.22	59.15	57.98
Grade C15; sulphate resisting cement	m³	64.28	62.10	60.88
Grade C20; cement to BS12	m³	61.73	59.64	58.48
Grade C20; sulphate resisting cement	m³	64.82	62.62	61.41
Grade C25; cement to BS12	m³	62.25	60.15	58.97
Grade C25; sulphate resisting cement	m³	65.36	63.16	61.92
Grade C30; cement to BS12	m³	62.77	60.65	59.48
Grade C30; sulphate resisting cement	m³	65.91	63.68	62.45
Grade C40; cement to BS12	m³	63.31	61.66	-
Grade C40; sulphate resisting cement	m³	66.47	64.23	-
Grade C50; cement to BS12	m³	63.84	61.68	-
Grade C50; sulphate resisting cement	m³	67.03	64.76	-

E IN SITU CONCRETE/LARGE PRECAST CONCRETE
Excluding overheads and profit

E05 IN SITU CONCRETE CONSTRUCTION GENERALLY - cont'd

MIXED CONCRETE PRICES (£/m³)

Prescribed mixes

Definition: "Mix for which the purchaser specifies the proportions of the constituents and is responsible for ensuring that these proportions will produce a concrete with the performance required".

NOTE: The following prices are for prescribed mix concrete ready for placing excluding any allowance for waste, discount or overheads and profit. Prices are based upon delivery to site within a 5 mile (8 km) radius of concrete mixing plant, using full loads.

| | | Aggregate | | |
| | | 10 mm | 20 mm | 40 mm |
Prescribed mix	Unit	£	£	£
Grade C7.5; cement to BS12	m³	62.09	60.09	59.45
Grade C7.5; sulphate resisting cement	m³	65.04	62.94	62.27
Grade C10; cement to BS12	m³	63.09	61.06	59.93
Grade C10; sulphate resisting cement	m³	68.14	63.96	62.78
Grade C15; cement to BS12	m³	63.61	61.56	60.41
Grade C15; sulphate resisting cement	m³	66.64	64.49	63.28
Grade C20; cement to BS12	m³	64.12	62.05	60.90
Grade C20; sulphate resisting cement	m³	67.18	65.00	63.80
Grade C25; cement to BS12	m³	64.63	62.55	61.39
Grade C25; sulphate resisting cement	m³	67.71	65.53	64.31
Grade C30; cement to BS12	m³	65.15	63.05	61.89
Grade C30; sulphate resisting cement	m³	68.26	66.05	64.83
Grade C40; cement to BS12	m³	65.68	63.56	-
Grade C40; sulphate resisting cement	m³	68.81	66.59	-
Grade C50; cement to BS12	m³	66.21	64.07	-
Grade C50; sulphate resisting cement	m³	69.37	67.12	-

E IN SITU CONCRETE/LARGE PRECAST CONCRETE
Excluding overheads and profit

MIXED CONCRETE PRICES (£/m³)

Designated mixes

Definition: "Mix produced in accordance with the specification given in section 5 of BS 5328: 2 : 1991 and requiring the producer to hold current product conformity certification based on product testing and surveillance coupled with approval of his quality system to BS 5750 : 1 (En 29001)".

NOTE: The following prices are for designated mix concrete ready for placing excluding any allowance for waste, discount or overheads and profit. Prices are based upon delivery to site within a 5 mile (8 km) radius of concrete mixing plant, using full loads.

		Aggregate		
		10 mm	20 mm	40 mm
Designated mix	**Unit**	**£**	**£**	**£**
Grade C7.5; cement to BS12	m³	59.09	57.09	56.45
Grade C7.5; sulphate resisting cement	m³	62.04	59.94	59.27
Grade C10; cement to BS12	m³	60.09	58.06	56.93
Grade C10; sulphate resisting cement	m³	65.14	60.96	59.78
Grade C15; cement to BS12	m³	60.61	58.56	57.41
Grade C15; sulphate resisting cement	m³	63.64	61.49	60.28
Grade C20; cement to BS12	m³	61.12	59.05	57.90
Grade C20; sulphate resisting cement	m³	64.18	62.00	60.80
Grade C25; cement to BS12	m³	61.63	59.55	58.39
Grade C25; sulphate resisting cement	m³	64.71	62.53	61.31
Grade C30; cement to BS12	m³	62.15	60.05	58.89
Grade C30; sulphate resisting cement	m³	65.26	63.05	61.83
Grade C40; cement to BS12	m³	62.68	60.56	-
Grade C40; sulphate resisting cement	m³	65.81	63.59	-
Grade C50; cement to BS12	m³	63.21	61.07	-
Grade C50; sulphate resisting cement	m³	66.37	64.12	-

E IN SITU CONCRETE/LARGE PRECAST CONCRETE
Excluding overheads and profit

E05 IN SITU CONCRETE CONSTRUCTION GENERALLY - cont'd

MIXED CONCRETE PRICES (£/m³)

Standard mixes

Definition: "Mix selected from the restricted list given in section 4 of BS 5328 : 2 : 1991 and made with a
a restricted range of materials".

NOTE: The following prices are for standard mix concrete ready for placing excluding any allowance for
waste, discount or overheads and profit. Prices are based upon delivery to site within a 5 mile (8 km)
radius of concrete mixing plant, using full loads.

Standard mix	Unit	£
GEN 0	m³	48.83
GEN 1	m³	50.10
GEN 2	m³	51.37
GEN 3	m³	52.64
GEN 4	m³	53.91
ST 1	m³	51.37
ST 2	m³	52.90
ST 3	m³	54.42
ST 4	m³	55.94
ST 5	m³	57.97

E IN SITU CONCRETE/LARGE PRECAST CONCRETE
Excluding overheads and profit

SITE MIXED CONCRETE

Site mixed	Unit	Aggregate		
		10 mm £	20 mm £	40 mm £
Mix 7.50 N/mm²; cement to BS12 (1:8)	m³	-	-	65.75
Mix 7.50 N/mm²; sulphate resisting cement (1:8)	m³	-	-	67.85
Mix 10.00 N/mm²; cement to BS12 (1:8)	m³	-	-	65.75
Mix 10.00 N/mm²; sulphate resisting cement (1:8)	m³	-	-	67.85
Mix 20.00 N/mm²; cement to BS12 (1:2:4)	m³	-	68.90	-
Mix 20.00 N/mm²; sulphate resisting cement (1:2:4)	m³	-	71.40	-
Mix 25.00 N/mm²; cement to BS12 (1:1:5:3)	m³	-	76.05	-
Mix 25.00 N/mm²; sulphate resisting cement (1:1:5:3)	m³	-	79.45	-

E IN SITU CONCRETE/LARGE PRECAST CONCRETE
Excluding overheads and profit

E05 IN SITU CONCRETE CONSTRUCTION GENERALLY - cont'd

MIXED CONCRETE PRICES (£/m³)

Add to the preceding prices for:	Unit	£
Rapid-hardening cement to BS 12	m³	3.50
Polypropylene fibre additive	m³	1.00
Air entrained concrete	m³	3.50
Water repellent additive	m³	3.75
Distance per mile in excess of 5 miles (8 km)	m³	0.80
Part loads per m³ below full load	m³	18.00

CEMENTS

Cement type:	Bulk	£
Ordinary Portland to BS12	t	84.55
Lightning high alumina	t	265.97
Sulfacrete sulphate resisting	t	101.52
Ferrocrete rapid hardening	t	95.88
Snowcrete white cement	t	153.71

CEMENT ADMIXTURES

Cement Admixture:	Unit	£
Febtone colorant - red, marigold, yellow, brown, black	kg	8.93
Febproof waterproof	5 litres	16.34
Febond PVA bonding agent	5 lites	16.28
Febspeed frostproofer and hardener	5 litres	5.78

NOTE: A discount of 7% has been applied to the above Mixed Concrete Prices before shrinkage factors (at plus 2½% (or 5% where poured on or against earth or unblinded hardcore)) and waste (at plus 7½%) have been added to arrive at the following material prices for measured works.

E IN SITU CONCRETE/LARGE PRECAST CONCRETE Excluding overheads and profit	PC £	Labour hours	Labour £	Material £	Unit	Total rate £
E IN SITU CONCRETE/LARGE PRECAST CONCRETE						
E05 IN SITU CONCRETE CONSTRUCTING GENERALLY						
Plain in situ ready mixed designated concrete; **C10 - 40 mm aggregate**						
Foundations	-	1.30	9.45	58.33	m³	**67.78**
Isolated foundations	-	1.50	10.90	58.33	m³	**69.23**
Beds						
thickness not exceeding 150 mm	-	1.75	12.72	58.33	m³	**71.05**
thickness 150 - 450 mm	-	1.25	9.09	58.33	m³	**67.42**
thickness exceeding 450 mm	-	1.00	7.27	58.33	m³	**65.60**
Filling hollow walls						
thickness not exceeding 150 mm	-	3.40	24.72	58.33	m³	**83.05**
Plain in situ ready mixed designated concrete; **C10 - 40 mm aggregate; poured on or against** **earth or unblinded hardcore**						
Foundations	-	1.35	9.81	59.76	m³	**69.57**
Isolated foundations	-	1.60	11.63	59.76	m³	**71.39**
Beds						
thickness not exceeding 150 mm	-	1.85	13.45	59.76	m³	**73.21**
thickness 150 - 450 mm	-	1.35	9.81	59.76	m³	**69.57**
thickness exceeding 450 mm	-	1.05	7.63	59.76	m³	**67.39**
Plain in situ ready mixed designated concrete; **C20 - 20 mm aggregate**						
Foundations	-	1.30	9.45	60.52	m³	**69.97**
Isolated foundations	-	1.50	10.90	60.52	m³	**71.42**
Beds						
thickness not exceeding 150 mm	-	1.90	13.81	60.52	m³	**74.33**
thickness 150 - 450 mm	-	1.30	9.45	60.52	m³	**69.97**
thickness exceeding 450 mm	-	1.00	7.27	60.52	m³	**67.79**
Filling hollow walls						
thickness not exceeding 150 mm	-	3.40	24.72	60.52	m³	**85.24**
Plain in situ ready mixed designated concrete; **C20 - 20 mm aggregate; poured on** **or against earth or unblinded hardcore**						
Foundations	-	1.35	9.81	61.99	m³	**71.80**
Isolated foundations	-	1.60	11.63	61.99	m³	**73.62**
Beds						
thickness not exceeding 150 mm	-	2.00	14.54	61.99	m³	**76.53**
thickness 150 - 450 mm	-	1.40	10.18	61.99	m³	**72.17**
thickness exceeding 450 mm	-	1.05	7.63	61.99	m³	**69.62**
Reinforced in situ ready mixed designated **concrete; C20 - 20 mm aggregate**						
Foundations	-	1.40	10.18	60.52	m³	**70.70**
Ground beams	-	2.80	20.36	60.52	m³	**80.88**
Isolated foundations	-	1.70	12.36	60.52	m³	**72.88**
Beds						
thickness not exceeding 150 mm	-	2.20	15.99	60.52	m³	**76.51**
thickness 150 - 450 mm	-	1.60	11.63	60.52	m³	**72.15**
thickness exceeding 450 mm	-	1.30	9.45	60.52	m³	**69.97**
Slabs						
thickness not exceeding 150 mm	-	3.50	25.45	60.52	m³	**85.97**
thickness 150 - 450 mm	-	2.80	20.36	60.52	m³	**80.88**
thickness exceeding 450 mm	-	2.50	18.18	60.52	m³	**78.70**

E IN SITU CONCRETE/LARGE PRECAST CONCRETE Excluding overheads and profit	PC £	Labour hours	Labour £	Material £	Unit	Total rate £
E05 IN SITU CONCRETE CONSTRUCTING **GENERALLY** - cont'd						
Reinforced in situ ready mixed designated **concrete; C20 - 20 mm aggregate** - cont'd						
Coffered and troughed slabs						
thickness 150 - 450 mm	-	3.20	23.26	60.52	m³	83.78
thickness exceeding 450 mm	-	2.80	20.36	60.52	m³	80.88
Extra over for sloping						
not exceeding 15 degrees	-	0.25	1.82	-	m³	1.82
over 15 degrees	-	0.50	3.63	-	m³	3.63
Walls						
thickness not exceeding 150 mm	-	3.70	26.90	60.52	m³	87.42
thickness 150 - 450 mm	-	2.95	21.45	60.52	m³	81.97
thickness exceeding 450 mm	-	2.60	18.90	60.52	m³	79.42
Beams						
isolated	-	4.00	29.08	60.52	m³	89.60
isolated deep	-	4.40	31.99	60.52	m³	92.51
attached deep	-	4.00	29.08	60.52	m³	89.60
Beam casings						
isolated	-	4.40	31.99	60.52	m³	92.51
isolated deep	-	4.80	34.90	60.52	m³	95.42
attached deep	-	4.40	31.99	60.52	m³	92.51
Columns	-	4.80	34.90	60.52	m³	95.42
Column casings	-	5.30	38.53	60.52	m³	99.05
Staircases	-	6.00	43.62	60.52	m³	104.14
Upstands	-	3.85	27.99	60.52	m³	88.51
Reinforced in situ ready mixed designated **concrete; C25 - 20 mm aggregate**						
Foundations	-	1.40	10.18	61.02	m³	71.20
Ground beams	-	2.80	20.36	61.02	m³	81.38
Isolated foundations	-	1.70	12.36	61.02	m³	73.38
Beds						
thickness not exceeding 150 mm	-	2.00	14.54	61.02	m³	75.56
thickness 150 - 450 mm	-	1.50	10.90	61.02	m³	71.92
thickness exceeding 450 mm	-	1.30	9.45	61.02	m³	70.47
Slabs						
thickness not exceeding 150 mm	-	3.30	23.99	61.02	m³	85.01
thickness 150 - 450 mm	-	2.75	19.99	61.02	m³	81.01
thickness exceeding 450 mm	-	2.50	18.18	61.02	m³	79.20
Coffered and troughed slabs						
thickness 150 - 450 mm	-	3.10	22.54	61.02	m³	83.56
thickness exceeding 450 mm	-	2.80	20.36	61.02	m³	81.38
Extra over for sloping						
not exceeding 15 degrees	-	0.25	1.82	-	m³	1.82
over 15 degrees	-	0.50	3.63	-	m³	3.63
Walls						
thickness not exceeding 150 mm	-	3.60	26.17	61.02	m³	87.19
thickness 150 - 450 mm	-	2.90	21.08	61.02	m³	82.10
thickness exceeding 450 mm	-	2.60	18.90	61.02	m³	79.92
Beams						
isolated	-	4.00	29.08	61.02	m³	90.10
isolated deep	-	4.40	31.99	61.02	m³	93.01
attached deep	-	4.00	29.08	61.02	m³	90.10
Beam casings						
isolated	-	4.40	31.99	61.02	m³	93.01
isolated deep	-	4.80	34.90	61.02	m³	95.92
attached deep	-	4.40	31.99	61.02	m³	93.01
Columns	-	4.80	34.90	61.02	m³	95.92
Column casings	-	5.30	38.53	61.02	m³	99.55
Staircases	-	6.00	43.62	61.02	m³	104.64

E IN SITU CONCRETE/LARGE PRECAST CONCRETE Excluding overheads and profit	PC £	Labour hours	Labour £	Material £	Unit	Total rate £
Upstands	-	3.85	27.99	61.02	m³	89.01
Reinforced in situ ready mixed designated **concrete; C30 - 20 mm aggregate**						
Foundations	-	1.40	10.18	61.54	m³	71.72
Ground beams	-	2.80	20.36	61.54	m³	81.90
Isolated foundations	-	1.70	12.36	61.54	m³	73.90
Beds						
thickness not exceeding 150 mm	-	2.20	15.99	61.54	m³	77.53
thickness 150 - 450 mm	-	1.60	11.63	61.54	m³	73.17
thickness exceeding 450 mm	-	1.30	9.45	61.54	m³	70.99
Slabs						
thickness not exceeding 150 mm	-	3.50	25.45	61.54	m³	86.99
thickness 150 - 450 mm	-	2.80	20.36	61.54	m³	81.90
thickness exceeding 450 mm	-	2.50	18.18	61.54	m³	79.72
Coffered and troughed slabs						
thickness 150 - 450 mm	-	3.20	23.26	61.54	m³	84.80
thickness exceeding 450 mm	-	2.80	20.36	61.54	m³	81.90
Extra over for sloping						
not exceeding 15 degrees	-	0.25	1.82	-	m³	1.82
over 15 degrees	-	0.50	3.63	-	m³	3.63
Walls						
thickness not exceeding 150 mm	-	3.70	26.90	61.54	m³	88.44
thickness 150 - 450 mm	-	2.95	21.45	61.54	m³	82.99
thickness exceeding 450 mm	-	2.60	18.90	61.54	m³	80.44
Beams						
isolated	-	4.00	29.08	61.54	m³	90.62
isolated deep	-	4.40	31.99	61.54	m³	93.53
attached deep	-	4.00	29.08	61.54	m³	90.62
Beam casings						
isolated	-	4.40	31.99	61.54	m³	93.53
isolated deep	-	4.80	34.90	61.54	m³	96.44
attached deep	-	4.40	31.99	61.54	m³	93.53
Columns	-	4.80	34.90	61.54	m³	96.44
Column casings	-	5.30	38.53	61.54	m³	100.07
Staircases	-	6.00	43.62	61.54	m³	105.16
Upstands	-	3.85	27.99	61.54	m³	89.53
Extra over vibrated concrete for						
Reinforcement content over 5%	-	0.55	4.00	-	m³	4.00
Grouting with cement:mortar (1:1)						
Stanchion bases						
10 mm thick	-	1.00	7.27	0.10	nr	7.37
25 mm thick	-	1.25	9.09	0.27	nr	9.36
Grouting with epoxy resin						
Stanchion bases						
10 mm thick	-	1.25	9.09	7.43	nr	16.52
25 mm thick	-	1.50	10.90	18.57	nr	29.47
Grouting with "Conbextra GP" cementitious **grout or other equal and approved**						
Stanchion bases						
10 mm thick	-	1.25	9.09	0.98	nr	10.07
25 mm thick	-	1.50	10.90	2.62	nr	13.52

E IN SITU CONCRETE/LARGE PRECAST CONCRETE Excluding overheads and profit	PC £	Labour hours	Labour £	Material £	Unit	Total rate £
E05 IN SITU CONCRETE CONSTRUCTING **GENERALLY** - cont'd						
Filling; plain in situ designated concrete; C20 **- 20 mm aggregate**						
Mortices	-	0.10	0.73	0.34	nr	**1.07**
Holes	-	0.25	1.82	71.66	m³	**73.48**
Chases exceeding 0.01 m²	-	0.20	1.45	71.66	m³	**73.11**
Chases not exceeding 0.01 m²	-	0.15	1.09	0.72	m	**1.81**
Sheeting to prevent moisture loss						
Building paper; lapped joints						
subsoil grade; horizontal on foundations	-	0.03	0.22	0.42	m²	**0.64**
standard grade; horizontal on slabs	-	0.05	0.36	0.60	m²	**0.96**
Polythene sheeting; lapped joints; horizontal on slabs						
250 microns; 0.25 mm thick	-	0.05	0.36	0.27	m²	**0.63**
"Visqueen" sheeting or other equal and approved; lapped joints; horizontal on slabs						
250 microns; 0.25 mm thick	-	0.05	0.36	0.23	m²	**0.59**
300 microns; 0.30 mm thick	-	0.06	0.44	0.30	m²	**0.74**
E20 FORMWORK FOR IN SITU CONCRETE						
NOTE: Generally all formwork based on four uses unless otherwise stated.						
Sides of foundations; basic finish						
Plain vertical						
height exceeding 1.00 m	-	1.60	17.92	7.44	m²	**25.36**
height exceeding 1.00 m; left in	-	1.40	15.68	17.92	m²	**33.60**
height not exceeding 250 mm	-	0.45	5.04	2.95	m	**7.99**
height not exceeding 250 mm; left in	-	0.45	5.04	5.21	m	**10.25**
height 250 - 500 mm	-	0.85	9.52	5.79	m	**15.31**
height 250 - 500 mm; left in	-	0.75	8.40	11.64	m	**20.04**
height 500 mm - 1.00 m	-	1.20	13.44	7.44	m	**20.88**
height 500 mm - 1.00 m; left in	-	1.15	12.88	17.92	m	**30.80**
Sides of foundations; polystyrene sheet formwork; **Cordek "Claymaster" or other equal and approved;** **50 mm thick**						
Plain vertical						
height exceeding 1.00 m; left in	-	0.32	3.58	6.99	m²	**10.57**
height not exceeding 250 mm; left in	-	0.10	1.12	1.75	m	**2.87**
height 250 - 500 mm; left in	-	0.17	1.90	3.50	m	**5.40**
height 500 mm - 1.00 m; left in	-	0.26	2.91	6.99	m	**9.90**
Sides of foundations; polystyrene sheet formwork; **Cordek "Claymaster" or other equal and approved;** **100 mm thick**						
Plain vertical						
height exceeding 1.00 m; left in	-	0.35	3.92	14.00	m²	**17.92**
height not exceeding 250 mm; left in	-	0.11	1.23	3.50	m	**4.73**
height 250 - 500 mm; left in	-	0.19	2.13	7.00	m	**9.13**
height 500 mm - 1.00 m; left in	-	0.29	3.25	14.00	m	**17.25**
Sides of ground beams and edges of beds; **basic finish**						
Plain vertical						
height exceeding 1.00 m	-	1.65	18.48	7.39	m²	**25.87**
height not exceeding 250 mm	-	0.50	5.60	2.90	m	**8.50**
height 250 - 500 mm	-	0.90	10.08	5.74	m	**15.82**
height 500 mm - 1.00 m	-	1.25	14.00	7.39	m	**21.39**

E IN SITU CONCRETE/LARGE PRECAST CONCRETE Excluding overheads and profit	PC £	Labour hours	Labour £	Material £	Unit	Total rate £
Edges of suspended slabs; basic finish						
Plain vertical						
height not exceeding 250 mm	-	0.75	8.40	3.00	m	**11.40**
height 250 - 500 mm	-	1.10	12.32	4.83	m	**17.15**
height 500 mm - 1.00 m	-	1.75	19.60	7.48	m	**27.08**
Sides of upstands; basic finish						
Plain vertical						
height exceeding 1.00 m	-	2.00	22.40	8.92	m²	**31.32**
height not exceeding 250 mm	-	0.63	7.06	3.10	m	**10.16**
height 250 - 500 mm	-	1.00	11.20	5.93	m	**17.13**
height 500 mm - 1.00 m	-	1.75	19.60	8.92	m	**28.52**
Steps in top surfaces; basic finish						
Plain vertical						
height not exceeding 250 mm	-	0.50	5.60	3.14	m	**8.74**
height 250 - 500 mm	-	0.80	8.96	5.98	m	**14.94**
Steps in soffits; basic finish						
Plain vertical						
height not exceeding 250 mm	-	0.55	6.16	2.47	m	**8.63**
height 250 - 500 mm	-	0.88	9.86	4.45	m	**14.31**
Machine bases and plinths; basic finish						
Plain vertical						
height exceeding 1.00 m	-	1.60	17.92	7.39	m²	**25.31**
height not exceeding 250 mm	-	0.50	5.60	2.90	m	**8.50**
height 250 - 500 mm	-	0.85	9.52	5.74	m	**15.26**
height 500 mm - 1.00 m	-	1.25	14.00	7.39	m	**21.39**
Soffits of slabs; basic finish						
Slab thickness not exceeding 200 mm						
horizontal; height to soffit not exceeding 1.50 m	-	1.80	20.16	6.85	m²	**27.01**
horizontal; height to soffit 1.50 - 3.00 m	-	1.75	19.60	6.95	m²	**26.55**
horizontal; height to soffit 1.50 - 3.00 m (based on 5 uses)	-	1.65	18.48	5.75	m²	**24.23**
horizontal; height to soffit 1.50 - 3.00 m (based on 6 uses)	-	1.60	17.92	4.96	m²	**22.88**
horizontal; height to soffit 3.00 - 4.50 m	-	1.70	19.04	7.19	m²	**26.23**
horizontal; height to soffit 4.50 - 6.00 m	-	1.80	20.16	7.44	m²	**27.60**
Slab thickness 200 - 300 mm						
horizontal; height to soffit 1.50 - 3.00 m	-	1.80	20.16	8.78	m²	**28.94**
Slab thickness 300 - 400 mm						
horizontal; height to soffit 1.50 - 3.00 m	-	1.85	20.72	9.69	m²	**30.41**
Slab thickness 400 - 500 mm						
horizontal; height to soffit 1.50 - 3.00 m	-	1.95	21.84	10.60	m²	**32.44**
Slab thickness 500 - 600 mm						
horizontal; height to soffit 1.50 - 3.00 m	-	2.10	23.52	10.60	m²	**34.12**
Extra over soffits of slabs for						
sloping not exceeding 15 degrees	-	0.20	2.24	-	m²	**2.24**
sloping exceeding 15 degrees	-	0.40	4.48	-	m²	**4.48**
Soffits of slabs; Expamet "Hy-Rib" permanent shuttering and reinforcement or other equal and approved; ref. 2411						
Slab thickness not exceeding 200 mm						
horizontal; height to soffit 1.50 - 3.00 m	-	1.50	16.80	15.21	m²	**32.01**

E IN SITU CONCRETE/LARGE PRECAST CONCRETE Excluding overheads and profit	PC £	Labour hours	Labour £	Material £	Unit	Total rate £
E20 FORMWORK FOR IN SITU CONCRETE - cont'd						
Soffits of slabs; Richard Lees "Ribdeck 60"						
steel deck permanent shuttering or other equal						
and approved; 0.90 mm gauge; shot-fired to						
frame (not included)						
Slab thickness not exceeding 200 mm						
horizontal; height to soffit 1.50 - 3.00 m	-	0.70	7.84	9.76	m²	**17.60**
horizontal; height to soffit 3.00 - 4.50 m	-	0.80	8.96	9.81	m²	**18.77**
horizontal; height to soffit 4.50 - 6.00 m	-	0.90	10.08	9.87	m²	**19.95**
Soffits of slabs; Richard Lees "Ribdeck 60"						
steel deck permanent shuttering or other equal						
and approved; 1.20 mm gauge; shot-fired to						
frame (not included)						
Slab thickness not exceeding 200 mm						
horizontal; height to soffit 1.50 - 3.00 m	-	0.80	8.96	11.94	m²	**20.90**
horizontal; height to soffit 3.00 - 4.50 m	-	0.90	10.08	11.75	m²	**21.83**
horizontal; height to soffit 4.50 - 6.00 m	-	1.05	11.76	11.83	m²	**23.59**
Soffits of slabs; Richard Lees "Super Holorib"						
steel deck permanent shuttering or other equal						
and approved; 0.90 mm gauge						
Slab thickness not exceeding 200 mm						
horizontal; height to soffit 1.50 - 3.00 m	-	0.70	7.84	14.93	m²	**22.77**
horizontal; height to soffit 3.00 - 4.50 m	-	0.80	8.96	15.42	m²	**24.38**
horizontal; height to soffit 4.50 - 6.00 m	-	0.90	10.08	15.90	m²	**25.98**
Soffits of slabs; Richard Lees "Super Holorib"						
steel deck permanent shuttering or other equal						
and approved; 1.20 mm gauge						
Slab thickness not exceeding 200 mm						
horizontal; height to soffit 1.50 - 3.00 m	-	0.80	8.96	17.32	m²	**26.28**
horizontal; height to soffit 3.00 - 4.50 m	-	0.80	8.96	18.05	m²	**27.01**
horizontal; height to soffit 4.50 - 6.00 m	-	1.05	11.76	18.54	m²	**30.30**
Soffits of landings; basic finish						
Slab thickness not exceeding 200 mm						
horizontal; height to soffit 1.50 - 3.00 m	-	1.80	20.16	7.32	m²	**27.48**
Slab thickness 200 - 300 mm						
horizontal; height to soffit 1.50 - 3.00 m	-	1.90	21.28	9.32	m²	**30.60**
Slab thickness 300 - 400 mm						
horizontal; height to soffit 1.50 - 3.00 m	-	1.95	21.84	10.33	m²	**32.17**
Slab thickness 400 - 500 mm						
horizontal; height to soffit 1.50 - 3.00 m	-	2.05	22.96	11.33	m²	**34.29**
Slab thickness 500 - 600 mm						
horizontal; height to soffit 1.50 - 3.00 m	-	2.20	24.64	11.33	m²	**35.97**
Extra over soffits of landings for						
sloping not exceeding 15 degrees	-	0.20	2.24	-	m²	**2.24**
sloping exceeding 15 degrees	-	0.40	4.48	-	m²	**4.48**
Soffits of coffered or troughed slabs; basic finish						
Cordek "Correx" trough mould or other equal and						
approved; 300 mm deep; ribs of mould at 600 mm						
centres and cross ribs at centres of bay; slab						
thickness 300 - 400 mm						
horizontal; height to soffit 1.50 - 3.00 m	-	2.50	28.00	11.21	m²	**39.21**
horizontal; height to soffit 3.00 - 4.50 m	-	2.60	29.12	11.45	m²	**40.57**
horizontal; height to soffit 4.50 - 6.00 m	-	2.70	30.24	11.59	m²	**41.83**
Top formwork; basic finish						
Sloping exceeding 15 degrees	-	1.50	16.80	5.37	m²	**22.17**

E IN SITU CONCRETE/LARGE PRECAST CONCRETE Excluding overheads and profit	PC £	Labour hours	Labour £	Material £	Unit	Total rate £
Walls; basic finish						
Vertical	-	1.80	20.16	8.78	m²	28.94
Vertical; height exceeding 3.00 m above floor level	-	2.20	24.64	9.02	m²	33.66
Vertical; interrupted	-	2.10	23.52	9.02	m²	32.54
Vertical; to one side only	-	3.50	39.20	11.09	m²	50.29
Battered	-	2.80	31.36	9.45	m²	40.81
Beams; basic finish						
Attached to slabs						
regular shaped; square or rectangular; height to soffit 1.50 - 3.00 m	-	2.20	24.64	8.48	m²	33.12
regular shaped; square or rectangular; height to soffit 3.00 - 4.50 m	-	2.30	25.76	8.78	m²	34.54
regular shaped; square or rectangular; height to soffit 4.50 - 6.00 m	-	2.40	26.88	9.02	m²	35.90
Attached to walls						
regular shaped; square or rectangular; height to soffit 1.50 - 3.00 m	-	2.30	25.76	8.48	m²	34.24
Isolated						
regular shaped; square or rectangular; height to soffit 1.50 - 3.00 m	-	2.40	26.88	8.48	m²	35.36
regular shaped; square or rectangular; height to soffit 3.00 - 4.50 m	-	2.50	28.00	8.78	m²	36.78
regular shaped; square or rectangular; height to soffit 4.50 - 6.00 m	-	2.60	29.12	9.02	m²	38.14
Extra over beams for						
regular shaped; sloping not exceeding 15 degrees	-	0.30	3.36	0.86	m²	4.22
regular shaped; sloping exceeding 15 degrees	-	0.60	6.72	1.73	m²	8.45
Beam casings; basic finish						
Attached to slabs						
regular shaped; square or rectangular; height to soffit 1.50 - 3.00 m	-	2.30	25.76	8.48	m²	34.24
regular shaped; square or rectangular; height to soffit 3.00 - 4.50 m	-	2.40	26.88	8.78	m²	35.66
Attached to walls						
regular shaped; square or rectangular; height to soffit 1.50 - 3.00 m	-	2.40	26.88	8.48	m²	35.36
Isolated						
regular shaped; square or rectangular; height to soffit 1.50 - 3.00 m	-	2.50	28.00	8.48	m²	36.48
regular shaped; square or rectangular; height to soffit 3.00 - 4.50 m	-	2.60	29.12	8.78	m²	37.90
Extra over beam casings for						
regular shaped; sloping not exceeding 15 degrees	-	0.30	3.36	0.86	m²	4.22
regular shaped; sloping exceeding 15 degrees	-	0.60	6.72	1.73	m²	8.45
Columns; basic finish						
Attached to walls						
regular shaped; square or rectangular; height to soffit 1.50 - 3.00 m	-	2.20	24.64	7.44	m²	32.08
Isolated						
regular shaped; square or rectangular; height to soffit 1.50 - 3.00 m	-	2.30	25.76	7.44	m²	33.20
regular shaped; circular; not exceeding 300 mm diameter; height to soffit 1.50 - 3.00 m	-	4.00	44.80	11.94	m²	56.74
regular shaped; circular; 300 - 600 mm diameter; height to soffit 1.50 - 3.00 m	-	3.75	42.00	10.60	m²	52.60
regular shaped; circular; 600 - 900 mm diameter; height to soffit 1.50 - 3.00 m	-	3.50	39.20	10.36	m²	49.56

E IN SITU CONCRETE/LARGE PRECAST CONCRETE Excluding overheads and profit	PC £	Labour hours	Labour £	Material £	Unit	Total rate £
E20 FORMWORK FOR IN SITU CONCRETE - cont'd						
Column casings; basic finish						
Attached to walls						
regular shaped; square or rectangular; height						
to soffit 1.50 - 3.00 m	-	2.30	25.76	7.44	m²	**33.20**
Isolated						
regular shaped; square or rectangular; height						
to soffit 1.50 - 3.00 m	-	2.40	26.88	7.44	m²	**34.32**
Recesses or rebates						
12 x 12 mm	-	0.07	0.78	0.07	m	**0.85**
25 x 25 mm	-	0.07	0.78	0.11	m	**0.89**
25 x 50 mm	-	0.07	0.78	0.15	m	**0.93**
50 x 50 mm	-	0.07	0.78	0.25	m	**1.03**
Nibs						
50 x 50 mm	-	0.55	6.16	0.92	m	**7.08**
100 x 100 mm	-	0.78	8.74	1.22	m	**9.96**
100 x 200 mm	-	1.04	11.65	2.21	m	**13.86**
Extra over a basic finish for fine formed finishes						
Slabs	-	0.35	3.92	-	m²	**3.92**
Walls	-	0.35	3.92	-	m²	**3.92**
Beams	-	0.35	3.92	-	m²	**3.92**
Columns	-	0.35	3.92	-	m²	**3.92**
Add to prices for basic formwork for						
Curved radius 6.00 m - 50%						
Curved radius 2.00 m - 100%						
Coating with retardant agent	-	0.02	0.22	0.41	m²	**0.63**
Wall kickers; basic finish						
Height 150 mm	-	0.50	5.60	2.14	m	**7.74**
Height 225 mm	-	0.65	7.28	2.64	m	**9.92**
Suspended wall kickers; basic finish						
Height 150 mm	-	0.63	7.06	2.17	m	**9.23**
Wall ends, soffits and steps in walls; basic finish						
Plain						
width exceeding 1.00 m	-	1.90	21.28	8.78	m²	**30.06**
width not exceeding 250 mm	-	0.60	6.72	2.22	m	**8.94**
width 250 - 500 mm	-	0.95	10.64	4.87	m	**15.51**
width 500 mm - 1.00 m	-	1.50	16.80	8.78	m	**25.58**
Openings in walls						
Plain						
width exceeding 1.00 m	-	2.10	23.52	8.78	m²	**32.30**
width not exceeding 250 mm	-	0.65	7.28	2.22	m	**9.50**
width 250 - 500 mm	-	1.10	12.32	4.87	m	**17.19**
width 500 mm - 1.00 m	-	1.70	19.04	8.78	m	**27.82**
Stairflights						
Width 1.00 m; 150 mm waist; 150 mm undercut risers						
string, width 300 mm	-	5.00	56.00	19.35	m	**75.35**
Width 2.00 m; 200 mm waist; 150 mm undercut risers						
string, width 350 mm	-	9.00	100.80	33.85	m	**134.65**

E IN SITU CONCRETE/LARGE PRECAST CONCRETE Excluding overheads and profit	PC £	Labour hours	Labour £	Material £	Unit	Total rate £
Mortices						
Girth not exceeding 500 mm						
depth not exceeding 250 mm; circular	-	0.15	1.68	0.74	nr	**2.42**
Holes						
Girth not exceeding 500 mm						
depth not exceeding 250 mm; circular	-	0.20	2.24	0.97	nr	**3.21**
depth 250 - 500 mm; circular	-	0.30	3.36	2.33	nr	**5.69**
Girth 500 mm - 1.00 m						
depth not exceeding 250 mm; circular	-	0.25	2.80	1.63	nr	**4.43**
depth 250 - 500 mm; circular	-	0.38	4.26	4.32	nr	**8.58**
Girth 1.00 - 2.00 m						
depth not exceeding 250 mm; circular	-	0.45	5.04	4.32	nr	**9.36**
depth 250 - 500 mm; circular	-	0.67	7.50	9.04	nr	**16.54**
Girth 2.00 - 3.00 m						
depth not exceeding 250 mm; circular	-	0.60	6.72	8.70	nr	**15.42**
depth 250 - 500 mm; circular	-	0.90	10.08	15.57	nr	**25.65**
E30 REINFORCEMENT FOR IN SITU CONCRETE						
Bar; BS 4449; hot rolled plain round mild steel bars						
40 mm diameter nominal size						
straight or bent	289.00	22.00	191.67	319.62	t	**511.29**
curved	317.90	22.00	191.67	349.96	t	**541.63**
32 mm diameter nominal size						
straight or bent	264.00	23.00	200.61	294.05	t	**494.66**
curved	290.40	23.00	200.61	321.77	t	**522.38**
25 mm diameter nominal size						
straight or bent	260.00	25.00	218.49	289.83	t	**508.32**
curved	286.00	25.00	218.49	317.13	t	**535.62**
20 mm diameter nominal size						
straight or bent	258.00	27.00	236.37	289.38	t	**525.75**
curved	283.80	27.00	236.37	316.47	t	**552.84**
16 mm diameter nominal size						
straight or bent	258.00	29.00	254.25	291.69	t	**545.94**
curved	283.80	29.00	254.25	318.78	t	**573.03**
12 mm diameter nominal size						
straight or bent	262.00	31.00	272.13	298.19	t	**570.32**
curved	288.20	31.00	272.13	325.71	t	**597.84**
10 mm diameter nominal size						
straight or bent	268.00	33.00	290.01	308.43	t	**598.44**
curved	294.80	33.00	290.01	336.57	t	**626.58**
8 mm diameter nominal size						
straight or bent	277.00	35.00	306.22	320.19	t	**626.41**
links	277.00	38.00	333.04	321.56	t	**654.60**
curved	304.70	35.00	306.22	349.28	t	**655.50**
6 mm diameter nominal size						
straight or bent	301.00	40.00	350.92	345.39	t	**696.31**
links	301.00	43.00	377.74	345.39	t	**723.13**
curved	331.10	40.00	350.92	377.00	t	**727.92**
Bar; BS 4449; hot rolled deformed high steel bars grade 460						
40 mm diameter nominal size						
straight or bent	263.00	22.00	191.67	292.32	t	**483.99**
curved	289.30	22.00	191.67	319.93	t	**511.60**
32 mm diameter nominal size						
straight or bent	259.00	23.00	200.61	288.80	t	**489.41**
curved	284.90	23.00	200.61	315.99	t	**516.60**

E IN SITU CONCRETE/LARGE PRECAST CONCRETE Excluding overheads and profit	PC £	Labour hours	Labour £	Material £	Unit	Total rate £
E30 REINFORCEMENT FOR IN SITU CONCRETE - cont'd						
Bar; BS 4449; hot rolled deformed high steel **bars grade 460** - cont'd						
25 mm diameter nominal size						
straight or bent	254.00	25.00	218.49	283.53	t	**502.02**
curved	279.40	25.00	218.49	310.20	t	**528.69**
20 mm diameter nominal size						
straight or bent	256.00	27.00	236.37	287.28	t	**523.65**
curved	281.60	27.00	236.37	314.16	t	**550.53**
16 mm diameter nominal size						
straight or bent	256.00	29.00	254.25	289.59	t	**543.84**
curved	281.60	29.00	254.25	316.47	t	**570.72**
12 mm diameter nominal size						
straight or bent	259.00	31.00	272.13	295.04	t	**567.17**
curved	284.90	31.00	272.13	322.24	t	**594.37**
10 mm diameter nominal size						
straight or bent	263.00	33.00	290.01	303.18	t	**593.19**
curved	289.30	33.00	290.01	330.80	t	**620.81**
8 mm diameter nominal size						
straight or bent	271.00	35.00	306.22	313.89	t	**620.11**
links	271.00	38.00	333.04	315.26	t	**648.30**
curved	298.10	35.00	306.22	342.35	t	**648.57**
Bar; stainless steel						
32 mm diameter nominal size						
straight or bent	2065.00	23.00	200.61	2081.85	t	**2282.46**
curved	2152.50	23.00	200.61	2169.35	t	**2369.96**
25 mm diameter nominal size						
straight or bent	2158.63	25.00	218.49	2175.46	t	**2393.95**
curved	2246.13	25.00	218.49	2262.96	t	**2481.45**
20 mm diameter nominal size						
straight or bent	1411.38	27.00	236.37	1429.86	t	**1666.23**
curved	1498.88	27.00	236.37	1517.36	t	**1753.73**
16 mm diameter nominal size						
straight or bent	1411.38	29.00	254.25	1432.17	t	**1686.42**
curved	1498.88	29.00	254.25	1519.67	t	**1773.92**
12 mm diameter nominal size						
straight or bent	1316.00	31.00	272.13	1339.10	t	**1611.23**
curved	1432.38	31.00	272.13	1455.48	t	**1727.61**
10 mm diameter nominal size						
straight or bent	1316.00	33.00	290.01	1343.03	t	**1633.04**
curved	1447.25	33.00	290.01	1474.28	t	**1764.29**
8 mm diameter nominal size						
straight or bent	1316.00	35.00	306.22	1345.34	t	**1651.56**
curved	1476.13	35.00	306.22	1505.47	t	**1811.69**
Fabric; BS 4483						
Ref A98 (1.54 kg/m^2)						
400 mm minimum laps	0.60	0.13	1.16	0.66	m^2	**1.82**
strips in one width; 600 mm width	0.60	0.16	1.43	0.66	m^2	**2.09**
strips in one width; 900 mm width	0.60	0.15	1.34	0.66	m^2	**2.00**
strips in one width; 1200 mm width	0.60	0.14	1.25	0.66	m^2	**1.91**
Ref A142 (2.22 kg/m^2)						
400 mm minimum laps	0.70	0.13	1.16	0.77	m^2	**1.93**
strips in one width; 600 mm width	0.70	0.16	1.43	0.77	m^2	**2.20**
strips in one width; 900 mm width	0.70	0.15	1.34	0.77	m^2	**2.11**
strips in one width; 1200 mm width	0.70	0.14	1.25	0.77	m^2	**2.02**

E IN SITU CONCRETE/LARGE PRECAST CONCRETE Excluding overheads and profit	PC £	Labour hours	Labour £	Material £	Unit	Total rate £
Ref A193 (3.02 kg/m^2)						
400 mm minimum laps	1.00	0.13	1.16	1.10	m^2	**2.26**
strips in one width; 600 mm width	1.00	0.16	1.43	1.10	m^2	**2.53**
strips in one width; 900 mm width	1.00	0.15	1.34	1.10	m^2	**2.44**
strips in one width; 1200 mm width	1.00	0.14	1.25	1.10	m^2	**2.35**
Ref A252 (3.95 kg/m^2)						
400 mm minimum laps	1.25	0.14	1.25	1.38	m^2	**2.63**
strips in one width; 600 mm width	1.25	0.17	1.52	1.38	m^2	**2.90**
strips in one width; 900 mm width	1.25	0.16	1.43	1.38	m^2	**2.81**
strips in one width; 1200 mm width	1.25	0.15	1.34	1.38	m^2	**2.72**
Ref A393 (6.16 kg/m^2)						
400 mm minimum laps	2.00	0.16	1.43	2.20	m^2	**3.63**
strips in one width; 600 mm width	2.00	0.19	1.70	2.20	m^2	**3.90**
strips in one width; 900 mm width	2.00	0.18	1.61	2.20	m^2	**3.81**
strips in one width; 1200 mm width	2.00	0.17	1.52	2.20	m^2	**3.72**
Ref B196 (3.05 kg/m^2)						
400 mm minimum laps	1.05	0.13	1.16	1.16	m^2	**2.32**
strips in one width; 600 mm width	1.05	0.16	1.43	1.16	m^2	**2.59**
strips in one width; 900 mm width	1.05	0.15	1.34	1.16	m^2	**2.50**
strips in one width; 1200 mm width	1.05	0.14	1.25	1.16	m^2	**2.41**
Ref B283 (3.73 kg/m^2)						
400 mm minimum laps	1.20	0.13	1.16	1.32	m^2	**2.48**
strips in one width; 600 mm width	1.20	0.16	1.43	1.32	m^2	**2.75**
strips in one width; 900 mm width	1.20	0.15	1.34	1.32	m^2	**2.66**
strips in one width; 1200 mm width	1.20	0.14	1.25	1.32	m^2	**2.57**
Ref B385 (4.53 kg/m^2)						
400 mm minimum laps	1.50	0.14	1.25	1.65	m^2	**2.90**
strips in one width; 600 mm width	1.50	0.17	1.52	1.65	m^2	**3.17**
strips in one width; 900 mm width	1.50	0.16	1.43	1.65	m^2	**3.08**
strips in one width; 1200 mm width	1.50	0.15	1.34	1.65	m^2	**2.99**
Ref B503 (5.93 kg/m^2)						
400 mm minimum laps	1.95	0.16	1.43	2.15	m^2	**3.58**
strips in one width; 600 mm width	1.95	0.19	1.70	2.15	m^2	**3.85**
strips in one width; 900 mm width	1.95	0.18	1.61	2.15	m^2	**3.76**
strips in one width; 1200 mm width	1.95	0.17	1.52	2.15	m^2	**3.67**
Ref B785 (8.14 kg/m^2)						
400 mm minimum laps	2.65	0.18	1.61	2.92	m^2	**4.53**
strips in one width; 600 mm width	2.65	0.22	1.97	2.92	m^2	**4.89**
strips in one width; 900 mm width	2.65	0.21	1.88	2.92	m^2	**4.80**
strips in one width; 1200 mm width	2.65	0.20	1.79	2.92	m^2	**4.71**
Ref B1131 (10.90 kg/m^2)						
400 mm minimum laps	3.50	0.20	1.79	3.85	m^2	**5.64**
strips in one width; 600 mm width	3.50	0.26	2.32	3.85	m^2	**6.17**
strips in one width; 900 mm width	3.50	0.24	2.15	3.85	m^2	**6.00**
strips in one width; 1200 mm width	3.50	0.22	1.97	3.85	m^2	**5.82**
Ref C385 (3.41 kg/m^2)						
400 mm minimum laps	1.15	0.13	1.16	1.26	m^2	**2.42**
strips in one width; 600 mm width	1.15	0.16	1.43	1.26	m^2	**2.69**
strips in one width; 900 mm width	1.15	0.15	1.34	1.26	m^2	**2.60**
strips in one width; 1200 mm width	1.15	0.14	1.25	1.26	m^2	**2.51**
Ref C503 (4.34 kg/m^2)						
400 mm minimum laps	1.45	0.14	1.25	1.59	m^2	**2.84**
strips in one width; 600 mm width	1.45	0.17	1.52	1.59	m^2	**3.11**
strips in one width; 900 mm width	1.45	0.16	1.43	1.59	m^2	**3.02**
strips in one width; 1200 mm width	1.45	0.15	1.34	1.59	m^2	**2.93**
Ref C636 (5.55 kg/m^2)						
400 mm minimum laps	1.95	0.15	1.34	2.15	m^2	**3.49**
strips in one width; 600 mm width	1.95	0.18	1.61	2.15	m^2	**3.76**
strips in one width; 900 mm width	1.95	0.17	1.52	2.15	m^2	**3.67**
strips in one width; 1200 mm width	1.95	0.16	1.43	2.15	m^2	**3.58**

E IN SITU CONCRETE/LARGE PRECAST CONCRETE Excluding overheads and profit	PC £	Labour hours	Labour £	Material £	Unit	Total rate £
E30 REINFORCEMENT FOR IN SITU CONCRETE - cont'd						
Fabric; BS 4483 - cont'd						
Ref C785 (6.72 kg/m²)						
400 mm minimum laps	2.25	0.15	1.34	2.48	m²	**3.82**
strips in one width; 600 mm width	2.25	0.18	1.61	2.48	m²	**4.09**
strips in one width; 900 mm width	2.25	0.17	1.52	2.48	m²	**4.00**
strips in one width; 1200 mm width	2.25	0.16	1.43	2.48	m²	**3.91**
Ref D49 (0.77 kg/m²)						
100 mm minimum laps; bent	0.75	0.26	2.32	0.82	m²	**3.14**
Ref D98 (1.54 kg/m²)						
200 mm minimum laps; bent	0.65	0.26	2.32	0.71	m²	**3.03**
E40 DESIGNED JOINTS IN IN SITU CONCRETE						
Formed; Fosroc Expandite "Flexcell" **impregnated fibreboard joint filler or** **other equal and approved**						
Width not exceeding 150 mm						
12.50 mm thick	-	0.15	1.68	1.15	m	**2.83**
20 mm thick	-	0.20	2.24	1.66	m	**3.90**
25 mm thick	-	0.20	2.24	1.89	m	**4.13**
Width 150 - 300 mm						
12.50 mm thick	-	0.20	2.24	1.97	m	**4.21**
20 mm thick	-	0.25	2.80	2.59	m	**5.39**
25 mm thick	-	0.25	2.80	2.99	m	**5.79**
Width 300 - 450 mm						
12.50 mm thick	-	0.25	2.80	2.96	m	**5.76**
20 mm thick	-	0.30	3.36	3.88	m	**7.24**
25 mm thick	-	0.30	3.36	4.48	m	**7.84**
Formed; Grace Servicised "Kork-pak" **waterproof bonded cork joint filler board or** **other equal and approved**						
Width not exceeding 150 mm						
10 mm thick	-	0.15	1.68	2.39	m	**4.07**
13 mm thick	-	0.15	1.68	2.42	m	**4.10**
19 mm thick	-	0.15	1.68	3.10	m	**4.78**
25 mm thick	-	0.15	1.68	3.52	m	**5.20**
Width 150 - 300 mm						
10 mm thick	-	0.20	2.24	4.44	m	**6.68**
13 mm thick	-	0.20	2.24	4.51	m	**6.75**
19 mm thick	-	0.20	2.24	5.87	m	**8.11**
25 mm thick	-	0.20	2.24	6.70	m	**8.94**
Width 300 - 450 mm						
10 mm thick	-	0.25	2.80	6.76	m	**9.56**
13 mm thick	-	0.25	2.80	6.86	m	**9.66**
19 mm thick	-	0.25	2.80	8.91	m	**11.71**
25 mm thick	-	0.25	2.80	10.15	m	**12.95**
Sealants; Fosroc Expandite "Pliastic 77" hot **poured rubberized bituminous compound or** **other equal and approved**						
Width 10 mm						
25 mm depth	-	0.18	2.02	0.71	m	**2.73**
Width 12.50 mm						
25 mm depth	-	0.19	2.13	0.87	m	**3.00**
Width 20 mm						
25 mm depth	-	0.20	2.24	1.41	m	**3.65**
Width 25 mm						
25 mm depth	-	0.21	2.35	1.74	m	**4.09**

E IN SITU CONCRETE/LARGE PRECAST CONCRETE Excluding overheads and profit	PC £	Labour hours	Labour £	Material £	Unit	Total rate £
Sealants; Fosroc Expandite "Thioflex 600" **gun grade two part polysulphide or other** **equal and approved**						
Width 10 mm						
depth 25 mm	-	0.06	0.67	2.69	m	**3.36**
Width 12.50 mm						
depth 25 mm	-	0.07	0.78	3.36	m	**4.14**
Width 20 mm						
depth 25 mm	-	0.08	0.90	5.38	m	**6.28**
Width 25 mm						
depth 25 mm	-	0.09	1.01	6.72	m	**7.73**
Sealants; Grace Servicised "Paraseal" **polysulphide compound or other equal and** **approved; priming with Grace Servicised** **"Servicised P" or other equal and approved**						
Width 10 mm						
25 mm depth	-	0.20	1.45	1.63	m	**3.08**
Width 13 mm						
25 mm depth	-	0.20	1.45	2.09	m	**3.54**
Width 19 mm						
25 mm depth	-	0.25	1.82	3.00	m	**4.82**
Width 25 mm						
25 mm depth	-	0.25	1.82	3.92	m	**5.74**
Waterstops						
PVC water stop; flat dumbbell type; heat welded joints; cast into concrete						
170 mm wide	2.16	0.25	2.23	2.33	m	**4.56**
flat angle	6.87	0.30	2.68	5.77	nr	**8.45**
vertical angle	9.88	0.30	2.68	8.85	nr	**11.53**
flat three way intersection	8.76	0.40	3.58	8.18	nr	**11.76**
vertical three way intersection	12.38	0.40	3.58	11.89	nr	**15.47**
four way intersection	9.56	0.50	4.47	9.47	nr	**13.94**
210 mm wide	2.81	0.25	2.23	3.02	m	**5.25**
flat angle	8.52	0.30	2.68	7.36	nr	**10.04**
vertical angle	9.40	0.30	2.68	8.25	nr	**10.93**
flat three way intersection	11.12	0.40	3.58	10.79	nr	**14.37**
vertical three way intersection	8.99	0.40	3.58	8.60	nr	**12.18**
four way intersection	12.18	0.50	4.47	12.63	nr	**17.10**
250 mm wide	3.72	0.30	2.68	3.98	m	**6.66**
flat angle	10.25	0.35	3.13	9.07	nr	**12.20**
vertical angle	10.56	0.35	3.13	9.39	nr	**12.52**
flat three way intersection	13.24	0.45	4.02	13.33	nr	**17.35**
vertical three way intersection	10.08	0.45	4.02	10.09	nr	**14.11**
four way intersection	14.70	0.55	4.92	16.01	nr	**20.93**
PVC water stop; centre bulb type; heat welded joints; cast into concrete						
160 mm wide	2.33	0.25	2.23	2.51	m	**4.74**
flat angle	7.07	0.30	2.68	5.87	nr	**8.55**
vertical angle	10.23	0.30	2.68	9.11	nr	**11.79**
flat three way intersection	8.97	0.40	3.58	8.33	nr	**11.91**
vertical three way intersection	9.80	0.40	3.58	9.18	nr	**12.76**
four way intersection	9.80	0.50	4.47	9.68	nr	**14.15**
210 mm wide	3.34	0.25	2.23	3.57	m	**5.80**
flat angle	8.99	0.30	2.68	7.59	nr	**10.27**
vertical angle	11.38	0.30	2.68	10.03	nr	**12.71**
flat three way intersection	11.52	0.40	3.58	11.07	nr	**14.65**
vertical three way intersection	10.89	0.40	3.58	10.42	nr	**14.00**
four way intersection	12.59	0.50	4.47	13.05	nr	**17.52**

E IN SITU CONCRETE/LARGE PRECAST CONCRETE Excluding overheads and profit	PC £	Labour hours	Labour £	Material £	Unit	Total rate £
E40 DESIGNED JOINTS IN IN SITU CONCRETE - cont'd						
Waterstops - cont'd						
PVC water stop; centre bulb type; heat welded joints; cast into concrete - cont'd						
260 mm wide	3.90	0.30	2.68	4.16	m	**6.84**
flat angle	10.47	0.35	3.13	9.23	nr	**12.36**
vertical angle	10.71	0.35	3.13	9.47	nr	**12.60**
flat three way intersection	13.51	0.45	4.02	13.59	nr	**17.61**
vertical three way intersection	10.29	0.45	4.02	10.29	nr	**14.31**
four way intersection	14.96	0.55	4.92	16.32	nr	**21.24**
325 mm wide	8.65	0.35	3.13	9.16	m	**12.29**
flat angle	21.41	0.40	3.58	20.37	nr	**23.95**
vertical angle	15.89	0.40	3.58	14.71	nr	**18.29**
flat three way intersection	24.18	0.50	4.47	26.88	nr	**31.35**
vertical three way intersection	15.41	0.50	4.47	17.88	nr	**22.35**
four way intersection	26.69	0.60	5.36	33.10	nr	**38.46**
E41 WORKED FINISHES/CUTTING TO IN SITU CONCRETE						
Worked finishes						
Tamping by mechanical means	-	0.03	0.22	0.08	m²	**0.30**
Power floating	-	0.17	1.24	0.27	m²	**1.51**
Trowelling	-	0.33	2.40	-	m²	**2.40**
Hacking						
by mechanical means	-	0.33	2.40	0.25	m²	**2.65**
by hand	-	0.70	5.09	-	m²	**5.09**
Lightly shot blasting surface of concrete	-	0.40	2.91	-	m²	**2.91**
Blasting surface of concrete						
to produce textured finish	-	0.70	5.09	0.52	m²	**5.61**
Wood float finish	-	0.13	0.95	-	m²	**0.95**
Tamped finish						
level or to falls	-	0.07	0.51	-	m²	**0.51**
to falls	-	0.10	0.73	-	m²	**0.73**
Spade finish	-	0.15	1.09	-	m²	**1.09**
Cutting chases						
Depth not exceeding 50 mm						
width 10 mm	-	0.33	2.40	0.69	m	**3.09**
width 50 mm	-	0.50	3.63	0.82	m	**4.45**
width 75 mm	-	0.66	4.80	0.93	m	**5.73**
Depth 50 - 100 mm						
width 75 mm	-	0.90	6.54	1.48	m	**8.02**
width 100 mm	-	1.00	7.27	1.55	m	**8.82**
width 100 mm; in reinforced concrete	-	1.50	10.90	2.40	m	**13.30**
Depth 100 - 150 mm						
width 100 mm	-	1.30	9.45	1.87	m	**11.32**
width 100 mm; in reinforced concrete	-	2.00	14.54	3.05	m	**17.59**
width 150 mm	-	1.60	11.63	2.09	m	**13.72**
width 150 mm; in reinforced concrete	-	2.40	17.45	3.40	m	**20.85**
Cutting rebates						
Depth not exceeding 50 mm						
width 50 mm	-	0.50	3.63	0.82	m	**4.45**
Depth 50 - 100 mm						
width 100 mm	-	1.00	7.27	1.55	m	**8.82**

E IN SITU CONCRETE/LARGE PRECAST CONCRETE Excluding overheads and profit	PC £	Labour hours	Labour £	Material £	Unit	Total rate £
NOTE: The following rates for cutting mortices and holes in reinforced concrete allow for diamond drilling.						
Cutting mortices						
Depth not exceeding 100 mm						
cross sectional size 20 mm diameter; making good	-	0.15	1.09	0.08	nr	1.17
cross sectional size 50 mm diameter; making good	-	0.17	1.24	0.10	nr	1.34
cross sectional size 150 x 150 mm; making good	-	0.35	2.54	0.27	nr	2.81
cross sectional size 300 x 300 mm; making good	-	0.70	5.09	0.58	nr	5.67
cross sectional size 50 mm diameter; in reinforced concrete; making good	-	-	-	-	nr	6.77
cross sectional size 50 - 75 mm diameter; in reinforced concrete; making good	-	-	-	-	nr	7.92
cross sectional size 75 - 100 mm diameter; in reinforced concrete; making good	-	-	-	-	nr	8.48
cross sectional size 100 - 125 mm diameter; in reinforced concrete; making good	-	-	-	-	nr	9.04
cross sectional size 125 - 150 mm diameter; in reinforced concrete; making good	-	-	-	-	nr	10.17
Depth 100 - 200 mm						
cross sectional size 50 mm diameter; in reinforced concrete; making good	-	-	-	-	nr	9.48
cross sectional size 50 - 75 mm diameter; in reinforced concrete; making good	-	-	-	-	nr	10.85
cross sectional size 75 - 100 mm diameter; in reinforced concrete; making good	-	-	-	-	nr	11.88
cross sectional size 100 - 125 mm diameter; in reinforced concrete; making good	-	-	-	-	nr	13.54
cross sectional size 125 - 150 mm diameter; in reinforced concrete; making good	-	-	-	-	nr	15.25
Depth 200 - 300 mm						
cross sectional size 50 mm diameter; in reinforced concrete; making good	-	-	-	-	nr	18.98
cross sectional size 50 - 75 mm diameter; in reinforced concrete; making good	-	-	-	-	nr	21.69
cross sectional size 75 - 100 mm diameter; in reinforced concrete; making good	-	-	-	-	nr	23.73
cross sectional size 100 - 125 mm diameter; in reinforced concrete; making good	-	-	-	-	nr	27.11
cross sectional size 125 - 150 mm diameter; in reinforced concrete; making good	-	-	-	-	nr	30.51
Depth exceeding 300 mm; 400 mm depth						
cross sectional size 50 mm diameter; in reinforced concrete; making good	-	-	-	-	nr	25.30
cross sectional size 50 - 75 mm diameter; in reinforced concrete; making good	-	-	-	-	nr	28.92
cross sectional size 75 - 100 mm diameter; in reinforced concrete; making good	-	-	-	-	nr	31.63
cross sectional size 100 - 125 mm diameter; in reinforced concrete; making good	-	-	-	-	nr	36.15
cross sectional size 125 - 150 mm diameter; in reinforced concrete; making good	-	-	-	-	nr	40.67

E IN SITU CONCRETE/LARGE PRECAST CONCRETE Excluding overheads and profit	PC £	Labour hours	Labour £	Material £	Unit	Total rate £
E41 WORKED FINISHES/CUTTING TO IN SITU CONCRETE - cont'd						
Cutting mortices - cont'd						
Depth exceeding 300 mm; 500 mm depth						
cross sectional size 50 mm diameter; in						
reinforced concrete; making good	-	-	-	-	nr	31.63
cross sectional size 50 - 75 mm diameter; in						
reinforced concrete; making good	-	-	-	-	nr	36.15
cross sectional size 75 - 100 mm diameter; in						
reinforced concrete; making good	-	-	-	-	nr	39.54
cross sectional size 100 - 125 mm diameter; in						
reinforced concrete; making good	-	-	-	-	nr	45.18
cross sectional size 125 - 150 mm diameter; in						
reinforced concrete; making good	-	-	-	-	nr	50.84
cross sectional size 200 x 150 mm; in						
reinforced concrete; making good	-	-	-	-	nr	135.54
Depth exceeding 300 mm; 600 mm depth						
cross sectional size 50 mm diameter; in						
reinforced concrete; making good	-	-	-	-	nr	37.96
cross sectional size 50 - 75 mm diameter; in						
reinforced concrete; making good	-	-	-	-	nr	43.38
cross sectional size 75 - 100 mm diameter; in						
reinforced concrete; making good	-	-	-	-	nr	47.44
cross sectional size 100 - 125 mm diameter; in						
reinforced concrete; making good	-	-	-	-	nr	54.23
cross sectional size 125 - 150 mm diameter; in						
reinforced concrete; making good	-	-	-	-	nr	61.01
Cutting holes						
Depth not exceeding 100 mm						
cross sectional size 50 mm diameter; making good	-	0.35	2.54	0.28	nr	2.82
cross sectional size 100 mm diameter; making good	-	0.40	2.91	0.32	nr	3.23
cross sectional size 150 x 150 mm; making good	-	0.45	3.27	0.36	nr	3.63
cross sectional size 300 x 300 mm; making good	-	0.55	4.00	0.44	nr	4.44
Depth 100 - 200 mm						
cross sectional size 50 mm diameter; making good	-	0.50	3.63	0.40	nr	4.03
cross sectional size 50 mm diameter; in reinforced concrete; making good	-	0.75	5.45	0.60	nr	6.05
cross sectional size 100 mm diameter; making good	-	0.60	4.36	0.48	nr	4.84
cross sectional size 100 mm diameter; in reinforced concrete; making good	-	0.90	6.54	0.72	nr	7.26
cross sectional size 150 x 150 mm; making good	-	0.75	5.45	0.60	nr	6.05
cross sectional size 150 x 150 mm; in reinforced concrete; making good	-	1.15	8.36	0.92	nr	9.28
cross sectional size 300 x 300 mm; making good	-	0.95	6.91	0.76	nr	7.67
cross sectional size 300 x 300 mm; in reinforced concrete; making good	-	1.45	10.54	1.16	nr	11.70
cross sectional size not exceeding 0.10 m²; in reinforced concrete; making good	-	-	-	-	nr	79.08
cross sectional size 0.10 - 0.20 m²; in reinforced concrete; making good	-	-	-	-	nr	158.15
cross sectional size 0.20 - 0.30 m²; in reinforced concrete; making good	-	-	-	-	nr	178.49

E IN SITU CONCRETE/LARGE PRECAST CONCRETE Excluding overheads and profit	PC £	Labour hours	Labour £	Material £	Unit	Total rate £
Depth 100 - 200 mm - cont'd						
cross sectional size 0.30 - 0.40 m²; in						
reinforced concrete; making good	-	-	-	-	nr	207.91
cross sectional size 0.40 - 0.50 m²; in						
reinforced concrete; making good	-	-	-	-	nr	238.35
cross sectional size 0.50 - 0.60 m²; in						
reinforced concrete; making good	-	-	-	-	nr	277.89
cross sectional size 0.60 - 0.70 m²; in						
reinforced concrete; making good	-	-	-	-	nr	317.44
cross sectional size 0.70 - 0.80 m²; in						
reinforced concrete; making good	-	-	-	-	nr	361.88
Depth 200 - 300 mm						
cross sectional size 50 mm diameter; making good	-	0.75	5.45	0.60	nr	6.05
cross sectional size 50 mm diameter; in reinforced concrete; making good	-	1.15	8.36	0.92	nr	9.28
cross sectional size 100 mm diameter; making good	-	0.90	6.54	0.72	nr	7.26
cross sectional size 100 mm diameter; in reinforced concrete; making good	-	1.35	9.81	1.08	nr	10.89
cross sectional size 150 x 150 mm; making good	-	1.10	8.00	0.88	nr	8.88
cross sectional size 150 x 150 mm; in reinforced concrete; making good	-	1.65	12.00	1.33	nr	13.33
cross sectional size 300 x 300 mm; making good	-	1.40	10.18	1.12	nr	11.30
cross sectional size 300 x 300 mm; in reinforced concrete; making good	-	2.10	15.27	1.69	nr	16.96
E42 ACCESSORIES CAST INTO IN SITU CONCRETE						
Foundation bolt boxes						
Temporary plywood; for group of 4 nr bolts						
75 x 75 x 150 mm	-	0.45	5.04	0.93	nr	5.97
75 x 75 x 250 mm	-	0.45	5.04	1.17	nr	6.21
Expanded metal; Expamet Building Products Ltd or other equal and approved						
75 mm diameter x 150 mm long	-	0.30	3.36	0.94	nr	4.30
75 mm diameter x 300 mm long	-	0.30	3.36	1.29	nr	4.65
100 mm diameter x 450 mm long	-	0.30	3.36	2.31	nr	5.67
Foundation bolts and nuts						
Black hexagon						
10 mm diameter x 100 mm long	-	0.25	2.80	0.46	nr	3.26
12 mm diameter x 120 mm long	-	0.25	2.80	0.71	nr	3.51
16 mm diameter x 160 mm long	-	0.30	3.36	1.96	nr	5.32
20 mm diameter x 180 mm long	-	0.30	3.36	2.29	nr	5.65
Masonry slots						
Galvanised steel; dovetail slots; 1.20 mm thick; 18G						
75 mm long	-	0.08	0.90	0.16	nr	1.06
100 mm long	-	0.08	0.90	0.18	nr	1.08
150 mm long	-	0.09	1.01	0.22	nr	1.23
225 mm long	-	0.10	1.12	0.31	nr	1.43
Galvanised steel; metal insert slots; Halfen Ltd or other equal and approved; 2.50 mm thick; end caps and foam filling						
41 x 41 mm; ref P3270	-	0.40	4.48	7.33	m	11.81
41 x 41 x 75 mm; ref P3249	-	0.10	1.12	1.49	nr	2.61
41 x 41 x 100 mm; ref P3250	-	0.10	1.12	1.81	nr	2.93
41 x 41 x 150 mm; ref P3251	-	0.10	1.12	2.22	nr	3.34

E IN SITU CONCRETE/LARGE PRECAST CONCRETE Excluding overheads and profit	PC £	Labour hours	Labour £	Material £	Unit	Total rate £
E42 ACCESSORIES CAST INTO IN SITU CONCRETE - cont'd						
Cramps						
Mild steel; once bent; one end shot fired into						
concrete; other end fanged and built into						
brickwork joint						
200 mm girth	-	0.15	1.70	0.40	nr	**2.10**
Column guards						
White nylon coated steel; "Rigifix" or other equal						
and approved; Huntley and Sparks Ltd; plugging;						
screwing to concrete; 1.50 mm thick						
75 x 75 x 1000 mm	-	0.80	8.96	15.51	nr	**24.47**
Galvanised steel; "Rigifix" or other equal and						
approved; Huntley and Sparks Ltd; 3 mm thick						
75 x 75 x 1000 mm	-	0.60	6.72	10.94	nr	**17.66**
Galvanised steel; "Rigifix" or other equal and						
approved; Huntley and Sparks Ltd; 4.50 mm thick						
75 x 75 x 1000 mm	-	0.60	6.72	14.70	nr	**21.42**
Stainless steel; "HKW" or other equal and						
approved; Halfen Ltd; 5 mm thick						
50 x 50 x 1500 mm	-	1.00	11.20	40.75	nr	**51.95**
50 x 50 x 2000 mm	-	1.20	13.44	57.41	nr	**70.85**
Channels						
Stainless steel; Halfen Ltd or other equal and approved						
ref 38/17/HTA	-	0.35	3.92	11.37	m	**15.29**
ref 41/22/HZA; 80 mm long; including "T"						
headed bolts and plate washers	-	0.10	1.12	7.79	nr	**8.91**
Channel ties						
Stainless steel; Halfen Ltd or other equal and approved						
ref HTS - B12; 150 mm projection; including						
insulation retainer	-	0.04	0.57	0.35	nr	**0.92**
ref HTS - B12; 200 mm projection; including						
insulation retainer	-	0.04	0.57	0.46	nr	**1.03**
E60 PRECAST/COMPOSITE CONCRETE DECKING						
Prestressed precast flooring planks; Bison						
"Drycast" or other equal and approved; cement:						
sand (1:3) grout between planks and on prepared						
bearings						
100 mm thick suspended slabs; horizontal						
600 mm wide planks	-	-	-	-	m²	**32.74**
1200 mm wide planks	-	-	-	-	m²	**31.06**
150 mm thick suspended slabs; horizontal						
400 mm wide planks	-	-	-	-	m²	**33.62**
1200 mm wide planks	-	-	-	-	m²	**32.38**

E IN SITU CONCRETE/LARGE PRECAST CONCRETE Excluding overheads and profit	PC £	Labour hours	Labour £	Material £	Unit	Total rate £
Prestressed precast concrete beam and **block floor; Bison "Housefloor" or other equal** **and approved; in situ concrete 30.00 N/mm² -** **10 mm aggregate in filling at wall abutments;** **cement :sand (1:6) grout brushed in between** **beams and blocks** 155 mm thick suspended slab at ground level; 440 mm x 215 mm x 100 mm blocks; horizontal beams at 510 mm centres; up to 3.30 m span						
with a superimposed load of 5.00 kN/m²	-	-	-	-	m²	17.73
beams at 285 mm centres; up to 4.35 m span						
with a superimposed load of 5.00 kN/m²	-	-	-	-	m²	20.71
Prestressed precast concrete structural **suspended floors; Bison "Hollowcore" or** **other equal and approved; supplied and fixed** **on hard level bearings, to areas of 500 m² per** **site visit; top surface screeding and ceiling** **finishes by others** Floors to dwellings, offices, car parks, shop retail floors, hospitals, school teaching rooms, staff rooms and the like; superimposed load of 5.00 kN/m²						
floor spans up to 3.00 m; 1200 mm x 150 mm	-	-	-	-	m²	31.95
floor spans up to 3.00 m; 400 mm x 150 mm	-	-	-	-	m²	33.62
floor spans 3.00 m - 6.00 m; 1200 mm x 150 mm	-	-	-	-	m²	32.38
floor spans 3.00 m - 6.00 m; 400 mm x 150 mm	-	-	-	-	m²	34.05
floor spans 6.00 m - 7.50 m; 1200 mm x 200 mm	-	-	-	-	m²	33.27
floor spans 7.50 m - 9.50 m; 1200 mm x 250 mm	-	-	-	-	m²	37.72
floor spans 9.50 m - 12.00 m; 1200 mm x 300 mm	-	-	-	-	m²	39.97
floor spans 12.00 m - 13.00 m; 1200 mm x 350 mm	-	-	-	-	m²	42.08
floor spans 13.00 m - 14.00 m; 1200 mm x 400 mm	-	-	-	-	m²	45.65
floor spans 14.00 m - 15.00 m; 1200 mm x 450 mm	-	-	-	-	m²	46.38
Floors to shop stockrooms, light warehousing, schools, churches or similar places of assembly, light factory accommodation, laboratories and the like; superimposed load of 8.50 kN/m²						
floor spans up to 3.00 m; 1200 mm x 150 mm	-	-	-	-	m²	32.00
floor spans 3.00 m - 6.00 m; 1200 mm x 200 mm	-	-	-	-	m²	33.32
floor spans 6.00 m - 7.50 m; 1200 mm x 250 mm	-	-	-	-	m²	37.77
Floors to heavy warehousing, factories, stores and the like; superimposed load of 12.50 kN/m²						
floor spans up to 3.00 m; 1200 mm x 150 mm	-	-	-	-	m²	32.06
floor spans 3.00 m - 6.00 m; 1200 mm x 250 mm	-	-	-	-	m²	37.82
Prestressed precast concrete staircase, supplied and fixed in conjunction with Bison "Hollowcore" flooring system or similar; comprising 2 nr 1100 mm wide flights with 7 nr 275 mm treads, 8 nr 185 mm risers and 150 mm waist; 1 nr 2200 mm x 1400 mm x 150 mm half landing and 1 nr top landing						
3.00 m storey height	-	-	-	-	nr	1453.54

E IN SITU CONCRETE/LARGE PRECAST CONCRETE Excluding overheads and profit	PC £	Labour hours	Labour £	Material £	Unit	Total rate £
E60 PRECAST/COMPOSITE CONCRETE **DECKING** - cont'd						
Composite floor comprising reinforced in situ **ready-mixed concrete 30.00 N/mm^2; on and** **including 1.20 mm thick "Super Holorib" steel** **deck permanent shutting or other equal and** **approved; complete with reinforcement to** **support imposed loading and A142 anti-crack mesh**						
150 mm thick suspended slab; 5.00 kN/m^2 loading						
1.50 m - 3.00 m high to soffit	-	1.55	14.56	27.11	m^2	**41.67**
3.00 m - 4.50 m high to soffit	-	1.55	14.56	28.21	m^2	**42.77**
4.50 m - 6.00 m high to soffit	-	1.80	17.36	28.63	m^2	**45.99**
200 mm thick suspended slab; 7.50 kN/m^2 loading						
1.50 m - 3.00 m high to soffit	-	1.59	14.85	30.12	m^2	**44.97**
3.00 m - 4.50 m high to soffit	-	1.59	14.85	31.22	m^2	**46.07**
4.50 m - 6.00 m high to soffit	-	1.84	17.65	31.63	m^2	**49.28**

F MASONRY Excluding overheads and profit	PC £	Labour hours	Labour £	Material £	Unit	Total rate £
F MASONRY						
F10 BRICK/BLOCK WALLING						
BASIC MORTAR PRICES						

Coloured mortar materials (£/tonne); (excluding cement)

light	38.75	medium	40.25
dark	48.75	extra dark	48.75

Mortar materials (£/tonne)

cement	75.50	lime	120.00
sand	13.45	white cement	140.00

Mortar materials (£/5 litres)

"Cemplas Super" mortar plasticiser	4.15

F MASONRY	PC £	Labour hours	Labour £	Material £	Unit	Total rate £
Common bricks; PC £167.20/1000; in cement mortar (1:3)						
Walls						
half brick thick	-	1.00	14.21	12.57	m²	26.78
half brick thick; building against other work; concrete	-	1.10	15.63	13.76	m²	29.39
half brick thick; building overhand	-	1.25	17.76	12.57	m²	30.33
half brick thick; curved; 6.00 m radii	-	1.30	18.47	12.57	m²	31.04
half brick thick; curved; 1.50 m radii	-	1.70	24.16	14.37	m²	38.53
one brick thick	-	1.70	24.16	25.14	m²	49.30
one brick thick; curved; 6.00 m radii	-	2.20	31.26	26.94	m²	58.20
one brick thick; curved; 1.50 m radii	-	2.75	39.08	27.53	m²	66.61
one and a half brick thick	-	2.30	32.68	37.71	m²	70.39
one and a half brick thick; battering	-	2.65	37.66	37.71	m²	75.37
two brick thick	-	2.80	39.79	50.28	m²	90.07
two brick thick; battering	-	3.30	46.89	50.28	m²	97.17
337 mm average thick; tapering, one side	-	2.90	41.21	37.71	m²	78.92
450 mm average thick; tapering, one side	-	3.75	53.29	50.28	m²	103.57
337 mm average thick; tapering, both sides	-	3.35	47.60	37.71	m²	85.31
450 mm average thick; tapering, both sides	-	4.20	59.68	50.87	m²	110.55
facework one side, half brick thick	-	1.10	15.63	12.57	m²	28.20
facework one side, one brick thick	-	1.80	25.58	25.14	m²	50.72
facework one side, one and a half brick thick	-	2.40	34.10	37.71	m²	71.81
facework one side, two brick thick	-	2.90	41.21	50.28	m²	91.49
facework both sides, half brick thick	-	1.20	17.05	12.57	m²	29.62
facework both sides, one brick thick	-	1.90	27.00	25.14	m²	52.14
facework both sides, one and a half brick thick	-	2.50	35.52	37.71	m²	73.23
facework both sides, two brick thick	-	3.00	42.63	50.28	m²	92.91
Isolated piers						
one brick thick	-	2.55	36.24	25.14	m²	61.38
two brick thick	-	4.00	56.84	50.87	m²	107.71
three brick thick	-	5.05	71.76	76.61	m²	148.37
Isolated casings						
half brick thick	-	1.30	18.47	12.57	m²	31.04
one brick thick	-	2.20	31.26	25.14	m²	56.40
Chimney stacks						
one brick thick	-	2.55	36.24	25.14	m²	61.38
two brick thick	-	4.00	56.84	50.87	m²	107.71
three brick thick	-	5.05	71.76	76.61	m²	148.37
Projections						
225 mm width; 112 mm depth; vertical	-	0.30	4.26	2.60	m	6.86
225 mm width; 225 mm depth; vertical	-	0.60	8.53	5.21	m	13.74
327 mm width; 225 mm depth; vertical	-	0.90	12.79	7.81	m	20.60
440 mm width; 225 mm depth; vertical	-	1.00	14.21	10.42	m	24.63

F MASONRY Excluding overheads and profit	PC £	Labour hours	Labour £	Material £	Unit	Total rate £
F10 BRICK/BLOCK WALLING - cont'd						
Common bricks; PC £167.20/1000; in cement **mortar (1:3)** - cont'd						
Closing cavities						
width of cavity 50 mm, closing with common brickwork half brick thick; vertical	-	0.30	4.26	0.64	m	4.90
width of cavity 50 mm, closing with common brickwork half brick thick; horizontal	-	0.30	4.26	1.92	m	6.18
width of cavity 50 mm, closing with common brickwork half brick thick; including damp proof course; vertical	-	0.40	5.68	1.37	m	7.05
width of cavity 50 mm, closing with common brickwork half brick thick; including damp proof course; horizontal	-	0.35	4.97	2.45	m	7.42
width of cavity 75 mm, closing with common brickwork half brick thick; vertical	-	0.30	4.26	0.93	m	5.19
width of cavity 75 mm, closing with common brickwork half brick thick; horizontal	-	0.30	4.26	2.82	m	7.08
width of cavity 75 mm, closing with common brickwork half brick thick; including damp proof course; vertical	-	0.40	5.68	1.66	m	7.34
width of cavity 75 mm, closing with common brickwork half brick thick; including damp proof course; horizontal	-	0.35	4.97	3.35	m	8.32
Bonding to existing						
half brick thick	-	0.30	4.26	0.69	m	4.95
one brick thick	-	0.45	6.39	1.38	m	7.77
one and a half brick thick	-	0.70	9.95	2.07	m	12.02
two brick thick	-	0.95	13.50	2.75	m	16.25
ADD or DEDUCT to walls for variation of £10.00/1000 in PC of common bricks						
half brick thick	-	-	-	0.65	m²	0.65
one brick thick	-	-	-	1.29	m²	1.29
one and a half brick thick	-	-	-	1.94	m²	1.94
two brick thick	-	-	-	2.58	m²	2.58
Common bricks; PC £167.20/1000; in gauged **mortar (1:1:6)**						
Walls						
half brick thick	-	1.00	14.21	12.37	m²	26.58
half brick thick; building against other work; concrete	-	1.10	15.63	13.43	m²	29.06
half brick thick; building overhand	-	1.25	17.76	12.37	m²	30.13
half brick thick; curved; 6.00 m radii	-	1.30	18.47	12.37	m²	30.84
half brick thick; curved; 1.50 m radii	-	1.70	24.16	14.17	m²	38.33
one brick thick	-	1.70	24.16	24.75	m²	48.91
one brick thick; curved; 6.00 m radii	-	2.20	31.26	26.55	m²	57.81
one brick thick; curved; 1.50 m radii	-	2.75	39.08	27.08	m²	66.16
one and a half brick thick	-	2.30	32.68	37.12	m²	69.80
one and a half brick thick; battering	-	2.65	37.66	37.12	m²	74.78
two brick thick	-	2.80	39.79	49.50	m²	89.29
two brick thick; battering	-	3.30	46.89	49.50	m²	96.39
337 average thick; tapering, one side	-	2.90	41.21	37.12	m²	78.33
450 average thick; tapering, one side	-	3.75	53.29	49.50	m²	102.79
337 average thick; tapering, both sides	-	3.35	47.60	37.12	m²	84.72
450 average thick; tapering, both sides	-	4.20	59.68	50.03	m²	109.71
facework one side, half brick thick	-	1.10	15.63	12.37	m²	28.00
facework one side, one brick thick	-	1.80	25.58	24.75	m²	50.33
facework one side, one and a half brick thick	-	2.40	34.10	37.12	m²	71.22
facework one side, two brick thick	-	2.90	41.21	49.50	m²	90.71
facework both sides, half brick thick	-	1.20	17.05	12.37	m²	29.42

F MASONRY Excluding overheads and profit	PC £	Labour hours	Labour £	Material £	Unit	Total rate £
Walls - cont'd						
facework both sides, one brick thick	-	1.90	27.00	24.75	m²	51.75
facework both sides, one and a half brick thick	-	2.50	35.52	37.12	m²	72.64
facework both sides, two brick thick	-	3.00	42.63	49.50	m²	92.13
Isolated piers						
one brick thick	-	2.55	36.24	24.75	m²	60.99
two brick thick	-	4.00	56.84	50.03	m²	106.87
three brick thick	-	5.05	71.76	75.31	m²	147.07
Isolated casings						
half brick thick	-	1.30	18.47	12.37	m²	30.84
one brick thick	-	2.20	31.26	24.75	m²	56.01
Chimney stacks						
one brick thick	-	2.55	36.24	24.75	m²	60.99
two brick thick	-	4.00	56.84	50.03	m²	106.87
three brick thick	-	5.05	71.76	75.31	m²	147.07
Projections						
225 mm width; 112 mm depth; vertical	-	0.30	4.26	2.58	m	6.84
225 mm width; 225 mm depth; vertical	-	0.60	8.53	5.16	m	13.69
337 mm width; 225 mm depth; vertical	-	0.90	12.79	7.75	m	20.54
440 mm width; 225 mm depth; vertical	-	1.00	14.21	10.33	m	24.54
Closing cavities						
width of cavity 50 mm, closing with common brickwork half brick thick; vertical	-	0.30	4.26	0.63	m	4.89
width of cavity 50 mm, closing with common brickwork half brick thick; horizontal	-	0.30	4.26	1.91	m	6.17
width of cavity 50 mm, closing with common brickwork half brick thick; including damp proof course; vertical	-	0.40	5.68	1.36	m	7.04
width of cavity 50 mm, closing with common brickwork half brick thick; including damp proof course; horizontal	-	0.35	4.97	2.44	m	7.41
width of cavity 75 mm, closing with common brickwork half brick thick; vertical	-	0.30	4.26	0.92	m	5.18
width of cavity 75 mm, closing with common brickwork half brick thick; horizontal	-	0.30	4.26	2.81	m	7.07
width of cavity 75 mm, closing with common brickwork half brick thick; including damp proof course; vertical	-	0.40	5.68	1.65	m	7.33
width of cavity 75 mm, closing with common brickwork half brick thick; including damp proof course; horizontal	-	0.35	4.97	3.34	m	8.31
Bonding to existing						
half brick thick	-	0.30	4.26	0.68	m	4.94
one brick thick	-	0.45	6.39	1.36	m	7.75
one and a half brick thick	-	0.70	9.95	2.04	m	11.99
two brick thick	-	0.95	13.50	2.71	m	16.21
Arches						
height on face 102 mm, width of exposed soffit 102 mm, shape of arch - segmental, one ring	-	1.70	18.53	7.29	m	25.82
height on face 102 mm, width of exposed soffit 215 mm, shape of arch - segmental, one ring	-	2.20	25.64	8.78	m	34.42
height on face 102 mm, width of exposed soffit 102 mm, shape of arch - semi-circular, one ring	-	2.15	24.93	7.29	m	32.22
height on face 102 mm, width of exposed soffit 215 mm, shape of arch - semi-circular, one ring	-	2.70	32.74	8.78	m	41.52
height on face 215 mm, width of exposed soffit 102 mm, shape of arch - segmental, two ring	-	2.15	24.93	8.59	m	33.52
height on face 215 mm, width of exposed soffit 215 mm, shape of arch - segmental, two ring	-	2.65	32.03	11.39	m	43.42
height on face 215 mm, width of exposed soffit 102 mm, shape of arch - semi-circular, two ring	-	2.90	35.58	8.59	m	44.17

| F MASONRY | PC | Labour | Labour | Material | | Total |
Excluding overheads and profit	£	hours	£	£	Unit	rate £
F10 BRICK/BLOCK WALLING - cont'd						
Common bricks; PC £167.20/1000; in gauged						
mortar (1:1:6) - cont'd						
ADD or DEDUCT to walls for variation of						
£10.00/1000 in PC of common bricks						
half brick thick	-	-	-	0.65	m²	0.65
one brick thick	-	-	-	1.29	m²	1.29
one and a half brick thick	-	-	-	1.94	m²	1.94
two brick thick	-	-	-	2.58	m²	2.58
Class A engineering bricks; PC £330.00/1000;						
in cement mortar (1:3)						
Walls						
half brick thick	-	1.10	15.63	22.97	m²	38.60
one brick thick	-	1.80	25.58	45.93	m²	71.51
one brick thick; building against other work	-	2.15	30.55	47.72	m²	78.27
one brick thick; curved; 6.00 m radii	-	2.40	34.10	45.93	m²	80.03
one and a half brick thick	-	2.40	34.10	68.90	m²	103.00
one and a half brick thick; building against other						
work	-	2.90	41.21	68.90	m²	110.11
two brick thick	-	3.00	42.63	91.87	m²	134.50
337 mm average thick; tapering, one side	-	3.10	44.05	68.90	m²	112.95
450 mm average thick; tapering, one side	-	4.00	56.84	91.87	m²	148.71
337 mm average thick; tapering, both sides	-	3.60	51.16	68.90	m²	120.06
450 mm average thick; tapering, both sides	-	4.55	64.66	92.46	m²	157.12
facework one side, half brick thick	-	1.20	17.05	22.97	m²	40.02
facework one side, one brick thick	-	1.90	27.00	45.93	m²	72.93
facework one side, one and a half brick thick	-	2.50	35.52	68.90	m²	104.42
facework one side, two brick thick	-	3.10	44.05	91.87	m²	135.92
facework both sides, half brick thick	-	1.30	18.47	22.97	m²	41.44
facework both sides, one brick thick	-	2.00	28.42	45.93	m²	74.35
facework both sides, one and a half brick thick	-	2.60	36.95	68.90	m²	105.85
facework both sides, two brick thick	-	3.20	45.47	91.87	m²	137.34
Isolated piers						
one brick thick	-	2.80	39.79	45.93	m²	85.72
two brick thick	-	4.40	62.52	92.46	m²	154.98
three brick thick	-	5.40	76.73	138.99	m²	215.72
Isolated casings						
half brick thick	-	1.40	19.89	22.97	m²	42.86
one brick thick	-	2.40	34.10	45.93	m²	80.03
Projections						
225 mm width; 112 mm depth; vertical	-	0.35	4.97	4.92	m	9.89
225 mm width; 225 mm depth; vertical	-	0.65	9.24	9.83	m	19.07
337 mm width; 225 mm depth; vertical	-	0.95	13.50	14.75	m	28.25
440 mm width; 225 mm depth; vertical	-	1.10	15.63	19.66	m	35.29
Bonding to existing						
half brick thick	-	0.35	4.97	1.27	m	6.24
one brick thick	-	0.50	7.11	2.53	m	9.64
one and a half brick thick	-	0.70	9.95	3.80	m	13.75
two brick thick	-	1.05	14.92	5.06	m	19.98
ADD or DEDUCT to walls for variation of						
£10.00/1000 in PC of bricks						
half brick thick	-	-	-	0.65	m²	0.65
one brick thick	-	-	-	1.29	m²	1.29
one and a half brick thick	-	-	-	1.94	m²	1.94
two brick thick	-	-	-	2.58	m²	2.58

F MASONRY Excluding overheads and profit	PC £	Labour hours	Labour £	Material £	Unit	Total rate £
Class B engineering bricks; PC £220.00/1000; **in cement mortar (1:3)**						
Walls						
half brick thick	–	1.10	15.63	15.92	m²	31.55
one brick thick	–	1.80	25.58	31.85	m²	57.43
one brick thick; building against other work	–	2.15	30.55	33.63	m²	64.18
one brick thick; curved; 6.00 m radii	–	2.40	34.10	31.85	m²	65.95
one and a half brick thick	–	2.40	34.10	47.77	m²	81.87
one and a half brick thick; building against other work	–	2.90	41.21	47.77	m²	88.98
two brick thick	–	3.00	42.63	63.69	m²	106.32
337 mm thick; tapering, one side	–	3.10	44.05	47.77	m²	91.82
450 mm thick; tapering, one side	–	4.00	56.84	63.69	m²	120.53
337 mm thick; tapering, both sides	–	3.60	51.16	47.77	m²	98.93
450 mm thick; tapering, both sides	–	4.55	64.66	64.29	m²	128.95
facework one side, half brick thick	–	1.20	17.05	15.92	m²	32.97
facework one side, one brick thick	–	1.90	27.00	31.85	m²	58.85
facework one side, one and a half brick thick	–	2.50	35.52	47.77	m²	83.29
facework one side, two brick thick	–	3.10	44.05	63.69	m²	107.74
facework both sides, half brick thick	–	1.30	18.47	15.92	m²	34.39
facework both sides, one brick thick	–	2.00	28.42	31.85	m²	60.27
facework both sides, one and a half brick thick	–	2.60	36.95	47.77	m²	84.72
facework both sides, two brick thick	–	3.20	45.47	63.69	m²	109.16
Isolated piers						
one brick thick	–	2.80	39.79	31.85	m²	71.64
two brick thick	–	4.40	62.52	64.29	m²	126.81
three brick thick	–	5.40	76.73	96.73	m²	173.46
Isolated casings						
half brick thick	–	1.40	19.89	15.92	m²	35.81
one brick thick	–	2.40	34.10	31.85	m²	65.95
Projections						
225 mm width; 112 mm depth; vertical	–	0.35	4.97	3.35	m	8.32
225 mm width; 225 mm depth; vertical	–	0.65	9.24	6.70	m	15.94
337 mm width; 225 mm depth; vertical	–	0.95	13.50	10.05	m	23.55
440 mm width; 225 mm depth; vertical	–	1.10	15.63	13.40	m	29.03
Bonding to existing						
half brick thick	–	0.35	4.97	0.87	m	5.84
one brick thick	–	0.50	7.11	1.75	m	8.86
one and a half brick thick	–	0.70	9.95	2.62	m	12.57
two brick thick	–	1.05	14.92	3.50	m	18.42
ADD or DEDUCT to walls for variation of £10.00/1000 in PC of bricks						
half brick thick	–	–	–	0.65	m²	0.65
one brick thick	–	–	–	1.29	m²	1.29
one and a half brick thick	–	–	–	1.94	m²	1.94
two brick thick	–	–	–	2.58	m²	2.58

| F MASONRY |
| Excluding overheads and profit |

F10 BRICK/BLOCK WALLING - cont'd

ALTERNATIVE FACING BRICK PRICES (£/1000)

	£		£

Ibstock facing bricks; 215 x 102.50 x 65 mm

Aldridge Brown Blend	314.00	Leicester Anglican Red Rustic	347.00
Ashdown Cottage Mixture	371.00	Leicester Red Stock	353.00
Ashdown Crowbridge Multi	452.00	Roughdales Red Multi Rustic	338.00
Ashdown Pevensey Multi	455.00	Roughdales Trafford Multi Rustic	318.00
Cattybrook Gloucestershire Golden	315.00	Stourbridge Kenilworth Multi	330.00
Chailey Stock	493.00	Stourbridge Pennine Pastone	324.00
Dorking Multi	384.00	Stratfford Red Rustic	245.00
Funton Second Hand Stock	509.00	Swanage Handmade Restoration	541.00
Himley Dark Brown Rustic	358.00	Tonbridge Handmade Multi	586.00
Himley Mixed Russet	305.00		
Holbrook Smooth Red	427.00		

Hanson Brick Ltd, London brand; 215 x 102.50 x 65 mm

Harvest Series		Country Wood Series	
- Autumn leaf	174.90	- Claydon Red Multi	182.60
- Burgundy Red	181.50	- Delph Autumn	176.00
- Dawn Red	182.60	- Longville Stone	177.10
- Hawthron Blend	173.80	- Morteyne Russet	185.90
- Honey Buff	176.00	- Nene Valley Stone	177.10
- Sunset Red	184.80	- Orton Multi Buff	177.10
Sovereign Series		Ridgeway Series	
- Georgian	182.60	- Brecken Grey	179.30
- Regency	195.80	- Ironstone	182.60
- Saxon Gold	198.00	- Milton Buff	191.40
- Tudor	209.00	- Windsor	184.80
Shire Series			
- Chiltern	209.00		
- Heather	209.00		
- Hereward Light	184.80		
- Sandfaced	204.60		

Breacon Hill Brick Company; 215 x 102.50 x 65 mm

Brown Flint Rustic	317.00	Buff Multi CS Textured	317.00
Charcoal Flint Textured	237.00	Dorset Buff Smooth	187.00
Dorset Golden Smooth	227.00	Golden Buff Flint Textured	237.00
Grey Black Flint Textured	237.00	Minster Autumn Gold	197.00
Minster Bracken Mixture	197.00	Minster Mixed Red	217.00
Oatmeal CS Plain	157.00	Oatmeal Flint Textured	192.00
Red Black Multi Flint Plain	317.00	Smoke Grey Multi CS Textured	317.00
Straw Flint Textured	237.00	Warm Brown Multi CS Textured	317.00
Wessex Brindle Buff	217.00	Wessex Brindle Red	217.00
Wessex Red Blend	202.00		

F MASONRY Excluding overheads and profit	PC £	Labour hours	Labour £	Material £	Unit	Total rate £
Facing bricks; sand faced; PC £130.00/1000 (unless otherwise stated); in gauged mortar (1:1:6)						
Walls						
facework one side, half brick thick; stretcher bond	-	1.30	18.47	9.97	m²	**28.44**
facework one side, half brick thick; flemish bond with snapped headers	-	1.50	21.32	9.97	m²	**31.29**
facework one side, half brick thick; stretcher bond; building against other work; concrete	-	1.40	19.89	11.04	m²	**30.93**
facework one side, half brick thick; flemish bond with snapped headers; building against other work; concrete	-	1.60	22.74	11.04	m²	**33.78**
facework one side, half brick thick; stretcher bond; building overhand	-	1.60	22.74	9.97	m²	**32.71**
facework one side, half brick thick; flemish bond with snapped headers; building overhand	-	1.80	25.58	9.97	m²	**35.55**
facework one side, half brick thick; stretcher bond; curved; 6.00 m radii	-	1.90	27.00	9.97	m²	**36.97**
facework one side, half brick thick; flemish bond with snapped headers; curved; 6.00 m radii	-	2.15	30.55	9.97	m²	**40.52**
facework one side, half brick thick; stretcher bond; curved; 1.50 m radii	-	2.40	34.10	9.97	m²	**44.07**
facework one side, half brick thick; flemish bond with snapped headers; curved; 1.50 m radii	-	2.80	39.79	9.97	m²	**49.76**
facework both sides, one brick thick; two stretcher skins tied together	-	2.25	31.97	20.76	m²	**52.73**
facework both sides, one brick thick; flemish bond	-	2.30	32.68	19.95	m²	**52.63**
facework both sides, one brick thick; two stretcher skins tied together; curved; 6.00 m radii	-	3.10	44.05	22.16	m²	**66.21**
facework both sides, one brick thick; flemish bond; curved; 6.00 m radii	-	3.20	45.47	21.35	m²	**66.82**
facework both sides, one brick thick; two stretcher skins tied together; curved; 1.50 m radii	-	3.85	54.71	24.09	m²	**78.80**
facework both sides, one brick thick; flemish bond; curved; 1.50 m radii	-	4.00	56.84	23.28	m²	**80.12**
Isolated piers						
facework both sides, one brick thick; two stretcher skins tied together	-	2.65	37.66	21.23	m²	**58.89**
facework both sides, one brick thick; flemish bond	-	2.70	38.37	21.23	m²	**59.60**
Isolated casings						
facework one side, half brick thick; stretcher bond	-	2.00	28.42	9.97	m²	**38.39**
facework one side, half brick thick; flemish bond with snapped headers	-	2.20	31.26	9.97	m²	**41.23**
Projections						
225 mm width; 112 mm depth; stretcher bond; vertical	-	0.30	4.26	2.05	m²	**6.31**
225 mm width; 112 mm depth; flemish bond with snapped headers; vertical	-	0.40	5.68	2.05	m²	**7.73**
225 mm width; 225 mm depth; flemish bond; vertical	-	0.65	9.24	4.10	m²	**13.34**
328 mm width; 112 mm depth; stretcher bond; vertical	-	0.60	8.53	3.08	m²	**11.61**
328 mm width; 112 mm depth; flemish bond with snapped headers; vertical	-	0.70	9.95	3.08	m²	**13.03**

F MASONRY Excluding overheads and profit	PC £	Labour hours	Labour £	Material £	Unit	Total rate £
F10 BRICK/BLOCK WALLING - cont'd						
Facing bricks; sand faced; PC £130.00/1000 (unless otherwise stated); in gauged mortar (1:1:6) - cont'd						
Projections - cont'd						
328 mm width; 225 mm depth; flemish bond; vertical	-	1.20	17.05	6.12	m²	23.17
440 mm width; 112 mm depth; stretcher bond; vertical	-	0.90	12.79	4.10	m²	16.89
440 mm width; 112 mm depth; flemish bond with snapped headers; vertical	-	0.95	13.50	4.10	m²	17.60
440 mm width; 225 mm depth; flemish bond; vertical	-	1.75	24.87	8.20	m²	33.07
Arches						
height on face 215 mm, width of exposed soffit 102 mm, shape of arch - flat	-	1.00	11.40	3.53	m	14.93
height on face 215 mm, width of exposed soffit 215 mm, shape of arch - flat	-	1.50	18.50	5.68	m	24.18
height on face 215 mm, width of exposed soffit 102 mm, shape of arch - segmental, one ring	-	1.90	20.75	8.06	m	28.81
height on face 215 mm, width of exposed soffit 215 mm, shape of arch - segmental, one ring	-	2.30	26.43	10.11	m	36.54
height on face 215 mm, width of exposed soffit 102 mm, shape of arch - semi-circular, one ring	-	2.90	34.96	8.06	m	43.02
height on face 215 mm, width of exposed soffit 215 mm, shape of arch - semi-circular, one ring	-	3.90	49.17	10.11	m	59.28
height on face 215 mm, width of exposed soffit 102 mm, shape of arch - segmental, two ring	-	2.35	27.14	8.06	m	35.20
height on face 215 mm, width of exposed soffit 215 mm, shape of arch - segmental, two ring	-	3.05	37.09	10.11	m	47.20
height on face 215 mm, width of exposed soffit 102 mm, shape of arch - semi-circular, two ring	-	3.90	49.17	8.06	m	57.23
height on face 215 mm, width of exposed soffit 215 mm, shape of arch - semi-circular, two ring	-	5.40	70.48	10.11	m	80.59
Arches; cut voussoirs; PC £162.00/100						
height on face 215 mm, width of exposed soffit 102 mm, shape of arch - segmental, one ring	-	1.95	21.46	28.34	m	49.80
height on face 215 mm, width of exposed soffit 215 mm, shape of arch - segmental, one ring	-	2.45	28.56	50.67	m	79.23
height on face 215 mm, width of exposed soffit 102 mm, shape of arch - semi-circular, one ring	-	2.20	25.01	28.34	m	53.35
height on face 215 mm, width of exposed soffit 215 mm, shape of arch - semi-circular, one ring	-	2.80	33.54	50.67	m	84.21
height on face 320 mm, width of exposed soffit 102 mm, shape of arch - segmental, one and a half ring	-	2.60	30.70	50.58	m	81.28
height on face 320 mm, width of exposed soffit 215 mm, shape of arch - segmental, one and a half ring	-	3.40	42.06	101.10	m	143.16
Arches; bullnosed specials; PC £103.50/100						
height on face 215 mm, width of exposed soffit 102 mm, shape of arch - flat	-	1.05	12.42	16.50	m	28.92
height on face 215 mm, width of exposed soffit 215 mm, shape of arch - flat	-	1.55	19.53	31.95	m	51.48
Bullseye windows; 600 mm diameter						
height on face 215 mm, width of exposed soffit 102 mm, two rings	-	5.00	64.80	6.63	nr	71.43
height on face 215 mm, width of exposed soffit 215 mm, two rings	-	7.00	93.22	11.19	nr	104.41

F MASONRY Excluding overheads and profit	PC £	Labour hours	Labour £	Material £	Unit	Total rate £
Bullseye windows; 600 mm diameter; cut voussoirs; PC £162.00/100						
height on face 215 mm, width of exposed soffit 102 mm, one ring	-	4.20	53.43	60.83	nr	**114.26**
height on face 215 mm, width of exposed soffit 215 mm, one ring	-	5.80	76.17	119.60	nr	**195.77**
Bullseye windows; 1200 mm diameter						
height on face 215 mm, width of exposed soffit 102 mm, two rings	-	7.80	104.59	16.87	nr	**121.46**
height on face 215 mm, width of exposed soffit 215 mm, two rings	-	11.20	152.90	26.48	nr	**179.38**
Bullseye windows; 1200 mm diameter; cut voussoirs PC £162.00/100						
height on face 215 mm, width of exposed soffit 102 mm, one ring	-	6.60	87.54	109.21	nr	**196.75**
height on face 215 mm, width of exposed soffit 215 mm, one ring	-	9.40	127.32	210.09	nr	**337.41**
ADD or DEDUCT for variation of £10.00/1000 in PC of facing bricks in 102 mm high arches with 215 mm soffit	-	-	-	0.29	m	**0.29**
Facework sills						
150 mm x 102 mm; headers on edge; pointing top and one side; set weathering; horizontal	-	0.55	7.82	2.05	m	**9.87**
150 mm x 102 mm; cant headers on edge; PC £103.50/100; pointing top and one side; set weathering; horizontal	-	0.60	8.53	15.02	m	**23.55**
150 mm x 102 mm; bullnosed specials; PC £103.50/100; headers on flat; pointing top and one side; horizontal	-	0.50	7.11	15.02	m	**22.13**
Facework copings						
215 mm x 102 mm; headers on edge; pointing top and both sides; horizontal	-	0.45	6.39	2.13	m	**8.52**
260 mm x 102 mm; headers on edge; pointing top and both sides; horizontal	-	0.70	9.95	3.13	m	**13.08**
215 mm x 102 mm; double bullnose specials headers on edge PC £103.50/100; pointing top and both sides; horizontal	-	0.50	7.11	15.10	m	**22.21**
260 mm x 102 mm; single bullnose specials headers on edge PC £103.50/100; pointing top and both sides; horizontal	-	0.70	9.95	30.00	m	**39.95**
ADD or DEDUCT for variation of £10.00/1000 in PC of facing bricks in copings 215 mm wide, 102 mm high	-	-	-	0.14	m	**0.14**
Extra over facing bricks for; facework ornamental bands and the like, plain bands; PC £150.00/1000						
flush; horizontal, 225 mm width; entirely of stretchers	-	0.20	2.84	0.29	m	**3.13**
Extra over facing bricks for; facework quoins; PC £150.00/1000						
flush; mean girth 320 mm	-	0.30	4.26	0.29	m	**4.55**
Bonding to existing						
facework one side, half brick thick; stretcher bond	-	0.50	7.11	0.55	m	**7.66**
facework one side, half brick thick; flemish bond with snapped headers	-	0.50	7.11	0.55	m	**7.66**
facework both sides, one brick thick; two stretcher skins tied together	-	0.70	9.95	1.09	m	**11.04**
facework both sides, one brick thick; flemish bond	-	0.70	9.95	1.09	m	**11.04**
ADD or DEDUCT for variation of £10.00/1000 in PC of facing bricks; in walls built entirely of facings; in stretcher or flemish bond						
half brick thick	-	-	-	0.65	m²	**0.65**
one brick thick	-	-	-	1.29	m²	**1.29**

F MASONRY Excluding overheads and profit	PC £	Labour hours	Labour £	Material £	Unit	Total rate £
F10 BRICK/BLOCK WALLING - cont'd						
Facing bricks; white sandlime; PC **£165.00/1000 in gauged mortar (1:1:6)** Walls						
facework one side, half brick thick; stretcher bond	-	1.30	18.47	12.23	m²	**30.70**
facework both sides, one brick thick; flemish bond	-	2.30	32.68	24.46	m²	**57.14**
ADD or DEDUCT for variation of £10.00/1000 in PC of facing bricks; in walls built entirely of facings; in stretcher or flemish bond						
half brick thick	-	-	-	0.65	m²	**0.65**
one brick thick	-	-	-	1.29	m²	**1.29**
Facing bricks; machine made facings; PC **£275.00/1000 (unless otherwise stated); in** **gauged mortar (1:1:6)** Walls						
facework one side, half brick thick; stretcher bond	-	1.30	18.47	19.33	m²	**37.80**
facework one side, half brick thick, flemish bond with snapped headers	-	1.50	21.32	19.33	m²	**40.65**
facework one side, half brick thick, stretcher bond; building against other work; concrete	-	1.40	19.89	20.39	m²	**40.28**
facework one side, half brick thick; flemish bond with snapped headers; building against other work; concrete	-	1.60	22.74	20.39	m²	**43.13**
facework one side, half brick thick, stretcher bond; building overhand	-	1.60	22.74	19.33	m²	**42.07**
facework one side, half brick thick; flemish bond with snapped headers; building overhand	-	1.80	25.58	19.33	m²	**44.91**
facework one side, half brick thick; stretcher bond; curved; 6.00 m radii	-	1.90	27.00	19.33	m²	**46.33**
facework one side, half brick thick; flemish bond with snapped headers; curved; 6.00 m radii	-	2.15	30.55	19.33	m²	**49.88**
facework one side, half brick thick; stretcher bond; curved; 1.50 m radii	-	2.40	34.10	22.28	m²	**56.38**
facework one side, half brick thick; flemish bond with snapped headers; curved; 1.50 m radii	-	2.80	39.79	22.28	m²	**62.07**
facework both sides, one brick thick; two stretcher skins tied together	-	2.25	31.97	39.47	m²	**71.44**
facework both sides, one brick thick; flemish bond	-	2.30	32.68	38.66	m²	**71.34**
facework both sides, one brick thick; two stretcher skins tied together; curved; 6.00 m radii	-	3.10	44.05	42.42	m²	**86.47**
facework both sides, one brick thick; flemish bond; curved; 6.00 m radii	-	3.20	45.47	41.61	m²	**87.08**
facework both sides, one brick thick; two stretcher skins tied together; curved; 1.50 m radii	-	3.85	54.71	45.91	m²	**100.62**
facework both sides, one brick thick; flemish bond; curved; 1.50 m radii	-	4.00	56.84	45.10	m²	**101.94**
Isolated piers						
facework both sides, one brick thick; two stretcher skins tied together	-	2.65	37.66	39.93	m²	**77.59**
facework both sides, one brick thick; flemish bond	-	2.70	38.37	39.93	m²	**78.30**

F MASONRY Excluding overheads and profit	PC £	Labour hours	Labour £	Material £	Unit	Total rate £
Isolated casings						
facework one side, half brick thick; stretcher bond	-	2.00	28.42	19.33	m²	47.75
facework one side, half brick thick; flemish bond with snapped headers	-	2.20	31.26	19.33	m²	50.59
Projections						
225 mm width; 112 mm depth; stretcher bond; vertical	-	0.30	4.26	4.13	m	8.39
225 mm width; 112 mm depth; flemish bond with snapped headers; vertical	-	0.40	5.68	4.13	m	9.81
225 mm width; 225 mm depth; flemish bond; vertical	-	0.65	9.24	8.25	m	17.49
328 mm width; 112 mm depth; stretcher bond; vertical	-	0.60	8.53	6.19	m	14.72
328 mm width; 112 mm depth; flemish bond with snapped headers; vertical	-	0.70	9.95	6.19	m	16.14
328 mm width; 225 mm depth; flemish bond; vertical	-	1.20	17.05	12.35	m	29.40
440 mm width; 112 mm depth; stretcher bond; vertical	-	0.90	12.79	8.25	m	21.04
440 mm width; 112 mm depth; flemish bond with snapped headers; vertical	-	0.95	13.50	8.25	m	21.75
440 mm width; 225 mm depth; flemish bond; vertical	-	1.75	24.87	16.51	m	41.38
Arches						
height on face 215 mm, width of exposed soffit 102 mm, shape of arch - flat	-	1.00	11.71	5.61	m	17.32
height on face 215 mm, width of exposed soffit 215 mm, shape of arch - flat	-	1.50	18.82	9.89	m	28.71
height on face 215 mm, width of exposed soffit 102 mm, shape of arch - segmental, one ring	-	1.90	20.75	10.14	m	30.89
height on face 215 mm, width of exposed soffit 215 mm, shape of arch segmental, one ring	-	2.30	26.43	14.27	m	40.70
height on face 215 mm, width of exposed soffit 102 mm, shape of arch - semi-circular, one ring	-	2.90	34.96	10.14	m	45.10
height on face 215 mm, width of exposed soffit 215 mm, shape of arch - semi-circular, one ring	-	3.90	49.17	14.27	m	63.44
height on face 215 mm, width of exposed soffit 102 mm, shape of arch - segmental, two ring	-	2.35	27.14	10.14	m	37.28
height on face 215 mm, width of exposed soffit 215 mm, shape of arch - segmental; two ring	-	3.05	37.09	14.27	m	51.36
height on face 215 mm, width of exposed soffit 102 mm, shape of arch - semi-circular, two ring	-	3.90	49.17	10.14	m	59.31
height on face 215 mm, width of exposed soffit 215 mm, shape of arch - semi-circular, two ring	-	5.40	70.48	14.27	m	84.75
Arches; cut voussoirs; PC £2570.00/1000						
height on face 215 mm, width of exposed soffit 102 mm, shape of arch - segmental, one ring	-	1.95	21.46	43.03	m	64.49
height on face 215 mm, width of exposed soffit 215 mm, shape of arch - segmental, one ring	-	2.45	28.56	80.06	m	108.62
height on face 215 mm, width of exposed soffit 102 mm, shape of arch - semi-circular, one ring	-	2.20	25.01	43.03	m	68.04
height on face 215 mm, width of exposed soffit 215 mm, shape of arch - semi-circular, one ring	-	2.80	33.54	80.06	m	113.60
height on face 320 mm, width of exposed soffit 102 mm, shape of arch - segmental, one and a half ring	-	2.60	30.70	79.98	m	110.68
height on face 320 mm, width of exposed soffit 215 mm, shape of arch - segmental, one and a half ring	-	3.40	42.06	159.88	m	201.94

F MASONRY Excluding overheads and profit	PC £	Labour hours	Labour £	Material £	Unit	Total rate £
F10 BRICK/BLOCK WALLING - cont'd						
Facing bricks; machine made facings; PC **£275.00/1000 (unless otherwise stated); in** **gauged mortar (1:1:6)** - cont'd						
Arches; bullnosed specials; PC £1186.00/1000						
height on face 215 mm, width of exposed soffit						
102 mm, shape of arch - flat	-	1.05	12.42	18.67	m	31.09
height on face 215 mm, width of exposed soffit						
215 mm, shape of arch - flat	-	1.55	19.53	36.33	m	55.86
Bullseye windows; 600 mm diameter						
height on face 215 mm, width of exposed soffit						
102 mm, two rings	-	5.00	64.80	10.99	nr	75.79
height on face 215 mm, width of exposed soffit						
215 mm, two rings	-	7.00	93.22	19.92	nr	113.14
Bullseye windows; 600 mm; cut voussoirs; PC £2570.00/1000						
height on face 215 mm, width of exposed soffit						
102 mm, one ring	-	4.20	53.43	99.41	nr	152.84
height on face 215 mm, width of exposed soffit						
215 mm, one ring	-	5.80	76.17	196.76	nr	272.93
Bullseye windows; 1200 mm diameter						
height on face 215 mm, width of exposed soffit						
102 mm, two rings	-	7.80	104.59	25.60	nr	130.19
height on face 215 mm, width of exposed soffit						
215 mm, two rings	-	11.20	152.90	43.94	nr	196.84
Bullseye windows; 1200 mm diameter; cut voussoirs; PC £2570.00/1000						
height on face 215 mm, width of exposed soffit						
102 mm, one ring	-	6.60	87.54	175.34	nr	262.88
height on face 215 mm, width of exposed soffit						
215 mm, one ring	-	9.40	127.32	342.36	nr	469.68
ADD or DEDUCT for variation of £10.00/1000 in PC of facing bricks in 102 mm high arches with						
215 mm soffit	-	-	-	0.29	m	0.29
Facework sills						
150 mm x 102 mm; headers on edge; pointing						
top and one side; set weathering; horizontal	-	0.55	7.82	4.13	m	11.95
150 mm x 102 mm; cant headers on edge; PC £1186.00/1000; pointing top and one side; set						
weathering; horizontal	-	0.60	8.53	17.18	m	25.71
150 mm x 102 mm; bullnosed specials; PC £1186.00/1000; headers on flat; pointing top						
and one side; horizontal	-	0.50	7.11	17.18	m	24.29
Facework copings						
215 mm x 102 mm; headers on edge; pointing						
top and both sides; horizontal	-	0.45	6.39	4.21	m	10.60
260 mm x 102 mm; headers on edge; pointing						
top and both sides; horizontal	-	0.70	9.95	6.25	m	16.20
215 mm x 102 mm; double bullnose specials; PC £1186.00/1000; headers on edge; pointing						
top and both sides; horizontal	-	0.50	7.11	17.26	m	24.37
260 mm x 102 mm; single bullnose specials; PC £1186.00/1000; headers on edge; pointing						
top and both sides; horizontal	-	0.70	9.95	34.33	m	44.28
ADD or DEDUCT for variation of £10.00/1000 in PC of facing bricks in copings 215 mm wide,						
102 mm high	-	-	-	0.14	m	0.14

F MASONRY Excluding overheads and profit	PC £	Labour hours	Labour £	Material £	Unit	Total rate £
Extra over facing bricks for; facework ornamental bands and the like, plain bands; PC £305.00/1000						
flush; horizontal; 225 mm width; entirely of stretchers	-	0.20	2.84	0.44	m	3.28
Extra over facing brick for; facework quoins; PC £305.00/1000						
flush; mean girth 320 mm	-	0.30	4.26	0.43	m	4.69
Bonding to existing						
facework one side, half brick thick; stretcher bond	-	0.50	7.11	1.06	m	8.17
facework one side, half brick thick; flemish bond with snapped headers	-	0.50	7.11	1.06	m	8.17
facework both sides, one brick thick; two stretcher skins tied together	-	0.70	9.95	2.13	m	12.08
facework both sides, one brick thick; flemish bond	-	0.70	9.95	2.13	m	12.08
ADD or DEDUCT for variation of £10.00/1000 in PC of facing bricks; in walls built entirely of facings; in stretcher or flemish bond						
half brick thick	-	-	-	0.65	m²	0.65
one brick thick	-	-	-	1.29	m²	1.29
Facing bricks; hand made; PC £450.00/1000 (unless otherwise stated); in gauged mortar (1:1:6)						
Walls						
facework one side, half brick thick; stretcher bond	-	1.30	18.47	30.61	m²	49.08
facework one side, half brick thick; flemish bond with snapped headers	-	1.50	21.32	30.61	m²	51.93
facework one side, half brick thick; stretcher bond; building against other work; concrete	-	1.40	19.89	31.67	m²	51.56
facework one side, half brick thick; flemish bond with snapped headers; building against other work; concrete	-	1.60	22.74	31.67	m²	54.41
facework one side, half brick thick; stretcher bond; building overhand	-	1.60	22.74	30.61	m²	53.35
facework one side, half brick thick; flemish bond with snapped headers; building overhand	-	1.80	25.58	30.61	m²	56.19
facework one side, half brick thick; stretcher bond; curved; 6.00 m radii	-	1.90	27.00	30.61	m²	57.61
facework one side, half brick thick; flemish bond with snapped headers; curved; 6.00 m radii	-	2.15	30.55	34.24	m²	64.79
facework one side, half brick thick; stretcher bond; curved; 1.50 m radii	-	2.40	34.10	30.61	m²	64.71
facework one side, half brick thick; flemish bond with snapped headers; curved; 1.50 m radii	-	2.80	39.79	36.66	m²	76.45
facework both sides, one brick thick; two stretcher skins tied together	-	2.25	31.97	62.04	m²	94.01
facework both sides, one brick thick; flemish bond	-	2.30	32.68	61.23	m²	93.91
facework both sides; one brick thick; two stretcher skins tied together; curved; 6.00 m radii	-	3.10	44.05	66.88	m²	110.93
facework both sides, one brick thick; flemish bond; curved; 6.00 m radii	-	3.20	45.47	66.07	m²	111.54
facework both sides, one brick thick; two stretcher skins tied together; curved; 1.50 m radii	-	3.85	54.71	72.25	m²	126.96
facework both sides, one brick thick; flemish bond; curved; 1.50 m radii	-	4.00	56.84	71.43	m²	128.27

F MASONRY Excluding overheads and profit	PC £	Labour hours	Labour £	Material £	Unit	Total rate £
F10 BRICK/BLOCK WALLING - cont'd						
Facing bricks; hand made; PC £450.00/1000 **(unless otherwise stated); in gauged mortar** **(1:1:6)** - cont'd						
Isolated piers						
facework both sides, one brick thick; two						
stretcher skins tied together	-	2.65	37.66	62.51	m²	**100.17**
facework both sides, one brick thick; flemish						
bond	-	2.70	38.37	62.51	m²	**100.88**
Isolated casings						
facework one side, half brick thick; stretcher						
bond	-	2.00	28.42	30.61	m²	**59.03**
facework one side, half brick thick; flemish						
bond with snapped headers	-	2.20	31.26	30.61	m²	**61.87**
Projections						
225 mm width; 112 mm depth; stretcher bond;						
vertical	-	0.30	4.26	6.64	m	**10.90**
225 mm width; 112 mm depth; flemish bond						
with snapped headers; vertical	-	0.40	5.68	6.64	m	**12.32**
225 mm width; 225 mm depth; flemish bond;						
vertical	-	0.65	9.24	13.27	m	**22.51**
328 mm width; 112 mm depth; stretcher bond;						
vertical	-	0.60	8.53	9.96	m	**18.49**
328 mm width; 112 mm depth; flemish bond						
with snapped headers; vertical	-	0.70	9.95	9.96	m	**19.91**
328 mm width; 225 mm depth; flemish bond;						
vertical	-	1.20	17.05	19.88	m	**36.93**
440 mm width; 112 mm depth; stretcher bond;						
vertical	-	0.90	12.79	13.27	m	**26.06**
440 mm width; 112 mm depth; flemish bond						
with snapped headers; vertical	-	0.95	13.50	13.27	m	**26.77**
440 mm width; 225 mm depth; flemish bond;						
vertical	-	1.75	24.87	26.54	m	**51.41**
Arches						
height on face 215 mm, width of exposed soffit						
102 mm, shape of arch - flat	-	1.00	11.71	8.12	m	**19.83**
height on face 215 mm, width of exposed soffit						
215 mm, shape of arch - flat	-	1.50	18.82	14.97	m	**33.79**
height on face 215 mm, width of exposed soffit						
102 mm, shape of arch - segmental, one ring	-	1.90	20.75	12.65	m	**33.40**
height on face 215 mm, width of exposed soffit						
215 mm, shape of arch - segmental, one ring	-	2.30	26.43	19.29	m	**45.72**
height on face 215 mm, width of exposed soffit						
102 mm, shape of arch - semi-circular, one ring	-	2.90	34.96	12.65	m	**47.61**
height on face 215 mm, width of exposed soffit						
215 mm, shape of arch - semi-circular, one ring	-	3.90	49.17	19.29	m	**68.46**
height on face 215 mm, width of exposed soffit						
102 mm, shape of arch - segmental, two ring	-	2.35	27.14	12.65	m	**39.79**
height on face 215 mm, width of exposed soffit						
215 mm, shape of arch - segmental, two ring	-	3.05	37.09	19.29	m	**56.38**
height on face 215 mm, width of exposed soffit						
102 mm, shape of arch - semi-circular, two ring	-	3.90	49.17	12.65	m	**61.82**
height on face 215 mm, width of exposed soffit						
215 mm, shape of arch - semi-circular, two ring	-	5.40	70.48	19.29	m	**89.77**
Arches; cut voussoirs; PC £2520.00/1000						
height on face 215 mm, width of exposed soffit						
102 mm, shape of arch - segmental, one ring	-	1.95	21.46	42.32	m	**63.78**
height on face 215 mm, width of exposed soffit						
215 mm, shape of arch - segmental, one ring	-	2.45	28.56	78.63	m	**107.19**
height on face 215 mm, width of exposed soffit						
102 mm, shape of arch - semi-circular, one ring	-	2.20	25.01	42.32	m	**67.33**

F MASONRY Excluding overheads and profit	PC £	Labour hours	Labour £	Material £	Unit	Total rate £
Arches; cut voussoirs; PC £2520.00/1000 - cont'd						
height one face 215 mm, width of exposed soffit 215 mm, shape of - arch semi-circular, one ring	-	2.80	33.54	78.63	m	112.17
height on face 320 mm, width of exposed soffit 102 mm, shape of arch - segmental, one and a half ring	-	2.60	30.70	78.54	m	109.24
height on face 320 mm, width of exposed soffit 215 mm, shape of arch - segmental, one and a half ring	-	3.40	42.06	157.02	m	199.08
Arches; bullnosed specials; PC £1160.00/1000						
height on face 215 mm, width of exposed soffit 102 mm, shape of arch - flat	-	1.05	12.42	18.30	m	30.72
height on face 215 mm, width of exposed soffit 215 mm, shape of arch - flat	-	1.55	19.53	35.58	m	55.11
Bullseye windows; 600 mm diameter						
height on face 215 mm, width of exposed soffit 102 mm, two ring	-	5.00	64.80	16.26	nr	81.06
height on face 215 mm, width of exposed soffit 215 mm, two ring	-	7.00	93.22	40.00	nr	133.22
Bullseye windows; 600 mm diameter; cut voussoirs; PC £2520.00/1000						
height on face 215 mm, width of exposed soffit 102 mm, one ring	-	4.20	53.43	97.53	nr	150.96
height on face 215 mm, width of exposed soffit 215 mm, one ring	-	5.80	76.17	193.00	nr	269.17
Bullseye windows; 1200 mm diameter						
height on face 215 mm, width of exposed soffit 102 mm, two ring	-	7.80	104.59	36.14	nr	140.73
height on face 215 mm, width of exposed soffit 215 mm, two ring	-	11.20	152.90	65.01	nr	217.91
Bullseye windows; 1200 mm diameter; cut voussoirs; PC £2520.00/1000						
height on face 215 mm, width of exposed soffit 102 mm, one ring	-	6.60	87.54	172.12	nr	259.66
height on face 215 mm, width of exposed soffit 215 mm, one ring	-	9.40	127.32	335.91	nr	463.23
ADD or DEDUCT for variation of £10.00/1000 in PC of facing bricks in 102 mm high arches with 215 mm soffit	-	-	-	0.29	m	0.29
Facework sills						
150 mm x 102 mm; headers on edge; pointing top and one side; set weathering; horizontal	-	0.55	7.82	6.64	m	14.46
150 mm x 102 mm; cant headers on edge; PC £1160.00/1000; pointing top and one side; set weathering; horizontal	-	0.60	8.53	16.81	m	25.34
150 mm x 102 mm; bullnosed specials; PC £1160.00/1000; headers on flat; pointing top and one side; horizontal	-	0.50	7.11	16.81	m	23.92
Facework copings						
215 mm x 102 mm; headers on edge; pointing top and both sides; horizontal	-	0.45	6.39	6.71	m	13.10
260 mm x 102 mm; headers on edge; pointing top and both sides; horizontal	-	0.70	9.95	10.01	m	19.96
215 mm x 102 mm; double bullnose specials; PC £1160.00/1000; headers on edge; pointing top and both sides; horizontal	-	0.50	7.11	16.89	m	24.00
260 mm x 102 mm; single bullnose specials; PC £1160.00/1000; headers on edge; pointing top and both sides; horizontal	-	0.70	9.95	33.59	m	43.54
ADD or DEDUCT for variation of £10.00/1000 in PC of facing bricks in copings 215 mm wide, 102 mm high	-	-	-	0.14	m	0.14

F MASONRY Excluding overheads and profit	PC £	Labour hours	Labour £	Material £	Unit	Total rate £
F10 BRICK/BLOCK WALLING - cont'd						
Facing bricks; hand made; PC £450.00/1000 (unless otherwise stated); in gauged mortar (1:1:6) - cont'd						
Extra over facing bricks for; facework ornamental bands and the like, plain bands; PC £490.00/1000						
flush; horizontal; 225 mm width; entirely of stretchers	-	0.20	2.84	0.57	m	**3.41**
Extra over facing bricks for; facework quoins; PC £490.00/1000						
flush mean girth 320 mm	-	0.30	4.26	0.57	m	**4.83**
Bonding ends to existing						
facework one side, half brick thick; stretcher bond	-	0.50	7.11	1.69	m	**8.80**
facework one side, half brick thick; flemish bond with snapped headers	-	0.50	7.11	1.69	m	**8.80**
facework both sides, one brick thick; two stretcher skins tied together	-	0.70	9.95	3.38	m	**13.33**
facework both sides, one brick thick; flemish bond	-	0.70	9.95	3.38	m	**13.33**
ADD or DEDUCT for variation of £10.00/1000 in PC of facing bricks; in walls built entirely of facings; in stretcher or flemish bond						
half brick thick	-	-	-	0.65	m²	**0.65**
one brick thick	-	-	-	1.29	m²	**1.29**
Facing bricks; slips 50 mm thick; PC £1050.00/1000; in gauged mortar (1:1:6) built up against concrete including flushing up at back (ties not included)						
Walls	-	2.00	28.42	69.27	m²	**97.69**
Edges of suspended slabs; 200 mm wide	-	0.60	8.53	13.85	m	**22.38**
Columns; 400 mm wide	-	1.20	17.05	27.71	m	**44.76**
Engineering bricks; PC £330.00/1000; and specials at PC £1186.00/1000; in cement mortar (1:3)						
Facework steps						
215 mm x 102 mm; all headers-on-edge; edges set with bullnosed specials; pointing top and one side; set weathering; horizontal	-	0.55	7.82	17.21	m	**25.03**
returned ends pointed	-	0.15	2.13	3.16	nr	**5.29**
430 mm x 102 mm; all headers-on-edge; edges set with bullnosed specials; pointing top and one side; set weathering; horizontal	-	0.80	11.37	22.12	m	**33.49**
returned ends pointed	-	0.20	2.84	3.98	nr	**6.82**

F MASONRY
Excluding overheads and profit

ALTERNATIVE BLOCK PRICES (£/m²)

Aerated concrete Durox "Supablocs"; 630 x 225 mm

	£		£		£
100 mm	7.20	140 mm	11.70	215 mm	17.15
130 mm	10.15	150 mm	12.00		

Hanson Conbloc blocks; 450 x 225 mm
Cream fair faced

	£		£		£
100 mm hollow	6.75	140 mm solid	11.03	215 mm hollow	13.70
100 mm solid	7.31	190 mm hollow	13.16		
140 mm hollow	9.32	190 mm solid	14.53		

"Fenlite"

100 mm solid; 3.5 N/mm²	5.27	100 mm solid; 7.00 N/mm²	5.54	140 mm solid; 3.50 N/mm²	7.64

Standard Dense

100 mm solid	5.10	140 mm hollow	7.20	190mm solid	10.00
140 mm solid	7.47	190 mm hollow	10.30	215mm hollow	9.82

Celcon "Standard" blocks; 450 x 225 mm

100 mm	7.55	140 mm	10.57	
125 mm	9.44	215 mm	16.23	

Forticrete painting quality blocks; 450 x 225 mm

100 mm solid	10.51	140 mm hollow	13.03	215 mm solid	21.82
100 mm hollow	9.44	190 mm solid	10.84	215 mm hollow	18.15
140 mm solid	15.21	190 mm hollow	17.30		

Tarmac "Topblocks"; 450 x 225 mm
3.50 N/mm² "Hemelite" blocks

100 mm solid	4.41	190 mm solid	9.04	215 mm solid	9.72

7.00 N/mm² "Hemelite" blocks

100 mm solid	4.73	190 mm solid	9.70	
140mm solid	6.78	215mm solid	10.43	

"Toplite" standard blocks

100 mm	6.77	150 mm	10.15	
140mm	9.48	215mm	14.57	

"Toplite" GTI (thermal) blocks

115 mm	8.03	130 mm	9.08	150 mm	10.48
125 mm	8.73	140 mm	9.78	215 mm	15.02

Discount of 0 - 20% available depending on quantity / status.

F MASONRY Excluding overheads and profit	PC £	Labour hours	Labour £	Material £	Unit	Total rate £
Lightweight aerated concrete blocks; **Thermalite "Shield"/"Turbo" blocks or** **other equal and approved; in gauged** **mortar (1:2:9)** Walls						
75 mm thick	4.90	0.45	6.39	5.65	m²	**12.04**
90 mm thick	5.89	0.45	6.39	6.79	m²	**13.18**
100 mm thick	6.53	0.50	7.11	7.53	m²	**14.64**
115 mm thick	7.80	0.50	7.11	8.97	m²	**16.08**
125 mm thick	8.49	0.50	7.11	9.76	m²	**16.87**
130 mm thick	8.82	0.50	7.11	10.14	m²	**17.25**
140 mm thick	9.50	0.55	7.82	10.93	m²	**18.75**
150 mm thick	10.19	0.55	7.82	11.72	m²	**19.54**
190 mm thick	12.90	0.60	8.53	14.84	m²	**23.37**
200 mm thick	13.57	0.60	8.53	15.61	m²	**24.14**
215 mm thick	14.59	0.60	8.53	16.78	m²	**25.31**
255 mm thick	17.99	0.75	10.66	20.66	m²	**31.32**

F MASONRY Excluding overheads and profit	PC £	Labour hours	Labour £	Material £	Unit	Total rate £
F10 BRICK/BLOCK WALLING - cont'd						
Lightweight aerated concrete blocks; Thermalite **"Shield"/"Turbo" blocks or other equal and approved;** **in gauged mortar (1:2:9)** - cont'd						
Isolated piers or chimney stacks						
190 mm thick	-	0.90	12.79	14.84	m²	27.63
215 mm thick	-	0.90	12.79	16.78	m²	29.57
255 mm thick	-	1.00	14.21	20.66	m²	34.87
Isolated casings						
75 mm thick	-	0.55	7.82	5.65	m²	13.47
90 mm thick	-	0.55	7.82	6.79	m²	14.61
100 mm thick	-	0.55	7.82	7.53	m²	15.35
115 mm thick	-	0.55	7.82	8.97	m²	16.79
125 mm thick	-	0.55	7.82	9.76	m²	17.58
140 mm thick	-	0.60	8.53	10.93	m²	19.46
Extra over for fair face; flush pointing						
walls; one side	-	0.05	0.71	-	m²	0.71
walls; both sides	-	0.10	1.42	-	m²	1.42
Closing cavities						
width of cavity 50 mm, closing with lightweight blockwork 100 mm thick; vertical	-	0.25	3.55	0.42	m	3.97
width of cavity 50 mm, closing with lightweight blockwork 100 mm thick; including damp proof course; vertical	-	0.30	4.26	1.15	m	5.41
width of cavity 75 mm, closing with lightweight blockwork 100 mm thick; vertical	-	0.25	3.55	0.61	m	4.16
width of cavity 75 mm, closing with lightweight blockwork 100 mm thick; including damp proof course; vertical	-	0.30	4.26	1.33	m	5.59
Bonding ends to common brickwork						
75 mm thick	-	0.10	1.42	0.65	m	2.07
90 mm thick	-	0.10	1.42	0.78	m	2.20
100 mm thick	-	0.15	2.13	0.86	m	2.99
115 mm thick	-	0.15	2.13	1.03	m	3.16
125 mm thick	-	0.25	3.55	1.12	m	4.67
130 mm thick	-	0.25	3.55	1.17	m	4.72
140 mm thick	-	0.25	3.55	1.26	m	4.81
150 mm thick	-	0.25	3.55	1.35	m	4.90
190 mm thick	-	0.30	4.26	1.70	m	5.96
200 mm thick	-	0.30	4.26	1.80	m	6.06
215 mm thick	-	0.35	4.97	1.94	m	6.91
255 mm thick	-	0.35	4.97	2.38	m	7.35
Lightweight smooth face aerated concrete blocks; **Thermalite "Smooth Face" blocks or other equal and** **approved; in gauged mortar (1:2:9); flush pointing** **one side**						
Walls						
100 mm thick	11.48	0.60	8.53	12.97	m²	21.50
140 mm thick	16.07	0.70	9.95	18.15	m²	28.10
150 mm thick	17.23	0.70	9.95	19.46	m²	29.41
190 mm thick	21.82	0.80	11.37	24.65	m²	36.02
200 mm thick	22.97	0.80	11.37	25.95	m²	37.32
215 mm thick	24.70	0.80	11.37	27.90	m²	39.27
Isolated piers or chimney stacks						
190 mm thick	-	1.00	14.21	24.65	m²	38.86
200 mm thick	-	1.00	14.21	25.95	m²	40.16
215 mm thick	-	1.00	14.21	27.90	m²	42.11

F MASONRY Excluding overheads and profit	PC £	Labour hours	Labour £	Material £	Unit	Total rate £
Isolated casings						
100 mm thick	-	0.75	10.66	12.97	m²	**23.63**
140 mm thick	-	0.80	11.37	18.15	m²	**29.52**
Extra over for fair face flush pointing						
walls; both sides	-	0.05	0.71	-	m²	**0.71**
Bonding ends to common brickwork						
100 mm thick	-	0.25	3.55	1.47	m	**5.02**
140 mm thick	-	0.25	3.55	2.07	m	**5.62**
150 mm thick	-	0.30	4.26	2.21	m	**6.47**
190 mm thick	-	0.35	4.97	2.79	m	**7.76**
200 mm thick	-	0.35	4.97	2.95	m	**7.92**
215 mm thick	-	0.35	4.97	3.17	m	**8.14**
Lightweight aerated high strength concrete block						
(7.00 N/mm²); Thermalite "High Strength" blocks or						
other equal and approved; in cement mortar (1:3)						
Walls						
100 mm thick	8.31	0.50	7.11	9.54	m²	**16.65**
140 mm thick	11.63	0.55	7.82	13.35	m²	**21.17**
150 mm thick	12.46	0.55	7.82	14.30	m²	**22.12**
190 mm thick	15.78	0.60	8.53	18.11	m²	**26.64**
200 mm thick	16.61	0.60	8.53	19.06	m²	**27.59**
215 mm thick	17.85	0.60	8.53	20.49	m²	**29.02**
Isolated piers or chimney stacks						
190 mm thick	-	0.90	12.79	18.11	m²	**30.90**
200 mm thick	-	0.90	12.79	19.06	m²	**31.85**
215 mm thick	-	0.90	12.79	20.49	m²	**33.28**
Isolated casings						
100 mm thick	-	0.55	7.82	9.54	m²	**17.36**
140 mm thick	-	0.60	8.53	13.35	m²	**21.88**
150 mm thick	-	0.60	8.53	14.30	m²	**22.83**
190 mm thick	-	0.75	10.66	18.11	m²	**28.77**
200 mm thick	-	0.75	10.66	19.06	m²	**29.72**
215 mm thick	-	0.75	10.66	20.49	m²	**31.15**
Extra over for flush pointing						
walls; one side	-	0.05	0.71	-	m²	**0.71**
walls; both sides	-	0.10	1.42	-	m²	**1.42**
Bonding ends to common brickwork						
100 mm thick	-	0.25	3.55	1.09	m	**4.64**
140 mm thick	-	0.25	3.55	1.54	m	**5.09**
150 mm thick	-	0.30	4.26	1.64	m	**5.90**
190 mm thick	-	0.35	4.97	2.08	m	**7.05**
200 mm thick	-	0.35	4.97	2.19	m	**7.16**
215 mm thick	-	0.35	4.97	2.36	m	**7.33**
Dense aggregate concrete blocks; "ARC						
Conbloc" or other equal and approved; in						
gauged mortar (1:2:9)						
Walls						
75 mm thick; solid	4.33	0.60	8.53	5.02	m²	**13.55**
100 mm thick; solid	4.81	0.75	10.66	5.63	m²	**16.29**
140 mm thick; solid	9.44	0.90	12.80	10.86	m²	**23.66**
140 mm thick; hollow	9.07	0.80	11.38	10.45	m²	**21.83**
190 mm thick; hollow	10.71	1.00	14.22	12.43	m²	**26.65**
215 mm thick; hollow	11.15	1.10	15.64	13.00	m²	**28.64**
Isolated piers or chimney stacks						
140 mm thick; hollow	-	1.10	15.64	10.45	m²	**26.09**
190 mm thick; hollow	-	1.45	20.62	12.43	m²	**33.05**
215 mm thick; hollow	-	1.65	23.46	13.00	m²	**36.46**

F MASONRY Excluding overheads and profit	PC £	Labour hours	Labour £	Material £	Unit	Total rate £
F10 BRICK/BLOCK WALLING - cont'd						
Dense aggregate concrete blocks; "ARC						
Conbloc" or other equal and approved; in						
gauged mortar (1:2:9) - cont'd						
Isolated casings						
75 mm thick; solid	-	0.75	10.66	5.02	m²	15.68
100 mm thick; solid	-	0.80	11.38	5.63	m²	17.01
140 mm thick; solid	-	1.00	14.22	10.86	m²	25.08
Extra over for fair face; flush pointing						
walls; one side	-	0.10	1.42	-	m²	1.42
walls; both sides	-	0.15	2.13	-	m²	2.13
Bonding ends to common brickwork						
75 mm thick solid	-	0.15	2.13	0.58	m	2.71
100 mm thick solid	-	0.25	3.56	0.65	m	4.21
140 mm thick solid	-	0.30	4.27	1.26	m	5.53
140 mm thick hollow	-	0.30	4.27	1.21	m	5.48
190 mm thick hollow	-	0.35	4.98	1.44	m	6.42
215 mm thick hollow	-	0.40	5.69	1.52	m	7.21
Dense aggregate concrete blocks; (7.00 N/mm²)						
Forticrete "Shepton Mallet Common" blocks or						
other equal and approved; in cement mortar (1:3)						
Walls						
75 mm thick; solid	6.41	0.60	8.53	7.35	m²	15.88
100 mm thick; hollow	7.48	0.75	10.66	8.63	m²	19.29
100 mm thick; solid	4.83	0.75	10.66	5.71	m²	16.37
140 mm thick; hollow	10.33	0.80	11.38	11.92	m²	23.30
140 mm thick; solid	7.40	0.90	12.80	8.69	m²	21.49
190 mm thick; hollow	13.71	1.00	14.22	15.83	m²	30.05
190 mm thick; solid	10.11	1.10	15.64	11.87	m²	27.51
215 mm thick; hollow	10.90	1.10	15.64	12.84	m²	28.48
215 mm thick; solid	10.78	1.25	17.77	12.71	m²	30.48
Dwarf support wall						
140 mm thick; solid	-	1.25	17.77	8.69	m²	26.46
190 mm thick; solid	-	1.45	20.62	11.87	m²	32.49
215 mm thick; solid	-	1.65	23.46	12.71	m²	36.17
Isolated piers or chimney stacks						
140 mm thick; hollow	-	1.10	15.64	11.92	m²	27.56
190 mm thick; hollow	-	1.45	20.62	15.83	m²	36.45
215 mm thick; hollow	-	1.65	23.46	12.84	m²	36.30
Isolated casings						
75 mm thick; solid	-	0.75	10.66	7.35	m²	18.01
100 mm thick; solid	-	0.80	11.38	5.71	m²	17.09
140 mm thick; solid	-	1.00	14.22	8.69	m²	22.91
Extra over for fair face; flush pointing						
walls; one side	-	0.10	1.42	-	m²	1.42
walls; both sides	-	0.15	2.13	-	m²	2.13
Bonding ends to common brickwork						
75 mm thick solid	-	0.15	2.13	0.83	m	2.96
100 mm thick solid	-	0.25	3.56	0.66	m	4.22
140 mm thick solid	-	0.30	4.27	1.01	m	5.28
190 mm thick solid	-	0.35	4.98	1.36	m	6.34
215 mm thick solid	-	0.40	5.69	1.47	m	7.16

F MASONRY Excluding overheads and profit	PC £	Labour hours	Labour £	Material £	Unit	Total rate £
Dense aggregate coloured concrete blocks; **Forticrete "Shepton Mallet Bathstone" or other** **equal and approved; in coloured gauged mortar** **(1:1:6); flush pointing one side**						
Walls						
100 mm thick hollow	16.69	0.80	11.38	17.97	m²	**29.35**
100 mm thick solid	20.22	0.80	11.38	21.68	m²	**33.06**
140 mm thick hollow	21.97	0.90	12.80	23.69	m²	**36.49**
140 mm thick solid	29.46	1.00	14.22	31.55	m²	**45.77**
190 mm thick hollow	27.92	1.10	15.64	30.15	m²	**45.79**
190 mm thick solid	40.45	1.25	17.77	43.31	m²	**61.08**
215 mm thick hollow	29.47	1.25	17.77	31.89	m²	**49.66**
215 mm thick solid	42.87	1.30	18.49	45.96	m²	**64.45**
Isolated piers or chimney stacks						
140 mm thick solid	-	1.35	19.20	31.55	m²	**50.75**
190 mm thick solid	-	1.50	21.33	43.31	m²	**64.64**
215 mm thick solid	-	1.70	24.17	45.96	m²	**70.13**
Extra over blocks for						
100 mm thick half lintel blocks; ref D14	-	0.25	3.56	16.57	m	**20.13**
140 mm thick half lintel blocks; ref H14	-	0.30	4.27	20.98	m	**25.25**
140 mm thick quoin blocks; ref H16	-	0.35	4.98	24.15	m	**29.13**
140 mm thick cavity closer blocks; ref H17	-	0.35	4.98	28.98	m	**33.96**
140 mm thick cill blocks; ref H21	-	0.30	4.27	17.20	m	**21.47**
190 mm thick half lintel blocks; ref A14	-	0.35	4.98	24.04	m	**29.02**
190 mm thick cill blocks; ref A21	-	0.35	4.98	17.89	m	**22.87**
"Astra-Glaze" satin-gloss glazed finish blocks or **other equal and approved; Forticrete Ltd;** **standard colours; in gauged mortar (1:1:6); joints** **raked out; gun applied latex grout to joints**						
Walls or partitions or skins of hollow walls						
100 mm thick; glazed one side	69.25	1.00	14.22	73.07	m²	**87.29**
extra; glazed square end return	9.14	0.40	5.69	23.27	m	**28.96**
150 mm thick; glazed one side	77.00	1.10	15.64	81.38	m²	**97.02**
extra; glazed square end return	14.69	0.50	7.11	48.59	m	**55.70**
200 mm thick; glazed one side	85.37	1.25	17.77	90.34	m²	**108.11**
extra; glazed square end return	-	0.55	7.82	69.34	m	**77.16**
100 mm thick; glazed both sides	99.00	1.20	17.06	104.31	m²	**121.37**
150 mm thick; glazed both sides	107.00	1.30	18.49	112.88	m²	**131.37**
100 mm thick lintel 200 mm high; glazed one side	-	0.90	9.67	19.77	m	**29.44**
150 mm thick lintel 200 mm high; glazed one side	-	1.00	11.09	23.97	m	**35.06**
200 mm thick lintel 200 mm high; glazed one side	-	1.35	14.50	22.99	m	**37.49**

F MASONRY Excluding overheads and profit	PC £	Labour hours	Labour £	Material £	Unit	Total rate £
F11 GLASS BLOCK WALLING						
NOTE: The following specialist prices for glass block walling assume standard blocks; panels of 50 m²; no fire rating; work in straight walls at ground level; and all necessary ancillary fixing; strengthening; easy access; pointing and expansion materials etc.						
Hollow glass block walling; Luxcrete sealed "Luxblocks" or other equal and approved; in cement mortar "Luxfix" joints or other equal and approved; reinforced with 6 mm diameter stainless steel rods; with "Luxfibre" or other equal and approved at head and jambs; pointed both sides with "Luxseal" mastic or other equal and approved						
Walls; facework both sides						
115 mm x 115 mm x 80 mm flemish blocks	-	-	-	-	m²	459.80
190 mm x 190 mm x 80 mm flemish; cross reeded or clear blocks	-	-	-	-	m²	214.22
240 mm x 240 mm x 80 mm flemish; cross reeded or clear blocks	-	-	-	-	m²	203.78
240 mm x 115 mm x 80 mm flemish or clear blocks	-	-	-	-	m²	323.95
F20 NATURAL STONE RUBBLE WALLING						
Cotswold Guiting limestone or other equal and approved; laid dry						
Uncoursed random rubble walling						
275 mm thick		2.24	29.14	28.04	m²	57.98
350 mm thick	-	2.66	34.33	36.69	m²	71.02
425 mm thick	-	3.03	38.81	44.56	m²	83.37
500 mm thick	-	3.40	43.28	52.43	m²	95.71
Cotswold Guiting limestone or other equal and approved; bedded; jointed and pointed in cement:lime mortar (1:2:9)						
Uncoursed random rubble walling; faced and pointed; both sides						
275 mm thick	-	2.14	27.70	31.94	m²	59.64
350 mm thick	-	2.36	30.01	40.64	m²	70.65
425 mm thick	-	2.58	32.32	49.35	m²	81.67
500 mm thick	-	2.80	34.64	58.06	m²	92.70
Coursed random rubble walling; rough dressed; faced and pointed one side						
114 mm thick	-	1.60	21.90	40.03	m²	61.93
150 mm thick	-	1.90	26.24	44.21	m²	70.45
Fair returns on walling						
114 mm wide	-	0.03	0.43	-	m	0.43
150 mm wide	-	0.04	0.57	-	m	0.57
275 mm wide	-	0.07	0.99	-	m	0.99
350 mm wide	-	0.09	1.28	-	m	1.28
425 mm wide	-	0.11	1.56	-	m	1.56
500 mm wide	-	0.13	1.85	-	m	1.85
Fair raking cutting or circular cutting						
114 mm thick	-	0.22	3.13	5.81	m	8.94
150 mm thick	-	0.27	3.84	6.38	m	10.22

F MASONRY Excluding overheads and profit	PC £	Labour hours	Labour £	Material £	Unit	Total rate £
Level uncoursed rubble walling for damp proof courses and the like						
275 mm wide	-	0.21	3.03	2.09	m	5.12
350 mm wide	-	0.22	3.17	2.61	m	5.78
425 mm wide	-	0.23	3.31	3.18	m	6.49
500 mm wide	-	0.24	3.46	3.76	m	7.22
Copings formed of rough stones; faced and pointed all round						
275 mm x 200 mm (average) high	-	0.60	8.00	7.55	m	15.55
350 mm x 250 mm (average) high	-	0.81	10.67	10.50	m	21.17
425 mm x 300 mm (average) high	-	1.05	13.70	14.51	m	28.21
500 mm x 300 mm (average) high	-	1.33	17.17	19.59	m	36.76
F22 CAST STONE ASHLAR WALLING DRESSINGS						
Reconstructed limestone walling; Bradstone 100 bed weathered "Cotswold" or "North Cerney" masonry blocks or other equal and approved; laid to pattern or course recommended; bedded; jointed and pointed in approved coloured cement:lime mortar (1:2:9)						
Walls; facing and pointing one side						
masonry blocks; random uncoursed	-	1.12	15.92	20.58	m²	36.50
extra; returned ends	-	0.40	5.68	22.04	m	27.72
extra; plain L shaped quoins	-	0.13	1.85	7.53	m	9.38
traditional walling; coursed squared	-	1.40	19.89	20.58	m²	40.47
squared random rubble	-	1.40	19.89	22.81	m²	42.70
squared coursed rubble (large module)	-	1.30	18.47	22.67	m²	41.14
squared coursed rubble (small module)	-	1.35	19.18	22.94	m²	42.12
squared and pitched rock faced walling; coursed	-	1.45	20.60	21.39	m²	41.99
rough hewn rockfaced walling; random	-	1.50	21.32	21.25	m²	42.57
extra; returned ends	-	0.16	2.27	-	m	2.27
Isolated piers or chimney stacks; facing and pointing one side						
masonry blocks; random uncoursed	-	1.55	22.03	20.58	m²	42.61
traditional walling; coursed squared	-	1.95	27.71	20.58	m²	48.29
squared random rubble	-	1.95	27.71	22.81	m²	50.52
squared coursed rubble (large module)	-	1.80	25.58	22.67	m²	48.25
squared coursed rubble (small module)	-	1.90	27.00	22.94	m²	49.94
squared and pitched rock faced walling; coursed	-	2.05	29.13	21.39	m²	50.52
rough hewn rockfaced walling; random	-	2.10	29.84	21.25	m²	51.09
Isolated casings; facing and pointing one side						
masonry blocks; random uncoursed	-	1.35	19.18	20.58	m²	39.76
traditional walling; coursed squared	-	1.70	24.16	20.58	m²	44.74
squared random rubble	-	1.70	24.16	22.81	m²	46.97
squared coursed rubble (large module)	-	1.55	22.03	22.67	m²	44.70
squared coursed rubble (small module)	-	1.65	23.45	22.94	m²	46.39
squared and pitched rock faced walling; coursed	-	1.75	24.87	21.39	m²	46.26
rough hewn rockfaced walling; random	-	1.80	25.58	21.25	m²	46.83
Fair returns 100 mm wide						
masonry blocks; random uncoursed	-	0.12	1.71	-	m²	1.71
traditional walling; coursed squared	-	0.15	2.13	-	m²	2.13
squared random rubble	-	0.15	2.13	-	m²	2.13
squared coursed rubble (large module)	-	0.14	1.99	-	m²	1.99
squared coursed rubble (small module)	-	0.14	1.99	-	m²	1.99
squared and pitched rock faced walling; coursed	-	0.15	2.13	-	m²	2.13
rough hewn rockfaced walling; random	-	0.16	2.27	-	m²	2.27
Fair raking cutting or circular cutting						
100 mm wide	-	0.18	2.56	-	m	2.56

F MASONRY Excluding overheads and profit	PC £	Labour hours	Labour £	Material £	Unit	Total rate £
F22 CAST STONE ASHLAR WALLING DRESSINGS - cont'd						
Reconstructed limestone dressings; "Bradstone Architectural" dressings in weathered "Cotswold" or "North Cerney" shades or other equal and approved; bedded, jointed and pointed in approved coloured cement:lime mortar (1:2:9)						
Copings; twice weathered and throated						
152 mm x 76 mm; type A	-	0.33	4.69	8.86	m	**13.55**
178 mm x 64 mm; type B	-	0.33	4.69	8.67	m	**13.36**
305 mm x 76 mm; type A	-	0.40	5.68	16.84	m	**22.52**
Extra for						
fair end	-	-	-	3.69	nr	**3.69**
returned mitred fair end	-	-	-	3.69	nr	**3.69**
Copings; once weathered and throated						
191 mm x 76 mm	-	0.33	4.69	9.61	m	**14.30**
305 mm x 76 mm	-	0.40	5.68	16.57	m	**22.25**
365 mm x 76 mm	-	0.40	5.68	17.80	m	**23.48**
Extra for						
fair end	-	-	-	3.69	nr	**3.69**
returned mitred fair end	-	-	-	3.69	nr	**3.69**
Chimney caps; four times weathered and throated; once holed						
553 mm x 553 mm x 76 mm	-	0.40	5.68	20.75	nr	**26.43**
686 mm x 686 mm x 76 mm	-	0.40	5.68	33.87	nr	**39.55**
Pier caps; four times weathered and throated						
305 mm x 305 mm	-	0.25	3.55	7.46	nr	**11.01**
381 mm x 381 mm	-	0.25	3.55	10.33	nr	**13.88**
457 mm x 457 mm	-	0.30	4.26	14.03	nr	**18.29**
533 mm x 533 mm	-	0.30	4.26	19.80	nr	**24.06**
Splayed corbels						
479 mm x 100 mm x 215 mm	-	0.15	2.13	9.65	nr	**11.78**
665 mm x 100 mm x 215 mm	-	0.20	2.84	15.47	nr	**18.31**
Air bricks						
300 mm x 140 mm x 76 mm	-	0.08	1.14	5.46	nr	**6.60**
100 mm x 140 mm lintels; rectangular; reinforced with mild steel bars						
not exceeding 1.22 m long	-	0.24	3.41	15.12	m	**18.53**
1.37 m - 1.67 m long	-	0.26	3.69	15.12	m	**18.81**
1.83 m - 1.98 m long	-	0.28	3.98	15.12	m	**19.10**
100 mm x 215 mm lintels; rectangular; reinforced with mild steel bars						
not exceeding 1.67 m long	-	0.26	3.69	20.34	m	**24.03**
1.83 m - 1.98 m long	-	0.28	3.98	20.34	m	**24.32**
2.13 m - 2.44 m long	-	0.30	4.26	20.34	m	**24.60**
2.59 m - 2.90 m long	-	0.32	4.55	20.34	m	**24.89**
197 mm x 67 mm sills to suit standard softwood windows; stooled at ends						
not exceeding 2.54 m long	-	0.30	4.26	23.82	m	**28.08**
Window surround; traditional with label moulding; for single light; sill 146 mm x 133 mm; jambs 146 mm x 146 mm; head 146 mm x 105 mm; including all dowels and anchors						
overall size 508 mm x 1479 mm	116.28	0.90	12.79	117.63	nr	**130.42**

F MASONRY Excluding overheads and profit	PC £	Labour hours	Labour £	Material £	Unit	Total rate £
Window surround; traditional with label moulding; three light; for windows 508 mm x 1219 mm; sill 146 mm x 133 mm; jambs 146 mm x 146 mm; head 146 mm x 103 mm; mullions 146 mm x 108 mm; including all dowels and anchors						
overall size 1975 mm x 1479 mm	252.00	2.35	33.39	255.36	nr	**288.75**
Door surround; moulded continuous jambs and head with label moulding; including all dowels and anchors						
door 839 mm x 1981 mm in 102 mm x 64 mm frame	216.00	1.65	23.45	216.67	nr	**240.12**
F30 ACCESSORIES/SUNDRY ITEMS FOR BRICK/BLOCK/STONE WALLING						
Forming cavities						
In hollow walls						
width of cavity 50 mm; polypropylene ties; three wall ties per m²	-	0.06	0.85	0.19	m²	**1.04**
width of cavity 50 mm; galvanised steel butterfly wall ties; three wall ties per m²	-	0.06	0.85	0.14	m²	**0.99**
width of cavity 50 mm; galvanised steel twisted wall ties; three wall ties per m²	-	0.06	0.85	0.28	m²	**1.13**
width of cavity 50 mm; stainless steel butterfly wall ties; three wall ties per m²	-	0.06	0.85	0.30	m²	**1.15**
width of cavity 50 mm; stainless steel twisted wall ties; three wall ties per m²	-	0.06	0.85	0.58	m²	**1.43**
width of cavity 75 mm; polypropylene ties; three wall ties per m²	-	0.06	0.85	0.19	m²	**1.04**
width of cavity 75 mm; galvanised steel butterfly wall ties; three wall ties per m²	-	0.06	0.85	0.18	m²	**1.03**
width of cavity 75 mm; galvanised steel twisted wall ties; three wall ties per m²	-	0.06	0.85	0.31	m²	**1.16**
width of cavity 75 mm; stainless steel butterfly wall ties; three wall ties per m²	-	0.06	0.85	0.42	m²	**1.27**
width of cavity 75 mm; stainless steel twisted wall ties; three wall ties per m²	-	0.06	0.85	0.64	m²	**1.49**
Damp proof courses						
"Pluvex No 1" (hessian based) damp proof course or other equal and approved; 200 mm laps; in gauged mortar (1:1:6)						
width exceeding 225 mm; horizontal	6.15	0.25	3.55	6.61	m²	**10.16**
width exceeding 225 mm; forming cavity gutters in hollow walls; horizontal	-	0.40	5.68	6.61	m²	**12.29**
width not exceeding 225 mm; horizontal	-	0.50	7.11	6.61	m²	**13.72**
width not exceeding 225 mm; vertical	-	0.75	10.66	6.61	m²	**17.27**
"Pluvex No 2" (fibre based) damp proof course or other equal and approved; 200 mm laps; in gauged mortar (1:1:6)						
width exceeding 225 mm; horizontal	4.13	0.25	3.55	4.44	m²	**7.99**
width exceeding 225 mm wide; forming cavity gutters in hollow walls; horizontal	-	0.40	5.68	4.44	m²	**10.12**
width not exceeding 225 mm; horizontal	-	0.50	7.11	4.44	m²	**11.55**
width not exceeding 225 mm; vertical	-	0.75	10.66	4.44	m²	**15.10**
"Ruberthene" polythylene damp proof course or other equal and approved; 200 mm laps; in gauged mortar (1:1:6)						
width exceeding 225 mm; horizontal	0.93	0.25	3.55	1.00	m²	**4.55**
width exceeding 225 mm; forming cavity gutters in hollow walls; horizontal	-	0.40	5.68	1.00	m²	**6.68**
width not exceeding 225 mm; horizontal	-	0.50	7.11	1.00	m²	**8.11**
width not exceeding 225 mm; vertical	-	0.75	10.66	1.00	m²	**11.66**

F MASONRY Excluding overheads and profit	PC £	Labour hours	Labour £	Material £	Unit	Total rate £
F30 ACCESSORIES/SUNDRY ITEMS FOR BRICK/BLOCK/STONE WALLING - cont'd						
Damp proof courses - cont'd						
"Permabit" bitumen polymer damp proof course or other equal and approved; 150 mm laps; in gauged mortar (1:1:6)						
width exceeding 225 mm; horizontal	5.27	0.25	3.55	5.67	m²	**9.22**
width exceeding 225 mm; forming cavity gutters in hollow walls; horizontal	-	0.40	5.68	5.67	m²	**11.35**
width not exceeding 225 mm; horizontal	-	0.50	7.11	5.67	m²	**12.78**
width not exceeding 225 mm; vertical	-	0.75	10.66	5.67	m²	**16.33**
"Hyload" (pitch polymer) damp proof course or other equal and approved; 150 mm laps; in gauged mortar (1:1:6)						
width exceeding 225 mm; horizontal	5.27	0.25	3.55	5.67	m²	**9.22**
width exceeding 225 mm; forming cavity gutters in hollow walls; horizontal	-	0.40	5.68	5.67	m²	**11.35**
width not exceeding 225 mm; horizontal	-	0.50	7.11	5.67	m²	**12.78**
width not exceeding 225 mm; vertical	-	0.75	10.66	5.67	m²	**16.33**
"Ledkore" grade A (bitumen based lead cored); damp proof course or other equal and approved; 200 mm laps; in gauged mortar (1:1;6)						
width exceeding 225 mm; horizontal	11.47	0.33	4.69	12.33	m²	**17.02**
width exceeding 225 mm; forming cavity gutters in hollow walls; horizontal	-	0.53	7.53	12.33	m²	**19.86**
width not exceeding 225 mm; horizontal	-	0.65	9.24	12.33	m²	**21.57**
width not exceeding 225 mm; vertical	-	0.90	12.79	12.33	m²	**25.12**
Milled lead damp proof course; PC £20.85/m²; BS 1178; 1.80 mm thick (code 4), 175 mm laps; in cement:lime mortar (1:2:9)						
width exceeding 225 mm; horizontal	-	2.00	28.42	20.86	m²	**49.28**
width not exceeding 225 mm; horizontal	-	3.00	42.63	20.86	m²	**63.49**
Two courses slates in cement mortar (1:3)						
width exceeding 225 mm; horizontal	-	1.50	21.32	9.21	m²	**30.53**
width exceeding 225 mm; vertical	-	2.25	31.97	9.21	m²	**41.18**
"Synthaprufe" damp proof membrane or other equal and approved; PC £43.85/25 litres; three coats brushed on						
width not exceeding 150 mm; vertical	-	0.34	2.19	5.53	m²	**7.72**
width 150 mm - 225 mm; vertical	-	0.32	2.06	5.53	m²	**7.59**
width 225 mm - 300 mm; vertical	-	0.30	1.94	5.53	m²	**7.47**
width exceeding 300 mm; vertical	-	0.28	1.81	5.53	m²	**7.34**
Joint reinforcement						
"Brickforce" galvanised steel joint reinforcement or other equal and approved						
width 40 mm; ref GBF40B	-	0.02	0.28	0.24	m	**0.52**
width 60 mm; ref GBF60B	-	0.03	0.43	0.27	m	**0.70**
width 100 mm; ref GBF100B	-	0.04	0.57	0.31	m	**0.88**
width 160 mm; ref GBF160B	-	0.05	0.71	0.39	m	**1.10**
"Brickforce" stainless steel joint reinforcement or other equal and approved						
width 40 mm; ref SBF40BRC	-	0.02	0.28	0.73	m	**1.01**
width 60 mm; ref SBF60BRC	-	0.03	0.43	0.77	m	**1.20**
width 100 mm; ref SBF100BRC	-	0.04	0.57	0.82	m	**1.39**
width 160 mm; ref SBF160BRC	-	0.05	0.71	0.86	m	**1.57**
"Wallforce" stainless steel joint reinforcement or other equal and approved						
width 210 mm; ref SWF40BSC	-	0.06	0.85	2.17	m	**3.02**
width 235 mm; ref SWF60BSC	-	0.07	0.99	2.23	m	**3.22**
width 250 mm; ref SWF100BSC	-	0.08	1.14	2.30	m	**3.44**
width 275 mm; ref SWF160BSC	-	0.09	1.28	2.35	m	**3.63**

F MASONRY Excluding overheads and profit	PC £	Labour hours	Labour £	Material £	Unit	Total rate £
Weather fillets						
Weather fillets in cement mortar (1:3)						
50 mm face width	-	0.12	1.71	0.04	m	1.75
100 mm face width	-	0.20	2.84	0.15	m	2.99
Angle fillets						
Angle fillets in cement mortar (1:3)						
50 mm face width	-	0.12	1.71	0.04	m	1.75
100 mm face width	-	0.20	2.84	0.15	m	2.99
Pointing in						
Pointing with mastic						
wood frames or sills	-	0.10	0.80	0.39	m	1.19
Pointing with polysulphide sealant						
wood frames or sills	-	0.10	0.80	1.18	m	1.98
Wedging and pinning						
To underside of existing construction with						
slates in cement mortar (1:3)						
width of wall - one brick thick	-	0.80	11.37	1.98	m	13.35
width of wall - one and a half brick thick	-	1.00	14.21	3.95	m	18.16
width of wall - two brick thick	-	1.20	17.05	5.93	m	22.98
Joints						
Hacking joints and faces of brickwork or						
blockwork						
to form key for plaster	-	0.26	1.68	-	m²	1.68
Raking out joint in brickwork or blockwork for						
turned-in edge of flashing						
horizontal	-	0.15	2.13	-	m	2.13
stepped	-	0.20	2.84	-	m	2.84
Raking out and enlarging joint in brickwork or						
blockwork for nib of asphalt						
horizontal	-	0.20	2.84	-	m	2.84
Cutting grooves in brickwork or blockwork						
for water bars and the like	-	0.25	1.61	0.44	m	2.05
for nib of asphalt; horizontal	-	0.25	1.61	0.44	m	2.05
Preparing to receive new walls						
top existing 215 mm wall	-	0.20	2.84	-	m	2.84
Cleaning and priming both faces; filling with						
pre-formed closed cell joint filler and pointing						
one side with polysulphide sealant; 12 mm						
deep						
expansion joints; 12 mm wide	-	0.25	2.93	2.35	m	5.28
expansion joints; 20 mm wide	-	0.30	3.33	3.44	m	6.77
expansion joints; 25 mm wide	-	0.35	3.72	4.14	m	7.86
Fire resisting horizontal expansion joints; filling						
with joint filler; fixed with high temperature slip						
adhesive; between top of wall and soffit						
wall not exceeding 215 mm wide; 10 mm wide						
joint with 30 mm deep filler (one hour fire seal)	-	0.25	3.55	4.39	m	7.94
wall not exceeding 215 mm wide; 10 mm wide						
joint with 30 mm deep filler (two hour fire seal)	-	0.25	3.55	4.39	m	7.94
wall not exceeding 215 mm wide; 20 mm wide						
joint with 45 mm deep filler (two hour fire seal)	-	0.30	4.26	6.71	m	10.97
wall not exceeding 215 mm wide; 30 mm wide						
joint with 75 mm deep filler (three hour fire						
seal)	-	0.35	4.97	16.36	m	21.33

F MASONRY Excluding overheads and profit	PC £	Labour hours	Labour £	Material £	Unit	Total rate £
F30 ACCESSORIES/SUNDRY ITEMS FOR BRICK/BLOCK/STONE WALLING - cont'd						
Joints - cont'd						
Fire resisting vertical expansion joints; filling						
with joint filler; fixed with high temperature slip						
adhesive; with polysulphide sealant one side;						
between end of wall and concrete						
wall not exceeding 215 mm wide; 20 mm wide						
joint with 45 mm deep filler (two hour fire seal)	-	0.40	5.06	9.07	m	14.13
Slate and tile sills						
Sills; two courses of machine made plain						
roofing tiles						
set weathering; bedded and pointed	-	0.60	8.53	3.70	m	12.23
Flue linings						
Flue linings; Marflex "ML 200" square refractory						
concrete flue linings or other equal and approved;						
rebated joints in flue joint mortar mix						
linings; ref MLS1U	-	0.30	4.26	13.58	m	17.84
bottom swivel unit; ref MLS2U	-	0.10	1.42	10.26	nr	11.68
45 degree bend; ref MLS4U	-	0.10	1.42	10.26	nr	11.68
90 mm offset liner; ref MLS5U	-	0.10	1.42	5.41	nr	6.83
70 mm offset liner; ref MLS6U	-	0.10	1.42	4.87	nr	6.29
57 mm offset liner; ref MLS7U	-	0.10	1.42	8.79	nr	10.21
pot; ref MLS9UR	-	0.10	1.42	19.57	nr	20.99
single cap unit; ref MLS10U	-	0.25	3.55	29.39	nr	32.94
double cap unit; ref MLS11U	-	0.30	4.26	26.93	nr	31.19
combined gather lintel; ref MLSUL4	-	0.30	4.26	26.62	nr	30.88
Air bricks						
Air bricks; red terracotta; building into prepared						
openings						
215 mm x 65 mm	-	0.08	1.14	1.03	nr	2.17
215 mm x 140 mm	-	0.08	1.14	1.43	nr	2.57
215 mm x 215 mm	-	0.08	1.14	3.87	nr	5.01
Gas flue blocks						
Gas flue system; Marflex "HP" or other equal and						
approved; concrete blocks built in; in flue joint mortar						
mix; cutting brickwork or blockwork around						
recess unit; ref HP1	-	0.10	1.42	4.01	nr	5.43
cover block; ref HP2	-	0.10	1.42	5.63	nr	7.05
222 mm standard block with nib; ref HP3	-	0.10	1.42	3.97	nr	5.39
112 mm standard block with nib; ref HP3112	-	0.10	1.42	3.97	nr	5.39
72 mm standard block with nib; ref HP372	-	0.10	1.42	3.97	nr	5.39
vent block; ref HP3BH	-	0.10	1.42	7.84	nr	9.26
222 mm standard block without nib; ref HP4	-	0.10	1.42	3.86	nr	5.28
112 mm standard block without nib; ref HP4112	-	0.10	1.42	3.86	nr	5.28
72 mm standard block without nib; ref HP472	-	0.10	1.42	3.86	nr	5.28
120 mm side offset block; ref HP5	-	0.10	1.42	4.66	nr	6.08
70 mm back offset block; ref HP6	-	0.10	1.42	11.49	nr	12.91
vertical exit block; ref HP7	-	0.10	1.42	7.73	nr	9.15
angled entry/exit block; ref HP8	-	0.10	1.42	7.73	nr	9.15
reverse rebate block; ref HP9	-	0.10	1.42	5.80	nr	7.22
corbel block; ref HP10	-	0.10	1.42	7.31	nr	8.73
lintel unit; ref HP11	-	0.10	1.42	6.93	nr	8.35

F MASONRY Excluding overheads and profit	PC £	Labour hours	Labour £	Material £	Unit	Total rate £
Proprietary items						
"Thermabate" cavity closers or other equal and						
approved; RMC Panel Products Ltd						
closing cavities; width of cavity 50 mm	-	0.15	2.13	4.53	m	**6.66**
closing cavities; width of cavity 75 mm	-	0.15	2.13	4.86	m	**6.99**
"Westbrick" cavity closers or other equal and approved;						
Manthorpe Building Products Ltd						
closing cavities; width of cavity 50 mm	-	0.15	2.13	4.41	m	**6.54**
"Type H cavicloser" or other equal and approved;						
uPVC universal cavity closer, insulator and damp						
proof course by Cavity Trays Ltd; built into cavity wall						
as work proceeds, complete with face closer and ties						
closing cavities; width of cavity 50 mm - 100						
mm"	-	0.08	1.14	4.70	m	**5.84**
"Type L" durropolyethelene lintel stop ends or other						
equal and approved; Cavity Trays Ltd; fixing to lintel						
with butyl anchoring strip; building in as the work proceeds						
adjusted to lintel as required	-	0.05	0.71	0.48	nr	**1.19**
"Type W" polypropylene weeps/vents or other equal						
and approved; Cavity Trays Ltd; built into cavity wall						
as work proceeds						
100/115 mm x 65 mm x 10 mm including lock fit						
wedges	-	0.05	0.71	0.37	nr	**1.08**
extra; extension duct 200/225 mm x 65 mm x 10						
mm	-	0.08	1.14	0.47	nr	**1.61**
"Type X" polypropylene abutment cavity tray or						
other equal and approved; Cavity Trays Ltd; built						
into facing brickwork as the work proceeds; complete						
with Code 4 flashing; intermediate/catchment tray						
with short leads (requiring soakers); to suit roof of						
17 - 20 degree pitch	-	0.06	0.85	4.09	nr	**4.94**
21 - 25 degree pitch	-	0.06	0.85	3.79	nr	**4.64**
26 - 45 degree pitch	-	0.06	0.85	3.63	nr	**4.48**
"Type X" polypropylene abutment cavity tray or						
other equal and approved; Cavity Trays Ltd; built						
into facing brickwork as the work proceeds; complete						
with Code 4 flashing; intermediate/catchment tray						
with long leads (suitable only for corrugated roof tiles);						
to suit roof of						
17 - 20 degree pitch	-	0.06	0.85	5.51	nr	**6.36**
21 - 25 degree pitch	-	0.06	0.85	5.06	nr	**5.91**
26 - 45 degree pitch	-	0.06	0.85	4.67	nr	**5.52**
"Type X" polypropylene abutment cavity tray or						
other equal and approved; Cavity Trays Ltd; built						
into facing brickwork as the work proceeds; complete						
with Code 4 flashing; ridge tray with short/long leads;						
to suit roof of						
17 - 20 degree pitch	-	0.06	0.85	9.28	nr	**10.13**
21 - 25 degree pitch	-	0.06	0.85	8.61	nr	**9.46**
26 - 45 degree pitch	-	0.06	0.85	7.65	nr	**8.50**
Serviciced "Bitu-thene" self-adhesive cavity flashing						
or other equal and approved; type "CA"; well lapped						
at joints; in gauged mortar (1:1:6)						
width exceeding 225 mm; horizontal	-	0.85	12.08	16.03	m²	**28.11**
"Expamet" stainless steel wall starters or other equal						
and approved; plugged and screwed						
to suit walls 60 mm - 75 mm thick	-	0.25	1.61	5.63	m	**7.24**
to suit walls 100 mm - 115 mm thick	-	0.25	1.61	6.20	m	**7.81**
to suit walls 125 mm - 180 mm thick	-	0.40	2.58	8.29	m	**10.87**
to suit walls 190 mm - 260 mm thick	-	0.50	3.23	10.59	m	**13.82**

F MASONRY Excluding overheads and profit	PC £	Labour hours	Labour £	Material £	Unit	Total rate £
F30 ACCESSORIES/SUNDRY ITEMS FOR BRICK/BLOCK/STONE WALLING - cont'd						
Proprietary items - cont'd						
Brickwork support angle welded to bracket ref. HC6C or other equal and approved; Halfen Ltd; to suit 75 mm cavity, support to brickwork 6000 mm high						
6 mm thick; bolting with M12 x 50 mm T head bolts to cast in channel (not included)	-	0.35	3.97	37.86	m	**41.83**
Slotted frame cramp; Halfen Ltd or other equal and approved; fixing by bolting (bolts measured elsewhere)						
ref. HTS - FH12; 150 mm projection	-	0.08	0.58	0.33	nr	**0.91**
Single expansion bolt, Halfen Ltd or other equal and approved; including washer						
8 mm diameter; ref SEB 8	-	0.12	1.36	1.23	nr	**2.59**
Head restraint fixings; sliding brick anchors with 500 mm long stem; 2 nr 100 mm projection HST brick anchor ties or other equal and approved; Halfen Ltd; fixing with bolts to concrete soffit (bolts not included)						
ref SBA/L	-	0.20	2.27	4.06	nr	**6.33**
Ties in walls; 200 mm long butterfly type; building into joints of brickwork or blockwork						
galvanised steel or polypropylene	-	0.03	0.43	0.08	nr	**0.51**
stainless steel	-	0.03	0.43	0.12	nr	**0.55**
Ties in walls; 20 mm x 3 mm x 200 mm long twisted wall type; building into joints of brickwork or blockwork						
galvanised steel	-	0.03	0.43	0.11	nr	**0.54**
stainless steel	-	0.03	0.43	0.24	nr	**0.67**
Anchors in walls; 25 mm x 3 mm x 100 mm long; one end dovetailed; other end building into joints of brickwork or blockwork						
galvanised steel	-	0.06	0.85	0.16	nr	**1.01**
stainless steel	-	0.06	0.85	0.25	nr	**1.10**
Fixing cramps; 25 mm x 3 mm x 250 mm long; once bent; fixed to back of frame; other end building into joints of brickwork or blockwork						
galvanised steel	-	0.06	0.85	0.12	nr	**0.97**
Chimney pots; red terracotta; plain or cannon-head; setting and flaunching in cement mortar (1:3)						
185 mm diameter x 300 mm long	14.64	1.80	25.58	15.83	nr	**41.41**
185 mm diameter x 600 mm long	26.07	2.00	28.42	27.26	nr	**55.68**
185 mm diameter x 900 mm long	47.52	2.00	28.42	48.71	nr	**77.13**
Galvanised steel lintels; "Catnic" or other equal and approved; built into brickwork or blockwork; "CN7" combined lintel; 143 mm high; for standard cavity walls						
750 mm long	17.60	0.25	3.55	17.63	nr	**21.18**
900 mm long	21.31	0.30	4.26	21.34	nr	**25.60**
1200 mm long	27.62	0.35	4.97	27.65	nr	**32.62**
1500 mm long	31.58	0.40	5.68	31.61	nr	**37.29**
1800 mm long	44.38	0.45	6.39	44.41	nr	**50.80**
2100 mm long	50.94	0.50	7.11	50.97	nr	**58.08**
Galvanised steel lintels; "Catnic" or other equal and approved; built into brickwork or blockwork; "CN8" combined lintel; 219 mm high; for standard cavity walls						
2400 mm long	62.45	0.60	8.53	62.48	nr	**71.01**
2700 mm long	70.88	0.70	9.95	70.91	nr	**80.86**
3000 mm long	98.14	0.80	11.37	98.17	nr	**109.54**
3300 mm long	109.55	0.90	12.79	109.58	nr	**122.37**
3600 mm long	120.22	1.00	14.21	120.25	nr	**134.46**
3900 mm long	156.40	1.10	15.63	156.43	nr	**172.06**
4200 mm long	171.51	0.50	7.11	171.54	nr	**178.65**

F MASONRY Excluding overheads and profit	PC £	Labour hours	Labour £	Material £	Unit	Total rate £
Galvanised steel lintels; "Catnic" or other equal and approved; built into brickwork or blockwork; "CN92" single lintel; for 75 mm internal walls						
900 mm long	2.77	0.30	4.26	2.79	nr	7.05
1050 mm long	3.17	0.30	4.26	3.19	nr	7.45
1200 mm long	3.59	0.35	4.97	3.61	nr	8.58
Galvanised steel lintels; "Catnic" or other equal and approved; built into brickwork or blockwork; "CN102" single lintel; for 100 mm internal walls						
900 mm long	3.41	0.30	4.26	3.43	nr	7.69
1050 mm long	4.02	0.30	4.26	4.04	nr	8.30
1200 mm long	4.43	0.35	4.97	4.45	nr	9.42
F31 PRECAST CONCRETE SILLS/LINTELS/ COPINGS/FEATURES						
Mix 20.00 N/mm² - 20 mm aggregate (1:2:4)						
Lintels; plate; prestressed bedded						
100 mm x 70 mm x 750 mm long	2.60	0.40	5.68	2.62	nr	8.30
100 mm x 70 mm x 900 mm long	3.10	0.40	5.68	3.12	nr	8.80
100 mm x 70 mm x 1050 mm long	3.65	0.40	5.68	3.67	nr	9.35
100 mm x 70 mm x 1200 mm long	4.15	0.40	5.68	4.17	nr	9.85
150 mm x 70 mm x 900 mm long	4.25	0.50	7.11	4.28	nr	11.39
150 mm x 70 mm x 1050 mm long	4.95	0.50	7.11	4.98	nr	12.09
150 mm x 70 mm x 1200 mm long	5.65	0.50	7.11	5.68	nr	12.79
220 mm x 70 mm x 900 mm long	6.55	0.60	8.53	6.59	nr	15.12
220 mm x 70 mm x 1200 mm long	8.70	0.60	8.53	8.74	nr	17.27
220 mm x 70 mm x 1500 mm long	10.90	0.70	9.95	10.94	nr	20.89
265 mm x 70 mm x 900 mm long	6.95	0.60	8.53	7.00	nr	15.53
265 mm x 70 mm x 1200 mm long	9.30	0.60	8.53	9.35	nr	17.88
265 mm x 70 mm x 1500 mm long	11.60	0.70	9.95	11.65	nr	21.60
265 mm x 70 mm x 1800 mm long	13.90	0.80	11.37	13.95	nr	25.32
Lintels; rectangular; reinforced with mild steel bars; bedded						
100 mm x 145 mm x 900 mm long	6.30	0.60	8.53	6.32	nr	14.85
100 mm x 145 mm x 1050 mm long	7.40	0.60	8.53	7.42	nr	15.95
100 mm x 145 mm x 1200 mm long	8.40	0.60	8.53	8.42	nr	16.95
225 mm x 145 mm x 1200 mm long	9.59	0.80	11.37	9.63	nr	21.00
225 mm x 225 mm x 1800 mm long	18.54	1.50	21.32	18.58	nr	39.90
Lintels; boot; reinforced with mild steel bars; bedded						
250 mm x 225 mm x 1200 mm long	15.39	1.20	17.05	15.43	nr	32.48
275 mm x 225 mm x 1800 mm long	20.61	1.80	25.58	20.65	nr	46.23
Padstones						
300 mm x 100 mm x 75 mm	3.15	0.30	4.26	3.17	nr	7.43
225 mm x 225 mm x 150 mm	4.77	0.40	5.68	4.80	nr	10.48
450 mm x 450 mm x 150 mm	12.60	0.60	8.53	12.72	nr	21.25
Mix 30.00 N/mm² - 20 mm aggregate (1:1:2)						
Copings; once weathered; once throated; bedded and pointed						
152 mm x 76 mm	3.83	0.70	9.95	4.08	m	14.03
178 mm x 64 mm	4.23	0.70	9.95	4.50	m	14.45
305 mm x 76 mm	7.11	0.80	11.37	7.60	m	18.97
extra for fair ends	-	-	-	3.60	nr	3.60
extra for angles	-	-	-	4.10	nr	4.10
Copings; twice weathered; twice throated; bedded and pointed						
152 mm x 76 mm	3.83	0.70	9.95	4.08	m	14.03
178 mm x 64 mm	4.19	0.70	9.95	4.46	m	14.41
305 mm x 76 mm	7.11	0.80	11.37	7.60	m	18.97
extra for fair ends	-	-	-	3.60	nr	3.60
extra for angles	-	-	-	4.10	nr	4.10

G STRUCTURAL CARCASSING/METAL/TIMBER

Excluding overheads and profit

G10 STRUCTURAL STEEL FRAMING

NOTE: The following basic prices are for basic quantities of BS EN10025 1993 grade 275 JR steel (over 10 tonnes of one quality, one serial size and one thickness in lengths between 6 m and 18.5 m, for delivery to one destination). Transport charges are shown in a separate schedule.

See page 185 for other extra charges.

Based on delivery Middlesbrough/Scunthorpe/Stoke-on-Trent Railway Stations - refer BS section availability at each location.

See page 186 for delivery charges.

Universal beams (kg/m)	£/tonne	Universal beams (kg/m)	£/tonne
1016 x 305 mm (222,249,272,314, 349,393,438,487)	450.00	356 x 171 mm (45,51,57,67)	400.00
914 x 419 mm (343,388)	440.00	356 x 127 mm (33,39)	400.00
914 x 305 mm (201,224,253,289)	435.00	305 x 165 mm (40,46,54)	395.00
838 x 292 mm (176,194,226)	430.00	305 x 127 mm (37,42,48)	395.00
762 x 267 mm (134,147,173,197)	430.00	305 x 102 mm (25,28,33)	395.00
686 x 254 mm (125,140,152,170)	430.00	254 x 146 mm (31,37,43)	380.00
610 x 305 mm (149,179,238)	420.00	254 x 102 mm (22,25,28)	380.00
610 x 229 mm (101,113,125,140)	420.00	203 x 133 mm (25,30)	340.00
533 x 210 mm (82,92,101,109,122)	405.00	203 x 102 mm (23)	360.00
457 x 191 mm (67,74,82,89,98)	395.00	178 x 102 mm (19)	330.00
457 x 152 mm (52,60,67,74,82)	395.00	152 x 89 mm (16)	370.00
406 x 178 mm (54,60,67,74)	400.00	127 x 76 mm (13)	390.00
406 x 140 mm (39,46)	400.00		

Universal columns (kg/m)	£/tonne	Universal columns (kg/m)	£/tonne
356 x 406 mm (235,287,340,393,467, 551, 634)	440.00	254 x 254 mm (73,89,107,132,167)	400.00
356 x 368 mm (129,153,177,202)	440.00	203 x 203 mm (46,52,60,71,86)	390.00
305 x 305 mm (97,118,137,158,198, 240,283)	420.00	152 x 152 mm (23,30,37)	360.00

Joists (kg/m)	£/tonne	Joists (kg/m)	£/tonne
254 x 203 mm (82.0)	385.00	114 x 114 mm (26.9)	365.00
203 x 152 mm (60.2)	400.00	102 x 102 mm (23.0)	365.00
203 x 152 mm (52.3)	375.00	102 x 44 mm (7.5)	325.00
152 x 127 mm (37.3)	375.00	89 x 89 mm (19.5)	365.00
127 x 114 mm (26.9,29.3)	365.00	76 x 76 mm (12.8)	415.00

Channels (kg/m)	£/tonne	Channels (kg/m)	£/tonne
430 x 100 mm (64.4)	445.00	200 x 90 mm (29.7)	415.00
380 x 100 mm (54.0)	445.00	200 x 75 mm (23.4)	335.00
300 x 100 mm (45.5)	415.00	180 x 90 mm (26.1)	405.00
300 x 90 mm (41.4)	415.00	180 x 75 mm (20.3)	335.00
260 x 90 mm (34.8)	415.00	150 x 90 mm (23.9)	405.00
260 x 75 mm (27.6)	415.00	150 x 75 mm (17.9)	335.00
230 x 90 mm (32.2)	415.00	125 x 65 mm (14.8)	335.00
230 x 75 mm (25.7)	415.00	100 x 50 mm (10.2)	330.00

G STRUCTURAL CARCASSING METAL/TIMBER
Excluding overheads and profit

Equal angles	£/tonne	Equal angles	£/tonne	Equal angles	£/tonne
200 x 200 x 16 mm	375.00	150 x 150 x 18 mm	370.00	100 x 100 x 12 mm	310.00
200 x 200 x 18 mm	375.00	120 x 120 x 8 mm	345.00	100 x 100 x 15 mm	310.00
200 x 200 x 20 mm	375.00	120 x 120 x 10 mm	345.00	90 x 90 x 6 mm	310.00
200 x 200 x 24 mm	375.00	120 x 120 x 12 mm	345.00	90 x 90 x 7 mm	310.00
150 x 150 x 10 mm	370.00	120 x 120 x 15 mm	345.00	90 x 90 x 8 mm	310.00
150 x 150 x 12 mm	370.00	100 x 100 x 8 mm	310.00	90 x 90 x 10 mm	310.00
150 x 150 x 15 mm	370.00	100 x 100 x 10 mm	310.00	90 x 90 x 12 mm	310.00

Unequal angles	£/tonne	Unequal angles	£/tonne	Unequal angles	£/tonne
200 x 150 x 12 mm	390.00	150 x 90 x 12 mm	370.00	125 x 75 x 12 mm	325.00
200 x 150 x 15 mm	390.00	150 x 90 x 15 mm	370.00	100 x 75 x 8 mm	320.00
200 x 150 x 18 mm	390.00	150 x 75 x 10 mm	360.00	100 x 75 x 10 mm	320.00
200 x 100 x 10 mm	385.00	150 x 75 x 12 mm	360.00	100 x 75 x 12 mm	320.00
200 x 100 x 12 mm	385.00	150 x 75 x 15 mm	360.00	100 x 65 x 7 mm	320.00
200 x 100 x 15 mm	385.00	125 x 75 x 8 mm	325.00	100 x 65 x 8 mm	320.00
150 x 90 x 10 mm	370.00	125 x 75 x 10 mm	325.00	100 x 65 x 10 mm	320.00

Add to the aforementioned prices for:

	Unit	£
Universal beams, columns, joists, channels and angles non-standard size	t	25.00
Quantity under 10 tonnes to 5 tonnes	t	10.00
under 5 tonnes to 2 tonnes	t	25.00
under 2 tonnes	t	50.00
Size lengths 3,000 mm to under 6,000 mm in 100 mm increments	t	15.00
lengths over 18,000 to 24,000 mm in 100 mm increments	t	5.00
lengths over 24,000 to 27,000 mm in 100 mm increments	t	10.00
lengths over 27,000 to 29,500 mm in 100 mm increments	t	60.00
Tees cut from universal beams and columns and joists		
weight per metre of rolled section before splitting		
up to 22 kg per metre	t	120.00
22 - 33 kg per metre	t	90.00
33 - 67 kg per metre	t	80.00
67 kg + per metre	t	75.00
impact testing within the specification	t	10.00
Shotblasting and priming		
Epoxy Zinc Phosphate primer to universal beams and columns		
Epoxy Zinc Phosphate primer to channels and angles	m²	2.60
Zinc rich epoxy primer to universal beams and columns	m²	2.70
Zinc rich epoxy primer to channels and angles	m²	3.60
	m²	3.50
Surface quality		
Specification of class D in respect of EN 10163-3: 1991	t	40.00

G STRUCTURAL/CARCASSING METAL/TIMBER
Excluding overheads and profit
G10 STRUCTRURAL STEEL FRAMING - cont'd

RADIAL DISTANCES MILES FROM BASING POINT	0. under 5 tonnes £/tonne	5. under 10 tonnes £/tonne	10. under 20 tonnes £/tonne	20. under and over £/tonne
Schedule IX - Iron and Steel				
up to 10	7.05	4.90	3.70	3.35
over 10 up to 15	7.75	5.30	4.15	3.70
over 15 up to 20	8.25	5.80	4.60	4.10
over 20 up to 25	8.75	6.20	4.95	4.55
over 25 up to 30	9.15	6.70	5.40	4.90
over 30 up to 35	9.60	7.10	5.75	5.30
over 35 up to 40	10.10	7.55	6.15	5.65
over 40 up to 45	10.50	8.00	6.55	6.05
over 45 up to 50	10.85	8.45	6.95	6.40
over 50 up to 60	11.40	9.05	7.50	6.95
over 60 up to 70	11.90	9.85	8.25	7.70
over 70 up to 80	12.70	10.60	8.95	8.45
over 80 up to 90	13.60	11.35	9.65	9.10
over 90 up to 100	14.40	12.10	10.35	9.85
over 100 up to 110	15.05	12.80	11.10	10.50
over 110 up to 120	15.60	13.50	11.75	11.20
over 120 up to 130	16.10	14.20	12.45	11.90
over 130 up to 140	16.70	14.90	13.10	12.55
over 140 up to 150	16.85	15.55	13.80	13.20
over 150 up to 160	17.25	16.25	14.45	13.90
over 160 up to 170	17.85	16.90	15.15	14.55
over 170 up to 180	18.30	17.55	15.75	15.20
over 180 up to 190	18.95	18.20	16.45	15.80
over 190 up to 200	19.55	18.85	17.10	16.20
over 200 up to 210	20.10	19.45	17.70	16.85
over 210 up to 220	20.70	20.10	18.35	17.40
over 220 up to 230	21.20	20.70	18.85	18.10
over 230 up to 240	22.00	21.30	19.35	18.60
over 240 up to 250	22.45	21.95	19.90	19.00
over 250 up to 275	23.35	22.95	20.75	20.00
over 275 up to 300	24.70	24.45	22.00	21.20
over 300 up to 325	25.95	25.90	23.25	22.55
over 325 up to 350	27.30	27.35	24.55	23.80
over 350 up to 375	28.65	28.75	25.60	25.20
over 375 up to 400	30.00	30.15	26.70	26.30

NOTE: The minimum charge under this schedule will be as for 2 tonnes.
Lengths over 14 metres and up to 18 metres will be subject to a surcharge of 20%.
Lengths over 18 metres and up to 24 metres will be subject to a surcharge of 40%.
Lengths over 24 metres will be subect to a surcharge of 70%.

Collection by customer from works will incur an extra cost of £3.00/tonne in addition to any additional transport charges between the basing point and the producing works.

G STRUCTURAL CARCASSING/METAL/TIMBER
Excluding overheads and profit

NOTE: The following basic prices are for basic quantities of 10 tonnes and over in one size, thickness, length,
       steelgrade and surface finish and include delivery to mainland of Great Britain to one destination.
       Additional costs for variations to these factors vary between sections and should be ascertained from the
       supplier.

       The following lists are not fully comprehensive and for alternative sections BS PLC price lists
       should be consulted.

Hot formed structural hollow section	Approx metres per tonne (m)	S276J2H Grade 43D £/100m	S355J2H Grade 50D £/100m
Circular (kg/m)			
21.30 x 3.20 mm (1.43)	700.00	82.13	-
26.90 x 3.20 mm (1.87)	535.00	107.40	-
33.70 x 3.20 mm (2.41)	415.00	138.41	-
33.70 x 4.00 mm (2.93)	342.00	169.90	-
42.40 x 3.20 mm (3.09)	324.00	176.61	-
42.40 x 4.00 mm (3.79)	264.00	218.72	-
48.30 x 3.20 mm (3.56)	281.00	203.48	223.82
48.30 x 4.00 mm (4.37)	229.00	252.19	277.41
48.30 x 5.00 mm (5.34)	188.00	308.17	338.98
60.30 x 3.20 mm (4.51)	222.00	257.77	283.55
60.30 x 4.00 mm (5.55)	181.00	332.78	366.06
60.30 x 5.00 mm (6.82)	147.00	408.93	449.82
76.10 x 3.20 mm (5.75)	174.00	328.65	361.51
76.10 x 4.00 mm (7.11)	141.00	426.32	468.95
76.10 x 5.00 mm (8.77)	115.00	525.85	578.43
88.90 x 3.20 mm (6.76)	148.00	386.37	425.01
88.90 x 4.00 mm (8.38)	120.00	502.46	552.71
88.90 x 5.00 mm (10.30)	97.10	617.59	679.35
114.30 x 3.60 mm (9.83)	102.00	589.41	648.35
114.30 x 5.00 mm (13.50)	74.10	809.46	890.41
114.30 x 6.30 mm (16.80)	59.60	1007.33	1108.06
139.70 x 5.00 mm (16.60)	60.30	1029.81	1132.80
139.70 x 6.30 mm (20.70)	48.40	1284.17	1412.59
139.70 x 8.00 mm (26.00)	38.50	1612.96	1774.27
139.70 x 10.00 mm (32.00)	31.30	2053.54	2258.88
168.30 x 5.00 mm (20.10)	49.80	1246.94	1371.64
168.30 x 6.30 mm (25.20)	39.70	1563.33	1719.67
168.30 x 8.00 mm (31.60)	31.70	1960.37	2156.42
168.30 x 10.00 mm (39.00)	25.70	2502.75	2753.01
168.30 x 12.50 mm (48.00)	20.80	3736.75	4110.43
193.70 x 5.00 mm (23.30)	42.90	1445.46	1590.02
193.70 x 6.30 mm (29.10)	34.40	1805.28	1985.81
193.70 x 8.00 mm (36.60)	27.30	2270.55	2497.62
193.70 x 10.00 mm (45.30)	22.10	2907.04	3197.73
193.70 x 12.50 mm (55.90)	17.90	4351.76	4786.94
219.10 x 5.00 mm (26.40)	37.90	1938.42	2132.28
219.10 x 6.30 mm (33.10)	30.20	2430.37	2673.42
219.10 x 8.00 mm (41.60)	24.10	3054.48	3359.95
219.10 x 10.00 mm (51.60)	19.40	3788.73	4167.63
219.10 x 12.50 mm (63.70)	15.70	5098.57	5606.24

G STRUCTURAL CARCASSING/METAL/TIMBER

Excluding overheads and profit

G10 STRUCTURAL STEEL FRAMING - cont'd

Hot formed structural hollow section	Approx metres per tonne (m)	S276J2H Grade 43D £/100m	S355J2H Grade 50D £/100m
Circular (kg/m) - cont'd			
219.10 x 16.00 mm (80.10)	12.50	6408.72	7049.60
244.50 x 6.30 mm (37.00)	27.10	2716.72	2988.42
244.50 x 8.00 mm (46.70)	21.50	3428.95	3771.87
244.50 x 10.00 mm (57.80)	17.40	4243.96	4668.39
244.50 x 12.50 mm (71.50)	14.00	5541.89	6096.09
244.50 x 16.00 mm (90.20)	11.10	7216.81	7938.50
273.00 x 6.30 mm (41.40)	24.20	3039.80	3343.80
273.00 x 8.00 mm (52.30)	19.10	3840.13	4224.17
273.00 x 10.00 mm (64.90)	15.40	4765.28	5241.84
273.00 x 12.50 mm (80.30)	12.50	6223.97	6846.38
273.00 x 16.00 mm (101.00)	9.91	8080.91	8889.01
323.90 x 6.30 mm (49.30)	20.30	3619.85	3981.86
323.90 x 8.00 mm (62.30)	16.10	4574.38	5031.85
323.90 x 10.00 mm (77.40)	12.90	5683.10	6251.44
323.90 x 12.50 mm (96.00)	10.40	7440.86	8184.96
323.90 x 16.00 mm (121.00)	8.27	9 681.09	10649.21
355.60 x 8.00 mm (68.60)	14.60	5036.96	5540.68
355.60 x 10.00 mm (85.30)	11.80	6255.81	6881.43
355.60 x 12.50 mm (106.00)	9.44	8215.95	9037.56
355.60 x 16.00 mm (134.00)	7.47	10721.21	11793.34
406.40 x 10.00 mm (97.80)	10.20	7180.96	7899.11
406.40 x 12.50 mm (121.00)	8.27	9378.59	10316.46
406.40 x 16.00 mm (154.00)	6.50	12321.39	13553.54
457.00 x 10.00 mm (110.00)	9.09	8076.75	8884.48
457.00 x 12.50 mm (137.00)	7.30	10618.73	11680.62
457.00 x 16.00 mm (174.00)	5.75	13921.57	15313.74
508.00 x 10.00 mm (123.00)	8.13	9031.28	9934.46
508.00 x 12.50 mm (153.00)	6.54	11858.88	13044.78
508.00 x 16.00 mm (194.00)	5.16	15521.75	17073.94
Square (kg/m)	346.00	169.30	186.23
40 x 40 x 2.50 mm (2.89)	293.30	200.03	220.03
40 x 40 x 3.00 mm (3.41)	277.00	212.21	233.43
40 x 40 x 3.20 mm (3.61)	227.80	258.59	284.45
40 x 40 x 4.00 mm (4.39)	189.40	313.09	344.40
40 x 40 x 5.00 mm (5.28)	271.70	215.11	236.62
50 x 50 x 2.50 mm (3.68)	229.90	254.53	279.99
50 x 50 x 3.00 mm (4.35)	216.50	270.19	297.21
50 x 50 x 3.20 mm (4.62)	177.30	331.65	364.81
50 x 50 x 4.00 mm (5.64)	146.00	404.12	444.53
50 x 50 x 5.00 mm (6.85)	120.30	492.25	541.48
50 x 50 x 6.30 mm (8.31)	189.00	309.61	340.57
60 x 60 x 3.00 mm (5.29)			

G STRUCTURAL CARCASSING/METAL/TIMBER

Excluding overheads and profit

Hot formed structural hollow section	Approx metres per tonne (m)	S276J2H Grade 43D £/100m	S355J2H Grade 50D £/100m
Square (kg/m) - cont'd			
60 x 60 x 3.20 mm (5.62)	177.90	328.75	361.62
60 x 60 x 4.00 mm (6.90)	145.00	423.94	466.33
60 x 60 x 5.00 mm (8.42)	118.80	519.44	571.38
60 x 60 x 6.30 mm (10.30)	97.10	638.65	702.51
60 x 60 x 8.00 mm (12.50)	80.00	778.55	856.40
70 x 70 x 3.00 mm (6.24)	160.30	353.46	388.81
70 x 70 x 3.60 mm (7.40)	135.10	440.45	484.49
70 x 70 x 5.00 mm (9.99)	100.10	614.32	675.75
70 x 70 x 6.30 mm (12.30)	81.30	760.30	836.32
70 x 70 x 8.00 mm (15.00)	66.70	930.61	1023.66
80 x 80 x 3.60 mm (8.53)	117.20	507.16	557.88
80 x 80 x 5.00 mm (11.60)	86.20	711.64	782.80
80 x 80 x 6.30 mm (14.20)	70.40	875.87	963.45
80 x 80 x 8.00 mm (17.50)	57.10	1082.67	1190.93
90 x 90 x 3.60 mm (9.66)	103.50	573.88	631.27
90 x 90 x 5.00 mm (13.10)	76.30	808.96	889.85
90 x 90 x 6.30 mm (16.20)	61.70	997.51	1097.26
90 x 90 x 8.00 mm (20.10)	49.80	1240.81	1364.88
100 x 100 x 4.00 mm (11.90)	84.00	688.84	757.72
100 x 100 x 5.00 mm (14.70)	68.00	900.20	990.21
100 x 100 x 6.30 mm (18.20)	54.90	1119.16	1231.07
100 x 100 x 8.00 mm (22.60)	44.20	1461.87	1608.06
100 x 100 x 10.00 mm (27.40)	36.50	1816.51	1998.17
120 x 120 x 4.00 mm (14.40)	69.40	912.60	1003.86
120 x 120 x 5.00 mm (17.80)	56.20	1132.88	1246.18
120 x 120 x 6.30 mm (22.20)	45.00	1403.52	1543.87
120 x 120 x 8.00 mm (27.60)	36.20	1755.97	1931.57
120 x 120 x 10.00 mm (33.70)	29.70	2226.69	2449.37
120 x 120 x 12.50 mm (40.90)	24.40	2708.49	2979.35
140 x 140 x 5.00 mm (21.00)	47.60	1327.99	1460.80
140 x 140 x 6.30 mm (26.10)	38.3 0	1655.27	1820.80
140 x 140 x 8.00 mm (32.60)	30.70	2070.68	2277.73
140 x 140 x 10.00 mm (40.00)	25.00	2630.36	2893.41
140 x 140 x 12.50 mm (48.70)	20.50	4411.34	4852.48
150 x 150 x 5.00 mm (22.60)	44.20	1442.24	1586.48
150 x 150 x 6.30 mm (28.10)	35.60	1798.04	1977.86
150 x 150 x 8.00 mm (35.10)	28.50	2249.14	2474.07
150 x 150 x 10.00 mm (43.10)	23.20	2865.65	3152.24
150 x 150 x 12.50 mm (52.70)	19.00	4758.90	5234.80
150 x 150 x 16.00 mm (65.20)	15.30	7879.20	8667.19
160 x 160 x 5.00 mm (24.10)	41.50	1820.20	2002.21
160 x 160 x 6.30 mm (30.10)	33.20	2279.01	2506.90
160 x 160 x 8.00 mm (37.60)	26.60	2850.65	3135.69
160 x 160 x 10.00 mm (46.30)	21.60	3512.54	3863.77
160 x 160 x 12.50 mm (56.60)	17.70	4549.39	5004.35

| G STRUCTURAL CARCASSING/METAL/TIMBER |
| Excluding overheads and profit |
| **G10 STRUCTURAL STEEL FRAMING** - cont'd |

Hot formed structural hollow section	Approx metres per tonne (m)	S276J2H Grade 43D £/100m	S355J2H Grade 50D £/100m
Square (kg/m) - cont'd			
160 x 160 x 16.50 mm (70.20)	14.20	6362.81	6999.06
180 x 180 x 5.00 mm (27.30)	36.60	2060.89	2266.97
180 x 180 x 6.30 mm (34.00)	29.40	2572.35	2829.57
180 x 180 x 8.00 mm (42.70)	23.40	3234.24	3557.65
180 x 180 x 10.00 mm (52.50)	19.00	3986.40	4385.01
180 x 180 x 12.50 mm (64.40)	15.50	5176.62	5694.31
180 x 180 x 16.00 mm (80.20)	12.50	7253.96	7979.32
200 x 200 x 5.00 mm (30.40)	32.90	2294.06	2523.45
200 x 200 x 6.30 mm (38.00)	26.30	2873.21	3160.52
200 x 200 x 8.00 mm (47.70)	21.00	3610.32	3971.33
200 x 200 x 10.00 mm (58.80)	17.00	4460.25	4906.24
200 x 200 x 12.50 mm (72.30)	13.80	5795.91	6375.53
200 x 200 x 16.00 mm (90.30)	11.10	8154.02	8969.38
250 x 250 x 6.30 mm (47.90)	20.90	3617.84	3979.60
250 x 250 x 8.00 mm (60.30)	16.60	4550.51	5005.53
250 x 250 x 10.00 mm (74.50)	13.40	5641.12	6205.20
250 x 250 x 12.50 mm (91.90)	10.90	7352.07	8087.31
250 x 250 x 16.00 mm (115.00)	8.70	10426.46	11469.04
300 x 300 x 6.30 mm (57.80)	17.30	4354.95	4790.41
300 x 300 x 8.00 mm (72.80)	13.70	5498.22	6048.00
300 x 300 x 10.00 mm (90.20)	11.10	6822.00	7504.16
300 x 300 x 12.50 mm (112.00)	8.93	8892.35	9781.63
300 x 300 x 16.00 mm (141.00)	7.09	12654.33	13919.69
350 x 350 x 8.00 mm (85.40)	11.70	6445.93	7090.48
350 x 350 x 10.00 mm (106.00)	9.43	7972.79	8770.02
350 x 350 x 12.50 mm (131.00)	7.63	10480.27	11528.35
350 x 350 x 16.00 mm (166.00)	6.02	14882.20	16370.34
400 x 400 x 10.00 mm (122.00)	8.20	9176.23	10093.79
400 x 400 x 12.50 mm (151.00)	6.62	12068.19	13275.07
400 x 400 x 16.00 mm (191.00)	5.24	17110.08	18820.99
Rectangular (kg/m)			
50 x 30 x 2.50 mm (2.89)	346.00	169.30	186.23
50 x 30 x 3.00 mm (3.41)	293.30	200.03	220.03
50 x 30 x 3.20 mm (3.61)	277.00	212.21	233.43
50 x 30 x 4.00 mm (4.39)	227.80	258.59	284.45
50 x 30 x 5.00 mm (5.28)	189.40	313.09	344.40
60 x 40 x 2.50 mm (3.68)	271.70	215.11	236.62
60 x 40 x 3.00 mm (4.35)	229.90	254.53	279.99
60 x 40 x 3.20 mm (4.62)	216.50	270.19	297.21
60 x 40 x 4.00 mm (5.64)	177.30	331.65	364.81
60 x 40 x 5.00 mm (6.85)	146.00	404.12	444.53
60 x 40 x 6.30 mm (8.31)	120.30	492.25	541.48
76.20 x 50.80 x 3.20 mm (5.97)	167.50	334.04	378.44

G STRUCTURAL CARCASSING/METAL/TIMBER			
Excluding overheads and profit			
Hot formed structural hollow section	**Approx metres per tonne (m)**	**S276J2H Grade 43D £/100m**	**S355J2H Grade 50D £/100m**
Rectangular (kg/m) - cont'd			
76.20 x 50.80 x 4.00 mm (7.34)	136.20	444.21	488.63
76.20 x 50.80 x 6.30 mm (11.00)	90.90	698.25	768.07
80 x 40 x 3.00 mm (5.29)	189.00	309.61	340.57
80 x 40 x 3.20 mm (5.62)	177.90	328.75	361.62
80 x 40 x 4.00 mm (6.90)	144.90	423.94	466.33
80 x 40 x 5.00 mm (8.42)	118.80	519.44	571.38
80 x 40 x 6.30 mm (10.30)	97.10	638.65	702.51
80 x 40 x 8.00 mm (12.50)	80.00	778.55	856.40
90 x 50 x 3.00 mm (6.24)	160.30	353.46	388.81
90 x 50 x 3.60 mm (7.40)	135.10	440.45	484.49
90 x 50 x 5.00 mm (9.99)	100.10	614.32	675.75
90 x 50 x 6.30 mm (12.30)	81.30	760.30	836.32
90 x 50 x 8.00 mm (15.00)	66.70	930.61	1023.66
100 x 50 x 3.00 mm (6.71)	149.00	379.92	417.91
100 x 50 x 3.20 mm (7.13)	140.30	404.12	444.53
100 x 50 x 4.00 mm (8.78)	113.90	523.10	575.41
100 x 50 x 5.00 mm (10.80)	92.60	662.98	729.28
100 x 50 x 6.30 mm (13.30)	75.20	815.04	896.54
100 x 50 x 8.00 mm (16.30)	61.30	1009.68	1110.64
100 x 60 x 3.00 mm (7.18)	139.30	406.37	447.00
100 x 60 x 3.60 mm (8.53)	117.20	507.16	557.88
100 x 60 x 5.00 mm (11.60)	86.20	711.64	782.80
100 x 60 x 6.30 mm (14.20)	70.40	875.87	963.45
100 x 60 x 8.00 mm (17.50)	57.10	1082.67	1190.93
120 x 60 x 3.60 mm (9.66)	103.50	573.88	631.27
120 x 60 x 5.00 mm (13.10)	76.30	808.96	889.85
120 x 60 x 6.30 mm (16.20)	61.70	997.51	1097.26
120 x 60 x 8.00 mm (20.10)	49.80	1240.81	1364.88
120 x 80 x 5.00 mm (14.70)	68.00	900.20	990.21
120 x 80 x 6.30 mm (18.20)	54.90	1119.16	1231.07
120 x 80 x 8.00 mm (22.60)	44.20	1461.87	1608.06
120 x 80 x 10.00 mm (27.40)	36.50	1816.51	1998.17
150 x 100 x 4.00 mm (15.10)	66.20	950.36	1045.40
150 x 100 x 5.00 mm (18.60)	53.80	1176.94	1294.64
150 x 100 x 6.30 mm (23.10)	43.30	1466.46	1613.11
150 x 100 x 8.00 mm (28.90)	34.60	1831.50	2014.65
150 x 100 x 10.00 mm (35.30)	28.30	2324.36	2556.80
150 x 100 x 12.50 mm (42.80)	23.40	2838.71	3122.59
160 x 80 x 4.00 mm (14.40)	69.40	912.60	1003.86
160 x 80 x 5.00 mm (17.80)	56.20	1132.88	1246.18
160 x 80 x 6.30 mm (22.20)	45.00	1403.52	1543.87
160 x 80 x 8.00 mm (27.60)	36.20	1755.97	1931.57
160 x 80 x 10.00 mm (33.70)	29.70	2226.69	2449.37
160 x 80 x 12.50 mm (40.90)	24.40	2708.49	2979.35
200 x 100 x 5.00 mm (22.60)	44.20	1442.24	1586.48

G STRUCTURAL CARCASSING/METAL/TIMBER

Excluding overheads and profit

G10 STRUCTURAL STEEL FRAMING - cont'd

Hot formed structural hollow section	Approx metres per tonne (m)	S276J2H Grade 43D £/100m	S355J2H Grade 50D £/100m
Rectangular (kg/m) - cont'd			
200 x 100 x 6.30 mm (28.10)	35.60	1798.04	1977.86
200 x 100 x 8.00 mm (35.10)	28.50	2249.14	2474.07
200 x 100 x 10.00 mm (43.10)	23.20	2865.65	3152.24
200 x 100 x 12.50 mm (52.70)	19.00	4758.90	5234.80
200 x 100 x 16.00 mm (65.20)	15.30	7879.20	8667.19
250 x 150 x 5.00 mm (30.40)	32.90	2294.06	2523.45
250 x 150 x 6.30 mm (38.00)	26.30	2873.21	3160.52
250 x 150 x 8.00 mm (47.70)	21.00	3610.32	3971.33
250 x 150 x 10.00 mm (58.80)	17.00	4460.25	4906.24
250 x 150 x 12.50 mm (72.30)	13.8 0	5795.91	6375.53
250 x 150 x 16.00 mm (90.30)	11.10	8154.02	8969.38
300 x 200 x 6.30 mm (47.90)	20.90	3617.84	3979.60
300 x 200 x 8.00 mm (60.30)	16.60	4550.51	5005.53
300 x 200 x 10.00 mm (74.50)	13.40	5641.12	6205.20
300 x 200 x 12.50 mm (91.90)	10.90	7352.07	8087.31
300 x 200 x 16.00 mm (115.00)	8.70	10426.46	11469.04
400 x 200 x 6.30 mm (57.80)	17.30	4354.95	4790.41
400 x 200 x 8.00 mm (72.80)	13.70	5498.22	6048.00
400 x 200 x 10.00 mm (90.20)	11.10	6822.00	7504.16
400 x 200 x 12.50 mm (112.00)	8.93	8892.35	9781.63
400 x 200 x 16.00 mm (141.00)	7.09	12654.33	13919.69
450 x 250 x 8.00 mm (85.40)	11.70	6445.93	7090.48
450 x 250 x 10.00 mm (106.00)	9.43	7972.79	8770.02
450 x 250 x 12.50 mm (131.00)	7.63	10480.27	11528.35
450 x 250 x 16.00 mm (166.00)	6.02	14882.20	16370.34
500 x 300 x 10.00 mm (122.00)	8.20	9176.23	1009 3.79
500 x 300 x 12.50 mm (151.00)	6.62	12068.19	13275.07
500 x 300 x 16.00 mm (191.00)	5.24	17110.08	18820.99

Add to the aforementioned prices for:

	Percentage extra %
Finish	
Self colour is suplied unless otherwise specified.	
Transit primer painted (All sections except for circular hollow sections over 200 mm diameter).	5.00
Test Certificates	
Test certificates will be charged at a rate of £25 per certificate.	

	Percentage extra %
G STRUCTURAL CARCASSING/METAL/TIMBER	
Excluding overheads and profit	

Add to the aforementioned prices for:

Quantity

- **Work despatches**
  Orders for the following hollow sections of one size, thickness, length, steel grade and surface finish.
  a)   circular hollow sections over 200 mm diameter
  b)   square hollow sections over 150 x 150 mm
  c)   rectangular hollow sections over 600 mm girth

	Percentage extra %
Order Quantity:	
4 tonnes to under 10 tonnes	15.00
2 tonnes to under 4 tonnes	20.00
1 tonne to under 2 tonnes	25.00
orders under 1 tonne are not supplied	

- **Warehouse despatches**
  Orders are for the following hollow sections in one steel grade, for delivery to one destination in one assignment.
  a)   circular hollow sections less than 200 mm diameter
  b)   square hollow sections up to and including 150 x 150 mm
  c)   rectangular hollow sections up to and including 600 mm girth

	Percentage extra %
Order Quantity:	
10 tonnes and over	7.50
4 tonnes to under 10 tonnes	10.00
2 tonnes to under 4 tonnes	12.50
1 tonne to under 2 tonnes	17.50
500 kg to under 1 tonne	22.50
250 kg to under 500 kg	35.00
100 kg to under 250 kg	50.00
under 100 kg	100.00

  a)   circular hollow sections over 200 mm diameter
  b)   square hollow sections over 150 x 150 mm
  c)   rectangular hollow sections over 600 mm girth

	Percentage extra %
Order Quantity:	
10 tonnes and over	12.50
4 tonnes to under 10 tonnes	15.00
2 tonnes to under 4 tonnes	20.00
1 tonne to under 2 tonnes	25.00
500 kg to under 1 tonne	45.00
250 kg to under 500 kg	75.00

G STRUCTURAL/CARCASSING METAL/TIMBER Excluding overheads and profit	PC £	Labour hours	Labour £	Material £	Unit	Total rate £
G10 STRUCTURAL STEEL FRAMING - cont'd						
Framing, fabrication; weldable steel; BS EN **10025: 1993 Grade S275; hot rolled structural** **steel sections; welded fabrication**						
Columns						
weight not exceeding 40 kg/m	-	-	-	-	t	800.00
weight not exceeding 40 kg/m; castellated	-	-	-	-	t	905.00
weight not exceeding 40 kg/m; curved	-	-	-	-	t	1100.00
weight not exceeding 40 kg/m; square hollow section	-	-	-	-	t	1200.00
weight not exceeding 40 kg/m; circular hollow section	-	-	-	-	t	1330.00
weight 40 - 100 kg/m	-	-	-	-	t	780.00
weight 40 - 100 kg/m; castellated	-	-	-	-	t	880.00
weight 40 - 100 kg/m; curved	-	-	-	-	t	1080.00
weight 40 - 100 kg/m; square hollow section	-	-	-	-	t	1175.00
weight 40 - 100 kg/m; circular hollow section	-	-	-	-	t	1305.00
weight exceeding 100 kg/m	-	-	-	-	t	770.00
weight exceeding 100 kg/m; castellated	-	-	-	-	t	865.00
weight exceeding 100 kg/m; curved	-	-	-	-	t	1060.00
weight exceeding 100 kg/m; square hollow section	-	-	-	-	t	1160.00
weight exceeding 100 kg/m; circular hollow section	-	-	-	-	t	1290.00
Beams						
weight not exceeding 40 kg/m	-	-	-	-	t	840.00
weight not exceeding 40 kg/m; castellated	-	-	-	-	t	955.00
weight not exceeding 40 kg/m; curved	-	-	-	-	t	1230.00
weight not exceeding 40 kg/m; square hollow section	-	-	-	-	t	1305.00
weight not exceeding 40 kg/m; circular hollow section	-	-	-	-	t	1500.00
weight 40 - 100 kg/m	-	-	-	-	t	820.00
weight 40 - 100 kg/m; castellated	-	-	-	-	t	925.00
weight 40 - 100 kg/m; curved	-	-	-	-	t	1205.00
weight 40 - 100 kg/m; square hollow section	-	-	-	-	t	1280.00
weight 40 - 100 kg/m; circular hollow section	-	-	-	-	t	1470.00
weight exceeding 100 kg/m	-	-	-	-	t	810.00
weight exceeding 100 kg/m; castellated	-	-	-	-	t	910.00
weight exceeding 100 kg/m; curved	-	-	-	-	t	1185.00
weight exceeding 100 kg/m; square hollow section	-	-	-	-	t	1265.00
weight exceeding 100 kg/m; circular hollow section	-	-	-	-	t	1450.00
Bracings						
weight not exceeding 40 kg/m	-	-	-	-	t	1075.00
weight not exceeding 40 kg/m; square hollow section	-	-	-	-	t	1500.00
weight not exceeding 40 kg/m; circular hollow section	-	-	-	-	t	1675.00
weight 40 - 100 kg/m	-	-	-	-	t	1050.00
weight 40 - 100 kg/m; square hollow section	-	-	-	-	t	1475.00
weight 40 - 100 kg/m; circular hollow section	-	-	-	-	t	1650.00
weight exceeding 100 kg/m	-	-	-	-	t	1020.00
weight exceeding 100 kg/m; square hollow section	-	-	-	-	t	1455.00
weight exceeding 100 kg/m; circular hollow section	-	-	-	-	t	1630.00

G STRUCTURAL/CARCASSING METAL/TIMBER Excluding overheads and profit	PC £	Labour hours	Labour £	Material £	Unit	Total rate £
Purlins and cladding rails						
weight not exceeding 40 kg/m	-	-	-	-	t	950.00
weight not exceeding 40 kg/m; square hollow section	-	-	-	-	t	1350.00
weight not exceeding 40 kg/m; circular hollow section	-	-	-	-	t	1500.00
weight 40 - 100 kg/m	-	-	-	-	t	925.00
weight 40 - 100 kg/m; square hollow section	-	-	-	-	t	1325.00
weight 40 - 100 kg/m; circular hollow section	-	-	-	-	t	1475.00
weight exceeding 100 kg/m	-	-	-	-	t	900.00
weight exceeding 100 kg/m; square hollow section	-	-	-	-	t	1300.00
weight exceeding 100 kg/m; circular hollow section	-	-	-	-	t	1450.00
Grillages						
weight not exceeding 40 kg/m	-	-	-	-	t	650.00
weight 40 - 100 kg/m	-	-	-	-	t	690.00
weight exceeding 100 kg/m	-	-	-	-	t	650.00
Trestles, towers and built up columns						
straight	-	-	-	-	t	1250.00
Trusses and built up girders						
straight	-	-	-	-	t	1250.00
curved	-	-	-	-	t	1600.00
Fittings	-	-	-	-	t	900.00
Framing, erection						
Trial erection	-	-	-	-	t	225.00
Permanent erection on site	-	-	-	-	t	180.00
Surface preparation						
At works						
blast cleaning	-	-	-	-	m²	1.65
Surface treatment						
At works						
galvanising	-	-	-	-	m²	10.00
grit blast and one coat zinc chromate primer	-	-	-	-	m²	2.45
touch up primer and one coat of two pack epoxy zinc phosphate primer	-	-	-	-	m²	3.00
On site						
"Nullifire" fire protection system	-	-	-	-	m²	33.50
G12 ISOLATED STRUCTURAL METAL MEMBERS						
Isolated structural member; weldable steel; BS EN 10025: 1993 Grade S275; hot rolled structural steel sections						
Plain member; beams						
weight not exceeding 40 kg/m	-	-	-	-	t	585.00
weight 40 - 100 kg/m	-	-	-	-	t	560.00
weight exceeding 100 kg/m	-	-	-	-	t	550.00

G STRUCTURAL/CARCASSING METAL/TIMBER Excluding overheads and profit	PC £	Labour hours	Labour £	Material £	Unit	Total rate £
G12 ISOLATED STRUCTURAL METAL MEMBERS - cont'd						
Metsec open web steel lattice beams or other equal and approved; in single members; raised 3.50 m above ground; ends built in Beams; one coat zinc phosphate primer at works						
200 mm deep; to span 5.00 m (7.69 kg/m); ref B22	-	0.20	2.88	23.63	m	**26.51**
300 mm deep; to span 7.00 m (10.26 kg/m); ref B30	-	0.25	3.60	31.64	m	**35.24**
350 mm deep; to span 8.50 m (10.60 kg/m); ref B35	-	0.25	3.60	32.61	m	**36.21**
350 mm deep; to span 10.00 m (12.76 kg/m); ref D35	-	0.30	4.32	39.96	m	**44.28**
450 mm deep; to span 13.00 m (25.44 kg/m); ref G50	-	0.50	7.21	62.96	m	**70.17**
Beams; galvanised						
200 mm deep; to span 5.00 m (7.69 kg/m); ref B22	-	0.20	2.88	25.96	m	**28.84**
300 mm deep; to span 7.00 m (10.26 kg/m); ref B30	-	0.25	3.60	34.77	m	**38.37**
350 mm deep; to span 8.50 m (10.60 kg/m); ref B35	-	0.25	3.60	35.84	m	**39.44**
350 mm deep; to span 10.00 m (12.76 kg/m); ref D35	-	0.30	4.32	43.93	m	**48.25**
450 mm deep; to span 13.00 m (25.44 kg/m); ref G50	-	0.50	7.21	69.23	m	**76.44**

G20 CARPENTRY/TIMBER FRAMING/FIRST FIXING

BASIC TIMBER PRICES

	£		£		£

Hardwood; Joinery quality (£/m³)

Agba	909.00	American White Ash	925.00	Beech	1006.00
Brazilian Mahogany	1371.00	European Oak	1700.00	Iroko	821.00
Maple	1634.00	Sapele	760.00	Teak	2000.00
Utile	963.00	W.A. Mahogany	705.00		

Softwood; Carcassing quality (£/m³)

2.00 - 4.80 m lengths	236.78	6 .00 - 9.00 m lengths	248.05	S. S. Grade	27.44
4.80 - 6.00 m lengths	225.50	G. S. Grade	14.28		

Joinery quality - (£/m³)   290.00

"Treatment" - (£/m³)

Pre-treatment of timber by vacuum/pressure impregnation,
excluding transport costs and any subsequent seasoning:
    interior work; minimum. salt retention 4.00 kg/m³   42.28
    exterior work; minimum salt retention 5.30 kg/m³   48.31

Pre-treatment of timber including flame proofing
all purposes; minimum salt retention 36.00 kg/m³   110.00

"Aquaseal" timber treatments - (£/25 litres)

"Timbershield"	26.10
"Longlife Wood Protector"	70.51

G STRUCTURAL/CARCASSING METAL/TIMBER Excluding overheads and profit	PC £	Labour hours	Labour £	Material £	Unit	Total rate £
Sawn softwood; untreated						
Floor members						
38 mm x 100 mm	-	0.12	1.36	0.85	m	**2.21**
38 mm x 150 mm	-	0.14	1.59	1.25	m	**2.84**
50 mm x 75 mm	-	0.12	1.36	0.84	m	**2.20**
50 mm x 100 mm	-	0.14	1.59	1.08	m	**2.67**
50 mm x 125 mm	-	0.14	1.59	1.32	m	**2.91**
50 mm x 150 mm	-	0.15	1.70	1.60	m	**3.30**
50 mm x 175 mm	-	0.15	1.70	1.84	m	**3.54**
50 mm x 200 mm	-	0.16	1.81	2.17	m	**3.98**
50 mm x 225 mm	-	0.16	1.81	2.50	m	**4.31**
50 mm x 250 mm	-	0.17	1.93	2.84	m	**4.77**
75 mm x 125 mm	-	0.16	1.81	1.98	m	**3.79**
75 mm x 150 mm	-	0.16	1.81	2.38	m	**4.19**
75 mm x 175 mm	-	0.16	1.81	2.79	m	**4.60**
75 mm x 200 mm	-	0.17	1.93	3.25	m	**5.18**
75 mm x 225 mm	-	0.17	1.93	3.74	m	**5.67**
75 mm x 250 mm	-	0.18	2.04	4.27	m	**6.31**
100 mm x 150 mm	-	0.22	2.49	3.25	m	**5.74**
100 mm x 200 mm	-	0.23	2.61	4.44	m	**7.05**
100 mm x 250 mm	-	0.25	2.83	6.16	m	**8.99**
100 mm x 300 mm	-	0.27	3.06	7.60	m	**10.66**
Wall or partition members						
25 mm x 25 mm	-	0.07	0.79	0.25	m	**1.04**
25 mm x 38 mm	-	0.07	0.79	0.32	m	**1.11**
25 mm x 75 mm	-	0.09	1.02	0.45	m	**1.47**
38 mm x 38 mm	-	0.09	1.02	0.37	m	**1.39**
38 mm x 50 mm	-	0.09	1.02	0.44	m	**1.46**
38 mm x 75 mm	-	0.12	1.36	0.64	m	**2.00**
38 mm x 100 mm	-	0.15	1.70	0.85	m	**2.55**
50 mm x 50 mm	-	0.12	1.36	0.59	m	**1.95**
50 mm x 75 mm	-	0.15	1.70	0.86	m	**2.56**
50 mm x 100 mm	-	0.18	2.04	1.10	m	**3.14**
50 mm x 125 mm	-	0.19	2.15	1.34	m	**3.49**
75 mm x 75 mm	-	0.18	2.04	1.45	m	**3.49**
75 mm x 100 mm	-	0.21	2.38	1.63	m	**4.01**
100 mm x 100 mm	-	0.21	2.38	2.16	m	**4.54**
Roof members; flat						
38 mm x 75 mm	-	0.14	1.59	0.64	m	**2.23**
38 mm x 100 mm	-	0.14	1.59	0.85	m	**2.44**
38 mm x 125 mm	-	0.14	1.59	1.06	m	**2.65**
38 mm x 150 mm	-	0.14	1.59	1.25	m	**2.84**
50 mm x 100 mm	-	0.14	1.59	1.08	m	**2.67**
50 mm x 125 mm	-	0.14	1.59	1.32	m	**2.91**
50 mm x 150 mm	-	0.15	1.70	1.60	m	**3.30**
50 mm x 175 mm	-	0.15	1.70	1.84	m	**3.54**
50 mm x 200 mm	-	0.16	1.81	2.17	m	**3.98**
50 mm x 225 mm	-	0.16	1.81	2.50	m	**4.31**
50 mm x 250 mm	-	0.17	1.93	2.84	m	**4.77**
75 mm x 150 mm	-	0.16	1.81	2.38	m	**4.19**
75 mm x 175 mm	-	0.16	1.81	2.79	m	**4.60**
75 mm x 200 mm	-	0.17	1.93	3.25	m	**5.18**
75 mm x 225 mm	-	0.17	1.93	3.74	m	**5.67**
75 mm x 250 mm	-	0.18	2.04	4.27	m	**6.31**
Roof members; pitched						
25 mm x 100 mm	-	0.12	1.36	0.59	m	**1.95**
25 mm x 125 mm	-	0.12	1.36	0.72	m	**2.08**
25 mm x 150 mm	-	0.15	1.70	0.92	m	**2.62**
25 mm x 175 mm	-	0.17	1.93	1.19	m	**3.12**
25 mm x 200 mm	-	0.18	2.04	1.39	m	**3.43**
38 mm x 100 mm	-	0.15	1.70	0.85	m	**2.55**
38 mm x 125 mm	-	0.15	1.70	1.06	m	**2.76**

G STRUCTURAL/CARCASSING METAL/TIMBER Excluding overheads and profit	PC £	Labour hours	Labour £	Material £	Unit	Total rate £
G20 CARPENTRY/TIMBER FRAMING/FIRST **FIXING** - cont'd						
Sawn softwood; untreated - cont'd						
Roof members; pitched - cont'd						
38 mm x 150 mm	-	0.15	1.70	1.25	m	**2.95**
50 mm x 50 mm	-	0.12	1.36	0.58	m	**1.94**
50 mm x 75 mm	-	0.15	1.70	0.84	m	**2.54**
50 mm x 100 mm	-	0.18	2.04	1.08	m	**3.12**
50 mm x 125 mm	-	0.18	2.04	1.32	m	**3.36**
50 mm x 150 mm	-	0.21	2.38	1.60	m	**3.98**
50 mm x 175 mm	-	0.21	2.38	1.84	m	**4.22**
50 mm x 200 mm	-	0.21	2.38	2.17	m	**4.55**
50 mm x 225 mm	-	0.21	2.38	2.50	m	**4.88**
75 mm x 100 mm	-	0.25	2.83	1.60	m	**4.43**
75 mm x 125 mm	-	0.25	2.83	1.98	m	**4.81**
75 mm x 150 mm	-	0.25	2.83	2.38	m	**5.21**
100 mm x 150 mm	-	0.30	3.40	3.27	m	**6.67**
100 mm x 175 mm	-	0.30	3.40	3.80	m	**7.20**
100 mm x 200 mm	-	0.30	3.40	4.44	m	**7.84**
100 mm x 225 mm	-	0.33	3.74	5.42	m	**9.16**
100 mm x 250 mm	-	0.33	3.74	6.16	m	**9.90**
Plates						
38 mm x 75 mm	-	0.12	1.36	0.64	m	**2.00**
38 mm x 100 mm	-	0.15	1.70	0.85	m	**2.55**
50 mm x 75 mm	-	0.15	1.70	0.86	m	**2.56**
50 mm x 100 mm	-	0.18	2.04	1.10	m	**3.14**
75 mm x 100 mm	-	0.21	2.38	1.63	m	**4.01**
75 mm x 125 mm	-	0.24	2.72	1.96	m	**4.68**
75 mm x 150 mm	-	0.27	3.06	2.36	m	**5.42**
Plates; fixing by bolting						
38 mm x 75 mm	-	0.22	2.49	0.64	m	**3.13**
38 mm x 100 mm	-	0.25	2.83	0.85	m	**3.68**
50 mm x 75 mm	-	0.25	2.83	0.86	m	**3.69**
50 mm x 100 mm	-	0.28	3.17	1.10	m	**4.27**
75 mm x 100 mm	-	0.31	3.51	1.63	m	**5.14**
75 mm x 125 mm	-	0.34	3.85	1.96	m	**5.81**
75 mm x 150 mm	-	0.37	4.19	2.36	m	**6.55**
Joist strutting; herringbone						
50 mm x 50 mm; depth of joist 150 mm	-	0.50	5.67	1.39	m	**7.06**
50 mm x 50 mm; depth of joist 175 mm	-	0.50	5.67	1.41	m	**7.08**
50 mm x 50 mm; depth of joist 200 mm	-	0.50	5.67	1.44	m	**7.11**
50 mm x 50 mm; depth of joist 225 mm	-	0.50	5.67	1.47	m	**7.14**
50 mm x 50 mm; depth of joist 250 mm	-	0.50	5.67	1.49	m	**7.16**
Joist strutting; block						
50 mm x 150 mm; depth of joist 150 mm	-	0.30	3.40	1.84	m	**5.24**
50 mm x 175 mm; depth of joist 175 mm	-	0.30	3.40	2.09	m	**5.49**
50 mm x 200 mm; depth of joist 200 mm	-	0.30	3.40	2.41	m	**5.81**
50 mm x 225 mm; depth of joist 225 mm	-	0.30	3.40	2.75	m	**6.15**
50 mm x 250 mm; depth of joist 250 mm	-	0.30	3.40	3.09	m	**6.49**
Cleats						
225 mm x 100 mm x 75 mm	-	0.20	2.27	0.42	nr	**2.69**
Extra for stress grading to above timbers						
general structural (GS) grade	-	-	-	13.43	m³	**13.43**
special structural (SS) grade	-	-	-	25.85	m³	**25.85**
Extra for protecting and flameproofing timber with "Celgard CF" protection or other equal and approved						
small sections	-	-	-	92.40	m³	**92.40**
large sections	-	-	-	88.20	m³	**88.20**

G STRUCTURAL/CARCASSING METAL/TIMBER Excluding overheads and profit	PC £	Labour hours	Labour £	Material £	Unit	Total rate £
Wrot surfaces						
plain; 50 mm wide	-	0.03	0.34	-	m	0.34
plain; 100 mm wide	-	0.04	0.45	-	m	0.45
plain; 150 mm wide	-	0.05	0.57	-	m	0.57
Sawn softwood; "Tanalised"						
Floor members						
38 mm x 75 mm	-	0.12	1.36	0.73	m	2.09
38 mm x 100 mm	-	0.12	1.36	0.97	m	2.33
38 mm x 150 mm	-	0.14	1.59	1.43	m	3.02
50 mm x 75 mm	-	0.12	1.36	0.96	m	2.32
50 mm x 100 mm	-	0.14	1.59	1.24	m	2.83
50 mm x 125 mm	-	0.14	1.59	1.51	m	3.10
50 mm x 150 mm	-	0.15	1.70	1.83	m	3.53
50 mm x 175 mm	-	0.15	1.70	2.12	m	3.82
50 mm x 200 mm	-	0.16	1.81	2.48	m	4.29
50 mm x 225 mm	-	0.16	1.81	2.85	m	4.66
50 mm x 250 mm	-	0.17	1.93	3.23	m	5.16
75 mm x 125 mm	-	0.16	1.81	2.27	m	4.08
75 mm x 150 mm	-	0.16	1.81	2.73	m	4.54
75 mm x 175 mm	-	0.16	1.81	3.20	m	5.01
75 mm x 200 mm	-	0.17	1.93	3.72	m	5.65
75 mm x 225 mm	-	0.17	1.93	4.27	m	6.20
75 mm x 250 mm	-	0.18	2.04	4.86	m	6.90
100 mm x 150 mm	-	0.22	2.49	3.72	m	6.21
100 mm x 200 mm	-	0.23	2.61	5.06	m	7.67
100 mm x 250 mm	-	0.25	2.83	6.94	m	9.77
100 mm x 300 mm	-	0.27	3.06	8.54	m	11.60
Wall or partition members						
25 mm x 25 mm	-	0.07	0.79	0.27	m	1.06
25 mm x 38 mm	-	0.07	0.79	0.35	m	1.14
25 mm x 75 mm	-	0.09	1.02	0.50	m	1.52
38 mm x 38 mm	-	0.09	1.02	0.41	m	1.43
38 mm x 50 mm	-	0.09	1.02	0.49	m	1.51
38 mm x 75 mm	-	0.12	1.36	0.73	m	2.09
38 mm x 100 mm	-	0.15	1.70	0.97	m	2.67
50 mm x 50 mm	-	0.12	1.36	0.67	m	2.03
50 mm x 75 mm	-	0.15	1.70	0.98	m	2.68
50 mm x 100 mm	-	0.18	2.04	1.26	m	3.30
50 mm x 125 mm	-	0.19	2.15	1.53	m	3.68
75 mm x 75 mm	-	0.18	2.04	1.63	m	3.67
75 mm x 100 mm	-	0.21	2.38	1.87	m	4.25
100 mm x 100 mm	-	0.21	2.38	2.47	m	4.85
Roof members; flat						
38 mm x 75 mm	-	0.14	1.59	0.73	m	2.32
38 mm x 100 mm	-	0.14	1.59	0.97	m	2.56
38 mm x 125 mm	-	0.14	1.59	1.21	m	2.80
38 mm x 150 mm	-	0.14	1.59	1.43	m	3.02
50 mm x 100 mm	-	0.14	1.59	1.24	m	2.83
50 mm x 125 mm	-	0.14	1.59	1.51	m	3.10
50 mm x 150 mm	-	0.15	1.70	1.83	m	3.53
50 mm x 175 mm	-	0.15	1.70	2.12	m	3.82
50 mm x 200 mm	-	0.16	1.81	2.48	m	4.29
50 mm x 225 mm	-	0.16	1.81	2.85	m	4.66
50 mm x 250 mm	-	0.17	1.93	3.23	m	5.16
75 mm x 150 mm	-	0.16	1.81	2.73	m	4.54
75 mm x 175 mm	-	0.16	1.81	3.20	m	5.01
75 mm x 200 mm	-	0.17	1.93	3.72	m	5.65
75 mm x 225 mm	-	0.17	1.93	4.27	m	6.20
75 mm x 250 mm	-	0.18	2.04	4.86	m	6.90

G STRUCTURAL/CARCASSING METAL/TIMBER Excluding overheads and profit	PC £	Labour hours	Labour £	Material £	Unit	Total rate £
G20 CARCENTRY/TIMBER FRAMING/FIRST FIXING - cont'd						
Sawn softwood; "Tanalised" - cont'd						
Roof members; pitched						
25 mm x 100 mm	-	0.12	1.36	0.66	m	**2.02**
25 mm x 125 mm	-	0.12	1.36	0.81	m	**2.17**
25 mm x 150 mm	-	0.15	1.70	1.04	m	**2.74**
25 mm x 175 mm	-	0.17	1.93	1.32	m	**3.25**
25 mm x 200 mm	-	0.18	2.04	1.55	m	**3.59**
38 mm x 100 mm	-	0.15	1.70	0.97	m	**2.67**
38 mm x 125 mm	-	0.15	1.70	1.21	m	**2.91**
38 mm x 150 mm	-	0.15	1.70	1.43	m	**3.13**
50 mm x 50 mm	-	0.12	1.36	0.65	m	**2.01**
50 mm x 75 mm	-	0.15	1.70	0.96	m	**2.66**
50 mm x 100 mm	-	0.18	2.04	1.24	m	**3.28**
50 mm x 125 mm	-	0.18	2.04	1.51	m	**3.55**
50 mm x 150 mm	-	0.21	2.38	1.83	m	**4.21**
50 mm x 175 mm	-	0.21	2.38	2.12	m	**4.50**
50 mm x 200 mm	-	0.21	2.38	2.48	m	**4.86**
50 mm x 225 mm	-	0.21	2.38	2.85	m	**5.23**
75 mm x 100 mm	-	0.25	2.83	1.83	m	**4.66**
75 mm x 125 mm	-	0.25	2.83	2.27	m	**5.10**
75 mm x 150 mm	-	0.25	2.83	2.73	m	**5.56**
100 mm x 150 mm	-	0.30	3.40	3.74	m	**7.14**
100 mm x 175 mm	-	0.30	3.40	4.34	m	**7.74**
100 mm x 200 mm	-	0.30	3.40	5.06	m	**8.46**
100 mm x 225 mm	-	0.33	3.74	6.12	m	**9.86**
100 mm x 250 mm	-	0.33	3.74	6.94	m	**10.68**
Plates						
38 mm x 75 mm	-	0.12	1.36	0.73	m	**2.09**
38 mm x 100 mm	-	0.15	1.70	0.97	m	**2.67**
50 mm x 75 mm	-	0.15	1.70	0.98	m	**2.68**
50 mm x 100 mm	-	0.18	2.04	1.26	m	**3.30**
75 mm x 100 mm	-	0.21	2.38	1.87	m	**4.25**
75 mm x 125 mm	-	0.24	2.72	2.26	m	**4.98**
75 mm x 150 mm	-	0.27	3.06	2.71	m	**5.77**
Plates; fixing by bolting						
38 mm x 75 mm	-	0.22	2.49	0.73	m	**3.22**
38 mm x 100 mm	-	0.25	2.83	0.97	m	**3.80**
50 mm x 75 mm	-	0.25	2.83	0.98	m	**3.81**
50 mm x 100 mm	-	0.28	3.17	1.26	m	**4.43**
75 mm x 100 mm	-	0.31	3.51	1.87	m	**5.38**
75 mm x 125 mm	-	0.34	3.85	2.26	m	**6.11**
75 mm x 150 mm	-	0.37	4.19	2.71	m	**6.90**
Joist strutting; herringbone						
50 mm x 50 mm; depth of joist 150 mm	-	0.50	5.67	1.55	m	**7.22**
50 mm x 50 mm; depth of joist 175 mm	-	0.50	5.67	1.58	m	**7.25**
50 mm x 50 mm; depth of joist 200 mm	-	0.50	5.67	1.61	m	**7.28**
50 mm x 50 mm; depth of joist 225 mm	-	0.50	5.67	1.64	m	**7.31**
50 mm x 50 mm; depth of joist 250 mm	-	0.50	5.67	1.67	m	**7.34**
Joist strutting; block						
50 mm x 150 mm; depth of joist 150 mm	-	0.30	3.40	2.08	m	**5.48**
50 mm x 175 mm; depth of joist 175 mm	-	0.30	3.40	2.37	m	**5.77**
50 mm x 200 mm; depth of joist 200 mm	-	0.30	3.40	2.73	m	**6.13**
50 mm x 225 mm; depth of joist 225 mm	-	0.30	3.40	3.10	m	**6.50**
50 mm x 250 mm; depth of joist 250 mm	-	0.30	3.40	3.48	m	**6.88**
Cleats						
225 mm x 100 mm x 75 mm	-	0.20	2.27	0.47	nr	**2.74**

G STRUCTURAL/CARCASSING METAL/TIMBER Excluding overheads and profit	PC £	Labour hours	Labour £	Material £	Unit	Total rate £
Extra for stress grading to above timbers						
general structural (GS) grade	-	-	-	13.43	m³	13.43
special structural (SS) grade	-	-	-	25.85	m³	25.85
Extra for protecting and flameproofing timber						
with "Celgard CF" protection or other equal and						
approved						
small sections	-	-	-	92.40	m³	92.40
large sections	-	-	-	88.20	m³	88.20
Wrot surfaces						
plain; 50 mm wide	-	0.03	0.34	-	m	0.34
plain; 100 mm wide	-	0.04	0.45	-	m	0.45
plain; 150 mm wide	-	0.05	0.57	-	m	0.57
Trussed rafters, stress graded sawn						
softwood pressure impregnated; raised						
through two storeys and fixed in position						
"W" type truss (Fink); 22.5 degree pitch; 450						
mm eaves overhang						
5.00 m span	-	1.60	18.14	22.03	nr	40.17
7.60 m span	-	1.75	19.84	30.68	nr	50.52
10.00 m span	-	2.00	22.68	43.99	nr	66.67
"W" type truss (Fink); 30 degree pitch; 450 mm						
eaves overhang						
5.00 m span	-	1.60	18.14	23.08	nr	41.22
7.60 m span	-	1.75	19.84	30.82	nr	50.66
10.00 m span	-	2.00	22.68	45.94	nr	68.62
"W" type truss (Fink); 45 degree pitch; 450 mm						
eaves overhang						
4.60 m span	-	1.60	18.14	24.94	nr	43.08
7.00 m span	-	1.75	19.84	32.73	nr	52.57
"Mono" type truss; 17.50 degree pitch; 450 mm						
eaves overhang						
3.30 m span	-	1.40	15.88	18.75	nr	34.63
5.60 m span	-	1.60	18.14	31.87	nr	50.01
7.00 m span	-	1.85	20.98	37.38	nr	58.36
"Mono" type truss; 30 degree pitch; 450 mm						
eaves overhang						
3.30 m span	-	1.40	15.88	19.57	nr	35.45
5.60 m span	-	1.60	18.14	31.75	nr	49.89
7.00 m span	-	1.85	20.98	41.10	nr	62.08
"Attic" type truss; 45 degree pitch; 450 mm						
eaves overhang						
5.00 m span	-	3.15	35.72	39.72	nr	75.44
7.60 m span	-	3.30	37.42	66.55	nr	103.97
9.00 m span	-	3.50	39.69	83.31	nr	123.00
"Moelven Toreboda" glulam timber beams or						
other equal and approved; Moelven Laminated						
Timber Structures; LB grade whitewood;						
pressure impregnated; phenbol resorcinol						
adhesive; clean planed finish; fixed						
Laminated roof members						
56 mm x 225 mm	-	0.55	6.24	6.39	m	12.63
66 mm x 315 mm	-	0.70	7.94	10.54	m	18.48
90 mm x 315 mm	-	0.90	10.21	14.38	m	24.59
90 mm x 405 mm	-	1.15	13.04	18.34	m	31.38
115 mm x 405 mm	-	1.45	16.44	23.61	m	40.05
115 mm x 495 mm	-	1.80	20.41	28.85	m	49.26
115 mm x 630 mm	-	2.20	24.95	36.72	m	61.67

G STRUCTURAL/CARCASSING METAL/TIMBER Excluding overheads and profit	PC £	Labour hours	Labour £	Material £	Unit	Total rate £
G20 CARPENTRY/TIMBER FRAMING/FIRST FIXING - cont'd						
"Masterboard" or other equal and approved; 6 mm thick						
Eaves, verge soffit boards, fascia boards and the like						
over 300 mm wide	5.31	0.70	7.94	6.09	m²	14.03
75 mm wide	-	0.21	2.38	0.47	m	2.85
150 mm wide	-	0.24	2.72	0.91	m	3.63
225 mm wide	-	0.28	3.18	1.36	m	4.54
300 mm wide	-	0.30	3.40	1.81	m	5.21
Plywood; external quality; 15 mm thick						
Eaves, verge soffit boards, fascia boards and the like						
over 300 mm wide	9.35	0.82	9.30	10.43	m²	19.73
75 mm wide	-	0.25	2.83	0.79	m	3.62
150 mm wide	-	0.29	3.29	1.57	m	4.86
225 mm wide	-	0.33	3.74	2.34	m	6.08
300 mm wide	-	0.37	4.20	3.11	m	7.31
Plywood; external quality; 18 mm thick						
Eaves, verge soffit boards, fascia boards and the like						
over 300 mm wide	11.17	0.82	9.30	12.39	m²	21.69
75 mm wide	-	0.25	2.83	0.94	m	3.77
150 mm wide	-	0.29	3.29	1.86	m	5.15
225 mm wide	-	0.33	3.74	2.78	m	6.52
300 mm wide	-	0.37	4.20	3.70	m	7.90
Plywood; marine quality; 18 mm thick						
Gutter boards; butt joints						
over 300 mm wide	8.32	0.93	10.55	9.33	m²	19.88
150 mm wide	-	0.33	3.74	1.40	m	5.14
225 mm wide	-	0.37	4.20	2.11	m	6.31
300 mm wide	-	0.41	4.65	2.80	m	7.45
Eaves, verge soffit boards, fascias boards and the like						
over 300 mm wide	-	0.82	9.30	9.33	m²	18.63
75 mm wide	-	0.25	2.83	0.71	m	3.54
150 mm wide	-	0.29	3.29	1.40	m	4.69
225 mm wide	-	0.33	3.74	2.09	m	5.83
300 mm wide	-	0.37	4.20	2.78	m	6.98
Plywood; marine quality; 25 mm thick						
Gutter boards; butt joints						
over 300 mm wide	11.56	1.00	11.34	12.81	m²	24.15
150 mm wide	-	0.35	3.97	1.92	m	5.89
225 mm wide	-	0.40	4.54	2.89	m	7.43
300 mm wide	-	0.45	5.10	3.84	m	8.94
Eaves, verge soffit boards, fascia boards and the like						
over 300 mm wide	-	0.88	9.98	12.81	m²	22.79
75 mm wide	-	0.26	2.95	0.97	m	3.92
150 mm wide	-	0.31	3.52	1.92	m	5.44
225 mm wide	-	0.31	3.52	2.87	m	6.39
300 mm wide	-	0.40	4.54	3.82	m	8.36

G STRUCTURAL/CARCASSING METAL/TIMBER Excluding overheads and profit	PC £	Labour hours	Labour £	Material £	Unit	Total rate £
Sawn softwood; untreated						
Gutter boards; butt joints						
19 mm thick; sloping	-	1.25	14.18	5.11	m²	19.29
19 mm thick; 75 mm wide	-	0.35	3.97	0.38	m	4.35
19 mm thick; 150 mm wide	-	0.40	4.54	0.74	m	5.28
19 mm thick; 225 mm wide	-	0.45	5.10	1.27	m	6.37
25 mm thick; sloping	-	1.25	14.18	6.54	m²	20.72
25 mm thick; 75 mm wide	-	0.35	3.97	0.47	m	4.44
25 mm thick; 150 mm wide	-	0.40	4.54	0.96	m	5.50
25 mm thick; 225 mm wide	-	0.45	5.10	1.68	m	6.78
Cesspools with 25 mm thick sides and bottom						
225 mm x 225 mm x 150 mm	-	1.20	13.61	1.29	nr	14.90
300 mm x 300 mm x 150 mm	-	1.40	15.88	1.64	nr	17.52
Individual supports; firrings						
50 mm wide x 36 mm average depth	-	0.15	1.70	0.83	m	2.53
50 mm wide x 50 mm average depth	-	0.15	1.70	1.07	m	2.77
50 mm wide x 75 mm average depth	-	0.15	1.70	1.36	m	3.06
Individual supports; bearers						
25 mm x 50 mm	-	0.10	1.13	0.38	m	1.51
38 mm x 50 mm	-	0.10	1.13	0.47	m	1.60
50 mm x 50 mm	-	0.10	1.13	0.61	m	1.74
50 mm x 75 mm	-	0.10	1.13	0.88	m	2.01
Individual supports; angle fillets						
38 mm x 38 mm	-	0.10	1.13	0.41	m	1.54
50 mm x 50 mm	-	0.10	1.13	0.61	m	1.74
75 mm x 75 mm	-	0.12	1.36	1.44	m	2.80
Individual supports; tilting fillets						
19 mm x 38 mm	-	0.10	1.13	0.19	m	1.32
25 mm x 50 mm	-	0.10	1.13	0.27	m	1.40
38 mm x 75 mm	-	0.10	1.13	0.46	m	1.59
50 mm x 75 mm	-	0.10	1.13	0.57	m	1.70
75 mm x 100 mm	-	0.15	1.70	1.08	m	2.78
Individual supports; grounds or battens						
13 mm x 19 mm	-	0.05	0.57	0.23	m	0.80
13 mm x 32 mm	-	0.05	0.57	0.25	m	0.82
25 mm x 50 mm	-	0.05	0.57	0.34	m	0.91
Individual supports; grounds or battens; plugged and screwed						
13 mm x 19 mm	-	0.15	1.70	0.25	m	1.95
13 mm x 32 mm	-	0.15	1.70	0.27	m	1.97
25 mm x 50 mm	-	0.15	1.70	0.36	m	2.06
Framed supports; open-spaced grounds or battens; at 300 mm centres one way						
25 mm x 50 mm	-	0.15	1.70	1.12	m²	2.82
25 mm x 50 mm; plugged and screwed	-	0.45	5.10	1.19	m²	6.29
Framed supports; at 300 mm centres one way and 600 mm centres the other way						
25 mm x 50 mm	-	0.75	8.51	1.68	m²	10.19
38 mm x 50 mm	-	0.75	8.51	2.16	m²	10.67
50 mm x 50 mm	-	0.75	8.51	2.86	m²	11.37
50 mm x 75 mm	-	0.75	8.51	4.20	m²	12.71
75 mm x 75 mm	-	0.75	8.51	7.16	m²	15.67
Framed supports; at 300 mm centres one way and 600 mm centres the other way; plugged and screwed						
25 mm x 50 mm	-	1.25	14.18	1.92	m²	16.10
38 mm x 50 mm	-	1.25	14.18	2.40	m²	16.58
50 mm x 50 mm	-	1.25	14.18	3.10	m²	17.28
50 mm x 75 mm	-	1.25	14.18	4.44	m²	18.62
75 mm x 75 mm	-	1.25	14.18	7.40	m²	21.58

G STRUCTURAL/CARCASSING METAL/TIMBER Excluding overheads and profit	PC £	Labour hours	Labour £	Material £	Unit	Total rate £
G20 CARPENTRY/TIMBER FRAMING/FIRST FIXING - cont'd						
Sawn softwood; untreated - cont'd						
Framed supports; at 500 mm centres both ways						
25 mm x 50 mm; to bath panels	-	0.90	10.21	2.18	m²	**12.39**
Framed supports; as bracketing and cradling around steelwork						
25 mm x 50 mm	-	1.40	15.88	2.37	m²	**18.25**
50 mm x 50 mm	-	1.50	17.01	4.03	m²	**21.04**
50 mm x 75 mm	-	1.60	18.14	5.91	m²	**24.05**
Sawn softwood; "Tanalised"						
Gutter boards; butt joints						
19 mm thick; sloping	-	1.25	14.18	5.70	m²	**19.88**
19 mm thick; 75 mm wide	-	0.35	3.97	0.42	m	**4.39**
19 mm thick; 150 mm wide	-	0.40	4.54	0.83	m	**5.37**
19 mm thick; 225 mm wide	-	0.45	5.10	1.40	m	**6.50**
25 mm thick; sloping	-	1.25	14.18	7.32	m²	**21.50**
25 mm thick; 75 mm wide	-	0.35	3.97	0.52	m	**4.49**
25 mm thick; 150 mm wide	-	0.40	4.54	1.08	m	**5.62**
25 mm thick; 225 mm wide	-	0.45	5.10	1.85	m	**6.95**
Cesspools with 25 mm thick sides and bottom						
225 mm x 225 mm x 150 mm	-	1.20	13.61	1.45	nr	**15.06**
300 mm x 300 mm x 150 mm	-	1.40	15.88	1.86	nr	**17.74**
Individual supports; firrings						
50 mm wide x 36 mm average depth	-	0.15	1.70	0.89	m	**2.59**
50 mm wide x 50 mm average depth	-	0.15	1.70	1.15	m	**2.85**
50 mm wide x 75 mm average depth	-	0.15	1.70	1.48	m	**3.18**
Individual supports; bearers						
25 mm x 50 mm	-	0.10	1.13	0.42	m	**1.55**
38 mm x 50 mm	-	0.10	1.13	0.53	m	**1.66**
50 mm x 50 mm		0.10	1.13	0.69	m	**1.82**
50 mm x 75 mm	-	0.10	1.13	1.00	m	**2.13**
Individual supports; angle fillets						
38 mm x 38 mm	-	0.10	1.13	0.43	m	**1.56**
50 mm x 50 mm	-	0.10	1.13	0.65	m	**1.78**
75 mm x 75 mm	-	0.12	1.36	1.53	m	**2.89**
Individual supports; tilting fillets						
19 mm x 38 mm	-	0.10	1.13	0.21	m	**1.34**
25 mm x 50 mm	-	0.10	1.13	0.29	m	**1.42**
38 mm x 75 mm	-	0.10	1.13	0.51	m	**1.64**
50 mm x 75 mm	-	0.10	1.13	0.63	m	**1.76**
75 mm x 100 mm	-	0.15	1.70	1.19	m	**2.89**
Individual supports; grounds or battens						
13 mm x 19 mm	-	0.05	0.57	0.24	m	**0.81**
13 mm x 32 mm	-	0.05	0.57	0.26	m	**0.83**
25 mm x 50 mm	-	0.05	0.57	0.38	m	**0.95**
Individual supports; grounds or battens; plugged and screwed						
13 mm x 19 mm	-	0.15	1.70	0.26	m	**1.96**
13 mm x 32 mm	-	0.15	1.70	0.28	m	**1.98**
25 mm x 50 mm	-	0.15	1.70	0.40	m	**2.10**
Framed supports; open-spaced grounds or battens; at 300 mm centres one way						
25 mm x 50 mm	-	0.15	1.70	1.25	m²	**2.95**
25 mm x 50 mm; plugged and screwed	-	0.45	5.10	1.32	m²	**6.42**

G STRUCTURAL/CARCASSING METAL/TIMBER Excluding overheads and profit	PC £	Labour hours	Labour £	Material £	Unit	Total rate £
Framed supports; at 300 mm centres one way and 600 mm centres the other way						
25 mm x 50 mm	-	0.75	8.51	1.87	m²	10.38
38 mm x 50 mm	-	0.75	8.51	2.46	m²	10.97
50 mm x 50 mm	-	0.75	8.51	3.25	m²	11.76
50 mm x 75 mm	-	0.75	8.51	4.79	m²	13.30
75 mm x 75 mm	-	0.75	8.51	8.04	m²	16.55
Framed supports; at 300 mm centres one way and 600 mm centres the other way; plugged and screwed						
25 mm x 50 mm	-	1.25	14.18	2.12	m²	16.30
38 mm x 50 mm	-	1.25	14.18	2.70	m²	16.88
50 mm x 50 mm	-	1.25	14.18	3.49	m²	17.67
50 mm x 75 mm	-	1.25	14.18	5.03	m²	19.21
75 mm x 75 mm	-	1.25	14.18	8.28	m²	22.46
Framed supports; at 500 mm centres both ways						
25 mm x 50 mm; to bath panels	-	0.90	10.21	2.44	m²	12.65
Framed supports; as bracketing and cradling around steelwork						
25 mm x 50 mm	-	1.40	15.88	2.65	m²	18.53
50 mm x 50 mm	-	1.50	17.01	4.57	m²	21.58
50 mm x 75 mm	-	1.60	18.14	6.73	m²	24.87
Wrought softwood						
Gutter boards; tongued and grooved joints						
19 mm thick; sloping	-	1.50	17.01	6.90	m²	23.91
19 mm thick; 75 mm wide	-	0.40	4.54	0.81	m	5.35
19 mm thick; 150 mm wide	-	0.45	5.10	1.01	m	6.11
19 mm thick; 225 mm wide	-	0.50	5.67	1.78	m	7.45
25 mm thick; sloping	-	1.50	17.01	8.45	m²	25.46
25 mm thick; 75 mm wide	-	0.40	4.54	1.13	m	5.67
25 mm thick; 150 mm wide	-	0.45	5.10	1.20	m	6.30
25 mm thick; 225 mm wide	-	0.50	5.67	2.27	m	7.94
Eaves, verge soffit baords, fascia boards and the like						
19 mm thick; over 300 mm wide	-	1.24	14.06	6.91	m²	20.97
19 mm thick; 150 mm wide; once grooved	-	0.20	2.27	1.24	m	3.51
25 mm thick; 150 mm wide; once grooved	-	0.20	2.27	1.50	m	3.77
25 mm thick; 175 mm wide; once grooved	-	0.22	2.49	1.72	m	4.21
32 mm thick; 225 mm wide; once grooved	-	0.25	2.83	3.01	m	5.84
Wrought softwood; "Tanalised"						
Gutter boards; tongued and grooved joints						
19 mm thick; sloping	-	1.50	17.01	7.49	m²	24.50
19 mm thick; 75 mm wide	-	0.40	4.54	0.85	m	5.39
19 mm thick; 150 mm wide	-	0.45	5.10	1.10	m	6.20
19 mm thick; 225 mm wide	-	0.50	5.67	1.92	m	7.59
25 mm thick; sloping	-	1.50	17.01	9.23	m²	26.24
25 mm thick; 75 mm wide	-	0.40	4.54	1.19	m	5.73
25 mm thick; 150 mm wide	-	0.45	5.10	1.32	m	6.42
25 mm thick; 225 mm wide	-	0.50	5.67	2.45	m	8.12
Eaves, verge soffit boards, fascia boards and the like						
19 mm thick; over 300 mm wide	-	1.24	14.06	7.50	m²	21.56
19 mm thick; 150 mm wide; once grooved	-	0.20	2.27	1.33	m	3.60
25 mm thick; 150 mm wide; once grooved	-	0.20	2.27	1.61	m	3.88
25 mm thick; 175 mm wide; once grooved	-	0.22	2.49	1.86	m	4.35
32 mm thick; 225 mm wide; once grooved	-	0.25	2.83	3.23	m	6.06

G STRUCTURAL/CARCASSING METAL/TIMBER Excluding overheads and profit	PC £	Labour hours	Labour £	Material £	Unit	Total rate £
G20 CARPENTRY/TIMBER FRAMING/FIRST **FIXING** - cont'd						
Straps; mild steel; galvanised						
Standard twisted vertical restraint; fixing						
to softwood and brick or blockwork						
30 mm x 2.5 mm x 400 mm girth	-	0.25	2.83	2.07	nr	4.90
30 mm x 2.5 mm x 600 mm girth	-	0.26	2.95	3.07	nr	6.02
30 mm x 2.5 mm x 800 mm girth	-	0.27	3.06	4.23	nr	7.29
30 mm x 2.5 mm x 1000 mm girth	-	0.30	3.40	5.48	nr	8.88
30 mm x 2.5 mm x 1200 mm girth	-	0.31	3.52	6.47	nr	9.99
Hangers; mild steel; galvanised						
Joist hangers 0.90 mm thick; The Expanded						
Metal Company Ltd "Speedy" or other equal and						
approved; for fixing to softwood; joist sizes						
50 mm wide; all sizes to 225 mm deep	0.67	0.12	1.36	0.78	nr	2.14
75 mm wide; all sizes to 225 mm deep	0.70	0.15	1.70	0.84	nr	2.54
100 mm wide; all sizes to 225 mm deep	0.75	0.18	2.04	0.93	nr	2.97
Joist hangers 2.50 mm thick; for building in;						
joist sizes						
50 mm x 100 mm	1.29	0.08	0.96	1.40	nr	2.36
50 mm x 125 mm	1.30	0.08	0.96	1.41	nr	2.37
50 mm x 150 mm	1.22	0.10	1.19	1.35	nr	2.54
50 mm x 175 mm	1.28	0.10	1.19	1.42	nr	2.61
50 mm x 200 mm	1.42	0.12	1.42	1.59	nr	3.01
50 mm x 225 mm	1.51	0.12	1.42	1.68	nr	3.10
75 mm x 150 mm	1.88	0.10	1.19	2.05	nr	3.24
75 mm x 175 mm	1.77	0.10	1.19	1.93	nr	3.12
75 mm x 200 mm	1.88	0.12	1.42	2.07	nr	3.49
75 mm x 225 mm	2.01	0.12	1.42	2.21	nr	3.63
75 mm x 250 mm	2.13	0.14	1.65	2.36	nr	4.01
100 mm x 200 mm	2.34	0.12	1.42	2.55	nr	3.97
Metal connectors; mild steel; galvanised						
Round toothed plate; for 10 mm or 12 mm						
diameter bolts						
38 mm diameter; single sided	-	0.02	0.23	0.19	nr	0.42
38 mm diameter; double sided	-	0.02	0.23	0.21	nr	0.44
50 mm diameter; single sided	-	0.02	0.23	0.20	nr	0.43
50 mm diameter; double sided	-	0.02	0.23	0.22	nr	0.45
63 mm diameter; single sided	-	0.02	0.23	0.29	nr	0.52
63 mm diameter; double sided	-	0.02	0.23	0.33	nr	0.56
75 mm diameter; single sided	-	0.02	0.23	0.43	nr	0.66
75 mm diameter; double sided	-	0.02	0.23	0.45	nr	0.68
framing anchor	-	0.15	1.70	0.34	nr	2.04
Bolts; mild steel; galvanised						
Fixing only bolts; 50 mm -200 mm long						
6 mm diameter	-	0.04	0.45	-	nr	0.45
8 mm diameter	-	0.04	0.45	-	nr	0.45
10 mm diameter	-	0.05	0.57	-	nr	0.57
12 mm diameter	-	0.05	0.57	-	nr	0.57
16 mm diameter	-	0.06	0.68	-	nr	0.68
20 mm diameter	-	0.06	0.68	-	nr	0.68
Bolts						
Expanding bolts; "Rawlbolt" projecting type or other equal						
and approved; The Rawlplug Company; plated; one nut;						
one washer						
6 mm diameter; ref M6 10P	-	0.10	1.13	0.50	nr	1.63
6 mm diameter; ref M6 25P	-	0.10	1.13	0.56	nr	1.69

G STRUCTURAL/CARCASSING METAL/TIMBER Excluding overheads and profit	PC £	Labour hours	Labour £	Material £	Unit	Total rate £
Expanding bolts; "Rawlbolt" projecting type or other equal and approved; The Rawlplug Company; plated; one nut; one washer - cont'd						
6 mm diameter; ref M6 60P	-	0.10	1.13	0.59	nr	1.72
8 mm diameter; ref M8 25P	-	0.10	1.13	0.66	nr	1.79
8 mm diameter; ref M8 60P	-	0.10	1.13	0.71	nr	1.84
10 mm diameter; ref M10 15P	-	0.10	1.13	0.86	nr	1.99
10 mm diameter; ref M10 30P	-	0.10	1.13	0.90	nr	2.03
10 mm diameter; ref M10 60P	-	0.10	1.13	0.94	nr	2.07
12 mm diameter; ref M12 15P	-	0.10	1.13	1.37	nr	2.50
12 mm diameter; ref M12 30P	-	0.10	1.13	1.48	nr	2.61
12 mm diameter; ref M12 75P	-	0.10	1.13	1.84	nr	2.97
16 mm diameter; ref M16 35P	-	0.10	1.13	3.52	nr	4.65
16 mm diameter; ref M16 75P	-	0.10	1.13	3.69	nr	4.82
Expanding bolts; "Rawlbolt" loose bolt type or other equal and approved; The Rawlplug Company; plated; one bolt; one washer						
6 mm diameter; ref M6 10L	-	0.10	1.13	0.50	nr	1.63
6 mm diameter; ref M6 25L	-	0.10	1.13	0.53	nr	1.66
6 mm diameter; ref M6 40L	-	0.10	1.13	0.53	nr	1.66
8 mm diameter; ref M8 25L	-	0.10	1.13	0.65	nr	1.78
8 mm diameter; ref M8 40L	-	0.10	1.13	0.69	nr	1.82
10 mm diameter; ref M10 10L	-	0.10	1.13	0.83	nr	1.96
10 mm diameter; ref M10 25L	-	0.10	1.13	0.86	nr	1.99
10 mm diameter; ref M10 50L	-	0.10	1.13	0.91	nr	2.04
10 mm diameter; ref M10 75L	-	0.10	1.13	0.94	nr	2.07
12 mm diameter; ref M12 10L	-	0.10	1.13	1.25	nr	2.38
12 mm diameter; ref M12 25L	-	0.10	1.13	1.37	nr	2.50
12 mm diameter; ref M12 40L	-	0.10	1.13	1.43	nr	2.56
12 mm diameter; ref M12 60L	-	0.10	1.13	1.51	nr	2.64
16 mm diameter; ref M16 30L	-	0.10	1.13	3.34	nr	4.47
16 mm diameter; ref M16 60L	-	0.10	1.13	3.62	nr	4.75
Truss clips; mild steel galvanised						
Truss clips; fixing to softwood; joist size						
38 mm wide	0.23	0.15	1.70	0.39	nr	2.09
50 mm wide	0.25	0.15	1.70	0.41	nr	2.11
Sole plate angles; mild steel galvanised						
Sole plate angle; fixing to softwood and concrete						
112 mm x 40 mm x 76 mm	0.30	0.20	2.27	0.98	nr	3.25
Chemical anchors						
"Kemfix" capsules and standard studs or other equal and approved; The Rawlplug Company; with nuts and washers; drilling masonry						
capsule ref 60-408; stud ref 60-448	-	0.27	3.06	1.18	nr	4.24
capsule ref 60-410; stud ref 60-454	-	0.30	3.40	1.33	nr	4.73
capsule ref 60-412; stud ref 60-460	-	0.34	3.86	1.62	nr	5.48
capsule ref 60-416; stud ref 60-472	-	0.37	4.20	2.55	nr	6.75
capsule ref 60-420; stud ref 60-478	-	0.39	4.42	3.88	nr	8.30
capsule ref 60-424; stud ref 60-484	-	0.43	4.88	5.77	nr	10.65
"Kemfix" capsules and stainless steel studs or other equal and approved; The Rawlplug Company; with nuts and washers; drilling masonry						
capsule ref 60-408; stud ref 60-905	-	0.27	3.06	2.09	nr	5.15
capsule ref 60-410; stud ref 60-910	-	0.30	3.40	2.79	nr	6.19
capsule ref 60-412; stud ref 60-915	-	0.34	3.86	3.83	nr	7.69
capsule ref 60-416; stud ref 60-920	-	0.37	4.20	6.52	nr	10.72
capsule ref 60-420; stud ref 60-925	-	0.39	4.42	10.07	nr	14.49
capsule ref 60-424; stud ref 60-930	-	0.43	4.88	16.28	nr	21.16

G STRUCTURAL/CARCASSING METAL/TIMBER Excluding overheads and profit	PC £	Labour hours	Labour £	Material £	Unit	Total rate £
G20 CARPENTRY/TIMBER FRAMING/FIRST FIXING - cont'd						
Chemical anchors						
"Kemfix" capsules and standard internal threaded sockets or other equal and approved; The Rawlplug Company; drilling masonry						
capsule ref 60-408; socket ref 60-650	-	0.27	3.06	1.22	nr	**4.28**
capsule ref 60-410; socket ref 60-656	-	0.30	3.40	1.48	nr	**4.88**
capsule ref 60-412; socket ref 60-662	-	0.34	3.86	1.84	nr	**5.70**
capsule ref 60-416; socket ref 60-668	-	0.37	4.20	2.53	nr	**6.73**
capsule ref 60-420; socket ref 60-674	-	0.39	4.42	3.05	nr	**7.47**
capsule ref 60-424; socket ref 60-676	-	0.43	4.88	4.95	nr	**9.83**
"Kemfix" capsules and stainless steel internal threaded sockets or other equal and approved; The Rawlplug Company; drilling masonry						
capsule ref 60-408; socket ref 60-943	-	0.27	3.06	2.30	nr	**5.36**
capsule ref 60-410; socket ref 60-945	-	0.30	3.40	2.61	nr	**6.01**
capsule ref 60-412; socket ref 60-947	-	0.34	3.86	3.01	nr	**6.87**
capsule ref 60-416; socket ref 60-949	-	0.37	4.20	4.28	nr	**8.48**
capsule ref 60-420; socket ref 60-951	-	0.39	4.42	5.17	nr	**9.59**
capsule ref 60-424; socket ref 60-955	-	0.43	4.88	9.46	nr	**14.34**
"Kemfix" capsules, perforated sleeves and standard studs or other equal and approved; The Rawlplug Company; in low density material; with nuts and washers; drilling masonry						
capsule ref 60-408; sleeve ref 60-538; stud ref 60-448	-	0.27	3.06	1.74	nr	**4.80**
capsule ref 60-410; sleeve ref 60-544; stud ref 60-454	-	0.30	3.40	1.92	nr	**5.32**
capsule ref 60-412; sleeve ref 60-550; stud ref 60-460	-	0.34	3.86	2.29	nr	**6.15**
capsule ref 60-416; sleeve ref 60-562; stud ref 60-472	-	0.37	4.20	3.37	nr	**7.57**
"Kemfix" capsules, perforated sleeves and stainless steel studs or other equal and approved; The Rawlplug Company; in low density material; with nuts and washers; drilling masonry						
capsule ref 60-408; sleeve ref 60-538; stud ref 60-905	-	0.27	3.06	2.65	nr	**5.71**
capsule ref 60-410; sleeve ref 60-544; stud ref 60-910	-	0.30	3.40	3.38	nr	**6.78**
capsule ref 60-412; sleeve ref 60-550; stud ref 60-915	-	0.34	3.86	4.51	nr	**8.37**
capsule ref 60-416; sleeve ref 60-562; stud ref 60-920	-	0.37	4.20	7.35	nr	**11.55**
"Kemfix" capsules, perforated sleeves and standard internal threaded sockets or other equal and approved; The Rawlplug Company; in low density material; with nuts and washers; drilling masonry						
capsule ref 60-408; sleeve ref 60-538; socket ref 60-650	-	0.27	3.06	1.78	nr	**4.84**
capsule ref 60-410; sleeve ref 60-544; socket ref 60-656	-	0.30	3.40	2.06	nr	**5.46**
capsule ref 60-412; sleeve ref 60-550; socket ref 60-662	-	0.34	3.86	2.52	nr	**6.38**
capsule ref 60-416; sleeve ref 60-562; socket ref 60-668	-	0.37	4.20	3.36	nr	**7.56**

G STRUCTURAL/CARCASSING METAL/TIMBER Excluding overheads and profit	PC £	Labour hours	Labour £	Material £	Unit	Total rate £
"Kemfix" capsules, perforated sleeves and stainless steel internal threaded sockets or other equal and approved; The Rawlplug Company; in low density material; drilling masonry						
capsule ref 60-408; sleeve ref 60-538; socket ref 60-943	-	0.27	3.06	2.86	nr	5.92
capsule ref 60-410; sleeve ref 60-544; socket ref 60-945	-	0.30	3.40	3.20	nr	6.60
capsule ref 60-412; sleeve ref 60-550; socket ref 60-947	-	0.34	3.86	3.69	nr	7.55
capsule ref 60-416; sleeve ref 60-562; socket ref 60-949	-	0.37	4.20	5.11	nr	9.31
G32 EDGE SUPPORTED/REINFORCED WOODWOOL SLAB DECKING						
Woodwool interlocking reinforced slabs; Torvale "Woodcelip" or other equal and approved; natural finish; fixing to timber or steel with galvanized nails or clips; flat or sloping						
50 mm thick slabs; type 503; maximum span 2100 mm						
1800 mm - 2100 mm lengths	13.50	0.50	5.67	14.35	m²	20.02
2400 mm lengths	14.15	0.50	5.67	15.03	m²	20.70
2700 mm - 3000 mm lengths	14.38	0.50	5.67	15.28	m²	20.95
75 mm thick slabs; type 751; maximum span 2100 mm						
1800 mm - 2400 mm lengths	20.23	0.55	6.24	21.45	m²	27.69
2700 mm - 3000 mm lengths	20.33	0.55	6.24	21.56	m²	27.80
75 mm thick slabs; type 752; maximum span 2100 mm						
1800 mm - 2400 mm lengths	20.18	0.55	6.24	21.40	m²	27.64
2700 mm - 3000 mm lengths	20.22	0.55	6.24	21.44	m²	27.68
75 mm thick slabs; type 753; maximum span 3600 mm						
2400 mm lengths	19.57	0.55	6.24	20.76	m²	27.00
2700 mm - 3000 mm lengths	20.43	0.55	6.24	21.66	m²	27.90
3300 mm - 3900 mm lengths	24.62	0.55	6.24	26.06	m²	32.30
extra for holes for pipes and the like	-	0.12	1.36	-	nr	1.36
100 mm thick slabs; type 1001; maximum span 3600 mm						
3000 mm lengths	26.95	0.60	6.80	28.54	m²	35.34
3300 mm - 3600 mm lengths	29.17	0.60	6.80	30.87	m²	37.67
100 mm thick slabs; type 1002; maximum span 3600 mm						
3000 mm lengths	26.31	0.60	6.80	27.87	m²	34.67
3300 mm - 3600 mm lengths	27.94	0.60	6.80	29.58	m²	36.38
100 mm thick slabs; type 1003; maximum span 4000 mm						
3000 mm - 3600 mm lengths	24.98	0.60	6.80	26.47	m²	33.27
3900 mm - 4000 mm lengths	24.98	0.60	6.80	26.47	m²	33.27
125 mm thick slabs; type 1252; maximum span 3000 mm						
2400 - 3000 lengths	28.43	0.60	6.80	30.09	m²	36.89
Extra over slabs for						
pre-screeded deck	-	-	-	0.94	m²	0.94
pre-screeded soffit	-	-	-	2.42	m²	2.42
pre-screeded deck and soffit	-	-	-	3.16	m²	3.16
pre-screeded and proofed deck	-	-	-	1.94	m²	1.94
pre-screeded and proofed deck plus pre-screeded soffit	-	-	-	4.51	m²	4.51
pre-felted deck (glass fibre)	-	-	-	2.67	m²	2.67
pre-felted deck plus pre-screeded soffit	-	-	-	5.08	m²	5.08

Keep your figures up to date, free of charge
Now available on the web at www.efnspon.com

This section, and most of the other information in this Price Book, is brought up to date every three months with the Price Book Updates, until the next annual edition.

The Updates are available free to all Price Book purchasers.

To ensure you receive your free copies, either complete the reply card from the centre of the book and return it to us or register via the website www.efnspon.com

The updates will also be available to download from the website.

Multilingual Dictionary of Architecture and Building Terms

Edited by Chris Grech, Whitby & Bird Partners, UK

'...four easy-reference dictionaries for the price of one.' **Building -**

*concentrates on terms used regularly by the whole construction team
*compact layout makes it easy to use
*this project has been developed with the support of Bovis Construction

With an increasingly mobile workforce internationally, the need for good communication becomes greater. This new dictionary lists over 2000 key terms used in building design and construction in English, French, German, Spanish and Italian. The emphasis is on terms used most regularly in the design office and day-to-day running of a building job on site.

April 1998 246x189: 482 pages
Hb: 0-419-19920-9: £55.00

To Order: Tel: +44 (0) 8700 768853, or +44 (0) 1264 343071
Fax: +44 (0) 1264 343005, or **Post:** E & FN Spon Customer Services,
ITPS Andover, Hants, SP10 5BE, UK

All orders must be pre-paid and will be sent free in the UK. Europe please add: £2.95 for the first book, thereafter £1.25 per book. ROW please add: Airmail £6.50 for the first book, thereafter £2.50 per book. Please add £12.50 delivery charge for items over £100.00.

H CLADDING/COVERING Excluding overheads and profit	PC £	Labour hours	Labour £	Material £	Unit	Total rate £
H CLADDING/COVERING						
H10 PATENT GLAZING						
Patent glazing; aluminium alloy bars 2.55 m **long at 622 mm centres; fixed to supports**						
Roof cladding						
glazing with 7 mm thick Georgian wired cast glass	-	-	-	-	m²	95.00
Associated code 4 lead flashings						
top flashing; 210 mm girth	-	-	-	-	m	30.30
bottom flashing; 240 mm girth	-	-	-	-	m	25.00
end flashing; 300 mm girth	-	-	-	-	m	55.00
Wall cladding						
glazing with 7 mm thick Georgian wired cast glass	-	-	-	-	m²	100.00
glazing with 6 mm thick plate glass	-	-	-	-	m²	90.00
Extra for aluminium alloy members						
38 mm x 38 mm x 3 mm angle jamb	-	-	-	-	m	10.50
pressed cill member	-	-	-	-	m	27.95
pressed channel head and PVC case	-	-	-	-	m	24.35
"Kawneer" window frame system or other **equal and approved; polyester powder coated** **glazing bars; glazed with double hermetically** **sealed units in toughened safety glass; one 6 mm** **thick air space; overall 18 mm thick**						
Vertical surfaces						

single tier; aluminium glazing bars at 850 mm
    centres x 890 mm long; timber supports at 890
    mm centres
	-	-	-	-	m²	160.00

"Kawneer" window frame system or other **equal and approved; polyester powder coated** **glazing bars; glazed with clear toughened safety** **glass; 10.70 mm thick**						
Vertical surfaces						

single tier; aluminium glazing bars at 850 mm
    centres x 890 mm long; timber supports at 890
    mm centres
	-	-	-	-	m²	150.00

H14 CONCRETE ROOFLIGHTS/PAVEMENT **LIGHTS**						
Reinforced concrete rooflights/pavement **lights; "Luxcrete" or other equal and approved;** **with glass lenses; supplied and fixed complete**						
Rooflights						
2.50 kN/m² loading; ref R254/125	-	-	-	-	m²	440.55
2.50 kN/m² loading; ref R200/90	-	-	-	-	m²	465.30
2.50 kN/m² loading; home office; double glazed	-	-	-	-	m²	480.15
Pavement lights						
20.00 kN/m²; pedestrian traffic; ref. P150/100	-	-	-	-	m²	386.10
60.00 kN/m²; vehicular traffic; ref. P165/165	-	-	-	-	m²	396.00
brass terrabond	-	-	-	-	m²	8.16
150 mm x 75 mm identification plates	-	-	-	-	m²	18.32
escape hatch	-	-	-	-	m²	3960.00

H CLADDING/COVERING Excluding overheads and profit	PC £	Labour hours	Labour £	Material £	Unit	Total rate £
H20 RIGID SHEET CLADDING						
"Resoplan" sheet or other equal and approved;						
Eternit UK Ltd; flexible neoprene gasket joints;						
fixing with stainless steel screws and coloured caps						
6 mm thick cladding to walls						
over 300 mm wide	-	2.10	23.81	46.73	m²	**70.54**
not exceeding 300 mm wide	-	0.70	7.94	16.35	m	**24.29**
Eternit 2000 "Glasal" sheet or other equal and						
approved; Eternit UK Ltd; flexible neoprene gasket						
joints; fixing with stainless steel screws and						
coloured caps						
7.50 mm thick cladding to walls						
over 300 mm wide	-	2.10	23.81	42.70	m²	**66.51**
not exceeding 300 mm wide	-	0.70	7.94	15.14	m	**23.08**
external angle trim	-	0.10	1.13	7.82	m	**8.95**
7.50 mm thick cladding to eaves, verge soffit boards,						
fascia boards or the like						
100 mm wide	-	0.50	5.67	7.33	m	**13.00**
200 mm wide	-	0.60	6.80	11.24	m	**18.04**
300 mm wide	-	0.70	7.94	15.14	m	**23.08**
H30 FIBRE CEMENT PROFILED SHEET						
CLADDING/COVERING/SIDING						
Asbestos-free corrugated sheets; Eternit						
"2000" or other equal and approved						
Roof cladding; sloping not exceeding 50						
degrees; fixing to timber purlins with drive						
screws						
"Profile 3"; natural grey	9.58	0.20	2.88	11.87	m²	**14.75**
"Profile 3"; coloured	11.49	0.20	2.88	13.88	m²	**16.76**
"Profile 6"; natural grey	8.45	0.25	3.60	10.62	m²	**14.22**
"Profile 6"; coloured	10.13	0.25	3.60	12.38	m²	**15.98**
"Profile 6"; natural grey; insulated 60 mm glass fibre						
infill; lining panel	-	0.45	6.48	25.64	m²	**32.12**
Roof cladding; sloping not exceeding 50						
degrees; fixing to steel purlins with hook bolts						
"Profile 3"; natural grey	-	0.25	3.60	12.76	m²	**16.36**
"Profile 3"; coloured	-	0.25	3.60	14.77	m²	**18.37**
"Profile 6"; natural grey	-	0.30	4.32	11.51	m²	**15.83**
"Profile 6"; coloured	-	0.30	4.32	13.27	m²	**17.59**
"Profile 6"; natural grey; insulated 60 mm glass fibre						
infill; lining panel	-	0.50	7.21	23.45	m²	**30.66**
Wall cladding; vertical; fixing to steel rails with						
hook bolts						
"Profile 3"; natural grey	-	0.30	4.32	12.76	m²	**17.08**
"Profile 3"; coloured	-	0.30	4.32	14.77	m²	**19.09**
"Profile 6"; natural grey	-	0.35	5.04	11.51	m²	**16.55**
"Profile 6"; coloured	-	0.35	5.04	13.27	m²	**18.31**
"Profile 6"; natural grey; insulated 60 mm glass fibre						
infill; lining panel	-	0.55	7.93	23.45	m²	**31.38**
raking cutting	-	0.15	2.16	-	m	**2.16**
holes for pipe and the like	-	0.15	2.16	-	nr	**2.16**
Accessories; to "Profile 3" cladding; natural grey						
eaves filler	-	0.10	1.44	9.22	m	**10.66**
vertical corrugation closer	-	0.12	1.73	9.22	m	**10.95**
apron flashing	-	0.12	1.73	9.27	m	**11.00**
plain wing or close fitting two piece adjustable						
capping to ridge	-	0.17	2.45	8.65	m	**11.10**
ventilating two piece adjustable capping to ridge	-	0.17	2.45	13.06	m	**15.51**

H CLADING/COVERING Excluding overheads and profit	PC £	Labour hours	Labour £	Material £	Unit	Total rate £
H30 FIBRE CEMENT PROFILED SHEET **CLADDING/COVERING/SIDING** - cont'd						
Asbestos-free corrugated sheets; Eternit **"2000" or other equal and approved** - cont'd						
Accessories; to "Profile 3" cladding; coloured						
eaves filler	-	0.10	1.44	11.51	m	12.95
vertical corrugation closer	-	0.12	1.73	11.51	m	13.24
apron flashing	-	0.12	1.73	11.56	m	13.29
plain wing or close fitting two piece adjustable						
capping to ridge	-	0.17	2.45	10.44	m	12.89
ventilating two piece adjustable capping to ridge	-	0.17	2.45	16.32	m	18.77
Accessories; to "Profile 6" cladding; natural grey						
eaves filler	-	0.10	1.44	6.83	m	8.27
vertical corrugation closer	-	0.12	1.73	6.83	m	8.56
apron flashing	-	0.12	1.73	7.35	m	9.08
underglazing flashing	-	0.12	1.73	7.02	m	8.75
plain cranked crown to ridge	-	0.17	2.45	13.79	m	16.24
plain wing or close fitting two piece adjustable						
capping to ridge	-	0.17	2.45	13.47	m	15.92
ventilating two piece adjustable capping to ridge	-	0.17	2.45	17.20	m	19.65
Accessories; to "Profile 6" cladding; coloured						
eaves filler	-	0.10	1.44	8.54	m	9.98
vertical corrugation closer	-	0.12	1.73	8.54	m	10.27
apron flashing	-	0.12	1.73	9.20	m	10.93
underglazing flashing	-	0.12	1.73	8.79	m	10.52
plain cranked crown to ridge	-	0.17	2.45	17.24	m	19.69
plain wing or close fitting two piece adjustable						
capping to ridge	-	0.17	2.45	16.84	m	19.29
ventilating two piece adjustable capping to ridge	-	0.17	2.45	21.52	m	23.97
H31 METAL PROFILED/FLAT SHEET **CLADDING/COVERING/SIDING**						
Galvanised steel strip troughed sheets; PMF **Strip Mill Products or other equal and approved;** **colorcoat "Plastisol" finish**						
Roof cladding; sloping not exceeding 50 degrees; fixing to steel purlins with plastic headed self-tapping screws						
0.70 mm thick type 12.5; 75 mm corrugated	6.50	0.35	5.04	9.56	m²	14.60
0.70 mm thick Long Rib 1000; 35 mm deep	6.70	0.40	5.76	9.78	m²	15.54
Wall cladding; vertical; fixing to steel rails with plastic headed self-tapping screws						
0.70 mm thick type 12.5; 75 mm corrugated	-	0.40	5.76	9.56	m²	15.32
0.70 mm thick Scan Rib 1000; 19 mm deep	-	0.45	6.48	9.35	m²	15.83
raking cutting	-	0.22	3.17	-	m	3.17
holes for pipes and the like	-	0.40	5.76	-	nr	5.76
Accessories; colorcoat silicone polyester finish						
0.90 mm thick standard flashings; bent to profile						
250 mm girth	-	0.20	2.88	3.66	m²	6.54
375 mm girth	-	0.22	3.17	5.41	m²	8.58
500 mm girth	-	0.24	3.46	6.81	m²	10.27
625 mm girth	-	0.30	4.32	8.20	m²	12.52
Galvanised steel profile sheet cladding; Kelsey **Roofing Industries Ltd or other equal and approved**						
Roof cladding; sloping not exceeding 50 degrees; fixing to steel purlins with plastic headed self-tapping screws						
0.70 mm thick	-	-	-	-	m²	12.30
0.70 mm thick; PVF2 coated soffit finish	-	-	-	-	m²	17.85

H CLADDING/COVERING Excluding overheads and profit	PC £	Labour hours	Labour £	Material £	Unit	Total rate £
Galvanised steel profile sheet cladding; Plannja Ltd **or other equal and approved; metallack coated finish**						
Roof cladding; sloping not exceeding 50						
degrees; fixing to steel purlins with plastic						
headed self-tapping screws						
0.72 mm thick "profile 20B"	-	-	-	-	m²	13.68
0.72 mm thick "profile TOP 40"	-	-	-	-	m²	14.40
0.72 mm thick "profile 45"	-	-	-	-	m²	15.66
extra over for 80 mm insulation and 0.40 mm						
thick coated inner lining sheet	-	-	-	-	m²	10.57
Wall cladding; vertical fixing to steel rails with						
plastic headed self-tapping screws						
0.60 mm thick "profile 20B"; corrugations vertical	-	-	-	-	m²	13.14
0.60 mm thick "profile 30"; corrugations vertical	-	-	-	-	m²	14.04
0.60 mm thick "profile TOP 40"; corrugations						
vertical	-	-	-	-	m²	14.90
0.60 mm thick "profile 60B"; corrugations vertical	-	-	-	-	m²	16.47
0.60 mm thick "profile 30"; corrugations horizontal	-	-	-	-	m²	14.40
0.60 mm thick "profile 60B"; corrugations						
horizontal	-	-	-	-	m²	17.73
extra for 80 mm insulation and 0.40 mm thick						
coated inner lining sheet	-	-	-	-	m²	10.98
Accessories for roof/vertical cladding; PVF2						
coated finish; 0.60 mm thick flashings; once bent						
250 mm girth	-	-	-	-	m	9.81
375 mm girth	-	-	-	-	m	11.88
500 mm girth	-	-	-	-	m	13.54
625 mm girth	-	-	-	-	m	15.03
extra bends	-	-	-	-	nr	0.18
profile fillers	-	-	-	-	m	0.63
Lightweight galvanised steel roof tiles; Decra **Roof Systems (UK) Ltd or other equal and** **approved; coated finish**						
Roof coverings	-	0.25	3.60	12.73	m²	16.33
Accessories for roof cladding						
pitched "D" ridge	-	0.10	1.44	6.83	m	8.27
barge cover (handed)	-	0.10	1.44	7.33	m	8.77
in line air vent	-	0.10	1.44	33.66	nr	35.10
in line soil vent	-	0.10	1.44	52.75	nr	54.19
gas flue terminal	-	0.20	2.88	69.62	nr	72.50
Standing seam aluminium roof cladding; **"Kal-zip" Hoogovens Aluminium Building** **Systems Ltd or other equal and approved;** **ref AA 3004 A1 Mn1 Mg1; standard natural** **aluminium stucco embossed finish**						
Roof coverings (lining sheets not included);						
sloping not exceeding 50 degrees; 305 mm						
wide units						
0.90 mm thick	-	-	-	-	m²	22.80
1.00 mm thick	-	-	-	-	m²	25.00
1.20 mm thick	-	-	-	-	m²	29.50
extra over for						
polyester coating	-	-	-	-	m²	5.15
PVF2 coating	-	-	-	-	m²	7.30
smooth curved	-	-	-	-	m²	27.40
factory formed tapered sheets	-	-	-	-	m²	32.75
non standard lengths	-	-	-	-	m²	1.35
raking cutting	-	-	-	-	m	5.70

H CLADDING/COVERING Excluding overheads and profit	PC £	Labour hours	Labour £	Material £	Unit	Total rate £
H31 METAL PROFILED/FLAT SHEET **CLADDING/COVERING/SIDING** - cont'd						
Standing seam aluminium roof cladding; **"Kal-zip" Hoogovens Aluminium Building** **Systems Ltd other equal and approved;** **ref AA 3004 A1 Mn1 Mg1; standard natural** **aluminium stucco embossed finish** - cont'd						
Accessories for roof coverings						
single skin PVC rooflights; 305 mm cover	-	-	-	-	m²	82.70
double skin PVC rooflights; 305 mm cover	-	-	-	-	m²	102.00
thermal insulation quilt; 60 mm thick	-	-	-	-	m²	1.30
thermal insulation quilt; 80 mm thick	-	-	-	-	m²	1.50
thermal insulation quilt; 100 mm thick	-	-	-	-	m²	1.65
thermal insulation quilt; 150 mm thick	-	-	-	-	m²	2.50
semi-rigid insulation slab; 30 mm thick; tissue faced	-	-	-	-	m²	5.10
semi-rigid insulation slab; 50 mm thick	-	-	-	-	m²	9.70
"Kal-Foil" vapour check	-	-	-	-	m²	2.70
Lining sheets; "Kal-bau" aluminium ref TR 30/150; natural aluminium stucco embossed finish; fixed to steel purlins with stainless steel screws						
0.70 mm gauge	-	-	-	-	m²	12.85
0.80 mm gauge	-	-	-	-	m²	14.40
0.90 mm gauge	-	-	-	-	m²	16.00
1.00 mm gauge	-	-	-	-	m²	17.50
1.20 mm gauge	-	-	-	-	m²	20.75
extra over for						
crimped curve	-	-	-	-	m²	5.50
perforated sheet	-	-	-	-	m²	2.95
Lining sheets; "Kal-bau" aluminium ref TR 35/200; natural aluminium stucco embossed finish; fixed to steel purlins with stainless steel screws						
0.70 mm gauge	-	-	-	-	m²	12.65
0.80 mm gauge	-	-	-	-	m²	14.20
0.90 mm gauge	-	-	-	-	m²	15.60
1.00 mm gauge	-	-	-	-	m²	17.30
1.20 mm gauge	-	-	-	-	m²	20.40
extra over for						
crimped curve	-	-	-	-	m²	5.40
perforated sheet	-	-	-	-	m²	2.95
Lining sheets; profiled steel; 915 mm cover; bright white polyester paint finish; fixed to steel purlins with stainless steel screws						
0.40 mm gauge	-	-	-	-	m²	4.15
0.55 mm gauge	-	-	-	-	m²	7.10
0.70 mm gauge	-	-	-	-	m²	8.25
extra over for						
crimped curve	-	-	-	-	m²	3.10
perforated sheet	-	-	-	-	m²	2.95
tapered 0.70 mm plain galvanised steel liner	-	-	-	-	m²	17.80
plastisol coating on external liners	-	-	-	-	m²	1.75
Lining sheets; profiled steel; 1000 mm cover; bright white polyester paint finish; fixed to steel purlins with stainless steel screws						
0.40 mm gauge	-	-	-	-	m²	5.90
0.55 mm gauge	-	-	-	-	m²	7.10
0.70 mm gauge	-	-	-	-	m²	8.25
extra over for						
crimped curve	-	-	-	-	m²	3.10
perforated sheet	-	-	-	-	m²	2.95
tapered 0.70 mm plain galvanised steel liner	-	-	-	-	m²	17.80
plastisol coating on external liners	-	-	-	-	m²	1.75

H CLADDING/COVERING Excluding overheads and profit	PC £	Labour hours	Labour £	Material £	Unit	Total rate £
Eaves detail for 305 mm wide "Kal-zip" roof cladding units; including high density polythylene foam fillers; 2 mm extruded alloy drip angle; fixed to Kalzip sheet using stainless steel blind rivets						
40 mm x 20 mm angle: single skin	-	-	-	-	m	5.80
70 mm x 30 mm angle: single skin	-	-	-	-	m	7.50
40 mm x 20 mm angle: double skin	-	-	-	-	m	7.10
70 mm x 30 mm angle: double skin	-	-	-	-	m	8.75
Verge detail for 305 mm wide "Kal-zip" roof cladding units						
2 mm extruded aluminium alloy gable closure section; fixed with stainless steel blind sealed rivets; gable end hook/verge clip fixed to ST clip with stainless steel screws and 2 mm extruded aluminium tolerance clip	-	-	-	-	m	7.80
Ridge detail for 305 mm wide "Kal-zip" roof cladding units						
abutment ridge including natural aluminium stucco embossed "U" type ridge closures fixed with stainless steel blind steel rivets; "U" type polythylene ridge fillers and 2 mm extruded aluminium aluminium alloy support Zed fixed with stainless steel blind sealed rivets; fixing with rivets through small seam of "Kal-zip" into ST clip using stainless steel blind sealed rivets	-	-	-	-	m	12.50
duo ridge including natural aluminium stucco embossed "U" type ridge closures fixed with stainless steel blind sealed rivets; "U" type polythylene ridge fillers and 2 mm extruded aluminium alloy support Zed fixed with stainless steel blind sealed rivets; fixing with rivets through small seam of "Kal-zip" into ST clip using stainless steel blind steel rivets	-	-	-	-	m	25.00
H32 PLASTICS PROFILED SHEET CLADDING/COVERING/SIDING						
Extended, hard skinned, foamed PVC-UE profiled sections; Swish Celuka or other equal and approved; Class 1 fire rated to BS 476; Part 7; 1987; in white finish						
Wall cladding; vertical; fixing to timber						
100 mm shiplap profiles; Code 001	-	0.38	4.31	30.08	m²	34.39
150 mm shiplap profiles; Code 002	-	0.35	3.97	26.72	m²	30.69
125 mm feather-edged profiles; Code C208	-	0.37	4.20	29.12	m²	33.32
Vertical angles	-	0.20	2.27	3.19	m	5.46
Raking cutting	-	0.15	1.70	-	m	1.70
Holes for pipes and the like	-	0.04	0.45	-	nr	0.45
H41 GLASS REINFORCED PLASTICS PANEL CLADDING/FEATURES						
Glass fibre translucent sheeting grade AB class 3						
Roof cladding; sloping not exceeding 50 degrees; fixing to timber purlins with drive screws; to suit						
"Profile 3" or other equal and approved	9.63	0.20	2.88	11.41	m²	14.29
"Profile 6" or other equal and approved	8.93	0.25	3.60	10.67	m²	14.27
Roof cladding; sloping not exceeding 50 degrees; fixing to timber purlins with hook bolts; to suit						
"Profile 3" or other equal and approved	9.63	0.25	3.60	12.29	m²	15.89
"Profile 6" or other equal and approved	8.93	0.30	4.32	11.56	m²	15.88
"Longrib 1000" or other equal and approved	8.89	0.30	4.32	11.52	m²	15.84

H CLADDING/COVERING
Excluding overheads and profit

H51 NATURAL STONE SLAB CLADDING FEATURES

BASIC NATURAL STONE BLOCK PRICES

Block prices

	(£/m3)		(£/m3)
Monks Park bed ht n.e. 300 mm	229.00	Beer Stone - all sizes	535.00
Monks Park bed 300 - 599 mm	327.00	Portland Stone n.e. 0.60 m³	216.00
Monks Park bed ht 600 mm +	327.00	Portland Stone 0.60 - 0.99 m³	405.00
Westwood Ground n.e. 0.60 m³	227.00	Portland Stone 1.00 m³ +	486.00
Westwood Ground 0.60 - 0.99 m³	327.00		
Westwood Ground 1.00 m³ +	327.00		

H CLADDING/COVERING Excluding overheads and profit	PC £	Labour hours	Labour £	Material £	Unit	Total rate £
Portland Whitbed limestone bedded and jointed in cement - lime - mortar (1:2:9); slurrying with weak lime and stone dust mortar; flush pointing and cleaning on completion (cramps etc. measured separately)						
Facework; one face plain and rubbed; bedded against backing						
50 mm thick stones	-	-	-	-	m²	143.50
63 mm thick stones	-	-	-	-	m²	184.50
75 mm thick stones	-	-	-	-	m²	184.50
100 mm thick stones	-	-	-	-	m²	210.00
Fair returns on facework						
50 mm wide	-	-	-	-	m	0.90
63 mm wide	-	-	-	-	m	1.30
75 mm wide	-	-	-	-	m	1.30
100 mm wide	-	-	-	-	m	1.70
Fair raking cutting on facework						
50 mm thick	-	-	-	-	m	13.70
63 mm thick	-	-	-	-	m	15.50
75 mm thick	-	-	-	-	m	17.40
100 mm thick	-	-	-	-	m	21.00
Copings; once weathered; and throated; rubbed; set horizontal or raking						
250 mm x 50 mm	-	-	-	-	m	99.80
extra for external angle	-	-	-	-	nr	15.10
extra for internal angle	-	-	-	-	nr	22.60
300 mm x 50 mm	-	-	-	-	m	100.10
extra for external angle	-	-	-	-	nr	18.10
extra for internal angle	-	-	-	-	nr	27.20
350 mm x 75 mm	-	-	-	-	m	138.40
extra for external angle	-	-	-	-	nr	21.10
extra for internal angle	-	-	-	-	nr	31.70
400 mm x 100 mm	-	-	-	-	m	164.00
extra for external angle	-	-	-	-	nr	24.10
extra for internal angle	-	-	-	-	nr	36.20
450 mm x 100 mm	-	-	-	-	m	179.40
extra for external angle	-	-	-	-	nr	27.20
extra for internal angle	-	-	-	-	nr	40.70
500 mm x 125 mm	-	-	-	-	m	220.40
extra for external angle	-	-	-	-	nr	30.10
extra for internal angle	-	-	-	-	nr	45.20

H CLADDING/COVERING Excluding overheads and profit	PC £	Labour hours	Labour £	Material £	Unit	Total rate £
Band courses; plain; rubbed; horizontal						
225 mm x 112 mm	-	-	-	-	m	67.90
300 mm x 112 mm	-	-	-	-	m	81.30
extra for stopped ends	-	-	-	-	nr	0.60
extra for external angles	-	-	-	-	nr	0.60
Band courses; moulded 100 mm girth on face;						
rubbed; horizontal						
125 mm x 75 mm	-	-	-	-	m	88.10
extra for stopped ends	-	-	-	-	nr	0.60
extra for external angles	-	-	-	-	nr	8.50
extra for internal angles	-	-	-	-	nr	17.00
150 mm x 75 mm	-	-	-	-	m	95.50
extra for stopped ends	-	-	-	-	nr	0.60
extra for external angles	-	-	-	-	nr	11.00
extra for internal angles	-	-	-	-	nr	21.80
200 mm x 100 mm	-	-	-	-	m	120.60
extra for stopped ends	-	-	-	-	nr	0.60
extra for external angles	-	-	-	-	nr	18.10
extra for internal angles	-	-	-	-	nr	36.20
250 mm x 150 mm	-	-	-	-	m	157.80
extra for stopped ends	-	-	-	-	nr	0.60
extra for external angles	-	-	-	-	nr	25.40
extra for internal angles	-	-	-	-	nr	44.50
300 mm x 250 mm	-	-	-	-	m	229.90
extra for stopped ends	-	-	-	-	nr	0.60
extra for external angles	-	-	-	-	nr	33.90
extra for internal angles	-	-	-	-	nr	59.40
Coping apex block; two sunk faces; rubbed						
650 mm x 450 mm x 225 mm	-	-	-	-	nr	251.10
Coping kneeler block; three sunk faces; rubbed						
350 mm x 350 mm x 375 mm	-	-	-	-	nr	188.60
450 mm x 450 mm x 375 mm	-	-	-	-	nr	264.50
Corbel; turned and moulded; rubbed						
225 mm x 225 mm x 375 mm	-	-	-	-	nr	134.20
Slab surrounds to openings; one face splayed;						
rubbed						
75 mm x 100 mm	-	-	-	-	m	50.40
75 mm x 200 mm	-	-	-	-	m	69.50
100 mm x 100 mm	-	-	-	-	m	58.20
125 mm x 100 mm	-	-	-	-	m	65.90
125 mm x 150 mm	-	-	-	-	m	78.20
175 mm x 175 mm	-	-	-	-	m	99.90
225 mm x 175 mm	-	-	-	-	m	117.00
300 mm x 175 mm	-	-	-	-	m	141.50
300 mm x 225 mm	-	-	-	-	m	175.30
Slab surrounds to openings; one face sunk						
splayed; rubbed						
75 mm x 100 mm	-	-	-	-	m	61.20
75 mm x 200 mm	-	-	-	-	m	80.30
100 mm x 100 mm	-	-	-	-	m	69.00
125 mm x 100 mm	-	-	-	-	m	76.70
125 mm x 150 mm	-	-	-	-	m	89.00
175 mm x 175 mm	-	-	-	-	m	110.70
225 mm x 175 mm	-	-	-	-	m	127.80
300 mm x 175 mm	-	-	-	-	m	152.30
300 mm x 225 mm	-	-	-	-	m	186.10
extra for throating	-	-	-	-	m	5.40
extra for rebates and grooves	-	-	-	-	m	16.10
extra for stooling	-	-	-	-	m	15.10

H CLADDING/COVERING Excluding overheads and profit	PC £	Labour hours	Labour £	Material £	Unit	Total rate £
H51 NATURAL STONE SLAB CLADDING **FEATURES** - cont'd						
Sundries - stone walling						
Coating backs of stones with brush applied						
cold bitumen solution; two coats						
limestone facework	-	0.20	1.45	1.84	m²	**3.29**
Cutting grooves in limestone masonry for						
water bars or the like	-	-	-	-	m	**5.00**
Mortices in limestone masonry for						
metal dowel	-	-	-	-	nr	**0.40**
metal cramp	-	-	-	-	nr	**0.90**
"Eurobrick" insulated brick cladding systems **or other equal and approved; extruded polystyrene** **foam insulation; brick slips bonded to insulation** **panels with "Eurobrick" gun applied adhesive or** **other equal and approved; pointing** **with formulated mortar grout**						
25 mm insulation to walls						
over 300 mm wide; fixing with proprietary						
screws and plates to timber	-	1.50	19.88	39.85	m²	**59.73**
50 mm insulation to walls						
over 300 mm wide; fixing with proprietary						
screws and plates; to timber	-	1.50	19.88	44.05	m²	**63.93**
Cramps and dowels; Ancon CCL Ltd's **"Hemax" range or other equal and approved;** **one end built into brickwork or set in slot in** **concrete; stainless steel**						
Dowel						
8 mm diameter x 75 mm long	0.17	0.05	0.71	0.18	nr	**0.89**
10 mm diameter x 150 mm long	0.49	0.05	0.71	0.51	nr	**1.22**
Pattern "J" tie						
25 mm x 3 mm x 100 mm	0.36	0.07	0.99	0.38	nr	**1.37**
Pattern "S" cramp; with two 20 mm turndowns						
(190 mm girth)						
25 mm x 3 mm x 150 mm	0.51	0.07	0.99	0.53	nr	**1.52**
Pattern "B" anchor; with 8 mm x 75 mm loose						
dowel						
25 mm x 3 mm x 150 mm	0.62	0.10	1.42	0.66	nr	**2.08**
Pattern "Q" tie						
25 mm x 3 mm x 200 mm	0.63	0.07	0.99	0.66	nr	**1.65**
38 mm x 3 mm x 250 mm	1.27	0.07	0.99	1.34	nr	**2.33**
Pattern "P" half twist tie						
25 mm x 3 mm x 200 mm	0.68	0.07	0.99	0.71	nr	**1.70**
38 mm x 3 mm x 250 mm	1.07	0.07	0.99	1.12	nr	**2.11**

H CLADDING/COVERING
Excluding overheads and profit

H60 CLAY/CONCRETE ROOF TILING

ALTERNATIVE TILE PRICES (£/1000)

	£		£		£
CLAY TILES; INTERLOCKING AND PANTILES					
Langley's "Sterreberg" pantiles					
Anthracite	1800.00	Deep Brown	1950.00	Natural Red/Rustic	1500.00
Sandtoft pantiles					
The Barrow Bold Roman	1265.00	Gaelic	760.00	County Interlocking	632.00
William Blyth pantiles					
Barco Bold Roll	575.00	Celtic (French)	660.00		
CONCRETE TILES; PLAIN AND INTERLOCKING					
Marley roof tiles					
Anglia Plus	582.00	Ludlow Plus	473.00		
Ludlow Major	667.00	Plain	296.00		
Redland roof tiles					
Redland 49	472.00	50 Double Roman	657.00		
Mini Stoneworld	719.00	Grovebury	694.00		

Discounts of 2½ - 15% available depending on quantity/status

H CLADDING/COVERING Excluding overheads and profit	PC £	Labour hours	Labour £	Material £	Unit	Total rate £
NOTE: The following items of tile roofing unless otherwise described, include for conventional fixing assuming normal exposure with appropriate nails and/or rivets or clips to pressure impregnated softwood battens fixed with galvanised nails; prices also include for all bedding and pointing at verges, beneath ridge tiles, etc.						
Clay interlocking pantiles; Sandtoft Goxhill "Tudor" red sand faced or other equal and approved; PC £1249.50/1000; 470 mm x 285 mm; to 100 mm lap; on 25 mm x 38 mm battens and type 1F reinforced underlay						
Roof coverings	-	0.40	5.76	15.40	m²	21.16
Extra over coverings for						
fixing every tile	-	0.08	1.15	0.98	m²	2.13
eaves course with plastic filler	-	0.30	4.32	6.39	m	10.71
verges; extra single undercloak course of plain tiles	-	0.30	4.32	3.25	m	7.57
open valleys; cutting both sides	-	0.18	2.59	5.25	m	7.84
ridge tiles	-	0.60	8.65	12.07	m	20.72
hips; cutting both sides	-	0.75	10.81	17.32	m	28.13
holes for pipes and the like	-	0.20	2.88	-	nr	2.88

H CLADDING/COVERING Excluding overheads and profit	PC £	Labour hours	Labour £	Material £	Unit	Total rate £
H60 PLAIN ROOF TILING - cont'd						
Clay pantiles; Sandtoft Goxhill "Old English"; red sand faced or other equal and approved; PC £556.75/ 1000; 342 mm x 241 mm; to 75 mm lap; on 25 mm x 38 mm battens and type 1F reinforced underlay						
Roof coverings	-	0.45	6.48	12.49	m²	**18.97**
Extra over coverings for						
fixing every tile	-	0.03	0.43	2.46	m²	**2.89**
other colours	-	-	-	0.50	m²	**0.50**
double course at eaves	-	0.33	4.76	3.16	m	**7.92**
verges; extra single undercloak course of plain tiles	-	0.30	4.32	7.18	m	**11.50**
open valleys; cutting both sides	-	0.18	2.59	2.34	m	**4.93**
ridge tiles; tile slips	-	0.60	8.65	16.75	m	**25.40**
hips; cutting both sides	-	0.75	10.81	19.09	m	**29.90**
holes for pipes and the like	-	0.20	2.88	-	nr	**2.88**
Clay pantiles; William Blyth's "Lincoln" natural or other equal and approved; 343 mm x 280 mm; to 75 mm lap; PC £738.00/1000; on 19 mm x 38 mm battens and type 1F reinforced underlay						
Roof coverings	-	0.45	6.48	15.15	m²	**21.63**
Extra over coverings for						
fixing every tile	-	0.03	0.43	2.46	m²	**2.89**
other colours	-	-	-	1.03	m²	**1.03**
double course at eaves	-	0.33	4.76	3.92	m	**8.68**
verges; extra single undercloak course of plain tiles	-	0.30	4.32	9.60	m	**13.92**
open valleys; cutting both sides	-	0.18	2.59	3.10	m	**5.69**
ridge tiles; tile slips	-	0.60	8.65	16.45	m	**25.10**
hips; cutting both sides	-	0.75	10.81	19.55	m	**30.36**
holes for pipes and the like	-	0.20	2.88	-	nr	**2.88**
Clay plain tiles; Hinton, Perry and Davenhill "Dreadnought" smooth red machine-made or other equal and approved; PC £201.25/1000; 265 mm x 165 mm; on 19 mm x 38 mm battens and type 1F reinforced underlay						
Roof coverings; to 64 mm lap	-	1.05	15.13	18.07	m²	**33.20**
Wall coverings; to 38 mm lap	-	1.25	18.01	15.47	m²	**33.48**
Extra over coverings for						
other colours	-	-	-	6.95	m²	**6.95**
ornamental tiles	-	-	-	10.42	m²	**10.42**
double course at eaves	-	0.25	3.60	2.18	m	**5.78**
verges	-	0.30	4.32	1.23	m	**5.55**
swept valleys; cutting both sides	-	0.65	9.37	26.26	m	**35.63**
bonnet hips; cutting both sides	-	0.80	11.53	26.32	m	**37.85**
external vertical angle tiles; supplementary nail fixings	-	0.40	5.76	29.40	m	**35.16**
half round ridge tiles	-	0.60	8.65	8.84	m	**17.49**
holes for pipes and the like	-	0.20	2.88	-	nr	**2.88**
Clay plain tiles; Keymer best hand-made sand-faced tiles or other equal and approved; PC £531.25/1000; 265 mm x 165 mm; on 25 mm x 38 mm battens and type 1F reinforced underlay						
Roof coverings; to 64 mm lap	-	1.05	15.13	38.86	m²	**53.99**
Wall coverings; to 38 mm lap	-	1.25	18.01	33.84	m²	**51.85**
Extra over coverings for						
ornamental tiles	-	-	-	5.35	m²	**5.35**
double course at eaves	-	0.25	3.60	4.25	m	**7.85**
verges	-	0.30	4.32	1.61	m	**5.93**
swept valleys; cutting both sides	-	0.65	9.37	30.41	m	**39.78**
bonnet hips; cutting both sides	-	0.80	11.53	30.47	m	**42.00**

H CLADDING/COVERING Excluding overheads and profit	PC £	Labour hours	Labour £	Material £	Unit	Total rate £
Extra over coverings - cont'd						
external vertical angle tiles; supplementary nail fixings	-	0.40	5.76	41.88	m	47.64
half round ridge tiles	-	0.60	8.65	9.32	m	17.97
holes for pipes and the like	-	0.20	2.88	-	nr	2.88
Concrete interlocking tiles; Marley "Bold Roll" granule						
finish tiles or other equal and approved; PC £597.55/						
1000; 420 mm x 330 mm; to 75 mm lap; on 25 mm x 38						
mm battens and type 1F reinforced underlay						
Roof coverings	-	0.35	5.04	8.36	m²	13.40
Extra over coverings for						
fixing every tile	-	0.03	0.43	0.41	m²	0.84
eaves; eaves filler	-	0.05	0.72	0.81	m	1.53
verges; 150 mm wide asbestos free strip undercloak	-	0.23	3.31	1.53	m	4.84
valley trough tiles; cutting both sides	-	0.55	7.93	15.62	m	23.55
segmental ridge tiles; tile slips	-	0.55	7.93	8.97	m	16.90
segmental hip tiles; tile slips; cutting both sides	-	0.70	10.09	10.86	m	20.95
dry ridge tiles; segmental including batten						
sections; unions and filler pieces	-	0.30	4.32	12.92	m	17.24
segmental mono-ridge tiles	-	0.55	7.93	12.16	m	20.09
gas ridge terminal	-	0.50	7.21	51.73	nr	58.94
holes for pipes and the like	-	0.20	2.88	-	nr	2.88
Concrete interlocking tiles; Marley "Ludlow Major"						
granule finish tiles or other equal and approved; PC						
£566.95/1000; 420 mm x 330 mm; to 75 mm lap; on 25						
mm x 38 mm battens and type 1F reinforced underlay						
Roof coverings	-	0.35	5.04	8.11	m²	13.15
Extra over coverings for						
fixing every tile	-	0.03	0.43	0.41	m²	0.84
eaves; eaves filler	-	0.05	0.72	0.32	m	1.04
verges; 150 mm wide asbestos free strip undercloak	-	0.23	3.31	1.53	m	4.84
dry verge system; extruded white pvc	-	0.15	2.16	7.19	m	9.35
segmental ridge cap to dry verge	-	0.03	0.43	2.35	m	2.78
valley trough tiles; cutting both sides	-	0.55	7.93	15.56	m	23.49
segmental ridge tiles	-	0.50	7.21	6.30	m	13.51
segmental hip tiles; cutting both sides	-	0.65	9.37	8.08	m	17.45
dry ridge tiles; segmental including batten						
sections; unions and filler pieces	-	0.30	4.32	12.92	m	17.24
segmental mono-ridge tiles	-	0.50	7.21	10.60	m	17.81
gas ridge terminal	-	0.50	7.21	51.73	nr	58.94
holes for pipes and the like	-	0.20	2.88	-	nr	2.88
Concrete interlocking tiles; Marley "Mendip" granule						
finish double pantiles or other equal and approved; PC						
£609.45/1000; 420 mm x 330 mm; to 75 mm lap; on 22						
mm x 38 mm battens and type 1F reinforced underlay						
Roof coverings	-	0.35	5.04	8.48	m²	13.52
Extra over coverings for						
fixing every tile	-	0.03	0.43	0.41	m²	0.84
eaves; eaves filler	-	0.03	0.43	0.56	m	0.99
verges; 150 mm wide asbestos free strip undercloak	-	0.23	3.31	1.53	m	4.84
dry verge system; extruded white pvc	-	0.15	2.16	7.19	m	9.35
segmental ridge cap to dry verge	-	0.03	0.43	2.35	m	2.78
valley trough tiles; cutting both sides	-	0.55	7.93	15.65	m	23.58
segmental ridge tiles	-	0.55	7.93	8.97	m	16.90
segmental hip tiles; cutting both sides	-	0.70	10.09	10.89	m	20.98
dry ridge tiles; segmental including batten						
sections; unions and filler pieces	-	0.30	4.32	12.92	m	17.24
segmental mono-ridge tiles	-	0.50	7.21	11.94	m	19.15
gas ridge terminal	-	0.50	7.21	51.73	nr	58.94
holes for pipes and the like	-	0.20	2.88	-	nr	2.88

H CLADDING/COVERING Excluding overheads and profit	PC £	Labour hours	Labour £	Material £	Unit	Total rate £
H60 PLAIN ROOF TILING - cont'd						
Concrete interlocking tiles; Marley "Modern" smooth finish tiles or other equal and approved; PC £566.95/ 1000; 420 mm x 220 mm; to 75 mm lap; on 25 mm x 38 mm battens and type 1F reinforced underlay						
Roof coverings	-	0.35	5.04	8.26	m²	**13.30**
Extra over coverings for						
fixing every tile	-	0.03	0.43	0.41	m²	**0.84**
verges; 150 mm wide asbestos free strip undercloak	-	0.23	3.31	1.53	m	**4.84**
dry verge system; extruded white pvc	-	0.20	2.88	7.19	m	**10.07**
"Modern" ridge cap to dry verge	-	0.03	0.43	2.35	m	**2.78**
valley trough tiles; cutting both sides	-	0.55	7.93	15.56	m	**23.49**
"Modern" ridge tiles	-	0.50	7.21	6.61	m	**13.82**
"Modern" hip tiles; cutting both sides	-	0.65	9.37	8.40	m	**17.77**
dry ridge tiles; "Modern"; including batten sections; unions and filler pieces	-	0.30	4.32	13.24	m	**17.56**
"Modern" mono-ridge tiles	-	0.50	7.21	10.60	m	**17.81**
gas ridge terminal	-	0.50	7.21	51.73	nr	**58.94**
holes for pipes and the like	-	0.20	2.88	-	nr	**2.88**
Concrete interlocking tiles; Marley "Wessex" smooth finish tiles or other equal and approved; PC £929.90/ 1000; 413 mm x 330 mm; to 75 mm lap; on 25 mm x 38 mm battens and type 1F reinforced underlay						
Roof coverings	-	0.35	5.04	12.03	m²	**17.07**
Extra over coverings for						
fixing every tile	-	0.03	0.43	0.41	m²	**0.84**
verges; 150 mm wide asbestos free strip undercloak	-	0.23	3.31	1.53	m	**4.84**
dry verge system; extruded white pvc	-	0.20	2.88	7.19	m	**10.07**
"Modern" ridge cap to dry verge	-	0.03	0.43	2.35	m	**2.78**
valley trough tiles; cutting both sides	-	0.55	7.93	16.32	m	**24.25**
"Modern" ridge tiles	-	0.50	7.21	6.61	m	**13.82**
"Modern" hip tiles; cutting both sides	-	0.65	9.37	9.54	m	**18.91**
dry ridge tiles; "Modern"; including batten sections; unions and filler pieces	-	0.30	4.32	13.24	m	**17.56**
"Modern" mono-ridge tiles	-	0.50	7.21	10.60	m	**17.81**
gas ridge terminal	-	0.50	7.21	51.73	nr	**58.94**
holes for pipes and the like	-	0.20	2.88	-	nr	**2.88**
Concrete interlocking slates; Redland "Delta" smooth finish tiles or other equal and approved; PC £1582.70/ 1000; 430 mm x 380 mm; to 75 mm lap; on 25 mm x 38 mm battens and type 1F reinforced underlay						
Roof coverings	-	0.35	5.04	15.90	m²	**20.94**
Extra over coverings for						
fixing every tile	-	0.03	0.43	0.41	m²	**0.84**
eaves; eaves filler	-	0.03	0.43	0.77	m	**1.20**
verges; extra single undercloak course of plain tiles	-	0.25	3.60	3.09	m	**6.69**
ambi-dry verge system	-	0.20	2.88	8.89	m	**11.77**
ambi-dry verge eave/ridge end piece	-	0.03	0.43	3.12	m	**3.55**
valley trough tiles; cutting both sides	-	0.60	8.65	27.09	m	**35.74**
"Delta" ridge tiles	-	0.50	7.21	13.28	m	**20.49**
"Delta" hip tiles; cutting both sides	-	0.65	9.37	18.26	m	**27.63**
"Delta" mono-ridge tiles	-	0.50	7.21	19.88	m	**27.09**
gas ridge terminal	-	0.50	7.21	98.20	nr	**105.41**
ridge vent with 110 mm diameter flexible adaptor	-	0.50	7.21	83.03	nr	**90.24**
holes for pipes and the like	-	0.20	2.88	-	nr	**2.88**

H CLADDING/COVERING Excluding overheads and profit	PC £	Labour hours	Labour £	Material £	Unit	Total rate £
Concrete interlocking tiles; Redland "Norfolk" smooth finish pantiles or other equal and approved; PC £413.95/1000; 381 mm x 229 mm; to 75 mm lap; on 25 mm x 38 mm battens and type 1F reinforced underlay						
Roof coverings	-	0.45	6.48	10.33	m²	16.81
Extra over coverings for						
fixing every tile	-	0.05	0.72	0.23	m²	0.95
eaves; eaves filler	-	0.05	0.72	0.96	m	1.68
verges; extra single undercloak course of plain tiles	-	0.30	4.32	5.52	m	9.84
valley trough tiles; cutting both sides	-	0.60	8.65	22.62	m	31.27
universal ridge tiles	-	0.50	7.21	9.82	m	17.03
universal hip tiles; cutting both sides	-	0.65	9.37	11.99	m	21.36
universal gas flue ridge tile	-	0.50	7.21	78.90	nr	86.11
universal ridge vent tile with 110 mm diameter						
adaptor	-	0.50	7.21	67.93	nr	75.14
holes for pipes and the like	-	0.20	2.88	-	nr	2.88
Concrete interlocking tiles; Redland "Regent" granule finish bold roll tiles or other equal and approved; PC £589.90/1000; 418 mm x 332 mm; to 75 mm lap; on 25 mm x 38 mm battens and type 1F reinforced underlay						
Roof coverings	-	0.35	5.04	8.47	m²	13.51
Extra over coverings for						
fixing every tile	-	0.04	0.58	0.58	m²	1.16
eaves; eaves filler	-	0.05	0.72	0.72	m	1.44
verges; extra single undercloak course of plain tiles	-	0.25	3.60	2.53	m	6.13
cloaked verge system	-	0.15	2.16	5.93	m	8.09
valley trough tiles; cutting both sides	-	0.55	7.93	22.30	m	30.23
universal ridge tiles	-	0.50	7.21	9.82	m	17.03
universal hip tiles; cutting both sides	-	0.65	9.37	11.67	m	21.04
dry ridge system; universal ridge tiles	-	0.25	3.60	30.21	m	33.81
universal half round mono-pitch ridge tiles	-	0.55	7.93	20.29	m	28.22
universal gas flue ridge tile	-	0.50	7.21	78.90	nr	86.11
universal ridge vent tile with 110 mm diameter						
adaptor	-	0.50	7.21	67.93	nr	75.14
holes for pipes and the like	-	0.20	2.88	-	nr	2.88
Concrete interlocking tiles; Redland "Renown" granule finish tiles or other equal and approved; PC £558.45/1000; 418 mm x 330 mm; to 75 mm lap; on 25 mm x 38 mm battens and type 1F reinforced underlay						
Roof coverings	-	0.35	5.04	8.15	m²	13.19
Extra over coverings for						
fixing every tile	-	0.03	0.43	0.27	m²	0.70
verges; extra single undercloak course of plain tiles	-	0.25	3.60	3.08	m	6.68
cloaked verge system	-	0.15	2.16	6.02	m	8.18
valley trough tiles; cutting both sides	-	0.55	7.93	22.20	m	30.13
universal ridge tiles	-	0.50	7.21	9.82	m	17.03
universal hip tiles; cutting both sides	-	0.65	9.37	11.58	m	20.95
dry ridge system; universal ridge tiles	-	0.25	3.60	30.21	m	33.81
universal half round mono-pitch ridge tiles	-	0.55	7.93	20.29	m	28.22
universal gas flue ridge tile	-	0.50	7.21	78.90	nr	86.11
universal ridge vent tile with 110 mm diameter						
adaptor	-	0.50	7.21	67.93	nr	75.14
holes for pipes and the like	-	0.20	2.88	-	nr	2.88

H CLADDING/COVERING Excluding overheads and profit	PC £	Labour hours	Labour £	Material £	Unit	Total rate £
H60 PLAIN ROOF TILING - cont'd						
Concrete interlocking tiles; Redland "Stonewold II" smooth finish tiles or other equal and approved; PC £1160.25/1000; 430 mm x 380 mm; to 75 mm lap; on 25 mm x 38 mm battens and type 1F reinforced underlay						
Roof coverings	-	0.35	5.04	14.41	m²	**19.45**
Extra over coverings for						
fixing every tile	-	0.03	0.43	0.92	m²	**1.35**
verges; extra single undercloak course of plain tiles	-	0.30	4.32	3.09	m	**7.41**
ambi-dry verge system	-	0.20	2.88	8.89	m	**11.77**
ambi-dry verge eave/ridge end piece	-	0.03	0.43	3.12	m	**3.55**
valley trough tiles; cutting both sides	-	0.55	7.93	24.10	m	**32.03**
universal angle ridge tiles	-	0.50	7.21	7.25	m	**14.46**
universal hip tiles; cutting both sides	-	0.65	9.37	10.90	m	**20.27**
dry ridge system; universal angle ridge tiles	-	0.25	3.60	19.17	m	**22.77**
universal mono-pitch angle ridge tiles	-	0.55	7.93	13.79	m	**21.72**
universal gas flue angle ridge tile	-	0.50	7.21	81.48	nr	**88.69**
universal angle ridge vent tile with 110 mm						
diameter adaptor	-	0.50	7.21	67.83	nr	**75.04**
holes for pipes and the like	-	0.20	2.88	-	nr	**2.88**
Concrete plain tiles; EN 490 and 491 group A; PC £250.75/1000; 267 mm x 165 mm; on 25 mm x 38 mm battens and type 1F reinforced underlay						
Roof coverings; to 64 mm lap	-	1.05	15.13	21.18	m²	**36.31**
Wall coverings; to 38 mm lap	-	1.25	18.01	18.22	m²	**36.23**
Extra over coverings for						
ornamental tiles	-	-	-	15.10	m²	**15.10**
double course at eaves	-	0.25	3.60	2.49	m	**6.09**
verges	-	0.33	4.76	1.01	m	**5.77**
swept valleys; cutting both sides	-	0.65	9.37	23.80	m	**33.17**
bonnet hips; cutting both sides	-	0.80	11.53	23.87	m	**35.40**
external vertical angle tiles; supplementary nail						
fixings	-	0.40	5.76	17.14	m	**22.90**
half round ridge tiles	-	0.50	7.21	6.31	m	**13.52**
third round hip tiles; cutting both sides	-	0.50	7.21	7.89	m	**15.10**
holes for pipes and the like	-	0.20	2.88	-	nr	**2.88**
Sundries						
Hip irons						
galvanised mild steel; fixing with screws	-	0.10	1.44	2.35	nr	**3.79**
"Rytons Clip strip" or other equal and approved; continuous soffit ventilator						
51 mm wide; plastic; code CS351	-	0.30	4.32	0.92	m	**5.24**
"Rytons over fascia ventilator" or other equal and approved; continuous eaves ventilator						
40 mm wide; plastic; code OFV890	-	0.10	1.44	1.65	m	**3.09**
"Rytons roof ventilator" or other equal and approved; to suit rafters at 600 mm centres						
250 mm deep x 43 mm high; plastic; code TV600	-	0.10	1.44	1.56	m	**3.00**
"Rytons push and lock ventilators" or other equal and approved; circular						
83 mm diameter; plastic; code PL235	-	0.05	0.57	0.24	nr	**0.81**
Fixing only						
lead soakers (supply cost not included)	-	0.08	0.85	-	nr	**0.85**
Pressure impregnated softwood counter battens; 25 mm x 50 mm						
450 mm centres	-	0.07	1.01	0.91	m²	**1.92**
600 mm centres	-	0.05	0.72	0.69	m²	**1.41**

H CLADDING/COVERING Excluding overheads and profit	PC £	Labour hours	Labour £	Material £	Unit	Total rate £
Underlay; BS 747 type 1B; bitumen felt **weighing 14 kg/10 m²; 75 mm laps** To sloping or vertical surfaces	0.49	0.03	0.43	0.96	m²	**1.39**
Underlay; BS 747 type 1F; reinforced bitumen **felt weighing 22.50 kg/10 m²; 75 mm laps** To sloping or vertical surfaces	0.92	0.03	0.43	1.42	m²	**1.85**
Underlay; Visqueen "Tilene 200P" or other equal **and approved; micro-perforated sheet; 75 mm laps** To sloping or vertical surfaces	0.46	0.03	0.43	0.96	m²	**1.39**
Underlay; "Powerlon 250 BM" or other equal and **approved; reinforced breather membrane; 75 mm laps** To sloping or vertical surfaces	0.54	0.03	0.43	1.04	m²	**1.47**
Underlay; "Anticon" or other equal and approved; **sarking membrane; Euroroof Ltd; polyethylene;** **75 mm laps** To sloping or vertical surfaces	-	0.03	0.43	1.34	m²	**1.77**
H61 FIBRE CEMENT SLATING						
Asbestos-free artificial slates; Eternit "2000" or other **equal and approved; to 75 mm lap; on 19 mm x 50 mm** **battens and type 1F reinforced underlay**						
Coverings; 400 mm x 200 mm slates						
roof coverings	-	0.80	11.53	23.10	m²	**34.63**
wall coverings	-	1.05	15.13	23.10	m²	**38.23**
Coverings; 500 mm x 250 mm slates						
roof coverings	-	0.65	9.37	20.98	m²	**30.35**
wall coverings	-	0.80	11.53	20.98	m²	**32.51**
Coverings; 600 mm x 300 mm slates						
roof coverings	-	0.50	7.21	18.46	m²	**25.67**
wall coverings	-	0.65	9.37	18.46	m²	**27.83**
Extra over slate coverings for						
double course at eaves	-	0.25	3.60	4.59	m	**8.19**
verges; extra single undercloak course	-	0.33	4.76	1.11	m	**5.87**
open valleys; cutting both sides	-	0.20	2.88	4.45	m	**7.33**
valley gutters; cutting both sides	-	0.55	7.93	18.89	m	**26.82**
half round ridge tiles	-	0.50	7.21	16.92	m	**24.13**
stop end	-	0.10	1.44	5.78	nr	**7.22**
roll top ridge tiles	-	0.60	8.65	18.41	m	**27.06**
stop end	-	0.10	1.44	8.62	nr	**10.06**
mono-pitch ridge tiles	-	0.50	7.21	21.63	m	**28.84**
stop end	-	0.10	1.44	26.02	nr	**27.46**
duo-pitch ridge tiles	-	0.50	7.21	17.48	m	**24.69**
stop end	-	0.10	1.44	19.11	nr	**20.55**
mitred hips; cutting both sides	-	0.20	2.88	4.45	m	**7.33**
half round hip tiles; cutting both sides	-	0.20	2.88	21.38	m	**24.26**
holes for pipes and the like	-	0.20	2.88	-	nr	**2.88**
H62 NATURAL SLATING						
NOTE: The following items of slate roofing unless otherwise described, include for conventional fixing assuming "normal exposure" with appropriate nails and/or rivets or clips to pressure impregnated softwood battens fixed with galvanised nails; prices also include for all bedding and pointing at verges; beneath verge tiles, etc.						

H CLADDING/COVERING Excluding overheads and profit	PC £	Labour hours	Labour £	Material £	Unit	Total rate £
H62 NATURAL SLATING - cont'd						
Natural slates; BS 680 Part 2; Welsh blue; **uniform size; to 75 mm lap; on 25 mm x 50** **mm battens and type 1F reinforced underlay**						
Coverings; 405 mm x 255 mm slates						
roof coverings	-	0.90	12.97	31.12	m²	**44.09**
wall coverings	-	1.15	16.57	31.12	m²	**47.69**
Coverings; 510 mm x 255 mm slates						
roof coverings	-	0.75	10.81	37.48	m²	**48.29**
wall coverings	-	0.90	12.97	37.48	m²	**50.45**
Coverings; 610 mm x 305 mm slates						
roof coverings	-	0.60	8.65	47.60	m²	**56.25**
wall coverings	-	0.75	10.81	47.60	m²	**58.41**
Extra over coverings for						
double course at eaves	-	0.30	4.32	12.50	m	**16.82**
verges; extra single undercloak course	-	0.42	6.05	7.31	m	**13.36**
open valleys; cutting both sides	-	0.22	3.17	28.92	m	**32.09**
blue/black glazed ware 152 mm half round						
ridge tiles	-	0.50	7.21	6.76	m	**13.97**
blue/black glazed ware 125 mm x 125 mm						
plain angle ridge tiles	-	0.50	7.21	6.76	m	**13.97**
mitred hips; cutting both sides	-	0.22	3.17	28.92	m	**32.09**
blue/black glazed ware 152 mm half round hip						
tiles; cutting both sides	-	0.70	10.09	35.68	m	**45.77**
blue/black glazed ware 125 mm x 125 mm						
plain angle hip tiles; cutting both sides	-	0.70	10.09	35.68	m	**45.77**
holes for pipes and the like	-	0.20	2.88	-	nr	**2.88**
Natural slates; Westmoreland green; PC **£1703.00/t; random lengths; 457 mm - 229** **mm proportionate widths to 75 mm lap; in** **diminishing courses; on 25 mm x 50 mm** **battens and type 1F underlay**						
Roof coverings	-	1.15	16.57	99.75	m²	**116.32**
Wall coverings	-	1.45	20.89	99.75	m²	**120.64**
Extra over coverings for						
double course at eaves	-	0.66	9.51	18.58	m	**28.09**
verges; extra single undercloak course slates						
152 mm wide		0.75	10.81	16.26	m	**27.07**
holes for pipes and the like	-	0.30	4.32	-	nr	**4.32**
H63 RECONSTRUCTED STONE SLATING/TILING						
Reconstructed stone slates; "Hardrow Slates" or **other equal and approved; standard colours; or** **similar; PC £729.30/1000; to 75 mm lap; on 25 mm x** **50 mm battens and type 1F reinforced underlay**						
Coverings; 457 mm x 305 mm slates						
roof coverings	-	0.80	11.53	17.44	m²	**28.97**
wall coverings	-	1.00	14.41	17.44	m²	**31.85**
Coverings; 457 mm x 457 mm slates						
roof coverings	-	0.65	9.37	17.22	m²	**26.59**
wall coverings	-	0.85	12.25	17.22	m²	**29.47**
Extra over 457 mm x 305 mm coverings for						
double course at eaves	-	0.30	4.32	3.14	m	**7.46**
verges; pointed	-	0.42	6.05	0.06	m	**6.11**
open valleys; cutting both sides	-	0.22	3.17	7.66	m	**10.83**
ridge tiles	-	0.50	7.21	22.47	m	**29.68**
hip tiles; cutting both sides	-	0.70	10.09	16.84	m	**26.93**
holes for pipes and the like	-	0.20	2.88	-	nr	**2.88**

H CLADDING/COVERING Excluding overheads and profit	PC £	Labour hours	Labour £	Material £	Unit	Total rate £
Reconstructed stone slates; "Hardrow Slates" or other equal and approved; green/oldstone colours; PC £729.30/1000; to 75 mm lap; on 25 mm x 50 mm battens and type 1F reinforced underlay						
Coverings; 457 mm x 305 mm slates						
roof coverings	-	0.80	11.53	17.44	m²	**28.97**
wall coverings	-	1.00	14.41	17.44	m²	**31.85**
Coverings; 457 mm x 457 mm slates						
roof coverings	-	0.65	9.37	17.22	m²	**26.59**
wall coverings	-	0.85	12.25	17.22	m²	**29.47**
Extra over 457 mm x 305 mm coverings for						
double course at eaves	-	0.30	4.32	3.14	m	**7.46**
verges; pointed	-	0.42	6.05	0.06	m	**6.11**
open valleys; cutting both sides	-	0.22	3.17	7.66	m	**10.83**
ridge tiles	-	0.50	7.21	22.47	m	**29.68**
hip tiles; cutting both sides	-	0.70	10.09	16.84	m	**26.93**
holes for pipes and the like	-	0.20	2.88	-	nr	**2.88**
Reconstructed stone slates; Bradstone "Cotswold" style or other equal and approved; PC £18.58/m²; random lengths 550 mm - 300 mm; proportional widths; to 80 mm lap; in diminishing courses; on 25 mm x 50 mm battens and type 1F reinforced underlay						
Roof coverings (all-in rate inclusive of eaves and verges)	-	1.05	15.13	23.78	m²	**38.91**
Extra over coverings for						
open valleys/mitred hips; cutting both sides	-	0.45	6.48	8.78	m²	**15.26**
ridge tiles	-	0.66	9.51	11.70	m	**21.21**
hip tiles; cutting both sides	-	1.05	15.13	19.84	m	**34.97**
holes for pipes and the like	-	0.30	4.32	-	nr	**4.32**
Reconstructed stone slates; Bradstone "Moordale" style or other equal and approved; PC £17.50/m²; random lengths 550 mm - 450 mm; proportional widths; to 80 mm lap; in diminishing course; on 25 mm x 50 mm battens and type 1F reinforced underlay						
Roof coverings (all-in rate inclusive of eaves and verges)	-	1.05	15.13	22.64	m²	**37.77**
Extra over coverings for						
open valleys/mitred hips; cutting both sides	-	0.45	6.48	8.27	m²	**14.75**
ridge tiles	-	0.66	9.51	11.70	m	**21.21**
holes for pipes and the like	-	0.30	4.32	-	nr	**4.32**
H64 TIMBER SHINGLING						
Red cedar sawn shingles preservative treated; PC £24.56/bundle; uniform length 400 mm; to 125 mm gauge; on 25 mm x 38 mm battens and type 1F reinforced underlay						
Roof coverings; 125 mm gauge, 2.28 m²/bundle	-	1.05	15.13	15.70	m²	**30.83**
Wall coverings; 190 mm gauge, 3.47 m²/bundle	-	0.80	11.53	10.70	m²	**22.23**
Extra over coverings for						
double course at eaves	-	0.20	2.88	1.47	m	**4.35**
open valleys; cutting both sides	-	0.20	2.88	2.77	m	**5.65**
pre-formed ridge capping	-	0.30	4.32	5.00	m	**9.32**
pre-formed hip capping; cutting both sides	-	0.50	7.21	7.77	m	**14.98**
double starter course to cappings	-	0.10	1.44	0.52	m	**1.96**
holes for pipes and the like	-	0.15	2.16	-	nr	**2.16**

H CLADDING/COVERING Excluding overheads and profit	PC £	Labour hours	Labour £	Material £	Unit	Total rate £
H71 LEAD SHEET COVERINGS/FLASHINGS						
Milled lead; BS 1178; PC £980.00/t						
1.32 mm thick (code 3) roof coverings						
flat	-	2.70	28.54	15.29	m²	**43.83**
sloping 10 - 50 degrees	-	3.00	31.71	15.29	m²	**47.00**
vertical or sloping over 50 degrees	-	3.30	34.88	15.29	m²	**50.17**
1.80 mm thick (code 4) roof coverings						
flat	-	2.90	30.65	20.86	m²	**51.51**
sloping 10 - 50 degrees	-	3.20	33.82	20.86	m²	**54.68**
vertical or sloping over 50 degrees	-	3.50	36.99	20.86	m²	**57.85**
1.80 mm thick (code 4) dormer coverings						
flat	-	3.40	35.94	20.86	m²	**56.80**
sloping 10 - 50 degrees	-	3.90	41.22	20.86	m²	**62.08**
vertical or sloping over 50 degrees	-	4.20	44.39	20.86	m²	**65.25**
2.24 mm thick (code 5) roof coverings						
flat	-	3.10	32.77	27.81	m²	**60.58**
sloping 10 - 50 degrees	-	3.40	35.94	27.81	m²	**63.75**
vertical or sloping over 50 degrees	-	3.70	39.11	27.81	m²	**66.92**
2.24 mm thick (code 5) dormer coverings						
flat	-	3.70	39.11	27.81	m²	**66.92**
sloping 10 - 50 degrees	-	4.10	43.34	27.81	m²	**71.15**
vertical or sloping over 50 degrees	-	4.50	47.56	27.81	m²	**75.37**
2.65 mm thick (code 6) roof coverings						
flat	-	3.30	34.88	30.70	m²	**65.58**
sloping 10 - 50 degrees	-	3.60	38.05	30.70	m²	**68.75**
vertical or sloping over 50 degrees	-	3.90	41.22	30.70	m²	**71.92**
2.65 mm thick (code 6) dormer coverings						
flat	-	4.00	42.28	30.70	m²	**72.98**
sloping 10 - 50 degrees	-	4.30	45.45	30.70	m²	**76.15**
vertical or sloping over 50 degrees	-	4.70	49.68	30.70	m²	**80.38**
3.15 mm thick (code 7) roof coverings						
flat	-	3.50	36.99	36.50	m²	**73.49**
sloping 10 - 50 degrees	-	3.80	40.17	36.50	m²	**76.67**
vertical or sloping over 50 degrees	-	4.10	43.34	36.50	m²	**79.84**
3.15 mm thick (code 7) dormer coverings						
flat	-	4.20	44.39	36.50	m²	**80.89**
sloping 10 - 50 degrees	-	4.50	47.56	36.50	m²	**84.06**
vertical or sloping over 50 degrees	-	4.90	51.79	36.50	m²	**88.29**
3.55 mm thick (code 8) roof coverings						
flat	-	3.70	39.11	41.13	m²	**80.24**
sloping 10 - 50 degrees	-	4.00	42.28	41.13	m²	**83.41**
vertical or sloping over 50 degrees	-	4.30	45.45	41.13	m²	**86.58**
3.55 mm thick (code 8) dormer coverings						
flat	-	4.50	47.56	41.13	m²	**88.69**
sloping 10 - 50 degrees	-	4.80	50.74	41.13	m²	**91.87**
vertical or sloping over 50 degrees	-	5.20	54.96	41.13	m²	**96.09**
Dressing over glazing bars and glass	-	0.33	3.49	-	m	**3.49**
Soldered dot	-	0.15	1.59	-	nr	**1.59**
Copper nailing; 75 mm centres	-	0.20	2.11	0.25	m	**2.36**
1.80 mm thick (code 4) lead flashings, etc.						
Flashings; wedging into grooves						
150 mm girth	-	0.80	8.46	3.25	m	**11.71**
240 mm girth	-	0.90	9.51	5.18	m	**14.69**
Stepped flashings; wedging into grooves						
180 mm girth	-	0.90	9.51	3.86	m	**13.37**
270 mm girth	-	1.00	10.57	5.79	m	**16.36**
Linings to sloping gutters						
390 mm girth	-	1.20	12.68	8.43	m	**21.11**
450 mm girth	-	1.30	13.74	9.65	m	**23.39**

H CLADDING/COVERING Excluding overheads and profit	PC £	Labour hours	Labour £	Material £	Unit	Total rate £
Cappings to hips or ridges						
450 mm girth	-	1.50	15.86	9.65	m	**25.51**
600 mm girth	-	1.60	16.91	12.91	m	**29.82**
Soakers						
200 mm x 200 mm	-	0.15	1.59	0.83	nr	**2.42**
300 mm x 300 mm	-	0.20	2.11	1.88	nr	**3.99**
Saddle flashings; at intersections of hips and ridges; dressing and bossing						
450 mm x 600 mm	-	1.80	19.03	5.79	nr	**24.82**
Slates; with 150 mm high collar						
450 mm x 450 mm; to suit 50 mm diameter pipe	-	1.70	17.97	4.99	nr	**22.96**
450 mm x 450 mm; to suit 100 mm diameter pipe	-	2.00	21.14	5.48	nr	**26.62**
2.24 mm thick (code 5) lead flashings, etc.						
Flashings; wedging into grooves						
150 mm girth	-	0.80	8.46	4.04	m	**12.50**
240 mm girth	-	0.90	9.51	6.41	m	**15.92**
Stepped flashings; wedging into grooves						
180 mm girth	-	0.90	9.51	4.83	m	**14.34**
270 mm girth	-	1.00	10.57	7.20	m	**17.77**
Linings to sloping gutters						
390 mm girth	-	1.20	12.68	10.45	m	**23.13**
450 mm girth	-	1.30	13.74	12.03	m	**25.77**
Cappings to hips or ridges						
450 mm girth	-	1.50	15.86	12.03	m	**27.89**
600 mm girth	-	1.60	16.91	16.07	m	**32.98**
Soakers						
200 mm x 200 mm	-	0.15	1.59	1.11	nr	**2.70**
300 mm x 300 mm	-	0.20	2.11	2.50	nr	**4.61**
Saddle flashings; at intersections of hips and ridges; dressing and bossing						
450 mm x 600 mm	-	1.80	19.03	7.22	nr	**26.25**
Slates; with 150 mm high collar						
450 mm x 450 mm; to suit 50 mm diameter pipe	-	1.70	17.97	6.22	nr	**24.19**
450 mm x 450 mm; to suit 100 mm diameter pipe	-	2.00	21.14	6.83	nr	**27.97**
H72 ALUMINIUM SHEET COVERINGS/FLASHINGS						
Aluminium roofing; commercial grade						
0.90 mm thick roof coverings						
flat	5.28	3.00	31.71	5.54	m²	**37.25**
sloping 10 - 50 degrees	-	3.30	34.88	5.54	m²	**40.42**
vertical or sloping over 50 degrees	-	3.60	38.05	5.54	m²	**43.59**
0.90 mm thick dormer coverings						
flat	-	3.60	38.05	5.54	m²	**43.59**
sloping 10 - 50 degrees	-	4.00	42.28	5.54	m²	**47.82**
vertical or sloping over 50 degrees	-	4.40	46.51	5.54	m²	**52.05**
Aluminium nailing; 75 mm spacing	-	0.20	2.11	0.23	m	**2.34**
0.90 mm commercial grade aluminium **flashings, etc.**						
Flashings; wedging into grooves						
150 mm girth	-	0.80	8.46	0.86	m	**9.32**
240 mm girth	-	0.90	9.51	1.40	m	**10.91**
300 mm girth	-	1.05	11.10	1.71	m	**12.81**
Stepped flashings; wedging into grooves						
180 mm girth	-	0.90	9.51	1.03	m	**10.54**
270 mm girth	-	1.00	10.57	1.59	m	**12.16**

H CLADDING/COVERING Excluding overheads and profit	PC £	Labour hours	Labour £	Material £	Unit	Total rate £
H72 ALUMINIUM SHEET COVERINGS/FLASHINGS - cont'd						
1.20 mm commercial grade aluminium **flashings; polyester powder coated**						
Flashings; fixed with self tapping screws						
170 mm girth	-	0.90	9.51	1.19	m	**10.70**
200 mm girth	-	0.95	10.04	1.57	m	**11.61**
280 mm girth	-	1.10	11.63	2.07	m	**13.70**
H73 COPPER STRIP SHEET COVERINGS/FLASHINGS						
Copper roofing; BS 2870						
0.56 mm thick (24 swg) roof coverings						
flat	16.68	3.20	33.82	17.51	m²	**51.33**
sloping 10 - 50 degrees	-	3.50	36.99	17.51	m²	**54.50**
vertical or sloping over 50 degrees	-	3.80	40.17	17.51	m²	**57.68**
0.56 mm thick (24 swg) dormer coverings						
flat	16.68	3.80	40.17	17.51	m²	**57.68**
sloping 10 - 50 degrees	-	4.20	44.39	17.51	m²	**61.90**
vertical or sloping over 50 degrees	-	4.60	48.62	17.51	m²	**66.13**
0.61 mm thick (23 swg) roof coverings						
flat	18.17	3.20	33.82	19.08	m²	**52.90**
sloping 10 - 50 degrees	-	3.50	36.99	19.08	m²	**56.07**
vertical or sloping over 50 degrees	-	3.80	40.17	19.08	m²	**59.25**
0.61 mm thick (23 swg) dormer coverings						
flat	18.17	3.80	40.17	19.08	m²	**59.25**
sloping 10 - 50 degrees	-	4.20	44.39	19.08	m²	**63.47**
vertical or sloping over 50 degrees	-	4.60	48.62	19.08	m²	**67.70**
Copper nailing; 75 mm spacing	-	0.20	2.11	0.25	m	**2.36**
0.56 mm thick copper flashings, etc.						
Flashings; wedging into grooves						
150 mm girth	-	0.80	8.46	2.75	m	**11.21**
240 mm girth	-	0.90	9.51	4.41	m	**13.92**
300 mm girth	-	1.05	11.10	5.52	m	**16.62**
Stepped flashings; wedging into grooves						
180 mm girth	-	0.90	9.51	3.33	m	**12.84**
270 mm girth	-	1.00	10.57	4.97	m	**15.54**
0.61 mm thick copper flashings, etc.						
Flashings; wedging into grooves						
150 mm girth	-	0.80	8.46	2.98	m	**11.44**
240 mm girth	-	0.90	9.51	4.81	m	**14.32**
300 mm girth	-	1.05	11.10	6.01	m	**17.11**
Stepped flashings; wedging into grooves						
180 mm girth	-	0.90	9.51	3.61	m	**13.12**
270 mm girth	-	1.00	10.57	5.41	m	**15.98**
H74 ZINC STRIP SHEET COVERINGS/FLASHINGS						
Zinc; BS 849						
0.80 mm thick roof coverings						
flat	11.99	3.20	33.82	12.59	m²	**46.41**
sloping 10 - 50 degrees	-	3.50	36.99	12.59	m²	**49.58**
vertical or sloping over 50 degrees	-	3.80	40.17	12.59	m²	**52.76**
0.80 mm thick (23 swg) dormer coverings						
flat	-	3.80	40.17	12.59	m²	**52.76**
sloping 10 - 50 degrees	-	4.20	44.39	12.59	m²	**56.98**
vertical or sloping over 50 degrees	-	4.60	48.62	12.59	m²	**61.21**

H CLADDING/COVERING Excluding overheads and profit	PC £	Labour hours	Labour £	Material £	Unit	Total rate £
0.80 mm thick zinc flashings, etc.						
Flashings; wedging into grooves						
150 mm girth	-	0.80	8.46	1.96	m	**10.42**
240 mm girth	-	0.90	9.51	3.16	m	**12.67**
300 mm girth	-	1.05	11.10	3.97	m	**15.07**
Stepped flashings; wedging into grooves						
180 mm girth	-	0.90	9.51	2.38	m	**11.89**
270 mm girth	-	1.00	10.57	3.56	m	**14.13**
H75 STAINLESS STEEL SHEET COVERINGS/ **FLASHINGS**						
Terne coated stainless steel roofing; **Eurocom Enterprise Ltd or other equal and** **approved**						
Roof coverings; "Uginox AME"; 0.40 mm thick						
flat; fixing with stainless steel screws to timber	13.68	1.00	14.41	18.83	m²	**33.24**
flat; including batten rolls; fixing with stainless						
steel screws to timber	-	1.00	14.41	20.14	m²	**34.55**
Roof coverings; "Uginox AE"; 0.40 mm thick						
flat; fixing with stainless steel screws to timber	11.40	1.00	14.41	16.05	m²	**30.46**
flat; including batten rolls; fixing with stainless						
steel screws to timber	-	1.00	14.41	17.32	m²	**31.73**
Wall coverings; "Uginox AME"; 0.40 mm thick						
vertical; coulisseau joints; fixing with stainless						
steel screws; to timber	-	0.90	12.97	17.66	m²	**30.63**
Wall coverings; "Uginox AE"; 0.40 mm thick						
vertical; coulisseau joints; fixing with stainless						
steel screws; to timber	-	0.90	12.97	14.95	m²	**27.92**
Flashings						
head abutments; swiss fold and cover						
flashings 150 mm girth	-	0.40	5.76	3.71	m	**9.47**
head abutments; manchester fold and cover						
flashings 150 mm girth	-	0.50	7.21	3.71	m	**10.92**
head abutments; soldered saddle flashings						
150 mm girth	-	0.50	7.21	4.21	m	**11.42**
head abutments; into brick wall with timber						
infill; cover flashings 150 mm girth	-	0.80	11.53	5.82	m	**17.35**
head abutments; into brick wall with soldered						
apron; cover flashings 150 mm girth	-	0.95	13.69	6.51	m	**20.20**
side abutments; "Uginox" stepped flashings						
170 mm girth	-	1.60	23.06	4.68	m	**27.74**
eaves flashings 140 mm girth; approned with						
single lock welts	-	0.35	5.04	6.69	m	**11.73**
eaves flashings 190 mm girth; approned with						
flashings and soldered strips	-	0.50	7.21	8.20	m	**15.41**
verge flashings 150 mm girth	-	0.25	3.60	6.88	m	**10.48**
Aprons						
fan aprons 250 mm girth	-	0.30	4.32	5.76	m	**10.08**
Ridges						
ridge with coulisseau closures	-	0.60	8.65	2.69	m	**11.34**
monoridge flanged apex (AME)	-	0.30	4.32	3.99	m	**8.31**
ridge with tapered timber infill and flat saddles	-	1.00	14.41	5.43	m	**19.84**
monoridge with timber infill and flat saddles	-	0.55	7.93	8.52	m	**16.45**
ventilated ridge with timber kerb and flat saddles	-	1.20	17.29	14.54	m	**31.83**
ventilated ridge with stainless steel brackets	-	0.90	12.97	25.15	m	**38.12**
Edges						
downstand	-	0.30	4.32	5.36	m	**9.68**
flanged	-	0.25	3.60	5.76	m	**9.36**

H CLADDING/COVERING Excluding overheads and profit	PC £	Labour hours	Labour £	Material £	Unit	Total rate £
H75 STAINLESS STEEL SHEET COVERINGS/ **FLASHINGS** - cont'd						
Terne coated stainless steel roofing; **Eurocom Enterprise Ltd or other equal and** **approved** - cont'd						
Gutters						
double lock welted valley gutters	-	1.05	15.13	8.85	m	**23.98**
eaves gutters; against masonry work	-	1.20	17.29	12.03	m	**29.32**
recessed valley gutters	-	0.90	12.97	17.00	m	**29.97**
recessed valley gutters with laplocks	-	1.10	15.85	20.05	m	**35.90**
secret	-	1.00	14.41	20.93	m	**35.34**
saddle expansion joints in gutters	-	1.00	14.41	7.24	m	**21.65**
H76 FIBRE BITUMEN THERMOPLASTIC SHEET **COVERINGS/FLASHINGS**						
Glass fibre reinforced bitumen strip slates; **"Ruberglas 105" or other equal and approved;** **1000 mm x 336 mm mineral finish; to external** **quality plywood boarding (boarding not included)**						
Roof coverings	9.76	0.25	3.60	10.67	m²	**14.27**
Wall coverings	-	0.40	5.76	10.67	m²	**16.43**
Extra over coverings for						
double course at eaves; felt soaker	-	0.20	2.88	7.50	m	**10.38**
verges; felt soaker	-	0.15	2.16	6.27	m	**8.43**
valley slate; cut to shape; felt soaker and cutting						
both sides	-	0.45	6.48	9.75	m	**16.23**
ridge slate; cut to shape	-	0.30	4.32	6.27	m	**10.59**
hip slate; cut to shape; felt soaker and cutting						
both sides	-	0.45	6.48	9.66	m	**16.14**
holes for pipes and the like	-	0.52	7.49	-	nr	**7.49**
"Evode Flashband Original" sealing strips and **flashings or other equal and approved ; special** **grey finish**						
Flashings; wedging at top if required; pressure bonded; flashband primer before application; to walls						
75 mm girth	-	0.18	1.90	1.35	m	**3.25**
100 mm girth	-	0.25	2.64	1.80	m	**4.44**
150 mm girth	-	0.33	3.49	2.92	m	**6.41**
225 mm girth	-	0.40	4.23	4.28	m	**8.51**
300 mm girth	-	0.45	4.76	5.59	m	**10.35**

J WATERPROOFING Excluding overheads and profit	PC £	Labour hours	Labour £	Material £	Unit	Total rate £
J WATERPROOFING						
J10 SPECIALIST WATERPROOF RENDERING						
"Sika" waterproof rendering or other equal **and approved; steel trowelled**						
20 mm work to walls; three coat; to concrete base						
over 300 mm wide	-	-	-	-	m²	30.00
not exceeding 300 mm wide	-	-	-	-	m²	45.00
25 mm work to walls; three coat; to concrete base						
over 300 mm wide	-	-	-	-	m²	35.00
not exceeding 300 mm wide	-	-	-	-	m²	55.00
40 mm work to walls; four coat; to concrete base						
over 300 mm wide	-	-	-	-	m²	53.00
not exceeding 300 mm wide	-	-	-	-	m²	80.00
J20 MASTIC ASPHALT TANKING/DAMP PROOF ** MEMBRANES**						
Mastic asphalt to BS 6925 Type T 1097						
13 mm thick one coat coverings to concrete base; flat; subsequently covered						
over 300 mm wide	-	-	-	-	m²	7.81
225 mm - 300 mm wide	-	-	-	-	m²	18.48
150 mm - 225 mm wide	-	-	-	-	m²	20.35
not exceeding 150 mm wide	-	-	-	-	m²	25.30
20 mm thick two coat coverings to concrete base; flat; subsequently covered						
over 300 mm wide	-	-	-	-	m²	11.22
225 mm - 300 mm wide	-	-	-	-	m²	20.57
150 mm - 225 mm wide	-	-	-	-	m²	22.44
not exceeding 150 mm wide	-	-	-	-	m²	27.39
30 mm thick three coat coverings to concrete base; flat; subsequently covered						
over 300 mm wide	-	-	-	-	m²	16.06
225 mm - 300 mm wide	-	-	-	-	m²	23.32
150 mm - 225 mm wide	-	-	-	-	m²	25.30
not exceeding 150 mm wide	-	-	-	-	m²	30.25
13 mm thick two coat coverings to brickwork base; vertical; subsequently covered						
over 300 mm wide	-	-	-	-	m²	31.24
225 mm - 300 mm wide	-	-	-	-	m²	38.06
150 mm - 225 mm wide	-	-	-	-	m²	44.99
not exceeding 150 mm wide	-	-	-	-	m²	58.30
20 mm thick three coat coverings to brickwork base; vertical; subsequently covered						
over 300 mm wide	-	-	-	-	m²	48.84
225 mm - 300 mm wide	-	-	-	-	m²	52.58
150 mm - 225 mm wide	-	-	-	-	m²	55.88
not exceeding 150 mm wide	-	-	-	-	m²	72.16
Turning into groove 20 mm deep	-	-	-	-	m	0.55
Internal angle fillets; subsequently covered	-	-	-	-	m	3.63

J WATERPROOFING Excluding overheads and profit	PC £	Labour hours	Labour £	Material £	Unit	Total rate £
J21 MASTIC ASPHALT ROOFING/INSULATION/ FINISHES						
Mastic asphalt to BS 6925 Type R 988						
20 mm thick two coat coverings; felt isolating						
membrane; to concrete (or timber) base; flat or						
to falls or slopes not exceeding 10 degrees						
from horizontal						
over 300 mm wide	-	-	-	-	m²	**11.11**
225 mm - 300 mm wide	-	-	-	-	m²	**20.35**
150 mm - 225 mm wide	-	-	-	-	m²	**22.55**
not exceeding 150 mm wide	-	-	-	-	m²	**27.28**
Add to the above for covering with:						
10 mm thick limestone chippings in hot						
bitumen	-	-	-	-	m²	**2.20**
coverings with solar reflective paint	-	-	-	-	m²	**1.98**
300 mm x 300 mm x 8 mm g.r.p. tiles in hot						
bitumen	-	-	-	-	m²	**29.04**
Cutting to line; jointing to old asphalt	-	-	-	-	m	**4.84**
13 mm thick two coat skirtings to brickwork						
base						
not exceeding 150 mm girth	-	-	-	-	m	**8.69**
150 mm - 225 mm girth	-	-	-	-	m	**10.01**
225 mm - 300 mm girth	-	-	-	-	m	**11.22**
13 mm thick three coat skirtings; expanded						
metal lathing reinforcement nailed to timber						
base						
not exceeding 150 mm girth	-	-	-	-	m	**13.75**
150 mm - 225 mm girth	-	-	-	-	m	**16.28**
225 mm - 300 mm girth	-	-	-	-	m	**18.92**
13 mm thick two coat fascias to concrete base						
not exceeding 150 mm girth	-	-	-	-	m	**8.69**
150 mm - 225 mm girth	-	-	-	-	m	**10.01**
20 mm thick two coat linings to channels to						
concrete base						
not exceeding 150 mm girth	-	-	-	-	m	**21.23**
150 mm - 225 mm girth	-	-	-	-	m	**22.55**
225 mm - 300 mm girth	-	-	-	-	m	**25.41**
20 mm thick two coat lining to cesspools						
250 mm x 150 mm x 150 mm deep	-	-	-	-	nr	**20.68**
Collars around pipes, standards and like members	-	-	-	-	nr	**10.01**
Accessories						
Eaves trim; extruded aluminium alloy; working						
asphalt into trim						
"Alutrim" type A roof edging or other equal and						
approved	-	-	-	-	m	**9.68**
extra; angle	-	-	-	-	nr	**5.39**
Roof screed ventilator - aluminium alloy						
"Extr-aqua-vent" or other equal and approved;						
set on screed over and including dished sinking;						
working collar around ventilator	-	-	-	-	nr	**18.70**
J30 LIQUID APPLIED TANKING/DAMP PROOF MEMBRANES						
Tanking and damp proofing						
"Synthaprufe" or other equal and approved; blinding						
with sand; horizontal on slabs						
two coats	-	0.20	1.45	2.58	m²	**4.03**
three coats	-	0.28	2.04	3.81	m²	**5.85**

J WATERPROOFING Excluding overheads and profit	PC £	Labour hours	Labour £	Material £	Unit	Total rate £
"Tretolastex 202T" or other equal and approved; on vertical surfaces of concrete						
two coats	-	0.20	1.45	0.42	m²	1.87
three coats	-	0.28	2.04	0.64	m²	2.68
One coat Vandex "Super" 0.75 kg/m² slurry or other equal and approved; one consolidating coat of Vandex "Premix" 1 kg/m² slurry or other equal and approved; horizontal on beds						
over 225 mm wide	-	0.35	2.54	2.35	m²	4.89
J40 FLEXIBLE SHEET TANKING/DAMP PROOF MEMBRANES						
Tanking and damp proofing						
"Bituthene" sheeting or other equal and approved; lapped joints; horizontal on slabs						
500 grade	-	0.10	0.73	2.18	m²	2.91
1000 grade	-	0.11	0.80	2.97	m²	3.77
heavy duty grade	-	0.13	0.95	4.31	m²	5.26
"Bituthene" sheeting or other equal and approved; lapped joints; dressed up vertical face of concrete						
1000 grade	-	0.18	1.31	2.97	m²	4.28
"Servi-pak" protection board or other equal and approved; butt jointed; taped joints; to horizontal surfaces						
3 mm thick	-	0.15	1.09	4.10	m²	5.19
6 mm thick	-	0.15	1.09	5.68	m²	6.77
12 mm thick	-	0.20	1.45	8.87	m²	10.32
"Servi-pak" protection board or other equal and approved; butt jointed; taped joints; to vertical surfaces						
3 mm thick	-	0.20	1.45	4.10	m²	5.55
6 mm thick	-	0.20	1.45	5.68	m²	7.13
12 mm thick	-	0.25	1.82	8.87	m²	10.69
"Bituthene" fillet or other equal and approved						
40 mm x 40 mm	-	0.10	0.73	3.91	m	4.64
"Bituthene" reinforcing strip or other equal and approved; 300 mm wide						
1000 grade	-	0.10	0.73	0.89	m	1.62
Expandite "Famflex" hot bitumen bonded waterproof tanking or other equal and approved; 150 mm laps						
horizontal; over 300 mm wide	-	0.40	2.91	9.50	m²	12.41
vertical; over 300 mm wide	-	0.65	4.73	9.50	m²	14.23
J41 BUILT UP FELT ROOF COVERINGS						
NOTE: The following items of felt roofing, unless otherwise described, include for conventional lapping, laying and bonding between layers and to base; and laying flat or to falls, crossfalls or to slopes not exceeding 10 degrees - but exclude any insulation etc.						
Felt roofing; BS 747; suitable for flat roofs						
Three layer coverings first layer type 3G; subsequent layers type 3B bitumen glass fibre based felt	-	-	-	-	m²	6.45
Extra over felt for covering with and bedding in hot bitumen						
13 mm thick stone chippings	-	-	-	-	m²	2.10
300 mm x 300 mm x 8 mm g.r.p. tiles	-	-	-	-	m²	35.50
working into outlet pipes and the like	-	-	-	-	m²	8.75
Skirtings; three layer; top layer mineral surfaced; dressed over tilting fillet; turned into groove						
not exceeding 200 mm girth	-	-	-	-	m	6.50
200 mm - 400 mm girth	-	-	-	-	m	7.75

J WATERPROOFING Excluding overheads and profit	PC £	Labour hours	Labour £	Material £	Unit	Total rate £
J41 BUILT UP FELT ROOF COVERINGS - cont'd						
Felt roofing; BS 747; suitable for flat roofs - cont'd						
Coverings to kerbs; three layer						
400 mm - 600 mm girth	-	-	-	-	m	16.35
Linings to gutters; three layer						
400 mm - 600 mm girth	-	-	-	-	m	11.10
Collars around pipes and the like; three layer						
mineral surface; 150 mm high						
not exceeding 55 mm nominal size	-	-	-	-	nr	7.30
55 mm - 110 mm nominal size	-	-	-	-	nr	7.30
Three layer coverings; two base layers type 5U						
bitumen polyester based felt; top layer type 5B						
polyester based mineral surfaced felt; 10 mm						
stone chipping covering; bitumen bonded	-	-	-	-	m²	13.55
Coverings to kerbs						
not exceeding 200 mm girth	-	-	-	-	m	8.55
200 mm - 400 mm girth	-	-	-	-	m	10.70
Outlets and dishing to gullies						
300 mm diameter	-	-	-	-	nr	8.75
"Andersons" high performance polyester-based **roofing system or other equal and approved**						
Two layer coverings; first layer HT 125 underlay; second						
layer HT 350; fully bonded to wood; fibre or cork base	-	-	-	-	m²	9.70
Extra over for						
top layer mineral surfaced	-	-	-	-	m²	1.90
13 mm thick stone chippings	-	-	-	-	m²	2.10
third layer of type 3B as underlay for concrete or						
screeded base	-	-	-	-	m²	1.90
working into outlet pipes and the like	-	-	-	-	nr	8.75
Skirtings; two layer; top layer mineral surfaced;						
dressed over tilting fillet; turned into groove						
not exceeding 200 mm girth	-	-	-	-	m	6.90
200 mm - 400 mm girth	-	-	-	-	m	8.30
Coverings to kerbs; two layer						
400 mm - 600 mm girth	-	-	-	-	m	19.30
Linings to gutters; three layer						
400 mm - 600 mm girth	-	-	-	-	m	14.15
Collars around pipes and the like; two layer; 150 mm high						
not exceeding 55 mm nominal size	-	-	-	-	nr	7.30
55 mm - 110 mm nominal size	-	-	-	-	nr	7.30
"Ruberglas 120 GP" high performance roofing or **other equal and approved**						
Two layer coverings; first and second layers						
"Ruberglas 120 GP"; fully bonded to wood, fibre						
or cork base	-	-	-	-	m²	6.00
Extra over for						
top layer mineral surfaced	-	-	-	-	m²	1.90
13 mm thick stone chippings	-	-	-	-	m²	2.10
third layer of "Rubervent 3G" as underlay for						
concrete or screeded base	-	-	-	-	m²	1.90
working into outlet pipes and the like	-	-	-	-	nr	8.75
Skirtings; two layer; top layer mineral surfaced;						
dressed over tilting fillet; turned into groove						
not exceeding 200 mm girth	-	-	-	-	m	6.00
200 mm - 400 mm girth	-	-	-	-	m	7.00
Coverings to kerbs; two layer						
400 mm - 600 mm girth	-	-	-	-	m	12.00
Linings to gutters; three layer						
400 mm - 600 mm girth	-	-	-	-	m	9.95

J WATERPROOFING Excluding overheads and profit	PC £	Labour hours	Labour £	Material £	Unit	Total rate £
Collars around pipes and the like; two layer, 150 mm high						
not exceeding 55 mm nominal size	-	-	-	-	nr	7.30
55 mm - 110 mm nominal size	-	-	-	-	nr	7.30
"Ruberfort HP 350" high performance roofing or						
other equal and approved						
Two layer coverings; first layer "Ruberfort HP						
180"; second layer "Ruberfort HP 350"; fully						
bonded; to wood; fibre or cork base	-	-	-	-	m²	9.30
Extra over for						
top layer mineral surfaced	-	-	-	-	m²	1.90
13 mm thick stone chippings	-	-	-	-	m²	2.10
third layer of "Rubervent 3G"; as underlay for						
concrete or screeded base	-	-	-	-	m²	1.90
working into outlet pipes and the like	-	-	-	-	nr	8.75
Skirtings; two layer; top layer mineral surface;						
dressed over tilting fillet; turned into groove						
not exceeding 200 mm girth	-	-	-	-	m	6.60
200 mm - 400 mm girth	-	-	-	-	m	7.85
Coverings to kerbs; two layer						
400 mm - 600 mm girth	-	-	-	-	m	18.60
Linings to gutters; three layer						
400 mm - 600 mm girth	-	-	-	-	m	13.40
Collars around pipes and the like; two layer; 150 mm high						
not exceeding 55 mm nominal size	-	-	-	-	nr	7.30
55 mm - 110 mm nominal size	-	-	-	-	nr	7.30
"Polybit 350" elastomeric roofing or other						
equal approved						
Two layer coverings; first layer "Polybit 180"; second layer						
"Polybit 350"; fully bonded to wood; fibre or cork base	-	-	-	-	m²	9.50
Extra over for						
top layer mineral surfaced	-	-	-	-	m²	1.90
13 mm thick stone chippings	-	-	-	-	m²	2.10
third layer of "Rubervent 3G" as underlay for						
concrete or screeded base	-	-	-	-	m²	1.90
working into outlet pipes and the like	-	-	-	-	nr	8.75
Skirtings; two layer; top layer mineral surfaced;						
dressed over tilting fillet; turned into groove						
not exceeding 200 mm girth	-	-	-	-	m	6.80
200 mm - 400 mm girth	-	-	-	-	m	8.10
Coverings to kerbs; two layer						
400 mm - 600 mm girth	-	-	-	-	m	19.00
Linings to gutters; three layer						
400 mm - 600 mm girth	-	-	-	-	m	13.80
Collars around pipes and the like; two layer; 150 mm high						
not exceeding 55 mm nominal size	-	-	-	-	nr	7.30
55 mm - 110 mm nominal size	-	-	-	-	nr	7.30
"Hyload 150 E" elastomeric roofing or other						
equal and approved						
Two layer coverings; first layer "Ruberglas 120 GHP";						
second layer "Hyload 150 E" fully bonded to wood; fibre						
or cork base	-	-	-	-	m²	19.40
Extra over for						
13 mm thick stone chippings	-	-	-	-	m²	2.10
third layer of "Rubervent 3G" as underlay for						
concrete or screeded base	-	-	-	-	m²	1.90
working into outlet pipes and the like	-	-	-	-	nr	8.75
Skirtings; two layer; dressed over tilting fillet;						
turned into groove						
200 mm - 400 mm girth	-	-	-	-	m	17.75

J WATERPROOFING Excluding overheads and profit	PC £	Labour hours	Labour £	Material £	Unit	Total rate £
J41 BUILT UP FELT ROOF COVERINGS - cont'd						
"Hyload 150 E" elastomeric roofing or other equal **and approved** - cont'd						
Coverings to kerbs; two layer						
400 mm - 600 mm girth	-	-	-	-	m	36.20
Linings to gutters; three layer						
400 mm - 600 mm girth	-	-	-	-	m	24.00
Collars around pipes and the like; two layer; 150 mm high						
not exceeding 55 mm nominal size	-	-	-	-	nr	7.30
55 mm - 110 mm nominal size	-	-	-	-	nr	7.30
Accessories						
Eaves trim; extruded aluminium alloy; working						
felt into trim						
"Alutrim" type F roof edging or other						
equal and approved	-	-	-	-	m	6.50
extra over for; external angle	-	-	-	-	nr	8.70
Roof screed ventilator - aluminium alloy						
"Extr-aqua-vent" or other equal and approved; set on						
screed over and including dished sinking and collar	-	-	-	-	nr	19.30
Insulation board underlays						
Vapour barrier						
reinforced; metal lined	-	-	-	-	m²	9.30
Cork boards; density 112 - 125 kg/m³						
60 mm thick	-	-	-	-	m²	12.15
Rockwool slab RW4 or other equal and approved						
60 mm thick	-	-	-	-	m²	14.80
Perlite boards or other equal and approved; density						
170 - 180 kg/m³						
60 mm thick	-	-	-	-	m²	19.30
Polyurethane boards; density 32 kg/m³						
30 mm thick	-	-	-	-	m²	7.60
35 mm thick	-	-	-	-	m²	8.15
50 mm thick	-	-	-	-	m²	8.90
Wood fibre boards; impregnated; density 220 - 350 kg/m³						
12.70 mm thick	-	-	-	-	m²	3.40
Insulation board overlays						
Dow "Roofmate SL" extruded polystyrene foam						
boards or other equal and approved						
50 mm thick	-	0.30	4.32	11.01	m²	15.33
75 mm thick	-	0.30	4.32	15.07	m²	19.39
Dow "Roofmate LG" extruded polystyrene foam boards						
or other equal and approved						
60 mm thick	-	0.30	4.32	19.76	m²	24.08
90 mm thick	-	0.30	4.32	22.43	m²	26.75
110 mm thick	-	0.30	4.32	24.78	m²	29.10
Dow "Roofmate PR" extruded polystyrene foam boards						
or other equal and approved						
90 mm thick	-	0.30	4.32	16.97	m²	21.29
120 mm thick	-	0.30	4.32	22.60	m²	26.92
J42 SINGLE LAYER PLASTICS ROOF COVERINGS						
"Trocal S" PVC roofing or other equal and approved						
Coverings	-	-	-	-	m²	13.65
Skirtings; dressed over metal upstands						
not exceeding 200 mm girth	-	-	-	-	m	10.55
200 mm - 400 mm girth	-	-	-	-	m	12.90

J WATERPROOFING Excluding overheads and profit	PC £	Labour hours	Labour £	Material £	Unit	Total rate £
Coverings to kerbs						
400 mm - 600 mm girth	-	-	-	-	m	23.65
Collars around pipes and the like; 150 mm high						
not exceeding 55 mm nominal size	-	-	-	-	nr	7.30
55 mm - 110 mm nominal size	-	-	-	-	nr	7.30
Accessories						
"Trocal" metal upstands or other equal and approved						
not exceeding 200 mm girth	-	-	-	-	m	7.70
200 mm - 400 mm girth	-	-	-	-	m	9.90
J43 PROPRIETARY ROOF DECKING WITH FELT FINISH						
"Bitumetal" flat roof construction or other equal and approved; fixing to timber, steel or concrete; flat or sloping; vapour check; 32 mm thick polyurethane insulation; 3G perforated felt underlay; two layers of glass fibre base felt roofing; stone chipping finish						
0.70 mm thick galvanized steel						
35 mm deep profiled decking; 2.38 m span	-	-	-	-	m²	28.00
46 mm deep profiled decking; 2.96 m span	-	-	-	-	m²	28.30
60 mm deep profiled decking; 3.74 m span	-	-	-	-	m²	29.20
100 mm deep profiled decking; 5.13 m span	-	-	-	-	m²	30.10
0.90 mm thick aluminium; mill finish						
35 mm deep profiled decking; 1.79 m span	-	-	-	-	m²	31.30
60 mm deep profiled decking; 2.34 m span	-	-	-	-	m²	32.60
"Bitumetal" flat roof construction or other equal and approved; fixing to timber, steel or concrete; flat or sloping; vapour check; 32 mm polyurethane insulation; 3G perforated felt underlay; two layers of polyester based roofing; stone chipping finish						
0.70 mm thick galvanised steel						
35 mm deep profiled decking; 2.38 m span	-	-	-	-	m²	31.25
46 mm deep profiled decking; 2.96 m span	-	-	-	-	m²	31.55
60 mm deep profiled decking; 3.74 m span	-	-	-	-	m²	32.45
100 mm deep profiled decking; 5.13 m span	-	-	-	-	m²	33.35
0.90 mm thick aluminium; mill finish						
35 mm deep profiled decking; 1.79 m span	-	-	-	-	m²	34.55
60 mm deep profiled decking; 2.34 m span	-	-	-	-	m²	35.85
"Plannja" flat roof construction or other equal and approved; fixing to timber; steel or concrete; flat or sloping; 3B vapour check; 32 mm thick polyurethene insulation; 3G perforated felt underlay; two layers of glass fibre bitumen felt roofing type 3B; stone chipping finish						
0.72 mm thick galvanised steel						
45 mm deep profiled decking; 3.12 m span	-	-	-	-	m²	30.60
70 mm deep profiled decking; 4.40 m span	-	-	-	-	m²	32.04
"Plannja" flat roof construction or other equal and approved; fixing to timber; steel or concrete; flat or sloping; 3B vapour check; 32 mm thick polyurethene insulation; 3G perforated felt underlay; one layer of "Andersons" HT 125 underlay or other equal and approved and HT 350 sanded; stone chipping finish						
0.72 mm thick galvanised steel						
45 mm deep profiled decking; 3.12 m span	-	-	-	-	m²	36.31
70 mm deep profiled decking; 4.40 m span	-	-	-	-	m²	37.80

K LININGS/SHEATHING/DRY PARTITIONING
Excluding overheads and profit

K10 PLASTERBOARD DRY LINING

ALTERNATIVE SHEET LINING MATERIAL PRICES

	£		£		£
Blockboard: Gaboon faced (£/10 m²)					
16 mm	113.20	22 mm	134.75	25 mm	150.90
18 mm Decorative faced (£/10 m²)					
Ash	150.00	Beech	134.75	Oak	140.15
Teak	156.30				
Edgings; self adhesive (£/50 m roll)					
22 mm Ash	10.65	22 mm Oak	10.65		
22 mm Beech	10.65				
Chipboard Standard Grade (£/10 m²)					
12 mm	23.75	16 mm	29.10	22 mm	40.95
25 mm	45.30				
Melamine faced (£/10 m²)					
12 mm	40.95	18 mm	48.50		
Laminboard; Birch faced (£/10 m²)					
18 mm	181.10	25 mm	237.15		
Medium density fibreboard (£/10 m²)					
6 mm	28.00	9 mm	36.65	19 mm	64.70
25 mm	84.10				
Plasterboard (£/100 m²)					
Wallboard plank					
9.50 mm	162.00	12.50 mm	185.00	19 mm	210.00
Industrial board					
12.50 mm	339.00				
Fireline board					
12.50 mm	211.00	15 mm	255.00		
Moisture Resistant Board					
9.50 mm	227.00				

Discounts of 0 - 20% available depending on quantity/status

K LININGS/SHEATHING/DRY PARTITIONING Excluding overheads and profit	PC £	Labour hours	Labour £	Material £	Unit	Total rate £
"Gyproc" laminated proprietary partitions or other equal and approved; two skins of gypsum plasterboard bonded to a centre core of plasterboard square edge plank 19 mm thick; fixing with nails to softwood perimeter battens (not included); joints filled with filler and joint tape; to receive direct decoration						
50 mm partition; two outer skins of 12.50 mm thick tapered edge wallboard						
height 2.10 m - 2.40 m	-	2.00	22.56	14.09	m	**36.65**
height 2.40 m - 2.70 m	-	2.60	29.30	16.13	m	**45.43**
height 2.70 m - 3.00 m	-	2.90	32.68	17.54	m	**50.22**
height 3.00 m - 3.30 m	-	3.20	36.05	18.95	m	**55.00**
height 3.30 m - 3.60 m	-	3.50	39.42	20.43	m	**59.85**
65 mm partition; two outer skins of 19 mm thick tapered edge wallboard						
height 2.10 m - 2.40 m	-	2.20	24.83	17.10	m	**41.93**
height 2.40 m - 2.70 m	-	2.80	31.57	19.34	m	**50.91**
height 2.70 m - 3.00 m	-	3.10	34.94	20.94	m	**55.88**
height 3.00 m - 3.30 m	-	3.45	38.88	22.54	m	**61.42**
height 3.30 m - 3.60 m	-	3.75	42.25	24.21	m	**66.46**

K LININGS/SHEATHING/DRY PARTITIONING Excluding overheads and profit	PC £	Labour hours	Labour £	Material £	Unit	Total rate £
"Gyproc" metal stud proprietary partitions or other equal and approved; comprising 48 mm wide metal stud frame; 50 mm wide floor channel plugged and screwed to concrete through 38 mm x 48 mm tanalised softwood sole plate						
Tapered edge panels; joints filled with joint filler and joint tape to receive direct decoration; 80 mm thick partition; one hour; one layer of 15 mm thick "Fireline" board or other equal and approved each side						
height 2.10 m - 2.40 m	-	4.20	47.51	16.33	m	**63.84**
height 2.40 m - 2.70 m	-	4.85	54.82	18.89	m	**73.71**
height 2.70 m - 3.00 m	-	5.40	61.03	20.78	m	**81.81**
height 3.00 m - 3.30 m	-	6.25	70.64	22.86	m	**93.50**
height 3.30 m - 3.60 m	-	6.85	77.41	24.65	m	**102.06**
height 3.60 m - 3.90 m	-	8.20	92.69	26.60	m	**119.29**
height 3.90 m - 4.20 m	-	8.80	99.46	28.55	m	**128.01**
angles	-	0.20	2.25	1.00	m	**3.25**
T-junctions	-	0.10	1.13	-	m	**1.13**
fair ends	-	0.20	2.25	0.38	m	**2.63**
Tapered edge panels; joints filled with joint filler and joint tape to receive direct decoration; 100 mm thick partition; two hour; two layers of 12.50 mm thick "Fireline" board or other equal and approved both sides						
height 2.10 m - 2.40 m	-	5.20	58.85	22.90	m	**81.75**
height 2.40 m - 2.70 m	-	5.98	67.63	26.30	m	**93.93**
height 2.70 m - 3.00 m	-	6.65	75.20	29.01	m	**104.21**
height 3.00 m - 3.30 m	-	6.63	74.94	31.91	m	**106.85**
height 3.30 m - 3.60 m	-	8.35	94.42	34.52	m	**128.94**
height 3.60 m - 3.90 m	-	8.20	92.69	37.33	m	**130.02**
height 3.90 m - 4.20 m	-	10.55	119.31	40.05	m	**159.36**
angles	-	0.30	3.39	1.09	m	**4.48**
T-junctions	-	0.10	1.13	-	m	**1.13**
fair ends	-	0.30	3.39	0.47	m	**3.86**
Gypsum plasterboard; BS 1230; plain grade tapered edge wallboard; fixing with nails; joints left open to receive "Artex" finish or other equal and approved; to softwood base						
9.50 mm board to ceilings						
over 300 mm wide	-	0.25	3.70	1.38	m²	**5.08**
9.50 mm board to beams						
girth not exceeding 600 mm	-	0.30	4.44	0.84	m²	**5.28**
girth 600 mm - 1200 mm	-	0.40	5.92	1.67	m²	**7.59**
12.50 mm board to ceilings						
over 300 mm wide	-	0.33	4.88	1.63	m²	**6.51**
12.50 mm board to beams						
girth not exceeding 600 mm	-	0.30	4.44	1.00	m²	**5.44**
girth 600 mm - 1200 mm	-	0.40	5.92	1.96	m²	**7.88**
Gypsum plasterboard to BS 1230; fixing with nails; joints filled with joint filler and joint tape to receive direct decoration; to softwood base						
Plain grade tapered edge wallboard						
9.50 mm board to walls						
wall height 2.40 m - 2.70 m	-	1.00	11.25	4.65	m	**15.90**
wall height 2.70 m - 3.00 m	-	1.15	12.94	5.17	m	**18.11**
wall height 3.00 m - 3.30 m	-	1.30	14.62	5.69	m	**20.31**
wall height 3.30 m - 3.60 m	-	1.50	16.88	6.24	m	**23.12**

K LININGS/SHEATHING/DRY PARTITIONING Excluding overheads and profit	PC £	Labour hours	Labour £	Material £	Unit	Total rate £
K10 PLASTERBOARD DRY LINING/PARTITIONS/ **CEILINGS** - cont'd						
Plain grade tapered edge wallboard - cont'd						
9.50 mm board to reveals and soffits of						
openings and recesses						
not exceeding 300 mm wide	-	0.20	2.25	0.95	m	3.20
300 mm - 600 mm wide	-	0.40	4.51	1.36	m	5.87
9.50 mm board to faces of columns - 4 nr						
not exceeding 600 mm total girth	-	0.50	5.63	1.94	m	7.57
600 mm - 1200 mm total girth	-	1.00	11.26	2.75	m	14.01
1200 mm - 1800 mm total girth	-	1.30	14.62	3.56	m	18.18
9.50 mm board to ceilings						
over 300 mm wide	-	0.42	4.73	1.72	m²	6.45
9.50 mm board to faces of beams - 3 nr						
not exceeding 600 mm total girth	-	0.60	6.76	1.91	m	8.67
600 mm - 1200 mm total girth	-	1.10	12.38	2.72	m	15.10
1200 mm - 1800 mm total girth	-	1.40	15.75	3.52	m	19.27
add for "Duplex" insulating grade or other						
equal and approved	-	-	-	0.40	m²	0.40
12.50 mm board to walls						
wall height 2.40 m - 2.70 m	-	1.05	11.82	5.26	m	17.08
wall height 2.70 m - 3.00 m	-	1.20	13.50	5.85	m	19.35
wall height 3.00 m - 3.30 m	-	1.35	15.19	6.44	m	21.63
wall height 3.30 m - 3.60 m	-	1.55	17.44	7.06	m	24.50
12.50 mm board to reveals and soffits of						
openings and recesses						
not exceeding 300 mm wide	-	0.20	2.25	1.04	m	3.29
300 mm - 600 mm wide	-	0.40	4.51	1.50	m	6.01
12.50 mm board to faces of columns - 4 nr						
not exceeding 600 mm total girth	-	0.50	5.63	2.12	m	7.75
600 mm - 1200 mm total girth	-	1.00	11.26	3.05	m	14.31
1200 mm - 1800 mm total girth	-	1.30	14.62	3.99	m	18.61
12.50 mm board to ceilings						
over 300 mm wide	-	0.44	4.96	1.95	m²	6.91
12.50 mm board to faces of beams - 3 nr						
not exceeding 600 mm total girth	-	0.60	6.76	2.07	m	8.83
600 mm - 1200 mm total girth	-	1.10	12.38	3.00	m	15.38
1200 mm - 1800 mm total girth	-	1.40	15.75	3.94	m	19.69
external angle; with joint tape bedded and						
covered with "Jointex" or other equal and						
approved	-	0.12	1.34	0.26	m	1.60
add for "Duplex" insulating grade or other equal						
and approved	-	-	-	0.40	m²	0.40
Tapered edge plank						
19 mm plank to walls						
wall height 2.40 m - 2.70 m	-	1.10	12.38	6.97	m	19.35
wall height 2.70 m - 3.00 m	-	1.30	14.64	7.74	m	22.38
wall height 3.00 m - 3.30 m	-	1.40	15.76	8.52	m	24.28
wall height 3.30 m - 3.60 m	-	1.65	18.58	9.33	m	27.91
19 mm plank to reveals and soffits of openings						
and recesses						
not exceeding 300 mm wide	-	0.22	2.48	1.23	m	3.71
300 mm - 600 mm wide	-	0.45	5.07	1.88	m	6.95
19 mm plank to faces of columns - 4 nr						
not exceeding 600 mm total girth	-	0.55	6.20	2.50	m	8.70
600 mm - 1200 mm total girth	-	1.05	11.82	3.81	m	15.63
1200 mm - 1800 mm total girth	-	1.35	15.19	5.13	m	20.32
19 mm plank to ceilings						
over 300 mm wide	-	0.46	5.19	2.58	m²	7.77

K LININGS/SHEATHING/DRY PARTITIONING Excluding overheads and profit	PC £	Labour hours	Labour £	Material £	Unit	Total rate £
19 mm plank to faces of beams - 3 nr						
not exceeding 600 mm total girth	-	0.65	7.33	2.44	m	**9.77**
600 mm - 1200 mm total girth	-	1.15	12.95	3.76	m	**16.71**
1200 mm - 1800 mm total girth	-	1.45	16.32	5.08	m	**21.40**
Thermal Board						
27 mm board to walls						
wall height 2.40 m - 2.70 m	-	1.15	12.95	13.04	m	**25.99**
wall height 2.70 m - 3.00 m	-	1.35	15.20	14.49	m	**29.69**
wall height 3.00 m - 3.30 m	-	1.45	16.33	15.95	m	**32.28**
wall height 3.30 m - 3.60 m	-	1.75	19.71	17.43	m	**37.14**
27 mm board to reveals and soffits of openings and recesses						
not exceeding 300 mm wide	-	0.23	2.59	1.91	m	**4.50**
300 mm - 600 mm wide	-	0.46	5.19	3.23	m	**8.42**
27 mm board to faces of columns - 4 nr						
not exceeding 600 mm total girth	-	0.56	6.31	3.85	m	**10.16**
600 mm - 1200 mm total girth	-	1.10	12.39	6.51	m	**18.90**
1200 mm - 1800 mm total girth	-	1.40	15.76	9.18	m	**24.94**
27 mm board to ceilings						
over 300 mm wide	-	0.50	5.64	4.83	m²	**10.47**
27 mm board to faces of beams - 3 nr						
not exceeding 600 mm total girth	-	0.60	6.77	3.79	m	**10.56**
600 mm - 1200 mm total girth	-	1.15	12.96	6.46	m	**19.42**
1200 mm - 1800 mm total girth	-	1.55	17.45	9.13	m	**26.58**
50 mm board to walls						
wall height 2.40 m - 2.70 m	-	1.15	12.95	12.93	m	**25.88**
wall height 2.70 m - 3.00 m	-	1.40	15.77	14.38	m	**30.15**
wall height 3.00 m - 3.30 m	-	1.55	17.46	15.82	m	**33.28**
wall height 3.30 m - 3.60 m	-	1.85	20.84	17.30	m	**38.14**
50 mm board to reveals and soffits of openings and recesses						
not exceeding 300 mm wide	-	0.25	2.82	1.90	m	**4.72**
300 mm - 600 mm wide	-	0.50	5.64	3.22	m	**8.86**
50 mm board to faces of columns - 4 nr						
not exceeding 600 mm total girth	-	0.60	6.77	3.87	m	**10.64**
600 mm - 1200 mm total girth	-	1.20	13.53	6.50	m	**20.03**
1200 mm - 1800 mm total girth	-	1.55	17.46	9.13	m	**26.59**
50 mm board to ceilings						
over 300 mm wide	-	0.53	5.98	4.79	m²	**10.77**
50 mm board to faces of beams - 3 nr						
not exceeding 600 mm total girth	-	0.63	7.11	3.90	m	**11.01**
600 mm - 1200 mm total girth	-	1.27	14.32	6.57	m	**20.89**
1200 mm - 1800 mm total girth	-	1.70	19.15	9.24	m	**28.39**
White plastic faced gypsum plasterboard to BS 1230; **industrial grade square edge wallboard; fixing with** **screws; butt joints; to softwood base**						
9.50 mm board to walls						
wall height 2.40 m - 2.70 m	-	0.70	7.94	7.06	m	**15.00**
wall height 2.70 m - 3.00 m	-	0.85	9.64	7.84	m	**17.48**
wall height 3.00 m - 3.30 m	-	1.00	11.34	8.61	m	**19.95**
wall height 3.30 m - 3.60 m	-	1.15	13.04	9.39	m	**22.43**
9.50 mm board to reveals and soffits of openings and recesses						
not exceeding 300 mm wide	-	0.15	1.70	0.81	m	**2.51**
300 mm - 600 mm wide	-	0.30	3.40	1.57	m	**4.97**
9.50 mm board to faces of columns - 4 nr						
not exceeding 600 mm total girth	-	0.40	4.54	1.71	m	**6.25**
600 mm - 1200 mm total girth	-	0.80	9.07	3.35	m	**12.42**
1200 mm - 1800 mm total girth	-	1.05	11.91	4.92	m	**16.83**

K LININGS/SHEATHING/DRY PARTITIONING Excluding overheads and profit	PC £	Labour hours	Labour £	Material £	Unit	Total rate £
K10 PLASTERBOARD DRY LINING/PARTITIONS/ CEILINGS - cont'd						
White plastic faced gypsum plasterboard to BS 1230; industrial grade square edge wallboard; fixing with screws; butt joints; to softwood base - cont'd						
12.50 mm board to walls						
wall height 2.40 m - 2.70 m	-	0.75	8.51	7.53	m	**16.04**
wall height 2.70 m - 3.00 m	-	0.90	10.21	8.36	m	**18.57**
wall height 3.00 m - 3.30 m	-	1.05	11.91	9.18	m	**21.09**
wall height 3.30 m - 3.60 m	-	1.20	13.61	10.01	m	**23.62**
12.50 mm board to reveals and soffits of openings and recesses						
not exceeding 300 mm wide	-	0.16	1.81	0.86	m	**2.67**
300 mm - 600 mm wide	-	0.32	3.63	1.67	m	**5.30**
12.50 mm board to faces of columns - 4 nr						
not exceeding 600 mm total girth	-	0.42	4.76	1.83	m	**6.59**
600 mm - 1200 mm total girth	-	0.84	9.53	3.57	m	**13.10**
1200 mm - 1800 mm total girth	-	1.10	12.47	5.25	m	**17.72**
Plasterboard jointing system; filling joint with jointing compounds						
To ceilings						
to suit 9.50 mm or 12.50 mm thick boards	-	0.10	1.13	1.29	m	**2.42**
Angle trim; plasterboard edge support system						
To ceilings						
to suit 9.50 mm or 12.50 mm thick boards	-	0.10	1.13	1.22	m	**2.35**
Two layers of gypsum plasterboard to BS 1230; plain grade square and tapered edge wallboard; fixing with nails; joints filled with joint filler and joint tape; top layer to receive direct decoration; to softwood base						
19 mm two layer board to walls						
wall height 2.40 m - 2.70 m	-	1.40	15.79	8.48	m	**24.27**
wall height 2.70 m - 3.00 m	-	1.60	18.04	9.44	m	**27.48**
wall height 3.00 m - 3.30 m	-	1.80	20.29	10.38	m	**30.67**
wall height 3.30 m - 3.60 m	-	2.10	23.68	11.36	m	**35.04**
19 mm two layer board to reveals and soffits of openings and recesses						
not exceeding 300 mm wide	-	0.30	3.39	1.43	m	**4.82**
300 mm - 600 mm wide	-	0.60	6.77	2.24	m	**9.01**
19 mm two layer board to faces of columns - 4 nr						
not exceeding 600 mm total girth	-	0.75	8.47	2.92	m	**11.39**
600 mm - 1200 mm total girth	-	1.45	16.36	4.56	m	**20.92**
1200 mm - 1800 mm total girth	-	1.80	20.29	6.19	m	**26.48**
25 mm two layer board to walls						
wall height 2.40 m - 2.70 m	-	1.50	16.92	9.59	m	**26.51**
wall height 2.70 m - 3.00 m	-	1.70	19.17	10.66	m	**29.83**
wall height 3.00 m - 3.30 m	-	1.90	21.43	11.74	m	**33.17**
wall height 3.30 m - 3.60 m	-	2.20	24.81	12.83	m	**37.64**
25 mm two layer board to reveals and soffits of openings and recesses						
not exceeding 300 mm wide	-	0.30	3.39	1.57	m	**4.96**
300 mm - 600 mm wide	-	0.60	6.77	2.49	m	**9.26**
25 mm two layer board to faces of columns - 4 nr						
not exceeding 600 mm total girth	-	0.75	8.47	3.21	m	**11.68**
600 mm - 1200 mm total girth	-	1.45	16.36	5.08	m	**21.44**
1200 mm - 1800 mm total girth	-	1.80	20.29	6.95	m	**27.24**

K LININGS/SHEATHING/DRY PARTITIONING Excluding overheads and profit	PC £	Labour hours	Labour £	Material £	Unit	Total rate £
Gyproc Dri-Wall dry lining system or other equal and approved; plain grade tapered edge wallboard; fixed to walls with adhesive; joints filled with joint filler and joint tape; to receive direct decoration						
9.50 mm board to walls						
wall height 2.40 m - 2.70 m	-	1.20	13.52	5.77	m	**19.29**
wall height 2.70 m - 3.00 m	-	1.38	15.54	6.40	m	**21.94**
wall height 3.00 m - 3.30 m	-	1.55	17.46	7.03	m	**24.49**
wall height 3.30 m - 3.60 m	-	1.80	20.28	7.70	m	**27.98**
9.50 mm board to reveals and soffits of openings and recesses						
not exceeding 300 mm wide	-	0.25	2.82	1.04	m	**3.86**
300 mm - 600 mm wide	-	0.50	5.64	1.57	m	**7.21**
9.50 mm board to faces of columns - 4 nr						
not exceeding 600 mm total girth	-	0.63	7.11	2.08	m	**9.19**
600 mm - 1200 mm total girth	-	1.23	13.87	3.22	m	**17.09**
1200 mm - 1800 mm total girth	-	1.55	17.46	4.18	m	**21.64**
Angle; with joint tape bedded and covered with "Jointex" or other equal and approved						
internal	-	0.06	0.67	0.26	m	**0.93**
external	-	0.12	1.34	0.26	m	**1.60**
Gyproc Dri-Wall M/F dry lining system or other equal and approved; mild steel firrings fixed to walls with adhesive; tapered edge wallboard screwed to firrings; joints filled with joint filler and joint tape						
12.50 mm board to walls						
wall height 2.40 m - 2.70 m	-	1.60	18.05	10.12	m	**28.17**
wall height 2.70 m - 3.00 m	-	1.83	20.65	11.23	m	**31.88**
wall height 3.00 m - 3.30 m	-	2.05	23.13	12.36	m	**35.49**
wall height 3.30 m - 3.60 m	-	2.40	27.08	13.52	m	**40.60**
12.50 mm board to reveals and soffits of openings and recesses						
not exceeding 300 mm wide	-	0.25	2.82	0.94	m	**3.76**
300 mm - 600 mm wide	-	0.50	5.64	1.36	m	**7.00**
add for one coat of "Drywall" top coat or other equal and approved	-	0.05	0.56	0.59	m²	**1.15**
Vermiculite gypsum cladding; "Vicuclad 900R" board or other equal and approved; fixed with adhesive; joints pointed in adhesive						
25 mm thick column linings, faces - 4; 2 hour fire protection rating						
not exceeding 600 mm girth	-	0.75	8.51	11.51	m	**20.02**
600 mm - 1200 mm girth	-	0.90	10.21	22.83	m	**33.04**
1200 mm - 1800 mm girth	-	1.25	14.18	34.15	m	**48.33**
30 mm thick beam linings, faces - 3; 2 hour fire protection rating						
not exceeding 600 mm girth	-	0.60	6.80	13.59	m	**20.39**
600 mm - 1200 mm girth	-	0.75	8.51	27.00	m	**35.51**
1200 mm - 1800 mm girth	-	0.90	10.21	40.40	m	**50.61**
Vermiculite gypsum cladding; "Vicuclad 1050R" board or other equal and approved; fixed with adhesive; joints pointed in adhesive						
55 mm thick column linings, faces - 4 ; 4 hour fire protection rating						
not exceeding 600 mm girth	-	0.90	10.21	30.31	m	**40.52**
600 mm - 1200 mm girth	-	1.10	12.47	60.44	m	**72.91**
1200 mm - 1800 mm girth	-	1.50	17.01	90.56	m	**107.57**

K LININGS/SHEATHING/DRY PARTITIONING Excluding overheads and profit	PC £	Labour hours	Labour £	Material £	Unit	Total rate £
K10 PLASTERBOARD DRY LINING/PARTITIONS/ **CEILINGS** - cont'd						
Vermiculite gypsum cladding; "Vicuclad 1050R" **board or other equal and approved; fixed with** **adhesive; joints pointed in adhesive** - cont'd						
60 mm thick beam linings, faces - 3; 4 hour fire protection rating						
not exceeding 600 mm girth	-	0.75	8.51	33.22	m	41.73
600 mm - 1200 mm girth	-	0.90	10.21	66.25	m	76.46
1200 mm - 1800 mm girth	-	1.10	12.47	99.28	m	111.75
Add to the above for						
plus 3% for work 3.50 m - 5.00 m high						
plus 6% for work 5.00 m - 6.50 m high						
plus 12% for work 6.50 m - 8.00 m high						
plus 18% for work over 8.00 m high						
Cutting and fitting around steel joints, angles, trunking, ducting, ventilators, pipes, tubes, etc						
over 2.00 m girth	-	0.45	5.10	-	m	5.10
not exceeding 0.30 m girth	-	0.30	3.40	-	nr	3.40
0.30 m - 1.00 m girth	-	0.40	4.54	-	nr	4.54
1.00 m - 2.00 m girth	-	0.55	6.24	-	nr	6.24
K11 RIGID SHEET FLOORING/SHEATHING/ **LININGS/CASING**						
Blockboard (Birch faced)						
Linings to walls 12 mm thick						
over 300 mm wide	-	0.47	5.33	8.77	m²	14.10
not exceeding 300 mm wide	-	0.31	3.52	2.64	m	6.16
holes for pipes and the like	-	0.04	0.45	-	nr	0.45
Two-sided 12 mm thick pipe casing; to softwood framing (not included)						
300 mm girth	-	0.75	8.51	2.70	m	11.21
600 mm girth	-	0.90	10.21	5.28	m	15.49
Three-sided 12 mm thick pipe casing; to softwood framing (not included)						
450 mm girth	-	1.00	11.34	4.05	m	15.39
900 mm girth	-	1.20	13.61	7.94	m	21.55
extra for 400 mm x 400 mm removable access panel; brass cups and screws; additional framing	-	1.00	11.34	0.68	nr	12.02
Lining to walls 18 mm thick						
over 300 mm wide	11.21	0.50	5.67	12.20	m²	17.87
not exceeding 300 mm wide	-	0.32	3.63	3.67	m	7.30
holes for pipes and the like	-	0.05	0.57	-	nr	0.57
Lining to walls 25 mm thick						
over 300 mm wide	14.59	0.54	6.12	15.87	m²	21.99
not exceeding 300 mm wide	-	0.35	3.97	4.76	m	8.73
holes for pipes and the like	-	0.06	0.68	-	nr	0.68
Chipboard (plain)						
Lining to walls 12 mm thick						
over 300 mm wide	1.79	0.38	4.31	2.07	m²	6.38
not exceeding 300 mm wide	-	0.22	2.49	0.63	m	3.12
holes for pipes and the like	-	0.03	0.34	-	nr	0.34
Lining to walls 15 mm thick						
over 300 mm wide	2.05	0.40	4.54	2.35	m²	6.89
not exceeding 300 mm wide	-	0.24	2.72	0.72	m	3.44
holes for pipes and the like	-	0.04	0.45	-	nr	0.45

K LININGS/SHEATHING/DRY PARTITIONING Excluding overheads and profit	PC £	Labour hours	Labour £	Material £	Unit	Total rate £
Two-sided 15 mm thick pipe casing; to						
softwood framing (not included)						
300 mm girth	-	0.60	6.80	0.77	m	7.57
600 mm girth	-	0.70	7.94	1.44	m	9.38
Three-sided 15 mm thick pipe casing; to						
softwood framing (not included)						
450 mm girth	-	1.25	14.18	1.16	m	15.34
900 mm girth	-	1.50	17.01	2.17	m	19.18
extra for 400 mm x 400 mm removable access						
panel; brass cups and screws; additional framing	-	1.00	11.34	0.68	nr	12.02
Lining to walls 18 mm thick						
over 300 mm wide	2.46	0.42	4.76	2.83	m²	7.59
not exceeding 300 mm wide	-	0.27	3.06	0.85	m	3.91
holes for pipes and the like	-	0.05	0.57	-	nr	0.57
Fire-retardant chipboard; Antivlam or other equal						
and approved; Class 1 spread of flame						
Lining to walls 12 mm thick						
over 300 mm wide	-	0.38	4.31	7.06	m²	11.37
not exceeding 300 mm wide	-	0.22	2.49	2.13	m	4.62
holes for pipes and the like	-	0.03	0.34	-	nr	0.34
Lining to walls 18 mm thick						
over 300 mm wide	-	0.42	4.76	9.32	m²	14.08
not exceeding 300 mm wide	-	0.27	3.06	2.81	m	5.87
holes for pipes and the like	-	0.05	0.57	-	nr	0.57
Lining to walls 22 mm thick						
over 300 mm wide	-	0.44	4.99	11.86	m²	16.85
not exceeding 300 mm wide	-	0.30	3.40	3.57	m	6.97
holes for pipes and the like	-	0.06	0.68	-	nr	0.68
Chipboard; melamine faced; white matt finish;						
laminated masking strips						
Lining to walls 15 mm thick						
over 300 mm wide	3.31	1.05	11.91	3.85	m²	15.76
not exceeding 300 mm wide	-	0.68	7.71	1.22	m	8.93
holes for pipes and the like	-	0.07	0.79	-	nr	0.79
Chipboard boarding and flooring						
Boarding to floors; butt joints						
18 mm thick	2.40	0.30	3.40	2.77	m²	6.17
22 mm thick	3.11	0.33	3.74	3.54	m²	7.28
Boarding to floors; tongued and grooved joints						
18 mm thick	2.54	0.32	3.63	2.92	m²	6.55
22 mm thick	3.11	0.35	3.97	3.54	m²	7.51
Boarding to roofs; butt joints						
18 mm thick	3.15	0.33	3.74	3.58	m²	7.32
Durabella "Westbourne" flooring system or other						
equal and approved; comprising 19 mm thick tongued						
and grooved chipboard panels secret nailed to						
softwood MK 10X-profiled foam backed						
battens at 600 mm centres; on concrete floor						
Flooring tongued and grooved joints						
63 mm thick overall; 44 mm x 54 mm nominal						
size battens	-	-	-	-	m²	15.25
75 mm thick overall; 56 mm x 54 mm nominal						
size battens	-	-	-	-	m²	16.75
Plywood flooring						
Boarding to floors; tongued and grooved joints						
15 mm thick	14.27	0.40	4.54	15.53	m²	20.07
18 mm thick	16.57	0.44	4.99	18.00	m²	22.99

K LININGS/SHEATHING/DRY PARTITIONING Excluding overheads and profit	PC £	Labour hours	Labour £	Material £	Unit	Total rate £
K11 RIGID SHEET FLOORING/SHEATHING/ **LININGS/CASING** - cont'd						
Plywood; external quality; 18 mm thick						
Boarding to roofs; butt joints						
flat to falls	11.17	0.40	4.54	12.20	m²	**16.74**
sloping	11.17	0.43	4.88	12.20	m²	**17.08**
vertical	11.17	0.57	6.46	12.20	m²	**18.66**
Plywood; external quality; 12 mm thick						
Boarding to roofs; butt joints						
flat to falls	7.45	0.40	4.54	8.20	m²	**12.74**
sloping	7.45	0.43	4.88	8.20	m²	**13.08**
vertical	7.45	0.57	6.46	8.20	m²	**14.66**
Glazed hardboard to BS 1142; on and including **38 mm x 38 mm sawn softwood framing**						
3.20 mm thick panel						
to side of bath	-	1.80	20.41	3.58	nr	**23.99**
to end of bath	-	0.70	7.94	0.97	nr	**8.91**
Insulation board to BS 1142						
Lining to walls 12 mm thick						
over 300 mm wide	1.33	0.24	2.72	1.59	m²	**4.31**
not exceeding 300 mm wide	-	0.14	1.59	0.49	m	**2.08**
holes for pipes and the like	-	0.01	0.11	-	nr	**0.11**
Lining to walls 18 mm thick						
over 300 mm wide	2.10	0.26	2.95	2.41	m²	**5.36**
not exceeding 300 mm wide	-	0.16	1.81	0.73	m	**2.54**
holes for pipes and the like	-	0.01	0.11	-	nr	**0.11**
Laminboard (Birch Faced); 18 mm thick						
Lining to walls						
over 300 mm wide	13.99	0.53	6.01	15.19	m²	**21.20**
not exceeding 300 mm wide	-	0.34	3.86	4.57	m	**8.43**
holes for pipes and the like	-	0.06	0.68	-	nr	**0.68**
Non-asbestos board; "Masterboard" or other equal **and approved; sanded finish**						
Lining to walls 6 mm thick						
over 300 mm wide	5.31	0.33	3.74	5.82	m²	**9.56**
not exceeding 300 mm wide	-	0.20	2.27	1.75	m	**4.02**
Lining to ceilings 6 mm thick						
over 300 mm wide	5.31	0.44	4.99	5.82	m²	**10.81**
not exceeding 300 mm wide	-	0.27	3.06	1.75	m	**4.81**
holes for pipes and the like	-	0.03	0.34	-	nr	**0.34**
Lining to walls 9 mm thick						
over 300 mm wide	10.96	0.36	4.08	11.90	m²	**15.98**
not exceeding 300 mm wide	-	0.20	2.27	3.57	m	**5.84**
Lining to ceilings 9 mm thick						
over 300 mm wide	10.96	0.45	5.10	11.90	m²	**17.00**
not exceeding 300 mm wide	-	0.29	3.29	3.57	m	**6.86**
holes for pipes and the like	-	0.04	0.45	-	nr	**0.45**
Non-asbestos board; "Supalux" or other equal **and approved; sanded finish**						
Lining to walls 6 mm thick						
over 300 mm wide	7.94	0.33	3.74	8.65	m²	**12.39**
not exceeding 300 mm wide	-	0.20	2.27	2.60	m	**4.87**
Lining to ceilings 6 mm thick						
over 300 mm wide	7.94	0.44	4.99	8.65	m²	**13.64**
not exceeding 300 mm wide	-	0.27	3.06	2.60	m	**5.66**

K LININGS/SHEATHING/DRY PARTITIONING Excluding overheads and profit	PC £	Labour hours	Labour £	Material £	Unit	Total rate £
Lining to walls 9 mm thick						
over 300 mm wide	11.81	0.36	4.08	12.81	m²	16.89
not exceeding 300 mm wide	-	0.20	2.27	3.85	m	6.12
Lining to ceilings 9 mm thick						
over 300 mm wide	11.81	0.45	5.10	12.81	m²	17.91
not exceeding 300 mm wide	-	0.29	3.29	3.85	m	7.14
holes for pipes and the like	-	0.04	0.45	-	nr	0.45
Lining to walls 12 mm thick						
over 300 mm wide	15.64	0.40	4.54	16.93	m²	21.47
not exceeding 300 mm wide	-	0.24	2.72	5.08	m	7.80
Lining to ceilings 12 mm thick						
over 300 mm wide	15.64	0.53	6.01	16.93	m²	22.94
not exceeding 300 mm wide	-	0.32	3.63	5.08	m	8.71
holes for pipes and the like	-	0.05	0.57	-	nr	0.57
Non-asbestos board; "Monolux 40" or other equal and approved; 6 mm x 50 mm "Supalux" cover fillets or other equal and approved one side						
Lining to walls 19 mm thick						
over 300 mm wide	28.38	0.70	7.94	31.81	m²	39.75
not exceeding 300 mm wide	-	0.50	5.67	10.67	m	16.34
Lining to walls 25 mm thick						
over 300 mm wide	34.02	0.75	8.51	37.87	m²	46.38
not exceeding 300 mm wide	34.02	0.53	6.01	12.49	m	18.50
Plywood (Far Eastern); internal quality						
Lining to walls 4 mm thick						
over 300 mm wide	1.59	0.37	4.20	1.86	m²	6.06
not exceeding 300 mm wide	-	0.24	2.72	0.57	m	3.29
Lining to ceilings 4 mm thick						
over 300 mm wide	1.59	0.50	5.67	1.86	m²	7.53
not exceeding 300 mm wide	-	0.32	3.63	0.57	m	4.20
holes for pipes and the like	-	0.03	0.34	-	nr	0.34
Lining to walls 6 mm thick						
over 300 mm wide	1.89	0.40	4.54	2.18	m²	6.72
not exceeding 300 mm wide	-	0.26	2.95	0.67	m	3.62
Lining to ceilings 6 mm thick						
over 300 mm wide	1.89	0.53	6.01	2.18	m²	8.19
not exceeding 300 mm wide	-	0.35	3.97	0.67	m	4.64
holes for pipes and the like	-	0.03	0.34	-	nr	0.34
Two-sided 6 mm thick pipe casings; to softwood framing (not included)						
300 mm girth	-	0.80	9.07	0.72	m	9.79
600 mm girth	-	1.00	11.34	1.33	m	12.67
Three-sided 6 mm thick pipe casing; to softwood framing (not included)						
450 mm girth	-	1.15	13.04	1.08	m	14.12
900 mm girth	-	1.35	15.31	2.01	m	17.32
Lining to walls 9 mm thick						
over 300 mm wide	2.76	0.43	4.88	3.12	m²	8.00
not exceeding 300 mm wide	-	0.28	3.18	0.95	m	4.13
Lining to ceilings 9 mm thick						
over 300 mm wide	2.76	0.57	6.46	3.12	m²	9.58
not exceeding 300 mm wide	-	0.37	4.20	0.95	m	5.15
holes for pipes and the like	-	0.04	0.45	-	nr	0.45
Lining to walls 12 mm thick						
over 300 mm wide	3.56	0.46	5.22	3.98	m²	9.20
not exceeding 300 mm wide	-	0.30	3.40	1.20	m	4.60
Lining to ceilings 12 mm thick						
over 300 mm wide	3.56	0.61	6.92	3.98	m²	10.90
not exceeding 300 mm wide	-	0.40	4.54	1.20	m	5.74
holes for pipes and the like	-	0.04	0.45	-	nr	0.45

K LININGS/SHEATHING/DRY PARTITIONING Excluding overheads and profit	PC £	Labour hours	Labour £	Material £	Unit	Total rate £
K11 RIGID SHEET FLOORING/SHEATHING/ LININGS/CASING - cont'd						
Plywood (Far Eastern); external quality						
Lining to walls 4 mm thick						
over 300 mm wide	2.87	0.37	4.20	3.24	m²	7.44
not exceeding 300 mm wide	-	0.24	2.72	0.98	m	3.70
Lining to ceilings 4 mm thick						
over 300 mm wide	2.87	0.50	5.67	3.24	m²	8.91
not exceeding 300 mm wide	-	0.32	3.63	0.98	m	4.61
holes for pipes and the like	-	0.03	0.34	-	nr	0.34
Lining to walls 6 mm thick						
over 300 mm wide	3.78	0.40	4.54	4.22	m²	8.76
not exceeding 300 mm wide	-	0.26	2.95	1.28	m	4.23
Lining to ceilings 6 mm thick						
over 300 mm wide	3.78	0.53	6.01	4.22	m²	10.23
not exceeding 300 mm wide	-	0.35	3.97	1.28	m	5.25
holes for pipes and the like	-	0.03	0.34	-	nr	0.34
Two-sided 6 mm thick pipe casings; to softwood framing (not included)						
300 mm girth	-	0.80	9.07	1.33	m	10.40
600 mm girth	-	1.00	11.34	2.55	m	13.89
Three-sided 6 mm thick pipe casing; to softwood framing (not included)						
450 mm girth	-	1.15	13.04	2.00	m	15.04
900 mm girth	-	1.35	15.31	3.85	m	19.16
Lining to walls 9 mm thick						
over 300 mm wide	5.03	0.43	4.88	5.56	m²	10.44
not exceeding 300 mm wide	-	0.28	3.18	1.68	m	4.86
Lining to ceilings 9 mm thick						
over 300 mm wide	5.03	0.57	6.46	5.56	m²	12.02
not exceeding 300 mm wide	-	0.37	4.20	1.68	m	5.88
holes for pipes and the like	-	0.04	0.45	-	nr	0.45
Lining to walls 12 mm thick						
over 300 mm wide	6.69	0.46	5.22	7.34	m²	12.56
not exceeding 300 mm wide	-	0.30	3.40	2.21	m	5.61
Lining to ceilings 12 mm thick						
over 300 mm wide	6.69	0.61	6.92	7.34	m²	14.26
not exceeding 300 mm wide	-	0.40	4.54	2.21	m	6.75
holes for pipes and the like	-	0.04	0.45	-	nr	0.45
Extra over wall linings fixed with nails for screwing	-	-	-	-	m²	1.40
Preformed white melamine faced plywood casings; Pendock Profiles Ltd or other equal and approved; to softwood battens (not included)						
Skirting trunking profile; plain butt joints in the running length						
45 mm x 150 mm; ref TK150	-	0.12	1.36	6.09	m	7.45
extra for stop end	-	0.05	0.57	5.05	nr	5.62
extra for external corner	-	0.10	1.13	6.24	nr	7.37
extra for internal corner	-	0.10	1.13	4.67	nr	5.80
Casing profiles						
150 mm x 150 mm; ref MX150/150; 5 mm thick	-	0.12	1.36	9.70	m	11.06
extra for stop end	-	0.05	0.57	3.97	nr	4.54
extra for external corner	-	0.10	1.13	14.73	nr	15.86
extra for internal corner	-	0.10	1.13	4.67	nr	5.80

K LININGS/SHEATHING/DRY PARTITIONING Excluding overheads and profit	PC £	Labour hours	Labour £	Material £	Unit	Total rate £
Woodwool unreinforced slabs; Torvale "Woodcemair"						
or other equal and approved; BS 1105 type SB;						
natural finish; fixing to timber or steel with						
galvanized nails or clips; flat or sloping						
50 mm thick slabs; type 500; 600 mm maximum span						
1800 mm - 2400 mm lengths	5.52	0.40	4.54	6.00	m²	**10.54**
2700 mm - 3000 mm lengths	5.65	0.40	4.54	6.14	m²	**10.68**
75 mm thick slabs; type 750; 900 mm maximum span						
2100 mm lengths	6.57	0.45	5.10	7.15	m²	**12.25**
2400 mm - 2700 mm lengths	6.67	0.45	5.10	7.25	m²	**12.35**
3000 mm lengths	6.68	0.45	5.10	7.26	m²	**12.36**
100 mm thick slabs; type 1000; 1200 mm maximum span						
3000 mm - 3600 mm lengths	9.10	0.50	5.67	9.76	m²	**15.43**
Internal quality American Cherry veneered						
plywood; 6 mm thick						
Lining to walls						
over 300 mm wide	4.79	0.44	4.99	5.26	m²	**10.25**
not exceeding 300 mm wide	-	0.29	3.29	1.60	m	**4.89**
"Tacboard" or other equal and approved; Eternit UK						
Ltd; fire resisting boards; butt joints; to softwood base						
Lining to walls; 6 mm thick						
over 300 mm wide	-	0.33	3.74	7.42	m²	**11.16**
not exceeding 300 mm wide	-	0.20	2.27	2.25	m	**4.52**
Lining to walls; 9 mm thick						
over 300 mm wide	-	0.36	4.08	14.94	m²	**19.02**
not exceeding 300 mm wide	-	0.22	2.49	4.50	m	**6.99**
Lining to walls; 12 mm thick						
over 300 wide	-	0.40	4.54	19.42	m²	**23.96**
not exceeding 300 mm wide	-	0.24	2.72	5.85	m	**8.57**
"Tacfire" or other equal and approved; Eternit UK Ltd;						
fire resisting boards						
Lining to walls; 6 mm thick						
over 300 mm wide	-	0.33	3.74	10.94	m²	**14.68**
not exceeding 300 mm wide	-	0.20	2.27	3.30	m	**5.57**
Lining to walls; 9 mm thick						
over 300 mm wide	-	0.36	4.08	16.69	m²	**20.77**
not exceeding 300 mm wide	-	0.22	2.49	5.03	m	**7.52**
Lining to walls; 12 mm thick						
over 300 mm wide	-	0.40	4.54	22.00	m²	**26.54**
not exceeding 300 mm wide	-	0.24	2.72	6.62	m	**9.34**
K14 GLASS REINFORCED GYPSUM LININGS/						
PANELLING/CASINGS/MOULDINGS						
Glass reinforced gypsum Glasroc Multi-board or other						
equal and approved; fixing with nails; joints filled with						
joint filler and joint tape; finishing with "Jointex" or						
other equal and approved to receive decoration; to						
softwood base						
10 mm board to walls						
wall height 2.40 m - 2.70 m	-	1.00	11.25	31.43	m	**42.68**
wall height 2.70 m - 3.00 m	-	1.15	12.94	34.93	m	**47.87**
wall height 3.00 m - 3.30 m	-	1.30	14.62	38.43	m	**53.05**
wall height 3.30 m - 3.60 m	-	1.50	16.88	41.95	m	**58.83**
12.50 mm board to walls						
wall height 2.40 m - 2.70 m	-	1.05	11.82	41.03	m	**52.85**
wall height 2.70 m - 3.00 m	-	1.20	13.50	45.59	m	**59.09**
wall height 3.00 m - 3.30 m	-	1.35	15.19	50.16	m	**65.35**
wall height 3.30 m - 3.60 m	-	1.55	17.44	54.75	m	**72.19**

K LININGS/SHEATHING/DRY PARTITIONING Excluding overheads and profit	PC £	Labour hours	Labour £	Material £	Unit	Total rate £
K20 TIMBER BOARD FLOORING/SHEATHING/ LININGS/CASINGS						
Sawn softwood; untreated						
Boarding to roofs; 150 mm wide boards; butt joints						
19 mm thick; flat; over 300 mm wide	-	0.45	5.10	4.82	m²	**9.92**
19 mm thick; flat; not exceeding 300 mm wide	-	0.30	3.40	1.47	m	**4.87**
19 mm thick; sloping; over 300 mm wide	-	0.50	5.67	4.82	m²	**10.49**
19 mm thick; sloping; not exceeding 300 mm wide	-	0.33	3.74	1.47	m	**5.21**
19 mm thick; sloping; laid diagonally; over 300 mm wide	-	0.63	7.14	4.82	m²	**11.96**
19 mm thick; sloping; laid diagonally; not exceeding 300 mm wide	-	0.40	4.54	1.47	m	**6.01**
25 mm thick; flat; over 300 mm wide	-	0.45	5.10	6.26	m²	**11.36**
25 mm thick; flat; not exceeding 300 mm wide	-	0.30	3.40	1.90	m	**5.30**
25 mm thick; sloping; over 300 mm wide	-	0.50	5.67	6.26	m²	**11.93**
25 mm thick; sloping; not exceeding 300 mm wide	-	0.33	3.74	1.90	m	**5.64**
25 mm thick; sloping; laid diagonally; over 300 mm wide	-	0.63	7.14	6.26	m²	**13.40**
25 mm thick; sloping; laid diagonally; not exceeding 300 mm wide	-	0.40	4.54	1.90	m	**6.44**
Boarding to tops or cheeks of dormers; 150 mm wide boards; butt joints						
19 mm thick; laid diagonally; over 300 mm wide	-	0.80	9.07	4.82	m²	**13.89**
19 mm thick; laid diagonally; not exceeding 300 mm wide	-	0.50	5.67	1.47	m	**7.14**
19 mm thick; laid diagonally; area not exceeding 1.00 m² irrespective of width	-	1.00	11.34	4.58	nr	**15.92**
Sawn softwood; "Tanalised"						
Boarding to roofs; 150 wide boards; butt joints						
19 mm thick; flat; over 300 mm wide	-	0.45	5.10	5.42	m²	**10.52**
19 mm thick; flat; not exceeding 300 mm wide	-	0.30	3.40	1.64	m	**5.04**
19 mm thick; sloping; over 300 mm wide	-	0.50	5.67	5.42	m²	**11.09**
19 mm thick; sloping; not exceeding 300 mm wide	-	0.33	3.74	1.64	m	**5.38**
19 mm thick; sloping; laid diagonally; over 300 mm wide	-	0.63	7.14	5.42	m²	**12.56**
19 mm thick; sloping; laid diagonally; not exceeding 300 mm wide	-	0.40	4.54	1.64	m	**6.18**
25 mm thick; flat; over 300 mm wide	-	0.45	5.10	7.04	m²	**12.14**
25 mm thick; flat; not exceeding 300 mm wide	-	0.30	3.40	2.13	m	**5.53**
25 mm thick; sloping; over 300 mm wide	-	0.50	5.67	7.04	m²	**12.71**
25 mm thick; sloping; not exceeding 300 mm wide	-	0.33	3.74	2.13	m	**5.87**
25 mm thick; sloping; laid diagonally; over 300 mm wide	-	0.63	7.14	7.04	m²	**14.18**
25 mm thick; sloping; laid diagonally; not exceeding 300 mm wide	-	0.40	4.54	2.13	m	**6.67**
Boarding to tops or cheeks of dormers; 150 mm wide boards; butt joints						
19 mm thick; laid diagonally; over 300 mm wide	-	0.80	9.07	5.42	m²	**14.49**
19 mm thick; laid diagonally; not exceeding 300 mm wide	-	0.50	5.67	1.64	m	**7.31**
19 mm thick; laid diagonally; area not exceeding 1.00 m² irrespective of width	-	1.00	11.34	5.17	nr	**16.51**

K LININGS/SHEATHING/DRY PARTITIONING Excluding overheads and profit	PC £	Labour hours	Labour £	Material £	Unit	Total rate £
Wrought softwood						
Boarding to floors; butt joints						
19 mm x 75 mm boards	-	0.60	6.80	5.80	m²	**12.60**
19 mm x 125 mm boards	-	0.55	6.24	6.39	m²	**12.63**
22 mm x 150 mm boards	-	0.50	5.67	6.85	m²	**12.52**
25 mm x 100 mm boards	-	0.55	6.24	7.39	m²	**13.63**
25 mm x 150 mm boards	-	0.50	5.67	7.93	m²	**13.60**
Boarding to floors; tongued and grooved joints						
19 mm x 75 mm boards	-	0.70	7.94	6.34	m²	**14.28**
19 mm x 125 mm boards	-	0.65	7.37	6.93	m²	**14.30**
22 mm x 150 mm boards	-	0.60	6.80	7.39	m²	**14.19**
25 mm x 100 mm boards	-	0.65	7.37	7.93	m²	**15.30**
25 mm x 150 mm boards	-	0.60	6.80	8.47	m²	**15.27**
Boarding to internal walls; tongued and grooved and V-jointed						
12 mm x 100 mm boards	-	0.80	9.07	5.59	m²	**14.66**
16 mm x 100 mm boards	-	0.80	9.07	7.49	m²	**16.56**
19 mm x 100 mm boards	-	0.80	9.07	8.40	m²	**17.47**
19 mm x 125 mm boards	-	0.75	8.51	8.87	m²	**17.38**
19 mm x 125 mm boards; chevron pattern	-	1.20	13.61	8.87	m²	**22.48**
25 mm x 125 mm boards	-	0.75	8.51	11.39	m²	**19.90**
12 mm x 100 mm boards; knotty pine	-	0.80	9.07	4.61	m²	**13.68**
Boarding to internal ceilings						
12 mm x 100 mm boards	-	1.00	11.34	5.59	m²	**16.93**
16 mm x 100 mm boards	-	1.00	11.34	7.49	m²	**18.83**
19 mm x 100 mm boards	-	1.00	11.34	8.40	m²	**19.74**
19 mm x 125 mm boards	-	0.95	10.77	8.87	m²	**19.64**
19 mm x 125 mm boards; chevron pattern	-	1.40	15.88	8.87	m²	**24.75**
25 mm x 125 mm boards	-	0.95	10.77	11.39	m²	**22.16**
12 mm x 100 mm boards; knotty pine	-	1.00	11.34	4.61	m²	**15.95**
Boarding to roofs; tongued and grooved joints						
19 mm thick; flat to falls	-	0.55	6.24	6.62	m²	**12.86**
19 mm thick; sloping	-	0.60	6.80	6.62	m²	**13.42**
19 mm thick; sloping; laid diagonally	-	0.78	8.79	6.62	m²	**15.41**
25 mm thick; flat to falls	-	0.55	6.24	7.98	m²	**14.22**
25 mm thick; sloping	-	0.60	6.80	7.98	m²	**14.78**
Boarding to tops or cheeks of dormers; tongued and grooved joints						
19 mm thick; laid diagonally	-	1.00	11.34	6.62	m²	**17.96**
Wrought softwood; "Tanalised"						
Boarding to roofs; tongued and grooved joints						
19 mm thick; flat to falls	-	0.55	6.24	7.21	m²	**13.45**
19 mm thick; sloping	-	0.60	6.80	7.21	m²	**14.01**
19 mm thick; sloping; laid diagonally	-	0.78	8.79	7.21	m²	**16.00**
25 mm thick; flat to falls	-	0.55	6.24	8.76	m²	**15.00**
25 mm thick; sloping	-	0.60	6.80	8.76	m²	**15.56**
Boarding to tops or cheeks of dormers; tongued and grooved joints						
19 mm thick; laid diagonally	-	1.00	11.34	7.21	m²	**18.55**
Wood strip; 22 mm thick; "Junckers" pre-treated or other equal and approved; tongued and grooved joints; pre-finished boards; level fixing to resilient battens; to cement and sand base						
Strip flooring; over 300 mm wide						
beech; prime	-	-	-	-	m²	**44.80**
beech; standard	-	-	-	-	m²	**42.25**
beech; sylvia squash	-	-	-	-	m²	**44.10**
oak; quality A	-	-	-	-	m²	**53.55**

K LININGS/SHEATHING/DRY PARTITIONING Excluding overheads and profit	PC £	Labour hours	Labour £	Material £	Unit	Total rate £
K20 TIMBER BOARD FLOORING/SHEATHING/ LININGS/CASINGS - cont'd						
Wrought hardwood						
Strip flooring to floors; 25 mm thick x 75 mm						
wide; tongue and grooved joints; secret fixing;						
surface sanded after laying						
american oak	-	-	-	-	m²	32.80
canadian maple	-	-	-	-	m²	35.30
gurjun	-	-	-	-	m²	32.10
iroko	-	-	-	-	m²	31.00
K32 FRAMED PANEL CUBICLE PARTITIONS						
Cubicle partitions; Armitage Shanks "Rapide" **range or other equal and approved; standard** **colours; standard ironmongery; assembling;** **screwing to floor and wall**						
Cubicle sets complete with doors						
range of 1 nr open ended cubicles; 1 nr panel;						
1 nr door	-	2.25	25.52	255.00	nr	280.52
range of 3 nr open ended cubicles; 3 nr panel;						
3 nr door	-	6.75	76.55	685.00	nr	761.55
range of 6 nr open ended cubicles; 6 nr panel;						
6 nr door	-	13.50	153.09	1315.00	nr	1468.09
K33 CONCRETE/TERRAZZO PARTITIONS						
Terrazzo faced partitions; polished on two **faces**						
Pre-cast reinforced terrazzo faced WC partitions						
38 mm thick; over 300 mm wide	-	-	-	-	m²	164.00
50 mm thick; over 300 mm wide	-	-	-	-	m²	178.50
Wall post; once rebated						
64 mm x 102 mm	-	-	-	-	m	99.00
64 mm x 152 mm	-	-	-	-	m	105.00
Centre post; twice rebated						
64 mm x 102 mm	-	-	-	-	m	105.00
64 mm x 152 mm	-	-	-	-	m	113.50
Lintel; once rebated						
64 mm x 102 mm	-	-	-	-	m	99.00
Pair of brass topped plates or sockets cast into						
posts for fixings (not included)	-	-	-	-	nr	21.50
Brass indicator bolt lugs cast into posts for						
fixings (not included)	-	-	-	-	nr	11.55
K40 DEMOUNTABLE SUSPENDED CEILINGS						
Suspended ceilings; Donn Products exposed **suspended ceiling system or other equal and** **approved; hangers plugged and screwed to concrete** **soffit; 600 mm x 600 mm x 15 mm Cape TAP Ceilings** **Ltd; "Solitude" tegular fissured tile or other equal** **and approved**						
Lining to ceilings; hangers average 400 mm long						
over 300 mm wide	-	0.35	3.62	7.24	m²	10.86

K LININGS/SHEATHING/DRY PARTITIONING Excluding overheads and profit	PC £	Labour hours	Labour £	Material £	Unit	Total rate £
Suspended ceilings, Gyproc M/F suspended **ceiling system or other equal and approved; hangers** **plugged and screwed to concrete soffit, 900 mm x** **1800 mm x 12.50 mm tapered edge wallboard infill;** **joints filled with joint filler and taped to receive direct** **direction** Lining to ceilings; hangers average 400 mm long						
over 300 mm wide	-	-	-	-	m²	21.00
not exceeding 300 mm wide in isolated strips	-	-	-	-	m	8.50
300 mm - 600 mm wide in isolated strips	-	-	-	-	m	13.50
Vertical bulkhead; including additional hangers						
over 300 mm wide	-	-	-	-	m²	23.00
not exceeding 300 mm wide in isolated strips	-	-	-	-	m	13.00
300 mm - 600 mm wide in isolated strips	-	-	-	-	m	18.00
Suspended ceilings; "Slimline" exposed suspended **ceiling system or other equal and approved; hangers** **plugged and screwed to concrete soffit, 600 mm x 600** **mm x 19 mm Treetex "Glacier" mineral tile** **infill or other equal and approved; PC £10.00/m²** Lining to ceilings; hangers average 400 mm long						
over 300 mm wide	-	-	-	-	m²	21.50
not exceeding 300 mm wide in isolated strips	-	-	-	-	m	9.00
300 mm - 600 mm wide in isolated strips	-	-	-	-	m	17.00
Edge detail 24 mm x 19 mm white finished angle edge trim	-	-	-	-	m	1.65
Cutting and fitting around pipes; not exceeding 0.30 m girth	-	-	-	-	nr	1.20
Suspended ceilings; "Z" demountable suspended **ceiling system or other equal and approved; hangers** **plugged and screwed to concrete soffit, 600 mm x 600** **mm x 19 mm "Echostop" glass reinforced** **fibrous plaster lightweight plain bevelled edge** **tiles or other equal and approved; PC £14.50/m²** Lining to ceilings; hangers average 400 mm long						
over 300 mm wide	-	-	-	-	m²	45.00
not exceeding 300 mm wide in isolated strips	-	-	-	-	m	15.50
Suspended ceilings; concealed galvanised **steel suspension system; hangers plugged** **and screwed to concrete soffit, 600 mm x 600 mm** **"Burgess" white stove enamelled perforated mild steel** **tiles or other equal and approved; PC £13.50/m²** Lining to ceilings; hangers average 400 mm long						
over 300 mm wide	-	-	-	-	m²	36.50
not exceeding 300 mm wide; in isolated strips	-	-	-	-	m	13.00

K LININGS/SHEATHING/DRY PARTITIONING Excluding overheads and profit	PC £	Labour hours	Labour £	Material £	Unit	Total rate £
K40 DEMOUNTABLE SUSPENDED CEILINGS - cont'd						
Suspended ceilings; concealed galvanised **steel "Trulok" suspension system or other equal** **and approved; hangers plugged and screwed to** **concrete; 300 mm x 300 mm x 18 mm Armstrong** **"Travertone" mineral ceiling tiles or other equal** **and approved; PC £16.50/m²**						
Linings to ceilings; hangers average 700 mm long						
over 300 mm wide	-	-	-	-	m²	43.50
over 300 mm wide; 3.50 m - 5.00 m high	-	-	-	-	m²	44.00
over 300 mm wide; in staircase areas or plant rooms	-	-	-	-	m²	45.00
not exceeding 300 mm wide; in isolated strips	-	-	-	-	m	15.00
300 mm - 600 mm wide; in isolated strips	-	-	-	-	m	26.50
Extra for cutting and fitting around modular downlighter including yoke	-	-	-	-	nr	4.00
Vertical bulkhead; including additional hangers						
over 300 mm wide	-	-	-	-	m²	45.00
not exceeding 300 mm wide; in isolated strips	-	-	-	-	m	20.00
300 mm - 600 mm wide; in isolated strips	-	-	-	-	m	32.00
24 mm x 19 mm white finished angle edge trim	-	-	-	-	m	1.60
Cutting and fitting around pipes; not exceeding 0.30 m girth	-	-	-	-	nr	1.20
Suspended ceilings; galvanised steel **suspension system; hangers plugged and** **screwed to concrete soffit, "Luxalon" stove** **enamelled aluminium linear panel ceiling type** **80B or other equal and approved, complete with** **mineral insulation; PC £19.00/m²**						
Linings to ceilings; hangers average 700 mm long						
over 300 mm wide	-	-	-	-	m²	45.00
not exceeding 300 mm wide; in isolated strips	-	-	-	-	m	15.50
K41 RAISED ACCESS FLOORS						
USG (UK) Ltd raised flooring systems or other **equal and approved; laid on or fixed to concrete floor**						
"Donn Products UK Ltd" full access system; 150 mm high overall; pedestal supports						
PSA light grade; steel finish	-	-	-	-	m²	35.00
PSA medium grade; steel finish	-	-	-	-	m²	40.00
PSA heavy grade; steel finish	-	-	-	-	m²	45.00
Extra for						
factory applied needlepunch carpet	-	-	-	-	m²	11.50
factory applied anti-static vinyl	-	-	-	-	m²	25.00
factory applied black PVC edge strips	-	-	-	-	m	3.00
ramps; 3.00 m x 1.40 m (no finish)	-	-	-	-	nr	550.00
steps (no finish)	-	-	-	-	m	30.00
forming cut-out for electrical boxes	-	-	-	-	nr	6.75

L WINDOWS/DOORS/STAIRS Excluding overheads and profit	PC £	Labour hours	Labour £	Material £	Unit	Total rate £
L WINDOWS/DOORS/STAIRS						
L10 WINDOWS/ROOFLIGHTS/SCREENS/ **LOUVRES**						
Standard windows; "treated" wrought **softwood; Rugby Joinery or other equal** **and approved**						
Side hung casement windows without glazing						
bars; with 140 mm wide softwood sills;						
opening casements and ventilators hung on						
rustproof hinges; fitted with aluminized						
lacquered finish casement stays and fasteners						
500 mm x 750 mm; ref N07V	35.92	0.70	7.94	36.11	nr	**44.05**
500 mm x 900 mm; ref N09V	37.34	0.80	9.07	37.53	nr	**46.60**
600 mm x 750 mm; ref 107V	45.07	0.80	9.07	45.26	nr	**54.33**
600 mm x 750 mm; ref 107C	48.20	0.80	9.07	48.39	nr	**57.46**
600 mm x 900 mm; ref 109V	45.25	0.90	10.21	45.44	nr	**55.65**
600 mm x 900 mm; ref 109C	49.31	0.80	9.07	49.50	nr	**58.57**
600 mm x 1050 mm; ref 109V	46.45	0.80	9.07	46.70	nr	**55.77**
600 mm x 1050 mm; ref 110V	49.55	1.00	11.34	49.80	nr	**61.14**
915 mm x 900 mm; ref 2NO9W	56.61	1.10	12.47	56.80	nr	**69.27**
915 mm x 1050 mm; ref 2N1OW	57.49	1.15	13.04	57.74	nr	**70.78**
915 mm x 1200 mm; ref 2N12W	62.53	1.20	13.61	62.78	nr	**76.39**
915 mm x 1350 mm; ref 2N13W	63.91	1.35	15.31	64.16	nr	**79.47**
915 mm x 1500 mm; ref 2N15W	64.85	1.40	15.88	65.16	nr	**81.04**
1200 mm x 750 mm; ref 2O7C	62.16	1.15	13.04	62.41	nr	**75.45**
1200 mm x 750 mm; ref 2O7CV	79.32	1.15	13.04	79.57	nr	**92.61**
1200 mm x 900 mm; ref 2O9C	63.74	1.20	13.61	63.99	nr	**77.60**
1200 mm x 900 mm; ref 2O9W	68.56	1.20	13.61	68.81	nr	**82.42**
1200 mm x 900 mm; ref 2O9CV	80.15	1.20	13.61	80.40	nr	**94.01**
1200 mm x 1050 mm; ref 210C	63.81	1.35	15.31	64.12	nr	**79.43**
1200 mm x 1050 mm; ref 210W	69.86	1.35	15.31	70.17	nr	**85.48**
1200 mm x 1050 mm; ref 210T	82.48	1.35	15.31	82.79	nr	**98.10**
1200 mm x 1050 mm; ref 210CV	80.26	1.35	15.31	80.57	nr	**95.88**
1200 mm x 1200 mm; ref 212C	66.54	1.45	16.44	66.92	nr	**83.36**
1200 mm x 1200 mm; ref 212W	71.31	1.45	16.44	71.69	nr	**88.13**
1200 mm x 1200 mm; ref 212TX	89.61	1.45	16.44	89.99	nr	**106.43**
1200 mm x 1200 mm; ref 212CV	83.02	1.45	16.44	83.40	nr	**99.84**
1200 mm x 1350 mm; ref 213W	72.89	1.55	17.58	73.27	nr	**90.85**
1200 mm x 1350 mm; ref 213CV	92.60	1.55	17.58	92.98	nr	**110.56**
1200 mm x 1500 mm; ref 215W	74.75	1.70	19.28	75.19	nr	**94.47**
1770 mm x 750 mm; ref 307CC	94.52	1.40	15.88	94.90	nr	**110.78**
1770 mm x 900 mm; ref 309CC	96.95	1.70	19.28	97.33	nr	**116.61**
1770 mm x 1050 mm; ref 310C	80.60	1.75	19.84	80.98	nr	**100.82**
1770 mm x 1050 mm; ref 310T	97.15	1.70	19.28	97.53	nr	**116.81**
1770 mm x 1050 mm; ref 310CC	97.35	1.40	15.88	97.73	nr	**113.61**
1770 mm x 1050 mm; ref 310WW	113.26	1.40	15.88	113.64	nr	**129.52**
1770 mm x 1200 mm; ref 312C	83.15	1.80	20.41	83.59	nr	**104.00**
1770 mm x 1200 mm; ref 312T	100.04	1.80	20.41	100.48	nr	**120.89**
1770 mm x 1200 mm; ref 312CC	101.12	1.80	20.41	101.56	nr	**121.97**
1770 mm x 1200 mm; ref 312WW	116.32	1.80	20.41	116.76	nr	**137.17**
1770 mm x 1200 mm; ref 312CVC	124.69	1.80	20.41	125.13	nr	**145.54**
1770 mm x 1350 mm; ref 313CC	114.87	1.90	21.55	115.31	nr	**136.86**
1770 mm x 1350 mm; ref 313WW	119.15	1.90	21.55	119.59	nr	**141.14**
1770 mm x 1350 mm; ref 313CVC	132.36	1.90	21.55	132.80	nr	**154.35**
1770 mm x 1500 mm; ref 315T	105.12	2.00	22.68	105.56	nr	**128.24**
2340 mm x 1050 mm; ref 410CWC	141.95	1.95	22.11	142.39	nr	**164.50**
2340 mm x 1200 mm; ref 412CWC	146.69	2.05	23.25	147.19	nr	**170.44**
2340 mm x 1350 mm; ref 413CWC	155.10	2.20	24.95	155.67	nr	**180.62**

L WINDOWS/DOORS/STAIRS Excluding overheads and profit	PC £	Labour hours	Labour £	Material £	Unit	Total rate £
L10 WINDOWS/ROOFLIGHTS/SCREENS/ LOUVRES - cont'd						
Standard windows; "treated" wrought softwood; Rugby Joinery or other equal and approved - cont'd						
Top hung casement windows; with 140 mm wide softwood sills; opening casements and ventilators hung on rustproof hinges; fitted with aluminized lacquered finish casement stays						
600 mm x 750 mm; ref 107A	52.07	0.80	9.07	52.26	nr	**61.33**
600 mm x 900 mm; ref 109A	53.86	0.90	10.21	54.05	nr	**64.26**
600 mm x 1050 mm; ref 110A	56.24	1.00	11.34	56.49	nr	**67.83**
915 mm x 750 mm; ref 2N07A	63.34	1.05	11.91	63.53	nr	**75.44**
915 mm x 900 mm; ref 2N09A	68.29	1.10	12.47	68.48	nr	**80.95**
915 mm x 1050 mm; ref 2N10A	70.94	1.15	13.04	71.19	nr	**84.23**
915 mm x 1350 mm; ref 2N13AS	81.07	1.35	15.31	81.38	nr	**96.69**
1200 mm x 750 mm; ref 207A	71.89	1.15	13.04	72.14	nr	**85.18**
1200 mm x 900 mm; ref 209A	76.39	1.20	13.61	76.64	nr	**90.25**
1200 mm x 1050 mm; ref 210A	79.01	1.35	15.31	79.32	nr	**94.63**
1200 mm x 1200 mm; ref 212A	81.54	1.45	16.44	81.85	nr	**98.29**
1200 mm x 1350 mm; ref 213AS	89.61	1.55	17.58	89.99	nr	**107.57**
1200 mm x 1500 mm; ref 215AS	92.20	1.70	19.28	92.58	nr	**111.86**
1770 mm x 1050 mm; ref 310AE	93.92	1.70	19.28	94.30	nr	**113.58**
1770 mm x 1200 mm; ref 312A	96.88	1.80	20.41	97.26	nr	**117.67**
High performance single light with canopy sash windows; ventilators; weather stripping; opening sashes and fanlights hung on rustproof hinges; fitted with aluminized lacquered espagnolette bolts						
600 mm x 900 mm; ref AL0609	121.61	0.90	10.21	121.80	nr	**132.01**
900 mm x 900 mm; ref AL0909	126.15	1.10	12.47	126.34	nr	**138.81**
900 mm x 1050 mm; ref AL0910	126.83	1.15	13.04	127.02	nr	**140.06**
900 mm x 1200 mm; ref AL0912	129.34	1.25	14.18	129.59	nr	**143.77**
900 mm x 1500 mm; ref AL0915	136.28	1.40	15.88	136.53	nr	**152.41**
1200 mm x 1050 mm; ref AL1210	146.99	1.35	15.31	147.24	nr	**162.55**
1200 mm x 1200 mm; ref AL1212	147.93	1.45	16.44	148.24	nr	**164.68**
1200 mm x 1500 mm; ref AL1215	167.01	1.70	19.28	167.39	nr	**186.67**
1500 mm x 1050 mm; ref AL1510	147.24	1.65	18.71	147.55	nr	**166.26**
1500 mm x 1200 mm; ref AL1512	154.61	1.70	19.28	154.92	nr	**174.20**
1500 mm x 1500 mm; ref AL1515	166.51	1.80	20.41	166.95	nr	**187.36**
1500 mm x 1650 mm; ref AL1516	171.86	1.90	21.55	172.24	nr	**193.79**
High performance double hung sash windows with glazing bars; solid frames; 63 mm x 175 mm softwood sills; standard flush external linings; spiral spring balances and sash catch						
635 mm x 1050 mm; ref VS0610B	204.74	2.00	22.68	204.99	nr	**227.67**
635 mm x 1350 mm; ref VS0613B	221.74	2.20	24.95	222.05	nr	**247.00**
635 mm x 1650 mm; ref VS0616B	236.89	2.45	27.78	237.27	nr	**265.05**
860 mm x 1050 mm; ref VS0810B	223.34	2.30	26.08	223.59	nr	**249.67**
860 mm x 1350 mm; ref VS0813B	241.75	2.60	29.48	242.06	nr	**271.54**
860 mm x 1650 mm; ref VS0816B	260.11	3.00	34.02	260.49	nr	**294.51**
1085 mm x 1050 mm; ref VS1010B	242.92	2.60	29.48	243.17	nr	**272.65**
1085 mm x 1350 mm; ref VS1013B	266.45	3.00	34.02	266.76	nr	**300.78**
1085 mm x 1650 mm; ref VS1016B	281.89	3.70	41.96	282.27	nr	**324.23**
1725 mm x 1050 mm; ref VS1710B	444.77	3.70	41.96	445.08	nr	**487.04**
1725 mm x 1350 mm; ref VS1713B	484.74	4.60	52.16	485.12	nr	**537.28**
1725 mm x 1650 mm; ref VS1716B	520.10	4.70	53.30	520.54	nr	**573.84**

L WINDOWS/DOORS/STAIRS Excluding overheads and profit	PC £	Labour hours	Labour £	Material £	Unit	Total rate £
Standard windows; Premdor Crosby or other equal						
and approved; Meranti; factory applied preservative						
stain base coat						
Side hung casement windows; 45 mm x 140						
mm hardwood sills; weather stripping; opening						
sashes on canopy hinges; fitted with fasteners;						
brown finish ironmongery						
630 mm x 750 mm; ref 107C	86.04	0.95	10.77	86.23	nr	**97.00**
630 mm x 900 mm; ref 109C	91.56	1.20	13.61	91.75	nr	**105.36**
630 mm x 900 mm; ref 109V	86.25	0.95	10.77	86.44	nr	**97.21**
630 mm x 1050 mm; ref 110V	87.60	1.30	14.74	87.79	nr	**102.53**
915 mm x 900 mm; ref 2N09W	106.08	1.50	17.01	106.33	nr	**123.34**
915 mm x 1050 mm; ref 2N10W	108.93	1.60	18.14	109.24	nr	**127.38**
915 mm x 1200 mm; ref 2N12W	111.81	1.70	19.28	112.12	nr	**131.40**
915 mm x 1350 mm; ref 2N13W	114.66	1.80	20.41	114.97	nr	**135.38**
915 mm x 1500 mm; ref 2N15W	117.78	1.90	21.55	118.16	nr	**139.71**
1200 mm x 900 mm; ref 209C	125.61	1.70	19.28	125.80	nr	**145.08**
1200 mm x 900 mm; ref 209W	123.63	1.70	19.28	123.82	nr	**143.10**
1200 mm x 1050 mm; ref 210C	132.93	1.80	20.41	133.12	nr	**153.53**
1200 mm x 1050 mm; ref 210W	126.51	1.80	20.41	126.70	nr	**147.11**
1200 mm x 1200 mm; ref 212C	143.61	1.95	22.11	143.86	nr	**165.97**
1200 mm x 1200 mm; ref 212W	129.36	1.95	22.11	129.61	nr	**151.72**
1200 mm x 1350 mm; ref 213W	132.24	2.10	23.81	132.49	nr	**156.30**
1200 mm x 1500 mm; ref 215W	135.39	2.20	24.95	135.64	nr	**160.59**
1770 mm x 1050 mm; ref 310C	161.70	2.25	25.52	162.01	nr	**187.53**
1770 mm x 1050 mm; ref 310CC	200.82	2.25	25.52	201.13	nr	**226.65**
1770 mm x 1200 mm; ref 312C	172.35	2.40	27.22	172.66	nr	**199.88**
1770 mm x 1200 mm ; ref 312CC	217.83	2.40	27.22	218.14	nr	**245.36**
2339 mm x 1200 mm; ref 412CMC	241.86	2.60	29.48	242.24	nr	**271.72**
Top hung casement windows; 45 mm x 140						
mm hardwood sills; weather stripping; opening						
sashes on canopy hinges; fitted with fasteners;						
brown finish ironmongery						
630 mm x 900 mm; ref 109A	84.90	0.95	10.77	85.09	nr	**95.86**
630 mm x 1050 mm; ref 110A	90.42	1.30	14.74	90.67	nr	**105.41**
915 mm x 900 mm; ref 2N09A	101.01	1.50	17.01	101.20	nr	**118.21**
915 mm x 1050 mm; ref 2N10A	106.53	1.60	18.14	106.78	nr	**124.92**
915 mm x 1200 mm; ref 2N12A	112.59	1.70	19.28	112.84	nr	**132.12**
915 mm x 1350 mm; ref 2N13D	132.00	1.80	20.41	132.31	nr	**152.72**
1200 mm x 900 mm; ref 209A	114.90	1.50	17.01	115.09	nr	**132.10**
1200 mm x 1050 mm; ref 210A	120.45	1.70	19.28	120.70	nr	**139.98**
1200 mm x 1200 mm; ref 212A	126.51	1.80	20.41	126.76	nr	**147.17**
1770 mm x 1050 mm; ref 310AE	147.30	1.90	21.55	147.61	nr	**169.16**
1770 mm x 1200 mm; ref 312AE	155.19	2.00	22.68	155.50	nr	**178.18**
Purpose made window casements; "treated"						
wrought softwood						
Casements; rebated; moulded - supply only						
38 mm thick	-	-	-	20.73	m²	**20.73**
50 mm thick	-	-	-	24.64	m²	**24.64**
Casements; rebated; moulded; in medium						
panes - supply only						
38 mm thick	-	-	-	30.29	m²	**30.29**
50 mm thick	-	-	-	37.46	m²	**37.46**
Casements; rebated; moulded; with						
semi-circular head - supply only						
38 mm thick	-	-	-	37.83	m²	**37.83**
50 mm thick	-	-	-	46.84	m²	**46.84**

L WINDOWS/DOORS/STAIRS Excluding overheads and profit	PC £	Labour hours	Labour £	Material £	Unit	Total rate £
L10 WINDOWS/ROOFLIGHTS/SCREENS/ LOUVRES - cont'd						
Purpose made window casements; "treated" wrought softwood - cont'd						
Casements; rebated; moulded; to bullseye window - supply only						
38 mm thick; 600 mm diameter	-	-	-	68.03	nr	**68.03**
38 mm thick; 900 mm diameter	-	-	-	100.91	nr	**100.91**
50 mm thick; 600 mm diameter	-	-	-	78.25	nr	**78.25**
50 mm thick; 900 mm diameter	-	-	-	116.01	nr	**116.01**
Fitting and hanging casements						
square or rectangular	-	0.50	5.67	-	nr	**5.67**
semi-circular	-	1.25	14.18	-	nr	**14.18**
bullseye	-	2.00	22.68	-	nr	**22.68**
Purpose made window casements; selected West African Mahogany						
Casements; rebated; moulded - supply only						
38 mm thick	-	-	-	34.89	m²	**34.89**
50 mm thick	-	-	-	45.49	m²	**45.49**
Casements; rebated; moulded; in medium panes - supply only						
38 mm thick	-	-	-	42.34	m²	**42.34**
50 mm thick	-	-	-	56.65	m²	**56.65**
Casements; rebated; moulded with semi-circular head - supply only						
38 mm thick	-	-	-	52.93	m²	**52.93**
50 mm thick	-	-	-	70.87	m²	**70.87**
Casements; rebated; moulded; to bullseye window - supply only						
38 mm thick; 600 mm diameter	-	-	-	114.57	nr	**114.57**
38 mm thick; 900 mm diameter	-	-	-	171.47	nr	**171.47**
50 mm thick; 600 mm diameter	-	-	-	131.75	nr	**131.75**
50 mm thick; 900 mm diameter	-	-	-	196.44	nr	**196.44**
Fitting and hanging casements						
square or rectangular	-	0.70	7.94	-	nr	**7.94**
semi-circular	-	1.70	19.28	-	nr	**19.28**
bullseye	-	2.70	30.62	-	nr	**30.62**
Purpose made window casements; American White Ash						
Casements; rebated; moulded - supply only						
38 mm thick	-	-	-	41.25	m²	**41.25**
50 mm thick	-	-	-	50.64	m²	**50.64**
Casements; rebated; moulded; in medium panes - supply only						
38 mm thick	-	-	-	53.45	m²	**53.45**
50 mm thick	-	-	-	64.24	m²	**64.24**
Casements; rebated; moulded with semi-circular head - supply only						
38 mm thick	-	-	-	66.83	m²	**66.83**
50 mm thick	-	-	-	80.31	m²	**80.31**
Casements; rebated; moulded; to bullseye window - supply only						
38 mm thick; 600 mm diameter	-	-	-	135.49	nr	**135.49**
38 mm thick; 900 mm diameter	-	-	-	202.44	nr	**202.44**
50 mm thick; 600 mm diameter	-	-	-	156.28	nr	**156.28**
50 mm thick; 900 mm diameter	-	-	-	233.00	nr	**233.00**

L WINDOWS/DOORS/STAIRS Excluding overheads and profit	PC £	Labour hours	Labour £	Material £	Unit	Total rate £
Fitting and hanging casements						
square or rectangular	-	0.70	7.94	-	nr	**7.94**
semi-circular	-	1.70	19.28	-	nr	**19.28**
bullseye	-	2.70	30.62	-	nr	**30.62**
Purpose made window frames; "treated"						
wrought softwood; prices indicated are for						
supply only as part of a complete window						
frame; the reader is referred to the previous						
pages for fixing costs for frames based on						
the overall window size						
Frames; rounded; rebated check grooved						
25 mm x 120 mm	-	-	-	6.32	m	**6.32**
50 mm x 75 mm	-	-	-	7.49	m	**7.49**
50 mm x 100 mm	-	-	-	9.16	m	**9.16**
50 mm x 125 mm	-	-	-	11.13	m	**11.13**
63 mm x 100 mm	-	-	-	11.41	m	**11.41**
75 mm x 150 mm	-	-	-	19.16	m	**19.16**
90 mm x 140 mm	-	-	-	24.73	m	**24.73**
Mullions and transoms; twice rounded, rebated						
and check grooved						
50 mm x 75 mm	-	-	-	9.19	m	**9.19**
50 mm x 100 mm	-	-	-	10.87	m	**10.87**
63 mm x 100 mm	-	-	-	13.11	m	**13.11**
75 mm x 150 mm	-	-	-	20.86	m	**20.86**
Sill; sunk weathered, rebated and grooved						
75 mm x 100 mm	-	-	-	19.21	m	**19.21**
75 mm x 150 mm	-	-	-	25.17	m	**25.17**
Add 5% to the above material prices for						
"selected" softwood for staining						
Purpose made window frames; selected						
West African Mahogany; prices given are for						
supply only as part of a complete window						
frame; the reader is referred to the previous						
pages for fixing costs for frames based on						
the overall window size						
Frames; rounded; rebated check grooved						
25 mm x 120 mm	-	-	-	10.90	m	**10.90**
50 mm x 75 mm	-	-	-	13.02	m	**13.02**
50 mm x 100 mm	-	-	-	16.12	m	**16.12**
50 mm x 125 mm	-	-	-	19.65	m	**19.65**
63 mm x 100 mm	-	-	-	20.11	m	**20.11**
75 mm x 150 mm	-	-	-	34.04	m	**34.04**
90 mm x 140 mm	-	-	-	44.14	m	**44.14**
Mullions and transoms; twice rounded, rebated						
and check grooved						
50 mm x 75 mm	-	-	-	15.56	m	**15.56**
50 mm x 100 mm	-	-	-	18.66	m	**18.66**
63 mm x 100 mm	-	-	-	22.65	m	**22.65**
75 mm x 150 mm	-	-	-	36.59	m	**36.59**
Sill; sunk weathered, rebated and grooved						
75 mm x 100 mm	-	-	-	32.36	m	**32.36**
75 mm x 150 mm	-	-	-	43.09	m	**43.09**

L WINDOWS/DOORS/STAIRS Excluding overheads and profit	PC £	Labour hours	Labour £	Material £	Unit	Total rate £
L10 WINDOWS/ROOFLIGHTS/SCREENS/ LOUVRES - cont'd						
Purpose made window frames; American White Ash; prices indicated are for supply only as part of a complete window frame; the reader is referred to the previous pages for fixing costs for frames based on the overall window size						
Frames; rounded; rebated check grooved						
25 mm x 120 mm	-	-	-	12.13	m	**12.13**
50 mm x 75 mm	-	-	-	14.56	m	**14.56**
50 mm x 100 mm	-	-	-	18.19	m	**18.19**
50 mm x 125 mm	-	-	-	22.24	m	**22.24**
63 mm x 100 mm	-	-	-	22.73	m	**22.73**
75 mm x 150 mm	-	-	-	38.71	m	**38.71**
90 mm x 140 mm	-	-	-	50.40	m	**50.40**
Mullions and transoms; twice rounded, rebated and check grooved						
50 mm x 75 mm	-	-	-	17.10	m	**17.10**
50 mm x 100 mm	-	-	-	20.73	m	**20.73**
63 mm x 100 mm	-	-	-	25.27	m	**25.27**
75 mm x 150 mm	-	-	-	41.25	m	**41.25**
Sill; sunk weathered, rebated and grooved						
75 mm x 100 mm	-	-	-	35.47	m	**35.47**
75 mm x 150 mm	-	-	-	47.79	m	**47.79**
Purpose made double hung sash windows; "treated" wrought softwood						
Cased frames of 100 mm x 25 mm grooved inner linings; 114 mm x 25 mm grooved outer linings; 125 mm x 38 mm twice rebated head linings; 125 mm x 32 mm twice rebated grooved pulley stiles; 150 mm x 13 mm linings; 50 mm x 19 mm parting slips; 25 mm x 19 mm inside beads; 150 mm x 75 mm Oak twice sunk weathered throated sill; 50 mm thick rebated and moulded sashes; moulded horns						
over 1.25 m² each; both sashes in medium panes; including spiral spring balances	151.74	2.25	25.52	210.57	m²	**236.09**
As above but with cased mullions	160.10	2.50	28.35	218.93	m²	**247.28**
Purpose made double hung sash windows; selected West African Mahogany						
Cased frames of 100 mm x 25 mm grooved inner linings; 114 mm x 25 mm grooved outer linings; 125 mm x 38 mm twice rebated head linings; 125 mm x 32 mm twice rebated grooved pulley stiles; 150 mm x 13 mm linings; 50 mm x 19 mm parting slips; 25 mm x 19 mm inside beads; 150 mm x 75 mm Oak twice sunk weathered throated sill; 50 mm thick rebated and moulded sashes; moulded horns						
over 1.25 m² each; both sashes in medium panes; including spiral sash balances	242.22	3.00	34.02	301.05	m²	**335.07**
As above but with cased mullions	255.53	3.33	37.76	314.36	m²	**352.12**

L WINDOWS/DOORS/STAIRS Excluding overheads and profit	PC £	Labour hours	Labour £	Material £	Unit	Total rate £
Purpose made double hung sash windows; **American White Ash** Cased frames of 100 mm x 25 mm grooved inner linings; 114 mm x 25 mm grooved outer linings; 125 mm x 38 mm twice rebated head linings; 125 mm x 32 mm twice rebated grooved pulley stiles; 150 mm x 13 mm linings; 50 mm x 19 mm parting slips; 25 mm x 19 mm inside beads; 150 mm x 75 mm Oak twice sunk weathered throated sill; 50 mm thick rebated and moulded sashes; moulded horns						
over 1.25 m² each; both sashes in medium panes; including spiral spring balances	262.68	3.00	34.02	321.51	m²	**355.53**
As above but with cased mullions	-	3.33	37.76	335.95	m²	**373.71**
Galvanised steel fixed, casement and fanlight **windows; Crittal "Homelight" range or other** **equal and approved; site glazing not included;** **fixed in position including lugs plugged and** **screwed to brickwork or blockwork**						
Basic fixed lights; including easy-glaze beads						
628 mm x 292 mm; ref ZNG5	16.22	1.20	13.61	16.35	nr	**29.96**
628 mm x 923 mm; ref ZNC5	23.10	1.20	13.61	23.29	nr	**36.90**
628 mm x 1513 mm; ref ZNDV5	32.89	1.20	13.61	33.20	nr	**46.81**
1237 mm x 292 mm; ref ZNG13	24.77	1.20	13.61	24.90	nr	**38.51**
1237 mm x 923 mm; ref ZNC13	32.06	1.75	19.84	32.25	nr	**52.09**
1237 mm x 1218 mm; ref ZND13	37.77	1.75	19.84	38.02	nr	**57.86**
1237 mm x 1513 mm; ref ZNDV13	41.41	1.75	19.84	41.72	nr	**61.56**
1846 mm x 292 mm; ref ZNG14	32.12	1.20	13.61	32.31	nr	**45.92**
1846 mm x 923 mm; ref ZNC14	39.58	1.75	19.84	39.89	nr	**59.73**
1846 mm x 1513 mm; ref ZNDV14	47.95	2.20	24.95	48.39	nr	**73.34**
Basic opening lights; including easy-glaze beads and weatherstripping						
628 mm x 292 mm; ref ZNG1	41.51	1.20	13.61	41.64	nr	**55.25**
1237 mm x 292 mm; ref ZNG13G	59.43	1.20	13.61	59.56	nr	**73.17**
1846 mm x 292 mm; ref ZNG4	102.85	1.20	13.61	103.10	nr	**116.71**
One piece composites; including easy-glaze beads and weatherstripping						
628 mm x 923 mm; ref ZNC5F	56.06	1.20	13.61	56.25	nr	**69.86**
628 mm x 1513 mm; ref ZNDV5F	66.23	1.20	13.61	66.54	nr	**80.15**
1237 mm x 923 mm; ref ZNC2F	109.49	1.75	19.84	109.68	nr	**129.52**
1237 mm x 1218 mm; ref ZND2F	127.52	1.75	19.84	127.77	nr	**147.61**
1237 mm x 1513 mm; ref ZNDV2V	151.51	1.75	19.84	151.82	nr	**171.66**
1846 mm x 923 mm; ref ZNC4F	167.73	1.75	19.84	168.04	nr	**187.88**
1846 mm x 1218 mm; ref ZND10F	159.80	2.20	24.95	160.18	nr	**185.13**
Reversible windows; including easy-glaze beads						
997 mm x 923 mm; ref NC13R	141.90	1.55	17.58	142.09	nr	**159.67**
997 mm x 1067 mm; ref NCO13R	150.28	1.55	17.58	150.47	nr	**168.05**
1237 mm x 923 mm; ref ZNC13R	156.41	2.30	26.08	156.60	nr	**182.68**
1237 mm x 1218 mm; ref ZND13R	170.63	2.30	26.08	170.88	nr	**196.96**
1237 mm x 1513 mm; ref ZNDV13RS	191.12	2.30	26.08	191.43	nr	**217.51**
Pressed steel sills; to suit above window widths						
628 mm long	9.75	0.35	3.97	9.75	nr	**13.72**
997 mm long	13.12	0.45	5.10	13.12	nr	**18.22**
1237 mm long	16.33	0.55	6.24	16.33	nr	**22.57**
1846 mm long	21.28	0.75	8.51	21.28	nr	**29.79**

L WINDOWS/DOORS/STAIRS Excluding overheads and profit	PC £	Labour hours	Labour £	Material £	Unit	Total rate £
L10 WINDOWS/ROOFLIGHTS/SCREENS/ **LOUVRES** - cont'd						
Factory finished steel fixed light; casement **and fanlight windows; Crittall polyester** **powder coated "Homelight" range or other** **equal and approved; site glazing not included;** **fixed in position; including lugs plugged and** **screwed to brickwork or blockwork**						
Basic fixed lights; including easy-glaze beads						
628 mm x 292 mm; ref ZNG5	20.16	1.20	13.61	20.29	nr	**33.90**
628 mm x 923 mm; ref ZNC5	28.71	1.20	13.61	28.90	nr	**42.51**
628 mm x 1513 mm; ref ZNDV5	40.89	1.20	13.61	41.20	nr	**54.81**
1237 mm x 292 mm; ref ZNG13	30.79	1.20	13.61	30.92	nr	**44.53**
1237 mm x 923 mm; ref ZNC13	39.84	1.75	19.84	40.03	nr	**59.87**
1237 mm x 1218 mm; ref ZND13	46.95	1.75	19.84	47.20	nr	**67.04**
1237 mm x 1513 mm; ref ZNDV13	51.45	1.75	19.84	51.76	nr	**71.60**
1846 mm x 292 mm; ref ZNG14	39.93	1.20	13.61	40.06	nr	**53.67**
1846 mm x 923 mm; ref ZNC14	49.20	1.75	19.84	49.39	nr	**69.23**
1846 mm x 1513 mm; ref ZNDV14	59.93	2.20	24.95	60.24	nr	**85.19**
Basic opening lights; including easy-glaze beads and weatherstripping						
628 mm x 292 mm; ref ZNG1	49.27	1.20	13.61	49.40	nr	**63.01**
1237 mm x 292 mm; ref ZNG13G	71.32	1.20	13.61	71.45	nr	**85.06**
1846 mm x 292 mm; ref ZNG4	122.75	1.20	13.61	122.87	nr	**136.48**
One piece composites; including easy-glaze beads and weatherstripping						
628 mm x 923 mm; ref ZNC5F	67.31	1.20	13.61	67.50	nr	**81.11**
628 mm x 1513 mm; ref ZNDV5F	79.94	1.20	13.61	80.25	nr	**93.86**
1237 mm x 923 mm; ref ZNC2F	130.71	1.75	19.84	130.90	nr	**150.74**
1237 mm x 1218 mm; ref ZND2F	152.63	1.75	19.84	152.83	nr	**172.67**
1237 mm x 1513 mm; ref ZNDV2V	181.39	1.75	19.84	181.70	nr	**201.54**
1846 mm x 923 mm; ref ZNC4F	200.00	1.75	19.84	200.19	nr	**220.03**
1846 mm x 1218 mm; ref ZND10F	191.97	2.20	24.95	192.28	nr	**217.23**
Reversible windows; including easy-glaze beads						
997 mm x 923 mm; ref NC13R	181.99	1.55	17.58	182.18	nr	**199.76**
997 mm x 1218 mm; ref NCO13R	192.77	1.55	17.58	192.96	nr	**210.54**
1237 mm x 923 mm; ref ZNC13R	200.66	2.30	26.08	200.85	nr	**226.93**
1237 mm x 1218 mm; ref ZND13R	218.99	2.30	26.08	219.24	nr	**245.32**
1237 mm x 1513 mm; ref ZNDV13RS	245.48	2.30	26.08	245.79	nr	**271.87**
Pressed steel sills; to suit above window widths						
628 mm long	12.08	0.35	3.97	12.08	nr	**16.05**
997 mm long	16.25	0.45	5.10	16.25	nr	**21.35**
1237 mm long	20.24	0.55	6.24	20.24	nr	**26.48**
1846 mm long	26.38	0.75	8.51	26.38	nr	**34.89**
uPVC windows to BS 2782; reinforced where **appropriate with aluminium alloy; including standard** **ironmongery; cills and glazing; fixed in** **position; including lugs plugged and screwed** **to brickwork or blockwork**						
Fixed light; including e.p.d.m. glazing gaskets and weather seals						
600 mm x 900 mm; single glazed	32.32	1.50	17.01	32.57	nr	**49.58**
600 mm x 900 mm; double glazed	42.50	1.50	17.01	42.75	nr	**59.76**

L WINDOWS/DOORS/STAIRS Excluding overheads and profit	PC £	Labour hours	Labour £	Material £	Unit	Total rate £
Casement/fixed light; including e.p.d.m. glazing gaskets and weather seals						
600 mm x 1200 mm; single glazed	72.05	1.75	19.84	72.36	nr	92.20
600 mm x 1200 mm; double glazed	86.09	1.75	19.84	86.40	nr	106.24
1200 mm x 1200 mm; single glazed	98.91	2.00	22.68	99.29	nr	121.97
1200 mm x 1200 mm; double glazed	135.43	2.00	22.68	135.81	nr	158.49
1800 mm x 1200 mm; single glazed	103.19	2.00	22.68	103.57	nr	126.25
1800 mm x 1200 mm; double glazed	144.78	2.00	22.68	145.16	nr	167.84
"Tilt & Turn" light; including e.p.d.m. glazing gaskets and weather seals						
1200 mm x 1200 mm; single glazed	102.97	2.00	22.68	103.35	nr	126.03
1200 mm x 1200 mm; double glazed	125.36	2.00	22.68	125.74	nr	148.42
Rooflights, skylights, roof windows and frames; pre-glazed; "treated" Nordic Red Pine and aluminium trimmed "Velux" windows or other equal and approved; type U flashings and soakers (for tiles and pantiles), and sealed double glazing unit (trimming opening not included)						
Roof windows						
550 mm x 780 mm; ref GGL-3000-102	126.14	2.00	22.68	126.36	nr	149.04
550 mm x 980 mm; ref GGL-3000-104	139.50	2.25	25.52	139.72	nr	165.24
660 mm x 1180 mm; ref GGL-3000-206	164.63	2.50	28.35	164.89	nr	193.24
780 mm x 980 mm; ref GGL-3000-304	158.35	2.50	28.35	158.61	nr	186.96
780 mm x 1400 mm; ref GGL-3000-308	190.55	2.50	28.35	190.90	nr	219.25
940 mm x 1600 mm; ref GGL-3000-410	229.28	3.00	34.02	229.68	nr	263.70
1140 mm x 1180 mm; ref GGL-3000-606	210.99	3.00	34.02	211.39	nr	245.41
1340 mm x 980 mm; ref GGL-3000-804	217.96	3.00	34.02	218.36	nr	252.38
1340 mm x 1400 mm; ref GGL-3000-808	259.08	3.00	34.02	259.48	nr	293.50
Rooflights, skylights, roof windows and frames; galvanised steel; plugged and screwed to concrete; or screwed to timber						
Rooflight; "Coxdome TPX" or other equal and approved; dome; galvanised steel; UV protected polycarbonate glazing; GRP splayed upstand; hit and miss vent						
600 mm x 600 mm	145.35	1.75	19.84	145.55	nr	165.39
900 mm x 600 mm	195.70	1.90	21.55	195.93	nr	217.48
900 mm x 900 mm	230.85	2.05	23.25	231.11	nr	254.36
1200 mm x 900 mm	266.00	2.20	24.95	266.30	nr	291.25
1200 mm x 1200 mm	328.70	2.35	26.65	329.03	nr	355.68
1800 mm x 1200 mm	475.95	2.50	28.35	476.31	nr	504.66
Rooflights, skylights, roof windows and frames; uPVC; plugged and screwed to concrete; or screwed to timber						
Rooflight; "Coxdome Universal Dome" or other equal and approved; acrylic double skin; dome						
600 mm x 600 mm	81.94	1.50	17.01	82.14	nr	99.15
900 mm x 600 mm	152.95	1.55	17.58	153.18	nr	170.76
900 mm x 900 mm	152.95	1.80	20.41	153.21	nr	173.62
1200 mm x 900 mm	185.72	1.95	22.11	186.02	nr	208.13
1200 mm x 1200 mm	234.89	2.10	23.81	235.22	nr	259.03
1500 mm x 1050 mm	442.46	2.20	24.95	442.82	nr	467.77
Louvres and frames; polyester powder coated aluminium; fixing in position including brackets						
Louvre; Gil Airvac "Plusaire 75SP" weatherlip or other equal and approved						
1250 mm x 675 mm	-	-	-	-	nr	220.00
2000 mm x 530 mm	-	-	-	-	nr	250.00

L WINDOWS/DOORS/STAIRS Excluding overheads and profit	PC £	Labour hours	Labour £	Material £	Unit	Total rate £
L20 DOORS/SHUTTERS/HATCHES						
Doors; standard matchboarded; wrought softwood						
Matchboarded, ledged and braced doors; 25 mm thick ledges and braces; 19 mm thick tongued, grooved and V-jointed boarding; one side vertical boarding						
762 mm x 1981mm	37.20	1.50	17.01	37.20	nr	**54.21**
838 mm x 1981mm	37.20	1.50	17.01	37.20	nr	**54.21**
Matchboarded, framed, ledged and braced doors; 44 mm thick overall; 19 mm thick tongued, grooved and V-jointed boarding; one side vertical boarding						
762 mm x 1981mm	45.60	1.80	20.41	45.60	nr	**66.01**
838 mm x 1981mm	45.60	1.80	20.41	45.60	nr	**66.01**
Doors; standard flush; softwood composition						
Flush door; internal quality; skeleton or cellular core; hardboard faced both sides; Premdor Crosby "Primaseal" or other equal and approved						
457 mm x 1981 mm x 35 mm	14.88	1.25	14.18	14.88	nr	**29.06**
533 mm x 1981 mm x 35 mm	14.88	1.25	14.18	14.88	nr	**29.06**
610 mm x 1981 mm x 35 mm	14.88	1.25	14.18	14.88	nr	**29.06**
686 mm x 1981 mm x 35 mm	14.88	1.25	14.18	14.88	nr	**29.06**
762 mm x 1981 mm x 35 mm	14.88	1.25	14.18	14.88	nr	**29.06**
838 mm x 1981 mm x 35 mm	15.63	1.25	14.18	15.63	nr	**29.81**
526 mm x 2040 mm x 40 mm	16.59	1.25	14.18	16.59	nr	**30.77**
626 mm x 2040 mm x 40 mm	16.59	1.25	14.18	16.59	nr	**30.77**
726 mm x 2040 mm x 40 mm	16.59	1.25	14.18	16.59	nr	**30.77**
826 mm x 2040 mm x 40 mm	16.59	1.25	14.18	16.59	nr	**30.77**
Flush door; internal quality; skeleton or cellular core; chipboard veneered; faced both sides; lipped on two long edges; Premdor Crosby "Popular" or other equal and approved						
457 mm x 1981 mm x 35 mm	21.39	1.25	14.18	21.39	nr	**35.57**
533 mm x 1981 mm x 35 mm	21.39	1.25	14.18	21.39	nr	**35.57**
610 mm x 1981 mm x 35 mm	21.39	1.25	14.18	21.39	nr	**35.57**
686 mm x 1981 mm x 35 mm	21.39	1.25	14.18	21.39	nr	**35.57**
762 mm x 1981 mm x 35 mm	21.39	1.25	14.18	21.39	nr	**35.57**
838 mm x 1981 mm x 35 mm	22.38	1.25	14.18	22.38	nr	**36.56**
526 mm x 2040 mm x 40 mm	23.52	1.25	14.18	23.52	nr	**37.70**
626 mm x 2040 mm x 40 mm	23.52	1.25	14.18	23.52	nr	**37.70**
726 mm x 2040 mm x 40 mm	23.52	1.25	14.18	23.52	nr	**37.70**
826 mm x 2040 mm x 40 mm	23.52	1.25	14.18	23.52	nr	**37.70**
Flush door; internal quality; skeleton or cellular core; Sapele faced both sides; lipped on all four edges; Premdor Crosby "Landscape Sapele" or other equal and approved						
457 mm x 1981 mm x 35 mm	23.25	1.35	15.31	23.25	nr	**38.56**
533 mm x 1981 mm x 35 mm	23.25	1.35	15.31	23.25	nr	**38.56**
610 mm x 1981 mm x 35 mm	23.25	1.35	15.31	23.25	nr	**38.56**
686 mm x 1981 mm x 35 mm	23.25	1.35	15.31	23.25	nr	**38.56**
762 mm x 1981 mm x 35 mm	23.25	1.35	15.31	23.25	unit	**38.56**
838 mm x 1981 mm x 35 mm	24.21	1.35	15.31	24.21	nr	**39.52**
526 mm x 2040 mm x 40 mm	25.08	1.35	15.31	25.08	nr	**40.39**
626 mm x 2040 mm x 40 mm	25.08	1.35	15.31	25.08	nr	**40.39**
726 mm x 2040 mm x 40 mm	25.08	1.35	15.31	25.08	nr	**40.39**
826 mm x 2040 mm x 40 mm	25.08	1.35	15.31	25.08	nr	**40.39**

L WINDOWS/DOORS/STAIRS Excluding overheads and profit	PC £	Labour hours	Labour £	Material £	Unit	Total rate £
Flush door; half-hour fire check (FD20); hardboard faced both sides; Premdor Crosby "Primaseal Fireshield" or other equal and approved						
762 mm x 1981 mm x 44 mm	35.82	1.75	19.84	35.82	nr	**55.66**
838 mm x 1981 mm x 44 mm	37.11	1.75	19.84	37.11	nr	**56.95**
726 mm x 2040 mm x 44 mm	38.01	1.75	19.84	38.01	nr	**57.85**
826 mm x 2040 mm x 44 mm	38.01	1.75	19.84	38.01	nr	**57.85**
Flush door; half-hour fire check (30/20); chipboard veneered; faced both sides; lipped on all four edges; Premdor Crosby "Popular Fireshield" or other equal and approved						
457 mm x 1981 mm x 44 mm	35.22	1.75	19.84	35.22	nr	**55.06**
533 mm x 1981 mm x 44 mm	35.22	1.75	19.84	35.22	nr	**55.06**
610 mm x 1981 mm x 44 mm	35.22	1.75	19.84	35.22	nr	**55.06**
686 mm x 1981 mm x 44 mm	35.22	1.75	19.84	35.22	nr	**55.06**
762 mm x 1981 mm x 44 mm	35.22	1.75	19.84	35.22	nr	**55.06**
838 mm x 1981 mm x 44 mm	36.69	1.75	19.84	36.69	nr	**56.53**
526 mm x 2040 mm x 44 mm	38.52	1.75	19.84	38.52	nr	**58.36**
626 mm x 2040 mm x 44 mm	38.52	1.75	19.84	38.52	nr	**58.36**
726 mm x 2040 mm x 44 mm	38.52	1.75	19.84	38.52	nr	**58.36**
826 mm x 2040 mm x 44 mm	38.52	1.75	19.84	38.52	nr	**58.36**
Flush door; half hour fire resisting "Leaderflush" (type B30) or other equal and approved; chipboard for painting; hardwood lipping two long edges						
526 mm x 2040 mm x 44 mm	81.08	1.85	20.98	81.08	nr	**102.06**
626 mm x 2040 mm x 44 mm	86.66	1.85	20.98	86.66	nr	**107.64**
726 mm x 2040 mm x 44 mm	86.88	1.85	20.98	86.88	nr	**107.86**
826 mm x 2040 mm x 44 mm	87.68	1.85	20.98	87.68	nr	**108.66**
Flush door; half-hour fire check (FD20); Sapele faced both sides; lipped on all four edges; Premdor Crosby "Landscape Sapele Fireshield" or other equal and approved						
686 mm x 1981 mm x 44 mm	48.96	1.85	20.98	48.96	nr	**69.94**
762 mm x 1981 mm x 44 mm	48.96	1.85	20.98	48.96	nr	**69.94**
838 mm x 1981 mm x 44 mm	50.22	1.85	20.98	50.22	nr	**71.20**
726 mm x 2040 mm x 44 mm	51.09	1.85	20.98	51.09	nr	**72.07**
826 mm x 2040 mm x 44 mm	51.09	1.85	20.98	51.09	nr	**72.07**
Flush door; half-hour fire resisting (30/30) Sapele faced both sides; lipped on all four edges						
610 mm x 1981 mm x 44 mm	57.20	1.85	20.98	57.20	nr	**78.18**
686 mm x 1981 mm x 44 mm	57.20	1.85	20.98	57.20	nr	**78.18**
762 mm x 1981 mm x 44 mm	57.20	1.85	20.98	57.20	nr	**78.18**
838 mm x 1981 mm x 44 mm	57.20	1.85	20.98	57.20	nr	**78.18**
726 mm x 2040 mm x 44 mm	57.20	1.85	20.98	57.20	nr	**78.18**
826 mm x 2040 mm x 44 mm	57.20	1.85	20.98	57.20	nr	**78.18**
Flush door; half-hour fire resisting "Leaderflush" (type B30) or other equal and approved; American light oak veneer; hardwood lipping all edges						
526 mm x 2040 mm x 44 mm	107.27	1.85	20.98	107.27	nr	**128.25**
626 mm x 2040 mm x 44 mm	115.68	1.85	20.98	115.68	nr	**136.66**
726 mm x 2040 mm x 44 mm	118.72	1.85	20.98	118.72	nr	**139.70**
826 mm x 2040 mm x 44 mm	121.74	1.85	20.98	121.74	nr	**142.72**
Flush door; one-hour fire check (60/45); plywood faced both sides; lipped on all four edges; Premdor Crosby "Popular Firemaster" or other equal and approved						
762 mm x 1981 mm x 54 mm	128.64	2.00	22.68	128.64	nr	**151.32**
838 mm x 1981 mm x 54 mm	133.41	2.00	22.68	133.41	nr	**156.09**
726 mm x 2040 mm x 54 mm	135.18	2.00	22.68	135.18	nr	**157.86**
826 mm x 2040 mm x 54 mm	135.18	2.00	22.68	135.18	nr	**157.86**

L WINDOWS/DOORS/STAIRS Excluding overheads and profit	PC £	Labour hours	Labour £	Material £	Unit	Total rate £
L20 DOORS/SHUTTERS/HATCHES - cont'd						
Doors; standard flush; softwood composition - cont'd						
Flush door; one-hour fire check (60/45); Sapele						
faced both sides; lipped on all four edges						
762 mm x 1981 mm x 54 mm	211.32	2.10	23.81	211.32	nr	235.13
838 mm x 1981 mm x 54 mm	211.32	2.10	23.81	211.32	nr	235.13
Flush door; one-hour fire resisting "Leaderflush"						
(type B60) or other equal and approved; Afrormosia						
veneer; hardwood lipping all edges including groove						
and "Leaderseal" intumescent strip or other equal						
and approved						
457 mm x 1981 mm x 54 mm	115.98	2.10	23.81	115.98	nr	139.79
533 mm x 1981 mm x 54 mm	118.61	2.10	23.81	118.61	nr	142.42
610 mm x 1981 mm x 54 mm	143.64	2.10	23.81	143.64	nr	167.45
686 mm x 1981 mm x 54 mm	147.19	2.10	23.81	147.19	nr	171.00
762 mm x 1981 mm x 54 mm	150.73	2.10	23.81	150.73	nr	174.54
838 mm x 1981 mm x 54 mm	165.75	2.10	23.81	165.75	nr	189.56
526 mm x 2040 mm x 54 mm	118.90	2.10	23.81	118.90	nr	142.71
626 mm x 2040 mm x 54 mm	145.90	2.10	23.81	145.90	nr	169.71
726 mm x 2040 mm x 54 mm	149.38	2.10	23.81	149.38	nr	173.19
826 mm x 2040 mm x 54 mm	153.75	2.10	23.81	153.75	nr	177.56
Flush door; external quality; skeleton or cellular						
core; plywood faced both sides; lipped on all						
four edges						
762 mm x 1981 mm x 54 mm	35.99	1.75	19.84	35.99	nr	55.83
838 mm x 1981 mm x 54 mm	37.25	1.75	19.84	37.25	nr	57.09
Flush door; external quality with standard glass						
opening; skeleton or cellular core; plywood						
faced both sides; lipped on all four edges;						
including glazing beads						
762 mm x 1981 mm x 54 mm	45.22	1.75	19.84	45.22	nr	65.06
838 mm x 1981 mm x 54 mm	46.40	1.75	19.84	46.40	nr	66.24
Doors; purpose made panelled; wrought						
softwood						
Panelled doors; one open panel for glass;						
including glazing beads						
686 mm x 1981 mm x 44 mm	51.00	1.75	19.84	51.00	nr	70.84
762 mm x 1981 mm x 44 mm	52.56	1.75	19.84	52.56	nr	72.40
838 mm x 1981 mm x 44 mm	54.10	1.75	19.84	54.10	nr	73.94
Panelled doors; two open panel for glass;						
including glazing beads						
686 mm x 1981 mm x 44 mm	70.53	1.75	19.84	70.53	nr	90.37
762 mm x 1981 mm x 44 mm	74.31	1.75	19.84	74.31	nr	94.15
838 mm x 1981 mm x 44 mm	78.00	1.75	19.84	78.00	nr	97.84
Panelled doors; four 19 mm thick plywood						
panels; mouldings worked on solid both sides						
686 mm x 1981 mm x 44 mm	97.36	1.75	19.84	97.36	nr	117.20
762 mm x 1981 mm x 44 mm	101.03	1.75	19.84	101.03	nr	120.87
838 mm x 1981 mm x 44 mm	106.52	1.75	19.84	106.52	nr	126.36
Panelled doors; six 25 mm thick panels raised						
and fielded; mouldings worked on solid both						
sides						
686 mm x 1981 mm x 44 mm	222.41	2.10	23.81	222.41	nr	246.22
762 mm x 1981 mm x 44 mm	231.66	2.10	23.81	231.66	nr	255.47
838 mm x 1981 mm x 44 mm	243.25	2.10	23.81	243.25	nr	267.06
rebated edges beaded	-	-	-	1.17	m	1.17
rounded edges or heels	-	-	-	0.59	m	0.59
weatherboard fixed to bottom rail	-	0.25	2.83	2.26	m	5.09
stopped groove for weatherboard	-	-	-	3.52	m	3.52

L WINDOWS/DOORS/STAIRS Excluding overheads and profit	PC £	Labour hours	Labour £	Material £	Unit	Total rate £
Doors; purpose made panelled; selected **West African Mahogany** Panelled doors; one open panel for glass; including glazing beads						
686 mm x 1981 mm x 50 mm	103.11	2.50	28.35	103.11	nr	**131.46**
762 mm x 1981 mm x 50 mm	106.52	2.50	28.35	106.52	nr	**134.87**
838 mm x 1981 mm x 50 mm	109.92	2.50	28.35	109.92	nr	**138.27**
686 mm x 1981 mm x 63 mm	125.49	2.75	31.18	125.49	nr	**156.67**
762 mm x 1981 mm x 63 mm	129.73	2.75	31.18	129.73	nr	**160.91**
838 mm x 1981 mm x 63 mm	133.96	2.75	31.18	133.96	nr	**165.14**
Panelled doors; 250 mm wide cross tongued intermediate rail; two open panels for glass; mouldings worked on the solid one side; 19 mm x 13 mm beads one side; fixing with brass cups and screws						
686 mm x 1981 mm x 50 mm	140.82	2.50	28.35	140.82	nr	**169.17**
762 mm x 1981 mm x 50 mm	147.77	2.50	28.35	147.77	nr	**176.12**
838 mm x 1981 mm x 50 mm	154.65	2.50	28.35	154.65	nr	**183.00**
686 mm x 1981 mm x 63 mm	169.27	2.75	31.18	169.27	nr	**200.45**
762 mm x 1981 mm x 63 mm	177.68	2.75	31.18	177.68	nr	**208.86**
838 mm x 1981 mm x 63 mm	186.06	2.75	31.18	186.06	nr	**217.24**
Panelled doors; four panels; (19 mm thick for 50 mm doors, 25 mm thick for 63 mm doors); mouldings worked on solid both sides						
686 mm x 1981 mm x 50 mm	179.43	2.50	28.35	179.43	nr	**207.78**
762 mm x 1981 mm x 50 mm	186.89	2.50	28.35	186.89	nr	**215.24**
838 mm x 1981 mm x 50 mm	196.24	2.50	28.35	196.24	nr	**224.59**
686 mm x 1981 mm x 63 mm	211.88	2.75	31.18	211.88	nr	**243.06**
762 mm x 1981 mm x 63 mm	220.74	2.75	31.18	220.74	nr	**251.92**
838 mm x 1981 mm x 63 mm	231.76	2.75	31.18	231.76	nr	**262.94**
Panelled doors; 150 mm wide stiles in one width; 430 mm wide cross tongued bottom rail; six panels raised and fielded one side; (19 mm thick for 50 mm doors, 25 mm thick for 63 mm doors); mouldings worked on solid both sides						
686 mm x 1981 mm x 50 mm	378.56	2.50	28.35	378.56	nr	**406.91**
762 mm x 1981 mm x 50 mm	394.34	2.50	28.35	394.34	nr	**422.69**
838 mm x 1981 mm x 50 mm	414.03	2.50	28.35	414.03	nr	**442.38**
686 mm x 1981 mm x 63 mm	466.20	2.75	31.18	466.20	nr	**497.38**
762 mm x 1981 mm x 63 mm	485.65	2.75	31.18	485.65	nr	**516.83**
838 mm x 1981 mm x 63 mm	509.92	2.75	31.18	509.92	nr	**541.10**
rebated edges beaded	-	-	-	1.76	m	**1.76**
rounded edges or heels	-	-	-	0.87	m	**0.87**
weatherboard fixed to bottom rail	-	0.33	3.74	5.04	m	**8.78**
stopped groove for weatherboard	-	-	-	4.31	m	**4.31**
Doors; purpose made panelled; American **White Ash** Panelled doors; one open panel for glass; including glazing beads						
686 mm x 1981 mm x 50 mm	115.47	2.50	28.35	115.47	nr	**143.82**
762 mm x 1981 mm x 50 mm	119.34	2.50	28.35	119.34	nr	**147.69**
838 mm x 1981 mm x 50 mm	123.21	2.50	28.35	123.21	nr	**151.56**
686 mm x 1981 mm x 63 mm	140.90	2.75	31.18	140.90	nr	**172.08**
762 mm x 1981 mm x 63 mm	145.77	2.75	31.18	145.77	nr	**176.95**
838 mm x 1981 mm x 63 mm	150.58	2.75	31.18	150.58	nr	**181.76**
Panelled doors; 250 mm wide cross tongued intermediate rail; two open panels for glass; mouldings worked on the solid one side; 19 mm x 13 mm beads one side; fixing with brass cups and screws						
686 mm x 1981 mm x 50 mm	157.13	2.50	28.35	157.13	nr	**185.48**

L WINDOWS/DOORS/STAIRS Excluding overheads and profit	PC £	Labour hours	Labour £	Material £	Unit	Total rate £
L20 DOORS/SHUTTERS/HATCHES - cont'd						
Doors; purpose made panelled; American						
White Ash - cont'd						
Panelled doors; 250 mm wide cross tongued intermediate						
rail; two open panels for glass; mouldings worked on the						
solid one side; 19 mm x 13 mm beads one side; fixing						
with brass cups and screws - cont'd						
762 mm x 1981 mm x 50 mm	165.00	2.50	28.35	165.00	nr	**193.35**
838 mm x 1981 mm x 50 mm	172.81	2.50	28.35	172.81	nr	**201.16**
686 mm x 1981 mm x 63 mm	189.65	2.75	31.18	189.65	nr	**220.83**
762 mm x 1981 mm x 63 mm	199.18	2.75	31.18	199.18	nr	**230.36**
838 mm x 1981 mm x 63 mm	208.68	2.75	31.18	208.68	nr	**239.86**
Panelled doors; four panels; (19 mm thick for						
50 mm doors, 25 mm thick for 63 mm doors);						
mouldings worked on solid both sides						
686 mm x 1981 mm x 50 mm	199.56	2.50	28.35	199.56	nr	**227.91**
762 mm x 1981 mm x 50 mm	207.85	2.50	28.35	207.85	nr	**236.20**
838 mm x 1981 mm x 50 mm	218.24	2.50	28.35	218.24	nr	**246.59**
686 mm x 1981 mm x 63 mm	237.14	2.75	31.18	237.14	nr	**268.32**
762 mm x 1981 mm x 63 mm	247.04	2.75	31.18	247.04	nr	**278.22**
838 mm x 1981 mm x 63 mm	259.39	2.75	31.18	259.39	nr	**290.57**
Panelled doors; 150 mm wide stiles in one width;						
430 mm wide cross tongued bottom rail; six panels						
raised and fielded one side; (19 mm thick for 50 mm						
doors, 25 mm thick for 63 mm doors); mouldings						
worked on solid both sides						
686 mm x 1981 mm x 50 mm	411.27	2.50	28.35	411.27	nr	**439.62**
762 mm x 1981 mm x 50 mm	428.42	2.50	28.35	428.42	nr	**456.77**
838 mm x 1981 mm x 50 mm	449.83	2.50	28.35	449.83	nr	**478.18**
686 mm x 1981 mm x 63 mm	507.63	2.75	31.18	507.63	nr	**538.81**
762 mm x 1981 mm x 63 mm	528.78	2.75	31.18	528.78	nr	**559.96**
838 mm x 1981 mm x 63 mm	555.24	2.75	31.18	555.24	nr	**586.42**
rebated edges beaded	-	-	-	1.76	m	**1.76**
rounded edges or heels	-	-	-	0.87	m	**0.87**
weatherboard fixed to bottom rail	-	0.33	3.74	5.53	m	**9.27**
stopped groove for weatherboard	-	-	-	4.31	m	**4.31**
Doors; galvanised steel "up and over" type garage						
doors; Catnic "Horizon 90" or other equal and						
approved; spring counter balanced; fixed to						
timber frame (not included)						
Garage door						
2135 mm x 1980 mm	164.25	4.00	45.36	164.51	nr	**209.87**
2135 mm x 2135 mm	184.50	4.00	45.36	184.76	nr	**230.12**
2400 mm x 2135 mm	223.50	4.00	45.36	223.81	nr	**269.17**
3965 mm x 2135 mm	588.75	6.00	68.04	589.37	nr	**657.41**
Doorsets; Anti-Vandal Security door and frame						
units; Bastion Security Ltd or other equal and						
approved; to BS 5051; factory primed; fixing with						
frame anchors to masonry; cutting mortices; external						
46 mm thick insulated door with birch grade plywood;						
sheet steel bonded into door core; 2 mm thick polyester						
coated laminate finish; hardwood lippings all edges; 95						
mm x 65 mm hardwood frame; polyester coated standard						
ironmongery; weather stripping all round; low						
projecting aluminium threshold; plugging; screwing						
for 980 mm x 2100 mm structural opening;						
single door sets; panic bolt	-	-	-	-	nr	**1200.00**
for 1830 mm x 2100 mm structural opening;						
double door sets; panic bolt	-	-	-	-	nr	**2000.00**

L WINDOWS/DOORS/STAIRS Excluding overheads and profit	PC £	Labour hours	Labour £	Material £	Unit	Total rate £
Doorsets; galvanised steel IG "Weatherbeater Original" door and frame units or other equal and approved; treated softwood frame, primed hardwood sill; fixing in position; plugged and screwed to brickwork or blockwork						
Door and frame						
762 mm x 1981 mm; ref IGD1	259.63	3.00	34.02	259.88	nr	**293.90**
Doorsets; steel door and frame units; Jandor Architectural Ltd or other equal and approved; polyester powder coated; ironmongery						
Single action door set; "Metset MD01" doors and "Metset MF" frames						
900 mm x 2100 mm	-	-	-	-	nr	**1540.00**
pair 1800 mm x 2100 mm	-	-	-	-	nr	**2090.00**
Rolling shutters and collapsible gates; steel counter shutters; Bolton Brady Ltd or other equal and approved; push-up, self-coiling; polyester power coated; fixing by bolting						
Shutters						
3000 mm x 1000 mm	-	-	-	-	nr	**835.00**
4000 mm x 1000 mm; in two panels	-	-	-	-	nr	**1450.00**
Rolling shutters and collapsible gates; galvanised steel; Bolton Brady Type 474 or other equal and approved; one hour fire resisting; self-coiling; activated by fusible link; fixing with bolts						
Rolling shutters and collapsible gates						
1000 mm x 2750 mm	-	-	-	-	nr	**1000.00**
1500 mm x 2750 mm	-	-	-	-	nr	**1050.00**
2400 mm x 2750 mm	-	-	-	-	nr	**1235.00**
Rolling shutters and collapsible gates; GRP vertically opening insulated panel shutter doors; electrically operated; Envirodoor Markus Ltd type HT40 or other equal and approved; manual over-ride, lock interlock, stop and return safety cage, "deadmans" down button, anti-flip device, photo-electric cell and beam deflectors; fixing by bolting						
Shutter doors						
3000 mm x 3000 mm; windows - 2 nr	-	-	-	-	nr	**6560.00**
4000 mm x 4000 mm; windows - 2 nr	-	-	-	-	nr	**8140.00**
5000 mm x 5000 mm; windows - 2 nr	-	-	-	-	nr	**9710.00**
Sliding/folding partitions; aluminium double glazed sliding patio doors; Crittal "Luminaire" or other equal and approved; white acrylic finish; with and including 18 mm thick annealed double glazing; fixed in position; including lugs plugged and screwed to brickwork or blockwork						
Patio doors						
1800 mm x 2100 mm; ref PF1821	920.50	2.50	28.35	921.25	nr	**949.60**
2400 m x 2100 mm; ref PF2421	1141.00	3.00	34.02	1141.75	nr	**1175.77**
2700 mm x 2100 mm; ref PF2721	1249.50	3.50	39.69	1250.25	nr	**1289.94**

L WINDOWS/DOORS/STAIRS Excluding overheads and profit	PC £	Labour hours	Labour £	Material £	Unit	Total rate £
L20 DOORS/SHUTTERS/HATCHES - cont'd						
Grilles; "Galaxy" nylon rolling counter grille or						
other equal and approved; Bolton Brady Ltd;						
colour, off-white; self-coiling; fixing by bolting						
Grilles						
3000 mm x 1000 mm	-	-	-	-	nr	755.00
4000 mm x 1000 mm	-	-	-	-	nr	1130.00
Door frames and door linings, sets; standard						
joinery; wrought softwood						
Internal door frame or lining composite sets for						
686 mm x 1981 mm door; all with loose stops						
unless rebated; "finished sizes"						
27 mm x 94 mm lining	22.00	0.80	9.07	22.25	nr	31.32
27 mm x 107 mm lining	23.14	0.80	9.07	23.39	nr	32.46
35 mm x 107 mm rebated lining	24.02	0.80	9.07	24.27	nr	33.34
27 mm x 121 mm lining	25.03	0.80	9.07	25.28	nr	34.35
27 mm x 121 mm lining with fanlight over	35.25	0.95	10.77	35.56	nr	46.33
27 mm x 133 mm lining	26.98	0.80	9.07	27.23	nr	36.30
35 mm x 133 mm rebated lining	27.72	0.80	9.07	27.97	nr	37.04
27 mm x 133 mm lining with fanlight over	37.88	0.95	10.77	38.19	nr	48.96
33 mm x 57 mm frame	17.72	0.80	9.07	17.97	nr	27.04
33 mm x 57 mm storey height frame	21.87	0.95	10.77	22.18	nr	32.95
33 mm x 57 mm frame with fanlight over	26.51	0.95	10.77	26.82	nr	37.59
33 mm x 64 mm frame	19.10	0.80	9.07	19.35	nr	28.42
33 mm x 64 mm storey height frame	23.41	0.95	10.77	23.72	nr	34.49
33 mm x 64 mm frame with fanlight over	27.98	0.95	10.77	28.29	nr	39.06
44 mm x 94 mm frame	29.60	0.92	10.43	29.85	nr	40.28
44 mm x 94 mm storey height frame	35.22	1.10	12.47	35.53	nr	48.00
44 mm x 94 mm frame with fanlight over	41.07	1.10	12.47	41.38	nr	53.85
44 mm x 107 mm frame	33.85	1.00	11.34	34.10	nr	45.44
44 mm x 107 mm storey height frame	39.66	1.10	12.47	39.97	nr	52.44
44 mm x 107 mm frame with fanlight over	45.25	1.10	12.47	45.56	nr	58.03
Internal door frame or lining composite sets for						
762 mm x 1981 mm door; all with loose stops						
unless rebated; "finished sizes"						
27 mm x 94 mm lining	22.00	0.80	9.07	22.25	nr	31.32
27 mm x 107 mm lining	23.14	0.80	9.07	23.39	nr	32.46
35 mm x 107 mm rebated lining	24.02	0.80	9.07	24.27	nr	33.34
27 mm x 121 mm lining	25.03	0.80	9.07	25.28	nr	34.35
27 mm x 121 mm lining with fanlight over	35.25	0.95	10.77	35.56	nr	46.33
27 mm x 133 mm lining	26.98	0.80	9.07	27.23	nr	36.30
35 mm x 133 mm rebated lining	27.72	0.80	9.07	27.97	nr	37.04
27 mm x 133 mm lining with fanlight over	37.88	0.95	10.77	38.19	nr	48.96
33 mm x 57 mm frame	17.72	0.80	9.07	17.97	nr	27.04
33 mm x 57 mm storey height frame	21.87	0.95	10.77	22.18	nr	32.95
33 mm x 57 mm frame with fanlight over	26.51	0.95	10.77	26.82	nr	37.59
33 mm x 64 mm frame	19.10	0.80	9.07	19.35	nr	28.42
33 mm x 64 mm storey height frame	23.41	0.95	10.77	23.72	nr	34.49
33 mm x 64 mm frame with fanlight over	27.98	0.95	10.77	28.29	nr	39.06
44 mm x 94 mm frame	29.60	0.92	10.43	29.85	nr	40.28
44 mm x 94 mm storey height frame	35.22	1.10	12.47	35.53	nr	48.00
44 mm x 94 mm frame with fanlight over	41.07	1.10	12.47	41.38	nr	53.85
44 mm x 107 mm frame	33.85	1.00	11.34	34.10	nr	45.44
44 mm x 107 mm storey height frame	39.66	1.10	12.47	39.97	nr	52.44
44 mm x 107 mm frame with fanlight over	45.25	1.10	12.47	45.56	nr	58.03

L WINDOWS/DOORS/STAIRS Excluding overheads and profit	PC £	Labour hours	Labour £	Material £	Unit	Total rate £
Internal door frame or lining composite sets for						
726 mm x 2040 mm door; with loose stops						
30 mm x 94 mm lining	25.66	0.80	9.07	25.91	nr	**34.98**
30 mm x 94 mm lining with fanlight over	36.56	0.95	10.77	36.87	nr	**47.64**
30 mm x 107 mm lining	30.17	0.80	9.07	30.42	nr	**39.49**
30 mm x 107 mm lining with fanlight over	41.21	0.95	10.77	41.52	nr	**52.29**
30 mm x 133 mm lining	33.81	0.80	9.07	34.06	nr	**43.13**
30 mm x 133 mm lining with fanlight over	44.44	0.95	10.77	44.75	nr	**55.52**
Internal door frame or lining composite sets for						
826 mm x 2040 mm door; with loose stops						
30 mm x 94 mm lining	25.66	0.80	9.07	25.91	nr	**34.98**
30 mm x 94 mm lining with fanlight over	36.56	0.95	10.77	36.87	nr	**47.64**
30 mm x 107 mm lining	30.17	0.80	9.07	30.42	nr	**39.49**
30 mm x 107 mm lining with fanlight over	41.21	0.95	10.77	41.52	nr	**52.29**
30 mm x 133 mm lining	33.81	0.80	9.07	34.06	nr	**43.13**
30 mm x 133 mm lining with fanlight over	44.44	0.95	10.77	44.75	nr	**55.52**
Door frames and door linings, sets; purpose **made; wrought softwood**						
Jambs and heads; as linings						
32 mm x 63 mm	-	0.17	1.93	3.58	m	**5.51**
32 mm x 100 mm	-	0.17	1.93	4.59	m	**6.52**
32 mm x 140 mm	-	0.17	1.93	5.88	m	**7.81**
Jambs and heads; as frames; rebated,						
rounded and grooved						
38 mm x 75 mm	-	0.17	1.93	4.55	m	**6.48**
38 mm x 100 mm	-	0.17	1.93	5.39	m	**7.32**
38 mm x 115 mm	-	0.17	1.93	6.28	m	**8.21**
38 mm x 140 mm	-	0.20	2.27	7.30	m	**9.57**
50 mm x 100 mm	-	0.20	2.27	6.79	m	**9.06**
50 mm x 125 mm	-	0.20	2.27	8.07	m	**10.34**
63 mm x 88 mm	-	0.20	2.27	7.77	m	**10.04**
63 mm x 100 mm	-	0.20	2.27	8.30	m	**10.57**
63 mm x 125 mm	-	0.20	2.27	9.91	m	**12.18**
75 mm x 100 mm	-	0.20	2.27	9.52	m	**11.79**
75 mm x 125 mm	-	0.22	2.49	11.78	m	**14.27**
75 mm x 150 mm	-	0.22	2.49	13.73	m	**16.22**
100 mm x 100 mm	-	0.25	2.83	12.38	m	**15.21**
100 mm x 150 mm	-	0.25	2.83	17.72	m	**20.55**
Mullions and transoms; in linings						
32 mm x 63 mm	-	0.12	1.36	5.85	m	**7.21**
32 mm x 100 mm	-	0.12	1.36	6.88	m	**8.24**
32 mm x 140 mm	-	0.12	1.36	8.08	m	**9.44**
Mullions and transoms; in frames; twice						
rebated, rounded and grooved						
38 mm x 75 mm	-	0.12	1.36	6.97	m	**8.33**
38 mm x 100 mm	-	0.12	1.36	7.81	m	**9.17**
38 mm x 115 mm	-	0.12	1.36	8.48	m	**9.84**
38 mm x 140 mm	-	0.14	1.59	9.51	m	**11.10**
50 mm x 100 mm	-	0.14	1.59	9.01	m	**10.60**
50 mm x 125 mm	-	0.14	1.59	10.41	m	**12.00**
63 mm x 88 mm	-	0.14	1.59	10.05	m	**11.64**
63 mm x 100 mm	-	0.14	1.59	10.57	m	**12.16**
75 mm x 100 mm	-	0.14	1.59	11.87	m	**13.46**
Add 5% to the above material prices for						
selected softwood for staining						

L WINDOWS/DOORS/STAIRS Excluding overheads and profit	PC £	Labour hours	Labour £	Material £	Unit	Total rate £
L20 DOORS/SHUTTERS/HATCHES - cont'd						
Door frames and door linings, sets; purpose **made; selected West African Mahogany**						
Jambs and heads; as linings						
32 mm x 63 mm	6.58	0.23	2.61	6.64	m	9.25
32 mm x 100 mm	8.57	0.23	2.61	8.63	m	11.24
32 mm x 140 mm	10.88	0.23	2.61	11.01	m	13.62
Jambs and heads; as frames; rebated,						
rounded and grooved						
38 mm x 75 mm	8.31	0.23	2.61	8.37	m	10.98
38 mm x 100 mm	10.07	0.23	2.61	10.13	m	12.74
38 mm x 115 mm	11.57	0.23	2.61	11.70	m	14.31
38 mm x 140 mm	13.38	0.27	3.06	13.51	m	16.57
50 mm x 100 mm	12.72	0.27	3.06	12.85	m	15.91
50 mm x 125 mm	15.32	0.27	3.06	15.45	m	18.51
63 mm x 88 mm	14.23	0.27	3.06	14.29	m	17.35
63 mm x 100 mm	15.77	0.27	3.06	15.83	m	18.89
63 mm x 125 mm	18.96	0.27	3.06	19.09	m	22.15
75 mm x 100 mm	18.18	0.27	3.06	18.31	m	21.37
75 mm x 125 mm	22.61	0.30	3.40	22.74	m	26.14
75 mm x 150 mm	26.54	0.30	3.40	26.67	m	30.07
100 mm x 100 mm	23.81	0.30	3.40	23.94	m	27.34
100 mm x 150 mm	34.54	0.30	3.40	34.67	m	38.07
Mullions and transoms; in linings						
32 mm x 63 mm	10.10	0.16	1.81	10.10	m	11.91
32 mm x 100 mm	12.07	0.16	1.81	12.07	m	13.88
32 mm x 140 mm	14.39	0.16	1.81	14.39	m	16.20
Mullions and transoms; in frames; twice						
rebated, rounded and grooved						
38 mm x 75 mm	12.01	0.16	1.81	12.01	m	13.82
38 mm x 100 mm	13.77	0.16	1.81	13.77	m	15.58
38 mm x 115 mm	15.09	0.16	1.81	15.09	m	16.90
38 mm x 140 mm	16.89	0.18	2.04	16.89	m	18.93
50 mm x 100 mm	16.22	0.18	2.04	16.22	m	18.26
50 mm x 125 mm	19.02	0.18	2.04	19.02	m	21.06
63 mm x 88 mm	17.75	0.18	2.04	17.75	m	19.79
63 mm x 100 mm	19.29	0.18	2.04	19.29	m	21.33
75 mm x 100 mm	21.88	0.18	2.04	21.88	m	23.92
Sills; once sunk weathered; once rebated, three						
times grooved						
63 mm x 175 mm	35.47	0.33	3.74	35.47	m	39.21
75 mm x 125 mm	32.13	0.33	3.74	32.13	m	35.87
75 mm x 150 mm	36.12	0.33	3.74	36.12	m	39.86
Door frames and door linings, sets; purpose **made; American White Ash**						
Jambs and heads; as linings						
32 mm x 63 mm	7.48	0.23	2.61	7.54	m	10.15
32 mm x 100 mm	9.81	0.23	2.61	9.87	m	12.48
32 mm x 140 mm	12.66	0.23	2.61	12.79	m	15.40
Jambs and heads; as frames; rebated,						
rounded and grooved						
38 mm x 75 mm	9.43	0.23	2.61	9.49	m	12.10
38 mm x 100 mm	11.58	0.23	2.61	11.64	m	14.25
38 mm x 115 mm	13.38	0.23	2.61	13.51	m	16.12
38 mm x 140 mm	15.46	0.27	3.06	15.59	m	18.65
50 mm x 100 mm	14.69	0.27	3.06	14.82	m	17.88
50 mm x 125 mm	17.79	0.27	3.06	17.92	m	20.98
63 mm x 88 mm	16.46	0.27	3.06	16.52	m	19.58

L WINDOWS/DOORS/STAIRS Excluding overheads and profit	PC £	Labour hours	Labour £	Material £	Unit	Total rate £
Jambs and heads; as frames; rebated,						
rounded and grooved - cont'd						
63 mm x 100 mm	18.28	0.27	3.06	18.34	m	21.40
63 mm x 125 mm	22.09	0.27	3.06	22.22	m	25.28
75 mm x 100 mm	21.14	0.27	3.06	21.27	m	24.33
75 mm x 125 mm	26.32	0.30	3.40	26.45	m	29.85
75 mm x 150 mm	30.99	0.30	3.40	31.12	m	34.52
100 mm x 100 mm	27.74	0.30	3.40	27.87	m	31.27
100 mm x 150 mm	40.49	0.30	3.40	40.62	m	44.02
Mullions and transoms; in linings						
32 mm x 63 mm	10.98	0.16	1.81	10.98	m	12.79
32 mm x 100 mm	13.33	0.16	1.81	13.33	m	15.14
32 mm x 140 mm	16.17	0.16	1.81	16.17	m	17.98
Mullions and transoms; in frames; twice						
rebated, rounded and grooved						
38 mm x 75 mm	13.13	0.16	1.81	13.13	m	14.94
38 mm x 100 mm	15.29	0.16	1.81	15.29	m	17.10
38 mm x 115 mm	16.89	0.16	1.81	16.89	m	18.70
38 mm x 140 mm	18.96	0.18	2.04	18.96	m	21.00
50 mm x 100 mm	18.19	0.18	2.04	18.19	m	20.23
50 mm x 125 mm	21.49	0.18	2.04	21.49	m	23.53
63 mm x 88 mm	20.01	0.18	2.04	20.01	m	22.05
63 mm x 100 mm	21.78	0.18	2.04	21.78	m	23.82
75 mm x 100 mm	24.83	0.18	2.04	24.83	m	26.87
Sills; once sunk weathered; once rebated, three						
times grooved						
63 mm x 175 mm	39.82	0.33	3.74	39.82	m	43.56
75 mm x 125 mm	35.84	0.33	3.74	35.84	m	39.58
75 mm x 150 mm	40.59	0.33	3.74	40.59	m	44.33
Door frames and door linings, sets; European						
Oak						
Sills; once sunk weathered; once rebated, three						
times grooved						
63 mm x 175 mm	70.20	0.33	3.74	70.20	m	73.94
75 mm x 125 mm	62.34	0.33	3.74	62.34	m	66.08
75 mm x 150 mm	71.46	0.33	3.74	71.46	m	75.20
Bedding and pointing frames						
Pointing wood frames or sills with mastic						
one side	-	0.10	0.80	0.39	m	1.19
both sides	-	0.20	1.59	0.78	m	2.37
Pointing wood frames or sills with polysulphide						
sealant						
one side	-	0.10	0.80	1.18	m	1.98
both sides	-	0.20	1.59	2.35	m	3.94
Bedding wood frames in cement mortar (1:3)						
and point						
one side	-	0.08	1.14	0.06	m	1.20
both sides	-	0.10	1.42	0.08	m	1.50
one side in mortar; other side in mastic	-	0.20	2.22	0.45	m	2.67

L WINDOWS/DOORS/STAIRS Excluding overheads and profit	PC £	Labour hours	Labour £	Material £	Unit	Total rate £
L30 STAIRS/WALKWAYS/BALUSTRADES						
Standard staircases; wrought softwood						
(parana pine)						
Stairs; 25 m thick treads with rounded nosings;						
9 mm thick plywood risers; 32 mm thick strings;						
bullnose bottom tread; 50 mm x 75 mm						
hardwood handrail; 32 mm square plain						
balusters; 100 mm square plain newel posts						
straight flight; 838 mm wide; 2676 mm going;						
2600 mm rise; with two newel posts	-	7.00	79.38	329.45	nr	**408.83**
straight flight with turn; 838 mm wide; 2676 mm						
going; 2600 mm rise; with two newel posts;						
three top treads winding	-	7.00	79.38	414.95	nr	**494.33**
dogleg staircase; 838 mm wide; 2676 mm						
going; 2600 mm rise; with two newel posts;						
quarter space landing third riser from top	-	7.00	79.38	351.95	nr	**431.33**
dogleg staircase; 838 mm wide; 2676 mm						
going; 2600 mm rise; with two newel posts; half						
space landing third riser from top	-	8.00	90.72	369.95	nr	**460.67**
Standard balustrades; wrought softwood						
Landing balustrade; 50 mm x 75 mm hardwood						
handrail; three 32 mm x 140 mm balustrade						
kneerails; two 32 mm x 50 mm stiffeners; one						
end of handrail jointed to newel post; other end						
built into wall; (newel post and mortices both						
not included)						
3.00 m long	-	2.75	31.18	112.50	nr	**143.68**
Landing balustrade; 50 mm x 75 mm hardwood						
handrail; 32 mm square plain balusters; one						
end of handrail jointed to newel post; other end						
built into wall; balusters housed in at bottom						
(newel post and mortices both not included)						
3.00 m long	-	4.00	45.36	67.50	nr	**112.86**
Hardwood staircases; purpose made;						
assembled at works						
Fixing only complete staircase including						
landings, balustrades, etc.						
plugging and screwing to brickwork or blockwork	-	15.00	170.10	1.58	nr	**171.68**
The following are supply only prices for						
purpose made staircase components in						
selected West African Mahogany supplied as						
part of an assembled staircase and may be						
used to arrive at a guide price for a complete						
hardwood staircase						
Board landings; cross-tongued joints; 100 mm						
x 50 mm sawn softwood bearers						
25 mm thick	-	-	-	75.53	m²	**75.53**
32 mm thick	-	-	-	92.63	m²	**92.63**
Treads; cross-tongued joints and risers;						
rounded nosings; tongued, grooved, glued and						
blocked together; one 175 mm x 50 mm sawn						
softwood carriage						
25 mm treads; 19 mm risers	-	-	-	93.53	m²	**93.53**
ends; quadrant	-	-	-	43.30	nr	**43.30**
ends; housed to hardwood	-	-	-	0.80	nr	**0.80**
32 mm treads; 25 mm risers	-	-	-	112.25	m²	**112.25**
ends; quadrant	-	-	-	55.65	nr	**55.65**
ends; housed to hardwood	-	-	-	0.80	nr	**0.80**

L WINDOWS/DOORS/STAIRS Excluding overheads and profit	PC £	Labour hours	Labour £	Material £	Unit	Total rate £
Winders; cross-tongued joints and risers in one width; rounded nosings; tongued, grooved glued and blocked together; one 175 mm x 50 mm sawn softwood carriage						
25 mm treads; 19 mm risers	-	-	-	102.87	m²	102.87
32 mm treads; 25 mm risers	-	-	-	123.48	m²	123.48
wide ends; housed to hardwood	-	-	-	1.60	nr	1.60
narrow ends; housed to hardwood	-	-	-	1.20	nr	1.20
Closed strings; in one width; 230 mm wide; rounded twice						
32 mm thick	-	-	-	19.83	m	19.83
38 mm thick	-	-	-	23.81	m	23.81
50 mm thick	-	-	-	31.45	m	31.45
Closed strings; cross-tongued joints; 280 mm wide; once rounded						
32 mm thick	-	-	-	34.70	m	34.70
extra for short ramp	-	-	-	17.35	nr	17.35
38 mm thick	-	-	-	39.38	m	39.38
extra for short ramp	-	-	-	19.72	nr	19.72
50 mm thick	-	-	-	48.77	m	48.77
extra for short ramp	-	-	-	24.43	nr	24.43
Closed strings; ramped; crossed tongued joints 280 mm wide; once rounded; fixing with screws; plugging 450 mm centres						
32 mm thick	-	-	-	38.20	m	38.20
38 mm thick	-	-	-	43.35	m	43.35
50 mm thick	-	-	-	53.64	m	53.64
Apron linings; in one width 230 mm wide						
19 mm thick	-	-	-	7.86	m	7.86
25 mm thick	-	-	-	9.51	m	9.51
Handrails; rounded						
40 mm x 50 mm	-	-	-	6.55	m	6.55
50 mm x 75 mm	-	-	-	8.19	m	8.19
63 mm x 87 mm	-	-	-	10.60	m	10.60
75 mm x 100 mm	-	-	-	12.87	m	12.87
Handrails; moulded						
40 mm x 50 mm	-	-	-	7.02	m	7.02
50 mm x 75 mm	-	-	-	8.67	m	8.67
63 mm x 87 mm	-	-	-	11.08	m	11.08
75 mm x 100 mm	-	-	-	13.36	m	13.36
Handrails; rounded; ramped						
40 mm x 50 mm	-	-	-	13.09	m	13.09
50 mm x 75 mm	-	-	-	16.40	m	16.40
63 mm x 87 mm	-	-	-	21.21	m	21.21
75 mm x 100 mm	-	-	-	21.00	m	21.00
Handrails; moulded; ramped						
40 mm x 50 mm	-	-	-	14.04	m	14.04
50 mm x 75 mm	-	-	-	17.36	m	17.36
63 mm x 87 mm	-	-	-	22.17	m	22.17
75 mm x 100 mm	-	-	-	26.70	m	26.70
Heading joints to handrail; mitred or raked						
overall size not exceeding 50 mm x 75 mm	-	-	-	22.40	nr	22.40
overall size not exceeding 75 mm x 100 mm	-	-	-	28.53	nr	28.53
Balusters; stiffeners						
25 mm x 25 mm	-	-	-	3.18	m	3.18
32 mm x 32 mm	-	-	-	3.69	m	3.69
50 mm x 50 mm	-	-	-	4.45	m	4.45
ends; housed	-	-	-	1.01	nr	1.01

L WINDOWS/DOORS/STAIRS Excluding overheads and profit	PC £	Labour hours	Labour £	Material £	Unit	Total rate £
L30 STAIRS/WALKWAYS/BALUSTRADES - cont'd						
The following are supply only prices for **purpose made staircase components in** **selected West African Mahogany supplied as** **part of an assembled staircase and may be** **used to arrive at a guide price for a complete** **hardwood staircase** - cont'd						
Sub rails						
32 mm x 63 mm	-	-	-	5.66	m	**5.66**
ends; framed joint to newel	-	-	-	4.07	nr	**4.07**
Knee rails						
32 mm x 140 mm	-	-	-	8.85	m	**8.85**
ends; framed joint to newel	-	-	-	4.07	nr	**4.07**
Newel posts						
50 mm x 100 mm; half newel	-	-	-	9.47	m	**9.47**
75 mm x 75 mm	-	-	-	10.23	m	**10.23**
100 mm x 100 mm	-	-	-	15.80	m	**15.80**
Newel caps; splayed on four sides						
62.50 mm x 125 mm x 50 mm	-	-	-	5.95	nr	**5.95**
100 mm x 100 mm x 50 mm	-	-	-	5.95	nr	**5.95**
125 mm x 125 mm x 50 mm	-	-	-	6.45	nr	**6.45**
The following are supply only prices for **purpose made staircase components in** **selected Oak; supplied as part of an** **assembled staircase**						
Board landings; cross-tongued joints; 100 mm x 50 mm sawn softwood bearers						
25 mm thick	-	-	-	158.87	m²	**158.87**
32 mm thick	-	-	-	195.83	m²	**195.83**
Treads; cross-tongued joints and risers; rounded nosings; tongued, grooved, glued and blocked together; one 175 mm x 50 mm sawn softwood carriage						
25 mm treads; 19 mm risers	-	-	-	173.00	m²	**173.00**
ends; quadrant	-	-	-	86.52	nr	**86.52**
ends; housed to hardwood	-	-	-	1.06	nr	**1.06**
32 mm treads; 25 mm risers	-	-	-	212.97	m²	**212.97**
ends; quadrant	-	-	-	106.50	nr	**106.50**
ends; housed to hardwood	-	-	-	1.06	nr	**1.06**
Winders; cross-tongued joints and risers in one width; rounded nosings; tongued, grooved glued and blocked together; one 175 mm x 50 mm sawn softwood carriage						
25 mm treads; 19 mm risers	-	-	-	190.31	m²	**190.31**
32 mm treads; 25 mm risers	-	-	-	234.28	m²	**234.28**
wide ends; housed to hardwood	-	-	-	2.13	nr	**2.13**
narrow ends; housed to hardwood	-	-	-	1.60	nr	**1.60**
Closed strings; in one width; 230 mm wide; rounded twice						
32 mm thick	-	-	-	41.80	m	**41.80**
38 mm thick	-	-	-	49.82	m	**49.82**
50 mm thick	-	-	-	65.84	m	**65.84**
Closed strings; cross-tongued joints; 280 mm wide; once rounded						
32 mm thick	-	-	-	66.79	m	**66.79**
extra for short ramp	-	-	-	33.39	nr	**33.39**
38 mm thick	-	-	-	76.61	m	**76.61**
extra for short ramp	-	-	-	38.30	nr	**38.30**
50 mm thick	-	-	-	96.40	m	**96.40**
extra for short ramp	-	-	-	48.21	nr	**48.21**

L WINDOWS/DOORS/STAIRS Excluding overheads and profit	PC £	Labour hours	Labour £	Material £	Unit	Total rate £
Closed strings; ramped; crossed tongued						
joints 280 mm wide; once rounded; fixing with						
screws; plugging 450 mm centres						
32 mm thick	-	-	-	73.48	m	73.48
38 mm thick	-	-	-	84.28	m	84.28
50 mm thick	-	-	-	106.04	m	106.04
Apron linings; in one width 230 mm wide						
19 mm thick	-	-	-	19.10	m	19.10
25 mm thick	-	-	-	24.00	m	24.00
Handrails; rounded						
40 mm x 50 mm	-	-	-	13.59	m	13.59
50 mm x 75 mm	-	-	-	18.52	m	18.52
63 mm x 87 mm	-	-	-	25.68	m	25.68
75 mm x 100 mm	-	-	-	32.44	m	32.44
Handrails; moulded						
40 mm x 50 mm	-	-	-	14.23	m	14.23
50 mm x 75 mm	-	-	-	19.15	m	19.15
63 mm x 87 mm	-	-	-	21.57	m	21.57
75 mm x 100 mm	-	-	-	33.08	m	33.08
Handrails; rounded; ramped						
40 mm x 50 mm	-	-	-	27.19	m	27.19
50 mm x 75 mm	-	-	-	37.03	m	37.03
63 mm x 87 mm	-	-	-	51.37	m	51.37
75 mm x 100 mm	-	-	-	64.89	m	64.89
Handrails; moulded; ramped						
40 mm x 50 mm	-	-	-	28.46	m	28.46
50 mm x 75 mm	-	-	-	38.30	m	38.30
63 mm x 87 mm	-	-	-	52.64	m	52.64
75 mm x 100 mm	-	-	-	66.17	m	66.17
Heading joints to handrail; mitred or raked						
overall size not exceeding 50 mm x 75 mm	-	-	-	34.25	nr	34.25
overall size not exceeding 75 mm x 100 mm	-	-	-	41.70	nr	41.70
Balusters; stiffeners						
25 mm x 25 mm	-	-	-	5.18	m	5.18
32 mm x 32 mm	-	-	-	6.66	m	6.66
50 mm x 50 mm	-	-	-	8.94	m	8.94
ends; housed	-	-	-	1.33	nr	1.33
Sub rails						
32 mm x 63 mm	-	-	-	11.41	m	11.41
ends; framed joint to newel	-	-	-	5.42	nr	5.42
Knee rails						
32 mm x 140 mm	-	-	-	20.81	m	20.81
ends; framed joint to newel	-	-	-	5.42	nr	5.42
Newel posts						
50 mm x 100 mm; half newel	-	-	-	22.71	m	22.71
75 mm x 75 mm	-	-	-	24.95	m	24.95
100 mm x 100 mm	-	-	-	41.53	m	41.53
Newel caps; splayed on four sides						
62.50 mm x 125 mm x 50 mm	-	-	-	8.64	nr	8.64
100 mm x 100 mm x 50 mm	-	-	-	8.64	nr	8.64
125 mm x 125 mm x 50 mm	-	-	-	10.12	nr	10.12
Spiral staircases, balustrades and handrails; mild						
steel; galvanised and polyester powder coated						
Staircase						
2080 mm diameter x 3695 mm high; 18 nr treads;						
16 mm diameter intermediate balusters; 1040 mm						
x 1350 mm landing unit with matching balustrade						
both sides; fixing with 16 mm diameter resin						
anchors to masonry at landing and with 12 mm						
diameter expanding bolts to concrete at base	-	-	-	-	nr	3150.00

L WINDOWS/DOORS/STAIRS Excluding overheads and profit	PC £	Labour hours	Labour £	Material £	Unit	Total rate £
L30 STAIRS/WALKWAYS/BALUSTRADES - cont'd						
Aluminium alloy folding loft ladders; "Zig Zag" stairways, model B or other equal and approved; Light Alloy Ltd; on and including plywood backboard; fixing with screws to timber lining (not included)						
Loft ladders						
ceiling height not exceeding 2500 mm; model 888801	-	1.00	11.34	438.52	nr	**449.86**
ceiling height not exceeding 2800 mm; model 888802	-	1.00	11.34	479.39	nr	**490.73**
ceiling height not exceeding 3100 mm; model 888803	-	1.00	11.34	521.03	nr	**532.37**
Flooring, balustrades and handrails; mild steel						
Chequer plate flooring; over 300 mm wide; bolted to steel supports						
6 mm thick	-	-	-	39.95	m²	**39.95**
8 mm thick	-	-	-	51.60	m²	**51.60**
Open grid steel flooring; Eurogrid Ltd; "Safeway" type D38 diamond pattern flooring or other equal and approved to steel supports at 1200 mm centres; galvanised; to BS 729 part 1						
30 mm x 5 mm sections; in one mat; fixing to 10 mm thick channels with type F5 clamps	-	-	-	97.50	m²	**97.50**
Balustrades; welded construction; 1070 mm high; galvanized; 50 mm x 50 mm x 3.20 mm rhs top rail; 38 mm x 13 mm bottom rail, 50 mm x 50 mm x 3.20 mm rhs standards at 1830 mm centres with base plate drilled and bolted to concrete; 13 mm x 13 mm balusters at 102 mm centres	-	-	-	95.00	m	**95.00**
Balusters; isolated; one end ragged and cemented in; one 76 mm x 25 mm x 6 mm flange plate welded on; ground to a smooth finish; countersunk drilled and tap screwed to underside of handrail						
19 mm square; 914 mm long bar	-	-	-	13.10	nr	**13.10**
Core-rails; joints prepared, welded and ground to a smooth finish; fixing on brackets (not included)						
38 mm x 10 mm flat bar	-	-	-	17.50	m	**17.50**
50 mm x 8 mm flat bar	-	-	-	16.75	m	**16.75**
Handrails; joints prepared, welded and ground to a smooth finish; fixing on brackets (not included)						
38 mm x 12 mm half oval bar	-	-	-	23.30	m	**23.30**
44 mm x 13 mm half oval bar	-	-	-	25.10	m	**25.10**
Handrail bracket; comprising 40 mm x 5 mm plate with mitred and welded angle; one end welded to 100 mm diameter x 5 mm backplate; three times holed and plugged and screwed to brickwork; other end scribed and welded to underside of handrail						
140 mm girth	-	-	-	13.85	nr	**13.85**
Holes						
Holes; countersunk; for screws or bolts						
6 mm diameter; 3 mm thick	-	-	-	0.70	nr	**0.70**
6 mm diameter; 6 mm thick	-	-	-	1.05	nr	**1.05**
8 mm diameter; 6 mm thick	-	-	-	1.05	nr	**1.05**
10 mm diameter; 6 mm thick	-	-	-	1.10	nr	**1.10**
12 mm diameter; 8 mm thick	-	-	-	1.40	nr	**1.40**
Balustrades; stainless steel BS 970 grade 316; TIG welded joints; mirror polished finish						
Raking balustrade; comprising 40 mm handrail on 40 mm standards at 1.00 m centres with two 16 mm diameter intermediate standards						
1.00 m high	-	-	-	525.00	m	**525.00**

L WINDOWS/DOORS/STAIRS
Excluding overheads and profit

L40 GENERAL GLAZING

BASIC GLASS PRICES (£/m²)

Trade cut prices - all to limiting sizes

	£		£		£		£
Ordinary transluscent/patterned glass							
2 mm	14.50	5 mm	30.00	12 mm	100.00	25 mm	215.00
3 mm	18.00	6 mm	35.00	15 mm	110.00		
4 mm	20.00	10 mm	70.00	19 mm	155.00		
Obscured ground sheet glass - extra on sheet glass prices							
PC £10.00/m²							
Patterned							
4 mm tinted	26.50	4 mm white	15.00	6 mm white	25.50		
Rough cast							
6 mm	20.00	10 mm	77.75				
Ordinary Georgian wired							
7 mm cast	21.15	6 mm polish	55.55				
Polycarbonate standard sheets							
2 mm	37.75	3 mm	55.55	4 mm	72.25	5 mm	89.00
6 mm	111.10	8 mm	144.50	10 mm	166.50	12 mm	211.00

SPECIAL GLASSES

"Antisun"; float; bronze grey							
4 mm	40.00	6 mm	55.55				
10 mm	127.75	12 mm	160.00				
"Cetuff" toughened							
- float							
4 mm	30.00	5 mm	35.55	6 mm	40.00	10 mm	77.75
12 mm	115.00						
- patterened							
6 mm rough	75.55	10 mm rough	110.00	4 mm white	35.00	6 mm white	45.00
Clear laminated							
- security							
7.50 mm	90.00	9.50 mm	95.00	11.50 mm	100.00		
- safety							
4.40 mm	45.00	5.40 mm	47.50	6.40 mm	50.00	6.80 mm	60.00
8.80 mm	75.00	10.80 mm	90.00				
"Permawal"							
- reflective							
6 mm	75.00	10 mm	110.00				
"Permasol"							
6 mm	105.00						
"Silvered"							
2 mm	27.50	3 mm	30.50	4 mm	33.50	6 mm	44.50
"Silvered tinted"							
4 mm bronze	52.50	6 mm bronze	72.50	4 mm grey	52.50	6 mm grey	72.50
"Venetian striped"							
4 mm	90.00	6 mm	100.00				

Trade discounts of 30 - 50% are usually available off the above prices. The following "measured rates" are provided by a glazing sub-contractor and assume in excess of 500 m², within 20 miles of the suppliers branch. Therefore deduction of "trade prices for cut sizes" from "measured rates" is not a reliable basis for identifying fixing costs.

L WINDOWS/DOORS/STAIRS Excluding overheads and profit	PC £	Labour hours	Labour £	Material £	Unit	Total rate £
L40 GENERAL GLAZING - cont'd						
Standard plain glass; BS 952; clear float; **panes area 0.15 m² - 4.00 m²**						
3 mm thick; glazed with						
putty or bradded beads	-	-	-	-	m²	19.52
bradded beads and butyl compound	-	-	-	-	m²	19.52
screwed beads	-	-	-	-	m²	22.11
screwed beads and butyl compound	-	-	-	-	m²	22.11
4 mm thick; glazed with						
putty or bradded beads	-	-	-	-	m²	20.54
bradded beads and butyl compound	-	-	-	-	m²	20.54
screwed beads	-	-	-	-	m²	23.13
screwed beads and butyl compound	-	-	-	-	m²	23.13
5 mm thick; glazed with						
putty or bradded beads	-	-	-	-	m²	24.65
bradded beads and butyl compound	-	-	-	-	m²	24.65
screwed beads	-	-	-	-	m²	27.24
screwed beads and butyl compound	-	-	-	-	m²	27.24
6 mm thick; glazed with						
putty or bradded beads	-	-	-	-	m²	25.67
bradded beads and butyl compound	-	-	-	-	m²	25.67
screwed beads	-	-	-	-	m²	28.26
screwed beads and butyl compound	-	-	-	-	m²	28.26
Standard plain glass; BS 952; white patterned; **panes area 0.15 m² - 4.00 m²**						
4 mm thick; glazed with						
putty or bradded beads	-	-	-	-	m²	23.13
bradded beads and butyl compound	-	-	-	-	m²	23.13
screwed beads	-	-	-	-	m²	25.67
screwed beads and butyl compound	-	-	-	-	m²	25.67
6 mm thick; glazed with						
putty or bradded beads	-	-	-	-	m²	28.26
bradded beads and butyl compound	-	-	-	-	m²	28.26
screwed beads	-	-	-	-	m²	30.85
screwed beads and butyl compound	-	-	-	-	m²	30.85
Standard plain glass; BS 952; rough cast; **panes area 0.15 m² - 4.00 m²**						
6 mm thick; glazed with						
putty or bradded beads	-	-	-	-	m²	30.85
bradded beads and butyl compound	-	-	-	-	m²	30.85
screwed beads	-	-	-	-	m²	33.39
screwed beads and butyl compound	-	-	-	-	m²	33.39
Standard plain glass; BS 952; Georgian wired **cast; panes area 0.15 m² - 4.00 m²**						
7 mm thick; glazed with						
putty or bradded beads	-	-	-	-	m²	33.39
bradded beads and butyl compound	-	-	-	-	m²	33.39
screwed beads	-	-	-	-	m²	36.08
screwed beads and butyl compound	-	-	-	-	m²	36.08
Extra for lining up wired glass	-	-	-	-	m²	2.59
Standard plain glass; BS 952; Georgian wired **polished; panes area 0.15 m² - 4.00 m²**						
6 mm thick; glazed with						
putty or bradded beads	-	-	-	-	m²	61.65
bradded beads and butyl compound	-	-	-	-	m²	61.65
screwed beads	-	-	-	-	m²	64.29
screwed beads and butyl compound	-	-	-	-	m²	64.29

L WINDOWS/DOORS/STAIRS Excluding overheads and profit	PC £	Labour hours	Labour £	Material £	Unit	Total rate £
Extra for lining up wired glass	-	-	-	-	m²	2.59
Special glass; BS 952; toughened clear float; panes area 0.15 m² - 4.00 m²						
4 mm thick; glazed with						
putty or bradded beads	-	-	-	-	m²	23.13
bradded beads and butyl compound	-	-	-	-	m²	23.13
screwed beads	-	-	-	-	m²	25.67
screwed beads and butyl compound	-	-	-	-	m²	25.67
5 mm thick; glazed with						
putty or bradded beads	-	-	-	-	m²	30.85
bradded beads and butyl compound	-	-	-	-	m²	30.85
screwed beads	-	-	-	-	m²	33.39
screwed beads and butyl compound	-	-	-	-	m²	33.39
6 mm thick; glazed with						
putty or bradded beads	-	-	-	-	m²	30.85
bradded beads and butyl compound	-	-	-	-	m²	30.85
screwed beads	-	-	-	-	m²	33.39
screwed beads and butyl compound	-	-	-	-	m²	33.39
10 mm thick; glazed with						
putty or bradded beads	-	-	-	-	m²	61.65
bradded beads and butyl compound	-	-	-	-	m²	61.65
screwed beads	-	-	-	-	m²	64.29
screwed beads and butyl compound	-	-	-	-	m²	64.29
Special glass; BS 952; clear laminated safety glass; panes area 0.15 m² - 4.00 m²						
4.40 mm thick; glazed with						
putty or bradded beads	-	-	-	-	m²	50.88
bradded beads and butyl compound	-	-	-	-	m²	50.88
screwed beads	-	-	-	-	m²	52.26
screwed beads and butyl compound	-	-	-	-	m²	52.26
5.40 mm thick; glazed with						
putty or bradded beads	-	-	-	-	m²	61.65
bradded beads and butyl compound	-	-	-	-	m²	61.65
screwed beads	-	-	-	-	m²	64.29
screwed beads and butyl compound	-	-	-	-	m²	64.29
6.40 mm thick; glazed with						
putty or bradded beads	-	-	-	-	m²	67.53
bradded beads and butyl compound	-	-	-	-	m²	67.53
screwed beads	-	-	-	-	m²	74.46
screwed beads and butyl compound	-	-	-	-	m²	74.46
Special glass; BS 952; "Pyran" half-hour fire resisting glass or other equal and approved						
6.50 mm thick rectangular panes; glazed with screwed hardwood beads and Sealmaster "Fireglaze" intumescent compound or other equal and approved to rebated frame						
300 mm x 400 mm pane	-	0.40	5.76	24.74	nr	30.50
400 mm x 800 mm pane	-	0.50	7.21	61.75	nr	68.96
500 mm x 1400 mm pane	-	0.80	11.53	130.89	nr	142.42
600 mm x 1800 mm pane	-	1.00	14.41	221.76	nr	236.17
Special glass; BS 952; "Pyrostop" one-hour fire resisting glass or other equal and approved						
15 mm thick regular panes; glazed with screwed hardwood beads and Sealmaster "Fireglaze" intumescent liner and compound or other equal and approved both sides						
300 mm x 400 mm pane	-	1.20	17.29	55.53	nr	72.82
400 mm x 800 mm pane	-	1.50	21.61	108.65	nr	130.26
500 mm x 1400 mm pane	-	2.00	28.82	214.85	nr	243.67
600 mm x 1800 mm pane	-	2.50	36.02	313.96	nr	349.98

L WINDOWS/DOORS/STAIRS Excluding overheads and profit	PC £	Labour hours	Labour £	Material £	Unit	Total rate £
L40 GENERAL GLAZING - cont'd						
Special glass; BS 952; clear laminated security glass 7.50 mm thick regular panes; glazed with screwed hardwood beads and "Intergens" intumescent strip or other equal and approved						
300 mm x 400 mm pane	-	0.40	5.76	15.13	nr	**20.89**
400 mm x 800 mm pane	-	0.50	7.21	36.49	nr	**43.70**
500 mm x 1400 mm pane	-	0.80	11.53	75.64	nr	**87.17**
600 mm x 1800 mm pane	-	1.00	14.41	136.36	nr	**150.77**
Mirror panels; BS 952; silvered; insulation backing 4 mm thick float; fixing with adhesive						
1000 mm x 1000 mm	-	-	-	-	nr	**134.13**
1000 mm x 2000 mm	-	-	-	-	nr	**254.38**
1000 mm x 4000 mm	-	-	-	-	nr	**490.25**
Glass louvres; BS 952; with long edges ground or smooth 6 mm thick float						
150 mm wide	-	-	-	-	m	**10.41**
7 mm thick Georgian wired cast						
150 mm wide	-	-	-	-	m	**14.34**
6 mm thick Georgian wire polished						
150 mm wide	-	-	-	-	m	**20.58**
Factory made double hermetically sealed units; to wood or metal with screwed or clipped beads Two panes; BS 952; clear float glass; 4 mm thick; 6 mm air space						
2.00 m² - 4.00 m²	-	-	-	-	m²	**43.94**
1.00 m² - 2.00 m²	-	-	-	-	m²	**43.94**
0.75 m² - 1.00 m²	-	-	-	-	m²	**43.94**
0.50 m² - 0.75 m²	-	-	-	-	m²	**43.94**
0.35 m² - 0.50 m²	-	-	-	-	m²	**43.94**
0.25 m² - 0.35 m²	-	-	-	-	m²	**43.94**
not exceeding 0.25 m²	-	-	-	-	nr	**11.10**
Two panes; BS 952; clear float glass; 6 mm thick; 6 mm air space						
2.00 m² - 4.00 m²	-	-	-	-	m²	**54.11**
1.00 m² - 2.00 m²	-	-	-	-	m²	**54.11**
0.75 m² - 1.00 m²	-	-	-	-	m²	**54.11**
0.50 m² - 0.75 m²	-	-	-	-	m²	**54.11**
0.35 m² - 0.50 m²	-	-	-	-	m²	**54.11**
0.25 m² - 0.35 m²	-	-	-	-	m²	**54.11**
not exceeding 0.25 m²	-	-	-	-	nr	**13.88**

M SURFACE FINISHES Excluding overheads and profit	PC £	Labour hours	Labour £	Material £	Unit	Total rate £
M SURFACE FINISHES						
M10 CEMENT:SAND/CONCRETE SCREEDS/ TOPPINGS						
Cement:sand (1:3); steel trowelled						
Work to floors; one coat; level and to falls not						
exceeding 15 degrees from horizontal; to						
concrete base; over 300 mm wide						
32 mm thick	-	0.29	3.25	1.90	m²	**5.15**
40 mm thick	-	0.31	3.47	2.38	m²	**5.85**
48 mm thick	-	0.33	3.69	2.86	m²	**6.55**
50 mm thick	-	0.34	3.80	2.98	m²	**6.78**
60 mm thick	-	0.37	4.14	3.57	m²	**7.71**
65 mm thick	-	0.40	4.48	3.87	m²	**8.35**
70 mm thick	-	0.41	4.59	4.17	m²	**8.76**
75 mm thick	-	0.42	4.70	4.46	m²	**9.16**
Add to the above for work to falls and crossfalls						
and to slopes						
not exceeding 15 degrees from horizontal	-	0.03	0.34	-	m²	**0.34**
over 15 degrees from horizontal	-	0.10	1.12	-	m²	**1.12**
water repellent additive incorporated in the mix	-	0.03	0.34	0.49	m²	**0.83**
oil repellent additive incorporated in the mix	-	0.08	0.90	3.43	m²	**4.33**
Cement:sand (1:3) beds and backings						
Work to floors; one coat level; to concrete base;						
screeded; over 300 mm wide						
25 mm thick	-	-	-	-	m²	**7.23**
50 mm thick	-	-	-	-	m²	**8.53**
75 mm thick	-	-	-	-	m²	**11.14**
100 mm thick	-	-	-	-	m²	**13.76**
Work to floors; one coat; level; to concrete base;						
steel trowelled; over 300 mm wide						
25 mm thick	-	-	-	-	m²	**7.23**
50 mm thick	-	-	-	-	m²	**8.53**
75 mm thick	-	-	-	-	m²	**11.14**
100 mm thick	-	-	-	-	m²	**13.76**
Fine concrete (1:4) beds and backings						
Work to floors; one coat; level; to concrete base;						
steel trowelled; over 300 mm wide						
50 mm thick	-	-	-	-	m²	**8.33**
75 mm thick	-	-	-	-	m²	**10.68**
Granolithic paving; cement and granite						
chippings 5 mm to dust (1:1:2); steel trowelled						
Work to floors; one coat; level; laid on concrete						
while green; over 300 mm wide						
20 mm thick	-	-	-	-	m²	**13.07**
25 mm thick	-	-	-	-	m²	**14.11**
Work to floors; two coat; laid on hacked						
concrete with slurry; over 300 mm wide						
38 mm thick	-	-	-	-	m²	**16.83**
50 mm thick	-	-	-	-	m²	**19.34**
75 mm thick	-	-	-	-	m²	**26.14**
Work to landings; one coat; level; laid on						
concrete while green; over 300 mm wide						
20 mm thick	-	-	-	-	m²	**14.64**
25 mm thick	-	-	-	-	m²	**15.68**

M SURFACE FINISHES Excluding overheads and profit	PC £	Labour hours	Labour £	Material £	Unit	Total rate £
M10 CEMENT:SAND/CONCRETE SCREEDS/ TOPPINGS - cont'd						
Granolithic paving; cement and granite chippings 5 mm to dust (1:1:2); steel trowelled - cont'd						
Work to landings; two coat; laid on hacked concrete with slurry; over 300 mm wide						
38 mm thick	-	-	-	-	m²	18.40
50 mm thick	-	-	-	-	m²	20.91
75 mm thick	-	-	-	-	m²	27.71
Add to the above over 300 mm wide for						
liquid hardening additive incorporated in the mix	-	0.05	0.56	0.58	m²	1.14
oil-repellent additive incorporated in the mix	-	0.08	0.90	3.43	m²	4.33
25 mm work to treads; one coat; to concrete base						
225 mm wide	-	0.90	12.97	6.25	m	19.22
275 mm wide	-	0.90	12.97	7.00	m	19.97
returned end	-	0.18	2.59	-	nr	2.59
13 mm skirtings; rounded top edge and coved bottom junction; to brickwork or blockwork base						
75 mm wide on face	-	0.55	7.93	0.30	m	8.23
150 mm wide on face	-	0.75	10.81	5.50	m	16.31
ends; fair	-	0.05	0.72	-	nr	0.72
angles	-	0.07	1.01	-	nr	1.01
13 mm outer margin to stairs; to follow profile of and with rounded nosing to treads and risers; fair edge and arris at bottom, to concrete base						
75 mm wide	-	0.90	12.97	3.00	m	15.97
angles	-	0.07	1.01	-	nr	1.01
13 mm wall string to stairs; fair edge and arris on top; coved bottom junction with treads and risers; to brickwork or blockwork base						
275 mm (extreme) wide	-	0.80	11.53	5.25	m	16.78
ends	-	0.05	0.72	-	nr	0.72
angles	-	0.07	1.01	-	nr	1.01
ramps	-	0.08	1.15	-	nr	1.15
ramped and wreathed corners	-	0.10	1.44	-	nr	1.44
13 mm outer string to stairs; rounded nosing on top at junction with treads and risers; fair edge and arris at bottom; to concrete base						
300 mm (extreme) wide	-	0.80	11.53	6.50	m	18.03
ends	-	0.05	0.72	-	nr	0.72
angles	-	0.07	1.01	-	nr	1.01
ramps	-	0.08	1.15	-	nr	1.15
ramps and wreathed corners	-	0.10	1.44	-	nr	1.44
19 mm thick skirtings; rounded top edge and coved bottom junction; to brickwork or blockwork base						
75 mm wide on face	-	0.55	7.93	5.50	m	13.43
150 mm wide on face	-	0.75	10.81	8.50	m	19.31
ends; fair	-	0.05	0.56	-	nr	0.56
angles	-	0.07	1.01	-	nr	1.01
19 mm riser; one rounded nosing; to concrete base						
150 mm high; plain	-	0.90	12.97	4.75	m	17.72
150 mm high; undercut	-	0.90	12.97	4.75	m	17.72
180 mm high; plain	-	0.90	12.97	6.50	m	19.47
180 mm high; undercut	-	0.90	12.97	6.50	m	19.47

M SURFACE FINISHES Excluding overheads and profit	PC £	Labour hours	Labour £	Material £	Unit	Total rate £
M11 MASTIC ASPHALT FLOORING/FLOOR UNDERLAYS						
Mastic asphalt flooring to BS 6925 Type F 1076; black						
20 mm thick; one coat coverings; felt isolating membrane; to concrete base; flat						
over 300 mm wide	-	-	-	-	m²	9.90
225 mm - 300 mm wide	-	-	-	-	m²	18.40
150 mm - 225 mm wide	-	-	-	-	m²	20.20
not exceeding 150 mm wide	-	-	-	-	m²	24.70
25 mm thick; one coat coverings; felt isolating membrane; to concrete base; flat						
over 300 mm wide	-	-	-	-	m²	11.50
225 mm - 300 mm wide	-	-	-	-	m²	19.60
150 mm - 225 mm wide	-	-	-	-	m²	21.40
not exceeding 150 mm wide	-	-	-	-	m²	25.90
20 mm three coat skirtings to brickwork base						
not exceeding 150 mm girth	-	-	-	-	m	9.90
150 mm - 225 mm girth	-	-	-	-	m	11.50
225 mm - 300 mm girth	-	-	-	-	m	13.00
Mastic asphalt flooring; acid-resisting; black						
20 mm thick; one coat coverings; felt isolating membrane; to concrete base flat						
over 300 mm wide	-	-	-	-	m²	11.60
225 mm - 300 mm wide	-	-	-	-	m²	21.20
150 mm - 225 mm wide	-	-	-	-	m²	21.90
not exceeding 150 mm wide	-	-	-	-	m²	26.40
25 mm thick; one coat coverings; felt isolating membrane; to concrete base; flat						
over 300 mm wide	-	-	-	-	m²	13.70
225 mm - 300 mm wide	-	-	-	-	m²	21.80
150 mm - 225 mm wide	-	-	-	-	m²	23.60
not exceeding 150 mm wide	-	-	-	-	m²	28.10
20 mm thick; three coat skirtings to brickwork base						
not exceeding 150 mm girth	-	-	-	-	m	10.20
150 mm - 225 mm girth	-	-	-	-	m	11.90
225 mm - 300 mm girth	-	-	-	-	m	13.50
Mastic asphalt flooring to BS 6925 Type F 1451; red						
20 mm thick; one coat coverings; felt isolating membrane; to concrete base; flat						
over 300 mm wide	-	-	-	-	m²	16.20
225 mm - 300 mm wide	-	-	-	-	m²	26.80
150 mm - 225 mm wide	-	-	-	-	m²	28.90
not exceeding 150 mm wide	-	-	-	-	m²	34.60
20 mm thick; three coat skirtings to brickwork base						
not exceeding 150 mm girth	-	-	-	-	m	12.70
150 mm - 225 mm girth	-	-	-	-	m	16.20
M12 TROWELLED BITUMEN/RESIN/RUBBER LATEXFLOORING						
Latex cement floor screeds; steel trowelled						
Work to floors; level; to concrete base; over 300 mm wide						
3 mm thick; one coat	-	-	-	-	m²	3.35
5 mm thick; two coats	-	-	-	-	m²	4.75

M SURFACE FINISHES Excluding overheads and profit	PC £	Labour hours	Labour £	Material £	Unit	Total rate £
M12 TROWELLED BITUMEN/RESIN/RUBBER LATEXFLOORING - cont'd						
Epoxy resin flooring; Altro "Altroflow 3000" or other equal and approved; steel trowelled						
Work to floors; level; to concrete base; over 300 mm wide						
3 mm thick; one coat	-	-	-	-	m²	20.86
Isocrete K screeds or other equal and approved; steel trowelled						
Work to floors; level; to concrete base; over 300 mm wide						
35 mm thick; plus polymer bonder coat	-	-	-	-	m²	11.08
40 mm thick	-	-	-	-	m²	9.78
45 mm thick	-	-	-	-	m²	10.03
50 mm thick	-	-	-	-	m²	10.30
Work to floors; to falls or cross-falls; to concrete base; over 300 mm wide						
55 mm (average) thick	-	-	-	-	m²	11.35
60 mm (average) thick	-	-	-	-	m²	11.87
65 mm (average) thick	-	-	-	-	m²	12.39
75 mm (average) thick	-	-	-	-	m²	13.44
90 mm (average) thick	-	-	-	-	m²	15.01
Bituminous lightweight insulating roof screeds						
"Bit-Ag" roof screed or other equal and approved; to falls or cross-falls; bitumen felt vapour barrier; over 300 mm wide						
75 mm (average) thick	-	-	-	-	m²	26.00
100 mm (average) thick	-	-	-	-	m²	33.00
M20 PLASTERED/RENDERED/ROUGHCAST COATINGS						
Cement:sand (1:3) beds and backings						
10 mm thick work to walls; one coat; to brickwork or blockwork base						
over 300 mm wide	-	-	-	-	m²	8.17
not exceeding 300 mm wide	-	-	-	-	m	4.08
13 mm thick; work to walls; two coats; to brickwork or blockwork base						
over 300 mm wide	-	-	-	-	m²	9.77
not exceeding 300 mm wide	-	-	-	-	m	4.89
15 mm thick work to walls; two coats; to brickwork or blockwork base						
over 300 mm wide	-	-	-	-	m²	10.55
not exceeding 300 mm wide	-	-	-	-	m	5.27
Cement:sand (1:3); steel trowelled						
13 mm thick work to walls; two coats; to brickwork or blockwork base						
over 300 mm wide	-	-	-	-	m²	9.52
not exceeding 300 mm wide	-	-	-	-	m	4.76
16 mm thick work to walls; two coats; to brickwork or blockwork base						
over 300 mm wide	-	-	-	-	m²	10.67
not exceeding 300 mm wide	-	-	-	-	m	5.34
19 mm thick work to walls; two coats; to brickwork or blockwork base						
over 300 mm wide	-	-	-	-	m²	11.81
not exceeding 300 mm wide	-	-	-	-	m	5.90

M SURFACE FINISHES Excluding overheads and profit	PC £	Labour hours	Labour £	Material £	Unit	Total rate £
ADD to above						
over 300 mm wide in water repellant cement	-	-	-	-	m²	2.41
finishing coat in colour cement	-	-	-	-	m²	5.57
Cement:lime:sand (1:2:9); steel trowelled						
19 mm thick work to walls; two coats; to						
brickwork or blockwork base						
over 300 mm wide	-	-	-	-	m²	11.94
not exceeding 300 mm wide	-	-	-	-	m	5.98
Cement:lime:sand (1:1:6); steel trowelled						
13 mm thick work to walls; two coats; to						
brickwork or blockwork base						
over 300 mm wide	-	-	-	-	m²	9.67
not exceeding 300 mm wide	-	-	-	-	m	4.83
Add to the above over 300 mm wide for						
waterproof additive	-	-	-	-	m²	1.65
19 mm thick work to ceilings; three coats; to						
metal lathing base						
over 300 mm wide	-	-	-	-	m²	14.66
not exceeding 300 mm wide	-	-	-	-	m	7.56
Sto External Render System; Type 4 or other **equal and approved; CCS Scotseal Ltd**						
10 mm thick Sto Fibrecoat; glassfibre						
reinforcing mesh; one coat Sto primer; to						
brickwork or blockwork base						
over 300 mm wide	-	0.83	13.47	21.85	m²	35.32
Plaster; first and finishing coats of "Carlite" **pre-mixed lightweight plaster or other** **equal and approved; steel trowelled**						
13 mm thick work to walls; two coats; to						
brickwork or blockwork base (or 10 mm thick						
work to concrete base)						
over 300 mm wide	-	-	-	-	m²	6.96
over 300 mm wide; in staircase areas or plant rooms	-	-	-	-	m²	8.02
not exceeding 300 mm wide	-	-	-	-	m	3.47
13 mm thick work to isolated piers or columns;						
two coats						
over 300 mm wide	-	-	-	-	m²	8.55
not exceeding 300 mm wide	-	-	-	-	m	4.28
10 mm thick work to ceilings; two coats; to						
concrete base						
over 300 mm wide	-	-	-	-	m²	7.45
over 300 wide; 3.50 m - 5.00 m high	-	-	-	-	m²	7.98
over 300 mm wide; in staircase areas or plant rooms	-	-	-	-	m²	8.51
not exceeding 300 mm wide	-	-	-	-	m	3.72
10 mm thick work to isolated beams; two coats;						
to concrete base						
over 300 mm wide	-	-	-	-	m²	9.05
over 300 mm wide; 3.50 m - 5.00 m high	-	-	-	-	m²	9.59
not exceeding 300 mm wide	-	-	-	-	m	4.52

M SURFACE FINISHES Excluding overheads and profit	PC £	Labour hours	Labour £	Material £	Unit	Total rate £
M20 PLASTERED/RENDERED/ROUGHCAST COATINGS - cont'd						
Plaster; first coat of "Thistle Hardwall" plaster or other equal and approved; finishing coat of "Thistle Multi Finish" plaster or other equal and approved; steel trowelled						
13 mm thick work to walls; two coats; to brickwork or blockwork base						
over 300 mm wide	-	-	-	-	m²	7.55
over 300 mm wide; in staircase areas or plant rooms	-	-	-	-	m²	8.67
not exceeding 300 mm wide	-	-	-	-	m	3.79
13 mm thick work to isolated columns; two coats						
over 300 mm wide	-	-	-	-	m²	9.23
not exceeding 300 mm wide	-	-	-	-	m	4.62
Plaster; one coat "Snowplast" plaster or other equal and approved; steel trowelled						
13 mm thick work to walls; one coat; to brickwork or blockwork base						
over 300 mm wide	-	-	-	-	m²	8.06
over 300 mm wide; in staircase areas or plant rooms	-	-	-	-	m²	9.18
not exceeding 300 mm wide	-	-	-	-	m	4.03
13 thick work to isolated columns; one coat						
over 300 mm wide	-	-	-	-	m²	9.73
not exceeding 300 mm wide	-	-	-	-	m	4.88
Plaster; first coat of cement:sand (1:3); finishing coat of "Thistle" class B plaster or other equal and approved; steel trowelled						
13 mm thick; work to walls; two coats; to brickwork or blockwork base						
over 300 mm wide	-	-	-	-	m²	7.71
over 300 mm wide; in staircase areas or plant rooms	-	-	-	-	m²	8.82
not exceeding 300 mm wide	-	-	-	-	m	3.86
13 mm thick work to isolated columns; two coats						
over 300 mm wide	-	-	-	-	m²	9.94
not exceeding 300 mm wide	-	-	-	-	m	4.97
Plaster; first coat of cement:lime:sand (1:1:6); finishing coat of "Multi Finish" plaster or other equal and approved; steel trowelled						
13 mm thick work to walls; two coats; to brickwork or blockwork base						
over 300 mm wide	-	-	-	-	m²	7.93
over 300 mm wide; in staircase areas or plant rooms	-	-	-	-	m²	9.05
not exceeding 300 mm wide	-	-	-	-	m	3.79
13 mm thick work to isolated columns; two coats						
over 300 mm wide	-	-	-	-	m²	9.23
not exceeding 300 mm wide	-	-	-	-	m	4.62

M SURFACE FINISHES Excluding overheads and profit	PC £	Labour hours	Labour £	Material £	Unit	Total rate £
Plaster; first coat of "Limelite" renovating plaster or other equal and approved; finishing coat of "Limelite" renovating plaster or other equal and approved; finishing coat of "Limelite" finishing plaster or other equal and approved; steel trowelled						
13 mm thick work to walls; two coats; to brickwork or blockwork base						
over 300 mm wide	-	-	-	-	m²	11.13
over 300 mm wide; in staircase areas or plant rooms	-	-	-	-	m²	12.25
not exceeding 300 mm wide	-	-	-	-	m	5.57
Dubbing out existing walls with undercoat plaster; average 6 mm thick						
over 300 mm wide	-	-	-	-	m²	3.35
not exceeding 300 mm wide	-	-	-	-	m	1.68
Dubbing out existing walls with undercoat plaster; average 12 mm thick						
over 300 mm wide	-	-	-	-	m²	6.69
not exceeding 300 mm wide	-	-	-	-	m	3.35
Plaster; first coat of "Thistle X-ray" plaster or other equal and approved; finishing coat of "Thistle X-ray" finishing plaster or other equal and approved; steel trowelled						
17 mm thick work to walls; two coats; to brickwork or blockwork base						
over 300 mm wide	-	-	-	-	m²	36.20
over 300 mm wide; in staircase areas or plant rooms	-	-	-	-	m²	37.31
not exceeding 300 mm wide	-	-	-	-	m	14.48
17 mm thick work to isolated columns; two coats						
over 300 mm wide	-	-	-	-	m²	39.54
not exceeding 300 mm wide	-	-	-	-	m	15.81
Plaster; one coat "Thistle" projection plaster or other equal and approved; steel trowelled						
13 mm thick work to walls; one coat; to brickwork or blockwork base						
over 300 mm wide	-	-	-	-	m²	7.77
over 300 mm wide; in staircase areas or plant rooms	-	-	-	-	m²	8.88
not exceeding 300 mm wide	-	-	-	-	m	3.88
10 mm thick work to isolated columns; one coat						
over 300 mm wide	-	-	-	-	m²	9.44
not exceeding 300 mm wide	-	-	-	-	m	4.72
Plaster; first, second and finishing coats of "Carlite" pre-mixed lightweight plaster or other equal and approved; steel trowelled						
13 mm thick work to ceilings; three coats to metal lathing base						
over 300 mm wide	-	-	-	-	m²	10.04
over 300 mm wide; in staircase areas or plant rooms	-	-	-	-	m²	11.16
not exceeding 300 mm wide	-	-	-	-	m	5.01
13 mm thick work to swept soffit of metal lathing arch former						
not exceeding 300 mm wide	-	-	-	-	m	6.69
300 mm - 400 mm wide	-	-	-	-	m	8.92
13 mm thick work to vertical face of metal lathing arch former						
not exceeding 0.50 m² per side	-	-	-	-	nr	9.49
0.50 m² - 1.00 m² per side	-	-	-	-	nr	14.23

M SURFACE FINISHES Excluding overheads and profit	PC £	Labour hours	Labour £	Material £	Unit	Total rate £
M20 PLASTERED/RENDERED/ROUGHCAST COATINGS - cont'd						
Squash court plaster, Prodorite Ltd; first coat "Formula Base" screed or other equal and approved; finishing coat "Formula 90" finishing plaster or other equal and approved; steel trowelled and finished with sponge float						
12 mm thick work to walls; two coats; to brickwork or blockwork base						
over 300 mm wide	-	-	-	-	m²	26.25
not exceeding 300 mm wide	-	-	-	-	m	13.15
demarcation lines on battens	-	-	-	-	m	3.80
"Cemrend" self-coloured render or other equal and approved; one coat; to brickwork or blockwork base						
20 mm thick work to walls; to brickwork or blockwork base						
over 300 mm wide	-	-	-	-	m²	25.00
not exceeding 300 mm wide	-	-	-	-	m	14.50
Tyrolean decorative rendering or other equal and approved; 13 mm thick first coat of cement: lime:sand (1:1:6); finishing three coats of "Cullamix'" or other equal and approved; applied with approved hand operated machine external						
To walls; four coats; to brickwork or blockwork base						
over 300 mm wide	-	-	-	-	m²	17.82
not exceeding 300 mm wide	-	-	-	-	m	8.91
Drydash (pebbledash) finish of Derbyshire Spar chippings or other equal and approved on and including cement:lime:sand (1:2:9) backing						
18 mm thick work to walls; two coats; to brickwork or blockwork base						
over 300 mm wide	-	-	-	-	m²	16.39
not exceeding 300 mm wide	-	-	-	-	m	8.21
Plaster; one coat "Thistle" board finish or other equal and approved; steel trowelled (prices included within plasterboard rates)						
3 mm thick work to walls or ceilings; one coat; to plasterboard base						
over 300 mm wide	-	-	-	-	m²	3.95
over 300 mm wide; in staircase areas or plant rooms	-	-	-	-	m²	4.50
not exceeding 300 mm wide	-	-	-	-	m	2.36
Plaster; one coat "Thistle" board finish or other equal and approved; steel trowelled 3 mm work to walls or ceilings; one coat on and including gypsum plasterboard; BS 1230; fixing with nails; 3 mm joints filled with plaster and jute scrim cloth; to softwood base; plain grade baseboard or lath with rounded edges						
9.50 mm thick boards to walls						
over 300 mm wide	-	1.05	7.98	2.19	m²	10.17
not exceeding 300 mm wide	-	0.40	3.18	0.40	m²	3.58
9.50 mm thick boards to walls; in staircase areas or plant rooms						
over 300 mm wide	-	1.15	8.78	2.19	m²	10.97
not exceeding 300 mm wide	-	0.50	3.98	0.40	m²	4.38

M SURFACE FINISHES Excluding overheads and profit	PC £	Labour hours	Labour £	Material £	Unit	Total rate £
9.50 mm thick boards to isolated columns						
over 300 mm wide	-	1.15	8.78	2.19	m²	10.97
not exceeding 300 mm wide	-	0.60	4.78	0.40	m²	5.18
9.50 mm thick boards to ceilings						
over 300 mm wide	-	0.96	7.26	2.19	m²	9.45
over 300 mm wide; 3.50 m - 5.00 m high	-	1.11	8.46	2.19	m²	10.65
not exceeding 300 mm wide	-	0.46	3.66	0.40	m²	4.06
9.50 mm thick boards to ceilings; in staircase areas or plant rooms						
over 300 mm wide	-	1.06	8.06	2.19	m²	10.25
not exceeding 300 mm wide	-	0.51	4.06	0.40	m²	4.46
9.50 mm thick boards to isolated beams						
over 300 mm wide	-	1.13	8.62	2.19	m²	10.81
not exceeding 300 mm wide	-	0.54	4.30	0.40	m²	4.70
add for "Duplex" insulating grade 12.50 mm thick boards to walls	-	-		0.40	m²	0.40
12.50 mm thick boards to walls; in staircase areas or plant rooms						
over 300 mm wide	-	1.09	8.30	2.38	m²	10.68
not exceeding 300 mm wide	-	0.52	4.14	0.45	m²	4.59
12.50 mm thick boards to isolated columns						
over 300 mm wide	-	1.13	8.62	2.38	m²	11.00
not exceeding 300 mm wide	-	0.54	4.30	0.45	m²	4.75
12.50 mm thick boards to ceilings						
over 300 mm wide	-	1.03	7.82	2.38	m²	10.20
over 300 mm wide; 3.50 m - 5.00 m high	-	1.15	8.78	2.38	m²	11.16
not exceeding 300 mm wide	-	0.49	3.90	0.45	m²	4.35
12.50 mm thick boards to ceilings; in staircase areas or plant rooms						
over 300 mm wide	-	1.15	8.78	2.38	m²	11.16
not exceeding 300 mm wide	-	0.55	4.38	0.45	m²	4.83
12.50 mm thick boards to isolated beams						
over 300 mm wide	-	1.24	9.49	2.38	m²	11.87
not exceeding 300 mm wide	-	0.61	4.86	0.45	m²	5.31
add for "Duplex" insulating grade 12.50 mm thick boards to walls	-	-		0.40	m²	0.40
Accessories						
"Expamet" render beads or other equal and approved; white PVC nosings; to brickwork or blockwork base						
external stop bead; ref 573	-	0.08	0.64	1.78	m	2.42
"Expamet" render beads or other equal and approved; stainless steel; to brickwork or blockwork base						
stop bead; ref 546	-	0.08	0.64	1.46	m	2.10
stop bead; ref 547	-	0.08	0.64	1.46	m	2.10
"Expamet" plaster beads or other equal and approved; galvanised steel; to brickwork or blockwork base						
angle bead; ref 550	-	0.09	0.72	0.58	m	1.30
architrave bead; ref 579	-	0.11	0.88	0.90	m	1.78
stop bead; ref 562	-	0.08	0.64	0.69	m	1.33
stop beads; ref 563	-	0.08	0.64	0.69	m	1.33
movement bead; ref 588	-	0.10	0.80	3.22	m	4.02
"Expamet" plaster beads or other equal and approved; stainless steel; to brickwork or blockwork base						
angle bead; ref 545	-	0.09	0.72	1.65	m	2.37
stop bead; ref 534	-	0.08	0.64	1.46	m	2.10
stop bead; ref 533	-	0.08	0.64	1.46	m	2.10
"Expamet" thin coat plaster beads or other equal and approved; galvanised steel; to timber base						
angle bead; ref 553	-	0.08	0.64	0.58	m	1.22
angle bead; ref 554	-	0.08	0.64	0.81	m	1.45
stop bead; ref 560	-	0.07	0.56	0.74	m	1.30

M SURFACE FINISHES Excluding overheads and profit	PC £	Labour hours	Labour £	Material £	Unit	Total rate £
M21 INSULATION WITH RENDERED FINISH						
"StoTherm" mineral external wall insulation system						
or other equal and approved; CCS Scotseal Ltd						
40 mm thick mineral wool; Sto Ground Coat F						
reinforcing coat; glassfibre reinforcing mesh;						
one coat Sto Primer; mechanical fixing using						
PVC intermediate tracks and T-splines; to						
brickwork or blockwork base						
over 300 mm wide	-	1.42	22.91	34.19	m²	57.10
40 mm thick mineral wool; Sto Ground Coat F						
reinforcing coat; glassfibre reinforcing mesh;						
one coat Sto Primer; fixing using adhesive; to						
brickwork or blockwork base						
over 300 mm wide	-	1.17	18.86	27.63	m²	46.49
100 mm thick mineral wool; Sto Ground Coat F						
reinforcing coat; glassfibre reinforcing mesh;						
one coat Sto Primer; mechanical fixing using						
PVC intermediate tracks and T-splines; to						
brickwork or blockwork base						
over 300 mm wide	-	1.42	22.91	44.27	m²	67.18
100 mm thick mineral wool; Sto Ground Coat F						
reinforcing coat; glassfibre reinforcing mesh;						
one coat So Primer; fixing using adhesive; to						
brickwork or blockwork base						
over 300 mm wide	-	1.17	18.86	38.81	m²	57.67
M22 SPRAYED MINERAL FIBRE COATINGS						
Prepare and apply by spray "Mandolite CP2"						
fire protection or other equal and approved						
on structural steel/metalwork						
16 mm thick (one hour) fire protection						
to walls and columns	-	-	-	-	m²	7.50
to ceilings and beams	-	-	-	-	m²	8.25
to isolated metalwork	-	-	-	-	m²	16.50
22 mm thick (one and a half hour) fire						
protection						
to walls and columns	-	-	-	-	m²	8.75
to ceilings and beams	-	-	-	-	m²	9.70
to isolated metalwork	-	-	-	-	m²	19.40
28 mm thick (two hour) fire protection						
to walls and columns	-	-	-	-	m²	10.20
to ceilings and beams	-	-	-	-	m²	11.15
to isolated metalwork	-	-	-	-	m²	22.30
52 mm thick (four hour) fire protection						
to walls and columns	-	-	-	-	m²	15.50
to ceilings and beams	-	-	-	-	m²	17.25
to isolated metalwork	-	-	-	-	m²	34.30
Prepare and apply by spray; cementitious "Pyrok						
WF26" render or other equal and approved; on						
expanded metal lathing (not included)						
15 mm thick						
to ceilings and beams	-	-	-	-	m²	23.75

M SURFACE FINISHES Excluding overheads and profit	PC £	Labour hours	Labour £	Material £	Unit	Total rate £
M30 METAL MESH LATHING/ANCHORED REINFORCEMENT FOR PLASTERED COATING						
Accessories						
Pre-formed galvanised expanded steel arch-frames; "Simpson's Strong-Tie" or other equal and approved; semi-circular; to suit walls up to 230 mm thick						
375 mm radius; for 800 mm opening; ref SC 750	16.32	0.50	3.60	16.73	nr	**20.33**
425 mm radius; for 850 mm opening; ref SC 850	17.17	0.50	3.60	17.60	nr	**21.20**
450 mm radius; for 900 mm opening; ref SC 900	18.29	0.50	3.60	18.75	nr	**22.35**
600 mm radius; for 1200 mm opening; ref SC 1200	19.84	0.50	3.60	20.34	nr	**23.94**
Lathing; Expamet "BB" expanded metal lathing or other equal and approved; BS 1369; 50 mm laps						
6 mm thick mesh linings to ceilings; fixing with staples; to softwood base; over 300 mm wide						
ref BB263; 0.500 mm thick	2.99	0.60	4.32	3.14	m²	**7.46**
ref BB264; 0.675 mm thick	3.49	0.60	4.32	3.67	m²	**7.99**
6 mm thick mesh linings to ceilings; fixing with wire; to steelwork; over 300 mm wide						
ref BB263; 0.500 mm thick	-	0.64	4.61	3.14	m²	**7.75**
ref BB264; 0.675 mm thick	-	0.64	4.61	3.67	m²	**8.28**
6 mm thick mesh linings to ceilings; fixing with wire; to steelwork; not exceeding 300 mm wide						
ref BB263; 0.500 mm thick	-	0.40	2.88	3.14	m²	**6.02**
ref BB264; 0.675 mm thick	-	0.40	2.88	3.67	m²	**6.55**
raking cutting	-	0.20	1.59	-	m	**1.59**
cutting and fitting around pipes; not exceeding 0.30 m girth	-	0.30	2.39	-	nr	**2.39**
Lathing; Expamet "Riblath" or "Spraylath" or other equal and approved stiffened expanded metal lathing or similar; 50 mm laps						
10 mm thick mesh lining to walls; fixing with nails; to softwood base; over 300 mm wide						
"Riblath" ref 269; 0.30 mm thick	3.75	0.50	3.60	4.01	m²	**7.61**
"Riblath" ref 271; 0.50 mm thick	4.31	0.50	3.60	4.61	m²	**8.21**
"Spraylath" ref 273; 0.50 mm thick	-	0.50	3.60	5.59	m²	**9.19**
10 mm thick mesh lining to walls; fixing with nails; to softwood base; not exceeding 300 mm wide						
"Riblath" ref 269; 0.30 mm thick	-	0.30	2.16	1.24	m²	**3.40**
"Riblath" ref 271; 0.50 mm thick	-	0.30	2.16	1.41	m²	**3.57**
"Spraylath" ref 273; 0.50 mm thick	-	0.30	2.16	1.74	m²	**3.90**
10 mm thick mesh lining to walls; fixing to brick or blockwork; over 300 mm wide						
"Red-rib" ref 274; 0.50 mm thick	4.76	0.40	2.88	5.48	m²	**8.36**
stainless steel "Riblath" ref 267; 0.30 mm thick	9.44	0.40	2.88	10.40	m²	**13.28**
10 mm thick mesh lining to ceilings; fixing with wire; to steelwork; over 300 mm wide						
"Riblath" ref 269; 0.30 mm thick	-	0.64	4.61	4.40	m²	**9.01**
"Riblath" ref 271; 0.50 mm thick	-	0.64	4.61	4.99	m²	**9.60**
"Spraylath" ref 273; 0.50 mm thick	-	0.64	4.61	5.97	m²	**10.58**

M SURFACE FINISHES Excluding overheads and profit	PC £	Labour hours	Labour £	Material £	Unit	Total rate £
M31 FIBROUS PLASTER						
Fibrous plaster; fixing with screws; plugging;						
countersinking; stopping; filling and pointing						
joints with plaster						
16 mm thick plain slab coverings to ceilings						
over 300 mm wide	-	-	-	-	m²	94.50
not exceeding 300 mm wide	-	-	-	-	m	30.45
Coves; not exceeding 150 mm girth						
per 25 mm girth	-	-	-	-	m	4.50
Coves; 150 mm - 300 mm girth						
per 25 mm girth	-	-	-	-	m	5.50
Cornices						
per 25 mm girth	-	-	-	-	m	5.50
Cornice enrichments						
per 25 mm girth; depending on degree of						
enrichments	-	-	-	-	m	6.70
Fibrous plaster; fixing with plaster wadding						
filling and pointing joints with plaster; to steel						
base						
16 mm thick plain slab coverings to ceilings						
over 300 mm wide	-	-	-	-	m²	94.50
not exceeding 300 mm wide	-	-	-	-	m	30.45
16 mm thick plain casings to stanchions						
per 25 mm girth	-	-	-	-	m	2.80
16 mm thick plain casings to beams						
per 25 mm girth	-	-	-	-	m	2.80
Gyproc cove or other equal and approved; fixing						
with adhesive; filling and pointing joints with						
plaster						
Coves						
125 mm girth	-	0.20	1.59	0.67	m	2.26
angles	-	0.04	0.32	0.42	nr	0.74

M40 STONE/CONCRETE/QUARRY/CERAMIC TILING/MOSAIC

ALTERNATIVE TILE MATERIALS

	£		£		£
Dennis Ruabon clay floor quarries (£/1000) excl. VAT					
Heather Brown					
150 x 150 x 12.50 mm	340.00	194 x 94 x 12.50 mm	360.00	194 x 194 x 12.50 mm	610.00
Red					
150 x 150 x 12.50 mm;		150 x 150 x 12.50 mm;			
square	260.00	hexagonal	390.00		

Daniel Platt heavy duty floor tiles (£/m²)					
"Ferrolite" flat; 100 x 100 x 9 mm					
Black	18.49	Cream mingled (M29)	15.05	Red	15.05
"Ferrolite" flat; 152 x 152 x 12 mm					
Black	26.02	Cream mingled (M29)	21.93	Chocolate	26.02
Red	20.64				
"Ferrundum" anti - slip; 152 x 152 x 12 mm					
Black	27.95	Cream mingled (M29)	23.65		

	£			£	
Marley floor tiles (£/m²); 300 x 300 mm					
"Europa" - 2.00 mm	5.10	"Heavy Duty Hi-Tech Dissipative"		29.95	
- 2.50 mm	6.25	"Travertine" - 2.50 mm		8.10	
"Marleyflex" - 2.00 mm	4.52	"Vylon Plus"		4.99	
- 2.50 mm	5.12				

M SURFACE FINISHES Excluding overheads and profit	PC £	Labour hours	Labour £	Material £	Unit	Total rate £
Clay floor quarries; BS 6431; class 1; Daniel Platt "Crown" tiles or other equal and approved; level bedding 10 mm thick and jointing in cement:sand (1:3); butt joints; straight both ways; flush pointing with grout; to cement:sand base						
Work to floors; over 300 mm wide						
150 mm x 150 mm x 12.50 mm thick; red	-	0.80	8.95	14.98	m²	**23.93**
150 mm x 150 mm x 12.50 mm thick; brown	-	0.80	8.95	18.14	m²	**27.09**
200 mm x 200 mm x 19 mm thick; brown	-	0.65	7.27	25.38	m²	**32.65**
Works to floors; in staircase areas or plant rooms						
150 mm x 150 mm x 12.50 mm thick; red	-	0.90	10.07	14.98	m²	**25.05**
150 mm x 150 mm x 12.50 mm thick; brown	-	0.90	10.07	18.14	m²	**28.21**
200 mm x 200 mm x 19 mm thick; brown	-	0.75	8.39	25.38	m²	**33.77**
Work to floors; not exceeding 300 mm wide						
150 mm x 150 mm x 12.50 mm thick; red	-	0.40	4.48	3.30	m	**7.78**
150 mm x 150 mm x 12.50 mm thick; brown	-	0.40	4.48	4.25	m	**8.73**
200 mm x 200 mm x 19 mm thick; brown	-	0.33	3.69	6.42	m	**10.11**
fair square cutting against flush edges of existing finishes	-	0.12	0.91	0.72	m	**1.63**
raking cutting	-	0.21	1.62	0.81	m	**2.43**
cutting around pipes; not exceeding 0.30 m girth	-	0.15	1.19	-	nr	**1.19**
extra for cutting and fitting into recessed manhole cover 600 mm x 600 mm	-	1.00	7.96	-	nr	**7.96**
Work to sills; 150 mm wide; rounded edge tiles						
150 mm x 150 mm x 12.50 mm thick; red	0.20	0.33	3.69	2.89	m	**6.58**
150 mm x 150 mm x 12.50 mm thick; brown	-	0.33	3.69	3.84	m	**7.53**
fitted end	-	0.15	1.19	-	nr	**1.19**
Coved skirtings; 138 mm high; rounded top edge						
150 mm x 138 mm x 12.50 mm thick; red	0.37	0.25	2.80	3.65	m	**6.45**
150 mm x 138 mm x 12.50 mm thick; brown	0.39	0.25	2.80	3.78	m	**6.58**
ends	-	0.05	0.40	-	nr	**0.40**
angles	-	0.15	1.19	1.33	nr	**2.52**
Glazed ceramic wall tiles; BS 6431; fixing with adhesive; butt joints; straight both ways; flush pointing with white grout; to plaster base						
Work to walls; over 300 mm wide						
152 mm x 152 mm x 5.50 mm thick; white	10.49	0.60	8.65	14.84	m²	**23.49**
152 mm x 152 mm x 5.50 mm thick; light colours	12.64	0.60	8.65	17.10	m²	**25.75**
152 mm x 152 mm x 5.50 mm thick; dark colours	15.61	0.60	8.65	20.22	m²	**28.87**
extra for RE or REX tile	-	-	-	5.68	m²	**5.68**
200 mm x 100 mm x 6.50 mm thick; white and light colours	11.94	0.60	8.65	16.36	m²	**25.01**
250 mm x 200 mm x 7.00 mm thick; white and light colours	13.81	0.60	8.65	18.33	m²	**26.98**
Work to walls; in staircase areas or plant rooms						
152 mm x 152 mm x 5.50 mm thick; white	-	0.67	9.65	14.84	m²	**24.49**
Work to walls; not exceeding 300 mm wide						
152 mm x 152 mm x 5.50 mm thick; white	-	0.30	4.32	4.41	m	**8.73**
152 mm x 152 mm x 5.50 mm thick; light colours	-	0.30	4.32	6.91	m	**11.23**
152 mm x 152 mm x 5.50 mm thick; dark colours	-	0.30	4.32	7.84	m	**12.16**
200 mm x 100 mm x 6.50 mm thick; white and light colours	-	0.30	4.32	4.86	m	**9.18**
250 mm x 200 mm x 7.00 mm thick; white and light colours	-	0.25	3.60	5.45	m	**9.05**
cutting around pipes; not exceeding 0.30 m girth	-	0.10	0.80	-	nr	**0.80**
Work to sills; 150 mm wide; rounded edge tiles						
152 mm x 152 mm x 5.50 mm thick; white	-	0.25	3.60	2.20	m	**5.80**
fitted end	-	0.10	0.80	-	nr	**0.80**

M SURFACE FINISHES Excluding overheads and profit	PC £	Labour hours	Labour £	Material £	Unit	Total rate £
M40 STONE/CONCRETE/QUARRY/CERAMIC **TILING/MOSAIC** - cont'd						
198 mm x 64.50 mm x 6 mm thick wall tiles; **fixing with adhesive; butt joints; straight both** **ways; flush pointing with white grout; to** **plaster base**						
Work to walls						
over 300 mm wide	21.25	1.80	25.94	26.14	m²	**52.08**
not exceeding 300 mm wide	-	0.70	10.09	7.80	m	**17.89**
20 mm x 20 mm x 5.50 mm thick glazed **mosaic wall tiles; fixing with adhesive; butt** **joints; straight both ways; flush pointing with** **white grout; to plaster base**						
Work to walls						
over 300 mm wide	25.50	1.90	27.38	31.27	m²	**58.65**
not exceeding 300 mm wide	-	0.75	10.81	11.07	m	**21.88**
50 mm x 50 mm x 5.50 mm thick slip resistant **mosaic floor tiles, Series 2 or other equal and** **approved; Langley London Ltd; fixing with** **adhesive; butt joints; straight both ways; flush** **pointing with white grout; to cement:sand base**						
Work to floors						
over 300 mm wide	14.84	1.90	21.26	20.87	m²	**42.13**
not exceeding 300 mm wide	-	0.75	8.39	7.71	m	**16.10**
Dakota mahogany granite cladding; polished **finish; jointed and pointed in coloured mortar** **(1:2:8)**						
20 mm work to floors; level; to cement:sand base						
over 300 mm wide	-	-	-	-	m²	**204.25**
20 mm x 300 mm treads; plain nosings	-	-	-	-	m	**99.75**
raking, cutting	-	-	-	-	m	**19.00**
polished edges	-	-	-	-	m	**33.25**
birdsmouth	-	-	-	-	m	**19.00**
20 mm thick work to walls; to cement:sand base						
over 300 mm wide	-	-	-	-	m²	**209.00**
not exceeding 300 mm wide	-	-	-	-	m	**85.50**
40 mm thick work to walls; to cement:sand base						
over 300 mm wide	-	-	-	-	m²	**346.75**
not exceeding 300 mm wide	-	-	-	-	m	**133.00**
Riven Welsh slate floor tiles; level; bedding 10 **mm thick and jointing in cement:sand (1:3);** **butt joints; straight both ways; flush pointing** **with coloured mortar; to cement:sand base**						
Work to floors; over 300 mm wide						
250 mm x 250 mm x 12 mm - 15 mm thick	-	0.60	8.65	30.45	m²	**39.10**
Work to floors; not exceeding 300 mm wide						
250 mm x 250 mm x 12 mm - 15 mm thick	-	0.30	4.32	9.20	m	**13.52**
Roman Travertine marble cladding; polished finish; **jointed and pointed in coloured mortar (1:2:8)**						
20 mm thick work to floors; level; to cement:sand base						
over 300 mm wide	-	-	-	-	m²	**133.00**
20 mm x 300 mm treads; plain nosings	-	-	-	-	m	**71.25**
raking cutting	-	-	-	-	m	**14.25**
polished edges	-	-	-	-	m	**14.25**
birdsmouth	-	-	-	-	m	**23.75**

M SURFACE FINISHES Excluding overheads and profit	PC £	Labour hours	Labour £	Material £	Unit	Total rate £
20 mm thick work to walls; to cement:sand base						
over 300 mm wide	-	-	-	-	m²	137.75
not exceeding 300 mm wide	-	-	-	-	m	57.00
40 mm thick work to walls; to cement and sand base						
over 300 mm wide	-	-	-	-	m²	209.00
not exceeding 300 mm wide	-	-	-	-	m	90.25

M41 TERRAZZO TILING/IN SITU TERRAZZO

Terrazzo tiles; BS 4131; aggregate size random ground grouted and polished to 80's grit finish; standard colour range; 3 mm joints symmetrical layout; bedding in 42 mm cement semi-dry mix (1:4); grouting with neat matching cement
300 mm x 300 mm x 28 mm (nominal),
"Quil-Terra Terrazzo" tile units or other equal
and approved; Quiligotti Contracts Ltd; hydraulically
pressed, mechanically vibrated, steam cured; to floors on
concrete base (not included); sealed with
"Quil-Shield" penetrating case hardener or other
equal and approved; 2 coats applied immediately
after final polishing

plain; laid level	-	-	-	-	m²	30.50
plain; to slopes exceeding 15 degrees from horizontal	-	-	-	-	m²	35.00
to small areas/toilets	-	-	-	-	m²	67.00
Accessories						
plastic division strips; 6 mm x 38 mm; set into floor tiling above crack inducing joints, to the nearest full tile module	-	-	-	-	m	2.05

Specially made terrazzo precast units; BS 4387; aggregate size random; standard colour range; 3 mm joints; grouting with neat matching cement
Standard size Quiligotti Tread and Riser square
combined terrazzo units (with riser cast down) or
other equal and approved; 280 mm wide; 150 mm
high; 40 mm thick; machine made; vibrated and fully
machine polished; incorporating 1 nr "Ferodo" anti-slip
insert ref OT/D or other equal and approved cast-in
during manufacture; one end polished only

fixed with cement:sand (1:4) mortar on prepared backgrounds (not included); grouted in neat tinted cement; wiped clean on completion of fixing	-	-	-	-	m	133.00

Standard size Quiligotti Tread square terrazzo units or
other equal and approved; 40 mm thick; 280 mm wide;
factory polished; incorporating 1 nr "Ferodo" anti-slip
insert ref OT/D or other equal and approved

fixed with cement:sand (1:4) mortar on prepared backgrounds (not included); grouted in neat tinted cement; wiped clean on completion of fixing	-	-	-	-	m	76.50

Standard size Quiligotti Riser square terrazzo units
or other equal and approved; 40 mm thick; 150 mm
high; factory polished

fixed with cemnt:sand (1:4) mortar on prepared backgrounds (not included); grouted in neat tinted cement; wiped clean on completion of fixing	-	-	-	-	m	59.00

M SURFACE FINISHES Excluding overheads and profit	PC £	Labour hours	Labour £	Material £	Unit	Total rate £
M41 TERRAZZO TILING/IN SITU TERRAZZO - cont'd						
Specially made terrazzo precast units; BS 4387; aggregate size random; standard colour range; 3 mm joints; grouting with neat matching cement - cont'd Standard size Quiligotti coved terrazzo skirting units or other equal and approved; 904 mm long; 150 mm high; nominal finish; 23 mm thick; with square top edge						
fixed with cement:sand (1:4) mortar on prepared backgrounds (by others); grouted in neat tinted cement; wiped clean on completion of fixing	-	-	-	-	m	39.50
extra over for special internal/external angle pieces to match	-	-	-	-	m	15.50
extra over for special polished ends	-	-	-	-	nr	5.15
M42 WOOD BLOCK/COMPOSITION BLOCK/PARQUET FLOORING						
Wood block; Vigers, Stevens & Adams "Vigerflex" or other equal and approved; 7.50 mm thick; level; fixing with adhesive; to cement:sand base Work to floors; over 300 mm wide						
"Maple 7"	-	0.50	5.59	15.61	m²	21.20
Wood blocks 25 mm thick; tongued and grooved joints; herringbone pattern; level; fixing with adhesive; to cement:sand base Work to floors; over 300 mm wide						
iroko	-	-	-	-	m²	33.45
"Maple 7" or other equal and approved	-	-	-	-	m²	34.15
french oak	-	-	-	-	m²	45.95
american oak	-	-	-	-	m²	43.75
fair square cutting against flush edges of existing finishings	-	-	-	-	m	4.35
extra for cutting and fitting into recessed duct covers 450 mm wide; lining up with adjoining work	-	-	-	-	nr	10.90
cutting around pipes; not exceeding 0.30 m girth	-	-	-	-	nr	1.85
extra for cutting and fitting into recessed manhole covers 600 mm x 600 mm; lining up with adjoining work	-	-	-	-	nr	8.00
Add to wood block flooring over 300 wide for						
sanding; one coat sealer; one coat wax polish	-	-	-	-	m²	3.60
sanding; two coats sealer; buffing with steel wool	-	-	-	-	m²	3.50
sanding; three coats polyurethane lacquer; buffing down between coats	-	-	-	-	m²	5.35
M50 RUBBER/PLASTICS/CORK/LINO/CARPET TILING/SHEETING						
Linoleum sheet; BS 6826; Forbo-Nairn Floors or other equal and approved; level; fixing with adhesive; butt joints; to cement:sand base Work to floors; over 300 mm wide						
2.50 mm thick; plain	-	0.40	4.48	10.99	m²	15.47
3.20 mm thick; marbled	-	0.40	4.48	11.71	m²	16.19

M SURFACE FINISHES Excluding overheads and profit	PC £	Labour hours	Labour £	Material £	Unit	Total rate £
Linoleum sheet; "Marmoleum Real" or other equal and approved; level; with welded seams; fixing with adhesive; to cement:sand base Work to floors; over 300 mm wide						
2.50 mm thick	-	0.50	5.59	9.44	m²	**15.03**
Vinyl sheet; Altro "Safety" range or other equal and approved; with welded seams; level; fixing with adhesive; to cement:sand base Work to floors; over 300 mm wide						
2.00 mm thick; "Marine T20"	-	0.60	6.71	12.58	m²	**19.29**
2.50 mm thick; "Classic D25"	-	0.70	7.83	14.49	m²	**22.32**
3.50 mm thick; "Stronghold"	-	0.80	8.95	21.18	m²	**30.13**
Slip resistant vinyl sheet; Forbo-Nairn "Surestep" or other equal and approved; level with welded seams; fixing with adhesive; to cement:sand base Work to floors; over 300 mm wide						
2.00 mm thick	-	0.50	5.59	11.28	m²	**16.87**
Vinyl sheet; heavy duty; Marley "HD" or other equal and approved; level; with welded seams; fixing with adhesive; level; to cement:sand base Work to floors; over 300 mm wide						
2.00 mm thick	-	0.45	5.04	6.64	m²	**11.68**
2.50 mm thick	-	0.50	5.59	7.45	m²	**13.04**
2.00 mm thick skirtings						
100 mm high	-	0.12	1.34	1.13	m	**2.47**
Vinyl sheet; "Gerflex" standard sheet or other equal and approved; "Classic" range; level; with welded seams; fixing with adhesive; to cement:sand base Work to floors; over 300 mm wide						
2.00 mm thick	-	0.50	5.59	5.67	m²	**11.26**
Vinyl sheet; "Armstrong Rhino Contract" or other equal and approved; level; with welded seams; fixing with adhesive; to cement:sand base Work to floors; over 300 mm wide						
2.50 mm thick	-	0.50	5.59	10.90	m²	**16.49**
Vinyl tiles; "Accoflex" or other equal and approved; level; fixing with adhesive; butt joints; straight both ways; to cement:sand base Work to floors; over 300 mm wide						
300 mm x 300 mm x 2.00 mm thick	-	0.25	2.80	3.54	m²	**6.34**
Vinyl semi-flexible tiles; "Arlon" or other equal and approved; level; fixing with adhesive; butt joints; straight both ways; to cement:sand base Work to floors; over 300 mm wide						
250 mm x 250 mm x 2.00 mm thick	-	0.25	2.80	3.73	m²	**6.53**
Vinyl semi-flexible tiles; Marley "Marleyflex" or other equal and approved; level; fixing with adhesive; butt joints; straight both ways; to cement:sand base Work to floors; over 300 mm wide						
300 mm x 300 mm x 2.00 mm thick	-	0.25	2.80	3.83	m²	**6.63**
300 mm x 300 mm x 2.50 mm thick	-	0.25	2.80	4.64	m²	**7.44**

M SURFACE FINISHES Excluding overheads and profit	PC £	Labour hours	Labour £	Material £	Unit	Total rate £
M50 RUBBER/PLASTICS/CORK/LINO/CARPET **TILING/SHEETING** - cont'd						
Vinyl semi-flexible tiles; "Vylon" or other equal and **approved; level; fixing with adhesive; butt joints;** **straight both ways; to cement:sand base** Work to floors; over 300 mm wide						
250 mm x 250 mm x 2.00 mm thick	-	0.28	3.13	3.90	m²	**7.03**
Vinyl tiles; anti-static; level; fixing with **adhesive; butt joints; straight both ways; to** **cement:sand base** Work to floors; over 300 mm wide						
457 mm x 457 mm x 2.00 mm thick	-	0.45	5.04	8.17	m²	**13.21**
Vinyl tiles; "Polyflex" or other equal and approved; **level; fixing with adhesive; butt joints; straight both** **ways; to cement:sand base** Work to floors; over 300 mm wide						
300 mm x 300 mm x 1.50 mm thick	-	0.25	2.80	3.37	m²	**6.17**
300 mm x 300 mm x 2.00 mm thick	-	0.25	2.80	3.68	m²	**6.48**
Vinyl tiles; "Polyflor XL" or other equal and approved; **level; fixing with adhesive; butt joints; straight both** **ways; to cement:sand base** Work to floors; over 300 mm wide						
300 mm x 300 mm x 2.00 mm thick	-	0.35	3.92	4.85	m²	**8.77**
Vinyl tiles; Marley "HD" or other equal and approved; **level; fixing with adhesive; butt joints; straight both** **ways; to cement:sand base** Work to floors; over 300 mm wide						
300 mm x 300 mm x 2.00 mm thick	-	0.35	3.92	6.64	m²	**10.56**
Thermoplastic tiles; Marley "Marleyflex" or other **equal and approved; level; fixing with adhesive; butt** **joints; straight both ways; to cement:sand base** Work to floors; over 300 mm wide						
300 mm x 300 mm x 2.00 mm thick; series 2	-	0.23	2.57	3.17	m²	**5.74**
300 mm x 300 mm x 2.00 mm thick; series 4	-	0.23	2.57	3.66	m²	**6.23**
Linoleum tiles; BS 6826; Forbo-Nairn Floors or other **equal and approved; level; fixing with adhesive; butt** **joints; straight both ways; to cement:sand base** Work to floors; over 300 mm wide						
2.50 mm thick (marble pattern)	-	0.30	3.36	11.97	m²	**15.33**
Cork tiles Wicanders "Cork-Master" or other equal **and approved; level; fixing with adhesive; butt joints;** **straight both ways; to cement:sand base** Work to floors; over 300 mm wide						
300 mm x 300 mm x 4.00 mm thick	-	0.40	4.48	16.60	m²	**21.08**
Rubber studded tiles; Altro "Mondopave" or other **equal and approved; level; fixing with adhesive; butt** **joints; straight to cement:sand base** Work to floors; over 300 mm wide						
500 mm x 500 mm x 2.50 mm thick; type MRB; black	-	0.60	6.71	20.48	m²	**27.19**
500 mm x 500 mm x 4.00 mm thick; type MRB; black	-	0.60	6.71	22.33	m²	**29.04**
Work to landings; over 300 mm wide						
500 mm x 500 mm x 4.00 mm thick; type MRB; black	-	0.80	8.95	22.33	m²	**31.28**

M SURFACE FINISHES Excluding overheads and profit	PC £	Labour hours	Labour £	Material £	Unit	Total rate £
4.00 mm thick to treads						
275 mm wide	-	0.50	5.59	6.64	m	12.23
4.00 mm thick to risers						
180 mm wide	-	0.60	6.71	4.70	m	11.41
Sundry floor sheeting underlays						
For floor finishings; over 300 mm wide						
building paper to BS 1521; class A; 75 mm lap						
(laying only)	-	0.06	0.39	-	m²	0.39
3.20 mm thick hardboard	-	0.20	2.88	1.03	m²	3.91
6.00 mm thick plywood	-	0.30	4.32	5.33	m²	9.65
Stair nosings						
Light duty hard aluminium alloy stair tread						
nosings; plugged and screwed in concrete						
57 mm x 32 mm	6.33	0.25	1.99	6.58	m	8.57
84 mm x 32 mm	8.76	0.30	2.39	9.07	m	11.46
Heavy duty aluminium alloy stair tread nosings;						
plugged and screwed to concrete						
60 mm x 32 mm	7.52	0.30	2.39	7.80	m	10.19
92 mm x 32 mm	10.33	0.35	2.79	10.68	m	13.47
Heavy duty carpet tiles; "Heuga 580 Olympic" **or other equal and approved; to cement:sand base**						
Work to floors						
over 300 mm wide	19.01	0.30	3.36	19.96	m²	23.32
Nylon needlepunch carpet; "Marleytex" or other equal **and approved; fixing; with adhesive; level; to cement**						
Work to floors						
over 300 mm wide	-	0.25	2.80	4.58	m²	7.38
M51 EDGE FIXED CARPETING						
Fitted carpeting; Wilton wool/nylon or other equal and **approved; 80/20 velvet pile; heavy domestic plain**						
Work to floors						
over 300 mm wide	31.49	0.40	2.91	34.64	m²	37.55
Work to treads and risers						
over 300 mm wide	-	0.80	5.82	34.64	m²	40.46
Underlay to carpeting						
Work to floors						
over 300 mm wide	2.96	0.08	0.58	3.11	m²	3.69
raking cutting	-	0.08	0.52	-	m	0.52
Sundries						
Carpet gripper fixed to floor; standard edging						
22 mm wide	-	0.05	0.32	0.15	m	0.47
M52 DECORATIVE PAPERS/FABRICS						
Lining paper; PC £1.75/roll; and hanging						
Plaster walls or columns						
over 300 mm girth	-	0.20	1.59	0.30	m²	1.89
Plaster ceilings or beams						
over 300 mm girth	-	0.25	1.99	0.30	m²	2.29
Decorative paper-backed vinyl wallpaper; PC **£9.50/roll; and hanging**						
Plaster walls or columns						
over 300 mm girth	-	0.25	1.99	1.69	m²	3.68

M SURFACE FINISHES
Excluding overheads and profit

M60 PAINTING/CLEAR FINISHING

BASIC PAINT PRICES (£/5 LITRE TIN)

	£		£		£
Paints					
"Dulux"					
- matt emulsion	19.84	oil based undercoat	23.09	"Sandtex" masonry paint	
- gloss	23.09	"Weathershield" gloss	34.50	- brilliant white	12.29
- eggshell gloss	33.84	"Weathershield" undercoat	34.50	- coloured	14.19
Primer/undercoats					
acrylic	13.97	water based	13.97	masonry sealer	15.86
red oxide	19.14	zinc phosphate	28.74	knotting solution	33.45
Special paints					
solar reflective aluminium	32.50	"Hammerite"	38.41	fire retardant	
anti-graffiti	101.25	"Smoothrite"	38.41	- undercoat	45.00
bituminous emulsion	4.90			- top coat	60.00

	£			£
Stains and Preservatives				
Cuprinol		Sikkens		
- "Clear"	15.00	- "Cetol HLS"		40.88
- "Boiled linseed oil"	16.01	- "Cetol TS"		60.46
Sadolin		- "Cetol Filter 7"		62.18
- "Holdex"	63.50	Protim Soliignum		
- "Extra"	60.00	- "Architectural"		53.10
- "New base"	33.50	- "Brown"		16.30
		- "Cedar"		25.27
Varnishes				
polyurethene	31.98			

M SURFACE FINISHES Excluding overheads and profit	PC £	Labour hours	Labour £	Material £	Unit	Total rate £
NOTE: The following prices include for preparing surfaces. Painting woodwork also includes for knotting prior to applying the priming coat and for all stopping of nail holes.						
PAINTING/CLEAR FINISHING - INTERNALLY						
One coat primer; on wood surfaces before fixing						
General surfaces						
over 300 mm girth	-	0.09	0.72	0.34	m²	**1.06**
isolated surfaces not exceeding 300 mm girth	-	0.03	0.24	0.13	m	**0.37**
isolated areas not exceeding 0.50 m²						
irrespective of girth	-	0.07	0.56	0.17	nr	**0.73**
One coat sealer; on wood surfaces before fixing						
General surfaces						
over 300 mm girth	-	0.11	0.88	0.57	m²	**1.45**
isolated surfaces not exceeding 300 mm girth	-	0.04	0.32	0.20	m	**0.52**
isolated surfaces not exceeding 0.50 m²						
irrespective of girth	-	0.09	0.72	0.27	nr	**0.99**
One coat of Sikkens "Cetol HLS" stain or other equal and approved; on wood surfaces before fixing						
General surfaces						
over 300 mm girth	-	0.12	0.96	0.63	m²	**1.59**
isolated surfaces not exceeding 300 mm girth	-	0.04	0.32	0.24	m	**0.56**
isolated surfaces not exceeding 0.50 m²						
irrespective of girth	-	0.09	0.72	0.30	nr	**1.02**

M SURFACE FINISHES Excluding overheads and profit	PC £	Labour hours	Labour £	Material £	Unit	Total rate £
One coat of Sikkens "Cetol TS" interior stain or other **equal and approved; on wood surfaces before fixing**						
General surfaces						
over 300 mm girth	-	0.12	0.96	0.90	m²	**1.86**
isolated surfaces not exceeding 300 mm girth	-	0.04	0.32	0.35	m	**0.67**
isolated areas not exceeding 0.50 m²;						
irrespective of girth	-	0.09	0.72	0.44	nr	**1.16**
One coat Cuprinol clear wood preservative or other **equal and approved; on wood surfaces before fixing**						
General surfaces						
over 300 mm girth	-	0.09	0.72	0.38	m²	**1.10**
isolated surfaces not exceeding 300 mm girth	-	0.03	0.24	0.14	m	**0.38**
isolated areas not exceeding 0.50 m²;						
irrespective of girth	-	0.06	0.48	0.18	nr	**0.66**
One coat HCC Protective Coatings Ltd "Permacor" **urethane alkyd gloss finishing coat or other equal** **and approved; on previously primed steelwork**						
Members of roof trusses						
over 300 mm girth	-	0.07	0.56	1.20	m²	**1.76**
Two coats emulsion paint						
Brick or block walls						
over 300 mm girth	-	0.20	1.59	0.86	m²	**2.45**
Cement render or concrete						
over 300 mm girth	-	0.19	1.51	0.76	m²	**2.27**
isolated surfaces not exceeding 300 mm girth	-	0.09	0.72	0.23	m	**0.95**
Plaster walls or plaster/plasterboard ceilings						
over 300 mm girth	-	0.17	1.35	0.73	m²	**2.08**
over 300 mm girth; in multi colours	-	0.23	1.83	0.89	m²	**2.72**
over 300 mm girth; in staircase areas	-	0.20	1.59	0.85	m²	**2.44**
cutting in edges on flush surfaces	-	0.07	0.56	-	m	**0.56**
Plaster/plasterboard ceilings						
over 300 mm girth; 3.50 m - 5.00 m high	-	0.20	1.59	0.74	m²	**2.33**
One mist and two coats emulsion paint						
Brick or block walls						
over 300 mm girth	-	0.18	1.43	1.12	m²	**2.55**
Cement render or concrete						
over 300 mm girth	-	0.18	1.43	1.04	m²	**2.47**
Plaster walls or plaster/plasterboard ceilings						
over 300 mm girth	-	0.17	1.35	1.04	m²	**2.39**
over 300 mm girth; in multi colours	-	0.24	1.91	1.05	m²	**2.96**
over 300 mm girth; in staircase areas	-	0.20	1.59	1.04	m²	**2.63**
cutting in edges on flush surfaces	-	0.08	0.64	-	m	**0.64**
Plaster/plasterboard ceilings						
over 300 mm girth; 3.50 m - 5.00 m high	-	0.20	1.59	1.04	m²	**2.63**
One coat "Tretol No 10" sealer" or other equal **and approved; two coats Tretol sprayed "Supercover** **Spraytone" emulsion paint or other equal and** **approved**						
Plaster walls or plaster/plasterboard ceilings						
over 300 mm girth	-	-	-	-	m²	**4.00**
Textured plastic; "Artex" or other equal and **approved finish**						
Plasterboard ceilings						
over 300 mm girth	-	0.21	1.67	1.45	m²	**3.12**
Concrete walls or ceilings						
over 300 mm girth	-	0.23	1.83	1.38	m²	**3.21**

M SURFACE FINISHES Excluding overheads and profit	PC £	Labour hours	Labour £	Material £	Unit	Total rate £
M60 PAINTING/CLEAR FINISHING - cont'd						
PAINTING/CLEAR FINISHING - INTERNALLY - cont'd						
One coat "Portabond" or other equal and approved; **one coat "Portaflek" or other equal and approved; on** **plaster surfaces; spray applied, masking adjacent** **surfaces**						
General surfaces						
over 300 mm girth	-	-	-	-	m²	8.00
extra for one coat standard "HD" glaze	-	-	-	-	m²	1.50
not exceeding 300 mm girth	-	-	-	-	m	3.50
Touch up primer; one undercoat and one **finishing coat of gloss oil paint; on wood** **surfaces**						
General surfaces						
over 300 mm girth	-	0.25	1.99	0.96	m²	2.95
isolated surfaces not exceeding 300 mm girth	-	0.10	0.80	0.32	m	1.12
isolated areas not exceeding 0.50 m²;						
irrespective of girth	-	0.19	1.51	0.50	nr	2.01
Glazed windows and screens						
panes; area not exceeding 0.10 m²	-	0.41	3.26	0.69	m²	3.95
panes; area 0.10 m² - 0.50 m²	-	0.33	2.63	0.55	m²	3.18
panes; area 0.50 m² - 1.00 m²	-	0.28	2.23	0.43	m²	2.66
panes; area over 1.00 m²	-	0.25	1.99	0.36	m²	2.35
Touch up primer; two undercoats and one **finishing coat of gloss oil paint; on wood** **surfaces**						
General surfaces						
over 300 mm girth	-	0.35	2.79	0.86	m²	3.65
isolated surfaces not exceeding 300 mm girth	-	0.14	1.11	0.34	m	1.45
isolated areas not exceeding 0.50 m²;						
irrespective of girth	-	0.26	2.07	0.49	nr	2.56
Glazed windows and screens						
panes; area not exceeding 0.10 m²	-	0.58	4.62	0.92	m²	5.54
panes; area 0.10 m² - 0.50 m²	-	0.46	3.66	0.73	m²	4.39
panes; area 0.50 m² - 1.00 m²	-	0.40	3.18	0.60	m²	3.78
panes; area over 1.00 m²	-	0.35	2.79	0.51	m²	3.30
Knot; one coat primer; stop; one undercoat **and one finishing coat of gloss oil paint; on** **wood surfaces**						
General surfaces						
over 300 mm girth	-	0.36	2.87	0.84	m²	3.71
isolated surfaces not exceeding 300 mm girth	-	0.14	1.11	0.28	m	1.39
isolated areas not exceeding 0.50 m²;						
irrespective of girth	-	0.27	2.15	0.55	nr	2.70
Glazed windows and screens						
panes; area not exceeding 0.10 m²	-	0.61	4.86	0.84	m²	5.70
panes; area 0.10 m² - 0.50 m²	-	0.49	3.90	0.71	m²	4.61
panes; area 0.50 m² - 1.00 m²	-	0.43	3.42	0.71	m²	4.13
panes; area over 1.00 m²	-	0.36	2.87	0.52	m²	3.39
Knot; one coat primer; stop; two undercoats and one **finishing coat of gloss oil paint; on wood surfaces**						
General surfaces						
over 300 mm girth	-	0.46	3.66	1.17	m²	4.83
isolated surfaces not exceeding 300 mm girth	-	0.19	1.51	0.41	m	1.92
isolated areas not exceeding 0.50 m²;						
irrespective of girth	-	0.35	2.79	0.66	nr	3.45

M SURFACE FINISHES Excluding overheads and profit	PC £	Labour hours	Labour £	Material £	Unit	Total rate £
Glazed windows and screens						
panes; area not exceeding 0.10 m²	-	0.77	6.13	1.10	m²	**7.23**
panes; area 0.10 m² - 0.50 m²	-	0.61	4.86	1.00	m²	**5.86**
panes; area 0.50 m² - 1.00 m²	-	0.54	4.30	0.91	m²	**5.21**
panes; area over 1.00 m²	-	0.46	3.66	0.67	m²	**4.33**
One coat primer; one undercoat and one						
finishing coat of gloss oil paint						
Plaster surfaces						
over 300 mm girth	-	0.32	2.55	1.08	m²	**3.63**
One coat primer; two undercoats and one						
finishing coat of gloss oil paint						
Plaster surfaces						
over 300 mm girth	-	0.43	3.42	1.37	m²	**4.79**
One coat primer; two undercoats and one						
finishing coat of eggshell paint						
Plaster surfaces						
over 300 mm girth	-	0.43	3.42	1.40	m²	**4.82**
Touch up primer; one undercoat and one						
finishing coat of gloss paint; on iron or steel						
surfaces						
General surfaces						
over 300 mm girth	-	0.25	1.99	0.65	m²	**2.64**
isolated surfaces not exceeding 300 mm girth	-	0.10	0.80	0.22	m	**1.02**
isolated areas not exceeding 0.50 m²;						
irrespective of girth	-	0.19	1.51	0.36	nr	**1.87**
Glazed windows and screens						
panes; area not exceeding 0.10 m²	-	0.41	3.26	0.68	m²	**3.94**
panes; area 0.10 m² - 0.50 m²	-	0.33	2.63	0.55	m²	**3.18**
panes; area 0.50 m² - 1.00 m²	-	0.28	2.23	0.41	m²	**2.64**
panes; area over 1.00 m²	-	0.25	1.99	0.35	m²	**2.34**
Structural steelwork						
over 300 mm girth	-	0.27	2.15	0.69	m²	**2.84**
Members of roof trusses						
over 300 mm girth	-	0.37	2.95	0.78	m²	**3.73**
Ornamental railings and the like; each side						
measured overall						
over 300 mm girth	-	0.43	3.42	0.87	m²	**4.29**
Iron or steel radiators						
over 300 mm girth	-	0.25	1.99	0.71	m²	**2.70**
Pipes or conduits						
over 300 mm girth	-	0.37	2.95	0.75	m²	**3.70**
not exceeding 300 mm girth	-	0.14	1.11	0.25	m	**1.36**
Touch up primer; two undercoats and one						
finishing coat of gloss oil paint; on iron or						
steel surfaces						
General surfaces						
over 300 mm girth	-	0.35	2.79	0.89	m²	**3.68**
isolated surfaces not exceeding 300 mm girth	-	0.14	1.11	0.35	m	**1.46**
isolated areas not exceeding 0.50 m²;						
irrespective of girth	-	0.26	2.07	0.52	nr	**2.59**
Glazed windows and screens						
panes; area not exceeding 0.10 m²	-	0.58	4.62	0.94	m²	**5.56**
panes; area 0.10 m² - 0.50 m²	-	0.46	3.66	0.78	m²	**4.44**
panes; area 0.50 m² - 1.00 m²	-	0.40	3.18	0.66	m²	**3.84**
panes; area over 1.00 m²	-	0.35	2.79	0.53	m²	**3.32**
Structural steelwork						
over 300 mm girth	-	0.39	3.10	0.92	m²	**4.02**

M SURFACE FINISHES Excluding overheads and profit	PC £	Labour hours	Labour £	Material £	Unit	Total rate £
M60 PAINTING/CLEAR FINISHING - cont'd						
PAINTING/CLEAR FINISHING - INTERNALLY - cont'd						
Touch up primer; two undercoats and one **finishing coat of gloss oil paint; on iron or** **steel surfaces** - cont'd						
Members of roof trusses						
over 300 mm girth	-	0.52	4.14	1.07	m²	**5.21**
Ornamental railings and the like; each side measured overall						
over 300 mm girth	-	0.59	4.70	1.16	m²	**5.86**
Iron or steel radiators						
over 300 mm girth	-	0.35	2.79	0.98	m²	**3.77**
Pipes or conduits						
over 300 mm girth	-	0.52	4.14	1.09	m²	**5.23**
not exceeding 300 mm girth	-	0.20	1.59	0.36	m	**1.95**
One coat primer; one undercoat and one **finishing coat of gloss oil paint; on iron or** **steel surfaces**						
General surfaces						
over 300 mm girth	-	0.25	1.99	0.65	m²	**2.64**
isolated surfaces not exceeding 300 mm girth	-	0.13	1.03	0.35	m	**1.38**
isolated areas not exceeding 0.50 m²; irrespective of girth	-	0.25	1.99	0.62	nr	**2.61**
Glazed windows and screens						
panes; area not exceeding 0.10 m²	-	0.54	4.30	1.00	m²	**5.30**
panes; area 0.10 m² - 0.50 m²	-	0.43	3.42	0.79	m²	**4.21**
panes; area 0.50 m² - 1.00 m²	-	0.37	2.95	0.68	m²	**3.63**
panes; area over 1.00 m²	-	0.32	2.55	0.62	m²	**3.17**
Structural steelwork						
over 300 mm girth	-	0.36	2.87	0.96	m²	**3.83**
Members of roof trusses						
over 300 mm girth	-	0.49	3.90	1.04	m²	**4.94**
Ornamental railings and the like; each side measured overall						
over 300 mm girth	-	0.55	4.38	1.23	m²	**5.61**
Iron or steel radiators						
over 300 mm girth	-	0.32	2.55	1.04	m²	**3.59**
Pipes or conduits						
over 300 mm girth	-	0.49	3.90	1.04	m²	**4.94**
not exceeding 300 mm girth	-	0.19	1.51	0.35	m	**1.86**
One coat primer; two undercoats and one **finishing coat of gloss oil paint; on iron or** **steel surfaces**						
General surfaces						
over 300 mm girth	-	0.43	3.42	1.19	m²	**4.61**
isolated surfaces not exceeding 300 mm girth	-	0.17	1.35	0.53	m	**1.88**
isolated areas not exceeding 0.50 m²; irrespective of girth	-	0.31	2.47	0.67	nr	**3.14**
Glazed windows and screens						
panes; area not exceeding 0.10 m²	-	0.69	5.49	1.22	m²	**6.71**
panes; area 0.10 m² - 0.50 m²	-	0.58	4.62	0.69	m²	**5.31**
panes; area 0.50 m² - 1.00 m²	-	0.49	3.90	0.84	m²	**4.74**
panes; area over 1.00 m²	-	0.43	3.42	0.72	m²	**4.14**
Structural steelwork						
over 300 mm girth	-	0.48	3.82	1.22	m²	**5.04**
Members of roof trusses						
over 300 mm girth	-	0.63	5.01	1.45	m²	**6.46**

M SURFACE FINISHES Excluding overheads and profit	PC £	Labour hours	Labour £	Material £	Unit	Total rate £
Ornamental railings and the like; each side measured overall						
over 300 mm girth	-	0.71	5.65	1.60	m²	**7.25**
Iron or steel radiators						
over 300 mm girth	-	0.43	3.42	1.30	m²	**4.72**
Pipes or conduits						
over 300 mm girth	-	0.64	5.09	1.47	m²	**6.56**
not exceeding 300 mm girth	-	0.26	2.07	0.47	m	**2.54**
Two coats of bituminous paint; on iron or **steel surfaces**						
General surfaces						
over 300 mm girth	-	0.25	1.99	0.26	m²	**2.25**
Inside of galvanized steel cistern						
over 300 mm girth	-	0.37	2.95	0.30	m²	**3.25**
Two coats bituminous paint; first coat blinded **with clean sand prior to second coat; on** **concrete surfaces**						
General surfaces						
over 300 mm girth	-	0.85	6.77	1.02	m²	**7.79**
Mordant solution; one coat HCC Protective Coatings **Ltd "Permacor Alkyd MIO" or other equal and** **approved; one coat "Permatex Epoxy Gloss" finishing** **coat or other equal and approved on galvanised** **steelwork**						
Structural steelwork						
over 300 mm girth	-	0.48	3.82	2.24	m²	**6.06**
One coat HCC Protective Coatings Ltd "Epoxy Zinc **Primer" or other equal and approved; two coats** **"Permacor Alkyd MIO" or other equal and approved;** **one coat "Permacor Epoxy Gloss" finishing coat or** **other equal and approved on steelwork**						
Structural steelwork						
over 300 mm girth	-	0.68	5.41	4.04	m²	**9.45**
Steel protection; HCC Protective Coatings Ltd **"Unitherm" or other equal and approved; two** **coats to steelwork**						
Structural steelwork						
over 300 mm girth	-	1.07	8.52	2.18	m²	**10.70**
Two coats epoxy resin sealer; HCC Protective **Coatings Ltd "Betonol" or other equal and approved;** **on concrete surfaces**						
General surfaces						
over 300 mm girth	-	0.21	1.67	3.12	m²	**4.79**
"Nitoflor Lithurin" floor hardener and dust proofer **or other equal and approved; Fosroc Expandite Ltd;** **two coats; on concrete surfaces**						
General surfaces						
over 300 mm girth	-	0.26	1.68	0.39	m²	**2.07**
Two coats of boiled linseed oil; on hardwood surfaces						
General surfaces						
over 300 mm girth	-	0.19	1.51	1.10	m²	**2.61**
isolated surfaces not exceeding 300 mm girth	-	0.08	0.64	0.36	m	**1.00**
isolated areas not exceeding 0.50 m²;						
irrespective of girth	-	0.14	1.11	0.64	nr	**1.75**

M SURFACE FINISHES Excluding overheads and profit	PC £	Labour hours	Labour £	Material £	Unit	Total rate £
M60 PAINTING/CLEAR FINISHING - cont'd						
PAINTING/CLEAR FINISHING - INTERNALLY - cont'd						
Two coats polyurethane varnish; on wood surfaces						
General surfaces						
over 300 mm girth	-	0.19	1.51	1.00	m²	**2.51**
isolated surfaces not exceeding 300 mm girth	-	0.08	0.64	0.37	m	**1.01**
isolated areas not exceeding 0.50 m²;						
irrespective of girth	-	0.14	1.11	0.12	nr	**1.23**
Three coats polyurethane varnish; on wood surfaces						
General surfaces						
over 300 mm girth	-	0.28	2.23	1.52	m²	**3.75**
isolated surfaces not exceeding 300 mm girth	-	0.11	0.88	0.47	m	**1.35**
isolated areas not exceeding 0.50 m²;						
irrespective of girth	-	0.21	1.67	0.85	nr	**2.52**
One undercoat; and one finishing coat; of "Albi" clear flame retardant surface coating; on wood surfaces						
General surfaces						
over 300 mm girth	-	0.37	2.95	2.09	m²	**5.04**
isolated surfaces not exceeding 300 mm girth	-	0.15	1.19	0.73	m	**1.92**
isolated areas not exceeding 0.50 m²;						
irrespective of girth	-	0.21	1.67	1.60	nr	**3.27**
Two undercoats; and one finishing coat; of "Albi" clear flame retardant surface coating or other equal and approved; on wood surfaces						
General surfaces						
over 300 mm girth	-	0.43	3.42	2.95	m²	**6.37**
isolated surfaces not exceeding 300 mm girth	-	0.22	1.75	1.07	m	**2.82**
isolated areas not exceeding 0.50 m²;						
irrespective of girth	-	0.36	2.87	1.63	nr	**4.50**
Seal and wax polish; dull gloss finish on wood surfaces						
General surfaces						
over 300 mm girth	-	-	-	-	m²	**7.33**
isolated surfaces not exceeding 300 mm girth	-	-	-	-	m	**3.31**
isolated areas not exceeding 0.50m²;						
irrespective of girth	-	-	-	-	nr	**5.13**
One coat of "Sadolin Extra" or other equal and approved; clear or pigmented; one further coat of "Holdex" clear interior silk matt lacquer or other equal and approved						
General surfaces						
over 300 mm girth	-	0.27	2.15	3.31	m²	**5.46**
isolated surfaces not exceeding 300 mm girth	-	0.11	0.88	1.55	m	**2.43**
isolated areas not exceeding 0.50 m²;						
irrespective of girth	-	0.20	1.59	1.61	nr	**3.20**
Glazed windows and screens						
panes; area not exceeding 0.10 m²	-	0.45	3.58	1.89	m²	**5.47**
panes; area 0.10 m² - 0.50 m²	-	0.36	2.87	1.76	m²	**4.63**
panes; area 0.50 m² - 1.00 m²	-	0.31	2.47	1.63	m²	**4.10**
panes; area over 1.00 m²	-	0.27	2.15	1.55	m²	**3.70**

M SURFACE FINISHES Excluding overheads and profit	PC £	Labour hours	Labour £	Material £	Unit	Total rate £
Two coats of "Sadolin Extra" or other equal and approved; clear or pigmented; two further coats of "Holdex" clear interior silk matt lacquer or other equal and approved						
General surfaces						
over 300 mm girth	-	0.43	3.42	6.11	m²	**9.53**
isolated surfaces not exceeding 300 mm girth	-	0.17	1.35	3.06	m	**4.41**
isolated areas not exceeding 0.50 m²;						
irrespective of girth	-	0.32	2.55	3.49	nr	**6.04**
Glazed windows and screens						
panes; area not exceeding 0.10 m²	-	0.71	5.65	3.74	m²	**9.39**
panes; area 0.10 m² - 0.50 m²	-	0.56	4.46	3.49	m²	**7.95**
panes; area 0.50 m² - 1.00 m²	-	0.49	3.90	3.23	m²	**7.13**
panes; area over 1.00 m²	-	0.43	3.42	3.06	m²	**6.48**
Two coats of Sikkens "Cetol TS" interior stain or other equal and approved; on wood surfaces						
General surfaces						
over 300 mm girth	-	0.20	1.59	1.62	m²	**3.21**
isolated surfaces not exceeding 300 mm girth	-	0.09	0.72	0.57	m	**1.29**
isolated areas not exceeding 0.50 m²;						
irrespective of girth	-	0.14	1.11	0.89	nr	**2.00**
Body in and wax polish; dull gloss finish; on hardwood surfaces						
General surfaces						
over 300 mm girth	-	-	-	-	m²	**8.47**
isolated surfaces not exceeding 300 mm girth	-	-	-	-	m	**3.82**
isolated areas not exceeding 0.50 m²;						
irrespective of girth	-	-	-	-	nr	**5.91**
Stain; body in and wax polish; dull gloss finish; on hardwood surfaces						
General surfaces						
over 300 mm girth	-	-	-	-	m²	**11.71**
isolated surfaces not exceeding 300 mm girth	-	-	-	-	m	**5.28**
isolated areas not exceeding 0.50 m²;						
irrespective of girth	-	-	-	-	nr	**8.21**
Seal; two coats of synthetic resin lacquer; decorative flatted finish; wire down, wax and burnish; on wood surfaces						
General surfaces						
over 300 mm girth	-	-	-	-	m²	**14.06**
isolated surfaces not exceeding 300 mm girth	-	-	-	-	m	**6.32**
isolated areas not exceeding 0.50 m²;						
irrespective of girth	-	-	-	-	nr	**9.85**
Stain; body in and fully French polish; full gloss finish; on hardwood surfaces						
General surfaces						
over 300 mm girth	-	-	-	-	m²	**16.16**
isolated surfaces not exceeding 300 mm girth	-	-	-	-	m	**7.28**
isolated areas not exceeding 0.50 m²;						
irrespective of girth	-	-	-	-	nr	**11.33**

M SURFACE FINISHES Excluding overheads and profit	PC £	Labour hours	Labour £	Material £	Unit	Total rate £
M60 PAINTING/CLEAR FINISHING - cont'd						
PAINTING/CLEAR FINISHING - INTERNALLY - cont'd						
Stain black; body in and fully French polish; **ebonized finish; on hardwood surfaces**						
General surfaces						
over 300 mm girth	-	-	-	-	m²	**27.72**
isolated surfaces not exceeding 300 mm girth	-	-	-	-	m	**11.54**
isolated areas not exceeding 0.50 m²;						
irrespective of girth	-	-	-	-	nr	**19.40**
PAINTING/CLEAR FINISHING - EXTERNALLY						
Two coats of cement paint, "Sandtex Matt" or **equal and approved**						
Brick or block walls						
over 300 mm girth	-	0.28	2.23	1.34	m²	**3.57**
Cement render or concrete walls						
over 300 mm girth	-	0.25	1.99	0.88	m²	**2.87**
Roughcast walls						
over 300 mm girth	-	0.43	3.42	0.88	m²	**4.30**
One coat sealer and two coats of external **grade emulsion paint, Dulux "Weathershield"** **or other equal and approved**						
Brick or block walls						
over 300 mm girth	-	0.46	3.66	5.41	m²	**9.07**
Cement render or concrete walls						
over 300 mm girth	-	0.38	3.02	3.61	m²	**6.63**
Concrete soffits						
over 300 mm girth	-	0.43	3.42	3.61	m²	**7.03**
One coat sealer (applied by brush) and two **coats of external grade emulsion paint, Dulux** **"Weathershield" or other equal and approved** **(spray applied)**						
Roughcast						
over 300 mm girth	-	0.31	2.47	7.30	m²	**9.77**
Two coat sealer and one coat of Anti-Graffiti **paint (spray applied)**						
Roughcast						
over 300 mm girth	-	0.31	2.47	29.07	m²	**31.54**
Two coats solar reflective aluminium paint; on **bituminous roofing**						
General surfaces						
over 300 mm girth	-	0.48	3.82	9.35	m²	**13.17**
Touch up primer; one undercoat and one finishing **coat of gloss oil paint; on wood surfaces**						
General surfaces						
over 300 mm girth	-	0.27	2.15	0.66	m²	**2.81**
isolated surfaces not exceeding 300 mm girth	-	0.12	0.96	0.20	m	**1.16**
isolated areas not exceeding 0.50 m²;						
irrespective of girth	-	0.20	1.59	0.39	nr	**1.98**
Glazed windows and screens						
panes; area not exceeding 0.10 m²	-	0.46	3.66	0.71	m²	**4.37**
panes; area 0.10 m² - 0.50 m²	-	0.37	2.95	0.59	m²	**3.54**
panes; area 0.50 m² - 1.00 m²	-	0.32	2.55	0.48	m²	**3.03**
panes; area over 1.00 m²	-	0.27	2.15	0.39	m²	**2.54**

M SURFACE FINISHES Excluding overheads and profit	PC £	Labour hours	Labour £	Material £	Unit	Total rate £
Glazed windows and screens; multi-coloured work						
panes; area not exceeding 0.10 m²	-	0.50	3.98	0.71	m²	4.69
panes; area 0.10 m² - 0.50 m²	-	0.41	3.26	0.61	m²	3.87
panes; area 0.50 m² - 1.00 m²	-	0.35	2.79	0.48	m²	3.27
panes; area over 1.00 m²	-	0.31	2.47	0.39	m²	2.86
Touch up primer; two undercoats and one **finishing coat of gloss oil paint; on wood** **surfaces**						
General surfaces						
over 300 mm girth	-	0.38	3.02	0.85	m²	3.87
isolated surfaces not exceeding 300 mm girth	-	0.16	1.27	0.23	m	1.50
isolated areas not exceeding 0.50 m²; irrespective of girth	-	0.29	2.31	0.47	nr	2.78
Glazed windows and screens						
panes; area not exceeding 0.10 m²	-	0.64	5.09	0.75	m²	5.84
panes; area 0.10 m² - 0.50 m²	-	0.64	5.09	0.63	m²	5.72
panes; area 0.50 m² - 1.00 m²	-	0.51	4.06	0.56	m²	4.62
panes; area over 1.00 m²	-	0.38	3.02	0.47	m²	3.49
Glazed windows and screens; multi-coloured work						
panes; area not exceeding 0.10 m²	-	0.73	5.81	0.75	m²	6.56
panes; area 0.10 m² - 0.50 m²	-	0.59	4.70	0.66	m²	5.36
panes; area 0.50 m² - 1.00 m²	-	0.51	4.06	0.56	m²	4.62
panes; area over 1.00 m²	-	0.44	3.50	0.47	m²	3.97
Knot; one coat primer; one undercoat and one **finishing coat of gloss oil paint; on wood** **surfaces**						
General surfaces						
over 300 mm girth	-	0.41	3.26	0.97	m²	4.23
isolated surfaces not exceeding 300 mm girth	-	0.17	1.35	0.31	m	1.66
isolated areas not exceeding 0.50 m²; irrespective of girth	-	0.31	2.47	0.57	nr	3.04
Glazed windows and screens						
panes; area not exceeding 0.10 m²	-	0.67	5.33	1.00	m²	6.33
panes; area 0.10 m² - 0.50 m²	-	0.54	4.30	0.90	m²	5.20
panes; area 0.50 m² - 1.00 m²	-	0.48	3.82	0.70	m²	4.52
panes; area over 1.00 m²	-	0.41	3.26	0.50	m²	3.76
Glazed windows and screens; multi-coloured work						
panes; area not exceeding 0.10 m²	-	0.73	5.81	1.00	m²	6.81
panes; area 0.10 m² - 0.50 m²	-	0.59	4.70	0.90	m²	5.60
panes; area 0.50 m² - 1.00 m²	-	0.52	4.14	0.69	m²	4.83
panes; area over 1.00 m²	-	0.44	3.50	0.49	m²	3.99
Knot; one coat primer; two undercoats and **one finishing coat of gloss oil paint; on wood** **surfaces**						
General surfaces						
over 300 mm girth	-	0.50	3.98	1.18	m²	5.16
isolated surfaces not exceeding 300 mm girth	-	0.20	1.59	0.42	m	2.01
isolated areas not exceeding 0.50 m²; irrespective of girth	-	0.38	3.02	0.74	nr	3.76
Glazed windows and screens						
panes; area not exceeding 0.10 m²	-	0.84	6.69	1.32	m²	8.01
panes; area 0.10 m² - 0.50 m²	-	0.67	5.33	1.17	m²	6.50
panes; area 0.50 m² - 1.00 m²	-	0.59	4.70	0.90	m²	5.60
panes; area over 1.00 m²	-	0.50	3.98	0.63	m²	4.61

M SURFACE FINISHES Excluding overheads and profit	PC £	Labour hours	Labour £	Material £	Unit	Total rate £
M60 PAINTING/CLEAR FINISHING - cont'd						
PAINTING/CLEAR FINISHING - EXTERNALLY - cont'd						
Knot; one coat primer; two undercoats and **one finishing coat of gloss oil paint; on wood** **surfaces** - cont'd						
Glazed windows and screens; multi-coloured work						
panes; area not exceeding 0.10 m^2	-	0.96	7.64	1.32	m^2	8.96
panes; area 0.10 m^2 - 0.50 m^2	-	0.78	6.21	1.18	m^2	7.39
panes; area 0.50 m^2 - 1.00 m^2	-	0.69	5.49	0.90	m^2	6.39
panes; area over 1.00 m^2	-	0.58	4.62	0.63	m^2	5.25
Touch up primer; one undercoat and one **finishing coat of gloss oil paint; on iron or** **steel surfaces**						
General surfaces						
over 300 mm girth	-	0.27	2.15	0.77	m^2	2.92
isolated surfaces not exceeding 300 mm girth	-	0.12	0.96	0.44	m	1.40
isolated areas not exceeding 0.50 m^2; irrespective of girth	-	0.20	1.59	0.40	nr	1.99
Glazed windows and screens						
panes; area not exceeding 0.10 m^2	-	0.46	3.66	0.82	m^2	4.48
panes; area 0.10 m^2 - 0.50 m^2	-	0.37	2.95	0.71	m^2	3.66
panes; area 0.50 m^2 - 1.00 m^2	-	0.32	2.55	0.60	m^2	3.15
panes; area over 1.00 m^2	-	0.27	2.15	0.45	m^2	2.60
Structural steelwork						
over 300 mm girth	-	0.31	2.47	0.81	m^2	3.28
Members of roof trusses						
over 300 mm girth	-	0.41	3.26	0.92	m^2	4.18
Ornamental railings and the like; each side measured overall						
over 300 mm girth	-	0.46	3.66	0.96	m^2	4.62
Eaves gutters						
over 300 mm girth	-	0.49	3.90	1.09	m^2	4.99
not exceeding 300 mm girth	-	0.20	1.59	0.36	m	1.95
Pipes or conduits						
over 300 mm girth	-	0.41	3.26	1.09	m^2	4.35
not exceeding 300 mm girth	-	0.16	1.27	0.36	m	1.63
Touch up primer; two undercoats and one **finishing coat of gloss oil paint; on iron or** **steel surfaces**						
General surfaces						
over 300 mm girth	-	0.38	3.02	1.05	m^2	4.07
isolated surfaces not exceeding 300 mm girth	-	0.15	1.19	0.28	m	1.47
isolated areas not exceeding 0.50 m^2; irrespective of girth	-	0.28	2.23	0.59	nr	2.82
Glazed windows and screens						
panes; area not exceeding 0.10 m^2	-	0.64	5.09	1.07	m^2	6.16
panes; area 0.10 m^2 - 0.50 m^2	-	0.51	4.06	0.92	m^2	4.98
panes; area 0.50 m^2 - 1.00 m^2	-	0.44	3.50	0.77	m^2	4.27
panes; area over 1.00 m^2	-	0.38	3.02	0.63	m^2	3.65
Structural steelwork						
over 300 mm girth	-	0.43	3.42	1.09	m^2	4.51
Members of roof trusses						
over 300 mm girth	-	0.58	4.62	1.23	m^2	5.85
Ornamental railings and the like; each side measured overall						
over 300 mm girth	-	0.65	5.17	1.28	m^2	6.45

M SURFACE FINISHES Excluding overheads and profit	PC £	Labour hours	Labour £	Material £	Unit	Total rate £
Eaves gutters						
over 300 mm girth	-	0.69	5.49	1.40	m²	**6.89**
not exceeding 300 mm girth	-	0.27	2.15	0.59	m	**2.74**
Pipes or conduits						
over 300 mm girth	-	0.58	4.62	1.40	m²	**6.02**
not exceeding 300 mm girth	-	0.23	1.83	0.48	m	**2.31**
One coat primer; one undercoat and one **finishing coat of gloss oil paint; on iron or** **steel surfaces**						
General surfaces						
over 300 mm girth	-	0.35	2.79	0.93	m²	**3.72**
isolated surfaces not exceeding 300 mm girth	-	0.14	1.11	0.24	m	**1.35**
isolated areas not exceeding 0.50 m²;						
irrespective of girth	-	0.27	2.15	0.49	nr	**2.64**
Glazed windows and screens						
panes; area not exceeding 0.10 m²	-	0.59	4.70	0.86	m²	**5.56**
panes; area 0.10 m² - 0.50 m²	-	0.48	3.82	0.75	m²	**4.57**
panes; area 0.50 m² - 1.00 m²	-	0.41	3.26	0.64	m²	**3.90**
panes; area over 1.00 m²	-	0.35	2.79	0.49	m²	**3.28**
Structural steelwork						
over 300 mm girth	-	0.40	3.18	0.98	m²	**4.16**
Members of roof trusses						
over 300 mm girth	-	0.52	4.14	1.09	m²	**5.23**
Ornamental railings and the like; each side						
measured overall						
over 300 mm girth	-	0.60	4.78	1.09	m²	**5.87**
Eaves gutters						
over 300 mm girth	-	0.63	5.01	1.28	m²	**6.29**
not exceeding 300 mm girth	-	0.26	2.07	0.44	m	**2.51**
Pipes or conduits						
over 300 mm girth	-	0.52	4.14	1.28	m²	**5.42**
not exceeding 300 mm girth	-	0.20	1.59	0.42	m	**2.01**
One coat primer; two undercoats and one **finishing coat of gloss oil paint; on iron or** **steel surfaces**						
General surfaces						
over 300 mm girth	-	0.46	3.66	1.21	m²	**4.87**
isolated surfaces not exceeding 300 mm girth	-	0.19	1.51	0.31	m	**1.82**
isolated areas not exceeding 0.50 m²;						
irrespective of girth	-	0.35	2.79	0.63	nr	**3.42**
Glazed windows and screens						
panes; area not exceeding 0.10 m²	-	0.77	6.13	1.11	m²	**7.24**
panes; area 0.10 m² - 0.50 m²	-	0.61	4.86	0.96	m²	**5.82**
panes; area 0.50 m² - 1.00 m²	-	0.54	4.30	0.82	m²	**5.12**
panes; area over 1.00 m²	-	0.46	3.66	0.63	m²	**4.29**
Structural steelwork						
over 300 mm girth	-	0.52	4.14	1.25	m²	**5.39**
Members of roof trusses						
over 300 mm girth	-	0.69	5.49	1.40	m²	**6.89**
Ornamental railings and the like; each side						
measured overall						
over 300 mm girth	-	0.78	6.21	1.40	m²	**7.61**
Eaves gutters						
over 300 mm girth	-	0.82	6.53	1.59	m²	**8.12**
not exceeding 300 mm girth	-	0.33	2.63	0.54	m	**3.17**
Pipes or conduits						
over 300 mm girth	-	0.69	5.49	1.59	m²	**7.08**
not exceeding 300 mm girth	-	0.27	2.15	0.53	m	**2.68**

M SURFACE FINISHES Excluding overheads and profit	PC £	Labour hours	Labour £	Material £	Unit	Total rate £
M60 PAINTING/CLEAR FINISHING - cont'd						
PAINTING/CLEAR FINISHING - EXTERNALLY - cont'd						
One coat of Andrews "Hammerite" paint or other **equal and approved; on iron or steel surfaces**						
General surfaces						
over 300 mm girth	-	0.16	1.27	1.01	m²	**2.28**
isolated surfaces not exceeding 300 mm girth	-	0.09	0.72	0.31	m	**1.03**
isolated areas not exceeding 0.50 m²;						
irrespective of girth	-	0.12	0.96	0.58	nr	**1.54**
Glazed windows and screens						
panes; area not exceeding 0.10 m²	-	0.27	2.15	0.76	m²	**2.91**
panes; area 0.10 m² - 0.50 m²	-	0.21	1.67	0.84	m²	**2.51**
panes; area 0.50 m² - 1.00 m²	-	0.20	1.59	0.75	m²	**2.34**
panes; area over 1.00 m²	-	0.16	1.27	0.75	m²	**2.02**
Structural steelwork						
over 300 mm girth		0.19	1.51	0.92	m²	**2.43**
Members of roof trusses						
over 300 mm girth	-	0.25	1.99	1.01	m²	**3.00**
Ornamental railings and the like; each side measured overall						
over 300 mm girth	-	0.28	2.23	1.01	m²	**3.24**
Eaves gutters						
over 300 mm girth	-	0.29	2.31	1.09	m²	**3.40**
not exceeding 300 mm girth	-	0.09	0.72	0.50	m	**1.22**
Pipes or conduits						
over 300 mm girth	-	0.28	2.23	0.92	m²	**3.15**
not exceeding 300 mm girth	-	0.09	0.72	0.42	m	**1.14**
Two coats of creosote; on wood surfaces						
General surfaces						
over 300 mm girth	-	0.17	1.35	0.16	m²	**1.51**
isolated surfaces not exceeding 300 mm girth	-	0.06	0.48	0.11	m	**0.59**
Two coats of "Solignum" wood preservative or **other equal and approved; on wood surfaces**						
General surfaces						
over 300 mm girth	-	0.15	1.19	0.87	m²	**2.06**
isolated surfaces not exceeding 300 mm girth	-	0.06	0.48	0.27	m	**0.75**
Three coats of polyurethane; on wood **surfaces**						
General surfaces						
over 300 mm girth	-	0.31	2.47	1.68	m²	**4.15**
isolated surfaces not exceeding 300 mm girth	-	0.12	0.96	0.83	m	**1.79**
isolated areas not exceeding 0.50 m²;						
irrespective of girth	-	0.23	1.83	0.96	nr	**2.79**
Two coats of "New Base" primer or other equal **and approved; and two coats of "Extra" or other** **equal and approved; Sadolin Ltd; pigmented; on** **wood surfaces**						
General surfaces						
over 300 mm girth	-	0.46	3.66	3.17	m²	**6.83**
isolated surfaces not exceeding 300 mm girth	-	0.28	2.23	1.09	m	**3.32**
Glazed windows and screens						
panes; area not exceeding 0.10 m²	-	0.77	6.13	2.26	m²	**8.39**
panes; area 0.10 m² - 0.50 m²	-	0.62	4.94	2.13	m²	**7.07**
panes; area 0.50 m² - 1.00 m²	-	0.54	4.30	2.00	m²	**6.30**
panes; area over 1.00 m²	-	0.46	3.66	1.61	m²	**5.27**

M SURFACE FINISHES Excluding overheads and profit	PC £	Labour hours	Labour £	Material £	Unit	Total rate £
Two coats Sikkens "Cetol Filter 7" exterior stain **or other equal and approved; on wood surfaces**						
General surfaces						
over 300 mm girth	-	0.20	1.59	2.64	m²	**4.23**
isolated surfaces not exceeding 300 mm girth	-	0.09	0.72	0.91	m	**1.63**
isolated areas not exceeding 0.50 m²;						
irrespective of girth	-	0.14	1.11	1.34	nr	**2.45**

Effective Speaking

Communicating in Speech

Christopher Turk, University of Wales College of Cardiff, UK

Effective Speaking provides the hard scientific information about audience psychology, text preparation, presentation methods, voice production, body language and persuasive advocacy which will help would-be speakers improve their performance. The emphasis throughout is on practical self-help, on methods which have been shown to work, with clear explanations of just why they are effective.

November 1985 171x108: 288pp
Pb: 0-419-13030-6: £15.99

Effective Writing

Improving Scientific, Technical and Business Communication

Christopher Turk, UK and John Kirkman, UK

Effective communication is vital to science, engineering and business management. This thoroughly updated second edition with a new chapter on the use of computers and word-processors gives clear, practical advice illustrated with real-life examples on how to select, organize and present information in reports, papers and other documents.

November 1988 234x156: 288pp
Pb: 0-419-14660-1: £14.99

To Order: Tel: +44 (0) 8700 768853, or +44 (0) 1264 343071
Fax: +44 (0) 1264 343005, or **Post:** E & FN Spon Customer Services, ITPS Andover, Hants, SP10 5BE, UK

All orders must be pre-paid and will be sent free in the UK. Europe please add: £2.95 for the first book, thereafter £1.25 per book. ROW please add: Airmail £6.50 for the first book, thereafter £2.50 per book. Please add £12.50 delivery charge for items over £100.00.

Marketing for Architects and Engineers

A new approach

Brian Richardson, Northern Architecture Centre Ltd, UK

Professional services marketing is a relatively new form of marketing that has been recognized only since the late 1980s. Most of the attempts to write about marketing for professional services have been a regurgitation of the traditional marketing approach that has evolved since the 1960s and have concentrated on minor differences and adjustments. In many ways, what is needed is a fresh approach which takes into account the complex political, social, economic, legislative and cultural backdrop and provides a way for design professionals, such as architects and engineers, to look to the future. This book does just that.

Contents: Introduction. Markets and marketing. Scenario planning. Synthesis marketing. Strategic mapping. A synthesis marketing programme. Architecture centres. Bibliography and references. Index.

November 1996: 234x156: 152pp
illus.25 line illus
Pb: 0-419-20290-0: £19.99

To Order: Tel: +44 (0) 8700 768853, or +44 (0) 1264 343071
Fax: +44 (0) 1264 343005, or **Post:** E & FN Spon Customer Services, ITPS Andover, Hants, SP10 5BE, UK

All orders must be pre-paid and will be sent free in the UK. Europe please add: £2.95 for the first book, thereafter £1.25 per book. ROW please add: Airmail £6.50 for the first book, thereafter £2.50 per book. Please add £12.50 delivery charge for items over £100.00.

N FURNITURE/EQUIPMENT Excluding overheads and profit	PC £	Labour hours	Labour £	Material £	Unit	Total rate £
N FURNITURE/EQUIPMENT						
N10/11 GENERAL FIXTURES/KITCHEN FITTINGS						
Fixing general fixtures						
NOTE: The fixing of general fixtures will vary considerably dependent upon the size of the fixture and the method of fixing employed. Prices for fixing like sized kitchen fittings may be suitable for certain fixtures, although adjustment to those rates will almost invariably be necessary and the reader is directed to section "G20" for information on bolts, plugging brickwork and blockwork, etc. which should prove useful in building up a suitable rate.						
The following supply only prices are for purpose made fittings components in various materials supplied as part of an assembled fitting and therefore may be used to arrive at a guide price for a complete fitting.						
Fitting components; blockboard						
Backs, fronts, sides or divisions; over 300 mm wide						
12 mm thick	-	-	-	32.31	m²	**32.31**
19 mm thick	-	-	-	41.69	m²	**41.69**
25 mm thick	-	-	-	54.76	m²	**54.76**
Shelves or worktops; over 300 mm wide						
19 mm thick	-	-	-	41.69	m²	**41.69**
25 mm thick	-	-	-	54.76	m²	**54.76**
Flush doors; lipped on four edges						
450 mm x 750 mm x 19 mm	-	-	-	22.64	nr	**22.64**
450 mm x 750 mm x 25 mm	-	-	-	27.73	nr	**27.73**
600 mm x 900 mm x 19 mm	-	-	-	33.66	nr	**33.66**
600 mm x 900 mm x 25 mm	-	-	-	41.09	nr	**41.09**
Fitting components; chipboard						
Backs, fronts, sides or divisions; over 300 mm wide						
6 mm thick	-	-	-	9.57	m²	**9.57**
9 mm thick	-	-	-	13.60	m²	**13.60**
12 mm thick	-	-	-	16.79	m²	**16.79**
19 mm thick	-	-	-	24.20	m²	**24.20**
25 mm thick	-	-	-	32.65	m²	**32.65**
Shelves or worktops; over 300 mm wide						
19 mm thick	-	-	-	24.20	m²	**24.20**
25 mm thick	-	-	-	32.65	m²	**32.65**
Flush doors; lipped on four edges						
450 mm x 750 mm x 19 mm	-	-	-	17.28	nr	**17.28**
450 mm x 750 mm x 25 mm	-	-	-	21.01	nr	**21.01**
600 mm x 900 mm x 19 mm	-	-	-	25.33	nr	**25.33**
600 mm x 900 mm x 25 mm	-	-	-	30.60	nr	**30.60**
Fitting components; Melamine faced chipboard						
Backs, fronts, sides or divisions; over 300 mm wide						
12 mm thick	-	-	-	23.05	m²	**23.05**
19 mm thick	-	-	-	31.25	m²	**31.25**
Shelves or worktops; over 300 mm wide						
19 mm thick	-	-	-	31.25	m²	**31.25**

N FURNITURE/EQUIPMENT Excluding overheads and profit	PC £	Labour hours	Labour £	Material £	Unit	Total rate £
Flush doors; lipped on four edges						
450 mm x 750 mm x 19 mm	-	-	-	21.45	nr	**21.45**
600 mm x 900 mm x 25 mm	-	-	-	31.55	nr	**31.55**
Fitting components; "Warerite Xcel" standard						
colour laminated chipboard type LD2 or other						
equal and approved						
Backs, fronts, sides or divisions; over 300 mm wide						
13.20 mm thick	-	-	-	61.84	m²	**61.84**
Shelves or worktops; over 300 mm wide						
13.20 mm thick	-	-	-	61.84	m²	**61.84**
Flush doors; lipped on four edges						
450 mm x 750 mm x 13.20 mm	-	-	-	30.36	m²	**30.36**
600 mm x 900 mm x 13.20 mm	-	-	-	45.65	m²	**45.65**
Fitting components; plywood						
Backs, fronts, sides or divisions; over 300 mm wide						
6 mm thick	-	-	-	15.86	m²	**15.86**
9 mm thick	-	-	-	21.54	m²	**21.54**
12 mm thick	-	-	-	27.13	m²	**27.13**
19 mm thick	-	-	-	39.58	m²	**39.58**
25 mm thick	-	-	-	53.40	m²	**53.40**
Shelves or worktops; over 300 mm wide						
19 mm thick	-	-	-	39.58	m²	**39.58**
25 mm thick	-	-	-	53.40	m²	**53.40**
Flush doors; lipped on four edges						
450 mm x 750 mm x 19 mm	-	-	-	21.65	nr	**21.65**
450 mm x 750 mm x 25 mm	-	-	-	26.92	nr	**26.92**
600 mm x 900 mm x 19 mm	-	-	-	32.24	nr	**32.24**
600 mm x 900 mm x 25 mm	-	-	-	39.94	nr	**39.94**
Fitting components; wrought softwood						
Backs, fronts, sides or divisions; cross-tongued						
joints; over 300 mm wide						
25 mm thick	-	-	-	38.07	m²	**38.07**
Shelves or worktops; cross-tongued joints; over						
300 mm wide						
25 mm thick	-	-	-	38.07	m²	**38.07**
Bearers						
19 mm x 38 mm	-	-	-	2.16	m	**2.16**
25 mm x 50 mm	-	-	-	2.70	m	**2.70**
50 mm x 50 mm	-	-	-	3.95	m	**3.95**
50 mm x 75 mm	-	-	-	5.28	m	**5.28**
Bearers; framed						
19 mm x 38 mm	-	-	-	4.23	m	**4.23**
25 mm x 50 mm	-	-	-	4.78	m	**4.78**
50 mm x 50 mm	-	-	-	6.02	m	**6.02**
50 mm x 75 mm	-	-	-	7.35	m	**7.35**
Framing to backs, fronts or sides						
19 mm x 38 mm	-	-	-	4.23	m	**4.23**
25 mm x 50 mm	-	-	-	4.78	m	**4.78**
50 mm x 50 mm	-	-	-	6.02	m	**6.02**
50 mm x 75 mm	-	-	-	7.35	m	**7.35**
Flush doors, softwood skeleton or cellular core;						
plywood facing both sides; lipped on four						
edges						
450 mm x 750 mm x 35 mm	-	-	-	21.38	nr	**21.38**
600 mm x 900 mm x 35 mm	-	-	-	34.05	nr	**34.05**
Add 5% to the above material prices for						
selected softwood staining						

N FURNITURE/EQUIPMENT Excluding overheads and profit	PC £	Labour hours	Labour £	Material £	Unit	Total rate £
N10/11 GENERAL FIXTURES/KITCHEN FITTINGS - cont'd						
Fitting components; selected West African Mahogany						
Bearers						
19 mm x 38 mm	-	-	-	3.62	m	3.62
25 mm x 50 mm	-	-	-	4.76	m	4.76
50 mm x 50 mm	-	-	-	7.32	m	7.32
50 mm x 75 mm	-	-	-	10.00	m	10.00
Bearers; framed						
19 mm x 38 mm	-	-	-	6.73	m	6.73
25 mm x 50 mm	-	-	-	7.88	m	7.88
50 mm x 50 mm	-	-	-	10.43	m	10.43
50 mm x 75 mm	-	-	-	13.11	m	13.11
Framing to backs, fronts or sides						
19 mm x 38 mm	-	-	-	6.73	m	6.73
25 mm x 50 mm	-	-	-	7.88	m	7.88
50 mm x 50 mm	-	-	-	10.43	m	10.43
50 mm x 75 mm	-	-	-	13.11	m	13.11
Fitting components; Iroko						
Backs, fronts, sides or divisions; cross-tongued joints; over 300 mm wide						
25 mm thick	-	-	-	85.52	m²	85.52
Shelves or worktops; cross-tongued joints; over 300 mm wide						
25 mm thick	-	-	-	85.52	m²	85.52
Draining boards; cross-tongued joints; over 300 mm wide						
25 mm thick	-	-	-	90.38	m²	90.38
stopped flutes	-	-	-	2.72	m	2.72
grooves; cross-grain	-	-	-	0.64	m	0.64
Bearers						
19 mm x 38 mm	-	-	-	4.40	m	4.40
25 mm x 50 mm	-	-	-	5.69	m	5.69
50 mm x 50 mm	-	-	-	8.67	m	8.67
50 mm x 75 mm	-	-	-	11.81	m	11.81
Bearers; framed						
19 mm x 38 mm	-	-	-	8.55	m	8.55
25 mm x 50 mm	-	-	-	9.84	m	9.84
50 mm x 50 mm	-	-	-	12.82	m	12.82
50 mm x 75 mm	-	-	-	15.96	m	15.96
Framing to backs, fronts or sides						
19 mm x 38 mm	-	-	-	8.55	m	8.55
25 mm x 50 mm	-	-	-	9.84	m	9.84
50 mm x 50 mm	-	-	-	12.82	m	12.82
50 mm x 75 mm	-	-	-	15.96	m	15.96
Fitting components; Teak						
Backs, fronts, sides or divisions; cross-tongued joints; over 300 mm wide						
25 mm thick	-	-	-	173.56	m²	173.56
Shelves or worktops; cross-tongued joints; over 300 mm wide						
25 mm thick	-	-	-	173.56	m²	173.56
Draining boards; cross-tongued joints; over 300 mm wide						
25 mm thick	-	-	-	177.19	m²	177.19
stopped flutes	-	-	-	2.72	m	2.72
grooves; cross-grain	-	-	-	0.64	m	0.64

N FURNITURE/EQUIPMENT Excluding overheads and profit	PC £	Labour hours	Labour £	Material £	Unit	Total rate £
Fixing kitchen fittings						
NOTE: Kitchen fittings vary considerably. PC supply prices for reasonable quantities for a moderately priced range of kitchen fittings (Rugby Joinery "Lambeth" range) have been shown but not extended.						
Fixing to backgrounds requiring plugging; including any pre-assembly						
Wall units						
300 mm x 580 mm x 300 mm	28.92	1.20	9.55	0.17	nr	**9.72**
300 mm x 720 mm x 300 mm	32.53	1.25	9.95	0.17	nr	**10.12**
600 mm x 580 mm x 300 mm	36.69	1.40	11.14	0.17	nr	**11.31**
600 mm x 720 mm x 300 mm	40.76	1.60	12.74	0.17	nr	**12.91**
Floor units with drawers						
600 mm x 900 mm x 500 mm	59.34	1.25	9.95	0.17	nr	**10.12**
600 mm x 900 mm x 600 mm	61.89	1.40	11.14	0.17	nr	**11.31**
1200 mm x 900 mm x 600 mm	110.66	1.70	13.53	0.17	nr	**13.70**
Sink units (excluding sink top)						
1000 mm x 900 mm x 600 mm	69.97	1.60	12.74	0.17	nr	**12.91**
1200 mm x 900 mm x 600 mm	77.27	1.80	14.33	0.17	nr	**14.50**
Laminated plastics worktops; single rolled edge; prices include for fixing						
28 mm thick; 600 mm wide	-	0.40	3.18	12.23	m	**15.41**
38 mm thick; 600 mm wide	-	0.40	3.18	19.41	m	**22.59**
extra for forming hole for inset sink	-	0.75	5.97	-	nr	**5.97**
extra for jointing strip at corner intersection of worktops	-	0.15	1.19	8.14	nr	**9.33**
extra for butt and scribe joint at corner intersection of worktops	-	4.50	35.82	-	nr	**35.82**
Lockers; The Welconstruct Company or other equal and approved						
Standard clothes lockers; steel body and door within reinforced 19G frame, powder coated finish, cam locks						
1 compartment; placing in position						
305 mm x 305 mm x 1830 mm	-	0.25	1.61	45.00	nr	**46.61**
305 mm x 460 mm x 1830 mm	-	0.25	1.61	54.60	nr	**56.21**
460 mm x 460 mm x 1830 mm	-	0.30	1.94	68.80	nr	**70.74**
610 mm x 460 mm x 1830 mm	-	0.30	1.94	82.80	nr	**84.74**
Compartment lockers; steel body and door within reinforced 19G frame, powder coated finish, cam locks						
2 compartments; placing in position						
305 mm x 305 mm x 1830 mm	-	0.25	1.61	60.50	nr	**62.11**
305 mm x 460 mm x 1830 mm	-	0.25	1.61	63.40	nr	**65.01**
460 mm x 460 mm x 1830 mm	-	0.30	1.94	75.10	nr	**77.04**
4 compartments; placing in position						
305 mm x 305 mm x 1830 mm	-	0.25	1.61	76.50	nr	**78.11**
305 mm x 460 mm x 1830 mm	-	0.25	1.61	81.80	nr	**83.41**
460 mm x 460 mm x 1830 mm	-	0.30	1.94	85.80	nr	**87.74**
Wet area lockers; galvanised steel 18/22G etched primed coating body, galvanised steel 18/20G reinforced door on non-ferrous hinges, powder coated finish, cam locks						
1 compartment; placing in position						
305 mm x 305 mm x 1830 mm	-	0.25	1.61	65.40	nr	**67.01**

N FURNITURE/EQUIPMENT Excluding overheads and profit	PC £	Labour hours	Labour £	Material £	Unit	Total rate £
N10/11 GENERAL FIXTURES/KITCHEN FITTINGS - cont'd						
Lockers; The Welconstruct Company or other **equal and approved** - cont'd Wet area lockers; galvanised steel 18/22G etched primed coating body, galvanised steel 18/20G reinforced door on non-ferrous hinges, powder coated finish, cam locks - cont'd						
2 compartments; placing in position						
305 mm x 305 mm x 1830 mm	-	0.25	1.61	84.75	nr	86.36
305 mm x 460 mm x 1830 mm	-	0.25	1.61	88.82	nr	90.43
4 compartments; placing in position						
305 mm x 305 mm x 1830 mm	-	0.25	1.61	107.20	nr	108.81
305 mm x 460 mm x 1830 mm	-	0.25	1.61	114.84	nr	116.45
Extra for						
coin operated lock; coin returned	-	-	-	34.35	nr	34.35
coin operated lock; coin retained	-	-	-	53.90	nr	53.90
Timber clothes lockers; veneered MDF finish, routed door, cam locks						
1 compartment; placing in position						
380 mm x 380 mm x 1830 mm	-	0.30	1.94	198.00	nr	199.94
4 compartments; placing in position						
380 mm x 380 mm x 1830 mm	-	0.30	1.94	297.00	nr	298.94
Shelving support systems; The Welconstruct **Company or other equal and approved** Rolled front shelving support systems; steel body; stove enamelled finish; assembling						
open initial bay; 5 shelves; placing in position						
915 mm x 305 mm x 1905 mm	-	0.75	5.45	61.24	nr	66.69
915 mm x 460 mm x 1905 mm	-	0.75	5.45	79.72	nr	85.17
open extension bay; 5 shelves; placing in position						
915 mm x 305 mm x 1905 mm	-	0.90	6.54	49.63	nr	56.17
915 mm x 460 mm x 1905 mm	-	0.90	6.54	63.95	nr	70.49
closed initial bay; 5 shelves; placing in position						
915 mm x 305 mm x 1905 mm	-	0.75	5.45	76.72	nr	82.17
915 mm x 460 mm x 1905 mm	-	0.75	5.45	95.20	nr	100.65
closed extension bay; 5 shelves; placing in position						
915 mm x 305 mm x 1905 mm	-	0.90	6.54	68.60	nr	75.14
915 mm x 460 mm x 1905 mm	-	0.90	6.54	82.91	nr	89.45
6 mm thick rectangular glass mirrors; silver **backed; fixed with chromium plated domed** **headed screws; to background requiring** **plugging**						
Mirror with polished edges						
365 mm x 254 mm	4.28	0.80	6.37	5.09	nr	11.46
400 mm x 300 mm	5.63	0.80	6.37	6.64	nr	13.01
560 mm x 380 mm	9.68	0.90	7.16	11.30	nr	18.46
640 mm x 460 mm	12.15	1.00	7.96	14.14	nr	22.10
Mirror with bevelled edges						
365 mm x 254 mm	7.42	0.80	6.37	8.70	nr	15.07
400 mm x 300 mm	8.78	0.80	6.37	10.26	nr	16.63
560 mm x 380 mm	14.40	0.90	7.16	16.73	nr	23.89
640 mm x 460 mm	18.00	1.00	7.96	20.87	nr	28.83

N FURNITURE/EQUIPMENT Excluding overheads and profit	PC £	Labour hours	Labour £	Material £	Unit	Total rate £
Door mats						
Entrance mats; "Tuftiguard type C" or other equal						
and approved; laying in position; 12 mm thick						
900 mm x 550 mm	181.90	0.50	3.23	90.95	nr	**94.18**
1200 mm x 750 mm	181.90	0.50	3.23	163.71	nr	**166.94**
2400 mm x 1200 mm	181.90	1.00	6.45	523.87	nr	**530.32**
Matwells						
Polished aluminium matwell; comprising 34						
mm x 26 mm x 6 mm angle rim; with brazed						
angles and lugs brazed on; to suit mat size						
914 mm x 560 mm	33.61	1.00	6.45	33.61	nr	**40.06**
1067 mm x 610 mm	36.92	1.00	6.45	36.92	nr	**43.37**
1219 mm x 762 mm	43.64	1.00	6.45	43.64	nr	**50.09**
Polished brass matwell; comprising 38 mm x						
38 mm x 6 mm angle rim; with brazed angles						
and lugs welded on; to suit mat size						
914 mm x 560 mm	99.52	1.00	6.45	99.52	nr	**105.97**
1067 mm x 610 mm	109.31	1.00	6.45	109.31	nr	**115.76**
1219 mm x 762 mm	129.21	1.00	6.45	129.21	nr	**135.66**
Internal blinds; Luxaflex Ltd or other						
equal and approved						
Roller blinds; Luxaflex "Safeweave RB"; fire						
resisting material; 1200 mm drop; fixing with						
screws						
1000 mm wide	38.00	1.00	6.45	38.00	nr	**44.45**
2000 mm wide	74.00	1.57	10.13	74.00	nr	**84.13**
3000 mm wide	112.00	2.13	13.74	112.00	nr	**125.74**
Roller blinds; Luxaflex "Plain RB"; plain type						
material; 1200 mm drop; fixing with screws						
1000 mm wide	24.00	1.00	6.45	24.00	nr	**30.45**
2000 mm wide	46.00	1.57	10.13	46.00	nr	**56.13**
3000 mm wide	68.00	2.13	13.74	68.00	nr	**81.74**
Roller blinds; Luxaflex "Dimout plain RB";						
blackout material; 1200 mm drop; fixing with						
screws						
1000 mm wide	38.00	1.00	6.45	38.00	nr	**44.45**
2000 mm wide	74.00	1.57	10.13	74.00	nr	**84.13**
3000 mm wide	112.00	2.13	13.74	112.00	nr	**125.74**
Roller blinds; Luxaflex "Lite-master Crank Op";						
100% blackout; 1200 mm drop; fixing with						
screws						
1000 mm wide	173.00	2.12	13.67	173.00	nr	**186.67**
2000 mm wide	246.00	2.97	19.16	246.00	nr	**265.16**
3000 mm wide	309.00	3.82	24.64	309.00	nr	**333.64**
Vertical louvre blinds; 89 mm wide louvres;						
Luxaflex "Finessa 3430" Group 0; 1200 mm						
drop; fixing with screws						
1000 mm wide	54.00	0.89	5.74	54.00	nr	**59.74**
2000 mm wide	93.00	1.40	9.03	93.00	nr	**102.03**
3000 mm wide	132.00	1.91	12.32	132.00	nr	**144.32**
Vertical louvre blinds; 127 mm wide louvres;						
"Finessa 3430" Group 0; 1200 mm drop; fixing						
with screws						
1000 mm wide	48.00	0.95	6.13	48.00	nr	**54.13**
2000 mm wide	80.00	1.46	9.42	80.00	nr	**89.42**
3000 mm wide	115.00	1.96	12.64	115.00	nr	**127.64**

N FURNITURE/EQUIPMENT Excluding overheads and profit	PC £	Labour hours	Labour £	Material £	Unit	Total rate £
N13 SANITARY APPLIANCES/FITTINGS						
NOTE: Sanitary fittings are largely a matter of selection and material prices vary considerably; the PC values given below are for "average quality".						
Sanitary fittings						
Sink; white fireclay; BS 1206; cast iron cantilever brackets						
610 mm x 455 mm x 205 mm	100.00	3.00	31.71	106.88	nr	**138.59**
610 mm x 455 mm x 255 mm	115.00	3.00	31.71	121.88	nr	**153.59**
760 mm x 455 mm x 255 mm	170.00	3.00	31.71	176.88	nr	**208.59**
Sink; stainless steel combined bowl and draining board; chain and self colour plug; to BS 3380						
1050 mm x 500 mm; with bowl 420 mm x 350 mm x 175 mm	115.00	1.75	18.50	115.00	nr	**133.50**
Sink; stainless steel combined bowl and double draining board; chain and self colour plug to BS 3380						
1550 mm x 500 mm; with bowl 420 mm x 350 mm x 200 mm	130.00	1.75	18.50	130.00	nr	**148.50**
Lavatory basin; vitreous china; BS 1188; 32 mm diameter chromium plated waste; chain, stay and plug; pair 13 mm diameter chromium plated easy clean pillar taps to BS 1010; painted cantilever brackets; plugged and screwed						
560 mm x 405 mm	55.00	2.30	24.31	55.00	nr	**79.31**
560 mm x 405 mm; coloured	65.00	2.30	24.31	65.00	nr	**89.31**
635 mm x 455 mm	75.00	2.30	24.31	75.00	nr	**99.31**
635 mm x 455 mm; coloured	85.00	2.30	24.31	85.00	nr	**109.31**
Lavatory basin and pedestal; vitreous china; BS 1188; 32 mm diameter chromium plated waste; chain, stay and plug; pair 13 mm diameter chromium plated easy clean pillar taps to BS 1010; pedestal; wall brackets; plugged and screwed						
560 mm x 405 mm	70.00	2.50	26.43	70.00	nr	**96.43**
560 mm x 405 mm; coloured	80.00	2.50	26.43	80.00	nr	**106.43**
635 mm x 455 mm	90.00	2.50	26.43	90.00	nr	**116.43**
635 mm x 455 mm; coloured	105.00	2.50	26.43	105.00	nr	**131.43**
Lavatory basin range; overlap joints; white glazed fireclay; 32 mm diameter chromium plated waste, chain, stay and plug; pair 13 mm diameter chromium plated easy clean pillar taps to BS 1010; painted cast iron cantilever brackets						
range of four; 506 mm x 405 mm	290.00	8.80	93.02	290.00	nr	**383.02**
add for each additional basin in range	-	2.00	21.14	75.00	nr	**96.14**
Drinking fountain; white glazed fireclay; 19 mm diameter chromium plated waste; self-closing non-concussive tap; regulating valve; plugged and screwed with chromium plated screws						
drinking fountain	160.00	2.50	26.43	160.00	nr	**186.43**
Bath; reinforced acrylic rectangular pattern; chromium plated overflow chain and plug; 40 mm diameter chromium plated waste; cast brass "P" trap with plain outlet and overflow connection; pair 20 mm diameter chromium plated easy clean pillar taps to BS 1010						
1700 mm long; white	180.00	3.50	36.99	180.00	nr	**216.99**
1700 mm long; coloured	200.00	3.50	36.99	200.00	nr	**236.99**

N FURNITURE/EQUIPMENT Excluding overheads and profit	PC £	Labour hours	Labour £	Material £	Unit	Total rate £
Bath; enamelled steel; medium gauge rectangular pattern; 40 mm diameter chromium plated overflow chain and plug; 40 mm diameter chromium plated waste; cast brass "P" trap with plain outlet and overflow connection; pair 20 mm diameter chromium plated easy clean pillar taps to BS 1010						
1700 mm long; white	275.00	3.50	36.99	275.00	nr	**311.99**
1700 mm long; coloured	295.00	3.50	36.99	295.00	nr	**331.99**
Shower tray; glazed fireclay with outlet and grated waste; chain and plug; bedding and pointing in waterproof cement mortar						
760 mm x 760 mm x 180 mm; white	110.00	3.00	31.71	110.00	nr	**141.71**
760 mm x 760 mm x 180 mm; coloured	170.00	3.00	31.71	170.00	nr	**201.71**
Shower fitting; riser pipe with mixing valve and shower rose; chromium plated; plugging and screwing mixing valve and pipe bracket						
15 mm diameter riser pipe; 127 mm diameter shower rose	220.00	5.00	52.85	220.00	nr	**272.85**
WC suite; high level; vitreous china pan; black plastic seat; 9 litre white vitreous china cistern and brackets; low pressure ball valve; galvanized steel flush pipe and clip; plugged and screwed; mastic joint to drain						
WC suite; white	160.00	3.30	34.88	160.00	nr	**194.88**
WC suite; coloured	200.00	3.30	34.88	200.00	nr	**234.88**
WC suite; low level; vitreous china pan; black plastic seat; 9 litre white vitreous china cistern and brackets; low pressure ball valve and plastic flush pipe; plugged and screwed; mastic joint to drain						
WC suite; white	105.00	3.00	31.71	105.00	nr	**136.71**
WC suite; coloured	135.00	3.00	31.71	135.00	nr	**166.71**
Bidet; vitreous china; chromium plated waste; mixer tap with hand wheels						
600 mm x 400 mm x 400 mm; white	180.00	3.50	36.99	180.00	nr	**216.99**
Slop sink; white glazed fireclay with hardwood pad; aluminium bucket grating; vitreous china cistern and porcelain enamelled brackets; galvanized steel flush pipe and clip; plugged and screwed; mastic joint to drain						
slop sink	555.00	3.50	36.99	555.00	nr	**591.99**
Bowl type wall urinal; white glazed vitreous china; white vitreous china automatic flushing cistern and brackets; 38 mm diameter chromium plated waste; chromium plated flush pipes and spreaders; cistern brackets and flush pipe plugged and screwed with chromium plated screws						
single; 455 mm x 380 mm x 330 mm	200.00	4.00	42.28	200.00	nr	**242.28**
range of two	275.00	7.50	79.28	275.00	nr	**354.28**
range of three	305.00	11.00	116.27	305.00	nr	**421.27**
add for each additional urinal	115.00	3.20	33.82	115.00	nr	**148.82**
add for divisions between urinals	40.00	0.75	7.93	40.00	nr	**47.93**
Bath screen; clear glass; chrome frame; plugged and screwed						
690 mm x 1340 mm	260.00	1.50	15.86	260.00	nr	**275.86**
N15 SIGNS/NOTICES						
Plain script; in gloss oil paint; on painted or varnished surfaces						
Capital letters; lower case letters or numerals						
per coat; per 25 mm high	-	0.10	0.80	-	nr	**0.80**
Stops						
per coat	-	0.03	0.24	-	nr	**0.24**

P BUILDING FABRIC SUNDRIES
Excluding overheads and profit

P10 SUNDRY INSULATION/PROOFING WORK/FIRESTOPS

ALTERNATIVE INSULATION PRICES

Insulation (£/m²)	£		£			£			£
EXPANDED POLYSTYRENE									
"Crown Wallmate"									
25 mm	3.86	30 mm	4.31	40 mm		4.64	50 mm		7.06
"Crown Wool"									
60 mm	1.91	80 mm	2.50	100 mm		2.98			
"Crown Dritherm" - part fill									
30 mm	1.97	50 mm	3.11	75 mm		4.13			
"Crown Sound Deadening Quilt"									
13 mm	2.09	25 mm	4.02						
"Crown Factoryclad"									
80 mm	2.71	90 mm	2.98	100 mm		3.23			

P BUILDING FABRIC SUNDRIES Excluding overheads and profit	PC £	Labour hours	Labour £	Material £	Unit	Total rate £
"Sisalkraft" building papers/vapour barriers						
or other equal and approved						
Building paper; 150 mm laps; fixed to softwood						
"Moistop" grade 728 (class A1F)	-	0.10	1.13	0.84	m²	**1.97**
Vapour barrier/reflective insulation 150 laps;						
fixed to softwood						
"Insulex" grade 714; single sided	-	0.10	1.13	1.05	m²	**2.18**
"Insulex" grade 714; double sided	-	0.10	1.13	1.50	m²	**2.63**
Mat or quilt insulation						
Glass fibre quilt; "Isowool 1000" or other equal						
and approved; laid loose between members at						
600 mm centres						
60 mm thick	2.01	0.21	2.38	2.01	m²	**4.39**
80 mm thick	2.63	0.23	2.61	2.63	m²	**5.24**
100 mm thick	3.13	0.25	2.83	3.13	m²	**5.96**
150 mm thick	4.80	0.30	3.40	4.80	m²	**8.20**
Mineral fibre quilt; "Isowool 1200" or other equal						
and approved; pinned vertically to softwood						
25 mm thick	1.66	0.14	1.59	1.66	m²	**3.25**
50 mm thick	2.73	0.15	1.70	2.73	m²	**4.43**
Glass fibre building roll; pinned vertically to						
softwood						
60 mm thick	1.53	0.15	1.70	1.61	m²	**3.31**
80 mm thick	2.00	0.16	1.81	2.10	m²	**3.91**
100 mm thick	2.38	0.17	1.93	2.50	m²	**4.43**
Glass fibre flanged building roll; paper faces;						
pinned vertically or to slope between timber						
framing						
60 mm thick	3.23	0.18	2.04	3.39	m²	**5.43**
80 mm thick	4.03	0.19	2.15	4.23	m²	**6.38**
100 mm thick	4.70	0.20	2.27	4.93	m²	**7.20**
Glass fibre aluminium foil faced roll; pinned to						
softwood						
80 mm thick	-	0.18	2.04	3.57	m²	**5.61**

P BUILDING FABRIC SUNDRIES Excluding overheads and profit	PC £	Labour hours	Labour £	Material £	Unit	Total rate £
Board or slab insulation						
Jablite expanded polystyrene board standard grade ISD						
or other equal and approved; fixed with adhesive						
25 mm thick	-	0.42	4.76	2.63	m²	**7.39**
40 mm thick	-	0.45	5.10	4.10	m²	**9.20**
50 mm thick	-	0.50	5.67	4.84	m²	**10.51**
Jablite expanded polystyrene board grade						
EHD(N) or other equal and approved						
100 mm thick	-	0.50	5.67	0.93	m²	**6.60**
"Styrofoam Floormate 350" extruded polystyrene						
foam or other equal and approved						
50 mm thick	-	0.50	5.67	10.17	m²	**15.84**
Fire stops						
Cape "Firecheck" channel or other equal and approved;						
intumescent coatings on cut mitres; fixing with brass cups						
and screws						
19 mm x 44 mm or 19 mm x 50 mm	7.61	0.60	6.80	8.30	m	**15.10**
"Sealmaster" intumescent fire and smoke seals or other						
equal and approved; pinned into groove in timber						
type N30; for single leaf half hour door	5.07	0.30	3.40	5.32	m	**8.72**
type N60; for single leaf one hour door	7.70	0.33	3.74	8.08	m	**11.82**
type IMN or IMP; for meeting or pivot stiles of						
pair of one hour doors; per stile	7.70	0.33	3.74	8.08	m	**11.82**
intumescent plugs in timber; including boring	-	0.10	1.13	0.25	nr	**1.38**
Rockwool fire stops or other equal and approved;						
between top of brick/block wall and concrete soffit						
25 mm deep x 112 mm wide	-	0.08	0.91	0.50	m	**1.41**
25 mm deep x 150 mm wide	-	0.10	1.13	0.67	m	**1.80**
50 mm deep x 225 mm wide	-	0.15	1.70	2.01	m	**3.71**
Fire protection compound						
Quelfire QF4, fire protection compound or other equal						
and approved; filling around pipes, ducts and the like;						
including all necessary formwork						
300 mm x 300 mm x 250 mm; pipes - 2	-	1.00	10.22	10.51	nr	**20.73**
500 mm x 500 mm x 250 mm; pipes - 2	-	1.25	12.04	31.53	nr	**43.57**
Fire barriers						
Rockwool fire barrier or other equal and approved;						
between top of suspended ceiling and concrete soffit						
one 50 mm layer x 900 mm wide; half hour	-	0.60	6.80	5.57	m²	**12.37**
two 50 mm layers x 900 mm wide; one hour	-	0.90	10.21	10.95	m²	**21.16**
Lamatherm fire barrier or other equal and approved;						
to void below raised access floors						
75 mm thick x 300 mm wide; half hour	-	0.18	2.04	12.57	m	**14.61**
75 mm thick x 600 mm wide; half hour	-	0.18	2.04	28.04	m	**30.08**
90 mm thick x 300 mm wide; half hour	-	0.18	2.04	15.66	m	**17.70**
90 mm thick x 600 mm wide; half hour	-	0.18	2.04	37.41	m	**39.45**
Dow Chemicals "Styrofoam 1B" or other equal and						
approved; cold bridging insulation fixed with						
adhesive to brick, block or concrete base						
Insulation to walls						
25 mm thick	-	0.34	3.86	4.85	m²	**8.71**
50 mm thick	-	0.36	4.08	8.90	m²	**12.98**
75 mm thick	-	0.38	4.31	13.27	m²	**17.58**
Insulation to isolated columns						
25 mm thick	-	0.41	4.65	4.85	m²	**9.50**
50 mm thick	-	0.44	4.99	8.90	m²	**13.89**
75 mm thick	-	0.47	5.33	13.27	m²	**18.60**

P BUILDING FABRIC SUNDRIES Excluding overheads and profit	PC £	Labour hours	Labour £	Material £	Unit	Total rate £
P10 SUNDRY INSULATION/PROOFING **WORK/FIRESTOPS** - cont'd						
Dow Chemicals "Styrofoam 1B" or other equal and **approved; cold bridging insulation fixed with** **adhesive to brick, block or concrete base** - cont'd						
Insulation to ceilings						
25 mm thick	-	0.36	4.08	4.85	m²	**8.93**
50 mm thick	-	0.39	4.42	8.90	m²	**13.32**
75 mm thick	-	0.42	4.76	13.27	m²	**18.03**
Insulation to isolated beams						
25 mm thick	-	0.44	4.99	4.85	m²	**9.84**
50 mm thick	-	0.47	5.33	8.90	m²	**14.23**
75 mm thick	-	0.50	5.67	13.27	m²	**18.94**
P11 FOAMED/FIBRE/BEAD CAVITY WALL **INSULATION**						
Injected insulation						
Cavity wall insulation; injecting 65 mm cavity with						
blown EPS granules	-	-	-	-	m²	**2.50**
blown mineral wool	-	-	-	-	m²	**2.25**
P20 UNFRAMED ISOLATED TRIMS/ **SKIRTINGS/SUNDRY ITEMS**						
Blockboard (Birch faced); 18 mm thick						
Window boards and the like; rebated; hardwood lipped on one edge						
18 mm x 200 mm	-	0.25	2.83	3.45	m	**6.28**
18 mm x 250 mm	-	0.28	3.18	4.05	m	**7.23**
18 mm x 300 mm	-	0.31	3.52	4.66	m	**8.18**
18 mm x 350 mm	-	0.34	3.86	5.26	m	**9.12**
returned and fitted ends	-	0.22	2.49	0.35	nr	**2.84**
Blockboard (Sapele veneered one side); 18 **mm thick**						
Window boards and the like; rebated; hardwood lipped on one edge						
18 mm x 200 mm	-	0.27	3.06	3.08	m	**6.14**
18 mm x 250 mm	-	0.30	3.40	3.59	m	**6.99**
18 mm x 300 mm	-	0.33	3.74	4.10	m	**7.84**
18 mm x 350 mm	-	0.36	4.08	4.61	m	**8.69**
returned and fitted ends	-	0.22	2.49	0.35	nr	**2.84**
Blockboard (American White Ash veneered **one side); 18 mm thick**						
Window boards and the like; rebated; hardwood lipped on one edge						
18 mm x 200 mm	-	0.27	3.06	3.52	m	**6.58**
18 mm x 250 mm	-	0.30	3.40	4.14	m	**7.54**
18 mm x 300 mm	-	0.33	3.74	4.76	m	**8.50**
18 mm x 350 mm	-	0.36	4.08	5.38	m	**9.46**
returned and fitted ends	-	0.22	2.49	0.35	nr	**2.84**
Medium density fibreboard primed profiles; **Balcas Kildare Ltd or other equal and approved**						
Window boards; rounded and rebated						
25 mm x 220 mm	-	0.30	3.40	3.72	m	**7.12**
25 mm x 245 mm	-	0.30	3.40	4.04	m	**7.44**

P BUILDING FABRIC SUNDRIES Excluding overheads and profit	PC £	Labour hours	Labour £	Material £	Unit	Total rate £
Skirtings						
14.50 mm x 45 mm; rounded	-	0.10	1.13	0.78	m	**1.91**
14.50 mm x 70 mm; rounded	-	0.10	1.13	1.06	m	**2.19**
14.50 mm x 95 mm; rounded	-	0.10	1.13	1.29	m	**2.42**
14.50 mm x 95 mm; moulded	-	0.10	1.13	1.29	m	**2.42**
14.50 mm x 120 mm; moulded	-	0.10	1.13	1.51	m	**2.64**
18 mm x 70 mm; moulded	-	0.10	1.13	1.19	m	**2.32**
18 mm x 145 mm; moulded	-	0.10	1.13	1.98	m	**3.11**
Dado rail						
18 mm x 58 mm; moulded	-	0.10	1.13	1.20	m	**2.33**
Wrought softwood						
Skirtings, picture rails, dado rails and the like; splayed or moulded						
19 mm x 50 mm; splayed	-	0.10	1.13	1.27	m	**2.40**
19 mm x 50 mm; moulded	-	0.10	1.13	1.39	m	**2.52**
19 mm x 75 mm; splayed	-	0.10	1.13	1.51	m	**2.64**
19 mm x 75 mm; moulded	-	0.10	1.13	1.62	m	**2.75**
19 mm x 100 mm; splayed	-	0.10	1.13	1.76	m	**2.89**
19 mm x 100 mm; moulded	-	0.10	1.13	1.86	m	**2.99**
19 mm x 150 mm; moulded	-	0.12	1.36	2.37	m	**3.73**
19 mm x 175 mm; moulded	-	0.12	1.36	2.60	m	**3.96**
22 mm x 100 mm; splayed	-	0.10	1.13	1.92	m	**3.05**
25 mm x 50 mm; moulded	-	0.10	1.13	1.56	m	**2.69**
25 mm x 75 mm; splayed	-	0.10	1.13	1.76	m	**2.89**
25 mm x 100 mm; splayed	-	0.10	1.13	2.06	m	**3.19**
25 mm x 150 mm; splayed	-	0.12	1.36	2.70	m	**4.06**
25 mm x 150 mm; moulded	-	0.12	1.36	2.81	m	**4.17**
25 mm x 175 mm; moulded	-	0.12	1.36	3.14	m	**4.50**
25 mm x 225 mm; moulded	-	0.14	1.59	3.77	m	**5.36**
returned ends	-	0.15	1.70	-	nr	**1.70**
mitres	-	0.10	1.13	-	nr	**1.13**
Architraves, cover fillets and the like; half round; splayed or moulded						
13 mm x 25 mm; half round	-	0.12	1.36	0.97	m	**2.33**
13 mm x 50 mm; moulded	-	0.12	1.36	1.25	m	**2.61**
16 mm x 32 mm; half round	-	0.12	1.36	1.06	m	**2.42**
16 mm x 38 mm; moulded	-	0.12	1.36	1.22	m	**2.58**
16 mm x 50 mm; moulded	-	0.12	1.36	1.33	m	**2.69**
19 mm x 50 mm; splayed	-	0.12	1.36	1.27	m	**2.63**
19 mm x 63 mm; splayed	-	0.12	1.36	1.40	m	**2.76**
19 mm x 75 mm; splayed	-	0.12	1.36	1.51	m	**2.87**
25 mm x 44 mm; splayed	-	0.12	1.36	1.44	m	**2.80**
25 mm x 50 mm; moulded	-	0.12	1.36	1.56	m	**2.92**
25 mm x 63 mm; splayed	-	0.12	1.36	1.58	m	**2.94**
25 mm x 75 mm; splayed	-	0.12	1.36	1.76	m	**3.12**
32 mm x 88 mm; moulded	-	0.12	1.36	2.42	m	**3.78**
38 mm x 38 mm; moulded	-	0.12	1.36	1.55	m	**2.91**
50 mm x 50 mm; moulded	-	0.12	1.36	2.06	m	**3.42**
returned ends	-	0.15	1.70	-	nr	**1.70**
mitres	-	0.10	1.13	-	nr	**1.13**
Stops; screwed on						
16 mm x 38 mm	-	0.10	1.13	0.95	m	**2.08**
16 mm x 50 mm	-	0.10	1.13	1.05	m	**2.18**
19 mm x 38 mm	-	0.10	1.13	1.01	m	**2.14**
25 mm x 38 mm	-	0.10	1.13	1.13	m	**2.26**
25 mm x 50 mm	-	0.10	1.13	1.30	m	**2.43**

P BUILDING FABRIC SUNDRIES Excluding overheads and profit	PC £	Labour hours	Labour £	Material £	Unit	Total rate £
P20 UNFRAMED ISOLATED TRIMS/ SKIRTINGS/SUNDRY ITEMS - cont'd						
Wrought softwood - cont'd						
Glazing beads and the like						
13 mm x 16 mm	-	0.05	0.57	0.70	m	**1.27**
13 mm x 19 mm	-	0.05	0.57	0.73	m	**1.30**
13 mm x 25 mm	-	0.05	0.57	0.78	m	**1.35**
13 mm x 25 mm; screwed	-	0.05	0.57	0.83	m	**1.40**
13 mm x 25 mm; fixing with brass cups and						
screws	-	0.10	1.13	1.04	m	**2.17**
16 mm x 25 mm; screwed	-	0.05	0.57	0.88	m	**1.45**
16 mm quadrant	-	0.05	0.57	0.85	m	**1.42**
19 mm quadrant or scotia	-	0.05	0.57	0.91	m	**1.48**
19 mm x 36 mm; screwed	-	0.05	0.57	1.03	m	**1.60**
25 mm x 38 mm; screwed	-	0.05	0.57	1.14	m	**1.71**
25 mm quadrant or scotia	-	0.05	0.57	1.04	m	**1.61**
38 mm scotia	-	0.05	0.57	1.47	m	**2.04**
50 mm scotia	-	0.05	0.57	1.98	m	**2.55**
Isolated shelves, worktops, seats and the like						
19 mm x 150 mm	-	0.16	1.81	2.24	m	**4.05**
19 mm x 200 mm	-	0.22	2.49	2.69	m	**5.18**
25 mm x 150 mm	-	0.16	1.81	2.69	m	**4.50**
25 mm x 200 mm	-	0.22	2.49	3.29	m	**5.78**
32 mm x 150 mm	-	0.16	1.81	3.18	m	**4.99**
32 mm x 200 mm	-	0.22	2.49	3.99	m	**6.48**
Isolated shelves, worktops, seats and the like; cross-tongued joints						
19 mm x 300 mm	-	0.28	3.18	10.45	m	**13.63**
19 mm x 450 mm	-	0.34	3.86	11.93	m	**15.79**
19 mm x 600 mm	-	0.40	4.54	17.36	m	**21.90**
25 mm x 300 mm	-	0.28	3.18	11.56	m	**14.74**
25 mm x 450 mm	-	0.34	3.86	13.45	m	**17.31**
25 mm x 600 mm	-	0.40	4.54	19.43	m	**23.97**
32 mm x 300 mm	-	0.28	3.18	12.67	m	**15.85**
32 mm x 450 mm	-	0.34	3.86	15.11	m	**18.97**
32 mm x 600 mm	-	0.40	4.54	21.67	m	**26.21**
Isolated shelves, worktops, seats and the like; slatted with 50 wide slats at 75 mm centres						
19 mm thick	-	1.33	15.08	8.08	m	**23.16**
25 mm thick	-	1.33	15.08	9.26	m	**24.34**
32 mm thick	-	1.33	15.08	10.29	m	**25.37**
Window boards, nosings, bed moulds and the like; rebated and rounded						
19 mm x 75 mm	-	0.18	2.04	1.76	m	**3.80**
19 mm x 150 mm	-	0.20	2.27	2.53	m	**4.80**
19 mm x 225 mm; in one width	-	0.26	2.95	3.25	m	**6.20**
19 mm x 300 mm; cross-tongued joints	-	0.30	3.40	10.76	m	**14.16**
25 mm x 75 mm	-	0.18	2.04	2.00	m	**4.04**
25 mm x 150 mm	-	0.20	2.27	3.00	m	**5.27**
25 mm x 225 mm; in one width	-	0.26	2.95	3.95	m	**6.90**
25 mm x 300 mm; cross-tongued joints	-	0.30	3.40	11.87	m	**15.27**
32 mm x 75 mm	-	0.18	2.04	2.28	m	**4.32**
32 mm x 150 mm	-	0.20	2.27	3.52	m	**5.79**
32 mm x 225 mm; in one width	-	0.26	2.95	4.76	m	**7.71**
32 mm x 300 mm; cross-tongued joints	-	0.30	3.40	13.01	m	**16.41**
38 mm x 75 mm	-	0.18	2.04	2.51	m	**4.55**
38 mm x 150 mm	-	0.20	2.27	3.98	m	**6.25**
38 mm x 225 mm; in one width	-	0.26	2.95	5.46	m	**8.41**
38 mm x 300 mm; cross-tongued joints	-	0.30	3.40	14.04	m	**17.44**
returned and fitted ends	-	0.15	1.70	-	nr	**1.70**

P BUILDING FABRIC SUNDRIES Excluding overheads and profit	PC £	Labour hours	Labour £	Material £	Unit	Total rate £
Handrails; mopstick						
50 mm diameter	-	0.25	2.83	3.03	m	5.86
Handrails; rounded						
44 mm x 50 mm	-	0.25	2.83	3.03	m	5.86
50 mm x 75 mm	-	0.27	3.06	3.72	m	6.78
63 mm x 87 mm	-	0.30	3.40	5.01	m	8.41
75 mm x 100 mm	-	0.35	3.97	5.61	m	9.58
Handrails; moulded						
44 mm x 50 mm	-	0.25	2.83	3.36	m	6.19
50 mm x 75 mm	-	0.27	3.06	4.06	m	7.12
63 mm x 87 mm	-	0.30	3.40	5.36	m	8.76
75 mm x 100 mm	-	0.35	3.97	5.97	m	9.94
Add 5% to the above material prices for						
selected softwood for staining						
Selected West African Mahogany						
Skirtings, picture rails, dado rails and the like;						
splayed or moulded						
19 mm x 50 mm; splayed	2.94	0.14	1.59	3.16	m	4.75
19 mm x 50 mm; moulded	3.10	0.14	1.59	3.33	m	4.92
19 mm x 75 mm; splayed	3.52	0.14	1.59	3.77	m	5.36
19 mm x 75 mm; moulded	3.69	0.14	1.59	3.95	m	5.54
19 mm x 100 mm; splayed	4.13	0.14	1.59	4.41	m	6.00
19 mm x 100 mm; moulded	4.29	0.14	1.59	4.58	m	6.17
19 mm x 150 mm; moulded	5.51	0.16	1.81	5.86	m	7.67
19 mm x 175 mm; moulded	6.33	0.16	1.81	6.72	m	8.53
22 mm x 100 mm; splayed	4.49	0.14	1.59	4.79	m	6.38
25 mm x 50 mm; moulded	3.49	0.14	1.59	3.74	m	5.33
25 mm x 75 mm; splayed	4.11	0.14	1.59	4.39	m	5.98
25 mm x 100 mm; splayed	4.89	0.14	1.59	5.21	m	6.80
25 mm x 150 mm; splayed	6.73	0.16	1.81	7.14	m	8.95
25 mm x 150 mm; moulded	6.89	0.16	1.81	7.31	m	9.12
25 mm x 175 mm; moulded	7.68	0.16	1.81	8.14	m	9.95
25 mm x 225 mm; moulded	9.24	0.18	2.04	9.78	m	11.82
returned ends	-	0.22	2.49	-	nr	2.49
mitres	-	0.15	1.70	-	nr	1.70
Architraves, cover fillets and the like; half round;						
splayed or moulded						
13 mm x 25 mm; half round	2.16	0.16	1.81	2.34	m	4.15
13 mm x 50 mm; moulded	2.70	0.16	1.81	2.91	m	4.72
16 mm x 32 mm; half round	2.38	0.16	1.81	2.58	m	4.39
16 mm x 38 mm; moulded	2.65	0.16	1.81	2.86	m	4.67
16 mm x 50 mm; moulded	2.90	0.16	1.81	3.12	m	4.93
19 mm x 50 mm; splayed	2.94	0.16	1.81	3.16	m	4.97
19 mm x 63 mm; splayed	3.25	0.16	1.81	3.49	m	5.30
19 mm x 75 mm; splayed	3.52	0.16	1.81	3.77	m	5.58
25 mm x 44 mm; splayed	3.33	0.16	1.81	3.57	m	5.38
25 mm x 50 mm; moulded	3.49	0.16	1.81	3.74	m	5.55
25 mm x 63 mm; splayed	3.72	0.16	1.81	3.98	m	5.79
25 mm x 75 mm; splayed	4.11	0.16	1.81	4.39	m	6.20
32 mm x 88 mm; moulded	5.79	0.16	1.81	6.16	m	7.97
38 mm x 38 mm; moulded	3.55	0.16	1.81	3.80	m	5.61
50 mm x 50 mm; moulded	4.89	0.16	1.81	5.21	m	7.02
returned ends	-	0.22	2.49	-	nr	2.49
mitres	-	0.15	1.70	-	nr	1.70
Stops; screwed on						
16 mm x 38 mm	2.33	0.15	1.70	2.45	m	4.15
16 mm x 50 mm	2.58	0.15	1.70	2.71	m	4.41
19 mm x 38 mm	2.50	0.15	1.70	2.63	m	4.33
25 mm x 38 mm	2.78	0.15	1.70	2.92	m	4.62
25 mm x 50 mm	3.16	0.15	1.70	3.32	m	5.02

P BUILDING FABRIC SUNDRIES Excluding overheads and profit	PC £	Labour hours	Labour £	Material £	Unit	Total rate £
P20 UNFRAMED ISOLATED TRIMS/ **SKIRTINGS/SUNDRY ITEMS** - cont'd						
Selected West African Mahogany - cont'd						
Glazing beads and the like						
13 mm x 16 mm	1.82	0.05	0.57	1.91	m	2.48
13 mm x 19 mm	1.87	0.05	0.57	1.96	m	2.53
13 mm x 25 mm	2.00	0.05	0.57	2.10	m	2.67
13 mm x 25 mm; screwed	1.82	0.08	0.91	2.05	m	2.96
13 mm x 25 mm; fixing with brass cups and						
screws	2.00	0.15	1.70	2.31	m	4.01
16 mm x 25 mm; screwed	2.07	0.08	0.91	2.31	m	3.22
16 mm quadrant	2.06	0.07	0.79	2.16	m	2.95
19 mm quadrant or scotia	2.18	0.07	0.79	2.29	m	3.08
19 mm x 36 mm; screwed	2.50	0.07	0.79	2.76	m	3.55
25 mm x 38 mm; screwed	2.78	0.07	0.79	3.05	m	3.84
25 mm quadrant or scotia	2.52	0.07	0.79	2.65	m	3.44
38 mm scotia	3.55	0.07	0.79	3.73	m	4.52
50 mm scotia	4.89	0.07	0.79	5.13	m	5.92
Isolated shelves; worktops, seats and the like						
19 mm x 150 mm	5.69	0.22	2.49	5.97	m	8.46
19 mm x 200 mm	6.84	0.30	3.40	7.18	m	10.58
25 mm x 150 mm	6.84	0.22	2.49	7.18	m	9.67
25 mm x 200 mm	8.35	0.30	3.40	8.77	m	12.17
32 mm x 150 mm	8.10	0.22	2.49	8.51	m	11.00
32 mm x 200 mm	10.12	0.30	3.40	10.63	m	14.03
Isolated shelves, worktops, seats and the like; cross-tongued joints						
19 mm x 300 mm	19.09	0.38	4.31	20.04	m	24.35
19 mm x 450 mm	22.74	0.45	5.10	23.88	m	28.98
19 mm x 600 mm	32.99	0.55	6.24	34.64	m	40.88
25 mm x 300 mm	21.75	0.38	4.31	22.84	m	27.15
25 mm x 450 mm	26.56	0.45	5.10	27.89	m	32.99
25 mm x 600 mm	38.07	0.55	6.24	39.97	m	46.21
32 mm x 300 mm	24.41	0.38	4.31	25.63	m	29.94
32 mm x 450 mm	30.47	0.45	5.10	31.99	m	37.09
32 mm x 600 mm	43.49	0.55	6.24	45.66	m	51.90
Isolated shelves, worktops, seats and the like; slatted with 50 mm wide slats at 75 mm centres						
19 mm thick	21.34	1.75	19.84	23.23	m²	43.07
25 mm thick	24.07	1.75	19.84	26.16	m²	46.00
32 mm thick	26.61	1.75	19.84	28.89	m²	48.73
Window boards, nosings, bed moulds and the like; rebated and rounded						
19 mm x 75 mm	3.92	0.24	2.72	4.29	m	7.01
19 mm x 150 mm	5.75	0.27	3.06	6.21	m	9.27
19 mm x 225 mm; in one width	7.54	0.36	4.08	8.09	m	12.17
19 mm x 300 mm; cross-tongued joints	18.98	0.40	4.54	20.10	m	24.64
25 mm x 75 mm	4.51	0.24	2.72	4.91	m	7.63
25 mm x 150 mm	6.94	0.27	3.06	7.46	m	10.52
25 mm x 225 mm; in one width	9.24	0.36	4.08	9.87	m	13.95
25 mm x 300 mm; cross-tongued joints	21.54	0.40	4.54	22.79	m	27.33
32 mm x 75 mm	5.19	0.24	2.72	5.62	m	8.34
32 mm x 150 mm	8.21	0.27	3.06	8.79	m	11.85
32 mm x 225 mm; in one width	11.25	0.36	4.08	11.98	m	16.06
32 mm x 300 mm; cross-tongued joints	24.20	0.40	4.54	25.58	m	30.12
38 mm x 75 mm	5.75	0.24	2.72	6.21	m	8.93
38 mm x 150 mm	9.35	0.27	3.06	9.99	m	13.05
38 mm x 225 mm ; in one width	12.97	0.36	4.08	13.79	m	17.87
38 mm x 300 mm; cross-tongued joints	26.59	0.40	4.54	28.09	m	32.63
returned and fitted ends	-	0.23	2.61	-	nr	2.61

P BUILDING FABRIC SUNDRIES Excluding overheads and profit	PC £	Labour hours	Labour £	Material £	Unit	Total rate £
Handrails; rounded						
44 mm x 50 mm	6.55	0.33	3.74	6.88	m	**10.62**
50 mm x 75 mm	8.19	0.36	4.08	8.60	m	**12.68**
63 mm x 87 mm	10.60	0.40	4.54	11.13	m	**15.67**
75 mm x 100 mm	12.87	0.45	5.10	13.51	m	**18.61**
Handrails; moulded						
44 mm x 50 mm	7.02	0.33	3.74	7.37	m	**11.11**
50 mm x 75 mm	8.67	0.36	4.08	9.10	m	**13.18**
63 mm x 87 mm	11.08	0.40	4.54	11.63	m	**16.17**
75 mm x 100 mm	13.36	0.45	5.10	14.03	m	**19.13**
American White Ash						
Skirtings, picture rails, dado rails and the like; splayed or moulded						
19 mm x 50 mm; splayed	3.30	0.14	1.59	3.54	m	**5.13**
19 mm x 50 mm; moulded	3.46	0.14	1.59	3.71	m	**5.30**
19 mm x 75 mm; splayed	4.11	0.14	1.59	4.39	m	**5.98**
19 mm x 75 mm; moulded	4.27	0.14	1.59	4.56	m	**6.15**
19 mm x 100 mm; splayed	4.89	0.14	1.59	5.21	m	**6.80**
19 mm x 100 mm; moulded	5.05	0.14	1.59	5.37	m	**6.96**
19 mm x 150 mm; moulded	6.62	0.16	1.81	7.03	m	**8.84**
19 mm x 175 mm; moulded	7.65	0.16	1.81	8.11	m	**9.92**
22 mm x 100 mm; splayed	5.39	0.14	1.59	5.74	m	**7.33**
25 mm x 50 mm; moulded	3.98	0.14	1.59	4.25	m	**5.84**
25 mm x 75 mm; splayed	4.84	0.14	1.59	5.16	m	**6.75**
25 mm x 100 mm; splayed	5.88	0.14	1.59	6.25	m	**7.84**
25 mm x 150 mm; splayed	8.21	0.16	1.81	8.70	m	**10.51**
25 mm x 150 mm; moulded	8.37	0.16	1.81	8.86	m	**10.67**
25 mm x 175 mm; moulded	9.39	0.16	1.81	9.94	m	**11.75**
25 mm x 225 mm; moulded	11.48	0.18	2.04	12.13	m	**14.17**
returned end	-	0.22	2.49	-	nr	**2.49**
mitres	-	0.15	1.70	-	nr	**1.70**
Architraves, cover fillets and the like; half round; splayed or moulded						
13 mm x 25 mm; half round	2.29	0.16	1.81	2.48	m	**4.29**
13 mm x 50 mm; moulded	2.96	0.16	1.81	3.18	m	**4.99**
16 mm x 32 mm; half round	2.57	0.16	1.81	2.77	m	**4.58**
16 mm x 38 mm; moulded	2.92	0.16	1.81	3.14	m	**4.95**
16 mm x 50 mm; moulded	3.23	0.16	1.81	3.47	m	**5.28**
19 mm x 50 mm; splayed	3.30	0.16	1.81	3.54	m	**5.35**
19 mm x 63 mm; splayed	3.73	0.16	1.81	3.99	m	**5.80**
19 mm x 75 mm; splayed	4.11	0.16	1.81	4.39	m	**6.20**
25 mm x 44 mm; splayed	3.82	0.16	1.81	4.09	m	**5.90**
25 mm x 50 mm; moulded	3.98	0.16	1.81	4.25	m	**6.06**
25 mm x 63 mm; splayed	4.33	0.16	1.81	4.62	m	**6.43**
25 mm x 75 mm; splayed	4.84	0.16	1.81	5.16	m	**6.97**
32 mm x 88 mm; moulded	7.04	0.16	1.81	7.47	m	**9.28**
38 mm x 38 mm; moulded	4.13	0.16	1.81	4.41	m	**6.22**
50 mm x 50 mm; moulded	5.88	0.16	1.81	6.25	m	**8.06**
returned end	-	0.22	2.49	-	nr	**2.49**
mitres	-	0.15	1.70	-	nr	**1.70**
Stops; screwed on						
16 mm x 38 mm	2.59	0.15	1.70	2.72	m	**4.42**
16 mm x 50 mm	2.92	0.15	1.70	3.07	m	**4.77**
19 mm x 38 mm	2.76	0.15	1.70	2.90	m	**4.60**
25 mm x 38 mm	3.13	0.15	1.70	3.29	m	**4.99**
25 mm x 50 mm	3.66	0.15	1.70	3.84	m	**5.54**

P BUILDING FABRIC SUNDRIES Excluding overheads and profit	PC £	Labour hours	Labour £	Material £	Unit	Total rate £
P20 UNFRAMED ISOLATED TRIMS/ **SKIRTINGS/SUNDRY ITEMS** - cont'd						
American White Ash - cont'd						
Glazing beads and the like						
13 mm x 16 mm	1.92	0.05	0.57	2.02	m	2.59
13 mm x 19 mm	1.99	0.05	0.57	2.09	m	2.66
13 mm x 25 mm	2.13	0.05	0.57	2.24	m	2.81
13 mm x 25 mm; screwed	2.13	0.08	0.91	2.37	m	3.28
13 mm x 25 mm; fixing with brass cups and						
screws	2.13	0.15	1.70	2.44	m	4.14
16 mm x 25 mm; screwed	2.23	0.08	0.91	2.48	m	3.39
16 mm quadrant	2.17	0.07	0.79	2.28	m	3.07
19 mm quadrant or scotia	2.34	0.07	0.79	2.46	m	3.25
19 mm x 36 mm; screwed	2.76	0.07	0.79	3.03	m	3.82
25 mm x 38 mm; screwed	3.13	0.07	0.79	3.42	m	4.21
25 mm quadrant or scotia	2.78	0.07	0.79	2.92	m	3.71
38 mm scotia	4.13	0.07	0.79	4.34	m	5.13
50 mm scotia	5.88	0.07	0.79	6.17	m	6.96
Isolated shelves, worktops, seats and the like						
19 mm x 150 mm	6.85	0.22	2.49	7.19	m	9.68
19 mm x 200 mm	8.35	0.30	3.40	8.77	m	12.17
25 mm x 150 mm	8.35	0.22	2.49	8.77	m	11.26
25 mm x 200 mm	10.32	0.30	3.40	10.84	m	14.24
32 mm x 150 mm	10.00	0.22	2.49	10.50	m	12.99
32 mm x 200 mm	12.64	0.30	3.40	13.27	m	16.67
Isolated shelves, worktops, seats and the like; cross-tongued joints						
19 mm x 300 mm	21.57	0.38	4.31	22.65	m	26.96
19 mm x 450 mm	26.40	0.45	5.10	27.72	m	32.82
19 mm x 600 mm	37.96	0.55	6.24	39.86	m	46.10
25 mm x 300 mm	25.06	0.38	4.31	26.31	m	30.62
25 mm x 450 mm	31.36	0.45	5.10	32.93	m	38.03
25 mm x 600 mm	44.61	0.55	6.24	46.84	m	53.08
32 mm x 300 mm	28.54	0.38	4.31	29.97	m	34.28
32 mm x 450 mm	36.52	0.45	5.10	38.35	m	43.45
32 mm x 600 mm	51.75	0.55	6.24	55.63	m	61.87
Isolated shelves, worktops, seats and the like; slatted with 50 wide slats at 75 mm centres						
19 mm thick	24.08	1.75	19.84	26.17	m²	46.01
25 mm thick	27.54	1.75	19.84	29.89	m²	49.73
32 mm thick	31.20	1.75	19.84	33.82	m²	53.66
Window boards, nosings, bed moulds and the like; rebated and rounded						
19 mm x 75 mm	4.48	0.24	2.72	4.88	m	7.60
19 mm x 150 mm	6.86	0.27	3.06	7.37	m	10.43
19 mm x 225 mm; in one width	9.21	0.36	4.08	9.84	m	13.92
19 mm x 300 mm; cross-tongued joints	21.51	0.40	4.54	22.76	m	27.30
25 mm x 75 mm	5.26	0.24	2.72	5.69	m	8.41
25 mm x 150 mm	8.46	0.27	3.06	9.05	m	12.11
25 mm x 225 mm; in one width	11.45	0.36	4.08	12.19	m	16.27
25 mm x 300 mm; cross-tongued joints	24.84	0.40	4.54	26.25	m	30.79
32 mm x 75 mm	6.13	0.24	2.72	6.61	m	9.33
32 mm x 150 mm	10.11	0.27	3.06	10.79	m	13.85
32 mm x 225 mm; in one width	-	0.36	4.08	14.99	m	19.07
32 mm x 300 mm; cross-tongued joints	28.33	0.40	4.54	29.92	m	34.46
38 mm x 75 mm	6.95	0.24	2.72	7.64	m	10.36
38 mm x 150 mm	11.63	0.27	3.06	12.38	m	15.44
38 mm x 225 mm; in one width	16.35	0.36	4.08	17.34	m	21.42
38 mm x 300 mm; cross-tongued joints	31.49	0.40	4.54	33.24	m	37.78
returned and fitted ends	-	0.23	2.61	-	nr	2.61

P BUILDING FABRIC SUNDRIES Excluding overheads and profit	PC £	Labour hours	Labour £	Material £	Unit	Total rate £
Handrails; rounded						
44 mm x 50 mm	7.52	0.33	3.74	7.90	m	11.64
50 mm x 75 mm	9.61	0.36	4.08	10.09	m	14.17
63 mm x 87 mm	13.86	0.40	4.54	14.55	m	19.09
75 mm x 100 mm	15.83	0.45	5.10	16.62	m	21.72
Handrails; moulded						
44 mm x 50 mm	8.01	0.33	3.74	8.41	m	12.15
50 mm x 75 mm	10.10	0.36	4.08	10.61	m	14.69
63 mm x 87 mm	14.34	0.40	4.54	15.06	m	19.60
75 mm x 100 mm	16.30	0.45	5.10	17.11	m	22.21
Pin-boards; medium board						
Sundeala "A" pin-board or other equal and approved; fixed with adhesive to backing (not included); over 300 mm wide						
6.40 mm thick	-	0.60	6.80	10.55	m²	17.35
Sundries on softwood/hardwood						
Extra over fixing with nails for						
gluing and pinning	-	0.02	0.23	0.05	m	0.28
masonry nails	-	-	-	-	m	0.24
steel screws	-	-	-	-	m	0.22
self-tapping screws	-	-	-	-	m	0.23
steel screws; gluing	-	-	-	-	m	0.40
steel screws; sinking; filling heads	-	-	-	-	m	0.50
steel screws; sinking; pellating over	-	-	-	-	m	1.10
brass cups and screws	-	-	-	-	m	1.35
Extra over for						
countersinking	-	-	-	-	m	0.20
pellating	-	-	-	-	m	0.95
Head or nut in softwood						
let in flush	-	-	-	-	nr	0.50
Head or nut; in hardwood						
let in flush	-	-	-	-	nr	0.75
let in over; pellated	-	-	-	-	nr	1.75
Metalwork; mild steel						
Angle section bearers; for building in						
150 mm x 100 mm x 6 mm	-	0.33	3.69	10.46	m	14.15
150 mm x 150 mm x 8 mm	-	0.35	3.92	16.37	m	20.29
200 mm x 200 mm x 12 mm	-	0.40	4.48	30.95	m	35.43
Metalwork; mild steel; galvanized						
Waterbars; groove in timber						
6 mm x 30 mm	-	0.50	5.67	4.39	m	10.06
6 mm x 40 mm	-	0.50	5.67	5.16	m	10.83
6 mm x 50 mm	-	0.50	5.67	6.89	m	12.56
Angle section bearers; for building in						
150 mm x 100 mm x 6 mm	-	0.33	3.69	13.54	m	17.23
150 mm x 150 mm x 8 mm	-	0.35	3.92	21.64	m	25.56
200 mm x 200 mm x 12 mm	-	0.40	4.48	43.35	m	47.83
Dowels; mortice in timber						
8 mm diameter x 100 mm long	-	0.05	0.57	0.07	nr	0.64
10 mm diameter x 50 mm long	-	0.05	0.57	0.20	nr	0.77
Cramps						
25 mm x 3 mm x 230 mm girth; one end bent, holed and screwed; other end fishtailed for building in	-	0.07	0.79	0.49	nr	1.28
Metalwork; stainless steel						
Angle section bearers; for building in						
150 mm x 100 mm x 6 mm	-	0.33	3.69	38.42	m	42.11
150 mm x 150 mm x 8 mm	-	0.35	3.92	60.99	m	64.91
200 mm x 200 mm x 12 mm	-	0.40	4.48	127.46	m	131.94

P BUILDING FABRIC SUNDRIES Excluding overheads and profit	PC £	Labour hours	Labour £	Material £	Unit	Total rate £
P21 IRONMONGERY						
NOTE: Ironmongery is largely a matter of selection and prices vary considerably; indicative prices for reasonable quantities of "standard quality" ironmongery are given below.						
Ironmongery; NT Laidlaw Ltd or other equal and **approved; standard ranges; to softwood**						
Bolts						
barrel; 100 mm x 32 mm; PAA	-	0.33	3.74	4.93	nr	8.67
barrel; 150 mm x 32 mm; PAA	-	0.42	4.76	5.64	nr	10.40
flush; 152 mm x 25 mm; SCP	-	0.60	6.80	11.46	nr	18.26
flush; 203 mm x 25 mm; SCP	-	0.60	6.80	12.62	nr	19.42
flush; 305 mm x 25 mm; SCP	-	0.60	6.80	17.08	nr	23.88
indicating; 76 mm x 41 mm; SAA	-	0.67	7.60	8.37	nr	15.97
indicating; coin operated; SAA	-	0.67	7.60	11.46	nr	19.06
panic; single; SVE	-	2.50	28.35	52.84	nr	81.19
panic; double; SVE	-	3.50	39.69	71.96	nr	111.65
necked tower; 152 mm; BJ	-	0.33	3.74	2.32	nr	6.06
necked tower; 203 mm; BJ	-	0.33	3.74	3.13	nr	6.87
mortice security; SCP	-	0.60	6.80	15.19	nr	21.99
garage door bolt; 305 mm	-	0.60	6.80	5.66	nr	12.46
monkey tail with knob; 305 mm x 19 mm; BJ	-	0.67	7.60	6.92	nr	14.52
monkey tail with bow; 305 mm x 19 mm; BJ	-	0.67	7.60	8.72	nr	16.32
Butts						
63 mm; light steel	-	0.25	2.83	0.57	pr	3.40
100 mm; light steel	-	0.25	2.83	1.00	pr	3.83
102 mm; SC	-	0.25	2.83	3.19	pr	6.02
102 mm double flap extra strong; SC	-	0.25	2.83	1.99	pr	4.82
76 mm x 51 mm; SC	-	0.25	2.83	2.30	pr	5.13
51 mm x 22 mm narrow suite S/D	-	0.25	2.83	1.93	pr	4.76
76 mm x 35 mm narrow suite S/D	-	0.25	2.83	2.69	pr	5.52
51 mm x 29 mm broad suite S/D	-	0.25	2.83	1.93	pr	4.76
76 mm x 41 mm broad suite S/D	-	0.25	2.83	2.59	pr	5.42
102 mm x 60 mm broad suite S/D	-	0.25	2.83	5.45	pr	8.28
102 mm x 69 mm lift-off (R/L hand)	-	0.25	2.83	2.89	pr	5.72
high security heavy butts F/pin; 100 mm x 94 mm; ball bearing; SSS	-	0.40	4.54	17.10	pr	21.64
"Hi-load" butts; 125 mm x 102 mm	-	0.30	3.40	39.19	pr	42.59
S/D rising butts (R/L hand); 102 mm x 67 mm; BRS	-	0.25	2.83	32.75	pr	35.58
ball bearing butts; 102 mm x 67 mm; SSS	-	0.25	2.83	7.66	pr	10.49
Catches						
ball catch; 13 mm diameter; BRS	-	0.33	3.74	0.46	nr	4.20
double ball catch; 50 mm; BRS	-	0.40	4.54	0.61	nr	5.15
57 mm x 38 mm cupboard catch; SCP	-	0.30	3.40	5.33	nr	8.73
14 mm x 35 mm magnetic catch; WHT	-	0.17	1.93	0.53	nr	2.46
adjustable nylon roller catch; WNY	-	0.25	2.83	1.41	nr	4.24
"Bales" catch; Nr 4; 41 mm x 16 mm; self colour brass; mortice	-	0.33	3.74	0.83	nr	4.57
"Bales" catch; Nr 8; 66 mm x 25 mm; self colour brass; mortice	-	0.35	3.97	1.84	nr	5.81
Door closers and furniture						
standard concealed overhead door closer (L/R hand); SIL	-	1.25	14.18	136.73	nr	150.91
light duty surface fixed door closer (L/R hand); SIL	-	1.00	11.34	58.12	nr	69.46
"Perkomatic" concealed door closer; BRS	-	0.67	7.60	67.25	nr	74.85
"Softline" adjustable size 2 - 4 overhead door closer; SIL	-	1.50	17.01	64.45	nr	81.46
"Centurion II" size 3 overhead door closer; SIL	-	1.25	14.18	29.97	nr	44.15
"Centurion II" size 4 overhead door closer; SIL	-	1.50	17.01	36.99	nr	54.00

P BUILDING FABRIC SUNDRIES Excluding overheads and profit	PC £	Labour hours	Labour £	Material £	Unit	Total rate £
Door closers and furniture - cont'd						
backcheck door closer size 3; SAA	-	1.25	14.18	76.76	nr	90.94
backcheck door closer size 4; SAA	-	1.50	17.01	80.25	nr	97.26
door selector; face fixing; SAA	-	0.60	6.80	57.54	nr	64.34
finger plate; 300 mm x 75 mm x 3 mm	-	0.17	1.93	3.32	nr	5.25
kicking plate; 1000 mm x 150 mm x 30 mm; PAA	-	0.25	2.83	9.64	nr	12.47
floor spring; single and double action; ZP	-	2.50	28.35	141.33	nr	169.68
lever furniture; 280 mm x 40 mm	-	0.25	2.83	18.99	pr	21.82
pull handle; 225 mm; back fixing; PAA	-	0.17	1.93	5.08	nr	7.01
pull handle; f/fix with cover rose; PAA	-	0.33	3.74	27.23	nr	30.97
letter plate; 330 mm x 76 mm; aluminium finish	-	1.33	15.08	6.89	nr	21.97
Latches						
102 mm mortice latch; SCP	-	1.25	14.18	5.80	nr	19.98
cylinder rim night latch; SC7	-	0.75	8.51	16.43	nr	24.94
Locks						
drawer or cupboard lock; 63 mm x 32 mm; SC	-	0.42	4.76	7.23	nr	11.99
mortice dead lock; 63 mm x 108 mm; SSS	-	0.75	8.51	9.31	nr	17.82
12 mm rebate conversion set to mortice dead lock	-	0.50	5.67	9.22	nr	14.89
rim lock; 140 mm x 73 mm; GYE	-	0.42	4.76	7.08	nr	11.84
rim dead lock; 92 mm x 74.5 mm; SCP	-	0.42	4.76	18.73	nr	23.49
upright mortice lock; 103 mm x 82 mm; 3 lever	-	0.83	9.41	9.59	nr	19.00
upright mortice lock; 103 mm x 82 mm; 5 lever	-	0.83	9.41	29.98	nr	39.39
Window furniture						
casement stay; 305 mm long; 2 pin; SAA	-	0.17	1.93	6.27	nr	8.20
casement fastener; standard; 113 mm; SAA	-	0.17	1.93	4.06	nr	5.99
cockspur fastener; ASV	-	0.33	3.74	6.86	nr	10.60
sash fastener; 65 mm; SAA	-	0.25	2.83	2.30	nr	5.13
Sundries						
numerals; SAA	-	0.08	0.91	0.65	nr	1.56
rubber door stop; SAA	-	0.08	0.91	0.97	nr	1.88
medium hot pressed cabin hook; 102 mm; CP	-	0.17	1.93	7.93	nr	9.86
medium hot pressed cabin hook; 203 mm; CP	-	0.17	1.93	10.48	nr	12.41
coat hook; SAA	-	0.08	0.91	1.06	nr	1.97
toilet roll holder; CP	-	0.17	1.93	13.89	nr	15.82
Ironmongery; NT Laidlaw Ltd or other equal and approved; standard ranges; to hardwood						
Bolts						
barrel; 100 mm x 32 mm; PAA	-	0.44	4.99	4.93	nr	9.92
barrel; 150 mm x 32 mm; PAA	-	0.56	6.35	5.64	nr	11.99
flush; 152 mm x 25 mm; SCP	-	0.80	9.07	11.46	nr	20.53
flush; 203 mm x 25 mm; SCP	-	0.80	9.07	12.62	nr	21.69
flush; 305 mm x 25 mm; SCP	-	0.80	9.07	17.08	nr	26.15
indicating; 76 mm x 41 mm; SAA	-	0.89	10.09	8.37	nr	18.46
indicating; coin operated; SAA	-	0.89	10.09	11.46	nr	21.55
panic; single	-	3.33	37.76	52.84	nr	90.60
panic; double	-	4.67	52.96	71.96	nr	124.92
necked tower; 152 mm; BJ	-	0.44	4.99	2.32	nr	7.31
necked tower; 203 mm; BJ	-	0.44	4.99	3.13	nr	8.12
mortice security; SCP	-	0.80	9.07	15.19	nr	24.26
garage door bolt; 305 mm	-	0.80	9.07	5.66	nr	14.73
monkey tail with knob; 305 mm x 19 mm; BJ	-	0.85	9.64	6.92	nr	16.56
monkey tail with bow; 305 mm x 19 mm; BJ	-	0.85	9.64	8.72	nr	18.36

P BUILDING FABRIC SUNDRIES Excluding overheads and profit	PC £	Labour hours	Labour £	Material £	Unit	Total rate £
P21 IRONMONGERY - cont'd						
Ironmongery; NT Laidlaw Ltd or other equal and approved; standard ranges; to hardwood - cont'd						
Butts						
63 mm; light steel	-	0.35	3.97	0.57	pr	**4.54**
100 mm; light steel	-	0.35	3.97	1.00	pr	**4.97**
102 mm; SC	-	0.35	3.97	3.19	pr	**7.16**
102 mm double flap extra strong; SC	-	0.35	3.97	1.99	pr	**5.96**
76 mm x 51 mm; SC	-	0.35	3.97	2.30	pr	**6.27**
51 mm x 22 mm narrow suite S/D	-	0.35	3.97	1.93	pr	**5.90**
76 mm x 35 mm narrow suite S/D	-	0.35	3.97	2.69	pr	**6.66**
51 mm x 29 mm broad suite S/D	-	0.35	3.97	1.93	pr	**5.90**
76 mm x 41 mm broad suite S/D	-	0.35	3.97	2.59	pr	**6.56**
102 mm x 60 mm broad suite S/D	-	0.35	3.97	5.45	pr	**9.42**
102 mm x 69 mm lift-off (R/L hand)	-	0.35	3.97	2.89	pr	**6.86**
high security heavy butts F/pin; 100 mm x 94 mm; ball bearing; SSS	-	0.45	5.10	17.10	pr	**22.20**
"Hi-load" butts; 125 mm x 102 mm	-	0.40	4.54	39.19	pr	**43.73**
S/D rising butts (R/L hand); 102 mm x 67 mm; BRS	-	0.35	3.97	32.75	pr	**36.72**
ball bearing butts; 102 mm x 67 mm; SSS	-	0.35	3.97	7.66	pr	**11.63**
Catches						
ball catch; 13 mm diameter; BRS	-	0.45	5.10	0.46	nr	**5.56**
double ball catch; 50 mm; BRS	-	0.47	5.33	0.61	nr	**5.94**
57 mm x 38 mm cupboard catch; SCP	-	0.40	4.54	5.33	nr	**9.87**
14 mm x 35 mm magnetic catch; WHT	-	0.23	2.61	0.53	nr	**3.14**
adjustable nylon roller catch; WNY	-	0.33	3.74	1.41	nr	**5.15**
"Bales" catch; Nr 4; 41 mm x 16 mm; self colour brass; mortice	-	0.44	4.99	0.83	nr	**5.82**
"Bales" catch; Nr 8; 66 mm x 25 mm; self colour brass; mortice	-	0.46	5.22	1.84	nr	**7.06**
Door closers and furniture						
standard concealed overhead door closer (L/R hand); SIL	-	1.67	18.94	136.73	nr	**155.67**
light duty surface fixed door closer (L/R hand); SIL	-	1.30	14.74	58.12	nr	**72.86**
"Perkomatic" concealed door closer; BRS	-	0.89	10.09	67.25	nr	**77.34**
"Softline" adjustable size 2 - 4 overhead door closer; SIL	-	2.00	22.68	64.45	nr	**87.13**
"Centurion II" size 3 overhead door closer; SIL	-	1.75	19.84	29.97	nr	**49.81**
"Centurion II" size 4 overhead door closer; SIL	-	2.00	22.68	36.99	nr	**59.67**
backcheck door closer size 3; SAA	-	1.75	19.84	76.76	nr	**96.60**
backcheck door closer size 4; SAA	-	2.00	22.68	80.25	nr	**102.93**
door selector; soffit fixing; SSS	-	0.67	7.60	26.49	nr	**34.09**
door selector; face fixing; SAA	-	0.80	9.07	57.54	nr	**66.61**
finger plate; 300 mm x 75 mm x 3 mm	-	0.23	2.61	3.32	nr	**5.93**
kicking plate; 1000 mm x 150 mm x 30 mm; PAA	-	0.44	4.99	9.64	nr	**14.63**
floor spring; single and double action; ZP	-	3.33	37.76	141.33	nr	**179.09**
lever furniture; 280 mm x 40 mm	-	0.33	3.74	18.99	pr	**22.73**
pull handle; 225 mm; back fixing; PAA	-	0.23	2.61	5.08	nr	**7.69**
pull handle; f/fix with cover rose; PAA	-	0.44	4.99	27.23	nr	**32.22**
letter plate; 330 mm x 76 mm; Aluminium finish	-	1.77	20.07	6.89	nr	**26.96**
Latches						
102 mm mortice latch; SCP	-	1.75	19.84	5.80	nr	**25.64**
cylinder rim night latch; SC7	-	1.00	11.34	16.43	nr	**27.77**
Locks						
drawer or cupboard lock; 63 mm x 32 mm; SC	-	0.56	6.35	7.23	nr	**13.58**
mortice dead lock; 63 mm x 108 mm; SSS	-	1.00	11.34	9.31	nr	**20.65**
12 mm rebate conversion set to mortice dead lock	-	0.75	8.51	9.22	nr	**17.73**
rim lock; 140 mm x 73 mm; GYE	-	0.56	6.35	7.08	nr	**13.43**
rim dead lock; 92 mm x 74.50 mm; SCP	-	0.56	6.35	18.73	nr	**25.08**
upright mortice lock; 103 mm x 82 mm; 3 lever	-	1.11	12.59	9.59	nr	**22.18**
upright mortice lock; 103 mm x 82 mm; 5 lever	-	1.11	12.59	29.98	nr	**42.57**

P BUILDING FABRIC SUNDRIES Excluding overheads and profit	PC £	Labour hours	Labour £	Material £	Unit	Total rate £
Window furniture						
casement stay; 305 mm long; 2 pin; SAA	-	0.23	2.61	6.27	nr	8.88
casement fastener; standard; 113 mm; SAA	-	0.23	2.61	4.06	nr	6.67
cockspur fastener; ASV	-	0.44	4.99	6.86	nr	11.85
sash fastener; 65 mm; SAA	-	0.33	3.74	2.30	nr	6.04
Sundries						
numerals; SAA	-	0.11	1.25	0.65	nr	1.90
rubber door stop; SAA	-	0.11	1.25	0.97	nr	2.22
medium hot pressed cabin hook; 102 mm; CP	-	0.23	2.61	7.93	nr	10.54
medium hot pressed cabin hook; 203 mm; CP	-	0.23	2.61	10.48	nr	13.09
coat hook; SAA	-	0.11	1.25	1.06	nr	2.31
toilet roll holder; CP	-	0.25	2.83	13.89	nr	16.72
Sliding door gear; Hillaldam Coburn Ltd or other **equal and approved; Commercial/Light industrial;** **for top hung timber/metal doors, weight not exceeding** **365 kg**						
Sliding door gear						
bottom guide; fixed to concrete in groove	13.60	0.50	5.67	13.60	m	19.27
top track	19.20	0.25	2.83	19.20	m	22.03
detachable locking bar and padlock	32.48	0.33	3.74	32.48	nr	36.22
hangers; timber doors	35.28	0.50	5.67	35.28	nr	40.95
hangers; metal doors	25.16	0.50	5.67	25.16	nr	30.83
head brackets; open, side fixing; bolting to masonry	3.76	0.50	5.67	5.92	nr	11.59
head brackets; open, soffit fixing; screwing to						
timber	2.84	0.35	3.97	2.88	nr	6.85
door guide to timber door	7.04	0.25	2.83	7.04	nr	9.87
door stop; rubber buffers; to masonry	19.36	0.75	8.51	19.36	nr	27.87
drop bolt; screwing to timber	36.16	0.50	5.67	36.16	nr	41.83
bow handle; to timber	7.80	0.25	2.83	7.80	nr	10.63
Sundries						
rubber door stop; plugged and screwed to concrete	4.80	0.10	1.13	4.80	nr	5.93
P30 TRENCHES/PIPEWAYS/PITS FOR BURIED **ENGINEERING SERVICES**						
Excavating trenches; by machine; grading bottoms; **earthwork support; filling with excavated material** **and compacting; disposal of surplus soil on site;** **spreading on site average 50 m**						
Services not exceeding 200 mm nominal size						
average depth of run not exceeding 0.50 m	-	0.30	1.97	1.13	m	3.10
average depth of run not exceeding 0.75 m	-	0.40	2.63	1.89	m	4.52
average depth of run not exceeding 1.00 m	-	0.85	5.59	3.60	m	9.19
average depth of run not exceeding 1.25 m	-	1.25	8.22	4.91	m	13.13
average depth of run not exceeding 1.50 m	-	1.60	10.53	6.41	m	16.94
average depth of run not exceeding 1.75 m	-	2.00	13.16	8.20	m	21.36
average depth of run not exceeding 2.00 m	-	2.30	15.13	9.38	m	24.51
Excavating trenches; by hand; grading bottoms; **earthwork support; filling with excavated material** **and compacting; disposal; of surplus soil on site;** **spreading on site average 50 m**						
Services not exceeding 200 mm nominal size						
average depth of run not exceeding 0.50 m	-	1.00	6.58	-	m	6.58
average depth of run not exceeding 0.75 m	-	1.50	9.87	-	m	9.87
average depth of run not exceeding 1.00 m	-	2.20	14.48	1.24	m	15.72
average depth of run not exceeding 1.25 m	-	3.10	20.40	1.71	m	22.11
average depth of run not exceeding 1.50 m	-	4.25	27.96	2.08	m	30.04
average depth of run not exceeding 1.75 m	-	5.60	36.85	2.51	m	39.36
average depth of run not exceeding 2.00 m	-	6.40	42.11	2.76	m	44.87

P BUILDING FABRIC SUNDRIES Excluding overheads and profit	PC £	Labour hours	Labour £	Material £	Unit	Total rate £
P30 TRENCHES/PIPEWAYS/PITS FOR BURIED ENGINEERING SERVICES - cont'd						
Stop cock pits, valve chambers and the like; excavating; half brick thick walls in common bricks in cement mortar (1:3); on in situ concrete designated mix C20 - 20 mm aggregate bed; 100 mm thick						
Pits						
100 mm x 100 mm x 750 mm deep; internal holes for one small pipe; polypropylene hinged box cover; bedding in cement mortar (1:3)	-	4.20	59.68	22.26	nr	**81.94**
P31 HOLES/CHASES/COVERS/SUPPORTS FOR SERVICES						
Builders' work for electrical installations; cutting away for and making good after electrician; including cutting or leaving all holes, notches, mortices, sinkings and chases, in both the structure and its coverings, for the following electrical points						
Exposed installation						
lighting points	-	0.30	2.41	-	nr	**2.41**
socket outlet points	-	0.50	4.17	-	nr	**4.17**
fitting outlet points	-	0.50	4.17	-	nr	**4.17**
equipment points or control gear points	-	0.70	5.94	-	nr	**5.94**
Concealed installation						
lighting points	-	0.40	3.29	-	nr	**3.29**
socket outlet points	-	0.70	5.94	-	nr	**5.94**
fitting outlet points	-	0.70	5.94	-	nr	**5.94**
equipment points or control gear points	-	1.00	8.35	-	nr	**8.35**
Builders' work for other services installations						
Cutting chases in brickwork						
for one pipe; not exceeding 55 mm nominal size; vertical	-	0.40	2.58	-	m	**2.58**
for one pipe; 55 mm - 110 mm nominal size; vertical	-	0.70	4.51	-	m	**4.51**
Cutting and pinning to brickwork or blockwork; ends of supports						
for pipes not exceeding 55 mm nominal size	-	0.20	2.84	-	nr	**2.84**
for cast iron pipes 55 mm - 110 mm nominal size	-	0.33	4.69	-	nr	**4.69**
Cutting holes for pipes or the like; not exceeding 55 mm nominal size						
half brick thick	-	0.33	2.40	-	nr	**2.40**
one brick thick	-	0.55	4.00	-	nr	**4.00**
one and a half brick thick	-	0.90	6.54	-	nr	**6.54**
100 mm blockwork	-	0.30	2.18	-	nr	**2.18**
140 mm blockwork	-	0.40	2.91	-	nr	**2.91**
215 mm blockwork	-	0.50	3.63	-	nr	**3.63**
Cutting holes for pipes or the like; 55 mm - 110 mm nominal size						
half brick thick	-	0.40	2.91	-	nr	**2.91**
one brick thick	-	0.70	5.09	-	nr	**5.09**
one and a half brick thick	-	1.10	8.00	-	nr	**8.00**
100 mm blockwork	-	0.35	2.54	-	nr	**2.54**
140 mm blockwork	-	0.50	3.63	-	nr	**3.63**
215 mm blockwork	-	0.60	4.36	-	nr	**4.36**

P BUILDING FABRIC SUNDRIES Excluding overheads and profit	PC £	Labour hours	Labour £	Material £	Unit	Total rate £
Cutting holes for pipes or the like; over 110 mm nominal size						
half brick thick	-	0.50	3.63	-	nr	3.63
one brick thick	-	0.85	6.18	-	nr	6.18
one and a half brick thick	-	1.35	9.81	-	nr	9.81
100 mm blockwork	-	0.45	3.27	-	nr	3.27
140 mm blockwork	-	0.60	4.36	-	nr	4.36
215 mm blockwork	-	0.75	5.45	-	nr	5.45
Add for making good fair face or facings one side						
pipe; not exceeding 55 mm nominal size	-	0.08	1.14	-	nr	1.14
pipe; 55 mm - 110 mm nominal size	-	0.10	1.42	-	nr	1.42
pipe; over 110 mm nominal size	-	0.12	1.71	-	nr	1.71
Add for fixing sleeve (supply not included)						
for pipe; small	-	0.15	2.13	-	nr	2.13
for pipe; large	-	0.20	2.84	-	nr	2.84
for pipe; extra large	-	0.30	4.26	-	nr	4.26
Cutting or forming holes for ducts; girth not exceeding 1.00 m						
half brick thick	-	0.60	4.36	-	nr	4.36
one brick thick	-	1.00	7.27	-	nr	7.27
one and a half brick thick	-	1.60	11.63	-	nr	11.63
100 mm blockwork	-	0.50	3.63	-	nr	3.63
140 mm blockwork	-	0.70	5.09	-	nr	5.09
215 mm blockwork	-	0.90	6.54	-	nr	6.54
Cutting or forming holes for ducts; girth 1.00 m - 2.00 m						
half brick thick	-	0.70	5.09	-	nr	5.09
one brick thick	-	1.20	8.72	-	nr	8.72
one and a half brick thick	-	1.90	13.81	-	nr	13.81
100 mm blockwork	-	0.60	4.36	-	nr	4.36
140 mm blockwork	-	0.80	5.82	-	nr	5.82
215 mm blockwork	-	1.00	7.27	-	nr	7.27
Cutting or forming holes for ducts; girth 2.00 m - 3.00 m						
half brick thick	-	1.10	8.00	-	nr	8.00
one brick thick	-	1.90	13.81	-	nr	13.81
one and a half brick thick	-	3.00	21.81	-	nr	21.81
100 mm blockwork	-	0.95	6.91	-	nr	6.91
140 mm blockwork	-	1.30	9.45	-	nr	9.45
215 mm blockwork	-	1.65	12.00	-	nr	12.00
Cutting or forming holes for ducts; girth 3.00 m - 4.00 m						
half brick thick	-	1.50	10.90	-	nr	10.90
one brick thick	-	2.50	18.18	-	nr	18.18
one and a half brick thick	-	4.00	29.08	-	nr	29.08
100 mm blockwork	-	1.10	8.00	-	nr	8.00
140 mm blockwork	-	1.50	10.90	-	nr	10.90
215 mm blockwork	-	1.90	13.81	-	nr	13.81
Mortices in brickwork						
for expansion bolt	-	0.20	1.45	-	nr	1.45
for 20 mm diameter bolt; 75 mm deep	-	0.15	1.09	-	nr	1.09
for 20 mm diameter bolt; 150 mm deep	-	0.25	1.82	-	nr	1.82
Mortices in brickwork; grouting with cement mortar (1:1)						
75 mm x 75 mm x 200 mm deep	-	0.30	2.18	0.12	nr	2.30
75 mm x 75 mm x 300 mm deep	-	0.40	2.91	0.17	nr	3.08
Holes in softwood for pipes, bars, cables and the like						
12 mm thick	-	0.04	0.45	-	nr	0.45
25 mm thick	-	0.06	0.68	-	nr	0.68
50 mm thick	-	0.10	1.13	-	nr	1.13
100 mm thick	-	0.15	1.70	-	nr	1.70

P BUILDING FABRIC SUNDRIES Excluding overheads and profit	PC £	Labour hours	Labour £	Material £	Unit	Total rate £
P31 HOLES/CHASES/COVERS/SUPPORTS FOR **SERVICES** - cont'd						
Builders' work for other services installations - cont'd						
Holes in hardwood for pipes, bars, cables and						
the like						
12 mm thick	-	0.06	0.68	-	nr	**0.68**
25 mm thick	-	0.09	1.02	-	nr	**1.02**
50 mm thick	-	0.15	1.70	-	nr	**1.70**
100 mm thick	-	0.22	2.49	-	nr	**2.49**
"SFD Screeduct" or other equal and						
approved; MDT Ducting Ltd; laid within						
floor screed; galvanised mild steel						
Floor ducting						
100 mm wide; 40 mm deep; ref SFD40/100/00	5.46	0.20	2.27	5.73	m	**8.00**
Extra for						
45 degree bend	5.94	0.10	1.13	6.24	nr	**7.37**
90 degree bend	4.75	0.10	1.13	4.99	nr	**6.12**
tee section	4.75	0.10	1.13	4.99	nr	**6.12**
cross over	6.17	0.10	1.13	6.48	nr	**7.61**
reducer; 100 mm - 50 mm	11.16	0.10	1.13	11.72	nr	**12.85**
connector / stop end	0.47	0.10	1.13	0.49	nr	**1.62**
divider	1.43	0.10	1.13	1.50	nr	**2.63**
ply cover 15 mm/16 mm thick WBP exterior						
grade	0.55	0.10	1.13	0.58	m	**1.71**
200 mm wide; 65 mm deep; ref SFD65/200/00	6.41	0.20	2.27	6.73	m	**9.00**
Extra for						
45 degree bend	8.31	0.10	1.13	8.73	nr	**9.86**
90 degree bend	6.41	0.10	1.13	6.73	nr	**7.86**
tee section	6.41	0.10	1.13	6.73	nr	**7.86**
cross over	8.79	0.10	1.13	9.23	nr	**10.36**
reducer; 200 mm - 100 mm	11.16	0.10	1.13	11.72	nr	**12.85**
connector / stop end	0.62	0.10	1.13	0.65	nr	**1.78**
divider	1.43	0.10	1.13	1.50	nr	**2.63**
ply cover 15 mm/16 mm thick WBP exterior						
grade	0.93	0.10	1.13	0.98	m	**2.11**

Q PAVING/PLANTING/FENCING/SITE FURNITURE Excluding overheads and profit	PC £	Labour hours	Labour £	Material £	Unit	Total rate £
Q PAVING/PLANTING/FENCING/SITE FURNITURE						
Q10 KERBS/EDGINGS/CHANNELS/PAVING ACCESSORIES						
Excavating; by machine						
Excavating trenches; to receive kerb foundations; average size						
300 mm x 100 mm	-	0.03	0.20	0.28	m	0.48
450 mm x 150 mm	-	0.03	0.20	0.57	m	0.77
600 mm x 200 mm	-	0.04	0.28	0.79	m	1.07
Excavating curved trenches; to receive kerb foundations; average size						
300 mm x 100 mm	-	0.02	0.13	0.47	m	0.60
450 mm x 150 mm	-	0.04	0.23	0.66	m	0.89
600 mm x 200 mm	-	0.05	0.32	0.85	m	1.17
Excavating; by hand						
Excavating trenches; to receive kerb foundations; average size						
150 mm x 50 mm	-	0.03	0.20	-	m	0.20
200 mm x 75 mm	-	0.07	0.46	-	m	0.46
250 mm x 100 mm	-	0.11	0.72	-	m	0.72
300 mm x 100 mm	-	0.14	0.92	-	m	0.92
Excavating curved trenches; to receive kerb foundations; average size						
150 mm x 50 mm	-	0.04	0.26	-	m	0.26
200 mm x 75 mm	-	0.08	0.53	-	m	0.53
250 mm x 100 mm	-	0.12	0.79	-	m	0.79
300 mm x 100 mm	-	0.15	0.99	-	m	0.99
Plain in situ ready mixed designated concrete; C7.5 - 40 mm aggregate; poured on or against earth or unblinded hardcore						
Foundations	52.50	1.25	9.09	59.26	m³	68.35
Blinding beds	52.50	1.85	13.45	59.26	m³	72.71
thickness not exceeding 150 mm						
Plain in situ ready mixed designated concrete; C10 - 40 mm aggregate; poured on or against earth or unblinded hardcore						
Foundations	52.50	1.25	9.09	59.26	m³	68.35
Blinding beds	52.50	1.85	13.45	59.26	m³	72.71
thickness not exceeding 150 mm						
Plain in situ ready mixed designated concrete; C20 - 20 mm aggregate; poured on or against earth or unblinded hardcore						
Foundations	54.92	1.25	9.09	61.99	m³	71.08
Blinding beds	54.92	1.85	13.45	61.99	m³	75.44
thickness not exceeding 150 mm						
Precast concrete kerbs, channels, edgings, etc.; BS 340; bedded, jointed and pointed in cement mortar (1:3); including haunching up one side with in situ ready mixed designated concrete C10 - 40 mm aggregate; to concrete base						
Edgings; straight; square edge, fig 12						
50 mm x 150 mm	-	0.25	2.80	2.24	m	5.04
50 mm x 200 mm	-	0.25	2.80	2.76	m	5.56
50 mm x 255 mm	-	0.25	2.80	2.87	m	5.67

Q PAVING/PLANTING/FENCING/SITE FURNITURE Excluding overheads and profit	PC £	Labour hours	Labour £	Material £	Unit	Total rate £
Q10 KERBS/EDGINGS/CHANNELS/PAVING **ACCESSORIES** - cont'd						
Precast concrete kerbs, channels, edgings, **etc.; BS 340; bedded, jointed and pointed in** **cement mortar (1:3); including haunching up** **one side with in situ ready mixed designated** **concrete C10 - 40 mm aggregate; to concrete** **base** - cont'd						
Kerbs; straight						
125 mm x 255 mm; fig 7	-	0.33	3.69	3.96	m	**7.65**
150 mm x 305 mm; fig 6	-	0.33	3.69	5.75	m	**9.44**
Kerbs; curved						
125 mm x 255 mm; fig 7	-	0.50	5.59	5.27	m	**10.86**
150 mm x 305 mm; fig 6	-	0.50	5.59	7.85	m	**13.44**
Channels; 255 x 125 mm; fig 8						
straight	-	0.33	3.69	3.96	m	**7.65**
curved	-	0.50	5.59	5.27	m	**10.86**
Quadrants; fig 14						
305 mm x 305 mm x 150 mm	-	0.35	3.92	5.93	nr	**9.85**
305 mm x 305 mm x 255 mm	-	0.35	3.92	6.35	nr	**10.27**
457 mm x 457 mm x 150 mm	-	0.40	4.48	7.40	nr	**11.88**
457 mm x 457 mm x 255 mm	-	0.40	4.48	7.40	nr	**11.88**
Q20 HARDCORE/GRANULAR/CEMENT BOUND **BASES/SUB-BASES TO ROADS/PAVINGS**						
Filling to make up levels; by machine						
Average thickness not exceeding 0.25 m						
obtained off site; hardcore	-	0.30	1.97	19.38	m³	**21.35**
obtained off site; granular fill type one	-	0.30	1.97	26.72	m³	**28.69**
obtained off site; granular fill type two	-	0.30	1.97	25.78	m³	**27.75**
Average thickness exceeding 0.25 m						
obtained off site; hardcore	-	0.26	1.71	16.67	m³	**18.38**
obtained off site; granular fill type one	-	0.26	1.71	26.60	m³	**28.31**
obtained off site; granular fill type two	-	0.26	1.71	25.65	m³	**27.36**
Filling to make up levels; hand						
Average thickness not exceeding 0.25 m						
obtained off site; hardcore	-	0.66	4.34	19.76	m³	**24.10**
obtained off site; sand	-	0.77	5.07	27.37	m³	**32.44**
Average thickness exceeding 0.25 m						
obtained off site; hardcore	-	0.55	3.62	16.90	m³	**20.52**
obtained off site; sand	-	0.65	4.28	27.07	m³	**31.35**
Surface treatments						
Compacting						
filling; blinding with sand	-	0.05	0.33	1.40	m²	**1.73**

Q PAVING/PLANTING/FENCING/SITE FURNITURE Excluding overheads and profit	PC £	Labour hours	Labour £	Material £	Unit	Total rate £
Q21 IN SITU CONCRETE ROADS/PAVINGS						
Reinforced in situ ready mixed designated **concrete; C10 - 40 mm aggregate**						
Roads; to hardcore base						
thickness not exceeding 150 mm	52.50	2.00	14.54	56.44	m³	**70.98**
thickness 150 mm - 450 mm	52.50	1.40	10.18	56.44	m³	**66.62**
Reinforced in situ ready mixed designated **concrete; C20 - 20 mm aggregate**						
Roads; to hardcore base						
thickness not exceeding 150 mm	54.92	2.00	14.54	59.04	m³	**73.58**
thickness 150 mm - 450 mm	54.92	1.40	10.18	59.04	m³	**69.22**
Reinforced in situ ready mixed designated **concrete; C25 - 20 mm aggregate**						
Roads; to hardcore base						
thickness not exceeding 150 mm	55.20	2.00	14.54	59.34	m³	**73.88**
thickness 150 mm - 450 mm	55.20	1.40	10.18	59.34	m³	**69.52**
Formwork; sides of foundations; basic finish						
Plain vertical						
height not exceeding 250 mm	-	0.42	4.70	1.31	m	**6.01**
height 250 mm - 500 mm	-	0.62	6.94	2.27	m	**9.21**
height 500 mm - 1.00 m	-	0.90	10.08	4.50	m	**14.58**
add to above for curved 6.00 m radii	-	0.04	0.45	0.18	m	**0.63**
Reinforcement fabric; BS 4483; lapped; in **roads, footpaths or pavings**						
Ref A142 (2.22 kg/m²)						
400 mm minimum laps	0.70	0.15	1.34	0.77	m²	**2.11**
Ref A193 (3.02 kg/m²)						
400 mm minimum laps	1.00	0.15	1.34	1.10	m²	**2.44**
Formed joints; Fosroc Expandite "Flexcell" **impreganted joint filler or other equal and** **approved**						
Width not exceeding 150 mm						
12.50 mm thick	-	0.15	1.68	1.52	m	**3.20**
25 mm thick	-	0.20	2.24	2.26	m	**4.50**
Width 150 - 300 mm						
12.50 mm thick	-	0.20	2.24	2.72	m	**4.96**
25 mm thick	-	0.20	2.24	3.74	m	**5.98**
Width 300 - 450 mm						
12.50 mm thick	-	0.25	2.80	4.08	m	**6.88**
25 mm thick	-	0.25	2.80	5.61	m	**8.41**
Sealants; Fosroc Expandite "Pliastic 77" hot **poured rubberized bituminous compound or** **other equal and approved**						
Width 25 mm						
25 mm depth	-	0.21	2.35	1.30	m	**3.65**
Concrete sundries						
Treating surfaces of unset concrete; grading to cambers; tamping with a 75 mm thick steel shod tamper	-	0.25	1.82	-	m²	**1.82**

Q PAVING/PLANTING/FENCING/SITE FURNITURE Excluding overheads and profit	PC £	Labour hours	Labour £	Material £	Unit	Total rate £
Q22 COATED MACADAM/ASPHALT 　　ROADS/PAVINGS						
In situ finishings; Associated Asphalt or other equal and approved						
NOTE: The prices for all in situ finishings to roads and footpaths include for work to falls, crossfalls or slopes not exceeding 15 degrees from horizontal; for laying on prepared bases (prices not included) and for rolling with an appropriate roller. The following rates are based on black bitumen macadam, except where stated. Red bitumen macadam rates are approximately 50% dearer.						
Fine graded wearing course; BS 4987; clause 2.7.7, tables 34 - 36; 14 mm nominal size pre-coated igneous rock chippings; tack coat of bitumen emulsion						
19 mm work to roads; one coat						
igneous aggregate	-	-	-	-	m²	**10.65**
Close graded bitumen macadam; BS 4987; 10 mm nominal size graded aggregate to clause 2.7.4 tables 34 - 36; tack coat of bitumen emulsion						
30 mm work to roads; one coat						
limestone aggregate	-	-	-	-	m²	**10.21**
igneous aggregate	-	-	-	-	m²	**10.29**
Bitumen macadam; BS 4987; 45 mm thick base course of 20 mm open graded aggregate to clause 2.6.1 tables 5 - 7; 20 mm thick wearing course of 6 mm nominal size medium graded aggregate to clause 2.7.6 tables 32 - 33						
65 mm work to pavements/footpaths; two coats						
limestone aggregate	-	-	-	-	m²	**11.90**
igneous aggregate	-	-	-	-	m²	**12.05**
add to last for 10 nominal size chippings; 　　　　sprinkled into wearing course	-	-	-	-	m²	**0.25**
Bitumen macadam; BS 4987; 50 mm nominal size graded aggregate to clause 2.6.2 tables 8 - 10						
75 mm work to roads; one coat						
limestone aggregate	-	-	-	-	m²	**12.60**
igneous aggregate	-	-	-	-	m²	**12.80**
Dense bitumen macadam; BS 4987; 50 mm thick base course of 20 mm graded aggregate to clause 2.6.5 tables 15 - 16; 200 pen. binder; 30 mm wearing course of 10 mm nominal size graded aggregate to clause 2.7.4 tables 26 - 28						
80 mm work to roads; two coats						
limestone aggregate	-	-	-	-	m²	**12.71**
igneous aggregate	-	-	-	-	m²	**12.88**

Q PAVING/PLANTING/FENCING/SITE FURNITURE Excluding overheads and profit	PC £	Labour hours	Labour £	Material £	Unit	Total rate £
Bitumen macadam; BS 4987; 50 mm thick base course of 20 mm nominal size graded aggregate to clause 2.6.1 tables 5 - 7; 25 mm thick wearing course of 10 mm nominal size graded aggregate to clause 2.7.2 tables 20 - 22 75 mm work to roads; two coats						
limestone aggregate	-	-	-	-	m²	**13.17**
igneous aggregate	-	-	-	-	m²	**13.37**
Dense bitumen macadam; BS 4987; 70 mm thick base course of 20 mm nominal size graded aggregate to clause 2.6.5 tables 15 - 16; 200 pen. binder; 30 mm wearing course of 10 mm nominal size graded aggregate to clause 2.7.4 tables 26 - 28 100 mm work to roads; two coats						
limestone aggregate	-	-	-	-	m²	**14.34**
igneous aggregate	-	-	-	-	m²	**14.56**
Dense bitumen macadam; BS 4987; 70 mm thick road base of 28 mm nominal size graded aggregate to clause 2.5.2 tables 3 - 4; 50 mm thick base course of 20 mm nominal size graded aggregate to clause 2.6.5 tables 15 - 16; 30 mm wearing course of 10 mm nominal size graded aggregate to clause 2.7.4 tables 26 - 28 150 mm work to roads; three coats						
limestone aggregate	-	-	-	-	m²	**23.22**
igneous aggregate	-	-	-	-	m²	**23.58**
Red bitumen macadam; BS 4987; 70 mm thick base course of 20 mm nominal size graded aggregate to clause 2.6.5 tables 15 - 16; 30 mm wearing course of 10 mm nominal size graded aggregate to clause 2.7.4 tables 26 - 28 100 mm work to roads; two coats						
limestone base; igneous wearing course	-	-	-	-	m²	**17.08**
igneous aggregate	-	-	-	-	m²	**17.25**
Q23 GRAVEL/HOGGIN/WOODCHIP ROADS/PAVINGS						
Two coat gravel paving; level and to falls; first layer course clinker aggregate and wearing layer fine gravel aggregate Pavings; over 300 mm wide						
50 mm thick	-	0.08	0.90	1.68	m²	**2.58**
63 mm thick	-	0.10	1.12	2.21	m²	**3.33**
Q25 SLAB/BRICK/BLOCK/SETT/COBBLE PAVINGS						
Artificial stone paving; Redland Aggregates "Texitone" or other equal and approved; to falls or crossfalls; bedding 25 mm thick in cement mortar (1:3); staggered joints; jointing in coloured cement mortar (1:3), brushed in; to sand base Pavings; over 300 mm wide						
450 mm x 600 mm x 50 mm thick; grey or coloured	2.80	0.45	5.04	13.34	m²	**18.38**
600 mm x 600 mm x 50 mm thick; grey or coloured	3.24	0.42	4.70	11.90	m²	**16.60**
750 mm x 600 mm x 50 mm thick; grey or coloured	3.78	0.39	4.36	11.28	m²	**15.64**
900 mm x 600 mm x 50 mm thick; grey or coloured	4.32	0.36	4.03	10.86	m²	**14.89**

Q PAVING/PLANTING/FENCING/SITE FURNITURE Excluding overheads and profit	PC £	Labour hours	Labour £	Material £	Unit	Total rate £
Q25 SLAB/BRICK/BLOCK/SETT/COBBLE PAVINGS - cont'd						
Brick paviors; 215 mm x 103 mm x 65 mm **rough stock bricks; PC £480.00/1000; to falls** **or crossfalls; bedding 10 mm thick in cement** **mortar (1:3); jointing in cement mortar (1:3);** **as work proceeds; to concrete base**						
Pavings; over 300 mm wide; straight joints both ways						
bricks laid flat	-	0.80	11.37	22.43	m²	**33.80**
bricks laid on edge	-	1.12	15.92	33.34	m²	**49.26**
Pavings; over 300 mm wide; laid to herringbone pattern						
bricks laid flat	-	1.00	14.21	22.43	m²	**36.64**
bricks laid on edge	-	1.40	19.89	33.34	m²	**53.23**
Add or deduct for variation of £10.00/1000 in PC of brick paviours						
bricks laid flat	-	-	-	0.45	m²	**0.45**
bricks laid on edge	-	-	-	0.68	m²	**0.68**
River washed cobble paving; 50 mm - 75 mm; **PC £70.00/t; to falls or crossfalls; bedding 13** **mm thick in cement mortar (1:3); jointing to a** **height of two thirds of cobbles in dry mortar** **(1:3); tightly butted, washed and brushed; to** **concrete**						
Pavings; over 300 mm wide						
regular	-	4.00	44.76	16.50	m²	**61.26**
laid to pattern	-	5.00	55.95	16.50	m²	**72.45**
Concrete paving flags; BS 7263; to falls or **crossfalls; bedding 25 mm thick in cement:** **sand mortar (1:4); butt joints straight both** **ways; jointing in cement:sand (1:3);** **brushed in; to sand base**						
Pavings; over 300 mm wide						
450 mm x 600 mm x 50 mm thick; grey	1.40	0.45	5.04	6.63	m²	**11.67**
450 mm x 600 mm x 60 mm thick; coloured	1.60	0.45	5.04	7.41	m²	**12.45**
600 mm x 600 mm x 50 mm thick; grey	1.59	0.42	4.70	5.83	m²	**10.53**
600 mm x 600 mm x 50 mm thick; coloured	1.84	0.42	4.70	6.56	m²	**11.26**
750 mm x 600 mm x 50 mm thick; grey	1.87	0.39	4.36	5.55	m²	**9.91**
750 mm x 600 mm x 50 mm thick; coloured	2.15	0.39	4.36	6.21	m²	**10.57**
900 mm x 600 mm x 50 mm thick; grey	2.10	0.36	4.03	5.27	m²	**9.30**
900 mm x 600 mm x 50 mm thick; coloured	2.41	0.36	4.03	5.88	m²	**9.91**
Concrete rectangular paving blocks; to falls **or crossfalls; bedding 50 mm thick in dry** **sharp sand; filling joints with sharp sand** **brushed in; on earth base**						
Pavings; "Keyblock" or other equal and approved; over 300 mm wide; straight joints both ways						
200 mm x 100 mm x 60 mm thick; grey	7.37	0.75	8.39	9.73	m²	**18.12**
200 mm x 100 mm x 60 mm thick; coloured	8.74	0.75	8.39	11.16	m²	**19.55**
200 mm x 100 mm x 80 mm thick; grey	7.93	0.80	8.95	10.48	m²	**19.43**
200 mm x 100 mm x 80 mm thick; coloured	9.34	0.80	8.95	11.96	m²	**20.91**
Pavings; "Keyblock" or other equal and approved; over 300 mm wide; laid to herringbone pattern						
200 mm x 100 mm x 60 mm thick; grey	-	0.95	10.63	9.73	m²	**20.36**
200 mm x 100 mm x 60 mm thick; coloured	-	0.95	10.63	11.16	m²	**21.79**
200 mm x 100 mm x 80 mm thick; grey	-	1.00	11.19	10.48	m²	**21.67**
200 mm x 100 mm x 80 mm thick; coloured	-	1.00	11.19	11.96	m²	**23.15**

Q PAVING/PLANTING/FENCING/SITE FURNITURE Excluding overheads and profit	PC £	Labour hours	Labour £	Material £	Unit	Total rate £
Extra for two row boundary edgings to herringbone pavings; 200 mm wide; including a 150 mm high ready mixed designated concrete C10 - 40 mm aggregate haunching to one side; blocks laid breaking joint						
200 mm x 100 mm x 60 mm; coloured	-	0.30	3.36	1.77	m	5.13
200 mm x 100 mm x 80 mm; coloured	-	0.30	3.36	1.82	m	5.18
Pavings; "Mount Sorrel" or other equal and approved; over 300 mm wide; straight joints both ways						
200 mm x 100 mm x 60 mm thick; grey	5.52	0.75	8.39	7.78	m²	16.17
200 mm x 100 mm x 60 mm thick; coloured	6.34	0.75	8.39	8.64	m²	17.03
200 mm x 100 mm x 80 mm thick; grey	6.56	0.80	8.95	9.04	m²	17.99
200 mm x 100 mm x 80 mm thick; coloured	7.54	0.80	8.95	10.07	m²	19.02
Pavings; "Pedesta" or other equal and approved; over 300 mm wide; straight joints both ways						
200 mm x 100 mm x 60 mm thick; grey	6.12	0.75	8.39	8.41	m²	16.80
200 mm x 100 mm x 60 mm thick; coloured	6.19	0.75	8.39	8.49	m²	16.88
200 mm x 100 mm x 80 mm thick; grey	7.13	0.80	8.95	9.64	m²	18.59
200 mm x 100 mm x 80 mm thick; coloured	7.52	0.80	8.95	10.05	m²	19.00
Pavings; "Intersett" or other equal and approved; over 300 mm wide; straight joints both ways						
200 mm x 100 mm x 60 mm thick; grey	8.05	0.75	8.39	10.44	m²	18.83
200 mm x 100 mm x 60 mm thick; coloured	8.94	0.75	8.39	11.37	m²	19.76
200 mm x 100 mm x 80 mm thick; grey	9.59	0.80	8.95	12.22	m²	21.17
200 mm x 100 mm x 80 mm thick; coloured	10.70	0.80	8.95	13.39	m²	22.34
Concrete rectangular paving blocks; to falls or crossfalls; 6 mm wide joints; symmetrical layout; bedding in 15 mm semi-dry cement mortar (1:4); jointing and pointing in cement: sand (1:4); on concrete base						
Pavings; "Trafica" or other equal and approved; over 300 mm wide						
400 mm x 400 mm x 65 mm; Standard; natural	1.33	0.48	5.37	9.67	m²	15.04
400 mm x 400 mm x 65 mm; Standard; buff	1.85	0.48	5.37	13.03	m²	18.40
400 mm x 400 mm x 65 mm; Saxon textured; natural	2.45	0.48	5.37	16.91	m²	22.28
400 mm x 400 mm x 65 mm; Saxon textured; buff	2.94	0.48	5.37	20.08	m²	25.45
400 mm x 400 mm x 65 mm; Perfecta; natural	2.98	0.48	5.37	20.34	m²	25.71
400 mm x 400 mm x 65 mm; Perfecta; buff	3.55	0.48	5.37	24.02	m²	29.39
450 mm x 450 mm x 70 mm; Standard; natural	2.19	0.46	5.15	12.28	m²	17.43
450 mm x 450 mm x 70 mm; Standard; buff	2.95	0.46	5.15	16.17	m²	21.32
450 mm x 450 mm x 70 mm; Saxon textured; natural	3.06	0.46	5.15	16.73	m²	21.88
450 mm x 450 mm x 70 mm; Saxon textured; buff	3.65	0.46	5.15	19.75	m²	24.90
450 mm x 450 mm x 70 mm; Perfecta; natural	3.67	0.46	5.15	19.85	m²	25.00
450 mm x 450 mm x 70 mm; Perfecta; buff	4.35	0.46	5.15	23.33	m²	28.48
450 mm x 450 mm x 100 mm; Standard; natural	4.85	0.48	5.37	25.89	m²	31.26
450 mm x 450 mm x 100 mm; Standard; buff	5.84	0.48	5.37	30.95	m²	36.32
450 mm x 450 mm x 100 mm; Saxon textured; natural	5.51	0.48	5.37	29.26	m²	34.63
450 mm x 450 mm x 100 mm; Saxon textured; buff	6.57	0.48	5.37	34.69	m²	40.06
450 mm x 450 mm x 100 mm; Perfecta; natural	5.95	0.48	5.37	31.52	m²	36.89
450 mm x 450 mm x 100 mm; Perfecta; buff	6.99	0.48	5.37	36.84	m²	42.21
York stone slab pavings; to falls or crossfalls; bedding 25 mm thick in cement:sand mortar (1:4); 5 mm wide joints; jointing in coloured cement mortar (1:3); brushed in; to sand base						
Pavings; over 300 mm wide						
50 mm thick; random rectangular pattern	53.00	0.75	10.66	55.77	m²	66.43
600 mm x 600 mm x 50 mm thick	63.00	0.42	5.97	66.02	m²	71.99
600 mm x 900 mm x 50 mm thick	65.00	0.36	5.12	68.07	m²	73.19

Q PAVING/PLANTING/FENCING/SITE FURNITURE Excluding overheads and profit	PC £	Labour hours	Labour £	Material £	Unit	Total rate £
Q25 SLAB/BRICK/BLOCK/SETT/COBBLE PAVINGS - cont'd						
Granite setts; BS 435; 200 mm x 100 mm x **100 mm; PC £115.00/t; standard "C" dressing;** **tightly butted to falls or crossfalls; bedding 25** **mm thick in cement mortar (1:3); filling joints** **with dry mortar (1:6); washed and brushed; on** **concrete base**						
Pavings; over 300 mm wide						
straight joints	-	1.60	17.90	34.60	m²	**52.50**
laid to pattern	-	2.00	22.38	34.60	m²	**56.98**
Two rows of granite setts as boundary edgings; 200 mm wide; including a 150 mm high ready mixed designated concrete C10 - 40 mm aggregate;						
haunching to one side; blocks laid breaking joint	-	0.70	7.83	7.98	m	**15.81**
Q26 SPECIAL SURFACINGS/PAVINGS FOR ** SPORT/GENERAL AMENITY**						
Sundries						
Line marking						
width not exceeding 300 mm	-	0.05	0.40	0.15	m	**0.55**
Q30 SEEDING/TURFING						
Vegetable soil						
Selected from spoil heaps; grading; prepared for turfing or seeding; to general surfaces						
average 75 mm thick	-	0.23	1.51	-	m²	**1.51**
average 100 mm thick	-	0.25	1.65	-	m²	**1.65**
average 125 mm thick	-	0.27	1.78	-	m²	**1.78**
average 150 mm thick	-	0.28	1.84	-	m²	**1.84**
average 175 mm thick	-	0.29	1.91	-	m²	**1.91**
average 200 mm thick	-	0.31	2.04	-	m²	**2.04**
Selected from spoil heaps; grading; prepared for turfing or seeding; to cuttings or embankments						
average 75 mm thick	-	0.26	1.71	-	m²	**1.71**
average 100 mm thick	-	0.28	1.84	-	m²	**1.84**
average 125 mm thick	-	0.30	1.97	-	m²	**1.97**
average 150 mm thick	-	0.32	2.11	-	m²	**2.11**
average 175 mm thick	-	0.33	2.17	-	m²	**2.17**
average 200 mm thick	-	0.35	2.30	-	m²	**2.30**
Imported vegetable soil						
Grading; prepared for turfing or seeding; to general surfaces						
average 75 thick	-	0.21	1.38	0.70	m²	**2.08**
average 100 thick	-	0.22	1.45	0.91	m²	**2.36**
average 125 thick	-	0.24	1.58	1.33	m²	**2.91**
average 150 thick	-	0.25	1.65	1.75	m²	**3.40**
average 175 thick	-	0.27	1.78	1.96	m²	**3.74**
average 200 thick	-	0.28	1.84	2.17	m²	**4.01**
Grading; preparing for turfing or seeding; to cuttings or embankments						
average 75 mm thick	-	0.23	1.51	0.70	m²	**2.21**
average 100 mm thick	-	0.25	1.65	0.91	m²	**2.56**
average 125 mm thick	-	0.27	1.78	1.33	m²	**3.11**
average 150 mm thick	-	0.28	1.84	1.75	m²	**3.59**
average 175 mm thick	-	0.29	1.91	1.96	m²	**3.87**
average 200 mm thick	-	0.31	2.04	2.17	m²	**4.21**

Q PAVING/PLANTING/FENCING/SITE FURNITURE Excluding overheads and profit	PC £	Labour hours	Labour £	Material £	Unit	Total rate £
Fertilizer; PC £7.75/25 kg						
Fertilizer 0.07 kg/m²; raking in						
general surfaces	-	0.04	0.26	0.02	m²	0.28
Selected grass seed; PC £62.50/25 kg						
Seeding; sowing at a rate of 0.042 kg/m²						
two applications; raking in						
general surfaces	-	0.07	0.46	0.21	m²	0.67
cuttings or embankments	-	0.08	0.53	0.21	m²	0.74
Preserved turf from stack on site						
Turfing						
general surfaces	-	0.20	1.32	-	m²	1.32
cuttings or embankments; shallow	-	0.22	1.45	-	m²	1.45
cuttings or embankments; steep; pegged	-	0.30	1.97	-	m²	1.97
Imported turf; selected meadow turf						
Turfing						
general surfaces	1.10	0.20	1.32	1.32	m²	2.64
cuttings or embankments; shallow	1.10	0.22	1.45	1.32	m²	2.77
cuttings or embankments; steep; pegged	1.10	0.30	1.97	1.32	m²	3.29
Q31 PLANTING						
Planting only						
Hedge plants						
height not exceeding 750 mm	-	0.25	1.65	-	nr	1.65
height 750 mm - 1.50 m	-	0.60	3.95	-	nr	3.95
Saplings						
height not exceeding 3.00 m	-	1.70	11.19	-	nr	11.19
Q40 FENCING						
NOTE: The prices for all fencing include for setting posts in position, to a depth not exceeding 0.60 m for fences not exceeding 1.40 m high and of 0.76 m for fences over 1.40 m high. The prices allow for excavating post holes; filling to within 150 mm of ground level with concrete and all backfilling.						
Strained wire fencing; BS 1722 Part 3; 4 mm diameter galvanized mild steel plain wire threaded through posts and strained with eye bolts						
Fencing; height 900 mm; three line; concrete posts at 2750 mm centres	-	-	-	-	m	7.30
Extra for						
end concrete straining post; one strut	-	-	-	-	nr	36.40
angle concrete straining post; two struts	-	-	-	-	nr	52.60
Fencing; height 1.07 m; five line; concrete posts at 2750 mm centres	-	-	-	-	m	10.50
Extra for						
end concrete straining post; one strut	-	-	-	-	nr	54.20
angle concrete straining post; two struts	-	-	-	-	nr	68.75
Fencing; height 1.20 m; six line; concrete posts at 2750 mm centres	-	-	-	-	m	10.75
Extra for						
end concrete straining post; one strut	-	-	-	-	nr	56.50
angle concrete straining post; two struts	-	-	-	-	nr	77.00
Fencing; height 1.40 m; seven line; concrete posts at 2750 mm centres	-	-	-	-	m	11.55
Extra for						
end concrete straining post; one strut	-	-	-	-	nr	60.40
angle concrete straining post; two struts	-	-	-	-	nr	82.80

Q PAVING/PLANTING/FENCING/SITE FURNITURE Excluding overheads and profit	PC £	Labour hours	Labour £	Material £	Unit	Total rate £
Q40 FENCING - cont'd						
Chain link fencing; BS 1722 Part 1; 3 mm diameter galvanized mild steel wire; 50 mm mesh; galvanized mild steel tying and line wire; three line wires threaded through posts and strained with eye bolts and winding brackets						
Fencing; height 900 mm; galvanized mild steel angle posts at 3 m centres	-	-	-	-	m	10.00
Extra for						
end steel straining post; one strut	-	-	-	-	nr	46.50
angle steel straining post; two struts	-	-	-	-	nr	62.50
Fencing; height 900 mm; concrete posts at 3.00 m centres	-	-	-	-	m	9.75
Extra for						
end concrete straining post; one strut	-	-	-	-	nr	42.50
angle concrete straining post; two struts	-	-	-	-	nr	58.50
Fencing; height 1.20 m; galvanized mild steel angle posts at 3 m centres	-	-	-	-	m	13.00
Extra for						
end steel straining post; one strut	-	-	-	-	nr	56.50
angle steel straining post; two struts	-	-	-	-	nr	74.75
Fencing; height 1.20 m; concrete posts at 3.00 m centres	-	-	-	-	m	11.75
Extra for						
end concrete straining post; one strut	-	-	-	-	nr	52.50
angle concrete straining post; two struts	-	-	-	-	nr	68.65
Fencing; height 1.80 m; galvanized mild steel angle posts at 3 m centres	-	-	-	-	m	16.45
Extra for						
end steel straining post; one strut	-	-	-	-	nr	74.75
angle steel straining post; two struts	-	-	-	-	nr	103.00
Fencing; height 1.80 m; concrete posts at 3.00 m centres	-	-	-	-	m	14.85
Extra for						
end concrete straining post; one strut	-	-	-	-	nr	68.65
angle concrete straining post; two struts	-	-	-	-	nr	95.00
Pair of gates and gate posts; gates to match galvanized chain link fencing, with angle framing, braces, etc., complete with hinges, locking bar, lock and bolts; two 100 mm x 100 mm angle section gate posts; each with one strut						
2.44 m x 0.90 m	-	-	-	-	nr	630.00
2.44 m x 1.20 m	-	-	-	-	nr	655.00
2.44 m x 1.80 m	-	-	-	-	nr	745.00
Chain link fencing; BS 1722 Part 1; 3 mm diameter plastic coated mild steel wire; 50 mm mesh; plastic coated mild steel tying and line wire; three line wires threaded through posts and strained with eye bolts and winding brackets						
Fencing; height 900 mm; galvanized mild steel angle posts at 3.00 m centres	-	-	-	-	m	10.50
Extra for						
end steel straining post; one strut	-	-	-	-	nr	46.50
angle steel straining post; two struts	-	-	-	-	nr	62.50
Fencing; height 900 mm; concrete posts at 3.00 m centres	-	-	-	-	m	10.20
Extra for						
end concrete straining post; one strut	-	-	-	-	nr	42.50
angle concrete straining post; two struts	-	-	-	-	nr	58.50

Q PAVING/PLANTING/FENCING/SITE FURNITURE Excluding overheads and profit	PC £	Labour hours	Labour £	Material £	Unit	Total rate £
Fencing; height 1.20 m; galvanized mild steel angle						
posts at 3.00 m centres	-	-	-	-	m	15.50
Extra for						
end steel straining post; one strut	-	-	-	-	nr	56.50
angle steel straining post; two struts	-	-	-	-	nr	75.00
Fencing; height 1.20 m; concrete posts at 3.00 m centres	-	-	-	-	m	12.25
Extra for						
end concrete straining post; one strut	-	-	-	-	nr	52.50
angle concrete straining post; two struts	-	-	-	-	nr	69.00
Fencing; height 1.80 m; galvanized mild steel angle						
posts at 3.00 m centres	-	-	-	-	m	18.00
Extra for						
end steel straining post; one strut	-	-	-	-	nr	75.00
angle steel straining post; two struts	-	-	-	-	nr	103.00
Fencing; height 1.80 m; concrete posts at 3.00 m centres	-	-	-	-	m	17.50
Extra for						
end concrete straining post; one strut	-	-	-	-	nr	69.00
angle concrete straining post; two struts	-	-	-	-	nr	95.00
Pair of gates and gate posts; gates to match						
plastic chain link fencing; with angle framing,						
braces, etc. complete with hinges, locking bar,						
lock and bolts; two 100 mm x 100 mm angle						
section gate posts; each with one strut						
2.44 m x 0.90 m	-	-	-	-	nr	640.00
2.44 m x 1.20 m	-	-	-	-	nr	665.00
2.44 m x 1.80 m	-	-	-	-	nr	760.00
Chain link fencing for tennis courts; BS 1722						
Part 13; 2.50 mm diameter galvanised mild wire; 45						
mm mesh; line and tying wires threaded						
through 45 mm x 45 mm x 5 mm galvanised						
mild steel angle standards, posts and struts;						
60 mm x 60 mm x 6 mm straining posts and						
gate posts; straining posts and struts						
strained with eye bolts and winding brackets						
Fencing to tennis court 36.00 m x 18.00 m; including						
gate 1.07 m x 1.98 m; complete with hinges,						
locking bar, lock and bolts						
height 2745 mm; standards at 3.00 m centres	-	-	-	-	nr	2040.00
height 3660 mm; standards at 2.50 m centres	-	-	-	-	nr	2780.00
Cleft chestnut pale fencing; BS 1722 Part 4;						
pales spaced 51 mm apart; on two lines of						
galvanized wire; 64 mm diameter posts; 76						
mm x 51 mm struts						
Fencing; height 900 mm; posts at 2.50 m centres	-	-	-	-	m	6.30
Extra for						
straining post; one strut	-	-	-	-	nr	11.50
corner straining post; two struts	-	-	-	-	nr	15.35
Fencing; height 1.05 m; posts at 2.50 m centres	-	-	-	-	m	7.00
Extra for						
straining post; one strut	-	-	-	-	nr	12.70
corner straining post; two struts	-	-	-	-	nr	16.90
Fencing; height 1.20 m; posts at 2.25 m centres	-	-	-	-	m	7.40
Extra for						
straining post; one strut	-	-	-	-	nr	13.90
corner straining post; two struts	-	-	-	-	nr	18.50
Fencing; height 1.35 m; posts at 2.25 m centres	-	-	-	-	m	7.90
Extra for						
straining post; one strut	-	-	-	-	nr	15.60
corner straining post; two struts	-	-	-	-	nr	20.70

Q PAVING/PLANTING/FENCING/SITE FURNITURE Excluding overheads and profit	PC £	Labour hours	Labour £	Material £	Unit	Total rate £
Q40 FENCING - cont'd						
Close boarded fencing; BS 1722 Part 5; 76 mm x 38 **mm softwood rails; 89 mm x 19 mm softwood pales** **lapped 13 mm; 152 mm x 25 mm softwood gravel** **boards; all softwood "treated"; posts at 3.00 m centres**						
Fencing; two rail; concrete posts						
height 1.00 m	-	-	-	-	m	26.40
height 1.20 m	-	-	-	-	m	28.00
Fencing; three rail; concrete posts						
height 1.40 m	-	-	-	-	m	35.40
height 1.60 m	-	-	-	-	m	36.80
height 1.80 m	-	-	-	-	m	38.40
Fencing; two rail; oak posts						
height 1.00 m	-	-	-	-	m	19.00
height 1.20 m	-	-	-	-	m	21.80
Fencing; three rail; oak posts						
height 1.40 m	-	-	-	-	m	24.50
height 1.60 m	-	-	-	-	m	27.90
height 1.80 m	-	-	-	-	m	31.10
Precast concrete slab fencing; 305 mm x 38 **mm x 1753 mm slabs; fitted into twice** **grooved concrete posts at 1830 mm centres**						
Fencing						
height 1.20 m	-	-	-	-	m	40.50
height 1.50 m	-	-	-	-	m	48.00
height 1.80 m	-	-	-	-	m	59.90
Mild steel unclimbable fencing; in rivetted panels **2440 mm long; 44 mm x 13 mm flat section top and** **bottom rails; two 44 mm x 19 mm flat section** **standards; one with foot plate; and 38 mm x 13 mm** **raking stay with foot plate; 20 mm diameter pointed** **verticals at 120 mm centres; two 44 mm x 19 mm** **supports 760 mm long with ragged ends to bottom rail;** **the whole bolted together; coated with red oxide** **primer; setting standards and stays in ground at 2440** **mm centres and supports at 815 mm centres**						
Fencing						
height 1.67 m	-	-	-	-	m	94.90
height 2.13 m	-	-	-	-	m	110.00
Pair of gates and gate posts, to match mild steel unclimbable fencing; with flat section framing, braces, etc., complete with locking bar, lock, handles, drop bolt, gate stop and holding back catches; two 102 mm x 102 mm hollow section gate posts with cap and foot plates						
2.44 m x 1.67 m	-	-	-	-	nr	840.00
2.44 m x 2.13 m	-	-	-	-	nr	980.00
4.88 m x 1.67 m	-	-	-	-	nr	1295.00
4.88 m x 2.13 m	-	-	-	-	nr	1655.00
PVC coated, galvanised mild steel high security **fencing; "Sentinal Sterling" fencing or other equal** **and approved; Twil Wire Products Ltd; 50 mm x 50 mm** **mesh; 3 mm/3.50 mm gauge wire; barbed edge - 1;** **"Sentinal Bi-steel" colour coated posts or other equal** **and approved at 2440 mm centres**						
Fencing						
height 1.80 m	-	1.00	6.58	27.80	m	34.38
height 2.10 m	-	1.25	8.22	31.55	m	39.77

R DISPOSAL SYSTEMS Excluding overheads and profit	PC £	Labour hours	Labour £	Material £	Unit	Total rate £
R DISPOSAL SYSTEMS						
R10 RAINWATER PIPEWORK/GUTTERS						
Aluminium pipes and fittings; BS 2997; ears **cast on; powder coated finish**						
63.50 mm diameter pipes; plugged and						
screwed	9.11	0.37	3.83	10.14	m	**13.97**
Extra for						
fittings with one end	-	0.22	2.28	5.25	nr	**7.53**
fittings with two ends	-	0.42	4.35	5.41	nr	**9.76**
fittings with three ends	-	0.60	6.21	7.19	nr	**13.40**
shoe	5.57	0.22	2.28	5.25	nr	**7.53**
bend	5.94	0.42	4.35	5.41	nr	**9.76**
single branch	7.75	0.60	6.21	7.19	nr	**13.40**
offset 228 mm projection	13.70	0.42	4.76	12.73	nr	**17.49**
offset 304 mm projection	15.28	0.42	4.35	14.35	nr	**18.70**
access pipe	16.93	-	-	15.01	nr	**15.01**
connection to clay pipes; cement:sand						
(1:2) joint	-	0.15	1.55	0.08	nr	**1.63**
76.50 mm diameter pipes; plugged and						
screwed	10.60	0.40	4.14	11.71	m	**15.85**
Extra for						
shoe	7.64	0.25	2.59	7.26	nr	**9.85**
bend	7.51	0.45	4.66	6.91	nr	**11.57**
single branch	9.33	0.65	6.73	8.65	nr	**15.38**
offset 228 mm projection	14.55	0.45	4.66	13.34	nr	**18.00**
offset 304 mm projection	16.76	0.45	4.66	15.60	nr	**20.26**
access pipe	18.50	-	-	16.23	nr	**16.23**
connection to clay pipes; cement:sand						
(1:2) joint	-	0.17	1.76	0.08	nr	**1.84**
100 mm diameter pipes; plugged and screwed	18.09	0.45	4.66	19.59	m	**24.25**
Extra for						
shoe	9.21	0.28	2.90	8.25	nr	**11.15**
bend	10.46	0.50	5.17	9.34	nr	**14.51**
single branch	12.49	0.75	7.76	10.99	nr	**18.75**
offset 228 mm projection	17.53	0.50	5.17	14.81	nr	**19.98**
offset 304 mm projection	19.46	0.50	5.17	16.78	nr	**21.95**
access pipe	21.92	-	-	17.79	nr	**17.79**
connection to clay pipes; cement:sand						
(1:2) joint	-	0.20	2.07	0.08	nr	**2.15**
Roof outlets; circular aluminium; with flat or						
domed grating; joint to pipe						
50 mm diameter	46.91	0.60	8.65	46.91	nr	**55.56**
75 mm diameter	61.47	0.65	9.37	61.47	nr	**70.84**
100 mm diameter	80.05	0.70	10.09	80.05	nr	**90.14**
150 mm diameter	102.56	0.75	10.81	102.56	nr	**113.37**
Roof outlets; d-shaped; balcony; with flat or						
domed grating; joint to pipe						
50 mm diameter	55.56	0.60	8.65	55.56	nr	**64.21**
75 mm diameter	63.86	0.65	9.37	63.86	nr	**73.23**
100 mm diameter	78.44	0.70	10.09	78.44	nr	**88.53**
Galvanized wire balloon grating; BS 416 for						
pipes or outlets						
50 mm diameter	1.38	0.07	1.01	1.38	nr	**2.39**
63 mm diameter	1.40	0.07	1.01	1.40	nr	**2.41**
75 mm diameter	1.49	0.07	1.01	1.49	nr	**2.50**
100 mm diameter	1.64	0.08	1.15	1.64	nr	**2.79**

R DISPOSAL SYSTEMS Excluding overheads and profit	PC £	Labour hours	Labour £	Material £	Unit	Total rate £
R10 RAINWATER PIPEWORK/GUTTERS - cont'd						
Aluminium gutters and fittings; BS 2997;						
powder coated finish						
100 mm half round gutters; on brackets;						
screwed to timber	8.35	0.35	3.97	11.05	m	**15.02**
Extra for						
stop end	2.26	0.16	1.81	4.47	nr	**6.28**
running outlet	5.02	0.33	3.74	5.09	nr	**8.83**
stop end outlet	4.46	0.16	1.81	6.02	nr	**7.83**
angle	4.63	0.33	3.74	3.94	nr	**7.68**
113 mm half round gutters; on brackets;						
screwed to timber	8.75	0.35	3.97	11.48	m	**15.45**
Extra for						
stop end	2.38	0.16	1.81	4.61	nr	**6.42**
running outlet	5.47	0.33	3.74	5.52	nr	**9.26**
stop end outlet	5.11	0.16	1.81	6.66	nr	**8.47**
angle	5.23	0.33	3.74	4.45	nr	**8.19**
125 mm half round gutters; on brackets;						
screwed to timber	9.83	0.40	4.54	13.76	m	**18.30**
Extra for						
stop end	2.90	0.18	2.04	6.19	nr	**8.23**
running outlet	5.92	0.35	3.97	5.90	nr	**9.87**
stop end outlet	5.44	0.18	2.04	7.97	nr	**10.01**
angle	5.80	0.35	3.97	5.88	nr	**9.85**
100 mm ogee gutters; on brackets; screwed to						
timber	10.42	0.37	4.20	14.12	m	**18.32**
Extra for						
stop end	2.38	0.17	1.93	2.94	nr	**4.87**
running outlet	5.88	0.35	3.97	5.39	nr	**9.36**
stop end outlet	4.56	0.17	1.93	6.74	nr	**8.67**
angle	4.96	0.35	3.97	3.50	nr	**7.47**
112 mm ogee gutters; on brackets; screwed to						
timber	11.58	0.42	4.76	15.56	m	**20.32**
Extra for						
stop end	2.56	0.17	1.93	3.13	nr	**5.06**
running outlet	5.95	0.35	3.97	5.37	nr	**9.34**
stop end outlet	5.11	0.17	1.93	7.39	nr	**9.32**
angle	5.90	0.35	3.97	4.26	nr	**8.23**
125 mm ogee gutters; on brackets; screwed to						
timber	12.79	0.42	4.76	17.09	m	**21.85**
Extra for						
stop end	2.79	0.19	2.15	3.37	nr	**5.52**
running outlet	6.52	0.37	4.20	5.85	nr	**10.05**
stop end outlet	5.80	0.19	2.15	8.24	nr	**10.39**
angle	6.89	0.37	4.20	5.07	nr	**9.27**
Cast iron pipes and fittings; EN 1462; ears						
cast on; joints						
65 mm pipes; primed; nailed to masonry	15.16	0.52	5.38	16.20	m	**21.58**
Extra for						
shoe	13.17	0.32	3.31	12.46	nr	**15.77**
bend	8.06	0.57	5.90	7.23	nr	**13.13**
single branch	15.54	0.72	7.45	14.40	nr	**21.85**
offset 225 mm projection	14.37	0.57	5.90	12.74	nr	**18.64**
offset 305 mm projection	16.82	0.57	5.90	14.93	nr	**20.83**
connection to clay pipes; cement:sand						
(1:2) joint	-	0.15	1.55	0.09	nr	**1.64**

R DISPOSAL SYSTEMS Excluding overheads and profit	PC £	Labour hours	Labour £	Material £	Unit	Total rate £
75 mm pipes; primed; nailed to masonry	15.16	0.55	5.69	16.36	m	22.05
Extra for						
shoe	13.17	0.35	3.62	12.52	nr	16.14
bend	9.80	1.20	13.01	9.06	nr	22.07
single branch	17.14	0.75	7.76	16.14	nr	23.90
offset 225 mm projection	14.37	0.60	6.21	12.79	nr	19.00
offset 305 mm projection	17.66	0.60	6.21	15.85	nr	22.06
connection to clay pipes; cement:sand						
(1:2) joint	-	0.17	1.76	0.09	nr	1.85
100 mm pipes; primed; nailed to masonry	20.36	0.60	6.21	22.00	m	28.21
Extra for						
shoe	17.16	0.40	4.14	16.28	nr	20.42
bend	13.83	0.65	6.73	12.86	nr	19.59
single branch	20.37	0.80	8.28	19.01	nr	27.29
offset 225 mm projection	28.21	0.65	6.73	26.32	nr	33.05
offset 305 mm projection	28.21	0.65	6.73	25.89	nr	32.62
connection to clay pipes; cement:sand						
(1:2) joint	-	0.20	2.07	0.08	nr	2.15
100 mm x 75 mm rectangular pipes; primed; nailing to masonry	58.24	0.60	6.21	61.78	m	67.99
Extra for						
shoe	49.35	0.40	4.14	46.09	nr	50.23
bend	46.99	0.65	6.73	43.67	nr	50.40
offset 225 mm projection	66.15	0.40	4.14	59.64	nr	63.78
offset 305 mm projection	70.71	0.40	4.14	63.09	nr	67.23
connection to clay pipes; cement:sand						
(1:2) joint	-	0.20	2.07	0.08	nr	2.15
Rainwater head; rectangular; for pipes						
65 mm diameter	17.98	0.57	5.90	18.67	nr	24.57
75 mm diameter	17.98	0.60	6.21	18.72	nr	24.93
100 mm diameter	24.83	0.65	6.73	25.85	nr	32.58
Rainwater head; octagonal; for pipes						
65 mm diameter	10.29	0.57	5.90	10.79	nr	16.69
75 mm diameter	11.69	0.60	6.21	12.28	nr	18.49
100 mm diameter	25.90	0.65	6.73	26.95	nr	33.68
Copper wire balloon grating; BS 416 for pipes or outlets						
50 mm diameter	1.68	0.07	0.72	1.68	nr	2.40
63 mm diameter	1.70	0.07	0.72	1.70	nr	2.42
75 mm diameter	1.91	0.07	0.72	1.91	nr	2.63
100 mm diameter	2.17	0.08	0.83	2.17	nr	3.00
Cast iron gutters and fittings; EN 1462						
100 mm half round gutters; primed; on brackets; screwed to timber	8.57	0.40	4.54	11.35	m	15.89
Extra for						
stop end	2.16	0.17	1.93	3.28	nr	5.21
running outlet	6.26	0.35	3.97	5.66	nr	9.63
angle	6.43	0.35	3.97	6.94	nr	10.91
115 mm half round gutters; primed; on brackets; screwed to timber	8.93	0.40	4.54	11.75	m	16.29
Extra for						
stop end	2.80	0.17	1.93	3.92	nr	5.85
running outlet	6.82	0.35	3.97	6.19	nr	10.16
angle	6.61	0.35	3.97	7.06	nr	11.03
125 mm half round gutters; primed; on brackets; screwed to timber	10.44	0.45	5.10	13.35	m	18.45
Extra for						
stop end	2.80	0.20	2.27	3.93	nr	6.20
running outlet	7.81	0.40	4.54	7.06	nr	11.60
angle	7.81	0.40	4.54	7.99	nr	12.53

R DISPOSAL SYSTEMS Excluding overheads and profit	PC £	Labour hours	Labour £	Material £	Unit	Total rate £
R10 RAINWATER PIPEWORK/GUTTERS - cont'd						
Cast iron gutters and fittings; EN 1462 - cont'd						
150 mm half round gutters; primed; on						
brackets; screwed to timber	17.86	0.50	5.67	20.79	m	**26.46**
Extra for						
stop end	3.73	0.22	2.49	6.26	nr	**8.75**
running outlet	13.50	0.45	5.10	12.20	nr	**17.30**
angle	14.25	0.45	5.10	13.74	nr	**18.84**
100 mm ogee gutters; primed; on brackets;						
screwed to timber	9.55	0.42	4.76	12.62	m	**17.38**
Extra for						
stop end	2.00	0.18	2.04	4.27	nr	**6.31**
running outlet	6.84	0.37	4.20	6.16	nr	**10.36**
angle	6.71	0.37	4.20	7.28	nr	**11.48**
115 mm ogee gutters; primed; on brackets;						
screwed to timber	10.51	0.42	4.76	13.66	m	**18.42**
Extra for						
stop end	2.64	0.18	2.04	4.92	nr	**6.96**
running outlet	7.27	0.37	4.20	6.51	nr	**10.71**
angle	7.27	0.37	4.20	7.67	nr	**11.87**
125 mm ogee gutters; primed; on brackets;						
screwed to timber	11.02	0.47	5.33	14.50	m	**19.83**
Extra for						
stop end	2.64	0.21	2.38	5.20	nr	**7.58**
running outlet	7.94	0.42	4.76	7.15	nr	**11.91**
angle	7.94	0.42	4.76	8.53	nr	**13.29**
3 mm thick galvanised heavy pressed steel						
gutters and fittings; joggle joints; BS 1091						
200 mm x 100 mm (400 mm girth) box gutter;						
screwed to timber	-	0.65	6.73	14.29	m	**21.02**
Extra for						
stop end	-	0.35	3.62	7.96	nr	**11.58**
running outlet	-	0.70	7.25	13.14	nr	**20.39**
stop end outlet	-	0.35	3.62	18.36	nr	**21.98**
angle	-	0.70	7.25	14.59	nr	**21.84**
381 mm boundary wall gutters (900 mm girth);						
bent twice; screwed to timber	-	0.65	6.73	23.45	m	**30.18**
Extra for						
stop end	-	0.40	4.14	13.51	nr	**17.65**
running outlet	-	0.70	7.25	18.09	nr	**25.34**
stop end outlet	-	0.35	3.62	25.52	nr	**29.14**
angle	-	0.70	7.25	21.35	nr	**28.60**
457 mm boundary wall gutters (1200 mm girth);						
bent twice; screwed to timber	-	0.75	7.76	31.23	m	**38.99**
Extra for						
stop end	-	0.40	4.14	17.37	nr	**21.51**
running outlet	-	0.80	8.28	26.12	nr	**34.40**
stop end outlet	-	0.40	4.14	27.78	nr	**31.92**
angle	-	0.80	8.28	28.82	nr	**37.10**
uPVC external rainwater pipes and fittings;						
BS 4576; slip-in joints						
50 mm pipes; fixing with pipe or socket						
brackets; plugged and screwed	2.14	0.30	3.10	3.04	m	**6.14**
Extra for						
shoe	1.27	0.20	2.07	1.63	nr	**3.70**
bend	1.48	0.30	3.10	1.84	nr	**4.94**
two bends to form offset 229 mm projection	1.48	0.30	3.10	2.97	nr	**6.07**
connection to clay pipes; cement:sand						
(1:2) joint	-	0.13	1.35	0.09	nr	**1.44**

R DISPOSAL SYSTEMS Excluding overheads and profit	PC £	Labour hours	Labour £	Material £	Unit	Total rate £
68 mm pipes; fixing with pipe or socket						
brackets; plugged and screwed	1.72	0.33	3.42	2.77	m	**6.19**
Extra for						
shoe	1.27	0.22	2.28	1.79	nr	**4.07**
bend	2.23	0.33	3.42	2.78	nr	**6.20**
single branch	3.90	0.44	4.55	4.49	nr	**9.04**
two bends to form offset 229 mm projection	2.23	0.33	3.42	4.76	nr	**8.18**
loose drain connector; cement:sand (1:2)						
joint	-	0.15	1.55	1.68	nr	**3.23**
110 mm pipes; fixing with pipe or socket						
brackets; plugged and screwed	3.70	0.36	3.73	5.71	m	**9.44**
Extra for						
shoe	4.05	0.24	2.48	4.66	nr	**7.14**
bend	5.71	0.36	3.73	6.37	nr	**10.10**
single branch	8.44	0.48	4.97	9.16	nr	**14.13**
two bends to form offset 229 mm projection	5.71	0.36	3.73	11.68	nr	**15.41**
loose drain connector; cement:sand (1:2)						
joint	-	0.35	3.62	6.57	nr	**10.19**
65 mm square pipes; fixing with pipe or socket						
brackets; plugged and screwed	1.89	0.33	3.42	3.00	m	**6.42**
Extra for						
shoe	1.39	0.22	2.28	1.91	nr	**4.19**
bend	1.52	0.33	3.42	2.05	nr	**5.47**
single branch	4.26	0.44	4.55	4.85	nr	**9.40**
two bends to form offset 229 mm projection	1.52	0.33	3.42	3.36	nr	**6.78**
drain connector; square to round; cement:						
sand (1:2) joint	-	0.35	3.62	2.19	nr	**5.81**
Rainwater head; rectangular; for pipes						
50 mm diameter	6.90	0.45	4.66	7.78	nr	**12.44**
68 mm diameter	5.57	0.47	4.86	6.76	nr	**11.62**
110 mm diameter	11.62	0.55	5.69	13.00	nr	**18.69**
65 mm square	5.57	0.47	4.86	6.75	nr	**11.61**
uPVC gutters and fittings; BS 4576						
76 mm half round gutters; on brackets screwed						
to timber	1.72	0.30	3.40	2.60	m	**6.00**
Extra for						
stop end	0.58	0.13	1.47	0.80	nr	**2.27**
running outlet	1.64	0.25	2.83	1.54	nr	**4.37**
stop end outlet	1.63	0.13	1.47	1.73	nr	**3.20**
angle	1.64	0.25	2.83	1.91	nr	**4.74**
112 mm half round gutters; on brackets						
screwed to timber	1.77	0.33	3.74	3.18	m	**6.92**
Extra for						
stop end	0.91	0.13	1.47	1.24	nr	**2.71**
running outlet	1.78	0.28	3.18	1.68	nr	**4.86**
stop end outlet	1.78	0.13	1.47	1.98	nr	**3.45**
angle	2.00	0.28	3.18	2.51	nr	**5.69**
170 mm half round gutters; on brackets;						
screwed to timber	3.42	0.33	3.74	5.76	m	**9.50**
Extra for						
stop end	1.54	0.16	1.81	2.15	nr	**3.96**
running outlet	3.43	0.31	3.52	3.23	nr	**6.75**
stop end outlet	3.27	0.16	1.81	3.63	nr	**5.44**
angle	4.47	0.31	3.52	5.43	nr	**8.95**
114 mm rectangular gutters; on brackets;						
screwed to timber	1.93	0.33	3.74	3.58	m	**7.32**
Extra for						
stop end	1.01	0.13	1.47	1.36	nr	**2.83**
running outlet	1.96	0.31	3.52	1.85	nr	**5.37**
stop end outlet	1.96	0.13	1.47	2.17	nr	**3.64**
angle	2.20	0.28	3.18	2.74	nr	**5.92**

R DISPOSAL SYSTEMS Excluding overheads and profit	PC £	Labour hours	Labour £	Material £	Unit	Total rate £
R11 FOUL DRAINAGE ABOVE GROUND						
Cast iron "Timesaver" pipes and fittings or other equal and approved; BS 416						
50 mm pipes; primed; 2.00 m lengths; fixing with expanding bolts; to masonry	11.56	0.55	5.69	18.37	m	**24.06**
Extra for						
fittings with two ends	-	0.55	5.69	12.70	nr	**18.39**
fittings with three ends	-	0.75	7.76	21.57	nr	**29.33**
bends; short radius	9.04	0.55	5.69	12.70	nr	**18.39**
access bends; short radius	22.29	0.55	5.69	26.29	nr	**31.98**
boss; 38 mm BSP	18.74	0.55	5.69	22.34	nr	**28.03**
single branch	13.62	0.75	7.76	22.11	nr	**29.87**
access pipe	21.76	0.55	5.69	24.41	nr	**30.10**
roof connector; for asphalt	24.79	0.55	5.69	29.03	nr	**34.72**
isolated "Timesaver" coupling joint	5.13	0.30	3.10	5.26	nr	**8.36**
connection to clay pipes; cement:sand (1:2) joint	-	0.13	1.35	0.08	nr	**1.43**
75 mm pipes; primed; 3.00 m lengths; fixing with standard brackets; plugged and screwed to masonry	11.31	0.55	5.69	18.38	m	**24.07**
75 mm pipes; primed; 2.00 m lengths; fixing with standard brackets; plugged and screwed to masonry	11.56	0.60	6.21	18.63	m	**24.84**
Extra for						
bends; short radius	9.04	0.60	6.21	13.27	nr	**19.48**
access bends; short radius	22.29	0.55	5.69	26.85	nr	**32.54**
boss; 38 mm BSP	18.74	0.60	6.21	23.21	nr	**29.42**
single branch	13.62	0.85	8.80	23.12	nr	**31.92**
double branch	22.52	1.10	11.38	38.06	nr	**49.44**
offset 115 mm projection	11.14	0.60	6.21	14.03	nr	**20.24**
offset 150 mm projection	11.14	0.60	6.21	13.66	nr	**19.87**
access pipe	21.76	0.60	6.21	24.73	nr	**30.94**
roof connector; for asphalt	28.26	0.60	6.21	32.85	nr	**39.06**
isolated "Timesaver" coupling joint	5.68	0.35	3.62	5.82	nr	**9.44**
connection to clay pipes; cement:sand (1:2) joint	-	0.15	1.55	0.08	nr	**1.63**
100 mm pipes; primed; 3.00 m lengths; fixing with standard brackets; plugged and screwed to masonry	13.67	0.60	6.21	25.96	m	**32.17**
100 mm pipes; primed; 2.00 m lengths; fixing with standard brackets; plugged and screwed to masonry	13.94	0.67	6.93	26.24	m	**33.17**
Extra for						
WC bent connector; 450 mm long tail	13.63	0.60	6.21	16.36	nr	**22.57**
bends; short radius	12.53	0.67	6.93	18.23	nr	**25.16**
access bends; short radius	26.49	0.67	6.93	32.54	nr	**39.47**
boss; 38 mm BSP	22.37	0.67	6.93	28.32	nr	**35.25**
single branch	19.36	1.00	10.35	31.58	nr	**41.93**
double branch	23.55	1.30	13.46	43.46	nr	**56.92**
offset 225 mm projection	18.00	0.67	6.93	21.94	nr	**28.87**
offset 300 mm projection	20.29	0.67	6.93	23.85	nr	**30.78**
access pipe	22.89	0.67	6.93	26.66	nr	**33.59**
roof connector; for asphalt	21.83	0.67	6.93	27.25	nr	**34.18**
roof connector; for roofing felt	69.83	0.67	6.93	76.45	nr	**83.38**
isolated "Timesaver" coupling joint	7.40	0.42	4.35	7.58	nr	**11.93**
transitional clayware socket; cement:sand (1:2) joint	14.86	0.40	4.14	22.90	nr	**27.04**
150 mm pipes; primed; 3.00 m lengths; fixing with standard brackets; plugged and screwed to masonry	28.55	0.75	7.76	52.55	m	**60.31**

R DISPOSAL SYSTEMS Excluding overheads and profit	PC £	Labour hours	Labour £	Material £	Unit	Total rate £
150 mm pipes; primed; 2.00 m lengths; fixing with						
standard brackets; plugged and screwed to						
masonry	28.60	0.83	8.59	52.60	m	**61.19**
Extra for						
bends; short radius	22.37	0.83	8.59	33.59	nr	**42.18**
access bends; short radius	37.63	0.83	8.59	49.24	nr	**57.83**
boss; 38 mm BSP	36.51	0.83	8.59	47.34	nr	**55.93**
single branch	45.43	1.20	12.42	68.80	nr	**81.22**
double branch	67.44	1.60	16.56	105.18	nr	**121.74**
access pipe	38.06	0.83	8.59	43.55	nr	**52.14**
roof connector; for asphalt	55.55	0.83	8.59	65.20	nr	**73.79**
isolated "Timesaver" coupling joint	-	0.50	5.17	15.17	nr	**20.34**
transitional clayware socket; cement:sand						
(1:2) joint	26.05	0.52	5.38	41.95	nr	**47.33**
Cast iron "Ensign" lightweight pipes and						
fittings or other equal and approved; EN 877						
50 mm pipes; primed; 3.00 m lengths; fixing with						
standard brackets; plugged and screwed to masonry	-	0.33	2.72	11.69	m	**14.41**
Extra for						
bends; short radius	-	0.29	2.37	9.31	nr	**11.68**
single branch	-	0.36	2.94	16.31	nr	**19.25**
access pipe	-	0.29	2.37	19.13	nr	**21.50**
70 mm pipes; primed; 3.00 m lengths; fixing with						
standard brackets; plugged and screwed to masonry	-	0.37	2.99	13.07	m	**16.06**
Extra for						
bends; short radius	-	0.32	2.61	10.39	nr	**13.00**
single branch	-	0.40	3.26	17.51	nr	**20.77**
access pipe	-	0.32	2.61	20.40	nr	**23.01**
100 mm pipes; primed; 3.00 m lengths; fixing with						
standard brackets; plugged and screwed to masonry	-	0.40	3.26	15.53	m	**18.79**
Extra for						
bends; short radius	-	0.35	2.86	12.79	nr	**15.65**
single branch	-	0.42	3.43	22.56	nr	**25.99**
double branch	-	0.50	4.08	33.06	nr	**37.14**
access pipe	-	0.35	2.86	23.22	nr	**26.08**
connector	-	0.23	1.84	21.42	nr	**23.26**
reducer	-	0.35	2.86	15.60	nr	**18.46**
Polypropylene (PP) waste pipes and fittings;						
BS 5254; push fit "O" - ring joints						
32 mm pipes; fixing with pipe clips; plugged and screwed	0.41	0.22	2.28	0.72	m	**3.00**
Extra for						
fittings with one end	-	0.16	1.66	0.37	nr	**2.03**
fittings with two ends	-	0.22	2.28	0.37	nr	**2.65**
fittings with three ends	-	0.30	3.10	0.37	nr	**3.47**
access plug	0.36	0.16	1.66	0.37	nr	**2.03**
double socket	0.36	0.15	1.55	0.37	nr	**1.92**
male iron to PP coupling	0.92	0.28	2.90	0.94	nr	**3.84**
sweep bend	0.36	0.22	2.28	0.37	nr	**2.65**
spigot bend	0.36	0.25	2.59	0.37	nr	**2.96**
40 mm pipes; fixing with pipe clips; plugged and screwed	0.50	0.22	2.28	0.82	m	**3.10**
Extra for						
fittings with one end	-	0.19	1.97	0.37	nr	**2.34**
fittings with two ends	-	0.30	3.10	0.37	nr	**3.47**
fittings with three ends	-	0.40	4.14	0.37	nr	**4.51**
access plug	0.36	0.19	1.97	0.37	nr	**2.34**
double socket	0.36	0.20	2.07	0.37	nr	**2.44**
universal connector	0.36	0.25	2.59	0.37	nr	**2.96**
sweep bend	0.36	0.30	3.10	0.37	nr	**3.47**
spigot bend	0.36	0.30	3.10	0.37	nr	**3.47**
reducer 40 mm - 32 mm	0.36	0.30	3.10	0.37	nr	**3.47**

R DISPOSAL SYSTEMS Excluding overheads and profit	PC £	Labour hours	Labour £	Material £	Unit	Total rate £
R11 FOUL DRAINAGE ABOVE GROUND - cont'd						
Polypropylene (PP) waste pipes and fittings;						
BS 5254; push fit "O" - ring joints - cont'd						
50 mm pipes; fixing with pipe clips; plugged and screwed	0.82	0.35	3.62	1.36	m	4.98
Extra for						
fittings with one end	-	0.21	2.17	0.68	nr	2.85
fittings with two ends	-	0.35	3.62	0.68	nr	4.30
fittings with three ends	-	0.47	4.86	0.68	nr	5.54
access plug	0.66	0.21	2.17	0.68	nr	2.85
double socket	0.66	0.23	2.38	0.68	nr	3.06
sweep bend	0.66	0.35	3.62	0.68	nr	4.30
spigot bend	0.66	0.35	3.62	0.68	nr	4.30
reducer 50 mm - 40 mm	0.66	0.35	3.62	0.68	nr	4.30
muPVC waste pipes and fittings; BS 5255;						
solvent welded joints						
32 mm pipes; fixing with pipe clips; plugged and screwed	1.19	0.25	2.59	1.69	m	4.28
Extra for						
fittings with one end	-	0.17	1.76	1.17	nr	2.93
fittings with two ends	-	0.25	2.59	1.00	nr	3.59
fittings with three ends	-	0.33	3.42	1.40	nr	4.82
access plug	1.01	0.17	1.76	1.17	nr	2.93
straight coupling	0.66	0.17	1.76	0.81	nr	2.57
expansion coupling	0.96	0.25	2.59	1.12	nr	3.71
male iron to muPVC coupling	0.82	0.38	3.93	0.91	nr	4.84
union coupling	2.27	0.25	2.59	2.46	nr	5.05
sweep bend	0.85	0.25	2.59	1.00	nr	3.59
spigot/socket bend	-	0.25	2.59	1.13	nr	3.72
sweep tee	1.20	0.33	3.42	1.40	nr	4.82
40 mm pipes; fixing with pipe clips; plugged and screwed	1.25	0.30	3.10	1.84	m	4.94
Extra for						
fittings with one end	-	0.19	1.97	1.35	nr	3.32
fittings with two ends	-	0.30	3.10	1.11	nr	4.21
fittings with three ends	-	0.40	4.14	1.72	nr	5.86
fittings with four ends	4.29	0.53	5.49	4.63	nr	10.12
access plug	1.19	0.19	1.97	1.35	nr	3.32
straight coupling	0.80	0.20	2.07	0.95	nr	3.02
expansion coupling	1.15	0.30	3.10	1.31	nr	4.41
male iron to muPVC coupling	0.97	0.38	3.93	1.06	nr	4.99
union coupling	2.99	0.30	3.10	3.20	nr	6.30
level invert taper	0.93	0.30	3.10	1.09	nr	4.19
sweep bend	0.94	0.30	3.10	1.11	nr	4.21
spigot/socket bend	1.08	0.30	3.10	1.24	nr	4.34
sweep tee	1.52	0.40	4.14	1.72	nr	5.86
sweep cross	4.29	0.53	5.49	4.63	nr	10.12
50 mm pipes; fixing with pipe clips; plugged and screwed	2.15	0.35	3.62	3.16	m	6.78
Extra for						
fittings with one end	-	0.21	2.17	2.10	nr	4.27
fittings with two ends	-	0.35	3.62	1.74	nr	5.36
fittings with three ends	-	0.47	4.86	3.24	nr	8.10
fittings with four ends	-	0.62	6.42	5.30	nr	11.72
access plug	1.92	0.21	2.17	2.10	nr	4.27
straight coupling	1.00	0.23	2.38	1.16	nr	3.54
expansion coupling	1.56	0.35	3.62	1.73	nr	5.35
male iron to muPVC coupling	1.40	0.45	4.66	1.50	nr	6.16
union coupling	4.67	0.35	3.62	4.92	nr	8.54
level invert taper	1.30	0.35	3.62	1.47	nr	5.09
sweep bend	1.57	0.35	3.62	1.74	nr	5.36
spigot/socket bend	2.55	0.35	3.62	2.75	nr	6.37
sweep tee	1.52	0.40	4.14	1.72	nr	5.86
sweep cross	4.94	0.62	6.42	5.30	nr	11.72

PRICE BOOKS
UPDATE REGISTRATION CARD

All four Spon Price Books – *Architects' and Builders'*, *Civil Engineering and Highway Works*, *Landscape and External Works* and *Mechanical and Electrical Services* – are supported by an updating service. Three Updates are issued during the year, in November, February and May. Each gives details of changes in prices of materials, wage rates and other significant items, with regional price level adjustments for Northern Ireland, Scotland and Wales and regions of England.

As a purchaser of a Spon Price Book you are entitled to this updating service for the 2000 edition – *free of charge*. Simply complete this registration card and return it to us – or register via the website www.efnspon.com. The updates will also be available to download from the website.

The updating service terminates with the publication of the next annual edition.

REGISTRATION CARD for Spon's Price Book Update   **2000**
Please print your details clearly

Name ....

(Please indicate membership of any professional body e.g. RICS, RIBA, CIoB etc.)

Position/Dept ....

Organisation ....

Address ....

....

.... Postcode ....

Tel: .... Fax: ....

E-mail address ....

FIND OUT MORE ABOUT OUR PUBLICATIONS

We publish a wide range of publications in several different formats – book, journal and electronic. This is undoubtedly one of the finest collection of technical publications available and there are sure to be several titles of real value to you in your work. Find out more and make sure your own personal library, or your company's information resource, is up-to-date.

Just tick the appropriate box(es) below, complete your name and address details and return this card to us - our address is printed on the reverse. We will be pleased to send you our current catalogues in the categories selected.

- ☐ **Architecture**
- ☐ **Planning**
- ☐ **Civil Engineering**
- ☐ **Building & Construction Management**
- ☐ **Environmental Engineering**
- ☐ **Occupational Safety & Health**
- ☐ **Landscape**
- ☐ **Journals** - inc. Journal of Architecture; Building Research & Information; Construction Management & Economics; Urban Design International
- ☐ **Other** - note any other areas of interest ....

....

E & FN SPON Marketing

11 New Fetter Lane
London
EC4P 4EE

R DISPOSAL SYSTEMS Excluding overheads and profit	PC £	Labour hours	Labour £	Material £	Unit	Total rate £
uPVC overflow pipes and fittings; solvent welded joints						
19 mm pipes; fixing with pipe clips; plugged and screwed	0.57	0.22	2.28	0.90	m	3.18
Extra for						
splay cut end	-	0.02	0.21	-	nr	0.21
fittings with one end	-	0.17	1.76	0.45	nr	2.21
fittings with two ends	-	0.17	1.76	0.62	nr	2.38
fittings with three ends	-	0.22	2.28	0.75	nr	3.03
straight connector	0.38	0.17	1.76	0.45	nr	2.21
female iron to uPVC coupling	-	0.20	2.07	0.86	nr	2.93
bend	0.55	0.17	1.76	0.62	nr	2.38
bent tank connector	0.89	0.20	2.07	0.92	nr	2.99
uPVC pipes and fittings; BS 4514; with solvent welded joints (unless otherwise described)						
82 mm pipes; fixing with holderbats; plugged and screwed	3.44	0.40	4.14	5.15	m	9.29
Extra for						
socket plug	2.68	0.20	2.07	3.09	nr	5.16
slip coupling; push fit	5.82	0.37	3.83	5.97	nr	9.80
expansion coupling	3.37	0.40	4.14	3.80	nr	7.94
sweep bend	4.73	0.40	4.14	5.19	nr	9.33
boss connector	2.77	0.27	2.79	3.18	nr	5.97
single branch	6.57	0.53	5.49	7.28	nr	12.77
access door	6.42	0.60	6.21	6.75	nr	12.96
connection to clay pipes; caulking ring and cement:sand (1:2) joint	4.51	0.37	3.83	4.87	nr	8.70
110 mm pipes; fixing with holderbats; plugged and screwed	3.50	0.44	4.55	5.38	m	9.93
Extra for						
socket plug	3.24	0.22	2.28	3.76	nr	6.04
slip coupling; push fit	7.28	0.40	4.14	7.46	nr	11.60
expansion coupling	3.40	0.44	4.55	3.93	nr	8.48
W.C. connector	5.19	0.29	3.00	5.56	nr	8.56
sweep bend	5.43	0.44	4.55	6.01	nr	10.56
W.C. connecting bend	7.75	0.29	3.00	8.18	nr	11.18
access bend	15.25	0.46	4.76	16.07	nr	20.83
boss connector	2.77	0.29	3.00	3.28	nr	6.28
single branch	8.56	0.58	6.00	9.46	nr	15.46
single branch with access	16.58	0.60	6.21	17.68	nr	23.89
double branch	20.86	0.73	7.56	22.30	nr	29.86
W.C. manifold	32.03	0.29	3.00	33.50	nr	36.50
access door	-	0.60	6.21	6.75	nr	12.96
access pipe connector	11.68	0.50	5.17	12.42	nr	17.59
connection to clay pipes; caulking ring and cement:sand (1:2) joint	-	0.42	4.35	1.69	nr	6.04
160 mm pipes; fixing with holderbats; plugged and screwed	8.98	0.50	5.17	13.73	m	18.90
Extra for						
socket plug	5.97	0.25	2.59	7.11	nr	9.70
slip coupling; push fit	18.64	0.45	4.66	19.11	nr	23.77
expansion coupling	10.24	0.50	5.17	11.49	nr	16.66
sweep bend	13.94	0.50	5.17	15.28	nr	20.45
boss connector	3.79	0.33	3.42	4.87	nr	8.29
single branch	44.56	0.66	6.83	47.14	nr	53.97
double branch	82.23	0.83	8.59	86.23	nr	94.82
access door	11.47	0.60	6.21	11.93	nr	18.14
access pipe connector	11.68	0.50	5.17	12.42	nr	17.59
connection to clay pipes; caulking ring and cement:sand (1:2) joint	-	0.50	5.17	2.85	nr	8.02

R DISPOSAL SYSTEMS Excluding overheads and profit	PC £	Labour hours	Labour £	Material £	Unit	Total rate £
R11 FOUL DRAINAGE ABOVE GROUND - cont'd						
uPVC pipes and fittings; BS 4514; with solvent welded joints (unless otherwise described) - cont'd						
Weathering apron; for pipe						
82 mm diameter	1.32	0.34	3.52	1.52	nr	5.04
110 mm diameter	1.56	0.38	3.93	1.84	nr	5.77
160 mm diameter	4.69	0.42	4.35	5.28	nr	9.63
Weathering slate; for pipe						
110 mm diameter	21.82	0.90	9.31	22.60	nr	31.91
Vent cowl; for pipe						
82 mm diameter	1.32	0.33	3.42	1.52	nr	4.94
110 mm diameter	1.34	0.33	3.42	1.61	nr	5.03
160 mm diameter	3.49	0.33	3.42	4.05	nr	7.47
Polypropylene ancillaries; screwed joint to waste fitting						
Tubular "S" trap; bath; shallow seal						
40 mm diameter	3.24	0.55	5.69	3.32	nr	9.01
Trap; "P"; two piece; 76 mm seal						
32 mm diameter	2.18	0.38	3.93	2.23	nr	6.16
40 mm diameter	2.51	0.45	4.66	2.57	nr	7.23
Trap; "S"; two piece; 76 mm seal						
32 mm diameter	2.77	0.38	3.93	2.84	nr	6.77
40 mm diameter	3.24	0.45	4.66	3.32	nr	7.98
Bottle trap; "P"; 76 mm seal						
32 diameter	2.43	0.38	3.93	2.49	nr	6.42
40 diameter	2.90	0.45	4.66	2.97	nr	7.63
Bottle trap; "S"; 76 mm seal						
32 diameter	2.93	0.38	3.93	3.00	nr	6.93
40 diameter	3.55	0.45	4.66	3.64	nr	8.30
R12 DRAINAGE BELOW GROUND						
NOTE: Prices for drain trenches are for excavating in "firm" soil and it has been assumed that earthwork support will only be required for trenches 1.00 m or more in depth.						
Excavating trenches; by machine; grading bottoms; earthwork support; filling with excavated material and compacting; disposal of surplus soil on site; spreading on site average 50 m						
Pipes not exceeding 200 mm nominal size						
average depth of trench 0.50 m	-	0.30	1.97	1.51	m	3.48
average depth of trench 0.75 m	-	0.40	2.63	2.26	m	4.89
average depth of trench 1.00 m	-	0.85	5.59	4.45	m	10.04
average depth of trench 1.25 m	-	1.25	8.22	5.10	m	13.32
average depth of trench 1.50 m	-	1.60	10.53	5.79	m	16.32
average depth of trench 1.75 m	-	2.00	13.16	6.44	m	19.60
average depth of trench 2.00 m	-	2.30	15.13	7.32	m	22.45
average depth of trench 2.25 m	-	2.85	18.75	9.19	m	27.94
average depth of trench 2.50 m	-	3.35	22.04	10.75	m	32.79
average depth of trench 2.75 m	-	3.70	24.35	11.97	m	36.32
average depth of trench 3.00 m	-	4.05	26.65	13.19	m	39.84
average depth of trench 3.25 m	-	4.40	28.95	14.03	m	42.98
average depth of trench 3.50 m	-	4.70	30.93	14.87	m	45.80

R DISPOSAL SYSTEMS Excluding overheads and profit	PC £	Labour hours	Labour £	Material £	Unit	Total rate £
Pipes exceeding 200 mm nominal size; 225 mm nominal size						
average depth of trench 0.50 m	-	0.30	1.97	1.51	m	**3.48**
average depth of trench 0.75 m	-	0.40	2.63	2.26	m	**4.89**
average depth of trench 1.00 m	-	0.85	5.59	4.45	m	**10.04**
average depth of trench 1.25 m	-	1.25	8.22	5.10	m	**13.32**
average depth of trench 1.50 m	-	1.60	10.53	5.79	m	**16.32**
average depth of trench 1.75 m	-	2.00	13.16	6.44	m	**19.60**
average depth of trench 2.00 m	-	2.30	15.13	7.32	m	**22.45**
average depth of trench 2.25 m	-	2.85	18.75	9.19	m	**27.94**
average depth of trench 2.50 m	-	3.35	22.04	10.75	m	**32.79**
average depth of trench 2.75 m	-	3.70	24.35	11.97	m	**36.32**
average depth of trench 3.00 m	-	4.05	26.65	13.19	m	**39.84**
average depth of trench 3.25 m	-	4.40	28.95	14.03	m	**42.98**
average depth of trench 3.50 m	-	4.70	30.93	14.87	m	**45.80**
Pipes exceeding 200 mm nominal size; 300 mm nominal size						
average depth of trench 0.75 m	-	0.48	3.16	2.83	m	**5.99**
average depth of trench 1.00 m	-	1.00	6.58	4.45	m	**11.03**
average depth of trench 1.25 m	-	1.35	8.88	5.29	m	**14.17**
average depth of trench 1.50 m	-	1.75	11.52	5.97	m	**17.49**
average depth of trench 1.75 m	-	2.00	13.16	6.63	m	**19.79**
average depth of trench 2.00 m	-	2.30	15.13	7.88	m	**23.01**
average depth of trench 2.25 m	-	2.85	18.75	9.57	m	**28.32**
average depth of trench 2.50 m	-	3.35	22.04	10.94	m	**32.98**
average depth of trench 2.75 m	-	3.70	24.35	12.16	m	**36.51**
average depth of trench 3.00 m	-	4.05	26.65	13.38	m	**40.03**
average depth of trench 3.25 m	-	4.40	28.95	14.60	m	**43.55**
average depth of trench 3.50 m	-	4.70	30.93	15.25	m	**46.18**
Pipes exceeding 200 mm nominal size; 375 mm nominal size						
average depth of trench 0.75 m	-	0.50	3.29	3.39	m	**6.68**
average depth of trench 1.00 m	-	1.05	6.91	5.01	m	**11.92**
average depth of trench 1.25 m	-	1.45	9.54	6.23	m	**15.77**
average depth of trench 1.50 m	-	1.85	12.17	6.73	m	**18.90**
average depth of trench 1.75 m	-	2.15	14.15	7.57	m	**21.72**
average depth of trench 2.00 m	-	2.45	16.12	8.07	m	**24.19**
average depth of trench 2.25 m	-	3.05	20.07	10.13	m	**30.20**
average depth of trench 2.50 m	-	3.65	24.02	11.69	m	**35.71**
average depth of trench 2.75 m	-	4.00	26.32	12.73	m	**39.05**
average depth of trench 3.00 m	-	4.35	28.62	13.76	m	**42.38**
average depth of trench 3.25 m	-	4.70	30.93	14.97	m	**45.90**
average depth of trench 3.50 m	-	5.05	33.23	16.01	m	**49.24**
Pipes exceeding 200 mm nominal size; 450 mm nominal size						
average depth of trench 0.75 m	-	0.55	3.62	3.39	m	**7.01**
average depth of trench 1.00 m	-	1.10	7.24	5.39	m	**12.63**
average depth of trench 1.25 m	-	1.60	10.53	6.61	m	**17.14**
average depth of trench 1.50 m	-	2.00	13.16	7.29	m	**20.45**
average depth of trench 1.75 m	-	2.30	15.13	7.95	m	**23.08**
average depth of trench 2.00 m	-	2.65	17.44	8.64	m	**26.08**
average depth of trench 2.25 m	-	3.30	21.71	10.51	m	**32.22**
average depth of trench 2.50 m	-	3.90	25.66	12.26	m	**37.92**
average depth of trench 2.75 m	-	4.30	28.29	13.48	m	**41.77**
average depth of trench 3.00 m	-	4.60	30.27	14.70	m	**44.97**
average depth of trench 3.25 m	-	5.00	32.90	16.11	m	**49.01**
average depth of trench 3.50 m	-	5.40	35.53	17.51	m	**53.04**
Pipes exceeding 200 mm nominal size; 600 mm nominal size						
average depth of trench 1.00 m	-	1.20	7.90	5.77	m	**13.67**
average depth of trench 1.25 m	-	1.70	11.19	6.98	m	**18.17**
average depth of trench 1.50 m	-	2.20	14.48	8.05	m	**22.53**

R DISPOSAL SYSTEMS Excluding overheads and profit	PC £	Labour hours	Labour £	Material £	Unit	Total rate £
R12 DRAINAGE BELOW GROUND - cont'd						
Excavating trenches; by machine; grading **bottoms; earthwork support; filling with** **excavated material and compacting;** **disposal of surplus soil on site;** **spreading on site average 50 m** - cont'd						
Pipes exceeding 200 mm nominal size; 600 mm nominal size - cont'd						
average depth of trench 1.75 m	-	2.50	16.45	8.51	m	24.96
average depth of trench 2.00 m	-	2.95	19.41	9.39	m	28.80
average depth of trench 2.25 m	-	3.55	23.36	11.64	m	35.00
average depth of trench 2.50 m	-	4.20	27.64	13.58	m	41.22
average depth of trench 2.75 m	-	4.65	30.60	15.18	m	45.78
average depth of trench 3.00 m	-	5.10	33.56	16.58	m	50.14
average depth of trench 3.25 m	-	5.50	36.19	17.80	m	53.99
average depth of trench 3.50 m	-	5.90	38.82	18.83	m	57.65
Pipes exceeding 200 mm nominal size; 900 mm nominal size						
average depth of trench 1.25 m	-	2.05	13.49	8.12	m	21.61
average depth of trench 1.50 m	-	2.60	17.11	9.18	m	26.29
average depth of trench 1.75 m	-	3.00	19.74	9.83	m	29.57
average depth of trench 2.00 m	-	3.35	22.04	11.28	m	33.32
average depth of trench 2.25 m	-	4.15	27.31	13.71	m	41.02
average depth of trench 2.50 m	-	4.90	32.24	15.84	m	48.08
average depth of trench 2.75 m	-	5.40	35.53	17.44	m	52.97
average depth of trench 3.00 m	-	5.90	38.82	19.04	m	57.86
average depth of trench 3.25 m	-	6.40	42.11	20.63	m	62.74
average depth of trench 3.50 m	-	6.90	45.40	22.04	m	67.44
Pipes exceeding 200 mm nominal size; 1200 mm nominal size						
average depth of trench 1.50 m	-	2.95	19.41	9.75	m	29.16
average depth of trench 1.75 m	-	3.45	22.70	11.34	m	34.04
average depth of trench 2.00 m	-	3.85	25.33	12.97	m	38.30
average depth of trench 2.25 m	-	4.70	30.93	15.79	m	46.72
average depth of trench 2.50 m	-	5.60	36.85	18.11	m	54.96
average depth of trench 2.75 m	-	6.15	40.47	20.08	m	60.55
average depth of trench 3.00 m	-	6.70	44.09	21.86	m	65.95
average depth of trench 3.25 m	-	7.30	48.03	23.65	m	71.68
average depth of trench 3.50 m	-	7.85	51.65	25.43	m	77.08
Extra over excavating trenches; irrespective of depth; breaking out existing materials						
brick	-	1.95	12.83	6.56	m³	19.39
concrete	-	2.75	18.09	9.06	m³	27.15
reinforced concrete	-	3.90	25.66	13.11	m³	38.77
Extra over excavating trenches; irrespective of depth; breaking out existing hard pavings; 75 mm thick						
tarmacadam	-	0.20	1.32	0.69	m²	2.01
Extra over excavating trenches; irrespective of depth; breaking out existing hard pavings; 150 mm thick						
concrete	-	0.40	2.63	1.54	m²	4.17
tarmacadam and hardcore	-	0.30	1.97	0.80	m²	2.77
Excavating trenches; by hand; grading bottoms; **earthwork support; filling with excavated material** **and compacting; disposal of surplus soil on site;** **spreading on site average 50 m**						
Pipes not exceeding 200 mm nominal size						
average depth of trench 0.50 m	-	1.00	6.58	-	m	6.58
average depth of trench 0.75 m	-	1.50	9.87	-	m	9.87
average depth of trench 1.00 m	-	2.20	14.48	1.24	m	15.72
average depth of trench 1.25 m	-	3.10	20.40	1.71	m	22.11

R DISPOSAL SYSTEMS Excluding overheads and profit	PC £	Labour hours	Labour £	Material £	Unit	Total rate £
Pipes not exceeding 200 mm nominal size - cont'd						
average depth of trench 1.50 m	-	4.25	27.96	2.08	m	30.04
average depth of trench 1.75 m	-	5.60	36.85	2.48	m	39.33
average depth of trench 2.00 m	-	6.40	42.11	2.79	m	44.90
average depth of trench 2.25 m	-	8.00	52.64	3.72	m	56.36
average depth of trench 2.50 m	-	9.60	63.17	4.34	m	67.51
average depth of trench 2.75 m	-	10.55	69.42	4.80	m	74.22
average depth of trench 3.00 m	-	11.50	75.67	5.27	m	80.94
average depth of trench 3.25 m	-	12.45	81.92	5.74	m	87.66
average depth of trench 3.50 m	-	13.40	88.17	6.20	m	94.37
Pipes exceeding 200 mm nominal size; 225 mm nominal size						
average depth of trench 0.50 m	-	1.00	6.58	-	m	6.58
average depth of trench 0.75 m	-	1.50	9.87	-	m	9.87
average depth of trench 1.00 m	-	2.20	14.48	1.24	m	15.72
average depth of trench 1.25 m	-	3.10	20.40	1.71	m	22.11
average depth of trench 1.50 m	-	4.25	27.96	2.08	m	30.04
average depth of trench 1.75 m	-	5.60	36.85	2.48	m	39.33
average depth of trench 2.00 m	-	6.40	42.11	2.79	m	44.90
average depth of trench 2.25 m	-	8.00	52.64	3.72	m	56.36
average depth of trench 2.50 m	-	9.60	63.17	4.34	m	67.51
average depth of trench 2.75 m	-	10.55	69.42	4.80	m	74.22
average depth of trench 3.00 m	-	11.50	75.67	5.27	m	80.94
average depth of trench 3.25 m	-	12.45	81.92	5.74	m	87.66
average depth of trench 3.50 m	-	13.40	88.17	6.20	m	94.37
Pipes exceeding 200 mm nominal size; 300 mm nominal size						
average depth of trench 0.75 m	-	1.75	11.52	-	m	11.52
average depth of trench 1.00 m	-	2.55	16.78	1.24	m	18.02
average depth of trench 1.25 m	-	3.60	23.69	1.71	m	25.40
average depth of trench 1.50 m	-	4.80	31.58	2.08	m	33.66
average depth of trench 1.75 m	-	5.60	36.85	2.48	m	39.33
average depth of trench 2.00 m	-	6.40	42.11	2.79	m	44.90
average depth of trench 2.25 m	-	8.00	52.64	3.72	m	56.36
average depth of trench 2.50 m	-	9.60	63.17	4.34	m	67.51
average depth of trench 2.75 m	-	10.55	69.42	4.80	m	74.22
average depth of trench 3.00 m	-	11.50	75.67	5.27	m	80.94
average depth of trench 3.25 m	-	12.45	81.92	5.74	m	87.66
average depth of trench 3.50 m	-	13.40	88.17	6.20	m	94.37
Pipes exceeding 200 mm nominal size; 375 mm nominal size						
average depth of trench 0.75 m	-	1.95	12.83	-	m	12.83
average depth of trench 1.00 m	-	2.85	18.75	1.24	m	19.99
average depth of trench 1.25 m	-	4.00	26.32	1.71	m	28.03
average depth of trench 1.50 m	-	5.33	35.07	2.08	m	37.15
average depth of trench 1.75 m	-	6.20	40.80	2.48	m	43.28
average depth of trench 2.00 m	-	7.10	46.72	2.79	m	49.51
average depth of trench 2.25 m	-	8.90	58.56	3.72	m	62.28
average depth of trench 2.50 m	-	10.70	70.41	4.34	m	74.75
average depth of trench 2.75 m	-	11.75	77.31	4.80	m	82.11
average depth of trench 3.00 m	-	12.80	84.22	5.27	m	89.49
average depth of trench 3.25 m	-	13.90	91.46	5.74	m	97.20
average depth of trench 3.50 m	-	15.00	98.70	6.20	m	104.90
Pipes exceeding 200 mm nominal size; 400 mm nominal size						
average depth of trench 0.75 m	-	2.20	14.48	-	m	14.48
average depth of trench 1.00 m	-	3.18	20.92	1.24	m	22.16
average depth of trench 1.25 m	-	4.47	29.41	1.71	m	31.12
average depth of trench 1.50 m	-	5.85	38.49	2.08	m	40.57
average depth of trench 1.75 m	-	6.82	44.88	2.48	m	47.36
average depth of trench 2.00 m	-	7.80	51.32	2.79	m	54.11
average depth of trench 2.25 m	-	9.78	64.35	3.72	m	68.07

R DISPOSAL SYSTEMS Excluding overheads and profit	PC £	Labour hours	Labour £	Material £	Unit	Total rate £
R12 DRAINAGE BELOW GROUND - cont'd						
Excavating trenches; by hand; grading bottoms; **earthwork support; filling with excavated material** **and compacting; disposal of surplus soil on site;** **spreading on site average 50 m** - cont'd						
Pipes exceeding 200 mm nominal size; 400 mm nominal size - cont'd						
average depth of trench 2.50 m	-	11.75	77.31	4.34	m	81.65
average depth of trench 2.75 m	-	12.93	85.08	4.80	m	89.88
average depth of trench 3.00 m	-	14.10	92.78	5.27	m	98.05
average depth of trench 3.25 m	-	15.25	100.34	5.74	m	106.08
average depth of trench 3.50 m	-	16.40	107.91	6.20	m	114.11
Pipes exceeding 200 mm nominal size; 600 mm nominal size						
average depth of trench 1.00 m	-	3.50	23.03	1.24	m	24.27
average depth of trench 1.25 m	-	5.00	32.90	1.71	m	34.61
average depth of trench 1.50 m	-	6.70	44.09	2.08	m	46.17
average depth of trench 1.75 m	-	7.75	50.99	2.48	m	53.47
average depth of trench 2.00 m	-	8.85	58.23	2.79	m	61.02
average depth of trench 2.25 m	-	9.95	65.47	3.72	m	69.19
average depth of trench 2.50 m	-	12.50	82.25	4.34	m	86.59
average depth of trench 2.75 m	-	13.35	87.84	4.80	m	92.64
average depth of trench 3.00 m	-	16.00	105.28	5.27	m	110.55
average depth of trench 3.25 m	-	17.33	114.03	5.74	m	119.77
average depth of trench 3.50 m	-	18.65	122.72	6.20	m	128.92
Pipes exceeding 200 mm nominal size; 900 mm nominal size						
average depth of trench 1.25 m	-	6.25	41.13	1.71	m	42.84
average depth of trench 1.50 m	-	8.25	54.28	2.08	m	56.36
average depth of trench 1.75 m	-	9.60	63.17	2.48	m	65.65
average depth of trench 2.00 m	-	10.95	72.05	2.79	m	74.84
average depth of trench 2.25 m	-	13.75	90.47	3.72	m	94.19
average depth of trench 2.50 m	-	16.55	108.90	4.34	m	113.24
average depth of trench 2.75 m	-	18.20	119.76	4.80	m	124.56
average depth of trench 3.00 m	-	19.80	130.28	5.27	m	135.55
average depth of trench 3.25 m	-	21.45	141.14	5.74	m	146.88
average depth of trench 3.50 m	-	23.10	152.00	6.20	m	158.20
Pipes exceeding 200 mm nominal size; 1200 mm nominal size						
average depth of trench 1.50 m	-	9.85	64.81	2.08	m	66.89
average depth of trench 1.75 m	-	11.45	75.34	2.48	m	77.82
average depth of trench 2.00 m	-	13.10	86.20	2.79	m	88.99
average depth of trench 2.25 m	-	16.43	108.11	3.72	m	111.83
average depth of trench 2.50 m	-	19.75	129.96	4.34	m	134.30
average depth of trench 2.75 m	-	21.70	142.79	4.80	m	147.59
average depth of trench 3.00 m	-	23.65	155.62	5.27	m	160.89
average depth of trench 3.25 m	-	25.58	168.32	5.74	m	174.06
average depth of trench 3.50 m	-	27.50	180.95	6.20	m	187.15
Extra over excavating trenches irrespective of depth; breaking out existing materials						
brick	-	3.00	19.74	4.70	m³	24.44
concrete	-	4.50	29.61	7.83	m³	37.44
reinforced concrete	-	6.00	39.48	10.96	m³	50.44
Extra over excavating trenches irrespective of depth; breaking out existing hard pavings, 75 mm thick						
tarmacadam	-	0.40	2.63	0.63	m²	3.26
Extra over excavating trenches irrespective of depth; breaking out existing hard pavings, 150 mm thick						
concrete	-	0.70	4.61	1.10	m²	5.71
tarmacadam and hardcore	-	0.50	3.29	0.78	m²	4.07

R DISPOSAL SYSTEMS Excluding overheads and profit	PC £	Labour hours	Labour £	Material £	Unit	Total rate £
Sand filling						
Beds; to receive pitch fibre pipes						
600 mm x 50 mm thick	-	0.08	0.53	0.62	m	**1.15**
700 mm x 50 mm thick	-	0.10	0.66	0.72	m	**1.38**
800 mm x 50 mm thick	-	0.12	0.79	0.83	m	**1.62**
Granular (shingle) filling						
Beds; 100 mm thick; to pipes						
100 mm nominal size	-	0.10	0.66	1.62	m	**2.28**
150 mm nominal size	-	0.10	0.66	1.89	m	**2.55**
225 mm nominal size	-	0.12	0.79	2.16	m	**2.95**
300 mm nominal size	-	0.14	0.92	2.43	m	**3.35**
375 mm nominal size	-	0.16	1.05	2.70	m	**3.75**
450 mm nominal size	-	0.18	1.18	2.97	m	**4.15**
600 mm nominal size	-	0.20	1.32	3.24	m	**4.56**
Beds; 150 mm thick; to pipes						
100 mm nominal size	-	0.14	0.92	2.43	m	**3.35**
150 mm nominal size	-	0.16	1.05	2.70	m	**3.75**
225 mm nominal size	-	0.18	1.18	2.97	m	**4.15**
300 mm nominal size	-	0.20	1.32	3.24	m	**4.56**
375 mm nominal size	-	0.24	1.58	4.05	m	**5.63**
450 mm nominal size	-	0.26	1.71	4.32	m	**6.03**
600 mm nominal size	-	0.30	1.97	5.13	m	**7.10**
Beds and benchings; beds 100 mm thick; to pipes						
100 nominal size	-	0.23	1.51	2.97	m	**4.48**
150 nominal size	-	0.25	1.65	2.97	m	**4.62**
225 nominal size	-	0.30	1.97	4.05	m	**6.02**
300 nominal size	-	0.35	2.30	4.59	m	**6.89**
375 nominal size	-	0.45	2.96	6.21	m	**9.17**
450 nominal size	-	0.52	3.42	7.02	m	**10.44**
600 nominal size	-	0.67	4.41	9.18	m	**13.59**
Beds and benchings; beds 150 mm thick; to pipes						
100 nominal size	-	0.25	1.65	3.24	m	**4.89**
150 nominal size	-	0.28	1.84	3.51	m	**5.35**
225 nominal size	-	0.35	2.30	4.86	m	**7.16**
300 nominal size	-	0.45	2.96	5.94	m	**8.90**
375 nominal size	-	0.52	3.42	7.02	m	**10.44**
450 nominal size	-	0.62	4.08	8.37	m	**12.45**
600 nominal size	-	0.74	4.87	10.80	m	**15.67**
Beds and coverings; 100 mm thick; to pipes						
100 nominal size	-	0.36	2.37	4.05	m	**6.42**
150 nominal size	-	0.45	2.96	4.86	m	**7.82**
225 nominal size	-	0.60	3.95	6.75	m	**10.70**
300 nominal size	-	0.72	4.74	8.10	m	**12.84**
375 nominal size	-	0.87	5.72	9.72	m	**15.44**
450 nominal size	-	1.02	6.71	11.61	m	**18.32**
600 nominal size	-	1.32	8.69	14.85	m	**23.54**
Beds and coverings; 150 mm thick; to pipes						
100 nominal size	-	0.54	3.55	5.94	m	**9.49**
150 nominal size	-	0.60	3.95	6.75	m	**10.70**
225 nominal size	-	0.78	5.13	8.64	m	**13.77**
300 nominal size	-	0.93	6.12	10.26	m	**16.38**
375 nominal size	-	1.08	7.11	12.15	m	**19.26**
450 nominal size	-	1.29	8.49	14.58	m	**23.07**
600 nominal size	-	1.56	10.26	17.54	m	**27.80**
Plain in situ ready mixed designated concrete; C10 - 40 mm aggregate						
Beds; 100 mm thick; to pipes						
100 mm nominal size	-	0.18	1.31	2.82	m	**4.13**
150 mm nominal size	-	0.18	1.31	2.82	m	**4.13**
225 mm nominal size	-	0.22	1.60	3.39	m	**4.99**

R DISPOSAL SYSTEMS Excluding overheads and profit	PC £	Labour hours	Labour £	Material £	Unit	Total rate £
R12 DRAINAGE BELOW GROUND - cont'd						
Plain in situ ready mixed designated concrete; C10						
- 40 mm aggregate - cont'd						
Beds; 100 mm thick; to pipes - cont'd						
300 mm nominal size	-	0.25	1.82	3.95	m	**5.77**
375 mm nominal size	-	0.29	2.11	4.51	m	**6.62**
450 mm nominal size	-	0.32	2.33	5.08	m	**7.41**
600 mm nominal size	-	0.36	2.62	5.64	m	**8.26**
900 mm nominal size	-	0.43	3.13	6.77	m	**9.90**
1200 mm nominal size	-	0.58	4.22	9.03	m	**13.25**
Beds; 150 mm thick; to pipes						
100 mm nominal size	-	0.25	1.82	3.95	m	**5.77**
150 mm nominal size	-	0.29	2.11	4.51	m	**6.62**
225 mm nominal size	-	0.32	2.33	5.08	m	**7.41**
300 mm nominal size	-	0.36	2.62	5.64	m	**8.26**
375 mm nominal size	-	0.43	3.13	6.77	m	**9.90**
450 mm nominal size	-	0.47	3.42	7.34	m	**10.76**
600 mm nominal size	-	0.54	3.93	8.47	m	**12.40**
900 mm nominal size	-	0.68	4.94	10.73	m	**15.67**
1200 mm nominal size	-	0.83	6.03	12.98	m	**19.01**
Beds and benchings; beds 100 mm thick; to pipes						
100 mm nominal size	-	0.36	2.62	5.08	m	**7.70**
150 mm nominal size	-	0.41	2.98	5.64	m	**8.62**
225 mm nominal size	-	0.49	3.56	6.77	m	**10.33**
300 mm nominal size	-	0.57	4.14	7.90	m	**12.04**
375 mm nominal size	-	0.73	5.31	10.16	m	**15.47**
450 mm nominal size	-	0.86	6.25	11.85	m	**18.10**
600 mm nominal size	-	1.10	8.00	15.24	m	**23.24**
900 mm nominal size	-	1.78	12.94	24.83	m	**37.77**
1200 mm nominal size	-	2.64	19.19	36.68	m	**55.87**
Beds and benchings; beds 150 mm thick; to pipes						
100 mm nominal size	-	0.41	2.98	5.64	m	**8.62**
150 mm nominal size	-	0.45	3.27	6.21	m	**9.48**
225 mm nominal size	-	0.57	4.14	7.90	m	**12.04**
300 mm nominal size	-	0.73	5.31	10.16	m	**15.47**
375 mm nominal size	-	0.86	6.25	11.85	m	**18.10**
450 mm nominal size	-	1.02	7.42	14.11	m	**21.53**
600 mm nominal size	-	1.30	9.45	18.06	m	**27.51**
900 mm nominal size	-	2.07	15.05	28.79	m	**43.84**
1200 mm nominal size	-	2.92	21.23	40.63	m	**61.86**
Beds and coverings; 100 mm thick; to pipes						
100 mm nominal size	-	0.54	3.93	6.77	m	**10.70**
150 mm nominal size	-	0.63	4.58	7.90	m	**12.48**
225 mm nominal size	-	0.90	6.54	11.29	m	**17.83**
300 mm nominal size	-	1.08	7.85	13.54	m	**21.39**
375 mm nominal size	-	1.31	9.52	16.36	m	**25.88**
450 mm nominal size	-	1.53	11.12	19.19	m	**30.31**
600 mm nominal size	-	1.98	14.39	24.83	m	**39.22**
900 mm nominal size	-	3.02	21.96	37.82	m	**59.78**
1200 mm nominal size	-	4.14	30.10	51.92	m	**82.02**
Beds and coverings; 150 mm thick; to pipes						
100 mm nominal size	-	0.81	5.89	10.16	m	**16.05**
150 mm nominal size	-	0.90	6.54	11.29	m	**17.83**
225 mm nominal size	-	1.17	8.51	14.67	m	**23.18**
300 mm nominal size	-	1.40	10.18	17.49	m	**27.67**
375 mm nominal size	-	1.62	11.78	20.32	m	**32.10**
450 mm nominal size	-	1.94	14.10	24.27	m	**38.37**
600 mm nominal size	-	2.34	17.01	29.35	m	**46.36**
900 mm nominal size	-	3.83	27.84	47.97	m	**75.81**
1200 mm nominal size	-	5.40	39.26	67.72	m	**106.98**

R DISPOSAL SYSTEMS Excluding overheads and profit	PC £	Labour hours	Labour £	Material £	Unit	Total rate £
Plain in situ ready mixed designated concrete;						
C20 - 40 mm aggregate						
Beds; 100 mm thick; to pipes						
100 mm nominal size	-	0.18	1.31	2.95	m	4.26
150 mm nominal size	-	0.18	1.31	2.95	m	4.26
225 mm nominal size	-	0.22	1.60	3.54	m	5.14
300 mm nominal size	-	0.25	1.82	4.14	m	5.96
375 mm nominal size	-	0.29	2.11	4.72	m	6.83
450 mm nominal size	-	0.32	2.33	5.32	m	7.65
600 mm nominal size	-	0.36	2.62	5.90	m	8.52
900 mm nominal size	-	0.43	3.13	7.08	m	10.21
1200 mm nominal size	-	0.58	4.22	9.45	m	13.67
Beds; 150 mm thick; to pipes						
100 mm nominal size	-	0.25	1.82	4.14	m	5.96
150 mm nominal size	-	0.29	2.11	4.72	m	6.83
225 mm nominal size	-	0.32	2.33	5.32	m	7.65
300 mm nominal size	-	0.36	2.62	5.90	m	8.52
375 mm nominal size	-	0.43	3.13	7.08	m	10.21
450 mm nominal size	-	0.47	3.42	7.68	m	11.10
600 mm nominal size	-	0.54	3.93	8.86	m	12.79
900 mm nominal size	-	0.68	4.94	11.22	m	16.16
1200 mm nominal size	-	0.83	6.03	13.58	m	19.61
Beds and benchings; beds 100 mm thick; to pipes						
100 mm nominal size	-	0.36	2.62	5.32	m	7.94
150 mm nominal size	-	0.41	2.98	5.90	m	8.88
225 mm nominal size	-	0.49	3.56	7.08	m	10.64
300 mm nominal size	-	0.57	4.14	8.27	m	12.41
375 mm nominal size	-	0.73	5.31	10.63	m	15.94
450 mm nominal size	-	0.86	6.25	12.40	m	18.65
600 mm nominal size	-	1.10	8.00	15.94	m	23.94
900 mm nominal size	-	1.78	12.94	25.98	m	38.92
1200 mm nominal size	-	2.64	19.19	38.37	m	57.56
Beds and benchings; beds 150 mm thick; to pipes						
100 mm nominal size	-	0.41	2.98	5.90	m	8.88
150 mm nominal size	-	0.45	3.27	6.49	m	9.76
225 mm nominal size	-	0.57	4.14	8.27	m	12.41
300 mm nominal size	-	0.73	5.31	10.63	m	15.94
375 mm nominal size	-	0.86	6.25	12.40	m	18.65
450 mm nominal size	-	1.02	7.42	14.76	m	22.18
600 mm nominal size	-	1.30	9.45	18.89	m	28.34
900 mm nominal size	-	2.07	15.05	30.11	m	45.16
1200 mm nominal size	-	2.92	21.23	42.51	m	63.74
Beds and coverings; 100 mm thick; to pipes						
100 mm nominal size	-	0.54	3.93	7.08	m	11.01
150 mm nominal size	-	0.63	4.58	8.27	m	12.85
225 mm nominal size	-	0.90	6.54	11.81	m	18.35
300 mm nominal size	-	1.08	7.85	14.17	m	22.02
375 mm nominal size	-	1.31	9.52	17.12	m	26.64
450 mm nominal size	-	1.53	11.12	20.07	m	31.19
600 mm nominal size	-	1.98	14.39	25.98	m	40.37
900 mm nominal size	-	3.02	21.96	39.56	m	61.52
1200 mm nominal size	-	4.14	30.10	54.32	m	84.42
Beds and coverings; 150 mm thick; to pipes						
100 mm nominal size	-	0.81	5.89	10.63	m	16.52
150 mm nominal size	-	0.90	6.54	11.81	m	18.35
225 mm nominal size	-	1.17	8.51	15.35	m	23.86
300 mm nominal size	-	1.40	10.18	18.30	m	28.48
375 mm nominal size	-	1.62	11.78	21.25	m	33.03
450 mm nominal size	-	1.94	14.10	25.38	m	39.48
600 mm nominal size	-	2.34	17.01	30.70	m	47.71
900 mm nominal size	-	3.83	27.84	50.18	m	78.02
1200 mm nominal size	-	5.40	39.26	70.85	m	110.11

R DISPOSAL SYSTEMS Excluding overheads and profit	PC £	Labour hours	Labour £	Material £	Unit	Total rate £
R12 DRAINAGE BELOW GROUND - cont'd						
NOTE: The following items unless otherwise described include for all appropriate joints/couplings in the running length. The prices for gullies and rainwater shoes, etc. include for appropriate joints to pipes and for setting on and surrounding accessory with site mixed in situ concrete 10.00 N/mm^2 - 40 mm aggregate (1:3:6).						
Cast iron "Timesaver" drain pipes and fittings or other equal and approved; BS 437; coated; with mechanical coupling joints						
75 mm pipes; laid straight	17.35	0.45	2.90	21.56	m	**24.46**
75 mm pipes; in runs not exceeding 3.00 m long	16.85	0.60	3.87	27.52	m	**31.39**
Extra for						
bend; medium radius	17.21	0.50	3.23	24.74	nr	**27.97**
single branch	23.92	0.70	4.51	39.62	nr	**44.13**
isolated "Timesaver" joint	9.59	0.30	1.94	9.83	nr	**11.77**
100 mm pipes; laid straight	18.02	0.50	3.23	22.93	m	**26.16**
100 mm pipes; in runs not exceeding 3.00 m long	17.38	0.68	4.39	30.06	m	**34.45**
Extra for						
bend; medium radius	21.55	0.60	3.87	31.06	nr	**34.93**
bend; medium radius with access	56.62	0.60	3.87	67.01	nr	**70.88**
bend; long radius	30.12	0.60	3.87	38.90	nr	**42.77**
rest bend	24.73	0.60	3.87	33.37	nr	**37.24**
diminishing pipe	18.03	0.60	3.87	26.51	nr	**30.38**
single branch	28.60	0.75	4.84	48.30	nr	**53.14**
single branch; with access	65.96	0.85	5.48	86.59	nr	**92.07**
double branch	43.08	0.95	6.13	73.43	nr	**79.56**
double branch; with access	78.28	0.95	6.13	109.51	nr	**115.64**
isolated "Timesaver" joint	11.52	0.35	2.26	11.81	nr	**14.07**
transitional pipe; for WC	16.41	0.50	3.23	28.63	nr	**31.86**
150 mm pipes; laid straight	33.94	0.60	3.87	40.50	m	**44.37**
150 mm pipes; in runs not exceeding 3.00 m long	32.40	0.82	5.29	48.32	m	**53.61**
Extra for						
bend; medium radius	49.59	0.70	4.51	59.78	nr	**64.29**
bend; medium radius with access	105.16	0.70	4.51	116.74	nr	**121.25**
bend; long radius	64.55	0.70	4.51	73.34	nr	**77.85**
diminishing pipe	28.10	0.70	4.51	35.97	nr	**40.48**
single branch	70.55	0.85	5.48	73.43	nr	**78.91**
isolated "Timesaver" joint	13.95	0.42	2.71	14.30	nr	**17.01**
Accessories in "Timesaver" cast iron or other equal and approved; with mechanical coupling joints						
Gully fittings; comprising low invert gully trap and round hopper						
75 mm outlet	18.03	0.90	5.80	31.27	nr	**37.07**
100 mm outlet	28.60	0.95	6.13	44.08	nr	**50.21**
150 mm outlet	71.16	1.30	8.38	90.78	nr	**99.16**
Add to above for bellmouth 300 mm high; circular plain grating						
100 mm nominal size; 200 mm grating	29.29	0.45	2.90	45.28	nr	**48.18**
100 mm nominal size; 100 mm horizontal inlet; 200 mm grating	36.41	0.45	2.90	52.58	nr	**55.48**
100 mm nominal size; 100 mm horizontal inlet; 200 mm grating	37.34	0.45	2.90	53.54	nr	**56.44**
Yard gully (Deans); trapped; galvanized sediment pan; 267 mm round heavy grating						
100 mm outlet	193.28	2.90	18.70	227.75	nr	**246.45**

R DISPOSAL SYSTEMS Excluding overheads and profit	PC £	Labour hours	Labour £	Material £	Unit	Total rate £
Yard gully (garage); trapless; galvanized sediment pan; 267 mm round heavy grating						
100 mm outlet	197.14	2.70	17.41	217.43	nr	**234.84**
Yard gully (garage); trapped; with rodding eye, galvanised perforated sediment pan; stopper; 267 mm round heavy grating						
100 mm outlet	366.66	2.70	17.41	427.66	nr	**445.07**
Grease trap; internal access; galvanized perforated bucket; lid and frame						
100 mm outlet; 20 gallon capacity	335.93	4.00	25.80	376.80	nr	**402.60**
Cast iron "Ensign" lightweight drain pipes and fittings **or other equal and approved; EN 877; ductile iron** **couplings**						
100 mm pipes; laid straight	-	0.20	1.63	16.78	m	**18.41**
Extra for						
bend; long radius	-	0.20	1.63	28.37	nr	**30.00**
single branch	-	0.25	2.06	28.66	nr	**30.72**
150 mm pipes; laid straight	-	0.24	1.96	33.26	m	**35.22**
Extra for						
bend; long radius	-	0.24	1.96	70.03	nr	**71.99**
single branch	-	0.30	2.45	63.07	nr	**65.52**
Extra strength vitrified clay pipes and fittings; **Hepworth "Supersleve" or other equal and approved;** **plain ends with push fit polypropylene flexible** **couplings**						
100 mm pipes; laid straight	4.11	0.20	1.29	4.32	m	**5.61**
Extra for						
bend	3.88	0.20	1.29	7.35	nr	**8.64**
access bend	25.56	0.20	1.29	30.11	nr	**31.40**
rest bend	8.76	0.20	1.29	12.47	nr	**13.76**
access pipe	22.20	0.20	1.29	26.28	nr	**27.57**
socket adaptor	4.11	0.17	1.10	6.10	nr	**7.20**
adaptor to "HepSeal" pipe	3.99	0.17	1.10	5.98	nr	**7.08**
saddle	8.23	0.75	4.84	10.73	nr	**15.57**
single junction	8.39	0.25	1.61	13.87	nr	**15.48**
single access junction	29.56	0.25	1.61	36.10	nr	**37.71**
150 mm pipes; laid straight	7.87	0.25	1.61	8.26	m	**9.87**
Extra for						
bend	7.99	0.24	1.55	14.12	nr	**15.67**
access bend	1.99	0.24	1.55	37.78	nr	**39.33**
rest bend	10.28	0.24	1.55	16.52	nr	**18.07**
taper pipe	11.72	0.24	1.55	16.34	nr	**17.89**
access pipe	28.84	0.24	1.55	35.40	nr	**36.95**
socket adaptor	7.75	0.20	1.29	11.31	nr	**12.60**
adaptor to "HepSeal" pipe	5.51	0.20	1.29	8.95	nr	**10.24**
saddle	11.72	0.90	5.80	16.09	nr	**21.89**
single junction	11.75	0.30	1.94	21.23	nr	**23.17**
single access junction	41.99	0.30	1.94	52.99	nr	**54.93**
Extra strength vitrified clay pipes and fittings; **Hepworth "HepSeal" or other equal and approved;** **socketed; with push-fit flexible joints**						
100 mm pipes; laid straight	7.16	0.27	1.74	7.52	m	**9.26**
Extra for						
bend	10.35	0.22	1.42	8.61	nr	**10.03**
rest bend	12.30	0.22	1.42	10.66	nr	**12.08**
stopper	3.90	0.14	0.90	4.09	nr	**4.99**
access pipe	21.65	0.24	1.55	19.73	nr	**21.28**
single junction	14.37	0.27	1.74	12.08	nr	**13.82**
double collar	9.21	0.18	1.16	9.67	nr	**10.83**

R DISPOSAL SYSTEMS Excluding overheads and profit	PC £	Labour hours	Labour £	Material £	Unit	Total rate £
R12 DRAINAGE BELOW GROUND - cont'd						
Extra strength vitrified clay pipes and fittings;						
Hepworth "HepSeal" or other equal and approved;						
socketed; with push-fit flexible joints - cont'd						
150 mm pipes; laid straight	9.30	0.32	2.06	9.77	m	11.83
Extra for						
bend	17.06	0.25	1.61	14.98	nr	16.59
rest bend	20.37	0.22	1.42	18.46	nr	19.88
stopper	5.82	0.16	1.03	6.11	nr	7.14
taper reducer	25.58	0.25	1.61	23.93	nr	25.54
access pipe	33.94	0.25	1.61	31.73	nr	33.34
saddle	8.95	0.81	5.22	9.40	nr	14.62
single junction	9.30	0.32	2.06	19.50	nr	21.56
single access junction	44.94	0.32	2.06	44.18	nr	46.24
double junction	44.32	0.48	3.10	41.65	nr	44.75
double collar	15.19	0.21	1.35	15.95	nr	17.30
225 mm pipes; laid straight	17.98	0.41	2.64	18.88	m	21.52
Extra for						
bend	34.82	0.32	2.06	30.90	nr	32.96
rest bend	48.50	0.32	2.06	45.26	nr	47.32
stopper	12.54	0.21	1.35	13.17	nr	14.52
taper reducer	39.34	0.32	2.06	35.64	nr	37.70
access pipe	85.94	0.32	2.06	82.69	nr	84.75
saddle	16.24	1.08	6.97	17.05	nr	24.02
single junction	52.35	0.41	2.64	47.42	nr	50.06
single access junction	102.75	0.41	2.64	100.34	nr	102.98
double junction	99.36	0.61	3.93	94.89	nr	98.82
double collar	33.20	0.27	1.74	34.86	nr	36.60
300 mm pipes; laid straight	28.10	0.54	3.48	29.50	m	32.98
Extra for						
bend	68.70	0.43	2.77	63.28	nr	66.05
rest bend	104.80	0.43	2.77	101.19	nr	103.96
stopper	28.15	0.27	1.74	29.56	nr	31.30
taper reducer	82.35	0.43	2.77	77.62	nr	80.39
saddle	80.44	1.44	9.29	84.46	nr	93.75
single junction	107.93	0.54	3.48	101.52	nr	105.00
double junction	210.95	0.81	5.22	206.75	nr	211.97
double collar	53.97	0.36	2.32	56.67	nr	58.99
400 mm pipes; laid straight	57.69	0.72	4.64	60.57	m	65.21
Extra for						
bend	216.76	0.58	3.74	209.43	nr	213.17
single unequal junction	203.10	0.72	4.64	189.03	nr	193.67
450 mm pipes; laid straight	74.93	0.90	5.80	78.68	m	84.48
Extra for						
bend	285.42	0.72	4.64	276.09	nr	280.73
single unequal junction	242.96	0.90	5.80	223.64	nr	229.44
British Standard quality vitrified clay pipes						
and fittings; socketed; cement and sand (1:2)						
joints						
100 mm pipes; laid straight	5.01	0.40	2.58	5.34	m	7.92
Extra for						
bend (short/medium/knuckle)	10.02	0.32	2.06	3.76	nr	5.82
bend (long/rest/elbow)	8.23	0.32	2.06	7.14	nr	9.20
single junction	9.20	0.40	2.58	7.66	nr	10.24
double junction	15.98	0.60	3.87	14.27	nr	18.14
double collar	6.04	0.27	1.74	6.42	nr	8.16

R DISPOSAL SYSTEMS Excluding overheads and profit	PC £	Labour hours	Labour £	Material £	Unit	Total rate £
150 mm pipes; laid straight	7.71	0.45	2.90	8.18	m	11.08
Extra for						
bend (short/medium/knuckle)	7.53	0.36	2.32	5.56	nr	7.88
bend (long/rest/elbow)	13.92	0.36	2.32	12.27	nr	14.59
taper	18.18	0.36	2.32	16.50	nr	18.82
single junction	15.23	0.45	2.90	12.85	nr	15.75
double junction	36.85	0.68	4.39	34.76	nr	39.15
double collar	10.06	0.30	1.94	10.64	nr	12.58
225 mm pipes; laid straight	15.27	0.55	3.55	16.23	m	19.78
Extra for						
bend (short/medium/knuckle)	23.58	0.44	2.84	20.05	nr	22.89
taper	38.39	0.36	2.32	35.12	nr	37.44
double collar	23.54	0.36	2.32	24.80	nr	27.12
300 mm pipes; laid straight	25.60	0.75	4.84	27.07	m	31.91
Extra for						
bend (short/medium/knuckle)	42.85	0.60	3.87	37.03	nr	40.90
double collar	46.66	0.40	2.58	49.13	nr	51.71
400 mm pipes; laid straight	49.34	1.00	6.45	52.08	m	58.53
450 mm pipes; laid straight	62.48	1.25	8.06	65.88	m	73.94
500 mm pipes; laid straight	78.14	1.45	9.35	82.34	m	91.69
Accessories in vitrified clay; set in concrete; **with polypropylene coupling joints to pipes**						
Rodding point; with oval aluminium plate						
100 mm nominal size	19.96	0.50	3.23	24.18	nr	27.41
Gully fittings; comprising low back trap and square hopper; 150 mm x 150 mm square gully grid						
100 mm nominal size	21.38	0.85	5.48	27.76	nr	33.24
Access gully; trapped with rodding eye and integral vertical back inlet; stopper; 150 mm x 150 mm square gully grid						
100 mm nominal size	27.86	0.65	4.19	32.46	nr	36.65
Inspection chamber; comprising base; 300 mm or 450 mm raising piece; integral alloy cover and frame; 100 mm inlets						
straight through; 2 nr inlets	81.03	2.00	12.90	89.32	nr	102.22
single junction; 3 nr inlets	87.43	2.20	14.19	98.13	nr	112.32
double junction; 4 nr inlets	94.87	2.40	15.48	108.03	nr	123.51
Accessories in polypropylene; cover set in **concrete; with coupling joints to pipes**						
Inspection chamber; 5 nr 100 mm inlets; cast iron cover and frame						
475 mm diameter x 585 mm deep	122.76	2.30	14.84	133.98	nr	148.82
475 mm diameter x 930 mm deep	143.12	2.50	16.13	155.36	nr	171.49
Accessories in vitrified clay; set in concrete; **with cement:sand (1:2) joints to pipes**						
Gully fittings; comprising low back trap and square hopper; square gully grid						
100 mm outlet; 150 mm x 150 mm grid	27.78	1.00	6.45	29.45	nr	35.90
150 mm outlet; 225 mm x 225 mm grid	50.24	1.00	6.45	53.04	nr	59.49
Yard gully (mud); trapped with rodding eye; galvanized square bucket; stopper; square hinged grate and frame						
100 mm outlet; 225 mm x 225 mm grid	71.42	3.00	19.35	75.34	nr	94.69
150 mm outlet; 300 mm x 300 mm grid	128.26	4.00	25.80	135.30	nr	161.10
Yard gully (garage); trapped with rodding eye; galvanized perforated round bucket; stopper; round hinged grate and frame						
100 mm outlet; 273 mm grid	71.43	3.00	19.35	95.66	nr	115.01
150 mm outlet; 368 mm grid	133.31	4.00	25.80	140.32	nr	166.12

R DISPOSAL SYSTEMS Excluding overheads and profit	PC £	Labour hours	Labour £	Material £	Unit	Total rate £
R12 DRAINAGE BELOW GROUND - cont'd						
Accessories in vitrified clay; set in concrete;						
with cement:sand (1:2) joints to pipes - cont'd						
Road gully; trapped with rodding eye and						
stopper (grate not included)						
300 mm x 600 mm x 100 mm outlet	49.68	3.30	21.29	65.22	nr	86.51
300 mm x 600 mm x 150 mm outlet	50.87	3.30	21.29	66.47	nr	87.76
400 mm x 750 mm x 150 mm outlet	59.00	4.00	25.80	81.78	nr	107.58
450 mm x 900 mm x 150 mm outlet	79.83	5.00	32.25	107.61	nr	139.86
Grease trap; with internal access; galvanized						
perforated bucket; lid and frame						
450 mm x 300 mm x 525 mm deep; 100 mm outlet	368.72	3.50	22.57	401.55	nr	424.12
600 mm x 450 mm x 600 mm deep; 100 mm outlet	467.98	4.20	27.09	510.88	nr	537.97
Interceptor; trapped with inspection arm; lever						
locking stopper; chain and staple; cement:						
sand (1:2) joints to pipes; building in, and cutting						
and fitting brickwork around						
100 mm outlet; 100 mm inlet	62.80	4.00	25.80	66.28	nr	92.08
150 mm outlet; 150 mm inlet	89.06	4.50	29.02	93.86	nr	122.88
225 mm outlet; 225 mm inlet	240.82	5.00	32.25	253.23	nr	285.48
Accessories; grates and covers						
Aluminium alloy gully grids; set in position						
120 mm x 120 mm	2.26	0.10	0.65	2.37	nr	3.02
150 mm x 150 mm	2.26	0.10	0.65	2.37	nr	3.02
225 mm x 225 mm	6.73	0.10	0.65	7.07	nr	7.72
100 mm diameter	2.26	0.10	0.65	2.37	nr	3.02
150 mm diameter	3.46	0.10	0.65	3.63	nr	4.28
225 mm diameter	7.53	0.10	0.65	7.91	nr	8.56
Aluminium alloy sealing plates and frames; set						
in cement:sand (1:3)						
150 mm x 150 mm	8.68	0.25	1.61	9.19	nr	10.80
225 mm x 225 mm	15.90	0.25	1.61	16.77	nr	18.38
140 mm diameter (for 100 mm)	7.08	0.25	1.61	7.51	nr	9.12
197 mm diameter (for 150 mm)	10.18	0.25	1.61	10.77	nr	12.38
273 mm diameter (for 225 mm)	16.29	0.25	1.61	17.18	nr	18.79
Coated cast iron heavy duty road gratings and frame;						
BS 497 Tables 6 and 7; bedding and pointing in cement:						
sand (1:3); one course half brick thick wall in						
semi-engineering bricks in cement mortar (1:3)						
445 mm x 400 mm; Grade A1, ref GA1-450 (90 kg)	90.45	2.50	16.13	94.74	nr	110.87
400 mm x 310 mm; Grade A2, ref GA2-325 (35 kg)	69.30	2.50	16.13	73.07	nr	89.20
500 mm x 310 mm; Grade A2, ref GA2-325 (65 kg)	94.50	2.50	16.13	98.90	nr	115.03
Vibrated concrete pipes and fittings; with						
flexible joints; BS 5911 Part 1						
300 mm pipes Class M; laid straight	11.69	0.70	4.51	12.27	m	16.78
Extra for						
bend; 22.50 degree	-	0.70	4.51	46.03	nr	50.54
bend; 45 degree	-	0.70	4.51	76.72	nr	81.23
junction; 300 mm x 100 mm	24.05	0.50	3.23	24.05	nr	27.28
450 mm pipes Class H; laid straight	25.16	1.10	7.09	26.42	m	33.51
Extra for						
bend; 22.50 degree	-	1.10	7.09	99.07	nr	106.16
bend; 45 degree	-	1.10	7.09	165.11	nr	172.20
junction; 450 mm x 150 mm	26.56	0.70	4.51	26.56	nr	31.07
600 mm pipes Class H; laid straight	33.97	1.60	10.32	35.67	m	45.99
Extra for						
bend; 22.50 degree	-	1.60	10.32	133.76	nr	144.08
bend; 45 degree	-	1.60	10.32	222.93	nr	233.25
junction; 600 mm x 150 mm	27.20	0.90	5.80	27.20	nr	33.00

R DISPOSAL SYSTEMS Excluding overheads and profit	PC £	Labour hours	Labour £	Material £	Unit	Total rate £
900 mm pipes Class H; laid straight	86.32	2.80	18.06	90.64	m	108.70
Extra for						
bend; 22.50 degree	-	2.80	18.06	339.88	nr	357.94
bend; 45 degree	-	2.80	18.06	566.48	nr	584.54
junction; 900 mm x 225 mm	46.33	1.10	7.09	46.33	nr	53.42
1200 mm pipes Class H; laid straight	110.97	4.00	25.80	116.52	m	142.32
Extra for						
bend; 22.50 degree	-	4.00	25.80	436.94	nr	462.74
bend; 45 degree	-	4.00	25.80	728.24	nr	754.04
junction; 300 mm x 100 mm	56.61	1.60	10.32	56.61	nr	66.93
Accessories in precast concrete; top set in						
with rodding eye and stopper; cement:						
sand (1:2) joint to pipe						
Concrete road gully; BS 5911; trapped with						
rodding eye and stopper; cement:sand						
(1:2) joint to pipe						
450 mm diameter x 1050 mm deep; 100 mm or						
150 mm outlet	26.77	4.75	30.64	41.85	nr	72.49
"Osmadrain" uPVC pipes and fittings or other						
equal and approved; BS 4660; with ring seal joints						
82 mm pipes; laid straight	3.23	0.16	1.03	3.39	m	4.42
Extra for						
bend; short radius	5.65	0.14	0.90	5.79	nr	6.69
spigot/socket bend	4.64	0.14	0.90	4.76	nr	5.66
adaptor	2.48	0.08	0.52	2.54	nr	3.06
single junction	7.18	0.19	1.23	7.36	nr	8.59
slip coupler	3.41	0.08	0.52	3.50	nr	4.02
100 mm pipes; laid straight	2.98	0.18	1.16	3.47	m	4.63
Extra for						
bend; short radius	7.29	0.16	1.03	7.28	nr	8.31
bend; long radius	11.80	0.16	1.03	11.16	nr	12.19
spigot/socket bend	6.16	0.16	1.03	7.91	nr	8.94
socket plug	2.95	0.05	0.32	3.02	nr	3.34
adjustable double socket bend	7.90	0.16	1.03	9.54	nr	10.57
adaptor to clay	6.30	0.10	0.65	6.35	nr	7.00
single junction	8.70	0.23	1.48	7.98	nr	9.46
sealed access junction	15.94	0.20	1.29	15.40	nr	16.69
slip coupler	3.41	0.10	0.65	3.50	nr	4.15
160 mm pipes; laid straight	6.58	0.23	1.48	7.53	m	9.01
Extra for						
bend; short radius	16.16	0.19	1.23	16.15	nr	17.38
spigot/socket bend	14.65	0.19	1.23	17.87	nr	19.10
socket plug	5.29	0.08	0.52	5.42	nr	5.94
adaptor to clay	12.76	0.13	0.84	12.75	nr	13.59
level invert taper	8.47	0.19	1.23	11.12	nr	12.35
single junction	26.45	0.26	1.68	27.11	nr	28.79
sealed access junction	41.88	0.24	1.55	42.93	nr	44.48
slip coupler	9.54	0.12	0.77	9.78	nr	10.55
uPVC Osma "Ultra-Rib" ribbed pipes and fittings or						
other equal and approved; WIS approval; with sealed						
ring push-fit joints						
150 mm pipes; laid straight	-	0.21	1.35	2.97	m	4.32
Extra for						
bend; short radius	8.63	0.18	1.16	8.67	nr	9.83
adaptor to 160 mm diameter upvc	10.13	0.11	0.71	10.03	nr	10.74
adaptor to clay	20.80	0.11	0.71	21.14	nr	21.85
level invert taper	3.78	0.19	1.23	3.34	nr	4.57
single junction	15.57	0.24	1.55	15.07	nr	16.62

R DISPOSAL SYSTEMS Excluding overheads and profit	PC £	Labour hours	Labour £	Material £	Unit	Total rate £
R12 DRAINAGE BELOW GROUND - cont'd						
uPVC Osma "Ultra-Rib" ribbed pipes and fittings or **other equal and approved; WIS approval; with sealed** **ring push-fit joints** - cont'd						
225 mm pipes; laid straight	6.48	0.24	1.55	6.81	m	**8.36**
Extra for						
bend; short radius	31.16	0.22	1.42	31.53	nr	**32.95**
adaptor to clay	25.92	0.14	0.90	25.75	nr	**26.65**
level invert taper	5.43	0.22	1.42	4.34	nr	**5.76**
single junction	46.34	0.29	1.87	45.46	nr	**47.33**
300 mm pipes; laid straight	9.72	0.35	2.26	10.21	m	**12.47**
Extra for						
bend; short radius	49.13	0.31	2.00	49.75	nr	**51.75**
adaptor to clay	68.17	0.15	0.97	68.65	nr	**69.62**
level invert taper	16.27	0.31	2.00	14.84	nr	**16.84**
single junction	98.75	0.40	2.58	98.15	nr	**100.73**
Interconnecting drainage channel; ACO Polymer **Products Ltd or other equal and approved;** **reinforced slotted galvanised steel grating** **ref 423/4; bedding and haunching in in** **situ concrete (not included)**						
100 mm wide						
laid level or to falls	-	0.50	3.23	40.26	m	**43.49**
extra for sump unit	-	1.50	9.68	87.80	nr	**97.48**
extra for end caps	-	0.10	0.65	4.72	nr	**5.37**
Interconnecting drainage channel; "Birco-lite" **ref 8012 or other equal and approved; Marshalls** **Plc; galvanised steel grating ref 8041 or other** **equal and approved; bedding and haunching in** **in situ concrete (not included)**						
100 mm wide						
laid level or to falls	-	0.50	3.23	39.04	m	**42.27**
extra for 100 mm diameter trapped outlet unit	-	1.50	9.68	64.61	nr	**74.29**
extra for end caps	-	0.10	0.65	3.72	nr	**4.37**
Accessories in uPVC; with ring seal joints to **pipes (unless otherwise described)**						
Cast iron access point						
110 mm diameter	17.59	0.81	5.22	18.03	nr	**23.25**
Rodding eye						
110 mm diameter	22.94	0.46	2.97	26.34	nr	**29.31**
Universal gulley fitting; comprising gulley trap, plain hopper						
150 mm x 150 mm grate	13.45	1.00	6.45	17.74	nr	**24.19**
Bottle gulley; comprising gulley with bosses closed; sealed access covers						
217 mm x 217 mm grate	22.91	0.84	5.42	27.45	nr	**32.87**
Shallow access pipe; light duty screw down access door assembly						
110 mm diameter	14.59	0.84	5.42	18.91	nr	**24.33**
Shallow access junction; 3 nr 110 mm inlets; light duty screw down access door assembly						
110 mm diameter	28.77	1.20	7.74	36.79	nr	**44.53**
Shallow inspection chamber; 250 mm diameter; 600 mm deep; sealed cover and frame						
4 nr 110 mm outlets/inlets	48.47	1.38	8.90	63.78	nr	**72.68**

R DISPOSAL SYSTEMS Excluding overheads and profit	PC £	Labour hours	Labour £	Material £	Unit	Total rate £
Universal inspection chamber; 450 mm diameter; single seal cast iron cover and frame; 4 nr 110 mm outlets/inlets						
500 mm deep	82.12	1.46	9.42	98.27	nr	107.69
730 mm deep	82.12	1.73	11.16	112.76	nr	123.92
960 mm deep	82.12	2.00	12.90	127.24	nr	140.14
Equal manhole base; 750 mm diameter						
6 nr 160 mm outlets/inlets	95.84	1.31	8.45	106.70	nr	115.15
Unequal manhole base; 750 mm diameter						
2 nr 160 mm, 4 nr 110 mm outlets/inlets	89.17	1.31	8.45	99.87	nr	108.32
Kerb to gullies; class B engineering bricks on edge to three sides in cement mortar (1:3) rendering in cement mortar (1:3) to top and two sides and skirting to brickwork 230 mm high; dishing in cement mortar (1:3) to gully; steel trowelled						
230 mm x 230 mm internally	-	1.50	9.68	1.07	nr	10.75
Excavating; by machine						
Manholes						
maximum depth not exceeding 1.00 m	-	0.21	1.38	3.96	m³	5.34
maximum depth not exceeding 2.00 m	-	0.23	1.51	4.34	m³	5.85
maximum depth not exceeding 4.00 m	-	0.27	1.78	5.09	m³	6.87
Excavating; by hand						
Manholes						
maximum depth not exceeding 1.00 m	-	3.30	21.71	-	m³	21.71
maximum depth not exceeding 2.00 m	-	3.90	25.66	-	m³	25.66
maximum depth not exceeding 4.00 m	-	5.00	32.90	-	m³	32.90
Earthwork support (average "risk" prices)						
Maximum depth not exceeding 1.00 m						
distance between opposing faces not exceeding 2.00 m	-	0.15	0.99	3.19	m²	4.18
Maximum depth not exceeding 2.00 m						
distance between opposing faces not exceeding 2.00 m	-	0.19	1.25	6.07	m²	7.32
Maximum depth not exceeding 4.00 m						
distance between opposing faces not exceeding 2.00 m	-	0.24	1.58	8.95	m²	10.53
Disposal; by machine						
Excavated material						
off site; to tip not exceeding 13 km (using lorries) including Landfill Tax based on inactive waste	-	-	-	13.50	m³	13.50
on site; depositing on site in spoil heaps; average 50 m distance	-	0.15	0.99	2.57	m³	3.56
Disposal; by hand						
Excavated material						
off site; to tip not exceeding 13 km (using orries) including Landfill Tax based on inactive waste	-	0.80	5.26	21.75	m³	27.01
on site; depositing in spoil heaps; average 50 m distance	-	1.30	8.55	-	m³	8.55
Filling to excavations; by machine						
Average thickness not exceeding 0.25 m						
arising from the excavations	-	0.15	0.99	1.89	m³	2.88
Filling to excavations; by hand						
Average thickness not exceeding 0.25 m						
arising from the excavations	-	1.00	6.58	-	m³	6.58

R DISPOSAL SYSTEMS Excluding overheads and profit	PC £	Labour hours	Labour £	Material £	Unit	Total rate £
R12 DRAINAGE BELOW GROUND - cont'd						
Plain in situ ready mixed designated concrete; C10						
- 40 mm aggregate						
Beds						
thickness not exceeding 150 mm	52.50	3.00	21.81	59.26	m³	**81.07**
thickness 150 - 450 mm	52.50	2.25	16.36	59.26	m³	**75.62**
thickness exceeding 450 mm	52.50	1.90	13.81	59.26	m³	**73.07**
Plain in situ ready mixed designated concrete; C20						
- 20 mm aggregate						
Beds						
thickness not exceeding 150 mm	54.92	3.00	21.81	61.99	m³	**83.80**
thickness 150 - 450 mm	54.92	2.25	16.36	61.99	m³	**78.35**
thickness exceeding 450 mm	54.92	1.90	13.81	61.99	m³	**75.80**
Plain in situ ready mixed designated concrete; C25						
- 20 mm aggregate (small quantities)						
Benching in bottoms						
150 mm - 450 mm average thickness	55.20	9.00	79.31	59.34	m³	**138.65**
Reinforced in situ ready mixed designated						
concrete; C20 - 20 mm aggregate; (small quantities)						
Isolated cover slabs						
thickness not exceeding 150 mm	54.92	7.00	50.89	59.04	m³	**109.93**
Reinforcement fabric to BS 4483; lapped; in						
beds or suspended slabs						
Ref A98 (1.54 kg/m²)						
400 mm minimum laps	0.60	0.12	1.07	0.66	m²	**1.73**
Ref A142 (2.22 kg/m²)						
400 mm minimum laps	0.70	0.12	1.07	0.77	m²	**1.84**
Ref A193 (3.02 kg/m²)						
400 mm minimum laps	1.00	0.12	1.07	1.10	m²	**2.17**
Formwork; basic finish						
Soffits of isolated cover slabs						
horizontal	-	2.85	31.92	6.85	m²	**38.77**
Edges of isolated cover slabs						
height not exceeding 250 mm	-	0.84	9.41	1.92	m	**11.33**
Precast concrete rectangular access and						
inspection chambers; "Hepworth" chambers						
or other equal and approved; comprising cover						
frame to receive manhole cover (not included)						
intermediate wall sections and base section with						
cut outs; bedding; jointing and pointing in cement						
mortar (1:3) on prepared bed						
Drainage chamber; size 600 mm x 450 mm						
internally; depth to invert						
600 mm deep	-	4.50	29.02	94.78	nr	**123.80**
900 mm deep	-	6.00	38.70	117.94	nr	**156.64**
Drainage chamber; 1200 mm x 750 mm						
reducing to 600 mm x 600 mm; no base unit;						
depth of invert						
1050 mm deep	-	7.50	48.38	169.31	nr	**217.69**
1650 mm deep	-	9.00	58.05	286.41	nr	**344.46**
2250 mm deep	-	11.00	70.95	402.91	nr	**473.86**

R DISPOSAL SYSTEMS Excluding overheads and profit	PC £	Labour hours	Labour £	Material £	Unit	Total rate £
Precast concrete circular manhole rings; **BS5911 Part 1; bedding, jointing and pointing** **in cement mortar (1:3) on prepared bed**						
Chamber or shaft rings; plain						
900 mm diameter	33.15	5.50	35.48	33.74	m	**69.22**
1050 mm diameter	39.52	6.50	41.92	40.71	m	**82.63**
1200 mm diameter	52.27	7.50	48.38	54.05	m	**102.43**
Chamber or shaft rings; reinforced						
1350 mm diameter	73.10	8.50	54.83	75.48	m	**130.31**
1500 mm diameter	85.00	9.50	61.27	88.57	m	**149.84**
1800 mm diameter	112.20	12.00	77.40	117.56	m	**194.96**
2100 mm diameter	152.15	15.00	96.75	159.29	m	**256.04**
extra for step irons built in	2.93	0.15	0.97	2.93	nr	**3.90**
Reducing slabs						
1200 mm diameter	58.65	6.00	38.70	59.84	nr	**98.54**
1350 mm diameter	79.90	9.50	61.27	82.28	nr	**143.55**
1500 mm diameter	93.50	11.00	70.95	96.47	nr	**167.42**
1800 mm diameter	133.45	14.00	90.30	138.21	nr	**228.51**
Heavy duty cover slabs; to suit rings						
900 mm diameter	30.60	3.00	19.35	31.20	nr	**50.55**
1050 mm diameter	38.67	3.50	22.57	39.38	nr	**61.95**
1200 mm diameter	52.70	4.00	25.80	53.89	nr	**79.69**
1350 mm diameter	73.95	4.50	29.02	75.73	nr	**104.75**
1500 mm diameter	85.85	5.00	32.25	88.23	nr	**120.48**
1800 mm diameter	123.25	6.00	38.70	126.55	nr	**165.25**
2100 mm diameter	246.50	7.00	45.15	250.96	nr	**296.11**
Common bricks; in cement mortar (1:3)						
Walls to manholes						
one brick thick	0.17	2.40	34.10	29.45	m²	**63.55**
one and a half brick thick	0.17	3.50	49.73	44.18	m²	**93.91**
Projections of footings						
two brick thick	0.17	4.90	69.63	58.91	m²	**128.54**
Class A engineering bricks; in cement mortar **(1:3)**						
Walls to manholes						
one brick thick	0.33	2.70	38.37	54.41	m²	**92.78**
one and a half brick thick	0.33	3.90	55.42	56.19	m²	**111.61**
Projections of footings						
two brick thick	0.33	5.50	78.16	108.81	m²	**186.97**
Class B engineering bricks; in cement mortar **(1:3)**						
Walls to manholes						
one brick thick	0.22	2.70	38.37	37.50	m²	**75.87**
one and a half brick thick	0.22	3.90	55.42	56.25	m²	**111.67**
Projections of footings						
two brick thick	0.22	5.50	78.16	75.00	m²	**153.16**
Brickwork sundries						
Extra over for fair face; flush smooth pointing						
manhole walls	-	0.20	2.84	-	m²	**2.84**
Building ends of pipes into brickwork; making good fair face or rendering						
not exceeding 55 mm nominal size	-	0.10	1.42	-	nr	**1.42**
55 mm - 110 mm nominal size	-	0.15	2.13	-	nr	**2.13**
over 110 mm nominal size	-	0.20	2.84	-	nr	**2.84**
Step irons; BS 1247; malleable; galvanized; building into joints						
general purpose pattern	-	0.15	2.13	4.15	nr	**6.28**

R DISPOSAL SYSTEMS Excluding overheads and profit	PC £	Labour hours	Labour £	Material £	Unit	Total rate £
R12 DRAINAGE BELOW GROUND - cont'd						
Cement:sand (1:3) in situ finishings; steel trowelled						
13 mm work to manhole walls; one coat; to						
brickwork base over 300 mm wide	-	0.70	9.95	1.19	m²	11.14
Cast iron inspection chambers; with bolted						
flat covers; BS 437; bedded in cement mortar						
(1:3); with mechanical coupling joints						
100 mm x 100 mm						
one branch	89.74	1.05	6.77	104.39	nr	111.16
one branch either side	112.28	1.55	10.00	139.30	nr	149.30
150 mm x 100 mm						
one branch	142.82	1.25	8.06	146.99	nr	155.05
one branch either side	156.02	1.80	11.61	172.92	nr	184.53
150 mm x 150 mm						
one branch	164.19	1.35	8.71	183.78	nr	192.49
one branch either side	179.63	1.90	12.26	213.91	nr	226.17
Access covers and frames; Drainage Systems or						
other equal and approved; coated; bedding frame						
in cement:sand (1:3); cover in grease and sand						
Grade A; light duty; rectangular single seal solid						
top						
450 mm x 450 mm; ref MC1-45/45	39.16	1.50	9.68	41.45	nr	51.13
600 mm x 450 mm; ref MC1-60/45	39.40	1.50	9.68	41.82	nr	51.50
600 mm x 600 mm; ref MC1-60/60	83.72	1.50	9.68	87.37	nr	97.05
Grade A; light duty; rectangular single seal						
recessed						
600 mm x 450 mm; ref MC1R-60/45	80.32	1.50	9.68	83.76	nr	93.44
600 mm x 600 mm; ref MC1R-60/60	110.92	1.50	9.68	115.25	nr	124.93
Grade A; light duty; rectangular double seal						
solid top						
450 mm x 450 mm; ref MC2-45/45	60.24	1.50	9.68	63.06	nr	72.74
600 mm x 450 mm; ref MC2-60/45	78.92	1.50	9.68	82.33	nr	92.01
600 mm x 600 mm; ref MC2-60/60	111.28	1.50	9.68	115.62	nr	125.30
Grade A; light duty; rectangular double seal						
recessed						
450 mm x 450 mm; ref MC2R-45/45	100.08	1.50	9.68	103.90	nr	113.58
600 mm x 450 mm; ref MC2R-60/45	119.28	1.50	9.68	123.70	nr	133.38
600 mm x 600 mm; ref MC2R-60/60	134.08	1.50	9.68	138.99	nr	148.67
Grade B; medium duty; circular single seal						
solid top						
300 mm diameter; ref MB2-50	115.92	2.00	12.90	120.11	nr	133.01
550 mm diameter; ref MB2-55	88.56	2.00	12.90	92.07	nr	104.97
600 mm diameter; ref MB2-60	77.36	2.00	12.90	80.59	nr	93.49
Grade B; medium duty; rectangular single seal						
solid top						
600 mm x 450 mm; ref MB2-60/45	69.44	2.00	12.90	72.61	nr	85.51
600 mm x 600 mm; ref MB2-60/60	88.96	2.00	12.90	92.74	nr	105.64
Grade B; medium duty; rectangular singular						
seal recessed						
600 mm x 450 mm; ref MB2R-60/45	118.48	2.00	12.90	122.88	nr	135.78
600 mm x 600 mm; ref MB2R-60/60	134.80	2.00	12.90	139.72	nr	152.62
Grade B; "Chevron"; medium duty; double						
triangular solid top						
600 mm x 600 mm; ref MB1-60/60	85.12	2.00	12.90	88.80	nr	101.70
Grade C; "Vulcan" heavy duty; single triangular						
solid top						
550 mm x 495 mm; ref MA-T	136.04	2.50	16.13	140.87	nr	157.00

R DISPOSAL SYSTEMS Excluding overheads and profit	PC £	Labour hours	Labour £	Material £	Unit	Total rate £
Grade C; "Chevron"; heavy duty double triangular solid top						
550 mm x 550 mm; ref MA-55	122.60	3.00	19.35	127.14	nr	**146.49**
600 mm x 600 mm; ref MA-60	140.00	3.00	19.35	145.06	nr	**164.41**
British Standard best quality vitrified clay channels; bedding and jointing in cement: sand (1:2)						
Half section straight						
100 mm diameter x 1.00 m long	3.34	0.80	5.16	3.51	nr	**8.67**
150 mm diameter x 1.00 m long	5.55	1.00	6.45	5.83	nr	**12.28**
225 mm diameter x 1.00 m long	12.49	1.30	8.38	13.11	nr	**21.49**
300 mm diameter x 1.00 m long	25.64	1.60	10.32	26.92	nr	**37.24**
Half section bend						
100 mm diameter	3.59	0.60	3.87	3.77	nr	**7.64**
150 mm diameter	5.93	0.75	4.84	6.23	nr	**11.07**
225 mm diameter	19.79	1.00	6.45	20.78	nr	**27.23**
300 mm diameter	40.36	1.20	7.74	42.38	nr	**50.12**
Half section taper straight						
150 mm - 100 mm diameter	14.96	0.70	4.51	15.71	nr	**20.22**
225 mm - 150 mm diameter	33.37	0.90	5.80	35.04	nr	**40.84**
300 mm - 225 mm diameter	132.39	1.10	7.09	139.01	nr	**146.10**
Half section taper bend						
150 mm - 100 mm diameter	22.76	0.90	5.80	23.90	nr	**29.70**
225 mm - 150 mm diameter	65.16	1.15	7.42	68.42	nr	**75.84**
300 mm - 225 mm diameter	132.39	1.40	9.03	139.01	nr	**148.04**
Three quarter section branch bend						
100 mm diameter	8.11	0.50	3.23	8.52	nr	**11.75**
150 mm diameter	14.09	0.75	4.84	14.79	nr	**19.63**
225 mm diameter	49.63	1.00	6.45	52.11	nr	**58.56**
300 mm diameter	103.01	1.33	8.58	108.16	nr	**116.74**
uPVC channels; with solvent weld or lip seal coupling joints; bedding in cement:sand						
Half section cut away straight; with coupling either end						
110 mm diameter	17.30	0.30	1.94	22.03	nr	**23.97**
160 mm diameter	29.84	0.40	2.58	41.01	nr	**43.59**
Half section cut away long radius bend; with coupling either end						
110 mm diameter	17.71	0.30	1.94	22.46	nr	**24.40**
160 mm diameter	43.81	0.40	2.58	55.68	nr	**58.26**
Channel adaptor to clay; with one coupling						
110 mm diameter	4.96	0.25	1.61	7.14	nr	**8.75**
160 mm diameter	10.69	0.33	2.13	16.07	nr	**18.20**
Half section bend						
110 mm diameter	6.44	0.33	2.13	6.97	nr	**9.10**
160 mm diameter	9.60	0.50	3.23	10.56	nr	**13.79**
Half section channel connector						
110 mm diameter	2.55	0.08	0.52	3.09	nr	**3.61**
160 mm diameter	6.34	0.10	0.65	7.61	nr	**8.26**
Half section channel junction						
110 mm diameter	7.21	0.50	3.23	7.78	nr	**11.01**
160 mm diameter	21.76	0.60	3.87	23.33	nr	**27.20**
Polypropylene slipper bend						
110 mm diameter	9.86	0.40	2.58	10.56	nr	**13.14**

R DISPOSAL SYSTEMS Excluding overheads and profit	PC £	Labour hours	Labour £	Material £	Unit	Total rate £
R12 DRAINAGE BELOW GROUND - cont'd						
Glass fibre septic tank; "Klargester" or other **equal and approved; fixing lockable manhole cover** **and frame; placing in position**						
3750 litre capacity; 2000 mm diameter; depth to invert						
1000 mm deep; standard grade	703.00	2.45	15.80	775.00	nr	790.80
1500 mm deep; heavy duty grade	885.00	2.75	17.74	957.00	nr	974.74
6000 litre capacity; 2300 mm diameter; depth to invert						
1000 mm deep; standard grade	1147.00	2.65	17.09	1236.00	nr	1253.09
1500 mm deep; heavy duty grade	1449.00	2.95	19.03	1538.00	nr	1557.03
9000 litre capacity; 2660 mm diameter; depth to invert						
1000 mm deep; standard grade	1652.00	2.85	18.38	1741.00	nr	1759.38
1500 mm deep; heavy duty grade	2091.00	3.15	20.32	2180.00	nr	2200.32
Glass fibre petrol interceptors; "Klargester" or **other equal and approved; placing in position**						
2000 litre capacity; 2370 mm x 1300 mm diameter; depth to invert						
1000 mm deep	805.00	2.70	17.41	805.00	nr	822.41
4000 litre capacity; 4370 mm x 1300 mm diameter; depth to invert						
1000 mm deep	1346.00	2.90	18.70	1346.00	nr	1364.70
R13 LAND DRAINAGE						
Excavating; by hand; grading bottoms; **earthwork support; filling to within 150 mm** **of surface with gravel rejects; remainder filled with** **excavated material and compacting; disposal** **of surplus soil on site; spreading on site average** **50 m**						
Pipes not exceeding 200 mm nominal size						
average depth of trench 0.75 m	-	1.70	11.19	6.87	m	18.06
average depth of trench 1.00 m	-	2.25	14.80	10.79	m	25.59
average depth of trench 1.25 m	-	3.15	20.73	13.50	m	34.23
average depth of trench 1.50 m	-	5.40	35.53	16.42	m	51.95
average depth of trench 1.75 m	-	6.40	42.11	19.14	m	61.25
average depth of trench 2.00 m	-	7.40	48.69	22.06	m	70.75
Disposal; by machine						
Excavated material						
off site; to tip not exceeding 13 km (using lorries); including Landfill Tax based on inactive waste	-	-	-	13.50	m³	13.50
Disposal; by hand						
Excavated material						
off site; to tip not exceeding 13 km (using lorries); including Landfill Tax based on inactive waste	-	0.80	5.26	21.75	m³	27.01
Vitrified clay perforated sub-soil pipes; BS 65; **Hepworth "Hepline" or other equal and approved**						
Pipes; laid straight						
100 mm diameter	4.50	0.22	1.42	4.72	m	6.14
150 mm diameter	8.18	0.27	1.74	8.59	m	10.33
225 mm diameter	15.02	0.36	2.32	15.77	m	18.09

S PIPED SUPPLY SYSTEMS Excluding overheads and profit	PC £	Labour hours	Labour £	Material £	Unit	Total rate £
S PIPED SUPPLY SYSTEMS						
S10/S11 HOT AND COLD WATER						
Copper pipes; EN1057:1996; capillary fittings						
15 mm pipes; fixing with pipe clips and screwed	0.58	0.37	3.83	0.68	m	4.51
Extra for						
made bend	-	0.15	1.55	-	nr	1.55
stop end	0.75	0.11	1.14	0.77	nr	1.91
straight coupling	0.13	0.17	1.76	0.13	nr	1.89
union coupling	3.72	0.17	1.76	3.81	nr	5.57
reducing coupling	1.08	0.17	1.76	1.11	nr	2.87
copper to lead connector	1.16	0.22	2.28	1.19	nr	3.47
imperial to metric adaptor	1.32	0.22	2.28	1.35	nr	3.63
elbow	0.25	0.17	1.76	0.26	nr	2.02
backplate elbow	2.85	0.35	3.62	2.92	nr	6.54
return bend	3.56	0.17	1.76	3.65	nr	5.41
tee; equal	0.42	0.25	2.59	0.43	nr	3.02
tee; reducing	2.77	0.25	2.59	2.84	nr	5.43
straight tap connector	1.32	0.51	5.28	1.35	nr	6.63
bent tap connector	1.35	0.68	7.04	1.38	nr	8.42
tank connector	3.25	0.25	2.59	3.33	nr	5.92
overflow bend	7.07	0.22	2.28	7.25	nr	9.53
22 mm pipes; fixing with pipe clips and screwed	1.17	0.43	4.45	1.29	m	5.74
Extra for						
made bend	-	0.20	2.07	-	nr	2.07
stop end	1.41	0.13	1.35	1.45	nr	2.80
straight coupling	0.37	0.22	2.28	0.38	nr	2.66
union coupling	5.96	0.22	2.28	6.11	nr	8.39
reducing coupling	1.24	0.22	2.28	1.27	nr	3.55
copper to lead connector	1.74	0.31	3.21	1.78	nr	4.99
elbow	0.59	0.22	2.28	0.60	nr	2.88
backplate elbow	6.00	0.44	4.55	6.15	nr	10.70
return bend	7.19	0.22	2.28	7.37	nr	9.65
tee; equal	1.21	0.33	3.42	1.24	nr	4.66
tee; reducing	1.03	0.33	3.42	1.06	nr	4.48
straight tap connector	1.51	0.17	1.76	1.55	nr	3.31
28 mm pipes; fixing with pipe clips and screwed	1.55	0.47	4.86	1.69	m	6.55
Extra for						
made bend	-	0.25	2.59	-	nr	2.59
stop end	2.23	0.15	1.55	2.29	nr	3.84
straight coupling	0.69	0.28	2.90	0.71	nr	3.61
reducing coupling	1.88	0.28	2.90	1.93	nr	4.83
union coupling	5.96	0.28	2.90	6.11	nr	9.01
copper to lead connector	2.36	0.39	4.04	2.42	nr	6.46
imperial to metric adaptor	2.57	0.39	4.04	2.63	nr	6.67
elbow	1.11	0.28	2.90	1.14	nr	4.04
return bend	10.92	0.28	2.90	11.19	nr	14.09
tee; equal	3.12	0.41	4.24	3.20	nr	7.44
35 mm pipes; fixing with pipe clips and screwed	3.80	0.54	5.59	4.05	m	9.64
Extra for						
made bend	-	0.30	3.10	-	nr	3.10
stop end	4.82	0.17	1.76	4.94	nr	6.70
straight coupling	2.28	0.33	3.42	2.34	nr	5.76
reducing coupling	4.48	0.33	3.42	4.59	nr	8.01
union coupling	11.40	0.33	3.42	11.69	nr	15.11
flanged connector	31.45	0.44	4.55	32.24	nr	36.79
elbow	4.54	0.33	3.42	4.65	nr	8.07
obtuse elbow	6.71	0.33	3.42	6.88	nr	10.30
tee; equal	7.80	0.46	4.76	8.00	nr	12.76
tank connector	8.55	0.46	4.76	8.76	nr	13.52

S PIPED SUPPLY SYSTEMS Excluding overheads and profit	PC £	Labour hours	Labour £	Material £	Unit	Total rate £
S10/S11 HOT AND COLD WATER - cont'd						
Copper pipes; EN1057:1996; capillary fittings - cont'd						
42 mm pipes; fixing with pipe clips; plugged and screwed	4.65	0.61	6.31	4.95	m	**11.26**
Extra for						
made bend	-	0.40	4.14	-	nr	**4.14**
stop end	7.40	0.19	1.97	7.58	nr	**9.55**
straight coupling	3.42	0.39	4.04	3.51	nr	**7.55**
reducing coupling	6.47	0.39	4.04	6.63	nr	**10.67**
union coupling	16.67	0.39	4.04	17.09	nr	**21.13**
flanged connector	37.58	0.50	5.17	38.52	nr	**43.69**
elbow	8.08	0.39	4.04	8.28	nr	**12.32**
obtuse elbow	11.82	0.39	4.04	12.12	nr	**16.16**
tee; equal	12.21	0.52	5.38	12.52	nr	**17.90**
tank connector	11.21	0.52	5.38	11.49	nr	**16.87**
54 mm pipes; fixing with pipe clips; plugged and screwed	5.99	0.67	6.93	6.36	m	**13.29**
Extra for						
made bend	-	0.55	5.69	-	nr	**5.69**
stop end	10.33	0.21	2.17	10.59	nr	**12.76**
straight coupling	7.05	0.44	4.55	7.23	nr	**11.78**
reducing coupling	10.05	0.44	4.55	10.30	nr	**14.85**
union coupling	31.70	0.44	4.55	32.49	nr	**37.04**
flanged connector	56.81	0.50	5.17	58.23	nr	**63.40**
elbow	16.54	0.44	4.55	16.95	nr	**21.50**
obtuse elbow	20.68	0.44	4.55	21.20	nr	**25.75**
tee; equal	23.08	0.57	5.90	23.66	nr	**29.56**
tank connector	17.12	0.57	5.90	17.55	nr	**23.45**
Copper pipes; EN1057:1996; compression fittings						
15 mm pipes; fixing with pipe clips; plugged and screwed	0.58	0.42	4.35	0.68	m	**5.03**
Extra for						
made bend	-	0.15	1.55	-	nr	**1.55**
stop end	1.46	0.10	1.03	1.50	nr	**2.53**
straight coupling	1.18	0.15	1.55	1.21	nr	**2.76**
reducing set	1.22	0.17	1.76	1.25	nr	**3.01**
male coupling	1.04	0.20	2.07	1.07	nr	**3.14**
female coupling	1.26	0.20	2.07	1.29	nr	**3.36**
90 degree bend	1.42	0.15	1.55	1.46	nr	**3.01**
90 degree backplate bend	3.42	0.30	3.10	3.51	nr	**6.61**
tee; equal	1.99	0.22	2.28	2.04	nr	**4.32**
tee; backplate	5.73	0.22	2.28	5.87	nr	**8.15**
tank coupling	3.38	0.22	2.28	3.46	nr	**5.74**
22 mm pipes; fixing with pipe clips; plugged and screwed	1.17	0.48	4.97	1.29	m	**6.26**
Extra for						
made bend	-	0.20	2.07	-	nr	**2.07**
stop end	2.12	0.12	1.24	2.17	nr	**3.41**
straight coupling	1.92	0.20	2.07	1.97	nr	**4.04**
reducing set	1.32	0.06	0.62	1.35	nr	**1.97**
male coupling	2.25	0.28	2.90	2.31	nr	**5.21**
female coupling	1.85	0.28	2.90	1.90	nr	**4.80**
90 degree bend	2.26	0.20	2.07	2.32	nr	**4.39**
tee; equal	3.30	0.30	3.10	3.38	nr	**6.48**
tee; reducing	4.68	0.30	3.10	4.80	nr	**7.90**
tank coupling	3.61	0.30	3.10	3.70	nr	**6.80**

S PIPED SUPPLY SYSTEMS Excluding overheads and profit	PC £	Labour hours	Labour £	Material £	Unit	Total rate £
28 mm pipes; fixing with pipe clips; plugged and screwed	1.55	0.52	5.38	1.69	m	7.07
Extra for						
made bend	-	0.25	2.59	-	nr	2.59
stop end	4.05	0.14	1.45	4.15	nr	5.60
straight coupling	3.88	0.25	2.59	3.98	nr	6.57
male coupling	2.75	0.35	3.62	2.82	nr	6.44
female coupling	3.57	0.35	3.62	3.66	nr	7.28
90 degree bend	5.02	0.25	2.59	5.15	nr	7.74
tee; equal	7.99	0.37	3.83	8.19	nr	12.02
tee; reducing	7.72	0.37	3.83	7.91	nr	11.74
tank coupling	6.20	0.37	3.83	6.36	nr	10.19
35 mm pipes; fixing with pipe clips; plugged and screwed	3.80	0.59	6.11	4.05	m	10.16
Extra for						
made bend	-	0.30	3.10	-	nr	3.10
stop end	6.25	0.16	1.66	6.41	nr	8.07
straight coupling	8.06	0.30	3.10	8.26	nr	11.36
male coupling	6.12	0.40	4.14	6.27	nr	10.41
female coupling	7.37	0.40	4.14	7.55	nr	11.69
tee; equal	14.16	0.42	4.35	14.51	nr	18.86
tee; reducing	13.83	0.42	4.35	14.18	nr	18.53
tank coupling	7.38	0.42	4.35	7.56	nr	11.91
42 mm pipes; fixing with pipe clips; plugged and screwed	4.65	0.66	6.83	4.95	m	11.78
Extra for						
made bend	-	0.40	4.14	-	nr	4.14
stop end	10.39	0.18	1.86	10.65	nr	12.51
straight coupling	10.60	0.35	3.62	10.87	nr	14.49
male coupling	9.19	0.45	4.66	9.42	nr	14.08
female coupling	9.89	0.45	4.66	10.14	nr	14.80
tee; equal	22.25	0.47	4.86	22.81	nr	27.67
tee; reducing	21.37	0.47	4.86	21.90	nr	26.76
54 mm pipes; fixing with pipe clips; plugged and screwed	5.99	0.72	7.45	6.36	m	13.81
Extra for						
made bend	-	0.55	5.69	-	nr	5.69
straight coupling	15.86	0.40	4.14	16.26	nr	20.40
male coupling	13.57	0.50	5.17	13.91	nr	19.08
female coupling	14.52	0.50	5.17	14.88	nr	20.05
tee; equal	35.76	0.52	5.38	36.65	nr	42.03
tee; reducing	35.76	0.52	5.38	36.65	nr	42.03
Copper, brass and gunmetal ancillaries; screwed joints to fittings						
Stopcock; brass/gunmetal capillary joints to copper						
15 mm nominal size	2.68	0.20	2.07	2.75	nr	4.82
22 mm nominal size	5.01	0.27	2.79	5.14	nr	7.93
28 mm nominal size	14.27	0.34	3.52	14.63	nr	18.15
Stopcock; brass/gunmetal compression joints to copper						
15 mm nominal size	3.66	0.18	1.86	3.75	nr	5.61
22 mm nominal size	6.43	0.24	2.48	6.59	nr	9.07
28 mm nominal size	16.75	0.30	3.10	17.17	nr	20.27
Stopcock; brass/gunmetal compression joints to polyethylene						
15 mm nominal size	9.72	0.26	2.69	9.96	nr	12.65
22 mm nominal size	10.01	0.33	3.42	10.26	nr	13.68
28 mm nominal size	15.04	0.40	4.14	15.42	nr	19.56

S PIPED SUPPLY SYSTEMS Excluding overheads and profit	PC £	Labour hours	Labour £	Material £	Unit	Total rate £
S10/S11 HOT AND COLD WATER - cont'd						
Copper, brass and gunmetal ancillaries; **screwed joints to fittings** - cont'd						
Gunmetal "Fullway" gate valve or other equal and approved; capillary joints to copper						
15 mm nominal size	8.38	0.20	2.07	8.59	nr	**10.66**
22 mm nominal size	9.70	0.27	2.79	9.94	nr	**12.73**
28 mm nominal size	13.51	0.34	3.52	13.85	nr	**17.37**
35 mm nominal size	30.14	0.41	4.24	30.89	nr	**35.13**
42 mm nominal size	37.70	0.47	4.86	38.64	nr	**43.50**
54 mm nominal size	54.67	0.53	5.49	56.04	nr	**61.53**
Brass gate valve; compression joints to copper						
15 mm nominal size	5.93	0.30	3.10	6.08	nr	**9.18**
22 mm nominal size	6.91	0.40	4.14	7.08	nr	**11.22**
28 mm nominal size	12.08	0.50	5.17	12.38	nr	**17.55**
Chromium plated; lockshield radiator valve; union outlet						
15 mm nominal size	5.26	0.22	2.28	5.39	nr	**7.67**
Water tanks/cisterns						
Polyethylene cold water feed and expansion cistern; BS 4213; with covers						
ref SC15; 68 litres	26.17	1.25	12.94	26.17	nr	**39.11**
ref SC25; 114 litres	30.53	1.45	15.01	30.53	nr	**45.54**
ref SC40; 182 litres	35.66	1.45	15.01	35.66	nr	**50.67**
ref SC50; 227 litres	49.61	1.95	20.18	49.61	nr	**69.79**
GRP cold water storage cistern; with covers						
ref 899.10; 30 litres	54.72	1.10	11.38	54.72	nr	**66.10**
ref 899.25; 68 litres	73.05	1.25	12.94	73.06	nr	**86.00**
ref 899.40; 114 litres	89.35	1.45	15.01	89.35	nr	**104.36**
ref 899.70; 227 litres	110.62	1.95	20.18	110.62	nr	**130.80**
Storage cylinders/calorifiers						
Copper cylinders; single feed coil indirect; BS 1566 Part 2; grade 3						
ref 2; 96 litres	-	2.00	20.70	144.67	nr	**165.37**
ref 3; 114 litres	92.04	2.25	23.29	92.04	nr	**115.33**
ref 7; 117 litres	90.83	2.50	25.88	90.83	nr	**116.71**
ref 8; 140 litres	102.83	3.00	31.05	102.83	nr	**133.88**
ref 9; 162 litres	131.35	3.50	36.23	131.35	nr	**167.58**
Combination copper hot water storage units; coil direct; BS 3198; (hot/cold)						
400 mm x 900 mm; 65/20 litres	106.90	2.80	28.98	106.90	nr	**135.88**
450 mm x 900 mm; 85/25 litres	110.10	3.90	40.37	110.10	nr	**150.47**
450 mm x 1075 mm; 115/25 litres	121.10	4.90	50.72	121.10	nr	**171.82**
450 mm x 1200 mm; 115/45 litres	128.93	5.50	56.92	128.93	nr	**185.85**
Combination copper hot water storage						
450 mm x 900 mm; 85/25 litres	138.06	4.40	45.54	138.06	nr	**183.60**
450 mm x 1200 mm; 115/45 litres	157.88	6.00	62.10	157.88	nr	**219.98**
Thermal insulation						
19 mm thick rigid mineral glass fibre sectional pipe lagging; plain finish; fixed with aluminium bands to steel or copper pipework; including working over pipe fittings						
around 15/15 pipes	4.43	0.07	0.72	4.65	m	**5.37**
around 20/22 pipes	4.76	0.10	1.03	5.00	m	**6.03**
around 25/28 pipes	5.15	0.11	1.14	5.41	m	**6.55**
around 32/35 pipes	5.71	0.12	1.24	6.00	m	**7.24**
around 40/42 pipes	6.05	0.13	1.35	6.35	m	**7.70**
around 50/54 pipes	7.01	0.15	1.55	7.36	m	**8.91**

S PIPED SUPPLY SYSTEMS Excluding overheads and profit	PC £	Labour hours	Labour £	Material £	Unit	Total rate £
19 mm thick rigid mineral glass fibre sectional pipe lagging; canvas or class O lacquered aluminium finish; fixed with aluminium bands to steel or copper pipework; including working over pipe fittings						
around 15/15 pipes	6.03	0.07	0.72	6.33	m	7.05
around 20/22 pipes	6.57	0.10	1.03	6.90	m	7.93
around 25/28 pipes	7.21	0.11	1.14	7.57	m	8.71
around 32/35 pipes	7.84	0.12	1.24	8.23	m	9.47
around 40/42 pipes	8.43	0.13	1.35	8.85	m	10.20
around 50/54 pipes	9.78	0.15	1.55	10.27	m	11.82
60 mm thick glass-fibre filled polyethylene insulating jackets for GRP or polyethylene cold water cisterns; complete with fixing bands; for cisterns size (supply not included)						
450 mm x 300 mm x 300 mm (45 litres)	-	0.40	4.14	-	nr	4.14
650 mm x 500 mm x 400 mm (91 litres)	-	0.60	6.21	-	nr	6.21
675 mm x 525 mm x 500 mm (136 litres)	-	0.70	7.25	-	nr	7.25
675 mm x 575 mm x 525 mm (182 litres)	-	0.80	8.28	-	nr	8.28
1000 mm x 625 mm x 525 mm (273 litres)	-	0.85	8.80	-	nr	8.80
1125 mm x 650 mm x 575 mm (341 litres)	-	0.85	8.80	-	nr	8.80
80 mm thick glass-fibre filled insulating jackets in flame retardant PVC to BS 1763; type 1B; segmental type for hot water cylinders; complete with fixing bands; for cylinders size (supply not included)						
400 mm x 900 mm; ref 2	-	0.33	3.42	-	nr	3.42
450 mm x 900 mm; ref 7	-	0.33	3.42	-	nr	3.42
450 mm x 1050 mm; ref 8	-	0.40	4.14	-	nr	4.14
450 mm x 1200 mm	-	0.50	5.17	-	nr	5.17
S13 PRESSURISED WATER						
Blue MDPE pipes; BS 6572; mains pipework; **no joints in the running length; laid in trenches** Pipes						
20 mm nominal size	0.48	0.11	1.14	0.49	m	1.63
25 mm nominal size	0.90	0.12	1.24	0.93	m	2.17
32 mm nominal size	1.02	0.13	1.35	1.05	m	2.40
50 mm nominal size	2.40	0.15	1.55	2.47	m	4.02
63 mm nominal size	3.90	0.16	1.66	4.02	m	5.68
Ductile iron bitumen coated pipes and fittings; **EN598; class K9; Stanton's "Tyton" water main** **pipes or other equal and approved; flexible joints**						
100 mm pipes; laid straight	13.65	0.60	3.87	19.03	m	22.90
Extra for						
bend; 45 degrees	31.35	0.60	3.87	42.33	nr	46.20
branch; 45 degrees; socketed	225.38	0.90	5.80	250.76	nr	256.56
tee	48.85	0.90	5.80	65.40	nr	71.20
flanged spigot	33.28	0.60	3.87	39.65	nr	43.52
flanged socket	32.58	0.60	3.87	38.91	nr	42.78
150 mm pipes; laid straight	20.55	0.70	4.51	26.71	m	31.22
Extra for						
bend; 45 degrees	53.55	0.70	4.51	66.50	nr	71.01
branch; 45 degrees; socketed	287.66	1.05	6.77	317.45	nr	324.22
tee	101.50	1.05	6.77	121.98	nr	128.75
flanged spigot	39.70	0.70	4.51	46.82	nr	51.33
flanged socket	51.86	0.70	4.51	59.59	nr	64.10

S PIPED SUPPLY SYSTEMS Excluding overheads and profit	PC £	Labour hours	Labour £	Material £	Unit	Total rate £
S13 PRESSURISED WATER - cont'd						
Ductile iron bitumen coated pipes and fittings; **EN598; class K9; Stanton's "Tyton" water main** **pipes or other equal and approved; flexible joints** - cont'd						
200 mm pipes; laid straight	27.77	1.00	6.45	36.33	m	**42.78**
Extra for						
bend; 45 degrees	96.65	1.00	6.45	115.83	nr	**122.28**
branch; 45 degrees; socketed	326.70	1.50	9.68	364.55	nr	**374.23**
tee	139.40	1.50	9.68	167.88	nr	**177.56**
flanged spigot	86.58	1.00	6.45	98.08	nr	**104.53**
flanged socket	82.02	1.00	6.45	93.29	nr	**99.74**
S32 NATURAL GAS						
Ductile iron bitumen coated pipes and fittings; BS **4772; class K9; Stanton's "Stanlock" gas main pipes** **or other equal and approved; bolted gland joints**						
100 mm pipes; laid straight	27.36	0.70	4.51	40.28	m	**44.79**
Extra for						
bend; 45 degrees	41.35	0.70	4.51	60.74	nr	**65.25**
tee	63.09	1.05	6.77	95.12	nr	**101.89**
flanged spigot	34.26	0.70	4.51	47.52	nr	**52.03**
flanged socket	33.79	0.70	4.51	47.03	nr	**51.54**
isolated "Stanlock" joint	11.00	0.35	2.26	11.55	nr	**13.81**
150 mm pipes; laid straight	41.67	0.90	5.80	60.23	m	**66.03**
Extra for						
bend; 45 degrees	59.70	0.90	5.80	87.40	nr	**93.20**
tee	105.63	1.35	8.71	152.10	nr	**160.81**
flanged spigot	39.70	0.90	5.80	58.16	nr	**63.96**
flanged socket	49.83	0.90	5.80	68.80	nr	**74.60**
isolated "Stanlock" joint	15.69	0.45	2.90	16.47	nr	**19.37**
200 mm pipes; laid straight	55.47	1.30	8.38	80.31	m	**88.69**
Extra for						
bend; 45 degrees	97.24	1.30	8.38	124.16	nr	**132.54**
tee	146.76	1.95	12.58	220.28	nr	**232.86**
flanged spigot	86.58	1.30	8.38	112.97	nr	**121.35**
flanged socket	77.10	1.30	8.38	103.02	nr	**111.40**
isolated "Stanlock" joint	21.01	0.65	4.19	22.06	nr	**26.25**

T MECHANICAL HEATING/COOLING ETC. SYSTEMS Excluding overheads and profit	PC £	Labour hours	Labour £	Material £	Unit	Total rate £
T MECHANICAL HEATING/COOLING ETC. SYSTEMS						
T10 GAS/OIL FIRED BOILERS						
Boilers						
Gas fired floor standing domestic boilers;						
cream or white; enamelled casing; 32 mm						
diameter BSPT female flow and return						
tappings; 102 mm diameter flue socket 13 mm						
diameter BSPT male draw-off outlet						
13.19 kW output (45,000 Btu/Hr)	-	5.00	52.85	438.37	nr	**491.22**
23.45 kW output (80,000 Btu/Hr)	-	5.00	52.85	563.61	nr	**616.46**
T31 LOW TEMPERATURE HOT WATER HEATING						
NOTE: The reader is referred to section						
"S10/S11 Hot and Cold Water" for rates for						
copper pipework which will equally apply to						
this section of work. For further and more						
detailed information the reader is advised to						
consult *Spon's Mechanical and Electrical*						
Services Price Book.						
Radiators; Myson Heat Emitters or other						
equal and approved						
"Premier HE" single panel type; steel; 690 mm						
high; wheelhead and lockshield valves						
540 mm long	20.60	2.00	21.14	31.51	nr	**52.65**
1149 mm long	41.64	2.25	23.78	52.55	nr	**76.33**
2165 mm long	79.12	2.50	26.43	90.03	nr	**116.46**
2978 mm long	120.92	2.75	29.07	131.89	nr	**160.96**

V ELECTRICAL SYSTEMS Excluding overheads and profit	PC £	Labour hours	Labour £	Material £	Unit	Total rate £
V ELECTRICAL SYSTEMS						
V21/V22 GENERAL LIGHTING AND LV POWER						
NOTE: The following items indicate approximate prices for wiring of lighting and power points complete, including accessories and socket outlets, but excluding lighting fittings. Consumer control units are shown separately. For a more detailed breakdown of these costs and specialist costs for a complete range of electrical items, reference should be made to *Spon's Mechanical and Electrical Services Price Book*.						
Consumer control units						
8-way 60 amp SP&N surface mounted insulated consumer control units fitted with miniature circuit breakers including 2.00 m long 32 mm screwed welded conduit with three runs of 16 mm² PVC cables ready for final connections	-	-	-	-	nr	**139.40**
extra for current operated ELCB of 30 mA tripping current	-	-	-	-	nr	**59.35**
As above but 100 amp metal cased consumer unit and 25 mm² PVC cables	-	-	-	-	nr	**157.25**
extra for current operated ELCB of 30 mA tripping current	-	-	-	-	nr	**130.55**
Final circuits						
Lighting points						
wired in PVC insulated and PVC sheathed cable in flats and houses; insulated in cavities and roof space; protected where buried by heavy gauge PVC conduit	-	-	-	-	nr	**50.45**
as above but in commercial property	-	-	-	-	nr	**62.30**
wired in PVC insulated cable in screwed welded conduit in flats and houses	-	-	-	-	nr	**106.80**
as above but in commercial property	-	-	-	-	nr	**130.55**
as above but in industrial property	-	-	-	-	nr	**148.30**
wired in MICC cable in flats and houses	-	-	-	-	nr	**89.00**
as above but in commercial property	-	-	-	-	nr	**106.80**
as above but in industrial property with PVC sheathed cable	-	-	-	-	nr	**125.60**
Single 13 amp switched socket outlet points						
wired in PVC insulated and PVC sheathed cable in flats and houses on a ring main circuit; protected where buried by heavy gauge PVC conduit	-	-	-	-	nr	**45.60**
as above but in commercial property	-	-	-	-	nr	**57.45**
wired in PVC insulated cable in screwed welded conduit throughout on a ring main circuit in flats and houses	-	-	-	-	nr	**80.10**
as above but in commercial property	-	-	-	-	nr	**91.95**
as above but in industrial property	-	-	-	-	nr	**106.80**
wired in MICC cable on a ring main circuit in flats and houses	-	-	-	-	nr	**80.10**
as above but in commercial property	-	-	-	-	nr	**94.90**
as above but in industrial property with PVC sheathed cable	-	-	-	-	nr	**121.65**

V ELECTRICAL SYSTEMS Excluding overheads and profit	PC £	Labour hours	Labour £	Material £	Unit	Total rate £
Cooker control units						
45 amp circuit including unit wired in PVC insulated and PVC sheathed cable; protected where buried by heavy gauge PVC conduit	-	-	-	-	nr	**109.80**
as above but wired in PVC insulated cable in screwed welded conduit	-	-	-	-	nr	**160.20**
as above but wired in MICC cable	-	-	-	-	nr	**180.95**

W SECURITY SYSTEMS Excluding overheads and profit	PC £	Labour hours	Labour £	Material £	Unit	Total rate £
W SECURITY SYSTEMS						
W20 LIGHTNING PROTECTION						
Lightning protection equipment						
Copper strip roof or down conductors fixed with bracket or saddle clips						
20 mm x 3 mm flat section	-	-	-	-	m	**12.75**
25 mm x 3 mm flat section	-	-	-	-	m	**14.25**
Aluminium strip roof or down conductors fixed with bracket or saddle clips						
20 mm x 3 mm flat section	-	-	-	-	m	**10.05**
25 mm x 3 mm flat section	-	-	-	-	m	**10.55**
Joints in tapes	-	-	-	-	nr	**7.85**
Bonding connections to roof and structural metalwork	-	-	-	-	nr	**44.15**
Testing points	-	-	-	-	nr	**21.60**
Earth electrodes						
16 mm diameter driven copper electrodes in 1220 mm long sectional lengths (minimum 2440 mm long overall)	-	-	-	-	nr	**119.00**
first 2440 mm length driven and tested 25 mm x 3 mm copper strip electrode in 457 mm deep prepared trench	-	-	-	-	m	**8.55**

PRICES FOR MEASURED WORK
- MINOR WORKS

INTRODUCTION

The "Prices for Measured Work - Minor Works" are intended to apply to a small project in the outer London area costing about £65,000 (excluding Preliminaries).

The format of this section follows that of the "Major Works" section with minor variations because of the different nature of the work, and reference should be made to the "Introduction" to that section on page 91.

It has been assumed that reasonable quantities of work are involved, equivalent to quantities for two houses, although clearly this would not apply to all trades and descriptions of work in a project of this value. Where smaller quantities of work are involved it will be necessary to adjust the prices accordingly.

For section "C Demolition/Alteration/Renovation" even smaller quantities have been assumed as can be seen from the stated "PC" of the materials involved.

Where work in an existing building is concerned it has been assumed that the building is vacated and that in all cases there is reasonable access and adequate storage space. Should this not be the case, and if any abnormal circumstances have to be taken into account, an allowance can be made either by a lump sum addition or by suitably modifying the percentage factor for overheads and profit. As for the major works section all rates exclude overheads and profit.

Labour rates are based upon typical gang costs divided by the number of primary working operatives for the trade concerned; and for general building work include an allowance for trade supervision, but exclude overheads and profit. The "Labour hours" column gives the total hours allocated to a particular item and the "Labour £" the consolidated cost of such labour. "Labour hours" have not always been given for "spot" items because of the inclusion of Sub-Contractor's labour.

The "Material Plant £" column includes the cost of removal of debris by skips or lorries. Alternative materials prices tables can be found in the appropriate "Prices for Measured Works - Major Works" section. As stated earlier, these prices are "list" prices before deduction of quantity discounts, and therefore can be substituted directly in place of "PC" figures given. The reader should bear in mind that although large orders are delivered free of charge, smaller orders generally attract a delivery or part load charge and this should be added to the alternative material price prior to substitution in a rate.

No allowance has been made for any Value Added Tax which will probably be payable on the majority of work of this nature.

DAVIS LANGDON & EVEREST

www.davislangdon.com

LONDON
Princes House
39 Kingsway
London WC2B 6TP
Tel : (020) 7 497 9000
Fax : (020) 7 497 8858
Email: london1@dle.co.uk

EDINBURGH
74 Great King Street
Edinburgh
EH3 6QU
Tel : (0131) 557 5306
Fax : (0131) 557 5704
Email: e-burgh1@dle.co.uk

MANCHESTER
Boulton House
Chorlton Street
Manchester M1 3HY
Tel : (0161) 2282011
Fax : (0161) 2286317
Email: manch1@dle.co.uk

PETERBOROUGH
Charterhouse
66 Broadway
Peterborough PE1 1SU
Tel: (01733) 343625
Fax: (01733) 349177
Email: p-boro@dle.co.uk

BIRMINGHAM
289 Woodbourne Road
Harborne
Birmingham B17 8BY
Tel : (0121) 4299511
Fax : (0121) 4292544
Email: bham1@dle.co.uk

GATESHEAD
11 Regent Terrace
Gateshead
Tyne and Wear NE8 1LU
Tel : (0191) 477 3844
Fax : (0191) 490 1742
Email: g-head1@dle.co.uk

MANCHESTER
Marshall House
2 Park Avenue, Sale
Cheshire M33 6HE
Tel : (0161) 9629431
Fax : (0161) 9620829
Email: manch2@dle.co.uk

PLYMOUTH
3 Russell Court
St Andrew Street
Plymouth PL1 2AX
Tel : (01752) 668372
Fax : (01752) 221219
Email: plymouth@dle.co.uk

BRISTOL
St Lawrence House
29/31 Broad Street
Bristol BS1 2HF
Tel : (0117) 9277832
Fax : (0117) 9251350
Email: bristol1@dle.co.uk

GLASGOW
Cumbrae House
15 Carlton Court
Glasgow G5 9JP
Tel : (0141) 429 6677
Fax : (0141) 429 2255
Email: glasgow1@dle.co.uk

MILTON KEYNES
6 Bassett Court
Newport Pagnell
Bucks MK16 OJN
Tel : (01908) 613777
Fax : (01908) 210642
Email: mkeynes@dle.co.uk

PORTSMOUTH
Kings House
4 Kings Road
Portsmouth PO5 3BQ
Tel : (023) 92815218
Fax : (023) 92827156
Email: ports1@dle.co.uk

CAMBRIDGE
36 Storey's Way
Cambridge
CB3 ODT
Tel : (01223) 351258
Fax : (01223) 321002
Email: camb1@dle.co.uk

LEEDS
Duncan House
14 Duncan Street
Leeds LS1 6DL
Tel : (0113) 2432481
Fax : (0113) 2424601
Email: leeds1@dle.co.uk

NORWICH
63 Thorpe Road
Norwich
NR1 1UD
Tel : (01603) 628194
Fax : (01603) 615928
Email: norwich1@dle.co.uk

SOUTHAMPTON
Brunswick House
Brunswick Place
Southampton
SO15 2AP
Tel : (023) 80333438
Fax : (023) 80226099

CARDIFF
4 Pierhead Street
Capital Waterside
Cardiff CF10 4QP
Tel : (029) 20497497
Fax : (029) 20497111
Email: cardiff1@dle.co.uk

LIVERPOOL
Cunard Building
Water Street
Liverpool L3 1JR
Tel : (0151) 2361992
Fax : (0151) 2275401
Email: dlelpool@compuserve.com

OXFORD
Avalon House
Marcham Road, Abingdon
Oxford OX14 1TZ
Tel : (01235) 555025
Fax : (01235) 554909
Email: oxford1@dle.co.uk

**DAVIS LANGDON
CONSULTANCY**
Princes House, 39 Kingsway
London WC2B 6TP
Tel : (020) 7 379 3322
Fax : (020) 7 379 3030
Email: gurrierin@dle-london.co.uk

with offices throughout Europe, the Middle East, Asia, Australia, Africa and the USA
which together form

DAVIS LANGDON & SEAH INTERNATIONAL

A PRELIMINARIES/CONTRACT CONDITIONS FOR MINOR WORKS

When pricing Preliminaries all factors affecting the execution of the works must be considered; some of the more obvious have already been mentioned above.

As mentioned in "A Preliminaries" in the "Prices for Measured Work - Major Works" section (page 97), the current trend is for Preliminaries to be priced at approximately 11 to 13%, but for alterations and additions work in particular, care must be exercised in ensuring that all adverse factors are covered. The reader is advised to identify systematically and separately price all preliminary items with cost/time implications in order to reflect as accurately as possible preliminary costs likely to stem from any particular scheme.

Where the Standard Form of Contract applies two clauses which will affect the pricing of Preliminaries should be noted.

(a)   Insurance of the works against Clause 22 Perils
        Clause 22C will apply whereby the Employer and not the Contractor effects the insurance.
(b)   Fluctuations
        An allowance for any shortfall in recovery of increased costs under whichever clause is contained in the Contract may be covered by the inclusion of a lump sum in the Preliminaries or by increasing the prices by a suitable percentage

ADDITIONS AND NEW WORKS WITHIN EXISTING BUILDINGS

Depending upon the contract size either the prices in "Prices for Measured Work - Major Works" or those prices in "Prices for Measured Work - Minor Works" will best apply.

It is likely, however, that conditions affecting the excavations for foundations might preclude the use of mechanical plant, and that it will be necessary to restrict prices to those applicable to hand excavation.

If, in any circumstances, less than what might be termed "normal quantities" are likely to be involved it is stressed that actual quotations should be invited from specialist Sub-contractors for these works.

JOBBING WORK

Jobbing work is outside the scope of this section and no attempt has been made to include prices for such work.

C DEMOLITION/ALTERATION/RENOVATION Excluding overheads and profit	PC £	Labour hours	Labour £	Material £	Unit	Total rate £
C DEMOLITION/ALTERATION/RENOVATION						
C20 DEMOLITION						
NOTE: Demolition rates vary considerably from one scheme to another, depending upon access, the type of construction, the method of demolition, whether there are any redundant materials etc. Therefore, it is advisable to obtain specific quotations for each scheme under consideration, however, the following rates (excluding scaffolding costs) for simple demolitions may be of some assistance for comparative purposes.						
Demolishing all structures						
Demolishing to ground level; single storey brick out-building; timber flat roofs; volume						
50 m³	-	-	-	-	m³	7.10
200 m³	-	-	-	-	m³	5.25
500 m³	-	-	-	-	m³	2.65
Demolishing to ground level; two storey brick out-building; timber joisted suspended floor and timber flat roofs; volume						
200 m³	-	-	-	-	m³	3.95
Demolishing parts of structures						
Breaking up concrete bed						
100 mm thick	-	0.54	3.93	1.73	m²	5.66
150 mm thick	-	0.80	5.82	3.52	m²	9.34
200 mm thick	-	1.08	7.85	3.46	m²	11.31
300 mm thick	-	1.60	11.63	5.08	m²	16.71
Breaking up reinforced concrete bed						
100 mm thick	-	0.60	4.36	1.98	m²	6.34
150 mm thick	-	0.90	6.54	2.92	m²	9.46
200 mm thick	-	1.20	8.72	3.95	m²	12.67
300 mm thick	-	1.80	13.09	5.93	m²	19.02
Demolishing reinforced concrete column or cutting away casing to steel column	-	12.00	87.24	26.80	m³	114.04
Demolishing reinforced concrete beam or cutting away casing to steel beam	-	14.00	101.78	29.35	m³	131.13
Demolishing reinforced concrete wall						
100 mm thick	-	1.20	8.72	2.66	m²	11.38
150 mm thick	-	1.80	13.09	3.98	m²	17.07
225 mm thick	-	2.70	19.63	6.00	m²	25.63
300 mm thick	-	3.60	26.17	8.03	m²	34.20
Demolishing reinforced concrete suspended slabs						
100 mm thick	-	1.00	7.27	2.47	m²	9.74
150 mm thick	-	1.50	10.90	3.60	m²	14.50
225 mm thick	-	2.25	16.36	5.41	m²	21.77
300 mm thick	-	3.00	21.81	7.30	m²	29.11
Breaking up concrete plinth; making good structures	-	4.60	33.44	17.20	m³	50.64
Breaking up precast concrete kerb	-	0.50	3.63	0.55	m	4.18
Removing precast concrete window sill; materials for re-use	-	1.60	11.63	-	m	11.63
Breaking up concrete hearth	-	1.80	13.09	0.92	nr	14.01

C DEMOLITION/ALTERATION/RENOVATION Excluding overheads and profit	PC £	Labour hours	Labour £	Material £	Unit	Total rate £
C20 DEMOLITION - cont'd						
Demolishing parts of structures - cont'd						
Demolishing external brick walls; in gauged mortar						
half brick thick	-	0.70	5.09	1.39	m²	6.48
two half brick thick skins	-	1.20	8.72	2.96	m²	11.68
one brick thick	-	1.20	8.72	2.96	m²	11.68
one and a half brick thick	-	1.70	12.36	4.62	m²	16.98
two brick thick	-	2.20	15.99	5.92	m²	21.91
add for plaster, render or pebbledash per side	-	0.10	0.73	0.28	m²	1.01
Demolishing external brick walls; in cement mortar						
half brick thick	-	1.05	7.63	1.39	m²	9.02
two half brick thick skins	-	1.75	12.72	2.96	m²	15.68
one brick thick	-	1.75	12.72	2.96	m²	15.68
one and a half brick thick	-	2.45	17.81	4.62	m²	22.43
two brick thick	-	3.15	22.90	5.92	m²	28.82
add for plaster, render or pebbledash per side	-	0.10	0.73	0.28	m²	1.01
Demolishing internal partitions; gauged mortar						
half brick thick	-	1.05	7.63	1.39	m²	9.02
one brick thick	-	1.80	13.09	2.96	m²	16.05
one and a half brick thick	-	2.55	18.54	4.62	m²	23.16
75 mm blockwork	-	0.70	5.09	1.02	m²	6.11
90 mm blockwork	-	0.75	5.45	1.20	m²	6.65
100 mm blockwork	-	0.80	5.82	1.39	m²	7.21
115 mm blockwork	-	0.85	6.18	1.39	m²	7.57
125 mm blockwork	-	0.90	6.54	1.48	m²	8.02
140 mm blockwork	-	0.95	6.91	1.57	m²	8.48
150 mm blockwork	-	1.00	7.27	1.76	m²	9.03
190 mm blockwork	-	1.18	8.58	2.22	m²	10.80
215 mm blockwork	-	1.30	9.45	2.40	m²	11.85
255 mm blockwork	-	1.50	10.90	2.87	m²	13.77
add for plaster per side	-	0.10	0.73	0.28	m²	1.01
Demolishing internal partitions; cement mortar						
half brick thick	-	1.60	11.63	1.39	m²	13.02
one brick thick	-	2.65	19.27	2.96	m²	22.23
one and a half brick thick	-	3.70	26.90	4.62	m²	31.52
add for plaster per side	-	0.10	0.73	0.28	m²	1.01
Breaking up brick plinths	-	4.00	29.08	9.25	m³	38.33
Demolishing bund walls or piers in cement mortar						
one brick thick	-	1.40	10.18	2.96	m²	13.14
Demolishing walls to roof ventilator housing						
one brick thick	-	1.60	11.63	2.96	m²	14.59
Demolishing brick chimney to 300 mm below						
roof level; sealing off flues with slates						
680 mm x 680 mm x 900 mm high above roof		12.50	96.08	15.47	nr	111.55
add for each additional 300 height	-	2.50	19.22	2.92	nr	22.14
680 mm x 1030 mm x 900 mm high above roof	-	18.81	144.59	22.52	nr	167.11
add for each additional 300 height	-	3.74	28.72	4.64	nr	33.36
1030 mm x 1030 mm x 900 mm high above roof	-	28.85	221.88	34.74	nr	256.62
add for each additional 300 height	-	5.65	43.50	7.38	nr	50.88
Demolishing brick chimney to 300 mm below						
roof level; sealing off flues with slates; piecing						
in "treated" sawn softwood rafters and making						
good roof coverings over to match existing						
(scaffolding excluded)						
680 mm x 680 mm x 900 mm high above roof	-	-	-	-	nr	145.00
add for each additional 300 mm height	-	-	-	-	nr	24.00
680 mm x 1030 mm x 900 mm high above roof	-	-	-	-	nr	215.00
add for each additional 300 mm height	-	-	-	-	nr	45.00
1030 mm x 1030 mm x 900 mm high above roof	-	-	-	-	nr	320.00
add for each additional 300 mm height	-	-	-	-	nr	105.00

C DEMOLITION/ALTERATION/RENOVATION Excluding overheads and profit	PC £	Labour hours	Labour £	Material £	Unit	Total rate £
Removing existing chimney pot; materials for re-use; demolishing defective chimney stack to roof level; re-building using 25% new facing bricks to match existing; providing new lead flashings; parge and core flues, resetting chimney pots including flaunching in cement:mortar (scaffolding excluded)						
680 mm x 680 mm x 900 mm high above roof	-	-	-	-	nr	330.00
add for each additional 300 mm height	-	-	-	-	nr	52.50
680 mm x 1030 mm x 900 mm high above roof	-	-	-	-	nr	500.00
add for each additional 300 mm height	-	-	-	-	nr	75.00
1030 mm x 1030 mm x 900 mm high above roof	-	-	-	-	nr	735.00
add for each additional 300 mm height	-	-	-	-	nr	110.00
Removing fireplace surround and hearth						
interior tiled	-	1.85	13.45	2.13	nr	15.58
cast iron; materials for re-use	-	3.10	22.54	-	nr	22.54
stone iron; materials for re-use	-	8.10	58.89	-	nr	58.89
Removing fireplace; filling in opening; plastering and extending skirtings; fixing air brick; breaking up hearth and re-screeding						
tiled	-	-	-	-	nr	120.00
cast iron; set aside	-	-	-	-	nr	115.00
stone; set aside	-	-	-	-	nr	190.00
Removing brick-on-edge coping; prepare walls for raising						
one brick thick	-	0.45	6.39	0.18	m	6.57
one and a half brick thick	-	0.60	8.53	0.28	m	8.81
Demolishing external stone walls in lime mortar						
300 mm thick	-	1.20	8.72	2.77	m²	11.49
400 mm thick	-	1.60	11.63	3.70	m²	15.33
600 mm thick	-	2.40	17.45	5.55	m²	23.00
Demolishing stone walls in lime mortar; clean off; set aside for re-use						
300 mm thick	-	1.80	13.09	0.92	m²	14.01
400 mm thick	-	2.40	17.45	1.20	m²	18.65
600 mm thick	-	3.60	26.17	1.85	m²	28.02
Demolishing metal partitions						
corrugated metal partition	-	0.35	2.54	0.28	m²	2.82
lightweight steel mesh security screen	-	0.50	3.63	0.46	m²	4.09
solid steel demountable partition	-	0.75	5.45	0.65	m²	6.10
glazed sheet demountable partition; including removal of glass	-	1.00	7.27	0.92	m²	8.19
Removing metal shutter door and track						
6.20 m x 4.60 m (12.60 m long track)	-	12.00	87.24	13.87	nr	101.11
12.40 m x 4.60 m (16.40 m long track)	-	15.00	109.05	27.74	nr	136.79
Removing roof timbers complete; including rafters, purlins, ceiling joists, plates, etc., (measured flat on plan)	-	0.33	2.72	1.02	m²	3.74
Removing softwood floor construction						
100 mm deep joists at ground level	-	0.25	1.82	0.18	m²	2.00
175 mm deep joists at first floor level	-	0.50	3.63	0.37	m²	4.00
125 mm deep joists at roof level	-	0.70	5.09	0.28	m²	5.37
Removing individual floor or roof members	-	0.27	2.25	0.18	m	2.43
Removing infected or decayed floor plates	-	0.37	3.10	0.18	m	3.28
Removing boarding; withdrawing nails						
25 mm thick softwood flooring; at ground floor level	-	0.37	2.97	0.28	m²	3.25
25 mm thick softwood flooring; at first floor level	-	0.63	5.19	0.28	m²	5.47
25 mm thick softwood roof boarding	-	0.74	6.11	0.28	m²	6.39
25 mm thick softwood gutter boarding	-	0.80	6.63	0.28	m²	6.91
22 mm thick chipboard flooring; at first floor level	-	0.37	2.97	0.28	m²	3.25

C DEMOLITION/ALTERATION/RENOVATION Excluding overheads and profit	PC £	Labour hours	Labour £	Material £	Unit	Total rate £
C20 DEMOLITION - cont'd						
Demolishing parts of structures - cont'd						
Removing tilting fillet or roll	-	0.15	1.25	0.09	m	1.34
Removing fascia or barge boards	-	0.60	4.97	0.09	m	5.06
Demolishing softwood stud partitions; including finishings both sides etc						
solid	-	0.45	3.27	0.92	m²	4.19
glazed; including removal of glass	-	0.60	4.36	0.92	m²	5.28
Removing windows and doors; and set aside or clear away						
single door	-	0.40	5.76	0.28	nr	6.04
single door and frame or lining	-	0.80	11.53	0.46	nr	11.99
pair of doors	-	0.70	10.09	0.55	nr	10.64
pair of doors and frame or lining	-	1.20	17.29	0.92	nr	18.21
extra for taking out floor spring box	-	0.75	10.81	0.18	nr	10.99
casement window and frame	-	1.20	17.29	0.46	nr	17.75
double hung sash window and frame	-	1.70	24.50	0.92	nr	25.42
pair of french windows and frame	-	4.00	57.64	1.39	nr	59.03
Removing double hung sash window and frame; remove and store for re-use elsewhere	-	2.40	34.58	-	nr	34.58
Demolishing staircase; including balustrades						
single straight flight	-	3.50	50.44	9.25	m	59.69
dogleg flight	-	5.00	72.05	13.87	m	85.92
C30 SHORING/FACADE RETENTION						
NOTE: The requirements for shoring and strutting for the formation of large openings are dependant upon a number of factors, for example, the weight of the superimposed structure to be supported, the number (if any) of windows above, the number of floors and the type of roof to be strutted, whether raking shores are required, the depth to a load- bearing surface, and the duration the support is to be in place. Prices, would therefore, be best built-up by assessing the use and waste of materials and the labour involved, including getting timber from and returning to a yard, cutting away and making good, overhead and profit. This method is considered a more practical way of pricing than endeavouring to price the work on a cubic metre basis of timber used, and has been adopted in preparing the prices of the examples which follow.						
Support of structures not to be demolished						
Strutting to window openings over proposed new openings	-	0.60	6.80	4.78	nr	11.58
Plates, struts, braces and hardwood wedges in supports to floors and roof of opening	-	1.20	13.61	13.99	nr	27.60
Dead shore and needle using die square timber with sole plates, braces, hardwood wedges and steel dogs	-	30.00	340.20	58.33	nr	398.53
Set of two raking shores using die square timber with 50 mm thick wall piece; hardwood wedges and steel dogs; including forming holes for needles and making good	-	36.00	408.24	58.90	nr	467.14
Cut holes through one brick wall for die square needle and make good; including facings externally and plaster internally	-	5.90	83.88	1.01	nr	84.89

C DEMOLITION/ALTERATION/RENOVATION Excluding overheads and profit	PC £	Labour hours	Labour £	Material £	Unit	Total rate £
C41 REPAIRING/RENOVATING/CONSERVING MASONRY						
Repairing/renovating plain/reinforced concrete work						
Reinstating plain concrete bed with site mixed in situ concrete; mix 20.00 N/mm² - 20 mm aggregate (1:2:4), where opening no longer required						
100 mm thick	-	0.48	4.20	7.00	m²	**11.20**
150 mm thick	-	0.78	6.38	10.49	m²	**16.87**
Reinstating reinforced concrete bed with site mixed in situ concrete; mix 20.00 N/mm² - 20 mm aggregate (1:2:4); including mesh reinforcement; where opening no longer required						
100 mm thick	-	0.71	5.87	8.92	m²	**14.79**
150 mm thick	-	0.98	7.83	12.42	m²	**20.25**
Reinstating reinforced concrete suspended floor with site mixed in situ concrete; mix 25.00 N/mm² - 20 mm aggregate (1:1.5:3); including mesh reinforcement and formwork; where opening no longer required						
150 mm thick	-	3.20	27.59	16.64	m²	**44.23**
225 mm thick	-	3.75	27.26	22.61	m²	**49.87**
300 mm thick	-	4.15	30.17	29.43	m²	**59.60**
Reinstating 150 mm x 150 mm x 150 mm perforation through concrete suspended slab; with site mixed in situ concrete; mix 20.00 N/mm² - 20 mm aggregate (1:2:4); including formwork; where opening no longer required	-	0.92	6.69	0.10	nr	**6.79**
Cleaning surfaces of concrete to receive new damp proof membrane	-	0.15	1.09	-	m²	**1.09**
Cleaning out existing minor crack and fill in with cement mortar mixed with bonding agent	-	0.33	2.40	0.60	m	**3.00**
Cleaning out existing crack to form 20 mm x 20 mm groove and fill in with fine cement mixed with bonding agent	-	0.66	4.80	2.60	m	**7.40**
Making good hole where existing pipe removed; 150 mm deep						
50 mm diameter	-	0.42	3.05	0.41	nr	**3.46**
100 mm diameter	-	0.55	4.00	0.50	nr	**4.50**
150 mm diameter	-	0.70	5.09	0.66	nr	**5.75**
Add for each additional 25 mm thick up to 300 mm thick						
50 mm diameter	-	0.09	0.65	0.07	nr	**0.72**
100 mm diameter	-	0.12	0.87	0.10	nr	**0.97**
150 mm diameter	-	0.15	1.09	0.13	nr	**1.22**
Repairing/renovating brick/blockwork						
Cutting out decayed, defective or cracked work and replacing with new common bricks PC £175.00/1000; in gauged mortar (1:1:6)						
half brick thick	-	5.25	74.60	14.07	m²	**88.67**
one brick thick	0.17	9.60	136.42	29.36	m²	**165.78**
one and a half brick thick	0.17	13.60	193.26	44.65	m²	**237.91**
two brick thick	0.17	17.40	247.25	59.94	m²	**307.19**
individual bricks; half brick thick	-	0.30	4.26	0.25	nr	**4.51**

C DEMOLITION/ALTERATION/RENOVATION Excluding overheads and profit	PC £	Labour hours	Labour £	Material £	Unit	Total rate £
C41 REPAIRING/RENOVATING/CONSERVING MASONRY - cont'd						
Repairing/renovating brick/blockwork - cont'd Cutting out decayed, defective or cracked work and replacing with new facing brickwork in gauged mortar (1:1:6); half brick thick; facing and pointing one side						
small areas; machine made facings PC £330.00/1000	0.33	7.30	103.73	25.14	m²	128.87
small areas; hand made facings PC £540.00/1000	0.54	7.30	103.73	39.36	m²	143.09
individual bricks; machine made facings PC £330.00/1000	0.33	0.45	6.39	0.42	nr	6.81
individual bricks; hand made facings PC £540.00/1000	0.54	0.45	6.39	0.64	nr	7.03
ADD or DEDUCT for variation of £10.00/1000 in PC of facing bricks; in flemish bond						
half brick thick	-	-	-	0.65	m²	0.65
Cutting out decayed, defective or cracked soldier arch and replacing with new; repointing to match existing						
machine made facings PC £330.00/1000	0.33	1.95	27.71	6.13	m	33.84
hand made facings PC £540.00/1000	0.54	1.95	27.71	9.75	m	37.46
Cutting out decayed, defective or cracked work in uncoursed stonework; replacing with cement mortar to match existing						
small areas; 300 mm thick wall	-	5.60	79.58	11.47	m²	91.05
small areas; 400 mm thick wall	-	7.00	99.47	15.51	m²	114.98
small areas; 600 mm thick wall	-	10.00	142.10	23.61	m²	165.71
Cutting out staggered cracks and repointing to match existing along brick joints	-	0.40	5.68	-	m	5.68
Cutting out raking cracks in brickwork; stitching in new common bricks and repointing to match existing						
half brick thick	0.17	3.20	45.47	6.49	m²	51.96
one brick thick	0.17	5.85	83.13	13.57	m²	96.70
one and a half brick thick	0.17	8.75	124.34	20.06	m²	144.40
Cutting out raking cracks in brickwork; stitching in new facing bricks; half brick thick; facing and pointing one side to match existing						
machine made facings PC £330.00/1000	0.33	4.80	68.21	10.93	m²	79.14
hand made facings PC £540.00/1000	0.54	4.80	68.21	17.02	m²	85.23
Cutting out raking cracks in cavity brickwork; stitching in new common bricks PC £175.00/1000 one side; facing bricks the other side; both skins half brick thick; facing and pointing one side to match existing						
machine made facings PC £330.00/1000	0.33	8.20	116.52	17.36	m²	133.88
hand made facings PC £540.00/1000	0.54	8.20	116.52	23.45	m²	139.97
Cutting away and replacing with new cement mortar (1:3); angle fillets; 50 mm face width	-	0.25	3.55	1.82	m	5.37

C DEMOLITION/ALTERATION/RENOVATION Excluding overheads and profit	PC £	Labour hours	Labour £	Material £	Unit	Total rate £
Cutting out ends of joists and plates from walls; making good in common bricks PC £175.00/1000; in cement mortar (1:3)						
175 mm deep joists; 400 mm centres	-	0.65	9.24	4.81	m	**14.05**
225 mm deep joists; 400 mm centres	-	0.80	11.37	5.57	m	**16.94**
Cutting and pinning to existing brickwork ends of joists	-	0.40	5.68	-	nr	**5.68**
Making good adjacent work; where intersecting wall removed						
half brick thick	-	0.30	4.26	0.61	m	**4.87**
one brick thick	-	0.40	5.68	1.22	m	**6.90**
100 blockwork	-	0.25	3.55	0.61	m	**4.16**
150 blockwork	-	0.29	4.12	0.61	m	**4.73**
215 blockwork	-	0.35	4.97	1.22	m	**6.19**
255 blockwork	-	0.39	5.54	1.22	m	**6.76**
Removing defective parapet wall; 600 mm high; with two courses of tiles and brick coping over; re-building in new facing bricks, tiles and coping stones						
one brick thick	-	6.66	94.64	42.71	m	**137.35**
Removing defective capping stones and haunching; replacing stones and re-haunching in cement mortar to match existing						
300 mm thick wall	-	1.35	19.18	3.37	m²	**22.55**
400 mm thick wall	-	1.50	21.32	4.05	m²	**25.37**
600 mm thick wall	-	1.75	24.87	6.07	m²	**30.94**
Cleaning surfaces; moss and lichen from walls	-	0.30	2.18	-	m²	**2.18**
Cleaning surfaces; lime mortar off brickwork; sort and stack for re-use	-	10.00	72.70	-	t	**72.70**
Repointing in cement mortar (1:1:6); to match existing						
raking out existing decayed joints in brickwork walls	-	0.75	10.66	0.61	m²	**11.27**
raking out existing decayed joints in chimney stacks	-	1.20	17.05	0.61	m²	**17.66**
raking out existing decayed joints in brickwork; re-wedging horizontal flashing	-	0.25	3.55	0.30	m	**3.85**
raking out existing decayed joints in brickwork; re-wedging stepped flashing	-	0.37	5.26	0.30	m	**5.56**
Repointing in cement mortar (1:3); to match existing						
raking out existing decayed joints in uncoursed stonework	-	1.20	17.05	0.67	m²	**17.72**
Making good hole where small pipe removed						
102 mm brickwork	-	0.20	1.45	0.07	nr	**1.52**
215 mm brickwork	-	0.20	1.45	0.07	nr	**1.52**
327 mm brickwork	-	0.20	1.45	0.07	nr	**1.52**
440 mm brickwork	-	0.20	1.45	0.07	nr	**1.52**
100 mm blockwork	-	0.20	1.45	0.07	nr	**1.52**
150 mm blockwork	-	0.20	1.45	0.07	nr	**1.52**
215 mm blockwork	-	0.20	1.45	0.07	nr	**1.52**
255 mm blockwork	-	0.20	1.45	0.07	nr	**1.52**
Making good hole and facings one side where small pipe removed						
102 mm brickwork	-	0.20	2.84	0.67	nr	**3.51**
215 mm brickwork	-	0.20	2.84	0.67	nr	**3.51**
327 mm brickwork	-	0.20	2.84	0.67	nr	**3.51**
440 mm brickwork	-	0.20	2.84	0.67	nr	**3.51**

C DEMOLITION/ALTERATION/RENOVATION Excluding overheads and profit	PC £	Labour hours	Labour £	Material £	Unit	Total rate £
C41 REPAIRING/RENOVATING/CONSERVING MASONRY - cont'd						
Repairing/renovating brick/blockwork - cont'd						
Making good hole where large pipe removed						
102 mm brickwork	-	0.30	2.18	0.07	nr	**2.25**
215 mm brickwork	-	0.45	3.27	0.24	nr	**3.51**
327 mm brickwork	-	0.60	4.36	0.40	nr	**4.76**
440 mm brickwork	-	0.75	5.45	0.51	nr	**5.96**
100 mm blockwork	-	0.30	2.18	0.07	nr	**2.25**
150 mm blockwork	-	0.35	2.54	0.13	nr	**2.67**
215 mm blockwork	-	0.40	2.91	0.17	nr	**3.08**
255 mm blockwork	-	0.45	3.27	0.24	nr	**3.51**
Making good hole and facings one side where large pipe removed						
half brick thick	-	0.27	3.84	0.67	nr	**4.51**
one brick thick	-	0.36	5.12	0.74	nr	**5.86**
one and a half brick thick	-	0.45	6.39	0.81	nr	**7.20**
two brick thick	-	0.54	7.67	1.08	nr	**8.75**
Making good hole where extra large pipe removed						
half brick thick	-	0.40	2.91	0.27	nr	**3.18**
one brick thick	-	0.60	4.36	0.57	nr	**4.93**
one and a half brick thick	-	0.80	5.82	1.01	nr	**6.83**
two brick thick	-	1.00	7.27	1.21	nr	**8.48**
100 mm blockwork	-	0.40	2.91	0.27	nr	**3.18**
150 mm blockwork	-	0.45	3.27	0.40	nr	**3.67**
215 mm blockwork	-	0.50	3.63	0.57	nr	**4.20**
255 mm blockwork	-	0.55	4.00	0.70	nr	**4.70**
Making good hole and facings one side where extra large pipe removed						
half brick thick	-	0.36	5.12	1.05	nr	**6.17**
one brick thick	-	0.48	6.82	1.28	nr	**8.10**
one and a half brick thick	-	0.60	8.53	1.62	nr	**10.15**
two brick thick	-	0.72	10.23	2.19	nr	**12.42**
C50 REPAIRING/RENOVATING/CONSERVING METAL						
Repairing metal						
Overhauling and repairing metal casement windows; adjusting and oiling ironmongery; bringing forward affected parts for redecoration	-	1.50	10.90	2.50	nr	**13.40**
C51 REPAIRING/RENOVATING/CONSERVING TIMBER						
Repairing timber						
Removing or punching in projecting nails; re-fixing softwood or hardwood flooring						
loose boards	-	0.15	1.70	-	m²	**1.70**
floorboards previously set aside	-	0.80	9.07	0.32	m²	**9.39**
Removing damaged softwood flooring; providing and fixing new 25 mm thick plain edge softwood boarding						
small areas	-	1.15	13.04	14.66	m²	**27.70**
individual boards 150 mm wide	-	0.30	3.40	1.46	m	**4.86**
Sanding down and resurfacing existing flooring; preparing, bodying in with shellac and wax polish						
softwood	-	-	-	-	m²	**8.72**
hardwood	-	-	-	-	m²	**8.21**

C DEMOLITION/ALTERATION/RENOVATION Excluding overheads and profit	PC £	Labour hours	Labour £	Material £	Unit	Total rate £
Fitting existing softwood skirting to new frames or architraves						
75 mm high	-	0.10	1.13	-	m	1.13
150 mm high	-	0.13	1.47	-	m	1.47
225 mm high	-	0.16	1.81	-	m	1.81
Piecing in new 25 mm x 150 mm moulded softwood skirtings to match existing where old removed; bringing forward for redecoration	-	0.38	3.63	3.42	m	7.05
Piecing in new 25 mm x 150 mm moulded softwood skirtings to match existing where socket outlet removed; bringing forward for redecoration	-	0.22	2.09	1.87	nr	3.96
Easing and adjusting softwood doors, oiling ironmongery; bringing forward affected parts for redecoration	-	0.77	8.33	0.43	nr	8.76
Removing softwood doors, easing and adjusting; re-hanging; oiling ironmongery; bringing forward affected parts for redecoration	-	1.20	13.10	0.57	nr	13.67
Removing mortice lock, piecing in softwood doors; bringing forward affected parts for redecoration	-	1.10	12.14	0.38	nr	12.52
Fixing only salvaged softwood door	-	1.60	18.14	-	nr	18.14
Removing softwood doors; planing 12 mm from bottom edge; re-hanging	-	1.20	13.61	-	nr	13.61
Removing softwood doors; altering ironmongery; piecing in and rebating frame and door; re-hanging on opposite stile; bringing forward affected parts for redecoration	-	2.65	29.21	0.75	nr	29.96
Removing softwood doors to prepare for fire upgrading; removing ironmongery; replacing existing beads with 25 mm x 38 mm hardwood screwed beads; repairing minor damaged areas; re-hanging on wider butt hinges; adjusting all ironmongery; sealing around frame in cement mortar; bringing forward affected parts for redecoration (replacing glass panes not included)	-	5.35	59.49	18.21	nr	77.70
Upgrading and facing up one side of flush doors with 9 mm thick "Supalux" or other equal and approved; screwing	-	1.25	14.18	32.64	nr	46.82
Upgrading and facing up one side of softwood panelled doors with 9 mm thick "Supalux" or other equal and approved; screwing; plasterboard infilling to recesses	-	2.70	30.62	34.50	nr	65.12
Taking off existing softwood doorstops; providing and screwing on new 25 mm x 38 mm doorstop; bringing forward for redecoration	-	0.22	2.09	1.58	nr	3.67
Cutting away defective 75 mm x 100 mm softwood external door frames; providing and splicing in new piece 300 mm long; bedding in cement mortar (1:3); pointing one side; bringing forward for redecoration	-	1.40	15.20	6.06	nr	21.26
Sealing roof trap flush with ceiling	-	0.60	6.80	2.60	nr	9.40
Easing and adjusting softwood casement windows, oiling ironmongery; bringing forward affected parts for redecoration	-	0.52	5.49	0.29	nr	5.78

C DEMOLITION/ALTERATION/RENOVATION Excluding overheads and profit	PC £	Labour hours	Labour £	Material £	Unit	Total rate £
C51 REPAIRING/RENOVATING/CONSERVING **TIMBER** - cont'd						
Repairing timber - cont'd						
Removing softwood casement windows; easing and adjusting; re-hanging; oiling ironmongery; bringing forward affected parts for redecoration	-	0.77	8.33	0.29	nr	8.62
Renewing solid mullion jambs or transoms of softwood casement windows to match existing; bringing forward affected parts for redecoration (taking off and re-hanging adjoining casements not included)	-	2.80	30.74	12.14	nr	42.88
Temporary linings 6 mm thick plywood infill to window while casement under repair	-	0.80	9.07	4.80	nr	13.87
Overhauling softwood double hung sash windows; easing, adjusting and oiling pulley wheels; re-hanging sashes on new hemp sash lines; re-assembling; bringing forward affected parts for redecoration	-	2.65	29.54	3.49	nr	33.03
Cutting away defective parts of softwood window sills; providing and splicing in new 75 mm x 100 mm weathered and throated pieces 300 mm long; bringing forward affected parts for redecoration	-	2.05	22.74	6.64	nr	29.38
Renewing broken stair nosings to treads or landings	-	1.80	20.41	2.63	nr	23.04
Cutting out infected or decayed structural members; shoring up adjacent work; providing and fixing new "treated" sawn softwood members pieced in						
Floors or flat roofs						
50 mm x 125 mm	-	0.40	4.54	1.96	m	6.50
50 mm x 150 mm	-	0.44	4.99	2.38	m	7.37
50 mm x 175 mm	-	0.48	5.44	2.77	m	8.21
Pitched roofs						
38 mm x 100 mm	-	0.36	4.08	1.19	m	5.27
50 mm x 100 mm	-	0.45	5.10	1.52	m	6.62
50 mm x 125 mm	-	0.50	5.67	1.88	m	7.55
50 mm x 150 mm	-	0.55	6.24	2.26	m	8.50
Kerbs bearers and the like						
50 mm x 75 mm	-	0.45	5.10	1.18	m	6.28
50 mm x 100 mm	-	0.56	6.35	1.52	m	7.87
75 mm x 100 mm	-	0.68	7.71	2.15	m	9.86
Scarfed joint; new to existing; over 450 mm^2	-	1.00	11.34	-	nr	11.34
Scarfed and bolted joint; new to existing; including bolt let in flush; over 450 mm^2	-	1.66	18.82	1.10	nr	19.92
C52 FUNGUS/BEETLE ERADICATION						
Treating existing timber						
Removing cobwebs, dust and roof insulation; de-frass; treat exposed joists/rafters with two coats of proprietary insecticide and fungicide; by spray application	-	-	-	-	m^2	6.90
Treating boarding with two coats of proprietary insecticide and fungicide; by spray application	-	-	-	-	m^2	3.00
Treating individual timbers with two coats proprietary insecticide and fungicide; by brush application						
boarding	-	-	-	-	m^2	3.35
structural members	-	-	-	-	m^2	3.35
skirtings	-	-	-	-	m	3.35

C DEMOLITION/ALTERATION/RENOVATION Excluding overheads and profit	PC £	Labour hours	Labour £	Material £	Unit	Total rate £
Lifting necessary floorboards; treating floors with two coats proprietary insecticide and fungicide; by spray application; re-fixing boards	-	-	-	-	m²	5.50
Treating surfaces of adjoining concrete or brickwork with two coats of dry rot fluid; by spray application	-	-	-	-	m²	2.90

C90 ALTERATIONS - SPOT ITEMS

Composite "spot" items

NOTE: Few exactly similar composite items of alteration works are encountered on different schemes; for this reason it is considered more accurate for the reader to build up the value of such items from individual prices in the following section. However, for estimating purposes, the following "spot" items have been prepared. Prices include for removal of debris from site but do not include for shoring, scaffolding or re-decoration, except where stated.

Removing fittings and fixtures						
Removing shelves, window boards and the like	-	0.33	2.40	0.09	m	2.49
Removing handrails and balustrades						
tubular handrailing and brackets	-	0.30	2.18	0.09	m	2.27
metal balustrades	-	0.50	3.63	0.28	m	3.91
Removing handrails and brackets	-	0.10	1.44	0.28	m	1.72
Removing sloping timber ramps in corridors; at changes of levels	-	2.00	28.82	1.39	nr	30.21
Removing bath panels and bearers	-	0.40	5.76	0.46	nr	6.22
Removing kitchen fittings						
wall units	-	0.45	6.48	1.39	nr	7.87
floor units	-	0.30	4.32	2.03	nr	6.35
larder units	-	0.40	5.76	4.62	nr	10.38
built-in cupboards	-	1.50	21.61	9.25	nr	30.86
Removing bathroom fittings; making good works disturbed						
toilet roll holder or soap dispenser	-	0.30	2.18	-	nr	2.18
towel holder	-	0.60	4.36	-	nr	4.36
mirror	-	0.65	4.73	-	nr	4.73
Removing pipe casings	-	0.30	4.32	0.37	m	4.69
Removing ironmongery; in preparation for re-decoration; and subsequently re-fixing; including providing any new screws necessary	-	0.25	3.60	0.09	nr	3.69
Removing, withdrawing nails, etc; making good holes						
carpet fixing strip from floors	-	0.05	0.36	-	m	0.36
curtain track from head of window	-	0.25	1.82	-	m	1.82
nameplates or numerals from face of door	-	0.50	3.63	-	nr	3.63
fly screen and frame from window	-	0.90	6.54	-	nr	6.54
small notice board and frame from walls	PC	0.89	6.47	-	nr	6.47
fire extinguisher and bracket from walls	-	1.25	9.09	-	nr	9.09
Removing plumbing and engineering installations						
Removing sanitary fittings and supports; temporarily capping off services; to receive new (not included)						
sink or lavatory basin	-	1.00	8.81	5.55	nr	14.36
bath	-	2.00	17.62	8.32	nr	25.94
WC suite	-	1.50	13.21	5.55	nr	18.76

C DEMOLITION/ALTERATION/RENOVATION Excluding overheads and profit	PC £	Labour hours	Labour £	Material £	Unit	Total rate £
C90 ALTERATIONS - SPOT ITEMS - cont'd						
Removing plumbing and engineering installations - cont'd						
Removing sanitary fittings and supports, complete with associated services, overflows and waste pipes; making good all holes and other works disturbed; bringing forward all surfaces ready for re-decoration						
sink or lavatory basin	-	4.00	35.24	7.70	nr	42.94
range of three lavatory basins	-	8.00	70.48	13.69	nr	84.17
bath	-	6.00	52.86	10.38	nr	63.24
WC suite	-	8.00	70.48	16.29	nr	86.77
2 stall urinal	-	16.00	140.96	14.77	nr	155.73
3 stall urinal	-	24.00	211.44	28.87	nr	240.31
4 stall urinal	-	32.00	281.92	42.75	nr	324.67
Removing taps	-	0.10	1.03	-	nr	1.03
Clearing blocked wastes without dismantling						
sinks	-	0.50	5.29	-	nr	5.29
WC traps	-	0.60	6.34	-	nr	6.34
Removing gutterwork and supports						
uPVC or asbestos	-	0.30	2.18	0.09	m	2.27
cast iron	-	0.35	2.54	0.18	m	2.72
Overhauling sections of rainwater gutterings; cutting out existing joints; adjusting brackets to correct falls; re-making joints						
100 mm diameter uPVC	-	0.25	2.83	0.02	m	2.85
100 mm diameter cast iron including bolt	-	0.90	10.21	0.07	m	10.28
Removing rainwater heads and supports						
uPVC or asbestos	-	0.29	2.11	0.09	nr	2.20
cast iron	-	0.40	2.91	0.18	nr	3.09
Removing pipework and supports						
uPVC or asbestos rainwater stack	-	0.30	2.18	0.09	m	2.27
cast iron rainwater stack	-	0.35	2.54	0.18	m	2.72
cast iron jointed soil stack	-	0.60	4.36	0.18	m	4.54
copper or steel water or gas pipework	-	0.15	1.09	0.09	m	1.18
cast iron rainwater shoe	-	0.08	0.58	0.09	m	0.67
Overhauling and re-making leaking joints in pipework						
100 mm diameter upvc	-	0.20	1.45	0.05	nr	1.50
100 mm diameter cast iron including bolt	-	0.80	5.82	0.15	nr	5.97
Cleaning out existing rainwater installations						
rainwater gutters	-	0.08	0.58	-	m	0.58
rainwater gully	-	0.20	1.45	-	nr	1.45
rainwater stack; including head, swan-neck and shoe (not exceeding 10 m long)	-	0.75	5.45	-	nr	5.45
Removing the following equipment and ancillaries; capping off services; making good works disturbed (excluding any draining down of system)						
expansion tank; 900 mm x 450 mm x 900 mm	-	1.80	15.86	3.70	nr	19.56
hot water cylinder; 450 mm diameter x 1050 mm high	-	1.20	10.57	1.57	nr	12.14
cold water tank; 1540 mm x 900 mm x 900 mm	-	2.40	21.14	11.37	nr	32.51
cast iron radiator	-	2.00	17.62	2.96	nr	20.58
gas water heater	-	4.00	35.24	1.85	nr	37.09
gas fire	-	2.00	17.62	2.40	nr	20.02
Removing cold water tanks and housing on roof; stripping out and capping off all associated piping; making good works disturbed and roof finishings						
1540 mm x 900 mm x 900 mm	-	12.00	105.72	14.15	nr	119.87

C DEMOLITION/ALTERATION/RENOVATION Excluding overheads and profit	PC £	Labour hours	Labour £	Material £	Unit	Total rate £
Turning off supplies; dismantling the following fittings; replacing washers; re-assembling and testing						
15 mm diameter tap	-	0.25	2.64	-	nr	**2.64**
15 mm diameter ball valve	-	0.35	3.70	-	nr	**3.70**
Turning off supplies; removing the following fittings; testing and replacing						
15 mm diameter ball valve	-	0.50	5.29	5.75	nr	**11.04**
Removing lagging from pipes						
up to 42 mm diameter	-	0.10	0.73	0.09	nr	**0.82**
Removing finishings						
Removing plasterboard wall finishings	-	0.40	2.91	-	m²	**2.91**
Removing wall finishings; cutting out and making good cracks						
plasterboard wall finishing	-	0.40	2.91	-	m²	**2.91**
decorative wallpaper and lining	-	0.21	1.53	0.15	m²	**1.68**
heavy wallpaper and lining	-	0.34	2.47	0.15	m²	**2.62**
Hacking off wall finishings						
plaster	-	0.20	1.45	0.46	m²	**1.91**
cement rendering or pebbledash	-	0.40	2.91	0.46	m²	**3.37**
wall tiling and screed	-	0.50	3.63	0.74	m²	**4.37**
Removing wall linings; including battening behind						
plain sheeting	-	0.30	2.18	0.37	m²	**2.55**
matchboarding	-	0.40	2.91	0.55	m²	**3.46**
Removing oak dado wall panel finishings; cleaning off and setting aside for re-use	-	0.65	9.37	-	m²	**9.37**
Removing defective or damaged plaster wall finishings; re-plastering walls with two coats of gypsum plaster; including dubbing out; jointing new to existing						
small areas	-	1.60	17.90	4.46	m²	**22.36**
isolated areas not exceeding 0.50 m²	-	1.15	12.87	2.23	nr	**15.10**
Making good plaster wall finishings with two coats of gypsum plaster where wall or partition removed; dubbing out; trimming back existing and fair jointing to new work						
150 mm wide	-	0.65	7.27	0.67	m	**7.94**
225 mm wide	-	0.80	8.95	1.00	m	**9.95**
300 mm wide	-	0.95	10.63	1.34	m	**11.97**
Removing defective or damaged damp plaster wall finishings, investigating and treating wall; re-plastering walls with two coats of "Thistle Renovating" plaster; including dubbing out; fair jointing to existing work						
small areas	-	1.70	19.02	3.90	m²	**22.92**
isolated areas not exceeding 0.50 m²	-	1.22	13.65	1.95	m²	**15.60**
Dubbing out in cement:sand; average 13 mm thick						
over 300 mm wide	-	0.50	5.59	0.88	m²	**6.47**
Making good plaster wall finishings with plasterboard and skim where wall or partition removed; trimming back existing and fair joint to new work						
150 mm wide	-	0.75	8.39	1.38	m	**9.77**
225 mm wide	-	0.90	10.07	1.60	m	**11.67**
300 mm wide	-	1.00	11.19	1.81	m	**13.00**
Cutting out; making good cracks in plaster wall finishings						
walls	-	0.25	2.80	0.15	m	**2.95**
ceilings	-	0.33	3.69	0.15	m	**3.84**

C DEMOLITION/ALTERATION/RENOVATION Excluding overheads and profit	PC £	Labour hours	Labour £	Material £	Unit	Total rate £
C90 ALTERATIONS - SPOT ITEMS - cont'd						
Removing finishings - cont'd						
Making good plaster wall finishings where						
items removed or holes left						
small pipe or conduit	-	0.07	0.78	0.07	nr	0.85
large pipe	-	0.10	1.12	0.15	nr	1.27
extra large pipe	-	0.15	1.68	0.69	nr	2.37
small recess; eg. electrical switch point	-	0.08	0.90	0.14	nr	1.04
Making good plasterboard and skim wall						
finishings where items removed or holes left						
small pipe or conduit	-	0.07	0.78	0.07	nr	0.85
large pipe	-	0.23	2.57	0.50	nr	3.07
extra large pipe	-	0.30	3.36	0.64	nr	4.00
Removing floor finishings						
carpet and underfelt	-	0.12	0.87	-	m²	0.87
linoleum sheet flooring	-	0.10	0.73	-	m²	0.73
carpet gripper	-	0.03	0.22	-	m	0.22
Removing floor finishings; preparing screed to						
receive new						
carpet and underfelt	-	0.66	4.80	-	m²	4.80
vinyl or thermoplastic tiles	-	0.85	6.18	-	m²	6.18
Removing woodblock floor finishings; cleaning						
off and setting aside for re-use	-	0.75	5.45	-	m²	5.45
Breaking up floor finishings						
floor screed	-	0.65	4.73	-	m²	4.73
granolithic flooring and screed	-	0.85	6.18	-	m²	6.18
terrazzo or ceramic floor tiles and screed	-	1.05	7.63	-	m²	7.63
Levelling and repairing floor finishings screed;						
5 mm thick						
screed; 5 mm thick; in small areas	-	0.50	5.59	5.98	m²	11.57
screed; 5 mm thick; in isolated areas not						
exceeding 0.50 m²	-	0.35	3.92	2.99	m²	6.91
Removing softwood skirtings, picture rails,						
dado rails, architraves and the like	-	0.10	0.73	-	m	0.73
Removing softwood skirtings; cleaning off and						
setting aside for re-use in making good	-	0.25	1.82	-	m	1.82
Breaking up paving						
asphalt	-	0.60	4.36	-	m²	4.36
Removing ceiling finishings						
plasterboard and skim; withdrawing nails	-	0.30	2.18	0.28	m²	2.46
wood lath and plaster; withdrawing nails	-	0.50	3.63	0.46	m²	4.09
suspended ceilings	-	0.75	5.45	0.46	m²	5.91
plaster moulded cornice; 25 mm girth	-	0.15	1.09	0.09	m	1.18
Removing part of plasterboard ceiling						
finishings to facilitate insertion of new steel						
beam	-	1.10	8.00	0.55	m	8.55
Removing ceiling linings; including battening						
behind						
plain sheeting	-	0.45	3.27	0.37	m²	3.64
matchboarding	-	0.60	4.36	0.55	m²	4.91
Removing defective or damaged ceiling plaster						
finishings; removing laths or cutting back						
boarding; preparing and fixing new						
plasterboard; applying one skim coat of						
gypsum plaster; fair jointing new to existing						
small areas	-	1.70	19.02	3.88	m²	22.90
isolated areas not exceeding 0.50 m²	-	1.22	13.65	2.15	m²	15.80

C DEMOLITION/ALTERATION/RENOVATION Excluding overheads and profit	PC £	Labour hours	Labour £	Material £	Unit	Total rate £
Removing coverings						
Removing roof coverings						
slates	-	0.50	3.63	0.18	m²	**3.81**
slates; set aside for re-use	-	0.60	4.36	-	m²	**4.36**
nibbed tiles	-	0.40	2.91	0.18	m²	**3.09**
nibbed tiles; set aside for re-use	-	0.50	3.63	-	m²	**3.63**
corrugated asbestos sheeting	-	0.40	2.91	0.18	m²	**3.09**
corrugated metal sheeting	-	0.40	2.91	0.18	m²	**3.09**
underfelt and nails	-	0.05	0.36	0.09	m²	**0.45**
three layer felt roofing; cleaning base off for new						
coverings	-	0.25	1.82	0.18	m²	**2.00**
sheet metal coverings	-	0.50	3.63	0.18	m²	**3.81**
Removing roof coverings; selecting and re-fixing; including providing 25% new; including nails, etc.						
asbestos-free artificial blue/black slates; 500 mm x 250 mm; PC £988.00/1000	-	1.10	15.85	6.73	m²	**22.58**
asbestos-free artificial blue/black slates; 600 mm x 300 mm; PC £1313.00/1000	-	1.00	14.41	5.72	m²	**20.13**
natural slates; Welsh blue 510 mm x 255 mm; PC £2100.00/1000	-	1.20	17.29	10.83	m²	**28.12**
natural slates; Welsh blue 600 mm x 300 mm; PC £4050.00/1000	-	1.05	15.13	13.76	m²	**28.89**
clay plain tiles "Dreadnought" machine made or other equal and approved; 265 mm x 165 mm; PC £230.00/1000	-	1.10	15.85	4.54	m²	**20.39**
concrete interlocking tiles; Marley "Ludlow Major" or other equal and approved; 413 mm x 330 mm; PC £667.00/1000	-	0.70	10.09	2.12	m²	**12.21**
concrete interlocking tiles; Redland "Renown" or other equal and approved; 417 mm x 330 mm; PC £657.00/1000	-	0.70	10.09	2.19	m²	**12.28**
Removing damaged roof coverings in area less than 10 m²; providing and fixing new; including nails, etc.						
asbestos-free artificial blue/black slates; 500 mm x 250 mm; PC £988.00/1000	-	1.35	19.45	21.45	m²	**40.90**
asbestos-free artificial blue/black slates; 600 mm x 300 mm; PC £1313.00/1000	-	1.25	18.01	18.91	m²	**36.92**
natural slates; Welsh blue 510 mm x 255 mm; PC £2100.00/1000	-	1.45	20.89	40.69	m²	**61.58**
natural slates; Welsh blue 600 mm x 300 mm; PC £4050.00/1000	-	1.30	18.73	52.88	m²	**71.61**
clay plain tiles "Dreadnought" machine made or other equal and approved; 265 mm x 165 mm; PC £230.00/1000	-	1.35	19.45	15.49	m²	**34.94**
concrete interlocking tiles; Marley "Ludlow Major" or other equal and approved; 413 mm x 330 mm; PC £667.00/1000	-	0.90	12.97	7.23	m²	**20.20**
concrete interlocking tiles; Redland "Renown" or other equal and approved; 417 mm x 330 mm; PC £657.00/1000	-	0.90	12.97	7.25	m²	**20.22**
Removing individual damaged roof coverings; providing and fixing new; including nails, etc.						
asbestos-free artificial blue/black slates; 500 mm x 250 mm; PC £988.00/1000	-	0.25	3.60	1.31	nr	**4.91**
asbestos-free artificial blue/black slates; 600 mm x 300 mm; PC £1313.00/1000	-	0.25	3.60	1.43	nr	**5.03**
natural slates; Welsh blue 510 mm x 255 mm; PC £2100.00/1000	-	0.30	4.32	2.25	nr	**6.57**
natural slates; Welsh blue 600 mm x 300 mm; PC £4050.00/1000	-	0.30	4.32	4.28	nr	**8.60**

C DEMOLITION/ALTERATION/RENOVATION Excluding overheads and profit	PC £	Labour hours	Labour £	Material £	Unit	Total rate £
C90 ALTERATIONS - SPOT ITEMS - cont'd						
Removing coverings - cont'd						
Removing individual damaged roof coverings;						
providing and fixing new; including nails, etc. - cont'd						
clay plain tiles "Dreadnought" machine made						
or other equal and approved; 265 mm x 165						
mm; PC £230.00/1000	-	0.15	2.16	0.26	nr	2.42
concrete interlocking tiles; Marley "Ludlow						
Major" or other equal and approved; 413 mm						
x 330 mm; PC £667.00/1000	-	0.20	2.88	0.72	nr	3.60
concrete interlocking tiles; Redland "Renown"						
or other equal and approved; 417 mm x 330						
mm; PC £657.00/1000	-	0.20	2.88	0.71	nr	3.59
Breaking up roof coverings						
asphalt	-	1.00	7.27	-	m²	7.27
Removing half round ridge or hip tile 300 mm						
long; providing and fixing new	-	0.50	7.21	3.18	nr	10.39
Removing defective metal flashings						
horizontal	-	0.20	1.45	0.18	m	1.63
stepped	-	0.25	1.82	0.09	m	1.91
Turning back bitumen felt and later dressing up						
face of new brickwork as skirtings; not						
exceeding 150 mm girth	-	1.00	10.84	0.11	m	10.95
Cutting out crack in asphalt roof coverings;						
making good to match existing						
20 mm thick two coat	-	1.65	13.13	-	m	13.13
Removing bitumen felt roof coverings and						
boarding to allow access for work to top of						
walls or beams beneath	-	0.80	5.82	-	m	5.82
Removing tiling battens; withdrawing nails	-	0.08	0.58	0.09	m²	0.67
Examining roof battens; re-nailing where loose;						
providing and fixing 25% new						
25 mm x 50 mm slating battens at 262 mm						
centres	-	0.08	1.15	0.55	m²	1.70
25 mm x 38 mm tiling battens at 100 mm						
centres	-	0.20	2.88	1.41	m²	4.29
Removing roof battens and nails; providing and						
fixing new "treated" softwood battens						
throughout						
25 mm x 50 mm slating battens at 262 mm						
centres	-	0.12	1.73	1.94	m²	3.67
25 mm x 38 mm tiling battens at 100 mm						
centres	-	0.25	3.60	4.30	m²	7.90
Removing underfelt and nails; providing and						
fixing new						
unreinforced felt	0.59	0.10	1.44	0.83	m²	2.27
reinforced felt	1.12	0.10	1.44	1.39	m²	2.83
Cutting openings or recesses						
Cutting openings or recesses through						
reinforced concrete walls						
150 mm thick	-	5.60	49.75	7.48	m²	57.23
225 mm thick	-	7.65	66.62	11.18	m²	77.80
300 mm thick	-	9.75	83.66	15.06	m²	98.72
Cutting openings or recesses through						
reinforced concrete suspended slabs						
150 mm thick	-	4.25	36.79	13.73	m²	50.52
225 mm thick	-	6.30	54.64	13.07	m²	67.71
300 mm thick	-	7.85	67.09	15.96	m²	83.05

C DEMOLITION/ALTERATION/RENOVATION Excluding overheads and profit	PC £	Labour hours	Labour £	Material £	Unit	Total rate £
Cutting openings or recesses through slated, boarded and timbered roof; 700 mm x 1100 mm; for new rooflight; including cutting structure and finishings; trimming timbers in rafters and making good roof coverings (kerb and rooflight not included)	-	-	-	-	nr	275.00
Cutting openings or recesses through brick or block walls or partitions; for lintels or beams above openings; in gauged mortar						
half brick thick	-	2.65	37.66	1.57	m²	39.23
one brick thick	-	4.40	62.52	3.14	m²	65.66
one and a half brick thick	-	6.15	87.39	4.72	m²	92.11
two brick thick	-	7.90	112.26	6.29	m²	118.55
75 mm blockwork	-	1.60	22.74	1.02	m²	23.76
90 mm blockwork	-	1.80	25.58	1.20	m²	26.78
100 mm blockwork	-	1.95	27.71	1.39	m²	29.10
115 mm blockwork	-	2.10	29.84	1.57	m²	31.41
125 mm blockwork	-	2.20	31.26	1.76	m²	33.02
140 mm blockwork	-	2.35	33.39	1.94	m²	35.33
150 mm blockwork	-	2.45	34.81	2.13	m²	36.94
190 mm blockwork	-	2.73	38.79	2.68	m²	41.47
215 mm blockwork	-	2.90	41.21	2.96	m²	44.17
255 mm blockwork	-	3.18	45.19	3.51	m²	48.70
Cutting openings or recesses through brick walls; for lintels or beams above openings; in cement mortar						
half brick thick	-	3.80	54.00	1.57	m²	55.57
one brick thick	-	6.30	89.52	3.14	m²	92.66
one and a half brick thick	-	8.80	125.05	4.72	m²	129.77
two brick thick	-	11.30	160.57	6.29	m²	166.86
Cutting openings or recesses through brick or block walls or partitions; for door or window openings; in gauged mortar						
half brick thick	-	1.35	19.18	1.57	m²	20.75
one brick thick	-	2.20	31.26	3.14	m²	34.40
one and a half brick thick	-	3.05	43.34	4.72	m²	48.06
two brick thick	-	3.95	56.13	6.29	m²	62.42
75 mm blockwork	-	0.80	11.37	1.02	m²	12.39
90 mm blockwork	-	0.92	13.07	1.20	m²	14.27
100 mm blockwork	-	1.00	14.21	1.39	m²	15.60
115 mm blockwork	-	1.06	15.06	1.57	m²	16.63
125 mm blockwork	-	1.10	15.63	1.76	m²	17.39
140 mm blockwork	-	1.16	16.48	1.94	m²	18.42
150 mm blockwork	-	1.20	17.05	2.13	m²	19.18
190 mm blockwork	-	1.32	18.76	2.68	m²	21.44
215 mm blockwork	-	1.45	20.60	2.96	m²	23.56
255 mm blockwork	-	1.60	22.74	3.51	m²	26.25
Cutting openings or recesses through brick or block walls or partitions; for door or window openings; in cement mortar						
half brick thick	-	1.90	27.00	1.57	m²	28.57
one brick thick	-	3.15	44.76	3.14	m²	47.90
one and a half brick thick	-	4.35	61.81	4.72	m²	66.53
two brick thick	-	5.65	80.29	6.29	m²	86.58
Cutting openings or recesses through faced wall 1200 mm x 1200 mm (1.44 m²) for new window; including cutting structure, quoining up jambs, cutting and pinning in suitable precast concrete boot lintel with galvanised steel angle bolted on to support, outer brick soldier course in facing bricks to match existing (new window and frame not included)						
one brick thick wall or two half brick thick skins	-	-	-	-	nr	370.00
one and a half brick thick wall	-	-	-	-	nr	390.00
two brick thick wall	-	-	-	-	nr	425.00

C DEMOLITION/ALTERATION/RENOVATION Excluding overheads and profit	PC £	Labour hours	Labour £	Material £	Unit	Total rate £
C90 ALTERATIONS - SPOT ITEMS - cont'd						
Cutting openings or recesses - cont'd						
Cutting openings or recesses through 100 mm						
thick softwood stud partition including framing						
studwork around, making good boarding and						
any plaster either side and extending floor						
finish through opening (new door and frame not						
included)						
single door and frame	-	-	-	-	nr	195.00
pair of doors and frame	-	-	-	-	nr	255.00
Cutting openings or recesses through internal						
plastered wall for single door and frame;						
including cutting structure, quoining or making						
good jambs, cutting and pinning in suitable						
precast concrete plate lintel(s), making good						
plasterwork up to new frame both sides and						
extending floor finish through new opening						
(new door and frame not included)						
150 mm reinforced concrete wall	-	-	-	-	nr	220.00
225 mm reinforced concrete wall	-	-	-	-	nr	300.00
half brick thick wall	-	-	-	-	nr	205.00
one brick thick wall or two half brick thick skins	-	-	-	-	nr	270.00
one and a half brick thick wall	-	-	-	-	nr	330.00
two brick thick wall	-	-	-	-	nr	400.00
100 mm block wall	-	-	-	-	nr	195.00
215 mm block wall	-	-	-	-	nr	252.00
Cutting openings or recesses through internal						
plastered wall for pair of doors and frame;						
including cutting structure, quoining or making						
good jambs, cutting and pinning in suitable						
precast concrete plate lintel(s), making good						
plasterwork up to new frame both sides and						
extending floor finish through new opening						
(new door and frame not included)						
150 mm reinforced concrete wall	-	-	-	-	nr	315.00
225 mm reinforced concrete wall	-	-	-	-	nr	405.00
half brick thick wall	-	-	-	-	nr	245.00
one brick thick wall or two half brick thick skins	-	-	-	-	nr	335.00
one and a half brick thick wall	-	-	-	-	nr	430.00
two brick thick wall	-	-	-	-	nr	515.00
100 mm block wall	-	-	-	-	nr	230.00
215 mm block wall	-	-	-	-	nr	310.00
Cutting back projections						
Cutting back brick projections flush with						
adjacent wall						
225 mm x 112 mm	-	0.30	4.26	0.09	m	4.35
225 mm x 225 mm	-	0.50	7.11	0.18	m	7.29
337 mm x 112 mm	-	0.70	9.95	0.28	m	10.23
450 mm x 225 mm	-	0.90	12.79	0.37	m	13.16
Cutting back chimney breasts flush with						
adjacent wall						
half brick thick	-	1.75	24.87	2.96	m²	27.83
one brick thick	-	2.35	33.39	4.62	m²	38.01
Filling in openings						
Removing doors and frames; making good						
plaster and skirtings across reveals and						
heads; leaving as blank openings						
single doors	-	-	-	-	nr	85.00
pair of doors	-	-	-	-	nr	95.00

C DEMOLITION/ALTERATION/RENOVATION Excluding overheads and profit	PC £	Labour hours	Labour £	Material £	Unit	Total rate £
Removing doors and frames in 100 mm thick softwood partitions; filling in openings with timber covered on both sides with boarding or lining to match existing; extending skirtings both sides						
single doors	-	-	-	-	nr	125.00
pair of doors	-	-	-	-	nr	170.00
Removing single doors and frames in internal walls; filling in openings with brickwork or blockwork; plastering walls and extending skirtings both sides						
half brick thick	-	-	-	-	nr	140.00
one brick thick	-	-	-	-	nr	200.00
one and a half brick thick	-	-	-	-	nr	250.00
two brick thick	-	-	-	-	nr	310.00
100 mm blockwork	-	-	-	-	nr	115.00
215 mm blockwork	-	-	-	-	nr	170.00
Removing pairs of doors and frames in internal walls; filling in openings with brickwork or blockwork; plastering walls and extend skirtings both sides						
half brick thick	-	-	-	-	nr	230.00
one brick thick	-	-	-	-	nr	320.00
one and a half brick thick	-	-	-	-	nr	415.00
two brick thick	-	-	-	▾	nr	500.00
100 mm blockwork	-	-	-	-	nr	200.00
215 mm blockwork	-	-	-	-	nr	265.00
Removing 825 mm x 1046 mm (1.16 m^2) sliding sash windows and frames in external faced walls; filling in openings with facing brickwork on outside to match existing and common brickwork on inside; plastering internally one brick thick or two half brick thick						
skins	-	-	-	-	nr	190.00
one and a half brick thick	-	-	-	-	nr	210.00
two brick thick	-	-	-	-	nr	245.00
Removing 825 mm x 1406 mm (1.16 m^2) curved headed sliding sashed windows in external stuccoed walls; filling in openings with common bricks; stucco on outside and plastering internally one brick thick or two half brick thick						
skins	-	-	-	-	nr	210.00
one and a half brick thick	-	-	-	-	nr	245.00
two brick thick	-	-	-	-	nr	300.00
Removing 825 mm x 1406 mm (1.16 m^2) curved headed sliding sash windows in external masonry faced brick walls; filling in openings with facing brickwork on outside and common brickwork on inside; plastering internally						
350 mm wall	-	-	-	-	nr	550.00
500 mm wall	-	-	-	-	nr	600.00
600 mm wall	-	-	-	-	nr	660.00

C DEMOLITION/ALTERATION/RENOVATION Excluding overheads and profit	PC £	Labour hours	Labour £	Material £	Unit	Total rate £
C90 ALTERATIONS - SPOT ITEMS - cont'd						
Filling in openings - cont'd						
Quoining up jambs in common bricks; PC						
£175.00/1000; in gauged mortar (1:1:6); as the						
work proceeds						
half brick thick or skin of hollow wall	-	1.00	14.21	3.24	m	17.45
one brick thick	-	1.50	21.32	6.48	m	27.80
one and a half brick thick	-	1.95	27.71	9.72	m	37.43
two brick thick	-	2.40	34.10	11.75	m	45.85
75 mm blockwork	-	0.63	8.95	3.48	m	12.43
90 mm blockwork	-	0.67	9.52	4.17	m	13.69
100 mm blockwork	-	0.70	9.95	4.59	m	14.54
115 mm blockwork	-	0.76	10.80	5.38	m	16.18
125 mm blockwork	-	0.80	11.37	6.10	m	17.47
140 mm blockwork	-	0.86	12.22	7.02	m	19.24
150 mm blockwork	-	0.90	12.79	7.74	m	20.53
190 mm blockwork	-	1.01	14.35	9.40	m	23.75
215 mm blockwork	-	1.08	15.35	10.43	m	25.78
225 mm blockwork	-	1.19	16.91	12.82	m	29.73
Closing at jambs with common brickwork half						
brick thick						
50 mm cavity; including lead-lined hessian						
based vertical damp proof course	-	0.40	5.68	5.44	m	11.12
Quoining up jambs in sand faced facings; PC						
£174.50/1000; in gauged mortar (1:1:6); facing						
and pointing one side to match existing						
half brick thick or skin of hollow wall	-	1.25	17.76	4.29	m	22.05
one brick thick	-	1.50	21.32	8.77	m	30.09
one and a half brick thick	-	2.30	32.68	13.01	m	45.69
two brick thick	-	2.80	39.79	17.35	m	57.14
Quoining up jambs in machine made facings;						
PC £330.00/1000; in gauged mortar (1:1:6);						
facing and pointing one side to match existing						
half brick thick or skin of hollow wall	-	1.25	17.76	7.16	m	24.92
one brick thick	-	1.50	21.32	13.09	m	34.41
one and a half brick thick	-	2.30	32.68	19.46	m	52.14
two brick thick	-	2.80	39.79	25.71	m	65.50
Quoining up jambs in hand made facings; PC						
£540.00/1000; in gauged mortar (1:1:6); facing						
and pointing one side to match existing						
half brick thick or skin of hollow wall	-	1.25	17.76	10.55	m	28.31
one brick thick	-	1.50	21.32	19.86	m	41.18
one and a half brick thick	-	2.30	32.68	29.62	m	62.30
two brick thick	-	2.80	39.79	39.25	m	79.04
Filling existing openings with common						
brickwork or blockwork in gauged mortar (1:1:6)						
(cutting and bonding not included)						
half brick thick	-	1.85	26.29	12.50	m²	38.79
one brick thick	-	3.05	43.34	26.22	m²	69.56
one and a half brick thick	-	4.20	59.68	39.33	m²	99.01
two brick thick	-	5.25	74.60	52.44	m²	127.04
75 mm blockwork	5.44	0.92	13.07	7.44	m²	20.51
90 mm blockwork	6.54	1.00	14.21	8.71	m²	22.92
100 mm blockwork	7.26	1.05	14.92	9.54	m²	24.46
115 mm blockwork	8.67	1.13	16.06	11.17	m²	27.23
125 mm blockwork	9.43	1.18	16.77	12.05	m²	28.82
140 mm blockwork	10.56	1.25	17.76	13.35	m²	31.11
150 mm blockwork	11.32	1.30	18.47	14.23	m²	32.70
190 mm blockwork	14.33	1.48	21.03	18.31	m²	39.34
215 mm blockwork	16.21	1.60	22.74	20.48	m²	43.22
255 mm blockwork	19.99	1.78	25.29	24.85	m²	50.14

C DEMOLITION/ALTERATION/RENOVATION Excluding overheads and profit	PC £	Labour hours	Labour £	Material £	Unit	Total rate £
Cutting and bonding ends to existing						
half brick thick	-	0.40	5.68	1.06	m	6.74
one brick thick	-	0.58	8.24	2.05	m	10.29
one and a half brick thick	-	0.86	12.22	2.49	m	14.71
two brick thick	-	1.25	17.76	3.85	m	21.61
75 mm blockwork	-	0.17	2.42	0.54	m	2.96
90 mm blockwork	-	0.21	2.98	0.67	m	3.65
100 mm blockwork	-	0.23	3.27	0.73	m	4.00
115 mm blockwork	-	0.25	3.55	0.88	m	4.43
125 mm blockwork	-	0.26	3.69	0.95	m	4.64
140 mm blockwork	-	0.28	3.98	1.04	m	5.02
150 mm blockwork	11.32	0.29	4.12	1.11	m	5.23
190 mm blockwork	14.33	0.36	5.12	1.47	m	6.59
215 mm blockwork	16.21	0.41	5.83	1.64	m	7.47
255 mm blockwork	19.99	0.48	6.82	1.97	m	8.79
half brick thick in facings; to match existing	0.33	0.60	8.53	3.21	m²	11.74
Extra over common brickwork for fair face; flush pointing						
walls and the like	-	0.20	2.84	-	m²	2.84
Extra over common bricks; PC £175.00/1000 for facing bricks in flemish bond; facing and pointing one side						
machine made facings; PC £330.00/1000	0.33	1.05	14.92	12.50	m²	27.42
hand made facings; PC £540.00/1000	0.54	1.05	14.92	29.43	m²	44.35
ADD or DEDUCT for variation of £10.00/1000 in PC for facing bricks; in flemish bond						
half brick thick	-	-	-	0.65	m²	0.65
Filling in openings to hollow walls with inner skin of common bricks PC £175.00/1000; 50 mm cavity and galvanised steel butterfly ties; outer skin of facings; all in gauged mortar (1:1:6); facing and pointing one side						
two half brick thick skins; outer skin sand faced facings	-	4.60	65.37	28.93	m²	94.30
two half brick thick skins; outer skin machine made facings	-	4.60	65.37	37.42	m²	102.79
two half brick thick skins; outer skin hand made facings	-	4.60	65.37	51.64	m²	117.01
Temporary screens						
Providing and erecting; maintaining; temporary dust proof screens; with 50 mm x 75 mm sawn softwood framing; covering one side with 12 mm thick plywood						
over 300 mm wide	-	0.80	9.07	8.07	m²	17.14
Providing and erecting; maintaining; temporary screen; with 50 mm x 100 mm sawn softwood framing; covering one side with 13 mm thick insulating board and other side with single layer of polythene sheet						
over 300 mm wide	-	1.00	11.34	13.49	m²	24.83
Providing and erecting; maintaining; temporary screen; with 50 mm x 100 mm sawn softwood framing; covering one side with 19 mm thick exterior quality plywood; softwood cappings; including three coats of gloss paint; clearing away						
over 300 mm wide	-	2.00	19.30	18.60	m²	37.90

D GROUNDWORK Excluding overheads and profit	PC £	Labour hours	Labour £	Material/ Plant £	Unit	Total rate £
D GROUNDWORK						
D20 EXCAVATING AND FILLING						
Site preparation						
Removing trees						
girth 600 mm - 1.50 m	-	22.00	144.76	-	nr	**144.76**
girth 1.50 - 3.00 m	-	38.50	253.33	-	nr	**253.33**
girth exceeding 3.00 m	-	55.00	361.90	-	nr	**361.90**
Removing tree stumps						
girth 600 mm - 1.50 m	-	1.10	7.24	35.59	nr	**42.83**
girth 1.50 m - 3.00 m	-	1.10	7.24	51.97	nr	**59.21**
girth exceeding 3.00 m	-	1.10	7.24	71.18	nr	**78.42**
Clearing site vegetation						
bushes, scrub, undergrowth, hedges and trees and tree stumps not exceeding 600 mm girth	-	0.04	0.29	-	m^2	**0.29**
Lifting turf for preservation						
stacking	-	0.39	2.53	-	m^2	**2.53**
Excavating; by machine						
Topsoil for preservation						
average depth 150 mm	-	0.03	0.20	1.08	m^2	**1.28**
add or deduct for each 25 mm variation in						
average depth	-	0.01	0.07	0.27	m^2	**0.34**
To reduce levels						
maximum depth not exceeding 0.25 m	-	0.07	0.46	1.36	m^3	**1.82**
maximum depth not exceeding 1.00 m	-	0.05	0.33	0.95	m^3	**1.28**
maximum depth not exceeding 2.00 m	-	0.07	0.46	1.36	m^3	**1.82**
maximum depth not exceeding 4.00 m	-	0.09	0.59	1.71	m^3	**2.30**
Basements and the like; commencing level exceeding 0.25 m below existing ground level						
maximum depth not exceeding 1.00 m	-	0.10	0.66	1.13	m^3	**1.79**
maximum depth not exceeding 2.00 m	-	0.07	0.46	0.85	m^3	**1.31**
maximum depth not exceeding 4.00 m	-	0.10	0.66	1.13	m^3	**1.79**
maximum depth not exceeding 6.00 m	-	0.11	0.72	1.42	m^3	**2.14**
maximum depth not exceeding 8.00 m	-	0.14	0.92	1.70	m^3	**2.62**
Pits						
maximum depth not exceeding 0.25 m	-	0.39	2.57	4.53	m^3	**7.10**
maximum depth not exceeding 1.00 m	-	0.34	2.24	3.97	m^3	**6.21**
maximum depth not exceeding 2.00 m	-	0.39	2.57	4.53	m^3	**7.10**
maximum depth not exceeding 4.00 m	-	0.42	2.76	5.10	m^3	**7.86**
maximum depth not exceeding 6.00 m	-	0.45	2.96	5.39	m^3	**8.35**
Extra over pit excavating for commencing level exceeding 0.25 m below existing ground level						
1.00 m below	-	0.04	0.26	0.57	m^3	**0.83**
2.00 m below	-	0.07	0.46	0.85	m^3	**1.31**
3.00 m below	-	0.08	0.53	1.13	m^3	**1.66**
4.00 m below	-	0.11	0.72	1.42	m^3	**2.14**

NOTE: Prices are applicable to excavating in firm soil. Multiplying factors for other soils are as follows:

	Mechanical	Hand
Clay	x 2.00	x 1.20
Compact gravel	x 3.00	x 1.50
Soft chalk	x 4.00	x 2.00
Hard rock	x 5.00	x 6.00
Running sand or silt	x 6.00	x 2.00

D GROUNDWORK Excluding overheads and profit	PC £	Labour hours	Labour £	Material/ Plant £	Unit	Total rate £
Trenches, width not exceeding 0.30 m						
maximum depth not exceeding 0.25 m	-	0.32	2.11	3.68	m³	5.79
maximum depth not exceeding 1.00 m	-	0.28	1.84	3.12	m³	4.96
maximum depth not exceeding 2.00 m	-	0.32	2.11	3.68	m³	5.79
maximum depth not exceeding 4.00 m	-	0.39	2.57	4.53	m³	7.10
maximum depth not exceeding 6.00 m	-	0.45	2.96	5.39	m³	8.35
Trenches, width exceeding 0.30 m						
maximum depth 0.25 m	-	0.29	1.91	3.40	m³	5.31
maximum depth 1.00 m	-	0.24	1.58	2.83	m³	4.41
maximum depth 2.00 m	-	0.29	1.91	3.40	m³	5.31
maximum depth 4.00 m	-	0.34	2.24	3.97	m³	6.21
maximum depth 6.00 m	-	0.42	2.76	5.10	m³	7.86
Extra over trench excavating for commencing level exceeding 0.25 m below existing ground level						
1.00 m below	-	0.04	0.26	0.57	m³	0.83
2.00 m below	-	0.07	0.46	0.85	m³	1.31
3.00 m below	-	0.08	0.53	1.13	m³	1.66
4.00 m below	-	0.11	0.72	1.42	m³	2.14
For pile caps and ground beams between piles						
maximum depth not exceeding 0.25 m	-	0.49	3.22	5.95	m³	9.17
maximum depth not exceeding 1.00 m	-	0.43	2.83	5.39	m³	8.22
maximum depth not exceeding 2.00 m	-	0.49	3.22	5.95	m³	9.17
To bench sloping ground to receive filling						
maximum depth not exceeding 0.25 m	-	0.11	0.72	1.42	m³	2.14
maximum depth not exceeding 1.00 m	-	0.08	0.53	1.70	m³	2.23
maximum depth not exceeding 2.00 m	-	0.11	0.72	1.42	m³	2.14
Extra over any types of excavating irrespective of depth						
excavating below ground water level	-	0.17	1.12	1.98	m³	3.10
next existing services	-	3.14	20.66	1.13	m³	21.79
around existing services crossing excavation	-	7.24	47.64	3.12	m³	50.76
Extra over any types of excavating irrespective of depth for breaking out existing materials						
rock	-	3.70	24.35	13.42	m³	37.77
concrete	-	3.14	20.66	9.67	m³	30.33
reinforced concrete	-	4.51	29.68	14.40	m³	44.08
brickwork, blockwork or stonework	-	2.25	14.80	7.34	m³	22.14
Extra over any types of excavating irrespective of depth for breaking out existing hard pavings, 75 mm thick						
coated macadam or asphalt	-	0.24	1.58	0.53	m²	2.11
Extra over any types of excavating irrespective of depth for breaking out existing hard pavings, 150 mm thick						
concrete	-	0.49	3.22	1.57	m²	4.79
reinforced concrete	-	0.73	4.80	2.04	m²	6.84
coated macadam or asphalt and hardcore	-	0.32	2.11	0.57	m²	2.68
Working space allowance to excavations						
reduce levels; basements and the like	-	0.10	0.66	1.13	m²	1.79
pits	-	0.24	1.58	3.12	m²	4.70
trenches	-	0.22	1.45	2.83	m²	4.28
pile caps and ground beams between piles	-	0.25	1.65	3.12	m²	4.77
Extra over excavating for working space for backfilling with special materials						
hardcore	-	0.17	1.12	14.42	m²	15.54
sand	-	0.17	1.12	22.11	m²	23.23
40 mm - 20 mm gravel	-	0.17	1.12	22.58	m²	23.70
plain in situ ready mixed designated concrete C7.5 - 40 mm aggregate	-	1.16	8.43	41.15	m²	49.58

D GROUNDWORK Excluding overheads and profit	PC £	Labour hours	Labour £	Material/ Plant £	Unit	Total rate £
D20 EXCAVATING AND FILLING - cont'd						
Excavating; by hand						
Topsoil for preservation						
average depth 150 mm	-	0.28	1.84	-	m²	**1.84**
add or deduct for each 25 mm variation in						
average depth	-	0.04	0.26	-	m²	**0.26**
To reduce levels						
maximum depth not exceeding 0.25 m	-	1.72	11.32	-	m³	**11.32**
maximum depth not exceeding 1.00 m	-	1.94	12.77	-	m³	**12.77**
maximum depth not exceeding 2.00 m	-	2.15	14.15	-	m³	**14.15**
maximum depth not exceeding 4.00 m	-	2.37	15.59	-	m³	**15.59**
Basements and the like; commencing level exceeding						
0.25 m below existing ground level						
maximum depth not exceeding 1.00 m	-	2.26	14.87	-	m³	**14.87**
maximum depth not exceeding 2.00 m	-	2.42	15.92	-	m³	**15.92**
maximum depth not exceeding 4.00 m	-	3.25	21.39	-	m³	**21.39**
maximum depth not exceeding 6.00 m	-	3.96	26.06	-	m³	**26.06**
maximum depth not exceeding 8.00 m	-	4.79	31.52	-	m³	**31.52**
Pits						
maximum depth not exceeding 0.25 m	-	2.53	16.65	-	m³	**16.65**
maximum depth not exceeding 1.00 m	-	2.75	18.09	-	m³	**18.09**
maximum depth not exceeding 2.00 m	-	3.30	21.71	-	m³	**21.71**
maximum depth not exceeding 4.00 m	-	4.18	27.50	-	m³	**27.50**
maximum depth not exceeding 6.00 m	-	5.17	34.02	-	m³	**34.02**
Extra over pit excavating for commencing level						
exceeding 0.25 m below existing ground level						
1.00 m below	-	0.49	3.22	-	m³	**3.22**
2.00 m below	-	1.05	6.91	-	m³	**6.91**
3.00 m below	-	1.54	10.13	-	m³	**10.13**
4.00 m below	-	2.03	13.36	-	m³	**13.36**
Trenches, width not exceeding 0.30 m						
maximum depth not exceeding 0.25 m	-	2.20	14.48	-	m³	**14.48**
maximum depth not exceeding 1.00 m	-	2.53	16.65	-	m³	**16.65**
maximum depth not exceeding 2.00 m	-	2.97	19.54	-	m³	**19.54**
maximum depth not exceeding 4.00 m	-	3.63	23.89	-	m³	**23.89**
maximum depth not exceeding 6.00 m	-	4.68	30.79	-	m³	**30.79**
Trenches, width exceeding 0.30 m						
maximum depth not exceeding 0.25 m	-	2.15	14.15	-	m³	**14.15**
maximum depth not exceeding 1.00 m	-	2.26	14.87	-	m³	**14.87**
maximum depth not exceeding 2.00 m	-	2.64	17.37	-	m³	**17.37**
maximum depth not exceeding 4.00 m	-	3.36	22.11	-	m³	**22.11**
maximum depth not exceeding 6.00 m	-	4.29	28.23	-	m³	**28.23**
Extra over trench excavating for commencing level						
exceeding 0.25 m below existing ground level						
1.00 m below	-	0.49	3.22	-	m³	**3.22**
2.00 m below	-	1.05	6.91	-	m³	**6.91**
3.00 m below	-	1.54	10.13	-	m³	**10.13**
4.00 m below	-	2.03	13.36	-	m³	**13.36**
For pile caps and ground beams between piles						
maximum depth not exceeding 0.25 m	-	3.30	21.71	-	m³	**21.71**
maximum depth not exceeding 1.00 m	-	3.52	23.16	-	m³	**23.16**
maximum depth not exceeding 2.00 m	-	4.18	27.50	-	m³	**27.50**
To bench sloping ground to receive filling						
maximum depth not exceeding 0.25 m	-	1.54	10.13	-	m³	**10.13**
maximum depth not exceeding 1.00 m	-	1.76	11.58	-	m³	**11.58**
maximum depth not exceeding 2.00 m	-	1.98	13.03	-	m³	**13.03**
Extra over any types of excavating irrespective of						
depth						
excavating below ground water level	-	0.39	2.57	-	m³	**2.57**
next existing services	-	1.10	7.24	-	m³	**7.24**
around existing services crossing excavation	-	2.20	14.48	-	m³	**14.48**

D GROUNDWORK Excluding overheads and profit	PC £	Labour hours	Labour £	Material/ Plant £	Unit	Total rate £
Extra over any types of excavating irrespective of depth for breaking out existing materials						
rock	-	5.50	36.19	5.89	m³	42.08
concrete	-	4.95	32.57	4.91	m³	37.48
reinforced concrete	-	6.60	43.43	6.87	m³	50.30
brickwork; blockwork or stonework	-	3.30	21.71	2.95	m³	24.66
Extra over any types of excavating irrespective of depth for breaking out existing hard pavings, 60 mm thick						
precast concrete paving slabs	-	0.33	2.17	-	m²	2.17
Extra over any types of excavating irrespective of depth for breaking out existing hard pavings, 75 mm thick						
coated macadam or asphalt	-	0.44	2.90	0.39	m²	3.29
Extra over any types of excavating irrespective of depth for breaking out existing hard pavings, 150 mm thick						
concrete	-	0.77	5.07	0.69	m²	5.76
reinforced concrete	-	0.99	6.51	0.98	m²	7.49
coated macadam or asphalt and hardcore	-	0.55	3.62	0.49	m²	4.11
Working space allowance to excavations						
reduce levels; basements and the like	-	2.53	16.65	-	m²	16.65
pits	-	2.64	17.37	-	m²	17.37
trenches	-	2.31	15.20	-	m²	15.20
pile caps and ground beams between piles	-	2.75	18.09	-	m²	18.09
Extra over excavation for working space for backfilling with special materials						
hardcore	-	0.88	5.79	12.52	m²	18.31
sand	-	0.88	5.79	20.21	m²	26.00
40 mm - 20 mm gravel	-	0.88	5.79	20.68	m²	26.47
plain in situ ready mixed designated concrete; C7.5 - 40 mm aggregate	-	1.21	8.80	39.25	m²	48.05
Excavating; by hand; inside existing buildings Basements and the like; commencing level exceeding 0.25 m below existing ground level						
maximum depth not exceeding 1.00 m	-	3.39	22.31	-	m³	22.31
maximum depth not exceeding 2.00 m	-	3.63	23.89	-	m³	23.89
maximum depth not exceeding 4.00 m	-	4.87	32.04	-	m³	32.04
maximum depth not exceeding 6.00 m	-	5.94	39.09	-	m³	39.09
maximum depth not exceeding 8.00 m	-	7.19	47.31	-	m³	47.31
Pits						
maximum depth not exceeding 0.25 m	-	3.79	24.94	-	m³	24.94
maximum depth not exceeding 1.00 m	-	4.13	27.18	-	m³	27.18
maximum depth not exceeding 2.00 m	-	4.95	32.57	-	m³	32.57
maximum depth not exceeding 4.00 m	-	6.27	41.26	-	m³	41.26
maximum depth not exceeding 6.00 m	-	7.75	50.99	-	m³	50.99
Extra over pit excavating for commencing level exceeding 0.25 m below existing ground level						
1.00 m below	-	0.73	4.80	-	m³	4.80
2.00 m below	-	1.57	10.33	-	m³	10.33
3.00 m below	-	2.31	15.20	-	m³	15.20
4.00 m below	-	3.04	20.00	-	m³	20.00
Trenches, width not exceeding 0.30 m						
maximum depth not exceeding 0.25 m	-	3.30	21.71	-	m³	21.71
maximum depth not exceeding 1.00 m	-	3.79	24.94	-	m³	24.94
maximum depth not exceeding 2.00 m	-	4.46	29.35	-	m³	29.35
maximum depth not exceeding 4.00 m	-	5.45	35.86	-	m³	35.86
maximum depth not exceeding 6.00 m	-	7.02	46.19	-	m³	46.19

D GROUNDWORK Excluding overheads and profit	PC £	Labour hours	Labour £	Material/ Plant £	Unit	Total rate £
D20 EXCAVATING AND FILLING - cont'd						
Excavating; by hand; inside existing buildings - cont'd						
Trenches, width exceeding 0.30 m						
maximum depth not exceeding 0.25 m	-	3.23	21.25	-	m³	**21.25**
maximum depth not exceeding 1.00 m	-	3.39	22.31	-	m³	**22.31**
maximum depth not exceeding 2.00 m	-	3.96	26.06	-	m³	**26.06**
maximum depth not exceeding 4.00 m	-	5.04	33.16	-	m³	**33.16**
maximum depth not exceeding 6.00 m	-	6.44	42.38	-	m³	**42.38**
Extra over trench excavating for commencing level						
exceeding 0.25 m below existing ground level						
1.00 m below	-	0.73	4.80	-	m³	**4.80**
2.00 m below	-	1.57	10.33	-	m³	**10.33**
3.00 m below	-	2.31	15.20	-	m³	**15.20**
4.00 m below	-	3.04	20.00	-	m³	**20.00**
Extra over any types of excavating irrespective of depth						
excavating below ground water level	-	0.59	3.88	-	m³	**3.88**
Extra over any types of excavating irrespective of						
depth for breaking out existing materials						
concrete	-	7.42	48.82	4.91	m³	**53.73**
reinforced concrete	-	9.90	65.14	6.87	m³	**72.01**
brickwork; blockwork or stonework	-	4.95	32.57	2.95	m³	**35.52**
Extra over any types of excavating irrespective of						
depth for breaking out existing hard pavings,						
150 mm thick						
concrete	-	1.16	7.63	0.69	m²	**8.32**
reinforced concrete	-	1.49	9.80	0.98	m²	**10.78**
Working space allowance to excavations						
pits	-	3.96	26.06	-	m²	**26.06**
trenches	-	3.47	22.83	-	m²	**22.83**
Earthwork support (average "risk" prices)						
Maximum depth not exceeding 1.00 m						
distance between opposing faces not						
exceeding 2.00 m	-	0.12	0.79	0.32	m²	**1.11**
distance between opposing faces 2.00 - 4.00 m	-	0.13	0.86	0.37	m²	**1.23**
distance between opposing faces exceeding						
4.00 m	-	0.14	0.92	0.47	m²	**1.39**
Maximum depth not exceeding 2.00 m						
distance between opposing faces not						
exceeding 2.00 m	-	0.14	0.92	0.37	m²	**1.29**
distance between opposing faces 2.00 - 4.00 m	-	0.15	0.99	0.47	m²	**1.46**
distance between opposing faces exceeding						
4.00 m	-	0.17	1.12	0.59	m²	**1.71**
Maximum depth not exceeding 4.00 m						
distance between opposing faces not						
exceeding 2.00 m	-	0.17	1.12	0.47	m²	**1.59**
distance between opposing faces 2.00 - 4.00 m	-	0.19	1.25	0.59	m²	**1.84**
distance between opposing faces exceeding						
4.00 m	-	0.21	1.38	0.75	m²	**2.13**
Maximum depth not exceeding 6.00 m						
distance between opposing faces not						
exceeding 2.00 m	-	0.21	1.38	0.56	m²	**1.94**
distance between opposing faces 2.00 - 4.00 m	-	0.23	1.51	0.75	m²	**2.26**
distance between opposing faces exceeding						
4.00 m	-	0.26	1.71	0.94	m²	**2.65**
Maximum depth not exceeding 8.00 m						
distance between opposing faces not						
exceeding 2.00 m	-	0.28	1.84	0.75	m²	**2.59**
distance between opposing faces 2.00 - 4.00 m	-	0.33	2.17	0.94	m²	**3.11**
distance between opposing faces exceeding						
4.00 m	-	0.40	2.63	1.12	m²	**3.75**

D GROUNDWORK Excluding overheads and profit	PC £	Labour hours	Labour £	Material/ Plant £	Unit	Total rate £
Earthwork support (open boarded)						
Maximum depth not exceeding 1.00 m						
distance between opposing faces not						
exceeding 2.00 m	-	0.33	2.17	0.66	m²	**2.83**
distance between opposing faces 2.00 - 4.00 m	-	0.37	2.43	0.75	m²	**3.18**
distance between opposing faces exceeding						
4.00 m	-	0.42	2.76	0.94	m²	**3.70**
Maximum depth not exceeding 2.00 m						
distance between opposing faces not						
exceeding 2.00 m	-	0.42	2.76	0.75	m²	**3.51**
distance between opposing faces 2.00 - 4.00 m	-	0.46	3.03	0.90	m²	**3.93**
distance between opposing faces exceeding						
4.00 m	-	0.53	3.49	1.12	m²	**4.61**
Maximum depth not exceeding 4.00 m						
distance between opposing faces not						
exceeding 2.00 m	-	0.53	3.49	0.85	m²	**4.34**
distance between opposing faces 2.00 - 4.00 m	-	0.59	3.88	1.04	m²	**4.92**
distance between opposing faces exceeding						
4.00 m	-	0.66	4.34	1.31	m²	**5.65**
Maximum depth not exceeding 6.00 m						
distance between opposing faces not						
exceeding 2.00 m	-	0.66	4.34	0.94	m²	**5.28**
distance between opposing faces 2.00 - 4.00 m	-	0.73	4.80	1.18	m²	**5.98**
distance between opposing faces exceeding						
4.00 m	-	0.84	5.53	1.50	m²	**7.03**
Maximum depth not exceeding 8.00 m						
distance between opposing faces not						
exceeding 2.00 m	-	0.88	5.79	1.22	m²	**7.01**
distance between opposing faces 2.00 - 4.00 m	-	0.99	6.51	1.41	m²	**7.92**
distance between opposing faces exceeding						
4.00 m	-	1.15	7.57	1.87	m²	**9.44**
Earthwork support (close boarded)						
Maximum depth not exceeding 1.00 m						
distance between opposing faces not						
exceeding 2.00 m	-	0.88	5.79	1.31	m²	**7.10**
distance between opposing faces 2.00 - 4.00 m	-	0.97	6.38	1.50	m²	**7.88**
distance between opposing faces exceeding						
4.00 m	-	1.07	7.04	1.87	m²	**8.91**
Maximum depth not exceeding 2.00 m						
distance between opposing faces not						
exceeding 2.00 m	-	1.10	7.24	1.50	m²	**8.74**
distance between opposing faces 2.00 - 4.00 m	-	1.21	7.96	1.79	m²	**9.75**
distance between opposing faces exceeding						
4.00 m	-	1.32	8.69	2.24	m²	**10.93**
Maximum depth not exceeding 4.00 m						
distance between opposing faces not						
exceeding 2.00 m	-	1.38	9.08	1.68	m²	**10.76**
distance between opposing faces 2.00 - 4.00 m	-	1.54	10.13	2.09	m²	**12.22**
distance between opposing faces exceeding						
4.00 m	-	1.71	11.25	2.62	m²	**13.87**
Maximum depth not exceeding 6.00 m						
distance between opposing faces not						
exceeding 2.00 m	-	1.72	11.32	1.87	m²	**13.19**
distance between opposing faces 2.00 - 4.00 m	-	1.87	12.30	2.35	m²	**14.65**
distance between opposing faces exceeding						
4.00 m	-	2.09	13.75	2.99	m²	**16.74**

D GROUNDWORK Excluding overheads and profit	PC £	Labour hours	Labour £	Material/ Plant £	Unit	Total rate £
D20 EXCAVATING AND FILLING - cont'd						
Earthwork support (close boarded) - cont'd						
Maximum depth not exceeding 8.00 m						
distance between opposing faces not						
exceeding 2.00 m	-	2.09	13.75	2.43	m²	**16.18**
distance between opposing faces 2.00 - 4.00 m	-	2.31	15.20	2.81	m²	**18.01**
distance between opposing faces exceeding						
4.00 m	-	2.64	17.37	3.37	m²	**20.74**
Extra over earthwork support for						
Curved	-	0.03	0.20	0.32	m²	**0.52**
Below ground water level	-	0.33	2.17	0.29	m²	**2.46**
Unstable ground	-	0.55	3.62	0.56	m²	**4.18**
Next to roadways	-	0.44	2.90	0.47	m²	**3.37**
Left in	-	0.72	4.74	13.09	m²	**17.83**
Earthwork support (average "risk" prices -						
inside existing buildings)						
Maximum depth not exceeding 1.00 m						
distance between opposing faces not						
exceeding 2.00 m	-	0.21	1.38	0.47	m²	**1.85**
distance between opposing faces 2.00 - 4.00 m	-	0.23	1.51	0.54	m²	**2.05**
distance between opposing faces exceeding						
4.00 m	-	0.26	1.71	0.66	m²	**2.37**
Maximum depth not exceeding 2.00 m						
distance between opposing faces not						
exceeding 2.00 m	-	0.26	1.71	0.54	m²	**2.25**
distance between opposing faces 2.00 - 4.00 m	-	0.29	1.91	0.71	m²	**2.62**
distance between opposing faces exceeding						
4.00 m	-	0.35	2.30	0.81	m²	**3.11**
Maximum depth not exceeding 4.00 m						
distance between opposing faces not						
exceeding 2.00 m	-	0.33	2.17	0.71	m²	**2.88**
distance between opposing faces 2.00 - 4.00 m	-	0.37	2.43	0.85	m²	**3.28**
distance between opposing faces exceeding						
4.00 m	-	0.41	2.70	0.99	m²	**3.69**
Maximum depth not exceeding 6.00 m						
distance between opposing faces not						
exceeding 2.00 m	-	0.41	2.70	0.80	m²	**3.50**
distance between opposing faces 2.00 - 4.00 m	-	0.45	2.96	0.99	m²	**3.95**
distance between opposing faces exceeding						
4.00 m	-	0.52	3.42	1.18	m²	**4.60**
Disposal; by machine						
Excavated material						
off site; to tip not exceeding 13 km (using						
lorries); including Landfill Tax based on inactive						
waste	-	-	-	15.75	m³	**15.75**
on site; depositing in spoil heaps; average 25						
m distance	-	-	-	0.81	m³	**0.81**
on site; spreading; average 25 m distance	-	0.25	1.65	0.54	m³	**2.19**
on site; depositing in spoil heaps; average 50						
m distance	-	-	-	1.36	m³	**1.36**
on site; spreading; average 50 m distance	-	0.25	1.65	1.08	m³	**2.73**
on site; depositing in spoil heaps; average 100						
m distance	-	-	-	2.44	m³	**2.44**
on site; spreading; average 100 m distance	-	0.25	1.65	1.63	m³	**3.28**
on site; depositing in spoil heaps; average 200						
m distance	-	-	-	3.52	m³	**3.52**
on site; spreading; average 200 m distance	-	0.25	1.65	2.17	m³	**3.82**

D GROUNDWORK Excluding overheads and profit	PC £	Labour hours	Labour £	Material/ Plant £	Unit	Total rate £
Disposal; by hand						
Excavated material						
off site; to tip not exceeding 13 km (using						
lorries); including Landfill Tax based on inactive						
waste	-	0.88	5.79	24.00	m³	**29.79**
on site; depositing in spoil heaps; average 25						
m distance	-	1.21	7.96	-	m³	**7.96**
on site; spreading; average 25 m distance	-	1.60	10.53	-	m³	**10.53**
on site; depositing in spoil heaps; average 50						
m distance		1.60	10.53	-	m³	**10.53**
on site; spreading; average 50 m distance	-	1.93	12.70	-	m³	**12.70**
on site; depositing in spoil heaps; average 100						
m distance		2.31	15.20	-	m³	**15.20**
on site; spreading; average 100 m distance		2.64	17.37	-	m³	**17.37**
on site; depositing in spoil heaps; average 200						
m distance		3.41	22.44	-	m³	**22.44**
on site; spreading; average 200 m distance	-	3.74	24.61	-	m³	**24.61**
Filling to excavations; by machine						
Average thickness not exceeding 0.25 m						
arising from the excavations	-	0.20	1.32	2.17	m³	**3.49**
obtained off site; hardcore	8.28	0.22	1.45	22.11	m³	**23.56**
obtained off site; granular fill type one	11.84	0.22	1.45	32.07	m³	**33.52**
obtained off site; granular fill type two	11.40	0.22	1.45	31.03	m³	**32.48**
Average thickness exceeding 0.25 m						
arising from the excavations	-	0.17	1.12	1.63	m³	**2.75**
obtained off site; hardcore	8.28	0.19	1.25	18.72	m³	**19.97**
obtained off site; granular fill type one	11.84	0.19	1.25	31.26	m³	**32.51**
obtained off site; granular fill type two	11.40	0.19	1.25	30.21	m³	**31.46**
Filling to make up levels; by machine						
Average thickness not exceeding 0.25 m						
arising from the excavations	-	0.29	1.91	2.43	m³	**4.34**
obtained off site; imported topsoil	9.90	0.29	1.91	12.88	m³	**14.79**
obtained off site; hardcore	8.28	0.33	2.17	22.21	m³	**24.38**
obtained off site; granular fill type one	11.84	0.33	2.17	32.18	m³	**34.35**
obtained off site; granular fill type two	11.40	0.33	2.17	31.13	m³	**33.30**
obtained off site; sand	11.84	0.33	2.17	32.18	m³	**34.35**
Average thickness exceeding 0.25 m						
arising from the excavations	-	0.24	1.58	1.75	m³	**3.33**
obtained off site; imported topsoil	9.90	0.24	1.58	12.19	m³	**13.77**
obtained off site; hardcore	8.28	0.29	1.91	18.71	m³	**20.62**
obtained off site; granular fill type one	11.84	0.29	1.91	31.25	m³	**33.16**
obtained off site; granular fill type two	11.40	0.29	1.91	30.21	m³	**32.12**
obtained off site; sand	11.84	0.29	1.91	31.25	m³	**33.16**
Filling to excavations; by hand						
Average thickness not exceeding 0.25 m						
arising from the excavations	-	1.35	8.88	-	m³	**8.88**
obtained off site; hardcore	8.28	1.46	9.61	19.93	m³	**29.54**
obtained off site; granular fill type one	11.84	1.73	11.38	28.00	m³	**39.38**
obtained off site; granular fill type two	11.40	1.73	11.38	26.96	m³	**38.34**
obtained off site; sand	11.84	1.73	11.38	28.00	m³	**39.38**

D GROUNDWORK Excluding overheads and profit	PC £	Labour hours	Labour £	Material/ Plant £	Unit	Total rate £
D20 EXCAVATING AND FILLING - cont'd						
Filling to excavations; by hand - cont'd						
Average thickness exceeding 0.25 m						
arising from the excavations	-	1.10	7.24	-	m³	7.24
obtained off site; hardcore	8.28	1.21	7.96	17.09	m³	25.05
obtained off site; granular fill type one	11.84	1.43	9.41	28.00	m³	37.41
obtained off site; granular fill type two	11.40	1.43	9.41	26.96	m³	36.37
obtained off site; sand	11.84	1.43	9.41	28.00	m³	37.41
Filling to make up levels; by hand						
Average thickness not exceeding 0.25 m						
arising from the excavations	-	1.49	9.80	4.15	m³	13.95
obtained off site; imported soil	9.90	1.49	9.80	14.05	m³	23.85
obtained off site; hardcore	8.28	1.85	12.17	25.09	m³	37.26
obtained off site; granular fill type one	11.84	1.97	12.96	33.49	m³	46.45
obtained off site; granular fill type two	11.40	1.97	12.96	32.45	m³	45.41
obtained off site; sand	11.84	1.97	12.96	33.49	m³	46.45
Average thickness exceeding 0.25 m						
arising from the excavations	-	1.21	7.96	3.37	m³	11.33
arising from on site spoil heaps; average 25 m						
distance; multiple handling	-	2.64	17.37	7.35	m³	24.72
obtained off site; imported soil	9.90	1.21	7.96	13.27	m³	21.23
obtained off site; hardcore	8.28	1.70	11.19	21.82	m³	33.01
obtained off site; granular fill type one	11.84	1.82	11.98	33.06	m³	45.04
obtained off site; granular fill type two	11.40	1.82	11.98	32.02	m³	44.00
obtained off site; sand	11.84	1.82	11.98	33.06	m³	45.04
Surface packing to filling						
To vertical or battered faces	-	0.20	1.32	0.19	m²	1.51
Surface treatments						
Compacting						
filling; blinding with sand	-	0.06	0.39	1.54	m²	1.93
bottoms of excavations	-	0.06	0.39	0.03	m²	0.42
Trimming						
sloping surfaces	-	0.20	1.32	-	m²	1.32
sloping surfaces; in rock	-	1.10	7.09	1.37	m²	8.46
Filter membrane; one layer; laid on earth to						
receive granular material						
"Terram 500" filter membrane or other equal and						
and approved; one layer; laid on earth	-	0.06	0.39	0.48	m²	0.87
"Terram 700" filter membrane or other equal and						
approved; one layer; laid on earth	-	0.06	0.39	0.51	m²	0.90
"Terram 1000" filter membrane or other equal and						
approved; one layer; laid on earth	-	0.06	0.39	0.54	m²	0.93
"Terram 2000" filter membrane or other equal and						
approved; one layer; laid on earth	-	0.06	0.39	1.13	m²	1.52
D50 UNDERPINNING						
Excavating; by machine						
Preliminary trenches						
maximum depth not exceeding 1.00 m	-	0.25	1.65	6.16	m³	7.81
maximum depth not exceeding 2.00 m	-	0.30	1.97	7.39	m³	9.36
maximum depth not exceeding 4.00 m	-	0.35	2.30	8.63	m³	10.93
Extra over preliminary trench excavating for						
breaking out existing hard pavings, 150 mm						
thick						
concrete	-	0.70	4.61	0.69	m²	5.30

D GROUNDWORK Excluding overheads and profit	PC £	Labour hours	Labour £	Material/ Plant £	Unit	Total rate £
Excavating; by hand						
Preliminary trenches						
maximum depth not exceeding 1.00 m	-	2.90	19.08	-	m³	**19.08**
maximum depth not exceeding 2.00 m	-	3.30	21.71	-	m³	**21.71**
maximum depth not exceeding 4.00 m	-	4.25	27.96	-	m³	**27.96**
Extra over preliminary trench excavating for						
breaking out existing hard pavings, 150 mm thick						
concrete	-	0.30	1.97	1.72	m²	**3.69**
Underpinning pits; commencing from 1.00 m						
below existing ground level						
maximum depth not exceeding 0.25 m	-	4.40	28.95	-	m³	**28.95**
maximum depth not exceeding 1.00 m	-	4.80	31.58	-	m³	**31.58**
maximum depth not exceeding 2.00 m	-	5.75	37.84	-	m³	**37.84**
Underpinning pits; commencing from 2.00 m						
below existing ground level						
maximum depth not exceeding 0.25 m	-	5.40	35.53	-	m³	**35.53**
maximum depth not exceeding 1.00 m	-	5.80	38.16	-	m³	**38.16**
maximum depth not exceeding 2.00 m	-	6.75	44.41	-	m³	**44.41**
Underpinning pits; commencing from 4.00 m						
below existing ground level						
maximum depth not exceeding 0.25 m	-	6.40	42.11	-	m³	**42.11**
maximum depth not exceeding 1.00 m	-	6.80	44.74	-	m³	**44.74**
maximum depth not exceeding 2.00 m	-	7.75	50.99	-	m³	**50.99**
Extra over any types of excavating irrespective of						
depth						
excavating below ground water level	-	0.35	2.30	-	m³	**2.30**
Earthwork support to preliminary trenches						
(open boarded - in 3.00 m lengths)						
Maximum depth not exceeding 1.00 m						
distance between opposing faces not						
exceeding 2.00 m	-	0.40	2.63	1.22	m²	**3.85**
Maximum depth not exceeding 2.00 m						
distance between opposing faces not						
exceeding 2.00 m	-	0.50	3.29	1.50	m²	**4.79**
Maximum depth not exceeding 4.00 m						
distance between opposing faces not						
exceeding 2.00 m	-	0.64	4.21	1.87	m²	**6.08**
Earthwork support to underpinning pits (open						
boarded - in 3.00 m lengths)						
Maximum depth not exceeding 1.00 m						
distance between opposing faces not						
exceeding 2.00 m	-	0.44	2.90	1.31	m²	**4.21**
Maximum depth not exceeding 2.00 m						
distance between opposing faces not						
exceeding 2.00 m	-	0.55	3.62	1.68	m²	**5.30**
Maximum depth not exceeding 4.00 m						
distance between opposing faces not						
exceeding 2.00 m	-	0.70	4.61	2.06	m²	**6.67**
Earthwork support to preliminary trenches						
(closed boarded - in 3.00 m lengths)						
Maximum depth not exceeding 1.00 m						
distance between opposing faces not						
exceeding 2.00 m		1.00	6.58	2.06	m²	**8.64**
Maximum depth not exceeding 2.00 m						
distance between opposing faces not						
exceeding 2.00 m	-	1.25	8.22	2.62	m²	**10.84**
Maximum depth not exceeding 4.00 m						
distance between opposing faces not						
exceeding 2.00 m	-	1.55	10.20	3.18	m²	**13.38**

D GROUNDWORK Excluding overheads and profit	PC £	Labour hours	Labour £	Material/ Plant £	Unit	Total rate £
D50 UNDERPINNING - cont'd						
Earthwork support to underpinning pits **(closed boarded - in 3.00 m lengths)**						
Maximum depth not exceeding 1.00 m						
distance between opposing faces not						
exceeding 2.00 m	-	1.10	7.24	2.24	m²	9.48
Maximum depth not exceeding 2.00 m						
distance between opposing faces not						
exceeding 2.00 m	-	1.38	9.08	2.81	m²	11.89
Maximum depth not exceeding 4.00 m						
distance between opposing faces not						
exceeding 2.00 m	-	1.70	11.19	3.55	m²	14.74
Extra over earthwork support for						
Left in	-	0.75	4.93	13.09	m²	18.02
Cutting away existing projecting foundations						
Concrete						
maximum width 150 mm; maximum depth 150 mm	-	0.16	1.05	0.13	m	1.18
maximum width 150 mm; maximum depth 225 mm	-	0.24	1.58	0.20	m	1.78
maximum width 150 mm; maximum depth 300 mm	-	0.32	2.11	0.27	m	2.38
maximum width 300 mm; maximum depth 300 mm	-	0.63	4.15	0.52	m	4.67
Masonry						
maximum width one brick thick; maximum depth						
one course high	-	0.05	0.33	0.04	m	0.37
maximum width one brick thick; maximum depth						
two courses high	-	0.14	0.92	0.12	m	1.04
maximum width one brick thick; maximum depth						
three courses high	-	0.27	1.78	0.22	m	2.00
maximum width one brick thick; maximum depth						
four courses high	-	0.45	2.96	0.37	m	3.33
Preparing the underside of the existing work to **receive the pinning up of the new work**						
Width of existing work						
380 mm	-	0.60	3.95	-	m	3.95
600 mm	-	0.80	5.26	-	m	5.26
900 mm	-	1.00	6.58	-	m	6.58
1200 mm	-	1.20	7.90	-	m	7.90
Disposal; by hand						
Excavated material						
off site; to tip not exceeding 13 km (using lorries); including Landfill Tax based on inactive waste	-	0.80	5.26	30.00	m³	35.26
Filling to excavations; by hand						
Average thickness exceeding 0.25 m						
arising from the excavations	-	1.00	6.58	-	m³	6.58
Surface treatments						
Compacting						
bottoms of excavations	-	0.06	0.39	0.03	m²	0.42
Plain in situ ready mixed designated concrete **C10 - 40 mm aggregate; poured against faces** **of excavation**						
Underpinning						
thickness not exceeding 150 mm	-	3.70	26.90	71.96	m³	98.86
thickness 150 - 450 mm	-	3.10	22.54	71.96	m³	94.50
thickness exceeding 450 mm	-	2.70	19.63	71.96	m³	91.59

D GROUNDWORK Excluding overheads and profit	PC £	Labour hours	Labour £	Material/ Plant £	Unit	Total rate £
Plain in situ ready mixed designated concrete **C20 - 20 mm aggregate; poured against faces** **of excavation**						
Underpinning						
thickness not exceeding 150 mm	-	3.70	26.90	75.28	m³	102.18
thickness 150 - 450 mm	-	3.10	22.54	75.28	m³	97.82
thickness exceeding 450 mm	-	2.70	19.63	75.28	m³	94.91
Extra for working around reinforcement	-	0.30	2.18	-	m³	2.18
Sawn formwork; sides of foundations in **underpinning**						
Plain vertical						
height exceeding 1.00 m	-	1.60	17.92	4.67	m²	22.59
height not exceeding 250 mm	-	0.55	6.16	1.34	m²	7.50
height 250 - 500 mm	-	0.85	9.52	2.50	m²	12.02
height 500 mm - 1.00 m	-	1.30	14.56	4.67	m²	19.23
Reinforcement bar; BS 4449; hot rolled plain **round mild steel bars**						
20 mm diameter nominal size						
bent	281.60	31.10	272.52	316.00	t	588.52
16 mm diameter nominal size						
bent	281.60	33.20	291.30	318.54	t	609.84
12 mm diameter nominal size						
bent	284.90	35.30	310.07	324.55	t	634.62
10 mm diameter nominal size						
bent	289.30	37.40	328.84	333.50	t	662.34
8 mm diameter nominal size						
bent	289.30	39.50	345.78	336.04	t	681.82
Reinforcement bar; BS 4461; cold worked **deformed high yield steel bars**						
20 mm diameter nominal size						
bent	281.60	31.10	272.52	316.00	t	588.52
16 mm diameter nominal size						
bent	281.60	33.20	291.30	318.54	t	609.84
12 mm diameter nominal size						
bent	284.90	35.30	310.07	324.55	t	634.62
10 mm diameter nominal size						
bent	289.30	37.40	328.84	333.50	t	662.34
8 mm diameter nominal size						
bent	289.30	39.50	345.78	336.04	t	681.82
Common bricks; PC £175.00/1000; in cement **mortar (1:3)**						
Walls in underpinning						
one brick thick	-	2.40	34.10	26.08	m²	60.18
one and a half brick thick	-	3.30	46.89	38.79	m²	85.68
two brick thick	-	4.10	58.26	54.26	m²	112.52
Class A engineering bricks; PC £353.00/1000; **in cement mortar (1:3)**						
Walls in underpinning						
one brick thick	-	2.40	34.10	48.01	m²	82.11
one and a half brick thick	-	3.30	46.89	71.68	m²	118.57
two brick thick	-	4.10	58.26	98.12	m²	156.38

D GROUNDWORK Excluding overheads and profit	PC £	Labour hours	Labour £	Material/ Plant £	Unit	Total rate £
D50 UNDERPINNING - cont'd						
Class B engineering bricks; PC £235.00/1000; **in cement mortar (1:3)**						
Walls in underpinning						
one brick thick	-	2.40	34.10	33.09	m²	67.19
one and a half brick thick	-	3.30	46.89	49.30	m²	96.19
two brick thick	-	4.10	58.26	68.28	m²	126.54
Add or deduct for variation of £10.00/1000 in PC						
of bricks						
one brick thick	-	-	-	1.29	m²	1.29
one and a half brick thick	-	-	-	1.94	m²	1.94
two brick thick	-	-	-	2.58	m²	2.58
"Pluvex" (hessian based) damp proof course **or other equal and approved; 200 mm laps; in** **cement mortar (1:3)**						
Horizontal						
width exceeding 225 mm	7.46	0.25	3.55	8.62	m²	12.17
width not exceeding 225 mm	7.46	0.50	7.11	8.82	m²	15.93
"Hyload" (pitch polymer) damp proof course or **other equal and approved; 150 mm laps; in** **cement mortar (1:3)**						
Horizontal						
width exceeding 225 mm	6.39	0.25	3.55	7.38	m²	10.93
width not exceeding 225 mm	6.39	0.50	7.11	7.56	m²	14.67
"Ledkore" grade A (bitumen based lead cored) **damp proof course or other equal and approved;** **200 mm laps; in cement mortar (1:3)**						
Horizontal						
width exceeding 225 mm	14.34	0.33	4.69	16.57	m²	21.26
width not exceeding 225 mm	14.34	0.66	9.38	16.96	m²	26.34
Two courses of slates in cement mortar (1:3)						
Horizontal						
width exceeding 225 mm	-	1.50	21.32	24.28	m²	45.60
width not exceeding 225 mm	-	2.50	35.52	24.83	m²	60.35
Wedging and pinning						
To underside of existing construction with						
slates in cement mortar (1:3)						
width of wall - half brick thick	-	1.10	15.63	5.72	m	21.35
width of wall - one brick thick	-	1.30	18.47	11.43	m	29.90
width of wall - one and a half brick thick	-	1.50	21.32	17.15	m	38.47

E IN SITU CONCRETE/LARGE PRECAST CONCRETE Excluding overheads and profit	PC £	Labour hours	Labour £	Material £	Unit	Total rate £
E IN SITU CONCRETE/LARGE PRECAST CONCRETE						
E05 IN SITU CONCRETE CONSTRUCTING GENERALLY						
Plain in situ ready mixed designated concrete; C10 - 40 mm aggregate						
Foundations	-	1.50	10.90	67.62	m³	**78.52**
Isolated foundations	-	1.75	12.72	67.62	m³	**80.34**
Beds						
thickness not exceeding 150 mm	-	2.05	14.90	67.62	m³	**82.52**
thickness 150 - 450 mm	-	1.40	10.18	67.62	m³	**77.80**
thickness exceeding 450 mm	-	1.15	8.36	67.62	m³	**75.98**
Filling hollow walls						
thickness not exceeding 150 mm	-	3.90	28.35	67.62	m³	**95.97**
Plain in situ ready mixed designated concrete; C10.00 - 40 mm aggregate; poured on or against earth or unblinded hardcore						
Foundations	-	1.55	11.27	69.27	m³	**80.54**
Isolated foundations	-	1.85	13.45	69.27	m³	**82.72**
Beds						
thickness not exceeding 150 mm	-	2.15	15.63	69.27	m³	**84.90**
thickness 150 - 450 mm	-	1.55	11.27	69.27	m³	**80.54**
thickness exceeding 450 mm	-	1.20	8.72	69.27	m³	**77.99**
Plain in situ ready mixed designated concrete; C20 - 20 mm aggregate						
Foundations	-	1.50	10.90	70.15	m³	**81.05**
Isolated foundations	-	1.75	12.72	70.15	m³	**82.87**
Beds						
thickness not exceeding 150 mm	-	2.20	15.99	70.15	m³	**86.14**
thickness 150 - 450 mm	-	1.50	10.90	70.15	m³	**81.05**
thickness exceeding 450 mm	-	1.15	8.36	70.15	m³	**78.51**
Filling hollow walls						
thickness not exceeding 150 mm	-	3.90	28.35	70.15	m³	**98.50**
Plain in situ ready mixed designated concrete; C20 - 20 mm aggregate; poured on or against earth or unblinded hardcore						
Foundations	-	1.55	11.27	71.86	m³	**83.13**
Isolated foundations	-	1.85	13.45	71.86	m³	**85.31**
Beds						
thickness not exceeding 150 mm	-	2.30	16.72	71.86	m³	**88.58**
thickness 150 - 450 mm	-	1.60	11.63	71.86	m³	**83.49**
thickness exceeding 450 mm	-	1.20	8.72	71.86	m³	**80.58**
Reinforced in situ ready mixed designated concrete; C20 - 20 mm aggregate						
Foundations	-	1.60	11.63	70.15	m³	**81.78**
Ground beams	-	3.20	23.26	70.15	m³	**93.41**
Isolated foundations	-	1.95	14.18	70.15	m³	**84.33**
Beds						
thickness not exceeding 150 mm	-	2.55	18.54	70.15	m³	**88.69**
thickness 150 - 450 mm	-	1.85	13.45	70.15	m³	**83.60**
thickness exceeding 450 mm	-	1.50	10.90	70.15	m³	**81.05**
Slabs						
thickness not exceeding 150 mm	-	4.05	29.44	70.15	m³	**99.59**
thickness 150 - 450 mm	-	3.20	23.26	70.15	m³	**93.41**
thickness exceeding 450 mm	-	2.90	21.08	70.15	m³	**91.23**

E IN SITU CONCRETE/LARGE PRECAST CONCRETE Excluding overheads and profit	PC £	Labour hours	Labour £	Material £	Unit	Total rate £
E05 IN SITU CONCRETE CONSTRUCTING **GENERALLY** - cont'd						
Reinforced in situ ready mixed designated **concrete; C20 - 20 mm aggregate** - cont'd						
Coffered and troughed slabs						
thickness 150 - 450 mm	-	3.70	26.90	70.15	m³	97.05
thickness exceeding 450 mm	-	3.20	23.26	70.15	m³	93.41
Extra over for sloping						
not exceeding 15 degrees	-	0.30	2.18	-	m³	2.18
over 15 degrees	-	0.60	4.36	-	m³	4.36
Walls						
thickness not exceeding 150 mm	-	4.25	30.90	70.15	m³	101.05
thickness 150 - 450 mm	-	3.40	24.72	70.15	m³	94.87
thickness exceeding 450 mm	-	3.00	21.81	70.15	m³	91.96
Beams						
isolated	-	4.60	33.44	70.15	m³	103.59
isolated deep	-	5.05	36.71	70.15	m³	106.86
attached deep	-	4.60	33.44	70.15	m³	103.59
Beam casings						
isolated	-	5.05	36.71	70.15	m³	106.86
isolated deep	-	5.50	39.98	70.15	m³	110.13
attached deep	-	5.05	36.71	70.15	m³	106.86
Columns	-	5.50	39.98	70.15	m³	110.13
Column casings	-	6.10	44.35	70.15	m³	114.50
Staircases	-	6.90	50.16	70.15	m³	120.31
Upstands	-	4.45	32.35	70.15	m³	102.50
Reinforced in situ ready mixed designated **concrete; C25 - 20 mm aggregate**						
Foundations	-	1.60	11.63	70.73	m³	82.36
Ground beams	-	3.20	23.26	70.73	m³	93.99
Isolated foundations	-	1.95	14.18	70.73	m³	84.91
Beds						
thickness not exceeding 150 mm	-	2.35	17.08	70.73	m³	87.81
thickness 150 - 450 mm	-	1.75	12.72	70.73	m³	83.45
thickness exceeding 450 mm	-	1.50	10.90	70.73	m³	81.63
Slabs						
thickness not exceeding 150 mm	-	3.85	27.99	70.73	m³	98.72
thickness 150 - 450 mm	-	3.15	22.90	70.73	m³	93.63
thickness exceeding 450 mm	-	2.90	21.08	70.73	m³	91.81
Coffered and troughed slabs						
thickness 150 - 450 mm	-	3.60	26.17	70.73	m³	96.90
thickness exceeding 450 mm	-	3.20	23.26	70.73	m³	93.99
Extra over for sloping						
not exceeding 15 degrees	-	0.30	2.18	-	m³	2.18
over 15 degrees	-	0.60	4.36	-	m³	4.36
Walls						
thickness not exceeding 150 mm	-	4.15	30.17	70.73	m³	100.90
thickness 150 - 450 mm	-	3.35	24.35	70.73	m³	95.08
thickness exceeding 450 mm	-	3.00	21.81	70.73	m³	92.54
Beams						
isolated	-	4.60	33.44	70.73	m³	104.17
isolated deep	-	5.05	36.71	70.73	m³	107.44
attached deep	-	4.60	33.44	70.73	m³	104.17
Beam casings						
isolated	-	5.05	36.71	70.73	m³	107.44
isolated deep	-	5.50	39.98	70.73	m³	110.71
attached deep	-	5.05	36.71	70.73	m³	107.44
Columns	-	5.50	39.98	70.73	m³	110.71
Column casings	-	6.10	44.35	70.73	m³	115.08
Staircases	-	6.90	50.16	70.73	m³	120.89

E IN SITU CONCRETE/LARGE PRECAST CONCRETE Excluding overheads and profit	PC £	Labour hours	Labour £	Material £	Unit	Total rate £
Upstands	-	4.45	32.35	70.73	m³	103.08
Reinforced in situ ready mixed designated **concrete; C30 - 20 mm aggregate**						
Foundations	-	1.60	11.63	71.33	m³	82.96
Ground beams	-	3.20	23.26	71.33	m³	94.59
Isolated foundations	-	1.95	14.18	71.33	m³	85.51
Beds						
thickness not exceeding 150 mm	-	2.55	18.54	71.33	m³	89.87
thickness 150 - 450 mm	-	1.85	13.45	71.33	m³	84.78
thickness exceeding 450 mm	-	1.50	10.90	71.33	m³	82.23
Slabs						
thickness not exceeding 150 mm	-	4.05	29.44	71.33	m³	100.77
thickness 150 - 450 mm	-	3.20	23.26	71.33	m³	94.59
thickness exceeding 450 mm	-	2.90	21.08	71.33	m³	92.41
Coffered and troughed slabs						
thickness 150 - 450 mm	-	3.70	26.90	71.33	m³	98.23
thickness exceeding 450 mm	-	3.20	23.26	71.33	m³	94.59
Extra over for sloping						
not exceeding 15 degrees	-	0.30	2.18	-	m³	2.18
over 15 degrees	-	0.60	4.36	-	m³	4.36
Walls						
thickness not exceeding 150 mm	-	4.25	30.90	71.33	m³	102.23
thickness 150 - 450 mm	-	3.40	24.72	71.33	m³	96.05
thickness exceeding 450 mm	-	3.00	21.81	71.33	m³	93.14
Beams						
isolated	-	4.60	33.44	71.33	m³	104.77
isolated deep	-	5.05	36.71	71.33	m³	108.04
attached deep	-	4.60	33.44	71.33	m³	104.77
Beam casings						
isolated	-	5.05	36.71	71.33	m³	108.04
isolated deep	-	5.50	39.98	71.33	m³	111.31
attached deep	-	5.05	36.71	71.33	m³	108.04
Columns	-	5.50	39.98	71.33	m³	111.31
Column casings	-	6.10	44.35	71.33	m³	115.68
Staircases	-	6.90	50.16	71.33	m³	121.49
Upstands	-	4.45	32.35	71.33	m³	103.68
Extra over vibrated concrete for						
Reinforcement content over 5%	-	0.63	4.60	-	m³	4.60
Grouting with cement:mortar (1:1)						
Stanchion bases						
10 mm thick	-	1.15	8.36	0.13	nr	8.49
25 mm thick	-	1.44	10.45	0.33	nr	10.78
Grouting with epoxy resin						
Stanchion bases						
10 mm thick	-	1.44	10.45	8.74	nr	19.19
25 mm thick	-	1.73	12.54	21.85	nr	34.39
Grouting with "Conbextra GP" cementitious **grout or other equal and approved**						
Stanchion bases						
10 mm thick	-	1.44	10.45	1.08	nr	11.53
25 mm thick	-	1.73	12.54	2.88	nr	15.42

E IN SITU CONCRETE/LARGE PRECAST CONCRETE Excluding overheads and profit	PC £	Labour hours	Labour £	Material £	Unit	Total rate £
E05 IN SITU CONCRETE CONSTRUCTING GENERALLY - cont'd						
Filling; plain ready mixed designated concrete; C20 - 20 mm aggregate						
Mortices	-	0.12	0.84	0.41	nr	**1.25**
Holes	-	0.29	2.09	84.48	m³	**86.57**
Chases exceeding 0.01 m²	-	0.23	1.67	84.48	m³	**86.15**
Chases not exceeding 0.01 m²	-	0.17	1.25	0.85	m	**2.10**
Sheeting to prevent moisture loss						
Building paper; lapped joints						
subsoil grade; horizontal on foundations	-	0.03	0.25	0.60	m²	**0.85**
standard grade; horizontal on slabs	-	0.06	0.42	0.86	m²	**1.28**
Polythene sheeting; lapped joints; horizontal on slabs						
250 microns; 0.25 mm thick	-	0.06	0.42	0.33	m²	**0.75**
"Visqueen" sheeting or other equal and approved; lapped joints; horizontal on slabs						
250 microns; 0.25 mm thick	-	0.06	0.42	0.27	m²	**0.69**
300 microns; 0.30 mm thick	-	0.07	0.50	0.36	m²	**0.86**
E20 FORMWORK FOR IN SITU CONCRETE						
NOTE: Generally all formwork based on four uses unless otherwise stated.						
Sides of foundations; basic finish						
Plain vertical						
height exceeding 1.00 m	-	1.84	20.61	7.67	m²	**28.28**
height exceeding 1.00 m; left in	-	1.61	18.03	18.48	m²	**36.51**
height not exceeding 250 mm	-	0.52	5.82	3.04	m	**8.86**
height not exceeding 250 mm; left in	-	0.52	5.82	5.37	m	**11.19**
height 250 - 500 mm	-	0.98	10.98	5.96	m	**16.94**
height 250 - 500 mm; left in	-	0.86	9.63	12.00	m	**21.63**
height 500 mm - 1.00 m	-	1.38	15.46	7.67	m	**23.13**
height 500 mm - 1.00 m ; left in	-	1.32	14.78	18.48	m	**33.26**
Sides of foundations; polystyrene sheet formwork; Cordek "Claymaster" or other equal and approved; 50 mm thick						
Plain vertical						
height exceeding 1.00 m; left in	-	0.37	4.14	7.70	m²	**11.84**
height not exceeding 250 mm; left in	-	0.12	1.34	1.92	m	**3.26**
height 250 - 500 mm; left in	-	0.20	2.24	3.85	m	**6.09**
height 500 mm - 1.00 m; left in	-	0.30	3.36	7.70	m	**11.06**
Sides of foundations; polystyrene sheet formwork; Cordek "Claymaster" or other equal and approved; 100 mm thick						
Plain vertical						
height exceeding 1.00 m; left in	-	0.40	4.48	15.39	m²	**19.87**
height not exceeding 250 mm; left in	-	0.13	1.46	3.85	m	**5.31**
height 250 - 500 mm; left in	-	0.22	2.46	7.70	m	**10.16**
height 500 mm - 1.00 m; left in	-	0.33	3.70	15.39	m	**19.09**
Sides of ground beams and edges of beds; basic finish						
Plain vertical						
height exceeding 1.00 m	-	1.90	21.28	7.62	m²	**28.90**
height not exceeding 250 mm	-	0.57	6.38	2.99	m	**9.37**
height 250 - 500 mm	-	1.03	11.54	5.91	m	**17.45**
height 500 mm - 1.00 m	-	1.44	16.13	7.62	m	**23.75**

E IN SITU CONCRETE/LARGE PRECAST CONCRETE Excluding overheads and profit	PC £	Labour hours	Labour £	Material £	Unit	Total rate £
Edges of suspended slabs; basic finish						
Plain vertical						
height not exceeding 250 mm	-	0.86	9.63	3.09	m	**12.72**
height 250 - 500 mm	-	1.26	14.11	4.98	m	**19.09**
height 500 mm - 1.00 m	-	2.01	22.51	7.72	m	**30.23**
Sides of upstands; basic finish						
Plain vertical						
height exceeding 1.00 m	-	2.30	25.76	9.20	m²	**34.96**
height not exceeding 250 mm	-	0.72	8.06	3.19	m	**11.25**
height 250 - 500 mm	-	1.15	12.88	6.11	m	**18.99**
height 500 mm - 1.00 m	-	2.01	22.51	9.20	m	**31.71**
Steps in top surfaces; basic finish						
Plain vertical						
height not exceeding 250 mm	-	0.57	6.38	3.24	m	**9.62**
height 250 - 500 mm	-	0.92	10.30	6.16	m	**16.46**
Steps in soffits; basic finish						
Plain vertical						
height not exceeding 250 mm	-	0.63	7.06	2.54	m	**9.60**
height 250 - 500 mm	-	1.01	11.31	4.58	m	**15.89**
Machine bases and plinths; basic finish						
Plain vertical						
height exceeding 1.00 m	-	1.84	20.61	7.62	m²	**28.23**
height not exceeding 250 mm	-	0.57	6.38	2.99	m	**9.37**
height 250 - 500 mm	-	0.98	10.98	5.91	m	**16.89**
height 500 mm - 1.00 m	-	1.44	16.13	7.62	m	**23.75**
Soffits of slabs; basic finish						
Slab thickness not exceeding 200 mm						
horizontal; height to soffit not exceeding 1.50 m	-	2.07	23.18	7.07	m²	**30.25**
horizontal; height to soffit 1.50 - 3.00 m	-	2.01	22.51	7.17	m²	**29.68**
horizontal; height to soffit 1.50 - 3.00 m (based on 5 uses)	-	1.90	21.28	5.94	m²	**27.22**
horizontal; height to soffit 1.50 - 3.00 m (based on 6 uses)	-	1.84	20.61	5.11	m²	**25.72**
horizontal; height to soffit 3.00 - 4.50 m	-	1.96	21.95	7.42	m²	**29.37**
horizontal; height to soffit 4.50 - 6.00 m	-	2.07	23.18	7.67	m²	**30.85**
Slab thickness 200 - 300 mm						
horizontal; height to soffit 1.50 - 3.00 m	-	2.07	23.18	9.05	m²	**32.23**
Slab thickness 300 - 400 mm						
horizontal; height to soffit 1.50 - 3.00 m	-	2.13	23.86	9.99	m²	**33.85**
Slab thickness 400 - 500 mm						
horizontal; height to soffit 1.50 - 3.00 m	-	2.24	25.09	10.93	m²	**36.02**
Slab thickness 500 - 600 mm						
horizontal; height to soffit 1.50 - 3.00 m	-	2.41	26.99	10.93	m²	**37.92**
Extra over soffits of slabs for						
sloping not exceeding 15 degrees	-	0.23	2.58	-	m²	**2.58**
sloping exceeding 15 degrees	-	0.46	5.15	-	m²	**5.15**
Soffits of slabs; Expamet "Hy-rib" permanent shuttering and reinforcement or other equal and approved; ref. 2411						
Slab thickness not exceeding 200 mm						
horizontal; height to soffit 1.50 - 3.00 m	-	1.73	19.38	19.01	m²	**38.39**

E IN SITU CONCRETE/LARGE PRECAST CONCRETE Excluding overheads and profit	PC £	Labour hours	Labour £	Material £	Unit	Total rate £
E20 FORMWORK FOR IN SITU CONCRETE - cont'd						
Soffits of slabs; Richard Lees "Ribdeck 60" **steel deck permanent shuttering or other** **equal and approved; 0.90 mm gauge; shot-fired** **to frame (not included)**						
Slab thickness not exceeding 200 mm						
horizontal; height to soffit 1.50 - 3.00 m	-	0.80	8.96	18.19	m²	**27.15**
horizontal; height to soffit 3.00 - 4.50 m	-	0.92	10.30	18.25	m²	**28.55**
horizontal; height to soffit 4.50 - 6.00 m	-	1.03	11.54	18.30	m²	**29.84**
Soffits of slabs; Richard Lees "Ribdeck 60" **steel deck permanent shuttering or other** **equal and approved; 1.20 mm gauge; shot-fired** **to frame (not included)**						
Slab thickness not exceeding 200 mm						
horizontal; height to soffit 1.50 - 3.00 m	-	0.92	10.30	21.93	m²	**32.23**
horizontal; height to soffit 3.00 - 4.50 m	-	1.03	11.54	21.74	m²	**33.28**
horizontal; height to soffit 4.50 - 6.00 m	-	1.21	13.55	21.83	m²	**35.38**
Soffits of slabs; Richard Lees "Super Holorib" **steel deck permanent shuttering or other equal** **and approved; 0.90 mm gauge**						
Slab thickness not exceeding 200 mm						
horizontal; height to soffit 1.50 - 3.00 m	-	0.80	8.96	24.73	m²	**33.69**
horizontal; height to soffit 3.00 - 4.50 m	-	0.92	10.30	25.23	m²	**35.53**
horizontal; height to soffit 4.50 - 6.00 m	-	1.03	11.54	25.73	m²	**37.27**
Soffits of slabs; Richard Lees "Super Holorib" **steel deck permanent shuttering or other equal** **and approved; 1.20 mm gauge**						
Slab thickness not exceeding 200 mm						
horizontal; height to soffit 1.50 - 3.00 m	-	0.92	10.30	29.29	m²	**39.59**
horizontal; height to soffit 3.00 - 4.50 m	-	0.92	10.30	30.04	m²	**40.34**
horizontal; height to soffit 4.50 - 6.00 m	-	1.21	13.55	30.54	m²	**44.09**
Soffits of landings; basic finish						
Slab thickness not exceeding 200 mm						
horizontal; height to soffit 1.50 - 3.00 m	-	2.07	23.18	7.55	m²	**30.73**
Slab thickness 200 - 300 mm						
horizontal; height to soffit 1.50 - 3.00 m	-	2.18	24.42	9.65	m²	**34.07**
Slab thickness 300 - 400 mm						
horizontal; height to soffit 1.50 - 3.00 m	-	2.24	25.09	10.65	m²	**35.74**
Slab thickness 400 - 500 mm						
horizontal; height to soffit 1.50 - 3.00 m	-	2.36	26.43	11.68	m²	**38.11**
Slab thickness 500 - 600 mm						
horizontal; height to soffit 1.50 - 3.00 m	-	2.53	28.34	11.68	m²	**40.02**
Extra over soffits of landings for						
sloping not exceeding 15 degrees	-	0.23	2.58	-	m²	**2.58**
sloping exceeding 15 degrees	-	0.46	5.15	-	m²	**5.15**
Soffits of coffered or troughed slabs; basic finish						
Cordek "Correx" trough mould or other equal and approved; 300 mm deep; ribs of mould at 600 mm centres and cross ribs at centres of bay; slab thickness 300 - 400 mm						
horizontal; height to soffit 1.50 - 3.00 m	-	2.88	32.26	11.85	m²	**44.11**
horizontal; height to soffit 3.00 - 4.50 m	-	2.99	33.49	12.10	m²	**45.59**
horizontal; height to soffit 4.50 - 6.00 m	-	3.11	34.83	12.25	m²	**47.08**
Top formwork; basic finish						
Sloping exceeding 15 degrees	-	1.73	19.38	5.54	m²	**24.92**

E IN SITU CONCRETE/LARGE PRECAST CONCRETE Excluding overheads and profit	PC £	Labour hours	Labour £	Material £	Unit	Total rate £
Walls; basic finish						
Vertical	-	2.07	23.18	9.05	m²	**32.23**
Vertical; height exceeding 3.00 m above floor level	-	2.53	28.34	9.30	m²	**37.64**
Vertical; interrupted	-	2.41	26.99	9.30	m²	**36.29**
Vertical; to one side only	-	4.03	45.14	11.43	m²	**56.57**
Vertical; exceeding 3.00 m high; inside stairwell	-	2.53	28.34	9.30	m²	**37.64**
Battered	-	3.22	36.06	9.75	m²	**45.81**
Beams; basic finish						
Attached to slabs						
regular shaped; square or rectangular; height to soffit 1.50 - 3.00 m	-	2.53	28.34	8.75	m²	**37.09**
regular shaped; square or rectangular; height to soffit 3.00 - 4.50 m	-	2.64	29.57	9.05	m²	**38.62**
regular shaped; square or rectangular; height to soffit 4.50 - 6.00 m	-	2.76	30.91	9.30	m²	**40.21**
Attached to walls						
regular shaped; square or rectangular; height to soffit 1.50 - 3.00 m	-	2.64	29.57	8.75	m²	**38.32**
Isolated						
regular shaped; square or rectangular; height to soffit 1.50 - 3.00 m	-	2.76	30.91	8.75	m²	**39.66**
regular shaped; square or rectangular; height to soffit 3.00 - 4.50 m	-	2.88	32.26	9.05	m²	**41.31**
regular shaped; square or rectangular; height to soffit 4.50 - 6.00 m	-	2.99	33.49	9.30	m²	**42.79**
Extra over beams for						
regular shaped; sloping not exceeding 15 degrees	-	0.35	3.92	0.89	m²	**4.81**
regular shaped; sloping exceeding 15 degrees	-	0.69	7.73	1.78	m²	**9.51**
Beam casings; basic finish						
Attached to slabs						
regular shaped; square or rectangular; height to soffit 1.50 - 3.00 m	-	2.64	29.57	8.75	m²	**38.32**
regular shaped; square or rectangular; height to soffit 3.00 - 4.50 m	-	2.76	30.91	9.05	m²	**39.96**
Attached to walls						
regular shaped; square or rectangular; height to soffit 1.50 - 3.00 m	-	2.76	30.91	8.75	m²	**39.66**
Isolated						
regular shaped; square or rectangular; height to soffit 1.50 - 3.00 m	-	2.88	32.26	8.75	m²	**41.01**
regular shaped; square or rectangular; height to soffit 3.00 - 4.50 m	-	2.99	33.49	9.05	m²	**42.54**
Extra over beam casings for						
regular shaped; sloping not exceeding 15 degrees	-	0.35	3.92	0.89	m²	**4.81**
regular shaped; sloping exceeding 15 degrees	-	0.69	7.73	1.78	m²	**9.51**
Columns; basic finish						
Attached to walls						
regular shaped; square or rectangular; height to soffit 1.50 - 3.00 m	-	2.53	28.34	7.67	m²	**36.01**
Isolated						
regular shaped; square or rectangular; height to soffit 1.50 - 3.00 m	-	2.64	29.57	7.67	m²	**37.24**
regular shaped; circular; not exceeding 300 mm diameter; height to soffit 1.50 - 3.00 m	-	4.60	51.52	12.31	m²	**63.83**
regular shaped; circular; 300 - 600 mm diameter; height to soffit 1.50 - 3.00 m	-	4.31	48.27	10.93	m²	**59.20**
regular shaped; circular; 600 - 900 mm diameter; height to soffit 1.50 - 3.00 m	-	4.03	45.14	10.68	m²	**55.82**

E IN SITU CONCRETE/LARGE PRECAST CONCRETE Excluding overheads and profit	PC £	Labour hours	Labour £	Material £	Unit	Total rate £
E20 FORMWORK FOR IN SITU CONCRETE - cont'd						
Column casings; basic finish						
Attached to walls						
regular shaped; square or rectangular; height						
to soffit; 1.50 - 3.00 m	-	2.64	29.57	7.67	m²	37.24
Isolated						
regular shaped; square or rectangular; height						
to soffit 1.50 - 3.00 m	-	2.76	30.91	7.67	m²	38.58
Recesses or rebates						
12 x 12 mm	-	0.08	0.90	0.07	m	0.97
25 x 25 mm	-	0.08	0.90	0.11	m	1.01
25 x 50 mm	-	0.08	0.90	0.15	m	1.05
50 x 50 mm	-	0.08	0.90	0.26	m	1.16
Nibs						
50 x 50 mm	-	0.63	7.06	0.93	m	7.99
100 x 100 mm	-	0.90	10.08	1.24	m	11.32
100 x 200 mm	-	1.20	13.44	2.26	m	15.70
Extra over a basic finish for fine formed finishes						
Slabs	-	0.38	4.26	-	m²	4.26
Walls	-	0.38	4.26	-	m²	4.26
Beams	-	0.38	4.26	-	m²	4.26
Columns	-	0.38	4.26	-	m²	4.26
Add to prices for basic formwork for						
Curved radius 6.00 m - 50%						
Curved radius 2.00 m - 100%						
Coating with retardant agent	-	0.02	0.22	0.45	m²	0.67
Wall kickers; basic finish						
Height 150 mm	-	0.57	6.38	2.21	m	8.59
Height 225 mm	-	0.75	8.40	2.72	m	11.12
Suspended wall kickers; basic finish						
Height 150 mm	-	0.72	8.06	1.80	m	9.86
Wall ends, soffits and steps in walls; basic finish						
Plain						
width exceeding 1.00 m	-	2.18	24.42	9.05	m²	33.47
width not exceeding 250 mm	-	0.69	7.73	2.29	m	10.02
width 250 - 500 mm	-	1.09	12.21	5.03	m	17.24
width 500 mm - 1.00 m	-	1.73	19.38	9.05	m	28.43
Openings in walls						
Plain						
width exceeding 1.00 m	-	2.41	26.99	9.05	m²	36.04
width not exceeding 250 mm	-	0.75	8.40	2.29	m	10.69
width 250 - 500 mm	-	1.26	14.11	5.03	m	19.14
width 500 mm - 1.00 m	-	1.96	21.95	9.05	m	31.00
Stairflights						
Width 1.00 m; 150 mm waist; 150 mm undercut risers						
string, width 300 mm	-	5.75	64.40	19.90	m	84.30
Width 2.00 m; 200 mm waist; 150 mm undercut risers						
string, width 350 mm	-	10.35	115.92	34.89	m	150.81

E IN SITU CONCRETE/LARGE PRECAST CONCRETE Excluding overheads and profit	PC £	Labour hours	Labour £	Material £	Unit	Total rate £
Mortices						
Girth not exceeding 500 mm						
depth not exceeding 250 mm; circular	-	0.17	1.90	0.76	nr	**2.66**
Holes						
Girth not exceeding 500 mm						
depth not exceeding 250 mm; circular	-	0.23	2.58	0.99	nr	**3.57**
depth 250 - 500 mm; circular	-	0.35	3.92	2.40	nr	**6.32**
Girth 500 mm - 1.00 m						
depth not exceeding 250 mm; circular	-	0.29	3.25	1.67	nr	**4.92**
depth 250 - 500 mm; circular	-	0.44	4.93	4.46	nr	**9.39**
Girth 1.00 - 2.00 m						
depth not exceeding 250 mm; circular	-	0.52	5.82	4.46	nr	**10.28**
depth 250 - 500 mm; circular	-	0.77	8.62	9.32	nr	**17.94**
Girth 2.00 - 3.00 m						
depth not exceeding 250 mm; circular	-	0.69	7.73	8.97	nr	**16.70**
depth 250 - 500 mm; circular	-	1.03	11.54	16.06	nr	**27.60**
E30 REINFORCEMENT FOR IN SITU CONCRETE						
Bar; BS 4449; hot rolled plain round mild steel bars						
40 mm diameter nominal size						
straight or bent	317.90	24.00	209.05	351.58	t	**560.63**
curved	346.80	24.00	209.05	381.92	t	**590.97**
32 mm diameter nominal size						
straight or bent	290.40	25.00	217.99	323.45	t	**541.44**
curved	316.80	25.00	217.99	351.17	t	**569.16**
25 mm diameter nominal size						
straight or bent	286.00	27.10	236.76	318.82	t	**555.58**
curved	312.00	27.10	236.76	346.12	t	**582.88**
20 mm diameter nominal size						
straight or bent	283.80	29.10	254.64	318.31	t	**572.95**
curved	309.60	29.10	254.64	345.40	t	**600.04**
16 mm diameter nominal size						
straight or bent	283.80	31.20	273.42	320.85	t	**594.27**
curved	309.60	31.20	273.42	347.94	t	**621.36**
12 mm diameter nominal size						
straight or bent	288.20	33.30	292.19	328.01	t	**620.20**
curved	314.40	33.30	292.19	355.52	t	**647.71**
10 mm diameter nominal size						
straight or bent	294.80	35.40	310.96	339.28	t	**650.24**
curved	321.60	35.40	310.96	367.42	t	**678.38**
8 mm diameter nominal size						
straight or bent	304.70	37.50	327.90	352.21	t	**680.11**
links	304.70	40.90	358.30	353.71	t	**712.01**
curved	332.40	37.50	327.90	381.30	t	**709.20**
6 mm diameter nominal size						
straight or bent	331.10	42.70	374.39	379.93	t	**754.32**
links	331.10	46.20	405.68	379.93	t	**785.61**
curved	361.20	42.70	374.39	411.54	t	**785.93**
Bar; BS 4449; hot rolled deformed high steel bars grade 460						
40 mm diameter nominal size						
straight or bent	289.30	24.00	209.05	321.55	t	**530.60**
curved	315.60	24.00	209.05	349.16	t	**558.21**
32 mm diameter nominal size						
straight or bent	284.90	25.00	217.99	317.68	t	**535.67**
curved	310.80	25.00	217.99	344.87	t	**562.86**

E IN SITU CONCRETE/LARGE PRECAST CONCRETE Excluding overheads and profit	PC £	Labour hours	Labour £	Material £	Unit	Total rate £
E30 REINFORCEMENT FOR IN SITU CONCRETE - cont'd						
Bar; BS 4449; hot rolled deformed high steel bars grade 460 - cont'd						
25 mm diameter nominal size						
straight or bent	279.40	27.10	236.76	311.89	t	**548.65**
curved	304.80	27.10	236.76	338.56	t	**575.32**
20 mm diameter nominal size						
straight or bent	281.60	29.10	254.64	316.00	t	**570.64**
curved	307.20	29.10	254.64	342.88	t	**597.52**
16 mm diameter nominal size						
straight or bent	281.60	31.20	273.42	318.54	t	**591.96**
curved	307.20	31.20	273.42	345.42	t	**618.84**
12 mm diameter nominal size						
straight or bent	284.90	33.30	292.19	324.55	t	**616.74**
curved	310.80	33.30	292.19	351.74	t	**643.93**
10 mm diameter nominal size						
straight or bent	289.30	35.40	310.96	333.50	t	**644.46**
curved	315.60	35.40	310.96	361.12	t	**672.08**
8 mm diameter nominal size						
straight or bent	298.10	37.50	327.90	345.28	t	**673.18**
links	298.10	40.90	358.30	346.78	t	**705.08**
curved	325.20	37.50	327.90	373.74	t	**701.64**
Bar; stainless steel						
32 mm diameter nominal size						
straight or bent	2401.30	25.00	217.99	2419.83	t	**2637.82**
curved	2503.05	25.00	217.99	2521.58	t	**2739.57**
25 mm diameter nominal size						
straight or bent	2510.17	27.10	236.76	2528.69	t	**2765.45**
curved	2611.92	27.10	236.76	2630.44	t	**2867.20**
20 mm diameter nominal size						
straight or bent	1641.23	29.10	254.64	1661.55	t	**1916.19**
curved	1742.98	29.10	254.64	1763.30	t	**2017.94**
16 mm diameter nominal size						
straight or bent	1641.23	31.20	273.42	1664.09	t	**1937.51**
curved	1742.98	31.20	273.42	1765.84	t	**2039.26**
12 mm diameter nominal size						
straight or bent	1530.32	33.30	292.19	1555.72	t	**1847.91**
curved	1665.65	33.30	292.19	1691.05	t	**1983.24**
10 mm diameter nominal size						
straight or bent	1530.32	35.40	310.96	1560.06	t	**1871.02**
curved	1682.95	35.40	310.96	1712.69	t	**2023.65**
8 mm diameter nominal size						
straight or bent	1530.32	37.50	327.90	1562.60	t	**1890.50**
curved	1716.52	37.50	327.90	1748.80	t	**2076.70**
Fabric; BS 4483						
Ref A98 (1.54 kg/m^2)						
400 mm minimum laps	0.66	0.14	1.25	0.73	m^2	**1.98**
strips in one width; 600 mm width	0.66	0.17	1.52	0.73	m^2	**2.25**
strips in one width; 900 mm width	0.66	0.16	1.43	0.73	m^2	**2.16**
strips in one width; 1200 mm width	0.66	0.15	1.34	0.73	m^2	**2.07**
Ref A142 (2.22 kg/m^2)						
400 mm minimum laps	0.77	0.14	1.25	0.85	m^2	**2.10**
strips in one width; 600 mm width	0.77	0.17	1.52	0.85	m^2	**2.37**
strips in one width; 900 mm width	0.77	0.16	1.43	0.85	m^2	**2.28**
strips in one width; 1200 mm width	0.77	0.15	1.34	0.85	m^2	**2.19**

E IN SITU CONCRETE/LARGE PRECAST CONCRETE Excluding overheads and profit	PC £	Labour hours	Labour £	Material £	Unit	Total rate £
Ref A193 (3.02 kg/m²)						
400 mm minimum laps	1.10	0.14	1.25	1.21	m²	**2.46**
strips in one width; 600 mm width	1.10	0.17	1.52	1.21	m²	**2.73**
strips in one width; 900 mm width	1.10	0.16	1.43	1.21	m²	**2.64**
strips in one width; 1200 mm width	1.10	0.15	1.34	1.21	m²	**2.55**
Ref A252 (3.95 kg/m²)						
400 mm minimum laps	1.38	0.15	1.34	1.52	m²	**2.86**
strips in one width; 600 mm width	1.38	0.18	1.61	1.52	m²	**3.13**
strips in one width; 900 mm width	1.38	0.17	1.52	1.52	m²	**3.04**
strips in one width; 1200 mm width	1.38	0.16	1.43	1.52	m²	**2.95**
Ref A393 (6.16 kg/m²)						
400 mm minimum laps	2.20	0.17	1.52	2.42	m²	**3.94**
strips in one width; 600 mm width	2.20	0.20	1.79	2.42	m²	**4.21**
strips in one width; 900 mm width	2.20	0.19	1.70	2.42	m²	**4.12**
strips in one width; 1200 mm width	2.20	0.18	1.61	2.42	m²	**4.03**
Ref B196 (3.05 kg/m²)						
400 mm minimum laps	1.16	0.14	1.25	1.28	m²	**2.53**
strips in one width; 600 mm width	1.16	0.17	1.52	1.28	m²	**2.80**
strips in one width; 900 mm width	1.16	0.16	1.43	1.28	m²	**2.71**
strips in one width; 1200 mm width	1.16	0.15	1.34	1.28	m²	**2.62**
Ref B283 (3.73 kg/m²)						
400 mm minimum laps	1.32	0.14	1.25	1.45	m²	**2.70**
strips in one width; 600 mm width	1.32	0.17	1.52	1.45	m²	**2.97**
strips in one width; 900 mm width	1.32	0.16	1.43	1.45	m²	**2.88**
strips in one width; 1200 mm width	1.32	0.15	1.34	1.45	m²	**2.79**
Ref B385 (4.53 kg/m²)						
400 mm minimum laps	1.65	0.15	1.34	1.81	m²	**3.15**
strips in one width; 600 mm width	1.65	0.18	1.61	1.81	m²	**3.42**
strips in one width; 900 mm width	1.65	0.17	1.52	1.81	m²	**3.33**
strips in one width; 1200 mm width	1.65	0.16	1.43	1.81	m²	**3.24**
Ref B503 (5.93 kg/m²)						
400 mm minimum laps	2.15	0.17	1.52	2.37	m²	**3.89**
strips in one width; 600 mm width	2.15	0.20	1.79	2.37	m²	**4.16**
strips in one width; 900 mm width	2.15	0.19	1.70	2.37	m²	**4.07**
strips in one width; 1200 mm width	2.15	0.18	1.61	2.37	m²	**3.98**
Ref B785 (8.14 kg/m²)						
400 mm minimum laps	2.92	0.20	1.79	3.21	m²	**5.00**
strips in one width; 600 mm width	2.92	0.24	2.15	3.21	m²	**5.36**
strips in one width; 900 mm width	2.92	0.23	2.06	3.21	m²	**5.27**
strips in one width; 1200 mm width	2.92	0.22	1.97	3.21	m²	**5.18**
Ref B1131 (10.90 kg/m²)						
400 mm minimum laps	3.85	0.22	1.97	4.24	m²	**6.21**
strips in one width; 600 mm width	3.85	0.28	2.50	4.24	m²	**6.74**
strips in one width; 900 mm width	3.85	0.26	2.32	4.24	m²	**6.56**
strips in one width; 1200 mm width	3.85	0.24	2.15	4.24	m²	**6.39**
Ref C385 (3.41 kg/m²)						
400 mm minimum laps	1.26	0.14	1.25	1.39	m²	**2.64**
strips in one width; 600 mm width	1.26	0.17	1.52	1.39	m²	**2.91**
strips in one width; 900 mm width	1.26	0.16	1.43	1.39	m²	**2.82**
strips in one width; 1200 mm width	1.26	0.15	1.34	1.39	m²	**2.73**
Ref C503 (4.34 kg/m²)						
400 mm minimum laps	1.59	0.15	1.34	1.75	m²	**3.09**
strips in one width; 600 mm width	1.59	0.18	1.61	1.75	m²	**3.36**
strips in one width; 900 mm width	1.59	0.17	1.52	1.75	m²	**3.27**
strips in one width; 1200 mm width	1.59	0.16	1.43	1.75	m²	**3.18**
Ref C636 (5.55 kg/m²)						
400 mm minimum laps	2.15	0.16	1.43	2.37	m²	**3.80**
strips in one width; 600 mm width	2.15	0.19	1.70	2.37	m²	**4.07**
strips in one width; 900 mm width	2.15	0.18	1.61	2.37	m²	**3.98**
strips in one width; 1200 mm width	2.15	0.17	1.52	2.37	m²	**3.89**

E IN SITU CONCRETE/LARGE PRECAST CONCRETE Excluding overheads and profit	PC £	Labour hours	Labour £	Material £	Unit	Total rate £
E30 REINFORCEMENT FOR IN SITU CONCRETE - cont'd						
Fabric; BS 4483 - cont'd						
Ref C785 (6.72 kg/m^2)						
400 mm minimum laps	2.48	0.16	1.43	2.73	m^2	**4.16**
strips in one width; 600 mm width	2.48	0.19	1.70	2.73	m^2	**4.43**
strips in one width; 900 mm width	2.48	0.18	1.61	2.73	m^2	**4.34**
strips in one width; 1200 mm width	2.48	0.17	1.52	2.73	m^2	**4.25**
Ref D49 (0.77 kg/m^2)						
100 mm minimum laps; bent	0.82	0.28	2.50	0.90	m^2	**3.40**
Ref D98 (1.54 kg/m^2)						
200 mm minimum laps; bent	0.72	0.28	2.50	0.79	m^2	**3.29**
E40 DESIGNED JOINTS IN IN SITU CONCRETE						
Formed; Fosroc Expandite "Flexcell" impregnated **fibreboard joint filler or other equal and approved**						
Width not exceeding 150 mm						
12.50 mm thick	-	0.17	1.90	1.23	m	**3.13**
20 mm thick	-	0.22	2.46	1.79	m	**4.25**
25 mm thick	-	0.22	2.46	2.04	m	**4.50**
Width 150 - 300 mm						
12.50 mm thick	-	0.22	2.46	2.10	m	**4.56**
20 mm thick	-	0.28	3.14	2.78	m	**5.92**
25 mm thick	-	0.28	3.14	3.22	m	**6.36**
Width 300 - 450 mm						
12.50 mm thick	-	0.28	3.14	3.15	m	**6.29**
20 mm thick	-	0.33	3.70	4.16	m	**7.86**
25 mm thick	-	0.33	3.70	4.83	m	**8.53**
Formed; Grace Servicised "Kork-pak" waterproof **bonded cork joint filler board or other equal and** **approved**						
Width not exceeding 150 mm						
10 mm thick	-	0.17	1.90	2.79	m	**4.69**
13 mm thick	-	0.17	1.90	2.83	m	**4.73**
19 mm thick	-	0.17	1.90	3.69	m	**5.59**
25 mm thick	-	0.17	1.90	4.20	m	**6.10**
Width 150 - 300 mm						
10 mm thick	-	0.22	2.46	5.26	m	**7.72**
13 mm thick	-	0.22	2.46	5.34	m	**7.80**
19 mm thick	-	0.22	2.46	7.05	m	**9.51**
25 mm thick	-	0.22	2.46	8.08	m	**10.54**
Width 300 - 450 mm						
10 mm thick	-	0.28	3.14	7.98	m	**11.12**
13 mm thick	-	0.28	3.14	8.10	m	**11.24**
19 mm thick	-	0.28	3.14	10.67	m	**13.81**
25 mm thick	-	0.28	3.14	12.21	m	**15.35**
Sealants; Fosroc Expandite "Pliastic 77" hot **poured rubberized bituminous compound or** **other equal and approved**						
Width 10 mm						
25 mm depth	-	0.20	2.24	0.78	m	**3.02**
Width 12.50 mm						
25 mm depth	-	0.21	2.35	0.96	m	**3.31**
Width 20 mm						
25 mm depth	-	0.22	2.46	1.56	m	**4.02**
Width 25 mm						
25 mm depth	-	0.23	2.58	1.91	m	**4.49**

E IN SITU CONCRETE/LARGE PRECAST CONCRETE Excluding overheads and profit	PC £	Labour hours	Labour £	Material £	Unit	Total rate £
Sealants; Fosroc Expandite "Thioflex 600" gun grade two part polysulphide or other equal and approved						
Width 10 mm						
25 mm depth	-	0.07	0.78	2.96	m	**3.74**
Width 12.50 mm						
25 mm depth	-	0.08	0.90	3.70	m	**4.60**
Width 20 mm						
25 mm depth	-	0.09	1.01	5.92	m	**6.93**
Width 25 mm						
25 mm depth	-	0.10	1.12	7.40	m	**8.52**
Sealants; Grace Servicised "Paraseal" polysulphide compound or other equal and approved; priming with Grace Servicised "Servicised P" or other equal and approved						
Width 10 mm						
25 mm depth	-	0.22	1.60	2.04	m	**3.64**
Width 13 mm						
25 mm depth	-	0.22	1.60	2.61	m	**4.21**
Width 19 mm						
25 mm depth	-	0.28	2.04	3.75	m	**5.79**
Width 25 mm						
25 mm depth	-	0.28	2.04	4.89	m	**6.93**
Waterstops						
PVC water stop; flat dumbbell type; heat welded joints; cast into concrete						
100 mm wide	1.98	0.22	1.97	2.15	m	**4.12**
flat angle	8.23	0.28	2.50	7.08	nr	**9.58**
vertical angle	12.39	0.28	2.50	11.34	nr	**13.84**
flat three way intersection	10.64	0.39	3.49	9.88	nr	**13.37**
vertical three way intersection	14.63	0.39	3.49	13.96	nr	**17.45**
four way intersection	11.01	0.49	4.38	10.58	nr	**14.96**
170 mm wide	2.96	0.28	2.50	3.19	m	**5.69**
flat angle	9.44	0.33	2.95	7.92	nr	**10.87**
vertical angle	13.58	0.33	2.95	12.17	nr	**15.12**
flat three way intersection	12.04	0.44	3.93	11.22	nr	**15.15**
vertical three way intersection	17.02	0.44	3.93	16.34	nr	**20.27**
four way intersection	13.15	0.55	4.92	13.01	nr	**17.93**
210 mm wide	3.87	0.28	2.50	4.13	m	**6.63**
flat angle	11.72	0.33	2.95	10.11	nr	**13.06**
vertical angle	12.92	0.33	2.95	11.34	nr	**14.29**
flat three way intersection	15.30	0.44	3.93	14.82	nr	**18.75**
vertical three way intersection	12.36	0.44	3.93	11.81	nr	**15.74**
four way intersection	16.75	0.55	4.92	17.34	nr	**22.26**
250 mm wide	5.12	0.33	2.95	5.45	m	**8.40**
flat angle	14.10	0.39	3.49	12.47	nr	**15.96**
vertical angle	14.52	0.39	3.49	12.91	nr	**16.40**
flat three way intersection	18.21	0.49	4.38	18.31	nr	**22.69**
vertical three way intersection	13.86	0.49	4.38	13.87	nr	**18.25**
four way intersection	20.21	0.61	5.45	21.99	nr	**27.44**
PVC water stop; centre bulb type; heat welded joints; cast into concrete						
160 mm wide	3.20	0.28	2.50	3.44	m	**5.94**
flat angle	9.73	0.33	2.95	8.07	nr	**11.02**
vertical angle	14.06	0.33	2.95	12.51	nr	**15.46**
flat three way intersection	12.33	0.44	3.93	11.44	nr	**15.37**
vertical three way intersection	13.48	0.44	3.93	12.61	nr	**16.54**
four way intersection	13.48	0.55	4.92	13.29	nr	**18.21**

E IN SITU CONCRETE/LARGE PRECAST CONCRETE Excluding overheads and profit	PC £	Labour hours	Labour £	Material £	Unit	Total rate £
E40 DESIGNED JOINTS IN IN SITU CONCRETE - cont'd						
Waterstops - cont'd						
PVC water stop; centre bulb type; heat welded						
joints; cast into concrete - cont'd						
210 mm wide	4.59	0.28	2.50	4.89	m	7.39
flat angle	12.37	0.33	2.95	10.42	nr	13.37
vertical angle	15.64	0.33	2.95	13.77	nr	16.72
flat three way intersection	15.84	0.44	3.93	15.21	nr	19.14
vertical three way intersection	14.97	0.44	3.93	14.31	nr	18.24
four way intersection	17.31	0.55	4.92	17.93	nr	22.85
260 mm wide	5.36	0.33	2.95	5.70	m	8.65
flat angle	14.40	0.39	3.49	12.68	nr	16.17
vertical angle	14.72	0.39	3.49	13.01	nr	16.50
flat three way intersection	18.57	0.49	4.38	18.67	nr	23.05
vertical three way intersection	14.15	0.49	4.38	14.13	nr	18.51
four way intersection	20.57	0.61	5.45	22.42	nr	27.87
325 mm wide	11.90	0.39	3.49	12.57	m	16.06
flat angle	29.43	0.44	3.93	28.00	nr	31.93
vertical angle	21.84	0.44	3.93	20.22	nr	24.15
flat three way intersection	33.25	0.55	4.92	36.94	nr	41.86
vertical three way intersection	21.18	0.55	4.92	24.57	nr	29.49
four way intersection	36.71	0.66	5.90	45.49	nr	51.39
E41 WORKED FINISHES/CUTTING TO IN SITU **CONCRETE**						
Worked finishes						
Tamping by mechanical means	-	0.03	0.22	0.09	m²	0.31
Power floating	-	0.19	1.38	0.30	m²	1.68
Trowelling	-	0.36	2.62	-	m²	2.62
Hacking						
by mechanical means	24.94	0.36	2.62	0.27	m²	2.89
by hand	-	0.77	5.60	-	m²	5.60
Lightly shot blasting surface of concrete	-	0.44	3.20	-	m²	3.20
Blasting surface of concrete						
to produce textured finish	-	0.77	5.60	0.58	m²	6.18
Wood float finish	-	0.14	1.02	-	m²	1.02
Tamped finish						
level or to falls	-	0.08	0.58	-	m²	0.58
to falls	-	0.11	0.80	-	m²	0.80
Spade finish	-	0.17	1.24	-	m²	1.24
Cutting chases						
Depth not exceeding 50 mm						
width 10 mm	-	0.36	2.62	0.77	m	3.39
width 50 mm	-	0.55	4.00	0.91	m	4.91
width 75 mm	-	0.73	5.31	1.04	m	6.35
Depth 50 - 100 mm						
width 75 mm	-	0.99	7.20	1.64	m	8.84
width 100 mm	-	1.10	8.00	1.73	m	9.73
width 100 mm; in reinforced concrete	-	1.65	12.00	2.67	m	14.67
Depth 100 - 150 mm						
width 100 mm	-	1.43	10.40	2.08	m	12.48
width 100 mm; in reinforced concrete	-	2.20	15.99	3.39	m	19.38
width 150 mm	-	1.76	12.80	2.33	m	15.13
width 150 mm; in reinforced concrete	-	2.64	19.19	3.78	m	22.97
Cutting rebates						
Depth not exceeding 50 mm						
width 50 mm	-	0.55	4.00	0.91	m	4.91

E IN SITU CONCRETE/LARGE PRECAST CONCRETE Excluding overheads and profit	PC £	Labour hours	Labour £	Material £	Unit	Total rate £
Depth 50 - 100 mm						
width 100 mm	-	1.10	8.00	1.73	m	9.73
NOTE: The following rates for cutting mortices						
and holes in reinforced concrete allow for						
diamond drilling.						
Cutting mortices						
Depth not exceeding 100 mm						
cross sectional size 20 mm diameter; making good	-	0.17	1.24	0.09	nr	1.33
cross sectional size 50 mm diameter; making good	-	0.19	1.38	0.12	nr	1.50
cross sectional size 150 x 150 mm; making good	-	0.39	2.84	0.30	nr	3.14
cross sectional size 300 x 300 mm; making good	-	0.77	5.60	0.64	nr	6.24
cross sectional size 50 mm diameter; in						
reinforced concrete; making good	-	-	-	-	nr	8.00
cross sectional size 50 - 75 mm diameter; in						
reinforced concrete; making good	-	-	-	-	nr	9.30
cross sectional size 75 - 100 mm diameter; in						
reinforced concrete; making good	-	-	-	-	nr	9.70
cross sectional size 100 - 125 mm diameter; in						
reinforced concrete; making good	-	-	-	-	nr	10.65
cross sectional size 125 - 150 mm diameter; in						
reinforced concrete; making good	-	-	-	-	nr	12.00
cross sectional size 150 x 150 mm; in						
reinforced concrete; making good	-	0.61	4.43	0.47	nr	4.90
cross sectional size 300 x 300 mm; in						
reinforced concrete; making good	-	1.15	8.36	0.90	nr	9.26
Depth 100 - 200 mm						
cross sectional size 50 mm diameter; in						
reinforced concrete; making good	-	-	-	-	nr	11.15
cross sectional size 50 - 75 mm diameter; in						
reinforced concrete; making good	-	-	-	-	nr	13.80
cross sectional size 75 - 100 mm diameter; in						
reinforced concrete; making good	-	-	-	-	nr	14.00
cross sectional size 100 - 125 mm diameter; in						
reinforced concrete; making good	-	-	-	-	nr	16.00
cross sectional size 125 - 150 mm diameter; in						
reinforced concrete; making good	-	-	-	-	nr	18.00
Depth 200 - 300 mm						
cross sectional size 50 mm diameter; in						
reinforced concrete; making good	-	-	-	-	nr	22.35
cross sectional size 50 - 75 mm diameter; in						
reinforced concrete; making good	-	-	-	-	nr	25.60
cross sectional size 75 - 100 mm diameter; in						
reinforced concrete; making good	-	-	-	-	nr	28.00
cross sectional size; 100 - 125 mm diameter; in						
reinforced concrete; making good	-	-	-	-	nr	31.95
cross sectional size; 125 - 150 mm diameter; in						
reinforced concrete; making good	-	-	-	-	nr	35.95
Depth exceeding 300 mm; 400 mm depth						
cross sectional size 50 mm diameter; in						
reinforced concrete; making good	-	-	-	-	nr	29.80
cross sectional size 50 - 75 mm diameter; in						
reinforced concrete; making good	-	-	-	-	nr	34.10
cross sectional size 75 - 100 mm diameter; in						
reinforced concrete; making good	-	-	-	-	nr	37.25
cross sectional size 100 - 125 mm diameter; in						
reinforced concrete; making good	-	-	-	-	nr	42.60
cross sectional size 125 - 150 mm diameter; in						
reinforced concrete; making good	-	-	-	-	nr	47.95

E IN SITU CONCRETE/LARGE PRECAST CONCRETE Excluding overheads and profit	PC £	Labour hours	Labour £	Material £	Unit	Total rate £
E41 WORKED FINISHES/CUTTING TO IN SITU CONCRETE - cont'd						
Cutting mortices - cont'd						
Depth exceeding 300 mm; 500 mm depth						
cross sectional size 50 mm diameter; in						
reinforced concrete; making good	-	-	-	-	nr	37.25
cross sectional size 50 - 75 mm diameter; in						
reinforced concrete; making good	-	-	-	-	nr	42.60
cross sectional size 75 - 100 mm diameter; in						
reinforced concrete; making good	-	-	-	-	nr	46.60
cross sectional size 100 - 125 mm diameter; in						
reinforced concrete; making good	-	-	-	-	nr	53.25
cross sectional size 125 - 150 mm diameter; in						
reinforced concrete; making good	-	-	-	-	nr	59.90
Depth exceeding 300 mm; 600 mm depth						
cross sectional size 50 mm diameter; in						
reinforced concrete; making good	-	-	-	-	nr	44.75
cross sectional size 50 - 75 mm diameter; in						
reinforced concrete; making good	-	-	-	-	nr	51.10
cross sectional size 75 - 100 mm diameter; in						
reinforced concrete; making good	-	-	-	-	nr	55.90
cross sectional size 100 - 125 mm diameter; in						
reinforced concrete; making good	-	-	-	-	nr	63.90
cross sectional size 125 - 150 mm diameter; in						
reinforced concrete; making good	-	-	-	-	nr	71.90
Cutting holes						
Depth not exceeding 100 mm						
cross sectional size 50 mm diameter; making						
good	-	0.39	2.84	0.31	nr	3.15
cross sectional size 50 mm diameter; in						
reinforced concrete; making good	-	0.61	4.43	0.49	nr	4.92
cross sectional size 100 mm diameter; making						
good	-	0.44	3.20	0.36	nr	3.56
cross sectional size 100 mm diameter; in						
reinforced concrete; making good	-	0.66	4.80	0.54	nr	5.34
cross sectional size 150 x 150 mm; making						
good	-	0.49	3.56	0.40	nr	3.96
cross sectional size 150 x 150 mm; in						
reinforced concrete; making good	-	0.77	5.60	0.62	nr	6.22
cross sectional size 300 x 300 mm; making						
good	-	0.61	4.43	0.49	nr	4.92
cross sectional size 300 x 300 mm; in						
reinforced concrete; making good	-	0.94	6.83	0.76	nr	7.59
Depth 100 - 200 mm						
cross sectional size 50 mm diameter; making						
good	-	0.55	4.00	0.45	nr	4.45
cross sectional size 50 mm diameter; in						
reinforced concrete; making good	-	0.83	6.03	0.67	nr	6.70
cross sectional size 100 mm diameter; making						
good	-	0.66	4.80	0.54	nr	5.34
cross sectional size 100 mm diameter; in						
reinforced concrete; making good	-	0.99	7.20	0.80	nr	8.00
cross sectional size 150 x 150 mm; making						
good	-	0.83	6.03	0.67	nr	6.70
cross sectional size 150 x 150 mm; in						
reinforced concrete; making good	-	1.26	9.16	1.03	nr	10.19
cross sectional size 300 x 300 mm; making						
good	-	1.05	7.63	0.85	nr	8.48
cross sectional size 300 x 300 mm; in						
reinforced concrete; making good	-	1.60	11.63	1.29	nr	12.92

E IN SITU CONCRETE/LARGE PRECAST CONCRETE Excluding overheads and profit	PC £	Labour hours	Labour £	Material £	Unit	Total rate £
Depth 100 - 200 mm - cont'd						
cross sectional size not exceeding 0.10 m²; in						
reinforced concrete; making good	-	-	-	-	nr	93.20
cross sectional size 0.10 m² - 0.20 m²; in						
reinforced concrete; making good	-	-	-	-	nr	186.35
cross sectional size 0.20 - 0.30 m²; in						
reinforced concrete; making good	-	-	-	-	nr	210.30
cross sectional size 0.30 - 0.40 m²; in						
reinforced concrete; making good	-	-	-	-	nr	244.95
cross sectional size 0.40 - 0.50 m²; in						
reinforced concrete; making good	-	-	-	-	nr	280.85
cross sectional size 0.50 - 0.60 m²; in						
reinforced concrete; making good	-	-	-	-	nr	327.45
cross sectional size 0.60 - 0.70 m²; in						
reinforced concrete; making good	-	-	-	-	nr	375.00
cross sectional size 0.70 - 0.80 m²; in						
reinforced concrete; making good	-	-	-	-	nr	430.00
Depth 200 - 300 mm						
cross sectional size 50 mm diameter; making good	-	0.83	6.03	0.67	nr	6.70
cross sectional size 50 mm diameter; in reinforced concrete; making good	-	1.26	9.16	1.03	nr	10.19
cross sectional size 100 mm diameter; making good	-	0.99	7.20	0.80	nr	8.00
cross sectional size 100 mm diameter; in reinforced concrete; making good	-	1.49	10.83	1.20	nr	12.03
cross sectional size 150 x 150 mm; making good	-	1.21	8.80	0.98	nr	9.78
cross sectional size 150 x 150 mm; in reinforced concrete; making good	-	1.82	13.23	1.47	nr	14.70
cross sectional size 300 x 300 mm; making good	-	1.54	11.20	1.25	nr	12.45
cross sectional size 300 x 300 mm; in reinforced concrete; making good	-	2.31	16.79	1.87	nr	18.66
E42 ACCESSORIES CAST INTO IN SITU CONCRETE						
Foundation bolt boxes						
Temporary plywood; for group of 4 nr bolts						
75 x 75 x 150 mm	-	0.49	5.49	0.93	nr	6.42
75 x 75 x 250 mm	-	0.49	5.49	1.17	nr	6.66
Expanded metal; Expamet Building Products Ltd or other equal and approved						
75 mm diameter x 150 mm long	-	0.33	3.70	1.25	nr	4.95
75 mm diameter x 300 mm long	-	0.33	3.70	1.72	nr	5.42
100 mm diameter x 450 mm long	-	0.33	3.70	3.08	nr	6.78
Foundation bolts and nuts						
Black hexagon						
10 mm diameter x 100 mm long	-	0.28	3.14	0.46	nr	3.60
12 mm diameter x 120 mm long	-	0.28	3.14	0.71	nr	3.85
16 mm diameter x 160 mm long	-	0.33	3.70	1.96	nr	5.66
20 mm diameter x 180 mm long	-	0.33	3.70	2.29	nr	5.99
Masonry slots						
Galvanised steel; dovetail slots; 1.20 mm thick; 18G						
75 mm long	-	0.09	1.01	0.21	nr	1.22
100 mm long	-	0.09	1.01	0.23	nr	1.24
150 mm long	-	0.10	1.12	0.28	nr	1.40
225 mm long	-	0.11	1.23	0.39	nr	1.62

E IN SITU CONCRETE/LARGE PRECAST CONCRETE Excluding overheads and profit	PC £	Labour hours	Labour £	Material £	Unit	Total rate £
E42 ACCESSORIES CAST INTO IN SITU **CONCRETE** - cont'd						
Masonry slots - cont'd						
Galvanised steel; metal insert slots; Halfen Ltd or other						
equal and approved; 2.50 mm thick; end caps and foam						
filling						
41 x 41 mm; ref P3270	-	0.44	4.93	8.04	m	**12.97**
41 x 41 mm x 75 mm; ref P3249	-	0.11	1.23	1.64	nr	**2.87**
41 x 41 mm x 100 mm; ref P3250	-	0.11	1.23	1.99	nr	**3.22**
41 x 41 mm x 150 mm; ref P3251	-	0.11	1.23	2.44	nr	**3.67**
Cramps						
Mild steel; once bent; one end shot fired into						
concrete; other end flanged and built into						
brickwork joint						
200 mm girth	-	0.17	1.93	0.46	nr	**2.39**
Column guards						
White nylon coated steel; "Rigifix" or other equal						
and approved; Huntley and Sparks Ltd; plugging;						
screwing to concrete; 1.50 mm thick						
75 x 75 x 1000 mm	-	0.88	9.86	17.19	nr	**27.05**
Galvanised steel; "Rigifix" or other equal and approved;						
Huntley and Sparks Ltd; 3 mm thick						
75 x 75 x 1000 mm	-	0.66	7.39	12.15	nr	**19.54**
Galvanised steel; "Rigifix" or other equal and approved;						
Huntley and Sparks Ltd; 4.50 mm thick						
75 x 75 x 1000 mm	-	0.66	7.39	16.33	nr	**23.72**
Stainless steel; "HKW" or other equal and approved;						
Halfen Ltd; 5 mm thick						
50 x 50 x 1500 mm	-	1.10	12.32	45.27	nr	**57.59**
50 x 50 x 2000 mm	-	1.32	14.78	63.77	nr	**78.55**
E60 PRECAST/COMPOSITE CONCRETE **DECKING**						
Prestressed precast flooring planks; Bison						
"Drycast" or other equal and approved;						
cement:sand (1:3) grout between planks and						
on prepared bearings						
100 mm thick suspended slabs; horizontal						
600 mm wide planks	-	-	-	-	m²	**36.67**
1200 mm wide planks	-	-	-	-	m²	**34.79**
150 mm thick suspended slabs; horizontal						
400 mm wide planks	-	-	-	-	m²	**37.65**
1200 mm wide planks	-	-	-	-	m²	**36.27**

F MASONRY Excluding overheads and profit	PC £	Labour hours	Labour £	Material £	Unit	Total rate £
F MASONRY						
F10 BRICK/BLOCK WALLING						
Common bricks; PC £175.00/1000; in cement mortar (1:3)						
Walls						
half brick thick	-	1.15	16.34	13.31	m²	**29.65**
half brick thick; building against other work;						
concrete	-	1.25	17.76	14.66	m²	**32.42**
half brick thick; building overhand	-	1.45	20.60	13.31	m²	**33.91**
half brick thick; curved; 6.00 m radii	-	1.50	21.32	13.31	m²	**34.63**
half brick thick; curved; 1.50 m radii	-	1.95	27.71	15.19	m²	**42.90**
one brick thick	-	1.95	27.71	26.62	m²	**54.33**
one brick thick; curved; 6.00 m radii	-	2.55	36.24	28.50	m²	**64.74**
one brick thick; curved; 1.50 m radii	-	3.15	44.76	29.18	m²	**73.94**
one and a half brick thick	-	2.65	37.66	39.93	m²	**77.59**
one and a half brick thick; battering	-	3.05	43.34	39.93	m²	**83.27**
two brick thick	-	3.20	45.47	53.24	m²	**98.71**
two brick thick; battering	-	3.80	54.00	53.24	m²	**107.24**
337 mm average thick; tapering, one side	-	3.35	47.60	39.93	m²	**87.53**
450 mm average thick; tapering, one side	-	4.30	61.10	53.24	m²	**114.34**
337 mm average thick; tapering, both sides	-	3.85	54.71	39.93	m²	**94.64**
450 mm average thick; tapering, both sides	-	4.85	68.92	53.92	m²	**122.84**
facework one side, half brick thick	-	1.25	17.76	13.31	m²	**31.07**
facework one side, one brick thick	-	2.05	29.13	26.62	m²	**55.75**
facework one side, one and a half brick thick	-	2.75	39.08	39.93	m²	**79.01**
facework one side, two brick thick	-	3.35	47.60	53.24	m²	**100.84**
facework both sides, half brick thick	-	1.40	19.89	13.31	m²	**33.20**
facework both sides, one brick thick	-	2.20	31.26	26.62	m²	**57.88**
facework both sides, one and a half brick thick	-	2.90	41.21	39.93	m²	**81.14**
facework both sides, two brick thick	-	3.45	49.02	53.24	m²	**102.26**
Isolated piers						
one brick thick	-	2.95	41.92	26.62	m²	**68.54**
two brick thick	-	4.60	65.37	53.92	m²	**119.29**
three brick thick	-	5.80	82.42	81.21	m²	**163.63**
Isolated casings						
half brick thick	-	1.50	21.32	13.31	m²	**34.63**
one brick thick	-	2.55	36.24	26.62	m²	**62.86**
Chimney stacks						
one brick thick	-	2.95	41.92	26.62	m²	**68.54**
two brick thick	-	4.60	65.37	53.92	m²	**119.29**
three brick thick	-	5.80	82.42	81.21	m²	**163.63**
Projections						
225 mm width; 112 mm depth; vertical	-	0.35	4.97	2.74	m	**7.71**
225 mm width; 225 mm depth; vertical	-	0.70	9.95	5.49	m	**15.44**
327 mm width; 225 mm depth; vertical	-	1.05	14.92	8.23	m	**23.15**
440 mm width; 225 mm depth; vertical	-	1.15	16.34	10.98	m	**27.32**
Closing cavities						
width of cavity 50 mm, closing with common						
brickwork half brick thick; vertical	-	0.35	4.97	0.68	m	**5.65**
width of cavity 50 mm, closing with common						
brickwork half brick thick; horizontal	-	0.35	4.97	2.02	m	**6.99**
width of cavity 50 mm, closing with common						
brickwork half brick thick; including damp proof						
course; vertical	-	0.46	6.54	1.56	m	**8.10**
width of cavity 50 mm, closing with common						
brickwork half brick thick; including damp proof						
course; horizontal	-	0.40	5.68	2.66	m	**8.34**
width of cavity 75 mm; closing with common						
brickwork half brick thick; vertical	-	0.35	4.97	0.98	m	**5.95**

F MASONRY Excluding overheads and profit	PC £	Labour hours	Labour £	Material £	Unit	Total rate £
F10 BRICK/BLOCK WALLING - cont'd						
Common bricks; PC £175.00/1000; in cement **mortar (1:3)** - cont'd						
Closing cavities - cont'd						
width of cavity 75 mm, closing with common brickwork half brick thick; horizontal	-	0.35	4.97	3.15	m	8.12
width of cavity 75 mm; closing with common brickwork half brick thick; including damp proof course; vertical	-	0.46	6.54	1.87	m	8.41
width of cavity 75 mm, closing with common brickwork half brick thick; including damp proof course; horizontal	-	0.40	5.68	3.79	m	9.47
Bonding to existing						
half brick thick	-	0.35	4.97	0.73	m	5.70
one brick thick	-	0.50	7.11	1.46	m	8.57
one and a half brick thick	-	0.80	11.37	2.18	m	13.55
two brick thick	-	1.10	15.63	2.91	m	18.54
ADD or DEDUCT to walls for variation of £10.00/1000 in PC of common bricks						
half brick thick	-	-	-	0.65	m²	0.65
one brick thick	-	-	-	1.29	m²	1.29
one and a half brick thick	-	-	-	1.94	m²	1.94
two brick thick	-	-	-	2.58	m²	2.58
Common bricks; PC £175.00/1000; in gauged **mortar (1:1:6)**						
Walls						
half brick thick	-	1.15	16.34	13.11	m²	29.45
half brick thick; building against other work; concrete	-	1.25	17.76	15.54	m²	33.30
half brick thick; building overhand	-	1.45	20.60	13.11	m²	33.71
half brick thick; curved; 6.00 m radii	-	1.50	21.32	13.11	m²	34.43
half brick thick; curved; 1.50 m radii	-	1.95	27.71	14.99	m²	42.70
one brick thick	-	1.95	27.71	26.22	m²	53.93
one brick thick; curved; 6.00 m radii	-	2.55	36.24	28.10	m²	64.34
one brick thick; curved; 1.50 m radii	-	3.15	44.76	28.71	m²	73.47
one and a half brick thick	-	2.65	37.66	39.33	m²	76.99
one and a half brick thick; battering	-	3.05	43.34	39.33	m²	82.67
two brick thick	-	3.20	45.47	52.44	m²	97.91
two brick thick; battering	-	3.80	54.00	52.44	m²	106.44
337 mm average thick; tapering, one side	-	3.35	47.60	39.33	m²	86.93
450 mm average thick; tapering, one side	-	4.30	61.10	52.44	m²	113.54
337 mm average thick; tapering both sides	-	3.85	54.71	39.33	m²	94.04
450 mm average thick; tapering both sides	-	4.85	68.92	53.05	m²	121.97
facework one side, half brick thick	-	1.25	17.76	13.11	m²	30.87
facework one side, one brick thick	-	2.05	29.13	26.22	m²	55.35
facework one side, one and a half brick thick	-	2.75	39.08	39.33	m²	78.41
facework one side, two brick thick	-	3.35	47.60	52.44	m²	100.04
facework both sides, half brick thick	-	1.40	19.89	13.11	m²	33.00
facework both sides, one brick thick	-	2.20	31.26	26.22	m²	57.48
facework both sides, one and a half brick thick	-	2.90	41.21	39.33	m²	80.54
facework both sides, two brick thick	-	3.45	49.02	52.44	m²	101.46
Isolated piers						
one brick thick	-	2.95	41.92	26.22	m²	68.14
two brick thick	-	4.60	65.37	53.05	m²	118.42
three brick thick	-	5.80	82.42	79.88	m²	162.30
Isolated casings						
half brick thick	-	1.50	21.32	13.11	m²	34.43
one brick thick	-	2.55	36.24	26.22	m²	62.46

F MASONRY Excluding overheads and profit	PC £	Labour hours	Labour £	Material £	Unit	Total rate £
Chimney stacks						
one brick thick	-	2.95	41.92	26.22	m²	68.14
two brick thick	-	4.60	65.37	53.05	m²	118.42
three brick thick	-	5.80	82.42	79.88	m²	162.30
Projections						
225 mm width; 112 mm depth; vertical	-	0.35	4.97	2.72	m	7.69
225 mm width; 225 mm depth; vertical	-	0.70	9.95	5.44	m	15.39
337 mm width; 225 mm depth; vertical	-	1.05	14.92	8.16	m	23.08
440 mm width; 225 mm depth; vertical	-	1.15	16.34	10.88	m	27.22
Closing cavities						
width of cavity 50 mm, closing with common brickwork half brick thick; vertical	-	0.35	4.97	0.67	m	5.64
width of cavity 50 mm, closing with common brickwork half brick thick; horizontal	-	0.35	4.97	2.01	m	6.98
width of cavity 50 mm, closing with common brickwork half brick thick; including damp proof course; vertical	-	0.46	6.54	1.55	m	8.09
width of cavity 50 mm, closing with common brickwork half brick thick; including damp proof course; horizontal	-	0.40	5.68	2.65	m	8.33
width of cavity 75 mm; closing with common brickwork half brick thick; vertical	-	0.35	4.97	0.97	m	5.94
width of cavity 75 mm, closing with common brickwork half brick thick; horizontal	-	0.35	4.97	3.14	m	8.11
width of cavity 75 mm, closing with common brickwork half brick thick; including damp proof course; vertical	-	0.46	6.54	1.86	m	8.40
width of cavity 75 mm, closing with common brickwork half brick thick; including damp proof course; horizontal	-	0.40	5.68	3.78	m	9.46
Bonding to existing						
half brick thick	-	0.35	4.97	0.72	m	5.69
one brick thick	-	0.50	7.11	1.44	m	8.55
one and a half brick thick	-	0.80	11.37	2.15	m	13.52
two brick thick	-	1.10	15.63	2.87	m	18.50
Arches						
height on face 102 mm, width of exposed soffit 102 mm, shape of arch - segmental, one ring	-	1.95	21.15	7.36	m	28.51
height on face 102 mm, width of exposed soffit 215 mm, shape of arch - segmental, one ring	-	2.55	29.67	8.93	m	38.60
height on face 102 mm, width of exposed soffit 102 mm, shape of arch - semi-circular, one ring	-	2.50	28.96	7.36	m	36.32
height on face 102 mm, width of exposed soffit 215 mm, shape of arch - semi-circular, one ring	-	3.10	37.49	8.93	m	46.42
height on face 215 mm, width of exposed soffit 102 mm, shape of arch - segmental, two ring	-	2.50	28.96	8.74	m	37.70
height on face 215 mm, width of exposed soffit 215 mm, shape of arch - segmental, two ring	-	3.05	36.78	11.68	m	48.46
height on face 215 mm, width of exposed soffit 102 mm, shape of arch semi-circular, two ring	-	3.35	41.04	8.74	m	49.78
height on face 215 mm, width of exposed soffit 215 mm, shape of arch - semi-circular, two ring	-	3.80	47.44	11.68	m	59.12
ADD or DEDUCT to walls for variation of £10.00/1000 in PC of common bricks						
half brick thick	-	-	-	0.65	m²	0.65
one brick thick	-	-	-	1.29	m²	1.29
one and a half brick thick	-	-	-	1.94	m²	1.94
two brick thick	-	-	-	2.58	m²	2.58

F MASONRY Excluding overheads and profit	PC £	Labour hours	Labour £	Material £	Unit	Total rate £
F10 BRICK/BLOCK WALLING - cont'd						
Class A engineering bricks; PC £353.00/1000; **in cement mortar (1:3)**						
Walls						
half brick thick	-	1.25	17.76	24.28	m²	42.04
one brick thick	-	2.05	29.13	48.55	m²	77.68
one brick thick; building against other work	-	2.45	34.81	50.57	m²	85.38
one brick thick; curved; 6.00 m radii	-	2.75	39.08	48.55	m²	87.63
one and a half brick thick	-	2.75	39.08	72.83	m²	111.91
one and a half brick thick; building against other						
work	-	3.35	47.60	72.83	m²	120.43
two brick thick	-	3.45	49.02	97.10	m²	146.12
337 mm average thick; tapering, one side	-	3.55	50.45	72.83	m²	123.28
450 mm average thick; tapering, one side	-	4.60	65.37	97.10	m²	162.47
337 mm average thick; tapering, both sides	-	4.15	58.97	72.83	m²	131.80
450 mm average thick; tapering, both sides	-	5.25	74.60	97.77	m²	172.37
facework one side, half brick thick	-	1.40	19.89	24.28	m²	44.17
facework one side, one brick thick	-	2.20	31.26	48.55	m²	79.81
facework one side, one and a half brick thick	-	2.90	41.21	72.83	m²	114.04
facework one side, two brick thick	-	3.55	50.45	97.10	m²	147.55
facework both sides, half brick thick	-	1.50	21.32	24.28	m²	45.60
facework both sides, one brick thick	-	2.30	32.68	48.55	m²	81.23
facework both sides, one and a half brick thick	-	3.00	42.63	72.83	m²	115.46
facework both sides, two brick thick	-	3.70	52.58	97.10	m²	149.68
Isolated piers						
one brick thick	-	3.20	45.47	48.55	m²	94.02
two brick thick	-	5.05	71.76	97.77	m²	169.53
three brick thick	-	6.20	88.10	147.00	m²	235.10
Isolated casings						
half brick thick	-	1.60	22.74	24.28	m²	47.02
one brick thick	-	2.75	39.08	48.55	m²	87.63
Projections						
225 mm width; 112 mm depth; vertical	-	0.40	5.68	5.18	m	10.86
225 mm width; 225 mm depth; vertical	-	0.75	10.66	10.36	m	21.02
337 mm width; 225 mm depth; vertical	-	1.10	15.63	15.54	m	31.17
440 mm width; 225 mm depth; vertical	-	1.25	17.76	20.72	m	38.48
Bonding to existing						
half brick thick	-	0.40	5.68	1.34	m	7.02
one brick thick	-	0.60	8.53	2.67	m	11.20
one and a half brick thick	-	0.80	11.37	4.01	m	15.38
two brick thick	-	1.20	17.05	5.35	m	22.40
ADD or DEDUCT to walls for variation of						
£10.00/1000 in PC of bricks						
half brick thick	-	-	-	0.65	m²	0.65
one brick thick	-	-	-	1.29	m²	1.29
one and a half brick thick	-	-	-	1.94	m²	1.94
two brick thick	-	-	-	2.58	m²	2.58
Class B engineering bricks; PC £235.00/1000; **in cement mortar (1:3)**						
Walls						
half brick thick	-	1.25	17.76	16.82	m²	34.58
one brick thick	-	2.05	29.13	33.63	m²	62.76
one brick thick; building against other work	-	2.45	34.81	35.66	m²	70.47
one brick thick; curved; 6.00 m radii	-	2.75	39.08	33.63	m²	72.71
one and a half brick thick	-	2.75	39.08	50.45	m²	89.53
one and a half brick thick; building against other						
work	-	3.35	47.60	50.45	m²	98.05
two brick thick	-	3.45	49.02	67.26	m²	116.28
337 mm average thick; tapering, one side	-	3.55	50.45	50.45	m²	100.90

F MASONRY Excluding overheads and profit	PC £	Labour hours	Labour £	Material £	Unit	Total rate £
Walls - cont'd						
450 mm average thick; tapering, one side	-	4.60	65.37	67.26	m²	**132.63**
337 mm average thick; tapering, both sides	-	4.15	58.97	50.45	m²	**109.42**
450 mm average thick; tapering, both sides	-	5.25	74.60	67.94	m²	**142.54**
facework one side, half brick thick	-	1.40	19.89	16.82	m²	**36.71**
facework one side, one brick thick	-	2.20	31.26	33.63	m²	**64.89**
facework one side, one and a half brick thick	-	2.90	41.21	50.45	m²	**91.66**
facework one side, two brick thick	-	3.55	50.45	67.26	m²	**117.71**
facework both sides, half brick thick	-	1.50	21.32	16.82	m²	**38.14**
facework both sides, one brick thick	-	2.30	32.68	33.63	m²	**66.31**
facework both sides, one and a half brick thick	-	3.00	42.63	50.45	m²	**93.08**
facework both sides, two brick thick	-	3.70	52.58	67.26	m²	**119.84**
Isolated piers						
one brick thick	-	3.20	45.47	33.63	m²	**79.10**
two brick thick	-	5.05	71.76	67.94	m²	**139.70**
three brick thick	-	6.20	88.10	102.24	m²	**190.34**
Isolated casings						
half brick thick	-	1.60	22.74	16.82	m²	**39.56**
one brick thick	-	2.75	39.08	33.63	m²	**72.71**
Projections						
225 mm width; 112 mm depth; vertical	-	0.40	5.68	3.52	m	**9.20**
225 mm width; 225 mm depth; vertical	-	0.75	10.66	7.05	m	**17.71**
337 mm width; 225 mm depth; vertical	-	1.10	15.63	10.57	m	**26.20**
440 mm width; 225 mm depth; vertical	-	1.25	17.76	14.09	m	**31.85**
Bonding to existing						
half brick thick	-	0.40	5.68	0.92	m	**6.60**
one brick thick	-	0.60	8.53	1.85	m	**10.38**
one and a half brick thick	-	0.80	11.37	2.77	m	**14.14**
two brick thick	-	1.20	17.05	3.69	m	**20.74**
ADD or DEDUCT to walls for variation of £10.00/1000 in PC of bricks						
half brick thick	-	-	-	0.65	m²	**0.65**
one brick thick	-	-	-	1.29	m²	**1.29**
one and a half brick thick	-	-	-	1.94	m²	**1.94**
two brick thick	-	-	-	2.58	m²	**2.58**
Facing bricks; sand faced; PC £155.00/1000 (unless otherwise stated); in gauged mortar (1:1:6)						
Walls						
facework one side, half brick thick; stretcher bond	-	1.50	21.32	11.17	m²	**32.49**
facework one side, half brick thick; flemish bond with snapped headers	-	1.75	24.87	11.17	m²	**36.04**
facework one side, half brick thick; stretcher bond; building against other work; concrete	-	1.60	22.74	12.39	m²	**35.13**
facework one side, half brick thick; flemish bond with snapped headers; building against other work; concrete	-	1.85	26.29	12.39	m²	**38.68**
facework one side, half brick thick; stretcher bond; building overhand	-	1.85	26.29	11.17	m²	**37.46**
facework one side, half brick thick; flemish bond with snapped headers; building overhand	-	2.05	29.13	11.17	m²	**40.30**
facework one side, half brick thick; stretcher bond; curved; 6.00 m radii	-	2.20	31.26	11.17	m²	**42.43**
facework one side, half brick thick; flemish bond with snapped headers; curved; 6.00 m radii	-	2.45	34.81	11.17	m²	**45.98**
facework one side, half brick thick; stretcher bond; curved; 1.50 m radii	-	2.75	39.08	11.17	m²	**50.25**
facework one side, half brick thick; flemish bond with snapped headers; curved; 1.50 m radii	-	3.20	45.47	11.17	m²	**56.64**

F MASONRY Excluding overheads and profit	PC £	Labour hours	Labour £	Material £	Unit	Total rate £
F10 BRICK/BLOCK WALLING - cont'd						
Facing bricks; sand faced; PC £155.00/1000 **(unless otherwise stated); in gauged mortar** **(1:1:6)** - cont'd						
Walls - cont'd						
facework both sides, one brick thick; two stretcher skins tied together	-	2.60	36.95	23.37	m²	60.32
facework both sides, one brick thick; flemish bond	-	2.65	37.66	22.35	m²	60.01
facework both sides, one brick thick; two stretcher skins tied together; curved; 6.00 m radii	-	3.55	50.45	24.92	m²	75.37
facework both sides, one brick thick; flemish bond; curved; 6.00 m radii	-	3.70	52.58	23.91	m²	76.49
facework both sides, one brick thick; two stretcher skins tied together; curved; 1.50 m radii	-	4.45	63.23	27.09	m²	90.32
facework both sides, one brick thick; flemish bond; curved; 1.50 m radii	-	4.60	65.37	26.08	m²	91.45
Isolated piers						
facework both sides, one brick thick; two stretcher skins tied together	-	3.05	43.34	23.95	m²	67.29
facework both sides, one brick thick; flemish bond	-	3.10	44.05	23.95	m²	68.00
Isolated casings						
facework one side, half brick thick; stretcher bond	-	2.30	32.68	11.17	m²	43.85
facework one side, half brick thick; flemish bond with snapped headers	-	2.55	36.24	11.17	m²	47.41
Projections						
225 mm width; 112 mm depth; stretcher bond; vertical	-	0.35	4.97	2.29	m	7.26
225 mm width; 112 mm depth; flemish bond with snapped headers; vertical	-	0.45	6.39	2.29	m	8.68
225 mm width; 225 mm depth; flemish bond; vertical	-	0.75	10.66	4.58	m	15.24
328 mm width; 112 mm depth; stretcher bond; vertical	-	0.70	9.95	3.44	m	13.39
328 mm width; 112 mm depth; flemish bond with snapped headers; vertical	-	0.80	11.37	3.44	m	14.81
328 mm width; 225 mm depth; flemish bond; vertical	-	1.40	19.89	6.84	m	26.73
440 mm width; 112 mm depth; stretcher bond; vertical	-	1.05	14.92	4.58	m	19.50
440 mm width; 112 mm depth; flemish bond with snapped headers; vertical	-	1.10	15.63	4.58	m	20.21
440 mm width; 225 mm depth; flemish bond; vertical	-	2.00	28.42	9.16	m	37.58
Arches						
height on face 215 mm, width of exposed soffit 102 mm, shape of arch - flat	-	1.15	13.53	3.78	m	17.31
height on face 215 mm, width of exposed soffit 215 mm, shape of arch - flat	-	1.70	21.34	6.19	m	27.53
height one face 215 mm, width of exposed soffit 102 mm, shape of arch - segmental, one ring	-	2.20	24.07	8.31	m	32.38
height on face 215 mm, width of exposed soffit 215 mm, shape of arch - segmental, one ring	-	2.65	30.47	10.58	m	41.05
height on face 215 mm, width of exposed soffit 102 mm, shape of arch - semi-circular, one ring	-	3.35	40.42	8.31	m	48.73

F MASONRY Excluding overheads and profit	PC £	Labour hours	Labour £	Material £	Unit	Total rate £
Arches - cont'd						
height on face 215 mm, width of exposed soffit 215 mm, shape of arch - semi-circular, one ring	-	4.50	56.76	10.58	m	**67.34**
height on face 215 mm, width of exposed soffit 102 mm, shape of arch - segmental, two ring	-	2.70	31.18	8.31	m	**39.49**
height on face 215 mm, width of exposed soffit 215 mm, shape of arch - segmental, two ring	-	3.50	42.55	10.58	m	**53.13**
height on face 215 mm, width of exposed soffit 102 mm, shape of arch - semi-circular, two ring	-	4.50	56.76	8.31	m	**65.07**
height on face 215 mm, width of exposed soffit 215 mm, shape of arch - semi-circular, two ring	-	6.20	80.91	10.58	m	**91.49**
Arches; cut voussoirs; PC £198.00/100						
height on face 215 mm, width of exposed soffit 102 mm, shape of arch - segmental, one ring	-	2.25	24.79	33.29	m	**58.08**
height on face 215 mm, width of exposed soffit 215 mm, shape of arch - segmental, one ring	-	2.80	32.60	60.54	m	**93.14**
height on face 215 mm, width of exposed soffit 102 mm, shape of arch - semi-circular, one ring	-	2.55	29.05	33.29	m	**62.34**
height on face 215 mm, width of exposed soffit 215 mm, shape of arch - semi-circular, one ring	-	3.20	38.28	60.54	m	**98.82**
height on face 320 mm, width of exposed soffit 102 mm, shape of arch - segmental, one and a half ring	-	3.00	35.44	60.47	m	**95.91**
height on face 320 mm, width of exposed soffit 215 mm, shape of arch - segmental, one and a half ring	-	3.90	48.23	121.71	m	**169.94**
Arches; bullnosed specials; PC £1265.00/1000						
height on face 215 mm, width of exposed soffit 102 mm, shape of arch - flat	-	1.20	14.24	19.83	m	**34.07**
height on face 215 mm, width of exposed soffit 215 mm, shape of arch - flat	-	1.75	22.05	38.69	m	**60.74**
Bullseye windows; 600 mm diameter						
height on face 215 mm, width of exposed soffit 102 mm, two rings	-	5.75	74.52	7.16	nr	**81.68**
height on face 215 mm, width of exposed soffit 215 mm, two rings	-	8.05	107.20	12.25	nr	**119.45**
Bullseye windows; 600 mm diameter; cut voussoirs; PC £198.00/100						
height on face 215 mm, width of exposed soffit 102 mm, one ring	-	4.85	61.73	73.83	nr	**135.56**
height on face 215 mm, width of exposed soffit 215 mm, one ring	-	6.65	87.31	145.59	nr	**232.90**
Bullseye windows; 1200 mm diameter						
height on face 215 mm, width of exposed soffit 102 mm, two rings	-	8.95	119.99	17.85	nr	**137.84**
height on face 215 mm, width of exposed soffit 215 mm, two rings	-	12.90	176.12	28.60	nr	**204.72**
Bullseye windows; 1200 mm diameter; cut voussoirs; PC £198.00/1000						
height on face 215 mm, width of exposed soffit 102 mm, one ring	-	7.60	100.81	131.50	nr	**232.31**
height on face 215 mm, width of exposed soffit 215 mm, one ring	-	10.80	146.28	254.68	nr	**400.96**
ADD or DEDUCT for variation of £10.00/1000 in PC of facing bricks in 102 mm high arches with 215 mm soffit	-	-	-	0.29	m	**0.29**
Facework sills						
150 mm x 102 mm; headers on edge; pointing top and one side; set weathering; horizontal	-	0.65	9.24	2.29	m	**11.53**
150 mm x 102 mm; cant headers on edge; PC £1265.00/1000; pointing top and one side; set weathering; horizontal	-	0.70	9.95	18.34	m	**28.29**

F MASONRY Excluding overheads and profit	PC £	Labour hours	Labour £	Material £	Unit	Total rate £
F10 BRICK/BLOCK WALLING - cont'd						
Facing bricks; sand faced; PC £155.00/1000 (unless otherwise stated); in gauged mortar (1:1:6) - cont'd						
Facework sills - cont'd						
150 mm x 102 mm; bullnosed specials; PC £1265.00/1000; headers on flat; pointing top and one side; horizontal	-	0.60	8.53	18.34	m	26.87
Facework copings						
215 mm x 102 mm; headers on edge; pointing top and both sides; horizontal	-	0.50	7.11	2.38	m	9.49
260 mm x 102 mm; headers on edge; pointing top and both sides; horizontal	-	0.80	11.37	3.50	m	14.87
215 mm x 102 mm; double bullnose specials; PC £1265.00/1000; headers on edge; pointing top and both sides; horizontal	-	0.60	8.53	18.44	m	26.97
260 mm x 102 mm; single bullnose specials; PC £1265.00/1000; headers on edge; pointing top and both sides; horizontal	-	0.80	11.37	36.65	m	48.02
ADD or DEDUCT for variation of £10.00/1000 in PC of facing bricks in copings 215 mm wide, 102 mm high	-	-	-	0.14	m	0.14
Extra over facing bricks for; facework ornamental bands and the like, plain bands; PC £165.00/1000						
flush; horizontal, 225 mm width; entirely of stretchers	-	0.25	3.55	0.29	m	3.84
Extra over facing bricks for; facework quoins; PC £165.00/1000						
flush; mean girth 320 mm	-	0.35	4.97	0.29	m	5.26
Bonding to existing						
facework one side, half brick thick; stretcher bond	-	0.60	8.53	0.61	m	9.14
facework one side, half brick thick, flemish bond with snapped headers	-	0.60	8.53	0.61	m	9.14
facework both sides, one brick thick; two stretcher skins tied together	-	0.80	11.37	1.22	m	12.59
facework both sides, one brick thick; flemish bond	-	0.80	11.37	1.22	m	12.59
ADD or DEDUCT for variation of £10.00/1000 in PC of facing bricks; in walls built entirely of facings; in stretcher or flemish bond						
half brick thick	-	-	-	0.65	m²	0.65
one brick thick	-	-	-	1.29	m²	1.29
Facing bricks; white sandlime; PC £180.00/1000 in gauged mortar (1:1:6)						
Walls						
facework one side, half brick thick; stretcher bond	-	1.50	21.32	13.43	m²	34.75
facework both sides, one brick thick; flemish bond	-	2.65	37.66	26.86	m²	64.52
ADD or DEDUCT for variation of £10.00/1000 in PC of facing bricks; in walls built entirely of facings; in stretcher or flemish bond						
half brick thick	-	-	-	0.65	m²	0.65
one brick thick	-	-	-	1.29	m²	1.29

F MASONRY Excluding overheads and profit	PC £	Labour hours	Labour £	Material £	Unit	Total rate £
Facing bricks; machine made facings; PC £330.00/1000 (unless otherwise stated); in gauged mortar (1:1:6)						
Walls						
facework one side, half brick thick; stretcher bond	-	1.50	21.32	23.11	m²	**44.43**
facework one side, half brick thick, flemish bond with snapped headers	-	1.75	24.87	23.11	m²	**47.98**
facework one side, half brick thick; stretcher bond; building against other work; concrete	-	1.60	22.74	24.32	m²	**47.06**
facework one side, half brick thick; flemish bond with snapped headers; building against other work; concrete	-	1.85	26.29	24.32	m²	**50.61**
facework one side, half brick thick, stretcher bond; building overhand	-	1.85	26.29	23.11	m²	**49.40**
facework one side, half brick thick; flemish bond with snapped headers; building overhand	-	2.05	29.13	23.11	m²	**52.24**
facework one side, half brick thick; stretcher bond; curved; 6.00 m radii	-	2.20	31.26	23.11	m²	**54.37**
facework one side, half brick thick; flemish bond with snapped headers; curved; 6.00 m radii	-	2.45	34.81	23.11	m²	**57.92**
facework one side, half brick thick; stretcher bond; curved; 1.50 m radii	-	2.75	39.08	26.66	m²	**65.74**
facework one side; half brick thick; flemish bond with snapped headers; curved; 1.50 m radii	-	3.20	45.47	26.66	m²	**72.13**
facework both sides, one brick thick; two stretcher skins tied together	-	2.60	36.95	47.23	m²	**84.18**
facework both sides, one brick thick; flemish bond	-	3.55	50.45	46.22	m²	**96.67**
facework both sides, one brick thick; two stretcher skins tied together; curved; 6.00 m radii	-	3.55	50.45	50.78	m²	**101.23**
facework both sides, one brick thick; flemish bond; curved; 6.00 m radii	-	3.70	52.58	49.76	m²	**102.34**
facework both sides, one brick thick; two stretcher skins tied together; curved; 1.50 m radii	-	4.45	63.23	54.93	m²	**118.16**
facework both sides, one brick thick; flemish bond; curved; 1.50 m radii	-	4.60	65.37	53.92	m²	**119.29**
Isolated piers						
facework both sides, one brick thick; two stretcher skins tied together	-	3.05	43.34	47.81	m²	**91.15**
facework both sides, one brick thick; flemish bond	-	3.10	44.05	47.81	m²	**91.86**
Isolated casings						
facework one side, half brick thick; stretcher bond	-	2.30	32.68	23.11	m²	**55.79**
facework one side, half brick thick; flemish bond with snapped headers	-	2.55	36.24	23.11	m²	**59.35**
Projections						
225 mm width; 112 mm depth; stretcher bond; vertical	-	0.35	4.97	4.94	m	**9.91**
225 mm width; 112 mm depth; flemish bond with snapped headers; vertical	-	0.45	6.39	4.94	m	**11.33**
225 mm width; 225 mm depth; flemish bond; vertical	-	0.75	10.66	9.89	m	**20.55**
328 mm width; 112 mm depth; stretcher bond; vertical	-	0.70	9.95	7.42	m	**17.37**
328 mm width; 112 mm depth; flemish bond with snapped headers; vertical	-	0.80	11.37	7.42	m	**18.79**

F MASONRY Excluding overheads and profit	PC £	Labour hours	Labour £	Material £	Unit	Total rate £
F10 BRICK/BLOCK WALLING - cont'd						
Facing bricks; machine made facings; PC £330.00/1000 (unless otherwise stated); in gauged mortar (1:1:6) - cont'd						
Projections - cont'd						
328 mm width; 225 mm depth; flemish bond; vertical	-	1.40	19.89	14.80	m	**34.69**
440 mm width; 112 mm depth; stretcher bond; vertical	-	1.05	14.92	9.89	m	**24.81**
440 mm width; 112 mm depth; flemish bond with snapped headers; vertical	-	1.10	15.63	9.89	m	**25.52**
440 mm width; 225 mm depth; flemish bond; vertical	-	2.00	28.42	19.77	m	**48.19**
Arches						
height on face 215 mm, width of exposed soffit 102 mm, shape of arch - flat	-	1.15	13.53	6.43	m	**19.96**
height on face 215 mm, width of exposed soffit 215 mm, shape of arch - flat	-	1.70	21.34	11.55	m	**32.89**
height on face 215 mm, width of exposed soffit 102 mm, shape of arch - segmental, one ring	-	2.20	24.07	10.96	m	**35.03**
height on face 215 mm, width of exposed soffit 215 mm, shape of arch - segmental, one ring	-	2.65	30.47	15.88	m	**46.35**
height on face 215 mm, width of exposed soffit 102 mm, shape of arch - semi-circular, one ring	-	3.35	40.42	10.96	m	**51.38**
height on face 215 mm, width of exposed soffit 215 mm, shape of arch - semi-circular, one ring	-	4.50	56.76	15.88	m	**72.64**
height on face 215 mm, width of exposed soffit 102 mm, shape of arch - segmental, two ring	-	2.70	31.18	10.96	m	**42.14**
height on face 215 mm, width of exposed soffit 215 mm, shape of arch - segmental, two ring	-	3.50	42.55	15.88	m	**58.43**
height on face 215 mm, width of exposed soffit 102 mm, shape of arch - semi-circular, two ring	-	4.50	56.76	10.96	m	**67.72**
height on face 215 mm, width of exposed soffit 215 mm, shape of arch - semi-circular, two ring	-	6.20	80.91	15.88	m	**96.79**
Arches; cut voussoirs; PC £2570.00/1000						
height on face 215 mm, width of exposed soffit 102 mm, shape of arch - segmental, one ring	-	2.25	24.79	43.06	m	**67.85**
height on face 215 mm, width of exposed soffit 215 mm, shape of arch - segmental, one ring	-	2.80	32.60	80.09	m	**112.69**
height on face 215 mm, width of exposed soffit 102 mm, shape of arch - semi-circular, one ring	-	2.55	29.05	43.06	m	**72.11**
height on face 215 mm, width of exposed soffit 215 mm, shape of arch - semi-circular, one ring	-	3.20	38.28	80.09	m	**118.37**
height on face 320 mm, width of exposed soffit 102 mm, shape of arch - segmental, one and a half ring	-	3.00	35.44	80.02	m	**115.46**
height on face 320 mm, width of exposed soffit 215 mm, shape of arch - segmental, one and a half ring	-	3.90	48.23	160.81	m	**209.04**
Arches; bullnosed specials; PC £1186.00/1000						
height on face 215 mm, width of exposed soffit 102 mm, shape of arch - flat	-	1.20	14.24	18.70	m	**32.94**
height on face 215 mm, width of exposed soffit 215 mm, shape of arch - flat	-	1.75	22.05	36.40	m	**58.45**
Bullseye windows; 600 mm diameter						
height on face 215 mm, width of exposed soffit 102 mm, two rings	-	5.75	74.52	12.73	nr	**87.25**
height on face 215 mm, width of exposed soffit 215 mm, two rings	-	8.05	107.20	23.39	nr	**130.59**

F MASONRY Excluding overheads and profit	PC £	Labour hours	Labour £	Material £	Unit	Total rate £
Bullseye windows; 600 mm diameter; cut voussoirs; PC £2570.00/1000						
height on face 215 mm, width of exposed soffit 102 mm, one ring	-	4.85	61.73	99.49	nr	**161.22**
height on face 215 mm, width of exposed soffit, 215 mm, one ring	-	6.65	87.31	196.92	nr	**284.23**
Bullseye windows; 1200 mm diameter						
height on face 215 mm, width of exposed soffit 102 mm, two rings	-	8.95	119.99	28.99	nr	**148.98**
height on face 215 mm, width of exposed soffit 215 mm, two rings	-	12.90	176.12	50.87	nr	**226.99**
Bullseye windows; 1200 mm diameter; cut voussoirs; PC £2570.00/1000						
height on face 215 mm, width of exposed soffit 102 mm, one ring	-	7.60	100.81	175.50	nr	**276.31**
height on face 215 mm, width of exposed soffit 215 mm, one ring	-	10.80	146.28	342.67	nr	**488.95**
ADD or DEDUCT for variation of £10.00/1000 in PC of facing bricks in 102 mm high arches with 215 mm soffit	-	-	-	0.29	m	**0.29**
Facework sills						
150 mm x 102 mm; headers on edge; pointing top and one side; set weathering; horizontal	-	0.65	9.24	4.94	m	**14.18**
150 mm x 102 mm; cant headers on edge; PC £1186.00/1000; pointing top and one side; set weathering; horizontal	-	0.70	9.95	17.21	m	**27.16**
150 mm x 102 mm; bullnosed specials; PC £1186.00/1000; headers on flat; pointing top and one side; horizontal	-	0.60	8.53	17.21	m	**25.74**
Facework copings						
215 mm x 102 mm; headers on edge; pointing top and both sides; horizontal	-	0.50	7.11	5.03	m	**12.14**
260 mm x 102 mm; headers on edge; pointing top and both sides; horizontal	-	0.80	11.37	7.48	m	**18.85**
215 mm x 102 mm; double bullnose specials; PC £1186.00/1000; headers on edge; pointing top and both sides; horizontal	-	0.60	8.53	17.30	m	**25.83**
260 mm x 102 mm; single bullnose specials; PC £1681.90/1000; headers on edge; pointing top and both sides; horizontal	-	0.80	11.37	39.82	m	**51.19**
ADD or DEDUCT for variation of £10.00/1000 in PC of facing bricks in copings 215 mm wide, 102 mm high	-	-	-	0.14	m	**0.14**
Extra over facing bricks for; facework ornamental bands and the like, plain bands; PC £360.00/1000						
flush; horizontal; 225 mm width; entirely of stretchers	-	0.25	3.55	0.44	m	**3.99**
Extra over facing bricks for; facework quoins; PC £360.00/1000						
flush; mean girth 320 mm	-	0.35	4.97	0.43	m	**5.40**
Bonding to existing						
facework one side, half brick thick; stretcher bond	-	0.60	8.53	1.27	m	**9.80**
facework one side, half brick thick; flemish bond with snapped headers	-	0.60	8.53	1.27	m	**9.80**
facework both sides, one brick thick; two stretcher skins tied together	-	0.80	11.37	2.55	m	**13.92**
facework both sides, one brick thick; flemish bond	-	0.80	11.37	2.55	m	**13.92**

F MASONRY Excluding overheads and profit	PC £	Labour hours	Labour £	Material £	Unit	Total rate £
F10 BRICK/BLOCK WALLING - cont'd						
Facing bricks; machine made facings; PC £330.00/1000 (unless otherwise stated); in gauged mortar (1:1:6) - cont'd						
ADD or DEDUCT for variation of £10.00/1000 in PC of facing bricks; in walls built entirely of facings; in stretcher or flemish bond						
half brick thick	-	-	-	0.65	m²	**0.65**
one brick thick	-	-	-	1.29	m²	**1.29**
Facing bricks; hand made; PC £540.00/1000 (unless otherwise stated); in gauged mortar (1:1:6)						
Walls						
facework one side, half brick thick; stretcher bond	-	1.50	21.32	36.65	m²	**57.97**
facework one side, half brick thick; flemish bond with snapped headers	-	1.75	24.87	36.65	m²	**61.52**
facework one side, half brick thick; stretcher bond; building against other work; concrete	-	1.60	22.74	37.87	m²	**60.61**
facework one side, half brick thick; flemish bond with snapped headers; building against other work; concrete	-	1.85	26.29	37.87	m²	**64.16**
facework one side, half brick thick; stretcher bond; building overhand	-	1.85	26.29	36.65	m²	**62.94**
facework one side, half brick thick; flemish bond with snapped headers; building overhand	-	2.05	29.13	36.65	m²	**65.78**
facework one side, half brick thick; stretcher bond; curved; 6.00 m radii	-	2.20	31.26	36.65	m²	**67.91**
facework one side, half brick thick; flemish bond with snapped headers; curved; 6.00 m radii	-	2.45	34.81	41.01	m²	**75.82**
facework one side; half brick thick; stretcher bond; curved; 1.50 m radii	-	2.75	39.08	36.65	m²	**75.73**
facework one side; half brick thick; flemish bond with snapped headers; curved; 1.50 m radii	-	3.20	45.47	43.91	m²	**89.38**
facework both sides, one brick thick; two stretcher skins tied together	-	2.60	36.95	74.32	m²	**111.27**
facework both sides; one brick thick; flemish bond	-	2.65	37.66	73.30	m²	**110.96**
facework both sides; one brick thick; two stretcher skins tied together; curved; 6.00 m radii	-	3.55	50.45	80.13	m²	**130.58**
facework both sides; one brick thick; flemish bond; curved; 6.00 m radii	-	3.70	52.58	79.11	m²	**131.69**
facework both sides; one brick thick; two stretcher skins tied together; curved; 1.50 m radii	-	4.45	63.23	86.54	m²	**149.77**
facework both sides; one brick thick; flemish bond; curved; 1.50 m radii	-	4.60	65.37	85.52	m²	**150.89**
Isolated piers						
facework both sides, one brick thick; two stretcher skins tied together	-	3.05	43.34	74.90	m²	**118.24**
facework both sides, one brick thick; flemish bond	-	3.10	44.05	74.90	m²	**118.95**
Isolated casings						
facework one side, half brick thick; stretcher bond	-	2.30	32.68	36.65	m²	**69.33**
facework one side, half brick thick; flemish bond with snapped headers	-	2.55	36.24	36.65	m²	**72.89**

F MASONRY Excluding overheads and profit	PC £	Labour hours	Labour £	Material £	Unit	Total rate £
Projections						
225 mm width; 112 mm depth; stretcher bond; vertical	-	0.35	4.97	7.95	m	12.92
225 mm width; 112 mm depth; flemish bond with snapped headers; vertical	-	0.45	6.39	7.95	m	14.34
225 mm width; 225 mm depth; flemish bond; vertical	-	0.75	10.66	15.91	m	26.57
328 mm width; 112 mm depth; stretcher bond; vertical	-	0.70	9.95	11.94	m	21.89
328 mm width; 112 mm depth; flemish bond with snapped headers; vertical	-	0.80	11.37	11.94	m	23.31
328 mm width; 225 mm depth; flemish bond; vertical	-	1.40	19.89	23.83	m	43.72
440 mm width; 112 mm depth; stretcher bond; vertical	-	1.05	14.92	15.91	m	30.83
440 mm width; 112 mm depth; flemish bond with snapped headers; vertical	-	1.10	15.63	15.91	m	31.54
440 mm width; 225 mm depth; flemish bond; vertical	-	2.00	28.42	31.81	m	60.23
Arches						
height on face 215 mm, width of exposed soffit 102 mm, shape of arch - flat	-	1.15	13.53	9.44	m	22.97
height on face 215 mm, width of exposed soffit 215 mm, shape of arch - flat	-	1.70	21.34	17.65	m	38.99
height on face 215 mm, width of exposed soffit 102 mm, shape of arch - segmental, one ring	-	2.20	24.07	13.97	m	38.04
height on face 215 mm, width of exposed soffit 215 mm, shape of arch - segmental, one ring	-	2.65	30.47	21.90	m	52.37
height on face 215 mm, width of exposed soffit 102 mm, shape of arch - semi-circular, one ring	-	3.35	40.42	13.97	m	54.39
height on face 215 mm, width of exposed soffit 215 mm, shape of arch - semi-circular, one ring	-	4.50	56.76	21.90	m	78.66
height on face 215 mm, width of exposed soffit 102 mm, shape of arch - segmental, two ring	-	2.70	31.18	13.97	m	45.15
height on face 215 mm, width of exposed soffit 215 mm, shape of arch - segmental, two ring	-	3.50	42.55	21.90	m	64.45
height on face 215 mm, width of exposed soffit 102 mm, shape of arch - semi-circular, two ring	-	4.50	56.76	13.97	m	70.73
height on face 215 mm, width of exposed soffit 215 mm, shape of arch - semi-circular, two ring	-	6.20	80.91	21.90	m	102.81
Arches; cut voussoirs; PC £2520.00/1000						
height on face 215 mm, width of exposed soffit 102 mm, shape of arch - segmental, one ring	-	2.25	24.79	42.35	m	67.14
height on face 215 mm, width of exposed soffit 215 mm, shape of arch - segmental, one ring	-	2.80	32.60	78.66	m	111.26
height on face 215 mm, width of exposed soffit 102 mm, shape of arch - semi-circular, one ring	-	2.55	29.05	42.35	m	71.40
height on face 215 mm, width of exposed soffit 215 mm, shape of arch - semi-circular, one ring	-	3.20	38.28	78.66	m	116.94
height on face 320 mm, width of exposed soffit 102 mm, shape of arch - segmental, one and a half ring	-	3.00	35.44	78.59	m	114.03
height on face 320 mm, width of exposed soffit 215 mm, shape of arch - segmental, one and a half ring	-	3.90	48.23	157.95	m	206.18
Arches; bullnosed specials; PC £1160.00/1000						
height on face 215 mm, width of exposed soffit 102 mm, shape of arch - flat	-	1.20	14.24	18.33	m	32.57
height on face 215 mm, width of exposed soffit 215 mm, shape of arch - flat	-	1.75	22.05	35.65	m	57.70

Prices for Measured Works - Minor Works

F MASONRY Excluding overheads and profit	PC £	Labour hours	Labour £	Material £	Unit	Total rate £
F10 BRICK/BLOCK WALLING - cont'd						
Facing bricks; hand made; PC £540.00/1000 **(unless otherwise stated); in gauged mortar** **(1:1:6)** - cont'd						
Bullseye windows; 600 mm diameter						
height on face 215 mm, width of exposed soffit						
102 mm, two ring	-	5.75	74.52	19.05	nr	93.57
height on face 215 mm, width of exposed soffit						
215 mm, two ring	-	8.05	107.20	46.97	nr	154.17
Bullseye windows; 600 mm diameter; cut						
voussoirs; PC £2520.00/1000						
height on face 215 mm, width of exposed soffit						
102 mm, one ring	-	4.85	61.73	97.61	nr	159.34
height on face 215 mm, width of exposed soffit						
215 mm, one ring	-	6.65	87.31	193.15	nr	280.46
Bullseye windows; 1200 mm diameter						
height on face 215 mm, width of exposed soffit						
102 mm, two ring	-	8.95	119.99	41.63	nr	161.62
height on face 215 mm, width of exposed soffit						
215 mm, two ring	-	12.90	176.12	76.16	nr	252.28
Bullseye windows; 1200 mm diameter; cut						
voussoirs; PC £2520.00/1000						
height on face 215 mm, width of exposed soffit						
102 mm, one ring	-	7.60	100.81	172.27	nr	273.08
height on face 215 mm, width of exposed soffit						
215 mm, one ring	-	10.80	146.28	336.22	nr	482.50
ADD or DEDUCT for variation of £10.00/1000 in PC of facing bricks in 102 mm high arches with 215 mm soffit	-	-	-	0.29	m	0.29
Facework sills						
150 mm x 102 mm; headers on edge; pointing top and one side; set weathering; horizontal	-	0.65	9.24	7.95	m	17.19
150 mm x 102 mm; cant headers on edge; PC £1160.00/1000; pointing top and one side; set weathering; horizontal	-	0.70	9.95	16.84	m	26.79
150 mm x 102 mm; bullnosed specials; PC £1160.00/1000; headers on flat; pointing top and one side; horizontal	-	0.60	8.53	16.84	m	25.37
Facework copings						
215 mm x 102 mm; headers on edge; pointing top and both sides; horizontal	-	0.50	7.11	8.04	m	15.15
260 mm x 102 mm; headers on edge; pointing top and both sides; horizontal	-	0.80	11.37	11.99	m	23.36
215 mm x 102 mm; double bullnose specials; PC £1160.00/1000; headers on edge; pointing top and both sides; horizontal	-	0.60	8.53	16.93	m	25.46
260 mm x 102 mm; single bullnose specials; PC £1160.00/1000; headers on edge; pointing top and both sides; horizontal	-	0.80	11.37	33.64	m	45.01
ADD or DEDUCT for variation of £10.00/1000 in PC of facing bricks in copings 215 mm wide, 102 mm high	-	-	-	0.14	m	0.14
Extra over facing bricks for; facework ornamental bands and the like, plain bands; PC £580.00/1000						
flush; horizontal; 225 mm width; entirely of stretchers	-	0.25	3.55	0.57	m	4.12

F MASONRY Excluding overheads and profit	PC £	Labour hours	Labour £	Material £	Unit	Total rate £
Extra over facing bricks for; facework quoins; PC £580.00/1000						
flush; mean girth 320 mm	-	0.35	4.97	0.57	m	5.54
Bonding ends to existing						
facework one side, half brick thick; stretcher bond	-	0.60	8.53	2.03	m	10.56
facework one side, half brick thick; flemish bond with snapped headers	-	0.60	8.53	2.03	m	10.56
facework both sides, one brick thick; two stretcher skins tied together	-	0.80	11.37	4.05	m	15.42
facework both sides, one brick thick; flemish bond	-	0.80	11.37	4.05	m	15.42
ADD or DEDUCT for variation of £10.00/1000 in PC of facing bricks; in walls built entirely of facings; in stretcher or flemish bond						
half brick thick	-	-	-	0.65	m²	0.65
one brick thick	-	-	-	1.29	m²	1.29
Facing bricks slips 50 mm thick; PC £1050.00/1000; in gauged mortar (1:1:6) built up against concrete including flushing up at back (ties not included)						
Walls	-	2.30	32.68	69.50	m²	102.18
Edges of suspended slabs; 200 mm wide	-	0.70	9.95	13.90	m	23.85
Columns; 400 mm wide	-	1.40	19.89	27.80	m	47.69
Engineering bricks; PC £353.00/1000; and specials at PC £1186.00/1000; in cement mortar (1:3)						
Facework steps						
215 mm x 102 mm; all headers-on-edge; edges set with bullnosed specials; pointing top and one side; set weathering; horizontal	-	0.65	9.24	17.24	m	26.48
returned ends pointed	-	0.15	2.13	3.76	nr	5.89
430 mm x 102 mm; all headers-on-edge; edges set with bullnosed specials; pointing top and one side; set weathering; horizontal	-	0.90	12.79	22.42	m	35.21
returned ends pointed	-	0.25	3.55	4.77	nr	8.32
Lightweight aerated concrete blocks; Thermalite "Shield"/"Turbo" blocks or other equal and approved; in gauged mortar (1:2:9)						
Walls						
75 mm thick	5.44	0.50	7.11	6.28	m²	13.39
90 mm thick	6.54	0.50	7.11	7.55	m²	14.66
100 mm thick	7.26	0.60	8.53	8.38	m²	16.91
115 mm thick	8.67	0.60	8.53	9.98	m²	18.51
125 mm thick	9.43	0.60	8.53	10.86	m²	19.39
130 mm thick	9.80	0.60	8.53	11.29	m²	19.82
140 mm thick	10.56	0.65	9.24	12.16	m²	21.40
150 mm thick	11.32	0.65	9.24	13.04	m²	22.28
190 mm thick	14.33	0.70	9.95	16.50	m²	26.45
200 mm thick	15.08	0.70	9.95	17.37	m²	27.32
215 mm thick	16.21	0.70	9.95	18.67	m²	28.62
255 mm thick	19.99	0.85	12.08	22.99	m²	35.07

F MASONRY Excluding overheads and profit	PC £	Labour hours	Labour £	Material £	Unit	Total rate £
F10 BRICK/BLOCK WALLING - cont'd						
Lightweight aerated concrete blocks; Thermalite "Shield"/"Turbo" blocks or other equal and approved; in gauged mortar (1:2:9) - cont'd						
Isolated piers or chimney stacks						
190 mm thick	-	1.05	14.92	16.50	m²	31.42
215 mm thick	-	1.05	14.92	18.67	m²	33.59
255 mm thick	-	1.15	16.34	22.99	m²	39.33
Isolated casings						
75 mm thick	-	0.65	9.24	6.28	m²	15.52
90 mm thick	-	0.65	9.24	7.55	m²	16.79
100 mm thick	-	0.65	9.24	8.38	m²	17.62
115 mm thick	-	0.65	9.24	9.98	m²	19.22
125 mm thick	-	0.65	9.24	10.86	m²	20.10
140 mm thick	-	0.70	9.95	12.16	m²	22.11
Extra over for fair face; flush pointing						
walls; one side	-	0.05	0.71	-	m²	0.71
walls; both sides	-	0.10	1.42	-	m²	1.42
Closing cavities						
width of cavity 50 mm, closing with lightweight blockwork 100 mm thick; vertical	-	0.29	4.12	0.47	m	4.59
width of cavity 50 mm, closing with lightweight blockwork 100 mm thick; including damp proof course; vertical	-	0.35	4.97	1.35	m	6.32
width of cavity 75 mm, closing with lightweight blockwork 100 mm thick; vertical	-	0.29	4.12	0.68	m	4.80
width of cavity 75 mm, closing with lightweight blockwork 100 mm thick; including damp proof course; vertical	-	0.35	4.97	1.56	m	6.53
Bonding ends to common brickwork						
75 mm thick	-	0.10	1.42	0.72	m	2.14
90 mm thick	-	0.10	1.42	0.87	m	2.29
100 mm thick	-	0.15	2.13	0.96	m	3.09
115 mm thick	-	0.15	2.13	1.15	m	3.28
125 mm thick	-	0.30	4.26	1.25	m	5.51
130 mm thick	-	0.30	4.26	1.30	m	5.56
140 mm thick	-	0.30	4.26	1.41	m	5.67
150 mm thick	-	0.30	4.26	1.50	m	5.76
190 mm thick	-	0.35	4.97	1.90	m	6.87
200 mm thick	-	0.35	4.97	2.00	m	6.97
215 mm thick	-	0.40	5.68	2.16	m	7.84
255 mm thick	-	0.40	5.68	2.65	m	8.33
Lightweight smooth face aerated concrete blocks; Thermalite "Smooth Face" blocks or other equal and approved; in gauged mortar (1:2:9); flush pointing one side						
Walls						
100 mm thick	12.76	0.70	9.95	14.43	m²	24.38
140 mm thick	17.86	0.80	11.37	20.19	m²	31.56
150 mm thick	19.14	0.80	11.37	21.64	m²	33.01
190 mm thick	24.24	0.90	12.79	27.40	m²	40.19
200 mm thick	25.52	0.90	12.79	28.85	m²	41.64
215 mm thick	27.44	0.90	12.79	31.02	m²	43.81
Isolated piers or chimney stacks						
190 mm thick	-	1.15	16.34	27.40	m²	43.74
200 mm thick	-	1.15	16.34	28.85	m²	45.19
215 mm thick	-	1.15	16.34	31.02	m²	47.36
Isolated casings						
100 mm thick	-	0.85	12.08	14.43	m²	26.51
140 mm thick	-	0.90	12.79	20.19	m²	32.98

F MASONRY Excluding overheads and profit	PC £	Labour hours	Labour £	Material £	Unit	Total rate £
Extra over for flush pointing						
walls; both sides	-	0.05	0.71	-	m²	0.71
Bonding ends to common brickwork						
100 mm thick	-	0.30	4.26	1.64	m	5.90
140 mm thick	-	0.30	4.26	2.30	m	6.56
150 mm thick	-	0.35	4.97	2.46	m	7.43
190 mm thick	-	0.40	5.68	3.11	m	8.79
200 mm thick	-	0.40	5.68	3.28	m	8.96
215 mm thick	-	0.40	5.68	3.53	m	9.21
Lightweight aerated high strength concrete block **(7.00 N/mm²); Thermalite "High Strength" blocks or** **other equal and approved; in cement mortar (1:3)**						
Walls						
100 mm thick	9.23	0.60	8.53	10.60	m²	19.13
140 mm thick	12.92	0.65	9.24	14.84	m²	24.08
150 mm thick	13.84	0.65	9.24	15.90	m²	25.14
190 mm thick	17.53	0.70	9.95	20.13	m²	30.08
200 mm thick	18.45	0.70	9.95	21.19	m²	31.14
215 mm thick	19.83	0.70	9.95	22.78	m²	32.73
Isolated piers or chimney stacks						
190 mm thick	-	1.05	14.92	20.13	m²	35.05
200 mm thick	-	1.05	14.92	21.19	m²	36.11
215 mm thick	-	1.05	14.92	22.78	m²	37.70
Isolated casings						
100 mm thick	-	0.65	9.24	10.60	m²	19.84
140 mm thick	-	0.70	9.95	14.84	m²	24.79
150 mm thick	-	0.70	9.95	15.90	m²	25.85
190 mm thick	-	0.85	12.08	20.13	m²	32.21
200 mm thick	-	0.85	12.08	21.19	m²	33.27
215 mm thick	-	0.85	12.08	22.78	m²	34.86
Extra over for flush pointing						
walls; one side	-	0.05	0.71	-	m²	0.71
walls; both sides	-	0.10	1.42	-	m²	1.42
Bonding ends to common brickwork						
100 mm thick	-	0.30	4.26	1.22	m	5.48
140 mm thick	-	0.30	4.26	1.71	m	5.97
150 mm thick	-	0.35	4.97	1.83	m	6.80
190 mm thick	-	0.40	5.68	2.31	m	7.99
200 mm thick	-	0.40	5.68	2.44	m	8.12
215 mm thick	-	0.40	5.68	2.63	m	8.31
Dense aggregate concrete blocks; "ARC Conbloc" or **other equal and approved; in gauged mortar (1:2:9)**						
Walls						
75 mm thick; solid	5.68	0.70	9.95	6.54	m²	16.49
100 mm thick; solid	6.31	0.85	12.09	7.33	m²	19.42
140 mm thick; solid	12.39	1.05	14.93	14.18	m²	29.11
140 mm thick; hollow	11.91	0.90	12.80	13.65	m²	26.45
190 mm thick; hollow	14.06	1.15	16.35	16.21	m²	32.56
215 mm thick; hollow	14.64	1.25	17.77	16.94	m²	34.71
Isolated piers or chimney stacks						
140 mm thick; hollow	-	1.25	17.77	13.65	m²	31.42
190 mm thick; hollow	-	1.65	23.46	16.21	m²	39.67
215 mm thick; hollow	-	1.90	27.02	16.94	m²	43.96
Isolated casings						
75 mm thick; solid	-	0.85	12.09	6.54	m²	18.63
100 mm thick; solid	-	0.90	12.80	7.33	m²	20.13
140 mm thick; solid	-	1.15	16.35	14.18	m²	30.53
Extra over for fair face; flush pointing						
walls; one side	-	0.10	1.42	-	m²	1.42
walls; both sides	-	0.15	2.13	-	m²	2.13

F MASONRY Excluding overheads and profit	PC £	Labour hours	Labour £	Material £	Unit	Total rate £
F10 BRICK/BLOCK WALLING - cont'd						
Dense aggregate concrete blocks; "ARC Conbloc" or **other equal and approved; in gauged mortar (1:2:9)** - cont'd						
Bonding ends to common brickwork						
75 mm thick solid	-	0.15	2.13	0.75	m	**2.88**
100 mm thick solid	-	0.30	4.27	0.85	m	**5.12**
140 mm thick solid	-	0.35	4.98	1.63	m	**6.61**
140 mm thick hollow	-	0.35	4.98	1.57	m	**6.55**
190 mm thick hollow	-	0.40	5.69	1.86	m	**7.55**
215 mm thick hollow	-	0.45	6.40	1.97	m	**8.37**
Dense aggregate concrete blocks; (7.00 N/mm²) **Forticrete "Shepton Mallet Common" blocks or** **other equal and approved; in cement mortar (1:3)**						
Walls						
75 mm thick; solid	6.57	0.70	9.95	7.56	m²	**17.51**
100 mm thick; hollow	7.67	0.85	12.09	8.89	m²	**20.98**
100 mm thick; solid	4.95	0.85	12.09	5.90	m²	**17.99**
140 mm thick; hollow	10.59	0.90	12.80	12.28	m²	**25.08**
140 mm thick; solid	7.59	1.05	14.93	8.98	m²	**23.91**
190 mm thick; hollow	14.06	1.15	16.35	16.32	m²	**32.67**
190 mm thick; solid	10.37	1.25	17.77	12.26	m²	**30.03**
215 mm thick; hollow	11.18	1.25	17.77	13.26	m²	**31.03**
215 mm thick; solid	11.06	1.45	20.62	13.13	m²	**33.75**
Dwarf support wall						
140 mm thick; solid	-	1.45	20.62	8.98	m²	**29.60**
190 mm thick; solid	-	1.65	23.46	12.26	m²	**35.72**
215 mm thick; solid	-	1.90	27.02	13.13	m²	**40.15**
Isolated piers or chimney stacks						
140 mm thick; hollow	-	1.25	17.77	12.28	m²	**30.05**
190 mm thick; hollow	-	1.65	23.46	16.32	m²	**39.78**
215 mm thick; hollow	-	1.90	27.02	13.26	m²	**40.28**
Isolated casings						
75 mm thick; solid	-	0.85	12.09	7.56	m²	**19.65**
100 mm thick; solid	-	0.90	12.80	5.90	m²	**18.70**
140 mm thick; solid	-	1.15	16.35	8.98	m²	**25.33**
Extra over for fair face; flush pointing						
walls; one side	-	0.10	1.42	-	m²	**1.42**
walls; both sides	-	0.15	2.13	-	m²	**2.13**
Bonding ends to common brickwork						
75 mm thick solid	-	0.15	2.13	0.86	m	**2.99**
100 mm thick solid	-	0.30	4.27	0.68	m	**4.95**
140 mm thick solid	-	0.35	4.98	1.04	m	**6.02**
190 mm thick solid	-	0.40	5.69	1.41	m	**7.10**
215 mm thick solid	-	0.45	6.40	1.53	m	**7.93**
Dense aggregate coloured concrete blocks; **Forticrete "Shepton Mallet Bathstone" or other** **equal and approved; in coloured gauged mortar** **(1:1:6); flush pointing one side**						
Walls						
100 mm thick hollow	17.12	0.90	12.80	18.49	m²	**31.29**
100 mm thick solid	20.74	0.90	12.80	22.29	m²	**35.09**
140 mm thick hollow	22.53	1.05	14.93	24.37	m²	**39.30**
140 mm thick solid	30.22	1.15	16.35	32.44	m²	**48.79**
190 mm thick hollow	28.64	1.25	17.77	31.03	m²	**48.80**
190 mm thick solid	41.49	1.45	20.62	44.52	m²	**65.14**
215 mm thick hollow	30.23	1.45	20.62	32.83	m²	**53.45**
215 mm thick solid	43.97	1.50	21.33	47.26	m²	**68.59**

F MASONRY Excluding overheads and profit	PC £	Labour hours	Labour £	Material £	Unit	Total rate £
Isolated piers or chimney stacks						
140 mm thick solid	-	1.55	22.04	32.44	m²	54.48
190 mm thick solid	-	1.75	24.89	44.52	m²	69.41
215 mm thick solid	-	1.95	27.73	47.26	m²	74.99
Extra over blocks for						
100 mm thick half lintel blocks ref D14	-	0.30	4.27	17.03	m	21.30
140 mm thick half lintel blocks ref H14	-	0.35	4.98	21.57	m	26.55
140 mm thick quoin blocks ref H16	-	0.40	5.69	24.76	m	30.45
140 mm thick cavity closer blocks ref H17	-	0.40	5.69	29.73	m	35.42
140 mm thick cill blocks ref H21	-	0.35	4.98	17.65	m	22.63
190 mm thick half lintel blocks ref A14	-	0.40	5.69	24.74	m	30.43
190 mm thick cill blocks ref A21	-	0.40	5.69	18.38	m	24.07
Astra-Glaze satin-gloss glazed finish blocks or other **equal and approved; Forticrete Ltd; standard** **colours; in gauged mortar (1:1:6); joints raked out;** **gun applied latex grout to joints**						
Walls						
100 mm thick; glazed one side	76.17	1.15	16.35	80.39	m²	96.74
extra; glazed square end return	10.05	0.45	6.40	25.59	m	31.99
150 mm thick; glazed one side	84.70	1.25	17.77	89.54	m²	107.31
extra; glazed square end return	16.16	0.60	8.53	53.46	m	61.99
200 mm thick; glazed one side	93.91	1.45	20.62	99.41	m²	120.03
extra; glazed square end return	-	0.65	9.24	76.28	m	85.52
100 mm thick; glazed both sides	108.90	1.40	19.91	114.75	m²	134.66
150 mm thick; glazed both sides	117.70	1.50	21.33	124.19	m²	145.52
100 mm thick lintel 200 mm high; glazed one side	-	1.05	11.18	21.41	m	32.59
150 mm thick lintel 200 mm high; glazed one side	-	1.20	13.31	25.73	m	39.04
200 mm thick lintel 200 mm high; glazed one side	-	1.55	16.72	24.12	m	40.84
F20 NATURAL STONE RUBBLE WALLING						
Cotswold Guiting limestone or other equal and **approved; laid dry**						
Uncoursed random rubble walling						
275 mm thick	-	2.55	33.18	33.64	m²	66.82
350 mm thick	-	3.05	39.31	42.81	m²	82.12
425 mm thick	-	3.50	44.72	51.99	m²	96.71
500 mm thick	-	3.90	49.77	61.17	m²	110.94
Cotswold Guiting limestone or other equal and **approved; bedded; jointed and pointed in cement:** **lime mortar (1:2:9)**						
Uncoursed random rubble walling; faced and						
pointed; both sides						
275 mm thick	-	2.45	31.73	37.20	m²	68.93
350 mm thick	-	2.70	34.27	47.33	m²	81.60
425 mm thick	-	3.00	37.52	57.48	m²	95.00
500 mm thick	-	3.20	39.69	67.63	m²	107.32
Coursed random rubble walling; rough						
dressed; faced and pointed one side						
114 mm thick	-	1.85	25.25	46.68	m²	71.93
150 mm thick	-	2.20	30.27	51.55	m²	81.82
Fair returns on walling						
114 mm wide	-	0.03	0.43	-	m	0.43
150 mm wide	-	0.05	0.71	-	m	0.71
275 mm wide	-	0.08	1.14	-	m	1.14
350 mm wide	-	0.10	1.42	-	m	1.42
425 mm wide	-	0.13	1.85	-	m	1.85
500 mm wide	-	0.15	2.13	-	m	2.13

F MASONRY Excluding overheads and profit	PC £	Labour hours	Labour £	Material £	Unit	Total rate £
F20 NATURAL STONE RUBBLE WALLING - cont'd						
Cotswold Guiting limestone; bedded; jointed **and pointed in cement - lime mortar (1:2:9)** - cont'd						
Fair raking cutting or circular cutting						
114 mm wide	-	0.25	3.56	6.78	m	**10.34**
150 mm wide	-	0.31	4.41	7.44	m	**11.85**
Level uncoursed rubble walling for damp proof courses and the like						
275 mm wide	-	0.24	3.46	2.43	m	**5.89**
350 mm wide	-	0.25	3.60	3.03	m	**6.63**
425 mm wide	-	0.26	3.75	3.70	m	**7.45**
500 mm wide	-	0.28	4.03	4.36	m	**8.39**
Copings formed of rough stones; faced and pointed all round						
275 mm x 200 mm (average) high	-	0.69	9.23	8.75	m	**17.98**
350 mm x 250 mm (average) high	-	0.93	12.26	12.17	m	**24.43**
425 mm x 300 mm (average) high	-	1.21	15.79	16.83	m	**32.62**
500 mm x 300 mm (average) high	-	1.53	19.76	22.73	m	**42.49**
F22 CAST STONE ASHLAR WALLING **DRESSINGS**						
Reconstructed limestone walling; "Bradstone **100 bed Weathered Cotswold" or "North Cerney"** **masonry blocks or other equal and approved; laid** **to pattern or course recommended; bedded; jointed** **and pointed in approved coloured cement:lime** **mortar (1:2:9)**						
Walls; facing and pointing one side						
masonry blocks; random uncoursed	-	1.29	18.33	21.41	m²	**39.74**
extra; returned ends	-	0.46	6.54	22.84	m	**29.38**
extra; plain L shaped quoins	-	0.15	2.13	7.84	m	**9.97**
traditional walling; coursed squared	-	1.61	22.88	21.41	m²	**44.29**
squared random rubble	-	1.61	22.88	23.81	m²	**46.69**
squared coursed rubble (large module)	-	1.49	21.17	23.65	m²	**44.82**
squared coursed rubble (small module)	-	1.55	22.03	23.96	m²	**45.99**
squared and pitched rock faced walling; coursed	-	1.67	23.73	22.34	m²	**46.07**
rough hewn rock faced walling; random	-	1.73	24.58	22.18	m²	**46.76**
extra; returned ends	-	0.18	2.56	-	m	**2.56**
Isolated piers or chimney stacks; facing and pointing one side						
masonry blocks; random uncoursed	-	1.78	25.29	21.41	m²	**46.70**
traditional walling; coursed squared	-	2.24	31.83	21.41	m²	**53.24**
squared random rubble	-	2.24	31.83	23.81	m²	**55.64**
squared coursed rubble (large module)	-	2.07	29.41	23.65	m²	**53.06**
squared coursed rubble (small module)	-	2.18	30.98	23.96	m²	**54.94**
squared and pitched rock faced walling; coursed	-	2.36	33.54	22.34	m²	**55.88**
rough hewn rock faced walling; random	-	2.41	34.25	22.18	m²	**56.43**
Isolated casings; facing and pointing one side						
masonry blocks; random uncoursed	-	1.55	22.03	21.41	m²	**43.44**
traditional walling; coursed squared	-	1.96	27.85	21.41	m²	**49.26**
squared random rubble	-	1.96	27.85	23.81	m²	**51.66**
squared coursed rubble (large module)	-	1.78	25.29	23.65	m²	**48.94**
squared coursed rubble (small module)	-	1.90	27.00	23.96	m²	**50.96**
squared and pitched rock faced walling; coursed	-	2.01	28.56	22.34	m²	**50.90**
rough hewn rock faced walling; random	-	2.07	29.41	22.18	m²	**51.59**
Fair returns 100 mm wide						
masonry blocks; random uncoursed	-	0.14	1.99	-	m²	**1.99**
traditional walling; coursed squared	-	0.17	2.42	-	m²	**2.42**
squared random rubble	-	0.17	2.42	-	m²	**2.42**

F MASONRY Excluding overheads and profit	PC £	Labour hours	Labour £	Material £	Unit	Total rate £
Fair returns 100 mm wide - cont'd						
squared coursed rubble (large module)	-	0.16	2.27	-	m²	2.27
squared coursed rubble (small module)	-	0.16	2.27	-	m²	2.27
squared and pitched rock faced walling;						
coursed	-	0.17	2.42	-	m²	2.42
rough hewn rock faced walling; random	-	0.18	2.56	-	m²	2.56
Fair raking cutting or circular cutting						
100 mm wide	-	0.21	2.98	-	m	2.98
Reconstructed limestone dressings;						
"Bradstone Architectural" dressings in						
weathered "Cotswold" or "North Cerney"						
shades or other equal and approved; bedded,						
jointed and pointed in approved coloured						
cement:lime mortar (1:2:9)						
Copings; twice weathered and throated						
152 mm x 76 mm; type A	-	0.38	5.40	9.84	m	15.24
178 mm x 64 mm; type B	-	0.38	5.40	9.63	m	15.03
305 mm x 76 mm; type A	-	0.46	6.54	18.73	m	25.27
Extra for						
fair end	-	-	-	4.10	nr	4.10
returned mitred fair end	-	-	-	4.10	nr	4.10
Copings; once weathered and throated						
191 mm x 76 mm	-	0.38	5.40	10.68	m	16.08
305 mm x 76 mm	-	0.46	6.54	18.41	m	24.95
365 mm x 76 mm	-	0.46	6.54	19.78	m	26.32
Extra for						
fair end	-	-	-	4.10	nr	4.10
returned mitred fair end	-	-	-	4.10	nr	4.10
Chimney caps; four times weathered and						
throated; once holed						
553 mm x 553 mm x 76 mm	-	0.46	6.54	23.06	nr	29.60
686 mm x 686 mm x 76 mm	-	0.46	6.54	37.64	nr	44.18
Pier caps; four times weathered and throated						
305 mm x 305 mm	-	0.29	4.12	8.30	nr	12.42
381 mm x 381 mm	-	0.29	4.12	11.49	nr	15.61
457 mm x 457 mm	-	0.35	4.97	15.60	nr	20.57
533 mm x 533 mm	-	0.35	4.97	22.00	nr	26.97
Splayed corbels						
479 mm x 100 mm x 215 mm	-	0.17	2.42	10.74	nr	13.16
665 mm x 100 mm x 215 mm	-	0.23	3.27	17.20	nr	20.47
Air bricks						
300 mm x 140 mm x 76 mm	-	0.09	1.28	6.08	nr	7.36
100 mm x 140 mm lintels; rectangular;						
reinforced with mild steel bars						
not exceeding 1.22 m long	-	0.28	3.98	16.80	m	20.78
1.37 m - 1.67 m long	-	0.30	4.26	16.80	m	21.06
1.83 m - 1.98 m long	-	0.32	4.55	16.80	m	21.35
100 mm x 215 mm lintels; rectangular;						
reinforced with mild steel bars						
not exceeding 1.67 m long	-	0.30	4.26	22.60	m	26.86
1.83 m - 1.98 m long	-	0.32	4.55	22.60	m	27.15
2.13 m - 2.44 m long	-	0.35	4.97	22.60	m	27.57
2.59 m - 2.90 m long	-	0.37	5.26	22.60	m	27.86
197 mm x 67 mm sills to suit standard						
softwood windows; stooled at ends						
not exceeding 2.54 m long	-	0.35	4.97	26.47	m	31.44
Window surround; traditional with label						
moulding; for single light; sill 146 mm x 133						
mm; jambs 146 mm x 146 mm; head 146 mm x						
105 mm; including all dowels and anchors						
overall size 508 mm x 1479 mm	129.20	1.03	14.64	130.75	nr	145.39

F MASONRY Excluding overheads and profit	PC £	Labour hours	Labour £	Material £	Unit	Total rate £
F22 CAST STONE ASHLAR WALLING DRESSINGS - cont'd						
Reconstructed limestone dressings; "Bradstone Architectural" dressings in weathered "Cotswold" or "North Cerney" shades or other equal and approved; bedded, jointed and pointed in approved coloured cement:lime mortar (1:2:9) - cont'd						
Window surround; traditional with label moulding; three light; for windows 508 mm x 1219 mm; sill 146 mm x 133 mm; jambs 146 mm x 146 mm; head 146 mm x 103 mm; mullions 146 mm x 108 mm; including all dowels and anchors						
overall size 1975 mm x 1479 mm	280.00	2.70	38.37	283.88	nr	**322.25**
Door surround; moulded continuous jambs and head with label moulding; including all dowels and anchors						
door 839 mm x 1981 mm in 102 mm x 64 mm frame	240.00	1.90	27.00	240.78	nr	**267.78**
F30 ACCESSORIES/SUNDRY ITEMS FOR BRICK/BLOCK/STONE WALLING						
Forming cavities						
In hollow walls						
width of cavity 50 mm; polypropylene ties; three wall ties per m²	-	0.07	0.99	0.25	m²	**1.24**
width of cavity 50 mm; galvanised steel butterfly wall ties; three wall ties per m²	-	0.07	0.99	0.22	m²	**1.21**
width of cavity 50 mm; galvanised steel twisted wall ties; three wall ties per m²	-	0.07	0.99	0.42	m²	**1.41**
width of cavity 50 mm; stainless steel butterfly wall ties; three wall ties per m²	-	0.07	0.99	0.46	m²	**1.45**
width of cavity 50 mm; stainless steel twisted wall ties; three wall ties per m²	-	0.07	0.99	0.82	m²	**1.81**
width of cavity 75 mm; polypropylene ties; three wall ties per m²	-	0.07	0.99	0.25	m²	**1.24**
width of cavity 75 mm; galvanised steel butterfly wall ties; three wall ties per m²	-	0.07	0.99	0.28	m²	**1.27**
width of cavity 75 mm; galvanised steel twisted wall ties; three wall ties per m²	-	0.07	0.99	0.46	m²	**1.45**
width of cavity 75 mm; stainless steel butterfly wall ties; three wall ties per m²	-	0.07	0.99	0.64	m²	**1.63**
width of cavity 75 mm; stainless steel twisted wall ties; three wall ties per m²	-	0.07	0.99	0.89	m²	**1.88**
Damp proof courses						
"Pluvex No 1" (hessian based) damp proof course or other equal and approved; 200 mm laps; in gauged mortar (1:1:6)						
width exceeding 225 mm; horizontal	7.46	0.29	4.12	8.02	m²	**12.14**
width exceeding 225 mm; forming cavity gutters in hollow walls; horizontal	-	0.46	6.54	8.02	m²	**14.56**
width not exceeding 225 mm; horizontal	-	0.57	8.10	8.02	m²	**16.12**
width not exceeding 225 mm; vertical	-	0.86	12.22	8.02	m²	**20.24**

F MASONRY Excluding overheads and profit	PC £	Labour hours	Labour £	Material £	Unit	Total rate £
"Pluvex No 2" (fibre based) damp proof course or other equal and approved; 200 mm laps; in gauged mortar (1:1:6)						
width exceeding 225 mm; horizontal	5.01	0.29	4.12	5.39	m²	9.51
width exceeding 225 mm; forming cavity gutters in hollow walls; horizontal	-	0.46	6.54	5.39	m²	11.93
width not exceeding 225 mm; horizontal	-	0.57	8.10	5.39	m²	13.49
width not exceeding 225 mm; vertical	-	0.86	12.22	5.39	m²	17.61
"Ruberthene" polyethylene damp proof course or other equal and approved; 200 mm laps; in gauged mortar (1:1:6)						
width exceeding 225 mm; horizontal	1.13	0.29	4.12	1.21	m²	5.33
width exceeding 225 mm; forming cavity gutters in hollow walls; horizontal	-	0.46	6.54	1.21	m²	7.75
width not exceeding 225 mm; horizontal	-	0.57	8.10	1.21	m²	9.31
width not exceeding 225 mm; vertical	-	0.86	12.22	1.21	m²	13.43
"Permabit" bitumen polymer damp proof course or other equal and approved; 150 mm laps; in gauged mortar (1:1:6)						
width exceeding 225 mm; horizontal	6.39	0.29	4.12	6.87	m²	10.99
width exceeding 225 mm; forming cavity gutters in hollow walls; horizontal	-	0.46	6.54	6.87	m²	13.41
width not exceeding 225 mm; horizontal	-	0.57	8.10	6.87	m²	14.97
width not exceeding 225 mm; vertical	-	0.86	12.22	6.87	m²	19.09
"Hyload" (pitch polymer) damp proof course or other equal and approved; 150 mm laps; in gauged mortar (1:1:6)						
width exceeding 225 mm; horizontal	6.39	0.29	4.12	6.87	m²	10.99
width exceeding 225 mm; forming cavity gutters in hollow walls; horizontal	-	0.46	6.54	6.87	m²	13.41
width not exceeding 225 mm; horizontal	-	0.57	8.10	6.87	m²	14.97
width not exceeding 225 mm; vertical	-	0.86	12.22	6.87	m²	19.09
"Ledkore" grade A (bitumen based lead cored); damp proof course or other equal and approved; 200 mm laps; in gauged mortar (1:1:6)						
width exceeding 225 mm; horizontal	14.34	0.38	5.40	15.42	m²	20.82
width exceeding 225 mm; forming cavity gutters in hollow walls; horizontal	-	0.61	8.67	15.42	m²	24.09
width not exceeding 225 mm; horizontal	-	0.73	10.37	15.42	m²	25.79
width not exceeding 225 mm; vertical	-	0.86	12.22	15.42	m²	27.64
Milled lead damp proof course; BS 1178; 1.80 mm thick (code 4), 175 mm laps; in cement: lime mortar (1:2:9)						
width exceeding 225 mm; horizontal	-	2.30	32.68	21.90	m²	54.58
width not exceeding 225 mm; horizontal	-	3.45	49.02	21.90	m²	70.92
Two courses slates in cement mortar (1:3)						
width exceeding 225 mm; horizontal	-	1.73	24.58	10.76	m²	35.34
width exceeding 225 mm; vertical	-	2.59	36.80	10.76	m²	47.56
"Peter Cox" chemical transfusion damp proof course system or other equal and approved						
half brick thick; horizontal	-	-	-	-	m	12.65
one brick thick; horizontal	-	-	-	-	m	25.25
one and a half brick thick; horizontal	-	-	-	-	m	38.00
Silicone injection damp-proofing 450 mm centres; making good brickwork						
half brick thick; horizontal	-	-	-	-	m	6.75
one brick thick; horizontal	-	-	-	-	m	12.50
one and a half brick thick; horizontal	-	-	-	-	m	16.00

F MASONRY Excluding overheads and profit	PC £	Labour hours	Labour £	Material £	Unit	Total rate £
F30 ACCESSORIES/SUNDRY ITEMS FOR BRICK/BLOCK/STONE WALLING - cont'd						
Damp proof courses - cont'd "Synthaprufe" damp proof membrane or other equal and approved; PC £53.15/25 litres; three coats brushed on						
width not exceeding 150 mm; vertical	-	0.39	2.52	6.70	m²	**9.22**
width 150 mm - 225 mm; vertical	-	0.37	2.39	6.70	m²	**9.09**
width 225 mm - 300 mm; vertical	-	0.35	2.26	6.70	m²	**8.96**
width exceeding 300 mm; vertical	-	0.32	2.06	6.70	m²	**8.76**
Joint reinforcement "Brickforce" galvanised steel joint reinforcement or other equal and approved						
width 40 mm; ref GBF40B	-	0.02	0.28	0.30	m	**0.58**
width 60 mm; ref GBF60B	-	0.03	0.43	0.33	m	**0.76**
width 100 mm; ref GBF100B	-	0.05	0.71	0.39	m	**1.10**
width 160 mm; ref GBF160B	-	0.06	0.85	0.48	m	**1.33**
"Brickforce" stainless steel joint reinforcement or other equal and approved						
width 40 mm; ref SBF40BRC	-	0.02	0.28	0.91	m	**1.19**
width 60 mm; ref SBF60BRC	-	0.03	0.43	0.97	m	**1.40**
width 100 mm; ref SBF100BRC	-	0.05	0.71	1.02	m	**1.73**
width 160 mm; ref SBF160BRC	-	0.06	0.85	1.07	m	**1.92**
"Wallforce" stainless steel joint reinforcement or other equal and approved						
width 210 mm; ref SWF40BSC	-	0.07	0.99	2.71	m	**3.70**
width 235 mm; ref SWF60BSC	-	0.08	1.14	2.78	m	**3.92**
width 250 mm; ref SWF100BSC	-	0.09	1.28	2.88	m	**4.16**
width 275 mm; ref SWF160BSC	-	0.10	1.42	2.95	m	**4.37**
Weather fillets Weather fillets in cement mortar (1:3)						
50 mm face width	-	0.14	1.99	0.04	m	**2.03**
100 mm face width	-	0.23	3.27	0.17	m	**3.44**
Angle fillets Angle fillets in cement mortar (1:3)						
50 mm face width	-	0.14	1.99	0.04	m	**2.03**
100 mm face width	-	0.23	3.27	0.17	m	**3.44**
Pointing in Pointing with mastic						
wood frames or sills	-	0.12	0.96	0.43	m	**1.39**
Pointing with polysulphide sealant						
wood frames or sills	-	0.12	0.96	1.29	m	**2.25**
Wedging and pinning To underside of existing construction with slates in cement mortar (1:3)						
width of wall - one brick thick	-	0.92	13.07	2.32	m	**15.39**
width of wall - one and a half brick thick	-	1.15	16.34	4.64	m	**20.98**
width of wall - two brick thick	-	1.38	19.61	6.96	m	**26.57**
Joints Hacking joints and faces of brickwork or blockwork						
to form key for plaster	-	0.30	1.94	-	m²	**1.94**
Raking out joint in brickwork or blockwork for turned-in edge of flashing						
horizontal	-	0.17	2.42	-	m	**2.42**
stepped	-	0.23	3.27	-	m	**3.27**

F MASONRY Excluding overheads and profit	PC £	Labour hours	Labour £	Material £	Unit	Total rate £
Raking out and enlarging joint in brickwork or blockwork for nib of asphalt						
horizontal	-	0.23	3.27	-	m	3.27
Cutting grooves in brickwork or blockwork						
for water bars and the like	-	0.29	1.87	0.49	m	2.36
for nib of asphalt; horizontal	-	0.29	1.87	0.49	m	2.36
Preparing to receive new walls						
top existing 215 mm wall	-	0.23	3.27	-	m	3.27
Cleaning and priming both faces; filling with pre-formed closed cell joint filler and pointing one side with polysulphide sealant; 12 mm deep						
expansion joints; 12 mm wide	-	0.29	3.37	2.58	m	5.95
expansion joints; 20 mm wide	-	0.34	3.77	3.78	m	7.55
expansion joints; 25 mm wide	-	0.40	4.25	4.56	m	8.81
Fire resisting horizontal expansion joints; filling with joint filler; fixed with high temperature slip adhesive; between top of wall and soffit						
wall not exceeding 215 mm wide; 10 mm wide joint with 30 mm deep filler (one hour fire seal)	-	0.29	4.12	5.86	m	9.98
wall not exceeding 215 mm wide; 10 mm wide joint with 30 mm deep filler (two hour fire seal)	-	0.29	4.12	5.86	m	9.98
wall not exceeding 215 mm wide; 20 mm wide joint with 45 mm deep filler (two hour fire seal)	-	0.35	4.97	8.96	m	13.93
wall not exceeding 215 mm wide; 30 mm wide joint with 75 mm deep filler (three hour fire seal)	-	0.40	5.68	21.82	m	27.50
Fire resisting vertical expansion joints; filling with joint filler; fixed with high temperature slip adhesive; with polysulphide sealant one side; between end of wall and concrete						
wall not exceeding 215 mm wide; 20 mm wide joint with 45 mm deep filler (two hour fire seal)	-	0.47	5.93	11.54	m	17.47
Slate and tile sills						
Sills; two courses of machine made plain roofing tiles						
set weathering; bedded and pointed	-	0.69	9.80	4.34	m	14.14
Flue linings						
Flue linings; Marflex "ML 200" square refractory concrete flue linings or other equal and approved; rebated joints in flue joint mortar mix						
linings; ref MLS1U	-	0.35	4.97	15.07	m	20.04
bottom swivel unit; ref MLS2U	-	0.12	1.71	11.67	nr	13.38
45 degree bend; ref MLS4U	-	0.12	1.71	11.67	nr	13.38
90 mm offset liner; ref MLS5U	-	0.12	1.71	6.15	nr	7.86
70 mm offset liner; ref MLS6U	-	0.12	1.71	5.54	nr	7.25
57 mm offset liner; ref MLS7U	-	0.12	1.71	10.00	nr	11.71
pot; ref MLSP83R	-	0.12	1.71	22.28	nr	23.99
single cap unit; ref MLS10U	-	0.29	4.12	33.46	nr	37.58
double cap unit; ref MLS11U	-	0.35	4.97	30.65	nr	35.62
combined gather lintel; ref MLSLUL4	-	0.35	4.97	30.30	nr	35.27
Air bricks						
Air bricks; red terracotta; building into prepared openings						
215 mm x 65 mm	-	0.09	1.28	1.79	nr	3.07
215 mm x 140 mm	-	0.09	1.28	2.47	nr	3.75
215 mm x 215 mm	-	0.09	1.28	6.73	nr	8.01

F MASONRY Excluding overheads and profit	PC £	Labour hours	Labour £	Material £	Unit	Total rate £
F30 ACCESSORIES/SUNDRY ITEMS FOR BRICK/BLOCK/STONE WALLING - cont'd						
Gas flue blocks						
Gas flue system; Marflex "HP" or other equal and						
approved; concrete blocks built in; in flue joint mortar						
mix; cutting brickwork or blockwork around						
recess; ref HP1	-	0.12	1.71	4.45	nr	6.16
cover; ref HP2	-	0.12	1.71	6.26	nr	7.97
222 mm standard block with nib; ref HP3	-	0.12	1.71	4.42	nr	6.13
112 mm standard block with nib; ref HP3112	-	0.12	1.71	4.42	nr	6.13
72 mm standard block with nib; ref HP372	-	0.12	1.71	4.42	nr	6.13
vent block; ref HP3BH	-	0.12	1.71	8.72	nr	10.43
222 mm standard block without nib; ref HP4	-	0.12	1.71	4.28	nr	5.99
112 mm standard block without nib; ref HP4112	-	0.12	1.71	4.28	nr	5.99
72 mm standard block without nib; ref HP472	-	0.12	1.71	4.28	nr	5.99
120 mm side offset block; ref HP5	-	0.12	1.71	5.18	nr	6.89
70 mm back offset block; ref HP6	-	0.12	1.71	12.77	nr	14.48
vertical exit block; ref HP7	-	0.12	1.71	8.59	nr	10.30
angled entry/exit block; ref HP8	-	0.12	1.71	8.59	nr	10.30
reverse rebate block; ref HP9	-	0.12	1.71	6.44	nr	8.15
corbel block; ref HP10	-	0.12	1.71	8.12	nr	9.83
lintel unit; ref HP11	-	0.12	1.71	7.70	nr	9.41
Proprietary items						
"Thermabate" cavity closers or other equal and						
approved; RMC Panel Products Ltd						
closing cavities; width of cavity 50 mm	-	0.17	2.42	5.03	m	7.45
closing cavities; width of cavity 75 mm	-	0.17	2.42	5.40	m	7.82
"Westbrick" cavity closers or other equal and						
approved; Manthorpe Building Products Ltd						
closing cavities; width of cavity 50 mm	-	0.17	2.42	5.04	m	7.46
"Type H cavicloser" or other equal and approved;						
uPVC universal cavity closer, insulator and damp-						
proof course by Cavity Trays Ltd; built into cavity wall						
as work proceeds, complete with face closer and ties						
closing cavities; width of cavity 50 mm - 100 mm	-	0.09	1.28	5.34	m	6.62
"Type L" durrpolyethelene lintel stop ends or						
other equal and approved; Cavity Trays Ltd; fixing						
to lintel with butyl anchoring strip; building in as the						
work proceeds						
adjusted to lintel as required	-	0.06	0.85	0.54	nr	1.39
"Type W" polypropylene weeps/vents or other equal						
and approved; Cavity Trays Ltd; built into cavity wall						
as work proceeds						
100 mm/115 mm x 65 mm x 10 mm including						
lock fit wedges	-	0.06	0.85	0.42	nr	1.27
extra; extension duct 200 mm/225 mm x 65 mm						
x 10 mm	-	0.09	1.28	0.53	nr	1.81
"Type X" polypropylene abutment cavity tray or						
other equal and approved; Cavity Trays Ltd; built into						
facing brickwork as the work proceeds; complete with						
Code 4 lead flashing; intermediate/catchment tray with						
short leads (requiring soakers); to suit roof of						
17 - 20 degree pitch	-	0.07	0.99	4.64	nr	5.63
21 - 25 degree pitch	-	0.07	0.99	4.30	nr	5.29
26 - 45 degree pitch	-	0.07	0.99	4.12	nr	5.11

F MASONRY Excluding overheads and profit	PC £	Labour hours	Labour £	Material £	Unit	Total rate £
"Type X" polypropylene abutment cavity tray or other equal and approved; Cavity Trays Ltd; built into facing brickwork as the work proceeds; complete with Code 4 lead flashing; intermediate/catchment tray with long leads (suitable only for corrugated roof tiles); to suit roof of						
17 - 20 degree pitch	-	0.07	0.99	6.26	nr	7.25
21 - 25 degree pitch	-	0.07	0.99	5.75	nr	6.74
26 - 45 degree pitch	-	0.07	0.99	5.31	nr	6.30
"Type X" polypropylene abutment cavity tray or other equal and approved; Cavity Trays Ltd; built into facing brickwork as the work proceeds; complete with Code 4 lead flashing; ridge tray with short/long leads; to suit roof of						
17 - 20 degree pitch	-	0.07	0.99	10.54	nr	11.53
21 - 25 degree pitch	-	0.07	0.99	9.78	nr	10.77
26 - 45 degree pitch	-	0.07	0.99	8.69	nr	9.68
Serviced "Bitu-thene" self-adhesive cavity flashing or other equal and approved; type "CA"; well lapped at joints; in gauged mortar (1:1:6)						
width exceeding 225 mm; horizontal	-	0.98	13.93	20.04	m²	33.97
"Expamet" stainless steel wall starters or other equal and approved; plugged and screwed						
to suit walls 60 mm - 75 mm thick	-	0.29	1.87	7.49	m	9.36
to suit walls 100 mm - 115 mm thick	-	0.29	1.87	8.24	m	10.11
to suit walls 125 mm - 180 mm thick	-	0.46	2.97	11.02	m	13.99
to suit walls 190 mm - 260 mm thick	-	0.57	3.68	14.08	m	17.76
Ties in walls; 200 mm long butterfly type; building into joints of brickwork or blockwork						
galvanised steel or polypropylene	-	0.03	0.43	0.10	nr	0.53
stainless steel	-	0.03	0.43	0.18	nr	0.61
Ties in walls; 20 mm x 3 mm x 200 mm long twisted wall type; building into joints of brickwork or blockwork						
galvanised steel	-	0.03	0.43	0.17	nr	0.60
stainless steel	-	0.03	0.43	0.33	nr	0.76
Anchors in walls; 25 mm x 3 mm x 100 mm long; one end dovetailed; other end building into joints of brickwork or blockwork						
galvanised steel	-	0.07	0.99	0.21	nr	1.20
stainless steel	-	0.07	0.99	0.33	nr	1.32
Fixing cramp 25 mm x 3 mm x 250 mm long; once bent; fixed to back of frame; other end building into joints of brickwork or blockwork						
galvanised steel	-	0.07	0.99	0.16	nr	1.15
Chimney pots; red terracotta; plain or cannon-head; setting and flaunching in cement mortar (1:3)						
185 mm diameter x 300 mm long	16.27	2.07	29.41	17.62	nr	47.03
185 mm diameter x 600 mm long	28.97	2.30	32.68	30.32	nr	63.00
185 mm diameter x 900 mm long	52.80	2.30	32.68	54.15	nr	86.83
Galvanized steel lintels; "Catnic" or other equal and approved; built into brickwork or blockwork; "CN7" combined lintel; 143 mm high; for standard cavity walls						
750 mm long	20.90	0.29	4.12	20.94	nr	25.06
900 mm long	25.31	0.35	4.97	25.35	nr	30.32
1200 mm long	32.79	0.40	5.68	32.83	nr	38.51
1500 mm long	42.37	0.46	6.54	42.41	nr	48.95
1800 mm long	52.70	0.52	7.39	52.74	nr	60.13
2100 mm long	60.50	0.57	8.10	60.54	nr	68.64

F MASONRY Excluding overheads and profit	PC £	Labour hours	Labour £	Material £	Unit	Total rate £
F30 ACCESSORIES/SUNDRY ITEMS FOR BRICK/BLOCK/STONE WALLING - cont'd						
Proprietary items - cont'd						
Galvanized steel lintels; "Catnic" or other equal and						
approved; built into brickwork or blockwork; "CN8"						
combined lintel; 219 mm high; for standard cavity walls						
2400 mm long	74.16	0.69	9.80	74.20	nr	84.00
2700 mm long	87.42	0.80	11.37	87.46	nr	98.83
3000 mm long	116.55	0.92	13.07	116.59	nr	129.66
3300 mm long	130.09	1.03	14.64	130.13	nr	144.77
3600 mm long	142.76	1.15	16.34	142.80	nr	159.14
3900 mm long	185.72	1.26	17.90	185.76	nr	203.66
4200 mm long	203.67	0.57	8.10	203.71	nr	211.81
Galvanized steel lintels; "Catnic" or other equal and						
approved; built into brickwork or blockwork; "CN92"						
single lintel; for 75 mm internal walls						
900 mm long	3.29	0.35	4.97	3.31	nr	8.28
1050 mm long	3.76	0.35	4.97	3.78	nr	8.75
1200 mm long	4.27	0.40	5.68	4.29	nr	9.97
Galvanized steel lintels; "Catnic" or other equal and						
approved; built into brickwork or blockwork; "CN102"						
single lintel; for 100 mm internal walls						
900 mm long	4.05	0.35	4.97	4.07	nr	9.04
1050 mm long	4.77	0.35	4.97	4.79	nr	9.76
1200 mm long	5.26	0.40	5.68	5.28	nr	10.96
F31 PRECAST CONCRETE SILLS/LINTELS/ COPINGS/FEATURES						
Mix 20.00 N/mm^2 - 20 mm aggregate (1:2:4)						
Lintels; plate; prestressed bedded						
100 mm x 70 mm x 750 mm long	2.86	0.46	6.54	2.88	nr	9.42
100 mm x 70 mm x 900 mm long	3.41	0.46	6.54	3.43	nr	9.97
100 mm x 70 mm x 1050 mm long	4.01	0.46	6.54	4.03	nr	10.57
100 mm x 70 mm x 1200 mm long	4.57	0.46	6.54	4.59	nr	11.13
150 mm x 70 mm x 900 mm long	4.67	0.57	8.10	4.70	nr	12.80
150 mm x 70 mm x 1050 mm long	5.45	0.57	8.10	5.48	nr	13.58
150 mm x 70 mm x 1200 mm long	6.22	0.57	8.10	6.24	nr	14.34
220 mm x 70 mm x 900 mm long	7.21	0.69	9.80	7.26	nr	17.06
220 mm x 70 mm x 1200 mm long	9.57	0.69	9.80	9.62	nr	19.42
220 mm x 70 mm x 1500 mm long	11.99	0.80	11.37	12.04	nr	23.41
265 mm x 70 mm x 900 mm long	7.65	0.69	9.80	7.70	nr	17.50
265 mm x 70 mm x 1200 mm long	10.23	0.69	9.80	10.28	nr	20.08
265 mm x 70 mm x 1500 mm long	12.76	0.80	11.37	12.81	nr	24.18
265 mm x 70 mm x 1800 mm long	15.29	0.92	13.07	15.34	nr	28.41
Lintels; rectangular; reinforced with mild steel						
bars; bedded						
100 mm x 145 mm x 900 mm long	6.93	0.69	9.80	6.95	nr	16.75
100 mm x 145 mm x 1050 mm long	8.14	0.69	9.80	8.16	nr	17.96
100 mm x 145 mm x 1200 mm long	9.24	0.69	9.80	9.26	nr	19.06
225 mm x 145 mm x 1200 mm long	11.71	0.92	13.07	11.76	nr	24.83
225 mm x 225 mm x 1800 mm long	22.66	1.73	24.58	22.71	nr	47.29
Lintels; boot; reinforced with mild steel bars;						
bedded						
250 mm x 225 mm x 1200 mm long	18.81	1.38	19.61	18.86	nr	38.47
275 mm x 225 mm x 1800 mm long	25.19	2.07	29.41	25.24	nr	54.65
Padstones						
300 mm x 100 mm x 75 mm	3.85	0.35	4.97	3.87	nr	8.84
225 mm x 225 mm x 150 mm	5.83	0.46	6.54	5.86	nr	12.40
450 mm x 450 mm x 150 mm	15.40	0.69	9.80	15.53	nr	25.33

F MASONRY Excluding overheads and profit	PC £	Labour hours	Labour £	Material £	Unit	Total rate £
Mix 30.00 N/mm² - 20 mm aggregate (1:1:2)						
Copings; once weathered; once throated;						
bedded and pointed						
152 mm x 76 mm	4.67	0.80	11.37	4.97	m	**16.34**
178 mm x 64 mm	5.17	0.80	11.37	5.50	m	**16.87**
305 mm x 76 mm	8.69	0.92	13.07	9.28	m	**22.35**
extra for fair ends	-	-	-	3.96	nr	**3.96**
extra for angles	-	-	-	4.51	nr	**4.51**
Copings; twice weathered; twice throated;						
bedded and pointed						
152 mm x 76 mm	4.67	0.80	11.37	4.97	m	**16.34**
178 mm x 64 mm	5.12	0.80	11.37	5.44	m	**16.81**
305 mm x 76 mm	8.69	0.92	13.07	9.28	m	**22.35**
extra for fair ends	-	-	-	3.96	nr	**3.96**
extra for angles	-	-	-	4.51	nr	**4.51**

G STRUCTURAL/CARCASSING METAL/TIMBER Excluding overheads and profit	PC £	Labour hours	Labour £	Material £	Unit	Total rate £
G STRUCTURAL/CARCASSING METAL/TIMBER						
G10 STRUCTURAL STEEL FRAMING						
Framing, fabrication; weldable steel; BS EN **10025: 1993 Grade S275; hot rolled structural** **steel sections; welded fabrication**						
Columns						
weight not exceeding 40 kg/m	-	-	-	-	t	860.00
weight not exceeding 40 kg/m; castellated	-	-	-	-	t	970.00
weight not exceeding 40 kg/m; curved	-	-	-	-	t	1180.00
weight not exceeding 40 kg/m; square hollow section	-	-	-	-	t	1290.00
weight not exceeding 40 kg/m; circular hollow section	-	-	-	-	t	1430.00
weight 40 - 100 kg/m	-	-	-	-	t	840.00
weight 40 - 100 kg/m; castellated	-	-	-	-	t	945.00
weight 40 - 100 kg/m; curved	-	-	-	-	t	1160.00
weight 40 - 100 kg/m; square hollow section	-	-	-	-	t	1265.00
weight 40 - 100 kg/m; circular hollow section	-	-	-	-	t	1400.00
weight exceeding 100 kg/m	-	-	-	-	t	825.00
weight exceeding 100 kg/m; castellated	-	-	-	-	t	930.00
weight exceeding 100 kg/m; curved	-	-	-	-	t	1140.00
weight exceeding 100 kg/m; square hollow section	-	-	-	-	t	1245.00
weight exceeding 100 kg/m; circular hollow section	-	-	-	-	t	1385.00
Beams						
weight not exceeding 40 kg/m	-	-	-	-	t	905.00
weight not exceeding 40 kg/m; castellated	-	-	-	-	t	1025.00
weight not exceeding 40 kg/m; curved	-	-	-	-	t	1320.00
weight not exceeding 40 kg/m; square hollow section	-	-	-	-	t	1400.00
weight not exceeding 40 kg/m; circular hollow section	-	-	-	-	t	1610.00
weight 40 - 100 kg/m	-	-	-	-	t	880.00
weight 40 - 100 kg/m; castellated	-	-	-	-	t	995.00
weight 40 - 100 kg/m; curved	-	-	-	-	t	1295.00
weight 40 - 100 kg/m; square hollow section	-	-	-	-	t	1375.00
weight 40 - 100 kg/m; circular hollow section	-	-	-	-	t	1580.00
weight exceeding 100 kg/m	-	-	-	-	t	870.00
weight exceeding 100 kg/m; castellated	-	-	-	-	t	980.00
weight exceeding 100 kg/m; curved	-	-	-	-	t	1275.00
weight exceeding 100 kg/m; square hollow section	-	-	-	-	t	1360.00
weight exceeding 100 kg/m; circular hollow section	-	-	-	-	t	1560.00
Bracings						
weight not exceeding 40 kg/m	-	-	-	-	t	1155.00
weight not exceeding 40 kg/m; square hollow section	-	-	-	-	t	1610.00
weight not exceeding 40 kg/m; circular hollow section	-	-	-	-	t	1800.00
weight 40 - 100 kg/m	-	-	-	-	t	1130.00
weight 40 - 100 kg/m; square hollow section	-	-	-	-	t	1585.00
weight 40 - 100 kg/m; circular hollow section	-	-	-	-	t	1775.00
weight exceeding 100 kg/m	-	-	-	-	t	1095.00
weight exceeding 100 kg/m; square hollow section	-	-	-	-	t	1565.00
weight exceeding 100 kg/m; circular hollow section	-	-	-	-	t	1750.00

G STRUCTURAL/CARCASSING METAL/TIMBER Excluding overheads and profit	PC £	Labour hours	Labour £	Material £	Unit	Total rate £
Purlins and cladding rails						
weight not exceeding 40 kg/m	-	-	-	-	t	1020.00
weight not exceeding 40 kg/m; square hollow section	-	-	-	-	t	1450.00
weight not exceeding 40 kg/m; circular hollow section	-	-	-	-	t	1610.00
weight 40 - 100 kg/m	-	-	-	-	t	995.00
weight 40 - 100 kg/m; square hollow section	-	-	-	-	t	1425.00
weight 40 - 100 kg/m; circular hollow section	-	-	-	-	t	1585.00
weight exceeding 100 kg/m	-	-	-	-	t	970.00
weight exceeding 100 kg/m; square hollow section	-	-	-	-	t	1400.00
weight exceeding 100 kg/m; circular hollow section	-	-	-	-	t	1565.00
Grillages						
weight not exceeding 40 kg/m	-	-	-	-	t	700.00
weight 40 - 100 kg/m	-	-	-	-	t	740.00
weight exceeding 100 kg/m	-	-	-	-	t	700.00
Trestles, towers and built up columns						
straight	-	-	-	-	t	1345.00
Trusses and built up girders						
straight	-	-	-	-	t	1345.00
curved	-	-	-	-	t	1720.00
Fittings	-	-	-	-	t	970.00
Framing, erection						
Trial erection	-	-	-	-	t	240.00
Permanent erection on site	-	-	-	-	t	195.00
Surface preparation						
At works						
blast cleaning	-	-	-	-	m²	1.85
Surface treatment						
At works						
galvanising	-	-	-	-	m²	12.00
grit blast and one coat zinc chromate primer	-	-	-	-	m²	3.20
touch up primer and one coat of two pack epoxy zinc phosphate primer	-	-	-	-	m²	3.85
On site						
"Nullifire" fire protection system	-	-	-	-	m²	36.85
G12 ISOLATED STRUCTURAL METAL MEMBERS						
Isolated structural member; weldable steel; BS EN 10025: 1993 Grade S275; hot rolled structural steel sections						
Plain member; beams						
weight not exceeding 40 kg/m	-	-	-	-	t	630.00
weight 40 - 100 kg/m	-	-	-	-	t	600.00
weight exceeding 100 kg/m	-	-	-	-	t	590.00
Metsec open web steel lattice beams; in single members; raised 3.50 m above ground; ends built in						
Beams; one coat zinc phosphate primer at works						
200 mm deep; to span 5.00 m (7.69 kg/m); ref B22	-	0.22	3.17	26.00	m	29.17
300 mm deep; to span 7.00 m (10.26 kg/m); ref B30	-	0.28	4.03	34.81	m	38.84
350 mm deep; to span 8.50 m (10.60 kg/m); ref B35	-	0.28	4.03	35.88	m	39.91
350 mm deep; to span 10.00 m (12.76 kg/m); ref D35	-	0.33	4.76	43.97	m	48.73
450 mm deep; to span 13.00 m (25.44 kg/m); ref G50	-	0.55	7.93	69.27	m	77.20

G STRUCTURAL/CARCASSING METAL/TIMBER Excluding overheads and profit	PC £	Labour hours	Labour £	Material £	Unit	Total rate £
G12 ISOLATED STRUCTURAL METAL MEMBERS - cont'd						
Metsec open web steel lattice beams; in single members; raised 3.50 m above ground; ends built in - cont'd						
Beams; galvanised						
200 mm deep; to span 5.00 m (7.69 kg/m); ref B22	-	0.22	3.17	29.08	m	**32.25**
300 mm deep; to span 7.00 m (10.26 kg/m); ref B30	-	0.28	4.03	38.95	m	**42.98**
350 mm deep; to span 8.50 m (10.60 kg/m); ref B35	-	0.28	4.03	40.14	m	**44.17**
350 mm deep; to span 10.00 m (12.76 kg/m); ref D35	-	0.33	4.76	49.21	m	**53.97**
450 mm deep; to span 13.00 m (25.44 kg/m); ref G50	-	0.55	7.93	77.54	m	**85.47**
G20 CARPENTRY/TIMBER FRAMING/FIRST FIXING						
Sawn softwood; untreated						
Floor members						
38 mm x 100 mm	-	0.13	1.47	1.04	m	**2.51**
38 mm x 150 mm	-	0.15	1.70	1.51	m	**3.21**
50 mm x 75 mm	-	0.13	1.47	1.03	m	**2.50**
50 mm x 100 mm	-	0.15	1.70	1.31	m	**3.01**
50 mm x 125 mm	-	0.15	1.70	1.60	m	**3.30**
50 mm x 150 mm	-	0.17	1.93	1.92	m	**3.85**
50 mm x 175 mm	-	0.17	1.93	2.24	m	**4.17**
50 mm x 200 mm	-	0.18	2.04	2.63	m	**4.67**
50 mm x 225 mm	-	0.18	2.04	3.04	m	**5.08**
50 mm x 250 mm	-	0.19	2.15	3.46	m	**5.61**
75 mm x 125 mm	-	0.18	2.04	2.40	m	**4.44**
75 mm x 150 mm	-	0.18	2.04	2.88	m	**4.92**
75 mm x 175 mm	-	0.18	2.04	3.38	m	**5.42**
75 mm x 200 mm	-	0.19	2.15	3.95	m	**6.10**
75 mm x 225 mm	-	0.19	2.15	4.55	m	**6.70**
75 mm x 250 mm	-	0.20	2.27	5.20	m	**7.47**
100 mm x 150 mm	-	0.24	2.72	3.95	m	**6.67**
100 mm x 200 mm	-	0.25	2.83	5.40	m	**8.23**
100 mm x 250 mm	-	0.28	3.18	7.48	m	**10.66**
100 mm x 300 mm	-	0.30	3.40	9.25	m	**12.65**
Wall or partition members						
25 mm x 25 mm	-	0.08	0.91	0.30	m	**1.21**
25 mm x 38 mm	-	0.08	0.91	0.38	m	**1.29**
25 mm x 75 mm	-	0.10	1.13	0.53	m	**1.66**
38 mm x 38 mm	-	0.10	1.13	0.45	m	**1.58**
38 mm x 50 mm	-	0.10	1.13	0.52	m	**1.65**
38 mm x 75 mm	-	0.13	1.47	0.77	m	**2.24**
38 mm x 100 mm	-	0.17	1.93	1.04	m	**2.97**
50 mm x 50 mm	-	0.13	1.47	0.71	m	**2.18**
50 mm x 75 mm	-	0.17	1.93	1.05	m	**2.98**
50 mm x 100 mm	-	0.20	2.27	1.33	m	**3.60**
50 mm x 125 mm	-	0.21	2.38	1.62	m	**4.00**
75 mm x 75 mm	-	0.20	2.27	1.76	m	**4.03**
75 mm x 100 mm	-	0.23	2.61	1.97	m	**4.58**
100 mm x 100 mm	-	0.23	2.61	2.61	m	**5.22**
Roof members; flat						
38 mm x 75 mm	-	0.15	1.70	0.77	m	**2.47**
38 mm x 100 mm	-	0.15	1.70	1.04	m	**2.74**
38 mm x 125 mm	-	0.15	1.70	1.29	m	**2.99**
38 mm x 150 mm	-	0.15	1.70	1.51	m	**3.21**
50 mm x 100 mm	-	0.15	1.70	1.31	m	**3.01**
50 mm x 125 mm	-	0.15	1.70	1.60	m	**3.30**
50 mm x 150 mm	-	0.17	1.93	1.92	m	**3.85**
50 mm x 175 mm	-	0.17	1.93	2.24	m	**4.17**

G STRUCTURAL/CARCASSING METAL/TIMBER Excluding overheads and profit	PC £	Labour hours	Labour £	Material £	Unit	Total rate £
Roof members; flat - cont'd						
50 mm x 200 mm	-	0.18	2.04	2.63	m	4.67
50 mm x 225 mm	-	0.18	2.04	3.04	m	5.08
50 mm x 250 mm	-	0.19	2.15	3.46	m	5.61
75 mm x 150 mm	-	0.18	2.04	2.88	m	4.92
75 mm x 175 mm	-	0.18	2.04	3.38	m	5.42
75 mm x 200 mm	-	0.19	2.15	3.95	m	6.10
75 mm x 225 mm	-	0.19	2.15	4.55	m	6.70
75 mm x 250 mm	-	0.20	2.27	5.20	m	7.47
Roof members; pitched						
25 mm x 100 mm	-	0.13	1.47	0.70	m	2.17
25 mm x 125 mm	-	0.13	1.47	0.87	m	2.34
25 mm x 150 mm	-	0.17	1.93	1.10	m	3.03
25 mm x 175 mm	-	0.19	2.15	1.45	m	3.60
25 mm x 200 mm	-	0.20	2.27	1.68	m	3.95
38 mm x 100 mm	-	0.17	1.93	1.04	m	2.97
38 mm x 125 mm	-	0.17	1.93	1.29	m	3.22
38 mm x 150 mm	-	0.17	1.93	1.51	m	3.44
50 mm x 50 mm	-	0.13	1.47	0.69	m	2.16
50 mm x 75 mm	-	0.17	1.93	1.03	m	2.96
50 mm x 100 mm	-	0.20	2.27	1.31	m	3.58
50 mm x 125 mm	-	0.20	2.27	1.60	m	3.87
50 mm x 150 mm	-	0.23	2.61	1.92	m	4.53
50 mm x 175 mm	-	0.23	2.61	2.24	m	4.85
50 mm x 200 mm	-	0.23	2.61	2.63	m	5.24
50 mm x 225 mm	-	0.23	2.61	3.04	m	5.65
75 mm x 100 mm	-	0.28	3.18	1.93	m	5.11
75 mm x 125 mm	-	0.28	3.18	2.40	m	5.58
75 mm x 150 mm	-	0.28	3.18	2.88	m	6.06
100 mm x 150 mm	-	0.33	3.74	3.97	m	7.71
100 mm x 175 mm	-	0.33	3.74	4.60	m	8.34
100 mm x 200 mm	-	0.33	3.74	5.40	m	9.14
100 mm x 225 mm	-	0.36	4.08	6.58	m	10.66
100 mm x 250 mm	-	0.36	4.08	7.48	m	11.56
Plates						
38 mm x 75 mm	-	0.13	1.47	0.77	m	2.24
38 mm x 100 mm	-	0.17	1.93	1.04	m	2.97
50 mm x 75 mm	-	0.17	1.93	1.05	m	2.98
50 mm x 100 mm	-	0.20	2.27	1.31	m	3.58
75 mm x 100 mm	-	0.23	2.61	1.97	m	4.58
75 mm x 125 mm	-	0.26	2.95	2.38	m	5.33
75 mm x 150 mm	-	0.29	3.29	2.87	m	6.16
Plates; fixing by bolting						
38 mm x 75 mm	-	0.23	2.61	0.77	m	3.38
38 mm x 100 mm	-	0.27	3.06	1.04	m	4.10
50 mm x 75 mm	-	0.27	3.06	1.05	m	4.11
50 mm x 100 mm	-	0.30	3.40	1.31	m	4.71
75 mm x 100 mm	-	0.33	3.74	1.97	m	5.71
75 mm x 125 mm	-	0.36	4.08	2.38	m	6.46
75 mm x 150 mm	-	0.39	4.42	2.87	m	7.29
Joist strutting; herringbone strutting						
50 mm x 50 mm; depth of joist 150 mm	-	0.55	6.24	1.63	m	7.87
50 mm x 50 mm; depth of joist 175 mm	-	0.55	6.24	1.66	m	7.90
50 mm x 50 mm; depth of joist 200 mm	-	0.55	6.24	1.69	m	7.93
50 mm x 50 mm; depth of joist 225 mm	-	0.55	6.24	1.73	m	7.97
50 mm x 50 mm; depth of joist 250 mm	-	0.55	6.24	1.76	m	8.00
Joist strutting; block						
50 mm x 150 mm; depth of joist 150 mm	-	0.33	3.74	2.17	m	5.91
50 mm x 175 mm; depth of joist 175 mm	-	0.33	3.74	2.49	m	6.23
50 mm x 200 mm; depth of joist 200 mm	-	0.33	3.74	2.88	m	6.62
50 mm x 225 mm; depth of joist 225 mm	-	0.33	3.74	3.28	m	7.02
50 mm x 250 mm; depth of joist 250 mm	-	0.33	3.74	3.70	m	7.44

G STRUCTURAL/CARCASSING METAL/TIMBER Excluding overheads and profit	PC £	Labour hours	Labour £	Material £	Unit	Total rate £
G20 CARPENTRY/TIMBER FRAMING/FIRST **FIXING** - cont'd						
Sawn softwood; untreated - cont'd						
Cleats						
225 mm x 100 mm x 75 mm	-	0.22	2.49	0.51	nr	3.00
Extra for stress grading to above timbers						
general structural (GS) grade	-	-	-	14.96	m³	14.96
special structural (SS) grade	-	-	-	28.80	m³	28.80
Extra for protecting and flameproofing timber						
with "Celgard CF" protection or other equal						
and approved						
small sections	-	-	-	115.50	m³	115.50
large sections	-	-	-	110.25	m³	110.25
Wrot surfaces						
plain; 50 mm wide	-	0.03	0.34	-	m	0.34
plain; 100 mm wide	-	0.04	0.45	-	m	0.45
plain; 150 mm wide	-	0.06	0.68	-	m	0.68
Sawn softwood; "Tanalised"						
Floor members						
38 mm x 75 mm	-	0.13	1.47	0.87	m	2.34
38 mm x 100 mm	-	0.13	1.47	1.17	m	2.64
38 mm x 150 mm	-	0.15	1.70	1.71	m	3.41
50 mm x 75 mm	-	0.13	1.47	1.16	m	2.63
50 mm x 100 mm	-	0.15	1.70	1.48	m	3.18
50 mm x 125 mm	-	0.15	1.70	1.82	m	3.52
50 mm x 150 mm	-	0.17	1.93	2.18	m	4.11
50 mm x 175 mm	-	0.17	1.93	2.55	m	4.48
50 mm x 200 mm	-	0.18	2.04	2.98	m	5.02
50 mm x 225 mm	-	0.18	2.04	3.43	m	5.47
50 mm x 250 mm	-	0.19	2.15	3.89	m	6.04
75 mm x 125 mm	-	0.18	2.04	2.73	m	4.77
75 mm x 150 mm	-	0.18	2.04	3.28	m	5.32
75 mm x 175 mm	-	0.18	2.04	3.83	m	5.87
75 mm x 200 mm	-	0.19	2.15	4.47	m	6.62
75 mm x 225 mm	-	0.19	2.15	5.14	m	7.29
75 mm x 250 mm	-	0.20	2.27	5.85	m	8.12
100 mm x 150 mm	-	0.24	2.72	4.47	m	7.19
100 mm x 200 mm	-	0.25	2.83	6.09	m	8.92
100 mm x 250 mm	-	0.28	3.18	8.35	m	11.53
100 mm x 300 mm	-	0.30	3.40	10.29	m	13.69
Wall or partition members						
25 mm x 25 mm	-	0.08	0.91	0.32	m	1.23
25 mm x 38 mm	-	0.08	0.91	0.42	m	1.33
25 mm x 75 mm	-	0.10	1.13	0.60	m	1.73
38 mm x 38 mm	-	0.10	1.13	0.49	m	1.62
38 mm x 50 mm	-	0.10	1.13	0.59	m	1.72
38 mm x 75 mm	-	0.13	1.47	0.87	m	2.34
38 mm x 100 mm	-	0.17	1.93	1.17	m	3.10
50 mm x 50 mm	-	0.13	1.47	0.80	m	2.27
50 mm x 75 mm	-	0.17	1.93	1.18	m	3.11
50 mm x 100 mm	-	0.20	2.27	1.50	m	3.77
50 mm x 125 mm	-	0.21	2.38	1.84	m	4.22
75 mm x 75 mm	-	0.20	2.27	1.95	m	4.22
75 mm x 100 mm	-	0.23	2.61	2.23	m	4.84
100 mm x 100 mm	-	0.23	2.61	2.96	m	5.57

G STRUCTURAL/CARCASSING METAL/TIMBER Excluding overheads and profit	PC £	Labour hours	Labour £	Material £	Unit	Total rate £
Roof members; flat						
38 mm x 75 mm	-	0.15	1.70	0.87	m	2.57
38 mm x 100 mm	-	0.15	1.70	1.17	m	2.87
38 mm x 125 mm	-	0.15	1.70	1.45	m	3.15
38 mm x 150 mm	-	0.15	1.70	1.71	m	3.41
50 mm x 100 mm	-	0.15	1.70	1.48	m	3.18
50 mm x 125 mm	-	0.15	1.70	1.82	m	3.52
50 mm x 150 mm	-	0.17	1.93	2.18	m	4.11
50 mm x 175 mm	-	0.17	1.93	2.55	m	4.48
50 mm x 200 mm	-	0.18	2.04	2.98	m	5.02
50 mm x 225 mm	-	0.18	2.04	3.43	m	5.47
50 mm x 250 mm	-	0.19	2.15	3.89	m	6.04
75 mm x 150 mm	-	0.18	2.04	3.28	m	5.32
75 mm x 175 mm	-	0.18	2.04	3.83	m	5.87
75 mm x 200 mm	-	0.19	2.15	4.47	m	6.62
75 mm x 225 mm	-	0.19	2.15	5.14	m	7.29
75 mm x 250 mm	-	0.20	2.27	5.85	m	8.12
Roof members; pitched						
25 mm x 100 mm	-	0.13	1.47	0.79	m	2.26
25 mm x 125 mm	-	0.13	1.47	0.97	m	2.44
25 mm x 150 mm	-	0.17	1.93	1.23	m	3.16
25 mm x 175 mm	-	0.19	2.15	1.60	m	3.75
25 mm x 200 mm	-	0.20	2.27	1.86	m	4.13
38 mm x 100 mm	-	0.17	1.93	1.17	m	3.10
38 mm x 125 mm	-	0.17	1.93	1.45	m	3.38
38 mm x 150 mm	-	0.17	1.93	1.71	m	3.64
50 mm x 50 mm	-	0.13	1.47	0.78	m	2.25
50 mm x 75 mm	-	0.17	1.93	1.16	m	3.09
50 mm x 100 mm	-	0.20	2.27	1.48	m	3.75
50 mm x 125 mm	-	0.20	2.27	1.82	m	4.09
50 mm x 150 mm	-	0.23	2.61	2.18	m	4.79
50 mm x 175 mm	-	0.23	2.61	2.55	m	5.16
50 mm x 200 mm	-	0.23	2.61	2.98	m	5.59
50 mm x 225 mm	-	0.23	2.61	3.43	m	6.04
75 mm x 100 mm	-	0.28	3.18	2.19	m	5.37
75 mm x 125 mm	-	0.28	3.18	2.73	m	5.91
75 mm x 150 mm	-	0.28	3.18	3.28	m	6.46
100 mm x 150 mm	-	0.33	3.74	4.49	m	8.23
100 mm x 175 mm	-	0.33	3.74	5.21	m	8.95
100 mm x 200 mm	-	0.33	3.74	6.09	m	9.83
100 mm x 225 mm	-	0.36	4.08	7.36	m	11.44
100 mm x 250 mm	-	0.36	4.08	8.35	m	12.43
Plates						
38 mm x 75 mm	-	0.13	1.47	0.87	m	2.34
38 mm x 100 mm	-	0.17	1.93	1.17	m	3.10
50 mm x 75 mm	-	0.17	1.93	1.18	m	3.11
50 mm x 100 mm	-	0.20	2.27	1.50	m	3.77
75 mm x 100 mm	-	0.23	2.61	2.23	m	4.84
75 mm x 125 mm	-	0.26	2.95	2.71	m	5.66
75 mm x 150 mm	-	0.29	3.29	3.26	m	6.55
Plates; fixing by bolting						
38 mm x 75 mm	-	0.23	2.61	0.87	m	3.48
38 mm x 100 mm	-	0.27	3.06	1.17	m	4.23
50 mm x 75 mm	-	0.27	3.06	1.18	m	4.24
50 mm x 100 mm	-	0.30	3.40	1.50	m	4.90
75 mm x 100 mm	-	0.33	3.74	2.23	m	5.97
75 mm x 125 mm	-	0.36	4.08	2.71	m	6.79
75 mm x 150 mm	-	0.39	4.42	3.26	m	7.68

G STRUCTURAL/CARCASSING METAL/TIMBER Excluding overheads and profit	PC £	Labour hours	Labour £	Material £	Unit	Total rate £
G20 CARPENTRY/TIMBER FRAMING/FIRST **FIXING** - cont'd						
Sawn softwood; "Tanalised" - cont'd						
Joist strutting; herringbone						
50 mm x 50 mm; depth of joist 150 mm	-	0.55	6.24	1.81	m	**8.05**
50 mm x 50 mm; depth of joist 175 mm	-	0.55	6.24	1.85	m	**8.09**
50 mm x 50 mm; depth of joist 200 mm	-	0.55	6.24	1.88	m	**8.12**
50 mm x 50 mm; depth of joist 225 mm	-	0.55	6.24	1.92	m	**8.16**
50 mm x 50 mm; depth of joist 250 mm	-	0.55	6.24	1.95	m	**8.19**
Joist strutting; block						
50 mm x 150 mm; depth of joist 150 mm	-	0.33	3.74	2.43	m	**6.17**
50 mm x 175 mm; depth of joist 175 mm	-	0.33	3.74	2.80	m	**6.54**
50 mm x 200 mm; depth of joist 200 mm	-	0.33	3.74	3.23	m	**6.97**
50 mm x 225 mm; depth of joist 225 mm	-	0.33	3.74	3.68	m	**7.42**
50 mm x 250 mm; depth of joist 250 mm	-	0.33	3.74	4.14	m	**7.88**
Cleats						
225 mm x 100 mm x 75 mm	-	0.22	2.49	0.56	nr	**3.05**
Extra for stress grading to above timbers						
general structural (GS) grade	-	-	-	14.96	m³	**14.96**
special structural (SS) grade	-	-	-	28.80	m³	**28.80**
Extra for protecting and flameproofing timber with "Celgard CF" protection or other equal and approved						
small sections	-	-	-	115.50	m³	**115.50**
large sections	-	-	-	110.25	m³	**110.25**
Wrot surfaces						
plain; 50 mm wide	-	0.03	0.34	-	m	**0.34**
plain; 100 mm wide	-	0.04	0.45	-	m	**0.45**
plain; 150 mm wide	-	0.06	0.68	-	m	**0.68**
Trussed rafters, stress graded sawn **softwood pressure impregnated; raised** **through two storeys and fixed in position** "W" type truss (Fink); 22.50 degree pitch; 450 mm eaves overhang						
5.00 m span	-	1.76	19.96	24.41	nr	**44.37**
7.60 m span	-	1.93	21.89	34.03	nr	**55.92**
10.00 m span	-	2.20	24.95	48.82	nr	**73.77**
"W" type truss (Fink); 30 degree pitch; 450 mm eaves overhang						
5.00 m span	-	1.76	19.96	25.58	nr	**45.54**
7.60 m span	-	1.93	21.89	34.18	nr	**56.07**
10.00 m span	-	2.20	24.95	50.98	nr	**75.93**
"W" type truss (Fink); 45 degree pitch; 450 mm eaves overhang						
4.60 m span	-	1.76	19.96	27.65	nr	**47.61**
7.00 m span	-	1.93	21.89	36.30	nr	**58.19**
"Mono" type truss; 17.50 degree pitch; 450 mm eaves overhang						
3.30 m span	-	1.54	17.46	20.77	nr	**38.23**
5.60 m span	-	1.76	19.96	35.35	nr	**55.31**
7.00 m span	-	2.03	23.02	41.47	nr	**64.49**
"Mono" type truss; 30 degree pitch; 450 mm eaves overhang						
3.30 m span	-	1.54	17.46	21.68	nr	**39.14**
5.60 m span	-	1.76	19.96	35.21	nr	**55.17**
7.00 m span	-	2.03	23.02	45.60	nr	**68.62**
"Attic" type truss; 45 degree pitch; 450 mm eaves overhang						
5.00 m span	-	3.47	39.35	44.07	nr	**83.42**
7.60 m span	-	3.63	41.16	73.88	nr	**115.04**

G STRUCTURAL/CARCASSING METAL/TIMBER Excluding overheads and profit	PC £	Labour hours	Labour £	Material £	Unit	Total rate £
"Moelven Toreboda" glulam timber beams or **other equal and approved; Moelven Laminated** **Timber Structures; LB grade whitewood; pressure** **impregnated; phenbol resorcinol adhesive; clean** **planed finish; fixed**						
Laminated roof beams						
56 mm x 225 mm	-	0.61	6.92	6.98	m	**13.90**
66 mm x 315 mm	-	0.77	8.73	11.52	m	**20.25**
90 mm x 315 mm	-	0.99	11.23	15.71	m	**26.94**
90 mm x 405 mm	-	1.26	14.29	20.05	m	**34.34**
115 mm x 405 mm	-	1.60	18.14	25.80	m	**43.94**
115 mm x 495 mm	-	1.98	22.45	31.53	m	**53.98**
115 mm x 630 mm	-	2.42	27.44	40.13	m	**67.57**
"Masterboard" or other equal and approved; 6 **mm thick**						
Eaves, verge soffit boards, fascia boards and the like						
over 300 mm wide	8.07	0.77	8.73	9.06	m²	**17.79**
75 mm wide	-	0.23	2.61	0.69	m	**3.30**
150 mm wide	-	0.26	2.95	1.36	m	**4.31**
225 mm wide	-	0.31	3.52	2.03	m	**5.55**
300 mm wide	-	0.33	3.74	2.70	m	**6.44**
Plywood; external quality; 15 mm thick						
Eaves, verge soffit boards, fascia boards and the like						
over 300 mm wide	10.39	0.90	10.21	11.55	m²	**21.76**
75 mm wide	-	0.28	3.18	0.88	m	**4.06**
150 mm wide	-	0.32	3.63	1.73	m	**5.36**
225 mm wide	-	0.36	4.08	2.59	m	**6.67**
300 mm wide	-	0.41	4.65	3.45	m	**8.10**
Plywood; external quality; 18 mm thick						
Eaves, verge soffit boards, fascia boards and the like						
over 300 mm wide	12.41	0.90	10.21	13.72	m²	**23.93**
75 mm wide	-	0.28	3.18	1.04	m	**4.22**
150 mm wide	-	0.32	3.63	2.06	m	**5.69**
225 mm wide	-	0.36	4.08	3.08	m	**7.16**
300 mm wide	-	0.41	4.65	4.10	m	**8.75**
Plywood; marine quality; 18 mm thick						
Gutter boards; butt joints						
over 300 mm wide	9.25	1.02	11.57	10.32	m²	**21.89**
150 mm wide	-	0.36	4.08	1.55	m	**5.63**
225 mm wide	-	0.41	4.65	2.33	m	**6.98**
300 mm wide	-	0.45	5.10	3.10	m	**8.20**
Eaves, verge soffit boards, fascia boards and the like						
over 300 mm wide	-	0.90	10.21	10.32	m²	**20.53**
75 mm wide	-	0.28	3.18	0.78	m	**3.96**
150 mm wide	-	0.32	3.63	1.55	m	**5.18**
225 mm wide	-	0.36	4.08	2.31	m	**6.39**
300 mm wide	-	0.41	4.65	3.08	m	**7.73**
Plywood; marine quality; 25 mm thick						
Gutter boards; butt joints						
over 300 mm wide	12.84	1.10	12.47	14.19	m²	**26.66**
150 mm wide	-	0.39	4.42	2.13	m	**6.55**
225 mm wide	-	0.44	4.99	3.20	m	**8.19**
300 mm wide	-	0.49	5.56	4.26	m	**9.82**

G STRUCTURAL/CARCASSING METAL/TIMBER Excluding overheads and profit	PC £	Labour hours	Labour £	Material £	Unit	Total rate £
G20 CARPENTRY/TIMBER FRAMING/FIRST FIXING - cont'd						
Plywood; marine quality; 25 mm thick - cont'd						
Eaves, verge soffit boards, fascia boards and						
the like						
over 300 mm wide	-	0.97	11.00	14.19	m²	25.19
75 mm wide	-	0.29	3.29	1.07	m	4.36
150 mm wide	-	0.34	3.86	2.13	m	5.99
225 mm wide	-	0.34	3.86	3.18	m	7.04
300 mm wide	-	0.44	4.99	4.24	m	9.23
Sawn softwood; untreated						
Gutter boards; butt joints						
19 mm thick; sloping	-	1.38	15.65	6.04	m²	21.69
19 mm thick; 75 mm wide	-	0.39	4.42	0.45	m	4.87
19 mm thick; 150 mm wide	-	0.44	4.99	0.88	m	5.87
19 mm thick; 225 mm wide	-	0.49	5.56	1.52	m	7.08
25 mm thick; sloping	-	1.38	15.65	7.76	m²	23.41
25 mm thick; 75 mm wide	-	0.39	4.42	0.55	m	4.97
25 mm thick; 150 mm wide	-	0.44	4.99	1.14	m	6.13
25 mm thick; 225 mm wide	-	0.49	5.56	2.02	m	7.58
Cesspools with 25 mm thick sides and bottom						
225 mm x 225 mm x 150 mm	-	1.32	14.97	1.55	nr	16.52
300 mm x 300 mm x 150 mm	-	1.54	17.46	1.97	nr	19.43
Individual supports; firrings						
50 mm wide x 36 mm average depth	-	0.17	1.93	0.97	m	2.90
50 mm wide x 50 mm average depth	-	0.17	1.93	1.25	m	3.18
50 mm wide x 75 mm average depth	-	0.17	1.93	1.62	m	3.55
Individual supports; bearers						
25 mm x 50 mm	-	0.11	1.25	0.44	m	1.69
38 mm x 50 mm	-	0.11	1.25	0.56	m	1.81
50 mm x 50 mm	-	0.11	1.25	0.73	m	1.98
50 mm x 75 mm	-	0.11	1.25	1.06	m	2.31
Individual supports; angle fillets						
38 mm x 38 mm	-	0.11	1.25	0.48	m	1.73
50 mm x 50 mm	-	0.11	1.25	0.73	m	1.98
75 mm x 75 mm	-	0.13	1.47	1.74	m	3.21
Individual supports; tilting fillets						
19 mm x 38 mm	-	0.11	1.25	0.23	m	1.48
25 mm x 50 mm	-	0.11	1.25	0.31	m	1.56
38 mm x 75 mm	-	0.11	1.25	0.55	m	1.80
50 mm x 75 mm	-	0.11	1.25	0.69	m	1.94
75 mm x 100 mm	-	0.17	1.93	1.29	m	3.22
Individual supports; grounds or battens						
13 mm x 19 mm	-	0.06	0.68	0.26	m	0.94
13 mm x 32 mm	-	0.06	0.68	0.30	m	0.98
25 mm x 50 mm	-	0.06	0.68	0.40	m	1.08
Individial supports; grounds or battens;						
plugged and screwed						
13 mm x 19 mm	-	0.17	1.93	0.28	m	2.21
13 mm x 32 mm	-	0.17	1.93	0.32	m	2.25
25 mm x 50 mm	-	0.17	1.93	0.42	m	2.35
Framed supports; open-spaced grounds or						
battens; at 300 mm centres one way						
25 mm x 50 mm	-	0.17	1.93	1.33	m²	3.26
25 mm x 50 mm; plugged and screwed	-	0.49	5.56	1.41	m²	6.97

G STRUCTURAL/CARCASSING METAL/TIMBER Excluding overheads and profit	PC £	Labour hours	Labour £	Material £	Unit	Total rate £
Framed supports; at 300 mm centres one way and 600 mm centres the other way						
25 mm x 50 mm	-	0.83	9.41	2.00	m²	11.41
38 mm x 50 mm	-	0.83	9.41	2.59	m²	12.00
50 mm x 50 mm	-	0.83	9.41	3.45	m²	12.86
50 mm x 75 mm	-	0.83	9.41	5.12	m²	14.53
75 mm x 75 mm	-	0.83	9.41	8.66	m²	18.07
Framed supports; at 300 mm centres one way and 600 mm centres the other way; plugged and screwed						
25 mm x 50 mm	-	1.38	15.65	2.24	m²	17.89
38 mm x 50 mm	-	1.38	15.65	2.83	m²	18.48
50 mm x 50 mm	-	1.38	15.65	3.69	m²	19.34
50 mm x 75 mm	-	1.38	15.65	5.36	m²	21.01
75 mm x 75 mm	-	1.38	15.65	8.91	m²	24.56
Framed supports; at 500 mm centres both ways						
25 mm x 50 mm; to bath panels	-	0.99	11.23	2.60	m²	13.83
Framed supports; as bracketing and cradling around steelwork						
25 mm x 50 mm	-	1.54	17.46	2.82	m²	20.28
50 mm x 50 mm	-	1.65	18.71	4.86	m²	23.57
50 mm x 75 mm	-	1.76	19.96	7.19	m²	27.15
Sawn softwood; "Tanalised"						
Gutter boards; butt joints						
19 mm thick; sloping	-	1.38	15.65	6.70	m²	22.35
19 mm thick; 75 mm wide	-	0.39	4.42	0.50	m	4.92
19 mm thick; 150 mm wide	-	0.44	4.99	0.98	m	5.97
19 mm thick; 225 mm wide	-	0.49	5.56	1.67	m	7.23
25 mm thick; sloping	-	1.38	15.65	8.63	m²	24.28
25 mm thick; 75 mm wide	-	0.39	4.42	0.62	m	5.04
25 mm thick; 150 mm wide	-	0.44	4.99	1.27	m	6.26
25 mm thick; 225 mm wide	-	0.49	5.56	2.21	m	7.77
Cesspools with 25 mm thick sides and bottom						
225 mm x 225 mm x 150 mm	-	1.32	14.97	1.73	nr	16.70
300 mm x 300 mm x 150 mm	-	1.54	17.46	2.21	nr	19.67
Individual supports; firrings						
50 mm wide x 36 mm average depth	-	0.17	1.93	1.04	m	2.97
50 mm wide x 50 mm average depth	-	0.17	1.93	1.34	m	3.27
50 mm wide x 75 mm average depth	-	0.17	1.93	1.75	m	3.68
Individual supports; bearers						
25 mm x 50 mm	-	0.11	1.25	0.49	m	1.74
38 mm x 50 mm	-	0.11	1.25	0.62	m	1.87
50 mm x 50 mm	-	0.11	1.25	0.82	m	2.07
50 mm x 75 mm	-	0.11	1.25	1.20	m	2.45
Individual supports; angle fillets						
38 mm x 38 mm	-	0.11	1.25	0.51	m	1.76
50 mm x 50 mm	-	0.11	1.25	0.78	m	2.03
75 mm x 75 mm	-	0.13	1.47	1.84	m	3.31
Individual supports; tilting fillets						
19 mm x 38 mm	-	0.11	1.25	0.24	m	1.49
25 mm x 50 mm	-	0.11	1.25	0.33	m	1.58
38 mm x 75 mm	-	0.11	1.25	0.60	m	1.85
50 mm x 75 mm	-	0.11	1.25	0.75	m	2.00
75 mm x 100 mm	-	0.17	1.93	1.42	m	3.35
Individual supports; grounds or battens						
13 mm x 19 mm	-	0.06	0.68	0.27	m	0.95
13 mm x 32 mm	-	0.06	0.68	0.31	m	0.99
25 mm x 50 mm	-	0.06	0.68	0.45	m	1.13

G STRUCTURAL/CARCASSING METAL/TIMBER Excluding overheads and profit	PC £	Labour hours	Labour £	Material £	Unit	Total rate £
G20 CARPENTRY/TIMBER FRAMING/FIRST FIXING - cont'd						
Sawn softwood; "Tanalised" - cont'd						
Individual supports; grounds or battens;						
plugged and screwed						
13 mm x 19 mm	-	0.17	1.93	0.29	m	**2.22**
13 mm x 32 mm	-	0.17	1.93	0.33	m	**2.26**
25 mm x 50 mm	-	0.17	1.93	0.47	m	**2.40**
Framed supports; open-spaced grounds or						
battens; at 300 mm centres one way						
25 mm x 50 mm	-	0.17	1.93	1.48	m²	**3.41**
25 mm x 50 mm; plugged and screwed	-	0.49	5.56	1.55	m²	**7.11**
Framed supports; at 300 mm centres one way						
and 600 mm centres the other way						
25 mm x 50 mm	-	0.83	9.41	2.22	m²	**11.63**
38 mm x 50 mm	-	0.83	9.41	2.92	m²	**12.33**
50 mm x 50 mm	-	0.83	9.41	3.88	m²	**13.29**
50 mm x 75 mm	-	0.83	9.41	5.77	m²	**15.18**
75 mm x 75 mm	-	0.83	9.41	9.64	m²	**19.05**
Framed supports; at 300 mm centres one way						
and 600 mm centres the other way; plugged						
and screwed						
25 mm x 50 mm	-	1.38	15.65	2.46	m²	**18.11**
38 mm x 50 mm	-	1.38	15.65	3.16	m²	**18.81**
50 mm x 50 mm	-	1.38	15.65	4.13	m²	**19.78**
50 mm x 75 mm	-	1.38	15.65	6.01	m²	**21.66**
75 mm x 75 mm	-	1.38	15.65	9.88	m²	**25.53**
Framed supports; at 500 mm centres both						
ways						
25 mm x 50 mm; to bath panels	-	0.99	11.23	2.89	m²	**14.12**
Framed supports; as bracketing and cradling						
around steelwork						
25 mm x 50 mm	-	1.54	17.46	3.13	m²	**20.59**
50 mm x 50 mm	-	1.65	18.71	5.46	m²	**24.17**
50 mm x 75 mm	-	1.76	19.96	8.10	m²	**28.06**
Wrought softwood						
Gutter boards; tongued and grooved joints						
19 mm thick; sloping	-	1.65	18.71	7.90	m²	**26.61**
19 mm thick; 75 mm wide	-	0.44	4.99	0.94	m	**5.93**
19 mm thick; 150 mm wide	-	0.49	5.56	1.16	m	**6.72**
19 mm thick; 225 mm wide	-	0.55	6.24	2.06	m	**8.30**
25 mm thick; sloping	-	1.65	18.71	9.67	m²	**28.38**
25 mm thick; 75 mm wide	-	0.44	4.99	1.30	m	**6.29**
25 mm thick; 150 mm wide	-	0.49	5.56	1.38	m	**6.94**
25 mm thick; 225 mm wide	-	0.55	6.24	2.63	m	**8.87**
Eaves, verge soffit boards, fascia boards and						
the like						
19 mm thick; over 300 mm wide	-	1.36	15.42	7.91	m²	**23.33**
19 mm thick; 150 mm wide; once grooved	-	0.22	2.49	1.41	m	**3.90**
25 mm thick; 150 mm wide; once grooved	-	0.22	2.49	1.71	m	**4.20**
25 mm thick; 175 mm wide; once grooved	-	0.24	2.72	1.98	m	**4.70**
32 mm thick; 225 mm wide; once grooved	-	0.28	3.18	3.47	m	**6.65**

G STRUCTURAL/CARCASSING METAL/TIMBER Excluding overheads and profit	PC £	Labour hours	Labour £	Material £	Unit	Total rate £
Wrought softwood; "Tanalised"						
Gutter boards; tongued and grooved joints						
19 mm thick; sloping	-	1.65	18.71	8.56	m²	27.27
19 mm thick; 75 mm wide	-	0.44	4.99	0.99	m	5.98
19 mm thick; 150 mm wide	-	0.49	5.56	1.26	m	6.82
19 mm thick; 225 mm wide	-	0.55	6.24	2.21	m	8.45
25 mm thick; sloping	-	1.65	18.71	10.54	m²	29.25
25 mm thick; 75 mm wide	-	0.44	4.99	1.37	m	6.36
25 mm thick; 150 mm wide	-	0.49	5.56	1.51	m	7.07
25 mm thick; 225 mm wide	-	0.55	6.24	2.82	m	9.06
Eaves, verge soffit boards, fascia boards and the like						
19 mm thick; over 300 mm wide	-	1.36	15.42	8.57	m²	23.99
19 mm thick; 150 mm wide; once grooved	-	0.22	2.49	1.51	m	4.00
25 mm thick; 150 mm wide; once grooved	-	0.22	2.49	1.84	m	4.33
25 mm thick; 175 mm wide; once grooved	-	0.24	2.72	2.13	m	4.85
32 mm thick; 225 mm wide; once grooved	-	0.28	3.18	3.72	m	6.90
Straps; mild steel; galvanised						
Straps; standard twisted vertical restraint; fixing to softwood and brick or blockwork						
30 mm x 2.50 mm x 400 mm girth	-	0.28	3.18	2.73	nr	5.91
30 mm x 2.50 mm x 600 mm girth	-	0.29	3.29	4.05	nr	7.34
30 mm x 2.50 mm x 800 mm girth	-	0.30	3.40	5.61	nr	9.01
30 mm x 2.50 mm x 1000 mm girth	-	0.33	3.74	7.26	nr	11.00
30 mm x 2.50 mm x 1200 mm girth	-	0.34	3.86	8.60	nr	12.46
Hangers; mild steel; galvanised						
Joist hangers 0.90 mm thick; The Expanded Metal Company Ltd "Speedy" or other equal and approved; for fixing to softwood; joist sizes						
50 mm wide; all sizes to 225 mm deep	0.89	0.13	1.47	1.03	nr	2.50
75 mm wide; all sizes to 225 mm deep	0.93	0.17	1.93	1.12	nr	3.05
100 mm wide; all sizes to 225 mm deep	1.00	0.20	2.27	1.25	nr	3.52
Joist hangers 2.50 mm thick; for building in; joist sizes						
50 mm x 100 mm	1.72	0.09	1.08	1.87	nr	2.95
50 mm x 125 mm	1.73	0.09	1.08	1.88	nr	2.96
50 mm x 150 mm	1.62	0.11	1.30	1.80	nr	3.10
50 mm x 175 mm	1.71	0.11	1.30	1.89	nr	3.19
50 mm x 200 mm	1.89	0.13	1.53	2.11	nr	3.64
50 mm x 225 mm	2.01	0.13	1.53	2.24	nr	3.77
75 mm x 150 mm	2.50	0.11	1.30	2.72	nr	4.02
75 mm x 175 mm	2.36	0.11	1.30	2.58	nr	3.88
75 mm x 200 mm	2.50	0.13	1.53	2.76	nr	4.29
75 mm x 225 mm	2.68	0.13	1.53	2.94	nr	4.47
75 mm x 250 mm	2.84	0.15	1.76	3.14	nr	4.90
100 mm x 200 mm	3.12	0.13	1.53	3.41	nr	4.94
Metal connectors; mild steel; galvanised						
Round toothed plate; for 10 mm or 12 mm diameter bolts						
38 mm diameter; single sided	-	0.02	0.23	0.25	nr	0.48
38 mm diameter; double sided	-	0.02	0.23	0.28	nr	0.51
50 mm diameter; single sided	-	0.02	0.23	0.27	nr	0.50
50 mm diameter; double sided	-	0.02	0.23	0.30	nr	0.53
63 mm diameter; single sided	-	0.02	0.23	0.39	nr	0.62
63 mm diameter; double sided	-	0.02	0.23	0.43	nr	0.66
75 mm diameter; single sided	-	0.02	0.23	0.58	nr	0.81
75 mm diameter; double sided	-	0.02	0.23	0.60	nr	0.83
framing anchor	-	0.17	1.93	0.45	nr	2.38

G STRUCTURAL/CARCASSING METAL/TIMBER Excluding overheads and profit	PC £	Labour hours	Labour £	Material £	Unit	Total rate £
G20 CARPENTRY/TIMBER FRAMING/FIRST **FIXING** - cont'd						
Bolts; mild steel; galvanised						
Fixing only bolts; 50 mm - 200 mm long						
6 mm diameter	-	0.04	0.45	-	nr	0.45
8 mm diameter	-	0.04	0.45	-	nr	0.45
10 mm diameter	-	0.06	0.68	-	nr	0.68
12 mm diameter	-	0.06	0.68	-	nr	0.68
16 mm diameter	-	0.07	0.79	-	nr	0.79
20 mm diameter	-	0.07	0.79	-	nr	0.79
Bolts						
Expanding bolts; "Rawlbolt" projecting type or						
other equal and approved; The Rawlplug						
Company; plated; one nut; one washer						
6 mm diameter; ref M6 10P	-	0.11	1.25	0.75	nr	2.00
6 mm diameter; ref M6 25P	-	0.11	1.25	0.84	nr	2.09
6 mm diameter; ref M6 60P	-	0.11	1.25	0.88	nr	2.13
8 mm diameter; ref M8 25P	-	0.11	1.25	1.00	nr	2.25
8 mm diameter; ref M8 60P	-	0.11	1.25	1.06	nr	2.31
10 mm diameter; ref M10 15P	-	0.11	1.25	1.30	nr	2.55
10 mm diameter; ref M10 30P	-	0.11	1.25	1.36	nr	2.61
10 mm diameter; ref M10 60P	-	0.11	1.25	1.42	nr	2.67
12 mm diameter; ref M12 15P	-	0.11	1.25	2.06	nr	3.31
12 mm diameter; ref M12 30P	-	0.11	1.25	2.22	nr	3.47
12 mm diameter; ref M12 75P	-	0.11	1.25	2.76	nr	4.01
16 mm diameter; ref M16 35P	-	0.11	1.25	5.27	nr	6.52
16 mm diameter; ref M16 75P	-	0.11	1.25	5.53	nr	6.78
Expanding bolts; "Rawlbolt" loose bolt type or						
other equal and approved; The Rawlplug						
Company; plated; one bolt; one washer						
6 mm diameter; ref M6 10L	-	0.11	1.25	0.75	nr	2.00
6 mm diameter; ref M6 25L	-	0.11	1.25	0.80	nr	2.05
6 mm diameter; ref M6 40L	-	0.11	1.25	0.80	nr	2.05
8 mm diameter; ref M8 25L	-	0.11	1.25	0.98	nr	2.23
8 mm diameter; ref M8 40L	-	0.11	1.25	1.04	nr	2.29
10 mm diameter; ref M10 10L	-	0.11	1.25	1.25	nr	2.50
10 mm diameter; ref M10 25L	-	0.11	1.25	1.29	nr	2.54
10 mm diameter; ref M10 50L	-	0.11	1.25	1.36	nr	2.61
10 mm diameter; ref M10 75L	-	0.11	1.25	1.41	nr	2.66
12 mm diameter; ref M12 10L	-	0.11	1.25	1.87	nr	3.12
12 mm diameter; ref M12 25L	-	0.11	1.25	2.06	nr	3.31
12 mm diameter; ref M12 40L	-	0.11	1.25	2.15	nr	3.40
12 mm diameter; ref M12 60L	-	0.11	1.25	2.27	nr	3.52
16 mm diameter; ref M16 30L	-	0.11	1.25	5.01	nr	6.26
16 mm diameter; ref M16 60L	-	0.11	1.25	5.42	nr	6.67
Truss clips; mild steel galvanised						
Truss clips; fixing to softwood; joist size						
38 mm wide	0.30	0.17	1.93	0.51	nr	2.44
50 mm wide	0.33	0.17	1.93	0.54	nr	2.47
Sole plate angles; mild steel; galvanised						
Sole plate angles; fixing to softwood and concrete						
112 mm x 40 mm x 76 mm	0.40	0.22	2.49	1.14	nr	3.63
Chemical anchors						
"Kemfix" capsules and standard studs or other equal and						
approved; The Rawlplug Company; with nuts and						
washers; drilling masonry						
capsule ref 60-408; stud ref 60-448	-	0.30	3.40	1.42	nr	4.82

G STRUCTURAL/CARCASSING METAL/TIMBER Excluding overheads and profit	PC £	Labour hours	Labour £	Material £	Unit	Total rate £
"Kemfix" capsules and standard studs or other equal and approved; The Rawlplug Company; with nuts and washers; drilling masonry - cont'd						
capsule ref 60-410; stud ref 60-454	-	0.33	3.74	1.59	nr	5.33
capsule ref 60-412; stud ref 60-460	-	0.37	4.20	1.94	nr	6.14
capsule ref 60-416; stud ref 60-472	-	0.41	4.65	3.05	nr	7.70
capsule ref 60-420; stud ref 60-478	-	0.43	4.88	4.66	nr	9.54
capsule ref 60-424; stud ref 60-484	-	0.47	5.33	6.92	nr	12.25
"Kemfix" capsules and stainless steel studs or other equal and approved; The Rawlplug Company; with nuts and washers; drilling masonry						
capsule ref 60-408; stud ref 60-905	-	0.30	3.40	2.50	nr	5.90
capsule ref 60-410; stud ref 60-910	-	0.33	3.74	3.35	nr	7.09
capsule ref 60-412; stud ref 60-915	-	0.37	4.20	4.60	nr	8.80
capsule ref 60-416; stud ref 60-920	-	0.41	4.65	7.83	nr	12.48
capsule ref 60-420; stud ref 60-925	-	0.43	4.88	12.08	nr	16.96
capsule ref 60-424; stud ref 60-930	-	0.47	5.33	19.54	nr	24.87
"Kemfix" capsules and standard internal threaded sockets or other equal and approved; The Rawlplug Company; drilling masonry						
capsule ref 60-408; socket ref 60-650	-	0.30	3.40	1.46	nr	4.86
capsule ref 60-410; socket ref 60-656	-	0.33	3.74	1.77	nr	5.51
capsule ref 60-412; socket ref 60-662	-	0.37	4.20	2.21	nr	6.41
capsule ref 60-416; socket ref 60-668	-	0.41	4.65	3.04	nr	7.69
capsule ref 60-420; socket ref 60-674	-	0.43	4.88	3.65	nr	8.53
capsule ref 60-424; socket ref 60-676	-	0.47	5.33	5.94	nr	11.27
"Kemfix" capsules and stainless steel internal threaded sockets or other equal and approved; The Rawlplug Company; drilling masonry						
capsule ref 60-408; socket ref 60-943	-	0.30	3.40	2.76	nr	6.16
capsule ref 60-410; socket ref 60-945	-	0.33	3.74	3.14	nr	6.88
capsule ref 60-412; socket ref 60-947	-	0.37	4.20	3.62	nr	7.82
capsule ref 60-416; socket ref 60-949	-	0.41	4.65	5.14	nr	9.79
capsule ref 60-420; socket ref 60-951	-	0.43	4.88	6.20	nr	11.08
capsule ref 60-424; socket ref 60-955	-	0.47	5.33	11.35	nr	16.68
"Kemfix" capsules, perforated sleeves and standard studs or other equal and approved; The Rawlplug Company; in low density material; with nuts and washers; drilling masonry						
capsule ref 60-408; sleeve ref 60-538 stud ref 60-448	-	0.30	3.40	2.09	nr	5.49
capsule ref 60-410; sleeve ref 60-544; stud ref 60-454	-	0.33	3.74	2.30	nr	6.04
capsule ref 60-412; sleeve ref 60-550; stud ref 60-460	-	0.37	4.20	2.75	nr	6.95
capsule ref 60-416; sleeve ref 60-562; stud ref 60-472	-	0.41	4.65	4.05	nr	8.70
"Kemfix" capsules, perforated sleeves and stainless steel studs or other equal and approved; The Rawlplug Company; in low density material; with nuts and washers; drilling masonry						
capsule ref 60-408; sleeve ref 60-538; stud ref 60-905	-	0.30	3.40	3.17	nr	6.57
capsule ref 60-410; sleeve ref 60-544; stud ref 60-910	-	0.33	3.74	4.05	nr	7.79
capsule ref 60-412; sleeve ref 60-550; stud ref 60-915	-	0.37	4.20	5.41	nr	9.61
capsule ref 60-416; sleeve ref 60-562; stud ref 60-920	-	0.41	4.65	8.82	nr	13.47
"Kemfix" capsules, perforated sleeves and standard internal threaded sockets or other equal and approved; The Rawlplug Company; in low density material; with nuts and washers; drilling masonry						
capsule ref 60-408; sleeve ref 60-538; socket ref 60-650	-	0.30	3.40	2.13	nr	5.53
capsule ref 60-410; sleeve ref 60-544; socket ref 60-656	-	0.33	3.74	2.48	nr	6.22
capsule ref 60-412; sleeve ref 60-550; socket ref 60-662	-	0.37	4.20	3.02	nr	7.22

G STRUCTURAL/CARCASSING METAL/TIMBER Excluding overheads and profit	PC £	Labour hours	Labour £	Material £	Unit	Total rate £
G20 CARPENTRY/TIMBER FRAMING/FIRST FIXING - cont'd						
Chemical anchors - cont'd						
"Kemfix" capsules, perforated sleeves and						
stainless steel internal threaded sockets or						
other equal and approved; The Rawlplug						
Company; in low density material; drilling						
masonry						
capsule ref 60-408; sleeve ref 60-538; socket ref 60-943	-	0.30	3.40	3.43	nr	**6.83**
capsule ref 60-410; sleeve ref 60-544; socket ref 60-945	-	0.33	3.74	3.84	nr	**7.58**
capsule ref 60-412; sleeve ref 60-550; socket ref 60-947	-	0.37	4.20	4.43	nr	**8.63**
capsule ref 60-416; sleeve ref 60-562; socket ref 60-949	-	0.41	4.65	6.13	nr	**10.78**
G32 EDGE SUPPORTED/REINFORCED WOODWOOL SLAB DECKING						
Woodwool interlocking reinforced slabs; Torvale "Woodcelip" or other equal and approved; natural finish; fixing to timber or steel with galvanized nails or clips; flat or sloping						
50 mm thick slabs; type 503; maximum span 2100 mm						
1800 mm - 2100 mm lengths	15.00	0.55	6.24	15.93	m²	**22.17**
2400 mm lengths	15.72	0.55	6.24	16.68	m²	**22.92**
2700 mm - 3000 mm lengths	15.98	0.55	6.24	16.96	m²	**23.20**
75 mm thick slabs; type 751; maximum span 2100 mm						
1800 mm - 2400 mm lengths	22.48	0.61	6.92	23.81	m²	**30.73**
2700 mm - 3000 mm lengths	22.59	0.61	6.92	23.93	m²	**30.85**
75 mm thick slabs; type 752; maximum span 2100 mm						
1800 mm - 2400 mm lengths	22.42	0.61	6.92	23.75	m²	**30.67**
2700 mm - 3000 mm lengths	22.47	0.61	6.92	23.80	m²	**30.72**
75 mm thick slabs; type 753; maximum span 3600 mm						
2400 mm lengths	21.75	0.61	6.92	23.05	m²	**29.97**
2700 mm - 3000 mm lengths	22.70	0.61	6.92	24.04	m²	**30.96**
3300 mm - 3900 mm lengths	27.35	0.61	6.92	28.93	m²	**35.85**
extra for holes for pipes and the like	-	0.13	1.47	-	nr	**1.47**
100 mm thick slabs; type 1001; maximum span 3600 mm						
3000 mm lengths	29.94	0.66	7.48	31.68	m²	**39.16**
3300 mm - 3600 mm lengths	32.41	0.66	7.48	34.27	m²	**41.75**
100 mm thick slabs; type 1002; maximum span 3600 mm						
3000 mm lengths	29.23	0.66	7.48	30.93	m²	**38.41**
3300 mm - 3600 mm lengths	31.04	0.66	7.48	32.83	m²	**40.31**
100 mm thick slabs; type 1003; maximum span 4000 mm						
3000 mm - 3600 mm lengths	27.76	0.66	7.48	29.39	m²	**36.87**
3900 mm - 4000 mm lengths	27.76	0.66	7.48	29.39	m²	**36.87**
125 mm thick slabs; type 1252; maximum span 3000 mm						
2400 mm - 3000 mm lengths	31.59	0.66	7.48	33.41	m²	**40.89**
Extra over slabs for						
pre-screeded deck	-	-	-	1.05	m²	**1.05**
pre-screeded soffit	-	-	-	2.69	m²	**2.69**
pre-screeded deck and soffit	-	-	-	3.51	m²	**3.51**
pre-screeded and proofed deck	-	-	-	2.16	m²	**2.16**
pre-screeded and proofed deck plus						
pre-screeded soffit	-	-	-	5.02	m²	**5.02**
pre-felted deck (glass fibre)	-	-	-	2.96	m²	**2.96**
pre-felted deck plus pre-screeded soffit	-	-	-	5.65	m²	**5.65**

Aluminium Design and Construction

John Dwight, Consultant, UK

*Clear and thorough examination of the subject
*Highly illustrated with drawings, photographs and tables

Aluminium Design and Construction address the metal's history and usage, wrought products, alloy selection and fabrication. The book also provides comprehensive rules for making structural calculations, together with the reasoning behind them. Extended coverage is given to key areas including: buckling failure, deflection, weld strength deflection, fatigue and adhesive bonding. The book also covers the design of extruded sections and local softening at welds.

Aluminium Design and Construction provides a clear and thorough examination of the subject. The text is highly illustrated with over 200 drawings, photographs and tables. This book is invaluable reading for structural designers, fabricators, architects and construction professionals.

Contents: Preface. Acknowledgements. About Aluminium. Manufacture. Fabrication. Aluminium Alloys and their sections. Limit State Design and Limiting Stresses. Heat-affected Zone Softening at Welds. Plate Elements in Compression. Beams. Tension and Compression Members. Calculation of Section Properties. Joints. Fatigue. References. Index.

December 1998 234x156 320pp
160 line, 20 halftone
Hb: 0-419-15710-7: £70.00

To Order: Tel: +44 (0) 8700 768853, or +44 (0) 1264 343071
Fax: +44 (0) 1264 343005, or Post: E & FN Spon Customer Services, ITPS Andover, Hants, SP10 5BE, UK

All orders must be pre-paid and will be sent free in the UK. Europe please add: £2.95 for the first book, thereafter £1.25 per book. ROW please add: Airmail £6.50 for the first book, thereafter £2.50 per book. Please add £12.50 delivery charge for items over £100.00.

Green Building Handbook: Volume 2

A guide to building products and their impact on the environment

Edited by Tom Woolley, Queens University of Belfast, UK and Sam Kimmins, Ethical Consumer Research Association, UK

From reviews of the Green Building Handbook: 'The Publisher is to be congratulated on this book' - **Building**

This new handbook provides a detailed reference for environmentally concerned purchasers of building products, and complements the first Green Building Handbook. Following the format of the original, this book discusses current issues in green building before moving on to consider eight building component types: Fencing Products, Flat Roofing Membranes, Glazing Products, Electrical Wiring, Adhesives, Straw Bale Building, Interior Decoration and Indoor Air Quality and Ventilation. Invaluable for the specifier, this companion handbook will be useful to all those interested in finding greener ways of designing and making buildings.

Contents: Part One. 1.Introduction: a discursive essay highlighting important trends in green building and explaining the rationale and methodology behind the handbook. Part Two. How to use the handbook. Key to product table headings. 2. Fencing products. 3. Flat roofing membranes. 4. Glazing products. 5. Electrical wiring. 6. Adhesives. 7. Straw bale building. 8. Interior decoration. 9. Indoor air quality and ventilation. Further reading. Useful information on relevant organizations. Index.

December 1999: 297x210: 152pp
Illus drawings and b+w photographs
Pb: 0-419-25380-7: £29.95

To Order: Tel: +44 (0) 8700 768853, or +44 (0) 1264 343071
Fax: +44 (0) 1264 343005, or Post: E & FN Spon Customer Services, ITPS Andover, Hants, SP10 5BE, UK

All orders must be pre-paid and will be sent free in the UK. Europe please add: £2.95 for the first book, thereafter £1.25 per book. ROW please add: Airmail £6.50 for the first book, thereafter £2.50 per book. Please add £12.50 delivery charge for items over £100.00.

H CLADDING/COVERING Excluding overheads and profit	PC £	Labour hours	Labour £	Material £	Unit	Total rate £
H CLADDING/COVERING						
H10 PATENT GLAZING						
Patent glazing; aluminium alloy bars 2.55 m **long at 622 mm centres; fixed to supports**						
Roof cladding						
glazing with 7 mm thick Georgian wired cast glass	-	-	-	-	m²	115.00
Associated code 4 lead flashings						
top flashing; 210 mm girth	-	-	-	-	m	37.75
bottom flashing; 240 mm girth	-	-	-	-	m	31.75
end flashing; 300 mm girth	-	-	-	-	m	65.00
Wall cladding						
glazing with 7 mm thick Georgian wired cast glass	-	-	-	-	m²	120.00
glazing with 6 mm thick plate glass	-	-	-	-	m²	110.00
Extra for aluminium alloy members						
38 mm x 38 mm x 3 mm angle jamb	-	-	-	-	m	13.00
pressed cill member	-	-	-	-	m	35.00
pressed channel head and PVC case	-	-	-	-	m	30.00
"Kawneer" window frame system or other equal **and approved; polyester powder coated glazing** **bars; glazed with double hermetically sealed units** **in toughened safety glass; one 6 mm thick air** **space; overall 18 mm thick**						
Vertical surfaces						
single tier; aluminium glazing bars at 850 mm centres x 890 mm long; timber supports at 890 mm centres	-	-	-	-	m²	200.00
"Kawneer" window frame system or other equal **and approved; polyester powder coated glazing** **bars; glazed with clear toughened safety glass;** **10.70 mm thick**						
Vertical surfaces						
single tier; aluminium glazing bars at 850 mm centres x 890 mm long; timber supports at 890 mm centres	-	-	-	-	m²	187.50
H20 RIGID SHEET CLADDING						
"Resoplan" sheet or other equal and approved; **Eternit UK Ltd; flexible neoprene gasket joints;** **fixing with stainless steel screws and coloured caps**						
6 mm thick cladding to walls						
over 300 mm wide	-	2.41	27.33	54.97	m²	82.30
not exceeding 300 mm wide	-	0.80	9.07	19.24	m	28.31
Eternit 2000 "Glasal" sheet or other equal and **approved; Eternit UK Ltd; flexible neoprene** **gasket joints; fixing with stainless steel screws** **and coloured caps**						
7.50 mm thick cladding to walls						
over 300 mm wide	-	2.41	27.33	50.24	m²	77.57
not exceeding 300 mm wide	-	0.80	9.07	17.81	m	26.88
external angle trim	-	0.12	1.36	9.20	m	10.56
7.50 mm thick cladding to eaves, verge soffit boards, fascia boards or the like						
100 mm wide	-	0.57	6.46	8.62	m	15.08
200 mm wide	-	0.69	7.82	13.22	m	21.04
300 mm wide	-	0.80	9.07	17.81	m	26.88

H CLADDING/COVERING Excluding overheads and profit	PC £	Labour hours	Labour £	Material £	Unit	Total rate £
H30 FIBRE CEMENT PROFILED SHEET **CLADDING/COVERING/SIDING**						
Asbestos-free corrugated sheets; Eternit **"2000" or other equal and approved**						
Roof cladding; sloping not exceeding 50 degrees; fixing to timber purlins with drive screws						
"Profile 3"; natural grey	11.27	0.23	3.31	13.12	m²	16.43
"Profile 3"; coloured	13.52	0.23	3.31	15.37	m²	18.68
"Profile 6"; natural grey	9.94	0.29	4.18	11.72	m²	15.90
"Profile 6"; coloured	11.92	0.29	4.18	13.70	m²	17.88
"Profile 6"; natural grey; insulated 60 mm glass fibre infill; lining panel	-	0.52	7.49	28.24	m²	35.73
Roof cladding; sloping not exceeding 50 degrees; fixing to steel purlins with hook bolts						
"Profile 3"; natural grey	-	0.29	4.18	14.01	m²	18.19
"Profile 3"; coloured	-	0.29	4.18	16.26	m²	20.44
"Profile 6"; natural grey	-	0.35	5.04	12.61	m²	17.65
"Profile 6"; coloured	-	0.35	5.04	14.59	m²	19.63
"Profile 6"; natural grey; insulated 60 mm glass fibre infill; lining panel	-	0.57	8.21	26.04	m²	34.25
Wall cladding; vertical; fixing to steel rails with hook bolts						
"Profile 3"; natural grey	-	0.35	5.04	14.01	m²	19.05
"Profile 3"; coloured	-	0.35	5.04	16.26	m²	21.30
"Profile 6"; natural grey	-	0.40	5.76	12.61	m²	18.37
"Profile 6"; coloured	-	0.40	5.76	14.59	m²	20.35
"Profile 6"; natural grey; insulated 60 mm glass fibre infill; lining panel	-	0.63	9.08	26.04	m²	35.12
raking cutting	-	0.17	2.45	-	m	2.45
holes for pipes and the like	-	0.17	2.45	-	nr	2.45
Accessories; to "Profile 3" cladding; natural grey						
eaves filler	-	0.12	1.73	10.32	m	12.05
vertical corrugation closer	-	0.14	2.02	10.32	m	12.34
apron flashing	-	0.14	2.02	10.38	m	12.40
plain wing or close fitting two piece adjustable capping to ridge	-	0.20	2.88	9.70	m	12.58
ventilating two piece adjustable capping to ridge	-	0.20	2.88	14.64	m	17.52
Accessories; to "Profile 3" cladding; coloured						
eaves filler	-	0.12	1.73	12.91	m	14.64
vertical corrugation closer	-	0.14	2.02	12.91	m	14.93
apron flashing	-	0.14	2.02	12.95	m	14.97
plain wing or close fitting two piece adjustable capping to ridge	-	0.20	2.88	11.69	m	14.57
ventilating two piece adjustable capping to ridge	-	0.20	2.88	18.28	m	21.16
Accessories; to "Profile 6" cladding; natural grey						
eaves filler	-	0.12	1.73	7.65	m	9.38
vertical corrugation closer	-	0.14	2.02	7.65	m	9.67
apron flashing	-	0.14	2.02	8.24	m	10.26
underglazing flashing	-	0.14	2.02	7.87	m	9.89
plain cranked crown to ridge	-	0.20	2.88	15.46	m	18.34
plain wing or close fitting two piece adjustable capping to ridge	-	0.20	2.88	15.10	m	17.98
ventilating two piece adjustable capping to ridge	-	0.20	2.88	19.27	m	22.15

H CLADDING/COVERING Excluding overheads and profit	PC £	Labour hours	Labour £	Material £	Unit	Total rate £
Accessories; to "Profile 6" cladding; coloured						
eaves filler	-	0.12	1.73	9.56	m	11.29
vertical corrugation closer	-	0.14	2.02	9.56	m	11.58
apron flashing	-	0.14	2.02	10.31	m	12.33
underglazing flashing	-	0.14	2.02	9.85	m	11.87
plain cranked crown to ridge	-	0.20	2.88	19.33	m	22.21
plain wing or close fitting two piece adjustable capping to ridge	-	0.20	2.88	18.87	m	21.75
ventilating two piece adjustable capping to ridge	-	0.20	2.88	24.12	m	27.00
H31 METAL PROFILED/FLAT SHEET CLADDING/COVERING/SIDING						
Lightweight galvanised steel roof tiles; Decra Roof Systems (UK) Ltd or other equal and approved; coated finish						
Roof coverings	-	0.28	4.03	14.98	m²	19.01
Accessories for roof cladding						
pitched "D" ridge	-	0.11	1.59	8.04	m	9.63
barge cover (handed)	-	0.11	1.59	8.62	m	10.21
in line air vent	-	0.11	1.59	39.60	nr	41.19
in line soil vent	-	0.11	1.59	62.06	nr	63.65
gas flue terminal	-	0.22	3.17	81.90	nr	85.07
H32 PLASTICS PROFILED SHEET CLADDING/COVERING/SIDING						
Extended, hard skinned, foamed PVC-UE profiled sections; Swish Celuka or other equal and approved; Class 1 fire rated to BS 476; Part 7; 1987; in white finish						
Wall cladding; vertical; fixing to timber						
100 mm shiplap profiles Code 001	-	0.42	4.76	37.45	m²	42.21
150 mm shiplap profiles Code 002	-	0.39	4.42	33.26	m²	37.68
125 mm feather-edged profiles Code C208	-	0.41	4.65	36.25	m²	40.90
Vertical angles	-	0.22	2.49	3.94	m	6.43
Raking cutting	-	0.17	1.93	-	m	1.93
Holes for pipes and the like	-	0.04	0.45	-	nr	0.45
H41 GLASS REINFORCED PLASTICS CLADDING/FEATURES						
Glass fibre translucent sheeting grade AB class 3						
Roof cladding; sloping not exceeding 50 degrees; fixing to timber purlins with drive screws; to suit						
"Profile 3"; or other equal and approved	12.38	0.23	3.31	14.33	m²	17.64
"Profile 6"; or other equal and approved	11.47	0.29	4.18	13.38	m²	17.56
Roof cladding; sloping not exceeding 50 degrees; fixing to timber purlins with hook bolts; to suit						
"Profile 3"; or other equal and approved	12.38	0.29	4.18	15.22	m²	19.40
"Profile 6"; or other equal and approved	11.47	0.35	5.04	14.27	m²	19.31
"Longrib 1000"; or other equal and approved	11.43	0.35	5.04	14.22	m²	19.26

H CLADDING/COVERING Excluding overheads and profit	PC £	Labour hours	Labour £	Material £	Unit	Total rate £
H60 PLAIN ROOF TILING						
NOTE: The following items of tile roofing unless otherwise described, include for conventional fixing assuming normal exposure with appropriate nails and/or rivets or clips to pressure impregnated softwood battens fixed with galvanised nails; prices also include for all bedding and pointing at verges, beneath ridge tiles, etc.						
Clay interlocking pantiles; Sandtoft Goxhill "Tudor" red sand faced or other equal and approved; PC £1470.00/1000; 470 mm x 285 mm; to 100 mm lap; on 25 mm x 38 mm battens and type 1F reinforced underlay						
Roof coverings	-	0.46	6.63	18.12	m²	24.75
Extra over coverings for						
fixing every tile	-	0.09	1.30	0.98	m²	2.28
eaves course with plastic filler	-	0.35	5.04	7.47	m	12.51
verges; extra single undercloak course of plain tiles	-	0.35	5.04	3.65	m	8.69
open valleys; cutting both sides	-	0.21	3.03	6.17	m	9.20
ridge tiles	-	0.69	9.94	13.83	m	23.77
hips; cutting both sides	-	0.86	12.39	20.00	m	32.39
holes for pipes and the like	-	0.23	3.31	-	nr	3.31
Clay pantiles; Sandtoft Goxhill "Old English"; red sand faced or other equal and approved; PC £655.00/1000; 342 mm x 241 mm; to 75 mm lap; on 25 mm x 38 mm battens and type 1F reinforced underlay						
Roof coverings	-	0.52	7.49	14.62	m²	22.11
Extra over coverings for						
fixing every tile	-	0.03	0.43	2.46	m²	2.89
other colours	-	-	-	0.59	m²	0.59
double course at eaves	-	0.38	5.48	3.57	m	9.05
verges; extra single undercloak course of plain tiles	-	0.35	5.04	8.28	m	13.32
open valleys; cutting both sides	-	0.21	3.03	2.75	m	5.78
ridge tiles; tile slips	-	0.69	9.94	19.33	m	29.27
hips; cutting both sides	-	0.86	12.39	22.08	m	34.47
holes for pipes and the like	-	0.23	3.31	-	nr	3.31
Clay pantiles; William Blyth's "Lincoln" natural or other equal and approved; 343 mm x 280 mm; to 75 mm lap; PC £820.00/1000; on 19 mm x 38 mm battens and type 1F reinforced underlay						
Roof coverings	-	0.52	7.49	16.96	m²	24.45
Extra over coverings for						
fixing every tile	-	0.03	0.43	2.46	m²	2.89
other colours	-	-	-	1.14	m²	1.14
double course at eaves	-	0.38	5.48	4.26	m	9.74
verges; extra single undercloak course of plain tiles	-	0.35	5.04	10.69	m	15.73
open valleys; cutting both sides	-	0.21	3.03	3.44	m	6.47
ridge tiles; tile slips	-	0.69	9.94	17.97	m	27.91
hips; cutting both sides	-	0.86	12.39	21.41	m	33.80
holes for pipes and the like	-	0.23	3.31	-	nr	3.31

H CLADDING/COVERING Excluding overheads and profit	PC £	Labour hours	Labour £	Material £	Unit	Total rate £
Clay plain tiles; Hinton, Perry and Davenhill "Dreadnought" smooth red machine-made or other equal and approved; PC £230.00/1000; 265 mm x 165 mm; on 19 mm x 38 mm battens and type 1F reinforced underlay						
Roof coverings; to 64 mm lap	-	1.21	17.44	20.79	m²	**38.23**
Wall coverings; to 38 mm lap	-	1.44	20.75	17.90	m²	**38.65**
Extra over coverings for						
other colours	-	-	-	7.94	m²	**7.94**
ornamental tiles	-	-	-	11.91	m²	**11.91**
double course at eaves	-	0.29	4.18	2.48	m	**6.66**
verges	-	0.35	5.04	1.25	m	**6.29**
swept valleys; cutting both sides	-	0.75	10.81	30.01	m	**40.82**
bonnet hips; cutting both sides	-	0.92	13.26	30.01	m	**43.27**
external vertical angle tiles; supplementary nail fixings	-	0.46	6.63	33.57	m	**40.20**
half round ridge tiles	-	0.69	9.94	9.76	m	**19.70**
holes for pipes and the like	-	0.23	3.31	-	nr	**3.31**
Clay plain tiles; Keymer best hand-made sand-faced tiles or other equal and approved; PC £625.00/1000; 265 mm x 165 mm; on 25 mm x 38 mm battens and type 1F reinforced underlay						
Roof coverings; to 64 mm lap	-	1.21	17.44	45.68	m²	**63.12**
Wall coverings; to 38 mm lap	-	1.44	20.75	39.88	m²	**60.63**
Extra over coverings for						
ornamental tiles	-	-	-	6.30	m²	**6.30**
double course at eaves	-	0.29	4.18	4.97	m	**9.15**
verges	-	0.35	5.04	1.73	m	**6.77**
swept valleys; cutting both sides	-	0.75	10.81	35.71	m	**46.52**
bonnet hips; cutting both sides	-	0.92	13.26	35.71	m	**48.97**
external vertical angle tiles; supplementary nail fixings	-	0.46	6.63	49.18	m	**55.81**
half round ridge tiles	-	0.69	9.94	10.59	m	**20.53**
holes for pipes and the like	-	0.23	3.31	-	nr	**3.31**
Concrete interlocking tiles; Marley "Bold Roll" granule finish tiles or other equal and approved; PC £703.00/1000; 420 mm x 330 mm; to 75 mm lap; on 25 mm x 38 mm battens and type 1F reinforced underlay						
Roof coverings	-	0.40	5.76	9.86	m²	**15.62**
Extra over coverings for						
fixing every tile	-	0.03	0.43	0.41	m²	**0.84**
eaves; eaves filler	-	0.06	0.86	0.91	m	**1.77**
verges; 150 mm wide asbestos free strip undercloak	-	0.26	3.75	1.68	m	**5.43**
valley trough tiles; cutting both sides	-	0.63	9.08	18.42	m	**27.50**
segmental ridge tiles; tile slips	-	0.63	9.08	10.50	m	**19.58**
segmental hip tiles; tile slips; cutting both sides	-	0.80	11.53	12.71	m	**24.24**
dry ridge tiles; segmental including batten sections; unions and filler pieces	-	0.35	5.04	15.21	m	**20.25**
segmental mono-ridge tiles	-	0.63	9.08	14.25	m	**23.33**
gas ridge terminal	-	0.57	8.21	60.64	nr	**68.85**
holes for pipes and the like	-	0.23	3.31	-	nr	**3.31**

H CLADDING/COVERING Excluding overheads and profit	PC £	Labour hours	Labour £	Material £	Unit	Total rate £
H60 PLAIN ROOF TILING - cont'd						
Concrete interlocking tiles; Marley "Ludlow Major" granule finish tiles or other equal and approved; PC £667.00/1000; 420 mm x 330 mm; to 75 mm lap; on 25 mm x 38 mm battens and type 1F reinforced underlay						
Roof coverings	-	0.40	5.76	9.56	m²	15.32
Extra over coverings for						
fixing every tile	-	0.03	0.43	0.41	m²	0.84
eaves; eaves filler	-	0.06	0.86	0.33	m	1.19
verges; 150 mm wide asbestos free strip undercloak	-	0.26	3.75	1.68	m	5.43
dry verge system; extruded white pvc	-	0.17	2.45	8.45	m	10.90
segmental ridge cap to dry verge	-	0.03	0.43	2.77	m	3.20
valley trough tiles; cutting both sides	-	0.63	9.08	18.35	m	27.43
segmental ridge tiles	-	0.57	8.21	7.35	m	15.56
segmental hip tiles; cutting both sides	-	0.75	10.81	9.45	m	20.26
dry ridge tiles; segmental including batten sections; unions and filler pieces	-	0.35	5.04	15.21	m	20.25
segmental mono-ridge tiles	-	0.57	8.21	12.41	m	20.62
gas ridge terminal	-	0.57	8.21	60.64	nr	68.85
holes for pipes and the like	-	0.23	3.31	-	nr	3.31
Concrete interlocking tiles; Marley "Mendip" granule finish double pantiles or other equal and approved; PC £717.00/1000; 420 mm x 330 mm; to 75 mm lap; on 22 mm x 38 mm battens and type 1F reinforced underlay						
Roof coverings	-	0.40	5.76	10.00	m²	15.76
Extra over coverings for						
fixing every tile	-	0.03	0.43	0.41	m²	0.84
eaves; eaves filler	-	0.03	0.43	0.66	m	1.09
verges; 150 mm wide asbestos free strip undercloak	-	0.26	3.75	1.68	m	5.43
dry verge system; extruded white pvc	-	0.17	2.45	8.45	m	10.90
segmental ridge cap to dry verge	-	0.03	0.43	2.77	m	3.20
valley trough tiles; cutting both sides	-	0.63	9.08	18.45	m	27.53
segmental ridge tiles	-	0.63	9.08	10.50	m	19.58
segmental hip tiles; cutting both sides	-	0.80	11.53	12.76	m	24.29
dry ridge tiles; segmental including batten sections; unions and filler pieces	-	0.35	5.04	15.21	m	20.25
segmental mono-ridge tiles	-	0.57	8.21	13.99	m	22.20
gas ridge terminal	-	0.57	8.21	60.64	nr	68.85
holes for pipes and the like	-	0.23	3.31	-	nr	3.31
Concrete interlocking tiles; Marley "Modern" smooth finish tiles or other equal and approved; PC £667.00/1000; 420 mm x 220 mm; to 75 mm lap; on 25 mm x 38 mm battens and type 1F reinforced underlay						
Roof coverings	-	0.40	5.76	9.76	m²	15.52
Extra over coverings for						
fixing every tile	-	0.03	0.43	0.41	m²	0.84
verges; 150 mm wide asbestos free strip undercloak	-	0.26	3.75	1.68	m	5.43
dry verge system; extruded white pvc	-	0.23	3.31	8.45	m	11.76
"Modern" ridge cap to dry verge	-	0.03	0.43	2.77	m	3.20
valley trough tiles; cutting both sides	-	0.63	9.08	18.35	m	27.43
"Modern" ridge tiles	-	0.57	8.21	7.72	m	15.93
"Modern" hip tiles; cutting both sides	-	0.75	10.81	9.82	m	20.63
dry ridge tiles; "Modern"; including batten sections; unions and filler pieces	-	0.35	5.04	15.58	m	20.62
"Modern" mono-ridge tiles	-	0.57	8.21	12.41	m	20.62
gas ridge terminal	-	0.57	8.21	60.64	nr	68.85
holes for pipes and the like	-	0.23	3.31	-	nr	3.31

H CLADDING/COVERING Excluding overheads and profit	PC £	Labour hours	Labour £	Material £	Unit	Total rate £
Concrete interlocking tiles; Marley "Wessex" smooth finish tiles or other equal and approved; PC £1094.00/1000; 413 mm x 330 mm; to 75 mm lap; on 25 mm x 38 mm battens and type 1F reinforced underlay						
Roof coverings	–	0.40	5.76	14.20	m²	19.96
Extra over coverings for						
fixing every tile	–	0.03	0.43	0.41	m²	0.84
verges; 150 mm wide asbestos free strip undercloak	–	0.26	3.75	1.68	m	5.43
dry verge system; extruded white pvc	–	0.23	3.31	8.45	m	11.76
"Modern" ridge cap to dry verge	–	0.03	0.43	2.77	m	3.20
valley trough tiles; cutting both sides	–	0.63	9.08	19.24	m	28.32
"Modern" ridge tiles	–	0.57	8.21	7.72	m	15.93
"Modern" hip tiles; cutting both sides	–	0.75	10.81	11.17	m	21.98
dry ridge tiles; "Modern"; including batten sections; unions and filler pieces	–	0.35	5.04	15.58	m	20.62
"Modern" mono-ridge tiles	–	0.57	8.21	12.41	m	20.62
gas ridge terminal	–	0.57	8.21	60.64	nr	68.85
holes for pipes and the like	–	0.23	3.31	–	nr	3.31
Concrete interlocking slates; Redland "Delta" smooth finish tiles or other equal and approved; PC £1862.00/1000; 430 mm x 380 mm; to 75 mm lap; on 25 mm x 38 mm battens and type 1F reinforced underlay						
Roof coverings	–	0.40	5.76	18.74	m²	24.50
Extra over coverings for						
fixing every tile	–	0.03	0.43	0.41	m²	0.84
eaves; eaves filler	–	0.03	0.43	0.90	m	1.33
verges; extra single undercloak course of plain tiles	–	0.29	4.18	3.51	m	7.69
ambi-dry verge system	–	0.23	3.31	10.46	m	13.77
ambi-dry verge eave/ridge end piece	–	0.03	0.43	3.67	m	4.10
valley trough tiles; cutting both sides	–	0.69	9.94	31.92	m	41.86
"Delta" ridge tiles	–	0.57	8.21	15.56	m	23.77
"Delta" hip tiles; cutting both sides	–	0.75	10.81	21.43	m	32.24
"Delta" mono-ridge tiles	–	0.57	8.21	23.33	m	31.54
gas ridge terminal	–	0.57	8.21	115.29	nr	123.50
ridge vent with 110 mm diameter flexible adaptor	–	0.57	8.21	97.44	nr	105.65
holes for pipes and the like	–	0.23	3.31	–	nr	3.31
Concrete interlocking tiles; Redland "Norfolk" smooth finish pantiles or other equal and approved; PC £487.00/1000; 381 mm x 229 mm; to 75 mm lap; on 25 mm x 38 mm battens and type 1F reinforced underlay						
Roof coverings	–	0.52	7.49	12.18	m²	19.67
Extra over coverings for						
fixing every tile	–	0.06	0.86	0.23	m²	1.09
eaves; eaves filler	–	0.06	0.86	1.13	m	1.99
verges; extra single undercloak course of plain tiles	–	0.35	5.04	6.37	m	11.41
valley trough tiles; cutting both sides	–	0.69	9.94	26.65	m	36.59
universal ridge tiles	–	0.57	8.21	11.49	m	19.70
universal hip tiles; cutting both sides	–	0.75	10.81	14.05	m	24.86
universal gas flue ridge tile	–	0.57	8.21	92.76	nr	100.97
universal ridge vent tile with 110 mm diameter adaptor	–	0.57	8.21	79.84	nr	88.05
holes for pipes and the like	–	0.23	3.31	–	nr	3.31

H CLADDING/COVERING Excluding overheads and profit	PC £	Labour hours	Labour £	Material £	Unit	Total rate £
H60 PLAIN ROOF TILING - cont'd						
Concrete interlocking tiles; Redland "Regent" granule finish bold roll tiles or other equal and approved; PC £694.00/1000; 418 mm x 332 mm; to 75 mm lap; on 25 mm x 38 mm battens and type 1F reinforced underlay						
Roof coverings	-	0.40	5.76	10.00	m²	15.76
Extra over coverings for						
fixing every tile	-	0.05	0.72	0.65	m²	1.37
eaves; eaves filler	-	0.06	0.86	0.85	m	1.71
verges; extra single undercloak course of plain tiles	-	0.29	4.18	2.85	m	7.03
cloaked verge system	-	0.17	2.45	6.96	m	9.41
valley trough tiles; cutting both sides	-	0.63	9.08	26.28	m	35.36
universal ridge tiles	-	0.57	8.21	11.49	m	19.70
universal hip tiles; cutting both sides	-	0.75	10.81	13.68	m	24.49
dry ridge system; universal ridge tiles	-	0.29	4.18	35.55	m	39.73
universal half round mono-pitch ridge tiles	-	0.63	9.08	23.81	m	32.89
universal gas flue ridge tile	-	0.57	8.21	92.76	nr	100.97
universal ridge vent tile with 110 mm diameter adaptor	-	0.57	8.21	79.84	nr	88.05
holes for pipes and the like	-	0.23	3.31	-	nr	3.31
Concrete interlocking tiles; Redland "Renown" granule finish tiles or other equal and approved; PC £657.00/1000; 418 mm x 330 mm; to 75 mm lap; on 25 mm x 38 mm battens and type 1F reinforced underlay						
Roof coverings	-	0.40	5.76	9.62	m²	15.38
Extra over coverings for						
fixing every tile	-	0.03	0.43	0.27	m²	0.70
verges; extra single undercloak course of plain tiles	-	0.29	4.18	3.50	m	7.68
cloaked verge system	-	0.17	2.45	7.07	m	9.52
valley trough tiles; cutting both sides	-	0.63	9.08	26.16	m	35.24
universal ridge tiles	-	0.57	8.21	11.49	m	19.70
universal hip tiles; cutting both sides	-	0.75	10.81	13.56	m	24.37
dry ridge system; universal ridge tiles	-	0.29	4.18	35.55	m	39.73
universal half round mono-pitch ridge tiles	-	0.63	9.08	23.81	m	32.89
universal gas flue ridge tile	-	0.57	8.21	92.76	nr	100.97
universal ridge vent tile with 110 mm diameter adaptor	-	0.57	8.21	79.84	nr	88.05
holes for pipes and the like	-	0.23	3.31	-	nr	3.31
Concrete interlocking tiles; Redland "Stonewold II" smooth finish tiles or other equal and approved; PC £1365.00/1000; 430 mm x 380 mm; to 75 mm lap; on 25 mm x 38 mm battens and type 1F reinforced underlay						
Roof coverings	-	0.40	5.76	16.98	m²	22.74
Extra over coverings for						
fixing every tile	-	0.03	0.43	1.03	m²	1.46
verges; extra single undercloak course of plain tiles	-	0.35	5.04	3.51	m	8.55
ambi-dry verge system	-	0.23	3.31	10.46	m	13.77
ambi-dry verge eave/ridge end piece	-	0.03	0.43	3.67	m	4.10
valley trough tiles; cutting both sides	-	0.63	9.08	28.39	m	37.47
universal angle ridge tiles	-	0.57	8.21	8.47	m	16.68
universal hip tiles; cutting both sides	-	0.75	10.81	12.77	m	23.58
dry ridge system; universal angle ridge tiles	-	0.29	4.18	22.55	m	26.73
universal monopitch angle ridge tiles	-	0.63	9.08	16.17	m	25.25
universal gas flue angle ridge tile	-	0.57	8.21	95.80	nr	104.01
universal angle ridge vent tile with 110 mm diameter adaptor	-	0.57	8.21	79.74	nr	87.95
holes for pipes and the like	-	0.23	3.31	-	nr	3.31

H CLADDING/COVERING Excluding overheads and profit	PC £	Labour hours	Labour £	Material £	Unit	Total rate £
Concrete plain tiles; EN 490 and 491 group A; **PC £295.00/1000; 267 mm x 165 mm; on 25** **mm x 38 mm battens and type 1F reinforced** **underlay**						
Roof coverings; to 64 mm lap	-	1.21	17.44	24.89	m²	42.33
Wall coverings; to 38 mm lap	-	1.44	20.75	21.51	m²	42.26
Extra over coverings for						
ornamental tiles	-	-	-	17.77	m²	17.77
double course at eaves	-	0.29	4.18	2.89	m	7.07
verges	-	0.38	5.48	1.02	m	6.50
swept valleys; cutting both sides	-	0.75	10.81	28.00	m	38.81
bonnet hips; cutting both sides	-	0.92	13.26	28.00	m	41.26
external vertical angle tiles; supplementary nail						
fixings	-	0.46	6.63	20.13	m	26.76
half round ridge tiles	-	0.57	8.21	7.07	m	15.28
third round hip tiles; cutting both sides	-	0.57	8.21	8.93	m	17.14
holes for pipes and the like	-	0.23	3.31	-	nr	3.31
Sundries						
Hip irons						
galvanised mild steel; fixing with screws	-	0.12	1.73	2.63	nr	4.36
"Rytons Clip strip" or other equal and approved; continuous soffit ventilator						
51 mm wide; plastic; code CS351	-	0.35	5.04	1.01	m	6.05
"Rytons over fascia ventilator" or other equal and approved; continuous eaves ventilator						
40 mm wide; plastic; code OFV890	-	0.12	1.73	1.80	m	3.53
"Rytons roof ventilator" or other equal and approved; to suit rafters at 600 mm centres						
250 mm deep x 43 mm high; plastic; code TV600	-	0.12	1.73	1.70	m	3.43
"Rytons push and lock ventilators" or other equal and approved; circular						
83 mm diameter; plastic; code PL235	-	0.06	0.68	0.26	nr	0.94
Fixing only						
lead soakers (supply cost given elsewhere)	-	0.09	0.95	-	nr	0.95
Pressure impregnated softwood counter battens; 25 mm x 50 mm						
450 mm centres	-	0.08	1.15	1.07	m²	2.22
600 mm centres	-	0.06	0.86	0.81	m²	1.67
Underlay; BS 747 type 1B; bitumen felt **weighing 14 kg/10m²; 75 mm laps**						
To sloping or vertical surfaces	0.59	0.03	0.43	1.07	m²	1.50
Underlay; BS 747 type 1F; reinforced bitumen **felt weighing 22.50 kg/10 m²; 75 mm laps**						
To sloping or vertical surfaces	1.12	0.03	0.43	1.63	m²	2.06
Underlay; Visqueen "Tilene 200P" or other equal and **approved; micro-perforated sheet; 75 mm laps**						
To sloping or vertical surfaces	0.49	0.03	0.43	0.99	m²	1.42
Underlay; "Powerlon 250 BM" or other equal and **approved; reinforced breather membrane; 75 mm** **laps**						
To sloping or vertical surfaces	0.59	0.03	0.43	1.10	m²	1.53
Underlay; "Anticon" sarking membrane or other **equal and approved; Euroroof Ltd; polyethylene;** **75 mm laps**						
To sloping or vertical surfaces	0.96	0.03	0.43	1.46	m²	1.89

H CLADDING/COVERING Excluding overheads and profit	PC £	Labour hours	Labour £	Material £	Unit	Total rate £
H61 FIBRE CEMENT SLATING						
Asbestos-free artificial slates; Eternit "2000" or						
other equal and approved; to 75 mm lap; on 19 mm						
x 50 mm battens and type 1F reinforced underlay						
Coverings; 400 mm x 200 mm slates						
roof coverings	-	0.92	13.26	27.05	m²	40.31
wall coverings	-	1.21	17.44	27.05	m²	44.49
Coverings; 500 mm x 250 mm slates						
roof coverings	-	0.75	10.81	24.60	m²	35.41
wall coverings	-	0.92	13.26	24.60	m²	37.86
Coverings; 600 mm x 300 mm slates						
roof coverings	-	0.57	8.21	21.67	m²	29.88
wall coverings	-	0.75	10.81	21.67	m²	32.48
Extra over slate coverings for						
double course at eaves	-	0.29	4.18	5.38	m	9.56
verges; extra single undercloak course	-	0.38	5.48	1.31	m	6.79
open valleys; cutting both sides	-	0.23	3.31	5.24	m	8.55
valley gutters; cutting both sides	-	0.63	9.08	22.25	m	31.33
half round ridge tiles	-	0.57	8.21	19.91	m	28.12
stop end	-	0.12	1.73	6.80	nr	8.53
roll top ridge tiles	-	0.69	9.94	21.67	m	31.61
stop end	-	0.12	1.73	10.14	nr	11.87
mono-pitch ridge tiles	-	0.57	8.21	25.44	m	33.65
stop end	-	0.12	1.73	30.61	nr	32.34
duo-pitch ridge tiles	-	0.57	8.21	20.56	m	28.77
stop end	-	0.12	1.73	22.48	nr	24.21
mitred hips; cutting both sides	-	0.23	3.31	5.24	m	8.55
half round hip tiles; cutting both sides	-	0.23	3.31	25.15	m	28.46
holes for pipes and the like	-	0.23	3.31	-	nr	3.31
H62 NATURAL SLATING						
NOTE: The following items of slate roofing						
unless otherwise described, include for						
conventional fixing assuming "normal						
exposure" with appropriate nails and/or rivets						
or clips to pressure impregnated softwood						
battens fixed with galvanised nails; prices						
also include for all bedding and pointing at						
verges, beneath verge tiles, etc.						
Natural slates; BS 680 Part 2; Welsh blue;						
uniform size; to 75 mm lap; on 25 mm x 50						
mm battens and type 1F reinforced underlay						
Coverings; 405 mm x 255 mm slates						
roof coverings	-	1.03	14.84	36.45	m²	51.29
wall coverings	-	1.32	19.02	36.45	m²	55.47
Coverings; 510 mm x 255 mm slates						
roof coverings	-	0.86	12.39	43.97	m²	56.36
wall coverings	-	1.03	14.84	43.97	m²	58.81
Coverings; 610 mm x 305 mm slates						
roof coverings	-	0.69	9.94	55.93	m²	65.87
wall coverings	-	0.86	12.39	55.93	m²	68.32
Extra over coverings for						
double course at eaves	-	0.35	5.04	14.68	m	19.72
verges; extra single undercloak course	-	0.48	6.92	8.59	m	15.51
open valleys; cutting both sides	-	0.25	3.60	34.02	m	37.62
blue/black glazed ware 152 mm half round						
ridge tiles	-	0.57	8.21	7.72	m	15.93
blue/black glazed ware 125 mm x 125 mm						
plain angle ridge tiles	-	0.57	8.21	7.72	m	15.93

H CLADDING/COVERING Excluding overheads and profit	PC £	Labour hours	Labour £	Material £	Unit	Total rate £
Extra over coverings for - cont'd						
mitred hips; cutting both sides	-	0.25	3.60	34.02	m	37.62
blue/black glazed ware 152 mm half round hip						
tiles; cutting both sides	-	0.80	11.53	41.74	m	53.27
blue/black glazed ware 125 mm x 125 mm						
plain angle hip tiles; cutting both sides	-	0.80	11.53	41.74	m	53.27
holes for pipes and the like	-	0.23	3.31	-	nr	3.31
Natural slates; Westmoreland green; PC						
£1703.00/t; random lengths; 457 mm - 229						
mm proportionate widths to 75 mm lap; in						
diminishing courses; on 25 mm x 50 mm						
battens and type 1F underlay						
Roof coverings	-	1.32	19.02	100.10	m²	119.12
Wall coverings	-	1.67	24.06	100.10	m²	124.16
Extra over coverings for						
double course at eaves	-	0.76	10.95	18.65	m	29.60
verges; extra single undercloak course slates						
152 mm wide	-	0.86	12.39	16.18	m	28.57
holes for pipes and the like	-	0.35	5.04	-	nr	5.04
H63 RECONSTRUCTED STONE SLATING/TILING						
Reconstructed stone slates; "Hardrow Slates"						
or other equal and approved; standard colours; or						
similar; PC £858.00/1000; to 75 mm lap; on 25 mm						
x 50 mm battens and type 1F reinforced underlay						
Coverings; 457 mm x 305 mm slates						
roof coverings	-	0.92	13.26	20.35	m²	33.61
wall coverings	-	1.15	16.57	20.35	m²	36.92
Coverings; 457 mm x 457 mm slates						
roof coverings	-	0.75	10.81	20.14	m²	30.95
wall coverings	-	0.98	14.12	20.14	m²	34.26
Extra over 457 mm x 305 mm coverings for						
double course at eaves	-	0.35	5.04	3.66	m	8.70
verges; pointed	-	0.48	6.92	0.06	m	6.98
open valleys; cutting both sides	-	0.25	3.60	9.01	m	12.61
ridge tiles	-	0.57	8.21	26.42	m	34.63
hip tiles; cutting both sides	-	0.80	11.53	19.81	m	31.34
holes for pipes and the like	-	0.23	3.31	-	nr	3.31
Reconstructed stone slates; "Hardrow Slates"						
or other equal and approved; green/oldstone						
colours; PC £858.00/1000; to 75 mm lap;						
on 25 mm x 50 mm battens and type 1F reinforced						
underlay						
Coverings; 457 mm x 305 mm slates						
roof coverings	-	0.92	13.26	20.35	m²	33.61
wall coverings	-	1.15	16.57	20.35	m²	36.92
Coverings; 457 mm x 457 mm slates						
roof coverings	-	0.75	10.81	20.14	m²	30.95
wall coverings	-	0.98	14.12	20.14	m²	34.26
Extra over 457 mm x 305 mm coverings for						
double course at eaves	-	0.35	5.04	3.66	m	8.70
verges; pointed	-	0.48	6.92	0.06	m	6.98
open valleys; cutting both sides	-	0.25	3.60	9.01	m	12.61
ridge tiles	-	0.57	8.21	26.42	m	34.63
hip tiles; cutting both sides	-	0.80	11.53	19.81	m	31.34
holes for pipes and the like	-	0.23	3.31	-	nr	3.31

H CLADDING/COVERING Excluding overheads and profit	PC £	Labour hours	Labour £	Material £	Unit	Total rate £
H63 RECONSTRUCTED STONE SLATING/TILING - cont'd						
Reconstructed stone slates; Bradstone "Cotswold" **style or other equal and approved; PC £20.65/m^2;** **random lengths 550 mm - 300 mm; proportional** **widths; to 80 mm lap; in diminishing courses; on** **25 mm x 50 mm battens and type 1F reinforced** **underlay**						
Roof coverings (all-in rate inclusive of eaves and verges)	-	1.21	17.44	26.54	m^2	**43.98**
Extra over coverings for						
open valleys/mitred hips; cutting both sides	-	0.52	7.49	9.76	m^2	**17.25**
ridge tiles	-	0.76	10.95	13.00	m	**23.95**
hip tiles; cutting both sides	-	1.21	17.44	22.06	m	**39.50**
holes for pipes and the like	-	0.35	5.04	-	nr	**5.04**
Reconstructed stone slates; Bradstone "Moordale" **style or other equal and approved; PC £19.45/m^2;** **random lengths 550 mm - 450 mm; proportional** **widths; to 80 mm lap; in diminishing course; on 25** **mm x 50 mm battens and type 1F reinforced underlay**						
Roof coverings (all-in rate inclusive of eaves and verges)	-	1.21	17.44	25.28	m^2	**42.72**
Extra over coverings for						
open valleys/mitred hips; cutting both sides	-	0.52	7.49	9.19	m^2	**16.68**
ridge tiles	-	0.76	10.95	13.00	m	**23.95**
holes for pipes and the like	-	0.35	5.04	-	nr	**5.04**
H64 TIMBER SHINGLING						
Red cedar sawn shingles preservative **treated; PC £32.75/bundle; uniform length 400** **mm; to 125 mm gauge; on 25 mm x 38 mm** **battens and type 1F reinforced underlay**						
Roof coverings; 125 mm gauge, 2.28 m^2/bundle	-	1.21	17.44	20.35	m^2	**37.79**
Wall coverings; 190 mm gauge, 3.47 m^2/bundle	-	0.92	13.26	13.83	m^2	**27.09**
Extra over coverings for						
double course at eaves	32.75	0.23	3.31	1.95	m	**5.26**
open valleys; cutting both sides	32.75	0.23	3.31	3.69	m	**7.00**
pre-formed ridge capping	-	0.35	5.04	6.66	m	**11.70**
pre-formed hip capping; cutting both sides	-	0.57	8.21	10.36	m	**18.57**
double starter course to cappings	-	0.12	1.73	0.69	m	**2.42**
holes for pipes and the like	-	0.17	2.45	-	nr	**2.45**
H71 LEAD SHEET COVERINGS/FLASHINGS						
Milled lead; BS 1178; PC £1029.00/t						
1.32 mm thick (code 3) roof coverings						
flat	-	3.11	32.87	16.06	m^2	**48.93**
sloping 10 - 50 degrees	-	3.45	36.47	16.06	m^2	**52.53**
vertical or sloping over 50 degrees	-	3.79	40.06	16.06	m^2	**56.12**
1.80 mm thick (code 4) roof coverings						
flat	-	3.33	35.20	21.90	m^2	**57.10**
sloping 10 - 50 degrees	-	3.68	38.90	21.90	m^2	**60.80**
vertical or sloping over 50 degrees	-	4.03	42.60	21.90	m^2	**64.50**

H CLADDING/COVERING Excluding overheads and profit	PC £	Labour hours	Labour £	Material £	Unit	Total rate £
1.80 mm thick (code 4) dormer coverings						
flat	-	3.91	41.33	21.90	m²	63.23
sloping 10 - 50 degrees	-	4.49	47.46	21.90	m²	69.36
vertical or sloping over 50 degrees	-	4.83	51.05	21.90	m²	72.95
2.24 mm thick (code 5) roof coverings						
flat	-	3.56	37.63	29.20	m²	66.83
sloping 10 - 50 degrees	-	3.91	41.33	29.20	m²	70.53
vertical or sloping over 50 degrees	-	4.25	44.92	29.20	m²	74.12
2.24 mm thick (code 5) dormer coverings						
flat	-	4.25	44.92	29.20	m²	74.12
sloping 10 - 50 degrees	-	4.71	49.78	29.20	m²	78.98
vertical or sloping over 50 degrees	-	5.17	54.65	29.20	m²	83.85
2.65 mm thick (code 6) roof coverings						
flat	-	3.79	40.06	32.24	m²	72.30
sloping 10 - 50 degrees	-	4.14	43.76	32.24	m²	76.00
vertical or sloping over 50 degrees	-	4.49	47.46	32.24	m²	79.70
2.65 mm thick (code 6) dormer coverings						
flat	-	4.60	48.62	32.24	m²	80.86
sloping 10 - 50 degrees	-	4.94	52.22	32.24	m²	84.46
vertical or sloping over 50 degrees	-	5.40	57.08	32.24	m²	89.32
3.15 mm thick (code 7) roof coverings						
flat	-	4.03	42.60	38.32	m²	80.92
sloping 10 - 50 degrees	-	4.37	46.19	38.32	m²	84.51
vertical or sloping over 50 degrees	-	4.71	49.78	38.32	m²	88.10
3.15 mm thick (code 7) dormer coverings						
flat	-	4.83	51.05	38.32	m²	89.37
sloping 10 - 50 degrees	-	5.17	54.65	38.32	m²	92.97
vertical or sloping over 50 degrees	-	5.64	59.61	38.32	m²	97.93
3.55 mm thick (code 8) roof coverings						
flat	-	4.25	44.92	43.19	m²	88.11
sloping 10 - 50 degrees	-	4.60	48.62	43.19	m²	91.81
vertical or sloping over 50 degrees	-	4.94	52.22	43.19	m²	95.41
3.55 mm thick (code 8) dormer coverings						
flat	-	5.17	54.65	43.19	m²	97.84
sloping 10 - 50 degrees	-	5.52	58.35	43.19	m²	101.54
vertical or sloping over 50 degrees	-	5.98	63.21	43.19	m²	106.40
Dressing over glazing bars and glass	-	0.38	4.02	-	m	4.02
Soldered dot	-	0.17	1.80	-	nr	1.80
Copper nailing; 75 mm centres	-	0.23	2.43	0.25	m	2.68
1.80 mm thick (code 4) lead flashings, etc.						
Flashings; wedging into grooves						
150 mm girth	-	0.92	9.72	3.41	m	13.13
240 mm girth	-	1.03	10.89	5.44	m	16.33
Stepped flashings; wedging into grooves						
180 mm girth	-	1.03	10.89	4.05	m	14.94
270 mm girth	-	1.15	12.16	6.08	m	18.24
Linings to sloping gutters						
390 mm girth	-	1.38	14.59	8.85	m	23.44
450 mm girth	-	1.49	15.75	10.14	m	25.89
750 mm girth	-	1.38	14.59	16.42	m	31.01
Cappings to hips or ridges						
450 mm girth	-	1.73	18.29	10.14	m	28.43
600 mm girth	-	1.84	19.45	13.56	m	33.01
Soakers						
200 mm x 200 mm	-	0.17	1.80	0.88	nr	2.68
300 mm x 300 mm	-	0.23	2.43	1.97	nr	4.40
Saddle flashings; at intersections of hips and ridges; dressing and bossing						
450 mm x 600 mm	-	2.07	21.88	6.08	nr	27.96

H CLADDING/COVERING Excluding overheads and profit	PC £	Labour hours	Labour £	Material £	Unit	Total rate £
H71 LEAD SHEET COVERINGS/FLASHINGS - cont'd						
1.80 mm thick (code 4) lead flashings, etc. - cont'd						
Slates; with 150 mm high collar						
450 mm x 450 mm; to suit 50 mm diameter pipe	-	1.96	20.72	5.24	nr	**25.96**
450 mm x 450 mm; to suit 100 mm diameter pipe	-	2.30	24.31	5.75	nr	**30.06**
2.24 mm (code 5) lead flashings, etc.						
Flashings; wedging into grooves						
150 mm girth	-	0.92	9.72	4.25	m	**13.97**
240 mm girth	-	1.03	10.89	6.73	m	**17.62**
Stepped flashings; wedging into grooves						
180 mm girth	-	1.03	10.89	5.06	m	**15.95**
270 mm girth	-	1.15	12.16	7.57	m	**19.73**
Linings to sloping gutters						
390 mm girth	-	1.38	14.59	10.98	m	**25.57**
450 mm girth	-	1.49	15.75	12.63	m	**28.38**
Cappings to hips or ridges						
450 mm girth	-	1.73	18.29	12.63	m	**30.92**
600 mm girth	-	1.84	19.45	16.88	m	**36.33**
Soakers						
200 mm x 200 mm	-	0.17	1.80	1.17	nr	**2.97**
300 mm x 300 mm	-	0.23	2.43	2.63	nr	**5.06**
Saddle flashings; at intersections of hips and ridges; dressing and bossing						
450 mm x 600 mm	-	2.07	21.88	7.58	nr	**29.46**
Slates; with 150 mm high collar						
450 mm x 450 mm; to suit 50 mm diameter pipe	-	1.96	20.72	6.53	nr	**27.25**
450 mm x 450 mm; to suit 100 mm diameter pipe	-	2.30	24.31	7.17	nr	**31.48**
H72 ALUMINIUM SHEET COVERINGS/FLASHINGS						
Aluminium roofing; commercial grade						
0.90 mm thick roof coverings						
flat	-	3.45	36.47	6.10	m²	**42.57**
sloping 10 - 50 degrees	-	3.80	40.17	6.10	m²	**46.27**
vertical or sloping over 50 degrees	-	4.15	43.87	6.10	m²	**49.97**
0.90 mm thick dormer coverings						
flat	-	4.15	43.87	6.10	m²	**49.97**
sloping 10 - 50 degrees	-	4.60	48.62	6.10	m²	**54.72**
vertical or sloping over 50 degrees	-	5.05	53.38	6.10	m²	**59.48**
Aluminium nailing; 75 mm spacing	-	0.23	2.43	0.23	m	**2.66**
0.90 mm commercial grade aluminium flashings, etc.						
Flashings; wedging into grooves						
150 mm girth	-	0.92	9.72	0.94	m	**10.66**
240 mm girth	-	1.05	11.10	1.53	m	**12.63**
300 mm girth	-	1.20	12.68	1.88	m	**14.56**
Stepped flashings; wedging into grooves						
180 mm girth	-	1.05	11.10	1.13	m	**12.23**
270 mm girth	-	1.15	12.16	1.74	m	**13.90**
1.20 mm commercial grade aluminium flashings; polyester powder coated						
Flashings; fixed with self tapping screws						
170 mm girth	-	1.05	11.10	1.30	m	**12.40**
200 mm girth	-	1.10	11.63	1.73	m	**13.36**
280 mm girth	-	1.25	13.21	2.28	m	**15.49**

H CLADDING/COVERING Excluding overheads and profit	PC £	Labour hours	Labour £	Material £	Unit	Total rate £
H73 COPPER STRIP/SHEET COVERINGS/ **FLASHINGS**						
Copper roofing; BS 2870						
0.56 mm thick (24 swg) roof coverings						
flat	18.35	3.70	39.11	19.27	m²	**58.38**
sloping 10 - 50 degrees	-	4.05	42.81	19.27	m²	**62.08**
vertical or sloping over 50 degrees	-	4.35	45.98	19.27	m²	**65.25**
0.56 mm thick (24 swg) dormer coverings						
flat	18.35	4.35	45.98	19.27	m²	**65.25**
sloping 10 - 50 degrees	-	4.85	51.26	19.27	m²	**70.53**
vertical or sloping over 50 degrees	-	5.30	56.02	19.27	m²	**75.29**
0.61 mm thick (23 swg) roof coverings						
flat	-	3.70	39.11	20.99	m²	**60.10**
sloping 10 - 50 degrees	-	4.05	42.81	20.99	m²	**63.80**
vertical or sloping over 50 degrees	-	4.35	45.98	20.99	m²	**66.97**
0.61 mm thick (23 swg) dormer coverings						
flat	-	4.35	45.98	20.99	m²	**66.97**
sloping 10 - 50 degrees	-	4.85	51.26	20.99	m²	**72.25**
vertical or sloping over 50 degrees	-	5.30	56.02	20.99	m²	**77.01**
Copper nailing; 75 mm spacing	-	0.23	2.43	0.25	m	**2.68**
0.56 mm thick copper flashings, etc.						
Flashings; wedging into grooves						
150 mm girth	-	0.92	9.72	3.02	m	**12.74**
240 mm girth	-	1.05	11.10	4.85	m	**15.95**
300 mm girth	-	1.20	12.68	6.08	m	**18.76**
Stepped flashings; wedging into grooves						
180 mm girth	-	1.05	11.10	3.66	m	**14.76**
270 mm girth	-	1.15	12.16	5.46	m	**17.62**
0.61 mm thick copper flashings, etc.						
Flashings; wedging into grooves						
150 mm girth	-	0.92	9.72	3.28	m	**13.00**
240 mm girth	-	1.05	11.10	5.29	m	**16.39**
300 mm girth	-	1.20	12.68	6.60	m	**19.28**
Stepped flashings; wedging into grooves						
180 mm girth	-	1.05	11.10	3.97	m	**15.07**
270 mm girth	-	1.15	12.16	5.95	m	**18.11**
H74 ZINC STRIP/SHEET COVERINGS/FLASHINGS						
Zinc; BS 849						
0.80 mm roof coverings						
flat	-	3.70	39.11	13.85	m²	**52.96**
sloping 10 - 50 degrees	-	4.05	42.81	13.85	m²	**56.66**
vertical or sloping over 50 degrees	-	4.35	45.98	13.85	m²	**59.83**
0.61 mm thick (23 swg) dormer coverings						
flat	-	4.35	45.98	13.85	m²	**59.83**
sloping 10 - 50 degrees	-	4.85	51.26	13.85	m²	**65.11**
vertical or sloping over 50 degrees	-	5.30	56.02	13.85	m²	**69.87**
0.80 mm thick zinc flashings, etc.						
Flashings; wedging into grooves						
150 mm girth	-	0.92	9.72	2.16	m	**11.88**
240 mm girth	-	1.05	11.10	3.48	m	**14.58**
300 mm girth	-	1.20	12.68	4.37	m	**17.05**
Stepped flashings; wedging into grooves						
180 mm girth	-	1.05	11.10	2.63	m	**13.73**
270 mm girth	-	1.15	12.16	3.92	m	**16.08**

H CLADDING/COVERING Excluding overheads and profit	PC £	Labour hours	Labour £	Material £	Unit	Total rate £
H75 STAINLESS STEEL SHEET COVERINGS/ FLASHINGS						
Terne coated stainless steel roofing; **Eurocom Enterprise Ltd or other equal and** **approved**						
Roof coverings; "Uginox AME"; 0.40 mm thick						
flat; fixing with stainless steel screws to timber	14.36	1.10	15.85	19.78	m²	35.63
flat; including batten rolls; fixing with stainless						
steel screws to timber	-	1.10	15.85	21.17	m²	37.02
Roof coverings; "Uginox AE"; 0.40 mm thick						
flat; fixing with stainless steel screws to timber	11.97	1.10	15.85	16.86	m²	32.71
flat; including batten rolls; fixing with stainless						
steel screws to timber	-	1.10	15.85	18.21	m²	34.06
Wall coverings; "Uginox AME"; 0.40 mm thick						
vertical; coulisseau joints; fixing with stainless						
steel screws to timber	-	0.99	14.27	18.58	m²	32.85
Wall coverings; "Uginox AE"; 0.40 mm thick						
vertical; coulisseau joints; fixing with stainless						
steel screws to timber	-	0.99	14.27	15.73	m²	30.00
Flashings						
head abutments; swiss fold and cover						
flashings 150 mm girth	-	0.44	6.34	3.90	m	10.24
head abutments; manchester fold and cover						
flashings 150 mm girth	-	0.55	7.93	3.90	m	11.83
head abutments; soldered saddle flashings						
150 mm girth	-	0.55	7.93	4.42	m	12.35
head abutments; into brick wall with timber						
infill; cover flashings 150 mm girth	-	0.88	12.68	6.12	m	18.80
head abutments; into brick wall with soldered						
apron; cover flashings 150 mm girth	-	1.05	15.13	6.85	m	21.98
side abutments; "Uginox" stepped flashings						
170 mm girth	-	1.76	25.36	4.91	m	30.27
eaves flashings 140 mm girth; approned with						
single lock welts	-	0.39	5.62	7.03	m	12.65
eaves flashings 190 mm girth; approned with						
flashings and soldered strips	-	0.55	7.93	8.61	m	16.54
verge flashings 150 mm girth	-	0.28	4.03	7.23	m	11.26
Aprons						
fan aprons 250 mm girth	-	0.30	4.32	6.05	m	10.37
Ridges						
ridge with coulisseau closures	-	0.66	9.51	2.82	m	12.33
monoridge flanged apex (AME)	-	0.33	4.76	4.19	m	8.95
ridge with tapered timber infill and flat saddles	-	1.10	15.85	5.70	m	21.55
monoridge with timber infill and flat saddles	-	0.61	8.79	8.94	m	17.73
ventilated ridge with timber kerb and flat						
saddles	-	1.32	19.02	15.27	m	34.29
ventilated ridge with stainless steel brackets	-	0.99	14.27	26.43	m	40.70
Edges						
downstand	-	0.33	4.76	5.63	m	10.39
flanged	-	0.28	4.03	6.05	m	10.08
Gutters						
double lock welted valley gutters	-	1.16	16.72	9.29	m	26.01
eaves gutters; against masonry work	-	1.32	19.02	12.64	m	31.66
recessed valley gutters	-	0.99	14.27	17.84	m	32.11
recessed valley gutters with laplocks	-	1.21	17.44	21.04	m	38.48
secret	-	1.10	15.85	21.97	m	37.82
saddle expansion joints in gutters	-	1.10	15.85	7.60	-	23.45

H CLADDING/COVERING Excluding overheads and profit	PC £	Labour hours	Labour £	Material £	Unit	Total rate £
H76 FIBRE BITUMEN THERMOPLASTIC SHEET COVERINGS/FLASHINGS						
Glass fibre reinforced bitumen strip slates; "Ruberglas 105" or other equal and approved; 1000 mm x 336 mm mineral finish; to external quality plywood boarding (boarding not included)						
Roof coverings	-	0.29	4.18	12.88	m²	17.06
Wall coverings	-	0.46	6.63	12.88	m²	19.51
Extra over coverings for						
double course at eaves; felt soaker	-	0.23	3.31	9.09	m	12.40
verges; felt soaker	-	0.17	2.45	7.60	m	10.05
valley slate; cut to shape; felt soaker and cutting						
both sides	-	0.52	7.49	11.79	m	19.28
ridge slate; cut to shape	-	0.35	5.04	7.60	m	12.64
hip slate; cut to shape; felt soaker and cutting						
both sides	-	0.52	7.49	11.70	m	19.19
holes for pipes and the like	-	0.60	8.65	-	nr	8.65
Evode "Flashband Original" sealing strips and flashings or other equal and approved; special grey finish						
Flashings; wedging at top if required; pressure bonded; flashband primer before application; to walls						
75 mm girth	-	0.19	2.01	1.35	m	3.36
100 mm girth	-	0.29	3.07	1.80	m	4.87
150 mm girth	-	0.38	4.02	2.92	m	6.94
225 mm girth	-	0.46	4.86	4.28	m	9.14
300 mm girth	-	0.52	5.50	5.59	m	11.09

J WATERPROOFING Excluding overheads and profit	PC £	Labour hours	Labour £	Material £	Unit	Total rate £
J WATERPROOFING						
J10 SPECIALIST WATERPROOF RENDERING						
"Sika" waterproof rendering or other equal and						
approved; steel trowelled						
20 mm work to walls; three coat; to concrete						
base						
over 300 mm wide	-	-	-	-	m²	33.70
not exceeding 300 mm wide	-	-	-	-	m²	52.80
25 mm work to walls; three coat; to concrete						
base						
over 300 mm wide	-	-	-	-	m²	38.20
not exceeding 300 mm wide	-	-	-	-	m²	60.70
40 mm work to walls; four coat; to concrete						
base						
over 300 mm wide	-	-	-	-	m²	58.50
not exceeding 300 mm wide	-	-	-	-	m²	89.90
J20 MASTIC ASPHALT TANKING/DAMP PROOF						
MEMBRANES						
Mastic asphalt to BS 6925 Type T 1097						
13 mm thick one coat coverings to concrete						
base; flat; subsequently covered						
over 300 mm wide	-	-	-	-	m²	10.65
225 mm - 300 mm wide	-	-	-	-	m²	25.20
150 mm - 225 mm wide	-	-	-	-	m²	27.75
not exceeding 150 mm wide	-	-	-	-	m²	34.50
20 mm thick two coat coverings to concrete						
base; flat; subsequently covered						
over 300 mm wide	-	-	-	-	m²	15.30
225 mm - 300 mm wide	-	-	-	-	m²	28.05
150 mm - 225 mm wide	-	-	-	-	m²	30.60
not exceeding 150 mm wide	-	-	-	-	m²	37.35
30 mm thick three coat coverings to concrete						
base; flat; subsequently covered						
over 300 mm wide	-	-	-	-	m²	21.90
225 mm - 300 mm wide	-	-	-	-	m²	31.80
150 mm - 225 mm wide	-	-	-	-	m²	34.50
not exceeding 150 mm wide	-	-	-	-	m²	41.25
13 mm thick two coat coverings to brickwork						
base; vertical; subsequently covered						
over 300 mm wide	-	-	-	-	m²	42.60
225 mm - 300 mm wide	-	-	-	-	m²	51.90
150 mm - 225 mm wide	-	-	-	-	m²	61.35
not exceeding 150 mm wide	-	-	-	-	m²	79.50
20 mm thick three coat coverings to brickwork						
base; vertical; subsequently covered						
over 300 mm wide	-	-	-	-	m²	66.60
225 mm - 300 mm wide	-	-	-	-	m²	71.70
150 mm - 225 mm wide	-	-	-	-	m²	76.20
not exceeding 150 mm wide	-	-	-	-	m²	98.40
Turning into groove 20 mm deep	-	-	-	-	m	0.75
Internal angle fillets; subsequently covered	-	-	-	-	m	4.95

J WATERPROOFING Excluding overheads and profit	PC £	Labour hours	Labour £	Material £	Unit	Total rate £
J21 MASTIC ASPHALT ROOFING/ INSULATION/FINISHES						
Mastic asphalt to BS 6925 Type R 988 20 mm thick two coat coverings; felt isolating membrane; to concrete (or timber) base; flat or to falls or slopes not exceeding 10 degrees from horizontal						
over 300 mm wide	-				m²	**15.15**
225 mm - 300 mm wide	-				m²	**27.75**
150 mm - 225 mm wide	-				m²	**30.75**
not exceeding 150 mm wide	-			-	m²	**37.20**
Add to the above for covering with:						
10 mm thick limestone chippings in hot bitumen	-			-	m²	**3.00**
coverings with solar reflective paint	-			-	m²	**2.70**
300 mm x 300 mm x 8 mm g.r.p. tiles in hot bitumen	-		-	-	m²	**39.60**
Cutting to line; jointing to old asphalt	-				m	**6.60**
13 mm thick two coat skirtings to brickwork base						
not exceeding 150 mm girth	-		-	-	m	**11.85**
150 mm - 225 mm girth	-				m	**13.65**
225 mm - 300 mm girth	-			-	m	**15.30**
13 mm thick three coat skirtings; expanded metal lathing reinforcement nailed to timber base						
not exceeding 150 mm girth	-		-	-	m	**18.75**
150 mm - 225 mm girth	-				m	**22.20**
225 mm - 300 mm girth	-			-	m	**25.80**
13 mm thick two coat fascias to concrete base						
not exceeding 150 mm girth	-		-	-	m	**11.85**
150 mm - 225 mm girth	-				m	**13.65**
20 mm thick two coat linings to channels to concrete base						
not exceeding 150 mm girth	-		-	-	m	**28.95**
150 mm - 225 mm girth	-		-	-	m	**30.75**
225 mm - 300 mm girth	-			-	m	**34.65**
20 mm thick two coat lining to cesspools						
250 mm x 150 mm x 150 mm deep	-				nr	**28.20**
Collars around pipes, standards and like members	-				nr	**13.65**
Accessories Eaves trim; extruded aluminium alloy; working asphalt into trim						
"Alutrim" type A roof edging or other equal and approved	-			-	m	**11.00**
extra; angle	-			-	nr	**6.13**
Roof screed ventilator - aluminium alloy "Extr-aqua-vent" or other equal and approved; set on screed over and including dished sinking; working collar around ventilator	-		-	-	nr	**21.25**
J30 LIQUID APPLIED TANKING/DAMP PROOF MEMBRANES						
Tanking and damp proofing "Synthaprufe" or other equal and approved; blinding with sand; horizontal on slabs						
two coats	-	0.22	1.60	2.98	m²	**4.58**
three coats	-	0.31	2.25	4.46	m²	**6.71**

J WATERPROOFING Excluding overheads and profit	PC £	Labour hours	Labour £	Material £	Unit	Total rate £
J30 LIQUID APPLIED TANKING/DAMP PROOF MEMBRANES - cont'd						
Tanking and damp proofing - cont'd "Tretolastex 202T" or other equal and approved; on vertical surfaces of concrete						
two coats	-	0.22	1.60	0.52	m²	**2.12**
three coats	-	0.31	2.25	0.78	m²	**3.03**
One coat Vandex "Super" 0.75 kg/m² slurry or other equal and approved; one consolidating coat of Vandex "Premix" 1 kg/m² slurry or other equal and approved; horizontal on beds						
over 225 mm wide	-	0.39	2.84	2.98	m²	**5.82**
J40 FLEXIBLE SHEET TANKING/DAMP PROOF MEMBRANES						
Tanking and damp proofing "Bituthene" sheeting or other equal and approved; lapped joints; horizontal on slabs						
500 grade	-	0.11	0.80	2.72	m²	**3.52**
1000 grade	-	0.12	0.87	3.71	m²	**4.58**
heavy duty grade	-	0.14	1.02	5.39	m²	**6.41**
"Bituthene" sheeting or other equal and approved; lapped joints; dressed up vertical face of concrete						
1000 grade	-	0.20	1.45	3.71	m²	**5.16**
"Servi-pak" protection board or other equal and approved; butt jointed; taped joints; to horizontal surfaces						
3 mm thick	-	0.17	1.24	5.13	m²	**6.37**
6 mm thick	-	0.17	1.24	7.09	m²	**8.33**
12 mm thick	-	0.22	1.60	11.08	m²	**12.68**
"Servi-pak" protection board or other equal and approved; butt jointed; taped joints; to vertical surfaces						
3 mm thick	-	0.22	1.60	5.13	m²	**6.73**
6 mm thick	-	0.22	1.60	7.09	m²	**8.69**
12 mm thick	-	0.28	2.04	11.08	m²	**13.12**
"Bituthene" fillet or other equal and approved						
40 mm x 40 mm	-	0.11	0.80	4.88	m	**5.68**
"Bituthene" reinforcing strip or other equal and approved; 300 mm wide						
1000 grade	-	0.11	0.80	1.11	m	**1.91**
Expandite "Famflex" hot bitumen bonded waterproof tanking or other equal and approved; 150 mm laps						
horizontal; over 300 mm wide	-	0.44	3.20	10.45	m²	**13.65**
vertical; over 300 mm wide	-	0.72	5.23	10.45	m²	**15.68**
J41 BUILT UP FELT ROOF COVERINGS						
NOTE: The following items of felt roofing, unless otherwise described, include for conventional lapping, laying and bonding between layers and to base; and laying flat or to falls, to crossfalls or to slopes not exceeding 10 degrees - but exclude any insulation etc.						
Felt roofing; BS 747; suitable for flat roofs Three layer coverings first layer type 3G; subsequent layers type 3B bitumen glass fibre based felt	-	-	-	-	m²	**6.85**

J WATERPROOFING Excluding overheads and profit	PC £	Labour hours	Labour £	Material £	Unit	Total rate £
Extra over felt for covering with and bedding in hot bitumen						
13 mm thick stone chippings	-	-	-	-	m²	2.25
300 mm x 300 mm x 8 mm g.r.p. tiles	-	-	-	-	m²	37.80
working into outlet pipes and the like	-	-	-	-	m²	9.30
Skirtings; three layer; top layer mineral surfaced; dressed over tilting fillet; turned into groove						
not exceeding 200 mm girth	-	-	-	-	m	6.90
200 mm - 400 mm girth	-	-	-	-	m	8.25
Coverings to kerbs; three layer						
400 mm - 600 mm girth	-	-	-	-	m	17.40
Linings to gutters; three layer						
400 mm - 600 mm girth	-	-	-	-	m	11.80
Collars around pipes and the like; three layer mineral surface; 150 mm high						
not exceeding 55 mm nominal size	-	-	-	-	nr	7.75
55 mm - 110 mm nominal size	-	-	-	-	nr	7.75
Three layer coverings; two base layers type 5U bitumen polyester based felt; top layer type 5B polyester based mineral surfaced felt; 10 mm stone chipping covering; bitumen bonded	-	-	-	-	m²	14.45
Coverings to kerbs						
not exceeding 200 mm girth	-	-	-	-	m	9.10
200 mm - 400 mm girth	-	-	-	-	m	11.40
Outlets and dishing to gullies						
300 mm diameter	-	-	-	-	nr	9.30
"Andersons" high performance polyester- based roofing system or other equal and approved						
Two layer coverings; first layer HT 125 underlay; second layer HT 350; fully bonded to wood; fibre or cork base	-	-	-	-	m²	10.35
Extra over for						
top layer mineral surfaced	-	-	-	-	m²	2.00
13 mm thick stone chippings	-	-	-	-	m²	2.25
third layer of type 3B as underlay for concrete or screeded base	-	-	-	-	m²	2.00
working into outlet pipes and the like	-	-	-	-	nr	9.30
Skirtings; two layer; top layer mineral surfaced; dressed over tilting fillet; turned into groove						
not exceeding 200 mm girth	-	-	-	-	m	7.35
200 mm - 400 mm girth	-	-	-	-	m	8.85
Coverings to kerbs; two layer						
400 mm - 600 mm girth	-	-	-	-	m	20.55
Linings to gutters; three layer						
400 mm - 600 mm girth	-	-	-	-	m	15.05
Collars around pipes and the like; two layer; 150 mm high						
not exceeding 55 mm nominal size	-	-	-	-	nr	7.75
55 mm - 110 mm nominal size	-	-	-	-	nr	7.75
"Ruberglas 120 GP" high performance roofing or other equal and approved						
Two layer coverings; first and second layers "Ruberglas 120 GP"; fully bonded to wood, fibre or cork base	-	-	-	-	m²	6.40
Extra over for						
top layer mineral surfaced	-	-	-	-	m²	2.00
13 mm thick stone chippings	-	-	-	-	m²	2.25
third layer of "Rubervent 3G" as underlay for concrete or screeded base	-	-	-	-	m²	2.00
working into outlet pipes and the like	-	-	-	-	nr	9.30

J WATERPROOFING Excluding overheads and profit	PC £	Labour hours	Labour £	Material £	Unit	Total rate £
J41 BUILT UP FELT ROOF COVERINGS - cont'd						
"Ruberglas 120 GP" high performance roofing or other equal and approved - cont'd						
Skirtings; two layer; top layer mineral surfaced; dressed over tilting fillet; turned into groove						
not exceeding 200 mm girth	-	-	-	-	m	6.40
200 mm - 400 mm girth	-	-	-	-	m	7.45
Coverings to kerbs; two layer						
400 mm - 600 mm girth	-	-	-	-	m	12.80
Linings to gutters; three layer						
400 mm - 600 mm girth	-	-	-	-	m	10.60
Collars around pipes and the like; two layer, 150 mm high						
not exceeding 55 mm nominal size	-	-	-	-	nr	7.75
55 mm - 110 mm nominal size	-	-	-	-	nr	7.75
"Ruberfort HP 350" high performance roofing or other equal and approved						
Two layer coverings; first layer "Ruberfort HP 180"; second layer "Ruberfort HP 350"; fully bonded; to wood; fibre or cork base	-	-	-	-	m²	9.90
Extra over for						
top layer mineral surfaced	-	-	-	-	m²	2.00
13 mm thick stone chippings	-	-	-	-	m²	2.25
third layer of "Rubervent 3G"; as underlay for concrete or screeded base	-	-	-	-	m²	2.00
working into outlet pipes and the like	-	-	-	-	nr	9.30
Skirtings; two layer; top layer mineral surface; dressed over tilting fillet; turned into groove						
not exceeding 200 mm girth	-	-	-	-	m	7.05
200 mm - 400 mm girth	-	-	-	-	m	8.35
Coverings to kerbs; two layer						
400 mm - 600 mm girth	-	-	-	-	m	19.80
Linings to gutters; three layer						
400 mm - 600 mm girth	-	-	-	-	m	14.25
Collars around pipes and the like; two layer; 150 mm high						
not exceeding 55 mm nominal size	-	-	-	-	nr	7.75
55 mm - 110 mm nominal size	-	-	-	-	nr	7.75
"Polybit 350" elastomeric roofing or other equal and approved						
Two layer coverings; first layer "Polybit 180"; second layer "Polybit 350"; fully bonded to wood; fibre or cork base	-	-	-	-	m²	10.10
Extra over for						
top layer mineral surfaced	-	-	-	-	m²	2.00
13 mm thick stone chippings	-	-	-	-	m²	2.25
third layer of "Rubervent 3G" as underlay for concrete or screeded base	-	-	-	-	m²	2.00
working into outlet pipes and the like	-	-	-	-	nr	9.30
Skirtings; two layer; top layer mineral surfaced; dressed over tilting fillet; turned into groove						
not exceeding 200 mm girth	-	-	-	-	m	7.25
200 mm - 400 mm girth	-	-	-	-	m	8.65
Coverings to kerbs; two layer						
400 mm - 600 mm girth	-	-	-	-	m	20.25
Linings to gutters; three layer						
400 mm - 600 mm girth	-	-	-	-	m	14.70
Collars around pipes and the like; two layer; 150 mm high						
not exceeding 55 mm nominal size	-	-	-	-	nr	7.75
55 mm - 110 mm nominal size	-	-	-	-	nr	7.75

J WATERPROOFING Excluding overheads and profit	PC £	Labour hours	Labour £	Material £	Unit	Total rate £
"Hyload 150 E" elastomeric roofing or other **equal and approved**						
Two layer coverings; first layer "Ruberglas 120 GHP"; second layer "Hyload 150 E" fully bonded						
to wood; fibre or cork base	-	-	-	-	m²	20.65
Extra over for						
13 mm thick stone chippings	-	-	-	-	m²	2.25
third layer of "Rubervent 3G" as underlay for						
concrete or screeded base	-	-	-	-	m²	2.00
working into outlet pipes and the like	-	-	-	-	nr	9.30
Skirtings; two layer; dressed over tilting fillet;						
turned into groove						
not exceeding 200 mm girth	-	-	-	-	m	11.60
200 mm - 400 mm girth	-	-	-	-	m	18.90
Coverings to kerbs; two layer						
400 mm - 600 mm girth	-	-	-	-	m	38.55
Linings to gutters; three layer						
400 mm - 600 mm girth	-	-	-	-	m	25.55
Collars around pipes and the like; two layer; 150 mm high						
not exceeding 55 mm nominal size	-	-	-	-	nr	7.75
55 mm - 110 mm nominal size	-	-	-	-	nr	7.75
Accessories						
Eaves trim; extruded aluminium alloy; working felt into trim						
"Alutrim" type F roof edging or other equal and						
approved	-	-	-	-	m	6.90
extra over for external angle	-	-	-	-	nr	9.25
Roof screed ventilator - aluminium alloy						
"Extr-aqua-vent" or other equal and approved; set on						
screed over and including dished sinking and collar	-	-	-	-	nr	20.55
Insulation board underlays						
Vapour barrier						
reinforced; metal lined	-	-	-	-	m²	9.90
Cork boards; density 112 - 125 kg/m³						
60 mm thick	-	-	-	-	m²	12.95
Rockwool; slab RW4 or other equal and approved						
60 mm thick	-	-	-	-	m²	15.75
Perlite boards or other equal and approved;						
density 170 - 180 kg/m³						
60 mm thick	-	-	-	-	m²	20.55
Polyurethane boards; density 32 kg/m³						
30 mm thick	-	-	-	-	m²	8.10
35 mm thick	-	-	-	-	m²	8.70
50 mm thick	-	-	-	-	m²	9.50
Wood fibre boards; impregnated; density 220 - 350 kg/m³						
12.70 mm thick	-	-	-	-	m²	3.60
Insulation board overlays						
Dow "Roofmate SL" extruded polystyrene foam						
boards or other equal and approved						
50 mm thick	-	0.35	5.04	12.49	m²	17.53
75 mm thick	-	0.35	5.04	17.09	m²	22.13
Dow "Roofmate LG" extruded polystyrene foam						
boards or other equal and approved						
60 mm thick	-	0.35	5.04	24.19	m²	29.23
90 mm thick	-	0.35	5.04	27.46	m²	32.50
110 mm thick	-	0.35	5.04	30.33	m²	35.37
Dow "Roofmate PR" extruded polystyrene foam boards						
or other equal and approved						
90 mm thick	-	0.35	5.04	19.25	m²	24.29
120 mm thick	-	0.35	5.04	25.63	m²	30.67

J WATERPROOFING Excluding overheads and profit	PC £	Labour hours	Labour £	Material £	Unit	Total rate £
J42 SINGLE LAYER PLASTICS ROOF COVERINGS						
"Trocal S" PVC roofing or other equal and approved						
Coverings	-	-	-	-	m²	**15.70**
Skirtings; dressed over metal upstands						
not exceeding 200 mm girth	-	-	-	-	m	**12.13**
200 mm - 400 mm girth	-	-	-	-	m	**14.84**
Coverings to kerbs						
400 mm - 600 mm girth	-	-	-	-	m	**27.20**
Collars around pipes and the like; 150 mm high						
not exceeding 55 mm nominal size	-	-	-	-	nr	**7.75**
55 mm - 110 mm nominal size	-	-	-	-	nr	**7.75**
Accessories						
"Trocal" metal upstands or other equal and approved						
not exceeding 200 mm girth	-	-	-	-	m	**8.86**
200 mm - 400 mm girth	-	-	-	-	m	**11.38**

K LININGS/SHEATHING/DRY PARTITIONING Excluding overheads and profit	PC £	Labour hours	Labour £	Material £	Unit	Total rate £
K LININGS/SHEATHING/DRY PARTITIONING						
K10 PLASTERBOARD DRY LINING/PARTITIONS/ CEILINGS						
"Gyproc" laminated proprietary partitions or other equal and approved; two skins of gypsum plasterboard bonded to a centre core of plasterboard square edge plank 19 mm thick; fixing with nails to softwood perimeter battens (not included); joints filled with filler and joint tape; to receive direct decoration 50 mm partition; two outer skins of 12.50 mm thick tapered edge wallboard						
height 2.10 m - 2.40 m	-	2.20	24.81	17.76	m	42.57
height 2.40 m - 2.70 m	-	2.85	32.12	20.34	m	52.46
height 2.70 m - 3.00 m	-	3.20	36.06	22.11	m	58.17
height 3.00 m - 3.30 m	-	3.50	39.43	23.89	m	63.32
height 3.30 m - 3.60 m	-	3.85	43.36	25.75	m	69.11
65 mm partition; two outer skins of 19 mm thick tapered edge wallboard						
height 2.10 m - 2.40 m	-	2.45	27.65	21.58	m	49.23
height 2.40 m - 2.70 m	-	3.05	34.39	24.39	m	58.78
height 2.70 m - 3.00 m	-	3.40	38.32	26.40	m	64.72
height 3.00 m - 3.30 m	-	3.80	42.83	28.42	m	71.25
height 3.30 m - 3.60 m	-	4.15	46.76	30.52	m	77.28
Labours and associated additional wrought softwood studwork Floor, wall or ceiling battens						
25 mm x 38 mm	-	0.13	1.47	0.36	m	1.83
Forming openings in 2400 mm high partition; 25 mm x 38 mm softwood framing						
900 mm x 2100 mm	-	0.55	6.24	2.02	nr	8.26
fair ends	-	0.22	2.48	0.41	m	2.89
angle	-	0.33	3.71	0.77	m	4.48
Cutting and fitting around steel joists, angles, trunking, ducting, ventilators, pipes, tubes, etc.						
over 2.00 m girth	-	0.10	1.13	-	nr	1.13
not exceeding 0.30 m girth	-	0.06	0.68	-	nr	0.68
0.30 m - 1.00 m girth	-	0.08	0.91	-	nr	0.91
1.00 m - 2.00 m girth	-	0.12	1.36	-	nr	1.36
"Gyproc" metal stud proprietary partitions or other equal and approved; comprising 48 mm wide metal stud frame; 50 mm wide floor channel plugged and screwed to concrete through 38 mm x 48 mm tanalised softwood sole plate Tapered edge panels; joints filled with joint filler and joint tape to receive direct decoration; 80 mm thick partition; one hour; one layer of 15 mm thick "Fireline" board or other equal and approved each side						
height 2.10 m - 2.40 m	-	4.65	52.60	20.52	m	73.12
height 2.40 m - 2.70 m	-	5.30	59.91	23.74	m	83.65
height 2.70 m - 3.00 m	-	5.95	67.24	26.13	m	93.37
height 3.00 m - 3.30 m	-	6.85	77.42	28.74	m	106.16
height 3.30 m - 3.60 m	-	7.55	85.32	31.00	m	116.32
height 3.60 m - 3.90 m	-	9.00	101.73	33.46	m	135.19
height 3.90 m - 4.20 m	-	9.65	109.07	35.92	m	144.99
angles	-	0.22	2.48	1.25	m	3.73
T-junctions	-	0.11	1.25	-	m	1.25
fair ends	-	0.22	2.48	0.47	m	2.95

K LININGS/SHEATHING/DRY PARTITIONING Excluding overheads and profit	PC £	Labour hours	Labour £	Material £	Unit	Total rate £
K10 PLASTERBOARD DRY LINING/PARTITIONS/ **CEILINGS** - cont'd						
"Gyproc" metal stud proprietary partitions or other **equal and approved; comprising 48 mm wide metal** **stud frame; 50 mm wide floor channel plugged and** **screwed to concrete through 38 mm x 48 mm** **tanalised softwood sole plate** - cont'd						
Tapered edge panels; joints filled with joint filler and joint tape to receive direct decoration; 100 mm thick partition; two hour; two layers of 12.50 mm thick "Fireline" board or other equal and approved both sides						
height 2.10 m - 2.40 m	-	5.75	65.07	28.82	m	**93.89**
height 2.40 m - 2.70 m	-	6.55	74.08	33.11	m	**107.19**
height 2.70 m - 3.00 m	-	7.35	83.12	36.52	m	**119.64**
height 3.00 m - 3.30 m	-	7.30	82.52	40.18	m	**122.70**
height 3.30 m - 3.60 m	-	9.20	104.03	43.47	m	**147.50**
height 3.60 m - 3.90 m	-	9.00	101.73	47.01	m	**148.74**
height 3.90 m - 4.20 m	-	11.60	131.18	50.44	m	**181.62**
angles	-	0.33	3.73	1.36	m	**5.09**
T-junctions	-	0.11	1.25	-	m	**1.25**
fair ends	-	0.33	3.73	0.59	m	**4.32**
Gypsum plasterboard; BS 1230; plain grade tapered **edge wallboard; fixing with nails; joints left open to** **receive "Artex" finish or other equal and approved;** **to softwood base**						
9.50 mm board to ceilings						
over 300 mm wide	-	0.28	4.14	1.74	m²	**5.88**
9.50 mm board to beams						
girth not exceeding 600 mm	-	0.33	4.88	1.06	m²	**5.94**
girth 600 mm - 1200 mm	-	0.44	6.51	2.11	m²	**8.62**
12.50 mm board to ceilings						
over 300 mm wide	-	0.36	5.32	2.06	m²	**7.38**
12.50 mm board to beams						
girth not exceeding 600 mm	-	0.33	4.88	1.27	m²	**6.15**
girth 600 mm - 1200 mm	-	0.44	6.51	2.47	m²	**8.98**
Gypsum plasterboard to BS 1230; fixing with **nails; joints filled with joint filler and joint tape** **to receive direct decoration; to softwood base**						
Plain grade tapered edge wallboard						
9.50 mm board to walls						
wall height 2.40 m - 2.70 m	-	1.10	12.38	5.86	m	**18.24**
wall height 2.70 m - 3.00 m	-	1.25	14.06	6.52	m	**20.58**
wall height 3.00 m - 3.30 m	-	1.45	16.31	7.17	m	**23.48**
wall height 3.30 m - 3.60 m	-	1.65	18.56	7.87	m	**26.43**
9.50 mm board to reveals and soffits of openings and recesses						
not exceeding 300 mm wide	-	0.22	2.48	1.20	m	**3.68**
300 mm - 600 mm wide	-	0.44	4.96	1.71	m	**6.67**
9.50 mm board to faces of columns - 4 nr						
not exceeding 600 mm total girth	-	0.56	6.31	2.43	m	**8.74**
600 mm - 1200 mm total girth	-	1.10	12.38	3.46	m	**15.84**
1200 mm - 1800 mm total girth	-	1.43	16.08	4.48	m	**20.56**
9.50 mm board to ceilings						
over 300 mm wide	-	0.46	5.18	2.17	m²	**7.35**
9.50 mm board to faces of beams - 3 nr						
not exceeding 600 mm total girth	-	0.66	7.43	2.39	m	**9.82**
600 mm - 1200 mm total girth	-	1.21	13.62	3.41	m	**17.03**
1200 mm - 1800 mm total girth	-	1.55	17.44	4.44	m	**21.88**

K LININGS/SHEATHING/DRY PARTITIONING Excluding overheads and profit	PC £	Labour hours	Labour £	Material £	Unit	Total rate £
12.50 mm board to walls						
wall height 2.40 m - 2.70 m	-	1.30	14.63	6.63	m	21.26
wall height 2.70 m - 3.00 m	-	1.45	16.32	7.37	m	23.69
wall height 3.00 m - 3.30 m	-	1.60	18.00	8.12	m	26.12
wall height 3.30 m - 3.60 m	-	1.90	21.38	8.89	m	30.27
12.50 mm board to reveals and soffits of openings and recesses						
not exceeding 300 mm wide	-	0.22	2.48	1.31	m	3.79
300 mm - 600 mm wide	-	0.44	4.96	1.89	m	6.85
12.50 mm board to faces of columns - 4 nr						
not exceeding 600 mm total girth	-	0.56	6.31	2.66	m	8.97
600 mm - 1200 mm total girth	-	1.10	12.38	3.84	m	16.22
1200 mm - 1800 mm total girth	-	1.43	16.08	5.02	m	21.10
12.50 mm board to ceilings						
over 300 mm wide	-	0.48	5.41	2.46	m²	7.87
12.50 mm board to faces of beams - 3 nr						
not exceeding 600 mm total girth	-	0.66	7.43	2.59	m	10.02
600 mm - 1200 mm total girth	-	1.21	13.62	3.78	m	17.40
1200 mm - 1800 mm total girth	-	1.55	17.44	4.96	m	22.40
external angle; with joint tape bedded and covered with "Jointex" or other equal and approved	-	0.13	1.45	0.32	m	1.77
add for "Duplex" insulating grade or other equal and approved	-	-	-	0.50	m²	0.50
Tapered edge plank						
19 mm plank to walls						
wall height 2.40 m - 2.70 m	-	1.20	13.51	8.78	m	22.29
wall height 2.70 m - 3.00 m	-	1.40	15.76	9.76	m	25.52
wall height 3.00 m - 3.30 m	-	1.55	17.44	10.75	m	28.19
wall height 3.30 m - 3.60 m	-	1.85	20.83	11.76	m	32.59
19 mm plank to reveals and soffits of openings and recesses						
not exceeding 300 mm wide	-	0.24	2.71	1.55	m	4.26
300 mm - 600 mm wide	-	0.50	5.64	2.37	m	8.01
19 mm plank to faces of columns - 4 nr						
not exceeding 600 mm total girth	-	0.61	6.88	3.14	m	10.02
600 mm - 1200 mm total girth	-	1.16	13.06	4.80	m	17.86
1200 mm - 1800 mm total girth	-	1.49	16.76	6.46	m	23.22
19 mm plank to ceilings						
over 300 mm wide	-	0.51	5.75	3.25	m²	9.00
19 mm plank to faces of beams - 3 nr						
not exceeding 600 mm total girth	-	0.72	8.12	3.07	m	11.19
600 mm - 1200 mm total girth	-	1.27	14.30	4.73	m	19.03
1200 mm - 1800 mm total girth	-	1.60	18.00	6.39	m	24.39
Thermal Board						
27 mm board to walls						
wall height 2.40 m - 2.70 m	-	1.25	14.08	16.46	m	30.54
wall height 2.70 m - 3.00 m	-	1.45	16.33	18.29	m	34.62
wall height 3.00 m - 3.30 m	-	1.60	18.02	20.13	m	38.15
wall height 3.30 m - 3.60 m	-	1.95	21.96	21.99	m	43.95
27 mm board to reveals and soffits of openings and recesses						
not exceeding 300 mm wide	-	0.25	2.82	2.40	m	5.22
300 mm - 600 mm wide	-	0.51	5.75	4.07	m	9.82
27 mm board to faces of columns - 4 nr						
not exceeding 600 mm total girth	-	0.62	6.99	4.84	m	11.83
600 mm - 1200 mm total girth	-	1.22	13.74	8.21	m	21.95
1200 mm - 1800 mm total girth	-	1.54	17.33	11.57	m	28.90
27 mm board to ceilings						
over 300 mm wide	-	0.55	6.20	6.10	m²	12.30

K LININGS/SHEATHING/DRY PARTITIONING Excluding overheads and profit	PC £	Labour hours	Labour £	Material £	Unit	Total rate £
K10 PLASTERBOARD DRY LINING/PARTITIONS/ **CEILINGS** - cont'd						
Thermal Board - cont'd						
27 mm board to faces of beams - 3 nr						
not exceeding 600 mm total girth	-	0.67	7.56	4.78	m	**12.34**
600 mm - 1200 mm total girth	-	1.27	14.31	8.14	m	**22.45**
1200 mm - 1800 mm total girth	-	1.71	19.25	11.51	m	**30.76**
50 mm board to walls						
wall height 2.40 m - 2.70 m	-	1.25	14.08	16.31	m	**30.39**
wall height 2.70 m - 3.00 m	-	1.50	16.90	18.15	m	**35.05**
wall height 3.00 m - 3.30 m	-	1.75	19.72	19.96	m	**39.68**
wall height 3.30 m - 3.60 m	-	2.05	23.10	21.82	m	**44.92**
50 mm board to reveals and soffits of openings						
and recesses						
not exceeding 300 mm wide	-	0.28	3.16	2.39	m	**5.55**
300 mm - 600 mm wide	-	0.55	6.20	4.05	m	**10.25**
50 mm board to faces of columns - 4 nr						
not exceeding 600 mm total girth	-	0.67	7.56	4.87	m	**12.43**
600 mm - 1200 mm total girth	-	1.33	14.99	8.19	m	**23.18**
1200 mm - 1800 mm total girth	-	1.71	19.26	11.52	m	**30.78**
50 mm board to ceilings						
over 300 mm wide	-	0.58	6.54	6.05	m²	**12.59**
50 mm board to faces of beams - 3 nr						
not exceeding 600 mm total girth	-	0.70	7.90	4.91	m	**12.81**
600 mm - 1200 mm total girth	-	1.40	15.78	8.28	m	**24.06**
1200 mm - 1800 mm total girth	-	1.88	21.18	11.65	m	**32.83**
White plastic faced gypsum plasterboard to						
BS 1230; industrial grade square edge						
wallboard; fixing with screws; butt joints; to						
softwood base						
9.50 mm board to walls						
wall height 2.40 m - 2.70 m	-	0.75	8.51	8.92	m	**17.43**
wall height 2.70 m - 3.00 m	-	0.95	10.77	9.90	m	**20.67**
wall height 3.00 m - 3.30 m	-	1.10	12.47	10.88	m	**23.35**
wall height 3.30 m - 3.60 m	-	1.25	14.18	11.85	m	**26.03**
9.50 mm board to reveals and soffits of						
openings and recesses						
not exceeding 300 mm wide	-	0.17	1.93	1.02	m	**2.95**
300 mm - 600 mm wide	-	0.33	3.74	1.98	m	**5.72**
9.50 mm board to faces of columns - 4 nr						
not exceeding 600 mm total girth	-	0.44	4.99	2.16	m	**7.15**
600 mm - 1200 mm total girth	-	0.88	9.98	4.22	m	**14.20**
1200 mm - 1800 mm total girth	-	1.15	13.04	6.21	m	**19.25**
12.50 mm board to walls						
wall height 2.40 m - 2.70 m	-	0.85	9.64	9.51	m	**19.15**
wall height 2.70 m - 3.00 m	-	1.00	11.34	10.56	m	**21.90**
wall height 3.00 m - 3.30 m	-	1.15	13.04	11.60	m	**24.64**
wall height 3.30 m - 3.60 m	-	1.30	14.74	12.64	m	**27.38**
12.50 mm board to reveals and soffits of						
openings and recesses						
not exceeding 300 mm wide	-	0.18	2.04	1.09	m	**3.13**
300 mm - 600 mm wide	-	0.35	3.97	2.12	m	**6.09**
12.50 mm board to faces of columns - 4 nr						
not exceeding 600 mm total girth	-	0.46	5.22	2.31	m	**7.53**
600 mm - 1200 mm total girth	-	0.92	10.43	4.51	m	**14.94**
1200 mm - 1800 mm total girth	-	1.21	13.72	6.63	m	**20.35**

K LININGS/SHEATHING/DRY PARTITIONING Excluding overheads and profit	PC £	Labour hours	Labour £	Material £	Unit	Total rate £
Plasterboard jointing system; filling joint with jointing compounds						
To ceilings						
to suit 9.50 mm or 12.50 mm thick boards	-	0.11	1.25	1.43	m	**2.68**
Angle trim; plasterboard edge support system						
To ceilings						
to suit 9.50 mm or 12.50 mm thick boards	-	0.11	1.25	1.35	m	**2.60**
Two layers of gypsum plasterboard to BS 1230; plain grade square and tapered edge wallboard; fixing with nails; joints filled with joint filler and joint tape; top layer to receive direct decoration; to softwood base						
19 mm two layer board to walls						
wall height 2.40 m - 2.70 m	-	1.55	17.48	10.69	m	**28.17**
wall height 2.70 m - 3.00 m	-	1.75	19.73	11.90	m	**31.63**
wall height 3.00 m - 3.30 m	-	2.00	22.55	13.09	m	**35.64**
wall height 3.30 m - 3.60 m	-	2.30	25.93	14.32	m	**40.25**
19 mm two layer board to reveals and soffits of openings and recesses						
not exceeding 300 mm wide	-	0.33	3.73	1.79	m	**5.52**
300 mm - 600 mm wide	-	0.66	7.45	2.81	m	**10.26**
19 mm two layer board to faces of columns - 4 nr						
not exceeding 600 mm total girth	-	0.83	9.37	3.67	m	**13.04**
600 mm - 1200 mm total girth	-	1.60	18.05	5.74	m	**23.79**
1200 mm - 1800 mm total girth	-	1.98	22.32	7.80	m	**30.12**
25 mm two layer board to walls						
wall height 2.40 m - 2.70 m	-	1.65	18.61	12.09	m	**30.70**
wall height 2.70 m - 3.00 m	-	1.85	20.87	13.45	m	**34.32**
wall height 3.00 m - 3.30 m	-	2.10	23.68	14.80	m	**38.48**
wall height 3.30 m - 3.60 m	-	2.45	27.63	16.18	m	**43.81**
25 mm two layer board to reveals and soffits of openings and recesses						
not exceeding 300 mm wide	-	0.33	3.73	1.97	m	**5.70**
300 mm - 600 mm wide	-	0.66	7.45	3.14	m	**10.59**
25 mm two layer board to faces of columns - 4 nr						
not exceeding 600 mm total girth	-	0.83	9.37	4.03	m	**13.40**
600 mm - 1200 mm total girth	-	1.60	18.05	6.40	m	**24.45**
1200 mm - 1800 mm total girth	-	1.98	22.32	8.76	m	**31.08**
Gyproc Dri-Wall dry lining system or other equal and approved; plain grade tapered edge wallboard; fixed to walls with adhesive; joints filled with joint filler and joint tape; to receive direct decoration						
9.50 mm board to walls						
wall height 2.40 m - 2.70 m	-	1.30	14.64	7.26	m	**21.90**
wall height 2.70 m - 3.00 m	-	1.50	16.90	8.06	m	**24.96**
wall height 3.00 m - 3.30 m	-	1.75	19.71	8.85	m	**28.56**
wall height 3.30 m - 3.60 m	-	2.00	22.53	9.69	m	**32.22**
9.50 mm board to reveals and soffits of openings and recesses						
not exceeding 300 mm wide	-	0.28	3.16	1.30	m	**4.46**
300 mm - 600 mm wide	-	0.55	6.20	1.97	m	**8.17**
9.50 mm board to faces of columns - 4 nr						
not exceeding 600 mm total girth	-	0.70	7.90	2.61	m	**10.51**
600 mm - 1200 mm total girth	-	1.36	15.33	4.05	m	**19.38**
1200 mm - 1800 mm total girth	-	1.71	19.26	5.26	m	**24.52**
Angle; with joint tape bedded and covered with "Jointex" or other equal and approved						
internal	-	0.07	0.78	0.32	m	**1.10**
external	-	0.13	1.45	0.32	m	**1.77**

K LININGS/SHEATHING/DRY PARTITIONING Excluding overheads and profit	PC £	Labour hours	Labour £	Material £	Unit	Total rate £
K10 PLASTERBOARD DRY LINING/PARTITIONS/ **CEILINGS** - cont'd						
Gyproc Dri-Wall M/F dry lining system or other **equal and approved; mild steel firrings fixed to** **walls with adhesive; tapered edge wallboard** **screwed to firrings; joints filled with joint filler** **and joint tape**						
12.50 mm board to walls						
wall height 2.40 m - 2.70 m	-	1.75	19.75	12.70	m	**32.45**
wall height 2.70 m - 3.00 m	-	2.00	22.57	14.09	m	**36.66**
wall height 3.00 m - 3.30 m	-	2.30	25.95	15.51	m	**41.46**
wall height 3.30 m - 3.60 m	-	2.65	29.90	16.96	m	**46.86**
12.50 mm board to reveals and soffits of openings and recesses						
not exceeding 300 mm wide	-	0.28	3.16	1.18	m	**4.34**
300 mm - 600 mm wide	-	0.55	6.20	1.71	m	**7.91**
add for one coat of "Dry-Wall" top coat or other equal and approved	-	0.06	0.67	0.70	m²	**1.37**
Vermiculite gypsum cladding; "Vicuclad 900R" **board or other equal and approved; fixed with** **adhesive; joints pointed in adhesive**						
25 mm thick column linings, faces - 4; 2 hour fire protection rating						
not exceeding 600 mm girth	-	0.83	9.41	13.54	m	**22.95**
600 mm - 1200 mm girth	-	0.99	11.23	26.89	m	**38.12**
1200 mm - 1800 mm girth	-	1.38	15.65	40.23	m	**55.88**
30 mm thick beam linings, faces - 3; 2 hour fire protection rating						
not exceeding 600 mm girth	-	0.66	7.48	16.06	m	**23.54**
600 mm - 1200 mm girth	-	0.83	9.41	31.94	m	**41.35**
1200 mm - 1800 mm girth	-	0.99	11.23	47.81	m	**59.04**
Vermiculite gypsum cladding; "Vicuclad 1050R" **board or other equal and approved; fixed with** **adhesive; joints pointed in adhesive**						
55 mm thick column linings, faces - 4 ; 4 hour fire protection rating						
not exceeding 600 mm girth	-	0.99	11.23	36.29	m	**47.52**
600 mm - 1200 mm girth	-	1.21	13.72	72.40	m	**86.12**
1200 mm - 1800 mm girth	-	1.65	18.71	108.50	m	**127.21**
60 mm thick beam linings, faces - 3; 4 hour fire protection rating						
not exceeding 600 mm girth	-	0.83	9.41	39.81	m	**49.22**
600 mm - 1200 mm girth	-	0.99	11.23	79.43	m	**90.66**
1200 mm - 1800 mm girth	-	1.21	13.72	119.05	m	**132.77**
Add to the above for						
plus 3% for work 3.50 m - 5.00 m high						
plus 6% for work 5.00 m - 6.50 m high						
plus 12% for work 6.50 m - 8.00 m high						
plus 18% for work over 8.00 m high						
Cutting and fitting around steel joints, angles, trunking, ducting, ventilators, pipes, tubes, etc.						
over 2.00 m girth	-	0.49	5.56	-	m	**5.56**
not exceeding 0.30 m girth	-	0.33	3.74	-	nr	**3.74**
0.30 m - 1.00 m girth	-	0.44	4.99	-	nr	**4.99**
1.00 m - 2.00 m girth	-	0.61	6.92	-	nr	**6.92**

K LININGS/SHEATHING/DRY PARTITIONING Excluding overheads and profit	PC £	Labour hours	Labour £	Material £	Unit	Total rate £
K11 RIGID SHEET FLOORING/SHEATHING/ **LININGS/CASING**						
Blockboard (Birch faced)						
Lining to walls 12 mm thick						
over 300 mm wide	8.91	0.52	5.90	9.73	m²	**15.63**
not exceeding 300 mm wide	-	0.34	3.86	2.93	m	**6.79**
holes for pipes and the like	-	0.04	0.45	-	nr	**0.45**
Two-sided 12 mm thick pipe casing; to						
softwood framing (not included)						
300 mm girth	-	0.85	9.64	2.99	m	**12.63**
600 mm girth	-	1.00	11.34	5.86	m	**17.20**
Three-sided 12 mm thick pipe casing; to						
softwood framing (not included)						
450 mm girth	-	1.10	12.47	4.48	m	**16.95**
900 mm girth	-	1.30	14.74	8.81	m	**23.55**
extra for 400 mm x 400 mm removable access						
panel; brass cups and screws; additional framing	-	1.10	12.47	0.73	nr	**13.20**
Lining to walls 18 mm thick						
over 300 mm wide	12.45	0.55	6.24	13.54	m²	**19.78**
not exceeding 300 mm wide	-	0.35	3.97	4.07	m	**8.04**
holes for pipes and the like	-	0.06	0.68	-	nr	**0.68**
Lining to walls 25 mm thick						
over 300 mm wide	16.21	0.59	6.69	17.62	m²	**24.31**
not exceeding 300 mm wide	-	0.39	4.42	5.28	m	**9.70**
holes for pipes and the like	-	0.07	0.79	-	nr	**0.79**
Chipboard (plain)						
Lining to walls 12 mm thick						
over 300 mm wide	1.99	0.42	4.76	2.29	m²	**7.05**
not exceeding 300 mm wide	-	0.24	2.72	0.70	m	**3.42**
holes for pipes and the like	-	0.03	0.34	-	nr	**0.34**
Lining to walls 15 mm thick						
over 300 mm wide	2.28	0.44	4.99	2.60	m²	**7.59**
not exceeding 300 mm wide	-	0.26	2.95	0.79	m	**3.74**
holes for pipes and the like	-	0.04	0.45	-	nr	**0.45**
Two-sided 15 mm thick pipe casing; to						
softwood framing (not included)						
300 mm girth	-	0.65	7.37	0.85	m	**8.22**
600 mm girth	-	0.75	8.51	1.58	m	**10.09**
Three-sided 15 mm thick pipe casing; to						
softwood framing (not included)						
450 mm girth	-	1.40	15.88	1.27	m	**17.15**
900 mm girth	-	1.65	18.71	2.39	m	**21.10**
extra for 400 mm x 400 mm removable access						
panel; brass cups and screws; additional framing	-	1.10	12.47	0.73	nr	**13.20**
Lining to walls 18 mm thick						
over 300 mm wide	2.73	0.46	5.22	3.13	m²	**8.35**
not exceeding 300 mm wide	-	0.30	3.40	0.94	m	**4.34**
holes for pipes and the like	-	0.06	0.68	-	nr	**0.68**
Fire-retardant chipboard; Antivlam or other equal						
and approved; Class 1 spread of flame						
Lining to walls 12 mm thick						
over 300 mm wide	-	0.42	4.76	8.45	m²	**13.21**
not exceeding 300 mm wide	-	0.24	2.72	2.55	m	**5.27**
holes for pipes and the like	-	0.03	0.34	-	nr	**0.34**
Lining to walls 18 mm thick						
over 300 mm wide	-	0.46	5.22	11.16	m²	**16.38**
not exceeding 300 mm wide	-	0.30	3.40	3.36	m	**6.76**
holes for pipes and the like	-	0.06	0.68	-	nr	**0.68**

K LININGS/SHEATHING/DRY PARTITIONING Excluding overheads and profit	PC £	Labour hours	Labour £	Material £	Unit	Total rate £
K11 RIGID SHEET FLOORING/SHEATHING/ LININGS/CASING - cont'd						
Fire-retardant chipboard; Antivlam or other equal and approved; Class 1 spread of flame - cont'd						
Lining to walls 22 mm thick						
over 300 mm wide	-	0.48	5.44	14.20	m²	**19.64**
not exceeding 300 mm wide	-	0.33	3.74	4.27	m	**8.01**
holes for pipes and the like	-	0.07	0.79	-	nr	**0.79**
Chipboard; melamine faced; white matt finish; laminated masking strips						
Lining to walls 15 mm thick						
over 300 mm wide	3.67	1.15	13.04	4.26	m²	**17.30**
not exceeding 300 mm wide	-	0.75	8.51	1.35	m	**9.86**
holes for pipes and the like	-	0.08	0.91	-	nr	**0.91**
Chipboard boarding and flooring						
Boarding to floors; butt joints						
18 mm thick	2.67	0.33	3.74	3.06	m²	**6.80**
22 mm thick	3.46	0.36	4.08	3.91	m²	**7.99**
Boarding to floors; tongued and grooved joints						
18 mm thick	2.82	0.35	3.97	3.22	m²	**7.19**
22 mm thick	3.46	0.39	4.42	3.91	m²	**8.33**
Boarding to roofs; butt joints						
18 mm thick	3.50	0.36	4.08	3.96	m²	**8.04**
Durabella "Westbourne" flooring system or other equal and approved; comprising 19 mm thick tongued and grooved chipboard panels secret nailed to softwood MK 10X-profiled foam backed battens at 600 mm centres; on concrete floor						
Flooring tongued and grooved joints						
63 mm thick overall; 44 mm x 54 mm nominal size battens	-	-	-	-	m²	**18.75**
75 mm thick overall; 56 mm x 54 mm nominal size battens	-	-	-	-	m²	**20.25**
Plywood flooring						
Boarding to floors; tongued and grooved joints						
15 mm thick	15.85	0.44	4.99	17.23	m²	**22.22**
18 mm thick	18.41	0.48	5.44	19.98	m²	**25.42**
Plywood; external quality; 18 mm thick						
Boarding to roofs; butt joints						
flat to falls	12.41	0.44	4.99	13.53	m²	**18.52**
sloping	12.41	0.47	5.33	13.53	m²	**18.86**
vertical	12.41	0.63	7.14	13.53	m²	**20.67**
Plywood; external quality; 12 mm thick						
Boarding to roofs; butt joints						
flat to falls	8.28	0.44	4.99	9.09	m²	**14.08**
sloping	8.28	0.47	5.33	9.09	m²	**14.42**
vertical	8.28	0.63	7.14	9.09	m²	**16.23**
Glazed hardboard to BS 1142; on and including 38 mm x 38 mm sawn softwood framing						
3.20 mm thick panel						
to side of bath	-	1.98	22.45	4.18	nr	**26.63**
to end of bath	-	0.77	8.73	1.15	nr	**9.88**

K LININGS/SHEATHING/DRY PARTITIONING Excluding overheads and profit	PC £	Labour hours	Labour £	Material £	Unit	Total rate £
Insulation board to BS 1142						
Lining to walls 12 mm thick						
over 300 mm wide	1.55	0.26	2.95	1.81	m²	**4.76**
not exceeding 300 mm wide	-	0.15	1.70	0.56	m	**2.26**
holes for pipes and the like	-	0.01	0.11	-	nr	**0.11**
Lining to walls 18 mm thick						
over 300 mm wide	2.44	0.29	3.29	2.77	m²	**6.06**
not exceeding 300 mm wide	-	0.18	2.04	0.84	m	**2.88**
holes for pipes and the like	-	0.01	0.11	-	nr	**0.11**
Laminboard (Birch Faced); 18 mm thick						
Lining to walls						
over 300 mm wide	15.54	0.58	6.58	16.86	m²	**23.44**
not exceeding 300 mm wide	-	0.37	4.20	5.07	m	**9.27**
holes for pipes and the like	-	0.07	0.79	-	nr	**0.79**
Non-asbestos board; "Masterboard" or other equal and approved; sanded finish						
Lining to walls 6 mm thick						
over 300 mm wide	8.07	0.36	4.08	8.79	m²	**12.87**
not exceeding 300 mm wide	-	0.22	2.49	2.64	m	**5.13**
Lining to ceilings 6 mm thick						
over 300 mm wide	8.07	0.48	5.44	8.79	m²	**14.23**
not exceeding 300 mm wide	-	0.30	3.40	2.64	m	**6.04**
holes for pipes and the like	-	0.03	0.34	-	nr	**0.34**
Lining to walls 9 mm thick						
over 300 mm wide	16.63	0.40	4.54	17.99	m²	**22.53**
not exceeding 300 mm wide	-	0.22	2.49	5.40	m	**7.89**
Lining to ceilings 9 mm thick						
over 300 mm wide	16.63	0.49	5.56	17.99	m²	**23.55**
not exceeding 300 mm wide	-	0.32	3.63	5.40	m	**9.03**
holes for pipes and the like	-	0.04	0.45	-	nr	**0.45**
Non-asbestos board; "Supalux" or other equal and approved; sanded finish						
Lining to walls 6 mm thick						
over 300 mm wide	12.05	0.36	4.08	13.07	m²	**17.15**
not exceeding 300 mm wide	-	0.22	2.49	3.92	m	**6.41**
Lining to ceilings 6 mm thick						
over 300 mm wide	12.05	0.48	5.44	13.07	m²	**18.51**
not exceeding 300 mm wide	-	0.30	3.40	3.92	m	**7.32**
holes for pipes and the like	-	0.03	0.34	-	nr	**0.34**
Lining to walls 9 mm thick						
over 300 mm wide	17.92	0.40	4.54	19.38	m²	**23.92**
not exceeding 300 mm wide	-	0.22	2.49	5.82	m	**8.31**
Lining to ceilings 9 mm thick						
over 300 mm wide	17.92	0.49	5.56	19.38	m²	**24.94**
not exceeding 300 mm wide	-	0.32	3.63	5.82	m	**9.45**
holes for pipes and the like	-	0.04	0.45	-	nr	**0.45**
Lining to walls 12 mm thick						
over 300 mm wide	23.73	0.44	4.99	25.62	m²	**30.61**
not exceeding 300 mm wide	-	0.26	2.95	7.69	m	**10.64**
Lining to ceilings 12 mm thick						
over 300 mm wide	23.73	0.58	6.58	25.62	m²	**32.20**
not exceeding 300 mm wide	-	0.35	3.97	7.69	m	**11.66**
holes for pipes and the like	-	0.06	0.68	-	nr	**0.68**

K LININGS/SHEATHING/DRY PARTITIONING Excluding overheads and profit	PC £	Labour hours	Labour £	Material £	Unit	Total rate £
K11 RIGID SHEET FLOORING/SHEATHING/ LININGS/CASING - cont'd						
Non-asbestos board; "Monolux 40" or other equal and approved; 6 mm x 50 mm "Supalux" cover fillets or other equal and approved one side						
Lining to walls 19 mm thick						
over 300 mm wide	43.06	0.77	8.73	48.21	m²	56.94
not exceeding 300 mm wide	-	0.55	6.24	16.18	m	22.42
Lining to walls 25 mm thick						
over 300 mm wide	51.61	0.83	9.41	57.40	m²	66.81
not exceeding 300 mm wide	-	0.58	6.58	18.94	m	25.52
Plywood (Far Eastern); internal quality						
Lining to walls 4 mm thick						
over 300 mm wide	1.77	0.41	4.65	2.05	m²	6.70
not exceeding 300 mm wide	-	0.26	2.95	0.63	m	3.58
Lining to ceilings 4 mm thick						
over 300 mm wide	1.77	0.55	6.24	2.05	m²	8.29
not exceeding 300 mm wide	-	0.35	3.97	0.63	m	4.60
holes for pipes and the like	-	0.03	0.34	-	nr	0.34
Lining to walls 6 mm thick						
over 300 mm wide	2.09	0.44	4.99	2.40	m²	7.39
not exceeding 300 mm wide	-	0.29	3.29	0.73	m	4.02
Lining to ceilings 6 mm thick						
over 300 mm wide	2.09	0.58	6.58	2.40	m²	8.98
not exceeding 300 mm wide	-	0.39	4.42	0.73	m	5.15
holes for pipes and the like	-	0.03	0.34	-	nr	0.34
Two-sided 6 mm thick pipe casings; to softwood framing (not included)						
300 mm girth	-	0.90	10.21	0.79	m	11.00
600 mm girth	-	1.10	12.47	1.47	m	13.94
Three-sided 6 mm thick pipe casing; to softwood framing (not included)						
450 mm girth	-	1.25	14.18	1.18	m	15.36
900 mm girth	-	1.50	17.01	2.22	m	19.23
Lining to walls 9 mm thick						
over 300 mm wide	3.06	0.47	5.33	3.45	m²	8.78
not exceeding 300 mm wide	-	0.31	3.52	1.05	m	4.57
Lining to ceilings 9 mm thick						
over 300 mm wide	3.06	0.63	7.14	3.45	m²	10.59
not exceeding 300 mm wide	-	0.41	4.65	1.05	m	5.70
holes for pipes and the like	-	0.04	0.45	-	nr	0.45
Lining to walls 12 mm thick						
over 300 mm wide	3.95	0.51	5.78	4.40	m²	10.18
not exceeding 300 mm wide	-	0.33	3.74	1.33	m	5.07
Lining to ceilings 12 mm thick						
over 300 mm wide	3.95	0.67	7.60	4.40	m²	12.00
not exceeding 300 mm wide	-	0.44	4.99	1.33	m	6.32
holes for pipes and the like	-	0.04	0.45	-	nr	0.45
Plywood (Far Eastern); external quality						
Lining to walls 4 mm thick						
over 300 mm wide	3.19	0.41	4.65	3.58	m²	8.23
not exceeding 300 mm wide	-	0.26	2.95	1.09	m	4.04
Lining to ceilings 4 mm thick						
over 300 mm wide	3.19	0.55	6.24	3.58	m²	9.82
not exceeding 300 mm wide	-	0.35	3.97	1.09	m	5.06
holes for pipes and the like	-	0.03	0.34	-	nr	0.34
Lining to walls 6 mm thick						
over 300 mm wide	4.20	0.44	4.99	4.67	m²	9.66
not exceeding 300 mm wide	-	0.29	3.29	1.41	m	4.70

K LININGS/SHEATHING/DRY PARTITIONING Excluding overheads and profit	PC £	Labour hours	Labour £	Material £	Unit	Total rate £
Lining to ceilings 6 mm thick						
over 300 mm wide	4.20	0.58	6.58	4.67	m²	11.25
not exceeding 300 mm wide	-	0.39	4.42	1.41	m	5.83
holes for pipes and the like	-	0.03	0.34	-	nr	0.34
Two-sided 6 mm thick pipe casings; to						
softwood framing (not included)						
300 mm girth	-	0.90	10.21	1.47	m	11.68
600 mm girth	-	1.10	12.47	2.82	m	15.29
Three-sided 6 mm thick pipe casing; to						
softwood framing (not included)						
450 mm girth	-	1.25	14.18	2.20	m	16.38
900 mm girth	-	1.50	17.01	4.26	m	21.27
Lining to walls 9 mm thick						
over 300 mm wide	5.59	0.47	5.33	6.17	m²	11.50
not exceeding 300 mm wide	-	0.31	3.52	1.86	m	5.38
Lining to ceilings 9 mm thick						
over 300 mm wide	5.59	0.63	7.14	6.17	m²	13.31
not exceeding 300 mm wide	-	0.41	4.65	1.86	m	6.51
holes for pipes and the like	-	0.04	0.45	-	nr	0.45
Lining to walls 12 mm thick						
over 300 mm wide	7.43	0.51	5.78	8.14	m²	13.92
not exceeding 300 mm wide	-	0.33	3.74	2.45	m	6.19
Lining to ceilings 12 mm thick						
over 300 mm wide	7.43	0.67	7.60	8.14	m²	15.74
not exceeding 300 mm wide	-	0.44	4.99	2.45	m	7.44
holes for pipes and the like	-	0.04	0.45	-	nr	0.45
Extra over wall linings fixed with nails for						
screwing	-	-	-	-	m²	1.54
Preformed white melamine faced plywood casings;						
Pendock Profiles Ltd or other equal and approved;						
to softwood battens (not included)						
Skirting trunking profile; plain butt joints in the						
running length						
45 mm x 150 mm; ref TK150	-	0.13	1.47	7.61	m	9.08
extra for stop end	-	0.06	0.68	6.32	nr	7.00
extra for external corner	-	0.11	1.25	7.80	nr	9.05
extra for internal corner	-	0.11	1.25	5.84	nr	7.09
Casing profiles						
150 mm x 150 mm ref MX150/150; 5 mm thick	-	0.13	1.47	12.12	m	13.59
extra for stop end	-	0.06	0.68	4.97	nr	5.65
extra for external corner	-	0.11	1.25	18.42	nr	19.67
extra for internal corner	-	0.11	1.25	5.84	nr	7.09
Woodwool unreinforced slabs; Torvale "Woodcemair"						
or other equal and approved; BS 1105 type SB;						
natural finish; fixing to timber or steel with galvanized						
nails or clips; flat or sloping						
50 mm thick slabs; type 500; 600 mm						
maximum span						
1800 mm - 2400 mm lengths	6.13	0.44	4.99	6.65	m²	11.64
2700 mm - 3000 mm lengths	6.28	0.44	4.99	6.80	m²	11.79
75 mm thick slabs; type 750; 900 mm						
maximum span						
2100 mm lengths	7.30	0.49	5.56	7.91	m²	13.47
2400 mm - 2700 mm lengths	7.41	0.49	5.56	8.03	m²	13.59
3000 mm lengths	7.42	0.49	5.56	8.04	m²	13.60
100 mm thick slabs; type 1000; 1200 mm						
maximum span						
3000 mm - 3600 mm lengths	10.11	0.55	6.24	10.82	m²	17.06

K LININGS/SHEATHING/DRY PARTITIONING Excluding overheads and profit	PC £	Labour hours	Labour £	Material £	Unit	Total rate £
K11 RIGID SHEET FLOORING/SHEATHING/ LININGS/CASING - cont'd						
Internal quality American Cherry veneered plywood; 6 mm thick						
Lining to walls						
over 300 mm wide	5.32	0.48	5.44	5.83	m²	**11.27**
not exceeding 300 mm wide	-	0.32	3.63	1.77	m	**5.40**
"Tacboard" or other equal and approved; Eternit UK Ltd; fire resisting boards; butt joints; to softwood base						
Lining to walls; 6 mm thick						
over 300 mm wide	-	0.36	4.08	8.96	m²	**13.04**
not exceeding 300 mm wide	-	0.22	2.49	2.71	m	**5.20**
Lining to walls; 9 mm thick						
over 300 mm wide	-	0.40	4.54	18.06	m²	**22.60**
not exceeding 300 mm wide	-	0.24	2.72	5.44	m	**8.16**
Lining to walls; 12 mm thick						
over 300 mm wide	-	0.44	4.99	23.48	m²	**28.47**
not exceeding 300 mm wide	-	0.26	2.95	7.07	m	**10.02**
"Tacfire" or other equal and approved; Eternit UK Ltd; fire resisting boards						
Lining to walls; 6 mm thick						
over 300 mm wide	-	0.36	4.08	13.22	m²	**17.30**
not exceeding 300 mm wide	-	0.22	2.49	3.99	m	**6.48**
Lining to walls; 9 mm thick						
over 300 mm wide	-	0.40	4.54	20.18	m²	**24.72**
not exceeding 300 mm wide	-	0.24	2.72	6.08	m	**8.80**
Lining to walls; 12 mm thick						
over 300 mm wide	-	0.44	4.99	26.60	m²	**31.59**
not exceeding 300 mm wide	-	0.26	2.95	8.00	m	**10.95**
K14 GLASS REINFORCED GYPSUM LININGS/ PANELLING/CASINGS/MOULDINGS						
Glass reinforced gypsum Glasroc Multi-board or other equal and approved; fixing with nails; joints filled with joint filler and joint tape; finishing with "Jointex" or other equal and approved to receive decoration; to softwood base						
10 mm board to walls						
wall height 2.40 m - 2.70 m	-	1.10	12.38	39.69	m	**52.07**
wall height 2.70 m - 3.00 m	-	1.25	14.06	44.11	m	**58.17**
wall height 3.00 m - 3.30 m	-	1.45	16.31	48.52	m	**64.83**
wall height 3.30 m - 3.60 m	-	1.65	18.56	52.97	m	**71.53**
12.50 mm board to walls						
wall height 2.40 m - 2.70 m	-	1.15	12.94	51.81	m	**64.75**
wall height 2.70 m - 3.00 m	-	1.30	14.63	57.57	m	**72.20**
wall height 3.00 m - 3.30 m	-	1.50	16.88	63.34	m	**80.22**
wall height 3.30 m - 3.60 m	-	1.70	19.13	69.13	m	**88.26**
K20 TIMBER BOARD FLOORING/SHEATHING/ LININGS/CASINGS						
Sawn softwood; untreated						
Boarding to roofs; 150 mm wide boards; butt joints						
19 mm thick; flat; over 300 mm wide	-	0.49	5.56	5.75	m²	**11.31**
19 mm thick; flat; not exceeding 300 mm wide	-	0.33	3.74	1.75	m	**5.49**
19 mm thick; sloping; over 300 mm wide	-	0.55	6.24	5.75	m²	**11.99**
19 mm thick; sloping; not exceeding 300 mm wide	-	0.36	4.08	1.75	m	**5.83**

K LININGS/SHEATHING/DRY PARTITIONING Excluding overheads and profit	PC £	Labour hours	Labour £	Material £	Unit	Total rate £
Boarding to roofs; 150 mm wide boards; butt joints - cont'd						
19 mm thick; sloping; laid diagonally; over 300 mm wide	-	0.69	7.82	5.75	m²	13.57
19 mm thick; sloping; laid diagonally; not exceeding 300 mm wide	-	0.44	4.99	1.75	m	6.74
25 mm thick; flat; over 300 mm wide	-	0.49	5.56	7.47	m²	13.03
25 mm thick; flat; not exceeding 300 mm wide	-	0.33	3.74	2.26	m	6.00
25 mm thick; sloping; over 300 mm wide	-	0.55	6.24	7.47	m²	13.71
25 mm thick; sloping; not exceeding 300 mm wide	-	0.36	4.08	2.26	m	6.34
25 mm thick; sloping; laid diagonally; over 300 mm wide	-	0.69	7.82	7.47	m²	15.29
25 mm thick; sloping; laid diagonally; not exceeding 300 mm wide	-	0.44	4.99	2.26	m	7.25
Boarding to tops or cheeks of dormers; 150 mm wide boards; butt joints						
19 mm thick; laid diagonally; over 300 mm wide	-	0.88	9.98	5.75	m²	15.73
19 mm thick; laid diagonally; not exceeding 300 mm wide	-	0.55	6.24	1.75	m	7.99
19 mm thick; laid diagonally; area not exceeding 1.00 m² irrespective of width	-	1.10	12.47	5.51	nr	17.98
Sawn softwood; "Tanalised"						
Boarding to roofs; 150 mm wide boards; butt joints						
19 mm thick; flat; over 300 mm wide	-	0.49	5.56	6.41	m²	11.97
19 mm thick; flat; not exceeding 300 mm wide	-	0.33	3.74	1.94	m	5.68
19 mm thick; sloping; over 300 mm wide	-	0.55	6.24	6.41	m²	12.65
19 mm thick; sloping; not exceeding 300 mm wide	-	0.36	4.08	1.94	m	6.02
19 mm thick; sloping; laid diagonally; over 300 mm wide	-	0.69	7.82	6.41	m²	14.23
19 mm thick; sloping; laid diagonally; not exceeding 300 mm wide	-	0.44	4.99	1.94	m	6.93
25 mm thick; flat; over 300 mm wide	-	0.49	5.56	8.35	m²	13.91
25 mm thick; flat; not exceeding 300 mm wide	-	0.33	3.74	2.52	m	6.26
25 mm thick; sloping; over 300 mm wide	-	0.55	6.24	8.35	m²	14.59
25 mm thick; sloping; not exceeding 300 mm wide	-	0.36	4.08	2.52	m	6.60
25 mm thick; sloping; laid diagonally; over 300 mm wide	-	0.69	7.82	8.35	m²	16.17
25 mm thick; sloping; laid diagonally; not exceeding 300 mm wide	-	0.44	4.99	2.52	m	7.51
Boarding to tops or cheeks of dormers; 150 mm wide boards; butt joints						
19 mm thick; laid diagonally; over 300 mm wide	-	0.88	9.98	6.41	m²	16.39
19 mm thick; laid diagonally; not exceeding 300 mm wide	-	0.55	6.24	1.94	m	8.18
19 mm thick; laid diagonally; area not exceeding 1.00 m² irrespective of width	-	1.10	12.47	6.17	nr	18.64
Wrought softwood						
Boarding to floors; butt joints						
19 mm x 75 mm boards	-	0.66	7.48	6.31	m²	13.79
19 mm x 125 mm boards	-	0.61	6.92	6.98	m²	13.90
22 mm x 150 mm boards	-	0.56	6.35	7.50	m²	13.85
25 mm x 100 mm boards	-	0.61	6.92	8.09	m²	15.01
25 mm x 150 mm boards	-	0.56	6.35	8.68	m²	15.03

K LININGS/SHEATHING/DRY PARTITIONING Excluding overheads and profit	PC £	Labour hours	Labour £	Material £	Unit	Total rate £
K20 TIMBER BOARD FLOORING/SHEATHING/ LININGS/CASINGS - cont'd						
Wrought softwood - cont'd						
25 mm boarding and bearers to floors; butt						
joints; in making good where partitions						
removed or openings formed (boards running						
in direction of partition)						
150 mm wide	-	0.30	3.40	1.58	m	**4.98**
225 mm wide	-	0.45	5.10	2.56	m	**7.66**
300 mm wide	-	0.60	6.80	3.12	m	**9.92**
25 mm boarding and bearers to floors; butt						
joints; in making good where partitions						
removed or openings formed (boards running						
at right angles to partition)						
150 mm wide	-	0.45	5.10	3.74	m	**8.84**
225 mm wide	-	0.70	7.94	4.95	m	**12.89**
300 mm wide	-	0.90	10.21	5.68	m	**15.89**
450 mm wide	-	1.35	15.31	7.45	m	**22.76**
Boarding to floors; tongued and grooved joints						
19 mm x 75 mm boards	-	0.77	8.73	6.91	m²	**15.64**
19 mm x 125 mm boards	-	0.72	8.16	7.58	m²	**15.74**
22 mm x 150 mm boards	-	0.67	7.60	8.09	m²	**15.69**
25 mm x 100 mm boards	-	0.72	8.16	8.68	m²	**16.84**
25 mm x 150 mm boards	-	0.67	7.60	9.28	m²	**16.88**
Boarding to internal walls; tongued and						
grooved and V-jointed						
12 mm x 100 mm boards	-	0.88	9.98	6.38	m²	**16.36**
16 mm x 100 mm boards	-	0.88	9.98	8.58	m²	**18.56**
19 mm x 100 mm boards	-	0.88	9.98	9.63	m²	**19.61**
19 mm x 125 mm boards	-	0.83	9.41	10.21	m²	**19.62**
19 mm x 125 mm boards; chevron pattern	-	1.32	14.97	10.21	m²	**25.18**
25 mm x 125 mm boards	-	0.83	9.41	13.13	m²	**22.54**
12 mm x 100 mm boards; knotty pine	-	0.88	9.98	5.24	m²	**15.22**
Boarding to internal ceilings						
12 mm x 100 mm boards	-	1.10	12.47	6.38	m²	**18.85**
16 mm x 100 mm boards	-	1.10	12.47	8.58	m²	**21.05**
19 mm x 100 mm boards	-	1.10	12.47	9.63	m²	**22.10**
19 mm x 125 mm boards	-	1.05	11.91	10.21	m²	**22.12**
19 mm x 125 mm boards; chevron pattern	-	1.54	17.46	10.21	m²	**27.67**
25 mm x 125 mm boards	-	1.05	11.91	13.13	m²	**25.04**
12 mm x 100 mm boards; knotty pine	-	1.10	12.47	5.24	m²	**17.71**
Boarding to roofs; tongued and grooved joints						
19 mm thick; flat to falls	-	0.61	6.92	7.62	m²	**14.54**
19 mm thick; sloping	-	0.66	7.48	7.62	m²	**15.10**
19 mm thick; sloping; laid diagonally	-	0.85	9.64	7.62	m²	**17.26**
25 mm thick; flat to falls	-	0.61	6.92	9.20	m²	**16.12**
25 mm thick; sloping	-	0.66	7.48	9.20	m²	**16.68**
Boarding to tops or cheeks of dormers;						
tongued and grooved joints						
19 mm thick; laid diagonally	-	1.10	12.47	7.62	m²	**20.09**
Wrought softwood; "Tanalised"						
Boarding to roofs; tongued and grooved joints						
19 mm thick; flat to falls	-	0.61	6.92	8.28	m²	**15.20**
19 mm thick; sloping	-	0.66	7.48	8.28	m²	**15.76**
19 mm thick; sloping; laid diagonally	-	0.85	9.64	8.28	m²	**17.92**
25 mm thick; flat to falls	-	0.61	6.92	10.07	m²	**16.99**
25 mm thick; sloping	-	0.66	7.48	10.07	m²	**17.55**
Boarding to tops or cheeks of dormers;						
tongued and grooved joints						
19 mm thick; laid diagonally	-	1.10	12.47	8.28	m²	**20.75**

K LININGS/SHEATHING/DRY PARTITIONING Excluding overheads and profit	PC £	Labour hours	Labour £	Material £	Unit	Total rate £
Wood strip; 22 mm thick; "Junckers" pre-treated or **other equal and approved; tongued and grooved** **joints; pre-finished boards; level fixing to** **resilient battens; to cement and sand base**						
Strip flooring; over 300 mm wide						
beech; prime	-	-	-	-	m²	50.40
beech; standard	-	-	-	-	m²	47.50
beech; sylvia squash	-	-	-	-	m²	50.00
oak; quality A	-	-	-	-	m²	60.15
Wrought hardwood						
Strip flooring to floors; 25 mm thick x 75 mm						
wide; tongue and grooved joints; secret fixing;						
surface sanded after laying						
american oak	-	-	-	-	m²	36.85
canadian maple	-	-	-	-	m²	39.70
gurjun	-	-	-	-	m²	36.15
iroko	-	-	-	-	m²	34.80

L WINDOWS/DOORS/STAIRS Excluding overheads and profit	PC £	Labour hours	Labour £	Material £	Unit	Total rate £
L WINDOWS/DOORS/STAIRS						
L10 WINDOWS/ROOFLIGHTS/SCREENS/ LOUVRES						
Standard windows; "treated" wrought softwood; **Rugby Joinery or other equal and approved** Side hung casement windows without glazing bars; with 140 mm wide softwood sills; opening casements and ventilators hung on rustproof hinges; fitted with aluminized lacquered finish casement stays and fasteners						
500 mm x 750 mm; ref N07V	47.90	0.75	8.51	48.09	nr	**56.60**
500 mm x 900 mm; ref N09V	49.78	0.90	10.21	49.97	nr	**60.18**
600 mm x 750 mm; ref 107V	60.10	0.90	10.21	60.29	nr	**70.50**
600 mm x 750 mm; ref 107C	64.27	0.90	10.21	64.46	nr	**74.67**
600 mm x 900 mm; ref 109V	60.33	1.00	11.34	60.52	nr	**71.86**
600 mm x 900 mm; ref 109C	65.75	0.90	10.21	65.94	nr	**76.15**
600 mm x 1050 mm; ref 109V	61.94	0.90	10.21	62.19	nr	**72.40**
600 mm x 1050 mm; ref 110V	66.06	1.10	12.47	66.31	nr	**78.78**
915 mm x 900 mm; ref 2NO9W	75.48	1.20	13.61	75.67	nr	**89.28**
915 mm x 1050 mm; ref 2N1OW	76.65	1.25	14.18	76.90	nr	**91.08**
915 mm x 1200 mm; ref 2N12W	83.38	1.30	14.74	83.63	nr	**98.37**
915 mm x 1350 mm; ref 2N13W	85.22	1.50	17.01	85.47	nr	**102.48**
915 mm x 1500 mm; ref 2N15W	86.47	1.55	17.58	86.78	nr	**104.36**
1200 mm x 750 mm; ref 2O7C	82.88	1.25	14.18	83.13	nr	**97.31**
1200 mm x 750 mm; ref 2O7CV	105.76	1.25	14.18	106.01	nr	**120.19**
1200 mm x 900 mm; ref 2O9C	84.99	1.30	14.74	85.24	nr	**99.98**
1200 mm x 900 mm; ref 2O9W	91.41	1.30	14.74	91.66	nr	**106.40**
1200 mm x 900 mm; ref 2O9CV	106.87	1.30	14.74	107.12	nr	**121.86**
1200 mm x 1050 mm; ref 210C	85.08	1.50	17.01	85.39	nr	**102.40**
1200 mm x 1050 mm; ref 210W	93.15	1.50	17.01	93.46	nr	**110.47**
1200 mm x 1050 mm; ref 210T	109.98	1.50	17.01	110.29	nr	**127.30**
1200 mm x 1050 mm; ref 210CV	107.02	1.50	17.01	107.33	nr	**124.34**
1200 mm x 1200 mm; ref 212C	88.72	1.60	18.14	89.10	nr	**107.24**
1200 mm x 1200 mm; ref 212W	95.08	1.60	18.14	95.46	nr	**113.60**
1200 mm x 1200 mm; ref 212TX	119.48	1.60	18.14	119.86	nr	**138.00**
1200 mm x 1200 mm; ref 212CV	110.69	1.60	18.14	111.07	nr	**129.21**
1200 mm x 1350 mm; ref 213W	97.19	1.70	19.28	97.57	nr	**116.85**
1200 mm x 1350 mm; ref 213CV	123.47	1.70	19.28	123.85	nr	**143.13**
1200 mm x 1500 mm; ref 215W	99.66	1.85	20.98	100.10	nr	**121.08**
1770 mm x 750 mm; ref 307CC	126.03	1.55	17.58	126.41	nr	**143.99**
1770 mm x 900 mm; ref 309CC	129.26	1.85	20.98	129.64	nr	**150.62**
1770 mm x 1050 mm; ref 310C	107.46	1.95	22.11	107.84	nr	**129.95**
1770 mm x 1050 mm; ref 310T	129.53	1.85	20.98	129.91	nr	**150.89**
1770 mm x 1050 mm; ref 310CC	129.80	1.55	17.58	130.18	nr	**147.76**
1770 mm x 1050 mm; ref 310WW	151.01	1.55	17.58	151.39	nr	**168.97**
1770 mm x 1200 mm; ref 312C	110.87	2.00	22.68	111.31	nr	**133.99**
1770 mm x 1200 mm; ref 312T	133.38	2.00	22.68	133.82	nr	**156.50**
1770 mm x 1200 mm; ref 312CC	134.82	2.00	22.68	135.26	nr	**157.94**
1770 mm x 1200 mm; ref 312WW	155.10	2.00	22.68	155.54	nr	**178.22**
1770 mm x 1200 mm; ref 312CVC	166.26	2.00	22.68	166.70	nr	**189.38**
1770 mm x 1350 mm; ref 313CC	153.16	2.10	23.81	153.60	nr	**177.41**
1770 mm x 1350 mm; ref 313WW	158.86	2.10	23.81	159.30	nr	**183.11**
1770 mm x 1350 mm; ref 313CVC	176.48	2.10	23.81	176.92	nr	**200.73**
1770 mm x 1500 mm; ref 315T	140.16	2.20	24.95	140.60	nr	**165.55**
2340 mm x 1050 mm; ref 410CWC	189.26	2.15	24.38	189.70	nr	**214.08**
2340 mm x 1200 mm; ref 412CWC	195.59	2.25	25.52	196.09	nr	**221.61**
2340 mm x 1350 mm; ref 413CWC	206.80	2.40	27.22	207.37	nr	**234.59**

L WINDOWS/DOORS/STAIRS Excluding overheads and profit	PC £	Labour hours	Labour £	Material £	Unit	Total rate £
Top hung casement windows; with 140 mm wide softwood sills; opening casements and ventilators hung on rustproof hinges; fitted with aluminized lacquered finish casement stays						
600 mm x 750 mm; ref 107A	69.42	0.90	10.21	69.61	nr	79.82
600 mm x 900 mm; ref 109A	71.81	1.00	11.34	72.00	nr	83.34
600 mm x 1050 mm; ref 110A	74.99	1.10	12.47	75.24	nr	87.71
915 mm x 750 mm; ref 2N07A	84.45	1.15	13.04	84.64	nr	97.68
915 mm x 900 mm; ref 2N09A	91.05	1.20	13.61	91.24	nr	104.85
915 mm x 1050 mm; ref 2N10A	94.59	1.25	14.18	94.84	nr	109.02
915 mm x 1350 mm; ref 2N13AS	108.10	1.50	17.01	108.41	nr	125.42
1200 mm x 750 mm; ref 207A	95.85	1.25	14.18	96.10	nr	110.28
1200 mm x 900 mm; ref 209A	101.86	1.30	14.74	102.11	nr	116.85
1200 mm x 1050 mm; ref 210A	105.35	1.50	17.01	105.66	nr	122.67
1200 mm x 1200 mm; ref 212A	108.72	1.60	18.14	109.03	nr	127.17
1200 mm x 1350 mm; ref 213AS	119.48	1.70	19.28	119.86	nr	139.14
1200 mm x 1500 mm; ref 215AS	122.94	1.85	20.98	123.32	nr	144.30
1770 mm x 1050 mm; ref 310AE	125.22	1.85	20.98	125.60	nr	146.58
1770 mm x 1200 mm; ref 312A	129.17	2.00	22.68	129.55	nr	152.23
High performance single light with canopy sash windows; ventilators; weather stripping; opening sashes and fanlights hung on rustproof hinges; fitted with aluminized lacquered espagnolette bolts						
600 mm x 900 mm; ref AL0609	162.14	1.00	11.34	162.33	nr	173.67
900 mm x 900 mm; ref AL0909	168.20	1.20	13.61	168.39	nr	182.00
900 mm x 1050 mm; ref AL0910	169.10	1.25	14.18	169.29	nr	183.47
900 mm x 1200 mm; ref AL0912	172.45	1.40	15.88	172.70	nr	188.58
900 mm x 1500 mm; ref AL0915	181.70	1.55	17.58	181.95	nr	199.53
1200 mm x 1050 mm; ref AL1210	195.98	1.50	17.01	196.23	nr	213.24
1200 mm x 1200 mm; ref AL1212	197.24	1.60	18.14	197.55	nr	215.69
1200 mm x 1500 mm; ref AL1215	222.68	1.85	20.98	223.06	nr	244.04
1500 mm x 1050 mm; ref AL1510	196.32	1.80	20.41	196.63	nr	217.04
1500 mm x 1200 mm; ref AL1512	206.15	1.85	20.98	206.46	nr	227.44
1500 mm x 1500 mm; ref AL1515	222.02	2.00	22.68	222.46	nr	245.14
1500 mm x 1650 mm; ref AL1516	229.14	2.10	23.81	229.52	nr	253.33
High performance double hung sash windows with glazing bars; solid frames; 63 mm x 175 mm softwood sills; standard flush external linings; spiral spring balances and sash catch						
635 mm x 1050 mm; ref VS0610B	272.98	2.20	24.95	273.23	nr	298.18
635 mm x 1350 mm; ref VS0613B	295.66	2.40	27.22	295.97	nr	323.19
635 mm x 1650 mm; ref VS0616B	315.85	2.70	30.62	316.23	nr	346.85
860 mm x 1050 mm; ref VS0810B	297.78	2.55	28.92	298.03	nr	326.95
860 mm x 1350 mm; ref VS0813B	322.33	2.85	32.32	322.64	nr	354.96
860 mm x 1650 mm; ref VS0816B	346.82	3.30	37.42	347.20	nr	384.62
1085 mm x 1050 mm; ref VS1010B	323.90	2.85	32.32	324.15	nr	356.47
1085 mm x 1350 mm; ref VS1013B	355.26	3.30	37.42	355.57	nr	392.99
1085 mm x 1650 mm; ref VS1016B	375.86	4.05	45.93	376.24	nr	422.17
1725 mm x 1050 mm; ref VS1710B	593.03	4.05	45.93	593.34	nr	639.27
1725 mm x 1350 mm; ref VS1713B	646.32	5.05	57.27	646.70	nr	703.97
1725 mm x 1650 mm; ref VS1716B	693.47	5.15	58.40	693.91	nr	752.31

L WINDOWS/DOORS/STAIRS Excluding overheads and profit	PC £	Labour hours	Labour £	Material £	Unit	Total rate £
L10 WINDOWS/ROOFLIGHTS/SCREENS/ LOUVRES - cont'd						
Standard windows; Premdor Crosby or other equal and approved; Meranti; factory applied preservative stain base coat						
Side hung casement windows; 45 mm x 140 mm hardwood sills; weather stripping; opening sashes on canopy hinges; fitted with fasteners; brown finish ironmongery						
630 mm x 750 mm; ref 107C	121.89	1.05	11.91	122.08	nr	133.99
630 mm x 900 mm; ref 109C	129.71	1.30	14.74	129.90	nr	144.64
630 mm x 900 mm; ref 109V	122.19	1.05	11.91	122.38	nr	134.29
630 mm x 1050 mm; ref 110V	124.10	1.45	16.44	124.29	nr	140.73
915 mm x 900 mm; ref 2N09W	150.28	1.65	18.71	150.53	nr	169.24
915 mm x 1050 mm; ref 2N10W	154.32	1.75	19.84	154.63	nr	174.47
915 mm x 1200 mm; ref 2N12W	158.40	1.85	20.98	158.71	nr	179.69
915 mm x 1350 mm; ref 2N13W	162.44	2.00	22.68	162.75	nr	185.43
915 mm x 1500 mm; ref 2N15W	166.86	2.10	23.81	167.24	nr	191.05
1200 mm x 900 mm; ref 209C	177.95	1.85	20.98	178.14	nr	199.12
1200 mm x 900 mm; ref 209W	175.14	1.85	20.98	175.33	nr	196.31
1200 mm x 1050 mm; ref 210C	188.32	2.00	22.68	188.51	nr	211.19
1200 mm x 1050 mm; ref 210W	179.22	2.00	22.68	179.41	nr	202.09
1200 mm x 1200 mm; ref 212C	203.45	2.15	24.38	203.70	nr	228.08
1200 mm x 1200 mm; ref 212W	183.26	2.15	24.38	183.51	nr	207.89
1200 mm x 1350 mm; ref 213W	187.34	2.30	26.08	187.59	nr	213.67
1200 mm x 1500 mm; ref 215W	191.80	2.40	27.22	192.05	nr	219.27
1770 mm x 1050 mm; ref 310C	229.07	2.50	28.35	229.38	nr	257.73
1770 mm x 1050 mm; ref 310CC	284.50	2.50	28.35	284.81	nr	313.16
1770 mm x 1200 mm; ref 312C	244.16	2.65	30.05	244.47	nr	274.52
1770 mm x 1200 mm; ref 312CC	308.59	2.65	30.05	308.90	nr	338.95
2339 mm x 1200 mm; ref 412CMC	342.63	2.85	32.32	343.01	nr	375.33
Top hung casement windows; 45 mm x 140 mm hardwood sills; weather stripping; opening sashes on canopy hinges; fitted with fasteners; brown finish ironmongery						
630 mm x 900 mm; ref 109A	120.28	1.05	11.91	120.47	nr	132.38
630 mm x 1050 mm; ref 110A	128.09	1.45	16.44	128.34	nr	144.78
915 mm x 900 mm; ref 2N09A	143.10	1.65	18.71	143.29	nr	162.00
915 mm x 1050 mm; ref 2N10A	150.92	1.75	19.84	151.17	nr	171.01
915 mm x 1200 mm; ref 2N12A	159.50	1.85	20.98	159.75	nr	180.73
915 mm x 1350 mm; ref 2N13D	187.00	2.00	22.68	187.31	nr	209.99
1200 mm x 900 mm; ref 209A	162.78	1.65	18.71	162.97	nr	181.68
1200 mm x 1050 mm; ref 210A	170.64	1.85	20.98	170.89	nr	191.87
1200 mm x 1200 mm; ref 212A	179.22	2.00	22.68	179.47	nr	202.15
1770 mm x 1050 mm; ref 310AE	208.68	2.10	23.81	208.99	nr	232.80
1770 mm x 1200 mm; ref 312AE	219.85	2.20	24.95	220.16	nr	245.11
Purpose made window casements; "treated" wrought softwood						
Casements; rebated; moulded - supply only						
38 mm thick	-	-	-	23.46	m²	23.46
50 mm thick	-	-	-	27.89	m²	27.89
Casements; rebated; moulded; in medium panes - supply only						
38 mm thick	-	-	-	34.27	m²	34.27
50 mm thick	-	-	-	42.39	m²	42.39
Casements; rebated; moulded; with semi-circular head - supply only						
38 mm thick	-	-	-	42.81	m²	42.81
50 mm thick	-	-	-	53.01	m²	53.01

L WINDOWS/DOORS/STAIRS Excluding overheads and profit	PC £	Labour hours	Labour £	Material £	Unit	Total rate £
Casements; rebated; moulded; to bullseye						
window - supply only						
38 mm thick; 600 mm diameter	-	-	-	76.98	nr	76.98
38 mm thick; 900 mm diameter	-	-	-	114.19	nr	114.19
50 mm thick; 600 mm diameter	-	-	-	88.55	nr	88.55
50 mm thick; 900 mm diameter	-	-	-	131.28	nr	131.28
Fitting and hanging casements						
square or rectangular	-	0.55	6.24	-	nr	6.24
semi-circular	-	1.40	15.88	-	nr	15.88
bullseye	-	2.20	24.95	-	nr	24.95
Purpose made window casements; selected						
West African Mahogany						
Casements; rebated; moulded - supply only						
38 mm thick	-	-	-	38.84	m²	38.84
50 mm thick	-	-	-	51.47	m²	51.47
Casements; rebated; moulded; in medium						
panes - supply only						
38 mm thick	-	-	-	47.91	m²	47.91
50 mm thick	-	-	-	64.10	m²	64.10
Casements; rebated; moulded with						
semi-circular head - supply only						
38 mm thick	-	-	-	59.90	m²	59.90
50 mm thick	-	-	-	80.19	m²	80.19
Casements; rebated; moulded; to bullseye						
window - supply only						
38 mm thick; 600 mm diameter	-	-	-	129.64	nr	129.64
38 mm thick; 900 mm diameter	-	-	-	194.04	nr	194.04
50 mm thick; 600 mm diameter	-	-	-	149.08	nr	149.08
50 mm thick; 900 mm diameter	-	-	-	222.29	nr	222.29
Fitting and hanging casements						
square or rectangular	-	0.75	8.51	-	nr	8.51
semi-circular	-	1.85	20.98	-	nr	20.98
bullseye	-	2.95	33.45	-	nr	33.45
Purpose made window casements; American						
White Ash						
Casements; rebated; moulded - supply only						
38 mm thick	-	-	-	46.68	m²	46.68
50 mm thick	-	-	-	57.35	m²	57.35
Casements; rebated; moulded; in medium						
panes - supply only						
38 mm thick	-	-	-	60.48	m²	60.48
50 mm thick	-	-	-	72.69	m²	72.69
Casements; rebated; moulded with						
semi-circular head - supply only						
38 mm thick	-	-	-	75.63	m²	75.63
50 mm thick	-	-	-	90.88	m²	90.88
Casements; rebated; moulded; to bullseye						
window - supply only						
38 mm thick; 600 mm diameter	-	-	-	153.32	nr	153.32
38 mm thick; 900 mm diameter	-	-	-	229.07	nr	229.07
50 mm thick; 600 mm diameter	-	-	-	176.84	nr	176.84
50 mm thick; 900 mm diameter	-	-	-	263.65	nr	263.65
Fitting and hanging casements						
square or rectangular	-	0.75	8.51	-	nr	8.51
semi-circular	-	1.85	20.98	-	nr	20.98
bullseye	-	2.95	33.45	-	nr	33.45

L WINDOWS/DOORS/STAIRS Excluding overheads and profit	PC £	Labour hours	Labour £	Material £	Unit	Total rate £
L10 WINDOWS/ROOFLIGHTS/SCREENS/ LOUVRES - cont'd						
Purpose made window frames; "treated" wrought softwood; prices indicated are for supply only as part of a complete window frame; the reader is referred to the previous pages for fixing costs for frames based on the overall window size						
Frames; rounded; rebated check grooved						
25 mm x 120 mm	-	-	-	7.15	m	**7.15**
50 mm x 75 mm	-	-	-	8.06	m	**8.06**
50 mm x 100 mm	-	-	-	9.87	m	**9.87**
50 mm x 125 mm	-	-	-	12.00	m	**12.00**
63 mm x 100 mm	-	-	-.	12.30	m	**12.30**
75 mm x 150 mm	-	-	-	20.65	m	**20.65**
90 mm x 140 mm	-	-	-	26.65	m	**26.65**
Mullions and transoms; twice rounded, rebated and check grooved						
50 mm x 75 mm	-	-	-	9.90	m	**9.90**
50 mm x 100 mm	-	-	-	11.71	m	**11.71**
63 mm x 100 mm	-	-	-	14.14	m	**14.14**
75 mm x 150 mm	-	-	-	22.49	m	**22.49**
Sill; sunk weathered, rebated and grooved						
75 mm x 100 mm	-	-	-	20.70	m	**20.70**
75 mm x 150 mm	-	-	-	27.12	m	**27.12**
Add 5% to the above material prices for "selected" softwood for staining						
Purpose made window frames; selected West African Mahogany; prices given are for supply only as part of a complete window frame; the reader is referred to the previous pages for fixing costs for frames based on the overall window size						
Frames; rounded; rebated check grooved						
25 mm x 120 mm	-	-	-	12.33	m	**12.33**
50 mm x 75 mm	-	-	-	14.03	m	**14.03**
50 mm x 100 mm	-	-	-	17.37	m	**17.37**
50 mm x 125 mm	-	-	-	21.18	m	**21.18**
63 mm x 100 mm	-	-	-	21.67	m	**21.67**
75 mm x 150 mm	-	-	-	36.69	m	**36.69**
90 mm x 140 mm	-	-	-	47.57	m	**47.57**
Mullions and transoms; twice rounded, rebated and check grooved						
50 mm x 75 mm	-	-	-	16.77	m	**16.77**
50 mm x 100 mm	-	-	-	20.10	m	**20.10**
63 mm x 100 mm	-	-	-	24.41	m	**24.41**
75 mm x 150 mm	-	-	-	39.43	m	**39.43**
Sill; sunk weathered, rebated and grooved						
75 mm x 100 mm	-	-	-	34.87	m	**34.87**
75 mm x 150 mm	-	-	-	46.44	m	**46.44**

L WINDOWS/DOORS/STAIRS Excluding overheads and profit	PC £	Labour hours	Labour £	Material £	Unit	Total rate £
Purpose made window frames; American White Ash; prices indicated are for supply only as part of a complete window frame; the reader is referred to the previous pages for fixing costs for frames based on the overall window size						
Frames; rounded; rebated check grooved						
25 mm x 120 mm	-	-	-	13.73	m	**13.73**
50 mm x 75 mm	-	-	-	15.70	m	**15.70**
50 mm x 100 mm	-	-	-	19.60	m	**19.60**
50 mm x 125 mm	-	-	-	23.96	m	**23.96**
63 mm x 100 mm	-	-	-	24.50	m	**24.50**
75 mm x 150 mm	-	-	-	41.72	m	**41.72**
90 mm x 140 mm	-	-	-	54.32	m	**54.32**
Mullions and transoms; twice rounded, rebated and check grooved						
50 mm x 75 mm	-	-	-	18.44	m	**18.44**
50 mm x 100 mm	-	-	-	22.34	m	**22.34**
63 mm x 100 mm	-	-	-	27.24	m	**27.24**
75 mm x 150 mm	-	-	-	44.46	m	**44.46**
Sill; sunk weathered, rebated and grooved						
75 mm x 100 mm	-	-	-	38.23	m	**38.23**
75 mm x 150 mm	-	-	-	51.50	m	**51.50**
Purpose made double hung sash windows; "treated" wrought softwood						
Cased frames of 100 mm x 25 mm grooved inner linings; 114 mm x 25 mm grooved outer linings; 125 mm x 38 mm twice rebated head linings; 125 mm x 32 mm twice rebated grooved pulley stiles; 150 mm x 13 mm linings; 50 mm x 19 mm partings slips; 25 mm x 19 mm inside beads; 150 mm x 75 mm Oak twice sunk weathered throated sill; 50 mm thick rebated and moulded sashes; moulded horns over 1.25 m² each; both sashes in medium panes; including spiral spring balances	171.71	2.50	28.35	240.48	m²	**268.83**
As above but with cased mullions	181.17	2.75	31.18	249.94	m²	**281.12**
Purpose made double hung sash windows; selected West African Mahogany						
Cased frames of 100 mm x 25 mm grooved inner linings; 114 mm x 25 mm grooved outer linings; 125 mm x 38 mm twice rebated head linings; 125 mm x 32 mm twice rebated grooved pulley stiles; 150 mm x 13 mm linings; 50 mm x 19 mm parting slips; 25 mm x 19 mm inside beads; 150 mm x 75 mm Oak twice sunk weathered throated sill; 50 mm thick rebated and moulded sashes; moulded horns over 1.25 m² each; both sashes in medium panes; including spiral sash balances	274.09	3.30	37.42	342.86	m²	**380.28**
As above but with cased mullions	289.15	3.65	41.39	357.92	m²	**399.31**

L WINDOWS/DOORS/STAIRS Excluding overheads and profit	PC £	Labour hours	Labour £	Material £	Unit	Total rate £
L10 WINDOWS/ROOFLIGHTS/SCREENS/ LOUVRES - cont'd						
Purpose made double hung sash windows; **American White Ash**						
Cased frames of 100 mm x 25 mm grooved						
inner linings; 114 mm x 25 mm grooved outer						
linings; 125 mm x 38 mm twice rebated head						
linings; 125 mm x 32 mm twice rebated						
grooved pulley stiles; 150 mm x 13 mm linings;						
50 mm x 19 mm parting slips; 25 mm x 19 mm						
inside beads; 150 mm x 75 mm Oak twice sunk						
weathered throated sill; 50 mm thick rebated						
and moulded sashes; moulded horns						
over 1.25 m² each; both sashes in medium						
panes; including spiral spring balances	297.24	3.30	37.42	366.01	m²	**403.43**
As above but with cased mullions	318.95	3.65	41.39	387.72	m²	**429.11**
Galvanised steel fixed, casement and fanlight **windows; Crittal "Homelight" range or other equal** **and approved; site glazing not included; fixed in** **position including lugs plugged and screwed to** **brickwork or blockwork**						
Basic fixed lights; including easy-glaze beads						
628 mm x 292 mm; ref ZNG5	20.85	1.30	14.74	20.98	nr	**35.72**
628 mm x 923 mm; ref ZNC5	29.70	1.30	14.74	29.89	nr	**44.63**
628 mm x 1513 mm; ref ZNDV5	42.29	1.30	14.74	42.60	nr	**57.34**
1237 mm x 292 mm; ref ZNG13	31.84	1.30	14.74	31.97	nr	**46.71**
1237 mm x 923 mm; ref ZNC13	41.22	1.95	22.11	41.41	nr	**63.52**
1237 mm x 1218 mm; ref ZND13	48.56	1.95	22.11	48.80	nr	**70.91**
1237 mm x 1513 mm; ref ZNDV13	53.23	1.95	22.11	53.54	nr	**75.65**
1846 mm x 292 mm; ref ZNG14	41.30	1.30	14.74	41.49	nr	**56.23**
1846 mm x 923 mm; ref ZNC14	50.89	1.95	22.11	51.20	nr	**73.31**
1846 mm x 1513 mm; ref ZNDV14	61.65	2.40	27.22	62.09	nr	**89.31**
Basic opening lights; including easy-glaze						
beads and weatherstripping						
628 mm x 292 mm; ref ZNG1	53.37	1.30	14.74	53.50	nr	**68.24**
1237 mm x 292 mm; ref ZNG13G	76.41	1.30	14.74	76.54	nr	**91.28**
1846 mm x 292 mm; ref ZNG4	132.24	1.30	14.74	132.49	nr	**147.23**
One piece composites; including easy-glaze						
beads and weatherstripping						
628 mm x 923 mm; ref ZNC5F	72.08	1.30	14.74	72.27	nr	**87.01**
628 mm x 1513 mm; ref ZNDV5F	85.16	1.30	14.74	85.47	nr	**100.21**
1237 mm x 923 mm; ref ZNC2F	140.77	1.95	22.11	140.96	nr	**163.07**
1237 mm x 1218 mm; ref ZND2F	163.95	1.95	22.11	164.20	nr	**186.31**
1237 mm x 1513 mm; ref ZNDV2V	194.80	1.95	22.11	195.11	nr	**217.22**
1846 mm x 923 mm; ref ZNC4F	215.65	1.95	22.11	215.96	nr	**238.07**
1846 mm x 1218 mm; ref ZND10F	205.45	2.40	27.22	205.83	nr	**233.05**
Reversible windows; including easy-glaze						
beads						
997 mm x 923 mm; ref NC13R	182.45	1.70	19.28	182.64	nr	**201.92**
997 mm x 1067 mm; ref NCO13R	193.21	1.70	19.28	193.40	nr	**212.68**
1237 mm x 923 mm; ref ZNC13R	201.10	2.55	28.92	201.29	nr	**230.21**
1237 mm x 1218 mm; ref ZND13R	219.38	2.55	28.92	219.63	nr	**248.55**
1237 mm x 1513 mm; ref ZNDV13RS	245.73	2.55	28.92	246.04	nr	**274.96**
Pressed steel sills; to suit above window						
widths						
628 mm long	12.54	0.40	4.54	12.54	nr	**17.08**
997 mm long	16.87	0.50	5.67	16.87	nr	**22.54**
1237 mm long	21.00	0.60	6.80	21.00	nr	**27.80**
1846 mm long	27.36	0.85	9.64	27.36	nr	**37.00**

L WINDOWS/DOORS/STAIRS Excluding overheads and profit	PC £	Labour hours	Labour £	Material £	Unit	Total rate £
Factory finished steel fixed light; casement **and fanlight windows; Crittall polyester** **powder coated "Homelight" range or other** **equal and approved; site glazing not included;** **fixed in position; including lugs plugged and** **screwed to brickwork or blockwork**						
Basic fixed lights; including easy-glaze beads						
628 mm x 292 mm; ref ZNG5	25.92	1.30	14.74	26.05	nr	**40.79**
628 mm x 923 mm; ref ZNC5	36.91	1.30	14.74	37.10	nr	**51.84**
628 mm x 1513 mm; ref ZNDV5	52.57	1.30	14.74	52.88	nr	**67.62**
1237 mm x 292 mm; ref ZNG13	39.59	1.30	14.74	39.72	nr	**54.46**
1237 mm x 923 mm; ref ZNC13	51.23	1.95	22.11	51.42	nr	**73.53**
1237 mm x 1218 mm; ref ZND13	60.36	1.95	22.11	60.61	nr	**82.72**
1237 mm x 1513 mm; ref ZNDV13	66.15	1.95	22.11	66.46	nr	**88.57**
1846 mm x 292 mm; ref ZNG14	51.34	1.30	14.74	51.47	nr	**66.21**
1846 mm x 923 mm; ref ZNC14	63.26	1.95	22.11	63.45	nr	**85.56**
1846 mm x 1513 mm; ref ZNDV14	77.06	2.40	27.22	77.37	nr	**104.59**
Basic opening lights; including easy-glaze beads and weatherstripping						
628 mm x 292 mm; ref ZNG1	63.35	1.30	14.74	63.48	nr	**78.22**
1237 mm x 292 mm; ref ZNG13G	91.70	1.30	14.74	91.83	nr	**106.57**
1846 mm x 292 mm; ref ZNG4	157.81	1.30	14.74	157.94	nr	**172.68**
One piece composites; including easy-glaze beads and weatherstripping						
628 mm x 923 mm; ref ZNC5F	86.54	1.30	14.74	86.73	nr	**101.47**
628 mm x 1513 mm; ref ZNDV5F	102.78	1.30	14.74	103.09	nr	**117.83**
1237 mm x 923 mm; ref ZNC2F	168.06	1.95	22.11	168.25	nr	**190.36**
1237 mm x 1218 mm; ref ZND2F	196.25	1.95	22.11	196.44	nr	**218.55**
1237 mm x 1513 mm; ref ZNDV2V	233.22	1.95	22.11	233.53	nr	**255.64**
1846 mm x 923 mm; ref ZNC4F	257.14	1.95	22.11	257.33	nr	**279.44**
1846 mm x 1218 mm; ref ZND10F	246.82	2.40	27.22	247.13	nr	**274.35**
Reversible windows; including easy-glaze beads						
997 mm x 923 mm; ref NC13R	233.98	1.70	19.28	234.17	nr	**253.45**
997 mm x 1218 mm; ref NCO13R	247.84	1.70	19.28	248.03	nr	**267.31**
1237 mm x 923 mm; ref ZNC13R	257.99	2.55	28.92	258.18	nr	**287.10**
1237 mm x 1218 mm; ref ZND13R	281.56	2.55	28.92	281.81	nr	**310.73**
1237 mm x 1513 mm; ref ZNDV13RS	315.62	2.55	28.92	315.93	nr	**344.85**
Pressed steel sills; to suit above window widths						
628 mm long	15.53	0.40	4.54	15.53	nr	**20.07**
997 mm long	20.90	0.50	5.67	20.90	nr	**26.57**
1237 mm long	26.02	0.60	6.80	26.02	nr	**32.82**
1846 mm long	33.91	0.85	9.64	33.91	nr	**43.55**
uPVC windows to BS 2782; reinforced where **appropriate with aluminium alloy; including** **standard ironmongery; cills and glazing; fixed in** **position; including lugs plugged and screwed** **to brickwork or blockwork**						
Fixed light; including e.p.d.m. glazing gaskets and weather seals						
600 mm x 900 mm; single glazed	33.94	1.65	18.71	34.19	nr	**52.90**
600 mm x 900 mm; double glazed	44.63	1.65	18.71	44.88	nr	**63.59**
Casement/fixed light; including e.p.d.m. glazing gaskets and weather seals						
600 mm x 1200 mm; single glazed	75.65	1.95	22.11	75.96	nr	**98.07**
600 mm x 1200 mm; double glazed	90.39	1.95	22.11	90.70	nr	**112.81**
1200 mm x 1200 mm; single glazed	103.86	2.20	24.95	104.24	nr	**129.19**
1200 mm x 1200 mm; double glazed	142.20	2.20	24.95	142.58	nr	**167.53**
1800 mm x 1200 mm; single glazed	108.35	2.20	24.95	108.73	nr	**133.68**
1800 mm x 1200 mm; double glazed	152.02	2.20	24.95	152.40	nr	**177.35**

L WINDOWS/DOORS/STAIRS Excluding overheads and profit	PC £	Labour hours	Labour £	Material £	Unit	Total rate £
L10 WINDOWS/ROOFLIGHTS/SCREENS/ LOUVRES - cont'd						
uPVC windows to BS 2782; reinforced where appropriate with aluminium alloy; including standard ironmongery; cills and glazing; fixed in position; including lugs plugged and screwed to brickwork or blockwork - cont'd						
"Tilt & Turn" light; including e.p.d.m. glazing gaskets and weather seals						
1200 mm x 1200 mm; single glazed	108.12	2.20	24.95	108.50	nr	**133.45**
1200 mm x 1200 mm; double glazed	131.63	2.20	24.95	132.01	nr	**156.96**
Rooflights, skylights, roof windows and frames; pre-glazed; "treated" Nordic Red Pine and aluminium trimmed "Velux" windows or other equal and approved; type U flashings and soakers (for tiles and pantiles), and sealed double glazing unit (trimming opening not included)						
Roof windows						
550 mm x 780 mm; ref GGL-3000-102	157.68	2.20	24.95	157.90	nr	**182.85**
550 mm x 980 mm; ref GGL-3000-104	174.38	2.50	28.35	174.60	nr	**202.95**
660 mm x 1180 mm; ref GGL-3000-206	205.79	2.75	31.18	206.05	nr	**237.23**
780 mm x 980 mm; ref GGL-3000-304	197.94	2.75	31.18	198.20	nr	**229.38**
780 mm x 1400 mm; ref GGL-3000-308	238.19	2.75	31.18	238.54	nr	**269.72**
940 mm x 1600 mm; ref GGL-3000-410	286.60	3.30	37.42	287.00	nr	**324.42**
1140 mm x 1180 mm; ref GGL-3000-606	263.74	3.30	37.42	264.14	nr	**301.56**
1340 mm x 980 mm; ref GGL-3000-804	272.45	3.30	37.42	272.85	nr	**310.27**
1340 mm x 1400 mm; ref GGL-3000-808	323.85	3.30	37.42	324.25	nr	**361.67**
Rooflights, skylights, roof windows and frames; galvanised steel; plugged and screwed to concrete; or screwed to timber						
Rooflight "Coxdome TPX" or other equal and approved; dome; galvanised steel; UV protected polycarbonate glazing; GRP splayed upstand; hit and miss vent						
600 mm x 600 mm	168.30	1.95	22.11	168.50	nr	**190.61**
900 mm x 600 mm	226.60	2.10	23.81	226.83	nr	**250.64**
900 mm x 900 mm	267.30	2.25	25.52	267.56	nr	**293.08**
1200 mm x 900 mm	308.00	2.40	27.22	308.30	nr	**335.52**
1200 mm x 1200 mm	380.60	2.60	29.48	380.93	nr	**410.41**
1800 mm x 1200 mm	551.10	2.75	31.18	551.46	nr	**582.64**
Rooflights, skylights, roof windows and frames; uPVC; plugged and screwed to concrete; or screwed to timber						
Rooflight; "Coxdome Universal Dome" or other equal and approved; acrylic double skin; dome						
600 mm x 600 mm	94.88	1.65	18.71	94.88	nr	**113.59**
900 mm x 600 mm	177.10	1.80	20.41	177.10	nr	**197.51**
900 mm x 900 mm	177.10	2.00	22.68	177.10	nr	**199.78**
1200 mm x 900 mm	215.05	2.15	24.38	215.05	nr	**239.43**
1200 mm x 1200 mm	271.98	2.30	26.08	271.98	nr	**298.06**
1500 mm x 1050 mm	512.33	2.40	27.22	512.33	nr	**539.55**

L WINDOWS/DOORS/STAIRS Excluding overheads and profit	PC £	Labour hours	Labour £	Material £	Unit	Total rate £
Louvres and frames; polyester powder coated aluminium; fixing in position including brackets						
Louvre; Gil Airvac "Plusaire 75SP" weatherlip or other equal and approved						
1250 mm x 675 mm	-	-	-	-	nr	235.00
2000 mm x 530 mm	-	-	-	-	nr	275.00
L20 DOORS/SHUTTERS/HATCHES						
Doors; standard matchboarded; wrought softwood						
Matchboarded, ledged and braced doors; 25 mm thick ledges and braces; 19 mm thick tongued, grooved and V-jointed boarding; one side vertical boarding						
762 mm x 1981 mm	52.70	1.65	18.71	52.70	nr	71.41
838 mm x 1981 mm	52.70	1.65	18.71	52.70	nr	71.41
Matchboarded, framed, ledged and braced doors; 44 mm thick overall; 19 mm thick tongued, grooved and V-jointed boarding; one side vertical boarding						
762 mm x 1981 mm	64.60	2.00	22.68	64.60	nr	87.28
838 mm x 1981 mm	64.60	2.00	22.68	64.60	nr	87.28
Doors; standard flush; softwood composition						
Flush door; internal quality; skeleton or cellular core; hardboard faced both sides; Premdor Crosby "Primaseal" or other equal and approved						
457 mm x 1981 mm x 35 mm	21.08	1.40	15.88	21.08	nr	36.96
533 mm x 1981 mm x 35 mm	21.08	1.40	15.88	21.08	nr	36.96
610 mm x 1981 mm x 35 mm	21.08	1.40	15.88	21.08	nr	36.96
686 mm x 1981 mm x 35 mm	21.08	1.40	15.88	21.08	nr	36.96
762 mm x 1981 mm x 35 mm	21.08	1.40	15.88	21.08	nr	36.96
838 mm x 1981 mm x 35 mm	22.14	1.40	15.88	22.14	nr	38.02
526 mm x 2040 mm x 40 mm	23.50	1.40	15.88	23.50	nr	39.38
626 mm x 2040 mm x 40 mm	23.50	1.40	15.88	23.50	nr	39.38
726 mm x 2040 mm x 40 mm	23.50	1.40	15.88	23.50	nr	39.38
826 mm x 2040 mm x 40 mm	23.50	1.40	15.88	23.50	nr	39.38
Flush door; internal quality; skeleton or cellular core; chipboard veneered; faced both sides; lipped on two long edges; Premdor Crosby "Popular" or other equal and approved						
457 mm x 1981 mm x 35 mm	30.30	1.40	15.88	30.30	nr	46.18
533 mm x 1981 mm x 35 mm	30.30	1.40	15.88	30.30	nr	46.18
610 mm x 1981 mm x 35 mm	30.30	1.40	15.88	30.30	nr	46.18
686 mm x 1981 mm x 35 mm	30.30	1.40	15.88	30.30	nr	46.18
762 mm x 1981 mm x 35 mm	30.30	1.40	15.88	30.30	nr	46.18
838 mm x 1981 mm x 35 mm	31.70	1.40	15.88	31.70	nr	47.58
526 mm x 2040 mm x 40 mm	33.32	1.40	15.88	33.32	nr	49.20
626 mm x 2040 mm x 40 mm	33.32	1.40	15.88	33.32	nr	49.20
726 mm x 2040 mm x 40 mm	33.32	1.40	15.88	33.32	nr	49.20
826 mm x 2040 mm x 40 mm	33.32	1.40	15.88	33.32	nr	49.20

L WINDOWS/DOORS/STAIRS Excluding overheads and profit	PC £	Labour hours	Labour £	Material £	Unit	Total rate £
L20 DOORS/SHUTTERS/HATCHES - cont'd						
Doors; standard flush; softwood composition - cont'd						
Flush door; internal quality; skeleton or cellular						
core; Sapele faced both sides; lipped on all four						
edges; Premdor Crosby "Landscape Sapele" or						
other equal and approved						
457 mm x 1981 mm x 35 mm	32.94	1.50	17.01	32.94	nr	49.95
533 mm x 1981 mm x 35 mm	32.94	1.50	17.01	32.94	nr	49.95
610 mm x 1981 mm x 35 mm	32.94	1.50	17.01	32.94	nr	49.95
686 mm x 1981 mm x 35 mm	32.94	1.50	17.01	32.94	nr	49.95
762 mm x 1981 mm x 35 mm	32.94	1.50	17.01	32.94	nr	49.95
838 mm x 1981 mm x 35 mm	34.30	1.50	17.01	34.30	nr	51.31
526 mm x 2040 mm x 40 mm	35.53	1.50	17.01	35.53	nr	52.54
626 mm x 2040 mm x 40 mm	35.53	1.50	17.01	35.53	nr	52.54
726 mm x 2040 mm x 40 mm	35.53	1.50	17.01	35.53	nr	52.54
826 mm x 2040 mm x 40 mm	35.53	1.50	17.01	35.53	nr	52.54
Flush door; half-hour fire check (FD20); hardboard						
faced both sides; Premdor Crosby "Primaseal						
Fireshield" or other equal and approved						
762 mm x 1981 mm x 44 mm	50.75	1.95	22.11	50.75	nr	72.86
838 mm x 1981 mm x 44 mm	52.57	1.95	22.11	52.57	nr	74.68
726 mm x 2040 mm x 44 mm	53.85	1.95	22.11	53.85	nr	75.96
826 mm x 2040 mm x 44 mm	53.85	1.95	22.11	53.85	nr	75.96
Flush door; half-hour fire check (30/20);						
chipboard veneered; faced both sides; lipped						
on all four edges; Premdor Crosby "Popular						
Fireshield" or other equal and approved						
457 mm x 1981 mm x 44 mm	49.90	1.95	22.11	49.90	nr	72.01
533 mm x 1981 mm x 44 mm	49.90	1.95	22.11	49.90	nr	72.01
610 mm x 1981 mm x 44 mm	49.90	1.95	22.11	49.90	nr	72.01
686 mm x 1981 mm x 44 mm	49.90	1.95	22.11	49.90	nr	72.01
762 mm x 1981 mm x 44 mm	49.90	1.95	22.11	49.90	nr	72.01
838 mm x 1981 mm x 44 mm	51.98	1.95	22.11	51.98	nr	74.09
526 mm x 2040 mm x 44 mm	54.57	1.95	22.11	54.57	nr	76.68
626 mm x 2040 mm x 44 mm	54.57	1.95	22.11	54.57	nr	76.68
726 mm x 2040 mm x 44 mm	54.57	1.95	22.11	54.57	nr	76.68
826 mm x 2040 mm x 44 mm	54.57	1.95	22.11	54.57	nr	76.68
Flush door; half hour fire resisting "Leaderflush"						
(type B30) or other equal and approved; chipboard						
for painting; hardwood lipping two long edges						
526 mm x 2040 mm x 44 mm	81.08	2.05	23.25	81.08	nr	104.33
626 mm x 2040 mm x 44 mm	86.66	2.05	23.25	86.66	nr	109.91
726 mm x 2040 mm x 44 mm	86.88	2.05	23.25	86.88	nr	110.13
826 mm x 2040 mm x 44 mm	87.68	2.05	23.25	87.68	nr	110.93
Flush door; half-hour fire check (FD20); Sapele						
faced both sides; lipped on all four edges;						
Premdor Crosby "Landscape Sapele						
Fireshield" or other equal and approved						
686 mm x 1981 mm x 44 mm	69.36	2.05	23.25	69.36	nr	92.61
762 mm x 1981 mm x 44 mm	69.36	2.05	23.25	69.36	nr	92.61
838 mm x 1981 mm x 44 mm	71.14	2.05	23.25	71.14	nr	94.39
726 mm x 2040 mm x 44 mm	72.38	2.05	23.25	72.38	nr	95.63
826 mm x 2040 mm x 44 mm	72.38	2.05	23.25	72.38	nr	95.63
Flush door; half-hour fire resisting (30/30)						
Sapele faced both sides; lipped on all four edges						
610 mm x 1981 mm x 44 mm	76.27	2.05	23.25	76.27	nr	99.52
686 mm x 1981 mm x 44 mm	76.27	2.05	23.25	76.27	nr	99.52
762 mm x 1981 mm x 44 mm	76.27	2.05	23.25	76.27	nr	99.52
838 mm x 1981 mm x 44 mm	76.27	2.05	23.25	76.27	nr	99.52
726 mm x 2040 mm x 44 mm	76.27	2.05	23.25	76.27	nr	99.52
826 mm x 2040 mm x 44 mm	76.27	2.05	23.25	76.27	nr	99.52

L WINDOWS/DOORS/STAIRS Excluding overheads and profit	PC £	Labour hours	Labour £	Material £	Unit	Total rate £
Flush door; half hour fire resisting "Leaderflush" (type B30) or other equal and approved; American light oak veneer; hardwood lipping all edges						
526 mm x 2040 mm x 44 mm	107.27	2.05	23.25	107.27	nr	**130.52**
626 mm x 2040 mm x 44 mm	115.68	2.05	23.25	115.68	nr	**138.93**
726 mm x 2040 mm x 44 mm	118.72	2.05	23.25	118.72	nr	**141.97**
826 mm x 2040 mm x 44 mm	121.74	2.05	23.25	121.74	nr	**144.99**
Flush door; one hour fire check (60/45); plywood faced both sides; lipped on all four edges; Premdor Crosby "Popular Firemaster" or other equal and approved						
762 mm x 1981 mm x 54 mm	182.24	2.20	24.95	182.24	nr	**207.19**
838 mm x 1981 mm x 54 mm	189.00	2.20	24.95	189.00	nr	**213.95**
726 mm x 2040 mm x 54 mm	191.50	2.20	24.95	191.50	nr	**216.45**
826 mm x 2040 mm x 54 mm	191.50	2.20	24.95	191.50	nr	**216.45**
Flush door; one hour fire check (60/45); Sapele faced both sides; lipped on all four edges						
762 mm x 1981 mm x 54 mm	299.37	2.30	26.08	299.37	nr	**325.45**
838 mm x 1981 mm x 54 mm	299.37	2.30	26.08	299.37	nr	**325.45**
Flush door; one hour fire resisting "Leaderflush" (type B60) or other equal and approved; Afrormosia veneer; hardwood lipping all edges including groove and "Leaderseal" intumescent strip or other equal and approved						
457 mm x 1981 mm x 54 mm	115.98	2.30	26.08	115.98	nr	**142.06**
533 mm x 1981 mm x 54 mm	118.61	2.30	26.08	118.61	nr	**144.69**
610 mm x 1981 mm x 54 mm	143.64	2.30	26.08	143.64	nr	**169.72**
686 mm x 1981 mm x 54 mm	147.19	2.30	26.08	147.19	nr	**173.27**
762 mm x 1981 mm x 54 mm	150.73	2.30	26.08	150.73	nr	**176.81**
838 mm x 1981 mm x 54 mm	165.75	2.30	26.08	165.75	nr	**191.83**
526 mm x 2040 mm x 54 mm	118.90	2.30	26.08	118.90	nr	**144.98**
626 mm x 2040 mm x 54 mm	145.90	2.30	26.08	145.90	nr	**171.98**
726 mm x 2040 mm x 54 mm	149.38	2.30	26.08	149.38	nr	**175.46**
826 mm x 2040 mm x 54 mm	153.75	2.30	26.08	153.75	nr	**179.83**
Flush door; external quality; skeleton or cellular core; plywood faced both sides; lipped on all four edges						
762 mm x 1981 mm x 54 mm	47.98	1.95	22.11	47.98	nr	**70.09**
838 mm x 1981 mm x 54 mm	49.66	1.95	22.11	49.66	nr	**71.77**
Flush door; external quality with standard glass opening; skeleton or cellular core; plywood faced both sides; lipped on all four edges; including glazing beads						
762 mm x 1981 mm x 54 mm	60.30	1.95	22.11	60.30	nr	**82.41**
838 mm x 1981 mm x 54 mm	61.87	1.95	22.11	61.87	nr	**83.98**
Doors; purpose made panelled; wrought softwood						
Panelled doors; one open panel for glass; including glazing beads						
686 mm x 1981 mm x 44 mm	57.71	1.95	22.11	57.71	nr	**79.82**
762 mm x 1981 mm x 44 mm	59.48	1.95	22.11	59.48	nr	**81.59**
838 mm x 1981 mm x 44 mm	61.22	1.95	22.11	61.22	nr	**83.33**
Panelled doors; two open panel for glass; including glazing beads						
686 mm x 1981 mm x 44 mm	79.81	1.95	22.11	79.81	nr	**101.92**
762 mm x 1981 mm x 44 mm	84.09	1.95	22.11	84.09	nr	**106.20**
838 mm x 1981 mm x 44 mm	88.27	1.95	22.11	88.27	nr	**110.38**
Panelled doors; four 19 mm thick plywood panels; mouldings worked on solid both sides						
686 mm x 1981 mm x 44 mm	110.17	1.95	22.11	110.17	nr	**132.28**
762 mm x 1981 mm x 44 mm	114.76	1.95	22.11	114.76	nr	**136.87**
838 mm x 1981 mm x 44 mm	120.54	1.95	22.11	120.54	nr	**142.65**

L WINDOWS/DOORS/STAIRS Excluding overheads and profit	PC £	Labour hours	Labour £	Material £	Unit	Total rate £
L20 DOORS/SHUTTERS/HATCHES - cont'd						
Doors; purpose made panelled; wrought						
softwood - cont'd						
Panelled doors; six 25 mm thick panels raised						
and fielded; mouldings worked on solid both						
sides						
686 mm x 1981 mm x 44 mm	251.68	2.30	26.08	251.68	nr	**277.76**
762 mm x 1981 mm x 44 mm	262.14	2.30	26.08	262.14	nr	**288.22**
838 mm x 1981 mm x 44 mm	275.25	2.30	26.08	275.25	nr	**301.33**
rebated edges beaded	-	-	-	1.32	m	**1.32**
rounded edges or heels	-	-	-	0.67	m	**0.67**
weatherboard fixed to bottom rail	-	0.30	3.40	2.56	m	**5.96**
stopped groove for weatherboard	-	-	-	3.98	m	**3.98**
Doors; purpose made panelled; selected						
West African Mahogany						
Panelled doors; one open panel for glass;						
including glazing beads						
686 mm x 1981 mm x 50 mm	116.68	2.75	31.18	116.68	nr	**147.86**
762 mm x 1981 mm x 50 mm	120.54	2.75	31.18	120.54	nr	**151.72**
838 mm x 1981 mm x 50 mm	124.39	2.75	31.18	124.39	nr	**155.57**
686 mm x 1981 mm x 63 mm	142.00	3.05	34.59	142.00	nr	**176.59**
762 mm x 1981 mm x 63 mm	146.80	3.05	34.59	146.80	nr	**181.39**
838 mm x 1981 mm x 63 mm	151.59	3.05	34.59	151.59	nr	**186.18**
Panelled doors; 250 mm wide cross tongued						
intermediate rail; two open panels for glass;						
mouldings worked on the solid one side; 19						
mm x 13 mm beads one side; fixing with brass						
cups and screws						
686 mm x 1981 mm x 50 mm	159.35	2.75	31.18	159.35	nr	**190.53**
762 mm x 1981 mm x 50 mm	167.22	2.75	31.18	167.22	nr	**198.40**
838 mm x 1981 mm x 50 mm	175.00	2.75	31.18	175.00	nr	**206.18**
686 mm x 1981 mm x 63 mm	191.54	3.05	34.59	191.54	nr	**226.13**
762 mm x 1981 mm x 63 mm	201.06	3.05	34.59	201.06	nr	**235.65**
838 mm x 1981 mm x 63 mm	210.54	3.05	34.59	210.54	nr	**245.13**
Panelled doors; four panels; (19 mm thick for						
50 mm doors, 25 mm thick for 63 mm doors);						
mouldings worked on solid both sides						
686 mm x 1981 mm x 50 mm	203.04	2.75	31.18	203.04	nr	**234.22**
762 mm x 1981 mm x 50 mm	211.48	2.75	31.18	211.48	nr	**242.66**
838 mm x 1981 mm x 50 mm	222.06	2.75	31.18	222.06	nr	**253.24**
686 mm x 1981 mm x 63 mm	239.76	3.05	34.59	239.76	nr	**274.35**
762 mm x 1981 mm x 63 mm	248.71	3.05	34.59	248.71	nr	**283.30**
838 mm x 1981 mm x 63 mm	262.26	3.05	34.59	262.26	nr	**296.85**
Panelled doors; 150 mm wide stiles in one						
width; 430 mm wide cross tongued bottom rail;						
six panels raised and fielded one side; (19 mm						
thick for 50 mm doors, 25 mm thick for 63 mm						
doors); mouldings worked on solid both sides						
686 mm x 1981 mm x 50 mm	428.37	2.75	31.18	428.37	nr	**459.55**
762 mm x 1981 mm x 50 mm	446.22	2.75	31.18	446.22	nr	**477.40**
838 mm x 1981 mm x 50 mm	468.51	2.75	31.18	468.51	nr	**499.69**
686 mm x 1981 mm x 63 mm	527.55	3.05	34.59	527.55	nr	**562.14**
762 mm x 1981 mm x 63 mm	549.55	3.05	34.59	549.55	nr	**584.14**
838 mm x 1981 mm x 63 mm	577.02	3.05	34.59	577.02	nr	**611.61**
rebated edges beaded	-	-	-	1.99	m	**1.99**
rounded edges or heels	-	-	-	0.99	m	**0.99**
weatherboard fixed to bottom rail	-	0.35	3.97	5.71	m	**9.68**
stopped groove for weatherboard	-	-	-	4.88	m	**4.88**

L WINDOWS/DOORS/STAIRS Excluding overheads and profit	PC £	Labour hours	Labour £	Material £	Unit	Total rate £
Doors; purpose made panelled; American White Ash						
Panelled doors; one open panel for glass; including glazing beads						
686 mm x 1981 mm x 50 mm	130.67	2.75	31.18	130.67	nr	**161.85**
762 mm x 1981 mm x 50 mm	135.04	2.75	31.18	135.04	nr	**166.22**
838 mm x 1981 mm x 50 mm	139.43	2.75	31.18	139.43	nr	**170.61**
686 mm x 1981 mm x 63 mm	159.44	3.05	34.59	159.44	nr	**194.03**
762 mm x 1981 mm x 63 mm	164.95	3.05	34.59	164.95	nr	**199.54**
838 mm x 1981 mm x 63 mm	170.40	3.05	34.59	170.40	nr	**204.99**
Panelled doors; 250 mm wide cross tongued intermediate rail; two open panels for glass; mouldings worked on the solid one side; 19 mm x 13 mm beads one side; fixing with brass cups and screws						
686 mm x 1981 mm x 50 mm	177.81	2.75	31.18	177.81	nr	**208.99**
762 mm x 1981 mm x 50 mm	186.71	2.75	31.18	186.71	nr	**217.89**
838 mm x 1981 mm x 50 mm	195.54	2.75	31.18	195.54	nr	**226.72**
686 mm x 1981 mm x 63 mm	214.60	3.05	34.59	214.60	nr	**249.19**
762 mm x 1981 mm x 63 mm	225.38	3.05	34.59	225.38	nr	**259.97**
838 mm x 1981 mm x 63 mm	236.13	3.05	34.59	236.13	nr	**270.72**
Panelled doors; four panels; (19 mm thick for 50 mm doors, 25 mm thick for 63 mm doors); mouldings worked on solid both sides						
686 mm x 1981 mm x 50 mm	225.81	2.75	31.18	225.81	nr	**256.99**
762 mm x 1981 mm x 50 mm	235.20	2.75	31.18	235.20	nr	**266.38**
838 mm x 1981 mm x 50 mm	246.96	2.75	31.18	246.96	nr	**278.14**
686 mm x 1981 mm x 63 mm	268.34	3.05	34.59	268.34	nr	**302.93**
762 mm x 1981 mm x 63 mm	279.54	3.05	34.59	279.54	nr	**314.13**
838 mm x 1981 mm x 63 mm	293.52	3.05	34.59	293.52	nr	**328.11**
Panelled doors; 150 mm wide stiles in one width; 430 mm wide cross tongued bottom rail; six panels raised and fielded one side; (19 mm thick for 50 mm doors, 25 mm thick for 63 mm doors); mouldings worked on solid both sides						
686 mm x 1981 mm x 50 mm	465.39	2.75	31.18	465.39	nr	**496.57**
762 mm x 1981 mm x 50 mm	484.79	2.75	31.18	484.79	nr	**515.97**
838 mm x 1981 mm x 50 mm	509.02	2.75	31.18	509.02	nr	**540.20**
686 mm x 1981 mm x 63 mm	574.43	3.05	34.59	574.43	nr	**609.02**
762 mm x 1981 mm x 63 mm	598.36	3.05	34.59	598.36	nr	**632.95**
838 mm x 1981 mm x 63 mm	628.29	3.05	34.59	628.29	nr	**662.88**
rebated edges beaded	-	-	-	1.99	m	**1.99**
rounded edges or heels	-	-	-	0.99	m	**0.99**
weatherboard fixed to bottom rail	-	0.35	3.97	6.26	m	**10.23**
stopped groove for weatherboard	-	-	-	4.88	m	**4.88**
Doors; galvanised steel "up and over" type garage doors; Catnic "Horizon 90" or other equal and approved; spring counterbalanced; fixed to timber frame (not included)						
Garage door						
2135 mm x 1980 mm	208.05	4.40	49.90	208.31	nr	**258.21**
2135 mm x 2135 mm	233.70	4.40	49.90	233.96	nr	**283.86**
2400 mm x 2135 mm	283.10	4.40	49.90	283.41	nr	**333.31**
3965 mm x 2135 mm	745.75	6.60	74.84	746.37	nr	**821.21**

L WINDOWS/DOORS/STAIRS Excluding overheads and profit	PC £	Labour hours	Labour £	Material £	Unit	Total rate £
L20 DOORS/SHUTTERS/HATCHES - cont'd						
Doorsets; galvanised steel IG "Weatherbeater Original" door and frame units or other equal and approved; treated softwood frame, primed hardwood sill; fixing in position; plugged and screwed to brickwork or blockwork						
Door and frame						
762 mm x 1981 mm; ref IGD1	324.54	3.30	37.42	324.79	nr	362.21
Doorsets; steel door and frame units; Jandor Architectural Ltd or other equal and approved; polyester powder coated; ironmongery						
Single action door set; "Metset MD01" doors and "Metset MF" frames						
900 mm x 2100 mm	-	-	-	-	nr	1694.00
pair 1800 mm x 2100 mm	-	-	-	-	nr	2299.00
Rolling shutters and collapsible gates; steel counter shutters; Bolton Brady Ltd or other equal and approved; push-up, self-coiling; polyester power coated; fixing by bolting						
Shutters						
3000 mm x 1000 mm	-	-	-	-	nr	870.00
4000 mm x 1000 mm; in two panels	-	-	-	-	nr	1500.00
Rolling shutters and collapsible gates; galvanised steel; Bolton Brady Type 474 or other equal and approved; one hour fibre resisting; self-coiling; activated by fusible link; fixing with bolts						
Rolling shutters and collapsible gates						
1000 mm x 2750 mm	-	-	-	-	nr	1050.00
1500 mm x 2750 mm	-	-	-	-	nr	1100.00
2400 mm x 2750 mm	-	-	-	-	nr	1300.00
Sliding/folding partitions; aluminium double glazed sliding patio doors; Crittal "Luminaire" or other equal and approved; white acrylic finish; with and including 18 mm thick annealed double glazing; fixed in position; including lugs plugged and screwed to brickwork or blockwork						
Patio doors						
1800 mm x 2100 mm; ref PF1821	1183.50	2.75	31.18	1184.25	nr	1215.43
2400 mm x 2100 mm; ref PF2421	1467.00	3.30	37.42	1467.75	nr	1505.17
2700 mm x 2100 mm; ref PF2721	1606.50	3.85	43.66	1607.25	nr	1650.91
Grilles; "Galaxy" nylon rolling counter grille or other equal and approved; Bolton Brady Ltd; colour, off-white; self-coiling; fixing by bolting						
Grilles						
3000 mm x 1000 mm	-	-	-	-	nr	790.00
4000 mm x 1000 mm	-	-	-	-	nr	1200.00

L WINDOWS/DOORS/STAIRS Excluding overheads and profit	PC £	Labour hours	Labour £	Material £	Unit	Total rate £
Door frames and door linings, sets; standard **joinery; wrought softwood**						
Internal door frame or lining composite sets for 686 mm x 1981 mm door; all with loose stops unless rebated; "finished sizes"						
27 mm x 94 mm lining	29.34	0.90	10.21	29.59	nr	**39.80**
27 mm x 107 mm lining	30.86	0.90	10.21	31.11	nr	**41.32**
35 mm x 107 mm rebated lining	32.02	0.90	10.21	32.27	nr	**42.48**
27 mm x 121 mm lining	33.37	0.90	10.21	33.62	nr	**43.83**
27 mm x 121 mm lining with fanlight over	47.00	1.05	11.91	47.31	nr	**59.22**
27 mm x 133 mm lining	35.98	0.90	10.21	36.23	nr	**46.44**
35 mm x 133 mm rebated lining	36.96	0.90	10.21	37.21	nr	**47.42**
27 mm x 133 mm lining with fanlight over	50.50	1.05	11.91	50.81	nr	**62.72**
33 mm x 57 mm frame	23.63	0.90	10.21	23.88	nr	**34.09**
33 mm x 57 mm storey height frame	29.16	1.05	11.91	29.47	nr	**41.38**
33 mm x 57 mm frame with fanlight over	35.34	1.05	11.91	35.65	nr	**47.56**
33 mm x 64 mm frame	25.47	0.90	10.21	25.72	nr	**35.93**
33 mm x 64 mm storey height frame	31.22	1.05	11.91	31.53	nr	**43.44**
33 mm x 64 mm frame with fanlight over	37.31	1.05	11.91	37.62	nr	**49.53**
44 mm x 94 mm frame	39.47	1.00	11.34	39.72	nr	**51.06**
44 mm x 94 mm storey height frame	46.96	1.20	13.61	47.27	nr	**60.88**
44 mm x 94 mm frame with fanlight over	54.76	1.20	13.61	55.07	nr	**68.68**
44 mm x 107 mm frame	45.14	1.10	12.47	45.39	nr	**57.86**
44 mm x 107 mm storey height frame	52.88	1.20	13.61	53.19	nr	**66.80**
44 mm x 107 mm frame with fanlight over	60.33	1.20	13.61	60.64	nr	**74.25**
Internal door frame or lining composite sets for 762 mm x 1981 mm door; all with loose stops unless rebated; "finished sizes"						
27 mm x 94 mm lining	29.34	0.90	10.21	29.59	nr	**39.80**
27 mm x 107 mm lining	30.86	0.90	10.21	31.11	nr	**41.32**
35 mm x 107 mm rebated lining	32.02	0.90	10.21	32.27	nr	**42.48**
27 mm x 121 mm lining	33.37	0.90	10.21	33.62	nr	**43.83**
27 mm x 121 mm lining with fanlight over	47.00	1.05	11.91	47.31	nr	**59.22**
27 mm x 133 mm lining	35.98	0.90	10.21	36.23	nr	**46.44**
35 mm x 133 mm rebated lining	36.96	0.90	10.21	37.21	nr	**47.42**
27 mm x 133 mm lining with fanlight over	50.50	1.05	11.91	50.81	nr	**62.72**
33 mm x 57 mm frame	23.63	0.90	10.21	23.88	nr	**34.09**
33 mm x 57 mm storey height frame	29.16	1.05	11.91	29.47	nr	**41.38**
33 mm x 57 mm frame with fanlight over	35.34	1.05	11.91	35.65	nr	**47.56**
33 mm x 64 mm frame	25.47	0.90	10.21	25.72	nr	**35.93**
33 mm x 64 mm storey height frame	31.22	1.05	11.91	31.53	nr	**43.44**
33 mm x 64 mm frame with fanlight over	37.31	1.05	11.91	37.62	nr	**49.53**
44 mm x 94 mm frame	39.47	1.00	11.34	39.72	nr	**51.06**
44 mm x 94 mm storey height frame	46.96	1.20	13.61	47.27	nr	**60.88**
44 mm x 94 mm frame with fanlight over	54.76	1.20	13.61	55.07	nr	**68.68**
44 mm x 107 mm frame	45.14	1.10	12.47	45.39	nr	**57.86**
44 mm x 107 mm storey height frame	52.88	1.20	13.61	53.19	nr	**66.80**
44 mm x 107 mm frame with fanlight over	60.33	1.20	13.61	60.64	nr	**74.25**
Internal door frame or lining composite sets for 726 mm x 2040 mm door; with loose stops						
30 mm x 94 mm lining	34.22	0.90	10.21	34.47	nr	**44.68**
30 mm x 94 mm lining with fanlight over	48.75	1.05	11.91	49.06	nr	**60.97**
30 mm x 107 mm lining	40.23	0.90	10.21	40.48	nr	**50.69**
30 mm x 107 mm lining with fanlight over	54.94	1.05	11.91	55.25	nr	**67.16**
30 mm x 133 mm lining	45.08	0.90	10.21	45.33	nr	**55.54**
30 mm x 133 mm lining with fanlight over	59.25	1.05	11.91	59.56	nr	**71.47**

L WINDOWS/DOORS/STAIRS Excluding overheads and profit	PC £	Labour hours	Labour £	Material £	Unit	Total rate £
L20 DOORS/SHUTTERS/HATCHES - cont'd						
Door frames and door linings, sets; standard joinery; wrought softwood - cont'd Internal door frame or lining composite sets for 826 mm x 2040 mm door; with loose stops						
30 mm x 94 mm lining	34.22	0.90	10.21	34.47	nr	**44.68**
30 mm x 94 mm lining with fanlight over	48.75	1.05	11.91	49.06	nr	**60.97**
30 mm x 107 mm lining	40.23	0.90	10.21	40.48	nr	**50.69**
30 mm x 107 mm lining with fanlight over	54.94	1.05	11.91	55.25	nr	**67.16**
30 mm x 133 mm lining	45.08	0.90	10.21	45.33	nr	**55.54**
30 mm x 133 mm lining with fanlight over	59.25	1.05	11.91	59.56	nr	**71.47**
Door frames and door linings, sets; purpose made; wrought softwood Jambs and heads; as linings						
32 mm x 63 mm	-	0.20	2.27	4.04	m	**6.31**
32 mm x 100 mm	-	0.20	2.27	5.19	m	**7.46**
32 mm x 140 mm	-	0.20	2.27	6.63	m	**8.90**
Jambs and heads; as frames; rebated, rounded and grooved						
38 mm x 75 mm	-	0.20	2.27	5.14	m	**7.41**
38 mm x 100 mm	-	0.20	2.27	6.09	m	**8.36**
38 mm x 115 mm	-	0.20	2.27	7.09	m	**9.36**
38 mm x 140 mm	-	0.20	2.27	8.25	m	**10.52**
50 mm x 100 mm	-	0.20	2.27	7.67	m	**9.94**
50 mm x 125 mm	-	0.20	2.27	9.12	m	**11.39**
63 mm x 88 mm	-	0.20	2.27	8.79	m	**11.06**
63 mm x 100 mm	-	0.20	2.27	9.38	m	**11.65**
63 mm x 125 mm	-	0.20	2.27	11.19	m	**13.46**
75 mm x 100 mm	-	0.20	2.27	10.75	m	**13.02**
75 mm x 125 mm	-	0.25	2.83	13.31	m	**16.14**
75 mm x 150 mm	-	0.25	2.83	15.52	m	**18.35**
100 mm x 100 mm	-	0.30	3.40	13.99	m	**17.39**
100 mm x 150 mm	-	0.30	3.40	20.04	m	**23.44**
Mullions and transoms; in linings						
32 mm x 63 mm	-	0.15	1.70	6.62	m	**8.32**
32 mm x 100 mm	-	0.15	1.70	7.78	m	**9.48**
32 mm x 140 mm	-	0.15	1.70	9.15	m	**10.85**
Mullions and transoms; in frames; twice rebated, rounded and grooved						
38 mm x 75 mm	-	0.15	1.70	7.89	m	**9.59**
38 mm x 100 mm	-	0.15	1.70	8.84	m	**10.54**
38 mm x 115 mm	-	0.15	1.70	9.60	m	**11.30**
38 mm x 140 mm	-	0.15	1.70	10.76	m	**12.46**
50 mm x 100 mm	-	0.15	1.70	10.19	m	**11.89**
50 mm x 125 mm	-	0.15	1.70	11.78	m	**13.48**
63 mm x 88 mm	-	0.15	1.70	11.37	m	**13.07**
63 mm x 100 mm	-	0.15	1.70	11.96	m	**13.66**
75 mm x 100 mm	-	0.15	1.70	13.43	m	**15.13**
Add 5% to the above material prices for selected softwood for staining						
Door frames and door linings, sets; purpose made; selected West African Mahogany Jambs and heads; as linings						
32 mm x 63 mm	7.45	0.25	2.83	7.51	m	**10.34**
32 mm x 100 mm	9.70	0.25	2.83	9.76	m	**12.59**
32 mm x 140 mm	12.31	0.25	2.83	12.44	m	**15.27**

L WINDOWS/DOORS/STAIRS Excluding overheads and profit	PC £	Labour hours	Labour £	Material £	Unit	Total rate £
Jambs and heads; as frames; rebated, rounded and grooved						
38 mm x 75 mm	9.41	0.25	2.83	9.47	m	12.30
38 mm x 100 mm	11.39	0.25	2.83	11.45	m	14.28
38 mm x 115 mm	13.09	0.25	2.83	13.22	m	16.05
38 mm x 140 mm	15.14	0.30	3.40	15.27	m	18.67
50 mm x 100 mm	14.37	0.30	3.40	14.50	m	17.90
50 mm x 125 mm	17.34	0.30	3.40	17.47	m	20.87
63 mm x 88 mm	16.10	0.30	3.40	16.16	m	19.56
63 mm x 100 mm	17.85	0.30	3.40	17.91	m	21.31
63 mm x 125 mm	21.46	0.30	3.40	21.59	m	24.99
75 mm x 100 mm	20.58	0.30	3.40	20.71	m	24.11
75 mm x 125 mm	25.59	0.35	3.97	25.72	m	29.69
75 mm x 150 mm	30.04	0.35	3.97	30.17	m	34.14
100 mm x 100 mm	26.94	0.35	3.97	27.07	m	31.04
100 mm x 150 mm	39.09	0.35	3.97	39.22	m	43.19
Mullions and transoms; in linings						
32 mm x 63 mm	11.43	0.20	2.27	11.43	m	13.70
32 mm x 100 mm	13.66	0.20	2.27	13.66	m	15.93
32 mm x 140 mm	16.29	0.20	2.27	16.29	m	18.56
Mullions and transoms; in frames; twice rebated, rounded and grooved						
38 mm x 75 mm	13.59	0.20	2.27	13.59	m	15.86
38 mm x 100 mm	15.58	0.20	2.27	15.58	m	17.85
38 mm x 115 mm	17.07	0.20	2.27	17.07	m	19.34
38 mm x 140 mm	19.11	0.20	2.27	19.11	m	21.38
50 mm x 100 mm	18.35	0.20	2.27	18.35	m	20.62
50 mm x 125 mm	21.52	0.20	2.27	21.52	m	23.79
63 mm x 88 mm	20.08	0.20	2.27	20.08	m	22.35
63 mm x 100 mm	21.82	0.20	2.27	21.82	m	24.09
75 mm x 100 mm	24.76	0.20	2.27	24.76	m	27.03
Sills; once sunk weathered; once rebated, three times grooved						
63 mm x 175 mm	40.14	0.35	3.97	40.14	m	44.11
75 mm x 125 mm	36.36	0.35	3.97	36.36	m	40.33
75 mm x 150 mm	40.87	0.35	3.97	40.87	m	44.84
Door frames and door linings, sets; purpose made; American White Ash						
Jambs and heads; as linings						
32 mm x 63 mm	8.46	0.25	2.83	8.52	m	11.35
32 mm x 100 mm	11.10	0.25	2.83	11.16	m	13.99
32 mm x 140 mm	14.33	0.25	2.83	14.46	m	17.29
Jambs and heads; as frames; rebated, rounded and grooved						
38 mm x 75 mm	10.67	0.25	2.83	10.73	m	13.56
38 mm x 100 mm	13.10	0.25	2.83	13.16	m	15.99
38 mm x 115 mm	15.14	0.25	2.83	15.27	m	18.10
38 mm x 140 mm	17.49	0.30	3.40	17.62	m	21.02
50 mm x 100 mm	16.62	0.30	3.40	16.75	m	20.15
50 mm x 125 mm	20.13	0.30	3.40	20.26	m	23.66
63 mm x 88 mm	18.63	0.30	3.40	18.69	m	22.09
63 mm x 100 mm	20.68	0.30	3.40	20.74	m	24.14
63 mm x 125 mm	24.99	0.30	3.40	25.12	m	28.52
75 mm x 100 mm	23.92	0.30	3.40	24.05	m	27.45
75 mm x 125 mm	29.79	0.35	3.97	29.92	m	33.89
75 mm x 150 mm	35.07	0.35	3.97	35.20	m	39.17
100 mm x 100 mm	31.39	0.35	3.97	31.52	m	35.49
100 mm x 150 mm	45.82	0.35	3.97	45.95	m	49.92

L WINDOWS/DOORS/STAIRS Excluding overheads and profit	PC £	Labour hours	Labour £	Material £	Unit	Total rate £
L20 DOORS/SHUTTERS/HATCHES - cont'd						
Door frames and door linings, sets; purpose made; American White Ash - cont'd						
Mullions and transoms; in linings						
32 mm x 63 mm	12.43	0.20	2.27	12.43	m	**14.70**
32 mm x 100 mm	15.08	0.20	2.27	15.08	m	**17.35**
32 mm x 140 mm	18.30	0.20	2.27	18.30	m	**20.57**
Mullions and transoms; in frames; twice rebated, rounded and grooved						
38 mm x 75 mm	14.86	0.20	2.27	14.86	m	**17.13**
38 mm x 100 mm	17.30	0.20	2.27	17.30	m	**19.57**
38 mm x 115 mm	19.11	0.20	2.27	19.11	m	**21.38**
38 mm x 140 mm	21.46	0.20	2.27	21.46	m	**23.73**
50 mm x 100 mm	20.59	0.20	2.27	20.59	m	**22.86**
50 mm x 125 mm	24.32	0.20	2.27	24.32	m	**26.59**
63 mm x 88 mm	22.64	0.20	2.27	22.64	m	**24.91**
63 mm x 100 mm	24.65	0.20	2.27	24.65	m	**26.92**
75 mm x 100 mm	28.10	0.20	2.27	28.10	m	**30.37**
Sills; once sunk weathered; once rebated, three times grooved						
63 mm x 175 mm	45.06	0.35	3.97	45.06	m	**49.03**
75 mm x 125 mm	40.56	0.35	3.97	40.56	m	**44.53**
75 mm x 150 mm	45.93	0.35	3.97	45.93	m	**49.90**
Door frames and door linings, sets; European Oak						
Sills; once sunk weathered; once rebated, three times grooved						
63 mm x 175 mm	79.43	0.35	3.97	79.43	m	**83.40**
75 mm x 125 mm	70.54	0.35	3.97	70.54	m	**74.51**
75 mm x 150 mm	80.86	0.35	3.97	80.86	m	**84.83**
Bedding and pointing frames						
Pointing wood frames or sills with mastic						
one side	-	0.10	0.80	0.43	m	**1.23**
both sides	-	0.20	1.59	0.86	m	**2.45**
Pointing wood frames or sills with polysulphide sealant						
one side	-	0.10	0.80	1.29	m	**2.09**
both sides	-	0.20	1.59	2.59	m	**4.18**
Bedding wood frames in cement mortar (1:3) and point						
one side	-	0.10	1.42	0.07	m	**1.49**
both sides	-	0.10	1.42	0.09	m	**1.51**
one side in mortar; other side in mastic	-	0.20	2.22	0.50	m	**2.72**
L30 STAIRS/WALKWAYS/BALUSTRADES						
Standard staircases; wrought softwood (parana pine)						
Stairs; 25 mm thick treads with rounded nosings; 9 mm thick plywood risers; 32 mm thick strings; bullnose bottom tread; 50 mm x 75 mm hardwood handrail; 32 mm square plain balusters; 100 mm square plain newel posts						
straight flight; 838 mm wide; 2676 mm going; 2600 mm rise; with two newel posts	-	7.70	87.32	365.95	nr	**453.27**
straight flight with turn; 838 mm wide; 2676 mm going; 2600 mm rise; with two newel posts; three top treads winding	-	7.70	87.32	460.95	nr	**548.27**

L WINDOWS/DOORS/STAIRS Excluding overheads and profit	PC £	Labour hours	Labour £	Material £	Unit	Total rate £
Stairs; 25 mm thick treads with rounded nosings; 9 mm thick plywood risers; 32 mm thick strings; bullnose bottom tread; 50 mm x 75 mm hardwood handrail; 32 mm square plain balusters; 100 mm square plain newel posts - cont'd						
dogleg staircase; 838 mm wide; 2676 mm going; 2600 mm rise; with two newel posts; quarter space landing third riser from top	-	7.70	87.32	390.95	nr	478.27
dogleg staircase; 838 mm wide; 2676 mm going; 2600 mm rise; with two newel posts; half space landing third riser from top	-	8.80	99.79	410.95	nr	510.74
Standard balustrades; wrought softwood						
Landing balustrade; 50 mm x 75 mm hardwood handrail; three 32 mm x 140 mm balustrade kneerails; two 32 mm x 50 mm stiffeners; one end of handrail jointed to newel post; other end built into wall; (newel post and mortices both not included)						
3.00 m long	-	3.05	34.59	125.00	nr	159.59
Landing balustrade; 50 mm x 75 mm hardwood handrail; 32 mm square plain balusters; one end of handrail jointed to newel post; other end built into wall; balusters housed in at bottom (newel post and mortices both not included)						
3.00 m long	-	4.40	49.90	75.00	nr	124.90
Hardwood staircases; purpose made; **assembled at works**						
Fixing only complete staircase including landings, balustrades, etc.						
plugging and screwing to brickwork or blockwork	-	16.50	187.11	1.58	nr	188.69
The following are supply only prices for **purpose made staircase components in** **selected West African Mahogany supplied as** **part of an assembled staircase and may be** **used to arrive at a guide price for a complete** **hardwood staircase**						
Board landings; cross-tongued joints; 100 mm x 50 mm sawn softwood bearers						
25 mm thick	-	-	-	85.47	m²	85.47
32 mm thick	-	-	-	104.81	m²	104.81
Treads; cross-tongued joints and risers; rounded nosings; tongued, grooved, glued and blocked together; one 175 mm x 50 mm sawn softwood carriage						
25 mm treads; 19 mm risers	-	-	-	105.83	m²	105.83
ends; quadrant	-	-	-	49.00	nr	49.00
ends; housed to hardwood	-	-	-	0.90	nr	0.90
32 mm treads; 25 mm risers	-	-	-	127.02	m²	127.02
ends; quadrant	-	-	-	62.97	nr	62.97
ends; housed to hardwood	-	-	-	0.90	nr	0.90
Winders; cross-tongued joints and risers in one width; rounded nosings; tongued, grooved glued and blocked together; one 175 mm x 50 mm sawn softwood carriage						
25 mm treads; 19 mm risers	-	-	-	116.40	m²	116.40
32 mm treads; 25 mm risers	-	-	-	139.73	m²	139.73
wide ends; housed to hardwood	-	-	-	1.81	nr	1.81
narrow ends; housed to hardwood	-	-	-	1.35	nr	1.35

L WINDOWS/DOORS/STAIRS Excluding overheads and profit	PC £	Labour hours	Labour £	Material £	Unit	Total rate £
L30 STAIRS/WALKWAYS/BALUSTRADES - cont'd						
The following are supply only prices for						
purpose made staircase components in						
selected West African Mahogany supplied as						
part of an assembled staircase and may be						
used to arrive at a guide price for a complete						
hardwood staircase - cont'd						
Closed strings; in one width; 230 mm wide;						
rounded twice						
32 mm thick	-	-	-	22.44	m	**22.44**
38 mm thick	-	-	-	26.94	m	**26.94**
50 mm thick	-	-	-	35.59	m	**35.59**
Closed strings; cross-tongued joints; 280 mm						
wide; once rounded						
32 mm thick	-	-	-	39.27	m	**39.27**
extra for short ramp	-	-	-	19.63	nr	**19.63**
38 mm thick	-	-	-	44.56	m	**44.56**
extra for short ramp	-	-	-	22.32	nr	**22.32**
50 mm thick	-	-	-	55.19	m	**55.19**
extra for short ramp	-	-	-	27.65	nr	**27.65**
Closed strings; ramped; crossed tongued						
joints 280 mm wide; once rounded; fixing with						
screws; plugging 450 mm centres						
32 mm thick	-	-	-	43.23	m	**43.23**
38 mm thick	-	-	-	49.05	m	**49.05**
50 mm thick	-	-	-	60.69	m	**60.69**
Apron linings; in one width 230 mm wide						
19 mm thick	-	-	-	8.89	m	**8.89**
25 mm thick	-	-	-	10.76	m	**10.76**
Handrails; rounded						
40 mm x 50 mm	-	-	-	7.41	m	**7.41**
50 mm x 75 mm	-	-	-	9.27	m	**9.27**
63 mm x 87 mm	-	-	-	12.00	m	**12.00**
75 mm x 100 mm	-	-	-	14.57	m	**14.57**
Handrails; moulded						
40 mm x 50 mm	-	-	-	7.94	m	**7.94**
50 mm x 75 mm	-	-	-	9.81	m	**9.81**
63 mm x 87 mm	-	-	-	12.53	m	**12.53**
75 mm x 100 mm	-	-	-	15.11	m	**15.11**
Handrails; rounded; ramped						
40 mm x 50 mm	-	-	-	14.81	m	**14.81**
50 mm x 75 mm	-	-	-	18.55	m	**18.55**
63 mm x 87 mm	-	-	-	24.00	m	**24.00**
75 mm x 100 mm	-	-	-	23.76	m	**23.76**
Handrails; moulded; ramped						
40 mm x 50 mm	-	-	-	15.89	m	**15.89**
50 mm x 75 mm	-	-	-	19.64	m	**19.64**
63 mm x 87 mm	-	-	-	25.09	m	**25.09**
75 mm x 100 mm	-	-	-	30.22	m	**30.22**
Heading joints to handrail; mitred or raked						
overall size not exceeding 50 mm x 75 mm	-	-	-	25.35	nr	**25.35**
overall size not exceeding 75 mm x 100 mm	-	-	-	32.28	nr	**32.28**

L WINDOWS/DOORS/STAIRS Excluding overheads and profit	PC £	Labour hours	Labour £	Material £	Unit	Total rate £
Balusters; stiffeners						
25 mm x 25 mm	-	-	-	3.60	m	3.60
32 mm x 32 mm	-	-	-	4.17	m	4.17
50 mm x 50 mm	-	-	-	5.03	m	5.03
ends; housed	-	-	-	1.14	nr	1.14
Sub rails						
32 mm x 63 mm	-	-	-	6.41	m	6.41
ends; framed joint to newel	-	-	-	4.60	nr	4.60
Knee rails						
32 mm x 140 mm	-	-	-	10.02	m	10.02
ends; framed joint to newel	-	-	-	4.60	nr	4.60
Newel posts						
50 mm x 100 mm; half newel	-	-	-	10.72	m	10.72
75 mm x 75 mm	-	-	-	11.58	m	11.58
100 mm x 100 mm	-	-	-	17.88	m	17.88
Newel caps; splayed on four sides						
52.50 mm x 125 mm x 50 mm	-	-	-	6.73	nr	6.73
100 mm x 100 mm x 50 mm	-	-	-	6.73	nr	6.73
125 mm x 125 mm x 50 mm	-	-	-	7.30	nr	7.30
The following are supply only prices for purpose made staircase components in selected Oak; supplied as part of an assembled staircase						
Board landings; cross-tongued joints; 100 mm x 50 mm sawn softwood bearers						
25 mm thick	-	-	-	179.77	m²	179.77
32 mm thick	-	-	-	221.60	m²	221.60
Treads; cross-tongued joints and risers; rounded nosings; tongued, grooved, glued and blocked together; one 175 mm x 50 mm sawn softwood carriage						
25 mm treads; 19 mm risers	-	-	-	195.77	m²	195.77
ends; quadrant	-	-	-	97.90	nr	97.90
ends; housed to hardwood	-	-	-	1.20	nr	1.20
32 mm treads; 25 mm risers	-	-	-	240.99	m²	240.99
ends; quadrant	-	-	-	120.52	nr	120.52
ends; housed to hardwood	-	-	-	1.20	nr	1.20
Winders; cross-tongued joints and risers in one width; rounded nosings; tongued, grooved glued and blocked together; one 175 mm x 50 mm sawn softwood carriage						
25 mm treads; 19 mm risers	-	-	-	215.35	m²	215.35
32 mm treads; 25 mm risers	-	-	-	265.11	m²	265.11
wide ends; housed to hardwood	-	-	-	2.41	nr	2.41
narrow ends; housed to hardwood	-	-	-	1.81	nr	1.81
Closed strings; in one width; 230 mm wide; rounded twice						
32 mm thick	-	-	-	47.30	m	47.30
38 mm thick	-	-	-	56.37	m	56.37
50 mm thick	-	-	-	74.51	m	74.51
Closed strings; cross-tongued joints; 280 mm wide; once rounded						
32 mm thick	-	-	-	75.58	m	75.58
extra for short ramp	-	-	-	37.79	nr	37.79
38 mm thick	-	-	-	86.69	m	86.69
extra for short ramp	-	-	-	43.34	nr	43.34
50 mm thick	-	-	-	109.08	m	109.08
extra for short ramp	-	-	-	54.56	nr	54.56

L WINDOWS/DOORS/STAIRS Excluding overheads and profit	PC £	Labour hours	Labour £	Material £	Unit	Total rate £
L30 STAIRS/WALKWAYS/BALUSTRADES - cont'd						
The following are supply only prices for						
purpose made staircase components in						
selected Oak; supplied as part of an						
assembled staircase - cont'd						
Closed strings; ramped; crossed tongued						
joints 280 mm wide; once rounded; fixing with						
screws; plugging 450 mm centres						
32 mm thick	-	-	-	83.15	m	**83.15**
38 mm thick	-	-	-	95.37	m	**95.37**
50 mm thick	-	-	-	119.99	m	**119.99**
Apron linings; in one width 230 mm wide						
19 mm thick	-	-	-	21.61	m	**21.61**
25 mm thick	-	-	-	27.15	m	**27.15**
Handrails; rounded						
40 mm x 50 mm	-	-	-	15.38	m	**15.38**
50 mm x 75 mm	-	-	-	20.95	m	**20.95**
63 mm x 87 mm	-	-	-	29.06	m	**29.06**
75 mm x 100 mm	-	-	-	36.71	m	**36.71**
Handrails; moulded						
40 mm x 50 mm	-	-	-	16.10	m	**16.10**
50 mm x 75 mm	-	-	-	21.67	m	**21.67**
63 mm x 87 mm	-	-	-	29.79	m	**29.79**
75 mm x 100 mm	-	-	-	37.43	m	**37.43**
Handrails; rounded; ramped						
40 mm x 50 mm	-	-	-	30.77	m	**30.77**
50 mm x 75 mm	-	-	-	41.90	m	**41.90**
63 mm x 87 mm	-	-	-	58.13	m	**58.13**
75 mm x 100 mm	-	-	-	73.43	m	**73.43**
Handrails; moulded; ramped						
40 mm x 50 mm	-	-	-	32.21	m	**32.21**
50 mm x 75 mm	-	-	-	43.34	m	**43.34**
63 mm x 87 mm	-	-	-	59.57	m	**59.57**
75 mm x 100 mm	-	-	-	74.87	m	**74.87**
Heading joints to handrail; mitred or raked						
overall size not exceeding 50 mm x 75 mm	-	-	-	38.75	nr	**38.75**
overall size not exceeding 75 mm x 100 mm	-	-	-	47.19	nr	**47.19**
Balusters; stiffeners						
25 mm x 25 mm	-	-	-	5.86	m	**5.86**
32 mm x 32 mm	-	-	-	7.54	m	**7.54**
50 mm x 50 mm	-	-	-	10.12	m	**10.12**
ends; housed	-	-	-	1.50	nr	**1.50**
Sub rails						
32 mm x 63 mm	-	-	-	12.91	m	**12.91**
ends; framed joint to newel	-	-	-	6.14	nr	**6.14**
Knee rails						
32 mm x 140 mm	-	-	-	23.55	m	**23.55**
ends; framed joint to newel	-	-	-	6.14	nr	**6.14**
Newel posts						
50 mm x 100 mm; half newel	-	-	-	25.70	m	**25.70**
75 mm x 75 mm	-	-	-	28.23	m	**28.23**
100 mm x 100 mm	-	-	-	47.00	m	**47.00**
Newel caps; splayed on four sides						
62.50 mm x 125 mm x 50 mm	-	-	-	9.77	nr	**9.77**
100 mm x 100 mm x 50 mm	-	-	-	9.77	nr	**9.77**
125 mm x 125 mm x 50 mm	-	-	-	11.45	nr	**11.45**

L WINDOWS/DOORS/STAIRS Excluding overheads and profit	PC £	Labour hours	Labour £	Material £	Unit	Total rate £
Aluminium alloy folding loft ladders; "Zig Zag" **stairways, model B or other equal and approved;** **Light Alloy Ltd; on and including plywood backboard;** **fixing with screws to timber lining (not included)** Loft ladders						
ceiling height not exceeding 2500 mm; model 888801	-	1.10	12.47	487.23	nr	**499.70**
ceiling height not exceeding 2800 mm; model 888802	-	1.10	12.47	532.64	nr	**545.11**
ceiling height not exceeding 3100 mm; model 888803	-	1.10	12.47	578.91	nr	**591.38**
Flooring, balustrades and handrails; mild steel						
Chequer plate flooring; over 300 mm wide; bolted to steel supports						
6 mm thick	-	-	-	43.95	m²	**43.95**
3 mm thick	-	-	-	56.76	m²	**56.76**
Open grid steel flooring; Eurogrid Ltd; "Safeway" type D38 diamond pattern flooring or other equal and approved; to steel supports at 1200 mm centres; galvanised; to BS 729 part 1						
30 mm x 5 mm sections; in one mat; fixing to 10 mm thick channels with type F5 clamps	-	-	-	107.25	m²	**107.25**
Balustrades; welded construction; 1070 mm high; galvanized; 50 mm x 50 mm x 3.20 mm rhs top rail; 38 mm x 13 mm bottom rail, 50 mm x 50 mm x 3.20 mm rhs standards at 1830 mm centres with base plate drilled and bolted to concrete; 13 mm x 13 mm balusters at 102 mm centres	-	-	-	104.50	m	**104.50**
Balusters; isolated; one end ragged and cemented in; one 76 mm x 25 mm x 6 mm flange plate welded on; ground to a smooth finish; countersunk drilled and tap screwed to underside of handrail						
19 mm square 914 mm long bar	-	-	-	14.41	nr	**14.41**
Core-rails; joints prepared, welded and ground to a smooth finish; fixing on brackets (not included)						
38 mm x 10 mm flat bar	-	-	-	19.25	m	**19.25**
50 mm x 8 mm flat bar	-	-	-	18.43	m	**18.43**
Handrails; joints prepared, welded and ground to a smooth finish; fixing on brackets (not included)						
38 mm x 12 mm half oval bar	-	-	-	25.63	m	**25.63**
44 mm x 13 mm half oval bar	-	-	-	27.61	m	**27.61**
Handrail bracket; comprising 40 mm x 5 mm plate with mitred welded angle; one end welded to 100 mm diameter x 5 mm backplate; three times holed and plugged and screwed to brickwork; other end scribed and welded to underside of handrail						
140 mm girth	-	-	-	15.23	nr	**15.23**

L WINDOWS/DOORS/STAIRS Excluding overheads and profit	PC £	Labour hours	Labour £	Material £	Unit	Total rate £
L30 STAIRS/WALKWAYS/BALUSTRADES - cont'd						
Holes						
Holes; countersunk; for screws or bolts						
6 mm diameter; 3 mm thick	-	-	-	0.77	nr	**0.77**
6 mm diameter; 6 mm thick	-	-	-	1.16	nr	**1.16**
8 mm diameter; 6 mm thick	-	-	-	1.16	nr	**1.16**
10 mm diameter; 6 mm thick	-	-	-	1.21	nr	**1.21**
12 mm diameter; 8 mm thick	-	-	-	1.54	nr	**1.54**
L40 GENERAL GLAZING						
Standard plain glass; BS 952; clear float;						
panes area 0.15 m² - 4.00 m²						
3 mm thick; glazed with						
putty or bradded beads	-	-	-	-	m²	**23.21**
bradded beads and butyl compound	-	-	-	-	m²	**23.21**
screwed beads	-	-	-	-	m²	**26.29**
screwed beads and butyl compound	-	-	-	-	m²	**26.29**
4 mm thick; glazed with						
putty or bradded beads	-	-	-	-	m²	**24.42**
bradded beads and butyl compound	-	-	-	-	m²	**24.42**
screwed beads	-	-	-	-	m²	**27.50**
screwed beads and butyl compound	-	-	-	-	m²	**27.50**
5 mm thick; glazed with						
putty or bradded beads	-	-	-	-	m²	**29.31**
bradded beads and butyl compound	-	-	-	-	m²	**29.31**
screwed beads	-	-	-	-	m²	**32.39**
screwed beads and butyl compound	-	-	-	-	m²	**32.39**
6 mm thick; glazed with						
putty or bradded beads	-	-	-	-	m²	**30.52**
bradded beads and butyl compound	-	-	-	-	m²	**30.52**
screwed beads	-	-	-	-	m²	**33.61**
screwed beads and butyl compound	-	-	-	-	m²	**33.61**
Standard plain glass; BS 952; white patterned;						
panes area 0.15 m² - 4.00 m²						
4 mm thick; glazed with						
putty or bradded beads	-	-	-	-	m²	**27.50**
bradded beads and butyl compound	-	-	-	-	m²	**27.50**
screwed beads	-	-	-	-	m²	**30.52**
screwed beads and butyl compound	-	-	-	-	m²	**30.52**
6 mm thick; glazed with						
putty or bradded beads	-	-	-	-	m²	**33.61**
bradded beads and butyl compound	-	-	-	-	m²	**33.61**
screwed beads	-	-	-	-	m²	**36.69**
screwed beads and butyl compound	-	-	-	-	m²	**36.69**
Standard plain glass; BS 952; rough cast;						
panes area 0.15 m² - 4.00 m²						
6 mm thick; glazed with						
putty or bradded beads	-	-	-	-	m²	**36.69**
bradded beads and butyl compound	-	-	-	-	m²	**36.69**
screwed beads	-	-	-	-	m²	**39.71**
screwed beads and butyl compound	-	-	-	-	m²	**39.71**

L WINDOWS/DOORS/STAIRS Excluding overheads and profit	PC £	Labour hours	Labour £	Material £	Unit	Total rate £
Standard plain glass; BS 952; Georgian wired cast; panes area 0.15 m² - 4.00 m²						
7 mm thick; glazed with						
putty or bradded beads	-	-	-	-	m²	39.71
bradded beads and butyl compound	-	-	-	-	m²	39.71
screwed beads	-	-	-	-	m²	42.90
screwed beads and butyl compound	-	-	-	-	m²	42.90
Extra for lining up wired glass	-	-	-	-	m²	3.08
Standard plain glass; BS 952; Georgian wired polished; panes area 0.15 m² - 4.00 m²						
6 mm thick; glazed with						
putty or bradded beads	-	-	-	-	m²	73.32
bradded beads and butyl compound	-	-	-	-	m²	73.32
screwed beads	-	-	-	-	m²	76.45
screwed beads and butyl compound	-	-	-	-	m²	76.45
Extra for lining up wired glass	-	-	-	-	m²	3.08
Special glass; BS 952; toughened clear float; panes area 0.15 m² - 4.00 m²						
4 mm thick; glazed with						
putty or bradded beads	-	-	-	-	m²	27.50
bradded beads and butyl compound	-	-	-	-	m²	27.50
screwed beads	-	-	-	-	m²	30.52
screwed beads and butyl compound	-	-	-	-	m²	30.52
5 mm thick; glazed with						
putty or bradded beads	-	-	-	-	m²	36.69
bradded beads and butyl compound	-	-	-	-	m²	36.69
screwed beads	-	-	-	-	m²	39.71
screwed beads and butyl compound	-	-	-	-	m²	39.71
6 mm thick; glazed with						
putty or bradded beads	-	-	-	-	m²	36.69
bradded beads and butyl compound	-	-	-	-	m²	36.69
screwed beads	-	-	-	-	m²	39.71
screwed beads and butyl compound	-	-	-	-	m²	39.71
10 mm thick; glazed with						
putty or bradded beads	-	-	-	-	m²	73.32
bradded beads and butyl compound	-	-	-	-	m²	73.32
screwed beads	-	-	-	-	m²	76.45
screwed beads and butyl compound	-	-	-	-	m²	76.45
Special glass; BS 952; clear laminated safety glass; panes area 0.15 m² - 4.00 m²						
4.40 mm thick; glazed with						
putty or bradded beads	-	-	-	-	m²	60.50
bradded beads and butyl compound	-	-	-	-	m²	60.50
screwed beads	-	-	-	-	m²	62.15
screwed beads and butyl compound	-	-	-	-	m²	62.15
5.40 mm thick; glazed with						
putty or bradded beads	-	-	-	-	m²	73.32
bradded beads and butyl compound	-	-	-	-	m²	73.32
screwed beads	-	-	-	-	m²	76.45
screwed beads and butyl compound	-	-	-	-	m²	76.45
6.40 mm thick; glazed with						
putty or bradded beads	-	-	-	-	m²	80.30
bradded beads and butyl compound	-	-	-	-	m²	80.30
screwed beads	-	-	-	-	m²	88.55
screwed beads and butyl compound	-	-	-	-	m²	88.55

L WINDOWS/DOORS/STAIRS Excluding overheads and profit	PC £	Labour hours	Labour £	Material £	Unit	Total rate £
L40 GENERAL GLAZING - cont'd						
Special glass; BS 952; "Pyran" half-hour fire resisting glass or other equal and approved						
6.50 mm thick rectangular panes; glazed with						
screwed hardwood beads and Sealmaster						
"Fireglaze" intumescent compound or other						
equal and approved to rebated frame						
300 mm x 400 mm pane	-	0.45	6.48	29.30	nr	35.78
400 mm x 800 mm pane	-	0.55	7.93	73.34	nr	81.27
500 mm x 1400 mm pane	-	0.90	12.97	155.64	nr	168.61
600 mm x 1800 mm pane	-	1.10	15.85	265.27	nr	281.12
Special glass; BS 952; "Pyrostop" one-hour fire resisting glass or other equal and approved						
15 mm thick regular panes; glazed with						
screwed hardwood beads and Sealmaster						
"Fireglaze" intumescent liner and compound						
or other equal and approved both sides						
300 mm x 400 mm pane	-	1.30	18.73	66.39	nr	85.12
400 mm x 800 mm pane	-	1.65	23.78	129.94	nr	153.72
500 mm x 1400 mm pane	-	2.20	31.70	256.81	nr	288.51
600 mm x 1800 mm pane	-	2.75	39.63	375.25	nr	414.88
Special glass; BS 952; clear laminated security glass						
7.50 mm thick regular panes; glazed with						
screwed hardwood beads and "Intergens"						
intumescent strip or other equal and approved						
300 mm x 400 mm pane	-	0.45	6.48	17.82	nr	24.30
400 mm x 800 mm pane	-	0.55	7.93	43.19	nr	51.12
500 mm x 1400 mm pane	-	0.90	12.97	89.70	nr	102.67
600 mm x 1800 mm pane	-	1.10	15.85	163.34	nr	179.19
Mirror panels; BS 952; silvered; insulation backing						
4 mm thick float; fixing with adhesive						
1000 mm x 1000 mm	-	-	-	-	nr	147.54
1000 mm x 2000 mm	-	-	-	-	nr	279.81
1000 mm x 4000 mm	-	-	-	-	nr	539.27
Glass louvres; BS 952; with long edges ground or smooth						
6 mm thick float						
150 mm wide	-	-	-	-	m	11.45
7 mm thick Georgian wired cast						
150 mm wide	-	-	-	-	m	15.77
6 mm thick Georgian wire polished						
150 mm wide	-	-	-	-	m	22.64
Factory made double hermetically sealed units; to wood or metal with screwed or clipped beads						
Two panes; BS 952; clear float glass; 4 mm						
thick; 6 mm air space						
2.00 m² - 4.00 m²	-	-	-	-	m²	48.33
1.00 m² - 2.00 m²	-	-	-	-	m²	48.33
0.75 m² - 1.00 m²	-	-	-	-	m²	48.33
0.50 m² - 0.75 m²	-	-	-	-	m²	48.33
0.35 m² - 0.50 m²	-	-	-	-	m²	48.33
0.25 m² - 0.35 m²	-	-	-	-	m²	48.33
not exceeding 0.25 m²	-	-	-	-	nr	12.21

L WINDOWS/DOORS/STAIRS Excluding overheads and profit	PC £	Labour hours	Labour £	Material £	Unit	Total rate £
Two panes; BS 952; clear float glass; 6 mm thick; 6 mm air space						
2.00 m² - 4.00 m²	-	-	-	-	m²	**59.52**
1.00 m² - 2.00 m²	-	-	-	-	m²	**59.52**
0.75 m² - 1.00 m²	-	-	-	-	m²	**59.52**
0.50 m² - 0.75 m²	-	-	-	-	m²	**59.52**
0.35 m² - 0.50 m²	-	-	-	-	m²	**59.52**
0.25 m² - 0.35 m²	-	-	-	-	m²	**59.52**
not exceeding 0.25 m²	-	-	-	-	nr	**15.26**

M SURFACE FINISHES Excluding overheads and profit	PC £	Labour hours	Labour £	Material £	Unit	Total rate £
M SURFACE FINISHES						
M10 CEMENT:SAND/CONCRETE SCREEDS/ **TOPPINGS**						
Cement:sand (1:3); steel trowelled						
Work to floors; one coat; level and to falls not						
exceeding 15 degrees from horizontal; to						
concrete base; over 300 mm wide						
32 mm thick	-	0.32	3.58	2.16	m²	5.74
40 mm thick	-	0.34	3.80	2.70	m²	6.50
48 mm thick	-	0.36	4.03	3.24	m²	7.27
50 mm thick	-	0.37	4.14	3.37	m²	7.51
60 mm thick	-	0.41	4.59	4.05	m²	8.64
65 mm thick	-	0.44	4.92	4.38	m²	9.30
70 mm thick	-	0.45	5.04	4.72	m²	9.76
75 mm thick	-	0.46	5.15	5.06	m²	10.21
Add to the above for work to falls and crossfalls						
and to slopes						
not exceeding 15 degrees from horizontal	-	0.03	0.34	-	m²	0.34
over 15 degrees from horizontal	-	0.11	1.23	-	m²	1.23
water repellent additive incorporated in the mix	-	0.03	0.34	0.54	m²	0.88
oil repellent additive incorporated in the mix	-	0.09	1.01	4.03	m²	5.04
Cement:sand (1:3); beds and backings						
Work to floors; one coat level; to concrete base;						
screeded; over 300 mm wide						
25 mm thick	-	-	-	-	m²	7.95
50 mm thick	-	-	-	-	m²	9.38
75 mm thick	-	-	-	-	m²	12.25
100 mm thick	-	-	-	-	m²	15.14
Work to floors; one coat; level; to concrete base;						
steel trowelled; over 300 mm wide						
25 mm thick	-	-	-	-	m²	7.95
50 mm thick	-	-	-	-	m²	9.38
75 mm thick	-	-	-	-	m²	12.25
100 mm thick	-	-	-	-	m²	15.14
Fine concrete (1:4); beds and backings						
Work to floors; one coat; level; to concrete base;						
steel trowelled; over 300 mm wide						
50 mm thick	-	-	-	-	m²	9.16
75 mm thick	-	-	-	-	m²	11.75
Granolithic paving; cement and granite						
chippings 5 mm to dust (1:1:2); steel trowelled						
Work to floors; one coat; level; laid on concrete						
while green; over 300 mm wide						
20 mm thick	-	-	-	-	m²	14.38
25 mm thick	-	-	-	-	m²	15.52
Work to floors; two coat; laid on hacked						
concrete with slurry; over 300 mm wide						
38 mm thick	-	-	-	-	m²	18.51
50 mm thick	-	-	-	-	m²	21.27
75 mm thick	-	-	-	-	m²	28.75
Work to landings; one coat; level; laid on						
concrete while green; over 300 mm wide						
20 mm thick	-	-	-	-	m²	16.10
25 mm thick	-	-	-	-	m²	17.25

M SURFACE FINISHES Excluding overheads and profit	PC £	Labour hours	Labour £	Material £	Unit	Total rate £
Work to landings; two coat; laid on hacked concrete with slurry; over 300 mm wide						
38 mm thick	-	-	-	-	m²	20.24
50 mm thick	-	-	-	-	m²	23.00
75 mm thick	-	-	-	-	m²	30.48
Add to the above over 300 mm wide for						
liquid hardening additive incorporated in the mix	-	0.06	0.67	0.63	m²	1.30
oil-repellent additive incorporated in the mix	-	0.09	1.01	4.03	m²	5.04
25 mm work to treads; one coat; to concrete base						
225 mm wide	-	0.99	14.27	6.88	m	21.15
275 mm wide	-	0.99	14.27	7.70	m	21.97
returned end	-	0.20	2.88	-	nr	2.88
13 mm skirtings; rounded top edge and coved bottom junction; to brickwork or blockwork base						
75 mm wide on face	-	0.61	8.79	0.33	m	9.12
150 mm wide on face	-	0.83	11.96	6.05	m	18.01
ends; fair	-	0.06	0.86	-	nr	0.86
angles	-	0.08	1.15	-	nr	1.15
13 mm outer margin to stairs; to follow profile of and with rounded nosing to treads and risers; fair edge and arris at bottom, to concrete base						
75 mm wide	-	0.99	14.27	3.30	m	17.57
angles	-	0.08	1.15	-	nr	1.15
13 mm wall string to stairs; fair edge and arris on top; coved bottom junction with treads and risers; to brickwork or blockwork base						
275 mm (extreme) wide	-	0.88	12.68	5.78	m	18.46
ends	-	0.06	0.86	-	nr	0.86
angles	-	0.08	1.15	-	nr	1.15
ramps	-	0.09	1.30	-	nr	1.30
ramped and wreathed corners	-	0.11	1.59	-	nr	1.59
13 mm outer string to stairs; rounded nosing on top at junction with treads and risers; fair edge and arris at bottom; to concrete base						
300 mm (extreme) wide	-	0.88	12.68	7.15	m	19.83
ends	-	0.06	0.86	-	nr	0.86
angles	-	0.08	1.15	-	nr	1.15
ramps	-	0.09	1.30	-	nr	1.30
ramps and wreathed corners	-	0.11	1.59	-	nr	1.59
19 mm thick skirtings; rounded top edge and coved bottom junction; to brickwork or blockwork base						
75 mm wide on face	-	0.61	8.79	6.05	m	14.84
150 mm wide on face	-	0.83	11.96	9.35	m	21.31
ends; fair	-	0.06	0.67	-	nr	0.67
angles	-	0.08	1.15	-	nr	1.15
19 mm risers; one rounded nosing; to concrete base						
150 mm high; plain	-	0.99	14.27	5.22	m	19.49
150 mm high; undercut	-	0.99	14.27	5.22	m	19.49
180 mm high; plain	-	0.99	14.27	7.15	m	21.42
180 mm high; undercut	-	0.99	14.27	7.15	m	21.42

M SURFACE FINISHES Excluding overheads and profit	PC £	Labour hours	Labour £	Material £	Unit	Total rate £
M11 MASTIC ASPHALT FLOORING/FLOOR **UNDERLAYS**						
Mastic asphalt flooring to BS 6925 Type F **1076; black**						
20 mm thick; one coat coverings; felt isolating						
membrane; to concrete base; flat						
over 300 mm wide	-	-	-	-	m²	14.85
225 mm - 300 mm wide	-	-	-	-	m²	27.60
150 mm - 225 mm wide	-	-	-	-	m²	30.30
not exceeding 150 mm wide	-	-	-	-	m²	37.05
25 mm thick; one coat coverings; felt isolating						
membrane; to concrete base; flat						
over 300 mm wide	-	-	-	-	m²	17.25
225 mm - 300 mm wide	-	-	-	-	m²	29.40
150 mm - 225 mm wide	-	-	-	-	m²	32.10
not exceeding 150 mm wide	-	-	-	-	m²	38.85
20 mm thick; three coat skirtings to brickwork						
base						
not exceeding 150 mm girth	-	-	-	-	m	14.85
150 mm - 225 mm girth	-	-	-	-	m	17.25
225 mm - 300 mm girth	-	-	-	-	m	19.50
Mastic asphalt flooring; acid-resisting; black						
20 mm thick; one coat coverings; felt isolating						
membrane; to concrete base flat						
over 300 mm wide	-	-	-	-	m²	17.40
225 mm - 300 mm wide	-	-	-	-	m²	31.80
150 mm - 225 mm wide	-	-	-	-	m²	32.85
not exceeding 150 mm wide	-	-	-	-	m²	39.60
25 mm thick; one coat coverings; felt isolating						
membrane; to concrete base; flat						
over 300 mm wide	-	-	-	-	m²	20.55
225 mm - 300 mm wide	-	-	-	-	m²	32.70
150 mm - 225 mm wide	-	-	-	-	m²	35.40
not exceeding 150 mm wide	-	-	-	-	m²	42.15
20 mm thick; three coat skirtings to brickwork						
base						
not exceeding 150 mm girth	-	-	-	-	m	15.30
150 mm - 225 mm girth	-	-	-	-	m	17.85
225 mm - 300 mm girth	-	-	-	-	m	20.25
Mastic asphalt flooring to BS 6925 Type F **1451; red**						
20 mm thick; one coat coverings; felt isolating						
membrane; to concrete base; flat						
over 300 mm wide	-	-	-	-	m²	24.30
225 mm - 300 mm wide	-	-	-	-	m²	40.20
150 mm - 225 mm wide	-	-	-	-	m²	43.35
not exceeding 150 mm wide	-	-	-	-	m²	51.90
20 mm thick; three coat skirtings to brickwork						
base						
not exceeding 150 mm girth	-	-	-	-	m	19.05
150 mm - 225 mm girth	-	-	-	-	m	24.30

M SURFACE FINISHES Excluding overheads and profit	PC £	Labour hours	Labour £	Material £	Unit	Total rate £
M12 TROWELLED BITUMEN/RESIN/RUBBER **LATEX FLOORING**						
Latex cement floor screeds; steel trowelled						
Work to floors; level; to concrete base; over 300						
mm wide						
3 mm thick; one coat	-	-	-	-	m²	**3.69**
5 mm thick; two coats	-	-	-	-	m²	**5.22**
Isocrete K screeds or other equal and approved;						
steel trowelled						
Work to floors; level; to concrete base; over 300						
mm wide						
35 mm thick; plus polymer bonder coat	-	-	-	-	m²	**12.19**
40 mm thick	-	-	-	-	m²	**10.76**
45 mm thick	-	-	-	-	m²	**11.03**
50 mm thick	-	-	-	-	m²	**11.33**
Work to floors; to falls or crossfalls; to concrete						
base; over 300 mm wide						
55 mm (average) thick	-	-	-	-	m²	**12.48**
60 mm (average) thick	-	-	-	-	m²	**13.06**
65 mm (average) thick	-	-	-	-	m²	**13.63**
75 mm (average) thick	-	-	-	-	m²	**14.78**
90 mm (average) thick	-	-	-	-	m²	**16.51**
Bituminous lightweight insulating roof						
screeds						
"Bit-Ag" roof screed or other equal and approved;						
to falls or crossfalls; bitumen felt vapour barrier;						
over 300 mm wide						
75 mm (average) thick	-	-	-	-	m²	**39.00**
100 mm (average) thick	-	-	-	-	m²	**49.50**
M20 PLASTERED/RENDERED/ROUGHCAST						
COATINGS						
Prepare and brush down 2 coats of "Unibond"						
bonding agent or other equal and approved						
Brick or block walls						
over 300 mm wide	-	0.17	1.90	0.79	m²	**2.69**
Concrete walls or ceilings						
over 300 mm wide	-	0.13	1.45	0.63	m²	**2.08**
Cement:sand (1:3) beds and backings						
10 mm thick work to walls; one coat; to						
brickwork or blockwork base						
over 300 mm wide	-	-	-	-	m²	**8.92**
not exceeding 300 mm wide	-	-	-	-	m	**4.45**
13 mm thick; work to walls; two coats; to						
brickwork or blockwork base						
over 300 mm wide	-	-	-	-	m²	**10.66**
not exceeding 300 mm wide	-	-	-	-	m	**5.33**
15 mm thick work to walls; two coats; to						
brickwork or blockwork base						
over 300 mm wide	-	-	-	-	m²	**11.51**
not exceeding 300 mm wide	-	-	-	-	m	**5.75**
Cement:sand (1:3); steel trowelled						
13 mm thick work to walls; two coats; to						
brickwork or blockwork base						
over 300 mm wide	-	-	-	-	m²	**10.39**
not exceeding 300 mm wide	-	-	-	-	m	**5.19**

M SURFACE FINISHES Excluding overheads and profit	PC £	Labour hours	Labour £	Material £	Unit	Total rate £
M20 PLASTERED/RENDERED/ROUGHCAST **COATINGS** - cont'd						
Cement:sand (1:3); steel trowelled - cont'd						
16 mm thick work to walls; two coats; to						
brickwork or blockwork base						
over 300 mm wide	-	-	-	-	m²	11.63
not exceeding 300 mm wide	-	-	-	-	m	5.83
19 mm thick work to walls; two coats; to						
brickwork or blockwork base						
over 300 mm wide	-	-	-	-	m²	12.88
not exceeding 300 mm wide	-	-	-	-	m	6.44
ADD to above						
over 300 mm wide in water repellant cement	-	-	-	-	m²	2.63
finishing coat in colour cement	-	-	-	-	m²	6.08
Cement:lime:sand (1:2:9); steel trowelled						
19 mm thick work to walls; two coats; to						
brickwork or blockwork base						
over 300 mm wide	-	-	-	-	m²	13.03
not exceeding 300 mm wide	-	-	-	-	m	6.52
Cement:lime:sand (1:1:6); steel trowelled						
13 mm thick work to walls; two coats; to						
brickwork or blockwork base						
over 300 mm wide	-	-	-	-	m²	10.55
not exceeding 300 mm wide	-	-	-	-	m	5.27
Add to the above over 300 wide for						
waterproof additive	-	-	-	-	m²	1.80
19 mm thick work to ceilings; three coats; to						
metal lathing base						
over 300 mm wide	-	-	-	-	m²	15.99
not exceeding 300 mm wide	-	-	-	-	m	8.24
Plaster; first and finishing coats of "Carlite" **pre-mixed lightweight plaster or other equal** **and approved; steel trowelled**						
13 mm thick work to walls; two coats; to						
brickwork or blockwork base (or 10 mm thick						
work to concrete base)						
over 300 mm wide	-	-	-	-	m²	7.59
over 300 mm wide; in staircase areas or plant						
rooms	-	-	-	-	m²	8.75
not exceeding 300 mm wide	-	-	-	-	m	3.78
13 mm thick work to isolated piers or columns;						
two coats						
over 300 mm wide	-	-	-	-	m²	9.33
not exceeding 300 mm wide	-	-	-	-	m	4.66
10 mm thick work to ceilings; two coats; to						
concrete base						
over 300 mm wide	-	-	-	-	m²	8.12
over 300 mm wide; 3.50 m - 5.00 m high	-	-	-	-	m²	8.70
over 300 mm wide; in staircase areas or plant						
rooms	-	-	-	-	m²	9.29
not exceeding 300 mm wide	-	-	-	-	m	4.06
10 mm thick work to isolated beams; two coats;						
to concrete base						
over 300 mm wide	-	-	-	-	m²	9.88
over 300 mm wide; 3.50 m - 5.00 m high	-	-	-	-	m²	10.46
not exceeding 300 mm wide	-	-	-	-	m	4.93

M SURFACE FINISHES Excluding overheads and profit	PC £	Labour hours	Labour £	Material £	Unit	Total rate £
Plaster; first coat of "Thistle Hardwall" plaster or other equal and approved; finishing coat of "Thistle Multi Finish" plaster or other equal and approved; steel trowelled						
13 mm thick work to walls; two coats; to						
brickwork or blockwork base						
over 300 mm wide	-	-	-	-	m²	8.24
over 300 mm wide; in staircase areas or plant						
rooms	-	-	-	-	m²	9.46
not exceeding 300 mm wide	-	-	-	-	m	4.13
13 mm thick work to isolated columns; two coats						
over 300 mm wide	-	-	-	-	m²	10.07
not exceeding 300 mm wide	-	-	-	-	m	5.04
Plaster; one coat "Snowplast" plaster or other equal and approved; steel trowelled						
13 mm thick work to walls; one coat; to						
brickwork or blockwork base						
over 300 mm wide	-	-	-	-	m²	8.79
over 300 mm wide; in staircase areas or plant						
rooms	-	-	-	-	m²	10.01
not exceeding 300 mm wide	-	-	-	-	m	4.40
13 mm thick work to isolated columns; one coat						
over 300 mm wide	-	-	-	-	m²	10.62
not exceeding 300 mm wide	-	-	-	-	m	5.32
Plaster; first coat of cement:sand (1:3); finishing coat of "Thistle" class B plaster or other equal and approved; steel trowelled						
13 mm thick; work to walls; two coats; to						
brickwork or blockwork base						
over 300 mm wide	-	-	-	-	m²	8.42
over 300 mm wide; in staircase areas or plant						
rooms	-	-	-	-	m²	9.63
not exceeding 300 mm wide	-	-	-	-	m	4.21
13 mm thick work to isolated columns; two coats						
over 300 mm wide	-	-	-	-	m²	10.85
not exceeding 300 mm wide	-	-	-	-	m	5.42
Plaster; first coat of cement:lime:sand (1:1:6); finishing coat of "Multi Finish" plaster or other equal and approved; steel trowelled						
13 mm thick work to walls; two coats; to						
brickwork or blockwork base						
over 300 mm wide	-	-	-	-	m²	8.65
over 300 mm wide; in staircase areas or plant						
rooms	-	-	-	-	m²	9.87
not exceeding 300 mm wide	-	-	-	-	m	4.13
13 mm thick work to isolated columns; two coats						
over 300 mm wide	-	-	-	-	m²	10.07
not exceeding 300 mm wide	-	-	-	-	m	5.04
Plaster; first coat of "Limelite" renovating plaster or other equal and approved; finishing coat of "Limelite" renovating plaster or other equal and approved; finishing coat of "Limelite" finishing plaster or other equal and approved; steel trowelled						
13 mm thick work to walls; two coats; to						
brickwork or blockwork base						
over 300 mm wide	-	-	-	-	m²	12.14
over 300 mm wide; in staircase areas or plant rooms	-	-	-	-	m²	13.36
not exceeding 300 mm wide	-	-	-	-	m	6.08

M SURFACE FINISHES Excluding overheads and profit	PC £	Labour hours	Labour £	Material £	Unit	Total rate £
M20 PLASTERED/RENDERED/ROUGHCAST **COATINGS** - cont'd						
Plaster; first coat of "Limelite" renovating plaster **or other equal and approved; finishing coat of** **"Limelite" renovating plaster or other equal and** **approved; finishing coat of "Limelite" finishing** **plaster or other equal and approved; steel trowelled** - cont'd						
Dubbing out existing walls with undercoat plaster; average 6 mm thick						
over 300 mm wide	-	-	-	-	m²	3.65
not exceeding 300 mm wide	-	-	-	-	m	1.83
Dubbing out existing walls with undercoat plaster; average 12 mm thick						
over 300 mm wide	-	-	-	-	m²	7.30
not exceeding 300 mm wide	-	-	-	-	m	3.65
Plaster; first coat of "Thistle X-ray" plaster or other **equal and approved; finishing coat of "Thistle X-ray"** **finishing plaster or other equal and approved;** **steel trowelled**						
17 mm thick work to walls; two coats; to brickwork or blockwork base						
over 300 mm wide	-	-	-	-	m²	39.49
over 300 mm wide; in staircase areas or plant rooms	-	-	-	-	m²	40.71
not exceeding 300 mm wide	-	-	-	-	m	15.80
17 mm thick work to isolated columns; two coats						
over 300 mm wide	-	-	-	-	m²	43.14
not exceeding 300 mm wide	-	-	-	-	m	17.25
Plaster, one coat "Thistle" projection plaster or other **equal and approved; steel trowelled**						
13 mm thick work to walls; one coat; to brickwork or blockwork base						
over 300 mm wide	-	-	-	-	m²	8.47
over 300 mm wide; in staircase areas or plant rooms	-	-	-	-	m²	9.68
not exceeding 300 mm wide	-	-	-	-	m	4.24
10 mm thick work to isolated columns; one coat						
over 300 mm wide	-	-	-	-	m²	10.30
not exceeding 300 mm wide	-	-	-	-	m	5.14
Plaster; first, second and finishing coats of "Carlite" **pre-mixed lightweight plaster or other equal and** **approved; steel trowelled**						
13 mm thick work to ceilings; three coats to metal lathing base						
over 300 mm wide	-	-	-	-	m²	10.95
over 300 mm wide; in staircase areas or plant rooms	-	-	-	-	m²	12.18
not exceeding 300 mm wide	-				m	5.47
13 mm thick work to swept soffit of metal lathing arch former						
not exceeding 300 mm wide	-	-	-	-	m	7.30
300 mm - 400 mm wide	-	-	-	-	m	9.73
13 mm thick work to vertical face of metal lathing arch former						
not exceeding 0.50 m² per side	-	-	-	-	nr	10.35
0.50 m² - 1.00 m² per side	-	-	-	-	nr	15.53

M SURFACE FINISHES Excluding overheads and profit	PC £	Labour hours	Labour £	Material £	Unit	Total rate £
"Tyrolean" decorative rendering or other equal and approved; 13 mm thick first coat of cement:lime: sand (1:1:6); finishing three coats of "Cullamix" or other equal and approved applied with approved hand operated machine external						
To walls; four coats; to brickwork or blockwork base						
over 300 mm wide	-	-	-	-	m²	19.44
not exceeding 300 mm wide	-	-	-	-	m	9.72
Drydash (pebbledash) finish of Derbyshire Spar chippings or other equal and approved on and including cement:lime:sand (1:2:9) backing						
18 mm thick work to walls; two coats; to brickwork or blockwork base						
over 300 mm wide	-	-	-	-	m²	17.88
not exceeding 300 mm wide	-	-	-	-	m	8.95
Plaster; one coat "Thistle" board finish or other equal and approved; steel trowelled (prices included within plasterboard rates)						
3 mm thick work to walls or ceilings; one coat; to plasterboard base						
over 300 mm wide	-	-	-	-	m²	4.31
over 300 mm wide; in staircase areas or plant rooms	-	-	-	-	m²	4.91
not exceeding 300 mm wide	-	-	-	-	m	2.57
Plaster; one coat "Thistle" board finish or other equal and approved; steel trowelled; 3 mm work to walls or ceilings; one coat on and including gypsum plasterboard; BS 1230; fixing with nails; 3 mm joints filled with plaster and jute scrim cloth; to softwood base; plain grade baseboard or lath with rounded edges						
9.50 mm thick boards to walls						
over 300 mm wide	-	1.16	8.81	2.81	m²	11.62
not exceeding 300 mm wide	-	0.45	3.58	0.50	m	4.08
9.50 mm thick boards to walls; in staircase areas or plant rooms						
over 300 mm wide	-	1.27	9.69	2.81	m²	12.50
not exceeding 300 mm wide	-	0.56	4.46	0.50	m	4.96
9.50 mm thick boards to isolated columns						
over 300 mm wide	-	1.27	9.69	2.81	m²	12.50
not exceeding 300 mm wide	-	0.67	5.33	0.50	m	5.83
9.50 mm thick boards to ceilings						
over 300 mm wide	-	1.07	8.09	2.81	m²	10.90
over 300 mm wide; 3.50 m - 5.00 m high	-	1.23	9.37	2.81	m²	12.18
not exceeding 300 mm wide	-	0.51	4.06	0.50	m	4.56
9.50 mm thick boards to ceilings; in staircase areas or plant rooms						
over 300 mm wide	-	1.18	8.97	2.81	m²	11.78
not exceeding 300 mm wide	-	0.56	4.46	0.50	m	4.96
9.50 mm thick boards to isolated beams						
over 300 mm wide	-	1.25	9.53	2.81	m²	12.34
not exceeding 300 mm wide	-	0.60	4.78	0.50	m	5.28
add for "Duplex" insulating grade 12.50 mm thick boards or other equal and approved to walls	-	-	-	0.50	m²	0.50
12.50 mm thick boards to walls; in staircase areas or plant rooms						
over 300 mm wide	-	1.21	9.21	3.04	m²	12.25
not exceeding 300 mm wide	-	0.57	4.54	0.57	m	5.11

M SURFACE FINISHES Excluding overheads and profit	PC £	Labour hours	Labour £	Material £	Unit	Total rate £
M20 PLASTERED/RENDERED/ROUGHCAST **COATINGS** - cont'd						
Plaster; one coat "Thistle" board finish or other **equal and approved; steel trowelled; 3 mm work** **to walls or ceilings; one coat on and including** **gypsum plasterboard; BS 1230; fixing with nails;** **3 mm joints filled with plaster and jute scrim cloth;** **to softwood base; plain grade baseboard or lath** **with rounded edges** - cont'd						
12.50 mm thick boards to isolated columns						
over 300 mm wide	-	1.25	9.53	3.04	m²	12.57
not exceeding 300 mm wide	-	0.60	4.78	0.57	m	5.35
12.50 mm thick boards to ceilings						
over 300 mm wide	-	1.14	8.65	3.04	m²	11.69
over 300 mm wide; 3.50 m - 5.00 m high	-	1.27	9.69	3.04	m²	12.73
not exceeding 300 mm wide	-	0.54	4.30	0.57	m	4.87
12.50 mm thick boards to ceilings; in staircase areas or plant rooms						
over 300 mm wide	-	1.27	9.69	3.04	m²	12.73
not exceeding 300 mm wide	-	0.61	4.86	0.57	m	5.43
12.50 mm thick boards to isolated beams						
over 300 wide	-	1.37	10.48	3.04	m²	13.52
not exceeding 300 mm wide	-	0.67	5.33	0.57	m	5.90
add for "Duplex" insulating grade 12.50 mm thick boards or other equal and approved to walls	-	-	-	0.50	m²	0.50
Accessories						
"Expamet" render beads or other equal and approved; white PVC nosings; to brickwork or blockwork base						
external stop bead; ref 573	-	0.09	0.72	2.38	m	3.10
"Expamet" render beads or other equal and approved; stainless steel; to brickwork or blockwork base						
stop bead; ref 546	-	0.09	0.72	1.95	m	2.67
stop bead; ref 547	-	0.09	0.72	1.95	m	2.67
"Expamet" plaster beads or other equal and approved; galvanised steel; to brickwork or blockwork base						
angle bead; ref 550	-	0.10	0.80	0.78	m	1.58
architrave bead; ref 579	-	0.12	0.96	1.20	m	2.16
stop bead; ref 562	-	0.09	0.72	0.91	m	1.63
stop beads; ref 563	-	0.09	0.72	0.91	m	1.63
movement bead; ref 588	-	0.11	0.88	4.29	m	5.17
"Expamet" plaster beads or other equal and approved; stainless steel; to brickwork or blockwork base						
angle bead; ref 545	-	0.10	0.80	2.20	m	3.00
stop bead; ref 534	-	0.09	0.72	1.95	m	2.67
stop bead; ref 533	-	0.09	0.72	1.95	m	2.67
"Expamet" thin coat plaster beads or other equal and approved; galvanised steel; to timber base						
angle bead; ref 553	-	0.09	0.72	0.77	m	1.49
angle bead; ref 554	-	0.09	0.72	1.07	m	1.79
stop bead; ref 560	-	0.08	0.64	0.98	m	1.62
M22 SPRAYED MINERAL FIBRE COATINGS						
Prepare and apply by spray "Mandolite CP2" **fire protection or other equal and approved on** **structural steel/metalwork**						
16 mm thick (one hour) fire protection						
to walls and columns	-	-	-	-	m²	8.30
to ceilings and beams	-	-	-	-	m²	9.10
to isolated metalwork	-	-	-	-	m²	18.25

M SURFACE FINISHES Excluding overheads and profit	PC £	Labour hours	Labour £	Material £	Unit	Total rate £
22 mm thick (one and a half hour) fire protection						
to walls and columns	-	-	-	-	m²	9.65
to ceilings and beams	-	-	-	-	m²	10.70
to isolated metalwork	-	-	-	-	m²	21.45
28 mm thick (two hour) fire protection						
to walls and columns	-	-	-	-	m²	11.25
to ceilings and beams	-	-	-	-	m²	12.35
to isolated metalwork	-	-	-	-	m²	24.65
52 mm thick (four hour) fire protection						
to walls and columns	-	-	-	-	m²	17.15
to ceilings and beams	-	-	-	-	m²	19.00
to isolated metalwork	-	-	-	-	m²	37.95
Prepare and apply by spray; cementitious "Pyrok WF26" render or other equal and approved; on expanded metal lathing (not included)						
15 mm thick						
to ceilings and beams	-	-	-	-	m²	26.30
M30 METAL MESH LATHING/ANCHORED REINFORCEMENT FOR PLASTERED COATING						
Accessories						
Pre-formed galvanised expanded steel arch-frames; "Simpson Strong-Tie" or other equal and approved; semi-circular; to suit walls up to 230 mm thick						
375 mm radius; for 800 mm opening; ref SC 750	21.92	0.56	4.03	22.47	nr	26.50
425 mm radius; for 850 mm opening; ref SC 850	23.06	0.56	4.03	23.64	nr	27.67
450 mm radius; for 900 mm opening; ref SC 900	24.57	0.56	4.03	25.18	nr	29.21
600 mm radius; for 1200 mm opening; ref SC 1200	26.65	0.56	4.03	27.32	nr	31.35
"Newlath" damp free lathing or other equal and approved; plugging and screwing to background at 250 mm centres each way						
Linings to walls						
over 300 mm wide	-	1.38	15.65	9.17	m²	24.82
not exceeding 300 mm wide	-	0.44	4.99	2.82	m²	7.81
Lathing; Expamet "BB" expanded metal lathing or other equal and approved; BS 1369; 50 mm laps						
6 mm thick mesh linings to ceilings; fixing with staples; to softwood base; over 300 mm wide						
ref BB263; 0.500 mm thick	3.98	0.66	4.76	4.18	m²	8.94
ref BB264; 0.675 mm thick	4.65	0.66	4.76	4.88	m²	9.64
6 mm thick mesh linings to ceilings; fixing with wire; to steelwork; over 300 mm wide						
ref BB263; 0.500 mm thick	-	0.70	5.04	4.18	m²	9.22
ref BB264; 0.675 mm thick	-	0.70	5.04	4.88	m²	9.92
6 mm thick mesh linings to ceilings; fixing with wire; to steelwork; not exceeding 300 mm wide						
ref BB263; 0.500 mm thick	-	0.44	3.17	4.18	m²	7.35
ref BB264; 0.675 mm thick	-	0.44	3.17	4.88	m²	8.05
raking cutting	-	0.22	1.75	-	m	1.75
cutting and fitting around pipes; not exceeding 0.30 m girth	-	0.33	2.63	-	nr	2.63

M SURFACE FINISHES Excluding overheads and profit	PC £	Labour hours	Labour £	Material £	Unit	Total rate £

M30 METAL MESH LATHING/ANCHORED
   REINFORCEMENT FOR PLASTERED
   COATING - cont'd						

Lathing; Expamet "Riblath" or "Spraylath" **stiffened expanded metal lathing or other** **equal and approved; 50 mm laps**						
10 mm thick mesh lining to walls; fixing with						
nails; to softwood base; over 300 mm wide						
"Riblath" ref 269; 0.30 mm thick	4.99	0.56	4.03	5.33	m²	9.36
"Riblath" ref 271; 0.50 mm thick	5.75	0.56	4.03	6.12	m²	10.15
"Spraylath" ref 273; 0.50 mm thick	-	0.56	4.03	7.43	m²	11.46
10 mm thick mesh lining to walls; fixing with						
nails; to softwood base; not exceeding 300 mm						
wide						
"Riblath" ref 269; 0.30 mm thick	-	0.34	2.45	1.63	m²	4.08
"Riblath" ref 271; 0.50 mm thick	-	0.34	2.45	1.87	m²	4.32
"Spraylath" ref 273; 0.50 mm thick	-	0.34	2.45	2.29	m²	4.74
10 mm thick mesh lining to walls; fixing to brick						
or blockwork; over 300 mm wide						
"Red-rib" ref 274; 0.50 mm thick	6.34	0.44	3.17	7.15	m²	10.32
stainless steel "Riblath" ref 267; 0.30 mm thick	12.59	0.44	3.17	13.71	m²	16.88
10 mm mesh lining to ceilings; fixing with						
wire; to steelwork; over 300 mm wide						
"Riblath" ref 269; 0.30 mm thick	-	0.70	5.04	5.71	m²	10.75
"Riblath" ref 271; 0.50 mm thick	-	0.70	5.04	6.50	m²	11.54
"Spraylath" ref 273; 0.50 mm thick	-	0.70	5.04	7.81	m²	12.85
M31 FIBROUS PLASTER						
Fibrous plaster; fixing with screws; plugging; **countersinking; stopping; filling and pointing** **joints with plaster**						
16 mm thick plain slab coverings to ceilings						
over 300 mm wide	-	-	-	-	m²	103.95
not exceeding 300 mm wide	-	-	-	-	m	33.49
Coves; not exceeding 150 mm girth						
per 25 mm girth	-	-	-	-	m	4.95
Coves; 150 mm - 300 mm girth						
per 25 mm girth	-	-	-	-	m	6.05
Cornices						
per 25 mm girth	-	-	-	-	m	6.05
Cornice enrichments						
per 25 mm girth; depending on degree of						
enrichments	-	-	-	-	m	7.37
Fibrous plaster; fixing with plaster wadding **filling and pointing joints with plaster; to steel** **base**						
16 mm thick plain slab coverings to ceilings						
over 300 mm wide	-	-	-	-	m²	103.95
not exceeding 300 mm wide	-	-	-	-	m	33.49
16 mm thick plain casings to stanchions						
per 25 mm girth	-	-	-	-	m	3.08
16 mm thick plain casings to beams						
per 25 mm girth	-	-	-	-	m	3.08
Gyproc cove or other equal and approved; fixing **with adhesive; filling and pointing joints with plaster**						
Coves						
125 mm girth	-	0.22	1.75	0.83	m	2.58
angles	-	0.04	0.32	0.52	nr	0.84

M SURFACE FINISHES Excluding overheads and profit	PC £	Labour hours	Labour £	Material £	Unit	Total rate £
M40 STONE/CONCRETE/QUARRY/CERAMIC TILING/MOSAIC						
Clay floor quarries; BS 6431; class 1; Daniel Platt "Crown" tiles or other equal and approved; level bedding 10 mm thick and jointing in cement: sand (1:3); butt joints; straight both ways; flush pointing with grout; to cement:sand base						
Work to floors; over 300 mm wide						
150 mm x 150 mm x 12.50 mm thick; red	-	0.88	9.85	22.10	m²	**31.95**
150 mm x 150 mm x 12.50 mm thick; brown	-	0.88	9.85	27.06	m²	**36.91**
200 mm x 200 mm x 19 mm thick; brown	-	0.72	8.06	39.29	m²	**47.35**
Works to floors; in staircase areas or plant rooms						
150 mm x 150 mm x 12.50 mm thick; red	-	0.99	11.08	22.10	m²	**33.18**
150 mm x 150 mm x 12.50 mm thick; brown	-	0.99	11.08	27.06	m²	**38.14**
200 mm x 200 mm x 19 mm thick; brown	-	0.83	9.29	39.29	m²	**48.58**
Work to floors; not exceeding 300 mm wide						
150 mm x 150 mm x 12.50 mm thick; red	-	0.44	4.92	5.28	m²	**10.20**
150 mm x 150 mm x 12.50 mm thick; brown	-	0.44	4.92	6.77	m²	**11.69**
200 mm x 200 mm x 19 mm thick; brown	-	0.36	4.03	10.44	m²	**14.47**
fair square cutting against flush edges of existing finishes	-	0.13	0.99	1.23	m	**2.22**
raking cutting	-	0.23	1.77	1.38	m	**3.15**
cutting around pipes; not exceeding 0.30 m girth	-	0.17	1.35	-	nr	**1.35**
extra for cutting and fitting into recessed manhole cover 600 mm x 600 mm	-	1.10	8.76	-	nr	**8.76**
Work to sills; 150 mm wide; rounded edge tiles						
150 mm x 150 mm x 12.50 mm thick; red	-	0.36	4.03	4.81	m	**8.84**
150 mm x 150 mm x 12.50 mm thick; brown	-	0.36	4.03	6.30	m	**10.33**
fitted end	-	0.17	1.35	-	m	**1.35**
Coved skirtings; 138 mm high; rounded top edge						
150 mm x 138 mm x 12.50 mm thick; red	-	0.28	3.13	5.40	m	**8.53**
150 mm x 138 mm x 12.50 mm thick; brown	-	0.28	3.13	5.67	m	**8.80**
ends	-	0.06	0.48	-	nr	**0.48**
angles	-	0.17	1.35	2.22	nr	**3.57**
Glazed ceramic wall tiles; BS 6431; fixing with adhesive; butt joints; straight both ways; flush pointing with white grout; to plaster base						
Work to walls; over 300 mm wide						
152 mm x 152 mm x 5.50 mm thick; white	11.66	0.66	9.51	16.07	m²	**25.58**
152 mm x 152 mm x 5.50 mm thick; light colours	14.04	0.66	9.51	18.57	m²	**28.08**
152 mm x 152 mm x 5.50 mm thick; dark colours	17.34	0.66	9.51	22.03	m²	**31.54**
extra for RE or REX tile	-	-	-	6.31	m²	**6.31**
200 mm x 100 mm x 6.50 mm thick; white and light colours	13.27	0.66	9.51	17.76	m²	**27.27**
250 mm x 200 mm x 7.00 mm thick; white and light colours	15.35	0.66	9.51	19.94	m²	**29.45**
Work to walls; in staircase areas or plant rooms						
152 mm x 152 mm x 5.50 mm thick; white	-	0.74	10.66	16.07	m²	**26.73**
Work to walls; not exceeding 300 mm wide						
152 mm x 152 mm x 5.50 mm thick; white	-	0.33	4.76	4.78	m	**9.54**
152 mm x 152 mm x 5.50 mm thick; light colours		0.33	4.76	7.35	m	**12.11**

M SURFACE FINISHES Excluding overheads and profit	PC £	Labour hours	Labour £	Material £	Unit	Total rate £
M40 STONE/CONCRETE/QUARRY/CERAMIC **TILING/MOSAIC** - cont'd						
Glazed ceramic wall tiles; BS 6431; fixing with **adhesive; butt joints; straight both ways; flush** **pointing with white grout; to plaster base** - cont'd						
Work to walls; not exceeding 300 mm wide - cont'd						
152 mm x 152 mm x 5.50 mm thick; dark						
colours	-	0.33	4.76	8.39	m	**13.15**
200 mm x 100 mm x 6.50 mm thick; white and						
light colours	-	0.33	4.76	5.28	m	**10.04**
250 mm x 200 mm x 7.00 mm thick; white and light						
colours	-	0.28	4.03	5.94	m	**9.97**
cutting around pipes; not exceeding 0.30 m						
girth	-	0.11	0.88	-	nr	**0.88**
Work to sills; 150 mm wide; rounded edge tiles						
152 mm x 152 mm x 5.50 mm thick; white	-	0.28	4.03	2.39	m	**6.42**
fitted end	-	0.11	0.88	-	nr	**0.88**
198 mm x 64.50 mm x 6 mm thick wall tiles; **fixing with adhesive; butt joints; straight both** **ways; flush pointing with white grout; to** **plaster base**						
Work to walls						
over 300 mm wide	25.00	1.98	28.53	30.07	m²	**58.60**
not exceeding 300 mm wide	-	0.77	11.10	8.98	m	**20.08**
20 mm x 20 mm x 5.50 mm thick glazed **mosaic wall tiles; fixing with adhesive; butt** **joints; straight both ways; flush pointing with** **white grout; to plaster base**						
Work to walls						
over 300 mm wide	30.00	2.09	30.12	36.00	m²	**66.12**
not exceeding 300 mm wide	-	0.83	11.96	12.49	m	**24.45**
50 mm x 50 mm x 5.50 mm thick slip resistant **mosaic floor tiles, Series 2 or other equal and** **approved; fixing with adhesive; butt joints;** **straight both ways; flush pointing with white** **grout; to cement:sand base**						
Work to floors						
over 300 mm wide	17.46	2.09	23.39	23.62	m²	**47.01**
not exceeding 300 mm wide	-	0.83	9.29	8.54	m	**17.83**
Riven Welsh slate floor tiles; level; bedding 10 **mm thick and jointing in cement:sand** **(1:3); butt joints; straight both ways; flush** **pointing with coloured mortar; to cement:** **sand base**						
Work to floors; over 300 mm wide						
250 mm x 250 mm x 12 mm - 15 mm thick	-	0.66	9.51	34.03	m²	**43.54**
Work to floors; not exceeding 300 mm wide						
250 mm x 250 mm x 12 mm - 15 mm thick	-	0.33	4.76	10.29	m	**15.05**

M SURFACE FINISHES Excluding overheads and profit	PC £	Labour hours	Labour £	Material £	Unit	Total rate £
M41 TERRAZZO TILING/ IN SITU TERRAZZO						
Terrazzo tiles BS 4131; aggregate size						
random ground grouted and polished to 80's						
grit finish; standard colour range; 3 mm joints						
symmetrical layout; bedding in 42 mm cement						
semi-dry mix (1:4); grouting with neat						
matching cement						
300 mm x 300 mm x 28 mm (nominal),						
"Quil-Terra Terrazzo" tile units or other equal						
and approved, Quilligotti Contracts Ltd; hydraulically						
pressed, mechanically vibrated, steam cured; to						
floors on concrete base (not included); sealed with						
"Quil-Shield" penetrating case hardener or other						
equal and approved; 2 nr coats applied immediately						
after final polishing						
plain; laid level	-	-	-	-	m²	36.45
plain; to slopes exceeding 15 degrees from						
horizontal	-	-	-	-	m²	41.55
to small areas/toilets	-	-	-	-	m²	74.15
Accessories						
plastic division strips 6 mm x 38 mm; set into						
floor tiling above crack inducing joints; to the						
nearest full tile module	-	-	-	-	m	2.05
M42 WOOD BLOCK/COMPOSITION						
BLOCK/PARQUET FLOORING						
Wood block; Vigers, Stevens & Adams "Vigerflex"						
or other equal and approved; 7.50 mm thick;						
level; fixing with adhesive; to cement:sand base						
Work to floors; over 300 mm wide						
"Maple 7"	-	0.55	6.15	17.35	m²	23.50
Wood blocks 25 mm thick; tongued and						
grooved joints; herringbone pattern; level;						
fixing with adhesive; to cement:sand base						
Work to floors; over 300 mm wide						
iroko	-	-	-	-	m²	37.60
"Maple 7" or other equal and approved	-	-	-	-	m²	38.50
french oak	-	-	-	-	m²	51.65
american oak	-	-	-	-	m²	49.25
fair square cutting against flush edges of						
existing finishings	-	-	-	-	m	4.95
extra for cutting and fitting into recessed duct						
covers 450 mm wide; lining up with adjoining						
work	-	-	-	-	m	12.30
cutting around pipes; not exceeding 0.30 m						
girth	-	-	-	-	nr	2.10
extra for cutting and fitting into recessed						
manhole covers 600 mm x 600 mm; lining up						
with adjoining work	-	-	-	-	nr	9.00
Add to wood block flooring over 300 mm wide						
for						
sanding; one coat sealer; one coat wax polish	-	-	-	-	m²	4.05
sanding; two coats sealer; buffing with steel						
wool	-	-	-	-	m²	3.95
sanding; three coats polyurethane lacquer;						
buffing down between coats	-	-	-	-	m²	6.05

M SURFACE FINISHES Excluding overheads and profit	PC £	Labour hours	Labour £	Material £	Unit	Total rate £
M50 RUBBER/PLASTICS/CORK/LINO/CARPET TILING/SHEETING						
Linoleum sheet; BS 6826; Forbo-Nairn floors or other equal and approved; level; fixing with adhesive; butt joints; to cement:sand base Work to floors; over 300 mm wide						
2.50 mm thick; plain	-	0.44	4.92	12.21	m²	**17.13**
3.20 mm thick; marbled	-	0.44	4.92	13.02	m²	**17.94**
Linoleum sheet; "Marmoleum Real" or other equal and approved; level; with welded seams; fixing with adhesive; to cement:sand base Work to floors; over 300 mm wide						
2.50 mm thick	-	0.55	6.15	10.49	m²	**16.64**
Vinyl sheet; Altro "Safety" range or other equal and approved; with welded seams; level; fixing with adhesive; to cement:sand base Work to floors; over 300 mm wide						
2.00 mm thick; "Marine T20"	-	0.66	7.39	15.12	m²	**22.51**
2.50 mm thick; "Classic D25"	-	0.77	8.62	17.55	m²	**26.17**
3.50 mm thick; "Stronghold"	-	0.88	9.85	25.49	m²	**35.34**
Slip resistant vinyl sheet; Forbo-Nairn "Surestep" or other equal and approved; level with welded seams; fixing with adhesive; to cement:sand base Work to floors; over 300 mm wide						
2.00 mm thick	-	0.55	6.15	13.34	m²	**19.49**
Vinyl sheet; heavy duty; Marley "HD" or other equal and approved; level; with welded seams; fixing with adhesive; level; to cement:sand base Work to floors; over 300 mm wide						
2.00 mm thick	-	0.49	5.48	9.50	m²	**14.98**
2.50 mm thick	-	0.55	6.15	10.65	m²	**16.80**
2.00 mm thick skirtings						
100 high	-	0.13	1.45	1.66	m	**3.11**
Vinyl sheet; "Gerflex" standard sheet or other equal and approved; "Classic" range; level; with welded seams; fixing with adhesive; to cement:sand base Work to floors; over 300 mm wide						
2.00 mm thick	-	0.55	6.15	7.05	m²	**13.20**
Vinyl sheet; "Armstrong Rhino Contract" or other equal and approved; level; with welded seams; fixing with adhesive; to cement:sand base Work to floors; over 300 mm wide						
2.50 mm thick	-	0.55	6.15	14.10	m²	**20.25**
Vinyl tiles; "Accoflex" or other equal and approved; level; fixing with adhesive; butt joints; straight both ways; to cement:sand base Work to floors; over 300 mm wide						
300 mm x 300 mm x 2.00 mm thick	-	0.28	3.13	4.10	m²	**7.23**

M SURFACE FINISHES Excluding overheads and profit	PC £	Labour hours	Labour £	Material £	Unit	Total rate £
Vinyl semi-flexible tiles; "Arlon" or other equal and approved; level; fixing with adhesive; butt joints; straight both ways; to cement:sand base Work to floors; over 300 mm wide						
250 mm x 250 mm x 2.00 mm thick	-	0.28	3.13	4.30	m²	**7.43**
Vinyl semi-flexible tiles; Marley "Marleyflex" or other equal and approved; level; fixing with adhesive; butt joints; straight both ways; to cement:sand base Work to floors; over 300 mm wide						
300 mm x 300 mm x 2.00 mm thick	-	0.28	3.13	5.47	m²	**8.60**
300 mm x 300 mm x 2.50 mm thick	-	0.28	3.13	6.63	m²	**9.76**
Vinyl semi-flexible tiles; "Vylon" or other equal and approved; level; fixing with adhesive; butt joints; straight both ways; to cement:sand base Work to floors; over 300 mm wide						
250 mm x 250 mm x 2.00 mm thick	-	0.31	3.47	5.58	m²	**9.05**
Vinyl tiles; anti-static; level; fixing with adhesive; butt joints; straight both ways; to cement:sand base Work to floors; over 300 mm wide						
457 mm x 457 mm x 2.00 mm thick	-	0.49	5.48	10.53	m²	**16.01**
Vinyl tiles; "Polyflex" or other equal and approved; level; fixing with adhesive; butt joints; straight both ways; to cement:sand base Work to floors; over 300 mm wide						
300 mm x 300 mm x 1.50 mm thick	-	0.28	3.13	4.36	m²	**7.49**
300 mm x 300 mm x 2.00 mm thick	-	0.28	3.13	4.77	m²	**7.90**
Vinyl tiles; "Polyflor XL" or other equal and approved; level; fixing with adhesive; butt joints; straight both ways; to cement:sand base Work to floors; over 300 mm wide						
300 mm x 300 mm x 2.00 mm thick	-	0.39	4.36	6.26	m²	**10.62**
Vinyl tiles; Marley "HD" or other equal and approved; level; fixing with adhesive; butt joints; straight both ways; to cement:sand base Work to floors; over 300 mm wide						
300 mm x 300 mm x 2.00 mm thick	-	0.39	4.36	9.50	m²	**13.86**
Thermoplastic tiles; Marley "Marleyflex" or other equal and approved; level; fixing with adhesive; butt joints; straight both ways; to cement:sand base Work to floors; over 300 mm wide						
300 mm x 300 mm x 2.00 mm thick; series 2	-	0.25	2.80	4.53	m²	**7.33**
300 mm x 300 mm x 2.00 mm thick; series 4	-	0.25	2.80	5.22	m²	**8.02**
Linoleum tiles; BS 6826; Forbo-Nairn Floors or other equal and approved; level; fixing with adhesive; butt joints; straight both ways; to cement:sand base Work to floors; over 300 mm wide						
2.50 mm thick (marble pattern)	-	0.33	3.69	13.30	m²	**16.99**

M SURFACE FINISHES Excluding overheads and profit	PC £	Labour hours	Labour £	Material £	Unit	Total rate £
M50 RUBBER/PLASTICS/CORK/LINO/CARPET **TILING/SHEETING** - cont'd						
Cork tiles Wicanders "Cork-Master" or other equal **and approved; level; fixing with adhesive; butt joints;** **straight both ways; to cement:sand base**						
Work to floors; over 300 mm wide						
300 mm x 300 mm x 4.00 mm thick	-	0.44	4.92	19.14	m²	**24.06**
Rubber studded tiles; Altro "Mondopave" or other **equal and approved; level; fixing with adhesive;** **butt joints; straight to cement:sand base**						
Work to floors; over 300 mm wide						
500 mm x 500 mm x 2.50 mm thick; type MRB; black	-	0.66	7.39	22.87	m²	**30.26**
500 mm x 500 mm x 4.00 mm thick; type MRB; black	-	0.66	7.39	24.99	m²	**32.38**
Work to landings; over 300 mm wide						
500 mm x 500 mm x 4.00 mm thick; type MRB; black	-	0.88	9.85	24.99	m²	**34.84**
4.00 mm thick to treads						
275 mm wide	-	0.55	6.15	7.44	m	**13.59**
4.00 mm thick to risers						
180 mm wide	-	0.66	7.39	5.23	m	**12.62**
Sundry floor sheeting underlays						
For floor finishings; over 300 mm wide						
building paper to BS 1521; class A; 75 mm lap (laying only)	-	0.07	0.45	-	m²	**0.45**
3.20 mm thick hardboard	-	0.22	3.17	1.11	m²	**4.28**
6.00 mm thick plywood	-	0.33	4.76	5.87	m²	**10.63**
Stair nosings						
Light duty hard aluminium alloy stair tread nosings; plugged and screwed in concrete						
57 mm x 32 mm	7.45	0.28	2.23	7.73	m	**9.96**
84 mm x 32 mm	10.30	0.33	2.63	10.65	m	**13.28**
Heavy duty aluminium alloy stair tread nosings; plugged and screwed to concrete						
60 mm x 32 mm	8.85	0.33	2.63	9.17	m	**11.80**
92 mm x 32 mm	12.15	0.39	3.10	12.55	m	**15.65**
Heavy duty carpet tiles; Heuga "580 Olympic" or **other equal and approved; to cement:sand base**						
Work to floors						
over 300 mm wide	22.57	0.33	3.69	23.70	m²	**27.39**
Nylon needlepunch carpet; "Marleytex" or other **equal and approved; fixing; with adhesive; level;** **to cement**						
Work to floors						
over 300 mm wide	-	0.28	3.13	6.54	m²	**9.67**
M51 EDGE FIXED CARPETING						
Fitted carpeting; Wilton wool/nylon or other equal **and approved; 80/20 velvet pile; heavy domestic** **plain; PC £34.81/m²**						
Work to floors						
over 300 mm wide	-	0.45	3.27	38.29	m²	**41.56**
Work to treads and risers						
over 300 mm wide	-	0.90	6.54	38.29	m²	**44.83**

M SURFACE FINISHES Excluding overheads and profit	PC £	Labour hours	Labour £	Material £	Unit	Total rate £
Underlay to carpeting; PC £3.36/m² Work to floors						
over 300 mm wide	-	0.09	0.65	3.53	m²	**4.18**
Sundries Carpet gripper fixed to floor; standard edging						
22 mm wide	-	0.06	0.39	0.16	m	**0.55**
M52 DECORATIVE PAPERS/FABRICS						
Lining paper; PC £2.00/roll; and hanging Plaster walls or columns						
over 300 mm girth	-	0.21	1.67	0.43	m²	**2.10**
Plaster ceilings or beams						
over 300 mm girth	-	0.26	2.07	0.43	m²	**2.50**
Decorative paper-backed vinyl wallpaper; **PC £10.00/roll; and hanging** Plaster walls or columns						
over 300 mm girth	-	0.26	2.07	1.96	m²	**4.03**
M60 PAINTING/CLEAR FINISHING						
PREPARATION OF EXISTING SURFACES - **INTERNALLY**						
NOTE: The prices for preparation given hereunder assume that existing surfaces are in fair condition and should be increased for badly dilapidated surfaces.						
Wash down walls; cut out and make good **cracks** Emulsion painted surfaces; including bringing						
forward bare patches	-	0.08	0.64	-	m²	**0.64**
Gloss painted surfaces	-	0.06	0.48	-	m²	**0.48**
Wash down ceilings; cut out and make good **cracks**						
Distempered surfaces	-	0.10	0.80	-	m²	**0.80**
Emulsion painted surfaces; including bringing						
forward bare patches	-	0.11	0.88	-	m²	**0.88**
Gloss painted surfaces	-	0.10	0.80	-	m²	**0.80**
Wash down plaster cornices; cut out and **make good cracks**						
Distempered surfaces	-	0.14	1.11	-	m²	**1.11**
Emulsion painted surfaces; including bringing						
forward bare patches	-	0.17	1.35	-	m²	**1.35**
Wash and rub down iron and steel surfaces; **bringing forward** General surfaces						
over 300 mm girth	-	0.13	1.03	-	m²	**1.03**
isolated surfaces not exceeding 300 mm girth	-	0.06	0.48	-	m²	**0.48**
isolated areas not exceeding 0.50 m² irrespective of girth	-	0.10	0.80	-	nr	**0.80**
Glazed windows and screens						
panes; area not exceeding 0.10 m²	-	0.22	1.75	-	m²	**1.75**
panes; area 0.10 m² - 0.50 m²	-	0.17	1.35	-	m²	**1.35**
panes; area 0.50 m² - 1.00 m²	-	0.14	1.11	-	m²	**1.11**
panes; area over 1.00 m²	-	0.13	1.03	-	m²	**1.03**

M SURFACE FINISHES Excluding overheads and profit	PC £	Labour hours	Labour £	Material £	Unit	Total rate £
M60 PAINTING/CLEAR FINISHING						
PREPARATION OF EXISTING SURFACES - INTERNALLY - cont'd						
Wash and rub down wood surfaces; prime bare patches; bringing forward						
General surfaces						
over 300 mm girth	-	0.20	1.59	-	m²	**1.59**
isolated surfaces not exceeding 300 mm girth	-	0.08	0.64	-	m²	**0.64**
isolated areas not exceeding 0.50 m²						
irrespective of girth	-	0.15	1.19	-	nr	**1.19**
Glazed windows and screens						
panes; area not exceeding 0.10 m²	-	0.33	2.63	-	m²	**2.63**
panes; area 0.10 m² - 0.50 m²	-	0.26	2.07	-	m²	**2.07**
panes; area 0.50 m² - 1.00 m²	-	0.21	1.67	-	m²	**1.67**
panes; area over 1.00 m²	-	0.20	1.59	-	m²	**1.59**
Wash down and remove paint with chemical stripper from iron, steel or wood surfaces						
General surfaces						
over 300 mm girth	-	0.60	4.78	-	m²	**4.78**
isolated surfaces not exceeding 300 mm girth	-	0.26	2.07	-	m²	**2.07**
isolated areas not exceeding 0.50 m²						
irrespective of girth	-	0.45	3.58	-	nr	**3.58**
Glazed windows and screens						
panes; area not exceeding 0.10 m²	-	1.28	10.19	-	m²	**10.19**
panes; area 0.10 m² - 0.50 m²	-	1.02	8.12	-	m²	**8.12**
panes; area 0.50 m² - 1.00 m²	-	0.88	7.00	-	m²	**7.00**
panes; area over 1.00 m²	-	0.77	6.13	-	m²	**6.13**
Burn off and rub down to remove paint from iron, steel or wood surfaces						
General surfaces						
over 300 mm girth	-	0.74	5.89	-	m²	**5.89**
isolated surfaces not exceeding 300 mm girth	-	0.34	2.71	-	m²	**2.71**
isolated areas not exceeding 0.50 m²						
irrespective of girth	-	0.56	4.46	-	nr	**4.46**
Glazed windows and screens						
panes; area not exceeding 0.10 m²	-	1.60	12.74	-	m²	**12.74**
panes; area 0.10 m² - 0.50 m²	-	1.28	10.19	-	m²	**10.19**
panes; area 0.50 m² - 1.00 m²	-	1.10	8.76	-	m²	**8.76**
panes; area over 1.00 m²	-	0.96	7.64	-	m²	**7.64**
PAINTING/CLEAR FINISHING - INTERNALLY						
NOTE: The following prices include for preparing surfaces. Painting woodwork also includes for knotting prior to applying the priming coat and for all stopping of nail holes.						
One coat primer; on wood surfaces before fixing						
General surfaces						
over 300 mm girth	-	0.11	0.88	0.40	m²	**1.28**
isolated surfaces not exceeding 300 mm girth	-	0.04	0.32	0.15	m	**0.47**
isolated areas not exceeding 0.50 m²						
irrespective of girth	-	0.08	0.64	0.20	nr	**0.84**

M SURFACE FINISHES Excluding overheads and profit	PC £	Labour hours	Labour £	Material £	Unit	Total rate £
One coat sealer; on wood surfaces before fixing						
General surfaces						
over 300 mm girth	-	0.13	1.03	0.67	m²	**1.70**
isolated surfaces not exceeding 300 mm girth	-	0.05	0.40	0.23	m	**0.63**
isolated areas not exceeding 0.50 m²						
irrespective of girth	-	0.10	0.80	0.32	nr	**1.12**
One coat of Sikkens "Cetol HLS" stain or other equal and approved; on wood surfaces before fixing						
General surfaces						
over 300 mm girth	-	0.14	1.11	0.74	m²	**1.85**
isolated surfaces not exceeding 300 mm girth	-	0.05	0.40	0.29	m	**0.69**
isolated areas not exceeding 0.50 m²						
irrespective of girth	-	0.10	0.80	0.35	nr	**1.15**
One coat of Sikkens "Cetol TS" interior stain or other equal and approved; on wood surfaces before fixing						
General surfaces						
over 300 mm girth	-	0.14	1.11	1.06	m²	**2.17**
isolated surfaces not exceeding 300 mm girth	-	0.05	0.40	0.41	m	**0.81**
isolated areas not exceeding 0.50 m²						
irrespective of girth	-	0.10	0.80	0.51	nr	**1.31**
One coat Cuprinol clear wood preservative or other equal and approved; on wood surfaces before fixing						
General surfaces						
over 300 mm girth	-	0.10	0.80	0.44	m²	**1.24**
isolated surfaces not exceeding 300 mm girth	-	0.04	0.32	0.16	m	**0.48**
isolated areas not exceeding 0.50 m²						
irrespective of girth	-	0.07	0.56	0.21	nr	**0.77**
One coat HCC Protective Coatings Ltd "Permacor" urethane alkyd gloss finishing coat or other equal and approved; on previously primed steelwork						
Members of roof trusses						
over 300 mm girth	-	0.09	0.68	1.35	m²	**2.03**
Two coats emulsion paint						
Brick or block walls						
over 300 mm girth	-	0.23	1.83	1.02	m²	**2.85**
Cement render or concrete						
over 300 mm girth	-	0.22	1.75	0.89	m²	**2.64**
isolated surfaces not exceeding 300 mm girth	-	0.11	0.88	0.27	m	**1.15**
Plaster walls or plaster/plasterboard ceilings						
over 300 mm girth	-	0.20	1.59	0.86	m²	**2.45**
over 300 mm girth; in multi colours	-	0.27	2.17	1.05	m²	**3.22**
over 300 mm girth; in staircase areas	-	0.23	1.83	0.99	m²	**2.82**
cutting in edges on flush surfaces	-	0.08	0.64	-	m	**0.64**
Plaster/plasterboard ceilings						
over 300 mm girth; 3.50 m - 5.00 m high	-	0.23	1.83	0.87	m²	**2.70**
One mist and two coats emulsion paint						
Brick or block walls						
over 300 mm girth	-	0.21	1.69	1.32	m²	**3.01**
Cement render or concrete						
over 300 mm girth	-	0.21	1.67	1.22	m²	**2.89**
Plaster walls or plaster/plasterboard ceilings						
over 300 mm girth	-	0.20	1.59	1.22	m²	**2.81**
over 300 mm girth; in multi colours	-	0.28	2.25	1.24	m²	**3.49**
over 300 mm girth; in staircase areas	-	0.23	1.83	1.22	m²	**3.05**
cutting in edges on flush surfaces	-	0.09	0.72	-	m	**0.72**

M SURFACE FINISHES Excluding overheads and profit	PC £	Labour hours	Labour £	Material £	Unit	Total rate £
M60 PAINTING/CLEAR FINISHING - cont'd						
PAINTING/CLEAR FINISHING - INTERNALLY - cont'd						
One mist and two coats emulsion paint - cont'd						
Plaster/plasterboard ceilings						
over 300 mm girth; 3.50 m - 5.00 m high	-	0.23	1.83	1.22	m²	3.05
One coat "Tretol No 10" sealer or other equal and approved; two coats Tretol sprayed "Supercover Spraytone" emulsion paint or other equal and approved						
Plaster walls or plaster/plasterboard ceilings						
over 300 mm girth	-	-	-	-	m²	4.40
Textured plastic; "Artex" finish or other equal and approved						
Plasterboard ceilings						
over 300 mm girth	-	0.25	1.99	1.70	m²	3.69
Concrete walls or ceilings						
over 300 mm girth	-	0.27	2.17	1.63	m²	3.80
One coat "Portabond" or other equal and approved; one coat "Portaflek" or other equal and approved; on plaster surfaces; spray applied, masking adjacent surfaces						
General surfaces						
over 300 mm girth	-	-	-	-	m²	8.80
extra for one coat standard "HD" glaze	-	-	-	-	m²	1.65
not exceeding 300 mm girth	-	-	-	-	m	3.85
Touch up primer; one undercoat and one finishing coat of gloss oil paint; on wood surfaces						
General surfaces						
over 300 mm girth	-	0.29	2.31	1.14	m²	3.45
isolated surfaces not exceeding 300 mm girth	-	0.12	0.96	0.38	m	1.34
isolated areas not exceeding 0.50 m²						
irrespective of girth	-	0.22	1.75	0.59	nr	2.34
Glazed windows and screens						
panes; area not exceeding 0.10 m²	-	0.48	3.82	0.81	m²	4.63
panes; area 0.10 m² - 0.50 m²	-	0.39	3.10	0.64	m²	3.74
panes; area 0.50 m² - 1.00 m²	-	0.33	2.63	0.51	m²	3.14
panes; area over 1.00 m²	-	0.29	2.31	0.43	m²	2.74
Touch up primer; two undercoats and one finishing coat of gloss oil paint; on wood surfaces						
General surfaces						
over 300 mm girth	-	0.41	3.26	1.01	m²	4.27
isolated surfaces not exceeding 300 mm girth	-	0.16	1.27	0.40	m	1.67
isolated areas not exceeding 0.50 m²						
irrespective of girth	-	0.30	2.39	0.57	nr	2.96
Glazed windows and screens						
panes; area not exceeding 0.10 m²	-	0.68	5.41	1.08	m²	6.49
panes; area 0.10 m² - 0.50 m²	-	0.54	4.30	0.86	m²	5.16
panes; area 0.50 m² - 1.00 m²	-	0.47	3.74	0.71	m²	4.45
panes; area over 1.00 m²	-	0.41	3.26	0.60	m²	3.86

M SURFACE FINISHES Excluding overheads and profit	PC £	Labour hours	Labour £	Material £	Unit	Total rate £
Knot; one coat primer; stop; one undercoat **and one finishing coat of gloss oil paint; on** **wood surfaces**						
General surfaces						
over 300 mm girth	-	0.42	3.36	0.99	m²	**4.35**
isolated surfaces not exceeding 300 mm girth	-	0.17	1.35	0.33	m	**1.68**
isolated areas not exceeding 0.50 m²						
irrespective of girth	-	0.32	2.55	0.64	nr	**3.19**
Glazed windows and screens						
panes; area not exceeding 0.10 m²	-	0.72	5.73	0.99	m²	**6.72**
panes; area 0.10 m² - 0.50 m²	-	0.58	4.62	0.84	m²	**5.46**
panes; area 0.50 m² - 1.00 m²	-	0.50	3.98	0.84	m²	**4.82**
panes; area over 1.00 m²	-	0.42	3.34	0.61	m²	**3.95**
Knot; one coat primer; stop; two undercoats **and one finishing coat of gloss oil paint; on** **wood surfaces**						
General surfaces						
over 300 mm girth	-	0.54	4.32	1.38	m²	**5.70**
isolated surfaces not exceeding 300 mm girth	-	0.22	1.75	0.48	m	**2.23**
isolated areas not exceeding 0.50 m²						
irrespective of girth	-	0.41	3.28	0.78	nr	**4.06**
Glazed windows and screens						
panes; area not exceeding 0.10 m²	-	0.90	7.16	1.29	m²	**8.45**
panes; area 0.10 m² - 0.50 m²	-	0.72	5.73	1.18	m²	**6.91**
panes; area 0.50 m² - 1.00 m²	-	0.63	5.01	1.07	m²	**6.08**
panes; area over 1.00 m²	-	0.54	4.30	0.79	m²	**5.09**
One coat primer; one undercoat and one **finishing coat of gloss oil paint**						
Plaster surfaces						
over 300 mm girth	-	0.38	3.02	1.28	m²	**4.30**
One coat primer; two undercoats and one **finishing coat of gloss oil paint**						
Plaster surfaces						
over 300 mm girth	-	0.50	3.98	1.61	m²	**5.59**
One coat primer; two undercoats and one **finishing coat of eggshell paint**						
Plaster surfaces						
over 300 mm girth	-	0.50	3.98	1.65	m²	**5.63**
Touch up primer; one undercoat and one **finishing coat of gloss paint; on iron or steel** **surfaces**						
General surfaces						
over 300 mm girth	-	0.29	2.31	0.77	m²	**3.08**
isolated surfaces not exceeding 300 mm girth	-	0.12	0.96	0.26	m	**1.22**
isolated areas not exceeding 0.50 m²						
irrespective of girth	-	0.22	1.75	0.43	nr	**2.18**
Glazed windows and screens						
panes; area not exceeding 0.10 m²	-	0.48	3.82	0.80	m²	**4.62**
panes; area 0.10 m² - 0.50 m²	-	0.39	3.10	0.65	m²	**3.75**
panes; area 0.50 m² - 1.00 m²	-	0.33	2.63	0.49	m²	**3.12**
panes; area over 1.00 m²	-	0.29	2.31	0.41	m²	**2.72**
Structural steelwork						
over 300 mm girth	-	0.32	2.55	0.81	m²	**3.36**
Members of roof trusses						
over 300 mm girth	-	0.43	3.42	0.91	m²	**4.33**

M SURFACE FINISHES Excluding overheads and profit	PC £	Labour hours	Labour £	Material £	Unit	Total rate £
M60 PAINTING/CLEAR FINISHING - cont'd						
PAINTING/CLEAR FINISHING - INTERNALLY - cont'd						
Touch up primer; one undercoat and one finishing coat of gloss paint; on iron or steel surfaces - cont'd						
Ornamental railings and the like; each side measured overall						
over 300 mm girth	-	0.50	3.98	1.03	m²	**5.01**
Iron or steel radiators						
over 300 mm girth	-	0.29	2.31	0.84	m²	**3.15**
Pipes or conduits						
over 300 mm girth	-	0.43	3.42	0.89	m²	**4.31**
not exceeding 300 mm girth	-	0.17	1.35	0.29	m	**1.64**
Touch up primer; two undercoats and one finishing coat of gloss oil paint; on iron or steel surfaces						
General surfaces						
over 300 mm girth	-	0.41	3.26	1.05	m²	**4.31**
isolated surfaces not exceeding 300 mm girth	-	0.16	1.27	0.42	m	**1.69**
isolated areas not exceeding 0.50 m²						
irrespective of girth	-	0.30	2.39	0.61	nr	**3.00**
Glazed windows and screens						
panes; area not exceeding 0.10 m²	-	0.68	5.41	1.11	m²	**6.52**
panes; area 0.10 m² - 0.50 m²	-	0.54	4.30	0.92	m²	**5.22**
panes; area 0.50 m² - 1.00 m²	-	0.47	3.74	0.78	m²	**4.52**
panes; area over 1.00 m²	-	0.41	3.26	0.62	m²	**3.88**
Structural steelwork						
over 300 mm girth	-	0.46	3.66	1.08	m²	**4.74**
Members of roof trusses						
over 300 mm girth	-	0.61	4.86	1.26	m²	**6.12**
Ornamental railings and the like; each side measured overall						
over 300 mm girth	-	0.69	5.49	1.36	m²	**6.85**
Iron or steel radiators						
over 300 mm girth	-	0.41	3.26	1.15	m²	**4.41**
Pipes or conduits						
over 300 mm girth	-	0.61	4.86	1.29	m²	**6.15**
not exceeding 300 mm girth	-	0.24	1.91	0.42	m	**2.33**
One coat primer; one undercoat and one finishing coat of gloss oil paint; on iron or steel surfaces						
General surfaces						
over 300 mm girth	-	0.29	2.31	0.77	m²	**3.08**
isolated surfaces not exceeding 300 mm girth	-	0.15	1.19	0.41	m	**1.60**
isolated areas not exceeding 0.50 m²						
irrespective of girth	-	0.29	2.31	0.73	nr	**3.04**
Glazed windows and screens						
panes; area not exceeding 0.10 m²	-	0.63	5.01	1.18	m²	**6.19**
panes; area 0.10 m² - 0.50 m²	-	0.50	3.98	0.93	m²	**4.91**
panes; area 0.50 m² - 1.00 m²	-	0.43	3.42	0.80	m²	**4.22**
panes; area over 1.00 m²	-	0.38	3.02	0.73	m²	**3.75**
Structural steelwork						
over 300 mm girth	-	0.42	3.34	1.13	m²	**4.47**
Members of roof trusses						
over 300 mm girth	-	0.57	4.56	1.23	m²	**5.79**
Ornamental railings and the like; each side measured overall						
over 300 mm girth	-	0.65	5.19	1.45	m²	**6.64**

M SURFACE FINISHES Excluding overheads and profit	PC £	Labour hours	Labour £	Material £	Unit	Total rate £
Iron or steel radiators						
over 300 mm girth	-	0.38	3.02	1.23	m²	4.25
Pipes or conduits						
over 300 mm girth	-	0.57	4.56	1.23	m²	5.79
not exceeding 300 mm girth	-	0.22	1.77	0.41	m	2.18
One coat primer; two undercoats and one						
finishing coat of gloss oil paint; on iron or						
steel surfaces						
General surfaces						
over 300 mm girth	-	0.50	3.98	1.40	m²	5.38
isolated surfaces not exceeding 300 mm girth	-	0.20	1.59	0.62	m	2.21
isolated areas not exceeding 0.50 m²						
irrespective of girth	-	0.36	2.87	0.79	nr	3.66
Glazed windows and screens						
panes; area not exceeding 0.10 m²	-	0.81	6.45	1.44	m²	7.89
panes; area 0.10 m² - 0.50 m²	-	0.68	5.41	0.81	m²	6.22
panes; area 0.50 m² - 1.00 m²	-	0.58	4.62	0.99	m²	5.61
panes; area over 1.00 m²	-	0.50	3.98	0.84	m²	4.82
Structural steelwork						
over 300 mm girth	-	0.56	4.46	1.44	m²	5.90
Members of roof trusses						
over 300 mm girth	-	0.74	5.89	1.71	m²	7.60
Ornamental railings and the like; each side						
measured overall						
over 300 mm girth	-	0.84	6.69	1.88	m²	8.57
Iron or steel radiators						
over 300 mm girth	-	0.50	3.98	1.53	m²	5.51
Pipes or conduits						
over 300 mm girth	-	0.75	5.97	1.73	m²	7.70
not exceeding 300 mm girth	-	0.30	2.39	0.55	m	2.94
Two coats of bituminous paint; on iron or						
steel surfaces						
General surfaces						
over 300 mm girth	-	0.29	2.33	0.30	m²	2.63
Inside of galvanized steel cistern						
over 300 mm girth	-	0.43	3.44	0.35	m²	3.79
Two coats bituminous paint; first coat blinded						
with clean sand prior to second coat; on						
concrete surfaces						
General surfaces						
over 300 mm girth	-	1.00	7.96	1.20	m²	9.16
Mordant solution; one coat HCC Protective						
Coatings Ltd "Permacor alkyd MIO" or other equal						
and approved; one coat "Permacor Epoxy Gloss"						
finishing coat or other equal and approved on						
galvanised steelwork						
Structural steelwork						
over 300 mm girth	-	0.56	4.48	2.63	m²	7.11
One coat HCC Protective Coatings Ltd						
"Permacor Epoxy Zinc Primer" or other equal						
and approved; two coats "Permacor alkyd MIO"						
or other equal and approved; one coat "Permatex						
Epoxy Gloss" finishing coat or other equal and						
approved on steelwork						
Structural steelwork						
over 300 mm girth	-	0.80	6.37	4.75	m²	11.12

M SURFACE FINISHES Excluding overheads and profit	PC £	Labour hours	Labour £	Material £	Unit	Total rate £
M60 PAINTING/CLEAR FINISHING - cont'd						
PAINTING/CLEAR FINISHING - INTERNALLY - cont'd						
Steel protection; HCC Protective Coatings Ltd "Unitherm" or other equal and approved; two coats to steelwork						
Structural steelwork						
over 300 mm girth	-	1.25	9.99	2.57	m²	**12.56**
Two coats epoxy resin sealer; HCC Protective Coatings Ltd "Betonol" or other equal and approved on concrete surfaces						
General surfaces						
over 300 mm girth	-	0.25	1.99	3.67	m²	**5.66**
"Nitoflor Lithurin" floor hardener and dust proofer or other equal and approved; Fosroc Expandite Ltd; two coats on concrete surfaces						
General surfaces						
over 300 mm girth	-	0.30	1.94	0.43	m²	**2.37**
Two coats of boiled linseed oil; on hardwood surfaces						
General surfaces						
over 300 mm girth	-	0.22	1.75	1.29	m²	**3.04**
isolated surfaces not exceeding 300 mm girth	-	0.09	0.72	0.42	m	**1.14**
isolated areas not exceeding 0.50 m²						
irrespective of girth	-	0.17	1.35	0.75	nr	**2.10**
Two coats polyurethane varnish; on wood surfaces						
General surfaces						
over 300 mm girth	-	0.22	1.77	1.18	m²	**2.95**
isolated surfaces not exceeding 300 mm girth	-	0.09	0.72	0.43	m	**1.15**
isolated areas not exceeding 0.50 m²						
irrespective of girth	-	0.17	1.35	0.14	nr	**1.49**
Three coats polyurethane varnish; on wood surfaces						
General surfaces						
over 300 mm girth	-	0.33	2.63	1.79	m²	**4.42**
isolated surfaces not exceeding 300 mm girth	-	0.13	1.03	0.55	m	**1.58**
isolated areas not exceeding 0.50 m²						
irrespective of girth	-	0.25	1.99	1.00	nr	**2.99**
One undercoat; and one finishing coat; of "Albi" clear flame retardant surface coating or other equal and approved; on wood surfaces						
General surfaces						
over 300 mm girth	-	0.43	3.42	2.61	m²	**6.03**
isolated surfaces not exceeding 300 mm girth	-	0.18	1.43	0.91	m	**2.34**
isolated areas not exceeding 0.50 m²						
irrespective of girth	-	0.25	1.99	1.99	nr	**3.98**
Two undercoats; and one finishing coat; of "Albi" clear flame retardant surface coating or other equal and approved; on wood surfaces						
General surfaces						
over 300 mm girth	-	0.51	4.06	3.68	m²	**7.74**
isolated surfaces not exceeding 300 mm girth	-	0.26	2.07	1.33	m	**3.40**
isolated areas not exceeding 0.50 m²						
irrespective of girth	-	0.42	3.34	2.03	nr	**5.37**

M SURFACE FINISHES Excluding overheads and profit	PC £	Labour hours	Labour £	Material £	Unit	Total rate £
Seal and wax polish; dull gloss finish on wood surfaces						
General surfaces						
over 300 mm girth	-	-	-	-	m²	8.21
isolated surfaces not exceeding 300 mm girth	-	-	-	-	m	3.71
isolated areas not exceeding 0.50 m²						
irrespective of girth	-	-	-	-	nr	5.75
One coat of "Sadolin Extra" or other equal and approved; clear or pigmented; one further coat of "Holdex" clear interior silk matt lacquer or other equal and approved						
General surfaces						
over 300 mm girth	-	0.32	2.55	4.28	m²	6.83
isolated surfaces not exceeding 300 mm girth	-	0.13	1.03	2.00	m	3.03
isolated areas not exceeding 0.50 m²						
irrespective of girth	-	0.24	1.91	2.08	nr	3.99
Glazed windows and screens						
panes; area not exceeding 0.10 m²	-	0.53	4.22	2.45	m²	6.67
panes; area 0.10 m² - 0.50 m²	-	0.42	3.34	2.28	m²	5.62
panes; area 0.50 m² - 1.00 m²	-	0.37	2.95	2.11	m²	5.06
panes; area over 1.00 m²	-	0.32	2.55	2.00	m²	4.55
Two coats of "Sadolins Extra" or other equal and approved; clear or pigmented; two further coats of "Holdex" clear interior silk matt lacquer or other equal and approved						
General surfaces						
over 300 mm girth	-	0.50	3.98	7.90	m²	11.88
isolated surfaces not exceeding 300 mm girth	-	0.20	1.59	3.95	m	5.54
isolated areas not exceeding 0.50 m²						
irrespective of girth	-	0.38	3.02	4.51	nr	7.53
Glazed windows and screens						
panes; area not exceeding 0.10 m²	-	0.83	6.61	4.84	m²	11.45
panes; area 0.10 m² - 0.50 m²	-	0.66	5.25	4.51	m²	9.76
panes; area 0.50 m² - 1.00 m²	-	0.58	4.62	4.17	m²	8.79
panes; area over 1.00 m²	-	0.50	3.98	3.95	m²	7.93
Two coats of Sikkens "Cetol TS" interior stain or other equal and approved; on wood surfaces						
General surfaces						
over 300 mm girth	-	0.23	1.83	1.91	m²	3.74
isolated surfaces not exceeding 300 mm girth	-	0.10	0.80	0.67	m	1.47
isolated areas not exceeding 0.50 m²						
irrespective of girth	-	0.17	1.35	1.04	nr	2.39
Body in and wax polish; dull gloss finish; on hardwood surfaces						
General surfaces						
over 300 mm girth	-	-	-	-	m²	9.49
isolated surfaces not exceeding 300 mm girth	-	-	-	-	m	4.28
isolated areas not exceeding 0.50 m²						
irrespective of girth	-	-	-	-	nr	6.62
Stain; body in and wax polish; dull gloss finish; on hardwood surfaces						
General surfaces						
over 300 mm girth	-	-	-	-	m²	13.12
isolated surfaces not exceeding 300 mm girth	-	-	-	-	m	5.91
isolated areas not exceeding 0.50 m²						
irrespective of girth	-	-	-	-	nr	9.20

M SURFACE FINISHES Excluding overheads and profit	PC £	Labour hours	Labour £	Material £	Unit	Total rate £
M60 PAINTING/CLEAR FINISHING - cont'd						
PAINTING/CLEAR FINISHING - INTERNALLY - cont'd						
Seal; two coats of synthetic resin lacquer; decorative flatted finish; wire down, wax and burnish; on wood surfaces						
General surfaces						
over 300 mm girth	-	-	-	-	m²	**15.75**
isolated surfaces not exceeding 300 mm girth	-	-	-	-	m	**7.08**
isolated areas not exceeding 0.50 m²						
irrespective of girth	-	-	-	-	nr	**11.03**
Stain; body in and fully French polish; full gloss finish; on hardwood surfaces						
General surfaces						
over 300 mm girth	-	-	-	-	m²	**18.10**
isolated surfaces not exceeding 300 mm girth	-	-	-	-	m	**8.15**
isolated areas not exceeding 0.50 m²						
irrespective of girth	-	-	-	-	nr	**12.69**
Stain; fill grain and fully French polish; full gloss finish; on hardwood surfaces						
General surfaces						
over 300 mm girth	-	-	-	-	m²	**24.83**
isolated surfaces not exceeding 300 mm girth	-	-	-	-	m	**11.17**
isolated areas not exceeding 0.50 m²						
irrespective of girth	-	-	-	-	nr	**17.39**
Stain black; body in and fully French polish; ebonized finish; on hardwood surfaces						
General surfaces						
over 300 mm girth	-	-	-	-	m²	**31.05**
isolated surfaces not exceeding 300 mm girth	-	-	-	-	m	**12.92**
isolated areas not exceeding 0.50 m²						
irrespective of girth	-	-	-	-	nr	**21.73**
PREPARATION OF EXISTING SURFACES - EXTERNALLY						
Wash and rub down iron and steel surfaces; bringing forward						
General surfaces						
over 300 mm girth	-	0.16	1.27	-	m²	**1.27**
isolated surfaces not exceeding 300 mm girth	-	0.06	0.48	-	m	**0.48**
isolated areas not exceeding 0.50 m²						
irrespective of girth	-	0.12	0.96	-	nr	**0.96**
Glazed windows and screens						
panes; area not exceeding 0.10 m²	-	0.26	2.07	-	m²	**2.07**
panes; area 0.10 m² - 0.50 m²	-	0.22	1.75	-	m²	**1.75**
panes; area 0.50 m² - 1.00 m²	-	0.18	1.43	-	m²	**1.43**
panes; area over 1.00 m²	-	0.16	1.27	-	m²	**1.27**
Wash and rub down wood surfaces; prime bare patches; bringing forward						
General surfaces						
over 300 mm girth	-	0.26	2.07	-	m²	**2.07**
isolated surfaces not exceeding 300 mm girth	-	0.10	0.80	-	m	**0.80**
isolated areas not exceeding 0.50 m²						
irrespective of girth	-	0.19	1.51	-	nr	**1.51**

M SURFACE FINISHES Excluding overheads and profit	PC £	Labour hours	Labour £	Material £	Unit	Total rate £
Glazed windows and screens						
panes; area not exceeding 0.10 m²	-	0.44	3.50	-	m²	3.50
panes; area 0.10 m² - 0.50 m²	-	0.35	2.79	-	m²	2.79
panes; area 0.50 m² - 1.00 m²	-	0.30	2.39	-	m²	2.39
panes; area over 1.00 m²	-	0.26	2.07	-	m²	2.07
Wash down and remove paint with chemical stripper from iron, steel or wood surfaces						
General surfaces						
over 300 mm girth	-	0.80	6.37	-	m²	6.37
isolated surfaces not exceeding 300 mm girth	-	0.36	2.87	-	m	2.87
isolated areas not exceeding 0.50 m² irrespective of girth	-	0.60	4.78	-	nr	4.78
Glazed windows and screens						
panes; area not exceeding 0.10 m²	-	1.71	13.61	-	m²	13.61
panes; area 0.10 m² - 0.50 m²	-	1.36	10.83	-	m²	10.83
panes; area 0.50 m² - 1.00 m²	-	1.18	9.39	-	m²	9.39
panes; area over 1.00 m²	-	1.02	8.12	-	m²	8.12
Burn off and rub down to remove paint from iron, steel or wood surfaces						
General surfaces						
over 300 mm girth	-	0.98	7.80	-	m²	7.80
isolated surfaces not exceeding 300 mm girth	-	0.45	3.58	-	m	3.58
isolated surfaces not exceeding 0.50 m²	-	0.74	5.89	-	nr	5.89
Glazed windows and screens						
panes; area not exceeding 0.10 m²	-	2.13	16.95	-	m²	16.95
panes; area 0.10 m² - 0.50 m²	-	1.70	13.53	-	m²	13.53
panes; area 0.50 m² - 1.00 m²	-	1.46	11.62	-	m²	11.62
panes; area over 1.00 m²	-	1.28	10.19	-	m²	10.19
PAINTING/CLEAR FINISHING - EXTERNALLY						
Two coats of cement paint, "Sandtex Matt" or other equal and approved						
Brick or block walls						
over 300 mm girth	-	0.33	2.63	1.57	m²	4.20
Cement render or concrete walls						
over 300 mm girth	-	0.29	2.31	1.04	m²	3.35
Roughcast walls						
over 300 mm girth	-	0.50	3.98	1.04	m²	5.02
One coat sealer and two coats of external grade emulsion paint, Dulux "Weathershield" or other equal and approved						
Brick or block walls						
over 300 mm girth	-	0.54	4.30	6.37	m²	10.67
Cement render or concrete walls						
over 300 mm girth	-	0.42	3.34	4.24	m²	7.58
Concrete soffits						
over 300 mm girth	-	0.50	3.98	4.24	m²	8.22
One coat sealer (applied by brush) and two coats of external grade emulsion paint, Dulux "Weathershield" or other equal and approved (spray applied)						
Roughcast						
over 300 mm girth	-	0.36	2.87	8.59	m²	11.46
Two coat sealer and one coat of Anti-Graffiti paint (spray applied)						
Roughcast						
over 300 mm girth	-	0.36	2.87	34.19	m²	37.06

M SURFACE FINISHES Excluding overheads and profit	PC £	Labour hours	Labour £	Material £	Unit	Total rate £
M60 PAINTING/CLEAR FINISHING - cont'd						
PAINTING/CLEAR FINISHING - EXTERNALLY - cont'd						
Two coats solar reflective aluminium paint; on bituminous roofing						
General surfaces						
over 300 mm girth	-	0.56	4.46	10.99	m²	**15.45**
Touch up primer; one undercoat and one finishing coat of gloss oil paint; on wood surfaces						
General surfaces						
over 300 mm girth	-	0.32	2.55	0.77	m²	**3.32**
isolated surfaces not exceeding 300 mm girth	-	0.14	1.11	0.24	m	**1.35**
isolated areas not exceeding 0.50 m²						
irrespective of girth	-	0.24	1.91	0.46	nr	**2.37**
Glazed windows and screens						
panes; area not exceeding 0.10 m²	-	0.54	4.30	0.83	m²	**5.13**
panes; area 0.10 m² - 0.50 m²	-	0.43	3.42	0.69	m²	**4.11**
panes; area 0.50 m² - 1.00 m²	-	0.38	3.02	0.57	m²	**3.59**
panes; area over 1.00 m²	-	0.32	2.55	0.46	m²	**3.01**
Glazed windows and screens; multi-coloured work						
panes; area not exceeding 0.10 m²	-	0.59	4.70	0.83	m²	**5.53**
panes; area 0.10 m² - 0.50 m²	-	0.48	3.82	0.72	m²	**4.54**
panes; area 0.50 m² - 1.00 m²	-	0.41	3.26	0.57	m²	**3.83**
panes; area over 1.00 m²	-	0.36	2.87	0.46	m²	**3.33**
Touch up primer; two undercoats and one finishing coat of gloss oil paint; on wood surfaces						
General surfaces						
over 300 mm girth	-	0.45	3.60	1.00	m²	**4.60**
isolated surfaces not exceeding 300 mm girth	-	0.18	1.45	0.28	m	**1.73**
isolated areas not exceeding 0.50 m²						
irrespective of girth	-	0.34	2.71	0.55	nr	**3.26**
Glazed windows and screens						
panes; area not exceeding 0.10 m²	-	0.75	5.97	0.89	m²	**6.86**
panes; area 0.10 m² - 0.50 m²	-	0.75	5.97	0.74	m²	**6.71**
panes; area 0.50 m² - 1.00 m²	-	0.60	4.78	0.66	m²	**5.44**
panes; area over 1.00 m²	-	0.45	3.58	0.55	m²	**4.13**
Glazed windows and screens; multi- coloured work						
panes; area not exceeding 0.10 m²	-	0.86	6.85	0.89	m²	**7.74**
panes; area 0.10 m² - 0.50 m²	-	0.69	5.49	0.78	m²	**6.27**
panes; area 0.50 m² - 1.00 m²	-	0.60	4.78	0.66	m²	**5.44**
panes; area over 1.00 m²	-	0.52	4.14	0.55	m²	**4.69**
Knot; one coat primer; one undercoat and one finishing coat of gloss oil paint; on wood surfaces						
General surfaces						
over 300 mm girth	-	0.48	3.82	1.14	m²	**4.96**
isolated surfaces not exceeding 300 mm girth	-	0.20	1.59	0.37	m	**1.96**
isolated areas not exceeding 0.50 m²						
irrespective of girth	-	0.36	2.87	0.67	nr	**3.54**
Glazed windows and screens						
panes; area not exceeding 0.10 m²	-	0.79	6.29	1.18	m²	**7.47**
panes; area 0.10 - 0.50 m²	-	0.63	5.01	1.06	m²	**6.07**
panes; area 0.50 - 1.00 m²	-	0.56	4.46	0.82	m²	**5.28**
panes; area over 1.00 m²	-	0.48	3.82	0.59	m²	**4.41**

M SURFACE FINISHES Excluding overheads and profit	PC £	Labour hours	Labour £	Material £	Unit	Total rate £
Glazed windows and screens; multi-coloured work						
panes; area not exceeding 0.10 m²	-	0.86	6.85	1.18	m²	8.03
panes; area 0.10 - 0.50 m²	-	0.69	5.49	1.06	m²	6.55
panes; area 0.50 - 1.00 m²	-	0.61	4.86	0.81	m²	5.67
panes; area over 1.00 m²	-	0.52	4.14	0.58	m²	4.72
Knot; one coat primer; two undercoats and one finishing coat of gloss oil paint; on wood surfaces						
General surfaces						
over 300 mm girth	-	0.59	4.70	1.39	m²	6.09
isolated surfaces not exceeding 300 mm girth	-	0.24	1.91	0.50	m	2.41
isolated areas not exceeding 0.50 m²						
irrespective of girth	-	0.45	3.58	0.87	nr	4.45
Glazed windows and screens						
panes; area not exceeding 0.10 m²	-	0.99	7.88	1.55	m²	9.43
panes; area 0.10 m² - 0.50 m²	-	0.79	6.29	1.38	m²	7.67
panes; area 0.50 m² - 1.00 m²	-	0.69	5.49	1.06	m²	6.55
panes; area over 1.00 m²	-	0.59	4.70	0.74	m²	5.44
Glazed windows and screens; multi-coloured work						
panes; area not exceeding 0.10 m²	-	1.13	8.99	1.55	m²	10.54
panes; area 0.10 m² - 0.50 m²	-	0.92	7.32	1.39	m²	8.71
panes; area 0.50 m² - 1.00 m²	-	0.81	6.45	1.06	m²	7.51
panes; area over 1.00 m²	-	0.68	5.41	0.74	m²	6.15
Touch up primer; one undercoat and one finishing coat of gloss oil paint; on iron or steel surfaces						
General surfaces						
over 300 mm girth	-	0.32	2.55	0.90	m²	3.45
isolated surfaces not exceeding 300 mm girth	-	0.14	1.11	0.51	m	1.62
isolated areas not exceeding 0.50 m²						
irrespective of girth	-	0.24	1.91	0.48	nr	2.39
Glazed windows and screens						
panes; area not exceeding 0.10 m²	-	0.54	4.30	0.97	m²	5.27
panes; area 0.10 m² - 0.50 m²	-	0.43	3.42	0.84	m²	4.26
panes; area 0.50 m² - 1.00 m²	-	0.38	3.02	0.71	m²	3.73
panes; area over 1.00 m²	-	0.32	2.55	0.53	m²	3.08
Structural steelwork						
over 300 mm girth	-	0.36	2.87	0.95	m²	3.82
Members of roof trusses						
over 300 mm girth	-	0.48	3.82	1.08	m²	4.90
Ornamental railings and the like; each side measured overall						
over 300 mm girth	-	0.54	4.30	1.13	m²	5.43
Eaves gutters						
over 300 mm girth	-	0.58	4.62	1.28	m²	5.90
not exceeding 300 mm girth	-	0.23	1.83	0.42	m	2.25
Pipes or conduits						
over 300 mm girth	-	0.48	3.82	1.28	m²	5.10
not exceeding 300 mm girth	-	0.19	1.51	0.42	m	1.93
Touch up primer; two undercoats and one finishing coat of gloss oil paint; on iron or steel surfaces						
General surfaces						
over 300 mm girth	-	0.45	3.58	1.23	m²	4.81
isolated surfaces not exceeding 300 mm girth	-	0.18	1.43	0.34	m	1.77
isolated areas not exceeding 0.50 m²						
irrespective of girth	-	0.33	2.63	0.69	nr	3.32

M SURFACE FINISHES Excluding overheads and profit	PC £	Labour hours	Labour £	Material £	Unit	Total rate £
M60 PAINTING/CLEAR FINISHING - cont'd						
PAINTING/CLEAR FINISHING - EXTERNALLY - cont'd						
Touch up primer; two undercoats and one **finishing coat of gloss oil paint; on iron or** **steel surfaces** - cont'd						
Glazed windows and screens						
panes; area not exceeding 0.10 m²	-	0.75	5.97	1.26	m²	**7.23**
panes; area 0.10 m² - 0.50 m²	-	0.60	4.78	1.08	m²	**5.86**
panes; area 0.50 m² - 1.00 m²	-	0.52	4.14	0.91	m²	**5.05**
panes; area over 1.00 m²	-	0.45	3.58	0.74	m²	**4.32**
Structural steelwork						
over 300 mm girth	-	0.51	4.06	1.28	m²	**5.34**
Members of roof trusses						
over 300 mm girth	-	0.68	5.41	1.45	m²	**6.86**
Ornamental railings and the like; each side measured overall						
over 300 mm girth	-	0.77	6.13	1.50	m²	**7.63**
Eaves gutters						
over 300 mm girth	-	0.81	6.45	1.65	m²	**8.10**
not exceeding 300 mm girth	-	0.32	2.55	0.69	m	**3.24**
Pipes or conduits						
over 300 mm girth	-	0.68	5.41	1.65	m²	**7.06**
not exceeding 300 mm girth	-	0.27	2.15	0.57	m	**2.72**
One coat primer; one undercoat and one **finishing coat of gloss oil paint; on iron or** **steel surfaces**						
General surfaces						
over 300 mm girth	-	0.41	3.26	1.10	m²	**4.36**
isolated surfaces not exceeding 300 mm girth	-	0.17	1.35	0.29	m	**1.64**
isolated areas not exceeding 0.50 m² irrespective of girth	-	0.32	2.55	0.57	nr	**3.12**
Glazed windows and screens						
panes; area not exceeding 0.10 m²	-	0.69	5.49	1.02	m²	**6.51**
panes; area 0.10 m² - 0.50 m²	-	0.56	4.46	0.89	m²	**5.35**
panes; area 0.50 m² - 1.00 m²	-	0.48	3.82	0.76	m²	**4.58**
panes; area over 1.00 m²	-	0.41	3.26	0.57	m²	**3.83**
Structural steelwork						
over 300 mm girth	-	0.47	3.74	1.15	m²	**4.89**
Members of roof trusses						
over 300 mm girth	-	0.61	4.86	1.28	m²	**6.14**
Ornamental railings and the like; each side measured overall						
over 300 mm girth	-	0.70	5.57	1.28	m²	**6.85**
Eaves gutters						
over 300 mm girth	-	0.74	5.89	1.50	m²	**7.39**
not exceeding 300 mm girth	-	0.30	2.39	0.52	m	**2.91**
Pipes or conduits						
over 300 mm girth	-	0.61	4.86	1.50	m²	**6.36**
not exceeding 300 mm girth	-	0.24	1.91	0.50	m	**2.41**
One coat primer; two undercoats and one finishing **coat of gloss oil paint; on iron or steel surfaces**						
General surfaces						
over 300 mm girth	-	0.54	4.30	1.43	m²	**5.73**
isolated surfaces not exceeding 300 mm girth	-	0.22	1.75	0.37	m	**2.12**
isolated areas not exceeding 0.50 m² irrespective of girth	-	0.41	3.26	0.74	nr	**4.00**

M SURFACE FINISHES Excluding overheads and profit	PC £	Labour hours	Labour £	Material £	Unit	Total rate £
Glazed windows and screens						
panes; area not exceeding 0.10 m²	-	0.90	7.16	1.30	m²	8.46
panes; area 0.10 m² - 0.50 m²	-	0.72	5.73	1.13	m²	6.86
panes; area 0.50 m² - 1.00 m²	-	0.63	5.01	0.96	m²	5.97
panes; area over 1.00 m²	-	0.54	4.30	0.74	m²	5.04
Structural steelwork						
over 300 mm girth	-	0.61	4.86	1.48	m²	6.34
Members of roof trusses						
over 300 mm girth	-	0.81	6.45	1.65	m²	8.10
Ornamental railings and the like; each side						
measured overall						
over 300 mm girth	-	0.92	7.32	1.65	m²	8.97
Eaves gutters						
over 300 mm girth	-	0.97	7.72	1.87	m²	9.59
not exceeding 300 mm girth	-	0.39	3.10	0.64	m	3.74
Pipes or conduits						
over 300 mm girth	-	0.81	6.45	1.87	m²	8.32
not exceeding 300 mm girth	-	0.32	2.55	0.62	m	3.17
One coat of Andrews "Hammerite" paint or other						
equal and approved; on iron or steel surfaces						
General surfaces						
over 300 mm girth	-	0.19	1.51	1.18	m²	2.69
isolated surfaces not exceeding 300 mm girth	-	0.10	0.80	0.36	m	1.16
isolated areas not exceeding 0.50 m²						
irrespective of girth	-	0.14	1.11	0.68	nr	1.79
Glazed windows and screens						
panes; area not exceeding 0.10 m²	-	0.32	2.55	0.90	m²	3.45
panes; area 0.10 m² - 0.50 m²	-	0.25	1.99	0.99	m²	2.98
panes; area 0.50 m² - 1.00 m²	-	0.23	1.83	0.89	m²	2.72
panes; area over 1.00 m²	-	0.19	1.51	0.89	m²	2.40
Structural steelwork						
over 300 mm girth	-	0.22	1.75	1.08	m²	2.83
Members of roof trusses						
over 300 mm girth	-	0.29	2.31	1.18	m²	3.49
Ornamental railings and the like; each side						
measured overall						
over 300 mm girth	-	0.33	2.63	1.18	m²	3.81
Eaves gutters						
over 300 mm girth	-	0.34	2.71	1.28	m²	3.99
not exceeding 300 mm girth	-	0.11	0.88	0.59	m	1.47
Pipes or conduits						
over 300 mm girth	-	0.33	2.63	1.08	m²	3.71
not exceeding 300 mm girth	-	0.11	0.88	0.49	m	1.37
Two coats of creosote; on wood surfaces						
General surfaces						
over 300 mm girth	-	0.20	1.59	0.19	m²	1.78
isolated surfaces not exceeding 300 mm girth	-	0.07	0.56	0.12	m	0.68
Two coats of "Solignum" wood preservative or						
other equal and approved; on wood surfaces						
General surfaces						
over 300 mm girth	-	0.18	1.43	1.11	m²	2.54
isolated surfaces not exceeding 300 mm girth	-	0.07	0.56	0.34	m	0.90
Three coats of polyurethane; on wood surfaces						
General surfaces						
over 300 mm girth	-	0.36	2.87	1.97	m²	4.84
isolated surfaces not exceeding 300 mm girth	-	0.14	1.11	0.97	m	2.08
isolated areas not exceeding 0.50 m²						
irrespective of girth	-	0.27	2.15	1.13	nr	3.28

M SURFACE FINISHES Excluding overheads and profit	PC £	Labour hours	Labour £	Material £	Unit	Total rate £
M60 PAINTING/CLEAR FINISHING - cont'd						
PAINTING/CLEAR FINISHING - EXTERNALLY - cont'd						
Two coats of "New Base" primer or other equal and approved; and two coats of "Extra" or other equal and approved; Sadolin Ltd; pigmented; on wood surfaces						
General surfaces						
over 300 mm girth	-	0.54	4.30	4.10	m²	**8.40**
isolated surfaces not exceeding 300 mm girth	-	0.33	2.63	1.40	m	**4.03**
Glazed windows and screens						
panes; area not exceeding 0.10 m²	-	0.91	7.24	2.92	m²	**10.16**
panes; area 0.10 m² - 0.50 m²	-	0.73	5.81	2.75	m²	**8.56**
panes; area 0.50 m² - 1.00 m²	-	0.63	5.01	2.58	m²	**7.59**
panes; area over 1.00 m²	-	0.54	4.30	2.07	m²	**6.37**
Two coats Sikkens "Cetol Filter 7" exterior stain or other equal and approved; on wood surfaces						
General surfaces						
over 300 mm girth	-	0.23	1.83	3.11	m²	**4.94**
isolated surfaces not exceeding 300 mm girth	-	0.10	0.80	1.07	m	**1.87**
isolated areas not exceeding 0.50 m²						
irrespective of girth	-	0.17	1.35	1.58	nr	**2.93**

N FURNITURE/EQUIPMENT Excluding overheads and profit	PC £	Labour hours	Labour £	Material £	Unit	Total rate £
N FURNITURE/EQUIPMENT						
N10/11 GENERAL FIXTURES/KITCHEN FITTINGS						
Fixing general fixtures						
NOTE: The fixing of general fixtures will vary considerably depending upon the size of the fixture and the method of fixing employed. Prices for fixing like sized kitchen fittings may be suitable for certain fixtures, although adjustment to those rates will almost invariably be necessary and the reader is directed to section "G20" for information on bolts, plugging brickwork and blockwork etc. which should prove useful in building up a suitable rate.						
The following supply only prices are for purpose made fittings components in various materials supplied as part of an assembled fitting and therefore may be used to arrive at a guide price for a complete fitting.						
Fitting components; blockboard						
Backs, fronts, sides or divisions; over 300 mm wide						
12 mm thick	-	-	-	36.56	m²	36.56
19 mm thick	-	-	-	47.17	m²	47.17
25 mm thick	-	-	-	61.96	m²	61.96
Shelves or worktops; over 300 mm wide						
19 mm thick	-	-	-	47.17	m²	47.17
25 mm thick	-	-	-	61.96	m²	61.96
Flush doors; lipped on four edges						
450 mm x 750 mm x 19 mm	-	-	-	25.62	nr	25.62
450 mm x 750 mm x 25 mm	-	-	-	31.38	nr	31.38
600 mm x 900 mm x 19 mm	-	-	-	38.09	nr	38.09
600 mm x 900 mm x 25 mm	-	-	-	46.49	nr	46.49
Fitting components; chipboard						
Backs, fronts, sides or divisions; over 300 mm wide						
6 mm thick	-	-	-	10.83	m²	10.83
9 mm thick	-	-	-	15.29	m²	15.29
12 mm thick	-	-	-	19.00	m²	19.00
19 mm thick	-	-	-	27.38	m²	27.38
25 mm thick	-	-	-	36.95	m²	36.95
Shelves or worktops; over 300 mm wide						
19 mm thick	-	-	-	27.38	m²	27.38
25 mm thick	-	-	-	36.95	m²	36.95
Flush doors; lipped on four edges						
450 mm x 750 mm x 19 mm	-	-	-	19.55	nr	19.55
450 mm x 750 mm x 25 mm	-	-	-	23.78	nr	23.78
600 mm x 900 mm x 19 mm	-	-	-	28.66	nr	28.66
600 mm x 900 mm x 25 mm	-	-	-	34.63	nr	34.63

N FURNITURE/EQUIPMENT Excluding overheads and profit	PC £	Labour hours	Labour £	Material £	Unit	Total rate £
N10/11 GENERAL FIXTURES/KITCHEN FITTINGS - cont'd						
Fitting components; Melamine faced chipboard						
Backs, fronts, sides or divisions; over 300 mm wide						
12 mm thick	-	-	-	26.08	m²	26.08
19 mm thick	-	-	-	35.36	m²	35.36
Shelves or worktops; over 300 mm wide						
19 mm thick	-	-	-	35.36	m²	35.36
Flush doors; lipped on four edges						
450 mm x 750 mm x 19 mm	-	-	-	24.27	nr	24.27
600 mm x 900 mm x 25 mm	-	-	-	35.70	nr	35.70
Fitting components; "Warerite Xcel" standard colour laminated chipboard type LD2 or other equal and approved						
Backs, fronts, sides or divisions; over 300 mm wide						
13.20 mm thick	-	-	-	69.97	m²	69.97
Shelves or worktops; over 300 mm wide						
13.20 mm thick	-	-	-	69.97	m²	69.97
Flush doors; lipped on four edges						
450 mm x 750 mm x 13.20 mm	-	-	-	34.36	nr	34.36
600 mm x 900 mm x 13.20 mm	-	-	-	51.65	nr	51.65
Fitting components; plywood						
Backs, fronts, sides or divisions; over 300 mm wide						
6 mm thick	-	-	-	17.94	m²	17.94
9 mm thick	-	-	-	24.37	m²	24.37
12 mm thick	-	-	-	30.70	m²	30.70
19 mm thick	-	-	-	44.78	m²	44.78
25 mm thick	-	-	-	60.43	m²	60.43
Shelves or worktops; over 300 mm wide						
19 mm thick	-	-	-	44.78	m²	44.78
25 mm thick	-	-	-	60.43	m²	60.43
Flush doors; lipped on four edges						
450 mm x 750 mm x 19 mm	-	-	-	24.50	nr	24.50
450 mm x 750 mm x 25 mm	-	-	-	30.47	nr	30.47
600 mm x 900 mm x 19 mm	-	-	-	36.49	nr	36.49
600 mm x 900 mm x 25 mm	-	-	-	45.19	nr	45.19
Fitting components; wrought softwood						
Backs, fronts, sides or divisions; cross-tongued joints; over 300 mm wide						
25 mm thick	-	-	-	43.08	m²	43.08
Shelves or worktops; cross-tongued joints; over 300 mm wide						
25 mm thick	-	-	-	43.08	m²	43.08
Bearers						
19 mm x 38 mm	-	-	-	2.44	m	2.44
25 mm x 50 mm	-	-	-	3.05	m	3.05
50 mm x 50 mm	-	-	-	4.47	m	4.47
50 mm x 75 mm	-	-	-	5.98	m	5.98
Bearers; framed						
19 mm x 38 mm	-	-	-	4.78	m	4.78
25 mm x 50 mm	-	-	-	5.41	m	5.41
50 mm x 50 mm	-	-	-	6.82	m	6.82
50 mm x 75 mm	-	-	-	8.32	m	8.32

N FURNITURE/EQUIPMENT Excluding overheads and profit	PC £	Labour hours	Labour £	Material £	Unit	Total rate £
Framing to backs, fronts or sides						
19 mm x 38 mm	-	-	-	4.78	m	4.78
25 mm x 50 mm	-	-	-	5.41	m	5.41
50 mm x 50 mm	-	-	-	6.82	m	6.82
50 mm x 75 mm	-	-	-	8.32	m	8.32
Flush doors, softwood skeleton or cellular core;						
plywood facing both sides; lipped on four edges						
450 mm x 750 mm x 35 mm	-	-	-	24.19	nr	24.19
600 mm x 900 mm x 35 mm	-	-	-	38.53	nr	38.53
Add 5% to the above materials prices for						
selected softwood for staining						
Fitting components; selected West African						
Mahogany						
Bearers						
19 mm x 38 mm	-	-	-	4.10	m	4.10
25 mm x 50 mm	-	-	-	5.39	m	5.39
50 mm x 50 mm	-	-	-	8.28	m	8.28
50 mm x 75 mm	-	-	-	11.32	m	11.32
Bearers; framed						
19 mm x 38 mm	-	-	-	7.61	m	7.61
25 mm x 50 mm	-	-	-	8.91	m	8.91
50 mm x 50 mm	-	-	-	11.80	m	11.80
50 mm x 75 mm	-	-	-	14.84	m	14.84
Framing to backs, fronts or sides						
19 mm x 38 mm	-	-	-	7.61	m	7.61
25 mm x 50 mm	-	-	-	8.91	m	8.91
50 mm x 50 mm	-	-	-	11.80	m	11.80
50 mm x 75 mm	-	-	-	14.84	m	14.84
Fitting components; Iroko						
Backs, fronts, sides or divisions; cross-tongued						
joints; over 300 mm wide						
25 mm thick	-	-	-	96.77	m²	96.77
Shelves or worktops; cross-tongued joints; over						
300 mm wide						
25 mm thick	-	-	-	96.77	m²	96.77
Draining boards; cross-tongued joints; over						
300 mm wide						
25 mm thick	-	-	-	102.28	m²	102.28
stopped flutes	-	-	-	3.07	m	3.07
grooves; cross-grain	-	-	-	0.72	m	0.72
Bearers						
19 mm x 38 mm	-	-	-	4.98	m	4.98
25 mm x 50 mm	-	-	-	6.44	m	6.44
50 mm x 50 mm	-	-	-	9.81	m	9.81
50 mm x 75 mm	-	-	-	13.36	m	13.36
Bearers; framed						
19 mm x 38 mm	-	-	-	9.68	m	9.68
25 mm x 50 mm	-	-	-	11.14	m	11.14
50 mm x 50 mm	-	-	-	14.51	m	14.51
50 mm x 75 mm	-	-	-	18.06	m	18.06
Framing to backs, fronts or sides						
19 mm x 38 mm	-	-	-	9.68	m	9.68
25 mm x 50 mm	-	-	-	11.14	m	11.14
50 mm x 50 mm	-	-	-	14.51	m	14.51
50 mm x 75 mm	-	-	-	18.06	m	18.06

N FURNITURE/EQUIPMENT Excluding overheads and profit	PC £	Labour hours	Labour £	Material £	Unit	Total rate £
N10/11 GENERAL FIXTURES/KITCHEN FITTINGS - cont'd						
Fitting components; Teak						
Backs, fronts, sides or divisions; cross-tongued joints; over 300 mm wide						
25 mm thick	-	-	-	196.39	m²	**196.39**
Shelves or worktops; cross-tongued joints; over 300 mm wide						
25 mm thick	-	-	-	196.39	m²	**196.39**
Draining boards; cross-tongued joints; over 300 mm wide						
25 mm thick	-	-	-	200.51	m²	**200.51**
stopped flutes	-	-	-	3.07	m	**3.07**
grooves; cross-grain	-	-	-	0.72	m	**0.72**
Fixing kitchen fittings						
NOTE: Kitchen fittings prices vary considerably. PC supply prices for reasonable quantities for a moderately priced range of kitchen fittings (Rugby Joinery "Lambeth" range) have been shown but not extended.						
Fixing to backgrounds requiring plugging; including any pre-assembly						
Wall units						
300 mm x 580 mm x 300 mm	38.56	1.30	10.35	0.17	nr	**10.52**
300 mm x 720 mm x 300 mm	43.37	1.40	11.14	0.17	nr	**11.31**
600 mm x 580 mm x 300 mm	48.92	1.55	12.34	0.17	nr	**12.51**
600 mm x 720 mm x 300 mm	54.35	1.75	13.93	0.17	nr	**14.10**
Floor units with drawers						
600 mm x 900 mm x 500 mm	79.12	1.40	11.14	0.17	nr	**11.31**
600 mm x 900 mm x 600 mm	82.52	1.55	12.34	0.17	nr	**12.51**
1200 mm x 900 mm x 600 mm	147.55	1.85	14.73	0.17	nr	**14.90**
Sink units (excluding sink top)						
1000 mm x 900 mm x 600 mm	93.30	1.75	13.93	0.17	nr	**14.10**
1200 mm x 900 mm x 600 mm	103.03	2.00	15.92	0.17	nr	**16.09**
Laminated plastics worktops; single rolled edge; prices include for fixing						
28 mm thick; 500 mm wide	-	0.44	3.50	22.36	m	**25.86**
38 mm thick; 600 mm wide	-	0.44	3.50	25.86	m	**29.36**
extra for forming hole for inset sink	-	0.83	6.61	-	nr	**6.61**
extra for jointing strip at corner intersection of worktops	-	0.17	1.35	10.86	nr	**12.21**
extra for butt and scribe joint at corner intersection of worktops	-	4.95	39.40	-	nr	**39.40**
Lockers; The Welconstruct Company or other equal and approved						
Standard clothes lockers; steel body and door within reinforced 19G frame, powder coated finish, cam locks						
1 compartment; placing in position						
305 mm x 305 mm x 1830 mm	-	0.25	1.61	47.25	nr	**48.86**
305 mm x 460 mm x 1830 mm	-	0.25	1.61	57.33	nr	**58.94**
460 mm x 460 mm x 1830 mm	-	0.30	1.94	72.24	nr	**74.17**
610 mm x 460 mm x 1830 mm	-	0.30	1.94	86.94	nr	**88.88**

N FURNITURE/EQUIPMENT Excluding overheads and profit	PC £	Labour hours	Labour £	Material £	Unit	Total rate £
Compartment lockers; steel body and door with reinforced 19G frame, powder coated finish, cam locks						
2 compartments; placing in position						
305 mm x 305 mm x 1830 mm	-	0.25	1.61	63.52	nr	65.13
305 mm x 460 mm x 1830 mm	-	0.25	1.61	66.57	nr	68.18
460 mm x 460 mm x 1830 mm	-	0.30	1.94	78.85	nr	80.78
4 compartments; placing in position						
305 mm x 305 mm x 1830 mm	-	0.25	1.61	80.33	nr	81.94
305 mm x 460 mm x 1830 mm	-	0.25	1.61	85.89	nr	87.50
460 mm x 460 mm x 1830 mm	-	0.30	1.94	90.09	nr	92.03
Wet area lockers; galvanised steel 18/22G etched primed coating body, galvanised steel 18/20G reinforced door on non-ferrous hinges, powder coated finish, cam locks						
1 compartment; placing in position						
305 mm x 305 mm x 1830 mm	-	0.25	1.61	70.98	nr	72.59
2 compartments; placing in position						
305 mm x 305 mm x 1830 mm	-	0.25	1.61	91.98	nr	93.59
305 mm x 460 mm x 1830 mm	-	0.25	1.61	96.39	nr	98.00
4 compartments; placing in position						
305 mm x 305 mm x 1830 mm	-	0.25	1.61	116.34	nr	117.95
305 mm x 460 mm x 1830 mm	-	0.25	1.61	124.64	nr	126.25
Extra for						
coin operated lock; coin returned	-	-	-	36.07	nr	36.07
coin operated lock; coin retained	-	-	-	56.59	nr	56.59
Timber clothes lockers; veneered MDF finish, routed door, cam locks						
1 compartment; placing in position						
380 mm x 380 mm x 1830 mm	-	0.30	1.94	207.90	nr	209.84
4 compartments; placing in position						
380 mm x 380 mm x 1830 mm	-	0.30	1.94	311.85	nr	313.79
Shelving support systems; The Welconstruct **Company or other equal and approved**						
Rolled front shelving support systems; steel body; stove enamelled finish; assembling						
open initial bay; 5 shelves; placing in position						
915 mm x 305 mm x 1905 mm	-	0.75	5.45	63.30	nr	68.75
915 mm x 460 mm x 1905 mm	-	0.75	5.45	82.40	nr	87.85
open extension bay; 5 shelves; placing in position						
915 mm x 305 mm x 1905 mm	-	0.90	6.54	51.30	nr	57.84
915 mm x 460 mm x 1905 mm	-	0.90	6.54	66.10	nr	72.64
closed initial bay; 5 shelves; placing in position						
915 mm x 305 mm x 1905 mm	-	0.75	5.45	79.30	nr	84.75
915 mm x 460 mm x 1905 mm	-	0.75	5.45	98.40	nr	103.85
closed extension bay; 5 shelves; placing in position						
915 mm x 305 mm x 1905 mm	-	0.90	6.54	70.90	nr	77.44
915 mm x 460 mm x 1905 mm	-	0.90	6.54	85.70	nr	92.24
6 mm thick rectangular glass mirrors; silver **backed; fixed with chromium plated domed** **headed screws; to background requiring** **plugging**						
Mirror with polished edges						
365 mm x 254 mm	5.22	0.88	7.00	5.39	nr	12.39
400 mm x 300 mm	-	0.88	7.00	7.05	nr	14.05
560 mm x 380 mm	11.82	0.99	7.88	11.99	nr	19.87
640 mm x 460 mm	14.85	1.10	8.76	15.02	nr	23.78

N FURNITURE/EQUIPMENT Excluding overheads and profit	PC £	Labour hours	Labour £	Material £	Unit	Total rate £
N10/11 GENERAL FIXTURES/KITCHEN FITTINGS - cont'd						
6 mm thick rectangular glass mirrors; silver **backed; fixed with chromium plated domed** **headed screws; to background requiring** **plugging** - cont'd						
Mirror with bevelled edges						
365 mm x 254 mm	9.07	0.88	7.00	9.24	nr	16.24
400 mm x 300 mm	10.72	0.88	7.00	10.89	nr	17.89
560 mm x 380 mm	17.60	0.99	7.88	17.77	nr	25.65
640 mm x 460 mm	22.00	1.10	8.76	22.17	nr	30.93
Door mats						
Entrance mats; "Tuftiguard type C" or other equal and approved; laying in position; 12 mm thick						
900 mm x 550 mm	200.09	0.55	3.55	100.05	nr	103.60
1200 mm x 750 mm	200.09	0.55	3.55	180.08	nr	183.63
2400 mm x 1200 mm	200.09	1.10	7.09	576.26	nr	583.35
Matwells						
Polished aluminium matwell; comprising 34 mm x 26 mm x 6 mm angle rim; with brazed angles and lugs brazed on; to suit mat size						
914 mm x 560 mm	36.97	1.10	7.09	36.97	nr	44.06
1067 mm x 610 mm	40.61	1.10	7.09	40.61	nr	47.70
1219 mm x 762 mm	48.00	1.10	7.09	48.00	nr	55.09
Polished brass matwell; comprising 38 mm x 38 mm x 6 mm angle rim; with brazed angles and lugs welded on; to suit mat size						
914 mm x 560 mm	109.47	1.10	7.09	109.47	nr	116.56
1067 mm x 610 mm	120.24	1.10	7.09	120.24	nr	127.33
1219 mm x 762 mm	142.13	1.10	7.09	142.13	nr	149.22
Internal blinds; Luxaflex Ltd or other equal and **approved**						
Roller blinds; Luxaflex "Safeweave RB"; fire resisting material; 1200 mm drop; fixing with screws						
1000 mm wide	41.80	1.10	7.09	41.80	nr	48.89
2000 mm wide	81.40	1.73	11.16	81.40	nr	92.56
3000 mm wide	123.20	2.34	15.09	123.20	nr	138.29
Roller blinds; Luxaflex "Plain RB"; plain type material; 1200 mm drop; fixing with screws						
1000 mm wide	26.40	1.10	7.09	26.40	nr	33.49
2000 mm wide	50.60	1.73	11.16	50.60	nr	61.76
3000 mm wide	74.80	2.34	15.09	74.80	nr	89.89
Roller blinds; Luxaflex "Dimout plain RB"; blackout material; 1200 mm drop; fixing with screws						
1000 mm wide	41.80	1.10	7.09	41.80	nr	48.89
2000 mm wide	81.40	1.73	11.16	81.40	nr	92.56
3000 mm wide	123.20	2.34	15.09	123.20	nr	138.29
Roller blinds; Luxaflex "Lite-master Crank Op"; 100% blackout; 1200 mm drop; fixing with screws						
1000 mm wide	190.30	2.33	15.03	190.30	nr	205.33
2000 mm wide	270.60	3.27	21.09	270.60	nr	291.69
3000 mm wide	339.90	4.20	27.09	339.90	nr	366.99
Vertical louvre blinds; 89 mm wide louvres; Luxaflex "Finessa 3430" Group 0; 1200 mm drop; fixing with screws						
1000 mm wide	59.40	0.98	6.32	59.40	nr	65.72
2000 mm wide	102.30	1.54	9.93	102.30	nr	112.23
3000 mm wide	145.20	2.10	13.54	145.20	nr	158.74

N FURNITURE/EQUIPMENT Excluding overheads and profit	PC £	Labour hours	Labour £	Material £	Unit	Total rate £
Vertical louvre blinds; 127 mm wide louvres; Luxaflex "Finessa 3420" Group 0; 1200 mm drop; fixing with screws						
1000 mm wide	52.80	1.05	6.77	52.80	nr	59.57
2000 mm wide	88.00	1.61	10.38	88.00	nr	98.38
3000 mm wide	126.50	2.16	13.93	126.50	nr	140.43

N13 SANITARY APPLIANCES/FITTINGS

NOTE: Sanitary fittings are largely a matter of selection material prices vary considerably; the PC values given below are for "average quality".

	PC £	Labour hours	Labour £	Material £	Unit	Total rate £
Sanitary fittings						
Sink; white glazed fireclay; BS 1206; cast iron cantilever brackets						
610 mm x 455 mm x 205 mm	105.00	3.60	38.05	112.22	nr	150.27
610 mm x 455 mm x 255 mm	120.00	3.60	38.05	127.22	nr	165.27
760 mm x 455 mm x 255 mm	180.00	3.60	38.05	187.22	nr	225.27
Sink; stainless steel combined bowl and draining board; chain and self colour plug; to BS 3380						
1050 mm x 500 mm with bowl 420 mm x 350 mm x 175 mm	120.00	2.10	22.20	120.00	nr	142.20
Sink; stainless steel combined bowl and double draining board; chain and self colour plug to BS 3380						
1550 mm x 500 mm with bowl 420 mm x 350 mm x 200 mm	145.00	2.10	22.20	145.00	nr	167.20
Lavatory basin; vitreous china; BS 1188; 32 mm diameter chromium plated waste; chain, stay and plug; pair 13 mm diameter chromium plated easy clean pillar taps to BS 1010; painted cantilever brackets; plugged and screwed						
560 mm x 405 mm	60.00	2.75	29.07	60.00	nr	89.07
560 mm x 405 mm; coloured	70.00	2.75	29.07	70.00	nr	99.07
635 mm x 455 mm	80.00	2.75	29.07	80.00	nr	109.07
635 mm x 455 mm; coloured	90.00	2.75	29.07	90.00	nr	119.07
Lavatory basin and pedestal; vitreous china; BS 1188; 32 mm diameter chromium plated waste; chain, stay and plug; pair 13 mm diameter chromium plated easy clean pillar taps to BS 1010; pedestal; wall brackets; plugged and screwed						
560 mm x 405 mm	75.00	3.00	31.71	75.00	nr	106.71
560 mm x 405 mm; coloured	85.00	3.00	31.71	85.00	nr	116.71
635 mm x 455 mm	95.00	3.00	31.71	95.00	nr	126.71
635 mm x 455 mm; coloured	110.00	3.00	31.71	110.00	nr	141.71
Lavatory basin range; overlap joints; white glazed fireclay; 32 mm diameter chromium plated waste, chain, stay and plug; pair 13 mm diameter chromium plated easy clean pillar taps to BS 1010; painted cast iron cantilever brackets						
range of four; 506 mm x 405 mm	305.00	10.55	111.51	305.00	nr	416.51
add for each additional basin in range	-	2.40	25.37	80.00	nr	105.37

N FURNITURE/EQUIPMENT Excluding overheads and profit	PC £	Labour hours	Labour £	Material £	Unit	Total rate £
N13 SANITARY APPLIANCES/FITTINGS - cont'd						
Sanitary fittings - cont'd						
Drinking fountain; white glazed fireclay; 19 mm diameter chromium plated waste; self-closing non-concussive tap; regulating valve; plugged and screwed with chromium plated screws						
drinking fountain	165.00	3.00	31.71	165.00	nr	**196.71**
Bath; reinforced acrylic rectangular pattern; chromium plated overflow chain and plug; 40 mm diameter chromium plated waste; cast brass "P" trap with plain outlet and overflow connection; pair 20 mm diameter chromium easy clean pillar taps to BS 1010						
1700 mm long; white	190.00	4.20	44.39	190.00	nr	**234.39**
1700 mm long; coloured	210.00	4.20	44.39	210.00	nr	**254.39**
Bath; enamelled steel; medium gauge rectangular pattern; 40 mm diameter chromium plated overflow chain and plug; 40 mm diameter chromium plated waste; cast brass "P" trap with plain outlet and overflow connection; pair 20 mm diameter chromium plated easy clean pillar taps to BS 1010						
1700 mm long; white	290.00	4.20	44.39	290.00	nr	**334.39**
1700 mm long; coloured	310.00	4.20	44.39	310.00	nr	**354.39**
Shower tray; glazed fireclay with outlet and grated waste; chain and plug; bedding and pointing in waterproof cement mortar						
760 mm x 760 mm x 180 mm; white	130.00	3.60	38.05	130.00	nr	**168.05**
760 mm x 760 mm x 180 mm; coloured	185.00	3.60	38.05	185.00	nr	**223.05**
Shower fitting; riser pipe with mixing valve and shower rose; chromium plated; plugging and screwing mixing valve and pipe bracket						
15 mm diameter riser pipe; 127 mm diameter shower rose	235.00	6.00	63.42	235.00	nr	**298.42**
WC suite; high level; vitreous china pan; black plastic seat; 9 litre white vitreous china cistern and brackets; low pressure ball valve; galvanized steel flush pipe and clip; plugged and screwed; mastic joint to drain						
WC suite; white	175.00	3.95	41.75	175.00	nr	**216.75**
WC suite; coloured	210.00	3.95	41.75	210.00	nr	**251.75**
WC suite; low level; vitreous china pan; black plastic seat; 9 litre white vitreous china cistern and brackets; low pressure ball valve and plastic flush pipe; plugged and screwed; mastic joint to drain						
WC suite; white	110.00	3.60	38.05	110.00	nr	**148.05**
WC suite; coloured	140.00	3.60	38.05	140.00	nr	**178.05**
Bidet; vitreous china; chromium plated waste; mixer tap with hand wheels						
600 mm x 400 mm x 400 mm; white	190.00	4.20	44.39	190.00	nr	**234.39**
Slop sink; white glazed fireclay with hardwood pad; aluminium bucket grating; vitreous china cistern and porcelain enamelled brackets; galvanized steel flush pipe and clip; plugged and screwed; mastic joint to drain						
slop sink	580.00	4.20	44.39	580.00	nr	**624.39**

N FURNITURE/EQUIPMENT Excluding overheads and profit	PC £	Labour hours	Labour £	Material £	Unit	Total rate £
Bowl type wall urinal; white glazed vitreous china; white vitreous china automatic flushing cistern and brackets; 38 mm diameter chromium plated waste; chromium plated flush pipes and spreaders; cistern brackets and flush pipe plugged and screwed with chromium plated screws						
single; 455 mm x 380 mm x 330 mm	210.00	4.80	50.74	210.00	nr	**260.74**
range of two	290.00	9.00	95.13	290.00	nr	**385.13**
range of three	325.00	13.20	139.52	325.00	nr	**464.52**
add for each additional urinal	120.00	3.85	40.69	120.00	nr	**160.69**
add for divisions between urinals	45.00	0.90	9.51	45.00	nr	**54.51**
Bath screen; clear glass; chrome frame; plugged and screwed						
690 mm x 1340 mm	275.00	1.80	19.03	275.00	nr	**294.03**

N15 SIGNS/NOTICES

**Plain script; in gloss oil paint; on painted or
varnished surfaces**

Capital letters; lower case letters or numerals						
per coat; per 25 mm high	-	0.11	0.88	-	nr	**0.88**
Stops						
per coat	-	0.03	0.24	-	nr	**0.24**

P BUILDING FABRIC SUNDRIES Excluding overheads and profit	PC £	Labour hours	Labour £	Material £	Unit	Total rate £
P BUILDING FABRIC SUNDRIES						
P10 SUNDRY INSULATION/PROOFING WORK/FIRESTOPS						
"Sisalkraft" building papers/vapour barriers or other equal and approved						
Building paper; 150 mm laps; fixed to softwood						
"Moistop" grade 728 (class A1F)	-	0.11	1.25	1.20	m²	**2.45**
Vapour barrier/reflective insulation 150 mm laps; fixed to softwood						
"Insulex" grade 714; single sided	-	0.11	1.25	1.50	m²	**2.75**
"Insulex" grade 714; double sided	-	0.11	1.25	2.15	m²	**3.40**
Mat or quilt insulation						
Glass fibre quilt; "Isowool 1000" or other equal and approved; laid loose between members at 600 mm centres						
60 mm thick	2.01	0.23	2.61	2.01	m²	**4.62**
80 mm thick	2.63	0.25	2.83	2.63	m²	**5.46**
100 mm thick	3.13	0.28	3.18	3.13	m²	**6.31**
150 mm thick	4.80	0.33	3.74	4.80	m²	**8.54**
Mineral fibre quilt; "Isowool 1200" or other equal and approved; pinned vertically to softwood						
25 mm thick	1.66	0.15	1.70	1.66	m²	**3.36**
50 mm thick	2.73	0.17	1.93	2.73	m²	**4.66**
Glass fibre building roll; pinned vertically to softwood						
60 mm thick	1.91	0.17	1.93	2.01	m²	**3.94**
80 mm thick	2.50	0.18	2.04	2.63	m²	**4.67**
100 mm thick	2.98	0.19	2.15	3.13	m²	**5.28**
Glass fibre flanged building roll; paper faces; pinned vertically or to slope between timber framing						
60 mm thick	4.04	0.20	2.27	4.24	m²	**6.51**
80 mm thick	5.04	0.21	2.38	5.29	m²	**7.67**
100 mm thick	5.88	0.22	2.49	6.17	m²	**8.66**
Glass fibre aluminium foil faced roll; pinned to softwood						
80 mm thick	-	0.20	2.27	4.46	m²	**6.73**
Board or slab insulation						
Jablite expanded polystyrene board standard grade ISD or other equal and approved; fixed with adhesive						
25 mm thick	-	0.46	5.22	3.18	m²	**8.40**
40 mm thick	-	0.49	5.56	5.28	m²	**10.84**
50 mm thick	-	0.55	6.24	6.33	m²	**12.57**
Jablite expanded polystyrene board grade EHD(N) or other equal and approved						
100 mm thick	-	0.55	6.24	1.33	m²	**7.57**
"Styrofoam Floormate 350" extruded polystyrene foam or other equal and approved						
50 mm thick	-	0.55	6.24	11.54	m²	**17.78**
Fire stops						
Cape "Firecheck" channel or other equal and approved; intumescent coatings on cut mitres; fixing with brass cups and screws						
19 mm x 44 mm or 19 mm x 50 mm	12.60	0.66	7.48	13.66	m	**21.14**

P BUILDING FABRIC SUNDRIES Excluding overheads and profit	PC £	Labour hours	Labour £	Material £	Unit	Total rate £
"Sealmaster" intumescent fire and smoke seals or						
other equal and approved; pinned into groove in timber						
type N30; for single leaf half hour door	6.33	0.33	3.74	6.65	m	10.39
type N60; for single leaf one hour door	9.62	0.36	4.08	10.10	m	14.18
type IMN or IMP; for meeting or pivot stiles of						
pair of one hour doors; per stile	9.62	0.36	4.08	10.10	m	14.18
intumescent plugs in timber; including boring	-	0.11	1.25	0.32	nr	1.57
Rockwool fire stops or other equal and approved;						
between top of brick/block wall and concrete soffit						
25 mm deep x 112 mm wide	-	0.09	1.02	0.69	m	1.71
25 mm deep x 150 mm wide	-	0.11	1.25	0.92	m	2.17
50 mm deep x 225 mm wide	-	0.17	1.93	2.77	m	4.70
Fire protection compound						
Quelfire "QF4" fire protection compound or other equal						
and approved; filling around pipes, ducts and the like;						
including all necessary formwork						
300 mm x 300 mm x 250 mm; pipes - 2	-	1.35	12.96	40.08	nr	53.04
Fire barriers						
Rockwool fire barrier or other equal and approved;						
between top of suspended ceiling and concrete soffit						
one 50 mm layer x 900 mm wide; half hour	-	0.66	7.48	7.66	m²	15.14
two 50 mm layers x 900 mm wide; one hour	-	0.99	11.23	15.05	m²	26.28
Lamatherm fire barrier or other equal and approved;						
to void below raised access floors						
75 mm thick x 300 mm wide; half hour	-	0.18	2.04	13.23	m	15.27
75 mm thick x 600 mm wide; half hour	-	0.18	2.04	29.50	m	31.54
90 mm thick x 300 mm wide; half hour	-	0.18	2.04	16.48	m	18.52
90 mm thick x 600 mm wide; half hour	-	0.18	2.04	39.38	m	41.42
Dow Chemicals "Styrofoam 1B" or other equal and						
approved; cold bridging insulation fixed with						
adhesive to brick, block or concrete base						
Insulation to walls						
25 mm thick	-	0.37	4.20	5.52	m²	9.72
50 mm thick	-	0.40	4.54	10.11	m²	14.65
75 mm thick	-	0.42	4.76	15.08	m²	19.84
Insulation to isolated columns						
25 mm thick	-	0.45	5.10	5.52	m²	10.62
50 mm thick	-	0.48	5.44	10.11	m²	15.55
75 mm thick	-	0.52	5.90	15.08	m²	20.98
Insulation to ceilings						
25 mm thick	-	0.40	4.54	5.52	m²	10.06
50 mm thick	-	0.43	4.88	10.11	m²	14.99
75 mm thick	-	0.46	5.22	15.08	m²	20.30
Insulation to isolated beams						
25 mm thick	-	0.48	5.44	5.52	m²	10.96
50 mm thick	-	0.52	5.90	10.11	m²	16.01
75 mm thick	-	0.55	6.24	15.08	m²	21.32
P11 FOAMED/FIBRE/BEAD CAVITY WALL **INSULATION**						
Injected insulation						
Cavity wall insulation; injecting 65 mm cavity						
with						
blown EPS granules	-	-	-	-	m²	3.00
blown mineral wool	-	-	-	-	m²	2.50

P BUILDING FABRIC SUNDRIES Excluding overheads and profit	PC £	Labour hours	Labour £	Material £	Unit	Total rate £
P20 UNFRAMED ISOLATED TRIMS/SKIRTINGS/ SUNDRY ITEMS						
Blockboard (Birch faced); 18 mm thick						
Window boards and the like; rebated;						
hardwood lipped on one edge						
18 mm x 200 mm	-	0.28	3.18	3.82	m	7.00
18 mm x 250 mm	-	0.31	3.52	4.48	m	8.00
18 mm x 300 mm	-	0.34	3.86	5.15	m	9.01
18 mm x 350 mm	-	0.37	4.20	5.82	m	10.02
returned and fitted ends	-	0.24	2.72	0.39	nr	3.11
Blockboard (Sapele veneered one side); 18 mm thick						
Window boards and the like; rebated;						
hardwood lipped on one edge						
18 mm x 200 mm	-	0.30	3.40	3.40	m	6.80
18 mm x 250 mm	-	0.33	3.74	3.97	m	7.71
18 mm x 300 mm	-	0.36	4.08	4.53	m	8.61
18 mm x 350 mm	-	0.40	4.54	5.10	m	9.64
returned and fitted ends	-	0.24	2.72	0.39	nr	3.11
Blockboard (American White Ash veneered one side); 18 mm thick						
Window boards and the like; rebated;						
hardwood lipped on one edge						
18 mm x 200 mm	-	0.30	3.40	3.89	m	7.29
18 mm x 250 mm	-	0.33	3.74	4.58	m	8.32
18 mm x 300 mm	-	0.36	4.08	5.27	m	9.35
18 mm x 350 mm	-	0.40	4.54	5.95	m	10.49
returned and fitted ends	-	0.24	2.72	0.39	nr	3.11
Medium density fibreboard primed profiles; Balcas Kildare Ltd or other equal and approved						
Window boards; rounded and rebated						
25 mm x 220 mm	-	0.33	3.74	4.07	m	7.81
25 mm x 245 mm	-	0.33	3.74	4.43	m	8.17
Skirtings						
14.50 mm x 45 mm; rounded	-	0.11	1.25	0.85	m	2.10
14.50 mm x 70 mm; rounded	-	0.11	1.25	1.15	m	2.40
14.50 mm x 95 mm; rounded	-	0.11	1.25	1.40	m	2.65
14.50 mm x 95 mm; moulded	-	0.11	1.25	1.40	m	2.65
14.50 mm x 120 mm; moulded	-	0.11	1.25	1.65	m	2.90
18 mm x 70 mm; moulded	-	0.11	1.25	1.29	m	2.54
18 mm x 145 mm; moulded	-	0.11	1.25	2.16	m	3.41
Dado rail						
18 mm x 58 mm; moulded	-	0.11	1.25	1.31	m	2.56
Wrought softwood						
Skirtings, picture rails, dado rails and the like;						
splayed or moulded						
19 mm x 50 mm; splayed	-	0.11	1.25	1.43	m	2.68
19 mm x 50 mm; moulded	-	0.11	1.25	1.57	m	2.82
19 mm x 75 mm; splayed	-	0.11	1.25	1.70	m	2.95
19 mm x 75 mm; moulded	-	0.11	1.25	1.83	m	3.08
19 mm x 100 mm; splayed	-	0.11	1.25	1.98	m	3.23
19 mm x 100 mm; moulded	-	0.11	1.25	2.09	m	3.34
19 mm x 150 mm; moulded	-	0.13	1.47	2.67	m	4.14
19 mm x 175 mm; moulded	-	0.13	1.47	2.93	m	4.40
22 mm x 100 mm; splayed	-	0.11	1.25	2.17	m	3.42

P BUILDING FABRIC SUNDRIES Excluding overheads and profit	PC £	Labour hours	Labour £	Material £	Unit	Total rate £
Skirtings, picture rails, dado rails and the like; splayed or moulded - cont'd						
25 mm x 50 mm; moulded	-	0.11	1.25	1.75	m	3.00
25 mm x 75 mm; splayed	-	0.11	1.25	1.98	m	3.23
25 mm x 100 mm; splayed	-	0.11	1.25	2.32	m	3.57
25 mm x 150 mm; splayed	-	0.13	1.47	3.05	m	4.52
25 mm x 150 mm; moulded	-	0.13	1.47	3.17	m	4.64
25 mm x 175 mm; moulded	-	0.13	1.47	3.54	m	5.01
25 mm x 225 mm; moulded	-	0.15	1.70	4.27	m	5.97
returned ends	-	0.17	1.93	-	nr	1.93
mitres	-	0.11	1.25	-	nr	1.25
Architraves, cover fillets and the like; half round; splayed or moulded						
13 mm x 25 mm; half round	-	0.13	1.47	1.09	m	2.56
13 mm x 50 mm; moulded	-	0.13	1.47	1.41	m	2.88
16 mm x 32 mm; half round	-	0.13	1.47	1.19	m	2.66
16 mm x 38 mm; moulded	-	0.13	1.47	1.38	m	2.85
16 mm x 50 mm; moulded	-	0.13	1.47	1.48	m	2.95
19 mm x 50 mm; splayed	-	0.13	1.47	1.43	m	2.90
19 mm x 63 mm; splayed	-	0.13	1.47	1.58	m	3.05
19 mm x 75 mm; splayed	-	0.13	1.47	1.70	m	3.17
25 mm x 44 mm; splayed	-	0.13	1.47	1.62	m	3.09
25 mm x 50 mm; moulded	-	0.13	1.47	1.75	m	3.22
25 mm x 63 mm; splayed	-	0.13	1.47	1.78	m	3.25
25 mm x 75 mm; splayed	-	0.13	1.47	1.98	m	3.45
32 mm x 88 mm; moulded	-	0.13	1.47	2.73	m	4.20
38 mm x 38 mm; moulded	-	0.13	1.47	1.74	m	3.21
50 mm x 50 mm; moulded	-	0.13	1.47	2.32	m	3.79
returned ends	-	0.17	1.93	-	nr	1.93
mitres	-	0.11	1.25	-	nr	1.25
Stops; screwed on						
16 mm x 38 mm		0.11	1.25	1.08	m	2.33
16 mm x 50 mm	-	0.11	1.25	1.19	m	2.44
19 mm x 38 mm	-	0.11	1.25	1.14	m	2.39
25 mm x 38 mm	-	0.11	1.25	1.26	m	2.51
25 mm x 50 mm	-	0.11	1.25	1.45	m	2.70
Glazing beads and the like						
13 mm x 16 mm	-	0.06	0.68	0.80	m	1.48
13 mm x 19 mm	-	0.06	0.68	0.84	m	1.52
13 mm x 25 mm	-	0.06	0.68	0.88	m	1.56
13 mm x 25 mm; screwed	-	0.06	0.68	0.93	m	1.61
13 mm x 25 mm; fixing with brass cups and screws	-	0.11	1.25	1.15	m	2.40
16 mm x 25 mm; screwed	-	0.06	0.68	0.98	m	1.66
16 mm quadrant	-	0.06	0.68	0.96	m	1.64
19 mm quadrant or scotia	-	0.06	0.68	1.04	m	1.72
19 mm x 36 mm; screwed	-	0.06	0.68	1.15	m	1.83
25 mm x 38 mm; screwed	-	0.06	0.68	1.28	m	1.96
25 mm quadrant or scotia	-	0.06	0.68	1.18	m	1.86
38 mm scotia	-	0.06	0.68	1.66	m	2.34
50 mm scotia	-	0.06	0.68	2.25	m	2.93
Isolated shelves, worktops, seats and the like						
19 mm x 150 mm	-	0.18	2.04	2.53	m	4.57
19 mm x 200 mm	-	0.24	2.72	3.03	m	5.75
25 mm x 150 mm	-	0.18	2.04	3.03	m	5.07
25 mm x 200 mm	-	0.24	2.72	3.72	m	6.44
32 mm x 150 mm	-	0.18	2.04	3.60	m	5.64
32 mm x 200 mm	-	0.24	2.72	4.51	m	7.23

P BUILDING FABRIC SUNDRIES Excluding overheads and profit	PC £	Labour hours	Labour £	Material £	Unit	Total rate £
P20 UNFRAMED ISOLATED TRIMS/SKIRTINGS/ **SUNDRY ITEMS** - cont'd						
Wrought softwood - cont'd						
Isolated shelves, worktops, seats and the like; cross-tongued joints						
19 mm x 300 mm	-	0.31	3.52	11.82	m	15.34
19 mm x 450 mm	-	0.37	4.20	13.50	m	17.70
19 mm x 600 mm	-	0.44	4.99	19.64	m	24.63
25 mm x 300 mm	-	0.31	3.52	13.08	m	16.60
25 mm x 450 mm	-	0.37	4.20	15.21	m	19.41
25 mm x 600 mm	-	0.44	4.99	21.98	m	26.97
32 mm x 300 mm	-	0.31	3.52	14.34	m	17.86
32 mm x 450 mm	-	0.37	4.20	17.10	m	21.30
32 mm x 600 mm	-	0.44	4.99	24.53	m	29.52
Isolated shelves, worktops, seats and the like; slatted with 50 mm wide slats at 75 mm centres						
19 mm thick	-	1.46	16.56	8.89	m	25.45
25 mm thick	-	1.46	16.56	10.21	m	26.77
32 mm thick	-	1.46	16.56	11.35	m	27.91
Window boards, nosings, bed moulds and the like; rebated and rounded						
19 mm x 75 mm	-	0.20	2.27	1.92	m	4.19
19 mm x 150 mm	-	0.22	2.49	2.76	m	5.25
19 mm x 225 mm; in one width	-	0.29	3.29	3.57	m	6.86
19 mm x 300 mm; cross-tongued joints	-	0.33	3.74	11.88	m	15.62
25 mm x 75 mm	-	0.20	2.27	2.19	m	4.46
25 mm x 150 mm	-	0.22	2.49	3.30	m	5.79
25 mm x 225 mm; in one width	-	0.29	3.29	4.36	m	7.65
25 mm x 300 mm; cross-tongued joints	-	0.33	3.74	13.10	m	16.84
32 mm x 75 mm	-	0.20	2.27	2.49	m	4.76
32 mm x 150 mm	-	0.22	2.49	3.88	m	6.37
32 mm x 225 mm; in one width	-	0.29	3.29	5.24	m	8.53
32 mm x 300 mm; cross-tongued joints	-	0.33	3.74	14.36	m	18.10
38 mm x 75 mm	-	0.20	2.27	2.76	m	5.03
38 mm x 150 mm	-	0.22	2.49	4.37	m	6.86
38 mm x 225 mm; in one width	-	0.29	3.29	6.02	m	9.31
38 mm x 300 mm; cross-tongued joints	-	0.33	3.74	15.50	m	19.24
returned and fitted ends	-	0.17	1.93	-	nr	1.93
Handrails; mopstick						
50 mm diameter	-	0.28	3.18	3.35	m	6.53
Handrails; rounded						
44 mm x 50 mm	-	0.28	3.18	3.35	m	6.53
50 mm x 75 mm	-	0.30	3.40	4.11	m	7.51
63 mm x 87 mm	-	0.33	3.74	5.54	m	9.28
75 mm x 100 mm	-	0.39	4.42	6.21	m	10.63
Handrails; moulded						
44 mm x 50 mm	-	0.25	2.83	3.73	m	6.56
50 mm x 75 mm	-	0.27	3.06	4.49	m	7.55
63 mm x 87 mm	-	0.30	3.40	5.92	m	9.32
75 mm x 100 mm	-	0.35	3.97	6.59	m	10.56
Add 5% to the above material prices for selected softwood for staining						

P BUILDING FABRIC SUNDRIES Excluding overheads and profit	PC £	Labour hours	Labour £	Material £	Unit	Total rate £
Selected West African Mahogany						
Skirtings, picture rails, dado rails and the like;						
splayed or moulded						
19 mm x 50 mm; splayed	3.32	0.15	1.70	3.56	m	**5.26**
19 mm x 50 mm; moulded	3.50	0.15	1.70	3.75	m	**5.45**
19 mm x 75 mm; splayed	3.99	0.15	1.70	4.27	m	**5.97**
19 mm x 75 mm; moulded	4.17	0.15	1.70	4.45	m	**6.15**
19 mm x 100 mm; splayed	4.68	0.15	1.70	4.99	m	**6.69**
19 mm x 100 mm; moulded	4.86	0.15	1.70	5.18	m	**6.88**
19 mm x 150 mm; moulded	6.23	0.18	2.04	6.62	m	**8.66**
19 mm x 175 mm; moulded	7.16	0.18	2.04	7.59	m	**9.63**
22 mm x 100 mm; splayed	5.08	0.15	1.70	5.41	m	**7.11**
25 mm x 50 mm; moulded	3.95	0.15	1.70	4.22	m	**5.92**
25 mm x 75 mm; splayed	4.65	0.15	1.70	4.96	m	**6.66**
25 mm x 100 mm; splayed	5.54	0.15	1.70	5.89	m	**7.59**
25 mm x 150 mm; splayed	7.61	0.18	2.04	8.07	m	**10.11**
25 mm x 150 mm; moulded	7.79	0.18	2.04	8.26	m	**10.30**
25 mm x 175 mm; moulded	8.69	0.18	2.04	9.20	m	**11.24**
25 mm x 225 mm; moulded	9.81	0.20	2.27	10.38	m	**12.65**
returned end	-	0.24	2.72	-	nr	**2.72**
mitres	-	0.17	1.93	-	nr	**1.93**
Architraves, cover fillets and the like; half round;						
splayed or moulded						
13 mm x 25 mm; half round	2.44	0.18	2.04	2.64	m	**4.68**
13 mm x 50 mm; moulded	3.05	0.18	2.04	3.28	m	**5.32**
16 mm x 32 mm; half round	2.70	0.18	2.04	2.91	m	**4.95**
16 mm x 38 mm; moulded	3.00	0.18	2.04	3.23	m	**5.27**
16 mm x 50 mm; moulded	3.28	0.18	2.04	3.52	m	**5.56**
19 mm x 50 mm; splayed	3.32	0.18	2.04	3.56	m	**5.60**
19 mm x 63 mm; splayed	3.68	0.18	2.04	3.94	m	**5.98**
19 mm x 75 mm; splayed	3.99	0.18	2.04	4.27	m	**6.31**
25 mm x 44 mm; splayed	3.76	0.18	2.04	4.02	m	**6.06**
25 mm x 50 mm; moulded	3.95	0.18	2.04	4.22	m	**6.26**
25 mm x 63 mm; splayed	4.21	0.18	2.04	4.50	m	**6.54**
25 mm x 75 mm; splayed	4.65	0.18	2.04	4.96	m	**7.00**
32 mm x 88 mm; moulded	6.55	0.18	2.04	6.95	m	**8.99**
38 mm x 88 mm; moulded	4.02	0.18	2.04	4.30	m	**6.34**
50 mm x 50 mm; moulded	5.54	0.18	2.04	5.89	m	**7.93**
returned end	-	0.24	2.72	-	nr	**2.72**
mitres	-	0.17	1.93	-	nr	**1.93**
Stops; screwed on						
16 mm x 38 mm	2.63	0.17	1.93	2.76	m	**4.69**
16 mm x 50 mm	2.92	0.17	1.93	3.07	m	**5.00**
19 mm x 38 mm	2.83	0.17	1.93	2.97	m	**4.90**
25 mm x 38 mm	3.15	0.17	1.93	3.31	m	**5.24**
25 mm x 50 mm	3.58	0.17	1.93	3.76	m	**5.69**
Glazing beads and the like						
13 mm x 16 mm	2.06	0.06	0.68	2.16	m	**2.84**
13 mm x 19 mm	2.12	0.06	0.68	2.23	m	**2.91**
13 mm x 25 mm	2.26	0.06	0.68	2.37	m	**3.05**
13 mm x 25 mm; screwed	2.06	0.09	1.02	2.30	m	**3.32**
13 mm x 25 mm; fixing with brass cups and						
screws	2.26	0.17	1.93	2.58	m	**4.51**
16 mm x 25 mm; screwed	2.34	0.09	1.02	2.59	m	**3.61**
16 mm quadrant	2.33	0.08	0.91	2.45	m	**3.36**
19 mm quadrant or scotia	2.47	0.08	0.91	2.59	m	**3.50**
19 mm x 36 mm; screwed	2.83	0.08	0.91	3.11	m	**4.02**
25 mm x 38 mm; screwed	3.15	0.08	0.91	3.44	m	**4.35**
25 mm quadrant or scotia	2.85	0.08	0.91	2.99	m	**3.90**
38 mm scotia	4.02	0.08	0.91	4.22	m	**5.13**
50 mm scotia	5.54	0.08	0.91	5.82	m	**6.73**

P BUILDING FABRIC SUNDRIES Excluding overheads and profit	PC £	Labour hours	Labour £	Material £	Unit	Total rate £
P20 UNFRAMED ISOLATED TRIMS/SKIRTINGS/ SUNDRY ITEMS - cont'd						
Selected West African Mahogany - cont'd						
Isolated shelves; worktops, seats and the like						
19 mm x 150 mm	6.44	0.24	2.72	6.76	m	**9.48**
19 mm x 200 mm	7.74	0.33	3.74	8.13	m	**11.87**
25 mm x 150 mm	7.74	0.24	2.72	8.13	m	**10.85**
25 mm x 200 mm	9.45	0.33	3.74	9.92	m	**13.66**
32 mm x 150 mm	9.17	0.24	2.72	9.63	m	**12.35**
32 mm x 200 mm	11.45	0.33	3.74	12.02	m	**15.76**
Isolated shelves, worktops, seats and the like; cross-tongued joints						
19 mm x 300 mm	21.60	0.42	4.76	22.68	m	**27.44**
19 mm x 450 mm	25.74	0.49	5.56	27.03	m	**32.59**
19 mm x 600 mm	37.33	0.61	6.92	39.20	m	**46.12**
25 mm x 300 mm	24.61	0.42	4.76	25.84	m	**30.60**
25 mm x 450 mm	30.06	0.49	5.56	31.56	m	**37.12**
25 mm x 600 mm	43.08	0.61	6.92	45.23	m	**52.15**
32 mm x 300 mm	27.62	0.42	4.76	29.00	m	**33.76**
32 mm x 450 mm	34.48	0.49	5.56	36.20	m	**41.76**
32 mm x 600 mm	49.21	0.61	6.92	51.67	m	**58.59**
Isolated shelves, worktops, seats and the like; slatted with 50 mm wide slats at 75 mm centres						
19 mm thick	24.14	1.93	21.89	25.63	m²	**47.52**
25 mm thick	27.24	1.93	21.89	28.89	m²	**50.78**
32 mm thick	30.11	1.93	21.89	31.90	m²	**53.79**
Window boards, nosings, bed moulds and the like; rebated and rounded						
19 mm x 75 mm	4.44	0.26	2.95	4.83	m	**7.78**
19 mm x 150 mm	6.50	0.30	3.40	7.00	m	**10.40**
19 mm x 225 mm; in one width	8.54	0.40	4.54	9.14	m	**13.68**
19 mm x 300 mm; cross-tongued joints	21.48	0.44	4.99	22.72	m	**27.71**
25 mm x 75 mm	5.11	0.26	2.95	5.54	m	**8.49**
25 mm x 150 mm	7.86	0.30	3.40	8.42	m	**11.82**
25 mm x 225 mm; in one width	10.46	0.40	4.54	11.15	m	**15.69**
25 mm x 300 mm; cross-tongued joints	24.37	0.44	4.99	25.76	m	**30.75**
32 mm x 75 mm	5.87	0.26	2.95	6.33	m	**9.28**
32 mm x 150 mm	9.29	0.30	3.40	9.93	m	**13.33**
32 mm x 225 mm; in one width	12.73	0.40	4.54	13.54	m	**18.08**
32 mm x 300 mm; cross-tongued joints	27.38	0.44	4.99	28.92	m	**33.91**
38 mm x 75 mm	6.50	0.26	2.95	7.00	m	**9.95**
38 mm x 150 mm	10.69	0.30	3.40	11.40	m	**14.80**
38 mm x 225 mm; in one width	14.67	0.40	4.54	15.57	m	**20.11**
38 mm x 300 mm; cross-tongued joints	30.09	0.44	4.99	31.77	m	**36.76**
returned and fitted ends	-	0.25	2.83	-	nr	**2.83**
Handrails; rounded						
44 mm x 50 mm	7.41	0.36	4.08	7.78	m	**11.86**
50 mm x 75 mm	9.27	0.40	4.54	9.73	m	**14.27**
63 mm x 87 mm	12.00	0.44	4.99	12.60	m	**17.59**
75 mm x 100 mm	14.57	0.49	5.56	15.30	m	**20.86**
Handrails; moulded						
44 mm x 50 mm	7.94	0.36	4.08	8.34	m	**12.42**
50 mm x 75 mm	9.81	0.40	4.54	10.30	m	**14.84**
63 mm x 87 mm	12.53	0.44	4.99	13.16	m	**18.15**
75 mm x 100 mm	15.11	0.49	5.56	15.87	m	**21.43**

P BUILDING FABRIC SUNDRIES Excluding overheads and profit	PC £	Labour hours	Labour £	Material £	Unit	Total rate £
American White Ash						
Skirtings, picture rails, dado rails and the like;						
splayed or moulded						
19 mm x 50 mm; splayed	3.73	0.15	1.70	3.99	m	5.69
19 mm x 50 mm; moulded	3.91	0.15	1.70	4.18	m	5.88
19 mm x 75 mm; splayed	4.65	0.15	1.70	4.96	m	6.66
19 mm x 75 mm; moulded	4.83	0.15	1.70	5.15	m	6.85
19 mm x 100 mm; splayed	5.54	0.15	1.70	5.89	m	7.59
19 mm x 100 mm; moulded	5.72	0.15	1.70	6.08	m	7.78
19 mm x 150 mm; moulded	7.49	0.18	2.04	7.94	m	9.98
19 mm x 175 mm; moulded	8.65	0.18	2.04	9.16	m	11.20
22 mm x 100 mm; splayed	6.10	0.15	1.70	6.48	m	8.18
25 mm x 50 mm; moulded	4.50	0.15	1.70	4.80	m	6.50
25 mm x 75 mm; splayed	5.48	0.15	1.70	5.83	m	7.53
25 mm x 100 mm; splayed	6.65	0.15	1.70	7.06	m	8.76
25 mm x 150 mm; splayed	9.29	0.18	2.04	9.83	m	11.87
25 mm x 150 mm; moulded	9.47	0.18	2.04	10.02	m	12.06
25 mm x 175 mm; moulded	10.62	0.18	2.04	11.23	m	13.27
25 mm x 225 mm; moulded	12.99	0.20	2.27	13.72	m	15.99
returned ends	-	0.24	2.72	-	nr	2.72
mitres	-	0.17	1.93	-	nr	1.93
Architraves, cover fillets and the like; half round;						
splayed or moulded						
13 mm x 25 mm; half round	2.59	0.18	2.04	2.80	m	4.84
13 mm x 50 mm; moulded	3.35	0.18	2.04	3.59	m	5.63
16 mm x 32 mm; half round	2.90	0.18	2.04	3.12	m	5.16
16 mm x 38 mm; moulded	3.30	0.18	2.04	3.54	m	5.58
16 mm x 50 mm; moulded	3.65	0.18	2.04	3.91	m	5.95
19 mm x 50 mm; splayed	3.73	0.18	2.04	3.99	m	6.03
19 mm x 63 mm; splayed	4.22	0.18	2.04	4.51	m	6.55
19 mm x 75 mm; splayed	4.65	0.18	2.04	4.96	m	7.00
25 mm x 44 mm; splayed	4.32	0.18	2.04	4.61	m	6.65
25 mm x 50 mm; moulded	4.50	0.18	2.04	4.80	m	6.84
25 mm x 63 mm; splayed	4.90	0.18	2.04	5.22	m	7.26
25 mm x 75 mm; splayed	5.48	0.18	2.04	5.83	m	7.87
32 mm x 88 mm; moulded	7.97	0.18	2.04	8.44	m	10.48
38 mm x 88 mm; moulded	4.68	0.18	2.04	4.99	m	7.03
50 mm x 50 mm; moulded	6.65	0.18	2.04	7.06	m	9.10
returned ends	-	0.24	2.72	-	nr	2.72
mitres	-	0.17	1.93	-	nr	1.93
Stops; screwed on						
16 mm x 38 mm	2.93	0.17	1.93	3.08	m	5.01
16 mm x 50 mm	3.30	0.17	1.93	3.47	m	5.40
19 mm x 38 mm	3.13	0.17	1.93	3.29	m	5.22
25 mm x 38 mm	3.55	0.17	1.93	3.73	m	5.66
25 mm x 50 mm	4.14	0.17	1.93	4.35	m	6.28
Glazing beads and the like						
13 mm x 16 mm	2.17	0.06	0.68	2.28	m	2.96
13 mm x 19 mm	2.25	0.06	0.68	2.36	m	3.04
13 mm x 25 mm	2.41	0.06	0.68	2.53	m	3.21
13 mm x 25 mm; screwed	2.41	0.09	1.02	2.67	m	3.69
13 mm x 25 mm; fixing with brass cups and						
screws	2.41	0.17	1.93	2.74	m	4.67
16 mm x 25 mm; screwed	2.53	0.09	1.02	2.79	m	3.81
16 mm quadrant	2.45	0.08	0.91	2.57	m	3.48
19 mm quadrant or scotia	2.64	0.08	0.91	2.77	m	3.68
19 mm x 36 mm; screwed	3.13	0.08	0.91	3.42	m	4.33
25 mm x 38 mm; screwed	3.55	0.08	0.91	3.86	m	4.77
25 mm quadrant or scotia	3.15	0.08	0.91	3.31	m	4.22
38 mm scotia	4.68	0.08	0.91	4.91	m	5.82
50 mm scotia	6.65	0.08	0.91	6.98	m	7.89

P BUILDING FABRIC SUNDRIES Excluding overheads and profit	PC £	Labour hours	Labour £	Material £	Unit	Total rate £
P20 UNFRAMED ISOLATED TRIMS/SKIRTINGS/ **SUNDRY ITEMS** - cont'd						
American White Ash - cont'd						
Isolated shelves, worktops, seats and the like						
19 mm x 150 mm	7.75	0.24	2.72	8.14	m	**10.86**
19 mm x 200 mm	9.45	0.33	3.74	9.92	m	**13.66**
25 mm x 150 mm	9.45	0.24	2.72	9.92	m	**12.64**
25 mm x 200 mm	11.67	0.33	3.74	12.25	m	**15.99**
32 mm x 150 mm	11.32	0.24	2.72	11.89	m	**14.61**
32 mm x 200 mm	14.31	0.33	3.74	15.03	m	**18.77**
Isolated shelves, worktops, seats and the like; cross-tongued joints						
19 mm x 300 mm	24.41	0.42	4.76	25.63	m	**30.39**
19 mm x 450 mm	29.87	0.49	5.56	31.36	m	**36.92**
19 mm x 600 mm	42.96	0.61	6.92	45.11	m	**52.03**
25 mm x 300 mm	28.36	0.42	4.76	29.78	m	**34.54**
25 mm x 450 mm	35.49	0.49	5.56	37.26	m	**42.82**
25 mm x 600 mm	50.48	0.61	6.92	53.00	m	**59.92**
32 mm x 300 mm	32.29	0.42	4.76	33.90	m	**38.66**
32 mm x 450 mm	41.32	0.49	5.56	43.39	m	**48.95**
32 mm x 600 mm	58.56	0.61	6.92	61.49	m	**68.41**
Isolated shelves, worktops, seats and the like; slatted with 50 mm wide slats at 75 mm centres						
19 mm thick	27.25	1.93	21.89	28.90	m²	**50.79**
25 mm thick	31.16	1.93	21.89	33.00	m²	**54.89**
32 mm thick	35.30	1.93	21.89	37.35	m²	**59.24**
Window boards, nosings, bed moulds and the like; rebated and rounded						
19 mm x 75 mm	5.07	0.26	2.95	5.49	m	**8.44**
19 mm x 150 mm	7.76	0.30	3.40	8.32	m	**11.72**
19 mm x 225 mm; in one width	10.43	0.40	4.54	11.12	m	**15.66**
19 mm x 300 mm; cross-tongued joints	24.34	0.44	4.99	25.73	m	**30.72**
25 mm x 75 mm	5.96	0.26	2.95	6.43	m	**9.38**
25 mm x 150 mm	9.57	0.30	3.40	10.22	m	**13.62**
25 mm x 225 mm; in one width	12.95	0.40	4.54	13.77	m	**18.31**
25 mm x 300 mm; cross-tongued joints	28.11	0.44	4.99	29.69	m	**34.68**
32 mm x 75 mm	6.93	0.26	2.95	7.45	m	**10.40**
32 mm x 150 mm	11.44	0.30	3.40	12.18	m	**15.58**
32 mm x 225 mm; in one width	-	0.40	4.54	16.93	m	**21.47**
32 mm x 300 mm; cross-tongued joints	32.06	0.44	4.99	33.83	m	**38.82**
38 mm x 75 mm	7.76	0.26	2.95	8.32	m	**11.27**
38 mm x 150 mm	13.16	0.30	3.40	13.99	m	**17.39**
38 mm x 225 mm; in one width	18.50	0.40	4.54	19.60	m	**24.14**
38 mm x 300 mm; cross-tongued joints	35.64	0.44	4.99	37.59	m	**42.58**
returned and fitted ends	-	0.25	2.83	-	nr	**2.83**
Handrails; rounded						
44 mm x 50 mm	8.51	0.36	4.08	8.94	m	**13.02**
50 mm x 75 mm	10.88	0.40	4.54	11.42	m	**15.96**
63 mm x 87 mm	15.68	0.44	4.99	16.46	m	**21.45**
75 mm x 100 mm	17.91	0.49	5.56	18.81	m	**24.37**
Handrails; moulded						
44 mm x 50 mm	9.06	0.36	4.08	9.51	m	**13.59**
50 mm x 75 mm	11.43	0.40	4.54	12.00	m	**16.54**
63 mm x 87 mm	16.22	0.44	4.99	17.03	m	**22.02**
75 mm x 100 mm	18.45	0.49	5.56	19.37	m	**24.93**

P BUILDING FABRIC SUNDRIES Excluding overheads and profit	PC £	Labour hours	Labour £	Material £	Unit	Total rate £
Pin-boards; medium board						
Sundeala "A" pin-board or other equal and						
approved; fixed with adhesive to backing						
(not included); over 300 mm wide						
6.40 mm thick	-	0.66	7.48	11.94	m²	**19.42**
Sundries on softwood/hardwood						
Extra over fixing with nails for						
gluing and pinning	-	0.02	0.23	0.05	m	**0.28**
masonry nails	-	-	-	-	m	**0.26**
steel screws	-	-	-	-	m	**0.24**
self-tapping screws	-	-	-	-	m	**0.25**
steel screws; gluing	-	-	-	-	m	**0.44**
steel screws; sinking; filling heads	-	-	-	-	m	**0.55**
steel screws; sinking; pellating over	-	-	-	-	m	**1.21**
brass cups and screws	-	-	-	-	m	**1.49**
Extra over for						
countersinking	-	-	-	-	m	**0.22**
pellating	-	-	-	-	m	**1.04**
Head or nut in softwood						
let in flush	-	-	-	-	nr	**0.55**
Head or nut; in hardwood						
let in flush	-	-	-	-	nr	**0.82**
let in over; pellated	-	-	-	-	nr	**1.93**
Metalwork; mild steel						
Angle section bearers; for building in						
150 mm x 100 mm x 6 mm	-	0.36	4.03	11.62	m	**15.65**
150 mm x 150 mm x 8 mm	-	0.39	4.36	18.19	m	**22.55**
200 mm x 200 mm x 12 mm	-	0.44	4.92	34.40	m	**39.32**
Metalwork; mild steel; galvanized						
Water bars; groove in timber						
6 mm x 30 mm	-	0.55	6.24	4.87	m	**11.11**
6 mm x 40 mm	-	0.55	6.24	5.72	m	**11.96**
6 mm x 50 mm	-	0.55	6.24	7.65	m	**13.89**
Angle section bearers; for building in						
150 mm x 100 mm x 6 mm	-	0.36	4.03	15.05	m	**19.08**
150 mm x 150 mm x 8 mm	-	0.39	4.36	24.05	m	**28.41**
200 mm x 200 mm x 12 mm	-	0.44	4.92	48.17	m	**53.09**
Dowels; mortice in timber						
8 mm diameter x 100 mm long	-	0.06	0.68	0.08	nr	**0.76**
10 mm diameter x 50 mm long	-	0.06	0.68	0.22	nr	**0.90**
Cramps						
25 mm x 3 mm x 230 mm girth; one end bent,						
holed and screwed to softwood; other end						
fishtailed for building in	-	0.08	0.91	0.55	nr	**1.46**
Metalwork; stainless steel						
Angle section bearers; for building in						
150 mm x 100 mm x 6 mm	-	0.36	4.03	42.68	m	**46.71**
150 mm x 150 mm x 8 mm	-	0.39	4.36	67.78	m	**72.14**
200 mm x 200 mm x 12 mm	-	0.44	4.92	141.62	m	**146.54**

P BUILDING FABRIC SUNDRIES Excluding overheads and profit	PC £	Labour hours	Labour £	Material £	Unit	Total rate £
P21 IRONMONGERY						
NOTE: Ironmongery is largely a matter of selection and prices vary considerably, indicative prices for reasonable quantities of "standard" quality ironmongery are given below.						
Ironmongery; NT Laidlaw Ltd or other equal and approved; standard ranges; to softwood						
Bolts						
barrel; 100 mm x 32 mm; PAA	-	0.33	3.74	5.48	nr	9.22
barrel; 150 mm x 32 mm; PAA	-	0.42	4.76	6.27	nr	11.03
flush; 152 mm x 25 mm; SCP	-	0.60	6.80	12.73	nr	19.53
flush; 203 mm x 25 mm; SCP	-	0.60	6.80	14.02	nr	20.82
flush; 305 mm x 25 mm; SCP	-	0.60	6.80	18.98	nr	25.78
indicating; 76 mm x 41 mm; SAA	-	0.67	7.60	9.30	nr	16.90
indicating; coin operated; SAA	-	0.67	7.60	12.73	nr	20.33
panic; single; SVE	-	2.50	28.35	58.71	nr	87.06
panic; double; SVE	-	3.50	39.69	79.96	nr	119.65
necked tower; 152 mm; BJ	-	0.33	3.74	2.58	nr	6.32
necked tower; 203 mm; BJ	-	0.33	3.74	3.48	nr	7.22
mortice security; SCP	-	0.60	6.80	16.88	nr	23.68
garage door bolt; 305 mm	-	0.60	6.80	6.29	nr	13.09
monkey tail with knob; 305 mm x 19 mm; BJ	-	0.67	7.60	7.69	nr	15.29
monkey tail with bow; 305 mm x 19 mm; BJ	-	0.67	7.60	9.69	nr	17.29
Butts						
63 mm; light steel	-	0.25	2.83	0.63	pr	3.46
100 mm; light steel	-	0.25	2.83	1.11	pr	3.94
102 mm; SC	-	0.25	2.83	3.55	pr	6.38
102 mm double flap extra strong; SC	-	0.25	2.83	2.21	pr	5.04
76 mm x 51 mm; SC	-	0.25	2.83	2.56	pr	5.39
51 mm x 22 mm narrow suite S/D	-	0.25	2.83	2.14	pr	4.97
76 mm x 35 mm narrow suite S/D	-	0.25	2.83	2.99	pr	5.82
51 mm x 29 mm broad suite S/D	-	0.25	2.83	2.14	pr	4.97
76 mm x 41 mm broad suite S/D	-	0.25	2.83	2.88	pr	5.71
102 mm x 60 mm broad suite S/D	-	0.25	2.83	6.05	pr	8.88
102 mm x 69 mm lift-off (R/L) hand	-	0.25	2.83	3.21	pr	6.04
high security heavy butts F/pin; 109 mm x 94 mm; ball bearing; SSS	-	0.40	4.54	19.00	pr	23.54
"Hi-load" butts; 125 mm x 102 mm	-	0.30	3.40	43.54	pr	46.94
S/D rising butts (R/L hand); 102 mm x 67 mm; BRS	-	0.25	2.83	36.39	pr	39.22
ball bearing butts; 102 mm x 67 mm; SSS	-	0.25	2.83	8.51	pr	11.34
Catches						
ball catch; 13 mm diameter; BRS	-	0.33	3.74	0.51	nr	4.25
double ball catch; 50 mm; BRS	-	0.40	4.54	0.68	nr	5.22
57 mm x 38 mm cupboard catch; SCP	-	0.30	3.40	5.92	nr	9.32
14 mm x 35 mm magnetic catch; WHT	-	0.17	1.93	0.59	nr	2.52
adjustable nylon roller catch; WNY	-	0.25	2.83	1.57	nr	4.40
"Bales" catch; Nr 4; 41 mm x 16 mm; self-colour brass; mortice	-	0.33	3.74	0.92	nr	4.66
"Bales" catch; Nr 8; 66 mm x 25 mm; self-colour brass; mortice	-	0.35	3.97	2.05	nr	6.02
Door closers and furniture						
standard concealed overhead door closer (L/R hand); SIL	-	1.25	14.18	151.92	nr	166.10
light duty surface fixed door closer (L/R hand); SIL	-	1.00	11.34	64.58	nr	75.92
"Perkomatic" concealed door closer; BRS	-	0.67	7.60	74.72	nr	82.32

P BUILDING FABRIC SUNDRIES Excluding overheads and profit	PC £	Labour hours	Labour £	Material £	Unit	Total rate £
Door closers and furniture - cont'd						
"Softline" adjustable size 2 - 4 overhead door closer; SIL	-	1.50	17.01	71.61	nr	88.62
"Centurion II" size 3 overhead door closer; SIL	-	1.25	14.18	33.30	nr	47.48
"Centurion II" size 4 overhead door closer; SIL	-	1.50	17.01	41.10	nr	58.11
backcheck door closer size 3; SAA	-	1.25	14.18	85.29	nr	99.47
backcheck door closer size 4; SAA	-	1.50	17.01	89.17	nr	106.18
door selector; face fixing; SAA	-	0.60	6.80	63.93	nr	70.73
finger plate; 300 mm x 75 mm x 3 mm	-	0.17	1.93	3.69	nr	5.62
kicking plate; 1000 mm x 150 mm x 30 mm; PAA	-	0.25	2.83	10.71	nr	13.54
floor spring; single and double action; ZP	-	2.50	28.35	157.03	nr	185.38
lever furniture; 280 mm x 40 mm	-	0.25	2.83	21.10	pr	23.93
pull handle; 225 mm; back fixing; PAA	-	0.17	1.93	5.64	nr	7.57
pull handle; f/fix with cover rose; PAA	-	0.33	3.74	30.26	nr	34.00
letter plate; 330 mm x 76 mm; aluminium finish	-	1.33	15.08	7.66	nr	22.74
Latches						
102 mm mortice latch; SCP	-	1.25	14.18	6.44	nr	20.62
cylinder rim night latch; SC7	-	0.75	8.51	18.25	nr	26.76
Locks						
drawer or cupboard lock; 63 mm x 32 mm; SC	-	0.42	4.76	8.03	nr	12.79
mortice dead lock; 63 mm x 108 mm; SSS	-	0.75	8.51	10.35	nr	18.86
12 mm rebate conversion set to mortice dead lock	-	0.50	5.67	10.25	nr	15.92
rim lock; 140 mm x 73 mm; GYE	-	0.42	4.76	7.87	nr	12.63
rim dead lock; 92 mm x 74.50 mm; SCP	-	0.42	4.76	20.81	nr	25.57
upright mortice lock; 103 mm x 82 mm; 3 lever	-	0.83	9.41	10.66	nr	20.07
upright mortice lock; 103 mm x 82 mm; 5 lever	-	0.83	9.41	33.31	nr	42.72
Window furniture						
casement stay; 305 mm long; 2 pin; SAA	-	0.17	1.93	6.97	nr	8.90
casement fastener; standard; 113 mm; SAA	-	0.17	1.93	4.51	nr	6.44
cockspur fastener; ASV	-	0.33	3.74	7.62	nr	11.36
sash fastener; 65 mm; SAA	-	0.25	2.83	2.56	nr	5.39
Sundries						
numerals; SAA	-	0.08	0.91	0.72	nr	1.63
rubber door stop; SAA	-	0.08	0.91	1.08	nr	1.99
medium hot pressed cabin hook; 102 mm; CP	-	0.17	1.93	8.81	nr	10.74
medium hot pressed cabin hook; 203 mm; CP	-	0.17	1.93	11.64	nr	13.57
coat hook; SAA	-	0.08	0.91	1.18	nr	2.09
toilet roll holder; CP	-	0.17	1.93	15.43	nr	17.36
Ironmongery; NT Laidlaw Ltd or other equal and approved; standard ranges; to hardwood						
Bolts						
barrel; 100 mm x 32 mm; PAA	-	0.44	4.99	5.48	nr	10.47
barrel; 150 mm x 32 mm; PAA	-	0.56	6.35	6.27	nr	12.62
flush; 152 mm x 25 mm; SCP	-	0.80	9.07	12.73	nr	21.80
flush; 203 mm x 25 mm; SCP	-	0.80	9.07	14.02	nr	23.09
flush; 305 mm x 25 mm; SCP	-	0.80	9.07	18.98	nr	28.05
indicating; 76 mm x 41 mm; SAA	-	0.89	10.09	9.30	nr	19.39
indicating; coin operated; SAA	-	0.89	10.09	12.73	nr	22.82
panic; single; SVE	-	3.33	37.76	58.71	nr	96.47
panic; double; SVE	-	4.67	52.96	79.96	nr	132.92
necked tower; 152 mm; BJ	-	0.44	4.99	2.58	nr	7.57
necked tower; 203 mm; BJ	-	0.44	4.99	3.48	nr	8.47
mortice security; SCP	-	0.80	9.07	16.88	nr	25.95
garage door bolt; 305 mm	-	0.80	9.07	6.29	nr	15.36
monkey tail with knob; 305 mm x 19 mm; BJ	-	0.85	9.64	7.69	nr	17.33
monkey tail with bow; 305 mm x 19 mm; BJ	-	0.85	9.64	9.69	nr	19.33

P BUILDING FABRIC SUNDRIES Excluding overheads and profit	PC £	Labour hours	Labour £	Material £	Unit	Total rate £
P21 IRONMONGERY - cont'd						
Iromongery; NT Laidlaw Ltd or other equal and approved; standard ranges; to hardwood - cont'd						
Butts						
63 mm; light steel	-	0.35	3.97	0.63	pr	4.60
100 mm; light steel	-	0.35	3.97	1.11	pr	5.08
102 mm; SC	-	0.35	3.97	3.55	pr	7.52
102 mm double flap extra strong; SC	-	0.35	3.97	2.21	pr	6.18
76 mm x 51 mm; SC	-	0.35	3.97	2.56	pr	6.53
51 mm x 22 mm narrow suite S/D	-	0.35	3.97	2.14	pr	6.11
76 mm x 35 mm narrow suite S/D	-	0.35	3.97	2.99	pr	6.96
51 mm x 29 mm broad suite S/D	-	0.35	3.97	2.14	pr	6.11
76 mm x 41 mm broad suite S/D	-	0.35	3.97	2.88	pr	6.85
102 mm x 60 mm broad suite S/D	-	0.35	3.97	6.05	pr	10.02
102 mm x 69 mm lift-off (R/L) hand	-	0.35	3.97	3.21	pr	7.18
high security heavy butts F/pin; 109 mm x 94 mm; ball bearing; SSS	-	0.45	5.10	19.00	pr	24.10
"Hi-load" butts; 125 mm x 102 mm	-	0.40	4.54	43.54	pr	48.08
S/D rising butts (R/L hand); 102 mm x 67 mm; BRS	-	0.35	3.97	36.39	pr	40.36
ball bearing butts; 102 mm x 67 mm; SSS	-	0.35	3.97	8.51	pr	12.48
Catches						
ball catch; 13 mm diameter; BRS	-	0.45	5.10	0.51	nr	5.61
double ball catch; 50 mm; BRS	-	0.47	5.33	0.68	nr	6.01
57 mm x 38 mm cupboard catch; SCP	-	0.40	4.54	5.92	nr	10.46
14 mm x 35 mm magnetic catch; WHT	-	0.23	2.61	0.59	nr	3.20
adjustable nylon roller catch; WNY	-	0.33	3.74	1.57	nr	5.31
"Bales" catch; Nr 4; 41 mm x 16 mm; self-colour brass; mortice	-	0.44	4.99	0.92	nr	5.91
"Bales" catch; Nr 8; 66 mm x 25 mm; self-colour brass; mortice		0.46	5.22	2.05	nr	7.27
Door closers and furniture						
standard concealed overhead door closer (L/R hand); SIL	-	1.67	18.94	151.92	nr	170.86
light duty surface fixed door closer (L/R hand); SIL	-	1.30	14.74	64.58	nr	79.32
"Perkomatic" concealed door closer; BRS	-	0.89	10.09	74.72	nr	84.81
"Softline" adjustable size 2 - 4 overhead door closer; SIL	-	2.00	22.68	71.61	nr	94.29
"Centurion II" size 3 overhead door closer; SIL	-	1.75	19.84	33.30	nr	53.14
"Centurion II" size 4 overhead door closer; SIL	-	2.00	22.68	41.10	nr	63.78
backcheck door closer size 3; SAA	-	1.75	19.84	85.29	nr	105.13
backcheck door closer size 4; SAA	-	2.00	22.68	89.17	nr	111.85
door selector; face fixing; SAA	-	0.80	9.07	63.93	nr	73.00
finger plate; 300 mm x 75 mm x 3 mm	-	0.23	2.61	3.69	nr	6.30
kicking plate; 1000 mm x 150 mm x 30 mm; PAA	-	0.44	4.99	10.71	nr	15.70
floor spring; single and double action; ZP	-	3.33	37.76	157.03	nr	194.79
lever furniture; 280 mm x 40 mm	-	0.33	3.74	21.10	pr	24.84
pull handle; 225 mm; back fixing; PAA	-	0.23	2.61	5.64	nr	8.25
pull handle; f/fix with cover rose; PAA	-	0.44	4.99	30.26	nr	35.25
letter plate; 330 mm x 76 mm; aluminium finish	-	1.77	20.07	7.66	nr	27.73
Latches						
102 mm mortice latch; SCP	-	1.75	19.84	6.44	nr	26.28
cylinder rim night latch; SC7	-	1.00	11.34	18.25	nr	29.59
Locks						
drawer or cupboard lock; 63 mm x 32 mm; SC		0.56	6.35	8.03	nr	14.38
mortice dead lock; 63 mm x 108 mm; SSS	-	1.00	11.34	10.35	nr	21.69
12 mm rebate conversion set to mortice dead lock	-	0.75	8.51	10.25	nr	18.76
rim lock; 140 mm x 73 mm; GYE	-	0.56	6.35	7.87	nr	14.22
rim dead lock; 92 mm x 74.50 mm; SCP	-	0.56	6.35	20.81	nr	27.16
upright mortice lock; 103 mm x 82 mm; 3 lever	-	1.11	12.59	10.66	nr	23.25
upright mortice lock; 103 mm x 82 mm; 5 lever	-	1.11	12.59	33.31	nr	45.90

P BUILDING FABRIC SUNDRIES Excluding overheads and profit	PC £	Labour hours	Labour £	Material £	Unit	Total rate £
Window furniture						
casement stay; 305 mm long; 2 pin; SAA	-	0.23	2.61	6.97	nr	9.58
casement fastener; standard; 113 mm; SAA	-	0.23	2.61	4.51	nr	7.12
cockspur fastener; ASV	-	0.44	4.99	7.62	nr	12.61
sash fastener; 65 mm; SAA	-	0.33	3.74	2.56	nr	6.30
Sundries						
numerals; SAA	-	0.11	1.25	0.72	nr	1.97
rubber door stop; SAA	-	0.11	1.25	1.08	nr	2.33
medium hot pressed cabin hook; 102 mm; CP	-	0.23	2.61	8.81	nr	11.42
medium hot pressed cabin hook; 203 mm; CP	-	0.23	2.61	11.64	nr	14.25
coat hook; SAA	-	0.11	1.25	1.18	nr	2.43
toilet roll holder; CP	-	0.25	2.83	15.43	nr	18.26
Sliding door gear; Hillaldam Coburn Ltd or other **equal and approved; Commercial/Light industrial;** **for top hung timber/metal doors, weight not** **exceeding 365 kg**						
Sliding door gear						
bottom guide; fixed to concrete in groove	17.85	0.50	5.67	17.85	m	23.52
top track	25.20	0.25	2.83	25.20	m	28.03
detachable locking bar and padlock	42.63	0.33	3.74	42.63	nr	46.37
hangers; timber doors	46.30	0.50	5.67	46.30	nr	51.97
hangers; metal doors	33.02	0.50	5.67	33.02	nr	38.69
head brackets; open, side fixing; bolting to masonry	4.94	0.50	5.67	8.08	nr	13.75
head brackets; open, soffit fixing; screwing to timber	3.73	0.35	3.97	3.77	nr	7.74
door guide to timber door	9.24	0.25	2.83	9.24	nr	12.07
door stop; rubber buffers; to masonry	25.41	0.75	8.51	25.41	nr	33.92
drop bolt; screwing to timber	47.46	0.50	5.67	47.46	nr	53.13
bow handle; to timber	10.24	0.25	2.83	10.24	nr	13.07
Sundries						
rubber door stop; plugged and screwed to concrete	5.40	0.10	1.13	5.40	nr	6.53
P30 TRENCHES/PIPEWAYS/PITS FOR BURIED **ENGINEERING SERVICES**						
Excavating trenches; by machine; grading bottoms; **earthwork support; filling with excavated material** **and compacting; disposal of surplus soil on site;** **spreading on site average 50 m**						
Services not exceeding 200 mm nominal size						
average depth of run 0.50 m	-	0.32	2.11	1.26	m	3.37
average depth of run 0.75 m	-	0.49	3.22	2.09	m	5.31
average depth of run 1.00 m	-	0.97	6.38	3.87	m	10.25
average depth of run 1.25 m	-	1.44	9.48	5.27	m	14.75
average depth of run 1.50 m	-	1.85	12.17	6.90	m	19.07
average depth of run 1.75 m	-	2.25	14.80	8.83	m	23.63
average depth of run 2.00 m	-	2.66	17.50	10.11	m	27.61
Excavating trenches; by hand; grading bottoms; **earthwork support; filling with excavated material** **and compacting; disposal; of surplus soil on site;** **spreading on site average 50 m**						
Services not exceeding 200 mm nominal size						
average depth of run 0.50 m	-	1.15	7.57	-	m	7.57
average depth of run 0.75 m	-	1.73	11.38	-	m	11.38
average depth of run 1.00 m	-	2.53	16.65	1.24	m	17.89
average depth of run 1.25 m	-	3.56	23.42	1.71	m	25.13
average depth of run 1.50 m	-	4.89	32.18	2.08	m	34.26
average depth of run 1.75 m	-	6.44	42.38	2.51	m	44.89
average depth of run 2.00 m	-	7.36	48.43	2.76	m	51.19

P BUILDING FABRIC SUNDRIES Excluding overheads and profit	PC £	Labour hours	Labour £	Material £	Unit	Total rate £
P30 TRENCHES/PIPEWAYS/PITS FOR BURIED ENGINEERING SERVICES - cont'd						
Stock cock pits, valve chambers and the like; excavating; half brick thick walls in common bricks in cement mortar (1:3); on in situ concrete designated mix C20 - 20 mm aggregate bed; 100 mm thick Pits						
100 mm x 100 mm x 750 mm deep; internal holes for one small pipe; polypropylene hinged box cover; bedding in cement mortar (1:3)	-	4.85	68.92	25.09	nr	**94.01**
P31 HOLES/CHASES/COVERS/SUPPORTS FOR SERVICES						
Builders' work for electrical installations; cutting away for and making good after electrician; including cutting or leaving all holes, notches, mortices, sinkings and chases, in both the structure and its coverings, for the following electrical points Exposed installation						
lighting points	-	0.35	2.83	-	nr	**2.83**
socket outlet points	-	0.58	4.83	-	nr	**4.83**
fitting outlet points	-	0.58	4.83	-	nr	**4.83**
equipment points or control gear points	-	0.81	6.88	-	nr	**6.88**
Concealed installation						
lighting points	-	0.46	3.77	-	nr	**3.77**
socket outlet points	-	0.81	6.88	-	nr	**6.88**
fitting outlet points	-	0.81	6.88	-	nr	**6.88**
equipment points or control gear points	-	1.15	9.60	-	nr	**9.60**
Builders' work for other services installations Cutting chases in brickwork						
for one pipe; not exceeding 55 mm nominal size; vertical	-	0.46	2.97	-	m	**2.97**
for one pipe; 55 mm - 110 mm nominal size; vertical	-	0.80	5.16	-	m	**5.16**
Cutting and pinning to brickwork or blockwork; ends of supports						
for pipes not exceeding 55 mm nominal size	-	0.23	3.27	-	nr	**3.27**
for cast iron pipes 55 mm - 110 mm nominal size	-	0.38	5.40	-	nr	**5.40**
Cutting holes for pipes or the like; not exceeding 55 mm nominal size						
half brick thick	-	0.38	2.76	-	nr	**2.76**
one brick thick	-	0.63	4.58	-	nr	**4.58**
one and a half brick thick	-	1.03	7.49	-	nr	**7.49**
100 mm blockwork	-	0.35	2.54	-	nr	**2.54**
140 mm blockwork	-	0.46	3.34	-	nr	**3.34**
215 mm blockwork	-	0.57	4.14	-	nr	**4.14**
Cutting holes for pipes or the like; 55 mm - 110 mm nominal size						
half brick thick	-	0.46	3.34	-	nr	**3.34**
one brick thick	-	0.80	5.82	-	nr	**5.82**
one and a half brick thick	-	1.26	9.16	-	nr	**9.16**
100 mm blockwork	-	0.40	2.91	-	nr	**2.91**
140 mm blockwork	-	0.57	4.14	-	nr	**4.14**
215 mm blockwork	-	0.69	5.02	-	nr	**5.02**

P BUILDING FABRIC SUNDRIES Excluding overheads and profit	PC £	Labour hours	Labour £	Material £	Unit	Total rate £
Cutting holes for pipes or the like; over 110 mm nominal size						
half brick thick	-	0.57	4.14	-	nr	4.14
one brick thick	-	0.98	7.12	-	nr	7.12
one and a half brick thick	-	1.55	11.27	-	nr	11.27
100 mm blockwork	-	0.52	3.78	-	nr	3.78
140 mm blockwork	-	0.69	5.02	-	nr	5.02
215 mm blockwork	-	0.86	6.25	-	nr	6.25
Add for making good fair face or facings one side						
pipe; not exceeding 55 mm nominal size	-	0.09	1.28	-	nr	1.28
pipe; 55 mm - 110 mm nominal size	-	0.12	1.71	-	nr	1.71
pipe; over 110 mm nominal size	-	0.14	1.99	-	nr	1.99
Add for fixing sleeve (supply not included)						
for pipe; small	-	0.17	2.42	-	nr	2.42
for pipe; large	-	0.23	3.27	-	nr	3.27
for pipe; extra large	-	0.35	4.97	-	nr	4.97
Cutting or forming holes for ducts; girth not exceeding 1.00 m						
half brick thick	-	0.69	5.02	-	nr	5.02
one brick thick	-	1.15	8.36	-	nr	8.36
one and a half brick thick	-	1.84	13.38	-	nr	13.38
100 mm blockwork	-	0.57	4.14	-	nr	4.14
140 mm blockwork	-	0.80	5.82	-	nr	5.82
215 mm blockwork	-	1.03	7.49	-	nr	7.49
Cutting or forming holes for ducts; girth 1.00 m - 2.00 m						
half brick thick	-	0.80	5.82	-	nr	5.82
one brick thick	-	1.38	10.03	-	nr	10.03
one and a half brick thick	-	2.18	15.85	-	nr	15.85
100 mm blockwork	-	0.69	5.02	-	nr	5.02
140 mm blockwork	-	0.92	6.69	-	nr	6.69
215 mm blockwork	-	1.15	8.36	-	nr	8.36
Cutting or forming holes for ducts; girth 2.00 m - 3.00 m						
half brick thick	-	1.26	9.16	-	nr	9.16
one brick thick	-	2.18	15.85	-	nr	15.85
one and a half brick thick	-	3.45	25.08	-	nr	25.08
100 mm blockwork	-	1.09	7.92	-	nr	7.92
140 mm blockwork	-	1.49	10.83	-	nr	10.83
215 mm blockwork	-	1.90	13.81	-	nr	13.81
Cutting or forming holes for ducts; girth 3.00 m - 4.00 m						
half brick thick	-	1.73	12.58	-	nr	12.58
one brick thick	-	2.88	20.94	-	nr	20.94
one and a half brick thick	-	4.60	33.44	-	nr	33.44
100 mm blockwork	-	1.26	9.16	-	nr	9.16
140 mm blockwork	-	1.73	12.58	-	nr	12.58
215 mm blockwork	-	2.18	15.85	-	nr	15.85
Mortices in brickwork						
for expansion bolt	-	0.23	1.67	-	nr	1.67
for 20 mm diameter bolt; 75 mm deep	-	0.17	1.24	-	nr	1.24
for 20 mm diameter bolt; 150 mm deep	-	0.29	2.11	-	nr	2.11
Mortices in brickwork; grouting with cement mortar (1:1)						
75 mm x 75 mm x 200 mm deep	-	0.35	2.54	-	nr	2.54
75 mm x 75 mm x 300 mm deep	-	0.46	3.34	-	nr	3.34

P BUILDING FABRIC SUNDRIES Excluding overheads and profit	PC £	Labour hours	Labour £	Material £	Unit	Total rate £
P31 HOLES/CHASES/COVERS/SUPPORTS FOR SERVICES - cont'd						
Builders' work for other services installations - cont'd						
Holes in softwood for pipes, bars, cables and						
the like						
12 mm thick	-	0.05	0.57	-	nr	**0.57**
25 mm thick	-	0.07	0.79	-	nr	**0.79**
50 mm thick	-	0.12	1.36	-	nr	**1.36**
100 mm thick	-	0.17	1.93	-	nr	**1.93**
Holes in hardwood for pipes, bars, cables and						
the like						
12 mm thick	-	0.07	0.79	-	nr	**0.79**
25 mm thick	-	0.10	1.13	-	nr	**1.13**
50 mm thick	-	0.17	1.93	-	nr	**1.93**
100 mm thick	-	0.25	2.83	-	nr	**2.83**
"SFD Screeduct" or other equal and						
approved; MDT Ducting Ltd; laid within						
floor screed; galvanised mild steel						
Floor ducting						
100 mm wide; 40 mm deep; ref SFD40/100/00	5.75	0.23	2.61	6.04	m	**8.65**
Extra for						
45 degree bend	6.25	0.12	1.36	6.56	nr	**7.92**
90 degree bend	5.00	0.12	1.36	5.25	nr	**6.61**
tee section	5.00	0.12	1.36	5.25	nr	**6.61**
cross over	6.50	0.12	1.36	6.83	nr	**8.19**
reducer; 100 mm - 50 mm	11.75	0.12	1.36	12.34	nr	**13.70**
connector / stop end	0.50	0.12	1.36	0.53	nr	**1.89**
divider	1.50	0.12	1.36	1.57	nr	**2.93**
ply cover 15 mm/16 mm thick WBP exterior						
grade	0.58	0.12	1.36	0.61	m	**1.97**
200 mm wide; 65 mm deep; ref SFD65/200/00	6.75	0.23	2.61	7.09	m	**9.70**
Extra for						
45 degree bend	8.75	0.12	1.36	9.19	nr	**10.55**
90 degree bend	6.75	0.12	1.36	7.09	nr	**8.45**
tee section	6.75	0.12	1.36	7.09	nr	**8.45**
cross over	9.25	0.12	1.36	9.71	nr	**11.07**
reducer; 200 mm - 100 mm	11.75	0.12	1.36	12.34	nr	**13.70**
connector / stop end	0.65	0.12	1.36	0.68	nr	**2.04**
divider	1.50	0.12	1.36	1.57	nr	**2.93**
ply cover 15 mm/16 mm thick WBP exterior						
grade	0.98	0.12	1.36	1.03	m	**2.39**

Q PAVING/PLANTING/FENCING/SITE FURNITURE Excluding overheads and profit	PC £	Labour hours	Labour £	Material £	Unit	Total rate £
Q PAVING/PLANTING/FENCING/SITE FURNITURE						
Q10 KERBS/EDGINGS/CHANNELS/PAVING ACCESSORIES						
Excavating; by machine						
Excavating trenches; to receive kerb foundations; average size						
300 mm x 100 mm	-	0.03	0.20	0.31	m	**0.51**
450 mm x 150 mm	-	0.03	0.20	0.63	m	**0.83**
600 mm x 200 mm	-	0.05	0.33	0.88	m	**1.21**
Excavating curved trenches; to receive kerb foundations; average size						
300 mm x 100 mm	-	0.02	0.13	0.52	m	**0.65**
450 mm x 150 mm	-	0.04	0.26	0.73	m	**0.99**
600 mm x 200 mm	-	0.06	0.39	0.94	m	**1.33**
Excavating; by hand						
Excavating trenches; to receive kerb foundations; average size						
150 mm x 50 mm	-	0.03	0.20	-	m	**0.20**
200 mm x 75 mm	-	0.08	0.53	-	m	**0.53**
250 mm x 100 mm	-	0.13	0.86	-	m	**0.86**
300 mm x 100 mm	-	0.16	1.05	-	m	**1.05**
Excavating curved trenches; to receive kerb foundations; average size						
150 mm x 50 mm	-	0.05	0.33	-	m	**0.33**
200 mm x 75 mm	-	0.09	0.59	-	m	**0.59**
250 mm x 100 mm	-	0.14	0.92	-	m	**0.92**
300 mm x 100 mm	-	0.17	1.12	-	m	**1.12**
Plain in situ ready mixed designated concrete; C7.5 - 40 mm aggregate; poured on or against earth or unblinded hardcore						
Foundations	60.85	1.44	10.47	68.69	m³	**79.16**
Blinding beds						
thickness not exceeding 150 mm	60.85	2.13	15.49	68.69	m³	**84.18**
Plain in situ ready mixed designated concrete; C10 - 40 mm aggregate; poured on or against earth or unblinded hardcore						
Foundations	60.85	1.44	10.47	68.69	m³	**79.16**
Blinding beds						
thickness not exceeding 150 mm	60.85	2.13	15.49	68.69	m³	**84.18**
Plain in situ ready mixed designated concrete; C20 - 20 mm aggregate; poured on or against earth or unblinded hardcore						
Foundations	63.66	1.44	10.47	71.86	m³	**82.33**
Blinding beds						
thickness not exceeding 150 mm	63.66	2.13	15.49	71.86	m³	**87.35**
Precast concrete kerbs, channels, edgings, etc.; BS 340; bedded, jointed and pointed in cement mortar (1:3); including haunching up one side with in situ ready mixed designated concrete C10 - 40 mm aggregate; to concrete base						
Edgings; straight; square edge, fig 12						
50 mm x 150 mm	-	0.29	3.25	2.53	m	**5.78**
50 mm x 200 mm	-	0.29	3.25	3.11	m	**6.36**
50 mm x 255 mm	-	0.29	3.25	3.22	m	**6.47**

Q PAVING/PLANTING/FENCING/SITE FURNITURE Excluding overheads and profit	PC £	Labour hours	Labour £	Material £	Unit	Total rate £
Q10 KERBS/EDGINGS/CHANNELS/PAVING ACCESSORIES - cont'd						
Precast concrete kerbs, channels, edgings, etc.; BS 340; bedded, jointed and pointed in cement mortar (1:3); including haunching up one side with in situ ready mixed designated concrete C10 - 40 mm aggregate; to concrete base - cont'd						
Kerbs; straight						
125 mm x 255 mm; fig 7	-	0.38	4.25	4.46	m	**8.71**
150 mm x 305 mm; fig 6	-	0.38	4.25	6.42	m	**10.67**
Kerbs; curved						
125 mm x 255 mm; fig 7	-	0.57	6.38	5.91	m	**12.29**
150 mm x 305 mm; fig 6	-	0.57	6.38	8.73	m	**15.11**
Channels; 255 mm x 125 mm; fig 8						
straight	-	0.38	4.25	4.46	m	**8.71**
curved	-	0.57	6.38	5.91	m	**12.29**
Quadrants; fig 14						
305 mm x 305 mm x 150 mm	-	0.40	4.48	6.55	nr	**11.03**
305 mm x 305 mm x 255 mm	-	0.40	4.48	7.02	nr	**11.50**
457 mm x 457 mm x 150 mm	-	0.46	5.15	8.18	nr	**13.33**
457 mm x 457 mm x 255 mm	-	0.46	5.15	8.18	nr	**13.33**
Q20 HARDCORE/GRANULAR/CEMENT BOUND BASES/SUB-BASES TO ROADS/PAVINGS						
Filling to make up levels; by machine						
Average thickness not exceeding 0.25 m						
obtained off site; hardcore	-	0.35	2.30	21.35	m³	**23.65**
obtained off site; granular fill type one	-	0.35	2.30	29.42	m³	**31.72**
obtained off site; granular fill type two	-	0.35	2.30	28.38	m³	**30.68**
Average thickness exceeding 0.25 m						
obtained off site; hardcore	-	0.30	1.97	18.37	m³	**20.34**
obtained off site; granular fill type one	-	0.30	1.97	29.28	m³	**31.25**
obtained off site; granular fill type two	-	0.30	1.97	28.24	m³	**30.21**
Filling to make up levels; by hand						
Average thickness not exceeding 0.25 m						
obtained off site; hardcore	-	0.76	5.00	21.78	m³	**26.78**
obtained off site; sand	-	0.89	5.86	30.14	m³	**36.00**
Average thickness exceeding 0.25 m						
obtained off site; hardcore	-	0.63	4.15	18.62	m³	**22.77**
obtained off site; sand	-	0.75	4.93	29.82	m³	**34.75**
Surface treatments						
Compacting						
filling; blinding with sand	-	0.06	0.39	1.54	m²	**1.93**
Q21 IN SITU CONCRETE ROADS/PAVINGS						
Reinforced in situ ready mixed designated concrete; C10 - 40 mm aggregate						
Roads; to hardcore base						
thickness not exceeding 150 mm	60.85	2.35	17.08	65.41	m³	**82.49**
thickness 150 mm - 450 mm	60.85	1.65	12.00	65.41	m³	**77.41**
Reinforced in situ ready mixed designated concrete; C20 - 20 mm aggregate						
Roads; to hardcore base						
thickness not exceeding 150 mm	63.66	2.35	17.08	68.43	m³	**85.51**
thickness 150 mm - 450 mm	63.66	1.65	12.00	68.43	m³	**80.43**

Q PAVING/PLANTING/FENCING/SITE FURNITURE Excluding overheads and profit	PC £	Labour hours	Labour £	Material £	Unit	Total rate £
Reinforced in situ ready mixed designated concrete; C25 - 20 mm aggregate						
Roads; to hardcore base						
thickness not exceeding 150 mm	63.98	2.35	17.08	68.78	m³	**85.86**
thickness 150 mm - 450 mm	63.98	1.65	12.00	68.78	m³	**80.78**
Formwork; sides of foundations; basic finish						
Plain vertical						
height not exceeding 250 mm	-	0.48	5.38	1.31	m	**6.69**
height 250 mm - 500 mm	-	0.71	7.95	2.27	m	**10.22**
height 500 mm - 1.00 m	-	1.03	11.54	4.50	m	**16.04**
add to above for curved 6.00 m radii	-	0.05	0.56	0.18	m	**0.74**
Reinforcement; fabric; BS 4483; lapped; in roads, footpaths or pavings						
Ref A142 (2.22 kg/m²)						
400 mm minimum laps	0.77	0.17	1.52	0.85	m²	**2.37**
Ref A193 (3.02 kg/m²)						
400 mm minimum laps	-	0.17	1.52	1.21	m²	**2.73**
Formed joints; Fosroc Expandite "Flexcell" impreganted joint filler or other equal and approved						
Width not exceeding 150 mm						
12.50 mm thick	-	0.17	1.90	1.60	m	**3.50**
25 mm thick	-	0.23	2.58	2.42	m	**5.00**
Width 150 - 300 mm						
12.50 mm thick	-	0.23	2.58	2.85	m	**5.43**
25 mm thick	-	0.23	2.58	3.97	m	**6.55**
Width 300 - 450 mm						
12.50 mm thick	-	0.29	3.25	4.27	m	**7.52**
25 mm thick	-	0.29	3.25	5.95	m	**9.20**
Sealants; Fosroc Expandite "Pliastic 77" hot poured rubberized bituminous compound or other equal and approved						
Width 25 mm						
25 mm depth	-	0.24	2.69	1.43	m	**4.12**
Concrete sundries						
Treating surfaces of unset concrete; grading to cambers; tamping with a 75 mm thick steel shod tamper	-	0.29	2.11	-	m²	**2.11**

Q PAVING/PLANTING/FENCING/SITE FURNITURE Excluding overheads and profit	PC £	Labour hours	Labour £	Material £	Unit	Total rate £
Q22 COATED MACADAM/ASPHALT ROADS/ PAVINGS						
In situ finishings; Associated Asphalt or other equal and approved						
NOTE: The prices for all in situ finishings to roads and footpaths include for work to falls, crossfalls or slopes not exceeding 15 degrees from horizontal; for laying on prepared bases (prices not included) and for rolling with an appropriate roller. The following rates are based on black bitumen macadam except where stated. Red bitumen macadam rates are approximately 50% dearer.						
Fine graded wearing course; BS 4987; clause 2.7.7, tables 34 - 36; 14 mm nominal size pre-coated igneous rock chippings; tack coat of bitumen emulsion						
19 mm work to roads; one coat						
igneous aggregate	-	-	-	-	m²	**13.85**
Close graded bitumen macadam; BS 4987; 10 mm nominal size graded aggregate to clause 2.7.4 tables 34 - 36; tack coat of bitumen emulsion						
30 mm work to roads; one coat						
limestone aggregate	-	-	-	-	m²	**13.27**
igneous aggregate	-	-	-	-	m²	**13.38**
Bitumen macadam; BS 4987; 45 mm thick base course of 20 mm open graded aggregate to clause 2.6.1 tables 5 - 7; 20 mm thick wearing course of 6 mm nominal size medium graded aggregate to clause 2.7.6 tables 32 - 33						
65 mm work to pavements/footpaths; two coats						
limestone aggregate	-	-	-	-	m²	**15.47**
igneous aggregate	-	-	-	-	m²	**15.67**
add to last for 10 nominal size chippings; sprinkled into wearing course	-	-	-	-	m²	**0.33**
Bitumen macadam; BS 4987; 50 mm nominal size graded aggregate to clause 2.6.2 tables 8 - 10						
75 mm work to roads; one coat						
limestone aggregate	-	-	-	-	m²	**16.38**
igneous aggregate	-	-	-	-	m²	**16.64**
Dense bitumen macadam; BS 4987; 50 mm thick base course of 20 mm graded aggregate to clause 2.6.5 tables 15 - 16; 200 pen. binder; 30 mm wearing course of 10 mm nominal size graded aggregate to clause 2.7.4 tables 26 - 28						
80 mm work to roads; two coats						
limestone aggregate	-	-	-	-	m²	**16.52**
igneous aggregate	-	-	-	-	m²	**16.74**

Q PAVING/PLANTING/FENCING/SITE FURNITURE Excluding overheads and profit	PC £	Labour hours	Labour £	Material £	Unit	Total rate £
Bitumen macadam; BS 4987; 50 mm thick **base course of 20 mm nominal size graded** **aggregate to clause 2.6.1 tables 5 - 7; 25 mm** **thick wearing course of 10 mm nominal size** **graded aggregate to clause 2.7.2 tables 20 -** **22**						
75 mm work to roads; two coats						
limestone aggregate	-	-	-	-	m²	**17.12**
igneous aggregate	-	-	-	-	m²	**17.38**
Dense bitumen macadam; BS 4987; 70 mm **thick base course of 20 mm nominal size** **graded aggregate to clause 2.6.5 tables 15 -** **16; 200 pen. binder; 30 mm wearing course of** **10 mm nominal size graded aggregate to** **clause 2.7.4 tables 26 - 28**						
100 mm work to roads; two coats						
limestone aggregate	-	-	-	-	m²	**18.64**
igneous aggregate	-	-	-	-	m²	**18.93**
Dense bitumen macadam; BS 4987; 70 mm thick **road base of 28 mm nominal size graded** **aggregate to clause 2.5.2 tables 3 - 4; 50 mm** **thick base course of 20 mm nominal size** **graded aggregate to clause 2.6.5 tables 15 -** **16; 30 mm wearing course of 10 mm nominal** **size graded aggregate to clause 2.7.4 tables** **26 - 28**						
150 mm work to roads; three coats						
limestone aggregate	-	-	-	-	m²	**30.19**
igneous aggregate	-	-	-	-	m²	**30.65**
Red bitumen macadam; BS 4987; 70 mm thick **base course of 20 mm nominal size graded** **aggregate to clause 2.6.5 tables 15 - 16; 30** **mm wearing course of 10 mm nominal size** **graded aggregate to clause 2.7.4 tables 26 -** **28**						
100 mm work to roads; two coats						
limestone base; igneous wearing course	-	-	-	-	m²	**22.20**
igneous aggregate	-	-	-	-	m²	**22.43**
Q23 GRAVEL/HOGGIN/WOODCHIP **ROADS/PAVINGS**						
Two coat gravel paving; level and to falls; first **layer course clinker aggregate and wearing** **layer fine gravel aggregate**						
Pavings; over 300 mm wide						
50 mm thick	-	0.09	1.01	1.85	m²	**2.86**
63 mm thick	-	0.11	1.23	2.42	m²	**3.65**

Q PAVING/PLANTING/FENCING/SITE FURNITURE Excluding overheads and profit	PC £	Labour hours	Labour £	Material £	Unit	Total rate £
Q25 SLAB/BRICK/BLOCK/SETT/COBBLE **PAVINGS**						
Artificial stone paving; Redland Aggregates **"Texitone" or other equal and approved; to** **falls or crossfalls; bedding 25 mm thick in cement** **mortar (1:3); staggered joints; jointing in coloured** **cement:mortar (1:3), brushed in; to sand base** Pavings; over 300 mm wide						
450 mm x 600 mm x 50 mm thick; grey or coloured	3.58	0.52	5.82	16.71	m²	**22.53**
600 mm x 600 mm x 50 mm thick; grey or coloured	4.14	0.48	5.37	14.87	m²	**20.24**
750 mm x 600 mm x 50 mm thick; grey or coloured	4.83	0.45	5.04	14.07	m²	**19.11**
900 mm x 600 mm x 50 mm thick; grey or coloured	5.52	0.41	4.59	13.53	m²	**18.12**
Brick paviors; 215 mm x 103 mm x 65 mm **rough stock bricks; PC £480.00/1000; to falls** **or crossfalls; bedding 10 mm thick in cement** **mortar (1:3); jointing in cement mortar (1:3);** **as work proceeds; to concrete base** Pavings; over 300 mm wide; straight joints both ways						
bricks laid flat	-	0.92	13.07	22.66	m²	**35.73**
bricks laid on edge	-	1.29	18.33	33.66	m²	**51.99**
Pavings; over 300 mm wide; laid to herringbone pattern						
bricks laid flat	-	1.15	16.34	22.66	m²	**39.00**
bricks laid on edge	-	1.61	22.88	33.66	m²	**56.54**
Add or deduct for variation of £10.00/1000 in PC of brick paviours						
bricks laid flat	-	-	-	0.45	m²	**0.45**
bricks laid on edge	-	-	-	0.68	m²	**0.68**
River washed cobble paving; 50 mm - 75 mm; **PC £80.00/t; to falls or crossfalls; bedding 13** **mm thick in cement mortar (1:3); jointing to a** **height of two thirds of cobbles in dry mortar** **(1:3); tightly butted, washed and brushed; to** **concrete** Pavings; over 300 mm wide						
regular	-	4.60	51.47	18.87	m²	**70.34**
laid to pattern	-	5.75	64.34	18.87	m²	**83.21**
Concrete paving flags; BS 7263; to falls or **crossfalls; bedding 25 mm thick in cement:** **sand mortar (1:4); butt joints straight both** **ways; jointing in cement:sand (1:3);** **brushed in; to sand base** Pavings; over 300 mm wide						
450 mm x 600 mm x 50 mm thick; grey	1.78	0.52	5.82	8.26	m²	**14.08**
450 mm x 600 mm x 60 mm thick; coloured	2.05	0.52	5.82	9.31	m²	**15.13**
600 mm x 600 mm x 50 mm thick; grey	2.04	0.48	5.37	7.30	m²	**12.67**
600 mm x 600 mm x 50 mm thick; coloured	2.35	0.48	5.37	8.20	m²	**13.57**
750 mm x 600 mm x 50 mm thick; grey	2.39	0.45	5.04	6.93	m²	**11.97**
750 mm x 600 mm x 50 mm thick; coloured	2.75	0.45	5.04	7.77	m²	**12.81**
900 mm x 600 mm x 50 mm thick; grey	2.68	0.41	4.59	6.56	m²	**11.15**
900 mm x 600 mm x 50 mm thick; coloured	3.08	0.41	4.59	7.34	m²	**11.93**

Q PAVING/PLANTING/FENCING/SITE FURNITURE Excluding overheads and profit	PC £	Labour hours	Labour £	Material £	Unit	Total rate £
Concrete rectangular paving blocks; to falls **or crossfalls; bedding 50 mm thick in dry** **sharp sand; filling joints with sharp sand** **brushed in; on earth base**						
Pavings; "Keyblock" or other equal and approved; over 300 mm wide; straight joints both ways						
200 mm x 100 mm x 65 mm thick; grey	8.11	0.86	9.62	10.81	m²	**20.43**
200 mm x 100 mm x 65 mm thick; coloured	9.61	0.86	9.62	12.38	m²	**22.00**
200 mm x 100 mm x 80 mm thick; grey	8.72	0.92	10.29	11.64	m²	**21.93**
200 mm x 100 mm x 80 mm thick; coloured	10.27	0.92	10.29	13.27	m²	**23.56**
Pavings; "Keyblock" or other equal and approved; over 300 mm wide; laid to herringbone pattern						
200 mm x 100 mm x 60 mm thick; grey	-	1.09	12.20	10.81	m²	**23.01**
200 mm x 100 mm x 60 mm thick; coloured	-	1.09	12.20	12.38	m²	**24.58**
200 mm x 100 mm x 80 mm thick; grey	-	1.15	12.87	11.64	m²	**24.51**
200 mm x 100 mm x 80 mm thick; coloured	-	1.15	12.87	13.27	m²	**26.14**
Extra for two row boundary edgings to herringbone pavings areas; 200 mm wide; including a 150 mm high ready mixed designated concrete C10 - 40 mm aggregate haunching to one side; blocks laid breaking joint						
200 mm x 100 mm x 65 mm; coloured	-	0.35	3.92	2.01	m	**5.93**
200 mm x 100 mm x 80 mm; coloured	-	0.35	3.92	2.06	m	**5.98**
Pavings; "Mount Sorrel" or other equal and approved; over 300 mm wide; straight joints both ways						
200 mm x 100 mm x 60 mm thick; grey	7.05	0.86	9.62	9.70	m²	**19.32**
200 mm x 100 mm x 60 mm thick; coloured	8.11	0.86	9.62	10.81	m²	**20.43**
200 mm x 100 mm x 80 mm thick; grey	8.38	0.92	10.29	11.28	m²	**21.57**
200 mm x 100 mm x 80 mm thick; coloured	9.64	0.92	10.29	12.61	m²	**22.90**
Pavings; "Pedesta" or other equal and approved; over 300 mm wide; straight joints both ways						
200 mm x 100 mm x 60 mm thick; grey	6.80	0.86	9.62	9.43	m²	**19.05**
200 mm x 100 mm x 60 mm thick; coloured	6.88	0.86	9.62	9.52	m²	**19.14**
200 mm x 100 mm x 80 mm thick; grey	7.92	0.92	10.29	10.80	m²	**21.09**
200 mm x 100 mm x 80 mm thick; coloured	8.36	0.92	10.29	11.26	m²	**21.55**
Pavings; "Intersett" or other equal and approved; over 300 mm wide; straight joints both ways						
200 mm x 100 mm x 60 mm thick; grey	8.45	0.86	9.62	11.17	m²	**20.79**
200 mm x 100 mm x 60 mm thick; coloured	9.39	0.86	9.62	12.15	m²	**21.77**
200 mm x 100 mm x 80 mm thick; grey	10.07	0.92	10.29	13.06	m²	**23.35**
200 mm x 100 mm x 80 mm thick; coloured	11.23	0.92	10.29	14.28	m²	**24.57**
Concrete rectangular paving blocks; to falls **or crossfalls; 6 mm wide joints; symmetrical** **layout; bedding in 15 mm semi-dry cement** **mortar (1:4); jointing and pointing in cement:** **sand (1:4); on concrete base**						
Pavings; "Trafica" or other equal and approved; over 300 mm wide						
400 mm x 400 mm x 65 mm; Standard; natural	1.46	0.55	6.15	10.67	m²	**16.82**
400 mm x 400 mm x 65 mm; Standard; buff	2.04	0.55	6.15	14.42	m²	**20.57**
400 mm x 400 mm x 65 mm; Saxon textured; natural	2.70	0.55	6.15	18.69	m²	**24.84**
400 mm x 400 mm x 65 mm; Saxon textured; buff	3.23	0.55	6.15	22.11	m²	**28.26**
400 mm x 400 mm x 65 mm; Perfecta; natural	3.28	0.55	6.15	22.44	m²	**28.59**
400 mm x 400 mm x 65 mm; Perfecta; buff	3.90	0.55	6.15	26.44	m²	**32.59**
450 mm x 450 mm x 70 mm; Standard; natural	2.41	0.53	5.93	13.56	m²	**19.49**
450 mm x 450 mm x 70 mm; Standard; buff	3.25	0.53	5.93	17.86	m²	**23.79**
450 mm x 450 mm x 70 mm; Saxon textured; natural	3.37	0.53	5.93	18.48	m²	**24.41**

Q PAVING/PLANTING/FENCING/SITE FURNITURE Excluding overheads and profit	PC £	Labour hours	Labour £	Material £	Unit	Total rate £
Q25 SLAB/BRICK/BLOCK/SETT/COBBLE PAVINGS - cont'd						
Concrete rectangular paving blocks; to falls or crossfalls; 6 mm wide joints; symmetrical layout; bedding in 15 mm semi-dry cement mortar (1:4); jointing and pointing in cement :sand (1:4); on concrete base - cont'd						
Pavings; "Trafica" or other equal and approved; over 300 mm wide - cont'd						
450 mm x 450 mm x 70 mm; Saxon textured; buff	4.01	0.53	5.93	21.75	m²	**27.68**
450 mm x 450 mm x 70 mm; Perfecta; natural	4.04	0.53	5.93	21.90	m²	**27.83**
450 mm x 450 mm x 70 mm; Perfecta; buff	4.78	0.53	5.93	25.69	m²	**31.62**
450 mm x 450 mm x 100 mm; Standard; natural	5.33	0.55	6.15	28.50	m²	**34.65**
450 mm x 450 mm x 100 mm; Standard; buff	6.42	0.55	6.15	34.08	m²	**40.23**
450 mm x 450 mm x 100 mm; Saxon textured; natural	6.06	0.55	6.15	32.24	m²	**38.39**
450 mm x 450 mm x 100 mm; Saxon textured; buff	7.23	0.55	6.15	38.23	m²	**44.38**
450 mm x 450 mm x 100 mm; Perfecta; natural	6.54	0.55	6.15	34.69	m²	**40.84**
450 mm x 450 mm x 100 mm; Perfecta; buff	7.69	0.55	6.15	40.58	m²	**46.73**
York stone slab pavings; to falls or crossfalls; bedding 25 mm thick in cement:sand mortar (1:4); 5 mm wide joints; jointing in coloured cement mortar (1:3); brushed in; to sand base						
Pavings; over 300 mm wide						
50 mm thick; random rectangular pattern	65.00	0.86	12.22	68.28	m²	**80.50**
600 mm x 600 mm x 50 mm thick	75.00	0.48	6.82	78.53	m²	**85.35**
600 mm x 900 mm x 50 mm thick	80.00	0.41	5.83	83.66	m²	**89.49**
Granite setts; BS 435; 200 mm x 100 mm x 100 mm; PC £145.00/t; standard "C" dressing; tightly butted to falls or crossfalls; bedding 25 mm thick in cement mortar (1:3); filling joints with dry mortar (1:6); washed and brushed; on concrete base						
Pavings; over 300 mm wide						
straight joints	-	1.84	20.59	43.23	m²	**63.82**
laid to pattern	-	2.30	25.74	43.23	m²	**68.97**
Two rows of granite setts as boundary edging; 200 mm wide; including a 150 mm high ready mixed designated concrete C10 - 40 mm aggregate; haunching to one side; blocks laid						
breaking joint	-	0.80	8.95	9.88	m	**18.83**
Q26 SPECIAL SURFACINGS/PAVINGS FOR SPORT/GENERAL AMENITY						
Sundries						
Line marking						
width not exceeding 300 mm	-	0.06	0.48	0.17	m	**0.65**

Q PAVING/PLANTING/FENCING/SITE FURNITURE Excluding overheads and profit	PC £	Labour hours	Labour £	Material £	Unit	Total rate £
Q30 SEEDING/TURFING						
Vegetable soil						
Selected from spoil heaps; grading; prepared						
for turfing or seeding; to general surfaces						
average 75 mm thick	-	0.25	1.65	-	m²	**1.65**
average 100 mm thick	-	0.27	1.78	-	m²	**1.78**
average 125 mm thick	-	0.29	1.91	-	m²	**1.91**
average 150 mm thick	-	0.31	2.04	-	m²	**2.04**
average 175 mm thick	-	0.32	2.11	-	m²	**2.11**
average 200 mm thick	-	0.34	2.24	-	m²	**2.24**
Selected from spoil heaps; grading; prepared						
for turfing or seeding; to cuttings or						
embankments						
average 75 mm thick	-	0.29	1.91	-	m²	**1.91**
average 100 mm thick	-	0.31	2.04	-	m²	**2.04**
average 125 mm thick	-	0.33	2.17	-	m²	**2.17**
average 150 mm thick	-	0.34	2.24	-	m²	**2.24**
average 175 mm thick	-	0.36	2.37	-	m²	**2.37**
average 200 mm thick	-	0.39	2.57	-	m²	**2.57**
Imported vegetable soil						
Grading; prepared for turfing or seeding; to						
general surfaces						
average 75 mm thick	-	0.23	1.51	0.77	m²	**2.28**
average 100 mm thick	-	0.25	1.65	1.00	m²	**2.65**
average 125 mm thick	-	0.26	1.71	1.46	m²	**3.17**
average 150 mm thick	-	0.28	1.84	1.93	m²	**3.77**
average 175 mm thick	-	0.29	1.91	2.16	m²	**4.07**
average 200 mm thick	-	0.31	2.04	2.39	m²	**4.43**
Grading; preparing for turfing or seeding; to						
cuttings or embankments						
average 75 mm thick	-	0.25	1.65	0.77	m²	**2.42**
average 100 mm thick	-	0.28	1.84	1.00	m²	**2.84**
average 125 mm thick	-	0.29	1.91	1.46	m²	**3.37**
average 150 mm thick	-	0.31	2.04	1.93	m²	**3.97**
average 175 mm thick	-	0.32	2.11	2.16	m²	**4.27**
average 200 mm thick	-	0.34	2.24	2.39	m²	**4.63**
Fertilizer; PC £7.75/25 kg						
Fertilizer 0.07 kg/m²; raking in						
general surfaces	-	0.04	0.26	0.02	m²	**0.28**
Selected grass seed; PC £62.50/25 kg						
Seeding; sowing at a rate of 0.042 kg/m²						
two applications; raking in						
general surfaces	-	0.08	0.53	0.23	m²	**0.76**
cuttings or embankments	-	0.09	0.59	0.23	m²	**0.82**
Preserved turf from stack on site						
Turfing						
general surfaces	-	0.22	1.45	-	m²	**1.45**
cuttings or embankments; shallow	-	0.24	1.58	-	m²	**1.58**
cuttings or embankments; steep; pegged	-	0.33	2.17	-	m²	**2.17**
Imported turf; selected meadow turf						
Turfing						
general surfaces	1.21	0.22	1.45	1.45	m²	**2.90**
cuttings or embankments; shallow	1.21	0.24	1.58	1.45	m²	**3.03**
cuttings or embankments; steep; pegged	1.21	0.33	2.17	1.45	m²	**3.62**

Q PAVING/PLANTING/FENCING/SITE FURNITURE Excluding overheads and profit	PC £	Labour hours	Labour £	Material £	Unit	Total rate £
Q31 PLANTING						
Planting only						
Hedge plants						
height not exceeding 750 mm	-	0.28	1.84	-	nr	**1.84**
height 750 mm - 1.50 m	-	0.66	4.34	-	nr	**4.34**
Saplings						
height not exceeding 3.00 m	-	1.87	12.30	-	nr	**12.30**
Q40 FENCING						
NOTE: The prices for all fencing include for setting posts in position, to a depth of 0.60 m for fences not exceeding 1.40 m high and of 0.76 m for fences over 1.40 m high. The prices allow for excavating post holes; filling to within 150 mm of ground level with concrete and all backfilling.						
Strained wire fencing; BS 1722 Part 3; 4 mm diameter galvanized mild steel plain wire threaded through posts and strained with eye bolts						
Fencing; height 900 mm; three line; concrete posts at 2750 mm centres	-	-	-	-	m	**8.00**
Extra for						
end concrete straining post; one strut	-	-	-	-	nr	**40.00**
angle concrete straining post; two struts	-	-	-	-	nr	**58.00**
Fencing; height 1.07 m; five line; concrete posts at 2750 mm centres	-	-	-	-	m	**11.50**
Extra for						
end concrete straining post; one strut	-	-	-	-	nr	**59.60**
angle concrete straining post; two struts	-	-	-	-	nr	**75.50**
Fencing; height 1.20 m; six line; concrete posts at 2750 mm centres	-	-	-	-	m	**12.00**
Extra for						
end concrete straining post; one strut	-	-	-	-	nr	**62.00**
angle concrete straining post; two struts	-	-	-	-	nr	**84.50**
Fencing; height 1.40 m; seven line; concrete posts at 2750 mm centres	-	-	-	-	m	**12.70**
Extra for						
end concrete straining post; one strut	-	-	-	-	nr	**66.50**
angle concrete straining post; two struts	-	-	-	-	nr	**91.00**
Chain link fencing; BS 1722 Part 1; 3 mm diameter galvanized mild steel wire; 50 mm mesh; galvanized mild steel tying and line wire; three line wires threaded through posts and strained with eye bolts and winding brackets						
Fencing; height 900 mm; galvanized mild steel angle posts at 3.00 m centres	-	-	-	-	m	**11.00**
Extra for						
end steel straining post; one strut	-	-	-	-	nr	**51.00**
angle steel straining post; two struts	-	-	-	-	nr	**69.00**
Fencing; height 900 mm; concrete posts at 3.00 m centres	-	-	-	-	m	**10.75**
Extra for						
end concrete straining post; one strut	-	-	-	-	nr	**46.70**
angle concrete straining post; two struts	-	-	-	-	nr	**64.50**

Q PAVING/PLANTING/FENCING/SITE FURNITURE Excluding overheads and profit	PC £	Labour hours	Labour £	Material £	Unit	Total rate £
Fencing; height 1.20 m; galvanized mild steel angle posts at 3.00 m centres	-	-	-	-	m	14.30
Extra for						
end steel straining post; one strut	-	-	-	-	nr	62.20
angle steel straining post; two struts	-	-	-	-	nr	82.20
Fencing; height 1.20 m; concrete posts at 3.00 m centres	-	-	-	-	m	13.00
Extra for						
end concrete straining post; one strut	-	-	-	-	nr	57.75
angle concrete straining post; two struts	-	-	-	-	nr	75.55
Fencing; height 1.80 m; galvanized mild steel angle posts at 3.00 m centres	-	-	-	-	m	18.00
Extra for						
end steel straining post; one strut	-	-	-	-	nr	82.15
angle steel straining post; two struts	-	-	-	-	nr	113.40
Fencing; height 1.80 m; concrete posts at 3.00 m centres	-	-	-	-	m	16.40
Extra for						
end concrete straining post; one strut	-	-	-	-	nr	75.55
angle concrete straining post; two struts	-	-	-	-	nr	105.00
Pair of gates and gate posts; gates to match galvanized chain link fencing, with angle framing, braces, etc., complete with hinges, locking bar, lock and bolts; two 100 mm x 100 mm angle section gate posts; each with one strut						
2.44 m x 0.90 m	-	-	-	-	nr	695.00
2.44 m x 1.20 m	-	-	-	-	nr	725.00
2.44 m x 1.80 m	-	-	-	-	nr	820.00
Chain link fencing; BS 1722 Part 1; 3 mm diameter plastic coated mild steel wire; 50 mm mesh; plastic coated mild steel tying and line wire; three line wires threaded through posts and strained with eye bolts and winding brackets						
Fencing; height 900 mm; galvanized mild steel angle posts at 3.00 m centres	-	-	-	-	m	11.50
Extra for						
end steel straining post; one strut	-	-	-	-	nr	51.15
angle steel straining post; two struts	-	-	-	-	nr	69.00
Fencing; height 900 mm; concrete posts at 3.00 m centres	-	-	-	-	m	11.25
Extra for						
end concrete straining post; one strut	-	-	-	-	nr	47.00
angle concrete straining post; two struts	-	-	-	-	nr	64.50
Fencing; height 1.20 m; galvanized mild steel angle posts at 3.00 m centres	-	-	-	-	m	16.85
Extra for						
end steel straining post; one strut	-	-	-	-	nr	62.20
angle steel straining post; two struts	-	-	-	-	nr	82.15
Fencing; height 1.20 m; concrete posts at 3.00 m centres	-	-	-	-	m	13.50
Extra for						
end concrete straining post; one strut	-	-	-	-	nr	57.75
angle concrete straining post; two struts	-	-	-	-	nr	75.55
Fencing; height 1.80 m; galvanized mild steel angle posts at 3.00 m centres	-	-	-	-	m	20.00
Extra for						
end steel straining post; one strut	-	-	-	-	nr	82.15
angle steel straining post; two struts	-	-	-	-	nr	113.50

Q PAVING/PLANTING/FENCING/SITE FURNITURE Excluding overheads and profit	PC £	Labour hours	Labour £	Material £	Unit	Total rate £
Q40 FENCING - cont'd						
Chain link fencing; BS 1722 Part 1; 3 mm diameter plastic coated mild steel wire; 50 mm mesh; plastic coated mild steel tying and line wire; three line wires threaded through posts and strained with eye bolts and winding brackets - cont'd						
Fencing; height 1.80 m; concrete posts at 3.00 m centres	-	-	-	-	m	**19.20**
Extra for						
end concrete straining post; one strut	-	-	-	-	nr	**75.55**
angle concrete straining post; two struts	-	-	-	-	nr	**105.00**
Pair of gates and gate posts; gates to match plastic chain link fencing; with angle framing, braces, etc. complete with hinges, locking bar, lock and bolts; two 100 mm x 100 mm angle section gate posts; each with one strut						
2.44 m x 0.90 m high	-	-	-	-	nr	**705.00**
2.44 m x 1.20 m high	-	-	-	-	nr	**735.00**
2.44 m x 1.80 m high	-	-	-	-	nr	**840.00**
Chain link fencing for tennis courts; BS 1722 Part 13; 2.50 mm diameter galvanised mild wire; 45 mm mesh; line and tying wires threaded through 45 mm x 45 mm x 5 mm galvanised mild steel angle standards, posts and struts; 60 mm x 60 mm x 6 mm straining posts and gate posts; straining posts and struts strained with eye bolts and winding brackets						
Fencing to tennis court 36.00 m x 18.00 m; including gate 1.07 m x 1.98 m complete with hinges, locking bar, lock and bolts						
height 2745 mm; standards at 3.00 m centres	-	-	-	-	nr	**2250.00**
height 3660 mm; standards at 2.50 m centres	-	-	-	-	nr	**3045.00**
Cleft chestnut pale fencing; BS 1722 Part 4; pales spaced 51 mm apart; on two lines of galvanized wire; 64 mm diameter posts; 76 mm x 51 mm struts						
Fencing; height 900 mm; posts at 2.50 m centres	-	-	-	-	m	**6.95**
Extra for						
straining post; one strut	-	-	-	-	nr	**12.65**
corner straining post; two struts	-	-	-	-	nr	**16.90**
Fencing; height 1.05 m; posts at 2.50 m centres	-	-	-	-	m	**7.70**
Extra for						
straining post; one strut	-	-	-	-	nr	**14.00**
corner straining post; two struts	-	-	-	-	nr	**18.60**
Fencing; height 1.20 m; posts at 2.25 m centres	-	-	-	-	m	**8.15**
Extra for						
straining post; one strut	-	-	-	-	nr	**15.30**
corner straining post; two struts	-	-	-	-	nr	**20.35**
Fencing; height 1.35 m; posts at 2.25 m centres	-	-	-	-	m	**8.70**
Extra for						
straining post; one strut	-	-	-	-	nr	**17.15**
corner straining post; two struts	-	-	-	-	nr	**22.75**

Q PAVING/PLANTING/FENCING/SITE FURNITURE Excluding overheads and profit	PC £	Labour hours	Labour £	Material £	Unit	Total rate £
Close boarded fencing; BS 1722 Part 5; 76 mm x 38 mm softwood rails; 89 mm x 19 mm softwood pales lapped 13 mm; 152 mm x 25 mm softwood gravel boards; all softwood "treated"; posts at 3.00 m centres						
Fencing; two rail; concrete posts						
height 1.00 m	-	-	-	-	m	29.05
height 1.20 m	-	-	-	-	m	30.80
Fencing; three rail; concrete posts						
height 1.40 m	-	-	-	-	m	39.00
height 1.60 m	-	-	-	-	m	40.50
height 1.80 m	-	-	-	-	m	42.25
Fencing; two rail; oak posts						
height 1.00 m	-	-	-	-	m	20.90
height 1.20 m	-	-	-	-	m	24.00
Fencing; three rail; oak posts						
height 1.40 m	-	-	-	-	m	26.95
height 1.60 m	-	-	-	-	m	30.70
height 1.80 m	-	-	-	-	m	34.20
Precast concrete slab fencing; 305 mm x 38 mm x 1753 mm slabs; fitted into twice grooved concrete posts at 1830 mm centres						
Fencing						
height 1.20 m	-	-	-	-	m	44.55
height 1.50 m	-	-	-	-	m	52.80
height 1.80 m	-	-	-	-	m	65.90
Mild steel unclimbable fencing; in rivetted panels 2440 mm long; 44 mm x 13 mm flat section top and bottom rails; two 44 mm x 19 mm flat section standards; one with foot plate, and 38 mm x 13 mm raking stay with foot plate; 20 mm diameter pointed verticals at 120 mm centres; two 44 mm x 19 mm supports 760 mm long with ragged ends to bottom rail; the whole bolted together; coated with red oxide primer; setting standards and stays in ground at 2440 mm centres and supports at 815 mm centres						
Fencing						
height 1.67 m	-	-	-	-	m	105.00
height 2.13 m	-	-	-	-	m	120.00
Pair of gates and gate posts, to match mild steel unclimbable fencing; with flat section framing, braces, etc., complete with locking bar, lock, handles, drop bolt, gate stop and holding back catches; two 102 mm x 102 mm hollow section gate posts with cap and foot plates						
2.44 m x 1.67 m	-	-	-	-	nr	925.00
2.44 m x 2.13 m	-	-	-	-	nr	1080.00
4.88 m x 1.67 m	-	-	-	-	nr	1425.00
4.88 m x 2.13 m	-	-	-	-	nr	1820.00
PVC coated, galvanised mild steel high security fencing; "Sentinel Sterling fencing" or other equal and approved; Twill Wire Products Ltd; 50 mm x 50 mm mesh; 3 mm/ 3.50 mm gauge wire; barbed edge - 1; "Sentinal Bi-steel" colour coated posts or other equal and approved; at 2440 mm centres						
Fencing						
height 1.80 m	-	1.10	7.24	31.58	m	38.82
height 2.10 m	-	1.10	7.24	35.05	m	42.29

R DISPOSAL SYSTEMS Excluding overheads and profit	PC £	Labour hours	Labour £	Material £	Unit	Total rate £
R DISPOSAL SYSTEMS						
R10 RAINWATER PIPEWORK/GUTTERS						
Aluminium pipes and fittings; BS 2997; ears cast on; powder coated finish						
63.50 mm diameter pipes; plugged and screwed	11.38	0.44	4.55	12.70	m	17.25
Extra for						
fittings with one end	-	0.26	2.69	6.59	nr	9.28
fittings with two ends	-	0.50	5.17	6.76	nr	11.93
fittings with three ends	-	0.72	7.45	8.98	nr	16.43
shoe	6.97	0.26	2.69	6.59	nr	9.28
bend	7.43	0.50	5.17	6.76	nr	11.93
single branch	9.68	0.72	7.45	8.98	nr	16.43
offset 228 mm projection	17.13	0.50	5.67	15.92	nr	21.59
offset 304 mm projection	19.10	0.50	5.17	17.94	nr	23.11
access pipe	21.16	-	-	18.75	nr	18.75
connection to clay pipes; cement:sand (1:2) joint	-	0.18	1.86	0.10	nr	1.96
76.50 mm diameter pipes; plugged and screwed	13.25	0.48	4.97	14.67	m	19.64
Extra for						
shoe	9.55	0.30	3.10	9.08	nr	12.18
bend	9.38	0.54	5.59	8.62	nr	14.21
single branch	11.66	0.78	8.07	10.81	nr	18.88
offset 228 mm projection	18.19	0.54	5.59	16.69	nr	22.28
offset 304 mm projection	20.95	0.54	5.59	19.53	nr	25.12
access pipe	23.12	-	-	20.28	nr	20.28
connection to clay pipes; cement:sand (1:2) joint	-	0.20	2.07	0.10	nr	2.17
100 mm diameter pipes; plugged and screwed	22.61	0.54	5.59	24.52	m	30.11
Extra for						
shoe	11.51	0.34	3.52	10.33	nr	13.85
bend	13.07	0.60	6.21	11.66	nr	17.87
single branch	15.62	0.90	9.31	13.75	nr	23.06
offset 228 mm projection	21.91	0.60	6.21	18.50	nr	24.71
offset 304 mm projection	24.33	0.60	6.21	20.98	nr	27.19
access pipe	27.40	-	-	22.23	nr	22.23
connection to clay pipes; cement:sand (1:2) joint	-	0.24	2.48	0.10	nr	2.58
Roof outlets; circular aluminium; with flat or domed grating; joint to pipe						
50 mm diameter	52.12	0.72	10.38	52.12	nr	62.50
75 mm diameter	68.30	0.78	11.24	68.30	nr	79.54
100 mm diameter	88.94	0.84	12.10	88.94	nr	101.04
150 mm diameter	113.95	0.90	12.97	113.95	nr	126.92
Roof outlets; d-shaped; balcony; with flat or domed grating; joint to pipe						
50 mm diameter	61.73	0.72	10.38	61.73	nr	72.11
75 mm diameter	70.96	0.78	11.24	70.96	nr	82.20
100 mm diameter	87.15	0.84	12.10	87.15	nr	99.25
Galvanized wire balloon grating; BS 416 for pipes or outlets						
50 mm diameter	1.52	0.08	1.15	1.52	nr	2.67
63 mm diameter	1.54	0.08	1.15	1.54	nr	2.69
75 mm diameter	1.64	0.08	1.15	1.64	nr	2.79
100 mm diameter	1.80	0.10	1.44	1.80	nr	3.24

R DISPOSAL SYSTEMS Excluding overheads and profit	PC £	Labour hours	Labour £	Material £	Unit	Total rate £
Aluminium gutters and fittings; BS 2997; **powder coated finish**						
100 mm half round gutters; on brackets; screwed to timber	10.44	0.42	4.76	13.85	m	**18.61**
Extra for						
stop end	2.83	0.19	2.15	5.64	nr	**7.79**
running outlet	6.27	0.40	4.54	6.39	nr	**10.93**
stop end outlet	5.58	0.19	2.15	7.58	nr	**9.73**
angle	5.79	0.40	4.54	4.95	nr	**9.49**
113 mm half round gutters; on brackets; screwed to timber	10.93	0.42	4.76	14.40	m	**19.16**
Extra for						
stop end	2.97	0.19	2.15	5.80	nr	**7.95**
running outlet	6.83	0.40	4.54	6.93	nr	**11.47**
stop end outlet	6.39	0.19	2.15	8.37	nr	**10.52**
angle	6.53	0.40	4.54	5.58	nr	**10.12**
125 mm half round gutters; on brackets; screwed to timber	12.28	0.48	5.44	17.26	m	**22.70**
Extra for						
stop end	3.62	0.22	2.49	7.79	nr	**10.28**
running outlet	7.39	0.42	4.76	7.39	nr	**12.15**
stop end outlet	6.79	0.22	2.49	10.00	nr	**12.49**
angle	7.25	0.42	4.76	7.38	nr	**12.14**
100 mm ogee gutters; on brackets; screwed to timber	13.02	0.44	4.99	17.69	m	**22.68**
Extra for						
stop end	2.98	0.20	2.27	3.71	nr	**5.98**
running outlet	7.35	0.42	4.76	6.75	nr	**11.51**
stop end outlet	5.70	0.20	2.27	8.46	nr	**10.73**
angle	6.20	0.42	4.76	4.37	nr	**9.13**
112 mm ogee gutters; on brackets; screwed to timber	14.48	0.50	5.67	19.46	m	**25.13**
Extra for						
stop end	3.19	0.20	2.27	3.93	nr	**6.20**
running outlet	7.44	0.42	4.76	6.72	nr	**11.48**
stop end outlet	6.38	0.20	2.27	9.25	nr	**11.52**
angle	7.38	0.42	4.76	5.33	nr	**10.09**
125 mm ogee gutters; on brackets; screwed to timber	15.99	0.50	5.67	21.39	m	**27.06**
Extra for						
stop end	3.49	0.23	2.61	4.24	nr	**6.85**
running outlet	8.14	0.44	4.99	7.32	nr	**12.31**
stop end outlet	7.25	0.23	2.61	10.33	nr	**12.94**
angle	8.62	0.44	4.99	6.34	nr	**11.33**
Cast iron pipes and fittings; EN 1462; ears **cast on; joints**						
65 mm pipes; primed; nailed to masonry	16.84	0.62	6.42	18.01	m	**24.43**
Extra for						
shoe	14.63	0.38	3.93	13.85	nr	**17.78**
bend	8.96	0.68	7.04	8.03	nr	**15.07**
single branch	17.27	0.86	8.90	16.01	nr	**24.91**
offset 225 mm projection	15.97	0.68	7.04	14.16	nr	**21.20**
offset 305 mm projection	18.69	0.68	7.04	16.59	nr	**23.63**
connection to clay pipes; cement:sand (1:2) joint	-	0.18	1.86	0.11	nr	**1.97**

R DISPOSAL SYSTEMS Excluding overheads and profit	PC £	Labour hours	Labour £	Material £	Unit	Total rate £
R10 RAINWATER PIPEWORK/GUTTERS - cont'd						
Cast iron pipes and fittings; EN 1462; ears						
cast on; joints - cont'd						
75 mm pipes; primed; nailed to masonry	16.84	0.66	6.83	18.20	m	25.03
Extra for						
shoe	14.63	0.42	4.35	13.91	nr	18.26
bend	10.89	1.44	15.62	10.08	nr	25.70
single branch	19.05	0.90	9.31	17.96	nr	27.27
offset 225 mm projection	15.97	0.72	7.45	14.22	nr	21.67
offset 305 mm projection	19.62	0.72	7.45	17.61	nr	25.06
connection to clay pipes; cement:sand						
(1:2) joint	-	0.20	2.07	0.11	nr	2.18
100 mm pipes; primed; nailed to masonry	22.62	0.72	7.45	24.48	m	31.93
Extra for						
shoe	19.07	0.48	4.97	18.10	nr	23.07
bend	15.37	0.78	8.07	14.31	nr	22.38
single branch	22.63	0.96	9.94	21.15	nr	31.09
offset 225 mm projection	31.34	0.78	8.07	29.25	nr	37.32
offset 305 mm projection	31.34	0.78	8.07	28.78	nr	36.85
connection to clay pipes; cement:sand						
(1:2) joint	-	0.24	2.48	0.10	nr	2.58
100 mm x 75 mm rectangular pipes; primed;						
nailing to masonry	64.71	0.72	7.45	68.68	m	76.13
Extra for						
shoe	54.83	0.48	4.97	51.22	nr	56.19
bend	52.21	0.78	8.07	48.53	nr	56.60
offset 225 mm projection	73.50	0.48	4.97	66.28	nr	71.25
offset 305 mm projection	78.57	0.48	4.97	70.11	nr	75.08
connection to clay pipes; cement:sand						
(1:2) joint	-	0.24	2.48	0.10	nr	2.58
Rainwater head; rectangular; for pipes						
65 mm diameter	19.98	0.68	7.04	20.74	nr	27.78
75 mm diameter	19.98	0.72	7.45	20.81	nr	28.26
100 mm diameter	27.59	0.78	8.07	28.73	nr	36.80
Rainwater head; octagonal; for pipes						
65 mm diameter	11.43	0.68	7.04	11.98	nr	19.02
75 mm diameter	12.99	0.72	7.45	13.64	nr	21.09
100 mm diameter	28.78	0.78	8.07	29.95	nr	38.02
Copper wire balloon grating; BS 416 for pipes						
or outlets						
50 mm diameter	1.85	0.08	0.83	1.85	nr	2.68
63 mm diameter	1.87	0.08	0.83	1.87	nr	2.70
75 mm diameter	2.10	0.08	0.83	2.10	nr	2.93
100 mm diameter	2.39	0.10	1.03	2.39	nr	3.42
Cast iron gutters and fittings; EN 1462						
100 mm half round gutters; primed; on						
brackets; screwed to timber	8.57	0.48	5.44	11.37	m	16.81
Extra for						
stop end	2.16	0.20	2.27	3.29	nr	5.56
running outlet	6.26	0.42	4.76	5.67	nr	10.43
angle	6.43	0.42	4.76	6.94	nr	11.70
115 mm half round gutters; primed; on						
brackets; screwed to timber	8.93	0.48	5.44	11.78	m	17.22
Extra for						
stop end	2.80	0.20	2.27	3.93	nr	6.20
running outlet	6.82	0.42	4.76	6.20	nr	10.96
angle	6.61	0.42	4.76	7.06	nr	11.82

R DISPOSAL SYSTEMS Excluding overheads and profit	PC £	Labour hours	Labour £	Material £	Unit	Total rate £
125 mm half round gutters; primed; on brackets; screwed to timber	10.44	0.54	6.12	13.38	m	**19.50**
Extra for						
stop end	2.80	0.24	2.72	3.93	nr	**6.65**
running outlet	7.81	0.48	5.44	7.06	nr	**12.50**
angle	7.81	0.48	5.44	7.99	nr	**13.43**
150 mm half round gutters; primed; on brackets; screwed to timber	17.86	0.60	6.80	20.83	m	**27.63**
Extra for						
stop end	3.73	0.26	2.95	6.26	nr	**9.21**
running outlet	13.50	0.54	6.12	12.21	nr	**18.33**
angle	14.25	0.54	6.12	13.75	nr	**19.87**
100 mm ogee gutters; primed; on brackets; screwed to timber	9.55	0.50	5.67	12.65	m	**18.32**
Extra for						
stop end	2.00	0.22	2.49	4.28	nr	**6.77**
running outlet	6.84	0.44	4.99	6.17	nr	**11.16**
angle	6.71	0.44	4.99	7.28	nr	**12.27**
115 mm ogee gutters; primed; on brackets; screwed to timber	10.51	0.50	5.67	13.68	m	**19.35**
Extra for						
stop end	2.64	0.22	2.49	4.92	nr	**7.41**
running outlet	7.27	0.44	4.99	6.52	nr	**11.51**
angle	7.27	0.44	4.99	7.67	nr	**12.66**
125 mm ogee gutters; primed; on brackets; screwed to timber	11.02	0.56	6.35	14.53	m	**20.88**
Extra for						
stop end	2.64	0.25	2.83	5.21	nr	**8.04**
running outlet	7.94	0.50	5.67	7.15	nr	**12.82**
angle	7.94	0.50	5.67	8.54	nr	**14.21**
3 mm thick galvanised heavy pressed steel **gutters and fittings; joggle joints; BS 1091**						
200 mm x 100 mm (400 mm girth) box gutter; screwed to timber	-	0.78	8.07	17.77	m	**25.84**
Extra for						
stop end	-	0.42	4.35	9.85	nr	**14.20**
running outlet	-	0.84	8.69	16.32	nr	**25.01**
stop end outlet	-	0.42	4.35	22.89	nr	**27.24**
angle	-	0.84	8.69	18.10	nr	**26.79**
381 mm boundary wall gutters (900 mm girth); bent twice; screwed to timber	-	0.78	8.07	29.25	m	**37.32**
Extra for						
stop end	-	0.48	4.97	16.79	nr	**21.76**
running outlet	-	0.84	8.69	22.45	nr	**31.14**
stop end outlet	-	0.42	4.35	31.77	nr	**36.12**
angle	-	0.84	8.69	26.40	nr	**35.09**
457 mm boundary wall gutters (1200 mm girth); bent twice; screwed to timber	-	0.90	9.31	38.97	m	**48.28**
Extra for						
stop end	-	0.48	4.97	21.61	nr	**26.58**
running outlet	-	0.96	9.94	32.48	nr	**42.42**
stop end outlet	-	0.48	4.97	34.64	nr	**39.61**
angle	-	0.96	9.94	35.71	nr	**45.65**

R DISPOSAL SYSTEMS Excluding overheads and profit	PC £	Labour hours	Labour £	Material £	Unit	Total rate £
R10 RAINWATER PIPEWORK/GUTTERS - cont'd						
uPVC external rainwater pipes and fittings; **BS 4576; slip-in joints**						
50 mm pipes; fixing with pipe or socket						
brackets; plugged and screwed	3.27	0.36	3.73	4.61	m	8.34
Extra for						
shoe	1.94	0.24	2.48	2.46	nr	4.94
bend	2.26	0.36	3.73	2.79	nr	6.52
two bends to form offset 229 mm projection	2.26	0.36	3.73	4.52	nr	8.25
connection to clay pipes; cement:sand						
(1:2) joint	-	0.16	1.66	0.11	nr	1.77
68 mm pipes; fixing with pipe or socket						
brackets; plugged and screwed	2.62	0.40	4.14	4.21	m	8.35
Extra for						
shoe	1.94	0.26	2.69	2.72	nr	5.41
bend	3.40	0.40	4.14	4.22	nr	8.36
single branch	5.94	0.53	5.49	6.82	nr	12.31
two bends to form offset 229 mm projection	3.40	0.40	4.14	7.23	nr	11.37
loose drain connector; cement:sand (1:2)						
joint	-	0.18	1.86	2.53	nr	4.39
110 mm pipes; fixing with pipe or socket						
brackets; plugged and screwed	5.63	0.43	4.45	8.68	m	13.13
Extra for						
shoe	6.17	0.29	3.00	7.09	nr	10.09
bend	8.70	0.43	4.45	9.68	nr	14.13
single branch	12.86	0.58	6.00	13.95	nr	19.95
two bends to form offset 229 mm projection	8.70	0.43	4.45	17.77	nr	22.22
loose drain connector; cement:sand (1:2)						
joint	-	0.42	4.35	9.98	nr	14.33
65 mm square pipes; fixing with pipe or socket						
brackets; plugged and screwed	2.89	0.40	4.14	4.56	m	8.70
Extra for						
shoe	2.11	0.26	2.69	2.89	nr	5.58
bend	2.32	0.40	4.14	3.11	nr	7.25
single branch	6.50	0.53	5.49	7.39	nr	12.88
two bends to form offset 229 mm projection	2.32	0.40	4.14	5.12	nr	9.26
drain connector; square to round; cement:						
sand (1:2) joint	-	0.42	4.35	3.32	nr	7.67
Rainwater head; rectangular; for pipes						
50 mm diameter	10.51	0.54	5.59	11.78	nr	17.37
68 mm diameter	8.49	0.56	5.80	10.23	nr	16.03
110 mm diameter	17.70	0.66	6.83	19.73	nr	26.56
65 mm square	8.49	0.56	5.80	10.22	nr	16.02
uPVC gutters and fittings; BS 4576						
76 mm half round gutters; on brackets screwed						
to timber	2.62	0.36	4.08	3.94	m	8.02
Extra for						
stop end	0.89	0.16	1.81	1.20	nr	3.01
running outlet	2.50	0.30	3.40	2.34	nr	5.74
stop end outlet	2.49	0.16	1.81	2.62	nr	4.43
angle	2.50	0.30	3.40	2.88	nr	6.28
112 mm half round gutters; on brackets						
screwed to timber	2.69	0.40	4.54	4.81	m	9.35
Extra for						
stop end	1.39	0.16	1.81	1.87	nr	3.68
running outlet	2.72	0.34	3.86	2.56	nr	6.42
stop end outlet	2.72	0.16	1.81	3.01	nr	4.82
angle	3.05	0.34	3.86	3.79	nr	7.65
170 mm half round gutters; on brackets;						
screwed to timber	5.22	0.40	4.54	8.75	m	13.29

R DISPOSAL SYSTEMS Excluding overheads and profit	PC £	Labour hours	Labour £	Material £	Unit	Total rate £
Extra for						
stop end	2.35	0.19	2.15	3.26	nr	**5.41**
running outlet	5.22	0.37	4.20	4.91	nr	**9.11**
stop end outlet	4.98	0.19	2.15	5.52	nr	**7.67**
angle	6.82	0.37	4.20	8.26	nr	**12.46**
114 mm rectangular gutters; on brackets;						
screwed to timber	2.94	0.40	4.54	5.37	m	**9.91**
Extra for						
stop end	1.54	0.16	1.81	2.06	nr	**3.87**
running outlet	2.98	0.37	4.20	2.81	nr	**7.01**
stop end outlet	2.98	0.16	1.81	3.30	nr	**5.11**
angle	3.35	0.34	3.86	4.16	nr	**8.02**
R11 FOUL DRAINAGE ABOVE GROUND						
Cast iron "Timesaver" pipes and fittings						
or other equal and approved; BS 416						
50 mm pipes; primed; 2.00 m lengths; fixing						
with expanding bolts; to masonry	12.84	0.66	6.83	21.12	m	**27.95**
Extra for						
fittings with two ends	-	0.66	6.83	14.12	nr	**20.95**
fittings with three ends	-	0.90	9.31	23.96	nr	**33.27**
bends; short radius	10.05	0.66	6.83	14.12	nr	**20.95**
access bends; short radius	24.77	0.66	6.83	29.21	nr	**36.04**
boss; 38 mm BSP	20.82	0.66	6.83	24.82	nr	**31.65**
single branch	15.13	0.90	9.31	24.56	nr	**33.87**
access pipe	24.18	0.66	6.83	27.12	nr	**33.95**
roof connector; for asphalt	27.54	0.66	6.83	32.25	nr	**39.08**
isolated "Timesaver" coupling joint	5.70	0.36	3.73	5.84	nr	**9.57**
connection to clay pipes; cement:sand						
(1:2) joint	-	0.16	1.66	0.10	nr	**1.76**
75 mm pipes; primed; 3.00 m lengths; fixing						
with standard brackets; plugged and screwed						
to masonry	12.57	0.66	6.83	20.41	m	**27.24**
75 mm pipes; primed; 2.00 m lengths; fixing						
with standard brackets; plugged and screwed						
to masonry	12.84	0.72	7.45	20.69	m	**28.14**
Extra for						
bends; short radius	10.05	0.72	7.45	14.75	nr	**22.20**
access bends; short radius	24.77	0.66	6.83	29.83	nr	**36.66**
boss; 38 mm BSP	20.82	0.72	7.45	25.79	nr	**33.24**
single branch	15.13	1.02	10.56	25.68	nr	**36.24**
double branch	25.02	1.32	13.66	42.29	nr	**55.95**
offset 115 mm projection	12.38	0.72	7.45	15.59	nr	**23.04**
offset 150 mm projection	12.38	0.72	7.45	15.18	nr	**22.63**
access pipe	24.18	0.72	7.45	27.48	nr	**34.93**
roof connector; for asphalt	31.40	0.72	7.45	36.50	nr	**43.95**
isolated "Timesaver" coupling joint	6.31	0.42	4.35	6.47	nr	**10.82**
connection to clay pipes; cement:sand						
(1:2) joint	-	0.18	1.86	0.10	nr	**1.96**
100 mm pipes; primed; 3.00 m lengths; fixing						
with standard brackets; plugged and screwed						
to masonry	15.19	0.72	7.45	28.84	m	**36.29**
100 mm pipes; primed; 2.00 m lengths; fixing						
with standard brackets; plugged and screwed						
to masonry	15.48	0.80	8.28	29.14	m	**37.42**

R DISPOSAL SYSTEMS Excluding overheads and profit	PC £	Labour hours	Labour £	Material £	Unit	Total rate £
R11 FOUL DRAINAGE ABOVE GROUND - cont'd						
Cast iron "Timesaver" pipes and fittings						
or other equal and approved; BS 416 - cont'd						
Extra for						
WC bent connector; 450 mm long tail	15.14	0.72	7.45	18.17	nr	25.62
bends; short radius	13.92	0.80	8.28	20.25	nr	28.53
access bends; short radius	29.43	0.80	8.28	36.15	nr	44.43
boss; 38 mm BSP	24.86	0.80	8.28	31.47	nr	39.75
single branch	21.51	1.20	12.42	35.08	nr	47.50
double branch	26.17	1.56	16.15	48.28	nr	64.43
offset 225 mm projection	20.00	0.80	8.28	24.37	nr	32.65
offset 300 mm projection	22.54	0.80	8.28	26.49	nr	34.77
access pipe	25.43	0.80	8.28	29.61	nr	37.89
roof connector; for asphalt	24.26	0.80	8.28	30.28	nr	38.56
roof connector; for roofing felt	77.59	0.80	8.28	84.95	nr	93.23
isolated "Timesaver" coupling joint	8.22	0.50	5.17	8.43	nr	13.60
transitional clayware socket; cement:sand						
(1:2) joint	16.51	0.48	4.97	25.44	nr	30.41
150 mm pipes; primed; 3.00 m lengths; fixing						
with standard brackets; plugged and screwed						
to masonry	31.72	0.90	9.31	58.37	m	67.68
150 mm pipes; primed; 2.00 m lengths; fixing						
with standard brackets; plugged and screwed						
to masonry	31.78	1.00	10.35	58.43	m	68.78
Extra for						
bends; short radius	24.86	1.00	10.35	37.33	nr	47.68
access bends; short radius	41.81	1.00	10.35	54.70	nr	65.05
boss; 38 mm BSP	40.57	1.00	10.35	52.60	nr	62.95
single branch	50.48	1.44	14.90	76.43	nr	91.33
double branch	74.93	1.92	19.87	116.85	nr	136.72
access pipe	42.29	1.00	10.35	48.39	nr	58.74
roof connector; for asphalt	61.72	1.00	10.35	72.44	nr	82.79
isolated "Timesaver" coupling joint	-	0.60	6.21	16.85	nr	23.06
transitional clayware socket; cement:sand						
(1:2) joint	28.94	0.62	6.42	46.61	nr	53.03
Cast iron "Ensign" lightweight pipes and						
fittings or other equal and approved; EN 877						
50 mm pipes; primed 3.00 m lengths; fixing with						
standard brackets; plugged and screwed to masonry	-	0.33	2.72	12.98	m	15.70
Extra for						
bends; short radius	-	0.29	2.37	10.35	nr	12.72
single branch	-	0.36	2.94	18.12	nr	21.06
access pipe	-	0.29	2.37	21.26	nr	23.63
70 mm pipes; primed 3.00 m lengths; fixing						
with standard brackets; plugged and screwed						
to masonry	-	0.37	2.99	14.51	m	17.50
Extra for						
bends; short radius	-	0.32	2.61	11.55	nr	14.16
single branch	-	0.40	3.26	19.46	nr	22.72
access pipe	-	0.32	2.61	22.67	nr	25.28
100 mm pipes; primed 3.00 m lengths; fixing						
with standard brackets; plugged and screwed						
to masonry	-	0.40	3.26	17.24	m	20.50
Extra for						
bends; short radius	-	0.35	2.86	14.20	nr	17.06
single branch	-	0.42	3.43	25.06	nr	28.49
double branch	-	0.50	4.08	36.72	nr	40.80
access pipe	-	0.35	2.86	25.79	nr	28.65
connector	-	0.23	1.84	23.79	nr	25.63
reducer	-	0.35	2.86	17.33	nr	20.19

R DISPOSAL SYSTEMS Excluding overheads and profit	PC £	Labour hours	Labour £	Material £	Unit	Total rate £
Polypropylene (PP) waste pipes and fittings; **BS 5254; push fit "O" - ring joints**						
32 mm pipes; fixing with pipe clips; plugged and screwed	0.63	0.26	2.69	1.09	m	**3.78**
Extra for						
fittings with one end	-	0.19	1.97	0.58	nr	**2.55**
fittings with two ends	-	0.26	2.69	0.58	nr	**3.27**
fittings with three ends	-	0.36	3.73	0.58	nr	**4.31**
access plug	0.57	0.19	1.97	0.58	nr	**2.55**
double socket	0.57	0.18	1.86	0.58	nr	**2.44**
male iron to PP coupling	1.42	0.34	3.52	1.46	nr	**4.98**
sweep bend	0.57	0.26	2.69	0.58	nr	**3.27**
spigot bend	0.57	0.30	3.10	0.58	nr	**3.68**
40 mm pipes; fixing with pipe clips; plugged and screwed	0.77	0.26	2.69	1.23	m	**3.92**
Extra for						
fittings with one end	-	0.23	2.38	0.58	nr	**2.96**
fittings with two ends	-	0.36	3.73	0.58	nr	**4.31**
fittings with three ends	-	0.48	4.97	0.58	nr	**5.55**
access plug	0.57	0.23	2.38	0.58	nr	**2.96**
double socket	0.57	0.24	2.48	0.58	nr	**3.06**
universal connector	0.57	0.30	3.10	0.58	nr	**3.68**
sweep bend	0.57	0.36	3.73	0.58	nr	**4.31**
spigot bend	0.57	0.36	3.73	0.58	nr	**4.31**
reducer 40 mm - 32 mm	0.57	0.36	3.73	0.58	nr	**4.31**
50 mm pipes; fixing with pipe clips; plugged and screwed	1.27	0.42	4.35	2.08	m	**6.43**
Extra for						
fittings with one end	-	0.25	2.59	1.05	nr	**3.64**
fittings with two ends	-	0.42	4.35	1.05	nr	**5.40**
fittings with three ends	-	0.56	5.80	1.05	nr	**6.85**
access plug	1.02	0.25	2.59	1.05	nr	**3.64**
double socket	1.02	0.28	2.90	1.05	nr	**3.95**
sweep bend	1.02	0.42	4.35	1.05	nr	**5.40**
spigot bend	1.02	0.42	4.35	1.05	nr	**5.40**
reducer 50 mm - 40 mm	1.02	0.42	4.35	1.05	nr	**5.40**
muPVC waste pipes and fittings; BS 5255; **solvent welded joints**						
32 mm pipes; fixing with pipe clips; plugged and screwed	1.82	0.30	3.10	2.55	m	**5.65**
Extra for						
fittings with one end	-	0.20	2.07	1.78	nr	**3.85**
fittings with two ends	-	0.30	3.10	1.53	nr	**4.63**
fittings with three ends	-	0.40	4.14	2.13	nr	**6.27**
access plug	1.54	0.20	2.07	1.78	nr	**3.85**
straight coupling	1.01	0.20	2.07	1.24	nr	**3.31**
expansion coupling	1.46	0.30	3.10	1.70	nr	**4.80**
male iron to muPVC coupling	1.26	0.46	4.76	1.39	nr	**6.15**
union coupling	3.46	0.30	3.10	3.75	nr	**6.85**
sweep bend	1.29	0.30	3.10	1.53	nr	**4.63**
spigot/socket bend	-	0.30	3.10	1.71	nr	**4.81**
sweep tee	1.83	0.40	4.14	2.13	nr	**6.27**
40 mm pipes; fixing with pipe clips; plugged and screwed	1.91	0.36	3.73	2.77	m	**6.50**

R DISPOSAL SYSTEMS Excluding overheads and profit	PC £	Labour hours	Labour £	Material £	Unit	Total rate £
R11 FOUL DRAINAGE ABOVE GROUND - cont'd						
muPVC waste pipes and fittings; BS 5255; **solvent welded joints** - cont'd						
Extra for						
fittings with one end	-	0.23	2.38	2.06	nr	**4.44**
fittings with two ends	-	0.36	3.73	1.68	nr	**5.41**
fittings with three ends	-	0.48	4.97	2.62	nr	**7.59**
fittings with four ends	6.54	0.64	6.62	7.06	nr	**13.68**
access plug	1.81	0.23	2.38	2.06	nr	**4.44**
straight coupling	1.22	0.24	2.48	1.45	nr	**3.93**
expansion coupling	1.75	0.36	3.73	2.00	nr	**5.73**
male iron to muPVC coupling	1.47	0.46	4.76	1.61	nr	**6.37**
union coupling	4.55	0.36	3.73	4.87	nr	**8.60**
level invert taper	1.42	0.36	3.73	1.66	nr	**5.39**
sweep bend	1.44	0.36	3.73	1.68	nr	**5.41**
spigot/socket bend	1.64	0.36	3.73	1.88	nr	**5.61**
sweep tee	2.31	0.48	4.97	2.62	nr	**7.59**
sweep cross	6.54	0.64	6.62	7.06	nr	**13.68**
50 mm pipes; fixing with pipe clips; plugged and screwed	3.28	0.42	4.35	4.79	m	**9.14**
Extra for						
fittings with one end	-	0.25	2.59	3.21	nr	**5.80**
fittings with two ends	-	0.42	4.35	2.66	nr	**7.01**
fittings with three ends	-	0.56	5.80	4.95	nr	**10.75**
fittings with four ends	-	0.74	7.66	8.06	nr	**15.72**
access plug	2.93	0.25	2.59	3.21	nr	**5.80**
straight coupling	1.52	0.28	2.90	1.76	nr	**4.66**
expansion coupling	2.38	0.42	4.35	2.64	nr	**6.99**
male iron to muPVC coupling	2.13	0.54	5.59	2.28	nr	**7.87**
union coupling	7.12	0.42	4.35	7.50	nr	**11.85**
level invert taper	1.98	0.42	4.35	2.23	nr	**6.58**
sweep bend	2.40	0.42	4.35	2.66	nr	**7.01**
spigot/socket bend	3.88	0.42	4.35	4.18	nr	**8.53**
sweep tee	2.31	0.48	4.97	2.62	nr	**7.59**
sweep cross	7.52	0.74	7.66	8.06	nr	**15.72**
uPVC overflow pipes and fittings; solvent **welded joints**						
19 mm pipes; fixing with pipe clips; plugged and screwed	0.87	0.26	2.69	1.37	m	**4.06**
Extra for						
splay cut end	-	0.02	0.21	-	nr	**0.21**
fittings with one end	-	0.20	2.07	0.70	nr	**2.77**
fittings with two ends	-	0.20	2.07	0.95	nr	**3.02**
fittings with three ends	-	0.26	2.69	1.17	nr	**3.86**
straight connector	0.58	0.20	2.07	0.70	nr	**2.77**
female iron to uPVC coupling	-	0.24	2.48	1.34	nr	**3.82**
bend	0.83	0.20	2.07	0.95	nr	**3.02**
bent tank connector	1.36	0.24	2.48	1.45	nr	**3.93**
uPVC pipes and fittings; BS 4514; with solvent **welded joints (unless otherwise described)**						
82 mm pipes; fixing with holderbats; plugged and screwed	5.24	0.48	4.97	7.82	m	**12.79**
Extra for						
socket plug	4.09	0.24	2.48	4.70	nr	**7.18**
slip coupling; push fit	8.86	0.44	4.55	9.08	nr	**13.63**
expansion coupling	5.13	0.48	4.97	5.77	nr	**10.74**
sweep bend	7.21	0.48	4.97	7.90	nr	**12.87**
boss connector	4.22	0.32	3.31	4.83	nr	**8.14**

R DISPOSAL SYSTEMS Excluding overheads and profit	PC £	Labour hours	Labour £	Material £	Unit	Total rate £
Extra for - cont'd						
single branch	10.01	0.64	6.62	11.07	nr	**17.69**
access door	9.78	0.72	7.45	10.28	nr	**17.73**
connection to clay pipes; caulking ring and						
cement:sand (1:2) joint	6.87	0.44	4.55	7.38	nr	**11.93**
110 mm pipes; fixing with holderbats; plugged						
and screwed	5.34	0.53	5.49	8.16	m	**13.65**
Extra for						
socket plug	4.94	0.26	2.69	5.72	nr	**8.41**
slip coupling; push fit	11.10	0.48	4.97	11.38	nr	**16.35**
expansion coupling	5.18	0.53	5.49	5.97	nr	**11.46**
W.C. connector	7.91	0.35	3.62	8.46	nr	**12.08**
sweep bend	8.27	0.53	5.49	9.14	nr	**14.63**
W.C. connecting bend	11.82	0.35	3.62	12.47	nr	**16.09**
access bend	23.23	0.55	5.69	24.47	nr	**30.16**
boss connector	4.22	0.35	3.62	4.99	nr	**8.61**
single branch	13.05	0.70	7.25	14.39	nr	**21.64**
single branch with access	25.26	0.72	7.45	26.91	nr	**34.36**
double branch	31.79	0.88	9.11	33.96	nr	**43.07**
W.C. manifold	48.80	0.35	3.62	51.04	nr	**54.66**
access door	-	0.72	7.45	10.28	nr	**17.73**
access pipe connector	17.80	0.60	6.21	18.91	nr	**25.12**
connection to clay pipes; caulking ring and						
cement:sand (1:2) joint	-	0.50	5.17	2.53	nr	**7.70**
160 mm pipes; fixing with holderbats; plugged						
and screwed	13.68	0.60	6.21	20.90	m	**27.11**
Extra for						
socket plug	9.10	0.30	3.10	10.80	nr	**13.90**
slip coupling; push fit	28.40	0.54	5.59	29.11	nr	**34.70**
expansion coupling	15.61	0.60	6.21	17.47	nr	**23.68**
sweep bend	21.25	0.60	6.21	23.26	nr	**29.47**
boss connector	5.77	0.40	4.14	7.39	nr	**11.53**
single branch	67.90	0.79	8.18	71.78	nr	**79.96**
double branch	125.30	1.00	10.35	131.33	nr	**141.68**
access door	17.47	0.72	7.45	18.16	nr	**25.61**
access pipe connector	17.80	0.60	6.21	18.91	nr	**25.12**
connection to clay pipes; caulking ring and						
cement:sand (1:2) joint	-	0.60	6.21	4.29	nr	**10.50**
Weathering apron; for pipe						
82 mm diameter	2.02	0.41	4.24	2.32	nr	**6.56**
110 mm diameter	2.38	0.46	4.76	2.80	nr	**7.56**
160 mm diameter	7.14	0.50	5.17	8.03	nr	**13.20**
Weathering slate; for pipe						
110 mm diameter	33.25	1.08	11.18	34.44	nr	**45.62**
Vent cowl; for pipe						
82 mm diameter	2.02	0.40	4.14	2.32	nr	**6.46**
110 mm diameter	2.04	0.40	4.14	2.45	nr	**6.59**
160 mm diameter	5.32	0.40	4.14	6.16	nr	**10.30**
Polypropylene ancillaries; screwed joint to **waste fitting**						
Tubular "S" trap; bath; shallow seal						
40 mm diameter	4.94	0.66	6.83	5.06	nr	**11.89**
Trap; "P"; two piece; 76 mm seal						
32 mm diameter	3.32	0.46	4.76	3.40	nr	**8.16**
40 mm diameter	3.83	0.54	5.59	3.93	nr	**9.52**
Trap; "S"; two piece; 76 mm seal						
32 mm diameter	4.22	0.46	4.76	4.33	nr	**9.09**
40 mm diameter	4.94	0.54	5.59	5.06	nr	**10.65**
Bottle trap; "P"; 76 mm seal						
32 mm diameter	3.70	0.46	4.76	3.79	nr	**8.55**
40 mm diameter	4.42	0.54	5.59	4.53	nr	**10.12**

R DISPOSAL SYSTEMS Excluding overheads and profit	PC £	Labour hours	Labour £	Material £	Unit	Total rate £
R11 FOUL DRAINAGE ABOVE GROUND - cont'd						
Polypropylene ancillaries; screwed joint to						
waste fitting - cont'd						
Bottle trap; "S"; 76 mm seal						
32 mm diameter	4.46	0.46	4.76	4.57	nr	**9.33**
40 mm diameter	5.42	0.54	5.59	5.56	nr	**11.15**
R12 DRAINAGE BELOW GROUND						
NOTE: Prices for drain trenches are for						
excavating in "firm" soil and it has been						
assumed that earthwork support will only be						
required for trenches 1.00 m or more in depth.						
Excavating trenches; by machine; grading bottoms;						
earthwork support; filling with excavated material						
and compacting; disposal of surplus soil on site;						
spreading on site average 50 m						
Pipes not exceeding 200 mm nominal size						
average depth of trench 0.50 m	-	0.32	2.11	1.68	m	**3.79**
average depth of trench 0.75 m	-	0.49	3.22	2.51	m	**5.73**
average depth of trench 1.00 m	-	0.96	6.32	4.80	m	**11.12**
average depth of trench 1.25 m	-	1.44	9.48	5.48	m	**14.96**
average depth of trench 1.50 m	-	1.85	12.17	6.21	m	**18.38**
average depth of trench 1.75 m	-	2.25	14.80	6.88	m	**21.68**
average depth of trench 2.00 m	-	2.66	17.50	7.82	m	**25.32**
average depth of trench 2.25 m	-	3.26	21.45	9.80	m	**31.25**
average depth of trench 2.50 m	-	3.86	25.40	11.46	m	**36.86**
average depth of trench 2.75 m	-	4.27	28.10	12.77	m	**40.87**
average depth of trench 3.00 m	-	4.66	30.66	14.07	m	**44.73**
average depth of trench 3.25 m	-	5.04	33.16	14.95	m	**48.11**
average depth of trench 3.50 m	-	5.39	35.47	15.84	m	**51.31**
Pipes exceeding 200 mm nominal size; 225 mm						
nominal size						
average depth of trench 0.50 m	-	0.32	2.11	1.68	m	**3.79**
average depth of trench 0.75 m	-	0.49	3.22	2.51	m	**5.73**
average depth of trench 1.00 m	-	0.96	6.32	4.80	m	**11.12**
average depth of trench 1.25 m	-	1.44	9.48	5.48	m	**14.96**
average depth of trench 1.50 m	-	1.85	12.17	6.21	m	**18.38**
average depth of trench 1.75 m	-	2.25	14.80	6.88	m	**21.68**
average depth of trench 2.00 m	-	2.66	17.50	7.82	m	**25.32**
average depth of trench 2.25 m	-	3.26	21.45	9.80	m	**31.25**
average depth of trench 2.50 m	-	3.86	25.40	11.46	m	**36.86**
average depth of trench 2.75 m	-	4.27	28.10	12.77	m	**40.87**
average depth of trench 3.00 m	-	4.66	30.66	14.07	m	**44.73**
average depth of trench 3.25 m	-	5.04	33.16	14.95	m	**48.11**
average depth of trench 3.50 m	-	5.39	35.47	15.84	m	**51.31**
Pipes; exceeding 200 mm nominal size; 300 mm						
nominal size						
average depth of trench 0.75 m	-	0.55	3.62	3.14	m	**6.76**
average depth of trench 1.00 m	-	1.12	7.37	4.80	m	**12.17**
average depth of trench 1.25 m	-	1.53	10.07	5.69	m	**15.76**
average depth of trench 1.50 m	-	2.01	13.23	6.42	m	**19.65**
average depth of trench 1.75 m	-	2.33	15.33	7.09	m	**22.42**
average depth of trench 2.00 m	-	2.66	17.50	8.45	m	**25.95**
average depth of trench 2.25 m	-	3.26	21.45	10.21	m	**31.66**
average depth of trench 2.50 m	-	3.86	25.40	11.67	m	**37.07**
average depth of trench 2.75 m	-	4.27	28.10	12.98	m	**41.08**
average depth of trench 3.00 m	-	4.66	30.66	14.28	m	**44.94**
average depth of trench 3.25 m	-	5.04	33.16	15.58	m	**48.74**
average depth of trench 3.50 m	-	5.39	35.47	16.26	m	**51.73**

R DISPOSAL SYSTEMS Excluding overheads and profit	PC £	Labour hours	Labour £	Material £	Unit	Total rate £
Extra over excavating trenches; irrespective of depth; breaking out existing materials						
brick	-	2.25	14.80	7.29	m³	22.09
concrete	-	3.14	20.66	10.07	m³	30.73
reinforced concrete	-	4.51	29.68	14.57	m³	44.25
Extra over excavating trenches; irrespective of depth; breaking out existing hard pavings; 75 mm thick						
tarmacadam	-	0.24	1.58	0.77	m²	2.35
Extra over excavating trenches; irrespective of depth; breaking out existing hard pavings; 150 mm thick						
concrete	-	0.49	3.22	1.71	m²	4.93
tarmacadam and hardcore	-	0.32	2.11	0.89	m²	3.00
Excavating trenches; by hand; grading bottoms; **earthwork support; filling with excavated material** **and compacting; disposal of surplus soil on site;** **spreading on site average 50 m**						
Pipes not exceeding 200 mm nominal size						
average depth of trench 0.50 m	-	1.10	7.24	-	m	7.24
average depth of trench 0.75 m	-	1.65	10.86	-	m	10.86
average depth of trench 1.00 m	-	2.42	15.92	1.24	m	17.16
average depth of trench 1.25 m	-	3.41	22.44	1.71	m	24.15
average depth of trench 1.50 m	-	4.68	30.79	2.08	m	32.87
average depth of trench 1.75 m	-	6.16	40.53	2.48	m	43.01
average depth of trench 2.00 m	-	7.04	46.32	2.79	m	49.11
average depth of trench 2.25 m	-	8.80	57.90	3.72	m	61.62
average depth of trench 2.50 m	-	10.56	69.48	4.34	m	73.82
average depth of trench 2.75 m	-	11.61	76.39	4.80	m	81.19
average depth of trench 3.00 m	-	12.65	83.24	5.27	m	88.51
average depth of trench 3.25 m	-	13.70	90.15	5.74	m	95.89
average depth of trench 3.50 m	-	14.74	96.99	6.20	m	103.19
Pipes exceeding 200 mm nominal size; 225 mm nominal size						
average depth of trench 0.50 m	-	1.10	7.24	-	m	7.24
average depth of trench 0.75 m	-	1.65	10.86	-	m	10.86
average depth of trench 1.00 m	-	2.42	15.92	1.24	m	17.16
average depth of trench 1.25 m	-	3.41	22.44	1.71	m	24.15
average depth of trench 1.50 m	-	4.68	30.79	2.08	m	32.87
average depth of trench 1.75 m	-	6.16	40.53	2.48	m	43.01
average depth of trench 2.00 m	-	7.04	46.32	2.79	m	49.11
average depth of trench 2.25 m	-	8.80	57.90	3.72	m	61.62
average depth of trench 2.50 m	-	10.56	69.48	4.34	m	73.82
average depth of trench 2.75 m	-	11.61	76.39	4.80	m	81.19
average depth of trench 3.00 m	-	12.65	83.24	5.27	m	88.51
average depth of trench 3.25 m	-	13.70	90.15	5.74	m	95.89
average depth of trench 3.50 m	-	14.74	96.99	6.20	m	103.19
Pipes exceeding 200 mm nominal size; 300 mm nominal size						
average depth of trench 0.75 m	-	1.93	12.70	-	m	12.70
average depth of trench 1.00 m	-	2.81	18.49	1.24	m	19.73
average depth of trench 1.25 m	-	3.96	26.06	1.71	m	27.77
average depth of trench 1.50 m	-	5.28	34.74	2.08	m	36.82
average depth of trench 1.75 m	-	6.16	40.53	2.48	m	43.01
average depth of trench 2.00 m	-	7.04	46.32	2.79	m	49.11
average depth of trench 2.25 m	-	8.80	57.90	3.72	m	61.62
average depth of trench 2.50 m	-	10.56	69.48	4.34	m	73.82
average depth of trench 2.75 m	-	11.61	76.39	4.80	m	81.19
average depth of trench 3.00 m	-	12.65	83.24	5.27	m	88.51
average depth of trench 3.25 m	-	13.70	90.15	5.74	m	95.89
average depth of trench 3.50 m	-	14.74	96.99	6.20	m	103.19

R DISPOSAL SYSTEMS Excluding overheads and profit	PC £	Labour hours	Labour £	Material £	Unit	Total rate £
R12 DRAINAGE BELOW GROUND - cont'd						
Excavating trenches; by hand; grading bottoms; **earthwork support; filling with excavated material** **and compacting; disposal of surplus soil on site;** **spreading on site average 50 m** - cont'd						
Extra over excavating trenches; irrespective of depth; breaking out existing materials						
brick	-	3.30	21.71	5.22	m³	26.93
concrete	-	4.95	32.57	8.70	m³	41.27
reinforced concrete	-	6.60	43.43	12.18	m³	55.61
Extra over excavating trenches; irrespective of depth; breaking out existing hard pavings; 75 mm thick						
tarmacadam	-	0.44	2.90	0.70	m²	3.60
Extra over excavating trenches; irrespective of depth; breaking out existing hard pavings; 150 mm thick						
concrete	-	0.77	5.07	1.22	m²	6.29
tarmacadam and hardcore	-	0.55	3.62	0.87	m²	4.49
Sand filling						
Beds; to receive pitch fibre pipes						
600 mm x 50 mm thick	-	0.09	0.59	0.72	m	1.31
700 mm x 50 mm thick	-	0.11	0.72	0.84	m	1.56
800 mm x 50 mm thick	-	0.13	0.86	0.96	m	1.82
Granular (shingle) filling						
Beds; 100 mm thick; to pipes						
100 mm nominal size	-	0.11	0.72	1.78	m	2.50
150 mm nominal size	-	0.11	0.72	2.08	m	2.80
225 mm nominal size	-	0.13	0.86	2.38	m	3.24
300 mm nominal size	-	0.15	0.99	2.67	m	3.66
Beds; 150 mm thick; to pipes						
100 mm nominal size	-	0.15	0.99	2.67	m	3.66
150 mm nominal size	-	0.18	1.18	2.97	m	4.15
225 mm nominal size	-	0.20	1.32	3.27	m	4.59
300 mm nominal size	-	0.22	1.45	3.56	m	5.01
Beds and benchings; beds 100 mm thick; to pipes						
100 mm nominal size	-	0.25	1.65	3.27	m	4.92
150 mm nominal size	-	0.28	1.84	3.27	m	5.11
225 mm nominal size	-	0.33	2.17	4.46	m	6.63
300 mm nominal size	-	0.39	2.57	5.05	m	7.62
Beds and benchings; beds 150 mm thick; to pipes						
100 mm nominal size	-	0.28	1.84	3.56	m	5.40
150 mm nominal size	-	0.31	2.04	3.86	m	5.90
225 mm nominal size	-	0.39	2.57	5.35	m	7.92
300 mm nominal size	-	0.49	3.22	6.53	m	9.75
Beds and coverings; 100 mm thick; to pipes						
100 mm nominal size	-	0.40	2.63	4.46	m	7.09
150 mm nominal size	-	0.49	3.22	5.35	m	8.57
225 mm nominal size	-	0.66	4.34	7.42	m	11.76
300 mm nominal size	-	0.79	5.20	8.91	m	14.11
Beds and coverings; 150 mm thick; to pipes						
100 mm nominal size	-	0.59	3.88	6.53	m	10.41
150 mm nominal size	-	0.66	4.34	7.42	m	11.76
225 mm nominal size	-	0.86	5.66	9.50	m	15.16
300 mm nominal size	-	1.02	6.71	11.29	m	18.00
Plain in situ ready mixed designated concrete; **C10 - 40 mm aggregate**						
Beds; 100 mm thick; to pipes						
100 mm nominal size	-	0.23	1.67	3.27	m	4.94
150 mm nominal size	-	0.23	1.67	3.27	m	4.94

R DISPOSAL SYSTEMS Excluding overheads and profit	PC £	Labour hours	Labour £	Material £	Unit	Total rate £
Beds; 100 mm thick; to pipes - cont'd						
225 mm nominal size	-	0.28	2.04	3.92	m	5.96
300 mm nominal size	-	0.31	2.25	4.58	m	6.83
Beds; 150 mm thick; to pipes						
100 mm nominal size	-	0.31	2.25	4.58	m	6.83
150 mm nominal size	-	0.36	2.62	5.23	m	7.85
225 mm nominal size	-	0.40	2.91	5.89	m	8.80
300 mm nominal size	-	0.45	3.27	6.54	m	9.81
Beds and benchings; beds 100 mm thick; to pipes						
100 mm nominal size	-	0.45	3.27	5.89	m	9.16
150 mm nominal size	-	0.51	3.71	6.54	m	10.25
225 mm nominal size	-	0.61	4.43	7.85	m	12.28
300 mm nominal size	-	0.71	5.16	9.16	m	14.32
Beds and benchings; beds 150 mm thick; to pipes						
100 mm nominal size	-	0.51	3.71	6.54	m	10.25
150 mm nominal size	-	0.56	4.07	7.19	m	11.26
225 mm nominal size	-	0.71	5.16	9.16	m	14.32
300 mm nominal size	-	0.91	6.62	11.77	m	18.39
Beds and coverings; 100 mm thick; to pipes						
100 mm nominal size	-	0.68	4.94	7.85	m	12.79
150 mm nominal size	-	0.79	5.74	9.16	m	14.90
225 mm nominal size	-	1.13	8.22	13.08	m	21.30
300 mm nominal size	-	1.35	9.81	15.70	m	25.51
Beds and coverings; 150 mm thick; to pipes						
100 mm nominal size	-	1.01	7.34	11.77	m	19.11
150 mm nominal size	-	1.13	8.22	13.08	m	21.30
225 mm nominal size	-	1.46	10.61	17.01	m	27.62
300 mm nominal size	-	1.75	12.72	20.28	m	33.00
Plain in situ ready mixed designated concrete; **C20 - 40 mm aggregate**						
Beds 100 mm thick; to pipes						
100 mm nominal size	-	0.23	1.67	3.42	m	5.09
150 mm nominal size	-	0.23	1.67	3.42	m	5.09
225 mm nominal size	-	0.28	2.04	4.11	m	6.15
300 mm nominal size	-	0.31	2.25	4.79	m	7.04
Beds; 150 mm thick; to pipes						
100 mm nominal size	-	0.31	2.25	4.79	m	7.04
150 mm nominal size	-	0.36	2.62	5.47	m	8.09
225 mm nominal size	-	0.40	2.91	6.16	m	9.07
300 mm nominal size	-	0.45	3.27	6.84	m	10.11
Beds and benchings; beds 100 mm thick; to pipes						
100 mm nominal size	-	0.45	3.27	6.16	m	9.43
150 mm nominal size	-	0.51	3.71	6.84	m	10.55
225 mm nominal size	-	0.61	4.43	8.21	m	12.64
300 mm nominal size	-	0.71	5.16	9.58	m	14.74
Beds and benchings; beds 150 mm thick; to pipes						
100 mm nominal size	-	0.51	3.71	6.84	m	10.55
150 mm nominal size	-	0.56	4.07	7.52	m	11.59
225 mm nominal size	-	0.71	5.16	9.58	m	14.74
300 mm nominal size	-	0.91	6.62	12.32	m	18.94
Beds and coverings; 100 mm thick; to pipes						
100 mm nominal size	-	0.68	4.94	8.21	m	13.15
150 mm nominal size	-	0.79	5.74	9.58	m	15.32
225 mm nominal size	-	1.13	8.22	13.69	m	21.91
300 mm nominal size	-	1.35	9.81	16.42	m	26.23
Beds and coverings; 150 mm thick; to pipes						
100 mm nominal size	-	1.01	7.34	12.32	m	19.66
150 mm nominal size	-	1.13	8.22	13.69	m	21.91
225 mm nominal size	-	1.46	10.61	17.79	m	28.40
300 mm nominal size	-	1.75	12.72	21.21	m	33.93

R DISPOSAL SYSTEMS Excluding overheads and profit	PC £	Labour hours	Labour £	Material £	Unit	Total rate £
R12 DRAINAGE BELOW GROUND - cont'd						
NOTE: The following items unless otherwise described include for all appropriate joints/ couplings in the running length. The prices for gullies and rainwater shoes, etc. include for appropriate joints to pipes and for setting on and surrounding accessory with site mixed in situ concrete 10.00 N/mm^2 - 40 mm aggregate (1:3:6)						
Cast iron "Timesaver" drain pipes and fittings or other equal and approved; BS 437; coated; with mechanical coupling joints						
75 mm pipes; laid straight	19.28	0.52	3.35	23.96	m	27.31
75 mm pipes; in runs not exceeding 3.00 m long	18.72	0.69	4.45	30.57	m	35.02
Extra for						
bend; medium radius	19.12	0.57	3.68	27.48	nr	31.16
single branch	26.58	0.80	5.16	44.02	nr	49.18
isolated "Timesaver" joint	10.65	0.35	2.26	10.92	nr	13.18
100 mm pipes; laid straight	20.02	0.57	3.68	25.48	m	29.16
100 mm pipes; in runs not exceeding 3.00 m long	19.32	0.78	5.03	33.40	m	38.43
Extra for						
bend; medium radius	23.95	0.69	4.45	34.52	nr	38.97
bend; medium radius with access	62.91	0.69	4.45	74.45	nr	78.90
bend; long radius	33.47	0.69	4.45	43.22	nr	47.67
rest bend	27.48	0.69	4.45	37.08	nr	41.53
diminishing pipe	20.03	0.69	4.45	29.45	nr	33.90
single branch	31.78	0.86	5.55	53.67	nr	59.22
single branch; with access	73.29	0.98	6.32	96.21	nr	102.53
double branch	47.87	1.09	7.03	81.60	nr	88.63
double branch; with access	86.98	1.09	7.03	121.68	nr	128.71
isolated "Timesaver" joint	12.80	0.40	2.58	13.12	nr	15.70
transitional pipe; for WC	18.23	0.57	3.68	31.81	nr	35.49
150 mm pipes; laid straight	37.71	0.69	4.45	44.99	m	49.44
150 mm pipes; in runs not exceeding 3.00 m long	36.00	0.94	6.06	53.69	m	59.75
Extra for						
bend; medium radius	55.10	0.80	5.16	66.43	nr	71.59
bend; medium radius with access	116.84	0.80	5.16	129.71	nr	134.87
bend; long radius	71.72	0.80	5.16	81.48	nr	86.64
diminishing pipe	31.22	0.80	5.16	39.97	nr	45.13
single branch	78.39	0.98	6.32	81.59	nr	87.91
isolated "Timesaver" joint	15.50	0.48	3.10	15.89	nr	18.99
Accessories in "Timesaver" cast iron or other equal and approved; with mechanical coupling joints						
Gully fittings; comprising low invert gully trap and round hopper						
75 mm outlet	20.03	1.03	6.64	34.87	nr	41.51
100 mm outlet	31.78	1.09	7.03	49.12	nr	56.15
150 mm outlet	79.07	1.49	9.61	101.04	nr	110.65
Add to above for; bellmouth 300 mm high; circular plain grating						
100 mm nominal size; 200 mm grating	32.55	0.52	3.35	50.32	nr	53.67
100 mm nominal size; 100 mm horizontal inlet; 200 mm grating	40.45	0.52	3.35	58.41	nr	61.76
100 mm nominal size; 100 mm horizontal inlet; 200 mm grating	41.49	0.52	3.35	59.48	nr	62.83
Yard gully (Deans); trapped; galvanized sediment pan; 267 mm round heavy grating						
100 mm outlet	214.75	3.33	21.48	253.23	nr	274.71

R DISPOSAL SYSTEMS Excluding overheads and profit	PC £	Labour hours	Labour £	Material £	Unit	Total rate £
Yard gully (garage); trapless; galvanized sediment pan; 267 mm round heavy grating						
100 mm outlet	219.05	3.11	20.06	241.75	nr	261.81
Yard gully (garage); trapped; with rodding eye, galvanised perforated sediment pan; stopper; 267 mm round heavy grating						
100 mm outlet	407.40	3.11	20.06	475.34	nr	495.40
Grease trap; internal access; galvanized perforated bucket; lid and frame						
100 mm outlet; 20 gallon capacity	373.26	4.60	29.67	419.10	nr	448.77
Cast iron "Ensign" lightweight pipes and fittings **or other equal and approved; EN 877; ductile** **iron couplings**						
100 mm pipes; laid straight	-	0.20	1.63	18.64	m	20.27
Extra for						
bend; long radius	-	0.20	1.63	31.52	nr	33.15
single branch	-	0.25	2.06	31.85	nr	33.91
150 mm pipes; laid straight	-	0.24	1.96	36.95	m	38.91
Extra for						
bend; long radius	-	0.24	1.96	77.81	nr	79.77
single branch	-	0.30	2.45	70.08	nr	72.53
Extra strength vitrified clay pipes and fittings; **Hepworth "Supersleve" or other equal and** **approved; plain ends with push fit** **polypropylene flexible couplings**						
100 mm pipes; laid straight	5.01	0.23	1.48	5.26	m	6.74
Extra for						
bend	4.73	0.23	1.48	8.97	nr	10.45
access bend	31.15	0.23	1.48	36.71	nr	38.19
rest bend	10.68	0.23	1.48	15.21	nr	16.69
access pipe	27.06	0.23	1.48	32.05	nr	33.53
socket adaptor	5.01	0.20	1.29	7.44	nr	8.73
adaptor to "HepSeal" pipe	4.87	0.20	1.29	7.30	nr	8.59
saddle	10.03	0.86	5.55	13.08	nr	18.63
single junction	10.23	0.29	1.87	16.93	nr	18.80
single access junction	36.03	0.29	1.87	44.02	nr	45.89
150 mm pipes; laid straight	9.59	0.29	1.87	10.07	m	11.94
Extra for						
bend	9.74	0.28	1.81	17.21	nr	19.02
access bend	2.43	0.28	1.81	46.07	nr	47.88
rest bend	12.53	0.28	1.81	20.14	nr	21.95
taper pipe	14.28	0.28	1.81	19.92	nr	21.73
access pipe	35.15	0.28	1.81	43.15	nr	44.96
socket adaptor	9.45	0.23	1.48	13.79	nr	15.27
adaptor to "HepSeal" pipe	6.72	0.23	1.48	10.92	nr	12.40
saddle	14.28	1.03	6.64	19.60	nr	26.24
single junction	14.32	0.35	2.26	25.89	nr	28.15
single access junction	51.18	0.35	2.26	64.59	nr	66.85
Extra strength vitrified clay pipes and fittings; **Hepworth "HepSeal" or other equal and approved;** **socketed; with push-fit flexible joints**						
100 mm pipes; laid straight	8.73	0.31	2.00	9.17	m	11.17
Extra for						
bend	12.62	0.25	1.61	10.50	nr	12.11
rest bend	14.99	0.25	1.61	12.99	nr	14.60
stopper	4.75	0.16	1.03	4.99	nr	6.02
access pipe	26.38	0.28	1.81	24.03	nr	25.84
single junction	17.51	0.31	2.00	14.72	nr	16.72
double collar	11.22	0.21	1.35	11.78	nr	13.13

R DISPOSAL SYSTEMS Excluding overheads and profit	PC £	Labour hours	Labour £	Material £	Unit	Total rate £
R12 DRAINAGE BELOW GROUND - cont'd						
Extra strength vitrified clay pipes and fittings; Hepworth "HepSeal" or other equal and approved; socketed; with push-fit flexible joints - cont'd						
150 mm pipes; laid straight	11.33	0.37	2.39	11.90	m	**14.29**
Extra for						
bend	20.80	0.29	1.87	18.27	nr	**20.14**
rest bend	24.82	0.25	1.61	22.49	nr	**24.10**
stopper	7.09	0.18	1.16	7.44	nr	**8.60**
taper reducer	31.17	0.29	1.87	29.16	nr	**31.03**
access pipe	41.37	0.29	1.87	38.68	nr	**40.55**
saddle	10.91	0.93	6.00	11.46	nr	**17.46**
single junction	11.33	0.37	2.39	23.76	nr	**26.15**
single access junction	54.78	0.37	2.39	53.85	nr	**56.24**
double junction	54.02	0.55	3.55	50.77	nr	**54.32**
double collar	18.52	0.24	1.55	19.45	nr	**21.00**
225 mm pipes; laid straight	21.91	0.47	3.03	23.01	m	**26.04**
Extra for						
bend	42.43	0.37	2.39	37.65	nr	**40.04**
rest bend	59.11	0.37	2.39	55.16	nr	**57.55**
stopper	15.28	0.24	1.55	16.04	nr	**17.59**
taper reducer	47.94	0.37	2.39	43.44	nr	**45.83**
access pipe	104.73	0.37	2.39	100.76	nr	**103.15**
saddle	19.79	1.24	8.00	20.78	nr	**28.78**
single junction	63.80	0.47	3.03	57.79	nr	**60.82**
single access junction	125.23	0.47	3.03	122.29	nr	**125.32**
double junction	121.09	0.70	4.51	115.64	nr	**120.15**
double collar	40.46	0.31	2.00	42.48	nr	**44.48**
300 mm pipes; laid straight	34.25	0.62	4.00	35.96	m	**39.96**
Extra for						
bend	83.72	0.49	3.16	77.12	nr	**80.28**
rest bend	127.72	0.49	3.16	123.32	nr	**126.48**
stopper	34.31	0.31	2.00	36.03	nr	**38.03**
taper reducer	100.37	0.49	3.16	94.60	nr	**97.76**
saddle	98.04	1.66	10.71	102.94	nr	**113.65**
single junction	131.54	0.62	4.00	123.73	nr	**127.73**
double junction	257.10	0.93	6.00	251.97	nr	**257.97**
double collar	65.77	0.41	2.64	69.06	nr	**71.70**
400 mm pipes; laid straight	70.31	0.83	5.35	73.83	m	**79.18**
Extra for						
bend	264.18	0.67	4.32	255.24	nr	**259.56**
single unequal junction	247.52	0.83	5.35	230.37	nr	**235.72**
450 mm pipes; laid straight	91.32	1.03	6.64	95.89	m	**102.53**
Extra for						
bend	347.86	0.83	5.35	336.49	nr	**341.84**
single unequal junction	296.11	1.03	6.64	272.56	nr	**279.20**
British Standard quality vitrified clay pipes and fittings; socketed; cement:sand (1:2) joints						
100 mm pipes; laid straight	6.10	0.46	2.97	6.50	m	**9.47**
Extra for						
bend (short/medium/knuckle)	12.21	0.37	2.39	4.58	nr	**6.97**
bend (long/rest/elbow)	10.03	0.37	2.39	8.71	nr	**11.10**
single junction	11.21	0.46	2.97	9.33	nr	**12.30**
double junction	19.47	0.69	4.45	17.38	nr	**21.83**
double collar	7.36	0.31	2.00	7.82	nr	**9.82**

R DISPOSAL SYSTEMS Excluding overheads and profit	PC £	Labour hours	Labour £	Material £	Unit	Total rate £
150 mm pipes; laid straight	9.40	0.52	3.35	9.96	m	13.31
Extra for						
bend (short/medium/knuckle)	9.17	0.41	2.64	6.76	nr	9.40
bend (long/rest/elbow)	16.96	0.41	2.64	14.94	nr	17.58
taper	22.16	0.41	2.64	20.11	nr	22.75
single junction	18.56	0.52	3.35	15.66	nr	19.01
double junction	44.89	0.78	5.03	42.34	nr	47.37
double collar	12.26	0.35	2.26	12.97	nr	15.23
225 mm pipes; laid straight	18.61	0.63	4.06	19.77	m	23.83
Extra for						
bend (short/medium/knuckle)	28.73	0.51	3.29	24.42	nr	27.71
taper	46.79	0.41	2.64	42.80	nr	45.44
double collar	28.69	0.41	2.64	30.22	nr	32.86
300 mm pipes; laid straight	31.20	0.86	5.55	32.99	m	38.54
Extra for						
bend (short/medium/knuckle)	52.22	0.69	4.45	45.12	nr	49.57
double collar	56.86	0.46	2.97	59.87	nr	62.84
400 mm pipes; laid straight	60.14	1.15	7.42	63.47	m	70.89
450 mm pipes; laid straight	76.15	1.44	9.29	80.28	m	89.57
500 mm pipes; laid straight	95.23	1.67	10.77	100.34	m	111.11
Accessories in vitrified clay; set in concrete; with polypropylene coupling joints to pipes						
Rodding point; with oval aluminium plate						
100 mm nominal size	24.33	0.57	3.68	29.41	nr	33.09
Gully fittings; comprising low back trap and square hopper; 150 mm x 150 mm square gully grid						
100 mm nominal size	26.06	0.98	6.32	33.78	nr	40.10
Access gully; trapped with rodding eye and integral vertical back inlet; stopper; 150 mm x 150 mm square gully grid						
100 mm nominal size	33.95	0.75	4.84	39.51	nr	44.35
Inspection chamber; comprising base; 300 mm or 450 mm raising piece; integral alloy cover and frame; 100 mm inlets						
straight through; 2 nr inlets	98.76	2.30	14.84	108.87	nr	123.71
single junction; 3 nr inlets	106.56	2.53	16.32	119.61	nr	135.93
double junction; 4 nr inlets	115.63	2.76	17.80	131.68	nr	149.48
Accessories in polypropylene; cover set in concrete; with coupling joints to pipes						
Inspection chamber; 5 nr 100 mm inlets; cast iron cover and frame						
475 mm diameter x 585 mm deep	149.61	2.64	17.03	162.99	nr	180.02
475 mm diameter x 930 mm deep	174.43	2.88	18.58	189.04	nr	207.62
Accessories in vitrified clay; set in concrete; with cement:sand (1:2) joints to pipes						
Gully fittings; comprising low back trap and square hopper; square gully grid						
100 mm outlet; 150 mm x 150 mm grid	33.86	1.15	7.42	35.88	nr	43.30
150 mm outlet; 225 mm x 225 mm grid	61.23	1.15	7.42	64.62	nr	72.04
Yard gully (mud); trapped with rodding eye; galvanized square bucket; stopper; square hinged grate and frame						
100 mm outlet; 225 mm x 225 mm grid	87.05	3.45	22.25	91.79	nr	114.04
150 mm outlet; 300 mm x 300 mm grid	156.32	4.60	29.67	164.87	nr	194.54

R DISPOSAL SYSTEMS Excluding overheads and profit	PC £	Labour hours	Labour £	Material £	Unit	Total rate £
R12 DRAINAGE BELOW GROUND - cont'd						
Accessories in vitrified clay; set in concrete;						
with cement:sand (1:2) joints to pipes - cont'd						
Yard gully (garage); trapped with rodding eye;						
galvanized perforated round bucket; stopper;						
round hinged grate and frame						
100 mm outlet; 273 mm grid	87.06	3.45	22.25	116.57	nr	**138.82**
150 mm outlet; 368 mm grid	162.47	4.60	29.67	170.99	nr	**200.66**
Road gully; trapped with rodding eye and						
stopper (grate not included)						
300 mm x 600 mm x 100 mm outlet	60.55	3.79	24.45	78.72	nr	**103.17**
300 mm x 600 mm x 150 mm outlet	62.00	3.79	24.45	80.24	nr	**104.69**
400 mm x 750 mm x 150 mm outlet	71.91	4.60	29.67	98.49	nr	**128.16**
450 mm x 900 mm x 150 mm outlet	97.30	5.75	37.09	129.73	nr	**166.82**
Grease trap; with internal access; galvanized						
perforated bucket; lid and frame						
450 mm x 300 mm x 525 mm deep; 100 mm						
outlet	449.38	4.03	25.99	488.53	nr	**514.52**
600 mm x 450 mm x 600 mm deep; 100 mm						
outlet	570.35	4.83	31.15	621.48	nr	**652.63**
Interceptor; trapped with inspection arm; lever						
locking stopper; chain and staple; cement:						
sand (1:2) joints to pipes; building in, and						
cutting and fitting brickwork around						
100 mm outlet; 100 mm inlet	76.54	4.60	29.67	80.77	nr	**110.44**
150 mm outlet; 150 mm inlet	108.55	5.17	33.35	114.38	nr	**147.73**
225 mm outlet; 225 mm inlet	293.49	5.75	37.09	308.63	nr	**345.72**
Accessories; grates and covers						
Aluminium alloy gully grids; set in position						
120 mm x 120 mm	2.76	0.12	0.77	2.90	nr	**3.67**
150 mm x 150 mm	2.76	0.12	0.77	2.90	nr	**3.67**
225 mm x 225 mm	8.20	0.12	0.77	8.61	nr	**9.38**
100 mm diameter	2.76	0.12	0.77	2.90	nr	**3.67**
150 mm diameter	4.21	0.12	0.77	4.42	nr	**5.19**
225 mm diameter	9.17	0.12	0.77	9.63	nr	**10.40**
Aluminium alloy sealing plates and frames; set						
in cement:sand (1:3)						
150 mm x 150 mm	10.58	0.29	1.87	11.20	nr	**13.07**
225 mm x 225 mm	19.37	0.29	1.87	20.43	nr	**22.30**
140 mm diameter (for 100 mm)	8.63	0.29	1.87	9.15	nr	**11.02**
197 mm diameter (for 150 mm)	12.40	0.29	1.87	13.11	nr	**14.98**
273 mm diameter (for 225 mm)	19.85	0.29	1.87	20.93	nr	**22.80**
Coated cast iron heavy duty road gratings and						
frame; BS 497 Tables 6 and 7; bedding and						
pointing in cement:sand (1:3); one course						
half brick thick wall in semi-engineering bricks						
in cement mortar (1:3)						
445 mm x 400 mm; Grade A1, ref GA1-450 (90						
kg)	100.50	2.88	18.58	105.19	nr	**123.77**
400 mm x 310 mm; Grade A2, ref GA2-325 (35						
kg)	77.00	2.88	18.58	81.10	nr	**99.68**
500 mm x 310 mm; Grade A2, ref GA2-325 (65						
kg)	105.00	2.88	18.58	109.80	nr	**128.38**

R DISPOSAL SYSTEMS Excluding overheads and profit	PC £	Labour hours	Labour £	Material £	Unit	Total rate £
Accessories in precast concrete; top set in **with rodding eye and stopper; cement:** **sand (1:2) joint to pipe** Concrete road gully; BS 5911; trapped with rodding eye and stopper; cement:sand (1:2) joint to pipe						
450 mm diameter x 1050 mm deep; 100 mm or 150 mm outlet	31.50	5.46	35.22	48.98	nr	84.20
"Osmadrain" uPVC pipes and fittings or other equal **and approved; BS 4660; with ring seal joints**						
82 mm pipes; laid straight	6.31	0.18	1.16	6.63	m	7.79
Extra for						
bend; short radius	11.02	0.15	0.97	11.30	nr	12.27
spigot/socket bend	9.05	0.15	0.97	9.28	nr	10.25
adaptor	4.83	0.09	0.58	4.95	nr	5.53
single junction	14.00	0.21	1.35	14.35	nr	15.70
slip coupler	6.65	0.09	0.58	6.82	nr	7.40
100 mm pipes; laid straight	5.80	0.20	1.29	6.75	m	8.04
Extra for						
bend; short radius	14.22	0.18	1.16	14.21	nr	15.37
bend; long radius	23.02	0.18	1.16	21.77	nr	22.93
spigot/socket bend	12.01	0.18	1.16	15.40	nr	16.56
socket plug	5.75	0.06	0.39	5.89	nr	6.28
adjustable double socket bend	15.41	0.18	1.16	18.58	nr	19.74
adaptor to clay	12.29	0.11	0.71	12.33	nr	13.04
single junction	16.96	0.25	1.61	15.56	nr	17.17
sealed access junction	31.07	0.22	1.42	30.02	nr	31.44
slip coupler	6.65	0.11	0.71	6.82	nr	7.53
160 mm pipes; laid straight	12.82	0.25	1.61	14.68	m	16.29
Extra for						
bend; short radius	31.51	0.21	1.35	31.49	nr	32.84
spigot/socket bend	28.57	0.21	1.35	34.84	nr	36.19
socket plug	10.32	0.09	0.58	10.58	nr	11.16
adaptor to clay	24.87	0.14	0.90	24.78	nr	25.68
level invert taper	16.52	0.21	1.35	21.69	nr	23.04
single junction	51.59	0.29	1.87	52.88	nr	54.75
sealed access junction	81.66	0.26	1.68	83.70	nr	85.38
slip coupler	18.60	0.13	0.84	19.07	nr	19.91
uPVC Osma "Ultra-Rib" ribbed pipes and **fittings or other equal and approved; WIS** **approval; with sealed ring push-fit joints**						
150 mm pipes; laid straight	-	0.23	1.48	5.78	m	7.26
Extra for						
bend; short radius	16.82	0.20	1.29	16.89	nr	18.18
adaptor to 160 diameter upvc	19.75	0.12	0.77	19.55	nr	20.32
adaptor to clay	40.56	0.12	0.77	41.23	nr	42.00
level invert taper	7.37	0.21	1.35	6.51	nr	7.86
single junction	30.36	0.26	1.68	29.38	nr	31.06
225 mm pipes; laid straight	12.65	0.26	1.68	13.28	m	14.96
Extra for						
bend; short radius	60.75	0.24	1.55	61.47	nr	63.02
adaptor to clay	50.54	0.15	0.97	50.21	nr	51.18
level invert taper	10.59	0.24	1.55	8.46	nr	10.01
single junction	90.36	0.32	2.06	88.64	nr	90.70
300 mm pipes; laid straight	18.96	0.39	2.52	19.91	m	22.43
Extra for						
bend; short radius	95.79	0.34	2.19	96.99	nr	99.18
adaptor to clay	132.92	0.17	1.10	133.85	nr	134.95
level invert taper	31.72	0.34	2.19	28.93	nr	31.12
single junction	192.57	0.44	2.84	191.41	nr	194.25

R DISPOSAL SYSTEMS Excluding overheads and profit	PC £	Labour hours	Labour £	Material £	Unit	Total rate £
R12 DRAINAGE BELOW GROUND - cont'd						
Interconnecting drainage channel; ACO						
Polymer Products Ltd or other equal and						
approved; reinforced slotted galvanised steel						
grating ref 423/4; bedding and haunching in						
in situ concrete (not included)						
100 mm wide						
laid level or to falls	-	0.55	3.55	49.19	m	**52.74**
extra for sump unit	-	1.65	10.64	112.36	nr	**123.00**
extra for end caps	-	0.11	0.71	5.50	nr	**6.21**
Interconnecting drainage channel; "Birco-lite"						
ref 8012 or other equal and approved; Marshalls						
Plc; galvanised steel grating ref 8041 or other						
wqual and approved; bedding and haunching in						
in situ concrete (not included)						
100 mm wide						
laid level or to falls	-	0.55	3.55	48.80	m	**52.35**
extra for 100 mm diameter trapped outlet unit	-	1.65	10.64	80.76	nr	**91.40**
extra for end caps	-	0.11	0.71	4.65	nr	**5.36**
Accessories in uPVC; with ring seal joints to						
pipes (unless otherwise described)						
Cast iron access point						
110 mm diameter	27.26	0.89	5.74	27.94	nr	**33.68**
Rodding eye						
110 mm diameter	35.56	0.51	3.29	39.72	nr	**43.01**
Universal gulley fitting; comprising gulley trap,						
plain hopper						
150 mm x 150 mm grate	20.84	1.10	7.09	25.94	nr	**33.03**
Bottle gulley; comprising gulley with bosses						
closed; sealed access covers						
217 mm x 217 mm grate	35.52	0.92	5.93	40.99	nr	**46.92**
Shallow access pipe; light duty screw down						
access door assembly						
110 mm diameter	22.61	0.92	5.93	27.77	nr	**33.70**
Shallow access junction; 3 nr 110 mm inlets;						
light duty screw down access door assembly						
110 mm diameter	44.60	1.32	8.51	56.36	nr	**64.87**
Shallow inspection chamber; 250 mm						
diameter; 600 mm deep; sealed cover and						
frame						
4 nr 110 mm outlets/inlets	75.12	1.52	9.80	93.35	nr	**103.15**
Universal inspection chamber; 450 mm						
diameter; single seal cast iron cover and frame;						
4 nr 110 mm outlets/inlets						
500 mm deep	127.29	1.61	10.38	146.82	nr	**157.20**
730 mm deep	127.29	1.90	12.26	168.19	nr	**180.45**
960 mm deep	127.29	2.20	14.19	189.55	nr	**203.74**
Equal manhole base; 750 mm diameter						
6 nr 160 mm outlets/inlets	148.55	1.44	9.29	162.08	nr	**171.37**
Unequal manhole base; 750 mm diameter						
2 nr 160 mm, 4 nr 110 mm outlets/inlets	138.21	1.44	9.29	151.48	nr	**160.77**
Kerb to gullies; class B engineering bricks on						
edge to three sides in cement mortar (1:3)						
rendering in cement mortar (1:3) to top and two						
sides and skirting to brickwork 230 mm high;						
dishing in cement mortar (1:3) to gully; steel						
trowelled						
230 mm x 230 mm internally	-	1.65	10.64	1.21	nr	**11.85**

R DISPOSAL SYSTEMS Excluding overheads and profit	PC £	Labour hours	Labour £	Material £	Unit	Total rate £
Excavating; by machine						
Manholes						
maximum depth not exceeding 1.00 m	-	0.24	1.58	4.40	m³	**5.98**
maximum depth not exceeding 2.00 m	-	0.26	1.71	4.82	m³	**6.53**
maximum depth not exceeding 4.00 m	-	0.31	2.04	5.66	m³	**7.70**
Excavating; by hand						
Manholes						
maximum depth not exceeding 1.00 m	-	3.80	25.00	-	m³	**25.00**
maximum depth not exceeding 2.00 m	-	4.50	29.61	-	m³	**29.61**
maximum depth not exceeding 4.00 m	-	5.75	37.84	-	m³	**37.84**
Earthwork support (average "risk" prices)						
Maximum depth not exceeding 1.00 m						
distance between opposing faces not exceeding 2.00 m	-	0.17	1.12	3.19	m²	**4.31**
Maximum depth not exceeding 2.00 m						
distance between opposing faces not exceeding 2.00 m	-	0.21	1.38	6.07	m²	**7.45**
Maximum depth not exceeding 4.00 m						
distance between opposing faces not exceeding 2.00 m	-	0.26	1.71	8.95	m²	**10.66**
Disposal; by machine						
Excavated material						
off site; to tip not exceeding 13 km (using lorries) including Landfill Tax based on inactive waste	-	-	-	15.75	m³	**15.75**
on site; depositing in spoil heaps; average 50 m distance	-	0.17	1.12	2.86	m³	**3.98**
Disposal; by hand						
Excavated material						
off site; to tip not exceeding 13 km (using lorries) including Landfill Tax based on inactive waste	-	0.88	5.79	24.00	m³	**29.79**
on site; depositing in spoil heaps; average 50 m distance	-	1.43	9.41	-	m³	**9.41**
Filling to excavations; by machine						
Average thickness not exceeding 0.25 m						
arising from the excavations	-	0.17	1.12	2.09	m³	**3.21**
Filling to excavations; by hand						
Average thickness not exceeding 0.25 m						
arising from the excavations	-	1.10	7.24	-	m³	**7.24**
Plain in situ ready mixed designated concrete; C10 - 40 mm aggregate						
Beds						
thickness not exceeding 150 mm	60.85	3.46	25.15	68.69	m³	**93.84**
thickness 150 mm - 450 mm	60.85	2.59	18.83	68.69	m³	**87.52**
thickness exceeding 450 mm	60.85	2.18	15.85	68.69	m³	**84.54**
Plain in situ ready mixed designated concrete; C20 - 20 mm aggregate						
Beds						
thickness not exceeding 150 mm	63.66	3.46	25.15	71.86	m³	**97.01**
thickness 150 mm - 450 mm	63.66	2.59	18.83	71.86	m³	**90.69**
thickness exceeding 450 mm	63.66	2.18	15.85	71.86	m³	**87.71**

R DISPOSAL SYSTEMS Excluding overheads and profit	PC £	Labour hours	Labour £	Material £	Unit	Total rate £
R12 DRAINAGE BELOW GROUND - cont'd						
Plain in situ ready mixed designated concrete; C25 - 20 mm aggregate (small quantities)						
Benching in bottoms						
150 mm - 450 mm average thickness	63.98	10.35	91.21	68.78	m³	**159.99**
Reinforced in situ ready mixed designated concrete; C20 - 20 mm aggregate; (small quantities)						
Isolated cover slabs						
thickness not exceeding 150 mm	63.66	8.05	58.52	68.43	m³	**126.95**
Reinforcement fabric to BS 4483; lapped; in beds or suspended slabs						
Ref A98 (1.54 kg/m²)						
400 mm minimum laps	0.66	0.14	1.25	0.73	m²	**1.98**
Ref A142 (2.22 kg/m²)						
400 mm minimum laps	0.77	0.14	1.25	0.85	m²	**2.10**
Ref A193 (3.02 kg/m²)						
400 mm minimum laps	1.10	0.14	1.25	1.21	m²	**2.46**
Formwork; basic finish						
Soffits of isolated cover slabs						
horizontal	-	3.28	36.74	6.85	m²	**43.59**
Edges of isolated cover slabs						
height not exceeding 250 mm	-	0.97	10.86	1.92	m	**12.78**
Precast concrete rectangular access and inspection chambers; "Hepworth" chambers or other equal and approved; comprising cover frame to receive manhole cover (not included) intermediate wall sections and base section with cut outs; bedding; jointing and pointing in cement mortar (1:3) on prepared bed						
Drainage chamber; size 600 mm x 450 mm internally; depth to invert						
600 mm deep	-	5.17	33.35	105.36	nr	**138.71**
900 mm deep	-	6.90	44.51	131.11	nr	**175.62**
Drainage chamber; 1200 mm x 750 mm reducing to 600 mm x 600 mm; no base unit; depth of invert						
1050 mm deep	-	8.63	55.66	188.19	nr	**243.85**
1650 mm deep	-	10.35	66.76	318.34	nr	**385.10**
2250 mm deep	-	12.65	81.59	447.81	nr	**529.40**
Common bricks; in cement mortar (1:3)						
Walls to manholes						
one brick thick	0.17	2.76	39.22	31.14	m²	**70.36**
one and a half brick thick	0.17	4.03	57.27	46.71	m²	**103.98**
Projections of footings						
two brick thick	0.17	5.64	80.14	62.27	m²	**142.41**
Class A engineering bricks; in cement mortar (1:3)						
Walls to manholes						
one brick thick	0.35	3.11	44.19	57.45	m²	**101.64**
one and a half brick thick	0.35	4.49	63.80	59.47	m²	**123.27**
Projections of footings						
two brick thick	0.35	6.32	89.81	114.90	m²	**204.71**
Class B engineering bricks; in cement mortar (1:3)						
Walls to manholes						
one brick thick	0.23	3.11	44.19	39.55	m²	**83.74**
one and a half brick thick	0.23	4.49	63.80	59.32	m²	**123.12**

R DISPOSAL SYSTEMS Excluding overheads and profit	PC £	Labour hours	Labour £	Material £	Unit	Total rate £
Projections of footings						
two brick thick	0.23	6.32	89.81	79.10	m²	**168.91**
Brickwork sundries						
Extra over for fair face; flush smooth pointing						
manhole walls	-	0.23	3.27	-	m²	**3.27**
Building ends of pipes into brickwork; making						
good fair face or rendering						
not exceeding 55 mm nominal size	-	0.12	1.71	-	nr	**1.71**
55 mm - 110 mm nominal size	-	0.17	2.42	-	nr	**2.42**
over 110 mm nominal size	-	0.23	3.27	-	nr	**3.27**
Step irons; BS 1247; malleable; galvanized;						
building into joints						
general purpose pattern	-	0.17	2.42	4.15	nr	**6.57**
Cement:sand (1:3) in situ finishings; steel						
trowelled						
13 mm work to manhole walls; one coat; to						
brickwork base over 300 mm wide	-	0.80	11.37	1.35	m²	**12.72**
Cast iron inspection chambers; with bolted						
flat covers; BS 437; bedded in cement mortar						
(1:3); with mechanical coupling joints						
100 mm x 100 mm						
one branch	99.71	1.20	7.74	116.00	nr	**123.74**
one branch either side	124.76	1.80	11.61	154.79	nr	**166.40**
150 mm x 100 mm						
one branch	158.69	1.45	9.35	163.33	nr	**172.68**
one branch either side	173.36	2.05	13.22	192.16	nr	**205.38**
150 mm x 150 mm						
one branch	182.43	1.55	10.00	204.23	nr	**214.23**
one branch either side	199.59	2.20	14.19	237.70	nr	**251.89**
Access covers and frames; Drainage						
Systems or other equal and approved;						
coated; bedding frame in cement:sand						
(1:3); cover in grease and sand						
Grade A; light duty; rectangular single seal solid top						
450 mm x 450 mm; ref MC1-45/45	48.95	1.75	11.29	51.57	nr	**62.86**
600 mm x 450 mm; ref MC1-60/45	49.25	1.75	11.29	52.00	nr	**63.29**
600 mm x 600 mm; ref MC1-60/60	104.65	1.75	11.29	108.90	nr	**120.19**
Grade A; light duty; rectangular single seal recessed						
600 mm x 450 mm; ref MC1R-60/45	100.40	1.75	11.29	104.42	nr	**115.71**
600 mm x 600 mm; ref MC1R-60/60	138.65	1.75	11.29	143.75	nr	**155.04**
Grade A; light duty; rectangular double seal solid top						
450 mm x 450 mm; ref MC2-45/45	75.30	1.75	11.29	78.58	nr	**89.87**
600 mm x 450 mm; ref MC2-60/45	98.65	1.75	11.29	102.63	nr	**113.92**
600 mm x 600 mm; ref MC2-60/60	139.10	1.75	11.29	144.21	nr	**155.50**
Grade A; light duty; rectangular double seal recessed						
450 mm x 450 mm; ref MC2R-45/45	125.10	1.75	11.29	129.62	nr	**140.91**
600 mm x 450 mm; ref MC2R-60/45	149.10	1.75	11.29	154.34	nr	**165.63**
600 mm x 600 mm; ref MC2R-60/60	167.60	1.75	11.29	173.42	nr	**184.71**
Grade B; medium duty; circular single seal solid top						
300 mm diameter; ref MB2-50	144.90	2.30	14.84	149.90	nr	**164.74**
550 mm diameter; ref MB2-55	110.70	2.30	14.84	114.84	nr	**129.68**
600 mm diameter; ref MB2-60	96.70	2.30	14.84	100.49	nr	**115.33**
Grade B; medium duty; rectangular single seal solid top						
600 mm x 450 mm; ref MB2-60/45	86.80	2.30	14.84	90.48	nr	**105.32**
600 mm x 600 mm; ref MB2-60/60	111.20	2.30	14.84	115.61	nr	**130.45**

R DISPOSAL SYSTEMS Excluding overheads and profit	PC £	Labour hours	Labour £	Material £	Unit	Total rate £
R12 DRAINAGE BELOW GROUND - cont'd						
Access covers and frames; Drainage Systems **or other equal and approved; coated; bedding** **frame in cement:sand (1:3); cover in grease and sand** - cont'd						
Grade B; medium duty; rectangular singular seal recessed						
600 mm x 450 mm; ref MB2R-60/45	148.10	2.30	14.84	153.32	nr	168.16
600 mm x 600 mm; ref MB2R-60/60	168.50	2.30	14.84	174.35	nr	189.19
Grade B; "Chevron"; medium duty; double triangular solid top						
600 mm x 600 mm; ref MB1-60/60	106.40	2.30	14.84	110.69	nr	125.53
Grade C; "Vulcan" heavy duty; single triangular solid top						
550 mm x 495 mm; ref MA-T	170.05	2.90	18.70	175.81	nr	194.51
Grade C; "Chevron"; heavy duty double triangular solid top						
550 mm x 550 mm; ref MA-55	153.25	3.45	22.25	158.64	nr	180.89
600 mm x 600 mm; ref MA-60	175.00	3.45	22.25	181.01	nr	203.26
British Standard best quality vitrified clay **channels; bedding and jointing in cement:** **sand (1:2)**						
Half section straight						
100 mm diameter x 1.00 m long	3.71	0.92	5.93	3.90	nr	9.83
150 mm diameter x 1.00 m long	6.17	1.15	7.42	6.48	nr	13.90
225 mm diameter x 1.00 m long	13.88	1.49	9.61	14.57	nr	24.18
300 mm diameter x 1.00 m long	28.49	1.84	11.87	29.91	nr	41.78
Half section bend						
100 mm diameter	3.99	0.69	4.45	4.19	nr	8.64
150 mm diameter	6.59	0.86	5.55	6.92	nr	12.47
225 mm diameter	21.99	1.15	7.42	23.09	nr	30.51
300 mm diameter	44.84	1.38	8.90	47.08	nr	55.98
Half section taper straight						
150 mm - 100 mm diameter	16.62	0.80	5.16	17.45	nr	22.61
225 mm - 150 mm diameter	37.08	1.03	6.64	38.93	nr	45.57
300 mm - 225 mm diameter	147.10	1.26	8.13	154.46	nr	162.59
Half section taper bend						
150 mm - 100 mm diameter	25.29	1.03	6.64	26.55	nr	33.19
225 mm - 150 mm diameter	72.40	1.32	8.51	76.02	nr	84.53
300 mm - 225 mm diameter	147.10	1.61	10.38	154.46	nr	164.84
Three quarter section branch bend						
100 mm diameter	9.01	0.57	3.68	9.46	nr	13.14
150 mm diameter	15.66	0.86	5.55	16.44	nr	21.99
225 mm diameter	55.15	1.15	7.42	57.91	nr	65.33
300 mm diameter	114.46	1.53	9.87	120.18	nr	130.05
uPVC channels; with solvent weld or lip seal **coupling joints; bedding in cement:sand**						
Half section cut away straight; with coupling either end						
110 mm diameter	26.37	0.35	2.26	33.57	nr	35.83
160 mm diameter	45.47	0.46	2.97	62.51	nr	65.48
Half section cut away long radius bend; with coupling either end						
110 mm diameter	26.98	0.35	2.26	34.21	nr	36.47
160 mm diameter	66.75	0.46	2.97	84.85	nr	87.82
Channel adaptor to clay; with one coupling						
110 mm diameter	7.55	0.29	1.87	10.87	nr	12.74
160 mm diameter	16.30	0.38	2.45	24.50	nr	26.95

R DISPOSAL SYSTEMS Excluding overheads and profit	PC £	Labour hours	Labour £	Material £	Unit	Total rate £
Half section bend						
110 mm diameter	9.81	0.38	2.45	10.61	nr	13.06
160 mm diameter	14.62	0.57	3.68	16.06	nr	19.74
Half section channel connector						
110 mm diameter	3.88	0.09	0.58	4.68	nr	5.26
160 mm diameter	9.66	0.12	0.77	11.57	nr	12.34
Half section channel junction						
110 mm diameter	10.99	0.57	3.68	11.84	nr	15.52
160 mm diameter	33.16	0.69	4.45	35.53	nr	39.98
Polypropylene slipper bend						
110 mm diameter	15.02	0.46	2.97	16.08	nr	19.05
Glass fibre septic tank; "Klargester" or other equal and approved; fixing lockable manhole cover and frame; placing in position						
3750 litre capacity; 2000 mm diameter; depth to invert						
1000 mm deep; standard grade	773.30	2.70	17.41	852.50	nr	869.91
1500 mm deep; heavy duty grade	973.50	3.05	19.67	1052.70	nr	1072.37
6000 litre capacity; 2300 mm diameter; depth to invert						
1000 mm deep; standard grade	1261.70	2.90	18.70	1359.60	nr	1378.30
1500 mm deep; heavy duty grade	1593.90	3.25	20.96	1691.80	nr	1712.76
9000 litre capacity; 2660 mm diameter; depth to invert						
1000 mm deep; standard grade	1817.20	3.15	20.32	1915.10	nr	1935.42
1500 mm deep; heavy duty grade	2300.10	3.45	22.25	2398.00	nr	2420.25
Glass fibre petrol interceptors; "Klargester" or other equal and approved; placing in position						
2000 litre capacity; 2370 mm x 1300 mm diameter; depth to invert						
1000 mm deep	885.50	2.95	19.03	885.50	nr	904.53
4000 litre capacity; 4370 mm x 1300 mm diameter; depth to invert						
1000 mm deep	1480.60	3.20	20.64	1480.60	nr	1501.24
R13 LAND DRAINAGE						
Excavating; by hand; grading bottoms; earthwork support; filling to within 150 mm of surface with gravel rejects; remainder filled with excavated material and compacting; disposal of surplus soil on site; spreading on site average 50 m						
Pipes not exceeding 200 mm nominal size						
average depth of trench 0.75 m	-	1.85	12.17	7.38	m	19.55
average depth of trench 1.00 m	-	2.50	16.45	11.66	m	28.11
average depth of trench 1.25 m	-	3.45	22.70	14.61	m	37.31
average depth of trench 1.50 m	-	5.95	39.15	17.79	m	56.94
average depth of trench 1.75 m	-	7.05	46.39	20.75	m	67.14
average depth of trench 2.00 m	-	8.15	53.63	23.92	m	77.55
Disposal; by machine						
Excavated material						
off site; to tip not exceeding 13 km (using lorries); including Landfill Tax based on inactive waste	-	-	-	15.75	m³	15.75
Disposal; by hand						
Excavated material						
off site; to tip not exceeding 13 km (using lorries); including Landfill Tax based on inactive waste	-	0.95	6.25	24.00	m³	30.25

R DISPOSAL SYSTEMS Excluding overheads and profit	PC £	Labour hours	Labour £	Material £	Unit	Total rate £
R13 LAND DRAINAGE - cont'd						
Vitrified clay perforated sub-soil pipes; BS 65;						
Hepworth "Hepline" or other equal and approved						
Pipes; laid straight						
100 mm diameter	5.48	0.25	1.61	5.75	m	**7.36**
150 mm diameter	9.96	0.31	2.00	10.46	m	**12.46**
225 mm diameter	18.31	0.41	2.64	19.23	m	**21.87**

S PIPED SUPPLY SYSTEMS Excluding overheads and profit	PC £	Labour hours	Labour £	Material £	Unit	Total rate £
S PIPED SUPPLY SYSTEMS						
S12 HOT AND COLD WATER (SMALL SCALE)						
Copper pipes; EN1057:1996; capillary fittings						
15 mm pipes; fixing with pipe clips and						
screwed	0.69	0.40	4.14	0.78	m	**4.92**
Extra for						
made bend	-	0.18	1.86	-	nr	**1.86**
stop end	1.07	0.13	1.35	1.10	nr	**2.45**
straight coupling	0.19	0.20	2.07	0.19	nr	**2.26**
union coupling	5.32	0.20	2.07	5.45	nr	**7.52**
reducing coupling	1.54	0.20	2.07	1.58	nr	**3.65**
copper to lead connector	1.65	0.26	2.69	1.69	nr	**4.38**
imperial to metric adaptor	1.89	0.26	2.69	1.94	nr	**4.63**
elbow	0.36	0.20	2.07	0.37	nr	**2.44**
backplate elbow	4.08	0.42	4.35	4.18	nr	**8.53**
return bend	5.09	0.20	2.07	5.22	nr	**7.29**
tee; equal	0.61	0.30	3.10	0.63	nr	**3.73**
tee; reducing	3.95	0.30	3.10	4.05	nr	**7.15**
straight tap connector	1.88	0.61	6.31	1.93	nr	**8.24**
bent tap connector	1.92	0.82	8.49	1.97	nr	**10.46**
tank connector	4.64	0.30	3.10	4.76	nr	**7.86**
overflow bend	10.09	0.26	2.69	10.34	nr	**13.03**
22 mm pipes; fixing with pipe clips and						
screwed	1.37	0.46	4.76	1.50	m	**6.26**
Extra for						
made bend	-	0.24	2.48	-	nr	**2.48**
stop end	2.02	0.16	1.66	2.07	nr	**3.73**
straight coupling	0.53	0.26	2.69	0.54	nr	**3.23**
union coupling	8.52	0.26	2.69	8.73	nr	**11.42**
reducing coupling	1.78	0.26	2.69	1.82	nr	**4.51**
copper to lead connector	2.49	0.37	3.83	2.55	nr	**6.38**
elbow	0.85	0.26	2.69	0.87	nr	**3.56**
backplate elbow	8.57	0.53	5.49	8.78	nr	**14.27**
return bend	10.27	0.26	2.69	10.53	nr	**13.22**
tee; equal	1.73	0.40	4.14	1.77	nr	**5.91**
tee; reducing	1.47	0.40	4.14	1.51	nr	**5.65**
straight tap connector	2.15	0.20	2.07	2.20	nr	**4.27**
tank connector	1.37	0.40	4.14	1.44	nr	**5.58**
28 mm pipes; fixing with pipe clips and						
screwed	1.82	0.50	5.17	1.98	m	**7.15**
Extra for						
made bend	-	0.30	3.10	-	nr	**3.10**
stop end	3.19	0.18	1.86	3.27	nr	**5.13**
straight coupling	0.98	0.34	3.52	1.00	nr	**4.52**
reducing coupling	2.69	0.34	3.52	2.76	nr	**6.28**
union coupling	8.52	0.34	3.52	8.73	nr	**12.25**
copper to lead connector	3.36	0.47	4.86	3.44	nr	**8.30**
imperial to metric adaptor	3.67	0.47	4.86	3.76	nr	**8.62**
elbow	1.59	0.34	3.52	1.63	nr	**5.15**
return bend	15.60	0.34	3.52	15.99	nr	**19.51**
tee; equal	4.45	0.49	5.07	4.56	nr	**9.63**
tank connector	1.82	0.49	5.07	1.92	nr	**6.99**
35 mm pipes; fixing with pipe clips and						
screwed	4.47	0.57	5.90	4.76	m	**10.66**
Extra for						
made bend	-	0.36	3.73	-	nr	**3.73**
stop end	6.89	0.20	2.07	7.06	nr	**9.13**
straight coupling	3.26	0.40	4.14	3.34	nr	**7.48**
reducing coupling	6.40	0.40	4.14	6.56	nr	**10.70**

S PIPED SUPPLY SYSTEMS Excluding overheads and profit	PC £	Labour hours	Labour £	Material £	Unit	Total rate £
S12 HOT AND COLD WATER (SMALL SCALE) - cont'd						
Copper pipes; EN1057:1996; capillary fittings - cont'd						
Extra for - cont'd						
union coupling	16.28	0.40	4.14	16.69	nr	20.83
flanged connector	44.92	0.53	5.49	46.04	nr	51.53
elbow	6.49	0.40	4.14	6.65	nr	10.79
obtuse elbow	9.58	0.40	4.14	9.82	nr	13.96
tee; equal	11.14	0.55	5.69	11.42	nr	17.11
tank connector	12.22	0.55	5.69	12.53	nr	18.22
42 mm pipes; fixing with pipe clips; plugged and screwed	5.47	0.64	6.62	5.81	m	12.43
Extra for						
made bend	-	0.48	4.97	-	nr	4.97
stop end	10.58	0.23	2.38	10.84	nr	13.22
straight coupling	4.88	0.47	4.86	5.00	nr	9.86
reducing coupling	9.25	0.47	4.86	9.48	nr	14.34
union coupling	23.82	0.47	4.86	24.42	nr	29.28
flanged connector	53.68	0.60	6.21	55.02	nr	61.23
elbow	11.55	0.47	4.86	11.84	nr	16.70
obtuse elbow	16.89	0.47	4.86	17.31	nr	22.17
tee; equal	17.44	0.62	6.42	17.88	nr	24.30
tank connector	16.01	0.62	6.42	16.41	nr	22.83
54 mm pipes; fixing with pipe clips; plugged and screwed	7.05	0.70	7.25	7.47	m	14.72
Extra for						
made bend	-	0.66	6.83	-	nr	6.83
stop end	14.76	0.25	2.59	15.13	nr	17.72
straight coupling	10.07	0.53	5.49	10.32	nr	15.81
reducing coupling	14.36	0.53	5.49	14.72	nr	20.21
union coupling	45.29	0.53	5.49	46.42	nr	51.91
flanged connector	81.15	0.60	6.21	83.18	nr	89.39
elbow	23.63	0.53	5.49	24.22	nr	29.71
obtuse elbow	29.54	0.53	5.49	30.28	nr	35.77
tee; equal	32.97	0.68	7.04	33.79	nr	40.83
tank connector	24.45	0.68	7.04	25.06	nr	32.10
Copper pipes; EN1057:1996; compression fittings						
15 mm pipes; fixing with pipe clips; plugged and screwed	0.69	0.45	4.66	0.78	m	5.44
Extra for						
made bend	-	0.18	1.86	-	nr	1.86
stop end	2.09	0.12	1.24	2.14	nr	3.38
straight coupling	1.68	0.18	1.86	1.72	nr	3.58
reducing set	1.75	0.20	2.07	1.79	nr	3.86
male coupling	1.48	0.24	2.48	1.52	nr	4.00
female coupling	1.80	0.24	2.48	1.84	nr	4.32
90 degree bend	2.03	0.18	1.86	2.08	nr	3.94
90 degree backplate bend	4.88	0.36	3.73	5.00	nr	8.73
tee; equal	2.84	0.26	2.69	2.91	nr	5.60
tee; backplate	8.18	0.26	2.69	8.38	nr	11.07
tank coupling	4.83	0.26	2.69	4.95	nr	7.64
22 mm pipes; fixing with pipe clips; plugged and screwed	1.37	0.51	5.28	1.50	m	6.78
Extra for						
made bend	-	0.24	2.48	-	nr	2.48
stop end	3.03	0.14	1.45	3.11	nr	4.56
straight coupling	2.74	0.24	2.48	2.81	nr	5.29
reducing set	1.88	0.07	0.72	1.93	nr	2.65
male coupling	3.22	0.34	3.52	3.30	nr	6.82

S PIPED SUPPLY SYSTEMS Excluding overheads and profit	PC £	Labour hours	Labour £	Material £	Unit	Total rate £
Extra for - cont'd						
female coupling	2.64	0.34	3.52	2.71	nr	6.23
90 degree bend	3.23	0.24	2.48	3.31	nr	5.79
tee; equal	4.71	0.36	3.73	4.83	nr	8.56
tee; reducing	6.69	0.36	3.73	6.86	nr	10.59
tank coupling	5.15	0.36	3.73	5.28	nr	9.01
28 mm pipes; fixing with pipe clips; plugged						
and screwed	1.82	0.55	5.69	1.98	m	7.67
Extra for						
made bend	-	0.30	3.10	-	nr	3.10
stop end	5.79	0.17	1.76	5.93	nr	7.69
straight coupling	5.54	0.30	3.10	5.68	nr	8.78
male coupling	3.93	0.42	4.35	4.03	nr	8.38
female coupling	5.10	0.42	4.35	5.23	nr	9.58
90 degree bend	7.17	0.30	3.10	7.35	nr	10.45
tee; equal	11.41	0.44	4.55	11.70	nr	16.25
tee; reducing	11.02	0.44	4.55	11.30	nr	15.85
tank coupling	8.86	0.44	4.55	9.08	nr	13.63
35 mm pipes; fixing with pipe clips; plugged						
and screwed	4.47	0.62	6.42	4.76	m	11.18
Extra for						
made bend	-	0.36	3.73	-	nr	3.73
stop end	8.92	0.19	1.97	9.14	nr	11.11
straight coupling	11.52	0.36	3.73	11.81	nr	15.54
male coupling	8.75	0.48	4.97	8.97	nr	13.94
female coupling	10.52	0.48	4.97	10.78	nr	15.75
tee; equal	20.23	0.50	5.17	20.74	nr	25.91
tee; reducing	19.76	0.50	5.17	20.25	nr	25.42
tank coupling	10.54	0.50	5.17	10.80	nr	15.97
42 mm pipes; fixing with pipe clips; plugged						
and screwed	5.47	0.69	7.14	5.81	m	12.95
Extra for						
made bend	-	0.48	4.97	-	nr	4.97
stop end	14.84	0.22	2.28	15.21	nr	17.49
straight coupling	15.14	0.42	4.35	15.52	nr	19.87
male coupling	13.13	0.54	5.59	13.46	nr	19.05
female coupling	14.13	0.54	5.59	14.48	nr	20.07
tee; equal	31.79	0.56	5.80	32.58	nr	38.38
tee; reducing	30.53	0.56	5.80	31.29	nr	37.09
54 mm pipes; fixing with pipe clips; plugged						
and screwed	7.05	0.75	7.76	7.47	m	15.23
Extra for						
made bend	-	0.66	6.83	-	nr	6.83
straight coupling	22.66	0.48	4.97	23.23	nr	28.20
male coupling	19.38	0.60	6.21	19.86	nr	26.07
female coupling	20.74	0.60	6.21	21.26	nr	27.47
tee; equal	51.08	0.62	6.42	52.36	nr	58.78
tee; reducing	51.08	0.62	6.42	52.36	nr	58.78
Copper, brass and gunmetal ancillaries;						
screwed joints to fittings						
Stopcock; brass/gunmetal capillary joints to						
copper						
15 mm nominal size	4.13	0.24	2.48	4.23	nr	6.71
22 mm nominal size	7.71	0.32	3.31	7.90	nr	11.21
28 mm nominal size	21.96	0.41	4.24	22.51	nr	26.75
Stopcock; brass/gunmetal compression joints						
to copper						
15 mm nominal size	5.62	0.22	2.28	5.76	nr	8.04
22 mm nominal size	9.89	0.29	3.00	10.14	nr	13.14
28 mm nominal size	25.77	0.36	3.73	26.41	nr	30.14

S PIPED SUPPLY SYSTEMS Excluding overheads and profit	PC £	Labour hours	Labour £	Material £	Unit	Total rate £
S12 HOT AND COLD WATER (SMALL SCALE) - cont'd						
Copper, brass and gunmetal ancillaries;						
screwed joints to fittings - cont'd						
Stopcock; brass/gunmetal compression joints						
to polyethylene						
15 mm nominal size	14.96	0.31	3.21	15.33	nr	18.54
22 mm nominal size	15.40	0.40	4.14	15.79	nr	19.93
28 mm nominal size	23.14	0.48	4.97	23.72	nr	28.69
Gunmetal "Fullway" gate valve or other equal and						
approved; capillary joints to copper						
15 mm nominal size	12.96	0.24	2.48	13.28	nr	15.76
22 mm nominal size	15.00	0.32	3.31	15.38	nr	18.69
28 mm nominal size	20.89	0.41	4.24	21.41	nr	25.65
35 mm nominal size	46.60	0.49	5.07	47.77	nr	52.84
42 mm nominal size	58.28	0.56	5.80	59.74	nr	65.54
54 mm nominal size	84.52	0.64	6.62	86.63	nr	93.25
Brass gate valve; compression joints to copper						
15 mm nominal size	9.17	0.36	3.73	9.40	nr	13.13
22 mm nominal size	10.68	0.48	4.97	10.95	nr	15.92
28 mm nominal size	18.67	0.60	6.21	19.14	nr	25.35
Chromium plated; lockshield radiator valve;						
union outlet						
15 mm nominal size	6.57	0.26	2.69	6.73	nr	9.42
Water tanks/cisterns						
Polyethylene cold water feed and expansion						
cistern; BS 4213; with covers						
ref SC15; 68 litres	43.62	1.50	15.53	43.62	nr	59.15
ref SC25; 114 litres	50.88	1.74	18.01	50.88	nr	68.89
ref SC40; 182 litres	59.43	1.74	18.01	59.43	nr	77.44
ref SC50; 227 litres	82.69	2.34	24.22	82.69	nr	106.91
GRP cold water storage cistern; with covers						
ref 899.10; 30 litres	103.28	1.32	13.66	103.28	nr	116.94
ref 899.25; 68 litres	138.16	1.50	15.53	138.16	nr	153.69
ref 899.40; 114 litres	169.13	1.74	18.01	169.13	nr	187.14
ref 899.70; 227 litres	209.30	2.34	24.22	209.30	nr	233.52
Storage cylinders/calorifiers						
Copper cylinders; single feed coil indirect; BS						
1566 Part 2; grade 3						
ref 2; 96 litres	-	2.40	24.84	160.74	nr	185.58
ref 3; 114 litres	102.27	2.70	27.95	102.27	nr	130.22
ref 7; 117 litres	100.92	3.00	31.05	100.92	nr	131.97
ref 8; 140 litres	114.26	3.60	37.26	114.26	nr	151.52
ref 9; 162 litres	145.94	4.20	43.47	145.94	nr	189.41
Combination copper hot water storage units;						
coil direct; BS 3198; (hot/cold)						
400 mm x 900 mm; 65/20 litres	118.78	3.36	34.78	118.78	nr	153.56
450 mm x 900 mm; 85/25 litres	122.33	4.68	48.44	122.33	nr	170.77
450 mm x 1075 mm; 115/25 litres	134.56	5.88	60.86	134.56	nr	195.42
450 mm x 1200 mm; 115/45 litres	143.25	6.60	68.31	143.25	nr	211.56
Combination copper hot water storage						
450 mm x 900 mm; 85/25 litres	153.40	5.28	54.65	153.40	nr	208.05
450 mm x 1200 mm; 115/45 litres	175.42	7.20	74.52	175.42	nr	249.94

S PIPED SUPPLY SYSTEMS Excluding overheads and profit	PC £	Labour hours	Labour £	Material £	Unit	Total rate £
Thermal insulation						
19 mm thick rigid mineral glass fibre sectional						
pipe lagging; plain finish; fixed with aluminium						
bands to steel or copper pipework; including						
working over pipe fittings						
around 15/15 pipes	5.90	0.08	0.83	6.20	m	7.03
around 20/22 pipes	6.34	0.12	1.24	6.66	m	7.90
around 25/28 pipes	6.87	0.13	1.35	7.21	m	8.56
around 32/35 pipes	7.62	0.14	1.45	8.00	m	9.45
around 40/42 pipes	8.07	0.16	1.66	8.47	m	10.13
around 50/54 pipes	9.35	0.18	1.86	9.82	m	11.68
19 mm thick rigid mineral glass fibre sectional						
pipe lagging; canvas or class O lacquered						
aluminium finish; fixed with aluminium bands						
to steel or copper pipework; including working						
over pipe fittings						
around 15/15 pipes	8.04	0.08	0.83	8.44	m	9.27
around 20/22 pipes	8.76	0.12	1.24	9.20	m	10.44
around 25/28 pipes	9.61	0.13	1.35	10.09	m	11.44
around 32/35 pipes	10.46	0.14	1.45	10.98	m	12.43
around 40/42 pipes	11.24	0.16	1.66	11.80	m	13.46
around 50/54 pipes	13.04	0.18	1.86	13.69	m	15.55
60 mm thick glass-fibre filled polyethylene						
insulating jackets for GRP or polyethylene cold						
water cisterns; complete with fixing bands; for						
cisterns size (supply not included)						
450 mm x 300 mm x 300 mm (45 litres)	-	0.48	4.97	-	nr	4.97
650 mm x 500 mm x 400 mm (91 litres)	-	0.72	7.45	-	nr	7.45
675 mm x 525 mm x 500 mm (136 litres)	-	0.84	8.69	-	nr	8.69
675 mm x 575 mm x 525 mm (182 litres)	-	0.96	9.94	-	nr	9.94
1000 mm x 625 mm x 525 mm (273 litres)	-	1.02	10.56	-	nr	10.56
1125 mm x 650 mm x 575 mm (341 litres)	-	1.02	10.56	-	nr	10.56
80 mm thick glass-fibre filled insulating jackets in flame						
retardant PVC to BS 1763; type 1B; segmental type for						
hot water cylinders; complete with fixing bands; for						
cylinders size (supply not included)						
400 mm x 900 mm; ref 2	-	0.40	4.14	-	nr	4.14
450 mm x 900 mm; ref 7	-	0.40	4.14	-	nr	4.14
450 mm x 1050 mm; ref 8	-	0.48	4.97	-	nr	4.97
450 mm x 1200 mm	-	0.60	6.21	-	nr	6.21
S13 PRESSURISED WATER						
Blue MDPE pipes; BS 6572; mains pipework;						
no joints in the running length; laid in trenches						
Pipes						
20 mm nominal size	0.72	0.13	1.35	0.74	m	2.09
25 mm nominal size	1.35	0.14	1.45	1.39	m	2.84
32 mm nominal size	1.53	0.16	1.66	1.58	m	3.24
50 mm nominal size	3.60	0.18	1.86	3.71	m	5.57
63 mm nominal size	5.85	0.19	1.97	6.03	m	8.00
Ductile iron bitumen coated pipes and fittings;						
EN598; class K9; Stanton's "Tyton" water main						
pipes or other equal and approved; flexible joints						
100 mm pipes; laid straight	15.35	0.72	4.64	21.41	m	26.05
Extra for						
bend; 45 degrees	35.27	0.72	4.64	47.62	nr	52.26
branch; 45 degrees; socketed	253.56	1.08	6.97	282.11	nr	289.08
tee	54.95	1.08	6.97	73.57	nr	80.54
flanged spigot	37.44	0.72	4.64	44.60	nr	49.24
flanged socket	36.66	0.72	4.64	43.79	nr	48.43

S PIPED SUPPLY SYSTEMS Excluding overheads and profit	PC £	Labour hours	Labour £	Material £	Unit	Total rate £
S13 PRESSURISED WATER - cont'd						
Ductile iron bitumen coated pipes and fittings; **EN598; class K9; Stanton's "Tyton" water main** **pipes or other equal and approved; flexible joints** **- cont'd**						
150 mm pipes; laid straight	23.12	0.84	5.42	30.05	m	35.47
Extra for						
bend; 45 degrees	60.25	0.84	5.42	74.81	nr	80.23
branch; 45 degrees; socketed	323.62	1.26	8.13	357.13	nr	365.26
tee	114.18	1.26	8.13	137.21	nr	145.34
flanged spigot	44.67	0.84	5.42	52.68	nr	58.10
flanged socket	58.34	0.84	5.42	67.03	nr	72.45
200 mm pipes; laid straight	31.24	1.20	7.74	40.88	m	48.62
Extra for						
bend; 45 degrees	108.73	1.20	7.74	130.32	nr	138.06
branch; 45 degrees; socketed	367.53	1.80	11.61	410.13	nr	421.74
tee	156.82	1.80	11.61	188.88	nr	200.49
flanged spigot	97.40	1.20	7.74	110.34	nr	118.08
flanged socket	92.27	1.20	7.74	104.96	nr	112.70
S32 NATURAL GAS						
Ductile iron bitumen coated pipes and fittings; EN **598; class K9; Stanton's "Stanlock" gas main pipes** **or other equal and approved; bolted gland joints**						
100 mm pipes; laid straight	30.78	0.80	5.16	45.32	m	50.48
Extra for						
bend; 45 degrees	46.52	0.80	5.16	68.34	nr	73.50
tee	70.97	1.21	7.80	107.02	nr	114.82
flanged spigot	38.54	0.80	5.16	53.47	nr	58.63
flanged socket	38.02	0.80	5.16	52.92	nr	58.08
isolated "Stanlock" joint	12.38	0.40	2.58	13.00	nr	15.58
150 mm pipes; laid straight	46.88	1.03	6.64	67.76	m	74.40
Extra for						
bend; 45 degrees	67.17	1.03	6.64	98.33	nr	104.97
tee	118.84	1.55	10.00	171.11	nr	181.11
flanged spigot	44.67	1.03	6.64	65.44	nr	72.08
flanged socket	56.06	1.03	6.64	77.40	nr	84.04
isolated "Stanlock" joint	17.65	0.52	3.35	18.53	nr	21.88
200 mm pipes; laid straight	62.41	1.49	9.61	90.34	m	99.95
Extra for						
bend; 45 degrees	109.39	1.49	9.61	139.67	nr	149.28
tee	165.10	2.24	14.45	247.79	nr	262.24
flanged spigot	97.40	1.49	9.61	127.08	nr	136.69
flanged socket	86.74	1.49	9.61	115.89	nr	125.50
isolated "Stanlock" joint	23.63	0.75	4.84	24.81	nr	29.65

T MECHANICAL HEATING/COOLING, ETC. SYSTEMS Excluding overheads and profit	PC £	Labour hours	Labour £	Material £	Unit	Total rate £
T MECHANICAL HEATING/COOLING, ETC. SYSTEMS						
T10 GAS/OIL FIRED BOILERS						
Boilers Gas fired floor standing domestic boilers; cream or white; enamelled casing; 32 mm diameter BSPT female flow and return tappings; 102 mm diameter flue socket 13 mm diameter BSPT male draw-off outlet						
13.19 kW output (45,000 Btu/Hr)	-	6.00	63.42	626.24	nr	**689.66**
23.45 kW output (80,000 Btu/Hr)	-	6.00	63.42	805.16	nr	**868.58**
T31 LOW TEMPERATURE HOT WATER HEATING						
NOTE: The reader is referred to section "S12 Hot and Cold Water (Small Scale)" for rates for copper pipework which will equally apply to this section of work. For further and more detailed information the reader is advised to consult *Spon's Mechanical and Electrical Services Price Book.*						
Radiators; Myson Heat Emitters or other equal and approved "Premier HE"; single panel type; steel; 690 mm high; wheelhead and lockshield valves						
540 mm long	25.75	2.40	25.37	39.34	nr	**64.71**
1149 mm long	52.05	2.70	28.54	65.64	nr	**94.18**
2165 mm long	98.90	3.00	31.71	112.49	nr	**144.20**
2978 mm long	151.15	3.30	34.88	164.81	nr	**199.69**

V ELECTRICAL SYSTEMS Excluding overheads and profit	PC £	Labour hours	Labour £	Material £	Unit	Total rate £
V ELECTRICAL SYSTEMS						
V21/V22 GENERAL LIGHTING AND LV POWER						
NOTE: The following items indicate approximate prices for wiring of lighting and power points complete, including accessories and socket outlets, but excluding lighting fittings. Consumer control units are shown separately. For a more detailed breakdown of these costs and specialist costs for a complete range of electrical items, reference should be made to *Spon's Mechanical and Electrical Services Price Book*.						
Consumer control units						
8-way 60 amp SP&N surface mounted insulated consumer control units fitted with miniature circuit breakers including 2.00 m long 32 mm screwed welded conduit with three runs of 16 mm^2 PVC cables ready for final connections	-	-	-	-	nr	147.00
extra for current operated ELCB of 30 mA tripping current	-	-	-	-	nr	62.30
As above but 100 amp metal cased consumer unit and 25 mm^2 PVC cables	-	-	-	-	nr	165.00
extra for current operated ELCB of 30 mA tripping current	-	-	-	-	nr	137.00
Final circuits						
Lighting points						
wired in PVC insulated and PVC sheathed cable in flats and houses; insulated in cavities and roof space; protected where buried by heavy gauge PVC conduit	-	-	-	-	nr	53.00
as above but in commercial property	-	-	-	-	nr	65.50
wired in PVC insulated cable in screwed welded conduit in flats and houses	-	-	-	-	nr	112.00
as above but in commercial property	-	-	-	-	nr	137.00
as above but in industrial property	-	-	-	-	nr	155.00
wired in MICC cable in flats and houses	-	-	-	-	nr	95.00
as above but in commercial property	-	-	-	-	nr	112.00
as above but in industrial property with PVC sheathed cable	-	-	-	-	nr	130.00
Single 13 amp switched socket outlet points						
wired in PVC insulated and PVC sheathed cable in flats and houses on a ring main circuit; protected where buried by heavy gauge PVC conduit	-	-	-	-	nr	50.00
as above but in commercial property	-	-	-	-	nr	60.00
wired in PVC insulated cable in screwed welded conduit throughout on a ring main circuit in flats and houses	-	-	-	-	nr	85.00
as above but in commercial property	-	-	-	-	nr	95.00
as above but in industrial property	-	-	-	-	nr	112.00
wired in MICC cable on a ring main circuit in flats and houses	-	-	-	-	nr	85.00
as above but in commercial property	-	-	-	-	nr	100.00
as above but in industrial property with PVC sheathed cable	-	-	-	-	nr	130.00

V ELECTRICAL SYSTEMS Excluding overheads and profit	PC £	Labour hours	Labour £	Material £	Unit	Total rate £
Cooker control units						
45 amp circuit including unit wired in PVC insulated and PVC sheathed cable; protected where buried by heavy gauge PVC conduit	-	-	-	-	nr	**115.00**
as above but wired in PVC insulated cable in screwed welded conduit	-	-	-	-	nr	**168.00**
as above but wired in MICC cable	-	-	-	-	nr	**190.00**

W SECURITY SYSTEMS Excluding overheads and profit	PC £	Labour hours	Labour £	Material £	Unit	Total rate £
W SECURITY SYSTEMS						
W20 LIGHTNING PROTECTION						
Lightning protection equipment						
Copper strip roof or down conductors fixed with bracket or saddle clips						
20 mm x 3 mm flat section	-	-	-	-	m	14.00
25 mm x 3 mm flat section	-	-	-	-	m	15.75
Aluminium strip roof or down conductors fixed with bracket or saddle clips						
20 mm x 3 mm flat section	-	-	-	-	m	11.00
25 mm x 3 mm flat section	-	-	-	-	m	11.65
Joints in tapes	-	-	-	-	nr	8.65
Bonding connections to roof and structural metalwork	-	-	-	-	nr	48.50
Testing points	-	-	-	-	nr	23.75
Earth electrodes						
16 mm diameter driven copper electrodes in 1220 mm long sectional lengths (minimum 2440 mm long overall)	-	-	-	-	nr	130.00
first 2440 mm length driven and tested 25 mm x 3 mm copper strip electrode in 457 mm deep prepared trench	-	-	-	-	m	9.50

Profiled Sheet Roofing and Cladding

A Guide to Good Practice

National Federation of Roofing Contractors

Edited by Nick Selves, J. Shanahan and Colin Sproul

This new edition of the NFRC's handbook, is intended as an accessible and practical guide to the application, design and installation of profiled sheeting for roof and wall cladding. It distills the knowledge of many of the leading experts in this area of construction with hands-on site experience.

Profiled Sheet Roofing and Cladding sets out principles whereby all necessary components can be successfully integrated to provide an external envelope meeting all the required performance standards. The special requirements of insulated structures are also considered. It contains up-to-date advice and information on the exceptional performance and developments which have occurred since the earlier second edition was published in 1991.

Contents: Chapter 1. Common Requirements for Light Weight Profiled Cladding. **Chapter 2.** Profiled Metal Roof and Wall Cladding. **Chapter 3.** Built-up Metal Roofing Systems **Chapter 4.** Composite Panels. **Chapter 5.** Fibre-Cement Sheeting. **Chapter 6.** Rooflights. **Chapter 7.** Fasteners and Fixings. **Chapter 8.** Sealants and Profile Fillers. **Chapter 9.** Rainwater Goods. **Chapter 10.** Construction, Safety and Maintenance.

May 1999: 297x210: 128pp
51 line drawings
Pb: 0-419-23940-5: £29.99

To Order: **Tel:** +44 (0) 8700 768853, or +44 (0) 1264 343071
Fax: +44 (0) 1264 343005, or **Post:** E & FN Spon Customer Services, ITPS Andover, Hants, SP10 5BE, UK

All orders must be pre-paid and will be sent free in the UK. Europe please add: £2.95 for the first book, thereafter £1.25 per book. ROW please add: Airmail £6.50 for the first book, thereafter £2.50 per book. Please add £12.50 delivery charge for items over £100.00.

PART IV

Approximate Estimating

This part of the book contains the following sections:

DAVIS LANGDON & EVEREST

LONDON
Princes House
39 Kingsway
London WC2B 6TP
Tel : (020) 7 497 9000
Fax : (020) 7 497 8858
Email: london1@dle.co.uk

EDINBURGH
74 Great King Street
Edinburgh
EH3 6QU
Tel : (0131) 557 5306
Fax : (0131) 557 5704
Email: e-burgh1@dle.co.uk

MANCHESTER
Boulton House
Chorlton Street
Manchester M1 3HY
Tel : (0161) 2282011
Fax : (0161) 2286317
Email: manch1@dle.co.uk

PETERBOROUGH
Charterhouse
66 Broadway
Peterborough PE1 1SU
Tel: (01733) 343625
Fax: (01733) 349177
Email: p-boro@dle.co.uk

BIRMINGHAM
289 Woodbourne Road
Harborne
Birmingham B17 8BY
Tel : (0121) 4299511
Fax : (0121) 4292544
Email: bham1@dle.co.uk

GATESHEAD
11 Regent Terrace
Gateshead
Tyne and Wear NE8 1LU
Tel : (0191) 477 3844
Fax : (0191) 490 1742
Email: g-head1@dle.co.uk

MANCHESTER
Marshall House
2 Park Avenue, Sale
Cheshire M33 6HE
Tel : (0161) 9629431
Fax : (0161) 9620829
Email: manch2@dle.co.uk

PLYMOUTH
3 Russell Court
St Andrew Street
Plymouth PL1 2AX
Tel : (01752) 668372
Fax : (01752) 221219
Email: plymouth@dle.co.uk

BRISTOL
St Lawrence House
29/31 Broad Street
Bristol BS1 2HF
Tel : (0117) 9277832
Fax : (0117) 9251350
Email: bristol1@dle.co.uk

GLASGOW
Cumbrae House
15 Carlton Court
Glasgow G5 9JP
Tel : (0141) 429 6677
Fax : (0141) 429 2255
Email: glasgow1@dle.co.uk

MILTON KEYNES
6 Bassett Court
Newport Pagnell
Bucks MK16 OJN
Tel : (01908) 613777
Fax : (01908) 210642
Email: mkeynes@dle.co.uk

PORTSMOUTH
Kings House
4 Kings Road
Portsmouth PO5 3BQ
Tel : (023) 92815218
Fax : (023) 92827156
Email: ports1@dle.co.uk

CAMBRIDGE
36 Storey's Way
Cambridge
CB3 ODT
Tel : (01223) 351258
Fax : (01223) 321002
Email: camb1@dle.co.uk

LEEDS
Duncan House
14 Duncan Street
Leeds LS1 6DL
Tel : (0113) 2432481
Fax : (0113) 2424601
Email: leeds1@dle.co.uk

NORWICH
63 Thorpe Road
Norwich
NR1 1UD
Tel : (01603) 628194
Fax : (01603) 615928
Email: norwich1@dle.co.uk

SOUTHAMPTON
Brunswick House
Brunswick Place
Southampton
SO15 2AP
Tel : (023) 80333438
Fax : (023) 80226099

CARDIFF
4 Pierhead Street
Capital Waterside
Cardiff CF10 4QP
Tel : (029) 20497497
Fax : (029) 20497111
Email: cardiff1@dle.co.uk

LIVERPOOL
Cunard Building
Water Street
Liverpool L3 1JR
Tel : (0151) 2361992
Fax : (0151) 2275401
Email: dlelpool@compuserve.com

OXFORD
Avalon House
Marcham Road, Abingdon
Oxford OX14 1TZ
Tel : (01235) 555025
Fax : (01235) 554909
Email: oxford1@dle.co.uk

**DAVIS LANGDON
CONSULTANCY**
Princes House, 39 Kingsway
London WC2B 6TP
Tel : (020) 7 379 3322
Fax : (020) 7 379 3030
Email: gurrierin@dle-london.co.uk

with offices throughout Europe, the Middle East, Asia, Australia, Africa and the USA
which together form

DAVIS LANGDON & SEAH INTERNATIONAL

Building Costs and Tender Prices

The tables which follow show the changes in building costs and tender prices since 1976.

To avoid confusion it is essential that the terms "building costs" and "tender prices" are clearly defined and understood. "Building costs" are the costs incurred by the builder in the course of his business, the principal ones being those for labour and materials. "Tender Price" is the price for which a builder offers to erect a building. This includes "building costs" but also takes into account market considerations such as the availability of labour and materials, and prevailing economic situation. This means that in "boom" periods, when there is a surfeit of building work to be done, "tender prices" may increase at a greater rate than "building costs", whilst in a period when work is scarce, "tender prices" may actually fall when "building costs" are rising.

Building costs

This table reflects the fluctuations since 1976 in wages and materials costs to the builder. In compiling the table, the proportion of labour to material has been assumed to be 40:60. The wages element has been assessed from a contract wages sheet revalued for each variation in labour costs, whilst the changes in the costs of materials have been based upon the indices prepared by the Department of Trade and Industry. No allowance has been made for changes in productivity, plus rates or hours worked which may occur in particular conditions and localities.

1976 = 100

Year	First quarter	Second quarter	Third quarter	Fourth quarter	Annual average
1976	93	97	104	107	100
1977	109	112	116	117	114
1978	118	120	127	129	123
1979	131	135	149	153	142
1980	157	161	180	181	170
1981	182	185	195	199	190
1982	203	206	214	216	210
1983	217	219	227	229	223
1984	230	232	239	241	236
1985	243	245	252	254	248
1986	256	258	266	267	262
1987	270	272	281	282	276
1988	284	286	299	302	293
1989	305	307	322	323	314
1990	326	329	346	347	337
1991	350	350	360	360	355
1992	361	362	367	368	365
1993	370	371	373	374	372
1994	376	379	385	388	382
1995	392	397	407	407	401
1996	407	408	414	414	411
1997	416	417	423	429	421
1998	430	431	448	447	439
1999	446 (P)	443 (P)	467 (F)	468 (F)	456 (F)

Note: P = Provisional   F = Forecast

671

Tender Prices

This table reflects the changes in tender prices since 1976. It indicates the level of pricing contained in the lowest competitive tenders for new work in the Greater London area (over £500,000 in value).

1976 = 100

Year	First quarter	Second quarter	Third quarter	Fourth quarter	Annual average
1976	97	98	102	103	100
1977	105	105	109	107	107
1978	113	116	126	139	124
1979	142	146	160	167	154
1980	179	200	192	188	190
1981	199	193	190	195	194
1982	191	188	195	195	192
1983	198	200	198	200	199
1984	205	206	214	215	210
1985	215	219	219	220	218
1986	221	226	234	234	229
1987	242	249	265	279	258
1988	289	299	321	328	309
1989	341	335	340	345	340
1990	320	315	312	290	309
1991	272	262	261	254	262
1992	250	248	241	233	243
1993	227	242	233	239	235
1994	239	247	266	256	252
1995	258	265	266	270	265
1996	265	262	270	270	267
1997	275	287	284	287	283
1998	305	312	318	318	313
1999	325	330 (P)	335 (F)	339 (F)	332 (F)

Note: P = Provisional   F = Forecast

Tender prices during 1998 rose by over 10%. The second quarter 1999 provisional index of 330 shows an increase of 3.80% over the fourth quarter 1998 and 5.80% over the year. Although provisional figures for new orders initially appeared to fall back (in constant 1995 prices) towards the end of 1998 and early in 1999, firmed up figures and recent price movements appear to reflect stronger order books and renewed confidence in the industry's medium term outlook. Other contributing factors include a 7 - 8% increase in "all-in" hourly rates in June 1999, the effect of the EEC's working Time Directive, which requires employer's to pay holiday pay based on average wages including bonuses, and a new Construction Industry Scheme which is likely to be introduced as from 1 August 1999.

DETR figures show that the total volume of construction output in 1998 was at its highest since 1991 and 1.60% higher than in 1997. New work output rose by 3.50%. The total volume of new orders in 1997 exceeded the 1996 total by 5.30% with the trend remaining upwards. The highest growth recorded in 1998 was in the private commercial sector, where new orders were 20.30% higher than in 1997. Other new work in the public sector (probably influenced by lottery/millennium funding was 16.70% higher in 1998 than in 1997. Total construction output is forecast to grow a further 2.00% in 1999 and 2.20% in 2000, led by the private commercial sector.

Our forecast for tender price inflation between second quarter 1999 and second quarter 2000 is for a rise in the range of 3.75% to 5.75%, with a further 4% to 7% in the following year.

Readers will be kept abreast of tender price movements in the free *Spon's Updates* and also in the "Tender Price Forecast" and "Cost Update" published quarterly in *Building* magazine.

TENDER PRICES / BUILDING COSTS / RETAIL PRICES

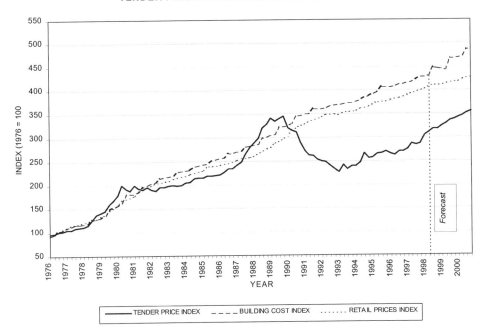

Regional Variations

As well as being aware of inflationary trends when preparing an estimate, it is also important to establish the appropriate price level for the project location.

Prices throughout this book reflect prices up to mid 2000 in Outer London. Prices in Inner London boroughs can be 5% to 15% higher while prices in the North and Yorkshire and Humberside may be 15% to 20% lower. Broad regional adjustment factors to assist with the preparation of initial estimates are shown in the table on the next page.

Over time, price differentials can change depending on regional workloads and local "hot spots". Workloads and prices have risen more strongly in Greater London and the South East over the last year or so than in most other regions. In the year to the first quarter 1999 prices in Greater London rose by 6% but in much of the North only by an average of 5%. Over the year to the 1st quarter 2000 this pattern is expected to be maintained with prices in London forecast to rise by 5% and slightly less, typically 4%, in the North. *Spon's Updates* and the "Tender Price Forecast" and "Cost Update" features in *Building* magazine will keep readers informed of the latest regional developments and changes as they occur.

The regional variations shown in the table on the next page are based on our forecast of price differentials in each of the economic planning regions in the fourth quarter 1999. The table shows the forecast fourth quarter 1999 tender price index for each region plus the recommended percentage adjustments required to the Major Works section of the Prices for Measured Work. (Prices in the book are at a Tender Price Index level of 350 for Outer London).

Region	Forecast fourth quarter 1999 tender price index	Percentage adjustment to *Major Works* section
Outer London	339	-3
Inner London	366	+5
East Anglia	292	-17
East Midlands	278	-20
Northern	282	-19
Northern Ireland	227	-35
North West	298	-15
Scotland	285	-18
South East	320	-9
South West	300	-14
Wales	278	-20
West Midlands	285	-18
Yorkshire and Humberside	282	-19

Special further adjustment to the above percentages may be necessary when considering city centre or very isolated locations.

The following example illustrates the adjustment of an estimate prepared using *Spon's A&B 2000*, to a price level that reflects the forecast Outer London market conditions for competitive tenders in the fourth quarter 1999:

				£
A	Value of items priced using Spon's A&B 2000 i.e. Tender Price Index 350			1,075,000
B	Adjustment to reduce value of A to forecast price level for fourth quarter 1999 i.e. Forecast Tender Price Index 339 $\frac{(339- 350)}{350} \times 100 = -3.14\%$			
	deduct 3.14%	say		-33,000
				1,042,000
C	Value of items priced using competitive quotations that reflect the market conditions in the fourth quarter 1999			400,000
				1,442,000
D	Allowance for preliminaries +11%	say		158,000
E	Total value of estimate at fourth quarter 1999 price levels		£	1,600,000

Alternatively, for a similar estimate in Scotland:

				£
A	Value of items priced using Spon's A&B 2000 i.e. Tender Price Index 350			1,075,000
B	Adjustment to reduce value of A to forecast price level for fourth quarter 1999 for Scotland (from regional variation table) i.e. Tender Price Index 285 $\frac{(285 - 350)}{350} \times 100 = -18.57\%$			
	deduct 18.57%	say		-200,000
				875,000
C	Value of items priced using competitive quotations that reflect the market conditions in the fourth quarter 1999			400,000
				1,275,000
D	Allowance for preliminaries +11%	say		140,000
E	Total value of estimate at fourth quarter 1999 price levels		£	1,415,000

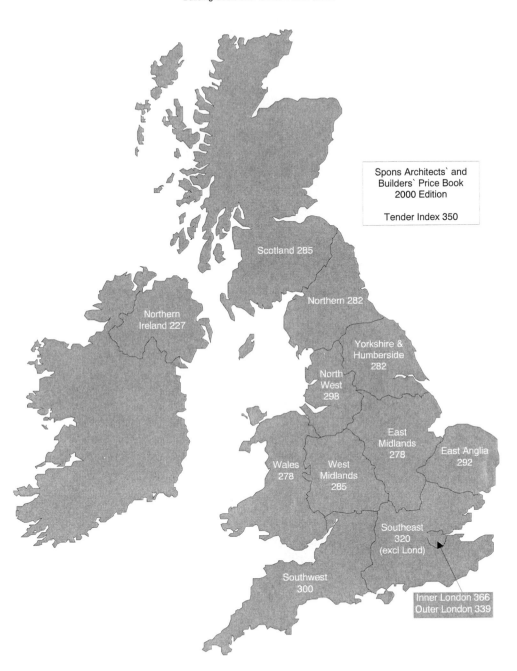

Spons Architects` and
Builders` Price Book
2000 Edition

Tender Index 350

Scotland 285

Northern Ireland 227

Northern 282

Yorkshire &
Humberside
282

North
West
298

East
Midlands
278

East Anglia
292

Wales
278

West
Midlands
285

Southeast
320
(excl Lond)

Southwest
300

Inner London 366
Outer London 339

NT Laidlaw ~ the total hardware specialist

NT Laidlaw is the UK's leading distributor of architectural hardware, backed by fully qualified staff who offer local representation and technical expertise to provide solutions to meet design criteria, building regulations and budget requirements.

NT Laidlaw offers fully co-ordinated ranges of hardware, door controls, locking systems, access control, hinges and accessories.

The NT Laidlaw programme includes:

Orbis:
a design classic for contemporary environments

Randi-line:
innovative designs in stainless steel from Scandinavia

Pennine:
classic co-ordinated hardware in polished aluminium

Arcus:
high impact coloured nylon door furniture and associated fittings

Centurion & Centurion Brass:
versatile aluminium contract quality hardware together with traditional and modern brassware

NT Laidlaw... The Total Hardware Specialist

NEWMAN TONKS

NT LAIDLAW

Pennine House Carrs Road Cheadle Cheshire SK8 2BW
Tel: 0161 491 4343 Fax: 0161 491 4355

Building Prices per Functional Units

Prices given under this heading are average prices, on a *fluctuating basis*, for typical buildings based on a tender price level index of 350 (1976 = 100). Unless otherwise stated, prices do not allow for external works, furniture, loose or special equipment and are, of course, exclusive of fees for professional services.

On certain types of buildings there exists a close relationship between its cost and the number of functional units that it accommodates. During the early stages of a project therefore an approximate estimate can be derived by multiplying the proposed unit of accommodation (i.e. hotel bedrooms, car parking spaces etc.) by an appropriate cost.

The following indicative unit areas and costs have been derived from historic data. It is emphasized that the prices must be treated with reserve, as they represent the average of prices from our records and cannot provide more than a rough guide to the cost of a building. There are limitations when using this method of estimating, for example, the functional areas and costs of football stadia are strongly influenced by the extent of front and back of house facilities housed within it, and these areas can vary considerably from scheme to scheme.

The areas may also be used as a "rule of thumb" in order to check on economy of designs. Where we have chosen not to show indicative areas, this is because either ranges are extensive or such figures may be misleading.

Costs have been expressed within a range, although this is not to suggest that figures outside this range will not be encountered, but simply that the calibre of such a type of building can itself vary significantly.

For assistance with the compilation of a closer estimate, or of a Cost Plan, the reader is directed to the *"Building Prices per Square Metre"* and *"Approximate Estimates"* sections. As elsewhere in this edition, prices do not include V.A.T., which is generally applied at the current rate to all non-domestic building (except those with charitable status).

Function:	Indicative functional unit area:	Indicative functional unit cost:
Utilities, civil engineering facilities (CI/SfB 1)		
Car parking - surface level	20 - 22 m²/car	£800 - £1,200/car
- ground level (under buildings)	22 - 24 m²/car	£1,500 - £3,000/car
- multi-storey	23 - 27 m²/car	£3,500 - £7,500/car
- semi-basement	27 - 30 m²/car	£8,000 - £11,000/car
- basement	28 - 37 m²/car	£11,000 - £18,000/car
Administrative, commercial protective service facilities (CI/SfB 3)		
Offices - air - low density cellular	15 m²/person	£7,500 - £15,000/person
conditioned - high density open plan	20 m²/person	£10,000 - £20,000/person
Health and welfare facilities (CI/SfB 4)		
Hospitals - district general	65 - 85 m²/bed	£60,000 - £90,000/bed
- teaching	120 + m²/bed	£80,000 - £110,000/bed
- private	75 - 100 m²/bed	£85,000 - £135,000/bed
Nursing - residential home	-	£18,000 - £35,000/bed
Homes - nursing home	-	£25,000 - £70,000/bed
Recreational facilities (CI/SfB 5)		
Football - basic stand	0.50 - 0.85 m²/seat	£450 - £700/seat
Stadia - stand plus basic facilities	0.85 - 1.28 m²/seat	£700 - £1,200/seat
- stand plus extensive facilities	1.00 - 1.30 m²/seat	£1,100 - £1,500/seat
- national stadia plus extensive facilities	1.20 - 1.80 m²/seat	£2,000 - £3,000/seat

Function:	Indicative functional unit area:	Indicative functional unit cost:
Recreational facilities (CI/SfB 5) - cont'd		
Theatres - theatre refurbishment	-	£7,000 - £10,000/seat
- workshop (fewer than 500 seats)	-	£3,000 - £8,000/seat
- more than 500 seats	-	£15,000 - £20,000/seat
Educational, scientific, information facilities (CI/SfB 7)		
Schools - nursery	3 - 5 m²/child	£3,000 - £7,000/child
- secondary	6 - 10 m²/child	£4,000 - £8,000/child
- boarding	10 - 12 m²/child	£6,000 - £12,000/child
- special	18 - 20 m²/child	£18,000 - £28,000/child
Residential facilities (CI/SfB 8)		
Housing - terraced; two bedroom	55 - 65 m²/gifa	£30,000 - £35,000/house
(Private - semi-detached; three bedroom	70 - 90 m²/gifa	£45,000 - £50,000/house
developer) - detached; four bedroom	90 - 100 m²/gifa	£60,000 - £90,000/house
- low rise flats; two bedroom	55 - 65 m²/gifa	£33,000 - £48,000/flat
- medium rise flat; two bedroom	55 - 65 m²/gifa	£40,000 - £55,000/flat
Hotels - budget roadside hotel - two to three storey lodge, excluding dining facilities	28 - 35 m²/bedroom	£25,000 - £33,000/bedroom
- budget city-centre hotel (office conversion) - four to six storeys, excluding dining facilities	32 - 38 m²/bedroom	£22,500 - £45,000/bedroom

Function:		Indicative functional unit area:	Indicative functional unit cost:
Residential facilities (CI/SfB 8) - cont'd			
Hotels - cont'd	- mid-range provincial hotel - two to three storeys, bedroom extension	33 - 40 m²/bedroom	£34,000 - £48,000/bedroom
	- budget city-centre hotel (new build) - four to six storeys, dining bar and facilities	35 - 45 m²/bedroom	£28,000 - £45,000/bedroom
	- city centre aparthotel - 4 to seven storeys, apartments with self-catering facilities	50 - 60 m²/bedroom	£45,000 - £70,000/bedroom
	- mid-range provincial hotel - two to three storeys, conference and leisure facilities	50 - 60 m²/bedroom	£55,000 - £85,000/bedroom
	- business town centre provincial hotel - four to six storeys, conference and wet leisure facilities	70 - 100 m²/bedroom	£95,000 - £135,000/bedroom
	- luxury city-centre hotel - multi-storey conference and wet leisure facilities	70 - 130 m²/bedroom	£135,000 - £200,000/bedroom
Hotel furniture, fittings and equipment	- budget hotel	-	£3,000 - £6,000/bedroom
	- mid-range hotel	-	£10,000 - £15,000/bedroom
	- luxury hotel	-	£25,000 - £60,000/bedroom
Students Residences	- large turnkey budget schemes (200 + units), simple design, open site; en suite accommodation	18 - 20 m²/bedroom	£10,000 - £18,000/bedroom

Function:	Indicative functional unit area:	Indicative functional unit cost:
Residential facilities (CI/SfB 8) - cont'd		
Students Residences - cont'd - smaller schemes (40 - 100 units) with mid range specifications, some with en suite bathroom and kitchen facilities	19 - 24 m²/bedroom	£18,000 - £30,000/bedroom
- smaller high quality courtyard schemes of collegiate style in restricted city centre sites	24 - 28 m²/bedroom	£30,000 - £50,000/bedroom

Effective Speaking

Communicating in Speech

Christopher Turk, University of Wales College of Cardiff, UK

Effective Speaking provides the hard scientific information about audience psychology, text preparation, presentation methods, voice production, body language and persuasive advocacy which will help would-be speakers improve their performance. The emphasis throughout is on practical self-help, on methods which have been shown to work, with clear explanations of just why they are effective.

November 1985 171x108: 288pp
Pb: 0-419-13030-6: £15.99

Effective Writing

Improving Scientific, Technical and Business Communication

Christopher Turk, UK and John Kirkman, UK

Effective communication is vital to science, engineering and business management. This thoroughly updated second edition with a new chapter on the use of computers and word-processors gives clear, practical advice illustrated with real-life examples on how to select, organize and present information in reports, papers and other documents.

November 1988 234x156: 288pp
Pb: 0-419-14660-1: £14.99

To Order: Tel: +44 (0) 8700 768853, or +44 (0) 1264 343071
Fax: +44 (0) 1264 343005, or **Post:** E & FN Spon Customer Services, ITPS Andover, Hants, SP10 5BE, UK

All orders must be pre-paid and will be sent free in the UK. Europe please add: £2.95 for the first book, thereafter £1.25 per book. ROW please add: Airmail £6.50 for the first book, thereafter £2.50 per book. Please add £12.50 delivery charge for items over £100.00.

Building Prices per Square Metre

Prices given under this heading are average prices, on a *fluctuating basis*, for typical buildings based on a tender price level index of 350 (1976 = 100). Unless otherwise stated, prices do not allow for external works, furniture, loose or special equipment and are, of course, exclusive of fees for professional services.

Prices are based upon the total floor area of all storeys, measured between external walls and without deduction for internal walls, columns, stairwells, liftwells and the like.

As in previous editions it is emphasized that the prices must be treated with reserve, as they represent the average of prices from our records and cannot provide more than a rough guide to the cost of a building.

In many instances normal commercial pressures together with a limited range of available specifications ensure that a single rate is sufficient to indicate the prevailing average price. However, where such restrictions do not apply a range has been given; this is not to suggest that figures outside this range will not be encountered, but simply that the calibre of such a type of building can itself vary significantly.

For assistance with the compilation of a closer estimate, or of a Cost Plan, the reader is directed to the *"Approximate Estimates"* sections. As elsewhere in this edition, prices do not include V.A.T., which is generally applied at the current rate to all non-domestic building (except those with charitable status).

Utilities, civil engineering facilities (CI/SfB 1)	Square metre excluding VAT £		
Surface car parking	40	to	55
Surface car parking; landscaped	65	to	90
Multi-storey car parks			
split level	195	to	255
split level with brick facades	215	to	295
flat slab	235	to	300
warped	240	to	275
Underground car parks			
partially underground under buildings; naturally ventilated	310	to	365
completely underground under buildings	400	to	605
completely underground with landscaped roof	660	to	785
Railway stations	1290	to	2190
Bus and coach stations	655	to	1095
Bus garages	625	to	685
Petrol stations			
minor refurbishment (£21,500 to £105,000 total cost)			
major refurbishment (£105,000 to £430,000 total cost)			
rebuild (£430,000 to £645,000 total cost)			
Garage showrooms	485	to	770
Garages, domestic	270	to	430
Airport facilities (excluding aprons)			
airport terminals	1185	to	2585
airport piers/satellites	1450	to	3230
apron/runway - varying infrastructure content	65	to	130
Airport campus facilities			
cargo handling bases	430	to	700
distribution centres	215	to	430

	Square metre excluding VAT £		

Utilities, civil engineering facilities (CI/SfB 1) - cont'd

Airport campus facilities - cont'd			
hangars (type C and D aircraft)	915	to	1075
hangars (type E aircraft)	1075	to	2690
TV, radio and video studios	795	to	1290
Telephone exchanges	650	to	1045
Telephone engineering centres	550	to	685
Branch Post Offices	685	to	930
Postal Delivery Offices/Sorting Offices	550	to	820
Mortuaries	1250	to	1735
Sub-stations	930	to	1395

Industrial facilities (CI/SfB 2)

Agricultural storage buildings	330	to	440
Factories			
for letting (incoming services only)	230	to	330
for letting (including lighting, power and heating)	305	to	425
nursery units (including lighting, power and heating)	375	to	565
workshops	430	to	695
maintenance/motor transport workshops	430	to	745
owner occupation-for light industrial use	385	to	565
owner occupation-for heavy industrial use	735	to	840
Factory/office buildings - high technology production			
for letting (shell and core only)	420	to	565
for letting (ground floor shell, first floor offices)	685	to	890
for owner occupation (controlled environment, fully finished)	890	to	1180
Laboratory workshops and offices	805	to	1010
Bi Light industrial/offices buildings			
economical shell, and core with heating only	375	to	660
medium shell and core with heating and ventilation	585	to	865
high quality shell and core with air-conditioning	765	to	1395
developers Category A fit out	305	to	525
tenants Category B fit out	135	to	420
High technology laboratory workshop centres, air conditioned	1865	to	2385
Distribution centres			
low bay; speculative	235	to	335
low bay; owner occupied	355	to	615
low bay; owner occupied and chilled	510	to	1025
high bay; owner occupied	575	to	835
Warehouses			
low bay (6 - 8 m high) for letting (no heating)	230	to	285
low bay for owner occupation (including heating)	275	to	490
high bay (9 - 18 m high) for owner occupation (including heating)	415	to	595
Cold stores, refrigerated stores	490	to	1115

Administrative, commercial protective service facilities (CI/SfB 3)

Embassies	1290	to	1865
County Courts	1145	to	1420
Magistrates Courts	870	to	1095
Civic offices			
non air conditioned	870	to	1095
fully air conditioned	1095	to	1290
Probation/Registrar Offices	635	to	915
Offices for letting			
low rise, non air conditioned	610	to	875
low rise, air conditioned	765	to	1035

Administrative, commercial protective service facilities (Cl/SfB 3)
- cont'd

			Square metre excluding VAT £

Owners for letting - cont'd			
medium rise, non air conditioned	735	to	965
medium rise, air conditioned	895	to	1205
high rise, non air conditioned	930	to	1205
high rise, air conditioned	1145	to	1685
Offices for owner occupation			
low rise, non air conditioned	705	to	920
low rise, air conditioned	875	to	1205
medium rise, non air conditioned	875	to	1095
medium rise, air conditioned	1145	to	1805
high rise, air conditioned	1465	to	2405
Offices, prestige			
medium rise	1435	to	2085
high rise	2085	to	2680
Large trading floors in medium rise offices	1940	to	2315
Two storey ancillary office accommodation to warehouses/factories	625	to	835
Fitting out offices			
basic fitting out including carpets, decorations, partitions and services	200	to	245
good quality fitting out including carpets, decorations, partitions, ceilings, furniture and services	400	to	480
high quality fitting out including raised floors and carpets, decorations, partitions, ceilings, furniture, air conditioning and electrical services	655	to	850
Office refurbishment			
basic refurbishment	335	to	490
good quality, including air conditioning	655	to	885
high quality, including air conditioning	1205	to	1615
Banks			
local	965	to	1205
city centre/head office	1385	to	1795
Building Society Branch Offices	885	to	1150
refurbishment	490	to	825
Shop shells			
small	415	to	535
large including department stores and supermarkets	360	to	500
Fitting out shell for small shop (including shop fittings)			
simple store	430	to	515
fashion store	820	to	1010
Fitting out shell for department store or supermarket			
excluding shop fittings	490	to	640
including shop fittings	735	to	1670
Retail Warehouses			
shell	275	to	405
fitting out	195	to	225
Supermarkets			
shell	270	to	645
supermarket fit-out	970	to	1290
hypermarket fit-out	430	to	860
Shopping centres			
malls including fitting out			
comfort cooled	2370	to	3770
air-conditioned	2690	to	4090
food court	2690	to	3875
factory outlet centre mall - enclosed	2150	to	3230
factory outlet centre mall - open	375	to	645
retail area shells, capped off services	540	to	860

Administrative, commercial protective service facilities (CI/SfB 3) - cont'd	Square metre excluding VAT £		
Shopping centres - cont'd			
landlord's back-up areas, management offices, plant rooms			
non air conditioned	620	to	690
excluding shop fittings	490	to	640
including shop fittings	735	to	1670
refurbishment			
mall; limited scope	755	to	1130
mall; comprehensive	1075	to	1615
*Ambulance stations	590	to	870
Ambulance controls centre	820	to	1205
Fire stations	875	to	1150
Police stations	785	to	1195
Prisons	1145	to	1395

Health and welfare facilities (CI/SfB 4)

*District hospitals	895	to	1205
Refurbishment	430	to	875
Hospice	930	to	1150
Private hospitals	865	to	1325
Pharmacies	830	to	1115
Hospital laboratories	1150	to	1685
Ward blocks	875	to	1095
Refurbishment	405	to	655
Geriatric units	895	to	1205
Psychiatric units	890	to	1035
Psycho-geriatric units	845	to	1240
Maternity units	890	to	1205
Operating theatres	955	to	1480
Outpatients/casualty units	980	to	1290
Hospital teaching centres	735	to	1040
*Health centres	840	to	1055
Welfare centres	895	to	1060
*Day centres	765	to	1060
Group practice surgeries	680	to	850
*Homes for the physically handicapped - houses	870	to	1040
*Homes for the mentally handicapped	705	to	975
Geriatric day hospital	765	to	1080
Accommodation for the elderly			
residential homes	540	to	860
nursing homes	755	to	1025
*Children's homes	575	to	875
*Homes for the aged	655	to	875
Refurbishment	255	to	610
*Observation and assessment units	650	to	1095

Recreational facilities (CI/SfB 5)

Public houses	785	to	1060
Kitchen blocks (including fitting out)	1290	to	1480
Dining blocks and canteens in shop and factory	765	to	1095
Restaurants	830	to	1205
Community centres	650	to	900
General purpose halls	650	to	900
Visitors' centres	870	to	1350
Youth clubs	605	to	895
Arts and drama centres	875	to	1010

Recreational facilities (CI/SfB 5) - cont'd	Square metre excluding VAT £		
Galleries			
refurbishment of historic building to create international standard gallery	2475	to	4090
international-standard art gallery	2050	to	2820
national-standard art gallery	1660	to	2050
independent commercial art gallery	895	to	1150
Arts and drama centres	875	to	1010
Theatres, including seating and stage equipment			
large - over 500 seats	1940	to	2690
studio/workshop - less than 500 seats	970	to	1615
refurbishment	1075	to	2155
Concert halls, including seating and stage equipment	1615	to	2640
Cinema			
shell	505	to	660
multiplex; shell only	645	to	915
fitting out including all equipment, air-conditioned	555	to	1010
Exhibition centres	1005	to	1350
Swimming pools			
international standard	1205	to	2170
local authority standard	975	to	1290
school standard	820	to	965
leisure pools, including wave making equipment	1940	to	2475
Ice rinks	905	to	1060
Rifle ranges	705	to	895
Leisure centres			
dry	645	to	915
extension to hotels (shell and fit-out - including pool)	1345	to	1885
wet and dry	1510	to	1940
Sports halls including changing	505	to	900
School gymnasiums	605	to	705
Squash courts	605	to	850
Indoor bowls halls	375	to	720
Bowls pavilions	605	to	745
Health and fitness clubs			
out-of-town (shell and fit-out - including pool)	860	to	1290
town centre (fit-out - excluding pool)	860	to	1350
Sports pavilions			
changing only	765	to	1040
social and changing	650	to	1120
Grandstands			
simple stands	490	to	575
first class stands with ancillary accommodation	870	to	1095
Football Stadia			
basic stand	375	to	755
medium quality including basic facilities	645	to	1185
high quality including extensive facilities	1185	to	1400
national stadium including extensive facilities	2155	to	3230
Clubhouses	645	to	875
Golf clubhouses			
up to 500 m²	925	to	1280
500 m² to 2000 m²	560	to	880
over 2000 m²	1465	to	1950

	Square metre excluding VAT £		

Religious facilities (CI/SfB 6)

Temples, mosques, synagogues	920	to	1290
Churches	785	to	1130
Mission halls, meeting houses	920	to	1205
Convents	850	to	965
Crematoria	1060	to	1235

Educational, scientific, information facilities (CI/SfB 7)

Nursery Schools	785	to	1155
*Primary/junior school	720	to	1055
*Secondary/middle schools	660	to	1055
*Secondary school and further education college buildings			
classrooms	690	to	860
laboratories	710	to	1075
craft design and technology	700	to	1075
music	1055	to	1240
*Extensions to schools			
classrooms	705	to	835
residential	745	to	835
laboratories	980	to	1060
School refurbishment	195	to	605
Sixth form colleges	735	to	925
*Special schools	645	to	925
*Polytechnics			
Students Union buildings	705	to	825
arts buildings	630	to	745
scientific laboratories	845	to	1060
*Training colleges	605	to	925
Management training centres	870	to	1180
*Universities			
arts buildings	785	to	975
science buildings	870	to	1125
College/University Libraries	735	to	1040
Laboratories and offices, low level servicing	785	to	985
Laboratories (specialist, controlled environment)	1205	to	2250
Computer buildings	1035	to	1550
Museums and art galleries			
national-standard museum	2050	to	3015
national-standard independent specialist museum (excluding fit-out)	1400	to	1725
regional, including full air conditioning	1085	to	1800
local, air conditioned	870	to	1235
conversion of existing warehouse to regional standard	845	to	1290
conversion of existing warehouse to local standard	735	to	1095
Learning resource centre			
economical	860	to	1070
high quality	1075	to	1615
Libraries			
branch	735	to	985
city centre	980	to	1155
collegiate; including fittings	1885	to	2260

Residential facilities (CI/SfB 8)

	Square metre excluding VAT £		
*Local authority and housing association schemes			
Bungalows			
semi-detached	555	to	655
terraced	470	to	590
Two storey housing			
detached	515	to	625
semi-detached	455	to	555
terraced	405	to	500
Three storey housing			
semi-detached	485	to	665
terraced	425	to	630
Flats			
low rise excluding lifts	535	to	665
medium rise excluding lifts	550	to	745
Sheltered housing with wardens' accommodation	550	to	795
Terraced blocks of garages	360	to	415
Private developments			
Single detached houses	625	to	875
Houses - two or three storey	410	to	575
High-quality apartments			
three-to-four storey villa	860	to	1025
multi-storey	1400	to	1615
Prestige-quality apartments			
multi-storey	1830	to	2425
Flats			
standard	535	to	655
Warehouse conversions to apartments	625	to	925
Rehabilitation			
housing	245	to	415
flats	375	to	605
Hotels (including fittings, furniture and equipment)			
luxury city-centre hotel - multi-storey conference and wet leisure facilities	1505	to	1830
business town centre/provincial hotel - 4-to-6 storeys, conference and wet leisure facilities	1075	to	1290
mid range provincial hotel - 2-to-3 storeys, conference and leisure facilities	1075	to	1345
mid-range provincial hotel - 2-to-3 storeys, bedroom extension	805	to	1185
city centre aparthotel - 4-to-7 storeys, apartments with self-catering facilities	860	to	1130
budget city-centre hotel - 4-to-6 storeys, dining and bar facilities	915	to	1025
budget city-centre hotel (office conversion) - 4-to-6 storeys, excluding dining facilities	700	to	1130
budget roadside hotel - 2-to-3 storey lodge, excluding dining facilities	860	to	970
Hotel accommodation facilities (excluding fittings, furniture and equipment)			
bedroom areas	590	to	840
front of house and reception	775	to	1025
restaurant areas	860	to	1290
bar areas	755	to	1185
function rooms/conference facilities	645	to	1185
dry leisure	590	to	700
wet leisure	1240	to	1615
*Students' residences			
large budget schemes with en-suite accommodation	700	to	915
smaller schemes (40 - 100 units) with mid-range specifications, some with en-suite bathroom and kitchen facilities	915	to	1185
smaller high-quality courtyard schemes, college style	1185	to	1725
Hostels	590	to	870

Common facilities, other facilities (CI/SfB 9)	Square metre excluding VAT £		
Conference centres	1225	to	1670
Public conveniences	1350	to	1925

* Refer also to *"Cost Limits and Allowances"* in following section.

Approximate Estimates

(incorporating Comparative Prices)

Estimating by means of priced approximate quantities is always more accurate than by using overall prices per square metre. Prices given in this section, which is arranged in elemental order, are derived from "Prices for Measured Works - Major Works" section, but also include for all incidental items and labours which are normally measured separately in Bills of Quantities. As in other sections, they have been established with a tender price index level of 350 (1976 = 100). They do not include for preliminaries, details of which are given in Part II and which in the current tendering climate currently amount to 11% of the value of measured work or fees for professional services.

Whilst every effort has been made to ensure the accuracy of these figures, they have been prepared for approximate estimating purposes and on no account should be used for the preparation of tenders.

Unless otherwise described, units denoted as m² refer to appropriate area unit (rather than gross floor) areas.

As elsewhere in this edition, prices do not include Value Added Tax, which should be applied at the current rate to all non-domestic building.

691

Item nr.	SPECIFICATIONS

1.0 SUBSTRUCTURE

ground floor plan area (unless otherwise described)

comprising:

Trench fill foundations
Strip foundations
Column bases
Pile caps
Strip or base foundations
Raft foundations
Piled foundations
Underpinning
Other foundations/Extras
Basements

Trench fill foundations
Machine excavation, disposal, plain in situ concrete 20.00 N/mm^2 - 20 mm aggregate (1:2:4) trench fill, 300 mm high brickwork in cement mortar (1:3), pitch polymer damp proof course

		Unit	450 x 760 mm £
	With common bricks PC £120.00/1000 in		
1.0.1	half brick wall	m	33.60
1.0.2	one brick wall	m	39.10
1.0.3	cavity wall	m	40.50
	With engineering bricks PC £210.00/1000 in		
1.0.4	one brick wall	m	44.60
1.0.5	cavity wall	m	46.00
	With facing bricks PC £130.000 in		
1.0.6	one brick wall	m	43.20
1.0.7	cavity wall	m	44.60
	With facing bricks PC £275.00/1000 in		
1.0.8	one brick wall	m	53.50
1.0.9	cavity wall	m	54.90

Strip foundations
Excavate trench, partial backfill, partial disposal, earthwork support (risk item), compact base of trench, plain insitu concrete 20.00 N/mm^2 - 20 mm aggregate (1:2:4) 250 mm thick, brickwork in cement mortar (1:3), pitch polymer damp proof course

	A = Wall thickness	A	Half brick
	B = Concrete footing width	B	350 mm wide
	C = Brick bonding	C	Stretcher
			£
	Hand excavation, depth of wall		
1.0.10	600 mm deep	m	38.40
1.0.11	900 mm deep	m	45.30
1.0.12	1200 mm deep	m	59.00
1.0.13	1500 mm deep	m	70.00
	Machine excavation, depth of wall		
1.0.14	600 mm deep	m	35.00
1.0.15	900 mm deep	m	41.90
1.0.16	1200 mm deep	m	52.20
1.0.17	1500 mm deep	m	59.00
	Extra over for three courses of facing bricks		
1.0.18	PC £110.00/1000	m	-
1.0.19	PC £150.00/1000	m	-
1.0.20	PC £275.00/1000	m	-

450 x 1000 mm £	600 x 760 mm £	600 x 1200 mm £	750 x 1200 mm £	750 x 1500 mm £	
40.50	40.50	59.00	73.40	91.30	1.0.1
47.40	47.40	67.30	80.30	98.10	1.0.2
48.70	48.70	68.60	80.30	98.10	1.0.3
51.50	51.50	70.00	83.70	98.10	1.0.4
53.50	53.50	73.40	83.70	105.00	1.0.5
50.10	51.50	70.00	83.70	98.10	1.0.6
51.50	54.20	73.40	83.70	105.00	1.0.7
61.80	61.80	80.30	94.70	111.90	1.0.8
63.10	63.10	83.70	94.70	111.90	1.0.9

COMMON BRICKS PC £100.00/1000		ENGINEERING BRICKS PC £175.00/1000		FACING BRICKS PC £110.00/1000		
One brick 600 mm wide English £	Cavity wall 750 mm wide Stretcher £	One brick 600 mm wide English £	Cavity wall 750 mm wide Stretcher £	One brick 600 mm wide English £	Cavity wall 750 mm wide Stretcher £	
59.70	65.20	66.60	70.00	63.10	64.80	1.0.10
73.40	87.80	83.70	98.10	75.50	89.90	1.0.11
94.71	111.90	111.90	126.30	105.00	116.70	1.0.12
111.90	133.10	133.10	153.70	126.30	146.90	1.0.13
52.20	59.70	59.70	70.00	59.70	66.60	1.0.14
70.00	76.90	82.40	91.30	76.90	82.40	1.0.15
83.70	98.10	98.80	111.90	98.10	111.90	1.0.16
98.10	115.30	118.70	133.10	111.90	123.50	1.0.17
0.14	0.21	-	-	-	-	1.0.18
0.69	1.24	-	-	-	-	1.0.19
2.06	4.19	1.24	2.40	-	-	1.0.20

Item nr.	SPECIFICATIONS	Unit	900 mm deep
1.0	**SUBSTRUCTURE - cont'd**		
	ground floor plan area (unless otherwise described)		
	Column bases		
	Excavate pit in firm ground, partial backfill, partial disposal, earthwork support, compact base of pit, plain insitu concrete 20.00 N/mm^2 - 20 mm aggregate (1:2:4), formwork		
	Hand excavation, base size		
1.0.21	600 mm x 600 mm x 300 mm	nr	42.50
1.0.22	900 mm x 900 mm x 450 mm	nr	78.20
1.0.23	1200 mm x 1200 mm x 450 mm	nr	129.00
1.0.24	1500 mm x 1500 mm x 600 mm	nr	228.50
	Machine excavation, base size		
1.0.25	600 mm x 600 mm x 300 mm	nr	35.70
1.0.26	900 mm x 900 mm x 450 mm	nr	71.40
1.0.27	1200 mm x 1200 mm x 450 mm	nr	108.20
1.0.28	1500 mm x 1500 mm x 600 mm	nr	200.40
	Excavate pit in firm ground by machine, partial backfill, partial disposal, earthwork support, compact base of pit, reinforced in situ concrete 20.00 N/mm^2 - 20 mm aggregate (1:2:4), formwork		
	Reinforcement at 50 kg/m^3 concrete, base size		
1.0.29	1750 mm x 1750 mm x 500 mm	nr	229.00
1.0.30	2000 mm x 2000 mm x 500 mm	nr	285.00
1.0.31	2200 mm x 2200 mm x 600 mm	nr	428.00
1.0.32	2400 mm x 2400 mm x 600 mm	nr	486.00
	Reinforcement at 75 kg/m^3 concrete, base size		
1.0.33	1750 mm x 1750 mm x 500 mm	nr	244.00
1.0.34	2000 mm x 2000 mm x 500 mm	nr	300.00
1.0.35	2200 mm x 2200 mm x 600 mm	nr	443.00
1.0.36	2400 mm x 2400 mm x 600 mm	nr	514.00
	Pile caps		
	Excavate pit in firm ground by machine, partial backfill partial disposal, earthwork support, compact base of pit, cut off top of pile and prepare reinforcement, reinforced insitu concrete 25.00 N/mm^2 - 20 mm aggregate (1:2:4), formwork		
	Reinforcement at 50 kg/m^3 concrete, cap size		
1.0.37	900 mm x 900 mm x 1400 mm; one pile	nr	-
1.0.38	2700 mm x 900 mm x 1400 mm; two piles	nr	-
1.0.39	2700 mm x 1475 mm x 1400 mm; three piles*	nr	-
1.0.40	2700 mm x 2700 mm x 1400 mm; four piles	nr	-
1.0.41	3700 mm x 2700 mm x 1400 mm; six piles	nr	-
	Reinforcement at 75 kg/m^3 concrete, cap size		
1.0.42	900 mm x 900 mm x 1400 mm; one pile	nr	-
1.0.43	2700 mm x 900 mm x 1400 mm; two piles	nr	-
1.0.44	2700 mm x 1475 mm x 1400 mm; three piles*	nr	-
1.0.45	2700 mm x 2700 mm x 1400 mm; four piles	nr	-
1.0.46	3700 mm x 2700 mm x 1400 mm; six piles	nr	-
	* = triangular on plan, overall dimensions given		
1.0.47	Additional cost of alternative strength concrete	m^3	-

		DEPTH OF PIT			Item nr
1200 mm deep £	1500 mm deep £	1800 mm deep £	2100 mm deep £	2500 mm deep £	
45.30	49.40	57.60	64.50	71.40	1.0.21
92.60	99.50	107.70	129.00	142.70	1.0.22
142.70	156.50	179.10	207.30	228.50	1.0.23
257.40	285.50	299.90	356.90	393.20	1.0.24
35.70	42.50	44.60	49.40	53.50	1.0.25
78.20	78.20	85.10	92.60	99.50	1.0.26
114.60	121.50	129.00	142.70	149.60	1.0.27
214.10	227.80	233.30	257.40	264.90	1.0.28
242.00	257.00	272.00	292.00	314.00	1.0.29
300.00	322.00	336.00	364.00	392.00	1.0.30
443.00	465.00	486.00	514.00	544.00	1.0.31
514.00	536.00	557.00	599.00	644.00	1.0.32
257.00	272.00	285.00	300.00	322.00	1.0.33
322.00	343.00	357.00	385.00	401.00	1.0.34
465.00	486.00	500.00	544.00	571.00	1.0.35
544.00	571.00	585.00	629.00	657.00	1.0.36

1500 mm deep £	1800 mm deep £	2100 mm deep £	2400 mm deep £		
228.00	231.00	242.00	249.00	-	1.0.37
571.00	567.00	585.00	599.00	-	1.0.38
1036.00	1040.00	1071.00	1106.00	-	1.0.39
1322.00	1358.00	1367.00	1428.00	-	1.0.40
1786.00	1820.00	1890.00	1925.00	-	1.0.41
228.00	233.00	242.00	256.00	-	1.0.42
571.00	581.00	606.00	627.00	-	1.0.43
1050.00	1085.00	1141.00	1176.00	-	1.0.44
1427.00	1455.00	1444.00	1498.00	-	1.0.45
1890.00	1932.00	2002.00	2030.00	-	1.0.46
30.00 N/mm^2 20 mm aggregate		40.00 N/mm^2 20 mm aggregate			
1.00	-	2.40	-	-	1.0.47

Item nr.	SPECIFICATIONS	Unit	RESIDENTIAL £ range £	
1.0	**SUBSTRUCTURE - cont'd**			
	ground floor plan area (unless otherwise described)			
	Strip or base foundations			
	Foundations in good ground; reinforced concrete bed: for one storey development			
1.0.48	shallow foundations	m²	-	-
1.0.49	deep foundations	m²	-	-
	Foundations in good ground; reinforced concrete bed: for two storey development			
1.0.50	shallow foundations	m²	-	-
1.0.51	deep foundations	m²	-	-
	Extra for			
1.0.52	each additional storey	m²	-	-
	Raft foundations			
	Raft on poor ground for development			
1.0.53	one storey high	m²	-	-
1.0.54	two storey high	m²	-	-
	Extra for			
1.0.55	each additional storey	m²	-	-
	Piled foundations			
	Foundations in poor ground; reinforced concrete slab and ground beams; for two storey residential development			
1.0.56	short bore piled	m²	122.00	- 163.00
1.0.57	fully piled	m²	150.00	- 187.00
	Foundations in poor ground; hollow ground floor; timber and boarding; for two storey residential			
1.0.58	short bore piled	m²	143.00	- 170.00
	Foundations in poor ground; reinforced concrete slab; for one storey commercial development			
1.0.59	short bore piles to columns only	m²	-	-
1.0.60	short bore piles	m²	-	-
1.0.61	fully piled	m²	-	-
	Foundations in poor ground; reinforced concrete slab and ground beams; for two storey commercial development			
1.0.62	short bore piles	m²	-	-
1.0.63	fully piled	m²	-	-
	Extra for			
1.0.64	each additional storey	m²	-	-
	Foundations in bad ground; inner city redevelopment; reinforced concrete slab and ground beams; for two storey commercial development			
1.0.65	fully piled	m²	-	-
	Underpinning			
	In stages not exceeding 1500 mm long from one side of existing wall and foundation, excavate preliminary trench by machine and underpinning pit by hand, partial backfill, partial disposal, earthwork support (open boarded), cutting away projecting foundations, prepare underside of existing, compact base of pit, plain in situ concrete 20.00 N/mm² - 20 mm aggregate (1:2:4), formwork, brickwork in cement mortar (1:3), pitch polymer damp proof course, wedge and pin to underside of existing with slates			
	With common bricks PC £100.00/1000, depth of underpinning			
1.0.66	900 mm high, one brick wall	m	-	
1.0.67	900 mm high, two brick wall	m	-	
1.0.68	1200 mm high, one brick wall	m	-	
1.0.69	1200 mm high, two brick wall	m	-	
1.0.70	1500 mm high, one brick wall	m	-	
1.0.71	1500 mm high, two brick wall	m	-	
1.0.72	1800 mm high, one brick wall	m	-	
1.0.73	1800 mm high, two brick wall	m	-	

INDUSTRIAL £ range £	RETAILING £ range £	LEISURE £ range £	OFFICES £ range £	HOTELS £ range £	Item nr.
42.50 - 57.30	49.40 - 71.40	49.80 - 71.40	- -	- -	1.0.48
71.40 - 85.40	78.20 - 100.20	71.40 - 85.40	- -	- -	1.0.49
49.80 - 78.20	57.30 - 85.40	50.40 - 85.40	57.30 - 85.40	57.30 - 85.40	1.0.50
78.20 - 121.80	85.40 - 121.80	85.40 - 121.80	85.40 - 121.80	85.40 - 121.80	1.0.51
17.20 - 19.90	14.40 - 18.50	14.40 - 18.50	14.40 - 18.50	14.40 - 18.50	1.0.52
57.30 - 99.50	64.50 - 99.50	71.40 - 113.20	- -	- -	1.0.53
92.30 - 135.90	106.40 - 150.00	106.40 - 150.00	106.40 - 146.90	106.40 - 146.90	1.0.54
17.20 - 19.90	14.40 - 18.50	14.40 - 18.50	14.40 - 18.50	14.40 - 18.50	1.0.55
- -	- -	- -	- -	- -	1.0.56
- -	- -	- -	- -	- -	1.0.57
- -	- -	- -	- -	- -	1.0.58
71.40 - 107.70	78.20 - 107.70	71.40 - 107.70	- -	- -	1.0.59
92.30 - 121.80	92.60 - 128.70	92.30 - 128.70	92.30 - 128.70	92.30 - 128.70	1.0.60
121.80 - 170.90	135.90 - 186.00	135.90 - 186.00	135.90 - 186.00	135.90 - 186.00	1.0.61
- -	107.70 - 135.90	107.70 - 134.50	107.70 - 135.90	107.70 - 135.90	1.0.62
- -	170.90 - 235.00	170.90 - 235.00	170.90 - 235.00	170.90 - 235.00	1.0.63
17.20 - 19.90	10.00 - 11.40	10.00 - 11.40	10.00 - 11.40	10.00 - 11.40	1.0.64
- -	200.00 - 292.70	- -	200.00 - 343.10	200.00 - 292.60	1.0.65

EXCAVATION COMMENCING AT

1.00 m below ground level	2.00 m below ground level	3.00 m below ground level	4.00 m below ground level		Item nr.
210.00	247.00	291.00	317.00	-	1.0.66
250.00	287.00	332.00	357.00	-	1.0.67
262.00	303.00	351.00	376.00	-	1.0.68
316.00	357.00	405.00	430.00	-	1.0.69
301.00	347.00	398.00	423.00	-	1.0.70
365.00	410.00	461.00	486.00	-	1.0.71
340.00	387.00	445.00	471.00	-	1.0.72
416.00	465.00	519.00	545.00	-	1.0.73

Item nr.	SPECIFICATIONS	Unit	

1.0   SUBSTRUCTURE - cont'd
                 ground floor plan area (unless otherwise described)

Underpinning - cont'd
With engineering bricks PC £210/1000, depth of underpinning

Item nr.	Specification	Unit	
1.0.74	900 mm high; one brick wall	m	-
1.0.75	900 mm high; two brick wall	m	-
1.0.76	1200 mm high; one brick wall	m	-
1.0.77	1200 mm high; two brick wall	m	-
1.0.78	1500 mm high; one brick wall	m	-
1.0.79	1500 mm high; two brick wall	m	-
1.0.80	1800 mm high; one brick wall	m	-
1.0.81	1800 mm high; two brick wall	m	-

Ground slabs
Mechanical excavation to reduce levels, disposal, level and compact, hardcore bed blinded with sand, 1200 gauge polythene damp proof membrane concrete 20.00 N/mm^2 - 20 mm aggregate (1:2:4) ground slab, tamped finish
Plain insitu concrete ground slab, thickness of hardcore bed

		Unit	150mm £
1.0.82	150 mm thick	m^2	27.30
1.0.83	175 mm thick	m^2	27.50
1.0.84	200 mm thick	m^2	28.70

Add to the foregoing prices for
Fabric reinforcement B.S. 4483, lapped

1.0.85	A142 (2.22kg/m^2) 1 layer	m^2	2.90
1.0.86	2 layers	m^2	4.30
1.0.87	A193 (3.02kg/m^2) 1 layer	m^2	2.90
1.0.88	2 layers	m^2	4.90
1.0.89	A252 (3.95kg/m^2) 1 layer	m^2	2.90
1.0.90	2 layers	m^2	5.80
1.0.91	A393 (6.16kg/m^2) 1 layer	m^2	4.30
1.0.92	2 layers	m^2	8.50

High yield steel bar reinforcement B.S. 4449 straight or bent, at a rate of

1.0.93	25 kg/m^3	m^2	2.90
1.0.94	50 kg/m^3	m^2	4.90
1.0.95	75 kg/m^3	m^2	7.10
1.0.96	100 kg/m^3	m^2	9.30

Alternative concrete mixes in lieu of 20.00 N/mm^2 20 mm aggregate (1:2:4)

1.0.97	25.00 N/mm^2	m^2	0.27
1.0.98	30.00 N/mm^2	m^2	0.38
1.0.99	40.00 N/mm^2	m^2	0.66

Other foundations/alternative slabs/extras

		Unit	RESIDENTIAL £ range £	
1.0.100	Cantilevered foundations in good ground; reinforced concrete slab for two storey commercial development	m^2	-	-
1.0.101	Underpinning foundations of existing buildings abutting site	m	-	-

Extra to substructure rates for

| 1.0.102 | watertight pool construction | m^2 | - | - |
| 1.0.103 | ice pad | m^2 | - | - |

Reinforced concrete bed including excavation and hardcore under

1.0.104	150 mm thick	m^2	18.50	- 25.70
1.0.105	200 mm thick	m^2	25.70	- 32.90
1.0.106	300 mm thick	m^2	-	-

EXCAVATION COMMENCING AT

1.00 m below ground level	2.00 m below ground level	3.00 m below ground level	4.00 m below ground level		Item nr.
220.00	258.00	302.00	328.00	-	1.0.74
270.00	307.00	351.00	376.00	-	1.0.75
276.00	318.00	365.00	391.00	-	1.0.76
340.00	382.00	431.00	457.00	-	1.0.77
320.00	362.00	415.00	439.00	-	1.0.78
398.00	456.00	494.00	519.00	-	1.0.79
361.00	410.00	465.00	490.00	-	1.0.80
456.00	504.00	559.00	583.00	-	1.0.81

THICKNESS OF CONCRETE SLAB

200 mm thick £	250 mm thick £	300 mm thick £	375 mm thick £	450 mm thick £	
28.80	32.90	34.30	39.80	44.60	1.0.82
30.20	32.90	35.70	41.20	46.00	1.0.83
30.20	34.30	35.70	42.50	46.00	1.0.84
2.90	2.90	2.90	2.90	2.90	1.0.85
4.30	4.30	4.90	4.90	4.90	1.0.86
2.90	2.90	2.90	2.90	3.60	1.0.87
4.90	5.80	5.80	5.80	5.80	1.0.88
3.60	3.60	3.60	4.30	4.30	1.0.89
5.80	6.50	6.50	6.50	7.10	1.0.90
4.30	4.30	4.30	4.90	4.90	1.0.91
8.50	8.50	8.50	8.50	8.50	1.0.92
3.60	4.30	5.80	7.10	7.80	1.0.93
6.50	8.50	10.00	12.90	15.00	1.0.94
10.00	12.20	14.40	18.50	21.30	1.0.95
12.90	15.80	18.50	24.20	28.70	1.0.96
0.36	0.45	0.54	0.69	0.81	1.0.97
0.51	0.63	0.75	0.95	1.13	1.0.98
0.89	1.10	1.32	1.65	1.98	1.0.99

INDUSTRIAL £ range £	RETAILING £ range £	LEISURE £ range £	OFFICES £ range £	HOTELS £ range £	
- -	242.00 - 316.00	242.00 - 316.00	242.00 - 316.00	242.00 - 316.00	1.0.100
- -	571.00 - 784.00	571.00 - 784.00	571.00 - 784.00	571.00 - 784.00	1.0.101
- -	- -	92.00 - 136.00	- -	- -	1.0.102
- -	- -	108.00 - 163.00	- -	- -	1.0.103
25.70 - 32.90	25.70 - 32.90	25.70 - 32.90	25.70 - 32.90	25.70 - 32.90	1.0.104
34.30 - 44.30	31.60 - 41.20	31.60 - 38.40	31.60 - 38.40	31.60 - 38.40	1.0.105
42.50 - 60.00	38.40 - 54.20	38.40 - 48.70	38.40 - 48.70	38.40 - 48.70	1.0.106

Item nr.	SPECIFICATIONS	Unit	RESIDENTIAL £ range £		
1.0	**SUBSTRUCTURE - cont'd**				
	ground floor plan area (unless otherwise described)				
	Other foundations/alternative slabs/extras - cont'd				
	Hollow ground floor with timber and boarding, including excavation, concrete and hardcore under				
1.0.107	300 mm deep	m²	30.90	-	39.10
	Extra for				
1.0.108	sound reducing quilt in screed	m²	2.70	-	3.80
1.0.109	50 mm insulation under slab and at edges	m²	2.70	-	4.80
1.0.110	75 mm insulation under slab and at edges	m²	-		-
1.0.111	suspended precast concrete slabs in lieu of in situ slab	m²	4.80	-	7.20
	Basement (excluding bulk excavation costs)				
	basement floor/wall area (as appropriate)				
	Reinforced concrete basement floors				
1.0.112	non-waterproofed	m²	-		-
1.0.113	waterproofed	m²	-		-
	Reinforced concrete basement walls				
1.0.114	non-waterproofed	m²	-		-
1.0.115	waterproofed	m²	-		-
1.0.116	sheet piled	m²	-		-
1.0.117	diaphragm walling	m²	-		-
	Extra for				
1.0.118	each additional basement level	%	-		-

Item nr.	SPECIFICATIONS	Unit	RESIDENTIAL £
2.0	**SUPERSTRUCTURE**		
2.1	**FRAME TO ROOF**		
	Roof plan area (unless otherwise described)		
	comprising:		
	Reinforced concrete frame		
	Steel frame		
	Other frames/extras		
	Reinforced Concrete Frame		20N/mm²- 20mm
	Reinforced insitu concrete column, bar reinforcement, formwork (assumed four uses)		Formwork Basic
	Reinforcement rate 180 kg /m³, column size		£
2.1.1	225 mm x 225 mm	m	33.00
2.1.2	300 mm x 300 mm	m	46.00
2.1.3	300 mm x 450 mm	m	65.00
2.1.4	300 mm x 600 mm	m	80.00
2.1.5	450 mm x 450 mm	m	82.00
2.1.6	450 mm x 600 mm	m	102.00
2.1.7	450 mm x 900 mm	m	141.00
	Reinforcement rate 200 kg /m³, column size		
2.1.8	225 mm x 225 mm	m	34.00
2.1.9	300 mm x 300 mm	m	48.00
2.1.10	300 mm x 450 mm	m	65.00
2.1.11	300 mm x 600 mm	m	81.00
2.1.12	450 mm x 450 mm	m	84.00
2.1.13	450 mm x 600 mm	m	104.00
2.1.14	450 mm x 900 mm	m	144.00

INDUSTRIAL £ range £	RETAILING £ range £	LEISURE £ range £	OFFICES £ range £	HOTELS £ range £	Item nr.
- -	- -	- -	- -	- -	1.0.107
2.70 - 4.80	2.70 - 4.80	2.70 - 4.80	2.70 - 4.80	2.70 - 4.80	1.0.108
4.50 - 6.50	4.50 - 6.50	4.50 - 6.50	4.50 - 6.50	4.50 - 6.50	1.0.109
5.50 - 8.20	5.50 - 8.20	5.50 - 8.20	5.50 - 8.20	5.50 - 8.20	1.0.110
11.70 - 14.80	9.60 - 11.70	9.60 - 11.70	9.60 - 11.70	9.60 - 11.70	1.0.111
- -	45.00 - 60.00	45.00 - 60.00	45.00 - 60.00	45.00 - 60.00	1.0.112
- -	60.00 - 82.00	60.00 - 82.00	60.00 - 82.00	60.00 - 82.00	1.0.113
- -	135.00 - 172.00	135.00 - 172.00	135.00 - 172.00	135.00 - 172.00	1.0.114
- -	156.00 - 195.00	156.00 - 195.00	156.00 - 195.00	156.00 - 195.00	1.0.115
- -	277.00 - 338.00	277.00 - 338.00	277.00 - 338.00	277.00 - 338.00	1.0.116
- -	306.00 - 360.00	306.00 - 360.00	306.00 - 360.00	306.00 - 360.00	1.0.117
- -	+ 20%	+ 20%	+ 20%	+ 20%	1.0.118

ALTERNATIVE MIXES AND FINISHES

aggregate (1:2:4), finish	30.00 N/mm^2 - 20 mm aggregate (1:1:2), Formwork finish		40.00 N/mm^2 - 20 mm aggregate Formwork finish		
Smooth £	Basic £	Smooth £	Basic £	Smooth £	
36.00	33.00	36.00	34.00	38.00	2.1.1
51.00	47.00	51.00	49.00	54.00	2.1.2
69.00	65.00	69.00	67.00	71.00	2.1.3
84.00	80.00	84.00	84.00	89.00	2.1.4
86.00	84.00	89.00	85.00	91.00	2.1.5
108.00	102.00	109.00	108.00	113.00	2.1.6
150.00	143.00	151.00	150.00	156.00	2.1.7
38.00	34.00	38.00	34.00	38.00	2.1.8
53.00	47.00	53.00	49.00	54.00	2.1.9
70.00	65.00	70.00	67.00	71.00	2.1.10
85.00	81.00	85.00	84.00	90.00	2.1.11
89.00	84.00	90.00	86.00	93.00	2.1.12
110.00	105.00	110.00	109.00	116.00	2.1.13
152.00	145.00	154.00	152.00	160.00	2.1.14

Approximate Estimates

Item nr.	SPECIFICATIONS	Unit	20N/mm^2 -20mm Formwork Basic £
2.1	**FRAME TO ROOF - cont'd**		
	roof plan area (unless otherwise described)		
	Reinforced Concrete Frame - cont'd		
	Reinforcement rate 220 kg /m^3, column size		
2.1.15	225 mm x 225 mm	m	34.00
2.1.16	300 mm x 300 mm	m	48.00
2.1.17	300 mm x 450 mm	m	66.00
2.1.18	300 mm x 600 mm	m	81.00
2.1.19	450 mm x 450 mm	m	84.00
2.1.20	450 mm x 600 mm	m	105.00
2.1.21	450 mm x 900 mm	m	147.00
	Reinforcement rate 240 kg /m^3, column size		
2.1.22	225 mm x 225 mm	m	34.00
2.1.23	300 mm x 300 mm	m	49.00
2.1.24	300 mm x 450 mm	m	67.00
2.1.25	300 mm x 600 mm	m	84.00
2.1.26	450 mm x 450 mm	m	85.00
2.1.27	450 mm x 600 mm	m	108.00
2.1.28	450 mm x 900 mm	m	150.00
	In situ concrete casing to steel column, formwork (assumed four uses), column size		
2.1.29	225 mm x 225 mm	m	32.00
2.1.30	300 mm x 300 mm	m	43.00
2.1.31	300 mm x 450 mm	m	58.00
2.1.32	300 mm x 600 mm	m	69.00
2.1.33	450 mm x 450 mm	m	71.00
2.1.34	450 mm x 600 mm	m	86.00
2.1.35	450 mm x 900 mm	m	120.00
	Reinforced in situ concrete isolated beams, bar reinforcement, formwork (assumed four uses)		
	Reinforcement rate 200 kg /m^3, beam size		
2.1.36	225 mm x 450 mm	m	58.00
2.1.37	225 mm x 600 mm	m	73.00
2.1.38	300 mm x 600 mm	m	84.00
2.1.39	300 mm x 900 mm	m	116.00
2.1.40	300 mm x 1200 mm	m	150.00
2.1.41	450 mm x 600 mm	m	108.00
2.1.42	450 mm x 900 mm	m	148.00
2.1.43	450 mm x 1200 mm	m	187.00
2.1.44	600 mm x 600 mm	m	132.00
2.1.45	600 mm x 900 mm	m	178.00
2.1.46	600 mm x 1200 mm	m	226.00
	Reinforcement rate 220 kg /m^3, beam size		
2.1.47	225 mm x 450 mm	m	59.00
2.1.48	225 mm x 600 mm	m	73.00
2.1.49	300 mm x 600 mm	m	84.00
2.1.50	300 mm x 900 mm	m	119.00
2.1.51	300 mm x 1200 mm	m	151.00
2.1.52	450 mm x 600 mm	m	109.00
2.1.53	450 mm x 900 mm	m	151.00
2.1.54	450 mm x 1200 mm	m	191.00
2.1.55	600 mm x 600 mm	m	133.00
2.1.56	600 mm x 900 mm	m	180.00
2.1.57	600 mm x 1200 mm	m	231.00
	Reinforcement rate 240 kg /m^3, beam size		
2.1.58	225 mm x 450 mm	m	60.00
2.1.59	225 mm x 600 mm	m	75.00
2.1.60	300 mm x 600 mm	m	85.00
2.1.61	300 mm x 900 mm	m	120.00
2.1.62	300 mm x 1200 mm	m	154.00
2.1.63	450 mm x 600 mm	m	110.00
2.1.64	450 mm x 900 mm	m	154.00
2.1.65	450 mm x 1200 mm	m	195.00

ALTERNATIVE MIXES AND FINISHES

aggregate (1:2:4) finish Smooth £	30.00 N/mm² - 20 mm aggregate (1:1:2), Formwork finish Basic £	Smooth £	40.00 N/mm² - 20 mm aggregate Formwork finish Basic £	Smooth £	Item nr.
38.00	34.00	38.00	36.00	39.00	2.1.15
53.00	49.00	53.00	51.00	54.00	2.1.16
70.00	66.00	70.00	69.00	73.00	2.1.17
86.00	82.00	86.00	85.00	91.00	2.1.18
91.00	85.00	91.00	89.00	94.00	2.1.19
112.00	106.00	113.00	112.00	119.00	2.1.20
155.00	148.00	156.00	155.00	164.00	2.1.21
38.00	34.00	38.00	36.00	39.00	2.1.22
54.00	49.00	54.00	51.00	56.00	2.1.23
71.00	67.00	71.00	70.00	75.00	2.1.24
89.00	84.00	89.00	86.00	91.00	2.1.25
91.00	86.00	93.00	91.00	98.00	2.1.26
113.00	108.00	115.00	113.00	120.00	2.1.27
156.00	152.00	159.00	156.00	168.00	2.1.28
34.00	32.00	34.00	33.00	36.00	2.1.29
46.00	45.00	46.00	46.00	49.00	2.1.30
63.00	59.00	63.00	60.00	65.00	2.1.31
75.00	70.00	77.00	73.00	80.00	2.1.32
78.00	71.00	78.00	77.00	82.00	2.1.33
95.00	89.00	94.00	93.00	101.00	2.1.34
128.00	120.00	129.00	128.00	136.00	2.1.35
62.00	59.00	63.00	60.00	65.00	2.1.36
78.00	73.00	80.00	77.00	82.00	2.1.37
89.00	84.00	90.00	86.00	93.00	2.1.38
124.00	119.00	125.00	121.00	129.00	2.1.39
156.00	151.00	159.00	156.00	167.00	2.1.40
113.00	108.00	115.00	113.00	120.00	2.1.41
156.00	150.00	156.00	156.00	165.00	2.1.42
198.00	190.00	199.00	198.00	210.00	2.1.43
140.00	133.00	140.00	140.00	145.00	2.1.44
189.00	179.00	190.00	190.00	199.00	2.1.45
237.00	230.00	240.00	241.00	253.00	2.1.46
63.00	59.00	63.00	60.00	65.00	2.1.47
80.00	75.00	81.00	78.00	82.00	2.1.48
89.00	85.00	91.00	88.00	93.00	2.1.49
126.00	121.00	128.00	124.00	132.00	2.1.50
161.00	152.00	162.00	158.00	167.00	2.1.51
115.00	110.00	117.00	115.00	121.00	2.1.52
158.00	152.00	161.00	158.00	167.00	2.1.53
200.00	194.00	205.00	203.00	213.00	2.1.54
141.00	136.00	143.00	141.00	148.00	2.1.55
192.00	185.00	195.00	195.00	202.00	2.1.56
242.00	233.00	246.00	248.00	257.00	2.1.57
65.00	60.00	65.00	62.00	65.00	2.1.58
81.00	77.00	81.00	78.00	84.00	2.1.59
91.00	86.00	92.00	89.00	95.00	2.1.60
128.00	122.00	129.00	126.00	133.00	2.1.61
163.00	155.00	165.00	162.00	170.00	2.1.62
119.00	112.00	121.00	117.00	124.00	2.1.63
162.00	155.00	163.00	162.00	170.00	2.1.64
206.00	196.00	209.00	207.00	215.00	2.1.65

Item nr.	SPECIFICATIONS	Unit	20N/mm^2 -20mm Formwork Basic £
2.1	**FRAME TO ROOF - cont'd**		
	roof plan area (unless otherwise described)		
	Reinforced Concrete Frame - cont'd		
	Reinforcement rate 240 kg /m^3, beam size - cont'd		
2.1.66	600 mm x 600 mm	m	136.00
2.1.67	600 mm x 900 mm	m	188.00
2.1.68	600 mm x 1200 mm	m	236.00
	In situ concrete casing to steel attached beams, formwork (assumed four uses), beam size		
2.1.69	225 mm x 450 mm	m	54.00
2.1.70	225 mm x 600 mm	m	67.00
2.1.71	300 mm x 600 mm	m	77.00
2.1.72	300 mm x 900 mm	m	104.00
2.1.73	300 mm x 1200 mm	m	132.00
2.1.74	450 mm x 600 mm	m	93.00
2.1.75	450 mm x 900 mm	m	128.00
2.1.76	450 mm x 1200 mm	m	159.00
2.1.77	600 mm x 600 mm	m	114.00
2.1.78	600 mm x 900 mm	m	150.00
2.1.79	600 mm x 1200 mm	m	188.00
	Steel		
	Fabricated steelwork B.S. 4360 grade 40 erected on site with bolted connections		
2.1.80	universal beams	tonne	-
2.1.81	rectangular section beams	tonne	-
2.1.82	composite beams	tonne	-
2.1.83	lattice beams	tonne	-
2.1.84	rectangular section columns	tonne	-
2.1.85	composite columns	tonne	-
2.1.86	roof trusses	tonne	-
2.1.87	smaller sections	tonne	-

Item nr.	SPECIFICATIONS	Unit	RESIDENTIAL £ range £	
	Other frames/extras			
	Space deck on steel frame			
2.1.88	unprotected	m^2	-	-
2.1.89	Exposed steel frame for tent/mast structures	m^2	-	-
	Columns and beams to 18.00 m high bay warehouse			
2.1.90	unprotected	m^2	-	-
	Columns and beams to mansard			
2.1.91	protected	m^2	-	-
	Feature columns and beams to glazed atrium roof			
2.1.92	unprotected	m^2	-	-

ALTERNATIVE MIXES AND FINISHES

aggregate (1:2:4) finish Smooth £	30.00 N/mm² - 20 mm aggregate (1:1:2), Formwork finish Basic £	Smooth £	40.00 N/mm² - 20 mm aggregate Formwork finish Basic £	Smooth £	Item nr.
144.00	137.00	145.00	144.00	151.00	2.1.66
195.00	189.00	198.00	198.00	207.00	2.1.67
248.00	237.00	251.00	251.00	262.00	2.1.68
58.00	54.00	59.00	56.00	60.00	2.1.69
71.00	67.00	73.00	70.00	77.00	2.1.70
82.00	77.00	82.00	80.00	85.00	2.1.71
113.00	106.00	113.00	110.00	119.00	2.1.72
141.00	133.00	143.00	140.00	148.00	2.1.73
100.00	93.00	102.00	100.00	107.00	2.1.74
136.00	129.00	137.00	136.00	145.00	2.1.75
169.00	162.00	172.00	170.00	181.00	2.1.76
122.00	115.00	124.00	122.00	128.00	2.1.77
159.00	152.00	162.00	162.00	170.00	2.1.78
198.00	191.00	200.00	202.00	214.00	2.1.79

STEEL FRAME

£	With galvanising £				Item nr.
1430.00	1630.00	-	-	-	2.1.80
1850.00	2050.00	-	-	-	2.1.81
1760.00	1960.00	-	-	-	2.1.82
1670.00	1870.00	-	-	-	2.1.83
1905.00	2110.00	-	-	-	2.1.84
1725.00	1930.00	-	-	-	2.1.85
1725.00	1930.00	-	-	-	2.1.86
1310.00	1515.00	-	-	-	2.1.87

INDUSTRIAL £ range £	RETAILING £ range £	LEISURE £ range £	OFFICES £ range £	HOTELS £ range £	Item nr.
107.00 - 214.00	115.00 - 214.00	115.00 - 214.00	115.00 - 214.00	- -	2.1.88
184.00 - 275.00	184.00 - 275.00	184.00 - 275.00	- -	- -	2.1.89
115.00 - 159.00	- -	- -	- -	- -	2.1.90
- -	77.00 - 106.00	80.00 - 115.00	80.00 - 115.00	80.00 - 115.00	2.1.91
- -	- -	- -	88.00 - 137.00	- -	2.1.92

Item nr.	SPECIFICATIONS	Unit	RESIDENTIAL £ range £
2.2	**FRAME & UPPER FLOORS (COMBINED)** **upper floor area** (unless otherwise described)		

comprising:

Softwood floors; no frame
Softwood floors; steel frame
Reinforced concrete floors; no frame
Reinforced concrete floors and frame
Reinforced concrete floors; steel frame
Precast concrete floors; no frame
Precast concrete floors; reinforced concrete frame
Precast concrete floors and frame
Precast concrete floors; steel frame
Other floor and frame constructions/extras

Softwood floors; no frame
Joisted floor; supported on layers; 22 mm thick chipboard t&g flooring;
herringbone strutting; no coverings or finishes

Item nr.	SPECIFICATIONS	Unit	£ low		£ high
2.2.1	150 mm x 50 mm thick joists	m²	20.00	-	24.00
2.2.2	175 mm x 50 mm thick joists	m²	23.00	-	27.00
2.2.3	200 mm x 50 mm thick joists	m²	24.00	-	27.00
2.2.4	225 mm x 50 mm thick joists	m²	25.00	-	28.00
2.2.5	250 mm x 50 mm thick joists	m²	27.00	-	30.00
2.2.6	275 mm x 50 mm thick joists	m²	30.00	-	34.00
2.2.7	Joisted floor; average depth; plasterboard; skim; emulsion; vinyl flooring and painted softwood skirtings	m²	47.00	-	60.00

Softwood construction; steel frame

2.2.8	Joisted floor; average depth; plasterboard; skim; emulsion; vinyl flooring and painted softwood skirtings	m²	-		-

Reinforced concrete floors; no frame
Suspended slab; no coverings or finishes

2.2.9	3.65 m span; 3.00 kN/m² loading	m²	40.00	-	42.00
2.2.10	4.25 m span; 3.00 kN/m² loading	m²	46.00	-	50.00
2.2.11	2.75 m span; 8.00 kN/m² loading	m²	-		-
2.2.12	3.35 m span; 8.00 kN/m² loading	m²	-		-
2.2.13	4.25 m span; 8.00 kN/m² loading	m²	-		-
	Suspended slab; no coverings or finishes				
2.2.14	150 mm thick	m²	46.00	-	59.00
2.2.15	225 mm thick	m²	69.00	-	82.00

Reinforced concrete floors and frame
Suspended slab; no coverings or finishes

2.2.16	up to six storeys	m²	-		-
2.2.17	seven to twelve storeys	m²	-		-
2.2.18	thirteen to eighteen storeys	m²	-		-
	Extra for				
2.2.19	section 20 fire regulations	m²	-		-
	Wide span suspended slab				
2.2.20	up to six storeys	m²	-		-

Reinforced concrete floors; steel frame
Suspended slab; average depth; "Holorib" permanent steel shuttering;
protected steel frame; no coverings or finishes

2.2.21	up to six storeys	m²	-		-
	Extra for				
2.2.22	spans 7.50 m to 15.00 m	m²	-		-
2.2.23	seven to twelve storeys	m²	-		-
	Extra for				
2.2.24	section 20 fire regulations	m²	-		-

INDUSTRIAL £ range £	RETAILING £ range £	LEISURE £ range £	OFFICES £ range £	HOTELS £ range £	Item nr.
- -	- -	- -	- -	- -	2.2.1
- -	- -	- -	- -	- -	2.2.2
- -	- -	- -	- -	- -	2.2.3
- -	- -	- -	- -	- -	2.2.4
- -	- -	- -	- -	- -	2.2.5
- -	- -	- -	- -	- -	2.2.6
- -	- -	- -	- -	- -	2.2.7
75.00 - 82.00	82.00 - 113.00	82.00 - 113.00	82.00 - 113.00	82.00 - 113.00	2.2.8
- -	- -	39.00 - 46.00	39.00 - 46.00	39.00 - 46.00	2.2.9
- -	- -	46.00 - 49.00	46.00 - 56.00	46.00 - 56.00	2.2.10
39.00 - 46.00	39.00 - 46.00	39.00 - 46.00	39.00 - 46.00	39.00 - 46.00	2.2.11
45.00 - 52.00	45.00 - 52.00	45.00 - 52.00	45.00 - 52.00	45.00 - 52.00	2.2.12
58.00 - 65.00	58.00 - 65.00	58.00 - 65.00	58.00 - 67.00	58.00 - 67.00	2.2.13
52.00 - 75.00	45.00 - 75.00	45.00 - 69.00	45.00 - 66.00	45.00 - 75.00	2.2.14
82.00 - 93.00	69.00 - 93.00	69.00 - 86.00	69.00 - 86.00	69.00 - 93.00	2.2.15
100.00 - 135.00	82.00 - 121.00	86.00 - 128.00	82.00 - 106.00	82.00 - 113.00	2.2.16
- -	- -	- -	106.00 - 165.00	- -	2.2.17
- -	- -	- -	165.00 - 210.00	- -	2.2.18
- -	- -	- -	7.00 - 10.00	- -	2.2.19
113.00 - 139.00	89.00 - 132.00	100.00 - 135.00	89.00 - 121.00	89.00 - 128.00	2.2.20
135.00 - 165.00	113.00 - 156.00	113.00 - 150.00	113.00 - 139.00	113.00 - 145.00	2.2.21
16.00 - 41.00	20.00 - 46.00	16.00 - 41.00	16.00 - 41.00	16.00 - 41.00	2.2.22
- -	- -	- -	128.00 - 195.00	- -	2.2.23
- -	- -	- -	16.00 - 20.00	- -	2.2.24

Item nr.	SPECIFICATIONS	Unit	RESIDENTIAL £ range £	
2.2	**FRAME & UPPER FLOORS (COMBINED) - cont'd**			
	upper floor area (unless otherwise described)			
	Reinforced concrete floors; steel frame - cont'd			
	Suspended slab; average depth; protected steel frame; no coverings or finishes			
2.2.25	up to six storeys	m²	-	-
2.2.26	seven to twelve storeys	m²	-	-
	Extra for			
2.2.27	section 20 fire regulations	m²	-	-
	Precast concrete floors; no frame			
	Suspended slab; 75 mm thick screed; no coverings or finishes			
2.2.28	3.00 m span; 5.00 kN/m² loading	m²	34.00 -	41.00
2.2.29	6.00 m span; 5.00 kN/m² loading	m²	34.00 -	43.00
2.2.30	7.50 m span; 8.50 kN/m² loading	m²	36.00 -	45.00
2.2.31	3.00 m span; 8.50 kN/m² loading	m²	-	-
2.2.32	6.00 m span; 8.50 kN/m² loading	m²	-	-
2.2.33	7.50 m span; 8.50 kN/m² loading	m²	-	-
2.2.34	3.00 m span; 12.50 kN/m² loading	m²	-	-
2.2.35	6.00 m span; 12.50 kN/m² loading	m²	-	-
2.2.36	Suspended slab; average depth; no coverings or finishes	m²	30.00 -	49.00
	Precast concrete floors; reinforced concrete frame			
2.2.37	Suspended slab; average depth; no coverings or finishes	m²	-	-
	Precast concrete floors and frame			
2.2.38	Suspended slab; average depth; no coverings or finishes	m²	-	-
	Precast concrete floors; steel frame			
	Suspended slabs; average depth; unprotected steel frame; no coverings or finishes			
2.2.39	up to three storeys	m²	-	-
	Suspended slabs; average depth; protected steel frame; no coverings or finishes			
2.2.40	up to six storeys	m²	-	-
2.2.41	seven to twelve storeys	m²	-	-
	Other floor and frame construction/extras			
2.2.42	Reinforced concrete cantilevered balcony	nr	1407 -	1887
2.2.43	Reinforced concrete cantilevered walkways	m²	-	-
2.2.44	Reinforced concrete walkways and supporting frame	m²	-	-
	Reinforced concrete core with steel umbrella frame			
2.2.45	twelve to twenty four storeys	m²	-	-
	Extra for			
2.2.46	wrought formwork	m²	2.80 -	3.50
2.2.47	sound reducing quilt in screed	m²	3.20 -	4.10
2.2.48	insulation to avoid cold bridging	m²	3.20 -	5.30

INDUSTRIAL £ range £	RETAILING £ range £	LEISURE £ range £	OFFICES £ range £	HOTELS £ range £	Item nr.
128.00 - 172.00	113.00 - 165.00	128.00 - 165.00	113.00 - 150.00	113.00 - 150.00	2.2.25
- -	- -	- -	128.00 - 210.00	- -	2.2.26
- -	- -	- -	16.00 - 19.00		2.2.27
- -	40.00 - 46.00	40.00 - 46.00	40.00 - 46.00	40.00 - 46.00	2.2.28
- -	40.00 - 48.00	40.00 - 48.00	40.00 - 46.00	45.00 - 48.00	2.2.29
	42.00 - 52.00	42.00 - 52.00	42.00 - 46.00	48.00 - 52.00	2.2.30
42.00 - 48.00	- -	- -	- -	- -	2.2.31
45.00 - 51.00	- -	- -	- -	- -	2.2.32
46.00 - 52.00	- -	- -	- -	- -	2.2.33
45.00 - 49.00	- -	- -	- -	- -	2.2.34
49.00 - 55.00	- -	- -	- -	- -	2.2.35
40.00 - 59.00	- -	- -	- -	- -	2.2.36
66.00 - 86.00	59.00 - 93.00	59.00 - 86.00	59.00 - 84.00	59.00 - 93.00	2.2.37
66.00 - 125.00	59.00 - 128.00	59.00 - 125.00	59.00 - 125.00	59.00 - 143.00	2.2.38
73.00 - 132.00	69.00 - 119.00	69.00 - 111.00	59.00 - 111.00	69.00 - 119.00	2.2.39
119.00 - 152.00	100.00 - 143.00	111.00 - 143.00	100.00 - 135.00	100.00 - 135.00	2.2.40
- -	- -	- -	128.00 - 195.00	- -	2.2.41
- -	- -	- -	- -	- -	2.2.42
- -	103.00 - 128.00	- -	- -	- -	2.2.43
- -	117.00 - 143.00	- -	- -	- -	2.2.44
- -	- -	- -	- -	- -	
- -	- -	- -	239.00 - 323.00	- -	2.2.45
2.80 - 3.40	2.80 - 6.00	2.80 - 6.00	2.80 - 6.00	2.80 - 7.30	2.2.46
3.00 - 5.30	3.00 - 5.30	3.00 - 5.30	3.00 - 5.30	3.00 - 5.30	2.2.47
5.30 - 7.30	5.30 - 7.30	5.30 - 7.30	5.30 - 7.30	5.30 - 7.30	2.2.48

Item nr.	SPECIFICATIONS	Unit	RESIDENTIAL £ range £
2.3	**ROOF**		
	roof plan area (Unless otherwise described)		

comprising:

Softwood flat roofs
Softwood trussed pitched roofs
Steel trussed pitch roofs
Concrete flat roofs
Flat roof decking and finishes
Roof claddings
Rooflights/patent glazing and glazed roofs
Comparative over/underlays
Comparative tiling and slating finishes/perimeter treatments
Comparative cladding finishes/perimeter treatments
Comparative waterproofing finishes/perimeter treatments

Softwood flat roofs
Structure only comprising roof joists; 100 mm x 50 mm wall plates;
herringbone strutting; 50 mm woodwool slabs; no coverings or finishes

Item nr.	SPECIFICATIONS	Unit	£ range £
2.3.1	150 mm x 50 mm joists	m^2	25.90 - 30.00
2.3.2	200 mm x 50 mm joists	m^2	30.20 - 33.00
2.3.3	250 mm x 50 mm joists	m^2	32.90 - 36.00

Structure only comprising roof joists; 100 mm x 50 mm wall plates;
herringbone strutting; 25 mm softwood boarding; no coverings or finishes

Item nr.	SPECIFICATIONS	Unit	£ range £
2.3.4	150 mm x 50 mm joists	m^2	29.00 - 33.00
2.3.5	200 mm x 50 mm joists	m^2	33.00 - 35.00
2.3.6	250 mm x 50 mm joists	m^2	35.00 - 39.00

Roof joists; average depth; 25 mm softwood boarding; PVC rainwater
goods; plasterboard; skim and emulsion

Item nr.	SPECIFICATIONS	Unit	£ range £
2.3.7	three layer felt and chippings	m^2	63.00 - 80.00
2.3.8	two coat asphalt and chippings	m^2	60.00 - 88.00

Softwood trussed pitched roofs
Structure only comprising 75 mm x 50 mm Fink roof trusses at 600 mm
centres (measured on plan)

Item nr.	SPECIFICATIONS	Unit	£ range £
2.3.9	22.50^0 pitch	m^2	12.00 - 15.00

Structure only comprising 100 mm x 38 mm Fink roof trusses at 600 mm
centres (measured on plan)

Item nr.	SPECIFICATIONS	Unit	£ range £
2.3.10	30^0 pitch	m^2	14.00 - 17.00
2.3.11	35^0 pitch	m^2	14.00 - 17.00
2.3.12	40^0 pitch	m^2	16.00 - 20.00

Structure only comprising 100 mm x 50 mm Fink roof trusses at 375 mm
centres (measured on plan)

Item nr.	SPECIFICATIONS	Unit	£ range £
2.3.13	30^0 pitch	m^2	24.00 - 27.00
2.3.14	35^0 pitch	m^2	24.00 - 27.00
2.3.15	40^0 pitch	m^2	26.00 - 30.00

Extra for

Item nr.	SPECIFICATIONS	Unit	£ range £
2.3.16	forming dormers	nr	351.00 - 491.00

Structure only for "Mansard" roof comprising 100 mm x 50 mm roof trusses
at 600 mm centres

Item nr.	SPECIFICATIONS	Unit	£ range £
2.3.17	70^0 pitch	m^2	18.00 - 24.00

Fink roof trusses; narrow span; 100 mm thick insulation; uPVC rainwater
goods; plasterboard; skim and emulsion

Item nr.	SPECIFICATIONS	Unit	£ range £
2.3.18	concrete interlocking tile coverings	m^2	59.00 - 78.00
2.3.19	clay pantile coverings	m^2	66.00 - 84.00
2.3.20	composition slate coverings	m^2	69.00 - 86.00
2.3.21	plain clay tile coverings	m^2	84.00 - 96.00
2.3.22	natural slate coverings	m^2	84.00 - 111.00
2.3.23	reconstructed stone coverings	m^2	70.00 - 118.00

INDUSTRIAL £ range £	RETAILING £ range £	LEISURE £ range £	OFFICES £ range £	HOTELS £ range £	Item nr.
- -	26.00 - 30.00	- -	26.00 - 30.00	26.00 - 30.00	2.3.1
- -	30.00 - 33.00	- -	30.00 - 33.00	30.00 - 33.00	2.3.2
- -	33.00 - 36.00	- -	33.00 - 36.00	33.00 - 36.00	2.3.3
- -	29.00 - 33.00	- -	29.00 - 33.00	29.00 - 33.00	2.3.4
- -	33.00 - 35.00	- -	33.00 - 35.00	33.00 - 35.00	2.3.5
- -	34.00 - 51.00	- -	34.00 - 52.00	34.00 - 40.00	2.3.6
- -	63.00 - 80.00	- -	63.00 - 80.00	63.00 - 80.00	2.3.7
- -	62.00 - 88.00	- -	62.00 - 88.00	62.00 - 88.00	2.3.8
- -	13.00 - 17.00	- -	13.00 - 17.00	13.00 - 17.00	2.3.9
- -	15.00 - 18.00	- -	15.00 - 18.00	15.00 - 19.00	2.3.10
- -	16.00 - 18.00	- -	16.00 - 18.00	16.00 - 20.00	2.3.11
- -	17.00 - 21.00	- -	17.00 - 21.00	17.00 - 22.00	2.3.12
- -	24.00 - 27.00	- -	24.00 - 27.00	24.00 - 29.00	2.3.13
- -	26.00 - 29.00	- -	26.00 - 29.00	26.00 - 30.00	2.3.14
- -	26.00 - 32.00	- -	26.00 - 32.00	26.00 - 33.00	2.3.15
- -	353.00 - 491.00	- -	353.00 - 491.00	353.00 - 491.00	2.3.16
- -	18.00 - 26.00	- -	18.00 - 26.00	18.00 - 26.00	2.3.17
- -	65.00 - 88.00	- -	65.00 - 93.00	71.00 - 97.00	2.3.18
- -	70.00 - 93.00	- -	70.00 - 97.00	75.00 - 103.00	2.3.19
- -	74.00 - 96.00	- -	74.00 - 102.00	80.00 - 108.00	2.3.20
- -	88.00 - 111.00	- -	88.00 - 117.00	93.00 - 122.00	2.3.21
- -	93.00 - 117.00	- -	93.00 - 121.00	97.00 - 128.00	2.3.22
- -	75.00 - 121.00	- -	75.00 - 126.00	81.00 - 132.00	2.3.23

Item nr.	SPECIFICATIONS	Unit	RESIDENTIAL £ range £
2.3	**ROOF - cont'd**		
	roof plan area (unless otherwise described)		
	Softwood trussed pitched roofs - cont'd		
	Monopitch roof trusses; 100 mm thick insulation; PVC rainwater goods; plasterboard; skim and emulsion		
2.3.24	concrete interlocking tile coverings	m^2	66.00 - 81.00
2.3.25	clay pantile coverings	m^2	70.00 - 86.00
2.3.26	composition slate coverings	m^2	74.00 - 91.00
2.3.27	plain clay tile coverings	m^2	86.00 - 103.00
2.3.28	natural slate coverings	m^2	93.00 - 111.00
2.3.29	reconstructed stone coverings	m^2	74.00 - 121.00
	Dormer roof trusses; 100 mm thick insulation; PVC rainwater goods; plasterboard; skim and emulsion		
2.3.30	concrete interlocking tile coverings	m^2	88.00 - 111.00
2.3.31	clay pantile coverings	m^2	93.00 - 118.00
2.3.32	composition slate coverings	m^2	96.00 - 133.00
2.3.33	plain clay tile coverings	m^2	110.00 - 133.00
2.3.34	natural slate coverings	m^2	117.00 - 136.00
2.3.35	reconstructed stone coverings	m^2	96.00 - 148.00
	Extra for		
2.3.36	end of terrace semi/detached configuration	m^2	24.00 - 26.00
2.3.37	hipped roof configuration	m^2	24.00 - 30.00
	Steel trussed pitched roofs		
	Fink roof trusses; wide span; 100 mm thick insulation		
2.3.38	concrete interlocking tile coverings	m^2	- -
2.3.39	clay pantile coverings	m^2	- -
2.3.40	composition slate coverings	m^2	- -
2.3.41	clay plain tile coverings	m^2	- -
2.3.42	natural slate coverings	m^2	- -
2.3.43	reconstructed stone coverings	m^2	- -
	Steel roof trusses and beams; thermal and acoustic insulation		
2.3.44	aluminium profiled composite cladding	m^2	- -
2.3.45	copper roofing on boarding	m^2	- -
	Steel roof and glulam beams; thermal and acoustic insulation		
2.3.46	aluminium profiled composite cladding	m^2	- -
	Concrete flat roofs		
	Structure only comprising reinforced concrete suspended slab; no coverings or finishes		
2.3.47	3.65 m span; 3.00 kN/m^2 loading	m^2	42.00 - 43.00
2.3.48	4.25 m span; 3.00 kN/m^2 loading	m^2	50.00 - 52.00
2.3.49	3.65 m span; 8.00 kN/m^2 loading	m^2	- -
2.3.50	4.25 m span; 8.00 kN/m^2 loading	m^2	- -
	Precast concrete suspended slab; average depth; 100 mm thick insulation; uPVC rainwater goods		
2.3.51	two coat asphalt coverings and chippings	m^2	- -
2.3.52	polyester roofing	m^2	- -
	Reinforced concrete or waffle suspended slabs; average depth; 100 mm thick insulation; uPVC rainwater goods		
2.3.53	two coat asphalt coverings and chippings	m^2	- -
2.3.54	two coat asphalt covering and paving slabs	m^2	- -
	Reinforced concrete slabs; on "Holorib" permanent steel shuttering; average depth; 100 mm thick insulation; uPVC rainwater goods		
2.3.55	two coat asphalt coverings and chippings	m^2	- -

INDUSTRIAL £ range £	RETAILING £ range £	LEISURE £ range £	OFFICES £ range £	HOTELS £ range £	Item nr.
-	70.00 - 93.00	-	70.00 - 96.00	77.00 - 103.00	2.3.24
-	77.00 - 96.00	-	77.00 - 103.00	81.00 - 111.00	2.3.25
-	81.00 - 103.00	-	81.00 - 111.00	84.00 - 117.00	2.3.26
-	93.00 - 118.00	-	93.00 - 121.00	96.00 - 126.00	2.3.27
-	96.00 - 121.00	-	96.00 - 126.00	103.00 - 133.00	2.3.28
-	80.00 - 126.00	-	80.00 - 133.00	86.00 - 136.00	2.3.29
-	93.00 - 121.00	-	93.00 - 126.00	96.00 - 133.00	2.3.30
-	96.00 - 126.00	-	96.00 - 133.00	103.00 - 136.00	2.3.31
-	99.00 - 133.00	-	99.00 - 136.00	107.00 - 143.00	2.3.32
-	117.00 - 143.00	-	117.00 - 148.00	121.00 - 152.00	2.3.33
-	121.00 - 148.00	-	121.00 - 152.00	126.00 - 159.00	2.3.34
-	103.00 - 152.00	-	103.00 - 159.00	110.00 - 165.00	2.3.35
-	-	-	-	-	2.3.36
-	-	-	-	-	2.3.37
-	110.00 - 143.00	107.00 - 136.00	110.00 - 150.00	118.00 - 154.00	2.3.38
-	118.00 - 150.00	110.00 - 143.00	118.00 - 154.00	124.00 - 162.00	2.3.39
-	107.00 - 152.00	118.00 - 150.00	121.00 - 156.00	129.00 - 165.00	2.3.40
-	136.00 - 167.00	132.00 - 159.00	135.00 - 172.00	141.00 - 181.00	2.3.41
-	141.00 - 172.00	136.00 - 167.00	141.00 - 181.00	150.00 - 187.00	2.3.42
-	132.00 - 187.00	125.00 - 181.00	132.00 - 194.00	136.00 - 199.00	2.3.43
167.00 - 199.00	152.00 - 187.00	150.00 - 181.00	152.00 - 170.00	-	2.3.44
-	167.00 - 206.00	170.00 - 206.00	180.00 - 199.00	-	2.3.45
-	167.00 - 222.00	159.00 - 217.00	167.00 - 214.00	-	2.3.46
-	-	40.00 - 48.00	40.00 - 48.00	40.00 - 48.00	2.3.47
-	-	46.00 - 50.00	46.00 - 56.00	46.00 - 56.00	2.3.48
45.00 - 52.00	45.00 - 52.00	45.00 - 52.00	45.00 - 52.00	45.00 - 52.00	2.3.49
56.00 - 65.00	56.00 - 65.00	55.00 - 65.00	55.00 - 65.00	55.00 - 65.00	2.3.50
75.00 - 106.00	69.00 - 114.00	69.00 - 108.00	69.00 - 106.00	69.00 - 114.00	2.3.51
80.00 - 93.00	77.00 - 106.00	77.00 - 100.00	77.00 - 92.00	77.00 - 103.00	2.3.52
82.00 - 108.00	77.00 - 119.00	77.00 - 114.00	77.00 - 106.00	77.00 - 119.00	2.3.53
114.00 - 143.00	108.00 - 152.00	108.00 - 145.00	108.00 - 143.00	108.00 - 155.00	2.3.54
77.00 - 92.00	69.00 - 103.00	69.00 - 100.00	69.00 - 92.00	55.00 - 103.00	2.3.55

Item nr.	SPECIFICATIONS	Unit	RESIDENTIAL	
			£ range £	
2.3	**ROOF - cont'd**			
	roof plan area (unless otherwise described)			
	Flat roof decking and finishes			
	Woodwool roof decking			
2.3.56	50 mm thick; two coat asphalt coverings to BS 5925 and chippings	m²	-	-
	Galvanised steel roof decking; 100 mm thick insulation; three layer felt roofing and chippings			
2.3.57	0.70 mm thick; 2.38 m span	m²	-	-
2.3.58	0.70 mm thick; 2.96 m span	m²	-	-
2.3.59	0.70 mm thick; 3.74 m span	m²	-	-
2.3.60	0.70 mm thick; 5.13 m span	m²	-	-
	Aluminium roof decking; 100 mm thick insulation; three layer felt roofing and chippings			
2.3.61	0.90 mm thick; 1.79 m span	m²	-	-
2.3.62	0.90 mm thick; 2.34 m span	m²	-	-
	Metal decking; 100 mm thick insulation; on wood/steel open lattice beams			
2.3.63	three layer felt roofing and chippings	m²	-	-
2.3.64	two layer high performance felt roofing and chippings	m²	-	-
2.3.65	two coats asphalt coverings and chippings	m²	-	-
	Metal decking to "Mansard"; excluding frame; 50 mm thick insulation; two coat asphalt coverings and chippings on decking			
2.3.66	natural slate covering to "Mansard" faces	m²	-	-
	Roof claddings			
	Non-asbestos profiled cladding			
2.3.67	"Profile 3"; natural	m²	-	-
2.3.68	"Profile 3"; coloured	m²	-	-
2.3.69	"Profile 6"; natural	m²	-	-
2.3.70	"Profile 6"; coloured	m²	-	-
2.3.71	"Profile 6"; natural; insulated; inner lining panel	m²	-	-
	Non-asbestos profiled cladding on steel purlins			
2.3.72	insulated	m²	-	-
2.3.73	insulated; with 10% translucent sheets	m²	-	-
2.3.74	insulated; plasterboard inner lining of metal tees	m²	-	-
	Asbestos cement profiled cladding on steel purlins			
2.3.75	insulated	m²	-	-
2.3.76	insulated; with 10% translucent sheets	m²	-	-
2.3.77	insulated; plasterboard inner lining on metal tees	m²	-	-
2.3.78	insulated; steel sheet liner on metal tees	m²	-	-
	PVF2 coated galvanised steel profiled cladding			
2.3.79	0.72 mm thick; "profile 20 B"	m²	-	-
2.3.80	0.72 mm thick; "profile TOP 40"	m²	-	-
2.3.81	0.72 mm thick "profile 45"	m²	-	-
	Extra for			
2.3.82	80 mm thick insulation and 0.40 mm thick coated inner lining sheet	m²	-	-
	PVF2 coated galvanised steel profiled cladding on steel purlins			
2.3.83	insulated	m²	-	-
2.3.84	insulated; plasterboard inner lining on metal tees	m²	-	
2.3.85	insulated; plasterboard inner lining on metal tees; with 1% fire vents	m²	-	-
2.3.86	insulated; plasterboard inner lining on metal tees; with 2.50% fire vents	m²	-	-
2.3.87	insulated; coloured inner lining panel	m²	-	-
2.3.88	insulated; coloured inner lining panel; with 1% fire vents	m²	-	-
2.3.89	insulated; coloured inner lining panel; with 2.50% fire vents	m²	-	-
2.3.90	insulated; sandwich panel	m²	-	-

INDUSTRIAL £ range £		RETAILING £ range £		LEISURE £ range £		OFFICES £ range £		HOTELS £ range £		Item nr.
32.00	- 44.00	34.00 -	43.00	36.00 -	45.00	32.00 -	45.00	36.00	45.00	2.3.56
35.00	- 45.00	35.00 -	45.00	35.00 -	45.00	35.00 -	45.00	35.00 -	45.00	2.3.57
36.00	- 47.00	36.00 -	47.00	36.00 -	47.00	36.00 -	47.00	36.00 -	47.00	2.3.58
38.00	- 47.00	38.00 -	47.00	38.00 -	47.00	38.00 -	47.00	38.00 -	47.00	2.3.59
39.00	- 49.00	39.00 -	49.00	39.00 -	49.00	39.00 -	49.00	39.00 -	49.00	2.3.60
43.00	- 52.00	43.00 -	52.00	43.00 -	52.00	43.00 -	52.00	43.00 -	52.00	2.3.61
44.00	- 55.00	44.00 -	55.00	44.00 -	55.00	44.00 -	55.00	44.00 -	55.00	2.3.62
66.00	- 81.00	70.00 -	82.00	70.00 -	82.00	70.00 -	82.00	70.00 -	85.00	2.3.63
69.00	- 82.00	70.00 -	82.00	70.00 -	88.00	70.00 -	88.00	70.00 -	88.00	2.3.64
66.00	- 86.00	66.00 -	88.00	66.00 -	88.00	66.00 -	88.00	70.00 -	95.00	2.3.65
-	-	121.00 -	196.00	110.00 -	181.00	110.00 -	181.00	119.00 -	210.00	2.3.66
11.30	- 14.10	-	-	-	-	-	-	-	-	2.3.67
12.60	- 15.40	-	-	-	-	-	-	-	-	2.3.68
12.60	- 15.40	-	-	-	-	-	-	-	-	2.3.69
14.10	- 15.40	-	-	-	-	-	-	-	-	2.3.70
22.30	- 29.50	-	-	-	-	-	-	-	-	2.3.71
22.30	- 28.10	-	-	-	-	-	-	-	-	2.3.72
25.00	- 29.50	-	-	-	-	-	-	-	-	2.3.73
36.40	- 42.50	-	-	-	-	-	-	-	-	2.3.74
22.30	- 26.80	-	-	-	-	-	-	-	-	2.3.75
25.00	- 29.50	-	-	-	-	-	-	-	-	2.3.76
35.00	- 42.50	-	-	-	-	-	-	-	-	2.3.77
34.30	- 42.50	-	-	-	-	-	-	-	-	2.3.78
15.40	- 20.20	20.90 -	28.10	20.90 -	28.10	-	-	-	-	2.3.79
15.40	- 18.90	20.20 -	26.40	20.20 -	26.40	-	-	-	-	2.3.80
16.80	- 22.30	22.30 -	29.50	22.30 -	29.50	-	-	-	-	2.3.81
10.10	- 11.30	10.10 -	11.30	10.10 -	11.30	-	-	-	-	2.3.82
27.10	- 36.40	30.90 -	40.50	30.90 -	40.50	-	-	-	-	2.3.83
40.50	- 52.50	43.90 -	57.60	43.90 -	57.60	-	-	-	-	2.3.84
47.40	- 65.90	53.20 -	71.40	53.20 -	71.40	-	-	-	-	2.3.85
59.00	- 76.90	65.90 -	82.40	65.90 -	82.40	-	-	-	-	2.3.86
41.90	- 53.90	47.40 -	59.00	47.40 -	59.00	-	-	-	-	2.3.87
47.40	- 59.00	53.20 -	65.90	53.20 -	65.90	-	-	-	-	2.3.88
59.00	- 76.90	64.50 -	76.90	64.50 -	76.90	-	-	-	-	2.3.89
87.80	- 135.90	112.50 -	153.70	112.50 -	153.70	-	-	-	-	2.3.90

Item nr.	SPECIFICATIONS	Unit	RESIDENTIAL £ range £	
2.3	**ROOF - cont'd**			
	roof plan area (unless otherwise described)			
	Roof claddings - cont'd			
	Pre-painted "Rigidal" aluminium profiled cladding			
2.3.91	0.70 mm thick; type WA6	m²	-	-
2.3.92	0.90 mm thick; type A7	m²	-	-
	PVF2 coated aluminium profiled cladding on steel purlins			
2.3.93	insulated; plasterboard inner lining on metal tees	m²	-	-
2.3.94	insulated; coloured inner lining panel	m²	-	-
	Rooflights/patent glazing and glazed roofs			
	Rooflights			
2.3.95	standard PVC	m²	-	-
2.3.96	feature/ventilating	m²	-	-
	Patent glazing; including flashings			
	standard aluminium georgian wired			
2.3.97	single glazed	m²	-	-
2.3.98	double glazed	m²	-	-
	purpose made polyester powder coated aluminium;			
2.3.99	double glazed low emissivity glass	m²	-	-
2.3.100	feature; to covered walkways	m²	-	-
	Glazed roofing on framing; to covered walkways			
2.3.101	feature; single glazed	m²	-	-
2.3.102	feature; double glazed barrel vault	m²	-	-
2.3.103	feature; very expensive	m²	-	-
	Comparative over/underlays			
	Roofing felt; unreinforced			
2.3.104	sloping (measured on face)	m²	1.13 -	1.40
	Roofing felt; reinforced			
2.3.105	sloping (measured on face)	m²	1.40 -	1.61
	Sloping (measured on plan)			
2.3.106	20⁰ pitch	m²	1.61 -	2.03
2.3.107	30⁰ pitch	m²	1.76 -	2.26
2.3.108	35⁰ pitch	m²	2.26 -	2.47
2.3.109	40⁰ pitch	m²	2.26 -	2.54
2.3.110	Building paper	m²	0.97 -	2.03
2.3.111	Vapour barrier	m²	1.47 -	4.39
	Insulation quilt; laid over ceiling joists			
2.3.112	80 mm thick	m²	2.75 -	3.02
2.3.113	100 mm thick	m²	3.29 -	3.50
2.3.114	150 mm thick	m²	4.53 -	5.01
2.3.115	200 mm thick	m²	6.04 -	6.59
	Wood fibre insulation boards; impregnated; density 220 - 350 kg/m³			
2.3.116	12.70 mm thick	m²	-	-
	Polystyrene insulation boards; fixed vertically with adhesive			
2.3.117	12 mm thick	m²	-	-
2.3.118	25 mm thick	m²	-	-
2.3.119	50 mm thick	m²	-	-
2.3.120	Limestone ballast	m²	-	-
	Polyurethane insulation boards; density 32 kg/m³			
2.3.121	30 mm thick	m²	-	-
2.3.122	35 mm thick	m²	-	-
2.3.123	50 mm thick	m²	-	-
	Cork insulation boards; density 112 - 125 kg/m³			
2.3.124	60 mm thick	m²	-	-
	Glass fibre insulation boards; density 120 - 130 kg/m²			
2.3.125	60 mm thick	m²	-	-
	Extruded polystyrene foam boards			
2.3.126	50 mm thick	m²	-	-
2.3.127	50 mm thick; with cement topping	m²	-	-
2.3.128	75 mm thick	m²	-	-

INDUSTRIAL £ range £	RETAILING £ range £	LEISURE £ range £	OFFICES £ range £	HOTELS £ range £	Item nr.
21.00 - 27.00	27.00 - 33.00	27.00 - 33.00	- -	- -	2.3.91
24.00 - 30.00	30.00 - 36.00	30.00 - 36.00	- -	- -	2.3.92
43.00 - 53.00	47.00 - 59.00	47.00 - 59.00	- -	- -	2.3.93
44.00 - 55.00	50.00 - 62.00	50.00 - 62.00	- -	- -	2.3.94
98.00 - 176.00	98.00 - 176.00	98.00 - 176.00	98.00 - 176.00	98.00 - 176.00	2.3.95
- -	176.00 - 323.00	176.00 - 323.00	176.00 - 323.00	176.00 - 323.00	2.3.96
126.00 - 176.00	133.00 - 176.00	133.00 - 176.00	133.00 - 176.00	140.00 - 196.00	2.3.97
147.00 - 189.00	161.00 - 203.00	161.00 - 203.00	161.00 - 203.00	176.00 - 224.00	2.3.98
176.00 - 210.00	189.00 - 224.00	189.00 - 224.00	189.00 - 224.00	196.00 - 246.00	2.3.99
- -	196.00 350.00	196.00 350.00	196.00 - 350.00	196.00 - 386.00	2.3.100
- -	273.00 - 406.00	273.00 - 406.00	273.00 - 406.00	301.00 - 447.00	2.3.101
- -	406.00 - 604.00	406.00 - 604.00	406.00 - 604.00	406.00 - 659.00	2.3.102
- -	604.00 - 755.00	604.00 - 755.00	604.00 - 755.00	604.00 - 803.00	2.3.103
- -	1.13 - 1.47	- -	1.13 - 1.47	1.13 - 1.47	2.3.104
- -	1.47 - 1.61	- -	1.47 - 1.61	1.47 - 1.61	2.3.105
- -	1.61 - 2.03	- -	1.61 - 2.03	1.61 - 2.03	2.3.106
- -	1.76 - 2.26	- -	1.76 - 2.26	1.76 - 2.26	2.3.107
- -	2.26 - 2.47	- -	2.26 - 2.47	2.26 - 2.47	2.3.108
- -	2.26 - 2.47	- -	2.26 - 2.47	2.26 - 2.54	2.3.109
- -	1.06 - 2.03	- -	1.06 - 2.03	1.06 - 2.03	2.3.110
- -	1.47 - 4.39	- -	1.47 - 4.39	1.47 - 4.39	2.3.111
- -	2.75 - 3.02	- -	2.75 - 3.02	2.75 - 3.02	2.3.112
- -	3.29 - 3.50	- -	3.29 - 3.50	1.13 - 3.50	2.3.113
- -	4.39 - 5.08	- -	4.39 - 5.08	1.13 - 5.08	2.3.114
- -	6.04 - 6.59	- -	6.04 - 6.59	1.13 - 6.59	2.3.115
- -	4.05 - 5.63	- -	- -	- -	2.3.116
4.40 - 5.40	4.40 - 5.40	4.40 - 5.40	4.40 - 5.40	4.40 - 5.40	2.3.117
5.40 - 6.30	5.40 - 6.30	5.40 - 6.30	5.40 - 6.30	5.40 - 6.30	2.3.118
6.30 - 7.50	6.30 - 7.50	6.30 - 7.50	6.30 - 7.50	6.30 - 7.50	2.3.119
4.40 - 7.50	4.40 - 7.50	4.40 - 7.50	4.40 - 7.50	4.40 - 7.50	2.3.120
6.30 - 7.50	6.30 - 7.50	6.30 - 7.50	6.30 - 7.50	6.30 - 7.50	2.3.121
7.50 - 7.90	7.50 - 7.90	7.50 - 7.90	7.50 - 7.90	7.50 - 7.90	2.3.122
8.80 - 10.10	8.80 - 10.10	8.80 - 10.10	8.80 - 10.10	8.80 - 10.10	2.3.123
7.90 - 11.00	7.90 - 11.00	7.90 - 11.00	7.90 - 11.00	7.90 - 11.00	2.3.124
11.70 - 14.10	11.70 - 14.10	11.70 - 14.10	11.70 - 14.10	11.70 - 14.10	2.3.125
11.00 - 12.60	11.00 - 12.60	11.00 - 12.60	11.00 - 12.60	11.00 - 12.60	2.3.126
17.80 - 20.20	17.80 - 20.20	17.80 - 20.20	17.80 - 20.20	17.80 - 20.20	2.3.127
14.40 - 16.10	14.40 - 16.10	14.40 - 16.10	14.40 - 16.10	14.40 - 16.10	2.3.128

Item nr.	SPECIFICATIONS	Unit	RESIDENTIAL £ range £	
2.3	**ROOF - cont'd**			
	roof plan area (unless otherwise described)			
	Comparative over/underlays - cont'd			
	"Perlite" insulation board; density 170 - 180 kg/m^3			
2.3.129	60 mm thick	m^2	-	-
	Foam glass insulation board; density 125 - 135 kg/m^3			
2.3.130	60 mm thick	m^2	-	-
	Screeds to receive roof coverings			
2.3.131	50 mm thick cement and sand screed	m^2	7.30 -	8.20
2.3.132	60 mm thick (average) "Isocrete K" screed; density 500 kg/m^3	m^2	7.80 -	8.50
2.3.133	75 mm thick lightweight bituminous screed and vapour barrier	m^2	12.30 -	14.10
2.3.134	100 mm thick lightweight bituminous screed and vapour barrier	m^2	15.00 -	16.80
	50 mm thick woodwool slabs; unreinforced			
2.3.135	sloping (measured on face)	m^2	7.80 -	10.10
	sloping (measured on plan)			
2.3.136	20^0 pitch	m^2	8.80 -	11.00
2.3.137	30^0 pitch	m^2	11.00 -	13.00
2.3.138	35^0 pitch	m^2	12.30 -	14.40
2.3.139	40^0 pitch	m^2	12.60 -	14.40
2.3.140	50 mm thick woodwool slabs; unreinforced; on and including steel purlins at			
	600 mm thick centres	m^2	13.60 -	16.50
2.3.141	sloping (measure on face)	m^2	8.80 -	11.00
	sloping (measured on plan)			
2.3.142	20^0 pitch	m^2	10.10 -	11.70
2.3.143	30^0 pitch	m^2	11.90 -	14.10
2.3.144	35^0 pitch	m^2	13.60 -	15.80
2.3.145	40^0 pitch	m^2	14.10 -	16.10
	25 mm thick "Tanalised" softwood boarding			
2.3.146	sloping (measured on face)	m^2	10.70 -	12.30
	sloping (measured on plan)			
2.3.147	20^0 pitch	m^2	11.60 -	13.30
2.3.148	30^0 pitch	m^2	14.10 -	16.10
2.3.149	35^0 pitch	m^2	15.40 -	17.50
2.3.150	40^0 pitch	m^2	16.80 -	18.20
	18 mm thick external quality plywood boarding			
2.3.151	sloping (measured on face)	m^2	13.60 -	16.50
	sloping (measured on plan)			
2.3.152	20^0 pitch	m^2	15.10 -	17.50
2.3.153	30^0 pitch	m^2	18.20 -	21.60
2.3.154	35^0 pitch	m^2	20.90 -	24.00
2.3.155	40^0 pitch	m^2	21.60 -	24.40
	Comparative tiling and slating finishes/perimeter treatments			
	(including underfelt, battening, eaves courses and ridges)			
	Concrete troughed interlocking tiles; 413 mm x 300 mm; 75 mm lap			
2.3.156	sloping (measured on face)	m^2	13.00 -	16.10
	sloping (measured on plan)			
2.3.157	30^0 pitch	m^2	16.80 -	19.90
2.3.158	35^0 pitch	m^2	18.90 -	21.30
2.3.159	40^0 pitch	m^2	20.20 -	21.60
	Concrete interlocking slates; 430 mm x 330 mm; 75 mm lap			
2.3.160	sloping (measured on face)	m^2	13.70 -	16.50
	sloping (measured on plan)			
2.3.161	30^0 pitch	m^2	14.80 -	20.60
2.3.162	35^0 pitch	m^2	19.60 -	22.30
2.3.163	40^0 pitch	m^2	20.20 -	22.60

INDUSTRIAL £ range £		RETAILING £ range £		LEISURE £ range £		OFFICES £ range £		HOTELS £ range £		Item nr.
11.90	- 13.00	11.90	- 13.00	11.90	- 13.00	11.90	- 13.00	11.90	- 13.00	2.3.129
15.10	- 17.50	15.10	- 17.50	15.10	- 17.50	15.10	- 17.50	15.10	- 17.50	2.3.130
-	-	7.30	- 8.20	-	-	7.30	- 8.20	7.30	- 8.20	2.3.131
-	-	7.80	- 8.60	-	-	7.80	- 8.50	7.80	- 8.60	2.3.132
-	-	12.60	- 14.10	-	-	12.60	- 14.10	12.60	- 14.10	2.3.133
-	-	14.40	- 16.80	-	-	14.40	- 16.80	14.40	- 16.80	2.3.134
7.80	- 10.10	-	-	-	-	7.80	- 10.10	-	-	2.3.135
8.90	- 11.00	-	-	-	-	8.90	- 11.00	-	-	2.3.136
11.30	- 13.30	-	-	-	-	11.30	- 13.30	-	-	2.3.137
12.60	- 14.40	-	-	-	-	12.60	- 14.40	-	-	2.3.138
12.60	- 14.80	-	-	-	-	12.60	- 14.80	-	-	2.3.139
13.70	- 16.50	-	-	-	-	13.70	- 16.50	-	-	2.3.140
-	-	8.90	- 11.00	-	-	8.90	- 11.00	8.90	- 11.00	2.3.141
-	-	10.10	- 12.00	-	-	10.10	- 12.00	10.10	- 12.00	2.3.142
-	-	12.00	- 14.10	-	-	12.00	- 14.10	12.00	- 14.10	2.3.143
-	-	13.60	- 15.40	-	-	13.60	- 15.40	13.60	- 15.40	2.3.144
-	-	14.10	- 16.10	-	-	14.10	- 16.10	14.10	- 16.10	2.3.145
-	-	10.40	- 12.30	-	-	10.40	- 12.30	10.40	- 12.30	2.3.146
-	-	11.30	- 13.30	-	-	11.30	- 13.30	11.30	- 13.30	2.3.147
-	-	14.10	- 16.10	-	-	14.10	- 16.10	14.10	- 16.10	2.3.148
-	-	15.80	- 17.50	-	-	15.80	- 17.50	15.80	- 17.50	2.3.149
-	-	16.50	- 18.20	-	-	16.50	- 18.20	16.50	- 18.20	2.3.150
-	-	13.60	- 16.50	-	-	13.60	- 16.50	13.60	- 16.50	2.3.151
-	-	15.10	- 17.50	-	-	15.10	- 17.50	15.10	- 17.50	2.3.152
-	-	18.20	- 20.90	-	-	18.20	- 20.90	18.20	- 20.90	2.3.153
-	-	20.90	- 23.70	-	-	20.90	- 23.70	20.90	- 23.70	2.3.154
-	-	20.90	- 24.00	-	-	20.90	- 24.00	20.90	- 24.00	2.3.155
-	-	13.00	- 16.10	-	-	13.00	- 16.10	13.00	- 16.10	2.3.156
-	-	16.80	- 20.20	-	-	16.80	- 20.20	16.80	- 20.20	2.3.157
-	-	18.90	- 21.60	-	-	18.90	- 21.60	18.90	- 21.60	2.3.158
-	-	20.20	- 22.30	-	-	20.20	- 22.30	20.20	- 22.30	2.3.159
-	-	13.70	- 16.10	-	-	13.70	- 16.10	13.70	- 16.10	2.3.160
-	-	17.50	- 20.20	-	-	17.50	- 20.20	17.50	- 20.20	2.3.161
-	-	19.60	- 22.30	-	-	19.60	- 22.30	19.60	- 22.30	2.3.162
-	-	20.20	- 22.30	-	-	20.20	- 22.30	20.20	- 22.30	2.3.163

Item nr.	SPECIFICATIONS	Unit	RESIDENTIAL £ range £
2.3	**ROOF - cont'd**		
	roof plan area (unless otherwise described)		
	Comparative tiling and slating finishes/perimeter treatments - cont'd		
	Glass fibre reinforced bitumen slates; 900 mm x 300 mm thick; fixed to boarding (not included)		
2.3.164	sloping (measured on face)	m²	12.60 - 15.10
	sloping (measured on plan)		
2.3.165	30° pitch	m²	16.10 - 18.20
2.3.166	35° pitch	m²	17.50 - 20.90
2.3.167	40° pitch	m²	18.90 - 23.00
	Concrete bold roll interlocking tiles; 418 mm x 332 mm; 75 mm lap		
2.3.168	sloping (measured on face)	m²	13.00 - 16.10
	sloping (measured on plan)		
2.3.169	30° pitch	m²	17.20 - 20.20
2.3.170	35° pitch	m²	18.90 - 21.60
2.3.171	40° pitch	m²	19.20 - 22.00
	Tudor clay pantiles; 470 mm x 285 mm; 100 mm lap		
2.3.172	sloping (measured on face)	m²	18.20 - 22.00
	sloping (measured on plan)		
2.3.173	30° pitch	m²	23.00 - 28.10
2.3.174	35° pitch	m²	25.70 - 31.20
2.3.175	40° pitch	m²	27.10 - 32.90
	Natural red pantiles; 337 mm x 241 mm; 76 mm head and 38 mm side laps		
2.3.176	sloping (measured on face)	m²	21.60 - 26.10
	sloping (measured on plan)		
2.3.177	30° pitch	m²	28.10 - 32.60
2.3.178	35° pitch	m²	30.50 - 35.00
2.3.179	40° pitch	m²	31.90 - 36.40
	Blue composition (non-asbestos) slates; 600 mm x 300 mm; 75 mm lap		
2.3.180	sloping (measured on face)	m²	22.30 - 27.50
2.3.181	sloping to mansard (measured on face)	m²	31.60 - 36.40
	sloping (measured on plan)		
2.3.182	30° pitch	m²	30.20 - 34.30
2.3.183	35° pitch	m²	32.60 - 37.10
2.3.184	40° pitch	m²	33.30 - 37.70
2.3.185	vertical to "Mansard"; including 18 mm thick blockboard (measured on face)	m²	45.30 - 54.20
2.3.186	sloping (measured on face)	m²	30.20 - 36.40
	sloping (measured on plan)		
2.3.187	30° pitch	m²	37.40 - 45.30
2.3.188	35° pitch	m²	41.90 - 50.40
2.3.189	40° pitch	m²	45.30 - 54.20
	Machine made clay plain tiles; 267 mm x 165 mm; 64 mm lap		
2.3.190	sloping (measured on face)	m²	34.00 - 40.50
	sloping (measured on plan)		
2.3.191	30° pitch	m²	42.20 - 50.40
2.3.192	35° pitch	m²	47.40 - 56.30
2.3.193	40° pitch	m²	51.10 - 60.40
	Black "Sterreberg" glazed interlocking pantiles; 355 mm x 240 mm; 76 mm head and 38 mm side laps		
2.3.194	sloping (measured on face)	m²	30.20 - 37.70
	sloping (measured on plan)		
2.3.195	30° pitch	m²	37.70 - 46.70
2.3.196	35° pitch	m²	42.50 - 52.80
2.3.197	40° pitch	m²	46.70 - 57.00

INDUSTRIAL £ range £	RETAILING £ range £	LEISURE £ range £	OFFICES £ range £	HOTELS £ range £	Item nr.
-	-	12.30 - 15.10	-	-	12.30 - 15.10	12.30 - 15.10	2.3.164

INDUSTRIAL £ range £	RETAILING £ range £	LEISURE £ range £	OFFICES £ range £	HOTELS £ range £	Item nr.
- -	12.30 - 15.10	- -	12.30 - 15.10	12.30 - 15.10	2.3.164
- -	16.10 - 17.80	- -	16.10 - 17.80	12.30 - 17.80	2.3.165
- -	17.20 - 20.90	- -	17.20 - 20.90	16.10 - 20.90	2.3.166
- -	18.90 - 22.60	- -	18.90 - 22.60	18.90 - 22.60	2.3.167
- -	13.00 - 16.10	- -	13.00 - 16.10	13.00 - 16.10	2.3.168
- -	16.80 - 20.20	- -	16.80 - 20.20	16.80 - 20.20	2.3.169
- -	18.90 - 21.60	- -	18.90 - 21.60	18.90 - 21.60	2.3.170
- -	19.20 - 22.30	- -	19.20 - 22.30	19.20 - 22.30	2.3.171
- -	18.50 - 22.30	- -	18.50 - 22.30	18.50 - 22.30	2.3.172
- -	23.00 - 28.10	- -	23.00 - 28.10	23.00 - 28.10	2.3.173
- -	25.70 - 31.20	- -	25.70 - 31.20	25.70 - 31.20	2.3.174
- -	27.10 - 32.90	- -	27.10 - 32.90	27.10 - 32.90	2.3.175
- -	21.60 - 26.40	- -	21.60 - 26.40	21.60 - 26.40	2.3.176
- -	28.10 - 32.90	- -	28.10 - 32.90	28.10 - 32.90	2.3.177
- -	30.50 - 35.30	- -	30.50 - 35.30	30.50 - 35.30	2.3.178
- -	31.60 - 36.00	- -	31.60 - 36.00	31.60 - 36.00	2.3.179
- -	22.30 - 27.50	- -	22.30 - 27.50	22.30 - 27.50	2.3.180
- -	31.60 - 36.40	- -	31.60 - 36.40	31.60 - 36.40	2.3.181
- -	29.50 - 34.30	- -	29.50 - 34.30	29.50 - 34.30	2.3.182
- -	32.30 - 37.10	- -	32.30 - 37.10	32.30 - 37.10	2.3.183
- -	33.30 - 37.70	- -	33.30 - 37.70	33.30 - 37.70	2.3.184
- -	45.30 - 54.20	- -	45.30 - 54.20	45.30 - 54.20	2.3.185
- -	30.20 - 36.40	- -	30.20 - 36.40	30.20 - 36.40	2.3.186
- -	37.40 - 45.60	- -	37.40 - 45.60	37.40 - 45.60	2.3.187
- -	41.90 - 50.40	- -	41.90 - 50.40	41.90 - 50.40	2.3.188
- -	45.30 - 54.20	- -	45.30 - 54.20	45.30 - 54.20	2.3.189
- -	34.00 - 40.10	- -	34.00 - 40.10	34.00 - 40.10	2.3.190
- -	42.20 - 50.40	- -	42.20 - 50.40	42.20 - 50.40	2.3.191
- -	47.40 - 56.30	- -	47.40 - 56.30	47.40 - 56.30	2.3.192
- -	51.10 - 60.40	- -	51.10 - 60.40	51.10 - 60.40	2.3.193
- -	31.60 - 37.70	- -	31.60 - 37.70	31.60 - 37.70	2.3.194
- -	37.70 - 46.70	- -	37.70 - 46.70	37.70 - 46.70	2.3.195
- -	42.50 - 52.80	- -	42.50 - 52.80	42.50 - 52.80	2.3.196
- -	46.70 - 57.00	- -	46.70 - 57.00	46.70 - 57.00	2.3.197

Item nr.	SPECIFICATIONS	Unit	RESIDENTIAL £ range £
2.3	**ROOF - cont'd**		
	roof plan area (unless otherwise described)		
	Comparative tiling and slating finishes/perimeter treatments - cont'd		
	Red cedar sawn shingles; 450 mm long; 125 mm lap		
2.3.198	sloping (measured on face)	m^2	35.00 - 43.20
	sloping (measured on plan)		
2.3.199	30^0 pitch	m^2	43.60 - 53.20
2.3.200	35^0 pitch	m^2	49.10 - 59.00
2.3.201	40^0 pitch	m^2	54.60 - 63.10
	Welsh natural slates; 510 mm x 255 mm; 76 mm lap		
2.3.202	sloping (measured on face)	m^2	37.70 - 44.60
	sloping (measured on plan)		
2.3.203	30^0 pitch	m^2	49.10 - 59.00
2.3.204	35^0 pitch	m^2	55.60 - 61.80
2.3.205	40^0 pitch	m^2	57.60 - 63.10
	Welsh slates; 610 mm x 305 mm; 76 mm lap		
2.3.206	sloping (measured on face)	m^2	39.10 - 44.60
	sloping (measured on plan)		
2.3.207	30^0 pitch	m^2	49.10 - 57.60
2.3.208	35^0 pitch	m^2	57.60 - 63.10
2.3.209	40^0 pitch	m^2	57.60 - 64.50
	Reconstructed stone slates; random slates; 80 mm lap		
2.3.210	sloping (measured on face)	m^2	23.70 - 44.60
	sloping (measured on plan)		
2.3.211	30^0 pitch	m^2	29.50 - 57.60
2.3.212	35^0 pitch	m^2	30.90 - 63.10
2.3.213	40^0 pitch	m^2	35.00 - 65.90
	Handmade sandfaced plain tiles; 267 mm x 165 mm; 64 mm lap		
2.3.214	sloping (measured on face)	m^2	49.10 - 60.40
	sloping (measured on plan)		
2.3.215	30^0 pitch	m^2	63.10 - 75.50
2.3.216	35^0 pitch	m^2	68.60 - 83.70
2.3.217	40^0 pitch	m^2	75.50 - 89.20
	Westmoreland green slates; random sizes; 76 mm lap		
2.3.218	sloping (measured on face)	m^2	100.20 - 116.70
	sloping (measured on plan)		
2.3.219	30^0 pitch	m^2	119.40 - 145.50
2.3.220	35^0 pitch	m^2	145.50 - 157.80
2.3.221	40^0 pitch	m^2	145.50 - 170.20
	perimeter length		
	Verges to sloping roofs; 250 mm x 25 mm painted softwood bargeboard		
2.3.222	6 mm thick "Masterboard" soffit lining 150 mm wide	m	12.30 - 14.80
2.3.223	19 mm x 150 mm painted soffit softwood	m	14.80 - 16.50
	Eaves to sloping roofs; 200 mm x 25 mm painted softwood fascia; 6 mm thick "Masterboard" soffit lining 225 mm wide		
2.3.224	100 mm uPVC gutter	m	16.80 - 22.60
2.3.225	150 mm uPVC gutter	m	21.30 - 27.50
2.3.226	100 mm cast iron gutter; decorated	m	26.80 - 31.90
2.3.227	150 mm cast iron gutter; decorated	m	32.60 - 37.70
	Eaves to sloping roofs; 200 mm x 25 mm painted softwood fascia; 19 mm x 225 mm painted softwood		
2.3.228	100 mm uPVC gutter	m	20.20 - 25.00
2.3.229	150 mm uPVC gutter	m	25.00 - 30.20
2.3.230	100 mm cast iron gutter; decorated	m	30.20 - 34.30
2.3.231	150 mm cast iron gutter; decorated	m	35.30 - 40.50

INDUSTRIAL £ range £	RETAILING £ range £	LEISURE £ range £	OFFICES £ range £	HOTELS £ range £	Item nr.
- -	35.00 - 43.20	- -	35.00 - 43.20	35.00 - 43.20	2.3.198
- -	43.20 - 53.20	- -	43.20 - 53.20	43.20 - 53.20	2.3.199
- -	49.10 - 59.00	- -	49.10 - 59.00	49.10 - 59.00	2.3.200
- -	53.20 - 64.50	- -	53.20 - 64.50	53.20 - 64.50	2.3.201
- -	37.70 - 44.60	- -	43.20 - 49.10	43.20 - 49.10	2.3.202
- -	49.10 - 59.00	- -	49.10 - 59.00	49.10 - 59.00	2.3.203
- -	56.30 - 61.80	- -	56.30 - 61.80	56.30 - 61.80	2.3.204
- -	57.60 - 63.10	- -	57.60 - 63.10	57.60 - 63.10	2.3.205
- -	39.10 - 44.60	- -	39.10 - 53.20	39.10 - 52.80	2.3.206
- -	49.10 - 57.60	- -	49.10 - 57.60	49.10 - 57.60	2.3.207
- -	56.30 - 63.10	- -	56.30 - 63.10	56.30 - 63.10	2.3.208
- -	57.60 - 64.50	- -	57.60 - 64.50	57.60 - 64.50	2.3.209
- -	23.70 - 44.60	- -	23.70 - 44.60	23.70 - 44.60	2.3.210
- -	29.50 - 57.60	- -	29.50 - 57.60	29.50 - 57.60	2.3.211
- -	30.90 - 63.10	- -	30.90 - 63.10	30.90 - 63.10	2.3.212
- -	35.00 - 65.90	- -	35.00 - 65.90	35.00 - 65.90	2.3.213
- -	49.10 - 60.40	- -	49.10 - 60.40	49.10 - 60.40	2.3.214
- -	61.80 - 76.90	- -	61.80 - 76.90	61.80 - 76.90	2.3.215
- -	70.00 - 85.10	- -	70.00 - 85.10	70.00 - 85.10	2.3.216
- -	74.10 - 87.80	- -	74.10 - 87.80	74.10 - 87.80	2.3.217
- -	100.20 - 116.70	- -	100.20 - 116.70	100.20 - 116.70	2.3.218
- -	119.40 - 145.50	- -	119.40 - 145.50	119.40 - 145.50	2.3.219
- -	145.50 - 157.80	- -	145.50 - 157.80	145.50 - 157.80	2.3.220
- -	151.00 - 170.20	- -	151.00 - 170.20	151.00 - 170.20	2.3.221
- -	11.90 - 14.80	- -	11.90 - 14.80	11.90 - 14.80	2.3.222
- -	14.40 - 16.50	- -	14.40 - 16.50	14.40 - 16.50	2.3.223
- -	17.20 - 22.60	- -	17.20 - 22.60	17.20 - 22.60	2.3.224
- -	21.30 - 27.50	- -	21.30 - 27.50	21.30 - 27.50	2.3.225
- -	26.80 - 31.90	- -	26.80 - 31.90	26.80 - 31.90	2.3.226
- -	32.60 - 37.70	- -	32.60 - 37.70	32.60 - 37.70	2.3.227
- -	20.20 - 25.40	- -	20.20 - 25.40	20.20 - 25.40	2.3.228
- -	25.00 - 30.20	- -	25.00 - 30.20	25.00 - 30.20	2.3.229
- -	30.20 - 34.00	- -	30.20 - 34.00	30.20 - 34.00	2.3.230
- -	35.30 - 40.80	- -	35.30 - 40.80	35.30 - 40.80	2.3.231

Item nr.	SPECIFICATIONS	Unit	RESIDENTIAL £ range £
2.3	**ROOF - cont'd**		
	roof plan area (unless otherwise described)		
	Comparative tiling and slating finishes/perimeter treatments - cont'd		
	Rainwater pipes; fixed to backgrounds; including offsets and shoe		
2.3.232	68 mm diameter uPVC	m	6.00 - 8.00
2.3.233	110 mm diameter uPVC	m	8.90 - 10.90
2.3.234	75 mm diameter cast iron; decorated	m	21.30 - 25.00
2.3.235	100 mm diameter cast iron; decorated	m	25.00 - 30.20
	Ridges		
2.3.236	concrete half round tiles	m	11.90 - 14.80
2.3.237	machine-made clay half round tiles	m	14.80 - 17.50
2.3.238	hand-made clay half round tiles	m	14.80 - 24.40
	Hips; including cutting roof tiles		
2.3.239	concrete half round tiles	m	15.40 - 20.20
2.3.240	machine-made clay half round tiles	m	22.00 - 24.40
2.3.241	hand-made clay half round tiles	m	22.00 - 25.70
2.3.242	hand-made clay bonnet hip tiles	m	35.30 - 40.10
	Comparative cladding finishes (including underfelt, labours, etc.)		
	0.91 mm thick aluminium roofing; commercial grade		
2.3.243	flat	m²	- -
	0.91 mm thick aluminium roofing; commercial grade; fixed to boarding		
2.3.244	sloping (measured on face)	m²	- -
	sloping (measured on plan)		
2.3.245	20⁰ pitch	m²	- -
2.3.246	30⁰ pitch	m²	- -
2.3.247	35⁰ pitch	m²	- -
2.3.248	40⁰ pitch	m²	- -
	0.81 mm thick zinc roofing		
2.3.249	flat	m²	- -
	0.81 mm thick zinc roofing; fixed to boarding (included)		
2.3.250	sloping (measured on face)	m²	- -
	sloping (measured on plan)		
2.3.251	20⁰ pitch	m²	- -
2.3.252	30⁰ pitch	m²	- -
2.3.253	35⁰ pitch	m²	- -
2.3.254	40⁰ pitch	m²	- -
	Copper roofing		
2.3.255	0.56 mm thick; flat	m²	- -
2.3.256	0.61 mm thick; flat	m²	- -
	Copper roofing; fixed to boarding (included)		
2.3.257	0.56 mm thick; sloping (measured on face)	m²	- -
	0.56 mm thick; sloping (measured on plan)		
2.3.258	20⁰ pitch	m²	- -
2.3.259	30⁰ pitch	m²	- -
2.3.260	35⁰ pitch	m²	- -
2.3.261	40⁰ pitch	m²	- -
2.3.262	0.61 mm thick; sloping (measured on face)	m²	- -
	0.61 mm thick; sloping (measured on plan)		
2.3.263	20⁰ pitch	m²	- -
2.3.264	30⁰ pitch	m²	- -
2.3.265	35⁰ pitch	m²	- -
2.3.266	40⁰ pitch	m²	- -
	Lead roofing		
2.3.267	code 4 sheeting; flat	m²	- -
2.3.268	code 5 sheeting; flat	m²	- -
2.3.269	code 6 sheeting; flat	m²	- -

INDUSTRIAL £ range £	RETAILING £ range £	LEISURE £ range £	OFFICES £ range £	HOTELS £ range £	Item nr.
- -	5.90 - 8.40	- -	5.90 - 8.40	5.90 - 8.40	2.3.232
- -	8.80 - 11.30	- -	8.80 - 11.30	8.80 - 11.30	2.3.233
- -	21.30 - 25.40	- -	21.30 - 25.40	21.30 - 25.40	2.3.234
- -	25.40 - 30.20	- -	25.40 - 30.20	25.40 - 30.20	2.3.235
- -	11.90 - 14.80	- -	11.90 - 14.80	11.90 - 14.80	2.3.236
- -	15.40 - 17.50	- -	15.40 - 17.50	15.40 - 17.50	2.3.237
- -	14.80 - 24.40	- -	14.80 - 24.40	14.80 - 24.40	2.3.238
- -	15.40 - 20.20	- -	15.40 - 20.20	15.40 - 20.20	2.3.239
- -	22.00 - 24.70	- -	22.00 - 24.70	22.00 - 24.70	2.3.240
- -	22.00 - 25.70	- -	22.00 - 25.70	22.00 - 25.70	2.3.241
- -	35.30 - 40.10	- -	35.30 - 40.10	35.30 - 40.10	2.3.242
- -	34.00 - 39.00	34.00 - 39.00	34.00 - 39.00	34.00 - 39.00	2.3.243
- -	36.00 - 43.00	36.00 - 43.00	36.00 - 43.00	36.00 - 43.00	2.3.244
- -	40.00 - 47.00	40.00 - 47.00	40.00 - 47.00	40.00 - 47.00	2.3.245
- -	49.00 - 56.00	49.00 - 56.00	49.00 - 56.00	49.00 - 56.00	2.3.246
- -	55.00 - 63.00	55.00 - 63.00	55.00 - 63.00	55.00 - 63.00	2.3.247
- -	58.00 - 63.00	58.00 - 63.00	58.00 - 63.00	58.00 - 63.00	2.3.248
- -	43.00 - 50.00	43.00 - 53.00	43.00 - 53.00	43.00 - 53.00	2.3.249
- -	47.00 - 55.00	47.00 - 55.00	47.00 - 55.00	47.00 - 55.00	2.3.250
- -	53.00 - 59.00	53.00 - 59.00	53.00 - 59.00	53.00 - 59.00	2.3.251
- -	66.00 - 70.00	66.00 - 70.00	66.00 - 70.00	66.00 - 70.00	2.3.252
- -	71.00 - 78.00	71.00 - 78.00	71.00 - 78.00	71.00 - 78.00	2.3.253
- -	75.00 - 82.00	75.00 - 82.00	75.00 - 82.00	75.00 - 82.00	2.3.254
- -	50.00 - 59.00	50.00 - 59.00	50.00 - 59.00	50.00 - 59.00	2.3.255
- -	55.00 - 60.00	55.00 - 60.00	55.00 - 60.00	55.00 - 60.00	2.3.256
- -	55.00 - 60.00	55.00 - 60.00	55.00 - 60.00	55.00 - 60.00	2.3.257
- -	60.00 - 66.00	60.00 - 66.00	60.00 - 66.00	60.00 - 66.00	2.3.258
- -	71.00 - 78.00	71.00 - 78.00	71.00 - 78.00	71.00 - 78.00	2.3.259
- -	82.00 - 88.00	82.00 - 88.00	82.00 - 88.00	82.00 - 88.00	2.3.260
- -	82.00 - 89.00	82.00 - 89.00	82.00 - 89.00	82.00 - 89.00	2.3.261
- -	58.00 - 65.00	58.00 - 65.00	58.00 - 65.00	58.00 - 65.00	2.3.262
- -	63.00 - 70.00	63.00 - 70.00	63.00 - 70.00	63.00 - 70.00	2.3.263
- -	77.00 - 82.00	77.00 - 82.00	77.00 - 82.00	77.00 - 82.00	2.3.264
- -	85.00 - 92.00	85.00 - 92.00	85.00 - 92.00	85.00 - 92.00	2.3.265
- -	88.00 - 95.00	88.00 - 95.00	88.00 - 95.00	88.00 - 95.00	2.3.266
- -	56.00 - 62.00	56.00 - 62.00	56.00 - 62.00	56.00 - 62.00	2.3.267
- -	66.00 - 71.00	66.00 - 71.00	66.00 - 71.00	66.00 - 71.00	2.3.268
- -	70.00 - 77.00	70.00 - 77.00	70.00 - 77.00	70.00 - 77.00	2.3.269

Item nr.	SPECIFICATIONS	Unit	RESIDENTIAL £ range £	
2.3	**ROOF - cont'd**			
	roof plan area (unless otherwise described)			
	Comparative cladding finishes (including underfelt, labours, etc.) - cont'd			
	Lead roofing; fixed to boarding (included)			
2.3.270	code 4 sheeting; sloping (measured on face)	m²	-	-
	code 4 sheeting; sloping (measured on plan)			
2.3.271	20⁰ pitch	m²	-	-
2.3.272	30⁰ pitch	m²	-	-
2.3.273	35⁰ pitch	m²	-	-
2.3.274	40⁰ pitch	m²	-	-
2.3.275	code 6 sheeting; sloping (measured on face)	m²	-	-
	code 6 sheeting; sloping (measured on plan)			
2.3.276	20⁰ pitch	m²	-	-
2.3.277	30⁰ pitch	m²	-	-
2.3.278	35⁰ pitch	m²	-	-
2.3.279	40⁰ pitch	m²	-	-
	code 6 sheeting; vertical to mansard; including			
2.3.280	insulation (measured on face)	m²	-	-
	Comparative waterproof finishes/perimeter treatments			
	Liquid applied coatings			
2.3.281	solar reflective paint	m²	-	-
2.3.282	spray applied bitumen	m²	-	-
2.3.283	spray applied co-polymer	m²	-	-
2.3.284	spray applied polyurethane	m²	-	-
	20 mm two coat asphalt roofing; laid flat; on felt underlay			
2.3.285	to BS 6925	m²	-	-
2.3.286	to BS 6577	m²	-	-
	Extra for			
2.3.287	solar reflective paint	m²	-	-
2.3.288	limestone chipping finish	m²	-	-
2.3.289	grp tiles in hot bitumen	m²	-	-
	20 mm two coat reinforced asphaltic compound; laid flat on felt underlay			
2.3.290	to BS 6577	m²	-	-
	Built-up bitumen felt roofing; laid flat			
2.3.291	three layer glass fibre roofing	m²	-	-
2.3.292	three layer asbestos based roofing	m²	-	-
	Extra for			
2.3.293	granite chipping finish	m²	-	-
	Built-up self-finished asbestos based bitumen felt roofing; laid sloping			
2.3.294	two layer roofing (measured on face)	m²	18.90 -	22.60
2.3.295	35⁰ pitch	m²	28.10 -	31.60
2.3.296	40⁰ pitch	m²	28.80 -	31.60
2.3.297	three layer roofing (measured on face)	m²	25.00 -	30.20
	three layer roofing (measured on plan)			
2.3.298	20⁰ pitch	m²	37.70 -	41.90
2.3.299	30⁰ pitch	m²	39.10 -	43.20
	Elastomeric single ply roofing; laid flat			
2.3.300	"EPDM" membrane; laid loose	m²	-	-
2.3.301	butyl rubber membrane; laid loose	m²	-	-
	Extra for			
2.3.302	ballast	m²	-	-

INDUSTRIAL £ range £	RETAILING £ range £	LEISURE £ range £	OFFICES £ range £	HOTELS £ range £	Item nr.
-	59.00 - 65.00	59.00 - 65.00	59.00 - 65.00	59.00 - 65.00	2.3.270
-	65.00 - 71.00	65.00 - 71.00	65.00 - 71.00	65.00 - 71.00	2.3.271
-	78.00 - 84.00	78.00 - 84.00	78.00 - 84.00	78.00 - 84.00	2.3.272
-	88.00 - 95.00	88.00 - 95.00	88.00 - 95.00	88.00 - 95.00	2.3.273
-	89.00 - 95.00	89.00 - 95.00	89.00 - 95.00	89.00 - 95.00	2.3.274
-	74.00 - 82.00	74.00 - 82.00	74.00 - 82.00	74.00 - 82.00	2.3.275
-	80.00 - 89.00	80.00 - 89.00	80.00 - 89.00	80.00 - 89.00	2.3.276
-	100.00 - 108.00	100.00 - 108.00	100.00 - 108.00	100.00 - 108.00	2.3.277
-	110.00 - 118.00	110.00 - 118.00	110.00 - 118.00	110.00 - 118.00	2.3.278
-	115.00 - 124.00	115.00 - 124.00	115.00 - 124.00	115.00 - 124.00	2.3.279
-	100.00 - 145.00	100.00 - 145.00	100.00 - 145.00	100.00 - 145.00	2.3.280
-	1.30 - 2.30	1.30 - 2.30	1.30 - 2.30	1.30 - 2.30	2.3.281
-	5.00 - 8.20	5.00 - 8.20	5.00 - 8.20	5.00 - 8.20	2.3.282
-	6.00 - 9.10	6.00 - 9.10	6.00 - 9.10	6.00 - 9.10	2.3.283
-	9.80 - 13.30	11.00 - 13.30	11.00 - 13.30	11.00 - 13.30	2.3.284
-	10.50 - 13.70	10.50 - 13.70	10.50 - 13.70	10.50 - 13.70	2.3.285
-	14.80 - 18.20	14.80 - 18.20	14.80 - 18.20	14.80 - 18.20	2.3.286
-	1.80 - 2.40	1.80 - 2.40	1.80 - 2.40	1.80 - 2.40	2.3.287
-	2.10 - 5.60	2.10 - 5.60	2.10 - 5.60	2.10 - 5.60	2.3.288
-	23.70 - 29.50	23.70 - 29.50	23.70 - 29.50	23.70 - 29.50	2.3.289
-	16.10 - 20.20	16.10 - 20.20	16.10 - 20.20	16.10 - 20.20	2.3.290
-	14.10 - 17.50	14.10 - 17.50	14.10 - 17.50	14.10 - 17.50	2.3.291
-	17.50 - 20.20	17.50 - 20.20	17.50 - 20.20	17.50 - 20.20	2.3.292
-	2.10 - 5.50	2.10 - 5.50	2.10 - 5.50	2.10 - 5.50	2.3.293
-	-	-	-	-	2.3.294
-	-	-	-	-	2.3.295
-	-	-	-	-	2.3.296
-	-	-	-	-	2.3.297
-	-	-	-	-	2.3.298
-	-	-	-	-	2.3.299
16.50 - 18.90	16.50 - 18.90	16.50 - 18.90	16.50 - 18.90	16.50 - 18.90	2.3.300
16.50 - 18.90	16.50 - 18.90	16.50 - 18.90	16.50 - 18.90	16.50 - 18.90	2.3.301
5.00 - 8.20	5.00 - 8.20	5.00 - 8.20	5.00 - 8.20	5.00 - 8.20	2.3.302

Item nr.	SPECIFICATIONS	Unit	RESIDENTIAL £ range £	
2.3	**ROOF - cont'd**			
	roof plan area (unless otherwise described)			
	Comparative waterproof finishes/perimeter treatments - cont'd			
	Thermoplastic single ply roofing; laid flat			
	uPVC membrane			
2.3.303	laid loose	m²	-	-
2.3.304	mechanically fixed	m²	-	-
2.3.305	fully adhered	m²	-	-
2.3.306	"CPE" membrane; laid loose	m²	-	-
2.3.307	"CPSG" membrane; fully adhered	m²	-	-
2.3.308	"PIB" membrane; laid loose	m²	-	-
	Extra for			
2.3.309	ballast	m²	-	-
	High performance built-up felt roofing; laid flat			
	three layer "Ruberglas 120 GP" felt roofing			
2.3.310	granite chipping finish	m²	-	-
	"Andersons" three layer self-finished polyester			
2.3.311	based bitumen felt roofing	m²	-	-
	Three layer polyester based modified bitumen felt roofing			
2.3.312	roofing	m²	-	-
	"Andersons" three layer polyester based bitumen			
2.3.313	felt roofing; granite chipping finish	m²	-	-
	Three layer metal faced glass cloth reinforced			
2.3.314	bitumen roofing	m²	-	-
	Three layer "Ruberfort HP 350" felt roofing; granite			
2.3.315	chipping finish	m²	-	-
	Three layer "Hyload 150E" elastomeric roofing; granite			
2.3.316	chipping finish	m²	-	-
	Three layer "Polybit 350" elastomeric roofing; granite		-	-
2.3.317	chipping finish	m²	-	-
	Torch on roofing; laid flat			
2.3.318	three layer polyester-based modified bitumen roofing	m²	-	-
2.3.319	two layer polymeric isotropic roofing	m²	-	-
	Extra for			
2.3.320	granite chipping finish	m²	-	-
	Edges to flat felt roofs; softwood splayed fillet;			
	280 mm x 25 mm painted softwood fascia; no gutter			
2.3.321	aluminium edge trim	m	23.70 -	25.40
	Edges to flat roofs; code 4 lead drip dressed into gutter; 230 mm x 25 mm			
	painted softwood fascia			
2.3.322	100 mm uPVC gutter	m	22.30 -	29.50
2.3.323	150 mm uPVC gutter	m	28.10 -	33.60
2.3.324	100 mm cast iron gutter; decorated	m	33.60 -	41.90
2.3.325	150 mm cast iron gutter; decorated	m	41.90 -	50.40
	Landcaped roofs			
	Vapour barrier, polyester-based elastomeric bitumen waterproofing and			
	vapour equalisation layer, copper lined bitumen membrane root barrier and			
	waterproofing layer, separation and slip layers, protection layer, 50 mm-			
2.3.326	thick drainage board, filter fleece, insulation, top soil and seed	m²	115.00 -	140.00

INDUSTRIAL £ range £	RETAILING £ range £	LEISURE £ range £	OFFICES £ range £	HOTELS £ range £	Item nr.
15.80 - 18.90	15.80 - 18.90	15.80 - 18.90	15.80 - 18.90	15.80 - 18.90	2.3.303
20.20 - 23.70	20.20 - 23.70	20.20 - 23.70	20.20 - 23.70	20.20 - 23.70	2.3.304
22.30 - 25.40	22.30 - 25.40	22.30 - 25.40	22.30 - 25.40	22.30 - 25.40	2.3.305
18.20 - 22.30	18.20 - 22.30	18.20 - 22.30	18.20 - 22.30	18.20 - 22.30	2.3.306
18.20 - 22.30	18.20 - 22.30	18.20 - 22.30	18.20 - 22.30	18.20 - 22.30	2.3.307
20.90 - 25.40	20.90 - 25.40	20.90 - 25.40	20.90 - 25.40	20.90 - 25.40	2.3.308
5.00 - 8.20	5.00 - 8.20	5.00 - 8.20	5.00 - 8.20	5.00 - 8.20	2.3.309
22.30 - 24.40	22.30 - 24.40	22.30 - 24.40	22.30 - 24.40	22.30 - 24.40	2.3.310
22.30 - 25.40	22.30 - 25.40	22.30 - 25.40	22.30 - 25.40	22.30 - 25.40	2.3.311
23.00 - 25.40	23.00 - 25.40	23.00 - 25.40	23.00 - 25.40	23.00 - 25.40	2.3.312
25.40 - 28.10	25.40 - 28.10	25.40 - 28.10	25.40 - 28.10	25.40 - 28.10	2.3.313
28.10 - 31.60	28.10 - 31.60	28.10 - 31.60	28.10 - 31.60	28.10 - 31.60	2.3.314
28.10 - 31.60	28.10 - 31.60	28.10 - 31.60	28.10 - 31.60	28.10 - 31.60	2.3.315
29.50 - 32.90	29.50 - 32.90	29.50 - 32.90	29.50 - 32.90	29.50 - 32.90	2.3.316
31.60 - 35.00	31.60 - 35.00	31.60 - 35.00	31.20 - 35.00	31.20 - 35.00	2.3.317
- -	20.20 - 24.00	20.20 - 24.00	20.20 - 24.00	20.20 - 24.00	2.3.318
- -	20.20 - 24.00	20.20 - 24.00	20.20 - 24.00	20.20 - 24.00	2.3.319
- -	1.90 - 5.10	1.90 - 5.10	1.90 - 5.10	1.90 - 5.10	2.3.320
- -	23.70 - 25.40	23.70 - 25.40	23.70 - 25.40	23.70 - 25.40	2.3.321
- -	22.30 - 29.50	- -	22.30 - 29.50	22.30 - 29.50	2.3.322
- -	28.10 - 34.30	- -	28.10 - 34.30	28.10 - 34.30	2.3.323
- -	33.60 - 41.90	- -	33.60 - 41.90	33.60 - 41.90	2.3.324
- -	41.90 - 53.20	- -	41.90 - 53.20	41.90 - 53.20	2.3.325
- -	- -	115.00 - 140.00	- -	- -	2.3.326

Item nr.	SPECIFICATIONS	Unit	RESIDENTIAL £ range £		
2.4	**STAIRS**				
	storey (unless otherwise described)				
	comprising:				
	Timber construction				
	Reinforced concrete construction				
	Metal construction				
	Comparative finishes/balustrading				
	Timber construction				
	Softwood staircase; softwood balustrades and hardwood handrail; plasterboard; skim and emulsion to soffit				
2.4.1	2.60 m rise; standard; straight flight	nr	504.00	-	763.00
2.4.2	2.60 m rise; standard; top three treads winding	nr	616.00	-	847.00
2.4.3	2.60 m rise; standard; dogleg	nr	707.00	-	896.00
	Oak staircase; balusters and handrails; plasterboard; skim and emulsion to soffit				
2.4.4	2.60 m rise; purpose-made; dogleg	nr	-		-
	plus or minus for				
2.4.5	each 300 mm variation in storey height	nr	-		-
	Reinforced concrete construction				
	Escape staircase; granolithic finish; mild steel balustrades and handrails				
2.4.6	3.00 m rise; dogleg	nr	2628	-	3363
	plus or minus for				
2.4.7	each 300 mm variation in storey height	nr	255.00	-	329.00
	Staircase; terrazzo finish; mild steel balustrades and handrails; plastered soffit; balustrades and staircase soffit decorated				
2.4.8	3.00 m rise; dogleg	nr	-		-
	plus or minus for				
2.4.9	each 300 mm variation in storey height	nr	-		-
	Staircase; terrazzo finish; stainless steel balustrades and handrails; plastered and decorated soffit				
2.4.10	3.00 m rise; dogleg	nr	-		-
	plus or minus for				
2.4.11	each 300 mm variation in storey height	nr	-		-
	Staircase; high quality finishes; stainless steel and glass balustrades; plastered and decorated soffit				
2.4.12	3.00 m rise; dogleg	nr	-		-
	plus or minus for				
2.4.13	each 300 mm variation in storey height	nr	-		-
	Metal construction				
	Steel access/fire ladder				
2.4.14	3.00 m high	nr	-		-
2.4.15	4.00 m high; epoxide finished	nr	-		-
	Light duty metal staircase; galvanised finish; perforated treads; no risers; balustrades and handrails; decorated				
2.4.16	3.00 m rise; spiral; 1548 mm diameter	nr	-		-
	plus or minus for				
2.4.17	each 300 mm variation in storey height	nr	-		-
2.4.18	3.00 m rise; spiral; 1936 mm diameter	nr	-		-
	plus or minus for				
2.4.19	each 300 mm variation in storey height	nr	-		-
2.4.20	3.00 m rise; spiral; 2072 mm diameter	nr	-		-
	plus or minus for				
2.4.21	each 300 mm variation in storey height	nr	-		-

INDUSTRIAL £ range £	RETAILING £ range £	LEISURE £ range £	OFFICES £ range £	HOTELS £ range £	Item nr.
- -	- -	- -	- -	- -	2.4.1
- -	- -	- -	- -	- -	2.4.2
- -	- -	- -	- -	- -	2.4.3
- -	- -	- -	- -	4550 - 6197	2.4.4
- -	- -	- -	- -	734.00 - 803.00	2.4.5
3747 - 4653	2628 - 4653	3603 - 4200	3603 - 4200	2628 - 5250	2.4.6
377.00 474.00	253.00 - 474.00	350.00 - 419.00	350.00 - 419.00	253.00 - 528.00	2.4.7
5250 - 6581	5250 - 7034	4934 - 6581	4934 - 6753	4056 - 7631	2.4.8
528.00 - 659.00	528.00 - 707.00	501.00 - 659.00	501.00 - 673.00	405.00 - 762.00	2.4.9
- -	5250 - 8544	5984 - 7871	5984 - 8612	5250 - 9134	2.4.10
- -	528.00 - 858.00	597.00 - 782.00	597.00 - 858.00	528.00 - 899.00	2.4.11
10500 - 11925	11618 - 12835	10500 - 11925	10150 - 11300	12353 - 13740	2.4.12
1050 - 1462	1160 - 1578	1050 - 1462	1016 - 1386	1235 - 1688	2.4.13
398.00 - 556.00	- -	405.00 - 419.00	- -	- -	2.4.14
- -	- -	556.00 - 954.00	- -	- -	2.4.15
1956 - 2381	- -	- -	- -	- -	2.4.16
196.00 - 240.00	- -	- -	- -	- -	2.4.17
2244 - 2800	- -	- -	- -	- -	2.4.18
224.00 - 281.00	- -	- -	- -	- -	2.4.19
2381 - 2800	- -	- -	- -	- -	2.4.20
237.00 - 280.00	- -	- -	- -	- -	2.4.21

Item nr.	SPECIFICATIONS	Unit	RESIDENTIAL £ range £	
2.4	**STAIRS - cont'd**			
	storey (unless otherwise described)			
	Metal construction - cont'd			
	Light duty metal staircase; galvanised finish; perforated treads; no risers; balustrades and handrails; decorated - cont'd			
2.4.22	3.00 m rise; straight; 760 mm wide	nr	-	-
	plus or minus for			
2.4.23	each 300 mm variation in storey height	nr	-	-
2.4.24	3.00 m rise; straight; 900 mm wide	nr	-	-
	plus or minus for			
2.4.25	each 300 mm variation in storey height	nr	-	-
2.4.26	3.00 m rise; straight; 1070 mm height	nr	-	-
	plus or minus for			
2.4.27	each 300 mm variation in storey height	nr	-	-
	Heavy duty cast iron staircase; perforated treads; no risers; balustrades and hand rails; decorated			
2.4.28	3.00 m rise; spiral; 1548 mm diameter	nr	-	-
	plus or minus for			
2.4.29	each 300 mm variation in storey height	nr	-	-
2.4.30	3.00 m rise; straight	nr	-	-
	plus or minus for			
2.4.31	each 300 mm variation in storey height	nr	-	-
	Feature metal staircase; galvanised finish perforated treads; no risers; decorated			
2.4.32	3.00 m rise; spiral; balustrades and handrails	nr	-	-
	plus or minus for			
2.4.33	each 300 mm variation in storey height	nr	-	-
2.4.34	3.00 m rise; dogleg; hardwood balustrades and handrails	nr	-	-
2.4.35	3.00 m rise; dogleg; stainless steel balustrades and handrails	nr	-	-
	Feature metal staircase; galvanised finish; concrete treads; balustrades and handrails; decorated			
2.4.36	3.00 m rise; dogleg	nr	-	-
	Feature metal staircase to water chute; steel springers; stainless steel treads in-filled with tiling; landings every one metre rise			
2.4.37	9.00 m rise; spiral	nr	-	-
	Galvanised steel catwalk; nylon coated balustrading			
2.4.38	450 mm wide	m	-	-
	Comparative finishes/balustrading			
	Finishes to treads and risers			
2.4.39	uPVC floor tiles including screeds	per storey	-	-
2.4.40	granolithic	per storey	-	-
2.4.41	heavy duty carpet	per storey	-	-
2.4.42	terrazzo	per storey	-	-
	Wall handrails			
2.4.43	uPVC covered mild steel rail on brackets	per storey	-	-
2.4.44	hardwood handrail on brackets	per storey	-	-
2.4.45	stainless steel handrail on brackets	per storey	-	-
	Balustrading and handrails			
2.4.46	mild steel balustrades and PVC covered handrails	per storey	-	-
2.4.47	mild steel balustrades and hardwood handrails	per storey	-	-
2.4.48	stainless steel balustrades and handrails	per storey	-	-
2.4.49	stainless steel and glass balustrades	per storey	-	-

INDUSTRIAL £ range £	RETAILING £ range £	LEISURE £ range £	OFFICES £ range £	HOTELS £ range £	Item nr.
4413 - 2800	- -	- -	- -	- -	2.4.22
224.00 - 280.00	- -	- -	- -	- -	2.4.23
2381 - 3013	- -	- -	- -	- -	2.4.24
253.00 - 302.00	- -	- -	- -	- -	2.4.25
2519 - 3013	- -	- -	- -	- -	2.4.26
253.00 - 301.00	- -	- -	- -	- -	2.4.27
3081 - 4063	- -	- -	- -	- -	2.4.28
307.00 - 405.00	- -	- -	- -	- -	2.4.29
3363 - 4550	- -	- -	- -	- -	2.4.30
336.00 - 453.00	- -	- -	- -	- -	2.4.31
- -	- -	4413 - 4763	- -	- -	2.4.32
- -	- -	441.00 - 476.00	- -	- -	2.4.33
- -	- -	4550 - 6300	- -	- -	2.4.34
- -	- -	5181 - 8402	- -	- -	2.4.35
- -	- -	7768 - 10500	- -	- -	2.4.36
- -	- -	25199 - 30799	- -	- -	2.4.37
217.00 - 273.00	- -	231.00 - 295.00	- -	- -	2.4.38
- -	528.00 - 741.00	528.00 - 741.00	528.00 - 741.00	528.00 - 741.00	2.4.39
- -	803.00 - 913.00	803.00 - 913.00	803.00 - 913.00	803.00 - 913.00	2.4.40
- -	1119 - 1400	1119 - 1400	1119 - 1400	1119 - 1400	2.4.41
- -	2244 - 2937	2244 - 2937	2244 - 2937	2244 - 2937	2.4.42
- -	210.00 - 336.00	210.00 - 336.00	210.00 - 336.00	210.00 - 336.00	2.4.43
- -	574.00 - 954.00	574.00 - 954.00	574.00 - 954.00	574.00 - 954.00	2.4.44
- -	2731 - 3637	2731 - 3637	2731 - 3637	2731 - 3637	2.4.45
- -	659.00 - 844.00	659.00 - 844.00	659.00 - 844.00	659.00 - 844.00	2.4.46
- -	1187 - 1681	1187 - 1681	1187 - 1681	1187 - 1681	2.4.47
- -	5044 - 6108	5044 - 6108	5044 - 4450	5044 - 6108	2.4.48
- -	4900 - 11186	6725 - 11186	6725 - 11186	6725 - 11186	2.4.49

Item nr.	SPECIFICATIONS	Unit	RESIDENTIAL £ range £		
2.5	**EXTERNAL WALLS**				
	external wall area (unless otherwise described)				
	comprising:				
	Timber framed walling				
	Brick/block walling				
	Reinforced concrete walling				
	Panelled walling				
	Wall claddings				
	Curtain/glazed walling				
	Comparative external finishes				
	Timber framed walling				
	Structure only comprising softwood studs at 400 mm x 600 mm centres; head and sole plates				
2.5.1	125 mm x 50 mm	m²	13.00	-	16.10
2.5.2	125 mm x 50 mm; one layer of double sided building paper	m²	15.40	-	19.20
	Softwood stud wall; vapour barrier and plasterboard inner lining; decorated				
2.5.3	uPVC weatherboard outer lining	m²	53.90	-	70.00
2.5.4	tile hanging on battens outer lining	m²	64.50	-	76.90
	Brick/block walling				
	Autoclaved aerated lightweight block walls				
2.5.5	100 mm thick	m²	16.10	-	17.50
2.5.6	140 mm thick	m²	18.90	-	23.00
2.5.7	190 mm thick	m²	26.10	-	30.20
	Dense aggregate block walls				
2.5.8	100 mm thick	m²	14.80	-	16.10
2.5.9	140 mm thick	m²	21.60	-	24.40
	Coloured dense aggregate masonry block walls				
2.5.10	100 mm thick; hollow	m²	27.50	-	30.20
2.5.11	100 mm thick; solid	m²	30.20	-	32.90
2.5.12	140 mm thick; hollow	m²	31.60	-	36.40
2.5.13	140 mm thick; solid	m²	41.90	-	44.60
	Common brick solid walls; bricks PC £120.00/1000				
2.5.14	half brick thick	m²	24.40	-	26.10
2.5.15	one brick thick	m²	41.90	-	44.60
2.5.16	one and a half brick thick	m²	59.00	-	64.50
	Add or deduct for				
	each variation of £10.00/1000 in PC value				
2.5.17	half brick thick	m²	0.60	-	1.00
2.5.18	one brick thick	m²	1.30	-	1.50
2.5.19	one and a half brick thick	m²	1.90	-	2.30
	Extra for				
2.5.20	fair face one side	m²	1.30	-	1.80
	Engineering brick walls; class B; bricks PC £175.00/1000				
2.5.21	half brick thick	m²	27.50	-	31.60
2.5.22	one brick thick	m²	51.80	-	57.60
	Facing brick walls; sand faced facings; bricks PC £130.00/1000				
2.5.23	half brick thick; pointed one side	m²	27.50	-	31.60
2.5.24	one brick thick; pointed both sides	m²	50.40	-	57.60
	Facing brick walls; machine-made facings; bricks PC £320.00/1000				
2.5.25	half brick thick; pointed one side	m²	41.90	-	44.60
2.5.26	half brick thick; built against concrete	m²	43.20	-	47.40
2.5.27	one brick thick; pointed both sides	m²	79.60	-	89.20
	Facing bricks solid walls; hand-made facings; bricks PC £525.00/1000				
2.5.28	half brick thick; pointed one side	m²	54.60	-	61.80
2.5.29	one brick thick; pointed both sides	m²	107.70	-	122.20

INDUSTRIAL £ range £	RETAILING £ range £	LEISURE £ range £	OFFICES £ range £	HOTELS £ range £	Item nr.
-	-	-	-	-	2.5.1
-	-	-	-	-	2.5.2
-	-	-	-	-	2.5.3
-	-	-	-	-	2.5.4
14.80 - 17.50	14.80 - 17.50	14.80 - 17.50	14.80 - 17.50	17.50 - 18.90	2.5.5
18.20 - 21.60	18.20 - 21.60	18.20 - 21.60	18.20 - 21.60	20.20 - 23.70	2.5.6
25.80 - 29.50	25.40 - 29.50	25.40 - 29.50	25.40 - 29.50	27.50 - 30.90	2.5.7
14.10 - 16.10	14.10 - 16.10	14.10 - 16.10	14.10 - 16.10	16.10 - 18.20	2.5.8
20.20 - 23.70	20.20 - 23.70	20.20 - 23.70	20.20 - 23.70	22.30 - 23.70	2.5.9
25.70 - 28.80	25.70 - 28.80	25.70 - 28.80	25.70 - 28.80	28.80 - 31.60	2.5.10
28.80 - 31.60	28.80 - 31.60	28.80 - 31.60	28.80 - 31.60	31.60 - 34.30	2.5.11
32.30 - 35.00	32.30 - 35.00	32.30 - 35.00	32.30 - 35.00	35.00 - 37.70	2.5.12
37.70 - 43.20	37.70 - 43.20	37.70 - 43.20	37.70 - 43.20	41.90 - 47.70	2.5.13
21.60 - 24.40	21.60 - 24.40	21.60 - 24.40	21.60 - 24.40	24.70 - 26.80	2.5.14
39.10 - 43.20	39.10 - 43.20	39.10 - 43.20	39.10 - 43.20	41.90 - 47.70	2.5.15
56.30 - 63.10	56.30 - 63.10	56.30 - 63.10	56.30 - 63.10	60.40 - 65.90	2.5.16
0.60 - 0.90	0.60 - 0.90	0.60 - 0.90	0.60 - 0.90	0.60 - 0.90	2.5.17
1.30 - 1.50	1.30 - 1.50	1.30 - 1.50	1.30 - 1.50	1.30 - 1.50	2.5.18
1.90 - 2.30	1.90 - 2.30	1.90 - 2.30	1.90 - 2.30	1.90 - 2.30	2.5.19
1.40 - 1.90	1.40 - 1.90	1.40 - 1.90	1.40 - 1.90	1.40 - 1.90	2.5.20
26.40 - 30.20	26.40 - 30.20	26.40 - 30.20	26.40 - 30.20	26.40 - 30.20	2.5.21
50.40 - 57.60	50.40 - 57.60	50.40 - 57.60	50.40 - 57.60	54.60 - 60.40	2.5.22
26.40 - 30.20	26.40 - 30.20	26.40 - 30.20	26.40 - 30.20	28.80 - 32.90	2.5.23
50.40 - 54.90	50.40 - 54.90	50.40 - 54.90	50.40 - 54.90	53.20 - 59.00	2.5.24
39.10 - 44.60	39.10 - 44.60	39.10 - 44.60	39.10 - 44.60	41.90 - 47.40	2.5.25
41.90 - 46.00	43.20 - 47.40	43.20 - 47.40	43.20 - 47.40	44.60 - 50.40	2.5.26
76.90 - 89.20	76.90 - 89.20	76.90 - 89.20	76.90 - 89.20	81.00 - 90.60	2.5.27
53.20 - 59.00	54.60 - 60.40	54.60 - 60.40	54.60 - 60.40	57.60 - 65.90	2.5.28
102.90 - 115.30	107.10 - 116.70	107.10 - 116.70	107.10 - 116.70	112.50 - 122.20	2.5.29

Item nr.	SPECIFICATIONS	Unit	RESIDENTIAL £ range £
2.5	**EXTERNAL WALLS - cont'd**		
	external wall area (unless otherwise described)		
	Brick/block walling - cont'd		
	Add or deduct for		
	each variation of £10.00/100 in PC value		
2.5.30	half brick thick	m²	0.60 - 1.00
2.5.31	one brick thick	m²	1.30 - 1.50
	Composite solid walls; facing brick on outside; bricks		
	PC £320.00/1000 and common brick on inside; bricks		
	PC £120.00/1000		
2.5.32	one brick thick; pointed one side	m²	63.00 - 70.00
	Extra for		
2.5.33	one and a half brick thick; pointed one side	m²	3.40 - 5.50
2.5.34	weather pointing as a separate operation	m²	82.00 - 85.00
	Composite cavity wall; block outer skin; 50 mm thick insulation; lightweight		
	block inner skin		
2.5.35	outer block rendered	m²	45.00 - 58.00
	outer block rendered; no insulation; inner skin		
2.5.36	insulating	m²	0.90 - 1.80
2.5.37	outer block roughcast	m²	0.40 - 1.80
2.5.38	coloured masonry outer block	m²	0.90 - 1.80
	Extra for		
2.5.39	heavyweight block inner skin	m²	1.80 - 2.70
2.5.40	fair face one side	m²	8.90 - 10.80
2.5.41	75 mm thick cavity insulation	m²	45.00 - 60.00
2.5.42	100 mm thick cavity insulation	m²	50.00 - 65.00
2.5.43	plaster and emulsion	m²	55.00 - 67.00
	Composite cavity wall; facing brick outer skin; 50 mm thick insulation;		
	plasterboard on stud inner skin; emulsion		
2.5.44	sand-faced facings; PC £130.00/1000	m²	53.00 - 63.00
2.5.45	machine-made facings; PC £320.00/1000	m²	66.00 - 74.00
2.5.46	hand-made facings; PC £525.00/1000	m²	78.00 - 88.00
	As above but with plaster on lightweight block inner skin; emulsion		
2.5.47	sand-faced facings; PC £130.00/1000	m²	47.00 - 60.00
2.5.48	machine-made facings; PC £320.00/1000	m²	63.00 - 73.00
2.5.49	hand-made facings; PC £525.00/1000	m²	73.00 - 86.00
	Add or deduct for		
2.5.50	each variation of £10.00/1000 in PC value	m²	0.60 - 0.90
	Extra for		
2.5.51	heavyweight block inner skin	m²	0.90 - 1.80
2.5.52	insulating block inner skin	m²	1.80 - 4.50
2.5.53	30 mm thick cavity wall slab	m²	2.00 - 5.00
2.5.54	50 mm thick cavity insulation	m²	2.50 - 3.00
2.5.55	75 mm thick cavity insulation	m²	3.50 - 4.00
2.5.56	100 mm thick cavity insulation	m²	4.50 - 5.00
2.5.57	weather-pointing as a separate operation	m²	3.50 - 5.60
2.5.58	purpose made feature course to windows	m²	4.50 - 9.00
	Composite cavity wall; facing brick outer skin; 50 mm thick insulation;		
	common brick inner skin; fair face on inside		
2.5.59	sand-faced facings; PC £130.00/1000	m²	52.00 - 65.00
2.5.60	machine-made facings; PC £320.00/1000	m²	66.00 - 77.00
2.5.61	hand-made facings; PC £525.00/1000	m²	80.00 - 91.00
	Composite cavity wall; facing brick outer skin; 50 mm thick insulation;		
	common brick inner skin; plaster and emulsion		
2.5.62	sand-faced facings; PC £130.00/1000	m²	59.00 - 70.00
2.5.63	machine-made facings; PC £320.00/1000	m²	74.00 - 84.00
2.5.64	hand-made facings; PC £525.00/1000	m²	86.00 - 100.00
2.5.65	Composite cavity wall; coloured masonry block; outer and		
	inner skins; fair faced both sides	m²	82.00 - 111.00

INDUSTRIAL £ range £	RETAILING £ range £	LEISURE £ range £	OFFICES £ range £	HOTELS £ range £	Item nr.
0.60 - 1.00	0.60 - 1.00	0.60 - 1.00	0.60 - 1.00	0.60 - 1.00	2.5.30
1.30 - 1.50	1.30 - 1.50	1.30 - 1.50	1.30 - 1.50	1.30 - 1.50	2.5.31
62.00 - 69.00	65.00 - 70.00	65.00 - 70.00	65.00 - 70.00	67.00 - 73.00	2.5.32
3.40 - 5.50	3.40 - 5.50	3.40 - 5.50	3.40 - 5.50	3.40 - 5.50	2.5.33
77.00 - 86.00	82.00 - 91.00	82.00 - 91.00	82.00 - 91.00	86.00 - 96.00	2.5.34
43.00 - 55.00	45.00 - 58.00	45.00 - 58.00	45.00 - 58.00	47.00 - 60.00	2.5.35
0.90 - 1.80	0.90 - 1.80	0.90 - 1.80	0.90 - 1.80	0.90 - 1.80	2.5.36
0.40 - 1.80	0.40 - 1.80	0.40 - 1.80	0.40 - 1.80	0.40 - 1.80	2.5.37
0.90 - 1.80	0.90 - 1.80	0.90 - 1.80	0.90 - 1.80	0.90 - 1.80	2.5.38
1.80 - 2.70	1.80 - 2.70	1.80 - 2.70	1.80 - 2.70	1.80 - 2.70	2.5.39
8.10 - 11.50	8.10 - 11.50	8.10 - 11.50	8.10 - 11.50	9.50 - 12.30	2.5.40
43.00 - 59.00	45.00 - 60.00	45.00 - 60.00	45.00 - 60.00	47.00 - 62.00	2.5.41
47.00 - 63.00	50.00 - 65.00	50.00 - 65.00	50.00 - 65.00	52.00 - 66.00	2.5.42
53.00 - 66.00	55.00 - 69.00	55.00 - 69.00	55.00 - 69.00	58.00 - 70.00	2.5.43
52.00 - 62.00	53.00 - 63.00	53.00 - 63.00	53.00 - 63.00	55.00 - 65.00	2.5.44
65.00 - 73.00	67.00 - 74.00	67.00 - 74.00	67.00 - 74.00	69.00 - 77.00	2.5.45
74.00 - 84.00	78.00 - 88.00	78.00 - 88.00	78.00 - 88.00	81.00 - 91.00	2.5.46
46.00 - 58.00	47.00 - 60.00	47.00 - 60.00	47.00 - 60.00	52.00 - 63.00	2.5.47
59.00 - 70.00	63.00 - 74.00	63.00 - 74.00	63.00 - 74.00	66.00 - 75.00	2.5.48
70.00 - 86.00	73.00 - 86.00	73.00 - 86.00	73.00 - 86.00	75.00 - 91.00	2.5.49
0.60 - 0.90	0.60 - 0.90	0.60 - 0.90	0.60 - 0.90	0.60 - 0.90	2.5.50
0.90 - 1.80	0.90 - 1.80	0.90 - 1.80	0.90 - 1.80	0.90 - 1.80	2.5.51
1.80 - 4.50	1.80 - 4.50	1.80 - 4.50	1.80 - 4.50	1.80 - 4.50	2.5.52
2.00 - 5.00	2.00 - 5.00	2.00 - 5.00	2.00 - 5.00	2.00 - 5.00	2.5.53
2.70 - 3.30	2.70 - 3.30	2.70 - 3.30	2.70 - 3.30	2.70 - 3.30	2.5.54
3.50 - 4.00	3.50 - 4.00	3.50 - 4.00	3.50 - 4.00	3.50 - 4.00	2.5.55
4.50 - 5.00	4.50 - 5.00	4.50 - 5.00	4.50 - 5.00	4.50 - 5.00	2.5.56
3.50 - 5.60	3.50 - 5.60	3.50 - 5.60	3.50 - 5.60	3.50 - 5.60	2.5.57
4.50 - 9.10	4.50 - 9.10	4.50 - 9.10	4.50 - 9.10	4.50 - 9.10	2.5.58
49.00 - 63.00	50.00 - 65.00	50.00 - 65.00	50.00 - 65.00	53.00 - 66.00	2.5.59
65.00 - 74.00	67.00 - 78.00	67.00 - 78.00	67.00 - 78.00	69.00 - 80.00	2.5.60
75.00 - 86.00	80.00 - 91.00	80.00 - 91.00	80.00 - 91.00	82.00 - 96.00	2.5.61
58.00 - 69.00	59.00 - 70.00	59.00 - 70.00	59.00 - 70.00	62.00 - 75.00	2.5.62
71.00 - 82.00	74.00 - 84.00	74.00 - 84.00	74.00 - 84.00	78.00 - 86.00	2.5.63
82.00 - 95.00	86.00 - 100.00	86.00 - 100.00	86.00 - 100.00	91.00 - 106.00	2.5.64
78.00 - 106.00	82.00 - 111.00	82.00 - 111.00	82.00 - 111.00	85.00 - 114.00	2.5.65

Item nr.	SPECIFICATIONS	Unit	RESIDENTIAL £ range £		
2.5	**EXTERNAL WALLS - cont'd**				
	external wall area (unless otherwise described)				
	Reinforced concrete walling				
	In situ reinforced concrete 25.00 N/mm^2; 13 kg/m^2 reinforcement; formwork both sides				
2.5.66	150 mm thick	m^2	69.00	-	84.00
2.5.67	225 mm thick	m^2	84.00	-	93.00
	Panelled walling				
	Precast concrete panels; including insulation; lining and fixings				
2.5.68	standard panels	m^2	-		-
2.5.69	standard panels; exposed aggregate finish	m^2	-		-
2.5.70	brick clad panels	m^2	-		-
2.5.71	reconstructed stone faced panels	m^2	-		-
2.5.72	natural stone faced panels	m^2	-		-
2.5.73	marble or granite faced panels	m^2	-		-
	GRP/laminate panels; including battens; back-up walls; plaster and emulsion				
2.5.74	melamine finished solid laminate panels	m^2	-		-
2.5.75	single skin panels	m^2	-		-
2.5.76	double skin panels	m^2	-		-
2.5.77	insulated sandwich panels	m^2	-		-
	Wall claddings				
	Non-asbestos profiled cladding				
2.5.78	"Profile 3"; natural	m^2	-		-
2.5.79	"Profile 3"; coloured	m^2	-		-
2.5.80	"Profile 6"; natural	m^2	-		-
2.5.81	"Profile 6"; coloured	m^2	-		-
2.5.82	insulated; inner lining of plasterboard	m^2	-		-
2.5.83	"Profile 6"; natural; insulated; inner lining panel	m^2	-		-
2.5.84	insulated; with 2.80 m high block inner skin; emulsion	m^2	-		-
2.5.85	insulated; with 2.80 m high block inner skin; plasterboard lining on metal tees; emulsion	m^2	-		-
	Asbestos cement profiled cladding on steel rails				
2.5.86	insulated; with 2.80 m high block inner skin; emulsion	m^2	-		-
2.5.87	Insulated; with 2.80 m high block inner skin plasterboard lining on metal tees; emulsion	m^2	-		-
	PVF2 coated galvanised steel profiled cladding				
2.5.88	0.60 mm thick; "profile 20B"; corrugations vertical	m^2	-		-
2.5.89	0.60 mm thick; "profile 30"; corrugations vertical	m^2	-		-
2.5.90	0.60 mm thick; "profile TOP 40"; corrugations vertical	m^2	-		-
2.5.91	0.60 mm thick; "profile 60B"; corrugations vertical	m^2	-		-
2.5.92	0.60 mm thick; "profile 30"; corrugations horizontal	m^2	-		-
2.5.93	0.60 mm thick; "profile 60B"; corrugations horizontal	m^2	-		-
	Extra for				
2.5.94	80 mm thick insulation and 0.40 mm thick coated inner lining	m^2	-		-
	PVF2 coated galvanised steel profiled cladding on steel rails				
2.5.95	insulated	m^2	-		-
2.5.96	2.80 m high insulating block inner skin; emulsion	m^2	-		-
	2.80 m high insulating block inner skin; plasterboard				
2.5.97	lining on metal tees; emulsion	m^2	-		-
2.5.98	insulated; coloured inner lining panel	m^2	-		-
	insulated; full-height insulating block inner skin;				
2.5.99	plaster and emulsion	m^2	-		-
2.5.100	insulated; metal sandwich panel system	m^2	-		-

INDUSTRIAL £ range £	RETAILING £ range £	LEISURE £ range £	OFFICES £ range £	HOTELS £ range £	Item nr.
69.00 - 84.00	69.00 - 84.00	69.00 - 84.00	69.00 - 84.00	69.00 - 84.00	2.5.66
84.00 - 93.00	84.00 - 93.00	84.00 - 93.00	84.00 - 93.00	84.00 - 93.00	2.5.67
89.00 - 135.00	92.00 - 135.00	92.00 - 135.00	92.00 - 135.00	92.00 - 145.00	2.5.68
135.00 - 189.00	147.00 - 189.00	147.00 - 189.00	147.00 - 189.00	147.00 - 203.00	2.5.69
176.00 - 224.00	189.00 - 224.00	189.00 - 224.00	189.00 - 224.00	189.00 - 237.00	2.5.70
- -	301.00 - 371.00	301.00 - 371.00	301.00 - 371.00	301.00 - 406.00	2.5.71
- -	419.00 - 528.00	419.00 - 528.00	419.00 - 528.00	419.00 - 563.00	2.5.72
- -	480.00 - 583.00	480.00 - 583.00	480.00 - 583.00	480.00 - 638.00	2.5.73
113.00 - 147.00	113.00 - 147.00	113.00 - 147.00	- -	- -	2.5.74
126.00 - 161.00	133.00 - 161.00	133.00 - 161.00	106.00 - 133.00	- -	2.5.75
176.00 - 210.00	183.00 - 210.00	183.00 - 210.00	161.00 - 203.00	- -	2.5.76
- -	210.00 - 268.00	210.00 - 268.00	203.00 - 254.00	203.00 - 254.00	2.5.77
14.80 - 16.80	- -	- -	- -	- -	2.5.78
16.10 - 18.20	- -	- -	- -	- -	2.5.79
16.10 - 18.20	- -	- -	- -	- -	2.5.80
16.80 - 18.90	- -	- -	- -	- -	2.5.81
28.80 - 36.40	- -	- -	- -	- -	2.5.82
28.80 - 36.40	- -	- -	- -	- -	2.5.83
25.00 - 28.80	- -	- -	- -	- -	2.5.84
34.30 - 40.50	- -	- -	- -	- -	2.5.85
25.00 - 28.10	- -	- -	- -	- -	2.5.86
32.90 - 39.10	- -	- -	- -	- -	2.5.87
20.20 - 25.00	25.00 - 31.60	25.00 - 31.60	- -	- -	2.5.88
20.20 - 25.00	25.00 - 31.60	25.00 - 31.60	- -	- -	2.5.89
18.90 - 23.70	23.70 - 30.20	23.70 - 30.20	- -	- -	2.5.90
23.70 - 29.50	29.50 - 34.00	29.50 - 34.30	- -	- -	2.5.91
20.90 - 26.80	26.80 - 32.90	26.80 - 32.90	- -	- -	2.5.92
23.70 - 30.20	30.20 - 36.40	30.20 - 36.40	- -	- -	2.5.93
11.30 - 11.90	11.30 - 11.90	11.30 - 11.90	- -	- -	2.5.94
33.00 - 43.00	- -	- -	- -	- -	2.5.95
42.00 - 50.00	- -	-	- -	- -	2.5.96
47.00 - 60.00	- -	- -	- -	- -	2.5.97
47.00 - 60.00	53.00 - 70.00	53.00 - 70.00	- -	- -	2.5.98
59.00 - 80.00	66.00 - 85.00	66.00 - 85.00	66.00 - 85.00	- -	2.5.99
119.00 - 183.00	140.00 - 189.00	133.00 - 183.00	154.00 - 183.00	- -	2.5.100

Item nr.	SPECIFICATIONS	Unit	RESIDENTIAL £ range £	
2.5	**EXTERNAL WALLS - cont'd**			
	external wall area (unless otherwise described)			
	Wall claddings - cont'd			
	PVF2 coated aluminium profiled cladding on steel rails			
2.5.101	insulated	m²	-	-
2.5.102	insulated; plasterboard lining on metal tees; emulsion	m²	-	-
2.5.103	insulated; coloured inner lining panel	m²	-	-
2.5.104	insulated; full-height insulating block inner skin; plaster and emulsion	m²	-	-
	Extra for			
2.5.105	heavyweight block inner skin	m²	-	-
2.5.106	insulated; aluminium sandwich panel system	m²	-	-
	insulated; aluminium sandwich panel system; on framing;			
2.5.107	on block inner skin; fair face one side	m²	-	-
	Other cladding systems			
	vitreous enamelled insulated steel sandwich panel system; with non-			
2.5.108	asbestos fibre insulating board on inner face	m²	-	-
2.5.109	Formalux sandwich panel system; with coloured lining tray; on steel	m²	-	-
	cladding rails			
2.5.110	aluminium over-cladding system rain screen	m²	-	-
2.5.111	natural stone cladding on full-height insulating block inner skin; plaster	m²	-	-
	and emulsion			
	Curtain/glazed walling			
	Single glazed polyester powder coated aluminium curtain walling			
2.5.112	economical; including part-height block back-up wall; plaster; emulsion	m²	-	-
	Extra over single 6 mm thick float glass for			
2.5.113	double glazing unit with two 6 mm thick float glass skins	m²	-	-
2.5.114	double glazing unit with one 6 mm thick "Antisun" skin			
	and one 6 mm thick float glass skin	m²	-	-
2.5.115	"Look-a-like non-vision spandrel panels"	m²	-	-
2.5.116	10% opening lights	m²	-	-
2.5.117	economical; including infill panels	m²	-	-
	Extra for			
2.5.118	50 mm thick insulation	m²	-	-
2.5.119	anodized finish in lieu of polyester powder coating	m²	-	-
2.5.120	bronze anodising in lieu of polyester powder coating	m²	-	-
2.5.121	good quality	m²	-	-
2.5.122	good quality; 35% opening lights	m²	-	-
	Extra over single 6 mm thick float glass for			
2.5.123	double glazing unit with "Low "E" and tinted glass"	m²	-	-
2.5.124	high quality	m²	-	-
2.5.125	high quality; fire rated	m²	-	-
	Extra over single 6 mm thick float glass for			
2.5.126	double glazing unit with tinted glass thermally broken	m²	-	-
2.5.127	50% granite panels	m²	-	-
	Suspended panelled glazing system (e.g. Planar)			
2.5.128	12 mm thick toughened float glass panels	m²	-	-
	Extra for			
	double glazing unit with one 12 mm thick tinted toughened skin and			
2.5.129	one 6 mm thick clear toughened skin	m²	-	-
2.5.130	solar control glass	m²	-	-
	supporting structure of aluminium; stainless steel or glass			
2.5.131	fins	m²	-	-
2.5.132	High quality structural glazing to entrance elevation	m²	-	-
	Lift surround of double glazed or laminated glass with aluminium or			
2.5.133	stainless steel framing	m²	-	-

INDUSTRIAL £ range £	RETAILING £ range £	LEISURE £ range £	OFFICES £ range £	HOTELS £ range £	Item nr.
38.00 - 48.00	- -	- -	- -	- -	2.5.101
50.00 - 59.00	- -	- -	- -	- -	2.5.102
53.00 - 66.00	59.00 - 74.00	59.00 - 74.00	- -	- -	2.5.103
70.00 - 88.00	74.00 - 95.00	74.00 - 95.00	74.00 - 100.00	- -	2.5.104
1.00 - 2.00	1.00 - 2.00	1.00 - 2.00	1.00 - 2.00	- -	2.5.105
100.20 - 133.10	133.10 - 167.40	133.10 - 182.50	140.00 - 182.50	- -	2.5.106
- -	154.00 - 259.00	- -	- -	- -	2.5.107
114.00 - 140.00	- -	- -	- -	- -	2.5.108
133.00 - 161.00	147.00 - 167.00	147.00 - 167.00	147.00 - 167.00	- -	2.5.109
167.00 - 189.00	- -	- -	- -	- -	2.5.110
- -	- -	- -	302.00 - 432.00	316.00 - 446.00	2.5.111
295.00 - 419.00	309.00 - 419.00	309.00 - 419.00	309.00 - 377.00	336.00 - 446.00	2.5.112
30.00 - 39.00	30.00 - 39.00	30.00 - 39.00	30.00 - 39.00	30.00 - 39.00	2.5.113
59.00 - 78.00	59.00 - 78.00	59.00 - 78.00	59.00 - 78.00	59.00 - 78.00	2.5.114
39.00 - 59.00	39.00 - 59.00	39.00 - 59.00	39.00 - 59.00	39.00 - 59.00	2.5.115
9.80 - 19.60	9.80 - 19.60	9.80 - 19.60	9.80 - 19.60	9.80 - 19.60	2.5.116
281.00 - 336.00	302.00 - 364.00	302.00 - 364.00	302.00 - 364.00	343.00 - 412.00	2.5.117
15.80 - 18.50	15.80 - 18.50	15.80 - 18.50	15.80 - 18.50	15.80 - 18.50	2.5.118
19.60 - 68.60	19.60 - 68.60	19.60 - 68.60	19.60 - 68.60	19.60 - 68.60	2.5.119
39.10 - 97.40	39.10 - 97.40	39.10 - 97.40	39.10 - 97.40	39.10 - 97.40	2.5.120
460.00 - 535.00	474.00 - 549.00	474.00 - 563.00	501.00 - 563.00	501.00 - 563.00	2.5.121
576.00 - 673.00	604.00 - 679.00	597.00 - 707.00	631.00 - 707.00	631.00 - 707.00	2.5.122
59.00 - 78.00	59.00 - 78.00	59.00 - 78.00	59.00 - 78.00	59.00 - 78.00	2.5.123
659.00 - 666.00	700.00 - 769.00	666.00 - 714.00	707.00 - 727.00	666.00 - 734.00	2.5.124
- -	- -	- -	1263 - 1887	- -	2.5.125
108.00 - 147.00	108.00 - 147.00	108.00 - 147.00	108.00 - 147.00	108.00 - 147.00	2.5.126
39.00 - 59.00	39.00 - 59.00	39.00 - 59.00	39.00 - 59.00	39.00 - 59.00	2.5.127
- -	446.00 - 522.00	446.00 - 522.00	446.00 - 522.00	- -	2.5.128
- -	167.00 - 176.00	167.00 - 176.00	167.00 - 176.00	- -	2.5.129
- -	70.00 - 217.00	70.00 - 217.00	70.00 - 217.00	- -	2.5.130
- -	91.00 - 199.00	91.00 - 199.00	91.00 - 199.00	- -	2.5.131
- -	631.00 - 988.00	631.00 - 988.00	631.00 - 988.00	- -	2.5.132
- -	1077 - 1187	1077 - 1187	1077 - 1187	- -	2.5.133

Item nr.	SPECIFICATIONS	Unit	RESIDENTIAL £ range £	
2.5	**EXTERNAL WALLS - cont'd**			
	external wall area (unless otherwise described)			
	Curtain/glazed walling - cont'd			
	Patent glazing systems; excluding opening lights and flashings			
	7 mm thick georgian wired cast glass, aluminium alloy bars spanning up			
2.5.134	to 3.00 m at 600 mm - 625 mm spacing	m²	-	-
	6.40 mm thick laminated safety glass polyester powder coated			
2.5.135	aluminium capped glazing bars up to 3.00 m at 600 - 625 mm spacing	m²	-	-
	Comparative external finishes			
	Comparative concrete wall finishes			
2.5.136	wrought formwork one side including rubbing down	m²	-	-
2.5.137	shotblasting to expose aggregate	m²	-	-
2.5.138	bush hammering to expose aggregate	m²	-	-
	Comparative insitu finishes			
2.5.139	two coats "Sandtex Matt" cement paint	m²	-	-
2.5.140	cement and sand plain face rendering	m²	-	-
2.5.141	three coat "Tyrolean" rendering; including backing	m²	-	-
2.5.142	"Mineralite" decorative rendering; including backing	m²	-	-
	Comparative claddings			
	25 mm thick tongued and grooved "Tanalised" softwood			
2.5.143	boarding; including battens	m²	-	-
	25 mm thick tongued and grooved western red cedar boarding including			
2.5.144	battens	m²	-	-
2.5.145	machine-made tiles; including battens	m²	-	-
2.5.146	best hand-made sand-faced tiles; including battens	m²	-	-
	20 mm x 20 mm thick mosaic glass or ceramic; in common colours;			
2.5.147	fixed on prepared surface	m²	-	-
2.5.148	75 mm thick Portland stone facing slabs and fixing; including clamps	m²	-	-
2.5.149	75 mm thick Ancaster stone facing slabs and fixing; including clamps	m²	-	-
	Comparative curtain wall finishes			
	Extra over aluminium mill finish for			
2.5.150	natural anodising	m²	-	-
2.5.151	polyester powder coating	m²	-	-
2.5.152	bronze anodising	m²	-	-
2.6	**WINDOWS AND EXTERNAL DOORS**			
	window and external door area (unless otherwise described)			
	comprising:			
	Softwood windows and external doors			
	Steel windows and external doors			
	Steel roller shutters			
	Hardwood windows and external doors			
	uPVC windows and external doors			
	Aluminium windows, entrance screens and doors			
	Stainless steel entrance screens and doors			
	Shop fronts, shutters and grilles			
	Softwood windows and external doors			
	Standard windows; painted			
2.6.1	single glazed	m²	161.00	- 210.00
2.6.2	double glazed	m²	210.00	- 253.00
	Purpose-made windows; painted			
2.6.3	single glazed	m²	210.00	- 268.00
2.6.4	double glazed	m²	268.00	- 336.00

INDUSTRIAL £ range £	RETAILING £ range £	LEISURE £ range £	OFFICES £ range £	HOTELS £ range £	Item nr.
97.00 - 108.00	97.00 - 108.00	108.00 - 118.00	108.00 - 118.00	118.00 - 128.00	2.5.134
- -	316.00 - 350.00	316.00 - 350.00	316.00 - 350.00	336.00 - 377.00	2.5.135
- -	2.40 - 4.70	2.40 - 4.70	2.40 - 4.70	2.40 - 4.70	2.5.136
- -	3.00 - 6.00	3.00 - 6.00	3.00 - 6.00	3.00 - 6.00	2.5.137
- -	9.50 - 13.20	9.50 - 13.20	9.50 - 13.20	9.50 - 13.20	2.5.138
- -	5.60 - 7.80	5.60 - 7.80	5.60 - 7.80	5.60 - 7.80	2.5.139
- -	9.80 - 14.80	9.80 - 14.80	9.80 - 14.80	9.80 - 14.80	2.5.140
- -	23.70 - 28.10	23.70 - 28.10	23.70 - 28.10	23.70 - 32.30	2.5.141
- -	47.40 - 54.90	47.40 - 54.90	47.40 - 54.90	50.40 - 61.80	2.5.142
- -	22.30 - 28.10	22.30 - 28.10	22.30 - 28.10	22.30 - 28.10	2.5.143
- -	26.40 - 33.60	26.40 - 33.60	26.40 - 33.60	26.40 - 33.60	2.5.144
- -	28.10 - 32.90	28.10 - 32.90	28.10 - 32.90	28.10 - 32.90	2.5.145
- -	34.30 - 37.70	34.30 - 37.70	34.30 - 37.70	34.30 - 37.70	2.5.146
- -	73.00 - 85.00	73.00 - 85.00	73.00 - 85.00	73.00 - 85.00	2.5.147
- -	- -	- -	281.00 - 350.00	295.00 - 384.00	2.5.148
- -	- -	- -	309.00 - 384.00	- -	2.5.149
- -	13.30 - 17.50	13.30 - 17.50	13.30 - 17.50	13.30 - 17.50	2.5.150
- -	17.50 - 29.50	17.50 - 29.50	17.50 - 29.50	17.50 - 28.10	2.5.151
- -	24.40 - 36.40	24.40 - 36.40	24.40 - 36.40	24.40 - 36.40	2.5.152
154.00 - 196.00	147.00 - 203.00	160.58 - 210.00	161.00 - 210.00	161.00 - 224.00	2.6.1
189.00 - 246.00	203.00 - 246.00	209.99 - 268.00	210.00 - 268.00	210.00 - 268.00	2.6.2
210.00 - 268.00	210.00 - 210.00	223.72 - 275.00	217.00 - 275.00	217.00 - 288.00	2.6.3
261.00 - 309.00	261.00 - 309.00	246.00 - 302.00	261.00 - 302.00	275.00 - 323.00	2.6.4

Item nr.	SPECIFICATIONS	Unit	RESIDENTIAL £ range £
2.6	**WINDOWS AND EXTERNAL DOORS - cont'd** **window and external door area** (unless otherwise described)		
	Softwood windows and external doors - cont'd Standard external softwood doors and hardwood frames; doors painted; including ironmongery		
2.6.5	two panelled door; plywood panels	nr	275.00 - 329.00
2.6.6	solid flush door	nr	309.00 - 357.00
2.6.7	two panelled door; glazed panels	nr	583.00 - 652.00
	heavy-duty solid flush door		
2.6.8	single leaf	nr	- -
2.6.9	double leaf	nr	- -
	Extra for		
2.6.10	emergency fire exit door	nr	- -
	Steel windows and external doors Standard windows		
2.6.11	single glazed; galvanised; painted	m^2	167.00 - 217.00
2.6.12	single glazed; powder-coated	m^2	176.00 - 224.00
2.6.13	double glazed; galvanised; painted	m^2	217.00 - 259.00
2.6.14	double glazed; powder coated	m^2	224.00 - 275.00
	Purpose-made windows		
2.6.15	double glazed; powder coated	m^2	- -
	Steel roller shutters Shutters; galvanised		
2.6.16	manual	m^2	- -
2.6.17	electric	m^2	- -
2.6.18	manual; insulated	m^2	- -
2.6.19	electric; insulated	m^2	- -
2.6.20	electric; insulated; fire-resistant	m^2	- -
	Hardwood windows and external doors Standard windows; stained or uVC coated		
2.6.21	single glazed	m^2	224.00 - 316.00
2.6.22	double glazed	m^2	288.00 - 364.00
	Purpose-made windows; stained or uPVC coated		
2.6.23	single glazed	m^2	259.00 - 350.00
2.6.24	double glazed	m^2	316.00 - 405.00
	uPVC windows and external doors Purpose-made windows		
2.6.25	double glazed	m^2	453.00 - 563.00
	Extra for		
2.6.26	tinted glass	m^2	- -
	Aluminium windows, entrance screens and doors Standard windows; anodised finish		
2.6.27	single glazed; horizontal sliding sash	m^2	- -
2.6.28	single glazed; vertical sliding slash	m^2	- -
2.6.29	single glazed; casement; in hardwood sub-frame	m^2	237.00 - 316.00
2.6.30	double glazed; vertical sliding slash	m^2	- -
2.6.31	double glazed; casement; in hardwood sub-frame	m^2	288.00 - 384.00
	Purpose-made windows		
2.6.32	single glazed	m^2	- -
2.6.33	double glazed	m^2	- -
2.6.34	double glazed; feature; with precast concrete surrounds m^2	m^2	- -
	Purpose-made entrance screens and doors		
2.6.35	double glazed	m^2	- -
	Purpose-made revolving door		
2.6.36	2000 mm diameter; double glazed	nr	- -

INDUSTRIAL £ range £	RETAILING £ range £	LEISURE £ range £	OFFICES £ range £	HOTELS £ range £	Item nr.
- -	- -	- -	- -	- -	2.6.5
405.00 - 714.00	323.00 - 364.00	323.00 - 364.00	323.00 - 364.00	329.00 - 377.00	2.6.6
- -	- -	- -	- -	- -	2.6.7
467.00 - 714.00	528.00 - 659.00	528.00 - 645.00	- -	- -	2.6.8
824.00 - 1173.00	1002.00 - 1119.00	1002.00 - 1119.00	- -	- -	2.6.9
- -	176.00 - 275.00	176.00 - 275.00	- -	- -	2.6.10
154.00 - 203.00	154.00 - 210.00	167.00 - 210.00	167.00 - 210.00	167.00 - 231.00	2.6.11
161.00 - 210.00	161.00 - 210.00	176.00 - 224.00	176.00 - 224.00	176.00 - 237.00	2.6.12
203.00 - 253.00	203.00 - 253.00	210.00 - 266.00	210.00 - 266.00	217.00 - 281.00	2.6.13
203.00 - 253.00	203.00 - 266.00	217.00 - 275.00	217.00 - 275.00	224.00 - 288.00	2.6.14
- -	288.00 - 364.00	288.00 - 364.00	288.00 - 364.00	230.00 - 384.00	2.6.15
167.00 - 217.00	154.00 - 203.00	154.00 - 210.00	- -	- -	2.6.16
203.00 - 288.00	189.00 - 281.00	189.00 - 281.00	- -	- -	2.6.17
281.00 - 329.00	259.00 - 316.00	259.00 - 316.00	- -	- -	2.6.18
316.00 - 398.00	302.00 - 384.00	302.00 - 384.00	- -	- -	2.6.19
762.00 - 913.00	734.00 - 913.00	734.00 - 913.00	- -	- -	2.6.20
288.00 - 350.00	288.00 - 350.00	288.00 - 350.00	288.00 - 350.00	302.00 - 364.00	2.6.21
364.00 - 439.00	364.00 - 439.00	364.00 - 439.00	364.00 - 439.00	364.00 - 377.00	2.6.22
350.00 - 405.00	350.00 - 405.00	350.00 - 405.00	350.00 - 405.00	350.00 - 439.00	2.6.23
405.00 - 494.00	405.00 - 494.00	405.00 - 494.00	405.00 - 494.00	405.00 - 515.00	2.6.24
419.00 - 467.00	419.00 - 467.00	419.00 - 467.00	419.00 - 467.00	419.00 - 467.00	2.6.25
21.00 - 29.00	21.00 - 29.00	21.00 - 29.00	21.00 - 29.00	21.00 - 29.00	2.6.26
203.00 - 246.00	203.00 - 246.00	203.00 - 246.00	203.00 - 246.00	203.00 - 259.00	2.6.27
316.00 - 377.00	316.00 - 377.00	316.00 - 377.00	316.00 - 377.00	316.00 - 384.00	2.6.28
- -	- -	- -	- -	- -	2.6.29
350.00 - 405.00	391.00 - 494.00	391.00 - 494.00	391.00 - 494.00	391.00 - 522.00	2.6.30
- -	- -	- -	- -	- -	2.6.31
203.00 - 288.00	203.00 - 288.00	203.00 - 288.00	203.00 - 288.00	203.00 - 288.00	2.6.32
453.00 - 549.00	453.00 - 549.00	453.00 - 549.00	453.00 - 549.00	453.00 - 563.00	2.6.33
- -	- -	1139.00 - 1716.00	- -	- -	2.6.34
- -	563.00 - 913.00	563.00 - 913.00	563.00 - 913.00	- -	2.6.35
- -	20176 - 25803	20176 - 25803	19860 - 25803	19860 - 25803	2.6.36

Item nr.	SPECIFICATIONS	Unit	RESIDENTIAL £ range £	
2.6	**WINDOWS AND EXTERNAL DOORS - cont'd** **window and external door area** (unless otherwise described)			
	Stainless steel entrance screens and doors Purpose-made screen; double glazed			
2.6.37	with manual doors	m²	-	-
2.6.38	with automatic doors	m²	-	-
	Purpose-made revolving door			
2.6.39	2000 mm diameter; double glazed	nr	-	-
	Shop fronts, shutters and grilles **shop front length**			
2.6.40	Temporary timber shop fronts	m	-	-
2.6.41	Grilles or shutters	m	-	-
2.6.42	Fire shutters; power-operated	m	-	-
	Shop front			
2.6.43	flat facade; glass in aluminium framing; manual centre doors only	m	-	-
2.6.44	flat facade; glass in aluminium framing; automatic centre doors only	m	-	-
2.6.45	hardwood and glass; including high enclosed window beds	m	-	-
2.6.46	high quality; marble or granite plasters and stair risers; window beds and backings; illuminated signs	m	-	-
2.7	**INTERNAL WALLS, PARTITIONS AND DOORS** **internal wall area** (unless otherwise described)			
	comprising:			
	Timber or metal stud partitions and doors **Brick/block partitions and doors** **Reinforced concrete walls** **Solid partitioning and doors** **Glazed partitioning and doors** **Special partitioning and doors** **WC/Changing cubicles** **Comparative doors/door linings/frames** **Perimeter treatments**			
	Timber or metal stud partitions and doors Structure only comprising softwood studs at 400 mm x 600 mm centres; head and sole plates			
2.7.1	100 mm x 38 mm	m²	10.00 -	12.60
	Softwood stud and plasterboard partitions			
2.7.2	57 mm thick "Paramount" dry partition	m²	18.50 -	20.60
2.7.3	65 mm thick "Paramount" dry partition	m²	20.60 -	22.60
2.7.4	50 mm thick laminated partition	m²	19.90 -	22.00
2.7.5	65 mm thick laminated partition	m²	23.00 -	25.00
2.7.6	65 mm thick laminated partition; emulsion both sides	m²	28.10 -	30.90
2.7.7	100 mm thick partition; taped joints; emulsion both sides	m²	30.90 -	35.70
2.7.8	100 mm thick partition; skim and emulsion both sides	m²	35.70 -	40.50
2.7.9	150 mm thick partition as party wall; skim and emulsion both sides	m²	42.50 -	50.40
	Metal stud and plasterboard partitions			
2.7.10	170 mm thick partition; one hour; taped joints; emulsion both sides	m²	-	-
2.7.11	200 mm thick partition; two hour; taped joints; emulsion both sides	m²	-	-
2.7.12	325 mm thick two layer partition; cavity insulation	m²	-	-
	Extra for			
2.7.13	curved work	m²	-	-

INDUSTRIAL £ range £	RETAILING £ range £	LEISURE £ range £	OFFICES £ range £	HOTELS £ range £	Item nr.
- -	913 - 1373	- -	- -	- -	2.6.37
- -	1132 - 1613	- -	- -	- -	2.6.38
- -	27725 - 34724	26141 - 32741	26141 - 32741	26141 - 32741	2.6.39
- -	37.10 - 52.50	- -	- -	- -	2.6.40
- -	453.00 - 913.00	- -	- -	- -	2.6.41
- -	803.00 - 1146.0	- -	- -	- -	2.6.42
- -	913 - 2100	- -	- -	- -	2.6.43
- -	1139 - 2553	- -	- -	- -	2.6.44
- -	3225 - 3912	- -	- -	- -	2.6.45
- -	3637 - 5044	- -	- -	- -	2.6.46
- -	- -	- -	- -	- -	2.7.1
- -	- -	- -	- -	- -	2.7.2
- -	- -	- -	- -	- -	2.7.3
- -	- -	- -	- -	- -	2.7.4
- -	- -	- -	- -	- -	2.7.5
- -	- -	- -	- -	- -	2.7.6
- -	- -	- -	- -	- -	2.7.7
- -	- -	- -	- -	- -	2.7.8
- -	- -	- -	- -	- -	2.7.9
36.00 - 44.00	38.00 - 47.00	38.00 - 47.00	38.00 - 47.00	40.00 - 47.00	2.7.10
50.00 - 56.00	53.00 - 58.00	53.00 - 58.00	53.00 - 58.00	55.00 - 59.00	2.7.11
85.00 - 119.00	91.00 - 124.00	91.00 - 124.00	91.00 - 124.00	91.00 - 124.00	2.7.12
+50%	+50%	+50%	+50%	+50%	2.7.13

Item nr.	SPECIFICATIONS	Unit	RESIDENTIAL £ range £		
2.7	**INTERNAL WALLS, PARTITIONS AND DOORS - cont'd**				
	internal wall area (unless otherwise described)				
	Timber or metal stud partitions and doors - cont'd				
	Metal stud and plasterboard partitions; emulsion both sides; softwood doors and frames; painted				
2.7.14	170 mm thick partition	m²	-		-
2.7.15	200 mm thick partition; insulated	m²	-		-
	Stud or plasterboard partitions; softwood doors and frames; painted				
2.7.16	partition; plaster and emulsion both sides	m²	60.00	-	77.00
	Extra for				
2.7.17	vinyl paper in lieu of emulsion	m²	4.00	-	6.00
2.7.18	hardwood doors and frames in lieu of softwood	m²	17.20	-	19.90
2.7.19	partition; plastered and vinyl both sides	m²	71.00	-	86.00
	Stud or plasterboard partitions; hardwood doors and frames				
2.7.20	partition; plaster and emulsion both sides	m²	77.00	-	96.00
2.7.21	partition; plaster and vinyl both sides	m²	88.00	-	108.00
	Brick/block partitions and doors				
	Autoclaved aerated/lightweight block partitions				
2.7.22	75 mm thick	m²	11.50	-	13.70
2.7.23	100 mm thick	m²	15.40	-	18.50
2.7.24	130 mm thick; insulating	m²	18.90	-	20.90
2.7.25	150 mm thick	m²	20.90	-	22.30
2.7.26	190 mm thick	m²	25.00	-	28.80
	Extra for				
2.7.27	fair face both sides	m²	2.00	-	4.00
2.7.28	curved work		+10%	-	+20%
2.7.29	average thickness; fair face both sides	m²	20.20	-	25.00
2.7.30	average thickness; fair face and emulsion both sides	m²	23.70	-	30.20
2.7.31	average thickness; plaster and emulsion both sides	m²	36.40	-	43.20
	Concrete block partitions				
2.7.32	to retail units	m²	-		-
	Dense aggregate block partitions				
2.7.33	average thickness; fair face both sides	m²	23.70	-	28.80
2.7.34	average thickness; fair face and emulsion both sides	m²	27.50	-	32.90
2.7.35	average thickness; plaster and emulsion both sides	m²	40.50	-	46.00
	Coloured dense aggregate masonry block partition				
2.7.36	fair face both sides	m²	-		-
	Common brick partitions; bricks PC £120.00/1000				
2.7.37	half brick thick	m²	21.60	-	23.70
2.7.38	half brick thick; fair face both sides	m²	23.70	-	28.80
2.7.39	half brick thick; fair face and emulsion both sides	m²	27.50	-	32.90
2.7.40	half brick thick; plaster and emulsion both sides	m²	39.10	-	50.40
2.7.41	one brick thick	m²	40.50	-	46.00
2.7.42	one brick thick; fair face and emulsion both sides	m²	43.20	-	50.40
2.7.43	one brick thick; fair face and emulsion both sides	m²	47.40	-	54.60
2.7.44	one brick thick; plaster and emulsion both sides	m²	59.00	-	70.00
2.7.45	Block partitions; softwood doors and frames; painted partition	m²	33.60	-	44.60
2.7.46	partition; fair faced both sides	m²	35.00	-	47.40
2.7.47	partition; fair face and emulsion both sides	m²	40.50	-	51.80
2.7.48	partition; plastered and emulsioned both sides	m²	53.20	-	67.30
	Block partitions; hardwood doors and frames;				
2.7.49	partition	m²	50.00	-	65.00
2.7.50	partition; plaster and emulsion both sides	m²	69.00	-	86.00
	Reinforced concrete walls				
	Walls				
2.7.51	150 mm thick	m²	70.00	-	84.00
2.7.52	150 mm thick; plaster and emulsion both sides	m²	93.30	-	112.50

INDUSTRIAL £ range £	RETAILING £ range £	LEISURE £ range £	OFFICES £ range £	HOTELS £ range £	Item nr.
47.00 - 65.00	50.00 - 67.00	50.00 - 67.00	50.00 - 67.00	50.00 - 69.00	2.7.14
65.00 - 78.00	66.00 - 81.00	66.00 - 81.00	66.00 - 81.00	66.00 - 86.00	2.7.15
59.00 - 74.00	62.00 - 77.00	62.00 - 77.00	62.00 - 77.00	62.00 - 81.00	2.7.16
-	4.50 - 6.30	4.50 - 6.30	4.50 - 6.30	4.50 - 10.20	2.7.17
17.50 - 19.90	17.50 - 19.90	17.50 - 19.90	17.50 - 19.90	17.50 - 26.80	2.7.18
50.00 - 84.00	70.00 - 86.00	70.00 - 86.00	70.00 - 86.00	77.00 - 102.00	2.7.19
75.00 - 92.00	77.00 - 96.00	77.00 - 96.00	77.00 - 96.00	77.00 - 102.00	2.7.20
102.00 - 100.00	88.00 - 108.00	88.00 - 108.00	88.00 - 108.00	88.00 - 122.00	2.7.21
11.50 - 13.00	11.50 - 13.70	11.50 - 13.70	11.50 - 14.80	13.00 - 15.10	2.7.22
14.10 - 17.50	14.80 - 18.20	14.80 - 18.20	14.80 - 18.20	16.10 - 18.90	2.7.23
17.50 - 20.20	18.90 - 21.60	18.90 - 21.60	18.90 - 21.60	20.20 - 23.00	2.7.24
19.60 - 21.60	20.20 - 22.30	20.20 - 22.30	20.20 - 22.30	21.60 - 22.30	2.7.25
23.70 - 27.50	25.00 - 28.80	25.00 - 28.80	25.00 - 28.80	25.00 - 29.50	2.7.26
2.10 - 4.50	2.10 - 4.50	2.10 - 4.50	2.10 - 4.50	2.10 - 4.50	2.7.27
+10% - +20%	+10% - +20%	+10% - +20%	+10% - +20%	+10% - +20%	2.7.28
20.20 - 23.70	15.80 - 25.00	21.60 - 25.00	21.60 - 25.00	22.30 - 26.80	2.7.29
23.70 - 30.20	23.70 - 30.20	23.70 - 30.20	23.70 - 30.20	25.40 - 31.60	2.7.30
35.70 - 41.90	36.40 - 43.20	36.40 - 43.20	36.40 - 43.20	37.70 - 46.00	2.7.31
-	32.30 - 36.40	-	-	-	2.7.32
23.70 - 27.50	24.00 - 28.80	24.00 - 28.80	24.00 - 28.80	24.00 - 30.20	2.7.33
26.80 - 32.90	27.50 - 32.90	27.50 - 32.90	27.50 - 32.90	28.80 - 34.30	2.7.34
39.10 - 43.20	40.50 - 46.00	40.50 - 46.00	40.50 - 46.00	40.50 - 47.40	2.7.35
-	-	44.60 - 54.60	-	-	2.7.36
20.20 - 23.00	21.60 - 23.70	21.60 - 23.70	21.60 - 23.70	22.30 - 25.00	2.7.37
22.30 - 27.50	23.70 - 28.80	23.70 - 28.80	23.70 - 28.80	23.70 - 30.20	2.7.38
26.40 - 32.90	27.50 - 32.90	27.50 - 32.90	27.50 - 32.90	28.80 - 34.30	2.7.39
37.70 - 49.10	39.10 - 50.40	39.10 - 50.40	39.10 - 50.40	40.50 - 54.60	2.7.40
39.10 - 43.20	40.50 - 46.00	40.50 - 46.00	40.50 - 46.00	43.20 - 47.40	2.7.41
41.90 - 47.40	43.20 - 50.40	43.20 - 50.40	43.20 - 50.40	44.60 - 50.40	2.7.42
44.60 - 51.80	47.40 - 54.60	47.40 - 54.60	47.40 - 54.60	50.40 - 57.30	2.7.43
57.30 - 65.90	58.70 - 68.60	58.70 - 68.60	58.70 - 68.60	63.10 - 72.70	2.7.44
32.30 - 43.20	33.60 - 44.60	33.60 - 44.60	33.60 - 44.60	35.00 - 46.00	2.7.45
33.60 - 44.60	35.00 - 47.40	35.00 - 47.40	35.00 - 47.40	37.70 - 47.40	2.7.46
37.70 - 50.40	40.50 - 51.80	40.50 - 51.80	40.50 - 51.80	41.90 - 51.80	2.7.47
51.80 - 64.50	53.20 - 67.30	53.20 - 67.30	53.20 - 67.30	53.20 - 70.00	2.7.48
49.10 - 61.80	50.40 - 64.50	50.40 - 64.50	50.40 - 64.50	54.60 - 66.00	2.7.49
66.00 - 84.00	69.00 - 86.00	69.00 - 86.00	69.00 - 82.00	65.00 - 82.00	2.7.50
70.00 - 82.00	70.00 - 82.00	70.00 - 82.00	70.00 - 82.00	70.00 - 82.00	2.7.51
93.00 - 113.00	93.00 - 113.00	93.00 - 113.00	93.00 - 113.00	93.00 - 113.00	2.7.52

Item nr.	SPECIFICATIONS	Unit	RESIDENTIAL £ range £	
2.7	**INTERNAL WALLS, PARTITION AND DOORS - cont'd**			
	internal wall area (unless otherwise described)			
	Solid partitioning and doors			
	Patent partitioning; softwood doors			
2.7.53	frame and sheet	m²	-	-
2.7.54	frame and panel	m²	-	-
2.7.55	panel to panel	m²	-	-
2.7.56	economical	m²	-	-
	Patent partitioning; hardwood doors			
2.7.57	economical	m²	-	-
	Demountable partitioning; hardwood doors			
2.7.58	medium quality; vinyl faced	m²	-	-
2.7.59	high quality; vinyl faced	m²	-	-
	Glazed partitioning and doors			
	Aluminium internal patent glazing			
2.7.60	single glazed	m²	-	-
2.7.61	double glazed	m²	-	-
	Demountable steel partitioning and doors			
2.7.62	medium quality	m²	-	-
2.7.63	high quality	m²	-	-
	Demountable aluminium/steel partitioning and doors			
2.7.64	high quality	m²	-	-
2.7.65	high quality; sliding	m²	-	-
	Stainless steel glazed manual doors and screens			
2.7.66	high quality; to inner lobby of malls	m²	-	-
	Special partitioning and doors			
	Demountable fire partitions			
2.7.67	enamelled steel; half hour	m²	-	-
2.7.68	stainless steel; half hour	m²	-	-
	Soundproof partitions; hardwood doors			
2.7.69	luxury veneered	m²	-	-
	Folding screens			
2.7.70	gym divider; electronically operated	m²	-	-
2.7.71	bar divider	m²	-	-
2.7.72	Squash court glass back wall and door	m²	-	-
	WC/Changing cubicles　　**each** (unless otherwise described)			
2.7.73	WC cubicles	nr	-	-
	Changing cubicles			
2.7.74	aluminium	nr	-	-
2.7.75	aluminium; textured glass and bench seating	nr	-	-
	Comparative doors/door linings/frames			
	Standard softwood doors; excluding ironmongery; linings and frames			
	40 mm thick flush; hollow core; painted			
2.7.76	726 mm x 2040 mm	nr	33.00 -	40.00
2.7.77	826 mm x 2040 mm	nr	33.00 -	40.00
	40 mm thick flush; hollow core; plywood faced; painted			
2.7.78	726 mm x 2040 mm	nr	40.00 -	50.00
2.7.79	826 mm x 2040 mm	nr	40.00 -	50.00
	40 mm thick flush; hollow core; sapele veneered hard board faced			
2.7.80	726 mm x 2040 mm	nr	33.00 -	40.00
2.7.81	826 mm x 2040 mm	nr	33.00 -	40.00
	40 mm thick flush; hollow core; teak veneered hard board faced			
2.7.82	726 mm x 2040 mm	nr	78.00 -	96.00
2.7.83	826 mm x 2040 mm	nr	78.00 -	96.00

INDUSTRIAL £ range £		RETAILING £ range £		LEISURE £ range £		OFFICES £ range £		HOTELS £ range £		Item nr.
45.00	- 88.00	50.00	- 91.00	50.00	- 91.00	50.00	- 91.00	50.00	- 111.00	2.7.53
38.00	- 70.00	40.00	- 73.00	40.00	- 73.00	40.00	- 73.00	40.00	- 91.00	2.7.54
56.00	- 119.00	60.00	- 125.00	60.00	- 125.00	60.00	- 125.00	60.00	- 140.00	2.7.55
60.00	- 77.00	65.00	- 82.00	65.00	- 82.00	65.00	- 82.00	65.00	- 102.00	2.7.56
66.00	- 81.00	66.00	- 86.00	66.00	- 86.00	66.00	- 86.00	66.00	- 91.00	2.7.57
86.00	- 113.00	91.00	- 113.00	91.00	- 113.00	91.00	- 113.00	91.00	- 122.00	2.7.58
114.00	- 159.00	114.00	- 159.00	114.00	- 159.00	114.00	- 159.00	119.00	- 173.00	2.7.59
77.00	- 106.00	-	-	-	-	-	-	-	-	2.7.60
130.00	- 162.00	-	-	-	-	-	-	-	-	2.7.61
140.00	- 176.00	-	-	-	-	140.00	- 189.00	-	-	2.7.62
176.00	- 217.00	-	-	-	-	189.00	- 224.00	-	-	2.7.63
-	-	-	-	210.00	- 377.00	-	-	301.00	- 377.00	2.7.64
-	-	-	-	504.00	- 616.00	-	-	-	-	2.7.65
-	-	301.00	- 806.00	-	-	-	-	-	-	2.7.66
315.00	- 476.00	364.00	- 511.00	364.00	- 511.00	364.00	- 511.00	-	-	2.7.67
-	-	637.00	- 806.00	637.00	- 806.00	637.00	- 806.00	-	-	2.7.68
161.00	- 217.00	176.00	- 246.00	176.00	- 246.00	176.00	- 246.00	176.00	- 266.00	2.7.69
-	-	-	-	119.00	- 133.00	-	-	-	-	2.7.70
-	-	-	-	316.00	- 357.00	-	-	-	-	2.7.71
-	-	-	-	210.00	- 250.00	-	-	-	-	2.7.72
224.00	- 350.00	231.00	- 350.00	231.00	- 350.00	224.00	- 497.00	280.00	- 497.00	2.7.73
-	-	-	-	273.00	- 497.00	-	-	-	-	2.7.74
-	-	-	-	454.00	- 596.00	-	-	-	-	2.7.75
33.00	- 40.00	33.00	- 40.00	33.00	- 40.00	33.00	- 40.00	33.00	- 40.00	2.7.76
33.00	- 40.00	33.00	- 40.00	33.00	- 40.00	33.00	- 40.00	33.00	- 40.00	2.7.77
40.00	- 50.00	40.00	- 50.00	40.00	- 50.00	40.00	- 50.00	40.00	- 50.00	2.7.78
40.00	- 50.00	40.00	- 50.00	40.00	- 50.00	40.00	- 50.00	40.00	- 50.00	2.7.79
33.00	- 40.00	33.00	- 40.00	33.00	- 40.00	33.00	- 40.00	24.00	- 40.00	2.7.80
33.00	- 40.00	33.00	- 40.00	33.00	- 40.00	33.00	- 40.00	33.00	- 40.00	2.7.81
78.00	- 95.00	78.00	- 95.00	78.00	- 95.00	78.00	- 95.00	78.00	- 95.00	2.7.82
78.00	- 95.00	78.00	- 95.00	78.00	- 95.00	78.00	- 95.00	78.00	- 95.00	2.7.83

Item nr.	SPECIFICATIONS	Unit	RESIDENTIAL £ range £	
2.7	**INTERNAL WALLS, PARTITION AND DOORS - cont'd**			
	each (unless otherwise described)			
	Comparative doors/door linings/ frames - cont'd			
	Standard softwood fire doors; excluding ironmongery; lining and frames			
	44 mm thick flush; half hour fire check; plywood faced; painted			
2.7.84	726 mm x 2040 mm	nr	50.00 -	56.00
2.7.85	826 mm x 2040 mm	nr	53.00 -	60.00
	44 mm thick flush; half hour fire check; plywood faced; painted			
2.7.86	726 mm x 2040 mm	nr	66.00 -	73.00
2.7.87	826 mm x 2040 mm	nr	67.00 -	75.00
	54 mm thick flush; one hour fire check; sapele veneered hardboard faced			
2.7.88	726 mm x 2040 mm	nr	203.00 -	224.00
2.7.89	826 mm x 2040 mm	nr	210.00 -	224.00
	54 mm thick flush; one hour fire check; sapele veneered hardboard faced			
2.7.90	726 mm x 2040 mm	nr	217.00 -	246.00
2.7.91	826 mm x 2040 mm	nr	224.00 -	253.00
	Purpose-made softwood doors; excluding ironmongery; linings and frames			
	44 mm thick four panel door; painted			
2.7.92	726 mm x 2040 mm	nr	113.00 -	126.00
2.7.93	826 mm x 2040 mm	nr	119.00 -	133.00
	50 mm thick four door panel; wax polished			
2.7.94	726 mm x 2040 mm	nr	217.00 -	246.00
2.7.95	826 mm x 2040 mm	nr	231.00 -	253.00
	Purpose-made softwood door frames/linings; painted including grounds			
	32 mm x 100 mm lining			
2.7.96	726 mm x 2040 mm opening	nr	67.00 -	75.00
2.7.97	826 mm x 2040 mm opening	nr	70.00 -	78.00
	32 mm x 140 mm lining			
2.7.98	726 mm x 2040 mm opening	nr	75.00 -	86.00
2.7.99	826 mm x 2040 mm opening	nr	77.00 -	88.00
	32 mm x 250 mm cross-tongued lining			
2.7.100	726 mm x 2040 mm opening	nr	99.00 -	114.00
2.7.101	826 mm x 2040 mm opening	nr	100.00 -	115.00
	32 mm x 375 mm cross-tongued lining			
2.7.102	726 mm x 2040 mm opening	nr	129.00 -	147.00
2.7.103	826 mm x 2040 mm opening	nr	133.00 -	147.00
	75 mm x 100 mm rebated frame			
2.7.104	726 mm x 2040 mm opening	nr	88.00 -	93.00
2.7.105	826 mm x 2040 mm opening	nr	92.00 -	97.00
	Purpose-made mahogany door frames/linings; wax polished including grounds			
	32 mm x 100 mm lining			
2.7.106	726 mm x 2040 mm opening	nr	91.00 -	97.00
2.7.107	826 mm x 2040 mm opening	nr	92.00 -	100.00
	32 mm x 140 mm lining			
2.7.108	726 mm x 2040 mm opening	nr	100.00 -	114.00
2.7.109	826 mm x 2040 mm opening	nr	103.00 -	115.00
	32 mm x 250 mm cross-tongued lining			
2.7.110	726 mm x 2040 mm opening	nr	115.00 -	124.00
2.7.111	826 mm x 2040 mm opening	nr	118.00 -	128.00
	32 mm x 375 mm cross-tongued lining			
2.7.112	726 mm x 2040 mm opening	nr	176.00 -	189.00
2.7.113	826 mm x 2040 mm opening	nr	176.00 -	196.00
	75 mm x 100 mm rebated frame			
2.7.114	726 mm x 2040 mm opening	nr	126.00 -	133.00
2.7.115	826 mm x 2040 mm opening	nr	126.00 -	133.00

INDUSTRIAL £ range £	RETAILING £ range £	LEISURE £ range £	OFFICES £ range £	HOTELS £ range £	Item nr.
50.00 - 56.00	50.00 - 56.00	50.00 - 56.00	50.00 - 56.00	50.00 - 56.00	2.7.84
53.00 - 60.00	53.00 - 60.00	53.00 - 60.00	53.00 - 60.00	53.00 - 60.00	2.7.85
65.00 - 73.00	65.00 - 73.00	65.00 - 73.00	65.00 - 73.00	65.00 - 73.00	2.7.86
67.00 - 75.00	67.00 - 75.00	67.00 - 75.00	67.00 - 75.00	67.00 - 75.00	2.7.87
203.00 - 224.00	203.00 - 224.00	203.00 - 224.00	203.00 - 224.00	203.00 - 224.00	2.7.88
210.00 - 224.00	210.00 - 224.00	210.00 - 224.00	210.00 - 224.00	210.00 - 224.00	2.7.89
217.00 - 246.00	217.00 - 246.00	217.00 - 246.00	217.00 - 246.00	217.00 - 246.00	2.7.90
224.00 - 253.00	224.00 - 253.00	224.00 - 253.00	224.00 - 253.00	224.00 - 253.00	2.7.91
113.00 - 126.00	113.00 - 126.00	113.00 - 126.00	113.00 - 126.00	113.00 - 126.00	2.7.92
119.00 - 133.00	119.00 - 133.00	119.00 - 133.00	119.00 - 133.00	119.00 - 133.00	2.7.93
217.00 - 246.00	217.00 - 246.00	217.00 - 246.00	217.00 - 246.00	217.00 - 246.00	2.7.94
224.00 - 253.00	224.00 - 253.00	224.00 - 253.00	224.00 - 253.00	224.00 - 253.00	2.7.95
67.00 - 75.00	67.00 - 75.00	67.00 - 75.00	67.00 - 75.00	67.00 - 75.00	2.7.96
70.00 - 78.00	70.00 - 78.00	70.00 - 78.00	70.00 - 78.00	70.00 - 78.00	2.7.97
74.00 - 86.00	74.00 - 86.00	74.00 - 86.00	74.00 - 86.00	74.00 - 86.00	2.7.98
77.00 - 89.00	77.00 - 89.00	77.00 - 89.00	77.00 - 89.00	77.00 - 89.00	2.7.99
99.00 - 114.00	99.00 - 114.00	99.00 - 114.00	99.00 - 114.00	99.00 - 114.00	2.7.100
100.00 - 115.00	100.00 - 115.00	100.00 - 115.00	100.00 - 115.00	100.00 - 115.00	2.7.101
136.00 - 141.00	136.00 - 141.00	136.00 - 141.00	136.00 - 141.00	136.00 - 141.00	2.7.102
136.00 - 145.00	136.00 - 145.00	136.00 - 145.00	136.00 - 145.00	136.00 - 145.00	2.7.103
88.00 - 93.00	88.00 - 93.00	88.00 - 93.00	88.00 - 93.00	88.00 - 93.00	2.7.104
93.00 - 99.00	93.00 - 99.00	93.00 - 99.00	93.00 - 99.00	93.00 - 99.00	2.7.105
92.00 - 99.00	92.00 - 99.00	92.00 - 99.00	92.00 - 99.00	92.00 - 99.00	2.7.106
93.00 - 100.00	93.00 - 100.00	93.00 - 100.00	93.00 - 100.00	93.00 - 100.00	2.7.107
100.00 - 114.00	100.00 - 114.00	100.00 - 114.00	100.00 - 114.00	100.00 - 114.00	2.7.108
103.00 - 115.00	103.00 - 115.00	103.00 - 115.00	103.00 - 115.00	103.00 - 115.00	2.7.109
114.00 - 124.00	114.00 - 124.00	114.00 - 124.00	114.00 - 124.00	114.00 - 124.00	2.7.110
119.00 - 130.00	119.00 - 130.00	119.00 - 130.00	119.00 - 130.00	119.00 - 130.00	2.7.111
167.00 - 189.00	167.00 - 189.00	167.00 - 189.00	167.00 - 189.00	167.00 - 189.00	2.7.112
176.00 - 196.00	176.00 - 196.00	176.00 - 196.00	176.00 - 196.00	176.00 - 196.00	2.7.113
126.00 - 133.00	126.00 - 133.00	126.00 - 133.00	126.00 - 133.00	126.00 - 133.00	2.7.114
126.00 - 133.00	126.00 - 133.00	126.00 - 133.00	126.00 - 133.00	126.00 - 133.00	2.7.115

Item nr.	SPECIFICATIONS	Unit	RESIDENTIAL £ range £	
2.7	**INTERNAL WALLS, PARTITION AND DOORS - cont'd**			
	each (unless otherwise described)			
	Comparative doors/door linings/frames - cont'd			
	Standard softwood doors and frames; including ironmongery and painting			
2.7.116	flush; hollow core	nr	167.00 -	210.00
2.7.117	flush; hollow core; hardwood faced	nr	167.00 -	224.00
	flush; solid core			
2.7.118	single leaf	nr	196.00 -	253.00
2.7.119	double leaf	nr	287.00 -	386.00
2.7.120	flush; solid core; hardwood faced	nr	203.00 -	266.00
2.7.121	four panel door	nr	287.00 -	350.00
	Purpose-made softwood doors and hardwood frames;			
	including ironmongery; painting and polishing flush			
	solid core; heavy duty			
2.7.122	single leaf	nr	-	-
2.7.123	double leaf	nr	-	-
	flush solid core; heavy duty; plastic laminate faced			
2.7.124	single leaf	nr	-	-
2.7.125	double leaf	nr	-	-
	Purpose-made softwood fire doors and hardwood frames; including			
	ironmongery; painting and polishing			
	flush; one hour fire resisting			
2.7.126	single leaf	nr	-	-
2.7.127	double leaf	nr	-	-
	flush; one hour fire resisting; plastic laminate faced			
2.7.128	single leaf	nr	-	-
2.7.128	double leaf	nr	-	-
	Purpose-made softwood doors and pressed steel frames;			
2.7.130	flush; half hour fire check; plastic laminate faced	nr	-	-
	Purpose-made mahogany doors and frames; including ironmongery and			
	polishing			
2.7.131	four panel door	nr	-	-
	Perimeter treatments			
	Precast concrete lintels; in block walls			
2.7.132	75 mm wide	nr	8.90 -	14.70
2.7.133	100 mm wide	nr	14.70 -	18.20
	Precast concrete lintels; in brick walls			
2.7.134	half brick thick	nr	14.70 -	18.20
2.7.135	one brick thick	nr	23.10 -	29.50
	Purpose-made softwood architraves; painted; including grounds			
	25 mm x 50 mm; to both sides of openings			
2.7.136	726 mm x 2040 mm opening	nr	66.00 -	71.00
2.7.137	826 mm x 2040 mm opening	nr	67.00 -	73.00
	Purpose-made mahogany architraves; wax polished; including grounds			
	25 mm x 50 mm; to both sides of openings			
2.7.138	726 mm x 2040 mm opening	nr	108.00 -	119.00
2.7.139	826 mm x 2040 mm opening	nr	108.00 -	119.00

INDUSTRIAL £ range £	RETAILING £ range £	LEISURE £ range £	OFFICES £ range £	HOTELS £ range £	Item nr.
167.00 - 210.00	167.00 - 210.00	167.00 - 210.00	167.00 - 210.00	167.00 - 210.00	2.7.116
167.00 - 224.00	167.00 - 224.00	167.00 - 224.00	167.00 - 224.00	167.00 - 224.00	2.7.117
196.00 - 253.00	196.00 - 253.00	196.00 - 253.00	196.00 - 253.00	196.00 - 253.00	2.7.118
287.00 - 386.00	287.00 - 386.00	209.00 - 386.00	287.00 - 386.00	287.00 - 386.00	2.7.119
203.00 - 266.00	203.00 - 266.00	203.00 - 266.00	203.00 - 266.00	203.00 - 266.00	2.7.120
287.00 - 350.00	287.00 - 350.00	287.00 - 350.00	287.00 - 350.00	287.00 - 350.00	2.7.121
483.00 - 567.00	483.00 - 567.00	352.00 - 567.00	483.00 - 567.00	483.00 - 567.00	2.7.122
657.00 - 840.00	657.00 - 840.00	657.00 - 840.00	657.00 - 840.00	657.00 - 840.00	2.7.123
587.00 - 666.00	587.00 - 666.00	587.00 - 666.00	587.00 - 666.00	587.00 - 666.00	2.7.124
813.00 - 910.00	813.00 - 910.00	813.00 - 910.00	813.00 - 910.00	813.00 - 910.00	2.7.125
637.00 - 714.00	637.00 - 714.00	637.00 - 714.00	637.00 - 714.00	637.00 - 714.00	2.7.126
813.00 - 994.00	813.00 - 994.00	813.00 - 994.00	813.00 - 994.00	813.00 - 994.00	2.7.127
791.00 - 867.00	791.00 - 867.00	791.00 - 867.00	791.00 - 867.00	791.00 - 867.00	2.7.128
1016.0 - 1098.0	1016.0 - 1098.0	1016.0 - 1098.0	1016.0 - 1098.0	1016.0 - 1098.00	2.7.129
734.00 - 883.00	734.00 - 883.00	734.00 - 883.00	734.00 - 883.00	734.00 - 883.00	2.7.130
609.00 - 714.00	609.00 - 714.00	609.00 - 714.00	609.00 - 714.00	609.00 - 714.00	2.7.131
6.70 - 10.60	6.70 - 10.60	6.70 - 10.60	6.70 - 10.60	6.70 - 10.60	2.7.132
8.40 - 11.90	8.40 - 11.90	8.40 - 11.90	8.40 - 11.90	8.40 - 11.90	2.7.133
8.40 - 11.90	8.40 - 11.90	8.40 - 11.90	8.40 - 11.90	8.40 - 11.90	2.7.134
12.90 - 15.80	12.90 - 15.80	12.90 - 15.80	12.90 - 15.80	12.90 - 15.80	2.7.135
66.00 - 71.00	66.00 - 71.00	66.00 - 71.00	66.00 - 71.00	66.00 - 71.00	2.7.136
67.00 - 73.00	67.00 - 73.00	67.00 - 73.00	67.00 - 73.00	67.00 - 69.00	2.7.137
108.00 - 119.00	108.00 - 119.00	108.00 - 119.00	108.00 - 119.00	108.00 - 119.00	2.7.138
110.00 - 119.00	110.00 - 119.00	110.00 - 119.00	110.00 - 119.00	110.00 - 119.00	2.7.139

Item nr.	SPECIFICATIONS	Unit	RESIDENTIAL £ range £		
3.1	**WALL FINISHES**				
	wall finish area (unless otherwise described)				
	comprising:				
	Sheet/board finishes				
	In situ wall finishes				
	Rigid tile/panel finishes				
	Sheet/board finishes				
	Dry plasterboard lining; taped joints; for direct decoration				
3.1.1	9.50 mm thick Gyproc Wallboard	m²	6.30	-	9.10
	Extra for				
3.1.2	insulating grade	m²	0.40	-	0.50
3.1.3	insulating grade; plastic faced	m²	1.40	-	1.70
3.1.4	12.50 mm thick Gyproc Wallboard (half-hour fire-resisting)	m²	7.00	-	10.20
	Extra for				
3.1.5	insulating grade	m²	0.50	-	0.60
3.1.6	insulating grade; plastic faced	m²	1.30	-	1.50
3.1.7	two layers of 12.50 mm thick Gyproc Wallboard (one-hour fire-resisting)	m²	12.60	-	16.10
3.1.8	9 mm thick Supalux (half-hour fire-resisting)	m²	12.60	-	16.10
	Dry plasterboard lining; taped joints; for direct decoration; fixed to wall on dabs				
3.1.9	9.50 mm thick Gyproc Wallboard	m²	7.00	-	10.20
	Dry plasterboard lining; taped joints; for direct decoration; including metal tees				
3.1.10	9.50 mm thick Gyproc Wallboard	m²	-		-
3.1.11	12.50 mm thick Gyproc Wallboard	m²	-		-
	Dry lining/sheet panelling; including battens; plugged to wall				
3.1.12	6.40 mm thick hardboard	m²	7.70	-	9.10
3.1.13	9.50 mm thick Gyproc Wallboard	m²	11.30	-	15.40
3.1.14	6 mm thick birch faced plywood	m²	12.60	-	14.80
3.1.15	6 mm thick WAM plywood	m²	15.40	-	18.20
3.1.16	15 mm thick chipboard	m²	11.30	-	12.60
3.1.17	15 mm thick melamine faced chipboard	m²	20.20	-	24.70
3.1.18	13.20 mm thick "Formica" faced chipboard	m²	27.10	-	40.50
	Timber boarding/panelling; on and including battens; plugged to wall				
3.1.19	12 mm thick softwood boarding	m²	17.50	-	22.60
3.1.20	25 mm thick softwood boarding	m²	25.00	-	28.10
3.1.21	hardwood panelling; t&g & v-jointed	m²	40.00	-	91.00
	In situ wall finishes				
	Extra over common brickwork for				
3.1.22	fair face and pointing both sides	m²	2.50	-	3.50
	Comparative finishes				
3.1.23	one mist and two coats emulsion paint	m²	2.00	-	3.00
3.1.24	multi-coloured gloss paint	m²	3.50	-	4.50
3.1.25	two coats of lightweight plaster	m²	7.00	-	9.10
3.1.26	9.50 mm thick Gyproc Wallboard and skim coat	m²	8.80	-	11.30
3.1.27	12.50 mm thick Gyproc Wallboard and skim coat	m²	10.20	-	12.60
3.1.28	two coats of "Thistle" plaster	m²	8.80	-	11.90
3.1.29	plaster and emulsion	m²	8.80	-	13.70
	Extra for				
3.1.30	gloss paint in lieu of emulsion	m²	1.50	-	1.80
3.1.31	two coat render and emulsion	m²	15.40	-	20.90
3.1.32	plaster and vinyl	m²	12.60	-	18.20
3.1.33	plaster and fabric	m²	12.60	-	27.50
3.1.34	squash court plaster "including markings"	m²	-		-
3.1.35	6 mm thick terrazzo wall lining; including backing	m²	-		-
3.1.36	glass reinforced gypsum	m²	-		-

INDUSTRIAL £ range £	RETAILING £ range £	LEISURE £ range £	OFFICES £ range £	HOTELS £ range £	Item nr.
5.90 - 9.10	5.90 - 9.10	5.90 - 9.10	5.90 - 9.10	5.90 - 9.10	3.1.1
0.40 - 0.60	0.40 - 0.60	0.40 - 0.60	0.40 - 0.60	0.40 - 0.60	3.1.2
1.50 - 1.70	1.50 - 1.70	1.50 - 1.70	1.50 - 1.70	1.50 - 1.70	3.1.3
7.00 - 9.50	7.00 - 10.20	7.00 - 10.20	7.00 - 10.20	7.70 - 11.90	3.1.4
0.50 - 0.60	0.50 - 0.60	0.50 - 0.60	0.50 - 0.60	0.50 - 0.60	3.1.5
1.30 - 1.50	1.30 - 1.50	1.30 - 1.50	1.30 - 1.50	1.30 - 1.50	3.1.6
11.90 - 16.10	12.60 - 16.10	12.60 - 16.10	12.60 - 16.10	13.30 - 18.90	3.1.7
11.90 - 16.10	12.60 - 16.10	12.60 - 16.10	12.60 - 16.10	13.30 - 18.90	3.1.8
6.30 - 9.50	7.00 - 10.20	7.00 - 10.20	7.00 - 10.20	7.70 - 10.80	3.1.9
15.40 - 17.80	- -	- -	- -	- -	3.1.10
16.10 - 18.90	- -	- -	- -	- -	3.1.11
7.70 - 9.10	7.70 - 9.10	7.70 - 9.10	7.70 - 9.10	8.40 - 10.20	3.1.12
11.30 - 14.80	11.30 - 15.40	11.30 - 15.40	11.30 - 15.40	12.60 - 16.10	3.1.13
11.90 - 14.10	12.60 - 14.80	12.60 - 14.80	12.60 - 14.80	13.30 - 16.10	3.1.14
14.80 - 18.20	15.40 - 18.90	15.40 - 18.90	15.40 - 18.90	16.10 - 18.90	3.1.15
11.30 - 12.60	11.30 - 12.60	11.30 - 12.60	11.30 - 12.60	12.60 - 14.10	3.1.16
18.90 - 23.30	20.20 - 24.70	20.20 - 24.70	20.20 - 24.70	20.90 - 25.40	3.1.17
25.70 - 39.10	27.50 - 40.50	27.50 - 40.50	27.50 - 40.50	27.50 - 44.60	3.1.18
17.50 - 22.60	17.50 - 22.60	17.50 - 22.60	17.50 - 22.60	18.90 - 24.00	3.1.19
24.40 - 26.80	25.00 - 28.10	25.00 - 28.10	25.00 - 28.10	25.70 - 29.50	3.1.20
40.00 - 91.00	40.00 - 91.00	40.00 - 91.00	30.00 - 91.00	45.00 - 101.00	3.1.21
2.50 - 3.50	2.50 - 3.50	2.50 - 3.50	2.50 - 3.50	2.50 - 3.50	3.1.22
2.00 - 3.00	2.00 - 3.00	2.00 - 3.00	2.00 - 3.00	2.00 - 3.00	3.1.23
3.50 - 4.50	3.50 - 4.50	3.50 - 4.50	3.50 - 4.50	3.50 - 4.50	3.1.24
6.30 - 9.10	7.00 - 9.10	7.00 - 9.10	7.00 - 9.10	7.70 - 10.20	3.1.25
8.40 - 10.50	9.10 - 11.30	9.10 - 11.30	9.10 - 11.30	9.50 - 11.90	3.1.26
9.50 - 11.90	10.20 - 11.90	10.20 - 11.90	10.20 - 11.90	10.40 - 11.90	3.1.27
9.10 - 11.90	9.10 - 11.90	9.10 - 11.90	9.10 - 11.90	9.50 - 11.90	3.1.28
8.40 - 12.60	9.10 - 13.70	9.10 - 13.70	9.10 - 13.70	10.20 - 16.10	3.1.29
1.50 - 1.80	1.50 - 1.80	1.50 - 1.80	1.50 - 1.80	1.50 - 1.80	3.1.30
14.80 - 20.20	15.40 - 20.90	15.40 - 20.90	15.40 - 20.90	16.10 - 22.30	3.1.31
- -	12.60 - 18.20	12.60 - 18.90	12.60 - 18.90	13.70 - 18.90	3.1.32
- -	12.60 - 27.50	12.60 - 27.50	12.60 - 27.50	14.10 - 29.50	3.1.33
- -	- -	18.00 - 22.00	- -	- -	3.1.34
- -	126.00 - 161.00	126.00 - 161.00	126.00 - 161.00	133.00 - 176.00	3.1.35
- -	113.00 - 176.00	113.00 - 176.00	113.00 - 176.00	126.00 - 183.00	3.1.36

Item nr.	SPECIFICATIONS	Unit	RESIDENTIAL £ range £	
3.1	**WALL FINISHES - cont'd**			
	wall finish area (unless otherwise described)			
	Rigid tile/panel finishes			
	Ceramic wall tiles; including backing			
3.1.37	economical	m²	16.80 -	30.90
3.1.38	medium quality	m²	30.90 -	54.60
3.1.39	high quality; to toilet blocks; kitchens and first aid rooms	m²	-	-
3.1.40	high quality; to changing areas, toilets, showers and fitness areas	m²	-	-
	Porcelain mosaic tiling; including backing to swimming pool lining; walls and			
3.1.41	floors	m²	-	-
	"Roman Travertine" marble wall linings; polished			
3.1.42	19 mm thick	m²	-	-
3.1.43	40 mm thick	m²	-	-
3.1.44	Metal mirror cladding panels	m²	-	-
3.2	**FLOOR FINISHES**			
	floor finish area (unless otherwise described)			
	comprising:			
	Sheet/board flooring			
	In situ screed and floor finishes			
	Rigid tile/slab finishes			
	Parquet/Wood block finishes			
	Flexible tiling/sheet finishes			
	Carpet tiles/Carpeting			
	Access floors and finishes			
	Perimeter treatments and sundries			
	Sheet/board flooring			
	Chipboard flooring; t&g joints			
3.2.1	18 mm thick	m²	6.30 -	7.70
3.2.2	22 mm thick	m²	7.70 -	9.10
	Wrought softwood flooring			
3.2.3	25 mm thick; butt joints	m²	14.10 -	15.40
3.2.4	25 mm thick; butt joints; cleaned off and polished	m²	16.10 -	18.90
3.2.5	25 mm thick; t&g joints	m²	14.80 -	18.20
3.2.6	25 mm thick; t&g joints; cleaned off and polished	m²	17.50 -	21.60
3.2.7	Wrought softwood t&g strip flooring; 25 mm thick; polished; including fillets	m²	21.60 -	27.50
3.2.8	maple	m²	-	-
3.2.9	gurjun	m²	-	-
3.2.10	iroko	m²	-	-
3.2.11	american oak	m²	-	-
	Wrought hardwood t&g strip flooring; 25 mm thick; polished; including fillets			
3.2.12	maple	m²	-	-
3.2.13	gurjun	m²	-	-
3.2.14	iroko	m²	-	-
3.2.15	american oak	m²	-	-
	Wrought hardwood t&g strip flooring; 25 mm thick; polished; including rubber pads			
3.2.16	maple	m²	-	-
	In situ screed and floor finishes			
	Extra over concrete floor for			
3.2.17	power floating	m²	-	-
3.2.18	power floating; surface hardener	m²	-	-

INDUSTRIAL £ range £		RETAILING £ range £		LEISURE £ range £		OFFICES £ range £		HOTELS £ range £		Item nr.
16.10	- 28.10	17.50	- 30.90	17.50	- 30.90	17.50	- 30.90	20.20	- 36.40	3.1.37
28.10	- 50.40	30.90	- 56.30	30.90	- 56.30	30.90	- 56.30	35.00	- 61.80	3.1.38
-	-	50.40	- 64.50	50.40	- 64.50	50.40	- 64.50	50.40	- 64.50	3.1.39
-	-	-	-	64.50	- 76.90	-	-	-	-	3.1.40
-	-	-	-	40.50	- 54.60	-	-	-	-	3.1.41
-	-	203.00	- 273.00	203.00	- 273.00	203.00	- 273.00	203.00	- 273.00	3.1.42
-	-	280.00	- 357.00	280.00	- 357.00	280.00	- 357.00	280.00	- 357.00	3.1.43
-	-	210.00	- 357.00	203.00	- 343.00	-	-	224.00	- 364.00	3.1.44
-	-	-	-	-	-	-	-	-	-	3.2.1
-	-	-	-	-	-	-	-	-	-	3.2.2
-	-	-	-	-	-	-	-	-	-	3.2.3
-	-	-	-	-	-	-	-	-	-	3.2.4
-	-	-	-	-	-	-	-	-	-	3.2.5
-	-	-	-	-	-	-	-	-	-	3.2.6
-	-	-	-	-	-	-	-	-	-	3.2.7
-	-	-	-	37.70	- 43.20	37.70	- 43.20	37.70	- 44.60	3.2.8
-	-	-	-	-	-	33.60	- 37.70	33.60	- 37.10	3.2.9
-	-	-	-	-	-	37.70	- 41.90	37.70	- 41.20	3.2.10
-	-	-	-	-	-	40.50	- 44.60	40.50	- 46.00	3.2.11
-	-	-	-	41.90	47.40	41.90	- 47.40	43.20	- 49.10	3.2.12
-	-	-	-	-	-	37.70	- 41.90	39.10	- 43.20	3.2.13
-	-	-	-	-	-	41.90	- 47.40	43.20	- 47.40	3.2.14
-	-	-	-	-	-	43.20	- 50.40	44.60	- 53.20	3.2.15
-	-	-	-	50.40	- 60.40	-	-	-	-	3.2.16
3.50	- 7.00	2.50	- 7.00	-	-	-	-	-	-	3.2.17
7.00	- 10.20	5.30	- 9.10	-	-	-	-	-	-	3.2.18

Item nr.	SPECIFICATIONS	Unit	RESIDENTIAL £ range £		
3.2	**FLOOR FINISHES - cont'd**				
	floor finish area (unless otherwise described)				
	Insitu screed and floor finishes - cont'd				
	Latex cement screeds				
3.2.19	3 mm thick; one coat	m²	-		-
3.2.20	5 mm thick; two coats	m²	-		-
3.2.21	Rubber latex non-slip solution and epoxy sealant	m²	-		-
	Cement and sand (1:3) screeds				
3.2.22	25 mm thick	m²	7.00	-	7.70
3.2.23	50 mm thick	m²	8.40	-	9.80
3.2.24	75 mm thick	m²	11.90	-	13.30
	Cement and sand (1:3) paving				
3.2.25	paving	m²	6.30	-	8.40
3.2.26	32 mm thick; surface hardener	m²	7.70	-	11.90
3.2.27	screed only (for subsequent finish)	m²	9.80	-	14.80
3.2.28	screed only (for subsequent finish); allowance for skirtings	m²	11.20	-	17.50
	Mastic asphalt paving				
3.2.29	20 mm thick; BS 1076; black	m²	-		-
3.2.30	20 mm thick; BS 1471; red	m²	-		-
	Granolithic				
3.2.31	20 mm thick	m²	-		-
3.2.32	25 mm thick	m²	-		-
3.2.33	25 mm thick; including screed	m²	-		-
3.2.34	38 mm thick; including screed	m²	-		-
	"Synthanite"; on and including building paper				
3.2.35	25 mm thick	m²	-		-
3.2.36	50 mm thick	m²	-		-
3.2.37	75 mm thick	m²	-		-
	Acrylic polymer floor finish				
3.2.38	10 mm thick	m²	-		-
	Epoxy floor finish				
3.2.39	1.50 mm - 2.00 mm thick	m²	-		-
3.2.40	5.00 mm - 6.00 mm thick	m²	-		-
	Polyester resin floor finish				
3.2.41	5.00 mm - 9.00 mm thick	m²	-		-
	Terrazzo paving; divided into squares with ebonite strip; polished				
3.2.42	16 mm thick	m²	-		-
3.2.43	16 mm thick; including screed	m²	-		-
	Rigid Tile/slab finishes				
	Quarry tile flooring				
3.2.44	150 mm x 150 mm x 12.50 mm thick; red	m²	-		-
3.2.45	150 mm x 150 mm x 12.50 mm thick; brown	m²	-		-
3.2.46	200 mm x 200 mm x 19 mm thick; brown	m²	-		-
3.2.47	average tiling	m²	-		-
3.2.48	tiling; including screed	m²	-		-
3.2.49	tiling; including screed and allowance for skirtings	m²	-		-
	Brick paving				
3.2.50	paving	m²	-		-
3.2.51	paving; including screed	m²	-		-
	Glazed ceramic tiled flooring				
3.2.52	100 mm x 100 mm x 9 mm thick; red	m²	-		-
3.2.53	150 mm x 150 mm x 12 mm thick; red	m²	-		-
3.2.54	100 mm x 100 mm x 9 mm thick; black	m²	-		-
3.2.55	150 mm x 150 mm x 12 mm thick; black	m²	-		-
3.2.56	150 mm x 150 mm x 12 mm thick; anti-slip	m²	-		-
3.2.57	fully vitrified	m²	-		-
3.2.58	fully vitrified; including screed	m²	-		-
3.2.59	fully vitrified; including screed and allowance for skirtings	m²	-		-
3.2.60	high quality; to service areas; kitchen and toilet blocks; including screed	m²	-		-

INDUSTRIAL £ range £	RETAILING £ range £	LEISURE £ range £	OFFICES £ range £	HOTELS £ range £	Item nr.
3.50 - 4.00	- -	- -	3.50 - 4.00	- -	3.2.19
4.70 - 5.40	- -	- -	4.70 - 5.30	- -	3.2.20
6.00 - 14.10	- -	- -	- -	- -	3.2.21
7.00 - 7.70	7.00 - 7.70	7.00 - 7.70	7.00 - 7.70	7.00 - 7.70	3.2.22
8.40 - 9.80	8.40 - 9.80	8.40 - 9.80	8.40 - 9.80	8.40 - 9.80	3.2.23
11.90 - 13.30	11.90 - 13.30	12.00 - 12.40	12.00 - 12.40	12.00 - 12.40	3.2.24
6.00 - 7.70	6.30 - 8.40	6.30 - 8.40	6.30 - 8.40	6.30 - 8.40	3.2.25
7.00 - 11.20	8.40 - 11.90	8.40 - 11.90	8.40 - 11.90	8.40 - 11.90	3.2.26
9.10 - 14.10	9.80 - 14.10	9.80 - 14.10	9.80 - 14.10	9.80 - 14.10	3.2.27
11.20 - 16.10	11.90 - 17.50	11.90 - 17.50	11.90 - 17.50	11.90 - 18.20	3.2.28
14.10 - 16.80	14.80 - 17.50	14.80 - 17.50	- -	- -	3.2.29
16.80 - 18.90	17.50 - 20.20	17.50 - 20.20	- -	- -	3.2.30
7.70 - 11.90	8.40 - 12.60	8.40 - 12.60	8.40 - 12.60	8.40 - 12.60	3.2.31
10.50 - 14.10	11.20 - 14.10	11.20 - 14.10	11.20 - 14.10	11.20 - 15.40	3.2.32
17.50 - 18.90	17.80 - 20.20	17.80 - 20.20	17.80 - 20.20	17.80 - 19.60	3.2.33
24.70 - 28.10	25.70 - 29.50	25.70 - 29.50	25.70 - 29.50	27.10 - 30.20	3.2.34
16.10 - 18.90	16.10 - 20.20	16.10 - 20.20	16.10 - 20.20	- -	3.2.35
22.30 - 25.70	23.70 - 27.50	23.70 - 27.50	23.70 - 27.50	- -	3.2.36
27.50 - 32.30	29.50 - 32.90	29.50 - 32.90	29.50 - 32.90	- -	3.2.37
16.10 - 20.20	16.80 - 21.60	16.80 - 21.60	16.80 - 21.60	- -	3.2.38
16.10 - 20.20	16.80 - 22.30	16.80 - 22.30	16.80 - 22.30	- -	3.2.39
32.90 - 37.70	33.60 - 38.40	33.60 - 38.40	33.60 - 38.40	- -	3.2.40
37.10 - 41.90	37.70 - 43.20	37.70 - 43.20	37.70 - 43.20	- -	3.2.41
- -	37.10 - 41.90	37.10 - 41.90	37.10 - 41.90	40.50 - 50.40	3.2.42
- -	54.60 - 63.10	54.60 - 63.10	54.60 - 63.10	58.70 - 72.70	3.2.43
20.20 - 22.30	20.90 - 23.00	20.90 - 23.00	20.90 - 23.00	20.90 - 24.40	3.2.44
24.40 - 28.10	25.70 - 28.80	25.70 - 28.80	25.70 - 28.80	27.10 - 30.20	3.2.45
30.20 - 33.60	30.90 - 34.30	30.90 - 34.30	30.90 - 34.30	32.30 - 35.70	3.2.46
20.20 - 33.60	20.90 - 34.30	20.90 - 34.30	20.90 - 34.30	20.90 - 35.70	3.2.47
28.80 - 43.20	30.20 - 44.60	30.20 - 44.60	30.20 - 44.60	30.90 - 44.60	3.2.48
38.40 - 53.20	40.50 - 54.60	40.50 - 54.60	40.80 - 54.60	40.50 - 55.90	3.2.49
- -	22.00 - 43.20	30.20 - 43.20	30.20 - 43.20	30.20 - 43.20	3.2.50
- -	37.70 - 54.60	37.70 - 54.60	37.70 - 54.60	37.70 - 54.60	3.2.51
- -	27.10 - 30.90	27.10 - 30.90	27.10 - 31.20	28.10 - 32.30	3.2.52
- -	23.70 - 27.10	23.70 - 27.10	23.70 - 27.10	24.40 - 28.80	3.2.53
- -	30.20 - 32.90	30.20 - 32.90	30.20 - 32.90	30.90 - 34.30	3.2.54
- -	24.40 - 30.20	24.40 - 30.20	24.40 - 30.20	25.00 - 30.90	3.2.55
- -	30.20 - 31.60	30.20 - 31.60	30.20 - 31.60	30.20 - 32.90	3.2.56
- -	31.60 - 44.60	31.60 - 44.60	31.60 - 44.60	32.30 - 47.70	3.2.57
- -	37.70 - 57.30	37.70 - 57.30	37.70 - 57.30	39.80 - 59.00	3.2.58
- -	43.20 - 68.60	43.20 - 68.60	43.20 - 68.60	43.20 - 72.70	3.2.59
- -	- -	60.00 - 70.00	- -	- -	3.2.60

Item nr.	SPECIFICATIONS	Unit	RESIDENTIAL £ range £
3.2	**FLOOR FINISHES - cont'd**		
	floor finish area (unless otherwise described)		
	Rigid Tile/slab finishes - cont'd		
	Glazed ceramic tile flooring - cont'd		
3.2.61	high quality; to foyer; fitness and bar areas; including screed	m^2	- -
3.2.62	high quality; to pool surround, bottoms, steps and changing room; including screed	m^2	- -
3.2.63	Porcelain mosaic paving; including screed to swimming pool lining; walls and floors	m^2	- -
	Extra for		
3.2.64	non-slip finish to pool lining; beach and changing areas and showers	m^2	- -
	Terrazzo tile flooring		
3.2.65	28 mm thick white "Sicilian" marble aggregate tiling	m^2	- -
3.2.66	tiling; including screed	m^2	- -
	York stone		
3.2.67	50 mm thick paving	m^2	- -
3.2.68	paving; including screed	m^2	- -
	Slate		
3.2.69	200 mm x 400 mm x 10 mm thick ; blue - grey	m^2	- -
3.2.70	otta riven	m^2	- -
3.2.71	otta boned (polished)	m^2	- -
	Portland stone		
3.2.72	50 mm thick paving	m^2	- -
	Fined sanded "Roman Travertine" marble		
3.2.73	20 mm thick paving	m^2	- -
3.2.74	paving; including screed	m^2	- -
3.2.75	paving; including screed and allowance for skirtings	m^2	- -
	Granite		
3.2.76	20 mm thick paving	m^2	- -
	Parquet/wood block finishes		
	Parquet flooring; polished		
3.2.77	8 mm thick gurjun "Feltwood"	m^2	20.20 - 23.00
	Wrought hardwood block floorings; 25 mm thick; polished; t&g joints herringbone pattern		
3.2.78	merbau	m^2	- -
3.2.79	iroko	m^2	- -
3.2.80	iroko; including screed	m^2	- -
3.2.81	oak	m^2	- -
3.2.82	oak; including screed	m^2	- -
	Composition block flooring		
3.2.83	174 mm x 57 mm blocks	m^2	- -
	Flexible tiling		
	Thermoplastic tile flooring		
3.2.84	2 mm thick (series 2)	m^2	6.00 - 7.00
3.2.85	2 mm thick (series 4)	m^2	6.00 - 7.00
3.2.86	2 mm thick; including screed	m^2	13.30 - 15.40
	Cork tile flooring		
3.2.87	3.20 mm thick	m^2	10.50 - 13.30
3.2.88	3.20 mm thick; including screed	m^2	18.90 - 25.00
3.2.89	6.30 mm thick	m^2	- -
3.2.90	6.30 mm thick; including screed	m^2	- -
	Vinyl floor tiling		
3.2.91	2 mm thick; semi-flexible tiles	m^2	6.30 - 9.10
3.2.92	2 mm thick; fully flexible tiles	m^2	6.00 - 8.40
3.2.93	2.50 mm thick; semi-flexible tiles	m^2	7.70 - 10.20
3.2.94	tiling; including screed	m^2	16.10 - 20.20
3.2.95	tiling; including screed and allowance for skirtings	m^2	17.50 - 23.70
3.2.96	tiling; anti-static	m^2	- -
3.2.97	tiling; anti-static; including screed	m^2	- -

INDUSTRIAL £ range £	RETAILING £ range £	LEISURE £ range £	OFFICES £ range £	HOTELS £ range £	Item nr.
- -	- -	63.00 - 73.00	- -	- -	3.2.61
- -	- -	66.00 - 77.00	- -	- -	3.2.62
- -	- -	40.50 - 54.60	- -	- -	3.2.63
- -	- -	1.10 - 2.00	- -	- -	3.2.64
- -	59.00 - 66.00	59.00 - 66.00	59.00 - 66.00	60.00 - 70.00	3.2.65
- -	75.50 - 85.00	75.00 - 85.00	75.00 - 85.00	78.00 - 91.00	3.2.66
- -	76.90 - 102.00	77.00 - 99.00	77.00 - 99.00	81.00 - 110.00	3.2.67
- -	83.70 - 111.00	84.00 - 111.00	84.00 - 111.00	89.00 - 124.00	3.2.68
- -	94.70 - 107.00	95.00 - 107.00	95.00 - 107.00	- -	3.2.69
- -	107.10 - 117.00	107.00 - 117.00	107.00 - 117.00	- -	3.2.70
- -	116.70 - 126.00	117.00 - 126.00	117.00 - 126.00	- -	3.2.71
- -	160.60 - 189.00	161.00 - 189.00	161.00 - 189.00	- -	3.2.72
- -	203.10 - 246.00	203.00 - 246.00	203.00 - 246.00	210.00 - 259.00	3.2.73
- -	210.00 - 259.00	210.00 - 258.00	210.00 - 259.00	217.00 - 266.00	3.2.74
- -	259.40 - 323.00	259.00 - 323.00	259.00 - 323.00	266.00 - 336.00	3.2.75
- -	280.00 - 329.00	280.00 - 329.00	280.00 - 329.00	280.00 - 357.00	3.2.76
- -	- -	- -	- -	- -	3.2.77
- -	41.90 - 49.10	41.90 - 49.10	41.90 - 49.10	43.20 - 49.10	3.2.78
- -	44.60 - 50.40	44.60 - 50.40	44.60 - 50.40	47.40 - 53.20	3.2.79
- -	53.20 - 64.50	53.20 - 64.50	53.20 - 64.50	53.20 - 64.50	3.2.80
- -	43.20 - 55.90	43.20 - 55.90	43.20 - 55.90	44.60 - 57.30	3.2.81
- -	51.80 - 63.10	51.80 - 63.10	51.80 - 63.10	53.20 - 63.10	3.2.82
- -	50.40 - 55.90	50.40 - 55.90	50.40 - 55.90	53.20 - 58.70	3.2.83
- -	- -	- -	- -	- -	3.2.84
- -	- -	- -	- -	- -	3.2.85
- -	- -	- -	- -	- -	3.2.86
- -	- -	- -	- -	- -	3.2.87
- -	- -	- -	- -	- -	3.2.88
- -	18.90 - 21.60	18.90 - 21.60	18.90 - 21.60	20.20 - 22.30	3.2.89
- -	25.00 - 32.90	25.00 - 32.90	25.00 - 32.90	25.70 - 34.30	3.2.90
- -	7.00 - 9.10	7.00 - 9.10	7.00 - 9.10	7.00 - 9.10	3.2.91
- -	6.30 - 8.40	6.30 - 8.40	6.30 - 8.40	6.30 - 8.40	3.2.92
- -	7.00 - 10.20	7.00 - 10.20	7.00 - 10.20	7.00 - 10.20	3.2.93
- -	16.10 - 20.20	16.10 - 20.20	16.10 - 20.20	16.10 - 20.20	3.2.94
- -	17.50 - 23.70	17.50 - 23.70	17.50 - 23.70	17.50 - 23.70	3.2.95
- -	29.50 - 33.60	29.50 - 33.60	29.50 - 33.60	29.50 - 33.60	3.2.96
- -	36.40 - 45.00	36.40 - 45.00	36.40 - 45.00	36.40 - 45.00	3.2.97

Item nr.	SPECIFICATIONS	Unit	RESIDENTIAL £ range £	
3.2	**FLOOR FINISHES - cont'd**			
	floor finish area (unless otherwise described)			
	Flexible tiling/sheet finishes - cont'd			
	Vinyl sheet flooring; heavy duty			
3.2.98	2 mm thick	m²	-	-
3.2.99	2.50 mm thick	m²	-	-
3.2.100	3 mm thick; needle felt backed	m²	-	-
3.2.101	3 mm thick; foam backed	m²	-	-
	Sheeting; including screed and allowance for skirtings			
3.2.102	Altro "Safety" flooring	m²	-	-
3.2.103	2 mm thick; Altro "Marine T20" flooring	m²	-	-
3.2.104	2.50 mm thick; Altro "Classic D25" flooring	m²	-	-
3.2.105	3.50 thick; Altro "Stronghold" flooring	m²	-	-
3.2.106	flooring	m²	-	-
3.2.107	flooring; including screed	m²	-	-
	Linoleum tile flooring			
3.2.108	3.20 mm thick; coloured	m²	-	-
3.2.109	3.20 mm thick; coloured; including screed	m²	-	-
	Linoleum sheet flooring			
3.2.110	3.20 mm thick; coloured	m²	-	-
3.2.111	3.20 mm thick; marbled; including screed	m²	-	-
	Rubber tile flooring; smooth; ribbed or studded tiles			
3.2.112	2.50 mm thick	m²	-	-
3.2.113	5 mm thick	m²	-	-
3.2.114	5 mm thick; including screed	m²	-	-
	Carpet tiles/Carpeting			
3.2.115	Underlay	m²	3.50 -	4.90
	Carpet tiles			
3.2.116	nylon needlepunch (stick down)	m²	9.10 -	11.20
3.2.117	80% animal hair; 20% wool cord	m²	-	-
3.2.118	100% wool	m²	-	-
3.2.119	80% wool; 20% nylon antistatic economical; including screed and allowance for	m²	-	-
3.2.120	skirtings	m²	-	-
3.2.121	good quality	m²	-	-
3.2.122	good quality; including screed	m²	-	-
3.2.123	good quality; including screed and allowance for skirtings	m²	-	-
	Carpet; including underlay			
3.2.124	nylon needlepunch	m²	-	-
3.2.125	100% acrylic; light duty	m²	11.90 -	14.80
3.2.126	80% animal hair; 20% wool cord	m²	-	-
3.2.127	open-weave matting poolside carpet (no underlay)	m²	-	-
3.2.128	80% wool; 20% acrylic; light duty	m²	-	-
3.2.129	100% acrylic; heavy duty	m²	-	-
3.2.130	cord	m²	-	-
3.2.131	100% wool	m²	-	-
3.2.132	good quality; including screed	m²	-	-
	good quality (grade 5); including screed and allowance			
3.2.133	for skirtings	m²	-	-
3.2.134	80% wool; 20% acrylic; heavy duty	m²	-	-
3.2.135	"Wilton"/pile carpet	m²	-	-
3.2.136	high quality; including screed	m²	-	-
3.2.137	high quality; including screed and allowance for skirtings	m²	-	-
	Access floors and finishes			
	Shallow void block and battened floors			
3.2.138	chipboard on softwood battens; partial access	m²	17.50 -	22.30
3.2.139	chipboard on softwood cradles (for uneven floors)	m²	20.90 -	24.40
	chipboard on softwood battens and cross battens;			
3.2.140	full access	m²	-	-

INDUSTRIAL £ range £	RETAILING £ range £	LEISURE £ range £	OFFICES £ range £	HOTELS £ range £	Item nr.
- -	11.20 - 12.60	11.20 - 12.60	11.20 - 12.60	11.20 - 12.60	3.2.98
- -	11.20 - 14.10	11.20 - 14.10	11.20 - 14.10	11.20 - 14.10	3.2.99
- -	7.70 - 10.20	7.70 - 10.20	7.70 - 10.20	7.70 - 10.20	3.2.100
- -	11.20 - 14.10	11.20 - 14.10	11.20 - 14.10	11.20 - 14.10	3.2.101
- -	20.90 - 25.40	20.90 - 25.40	20.90 - 25.40	20.90 - 25.40	3.2.102
- -	16.10 - 20.20	16.10 - 20.20	16.10 - 20.20	- -	3.2.103
- -	20.20 - 23.70	20.20 - 23.70	20.20 - 23.70	- -	3.2.104
- -	25.40 - 29.50	25.40 - 29.50	25.40 - 29.50	- -	3.2.105
- -	16.10 - 30.20	16.10 - 30.20	16.10 - 30.20	- -	3.2.106
- -	23.70 - 40.50	23.70 - 40.50	23.70 - 40.50	- -	3.2.107
- -	12.60 - 14.80	12.60 - 14.80	12.60 - 14.80	- -	3.2.108
- -	20.20 - 27.50	20.20 - 27.50	20.20 - 27.50	- -	3.2.109
- -	13.30 - 14.80	13.30 - 17.50	13.30 - 17.50	- -	3.2.110
- -	20.90 - 27.50	20.90 - 27.50	20.90 - 27.50	- -	3.2.111
- -	20.20 - 23.70	20.20 - 23.70	20.20 - 23.70	- -	3.2.112
- -	23.70 - 27.50	23.70 - 27.50	23.70 - 27.50	- -	3.2.113
- -	31.80 - 40.50	32.30 - 40.50	32.30 - 40.50	- -	3.2.114
- -	3.50 - 4.90	3.50 - 4.90	3.50 - 4.90	- -	3.2.115
- -	9.10 - 11.20	9.10 - 11.20	9.10 - 11.20	- -	3.2.116
- -	16.10 - 18.20	16.10 - 18.20	16.10 - 18.20	- -	3.2.117
- -	22.30 - 27.50	22.30 - 27.50	22.30 - 27.50	- -	3.2.118
- -	23.70 - 32.90	23.70 - 32.90	23.70 - 32.90	- -	3.2.119
- -	24.40 - 27.50	24.40 - 27.50	24.40 - 27.50	- -	3.2.120
- -	22.30 - 32.90	22.30 - 32.90	22.30 - 32.90	22.30 - 36.40	3.2.121
- -	30.20 - 40.50	30.20 - 40.50	30.20 - 40.50	30.20 - 44.60	3.2.122
- -	33.60 - 44.60	33.60 - 44.60	33.60 - 44.60	33.60 - 50.40	3.2.123
- -	11.90 - 14.80	11.90 - 14.80	11.90 - 14.80	- -	3.2.124
- -	15.40 - 18.20	15.40 - 18.20	15.40 - 18.20	- -	3.2.125
- -	18.90 - 23.70	18.90 - 23.70	18.90 - 23.70	- -	3.2.126
- -	- -	16.10 - 20.20	- -	- -	3.2.127
- -	23.70 - 30.90	23.70 - 30.90	23.70 - 30.90	- -	3.2.128
- -	24.40 - 29.50	24.40 - 29.50	24.40 - 29.50	- -	3.2.129
- -	- -	29.50 - 32.90	- -	- -	3.2.130
- -	29.50 - 38.40	29.50 - 38.40	29.50 - 38.40	29.50 - 41.20	3.2.131
- -	36.40 - 50.40	36.40 - 50.40	36.40 - 50.40	37.70 - 54.60	3.2.132
- -	37.70 - 53.20	37.70 - 53.20	37.70 - 53.20	41.20 - 56.30	3.2.133
- -	38.40 - 45.60	38.40 - 45.60	38.40 - 45.60	41.20 - 48.40	3.2.134
- -	41.90 - 46.30	41.90 - 46.30	41.90 - 46.30	43.20 - 48.40	3.2.135
- -	50.40 - 59.00	50.40 - 59.00	50.40 - 59.00	53.20 - 60.40	3.2.136
- -	53.20 - 60.40	53.20 - 60.40	53.20 - 60.40	54.90 - 65.90	3.2.137
- -	- -	- -	17.50 - 22.30	- -	3.2.138
- -	- -	- -	20.90 - 24.40	- -	3.2.139
- -	- -	- -	26.10 - 28.80	- -	3.2.140

Item nr.	SPECIFICATIONS	Unit	RESIDENTIAL £ range £	
3.2	**FLOOR FINISHES - cont'd**			
	floor finish area (unless otherwise described)			
	Access floors and finishes - cont'd			
	Shallow void block and battened floors - cont'd			
3.2.141	fibre and particle board; on lightweight concrete pedestal blocks	m^2	-	-
	Shallow void block and battened floors; including carpet-tile finish			
3.2.142	fibre and particle board; on lightweight concrete pedestal blocks	m^2	-	-
	Access floors; excluding finish			
	600 mm x 600 mm chipboard panels faced both sides with galvanised steel sheet; on adjustable steel/aluminium pedestals; cavity 100 mm - 300 mm high			
3.2.143	light grade duty	m^2	-	-
3.2.144	medium grade duty	m^2	-	-
3.2.145	heavy grade duty	m^2	-	-
3.2.146	extra heavy grade duty	m^2	-	-
	600 mm x 600 mm chipboard panels faced both sides with galvanised steel sheet; on adjustable steel/aluminium pedestals; cavity 300 mm - 600 mm high			
3.2.147	medium grade duty	m^2	-	-
3.2.148	heavy grade duty	m^2	-	-
3.2.149	extra heavy grade duty	m^2	-	-
	Access floor with medium quality carpeting			
3.2.150	"Durabella" suspended floors	m^2	-	-
3.2.151	"Buroplan" partial access raised floor	m^2	-	-
3.2.152	"Pedestal" partial access raised floor	m^2	-	-
3.2.153	modular floor; 100% access raised floor	m^2	-	-
	Access floor with high quality carpeting			
3.2.154	computer loading; 100% access raised floor	m^2	-	-
	Common floor coverings bonded to access floor panels			
3.2.155	heavy-duty fully flexible vinyl; to BS 3261; type A	m^2	-	-
3.2.156	fibre-bonded carpet	m^2	-	-
3.2.157	high-pressure laminate; to BS 2794; class D	m^2	-	-
3.2.158	anti-static grade fibre-bonded carpet	m^2	-	-
3.2.159	anti-static grade sheet PVC; to BS 3261	m^2	-	-
3.2.160	low loop tufted carpet	m^2	-	-
	Cavity fire barriers within access floors			
3.2.161	half-hour fire rating	m	-	-
3.2.162	one-hour fire rating	m	-	-
3.2.163	one-and-a-half hour fire rating	m	-	-
	Perimeter treatments and sundries			
	Comparative skirtings			
3.2.164	25 mm x 75 mm softwood skirting; painted; including grounds	m	7.30 -	8.70
3.2.165	25 mm x 100 mm mahogany skirting; polished; including grounds	m	10.40 -	11.60
3.2.166	12.50 mm x 150 mm quarry tile skirting; including backing	m	10.50 -	13.00
3.2.167	13 mm x 75 mm granolithic skirting; including backing	m	14.80 -	17.50
3.2.168	6 mm x 75 mm terrazzo; including backing	m	25.70 -	30.00
3.2.169	Entrance matting in aluminium-framed matwell	m^2	-	-

INDUSTRIAL £ range £		RETAILING £ range £		LEISURE £ range £		OFFICES £ range £		HOTELS £ range £		Item nr.
-	-	-	-	-	-	24.40	- 30.20	-	-	3.2.141
-	-	-	-	-	-	36.40	- 41.90	-	-	3.2.142
-	-	-	-	-	-	32.90	- 39.10	-	-	3.2.143
-	-	-	-	-	-	37.70	- 43.90	-	-	3.2.144
-	-	-	-	-	-	47.40	- 59.70	-	-	3.2.145
-	-	-	-	-	-	53.20	- 59.70	-	-	3.2.146
-	-	-	-	-	-	43.00	- 49.00	-	-	3.2.147
-	-	-	-	-	-	49.00	- 60.00	-	-	3.2.148
-	-	-	-	-	-	55.00	- 60.00	-	-	3.2.149
-	-	-	-	-	-	47.00	- 52.00	-	-	3.2.150
-	-	-	-	-	-	53.00	- 60.00	-	-	3.2.151
-	-	-	-	-	-	60.00	- 74.00	-	-	3.2.152
-	-	-	-	-	-	78.00	- 100.00	-	-	3.2.153
-	-	-	-	-	-	88.00	- 130.00	-	-	3.2.154
-	-	-	-	-	-	6.00	- 16.80	-	-	3.2.155
-	-	-	-	-	-	6.30	- 12.30	-	-	3.2.156
-	-	-	-	-	-	6.30	- 18.90	-	-	3.2.157
-	-	-	-	-	-	7.70	- 13.00	-	-	3.2.158
-	-	-	-	-	-	10.80	- 16.80	-	-	3.2.159
-	-	-	-	-	-	13.00	- 18.90	-	-	3.2.160
6.70	- 8.00	7.30	- 8.70	7.30	- 8.70	7.30	- 8.70	8.70	- 9.30	3.2.161
10.00	- 11.30	10.40	- 11.60	10.40	- 11.60	10.40	- 11.60	11.00	- 12.30	3.2.162
9.80	- 12.30	10.50	- 13.00	10.50	- 13.00	10.50	- 13.00	10.80	- 13.00	3.2.163
14.10	- 17.50	14.80	- 17.50	14.80	- 17.50	14.80	- 17.50	15.40	- 18.90	3.2.164
-	-	26.10	- 30.20	26.10	- 30.20	26.10	- 30.20	27.50	- 31.60	3.2.165
-	-	246.00	- 350.00	237.00	- 323.00	237.00	- 329.00	237.00	- 329.00	3.2.166

Item nr.	SPECIFICATIONS	Unit	RESIDENTIAL £ range £	
3.3	**CEILING FINISHES**			
	ceiling finish area (unless otherwise described)			
	comprising:			
	In situ board finishes			
	Suspended and integrated ceilings			
	In situ/board finishes			
	Decoration only to soffits			
3.3.1	to exposed steelwork	m^2	-	-
3.3.2	to concrete soffits	m^2	2.00 -	3.00
3.3.3	one mist and two coats emulsion paint; to plaster/plasterboard	m^2	2.00 -	3.00
	Plaster to soffits			
3.3.4	lightweight plaster	m^2	7.00 -	9.50
3.3.5	plaster and emulsion	m^2	9.50 -	14.10
	Extra for			
3.3.6	gloss paint in lieu of emulsion	m^2	1.50 -	1.80
	Plasterboard to soffits			
3.3.7	9.50 mm Gyproc lath and skim coat	m^2	10.20 -	11.90
3.3.8	9.50 mm Gyproc insulating lath and skim coat	m^2	10.50 -	11.90
3.3.9	plasterboard, skim and emulsion	m^2	11.90 -	14.80
	Extra for			
3.3.10	gloss paint in lieu of emulsion	m^2	1.50 -	1.80
3.3.11	plasterboard and "Artex"	m^2	8.40 -	10.20
3.3.12	plasterboard; "Artex" and emulsion	m^2	10.20 -	12.60
3.3.13	plaster and emulsion; including metal lathing	m^2	16.10 -	22.30
	Other board finishes; with fire-resisting properties; excluding decoration			
3.3.14	12.50 mm thick Gyproc "Fireline"; half hour	m^2	-	-
3.3.15	6 mm thick "Supalux"; half hour	m^2	-	-
3.3.16	two layers of 12.50 mm thick Gyproc "Wallboard"; half hour	m^2	-	-
3.3.17	two layers of 12.50 mm thick Gyproc "Fireline"; one hour	m^2	-	-
3.3.18	9 mm thick "Supalux"; one hour; on fillets	m^2	-	-
	Specialist plasters; to soffits			
3.3.19	sprayed acoustic plaster; self-finished	m^2	-	-
3.3.20	rendering; "Tyrolean" finish	m^2	-	-
	Other ceiling finishes			
3.3.21	50 mm thick wood wool slabs as permanent lining	m^2	-	-
3.3.22	12 mm thick pine t&g boarding	m^2	12.60 -	15.40
3.3.23	16 mm thick softwood t&g boardings	m^2	15.40 -	18.20
	Suspended and integrated ceilings			
	Suspended ceiling			
3.3.24	economical; exposed grid	m^2	-	-
3.3.25	jointless; plasterboard	m^2	-	-
3.3.26	semi-concealed grid	m^2	-	-
3.3.27	medium quality; "Minatone"; concealed grid	m^2	-	-
3.3.28	high quality; "Travertone"; concealed grid	m^2	-	-
	Other suspended ceilings			
3.3.29	metal linear strip; "Dampa"/"Luxalon"	m^2	-	-
3.3.30	metal tray	m^2	-	-
3.3.31	egg-crate	m^2	-	-
3.3.32	open grid; "Formalux"/"Dimension"	m^2	-	-
	Integrated ceilings			
3.3.33	coffered; with steel surfaces	m^2	-	-

INDUSTRIAL £ range £	RETAILING £ range £	LEISURE £ range £	OFFICES £ range £	HOTELS £ range £	Item nr.
2.40 - 3.50	2.00 - 3.00	- -	- -	- -	3.3.1
2.00 - 3.00	2.00 - 3.00	2.00 - 3.00	2.00 - 3.00	2.00 - 3.00	3.3.2
2.00 - 3.00	2.00 - 3.00	2.00 - 3.00	2.00 - 3.00	2.00 - 3.00	3.3.3
7.00 - 9.10	7.00 - 9.10	7.00 - 9.10	7.00 - 9.10	7.00 - 9.10	3.3.4
9.10 - 13.70	9.50 - 14.40	9.50 - 14.40	9.50 - 14.40	10.80 - 16.10	3.3.5
1.50 - 1.80	1.50 - 1.80	1.50 - 1.80	1.50 - 1.80	1.50 - 1.80	3.3.6
9.50 - 11.90	10.20 - 11.90	10.20 - 11.90	10.20 - 11.90	10.80 - 11.90	3.3.7
10.20 - 11.90	10.80 - 11.90	10.80 - 11.90	10.80 - 11.90	10.80 - 12.60	3.3.8
10.80 - 14.40	11.90 - 14.80	11.90 - 14.80	11.90 - 14.80	11.90 - 15.40	3.3.9
1.50 - 1.80	1.50 - 1.80	1.50 - 1.80	1.50 - 1.80	1.50 - 1.80	3.3.10
7.00 - 9.50	7.70 - 10.20	7.70 - 10.20	7.70 - 10.20	8.40 - 10.80	3.3.11
9.50 - 11.90	10.20 - 12.60	10.20 - 12.60	10.20 - 12.60	10.80 - 13.30	3.3.12
15.40 - 22.30	16.10 - 22.30	16.10 - 22.30	16.10 - 22.30	16.10 - 22.30	3.3.13
7.70 - 10.20	8.40 - 10.20	8.40 - 10.20	8.40 - 10.20	8.80 - 11.30	3.3.14
10.20 - 11.30	10.80 - 11.90	10.80 - 11.90	10.80 - 11.90	13.30 - 14.10	3.3.15
11.30 - 13.00	11.90 - 13.70	11.90 - 13.70	11.90 - 13.70	11.90 - 14.10	3.3.16
13.00 - 15.40	13.70 - 16.10	13.70 - 16.10	13.70 - 16.10	14.10 - 16.10	3.3.17
14.80 - 18.20	14.80 - 18.20	14.80 - 18.20	14.80 - 18.20	16.10 - 18.90	3.3.18
20.20 - 28.10	- -	- -	- -	- -	3.3.19
- -	- -	20.90 - 30.20	- -	- -	3.3.20
- -	- -	- -	9.50 - 11.90	- -	3.3.21
- -	12.60 - 15.40	12.60 - 15.40	12.60 - 15.40	13.00 - 16.10	3.3.22
- -	16.10 - 18.20	16.10 - 18.20	16.10 - 18.20	16.10 - 18.20	3.3.23
16.10 - 21.60	17.50 - 22.30	17.50 - 22.30	17.50 - 22.30	17.50 - 25.40	3.3.24
20.20 - 25.40	20.90 - 27.50	20.90 - 27.50	20.90 - 27.50	20.90 - 30.20	3.3.25
21.60 - 27.50	23.70 - 30.20	23.70 - 30.20	23.70 - 30.20	23.70 - 32.30	3.3.26
23.70 - 32.30	24.40 - 34.30	24.40 - 34.30	24.40 - 34.30	24.40 - 36.40	3.3.27
27.10 - 35.00	29.50 - 36.40	29.50 - 36.40	29.50 - 36.40	29.50 - 39.80	3.3.28
30.00 - 38.00	32.00 - 40.00	32.00 - 40.00	32.00 - 40.00	- -	3.3.29
31.00 - 40.00	34.00 - 40.00	34.00 - 40.00	34.00 - 40.00	- -	3.3.30
34.00 - 71.00	36.00 - 73.00	36.00 - 73.00	36.00 - 73.00	- -	3.3.31
62.00 - 75.00	63.00 - 78.00	63.00 - 78.00	63.00 - 78.00	- -	3.3.32
70.00 - 117.00	70.00 - 117.00	70.00 - 117.00	70.00 - 117.00	- -	3.3.33

Item nr.	SPECIFICATIONS	Unit	RESIDENTIAL £ range £		
3.3	**CEILING FINISHES - cont'd**				
	ceiling finish area (unless otherwise described)				
3.4	**DECORATIONS**				
	surface area (unless otherwise described)				
	comprising:				
	Comparative wall and ceiling finishes				
	Comparative steel/metalwork finishes				
	Comparative woodwork finishes				
	Comparative wall and ceiling finishes				
	Emulsion				
3.4.1	two coats	m²	1.40	-	1.80
3.4.2	one mist and two coats	m²	1.80	-	2.50
	"Artex" plastic compound				
3.4.3	one coat; textured	m²	2.30	-	3.20
3.4.4	Wall paper	m²	3.20	-	5.10
3.4.5	Hessian wall coverings	m²	-		-
	Gloss				
3.4.6	primer and two coats	m²	2.70	-	3.70
3.4.7	primer and three coats	m²	3.70	-	4.60
	Comparative steel/metalwork finishes				
	Primer				
3.4.8	only	m²	-		-
3.4.9	grit blast and one coat zinc chromate primer	m²	-		-
3.4.10	touch up primer and one coat of two pack epoxy zinc phosphate primer	m²	-		-
	Gloss				
3.4.11	three coats	m²	3.70	-	4.50
	Sprayed mineral fibre				
3.4.12	one hour	m²	-		-
3.4.13	two hour	m²	-		-
	Sprayed vermiculite cement				
3.4.14	one hour	m²	-		-
3.4.15	two hour	m²	-		-
	Intumescent coating with decorative top seal				
3.4.16	half hour	m²	-		-
3.4.17	one hour	m²	-		-
	Comparative woodwork finishes				
	Primer				
3.4.18	only	m²	1.10	-	1.10
	Gloss				
3.4.19	two coats; touch up primer	m²	2.00	-	2.30
3.4.20	three costs; touch up primer	m²	2.70	-	3.40
3.4.21	primer and two coat	m²	3.20	-	3.70
3.4.22	primer and three coat	m²	4.10	-	4.50
	Polyurethene lacquer				
3.4.23	two coats	m²	2.00	-	2.50
3.4.24	three coats	m²	3.20	-	3.70
	Flame-retardant paint				
3.4.25	three coats	m²	4.70	-	6.00
	Polish				
3.4.26	wax polish; seal	m²	5.10	-	7.00
3.4.27	wax polish; stain and body-in	m²	8.60	-	9.90
3.4.28	french polish; stain and body-in	m²	12.70	-	15.40

1.40	-	1.80	1.40	-	1.80	1.40	-	1.80	1.40	-	1.80	1.40	-	1.80	3.4.1

1.40 - 1.80	1.40 - 1.80	1.40 - 1.80	1.40 - 1.80	1.40 - 1.80	3.4.1
1.80 - 2.50	1.80 - 2.50	1.80 - 2.50	1.80 - 2.50	1.80 - 2.50	3.4.2
2.40 - 3.20	2.40 - 3.20	2.30 - 3.20	2.40 - 3.20	2.40 - 3.20	3.4.3
3.20 - 5.50	3.20 - 5.50	3.20 - 5.50	3.20 - 5.50	3.20 - 8.20	3.4.4
- -	7.00 - 10.20	7.00 - 10.20	7.00 - 10.20	8.00 - 12.50	3.4.5
2.70 - 3.70	2.70 - 3.70	2.70 - 3.70	2.70 - 3.70	2.70 - 3.70	3.4.6
3.70 - 4.50	3.70 - 4.50	3.70 - 4.50	3.70 - 4.50	3.70 - 4.50	3.4.7
0.60 - 1.10	- -	- -	- -	- -	3.4.8
1.20 - 1.80	- -	- -	- -	- -	3.4.9
1.60 - 2.00	- -	- -	- -	- -	3.4.10
- -	- -	- -	- -	- -	3.4.11
7.00 - 10.80	- -	- -	- -	- -	3.4.12
11.70 - 14.10	- -	- -	- -	- -	3.4.13
8.00 - 11.80	- -	- -	- -	- -	3.4.14
9.50 - 14.10	- -	- -	- -	- -	3.4.15
12.70 - 14.10	12.70 - 14.10	12.70 - 14.10	- -	- -	3.4.16
20.20 - 24.70	20.20 - 24.70	20.20 - 24.70	- -	- -	3.4.17
1.00 - 1.20	1.00 - 1.20	1.00 - 1.20	1.00 - 1.20	1.00 - 1.20	3.4.18
2.00 - 2.30	2.00 - 2.30	2.00 - 2.30	2.00 - 2.30	2.00 - 2.30	3.4.19
2.70 - 3.50	2.70 - 3.50	2.70 - 3.50	2.70 - 3.50	2.70 - 3.50	3.4.20
3.20 - 3.70	3.20 - 3.70	3.20 - 3.70	3.20 - 3.70	3.20 - 3.70	3.4.21
4.10 - 4.50	4.10 - 4.50	4.10 - 4.50	4.10 - 4.50	4.10 - 4.50	3.4.22
2.00 - 2.50	2.00 - 2.30	2.00 - 2.50	2.00 - 2.50	2.00 - 2.50	3.4.23
3.20 - 3.70	3.20 - 3.70	3.20 - 3.70	3.20 - 3.70	3.20 - 3.70	3.4.24
4.70 - 5.70	4.70 - 5.70	4.70 - 5.70	4.70 - 5.70	4.70 - 5.70	3.4.25
4.70 - 5.70	4.70 - 7.00	4.70 - 7.00	4.80 - 7.00	4.70 - 7.00	3.4.26
8.60 - 9.90	8.60 - 9.90	8.60 - 9.90	8.60 - 9.90	8.60 - 9.90	3.4.27
12.70 - 15.40	12.70 - 15.40	12.70 - 15.40	12.70 - 15.40	12.70 - 15.40	3.4.28

Item nr.	SPECIFICATIONS	Unit	RESIDENTIAL £ range £
4.1	**FITTINGS AND FURNISHINGS**		
	gross internal area or individual units		
	comprising:		
	Residential fittings		
	Comparative fittings/sundries		
	Industrial/Office furniture, fittings and equipment		
	Retail furniture, fittings and equipment		
	Leisure furniture, fittings and equipment		
	Hotel furniture, fittings and equipment		
	Residential fittings		
	Kitchen fittings for residential units		
4.1.1	one person flat/bed-sit	nr	453.00 - 913.00
4.1.2	two person flat/house	nr	611.00 - 1544.0
4.1.3	three person flat/house	nr	733.00 - 2127.0
4.1.4	four person house	nr	782.00 - 2730.0
4.1.5	five person house	nr	1016.00 - 5043.0
	Comparative residential fittings/sundries		
	Individual kitchen fittings		
4.1.6	600 mm x 600 mm x 300 mm wall unit	nr	56.30 - 67.30
4.1.7	1200 mm x 900 mm x 300 mm wall unit	nr	89.20 - 102.90
4.1.8	500 mm x 900 mm x 600 mm floor unit	nr	89.20 - 102.90
4.1.9	600 mm x 500 mm x 195 mm store cupboard	nr	133.10 - 146.90
4.1.10	1200 mm x 900 mm x 600 mm sink unit (excluding top)	nr	133.10 - 146.90
	Comparative wrought softwood shelving		
4.1.11	25 mm x 225 mm including black japanned brackets	m	8.60 - 10.00
4.1.12	25 mm thick slatted shelving; including bearers	m^2	35.70 - 39.80
4.1.13	25 mm thick cross-tongued shelving; including bearers	m^2	45.30 - 50.40
	Industrial/Office furniture, fittings and equipment		
	Reception desk, shelves and cupboards for general areas		
4.1.14	economical	m^2	- -
4.1.15	medium quality	m^2	- -
4.1.16	high quality	m^2	- -
	Extra for		
4.1.17	high quality finishes to reception areas	m^2	- -
4.1.18	full kitchen equipment (one cover/20 m^2)	m^2	- -
	Furniture and fittings to general office areas		
4.1.19	economical	m^2	- -
4.1.20	medium quality	m^2	- -
4.1.21	high quality	m^2	- -
	Retail fitting out, furniture, fittings and equipment		
	Mall furniture, etc.		
4.1.22	minimal provision	m^2	- -
4.1.23	good provision	m^2	- -
4.1.24	internal planting	m^2	- -
4.1.25	glazed metal balustrades to voids	m^2	- -
4.1.26	feature pond and fountain	m^2	- -
4.1.27	Fitting out a retail warehouse	m^2	- -
	Fitting out shell for small shop (including shop fittings)		
4.1.28	simple store	m^2	- -
4.1.29	fashion store	m^2	- -
	Fitting out shell for department store or supermarket		
4.1.30	excluding shop fittings	m^2	- -
4.1.31	including shop fittings	m^2	- -

INDUSTRIAL £ range £	RETAILING £ range £	LEISURE £ range £	OFFICES £ range £	HOTELS £ range £	Item nr.
- -	- -	- -	- -	- -	4.1.1
- -	- -	- -	- -	- -	4.1.2
- -	- -	- -	- -	- -	4.1.3
- -	- -	- -	- -	- -	4.1.4
- -	- -	- -	- -	- -	4.1.5
- -	- -	- -	- -	- -	4.1.6
- -	- -	- -	- -	- -	4.1.7
- -	- -	- -	- -	- -	4.1.8
- -	- -	- -	- -	- -	4.1.9
- -	- -	- -	- -	- -	4.1.10
8.70 - 10.00	8.70 - 10.00	8.70 - 10.00	8.70 - 10.00	8.70 - 10.00	4.1.11
33.60 - 39.80	33.60 - 39.80	33.60 - 39.80	33.60 - 39.80	33.60 - 39.80	4.1.12
45.30 - 50.40	45.30 - 50.40	45.30 - 50.40	45.30 - 50.40	45.30 - 50.40	4.1.13
2.80 - 6.30	- -	- -	4.70 - 9.70	- -	4.1.14
5.00 - 10.00	- -	- -	7.30 - 13.30	- -	4.1.15
8.00 - 15.40	- -	- -	11.30 - 17.90	- -	4.1.16
- -	- -	- -	5.00 - 7.30	- -	4.1.17
7.30 - 8.70	- -	- -	8.00 - 10.00	- -	4.1.18
- -	- -	- -	6.00 - 8.00	- -	4.1.19
- -	- -	- -	8.00 - 12.60	- -	4.1.20
- -	- -	- -	14.10 - 20.70	- -	4.1.21
- -	7.30 - 14.10	- -	- -	- -	4.1.22
- -	30.90 - 36.40	- -	- -	- -	4.1.23
- -	16.10 - 20.70	- -	- -	- -	4.1.24
- -	542.20 - 686.30	- -	- -	- -	4.1.25
- -	30100 - 46200	- -	- -	- -	4.1.26
- -	188.70 - 216.90	- -	- -	- -	4.1.27
- -	473.50 - 542.20	- -	- -	- -	4.1.28
- -	713.70 - 1015.7	- -	- -	- -	4.1.29
- -	501.00 - 679.40	- -	- -	- -	4.1.30
- -	713.70 - 1015.7	- -	- -	- -	4.1.31

Item nr.	SPECIFICATIONS	Unit	RESIDENTIAL £ range £	
4.1	**FITTINGS AND FURNISHINGS - cont'd**			
	gross internal area or internal units			
	(unless otherwise described)			
	Retail fitting out, furniture, fittings and			
	equipment - cont'd			
	Special fittings/equipment			
4.1.32	refrigerated installation for cold stores; display fittings in food stores	m²	-	-
4.1.33	food court furniture; fittings and special finishes (excluding catering	m²	-	-
	display units)			
4.1.34	bakery ovens	nr	-	-
4.1.35	refuse compactors	nr	-	-
	Leisure furniture, fittings and equipment			
	General fittings			
4.1.36	internal planting	m²	-	-
4.1.37	signs, notice-boards, shelving, fixed seating, curtains and blinds	m²	-	-
4.1.38	electric hand-dryers, incinerators, mirrors	m²	-	-
	Specific fittings			
4.1.39	lockers, coin return locks	nr	-	-
4.1.40	kitchen units; excluding equipment	nr	-	-
4.1.41	folding sun bed	nr	-	-
4.1.42	security grille	nr	-	-
4.1.43	entrance balustrading and control turnstile	nr	-	-
4.1.44	sports nets, screens etc in a medium sized sports hall reception	nr	-	-
	counter, fittings and reception counter			
4.1.45	screen	nr	-	-
4.1.46	bar and fittings	nr	-	-
4.1.47	telescopic seatings	nr	-	-
	Swimming pool fittings			
4.1.48	metal balustrades to pool areas	m	-	-
4.1.49	skimmer grilles to pool edge	nr	-	-
	stainless steel pool access ladder			
4.1.50	1700 mm high	nr	-	-
4.1.51	2500 mm high	nr	-	-
4.1.52	stainless steel tube ladders and fixing sockets to pool	nr	-	-
4.1.53	level deck starting blocks	nr	-	-
4.1.54	turning boards and brackets	nr	-	-
4.1.55	backstroke warning set and infill tubes	nr	-	-
4.1.56	false start equipment set including infill tubes	nr	-	-
4.1.57	set of four 25 m lane rope sets; storage trolley and flush deck			
	level adaptors	nr	-	..
4.1.58	electrically operated cover to pool	nr	-	-
	Leisure pool fittings			
4.1.59	stainless steel lighting post	nr	-	-
4.1.60	water cannons	nr	-	-
4.1.61	fountain or water sculpture	nr	-	-
4.1.62	loudspeaker tower	nr	-	-
	grp water chute; 65.00 m - 80.00 m long; steel supports;			
4.1.63	spiral stairs and balustrading	nr	-	-
	Sports halls			
4.1.64	administration areas	m²	-	-
4.1.65	aerobic dance studios	m²	-	-
4.1.66	badminton courts	m²	-	-
4.1.67	bowls halls	m²	-	-
4.1.68	cafe/restaurant areas	seat	-	-
4.1.69	changing rooms/WCs	m²	-	-
4.1.70	circulation areas	m²	-	-
4.1.71	creche areas	m²	-	-
4.1.72	fitness areas	m²	-	-
4.1.73	indoor cricket	m²	-	-
4.1.74	rifle ranges	m²	-	-
4.1.75	reception areas	m²	-	-
4.1.76	school gymnasium (no changing)	m²	-	-
4.1.77	sports halls (with changing)	m²	-	-
4.1.78	squash courts	m²	-	-

INDUSTRIAL £ range £	RETAILING £ range £	LEISURE £ range £	OFFICES £ range £	HOTELS £ range £	Item nr.
- -	19.90 - 61.10	- -	- -	- -	4.1.32
- -	645.00 - 700.00	- -	- -	- -	4.1.33
- -	8125 - 12250	- -	- -	- -	4.1.34
- -	8681 - 15956	- -	- -	- -	4.1.35
- -	- -	12.60 - 15.40	- -	- -	4.1.36
- -	- -	8.70 - 10.00	- -	- -	4.1.37
- -	- -	2.30 - 3.40	- -	- -	4.1.38
- -	- -	95.00 - 140.00	- -	- -	4.1.39
- -	- -	1681 - 2244	- -	- -	4.1.40
- -	- -	4063 - 4475	- -	- -	4.1.41
- -	- -	5600 - 7988	- -	- -	4.1.42
- -	- -	10225 - 11200	- -	- -	4.1.43
- -	- -	14000 - 16800	- -	- -	4.1.44
- -	- -	16800 - 28000	- -	- -	4.1.45
- -	- -	28000 - 33627	- -	- -	4.1.46
- -	- -	39200 - 44800	- -	- -	4.1.47
- -	- -	280.00 - 453.00	- -	- -	4.1.48
- -	- -	224.00 - 287.00	- -	- -	4.1.49
- -	- -	844.00 - 928.00	- -	- -	4.1.50
- -	- -	920.00 - 1055.0	- -	- -	4.1.51
- -	- -	375.00 - 425.00	- -	- -	4.1.52
- -	- -	525.00 - 575.00	- -	- -	4.1.53
- -	- -	350.00 - 400.00	- -	- -	4.1.54
- -	- -	400.00 - 450.00	- -	- -	4.1.55
- -	- -	200.00 - 250.00	- -	- -	4.1.56
- -	- -	2500.0 - 2800.0	- -	- -	4.1.57
- -	- -	6000 - 10000	- -	- -	4.1.58
- -	- -	113.00 - 140.00	- -	- -	4.1.59
- -	- -	769.00 - 1016.0	- -	- -	4.1.60
- -	- -	3088 - 15441	- -	- -	4.1.61
- -	- -	3925 - 4625	- -	- -	4.1.62
- -	- -	95508 - 106008	- -	- -	4.1.63
- -	- -	115.00 - 230.00	- -	- -	4.1.64
- -	- -	58.00 - 80.00	- -	- -	4.1.65
- -	- -	23.00 - 35.00	- -	- -	4.1.66
- -	- -	12.00 - 23.00	- -	- -	4.1.67
- -	- -	1250 - 1450	- -	- -	4.1.68
- -	- -	58.00 - 115.00	- -	- -	4.1.69
- -	- -	6.00 - 12.00	- -	- -	4.1.70
- -	- -	46.00 - 70.00	- -	- -	4.1.71
- -	- -	460.00 - 690.00	- -	- -	4.1.72
- -	- -	12.00 - 23.00	- -	- -	4.1.73
- -	- -	12.00 - 23.00	- -	- -	4.1.74
- -	- -	115.00 - 230.00	- -	- -	4.1.75
- -	- -	46.00 - 58.00	- -	- -	4.1.76
- -	- -	23.00 - 46.00	- -	- -	4.1.77
- -	- -	6.00 - 12.00	- -	- -	4.1.78

Item nr.	SPECIFICATIONS	Unit	RESIDENTIAL £ range £	
4.1	**FITTINGS AND FURNISHINGS - cont'd**			
	gross internal area or internal units (unless otherwise described)			
	Leisure furniture, fittings and equipment - cont'd			
	Sports halls - cont'd			
4.1.79	table tennis	m²	-	-
4.1.80	tennis courts	m²	-	-
4.1.81	viewing areas	m²	-	-
	Football stadia			
4.1.82	facilities to basic stand	m²	-	-
	Theatres			
	Stage engineering equipment to large-scale modern touring theatre			
4.1.83	flying	nr	-	-
4.1.84	safety curtains and fire doors	nr	-	-
4.1.85	lighting access	nr	-	-
4.1.86	stage/pit lifts	nr	-	-
4.1.87	hoists	nr	-	-
4.1.88	curtains and masking	nr	-	-
	Stage engineering equipment to medium-scale modern repertory touring theatre			
4.1.89	flying	nr	-	-
4.1.90	safety curtains and fire doors	nr	-	-
4.1.91	lighting access	nr	-	-
4.1.92	stage/pit lifts	nr	-	-
4.1.93	hoists	nr	-	-
4.1.94	curtains and masking	nr		
	Museums and art galleries	nr	-	-
	Display and retail areas			
4.1.95	display cases and lighting, finishes	m²	-	-
4.1.96	display fittings and power	m²	-	-
4.1.97	interactive display	m²	-	-
4.1.98	ticketing and retail	m²	-	-
4.1.99	display case (to 1.50 m x 1.50 m)	nr	-	-
4.1.100	fibre optic lighting to display case	nr	-	-
4.1.101	interactive "hands on" feature	nr	-	-
4.1.102	interactive video installations			
4.1.103	video wall	nr	-	-
4.1.104	video monitor hardware	nr	-	-
4.1.105	AV installation to cinema	nr	-	-
	Aviation			
	Airport passenger lounges			
4.1.106	international airport	m²	-	-
4.1.107	domestic airport	m²	-	-
4.1.108	allowance for furniture	m²	-	-
4.1.109	baggage handling facilities	m²	-	-
	Education			
	Schools and colleges			
4.1.110	general teaching	m²	-	-
4.1.111	laboratories	m²	-	-
4.1.112	information technology and business studies	m²	-	-
4.1.113	design and technology	m²	-	-
4.1.114	art and design	m²	-	-
4.1.115	library resource centre	m²	-	-
4.1.116	circulation	m²	-	-
4.1.117	laboratory preparation	m²	-	-
4.1.118	staff accommodation	m²	-	-

INDUSTRIAL		RETAILING		LEISURE			OFFICES		HOTELS		Item nr.
£	range £	£	range £	£	range	£	£	range £	£	range £	
-	-	-	-	6.00	-	12.00	-	-	-	-	4.1.79
-	-	-	-	6.00	-	12.00	-	-	-	-	4.1.80
-	-	-	-	12.00	-	115.00	-	-	-	-	4.1.81
-	-	-	-	230.00	-	360.00	-	-	-	-	4.1.82
-	-	-	-	390000	-	455000	-	-	-	-	4.1.83
-	-	-	-	350000	-	415000	-	-	-	-	4.1.84
-	-	-	-	235000	-	275000	-	-	-	-	4.1.85
-	-	-	-	260000	-	325000	-	-	-	-	4.1.86
-	-	-	-	195000	-	220000	-	-	-	-	4.1.87
-	-	-	-	300000	-	340000	-	-	-	-	4.1.88
-	-	-	-	170000	-	195000	-	-	-	-	4.1.89
-	-	-	-	80000	-	115000	-	-	-	-	4.1.90
-	-	-	-	195000	-	220000	-	-	-	-	4.1.91
-	-	-	-	90000	-	130000	-	-	-	-	4.1.92
-	-	-	-	40000	-	65000	-	-	-	-	4.1.93
-	-	-	-	25000	-	65000	-	-	-	-	4.1.94
-	-	-	-	2400	-	4800	-	-	-	-	4.1.95
-	-	-	-	1200	-	2160	-	-	-	-	4.1.96
-	-	-	-	1800	-	3000	-	-	-	-	4.1.97
-	-	-	-	1200	-	1800	-	-	-	-	4.1.98
-	-	-	-	3600	-	18000	-	-	-	-	4.1.99
-	-	-	-	840	-	1200	-	-	-	-	4.1.100
-	-	-	-	8400	-	12000	-	-	-	-	4.1.101
-	-	-	-	300000	-	420000	-	-	-	-	4.1.102
-	-	-	-	4200	-	6000	-	-	-	-	4.1.103
-	-	-	-	120000	-	420000	-	-	-	-	4.1.104
-	-	-	-	1240	-	1400	-	-	-	-	4.1.106
-	-	-	-	700	-	1190	-	-	-	-	4.1.107
-	-	-	-	195	-	345	-	-	-	-	4.1.108
-	-	-	-	1835	-	2270	-	-	-	-	4.1.109
-	-	-	-	115	-	180	-	-	-	-	4.1.110
-	-	-	-	150	-	250	-	-	-	-	4.1.111
-	-	-	-	325	-	460	-	-	-	-	4.1.112
-	-	-	-	315	-	355	-	-	-	-	4.1.113
-	-	-	-	210	-	250	-	-	-	-	4.1.114
-	-	-	-	355	-	400	-	-	-	-	4.1.115
-	-	-	-	35	-	60	-	-	-	-	4.1.116
-	-	-	-	325	-	375	-	-	-	-	4.1.117
-	-	-	-	380	-	400	-	-	-	-	4.1.118

Item nr.	SPECIFICATIONS	Unit	RESIDENTIAL £ range £
5.1	**SANITARY AND DISPOSAL INSTALLATIONS** **gross internal area** (unless otherwise described)		
	comprising:		
	Comparative sanitary fittings/sundries **Sanitary and disposal installations**		
	Comparative sanitary fittings/sundries Note: Material prices vary considerably, the following composite rates are based on "average" prices for mid priced fittings: Individual sanitary appliances (including fittings) lavatory basins; vitreous china; chromium plated taps; waste; chain and plug; cantilever brackets		
5.1.1	white	nr	154.00 - 175.00
5.1.2	coloured	nr	175.00 - 210.00
	low level WC's; vitreous china pan and cistern; black plastic seat; low pressure ball valve; plastic flush pipe; fixing brackets - on ground floor		
5.1.3	white	nr	133.00 - 154.00
5.1.4	coloured	nr	168.00 - 182.00
	- one of a range; on upper floors		
5.1.5	white	nr	253.00 - 287.00
5.1.6	coloured	nr	287.00 - 316.00
	Extra for bowl type wall urinal; white glazed vitreous china flushing cistern; chromium plated flush pipes and spreaders; fixing brackets		
5.1.7	white	nr	- -
	shower tray; glazed fireclay; chromium plated waste; chain and plug; riser pipe; rose and mixing valve		
5.1.8	white	nr	- -
5.1.9	coloured	nr	350.00 - 406.00
	sink; glazed fireclay; chromium plated waste; chain and plug; fixing		
5.1.10	white	nr	393.00 - 434.00
	sink; stainless steel; chromium plated waste; chain and self coloured		
5.1.11	single drainer	nr	- -
5.1.12	double drainer	nr	168.00 - 210.00
	bath; reinforced acrylic; chromium plated taps; overflow; waste; chain and plug; "P" trap and overflow connections		
5.1.13	white	nr	196.00 - 309.00
5.1.14	coloured	nr	253.00 - 309.00
	bath; enamelled steel; chromium plated taps; overflow; waste; chain and plug; "P" trap and overflow connections		
5.1.15	white	nr	280.00 - 336.00
5.1.16	coloured	nr	309.00 - 364.00
	Soil waste stacks; 3.15 m storey height; branch and connection to drain		
5.1.17	110 mm diameter PVC	nr	224.00 - 253.00
	Extra for		
5.1.18	additional floors	nr	112.00 - 126.00
5.1.19	100 mm diameter cast iron; decorated	nr	- -
	Extra for		
5.1.20	additional floors	nr	- -

INDUSTRIAL £ range £	RETAILING £ range £	LEISURE £ range £	OFFICES £ range £	HOTELS £ range £	Item nr.
133.00 - 168.00	154.00 - 210.00	154.00 - 210.00	154.00 - 210.00	154.00 - 253.00	5.1.1
- -	- -	175.00 - 247.00	175.00 - 247.00	175.00 - 247.00	5.1.2
126.00 - 154.00	133.00 - 154.00	133.00 - 154.00	133.00 - 154.00	133.00 - 182.00	5.1.3
- -	- -	168.00 - 210.00	168.00 - 210.00	168.00 - 231.00	5.1.4
246.00 - 288.00	253.00 - 287.00	253.00 - 287.00	253.00 - 287.00	253.00 - 309.00	5.1.5
- -	- -	287.00 - 323.00	287.00 - 336.00	287.00 - 357.00	5.1.6
112.00 - 133.00	126.00 - 154.00	126.00 - 154.00	126.00 - 154.00	126.00 - 154.00	5.1.7
329.00 - 371.00	357.00 - 405.00	357.00 - 405.00	357.00 - 405.00	357.00 - 405.00	5.1.8
- -	- -	357.00 - 432.00	357.00 - 453.00	357.00 - 666.00	5.1.9
168.00 - 210.00	168.00 - 287.00	- -	168.00 - 287.00	- -	5.1.10
- -	- -	- -	- -	- -	5.1.11
- -	- -	- -	- -	- -	5.1.12
- -	- -	- -	- -	253.00 - 364.00	5.1.13
- -	- -	- -	- -	253.00 - 364.00	5.1.14
- -	- -	- -	- -	280.00 - 391.00	5.1.15
- -	- -	- -	- -	307.00 - 405.00	5.1.16
224.00 - 253.00	224.00 - 253.00	224.00 - 253.00	224.00 - 253.00	224.00 - 253.00	5.1.17
112.00 - 133.00	112.00 - 133.00	112.00 - 133.00	112.00 - 133.00	113.00 - 133.00	5.1.18
453.00 - 480.00	453.00 - 480.00	453.00 - 480.00	453.00 - 480.00	453.00 - 480.00	5.1.19
224.00 - 253.00	224.00 - 253.00	224.00 - 253.00	224.00 - 253.00	224.00 - 253.00	5.1.20

Item nr.	SPECIFICATIONS	Unit	RESIDENTIAL £ range £
5.1	**SANITARY AND DISPOSAL INSTALLATIONS** **gross internal area** (unless otherwise described)		
	Sanitary and disposal installations Residential units		
5.1.21	range including WC; wash handbasin; bath	nr	1119 - 1887
5.1.22	range including WC; wash handbasin; bidet; bath	nr	1400 - 2244
5.1.23	and kitchen sink	nr	1681 - 2493
5.1.24	range including two WC's; two wash handbasins; bidet bath and kitchen sink	nr	2099 - 2906
	Extra for		
5.1.25	rainwater pipe per storey	nr	50.40 - 63.10
5.1.26	soil pipe per storey	nr	112.00 - 126.00
5.1.27	shower over bath	nr	280.00 - 398.00
	Industrial buildings warehouse		
5.1.28	minimum provision	m²	- -
5.1.29	high provision	m²	- -
	production unit		
5.1.30	minimum provision	m²	- -
5.1.31	minimum provision; area less than 1000 m²	m²	- -
5.1.32	high provision	m²	- -
	Retailing outlets		
5.1.33	to superstore	m²	- -
5.1.34	to shopping centre malls; public conveniences; branch connections to shop shells	m²	- -
5.1.35	fitting out public conveniences in shopping mall block	m²	- -
5.1.36	Leisure buildings	m²	- -
	Office and industrial office buildings		
5.1.37	speculative; low rise; area less than 1000 m²	m²	- -
5.1.38	speculative; low rise	m²	- -
5.1.39	speculative; medium rise; area less than 1000 m²	m²	- -
5.1.40	speculative; medium rise	m²	- -
5.1.41	speculative; high rise	m²	- -
5.1.42	owner-occupied; low rise; area less than 1000 m²	m²	- -
5.1.43	owner-occupied; low rise	m²	- -
5.1.44	owner-occupied; medium rise; area less than 1000 m²	m²	- -
5.1.45	owner-occupied; medium rise	m²	- -
5.1.46	owner-occupied; high rise	m²	- -
	Hotels		
5.1.47	WC; bath; shower; basin to each bedroom; sanitary accommodation to public areas	m²	- -
5.20	**WATER INSTALLATIONS** **gross internal area**		
	Hot and cold water installations		
5.2.1	Complete installations	m²	11.90 - 21.00
5.2.2	To mall public conveniences; branch connections to shop shells	m²	- -

INDUSTRIAL £ range £	RETAILING £ range £	LEISURE £ range £	OFFICES £ range £	HOTELS £ range £	Item nr.
- -	- -	- -	- -	- -	5.1.21
- -	- -	- -	- -	- -	5.1.22
- -	- -	- -	- -	- -	5.1.23
- -	- -	- -	- -	- -	5.1.24
- -	- -	- -	- -	- -	5.1.25
- -	- -	- -	- -	- -	5.1.26
- -	- -	- -	- -	- -	5.1.27
7.30 - 10.20	- -	- -	- -	- -	5.1.28
10.20 - 15.40	- -	- -	- -	- -	5.1.29
10.20 - 15.40	- -	- -	- -	- -	5.1.30
11.90 - 20.60	- -	- -	- -	- -	5.1.31
11.30 - 18.20	- -	- -	- -	- -	5.1.32
- -	2.60 - 6.30	- -	- -	- -	5.1.33
- -	5.10 - 8.20	- -	- -	- -	5.1.34
- -	3816 - 6128	- -	- -	- -	5.1.35
- -	- -	8.70 - 11.20	- -	- -	5.1.36
3.80 - 9.50	- -	- -	3.80 - 9.50	- -	5.1.37
7.00 - 12.60	- -	- -	6.70 - 12.60	- -	5.1.38
- -	- -	- -	7.30 - 13.30	- -	5.1.39
- -	- -	- -	10.00 - 15.40	- -	5.1.40
- -	- -	- -	10.00 - 15.40	- -	5.1.41
- -	- -	- -	6.30 - 12.60	- -	5.1.42
6.30 - 12.60	- -	- -	10.00 - 15.40	- -	5.1.43
10.00 - 15.40	- -	- -	10.00 - 15.40	- -	5.1.44
- -	- -	- -	11.90 - 17.50	- -	5.1.45
- -	- -	- -	14.10 - 19.60	- -	5.1.46
- -	- -	- -	- -	17.50 - 43.20	5.1.47
5.00 - 13.30	- -	16.10 - 23.00	9.10 - 13.30	25.40 - 30.90	5.2.1
- -	3.60 - 6.30	- -	- -	- -	5.2.2

Item nr.	SPECIFICATIONS	Unit	RESIDENTIAL £ range £	
5.3	**HEATING, AIR-CONDITIONING AND VENTILATING INSTALLATIONS** **gross internal area serviced** (unless otherwise described)			
	comprising:			
	Solid fuel radiator heating **Gas or oil-fired radiator heating** **Gas or oil-fired convector heating** **Electric and under floor heating** **Hot air systems** **Ventilation systems** **Heating and ventilation systems** **Comfort cooling systems** **Full air-conditioning systems**			
	Solid fuel radiator heating			
5.3.1	Chimney stack; hearth and surround to independent residential unit	nr	1544 -	1819
	Chimney; hot water service and central heating for			
5.3.2	two radiators	nr	2244 -	2656
5.3.3	three radiators	nr	2656 -	2951
5.3.4	four radiators	nr	2951 -	3253
5.3.5	five radiators	nr	3253 -	3569
5.3.6	six radiators	nr	3569 -	3884
5.3.7	seven radiators	nr	3884 -	4550
	Gas or oil-fired radiator heating			
	Gas-fired hot water service and central heating for			
5.3.8	three radiators	nr	1681 -	2381
5.3.9	four radiators	nr	2381 -	2594
5.3.10	five radiators	nr	2594 -	2766
5.3.11	six radiators	nr	2766 -	2951
5.3.12	seven radiators	nr	3081 -	3500
	Oil-fired hot water service, tank and central heating for			
5.3.13	seven radiators	nr	2747 -	3622
5.3.14	ten radiators	nr	3065 -	3001
5.3.15	LPHW radiator system	m^2	23.00 -	35.50
5.3.16	speculative; area less than 1000 m^2	m^2	-	-
5.3.17	speculative	m^2	-	-
5.3.18	owner-occupied; area less than 1000 m^2	m^2	-	-
5.3.19	owner-occupied	m^2	-	-
5.3.20	LPHW radiant panel system	m^2	-	-
5.3.21	speculative; less than 1000 m^2	m^2	-	-
5.3.22	speculative	m^2	-	-
5.3.23	LPHW fin tube heating	m^2	-	-
	Gas or oil-fired convector heating			
5.3.24	LPHW convector system	m^2	-	-
5.3.25	speculative; area less than 1000 m^2	m^2	-	-
5.3.26	speculative	m^2	-	-
5.3.27	owner-occupied; area less than 1000 m^2	m^2	-	-
5.3.28	owner-occupied	m^2	-	-
	LPHW sill-line convector system			
5.3.29	owner-occupied	m^2	-	-
	Electric and under floor heating			
5.3.30	Panel heaters	m^2	-	-
5.3.31	Skirting heaters	m^2	-	-
5.3.32	Storage heaters	m^2	-	-
5.3.33	Underfloor heating in changing areas	m^2	-	-

INDUSTRIAL £ range £			RETAILING £ range £			LEISURE £ range £			OFFICES £ range £			HOTELS £ range £			Item nr.
-	-		-	-		-	-		-	-		-	-		5.3.1
-	-		-	-		-	-		-	-		-	-		5.3.2
-	-		-	-		-	-		-	-		-	-		5.3.3
-	-		-	-		-	-		-	-		-	-		5.3.4
-	-		-	-		-	-		-	-		-	-		5.3.5
-	-		-	-		-	-		-	-		-	-		5.3.6
-	-		-	-		-	-		-	-		-	-		5.3.7
-	-		-	-		-	-		-	-		-	-		5.3.8
-	-		-	-		-	-		-	-		-	-		5.3.9
-	-		-	-		-	-		-	-		-	-		5.3.10
-	-		-	-		-	-		-	-		-	-		5.3.11
-	-		-	-		-	-		-	-		-	-		5.3.12
-	-		-	-		-	-		-	-		-	-		5.3.13
-	-		-	-		-	-		-	-		-	-		5.3.14
33.60	-	47.70	33.60	-	47.70	41.90	-	54.60	-		-	50.40	-	70.00	5.3.15
-	-		-	-		-	-		41.20	-	51.80	-	-		5.3.16
-	-		-	-		-	-		44.60	-	61.80	-	-		5.3.17
-	-		-	-		-	-		44.60	-	60.40	-	-		5.3.18
-	-		-	-		-	-		47.40	-	67.30	-	-		5.3.19
-	-		40.50	-	61.80	50.40	-	61.80	-		-	-	-		5.3.20
44.60	-	53.20	-	-		-	-		-		-	-	-		5.3.21
46.00	-	54.60	-	-		-	-		-		-	-	-		5.2.22
59.00	-	86.80	-	-		-	-		-		-	-	-		5.2.23
35.00	-	46.00	34.00	-	64.50	44.60	-	57.60	-		-	59.00	-	74.10	5.3.24
-	-		-	-		-	-		46.00	-	54.60	-	-		5.3.25
-	-		-	-		-	-		47.40	-	64.50	-	-		5.3.26
-	-		-	-		-	-		50.40	-	61.80	-	-		5.3.27
-	-		-	-		-	-		56.30	-	70.00	-	-		5.3.28
-	-		-	-		-	-		72.70	-	101.60	-	-		5.3.29
-	-		-	-		-	-		10.00	-	13.30	-	-		5.3.30
-	-		-	-		-	-		15.40	-	20.60	-	-		5.3.31
-	-		-	-		-	-		17.80	-	24.00	-	-		5.3.32
-	-		-	-		38.40	-	49.10	-		-	-	-		5.3.33

Item nr.	SPECIFICATIONS	Unit	RESIDENTIAL £ range £
5.3	**HEATING, AIR-CONDITIONING AND VENTILATING INSTALLATIONS - cont'd**		
	gross internal area serviced (unless otherwise described)		
	Hot air systems		
	Hot water service and ducted hot air heating to		
5.3.34	three rooms	nr	1544 - 1990
5.3.35	five rooms	nr	2059 - 2347
5.3.36	"Elvaco" warm air heating	m^2	- -
5.3.37	Gas-fired hot air space heating	m^2	- -
5.3.38	Warm air curtains; 1.60 m long electrically-operated	nr	- -
5.3.39	Hot water-operated; including supply pipework	nr	- -
	Ventilation system		
	Local ventilation to		
5.3.40	WC's	nr	168.10 - 223.70
5.3.41	toilet areas	m^2	- -
5.3.42	bathroom and toilet areas	m^2	- -
5.3.43	Air extract system	m^2	- -
5.3.44	Air supply and extract system	m^2	- -
5.3.45	Service yard vehicle extract system	m^2	- -
	Heating and ventilation systems		
5.3.46	Space heating and ventilation - economical	m^2	- -
5.3.47	Heating and ventilation	m^2	- -
5.3.48	Warm air heating and ventilation	m^2	- -
5.3.49	Hot air heating and ventilation to shopping malls; including automatic remote vents in rooflights	m^2	- -
	Extra for		
5.3.50	comfort cooling	m^2	- -
5.3.51	full air-conditioning	m^2	- -
	Comfort cooling systems		
5.3.52	Fan coil/induction systems	m^2	- -
5.3.53	speculative; area less than 1000 m^2	m^2	- -
5.3.54	speculative	m^2	- -
5.3.55	owner-occupied; area less than 1000 m^2	m^2	- -
5.3.56	owner-occupied	m^2	- -
5.3.57	"VAV" system	m^2	- -
5.3.58	speculative; area less than 1000 m^2	m^2	- -
5.3.59	speculative	m^2	- -
5.3.60	owner-occupied; area less than 1000 m^2	m^2	- -
5.3.61	owner-occupied	m^2	- -
	Stand-alone air-conditioning unit systems		
5.3.62	air supply and extract	m^2	- -
5.3.63	air supply and extract; including heat re-claim	m^2	- -
	Extra for		
5.3.64	automatic control installation	m^2	- -
5.3.65	Full air-conditioning with dust and humidity control	m^2	- -
5.3.66	Fan coil/induction systems	m^2	- -
5.3.67	speculative; area less than 1000 m^2	m^2	- -
5.3.68	speculative	m^2	- -
5.3.69	owner-occupied; area less than 1000 m^2	m^2	- -
5.3.70	owner-occupied	m^2	- -
5.3.71	"VAV" system	m^2	- -
5.3.72	speculative; area less than 1000 m^2	m^2	- -
5.3.73	speculative	m^2	- -
5.3.74	owner-occupied; area less than 1000 m^2	m^2	- -
5.3.75	owner-occupied	m^2	- -

INDUSTRIAL £ range £	RETAILING £ range £	LEISURE £ range £	OFFICES £ range £	HOTELS £ range £	Item nr.
- -	- -	- -	- -	- -	5.3.34
- -	- -	- -	- -	- -	5.3.35
- -	- -	- -	54.60 - 70.00	- -	5.3.36
20.60 - 40.50	- -	- -	- -	- -	5.3.37
- -	1681 - 2278	- -	- -	- -	5.3.38
- -	3397 - 3843	- -	- -	- -	5.3.39
- -	- -	- -	- -	- -	5.3.40
- -	- -	- -	3.10 - 7.50	- -	5.3.41
- -	- -	- -	- -	17.20 - 17.50	5.3.42
- -	28.10 - 37.70	28.10 - 37.70	28.10 - 37.70	30.90 - 40.50	5.3.43
- -	- -	- -	40.50 - 61.80	- -	5.3.44
- -	28.10 - 37.70	- -	- -	- -	5.3.45
17.20 - 39.10	18.50 - 34.00	- -	- -	- -	5.3.46
44.60 - 56.30	- -	- -	- -	- -	5.3.47
- -	84.00 - 107.00	84.00 - 107.00	84.00 - 107.00	91.00 - 126.30	5.3.48
- -	73.00 - 95.00	- -	- -	- -	5.3.49
- -	63.10 - 91.00	- -	- -	- -	5.3.50
- -	73.00 - 133.00	- -	- -	- -	5.3.51
- -	- -	- -	- -	126.00 - 175.00	5.3.52
- -	- -	- -	126.00 - 114.00	126.00 - 175.00	5.3.53
- -	- -	- -	133.00 - 161.00	- -	5.3.54
- -	- -	- -	133.00 - 168.00	- -	5.3.55
- -	- -	- -	140.00 - 175.00	- -	5.3.56
- -	126.00 - 175.00	- -	- -	154.00 - 224.00	5.3.57
- -	- -	- -	140.00 - 210.00	- -	5.3.58
- -	- -	- -	147.00 - 210.00	- -	5.3.59
- -	- -	- -	154.00 - 217.00	- -	5.3.60
- -	- -	- -	154.00 - 224.00	- -	5.3.61
- -	- -	105.00 - 140.00	- -	- -	5.3.62
- -	- -	119.00 - 154.00	- -	- -	5.3.63
- -	- -	10.00 - 30.90	- -	- -	5.3.64
126.00 - 210.00	- -	- -	- -	- -	5.3.65
- -	140.00 - 210.00	- -	- -	147.00 - 224.00	5.3.66
- -	- -	- -	133.00 - 168.00	- -	5.3.67
- -	- -	- -	133.00 - 189.00	- -	5.3.68
- -	- -	- -	140.00 - 210.00	- -	5.3.69
- -	- -	- -	147.00 - 224.00	- -	5.3.70
- -	- -	- -	- -	168.00 - 253.00	5.3.71
- -	- -	- -	161.00 - 210.00	- -	5.3.72
- -	- -	- -	168.00 - 224.00	- -	5.3.73
- -	- -	- -	168.00 - 244.00	- -	5.3.74
- -	- -	- -	168.00 - 253.00	- -	5.3.75

Item nr.	SPECIFICATIONS	Unit	RESIDENTIAL £ range £		
5.4	**ELECTRICAL INSTALLATIONS**				
	gross internal area serviced (unless otherwise described)				
	comprising:				
	Mains and sub-mains switchgear and distribution				
	Lighting installation				
	Lighting and power installation				
	Comparative fittings/rates per point				
	Mains and sub-mains switchgear and distribution				
5.4.1	Mains intake only	m²	-		-
5.4.2	Mains switchgear only	m²	2.00	-	3.40
	Mains and sub-mains distribution				
5.4.3	to floors only	m²	-		-
5.4.4	to floors; including small power and supplies to equipment	m²	-		-
	to floors; including lighting and power to landlords areas and supplies to				
5.4.5	equipment	m²	-		-
5.4.6	to floors; including power, communication and supplies to equipment	m²	-		-
5.4.7	to shop units; including fire alarms and telephone distribution	m²	-		-
	Lighting installation				
	Lighting to				
5.4.8	warehouse area	m²	-		-
5.4.9	production area	m²	-		-
5.4.10	General lighting; including luminaries	m²	-		-
5.4.11	Emergency lighting	m²	-		-
5.4.12	standby generators only	m²	-		-
5.4.13	Underwater lighting	m²	-		-
	Lighting and power installations				
	Lighting and power to residential units				
5.4.14	one person flat/bed-sit	nr	769	-	1194
5.4.15	two person flat/house	nr	913	-	1681
5.4.16	three person flat/house	nr	1050	-	2031
5.4.17	four person house	nr	1263	-	3081
5.4.18	five/six person house	nr	1544	-	3081
	Extra for				
5.4.19	intercom	nr	307.50	-	350.00
	Lighting and power to industrial buildings				
5.4.20	warehouse area	m²	-		-
5.4.21	production area	m²	-		-
5.4.22	production area; high provision	m²	-		-
5.4.23	office area	m²	-		-
5.4.24	office area; high provision	m²	-		-
	Lighting and power to retail outlets				
5.4.25	shopping mall and landlords' areas	m²	-		-
	Lighting and power to offices				
5.4.26	speculative office areas; average standard	m²	-		-
5.4.27	speculative office areas; high standard	m²	-		-
5.4.28	owner-occupied office areas; average standard	m²	-		-
5.4.29	owner-occupied office areas; high standard	m²	-		-
	Comparative fittings/rates per point				
5.4.30	Consumer control unit	nr	126.30	-	140.00
	Fittings; excluding lamps or light fittings				
5.4.31	lighting point; PVC cables	nr	39.80	-	43.20
5.4.32	lighting point; PVC cables in screwed conduits	nr	85.10	-	93.30
5.4.33	lighting point; MICC cables	nr	72.70	-	78.20

INDUSTRIAL £ range £		RETAILING £ range £		LEISURE £ range £		OFFICES £ range £		HOTELS £ range £		Item nr.
1.40 -	2.50	-	-	-	-	-	-	-	-	5.4.1
3.40 -	6.70	3.10 -	7.00	-	-	-	-	-	-	5.4.2
3.80 -	7.30	-	-	15.40 -	28.10	11.30 -	19.60	-	-	5.4.3
-	-	-	-	11.20 -	13.30	-	-	-	-	5.4.4
7.30 -	17.50	-	-	-	-	28.10 -	46.00	-	-	5.4.5
-	-	-	-	-	-	-	-	46.00 -	65.90	5.4.6
-	-	4.50 -	11.20	-	-	-	-	-	-	5.4.7
16.10 -	30.90	-	-	-	-	-	-	-	-	5.4.8
19.60 -	34.30	-	-	-	-	-	-	-	-	5.4.9
-	-	-	-	19.60 -	33.60	-	-	17.50	28.10	5.4.10
-	-	-	-	7.30 -	11.20	-	-	3.10	5.60	5.4.11
2.00 -	8.00	2.00 -	8.00	2.00 -	8.00	2.00 -	8.00	2.00	8.00	5.4.12
-	-	-	-	5.10 -	10.00	-	-	-	-	5.4.13
-	-	-	-	-	-	-	-	-	-	5.4.14
-	-	-	-	-	-	-	-	-	-	5.4.15
-	-	-	-	-	-	-	-	-	-	5.4.16
-	-	-	-	-	-	-	-	-	-	5.4.17
-	-	-	-	-	-	-	-	-	-	5.4.18
-	-	-	-	-	-	-	-	-	-	5.4.19
30.90 -	50.40	-	-	-	-	-	-	-	-	5.4.20
35.00 -	56.30	-	-	-	-	-	-	-	-	5.4.21
50.40 -	65.90	-	-	-	-	-	-	-	-	5.4.22
75.50 -	90.60	-	-	-	-	-	-	-	-	5.4.23
100.90 -	120.80	-	-	-	-	-	-	-	-	5.4.24
-	-	50.40 -	85.80	-	-	-	-	-	-	5.4.25
-	-	-	-	-	-	67.30 -	94.70	-	-	5.4.26
-	-	-	-	-	-	85.10 -	100.90	-	-	5.4.27
-	-	-	-	-	-	90.60 -	120.80	-	-	5.4.28
-	-	-	-	-	-	106.40 -	133.10	-	-	5.4.29
-	-	-	-	-	-	-	-	-	-	5.4.30
-	-	44.60 -	50.40	44.60 -	50.40	44.60 -	50.40	44.60 -	50.40	5.4.31
120.80 -	133.10	99.50 -	113.20	99.50 -	113.20	99.50 -	113.20	99.50 -	113.20	5.4.32
99.50 -	113.20	87.20 -	95.40	87.20 -	95.40	87.20 -	95.40	87.20 -	95.40	5.4.33

Item nr.	SPECIFICATIONS	Unit	RESIDENTIAL £ range £		
5.4	**ELECTRICAL INSTALLATIONS - cont'd**				
	gross internal area serviced				
	Comparative fittings/rates per point - cont'd				
	Switch socket outlet; PVC cables				
5.4.34	single	nr	42.00	-	47.00
5.4.35	double	nr	50.00	-	58.00
	Switch socket outlet; PVC cables in screwed conduit				
5.4.36	single	nr	66.00	-	70.00
5.4.37	double	nr	69.00	-	77.00
	Switch socket outlet; MICC cables				
5.4.38	single	nr	66.00	-	70.00
5.4.39	double	nr	70.00	-	78.00
5.4.40	Immersion heater point (excluding heater)	nr	62.00	-	70.00
5.4.41	Cooker point; including control unit	nr	87.20	-	140.00
5.5	**GAS INSTALLATION**				
5.5.1	Connection charge	nr	453.00	-	576.00
	Supply to heaters within shopping mall and capped off				
5.5.2	Supply to shop shells	m²	-		-
5.6	**LIFT AND CONVEYOR INSTALLATIONS**				
	lift or escalator (unless otherwise described)				
	comprising:				
	Passenger lifts				
	Escalators				
	Goods lift				
	Dock levellers				
	Electro-hydraulic passenger lifts				
	Eight to twelve person lifts				
5.6.1	8 person; 0.30 m/sec ; 2 - 3 levels	nr	-		-
5.6.2	8 person; 0.63 m/sec ; 3 - 5 levels	nr	-		-
5.6.3	8 person; 1.50 m/sec ; 3 levels	nr	-		-
5.6.4	8 person; 1.60 m/sec ; 6 - 9 levels	nr	-		-
5.6.5	10 person; 0.63 m/sec ; 2 - 4 levels	nr	-		-
5.6.6	10 person; 1.00 m/sec ; 2 levels	nr	-		-
5.6.7	10 person; 1.00 m/sec ; 3 - 6 levels	nr	-		-
5.6.8	10 person; 1.00 m/sec ; 3 - 6 levels	nr	-		-
5.6.9	10 person; 1.60 m/sec ; 4 levels	nr	-		-
5.6.10	10 person; 1.60 m/sec ; 10 levels	nr	-		-
5.6.11	10 person; 1.60 m/sec ; 13 levels	nr	-		-
5.6.12	10 person; 2.50 m/sec ; 18 levels	nr	-		-
5.6.13	12 person; 1.00 m/sec ; 2 - 3 levels	nr	-		-
5.6.14	12 person; 1.00 m/sec ; 3 - 6 levels	nr	-		-
	Thirteen person lifts				
5.6.15	13 person; 0.30 m/sec ; 2 - 3 levels	nr	-		-
5.6.16	13 person; 0.63 m/sec ; 4 levels	nr	-		-
5.6.17	13 person; 1.00 m/sec ; 2 levels	nr	-		-
5.6.18	13 person; 1.00 m/sec ; 2 - 3 levels	nr	-		-
5.6.19	13 person; 1.00 m/sec ; 3 - 6 levels	nr	-		-
5.6.20	13 person; 1.60 m/sec ; 7 - 11 levels	nr	-		-
5.6.21	13 person; 2.50 m/sec ; 7 - 11 levels	nr	-		-
5.6.22	13 person; 2.50 m/sec ; 12 - 15 levels	nr	-		-
	Sixteen person lifts				
5.6.23	16 person; 1.00 m/sec ; 2 levels	nr	-		-
5.6.24	16 person; 1.00 m/sec ; 3 levels	nr	-		-
5.6.25	16 person; 1.00 m/sec ; 3 - 6 levels	nr	-		-
5.6.26	16 person; 1.60 m/sec ; 3 - 6 levels	nr	-		-
5.6.27	16 person; 1.60 m/sec ; 7 - 11 levels	nr	-		-
5.6.28	16 person; 2.50 m/sec ; 7 - 11 levels	nr	-		-
5.6.29	16 person; 2.50 m/sec ; 12 - 15 levels	nr	-		-
5.6.30	16 person; 3.50 m/sec ; 12 - 15 levels	nr	-		-

INDUSTRIAL £ range £		RETAILING £ range £		LEISURE £ range £		OFFICES £ range £		HOTELS £ range £		Item nr.
-	-	52.00	56.00	52.00	56.00	52.00	56.00	52.00	56.00	5.4.34
100.00	109.00	62.00	67.00	62.00	67.00	62.00	67.00	62.00	67.00	5.4.35
80.00	89.00	73.00	75.00	73.00	75.00	73.00	75.00	73.00	75.00	5.4.36
91.00	98.00	78.00	87.00	78.00	87.00	78.00	87.00	78.00	87.00	5.4.37
85.00	89.00	73.00	77.00	73.00	77.00	73.00	77.00	73.00	77.00	5.4.38
91.00	114.00	78.00	88.00	78.00	88.00	78.00	88.00	78.00	88.00	5.4.39
-	-	-	-	-	-	-	-	-	-	5.4.40
-	-	-	-	-	-	-	-	-	-	5.4.41
-	-	-	-	-	-	-	-	-	-	5.5.1
-	-	5.63	8.58	-	-	-	-	-	-	5.5.2
-	-	-	-	27695	38500	25900	38500	-	-	5.6.1
-	-	-	-	-	-	47971	66500	-	-	5.6.2
64417	79814	-	-	-	-	-	-	-	-	5.6.3
-	-	-	-	-	-	85750	102941	-	-	5.6.4
-	-	-	-	-	-	57029	74529	-	-	5.6.5
-	-	-	-	-	-	47971	53186	-	-	5.6.6
-	-	-	-	-	-	65127	82628	-	-	5.6.7
-	-	-	-	-	-	69314	86471	-	-	5.6.8
-	-	-	-	-	-	69314	88804	-	-	5.6.9
-	-	-	-	-	-	95873	109186	-	-	5.6.10
-	-	-	-	-	-	109941	126343	-	-	5.6.11
-	-	-	-	-	-	192843	210493	-	-	5.6.12
64417	78943	-	-	-	-	-	-	-	-	5.6.13
-	-	-	-	-	-	-	-	73717	90686	5.6.14
-	-	-	-	-	-	30471	39941	-	-	5.6.15
-	-	-	-	-	-	65127	81255	-	-	5.6.16
-	-	76160	85528	-	-	-	-	-	-	5.6.17
64417	84170	-	-	-	-	-	-	-	-	5.6.18
-	-	-	-	-	-	65127	86471	73717	95166	5.6.19
-	-	-	-	-	-	85098	106373	92044	105928	5.6.20
-	-	-	-	-	-	136843	155103	-	-	5.6.21
-	-	-	-	-	-	155103	170368	-	-	5.6.22
-	-	72359	92044	-	-	-	-	-	-	5.6.23
-	-	85528	98696	-	-	-	-	-	-	5.6.24
-	-	-	-	-	-	74529	95941	-	-	5.6.25
-	-	-	-	-	-	79814	101157	-	-	5.6.26
-	-	-	-	-	-	109941	126412	-	-	5.6.27
-	-	-	-	-	-	143500	164539	-	-	5.6.28
-	-	-	-	-	-	163180	190740	-	-	5.6.29
-	-	-	-	-	-	171055	197324	-	-	5.6.30

Item nr.	SPECIFICATIONS	Unit	RESIDENTIAL £ range £	
5.6	**LIFT AND CONVEYOR INSTALLATIONS -cont'd**			
	lift or escalator (unless otherwise described)			
	Electro-hydraulic passenger lifts - cont'd			
	Twenty one person lifts			
5.6.31	21 person/bed; 0.40 m/sec ; 3 levels	nr	-	-
5.6.32	21 person; 0.60 m/sec ; 2 levels	nr	-	-
5.6.33	21 person; 1.00 m/sec ; 4 levels	nr	-	-
5.6.34	21 person; 1.60 m/sec ; 4 levels	nr	-	-
5.6.35	21 person; 1.60 m/sec ; 7 - 11 levels	nr	-	-
5.6.36	21 person; 1.60 m/sec ; 10 levels	nr	-	-
5.6.37	21 person; 1.60 m/sec ; 13 levels	nr	-	-
5.6.38	21 person; 2.50 m/sec ; 7 - 11 levels	nr	-	-
5.6.39	21 person; 2.50 m/sec ; 12 - 15 levels	nr	-	-
5.6.40	21 person; 2.50 m/sec ; 18 levels	nr	-	-
5.6.41	21 person; 3.50 m/sec ; 12 - 15 levels	nr	-	-
	Extra for			
5.6.42	enhanced finish to car	nr	-	-
5.6.43	glass backed observation car	nr	-	-
	Ten person wall climber lifts			
5.6.44	10 person; 0.50 m/sec ; 2 levels	nr	-	-
	Escalators			
	30^0 Escalator; 0.50 m/sec; enamelled steel glass balustrades			
5.6.45	3.50 m rise; 600 mm step width	nr	-	-
5.6.46	3.50 m rise; 800 mm step width	nr	-	-
5.6.47	3.50 m rise; 1000 mm step width	nr	-	-
	Extra for			
5.6.48	enhanced finish	nr	-	-
5.6.49	4.40 m rise; 800 mm step width	nr	-	-
5.6.50	4.40 m rise; 1000 mm step width	nr	-	-
5.6.51	5.20 m rise; 800 mm step width	nr	-	-
5.6.52	5.20 m rise; 1000 mm step width	nr	-	-
5.6.53	6.00 m rise; 800 mm step width	nr	-	-
5.6.54	6.00 m rise; 1000 mm step width	nr	-	-
	Extras (per escalator)			
5.6.55	under step lighting	nr	-	-
5.6.56	under handrail lighting	nr	-	-
5.6.57	stainless steel balustrades	nr	-	-
5.6.58	mirror glass cladding to sides and soffits	nr	-	-
5.6.59	heavy duty chairs	nr	-	-
	Goods lifts			
5.6.60	Hoist	nr	-	-
	Kitchen service hoist			
5.6.61	50 kg; 2 levels	nr	-	-
	Electric heavy duty goods lifts			
5.6.62	500 kg; 2 levels	nr	-	-
5.6.63	500 kg; 2 - 3 levels	nr	-	-
5.6.64	500 kg; 5 levels	nr	-	-
5.6.65	1000 kg; 2 levels	nr	-	-
5.6.66	1000 kg; 2 - 3 levels	nr	-	-
5.6.67	1000 kg; 5 levels	nr	-	-
5.6.68	1500 kg; 3 levels	nr	-	-
5.6.69	1500 kg; 4 levels	nr	-	-
5.6.70	1500 kg; 7 levels	nr	-	-
5.6.71	2000 kg; 2 levels	nr	-	-
5.6.72	2000 kg; 3 levels	nr	-	-
5.6.73	3000 kg; 2 levels	nr	-	-
5.6.74	3000 kg; 3 levels	nr	-	-
	Oil hydraulic heavy duty goods lifts			
5.6.75	500 kg; 3 levels	nr	-	-
5.6.76	1000 kg; 3 levels	nr	-	-
5.6.77	2000 kg; 3 levels	nr	-	-
5.6.78	3500 kg; 4 levels	nr	-	-

INDUSTRIAL £ range £		RETAILING £ range £		LEISURE £ range £		OFFICES £ range £		HOTELS £ range £		Item nr.
-	-	-	-	-	-	54559	- 61250	-	-	5.6.31
-	-	-	-	-	-	78407	- 95907	-	-	5.6.32
-	-	-	-	-	-	93093	- 109976	-	-	5.6.33
-	-	-	-	-	-	82525	- 95907	-	-	5.6.34
-	-	-	-	-	-	109976	- 123186	-	-	5.6.35
-	-	-	-	-	-	123873	- 135757	-	-	5.6.36
-	-	-	-	-	-	135757	- 150294	-	-	5.6.37
-	-	-	-	-	-	156814	- 185981	-	-	5.6.38
-	-	-	-	-	-	176716	- 206226	-	-	5.6.39
-	-	-	-	-	-	212745	- 232647	-	-	5.6.40
-	-	-	-	-	-	199363	- 219264	-	-	5.6.41
-	-	-	-	-	-	-	-	10500	- 11186	5.6.42
-	-	-	-	-	-	-	-	11873	- 21275	5.6.43
-	-	172941	- 216872	-	-	172941	- 219265	172941	- 219265	5.6.44
-	-	-	-	-	-	57098	- 70343	-	-	5.6.45
-	-	-	-	-	-	61250	- 74529	-	-	5.6.46
-	-	82628	- 109118	66569	- 79745	66569	- 79745	68628	- 96628	5.6.47
-	-	24500	- 34657	17157	- 23745	17157	- 23745	24500	- 37127	5.6.48
-	-	68628	- 86471	-	-	-	-	-	-	5.6.49
-	-	78407	- 92990	-	-	-	-	-	-	5.6.50
-	-	73088	- 89902	-	-	-	-	-	-	5.6.51
-	-	82696	- 98137	-	-	-	-	-	-	5.6.52
-	-	77549	- 92990	-	-	-	-	-	-	5.6.53
-	-	86471	- 102941	-	-	-	-	-	-	5.6.54
-	-	384	- 526	-	-	-	-	-	-	5.6.55
-	-	1544	- 3020	-	-	-	-	-	-	5.6.56
-	-	1681	- 3328	-	-	-	-	-	-	5.6.57
-	-	11907	- 14686	-	-	-	-	-	-	5.6.58
-	-	14686	- 20657	-	-	-	-	-	-	5.6.59
5971	- 21275	-	-	-	-	-	-	-	-	5.6.60
-	-	-	-	7000	- 7686	-	-	-	-	5.6.61
-	-	51814	- 58814	-	-	50441	- 58814	50441	- 58814	5.6.62
22647	- 31843	-	-	-	-	-	-	-	-	5.6.63
-	-	-	-	-	-	61216	- 77000	-	-	5.6.64
-	-	49000	- 66569	-	-	54559	- 66569	56000	- 63686	5.6.65
29373	- 39941	-	-	-	-	-	-	-	-	5.6.66
-	-	-	-	-	-	-	-	66569	- 76314	5.6.67
61216	- 73157	-	-	-	-	69314	- 82628	-	-	5.6.68
-	-	-	-	-	-	74529	- 89216	-	-	5.6.69
-	-	-	-	-	-	89216	- 102529	-	-	5.6.70
-	-	-	-	-	-	69314	- 82628	-	-	5.6.71
-	-	-	-	-	-	82628	- 95941	-	-	5.6.72
-	-	-	-	-	-	74529	- 89216	-	-	5.6.73
-	-	-	-	-	-	93059	- 109941	-	-	5.6.74
69314	- 82628	-	-	-	-	-	-	-	-	5.6.75
73157	- 86471	-	-	-	-	-	-	-	-	5.6.76
85098	- 98412	-	-	-	-	-	-	-	-	5.6.77
75902	- 89216	-	-	-	-	-	-	-	-	5.6.78

Item nr.	SPECIFICATIONS	Unit	RESIDENTIAL £ range £	
5.6	**LIFT AND CONVEYOR INSTALLATIONS - cont'd** **lift or escalator** (unless otherwise described)			
	Dock levellers			
5.6.79	Dock levellers	nr	-	-
5.6.80	Dock leveller and canopy	nr	-	-
5.7	**PROTECTIVE, COMMUNICATION AND SPECIAL INSTALLATIONS** **gross internal area served** (unless otherwise described)			
	comprising:			
	Fire fighting/protective installations **Security/communication installations** **Special installations**			
	Fire fighting/protective installations Fire alarms/appliances			
5.7.1	loose fire fighting equipment	m^2	-	-
5.7.2	smoke detectors; alarms and controls	m^2	-	-
5.7.3	hosereels; dry risers and extinguishers	m^2	-	-
	Sprinkler installations landlords areas; supply to shop shells; including fire alarms; appliances			
5.7.4	etc.	m^2	-	-
5.7.5	single level sprinkler systems, alarms and smoke detectors; low hazard	m^2	-	-
	Extra for			
5.7.6	ordinary hazard	m^2	-	-
5.7.7	single level sprinkler systems; alarms and smoke detectors; ordinary hazard	m^2	-	-
5.7.8	double level sprinkler systems; alarms and smoke detectors; high hazard	m^2	-	-
	Smoke vents			
5.7.9	automatic smoke vents over glazed shopping mall	m^2	-	-
5.7.10	smoke control ventilation to atria	m^2	-	-
5.7.11	Lightning protection			
	Security/communication installations			
5.7.12	Clock installation	m^2	-	-
5.7.13	Security alarm system	m^2	-	-
5.7.14	Telephone system	m^2	-	-
5.7.15	Public address, television aerial and clocks	m^2	-	-
5.7.16	Closed-circuit television	m^2	-	-
5.7.17	Public address system	m^2	-	-
5.7.18	Closed-circuit television and public address system	m^2	-	-
	Special installations Window cleaning equipment			
5.7.19	twin track	m	-	-
5.7.20	manual trolley/cradle	nr	-	-
5.7.21	automatic trolley/cradle	nr	-	-
5.7.22	Refrigeration installation for ice rinks	ice area m^2	-	-
5.7.23	Pool water treatment installation	pool area m^2	-	-
5.7.24	Laundry chute	nr	-	-
5.7.25	Sauna	nr	-	-
5.7.26	Jacuzzi installation	nr	-	-
5.7.27	Wave machine; four chamber wave generation equipment	nr	-	-
	Swimming pool; size 13.00 m x 6.00 m			
5.7.28	Extra over cost including structure; finishings, ventilation; heating and filtration	m^2	-	-

INDUSTRIAL £ range £		RETAILING £ range £		LEISURE £ range £		OFFICES £ range £		HOTELS £ range £		Item nr.
7309	17500	7453	17500	-	-	-	-	7309	17500	5.6.79
10500	24157	10500	24157	-	-	-	-	-	-	5.6.80
-	-	-	-	0.16	0.27	-	-	-	-	5.7.1
2.53	5.01	2.53	5.01	5.01	6.31	2.53	5.01	5.63	10.09	5.7.2
3.91	9.40	4.46	9.40	-	-	4.46	9.40	4.32	8.72	5.7.3
-	-	7.34	13.31	-	-	-	-	-	-	5.7.4
9.26	14.07	10.02	14.07	-	-	-	-	-	-	5.7.5
3.91	5.01	3.91	5.01	-	-	-	-	-	-	5.7.6
13.31	18.53	14.07	18.53	-	-	11.87	17.50	10.50	16.81	5.7.7
19.90	25.39	22.30	26.42	-	-	19.90	25.39	-	-	5.7.8
-	-	14.07	22.65	-	-	-	-	-	-	5.7.9
-	-	-	-	-	-	43.24	50.44	43.24	54.56	5.7.10
0.49	0.63	0.97	1.96	0.49	0.63	0.70	1.33	0.70	1.33	5.7.11
-	-	-	-	0.12	0.97	-	-	-	-	5.7.12
-	-	-	-	1.40	2.03	1.40	2.03	-	-	5.7.13
-	-	-	-	0.77	1.67	0.77	1.67	-	-	5.7.14
1.96	3.07	-	-	2.24	3.36	-	-	1.96	4.27	5.7.15
-	-	3.09	3.71	3.09	3.71	-	-	-	-	5.7.16
-	-	7.96	9.40	7.96	9.40	-	-	-	-	5.7.17
-	-	18.53	36.37	11.19	13.31	-	-	-	-	5.7.18
-	-	113.00	133.00	-	-	100.00	119.00	109.00	126.00	5.7.19
-	-	7316	8750	-	-	7316	8750	7000	8400	5.7.20
-	-	16127	20657	-	-	17157	20657	16814	20657	5.7.21
-	-	-	-	393.00	456.00	-	-	-	-	5.7.22
-	-	-	-	393.00	425.00	-	-	-	-	5.7.23
-	-	-	-	9985	12250	-	-	-	-	5.7.24
-	-	-	-	-	-	-	-	9831	12060	5.7.25
-	-	-	-	11209	15203	-	-	5891	12060	5.7.26
-	-	-	-	37161	52364	-	-	-	-	5.7.27
-	-	-	-	-	-	-	-	758.00	864.00	5.7.28

Item nr.	SPECIFICATIONS	Unit	RESIDENTIAL £ range £	
5.7	**PROTECTIVE, COMMUNICATION AND SPECIAL INSTALLATIONS - cont'd** **gross internal area served** (unless otherwise described)			
5.8	**BUILDERS' WORK IN CONNECTION WITH SERVICES** **gross internal area**			
	General builders work to			
5.8.1	main supplies, lighting and power to landlords areas	m²	-	-
5.8.2	central heating and electrical installation	m²	-	-
5.8.3	space heating and electrical installation	m²	-	-
5.8.4	central heating, electrical and lift installations	m²	-	-
5.8.5	space heating, electrical and ventilation installations	m²	-	-
5.8.6	air-conditioning	m²	-	-
5.8.7	air-conditioning and electrical installation	m²	-	-
5.8.8	air conditioning, electrical and lift installations	m²	-	-
	General builders work, including allowance for plant rooms; to			
5.8.9	central heating and electrical installations	m²	-	-
5.8.10	central heating, electrical and lift installations	m²	-	-
5.8.11	air-conditioning	m²	-	-
5.8.12	air-conditioning and electrical installation	m²	-	-
5.8.13	air-conditioning, electrical and lift installations	m²	-	-

INDUSTRIAL £ range £	RETAILING £ range £	LEISURE £ range £	OFFICES £ range £	HOTELS £ range £	Item nr.
1.40 - 4.00	- -	- -	- -	- -	5.8.1
2.90 - 9.70	4.70 - 10.80	4.70 - 10.80	7.00 - 10.80	7.00 - 10.80	5.8.2
3.80 - 10.80	6.30 - 11.20	6.30 - 11.20	8.10 - 11.20	8.10 - 11.20	5.8.3
4.20 - 11.20	7.00 - 11.90	7.00 - 11.90	9.50 - 12.60	9.50 - 12.60	5.8.4
6.30 - 14.80	9.50 - 16.10	9.50 - 17.50	13.30 - 17.50	13.30 - 17.50	5.8.5
10.60 - 16.50	12.60 - 17.50	12.60 - 17.50	15.10 - 19.60	15.10 - 19.60	5.8.6
11.90 - 17.50	14.80 - 19.60	14.80 - 19.60	16.80 - 21.70	16.80 - 21.70	5.8.7
13.30 - 19.60	16.10 - 21.70	16.10 - 21.70	18.90 - 23.10	18.90 - 23.10	5.8.8
- -	18.90 - 23.80	18.90 - 23.80	23.80 - 29.50	23.80 - 29.50	5.8.9
- -	23.80 - 29.50	23.80 - 29.50	29.50 - 33.60	29.50 - 33.60	5.8.10
- -	33.60 - 39.10	33.60 - 39.10	43.20 - 47.40	43.20 - 47.40	5.8.11
- -	43.20 - 47.40	43.20 - 47.40	53.20 - 59.00	53.20 - 59.00	5.8.12
- -	53.20 - 59.00	53.20 - 59.00	61.80 - 68.60	61.80 - 68.60	5.8.13

Keep your figures up to date, free of charge
Now available on the web at www.efnspon.com

This section, and most of the other information in this Price Book, is brought up to date every three months with the Price Book Updates, until the next annual edition.

The Updates are available free to all Price Book purchasers.

To ensure you receive your free copies, either complete the reply card from the centre of the book and return it to us or register via the website www.efnspon.com

The updates will also be available to download from the website.

Item nr.	SPECIFICATIONS	Unit	ALL AREAS £ range £	

6.1   **SITE WORK**

surface area (unless otherwise described)

comprising:

Preparatory excavation and sub-bases	**Roadbridges**
Seeded and planted areas	**Underpasses**
Sports Pitches	**Roundabouts**
Parklands	**Guard rails and parking bollards,**
Paved areas	**etc.**
Car parking alternatives	**Street furniture**
Roads and barriers	**Playground equipment**
Road Crossing	**Fencing and screen walls, ancillary**
Footbridges	**buildings etc.**

Preparatory excavation and sub-bases
Excavating

6.1.1	top soil; average 150 mm deep	m^2	0.77	-	1.40
	top soil; average 225 mm deep; preserving in spoil heaps				
6.1.2	by machine	m^2	1.40	-	1.89
6.1.3	by hand	m^2	3.43	-	5.35
	to reduce levels; not exceeding 0.25 m deep				
6.1.4	by machine	m^3	2.17	-	2.40
6.1.5	by hand	m^3	9.47	-	10.50
6.1.6	to form new foundation levels and contours	m^3	2.37	-	10.91
	Filling; imported top soil				
6.1.7	150 mm thick; spread and levelled for planting	m^2	4.39	-	5.08
	Comparative sub-bases/beds				
6.1.8	50 mm thick; sand	m^2	1.54	-	1.67
6.1.9	75 mm thick; ashes	m^2	1.33	-	1.54
6.1.10	75 mm thick; sand	m^2	2.17	-	2.37
6.1.11	50 mm thick; blinding concrete (1:8)	m^2	2.53	-	2.81
6.1.12	100 mm thick; granular fill	m^2	2.53	-	2.81
6.1.13	150 mm thick; granular fill	m^2	3.98	-	4.19
6.1.14	75 mm thick; blinding concrete (1:3:6)	m^2	3.77	-	4.19

Seeded and planted areas
Plant supply, planting, maintenance and 12 months guarantee

6.1.15	seeded areas	m^2	2.53	-	5.08
6.1.16	turfed areas	m^2	3.29	-	6.59
	Planted areas (per m^2 of surface area)				
6.1.17	herbaceous plants	m^2	2.81	-	3.77
6.1.18	climbing plants	m^2	3.77	-	6.59
6.1.19	general planting	m^2	8.44	-	17.16
6.1.20	woodland	m^2	12.76	-	25.53
6.1.21	shrubbed planting	m^2	16.81	-	47.01
6.1.22	dense planting	m^2	21.00	-	41.86
6.1.23	shrubbed area including allowance for small trees	m^2	25.25	-	59.02
	Trees				
6.1.24	advanced nursery stock trees (12 - 20 cm girth)	tree	104.00	-	126.00
	semi-mature trees; 5 - 8 m high				
6.1.25	coniferous	tree	336.00	-	847.00
6.1.26	deciduous	tree	511.00	-	1400.00

Item nr.	SPECIFICATIONS	Unit	ALL AREAS £ range £
6.1	**SITE WORK - cont'd**		
	surface area (unless otherwise described)		
	Sports pitches		
	Costs include for cultivating ground, bringing to appropriate levels for the specified game, applying fertiliser, weedkiller, seeding and rolling and white line marking with nets, posts, etc. as required		
6.1.27	football pitch (114 m x 72 m)	nr	12181
6.1.28	cricket outfield (160 m x 142 m)	nr	41451
6.1.29	cricket square (20 m x 20m) including imported marl or clay loam, bringing to accurate levels, seeding with cricket square type grass	nr	3775
6.1.30	bowling green (38 m x 38 m) rink including French drain and gravel path on four sides	nr	14995
6.1.31	grass tennis courts 1 court (35 m x 17 m) including bringing to accurate levels, chain link perimeter fencing and gate, tennis posts and net	nr	15270
6.1.32	two grass tennis courts (35 m x 32 m) ditto	pair	25907
6.1.33	artificial surface tennis courts (35 m x 17 m) including chain link fencing, gate, posts and net	nr	12044
6.1.34	two courts (45 m x 32 m) ditto	pair	22544
6.1.35	artificial football pitch, including sub-base, bitumen macadam open textured base and heavy duty "Astroturf" type carpet	nr	238000
6.1.36	golf-putting green	hole	1222
6.1.37	pitch and putt course	hole	3775 - 5730
6.1.38	full length golf course, full specifications including watering system	hole	13353 - 25299
6.1.39	championship golf course	hole	up to 93882
	Parklands		
	NOTE: Work on parklands will involve different techniques of earth shifting and cultivation. The following rates include for normal surface excavation, they include for the provision of any land drainage.		
6.1.40	Parklands, including cultivating ground, applying fertiliser, etc and seeding with parks type grass	ha	11632
6.1.41	General sports field	ha	13863
	Lakes including excavation average 10 m deep, laying 1.50 mm thick butyl rubber sheet and spreading top soil evenly on top 300 mm deep		
6.1.42	under 1 hectare in area	ha	254745
6.1.43	between 1 and 5 hectare in area	ha	238000
6.1.44	Extra for planting aquatic plants in lake top soil	m²	38.00
	Land drainage		
	NOTE: If land drainage is required on a project, the propensity of the land to flood will decide the spacing of the land drains. Costs include for excavation and backfilling of trenches and laying agricultural clay drain pipes with 75 mm diameter lateral runs average 600 mm deep, and 100 mm diameter main runs average 750 mm deep.		
	land drainage to parkland with laterals at		
6.1.45	30 m centres and main runs at 100 m centres	ha	2402
	land drainage to sportsfields with laterals at		
6.1.46	10 m centres and main runs at 33 m centres	ha	7000

Item nr.	SPECIFICATIONS	Unit	ALL AREAS £ range £		
6.1	**SITE WORK - cont'd**				
	surface area (unless otherwise described)				
	Paved areas				
	Gravel paving rolled to falls and cambers				
6.1.47	50 mm thick	m^2	1.80	-	2.30
6.1.48	paving on sub-base; including excavation	m^2	6.60	-	9.50
	Cold bitumen emulsion paving; in three layers				
6.1.49	25 mm thick	m^2	3.30	-	4.20
	Tarmacadam paving; two layers; limestone or igneous chipping finish				
6.1.50	65 mm thick	m^2	5.10	-	6.30
6.1.51	paving on sub-base; including excavation	m^2	12.20	-	17.50
	Precast concrete paving slabs				
6.1.52	50 mm thick	m^2	7.30	-	15.40
6.1.53	50 mm thick "Texitone" slabs	m^2	10.50	-	14.40
6.1.54	slabs on sub-base; including excavation	m^2	16.80	-	24.00
	Precast concrete block paviours				
6.1.55	65 mm thick "Keyblock" grey paving	m^2	14.10	-	17.50
6.1.56	65 mm thick "Mount Sorrel" grey paving	m^2	14.10	-	16.80
6.1.57	65 mm thick "Intersett" paving	m^2	14.80	-	17.50
6.1.58	60 mm thick "Pedesta" paving	m^2	11.80	-	17.50
6.1.59	paviours on sub-base; including excavation	m^2	20.20	-	28.80
	Brick paviours				
	229 mm x 114 mm x 38 mm paving bricks				
6.1.60	laid flat	m^2	23.00	-	28.80
6.1.61	laid to herringbone pattern	m^2	37.70	-	41.90
6.1.62	paviours on sub-base; including excavation	m^2	43.20	-	50.40
	Granite setts				
6.1.63	200 mm x 100 mm x 100 mm setts	m^2	59.00	-	64.50
6.1.64	setts on sub-base; including excavation	m^2	71.40	-	76.90
	York stone slab paving				
6.1.65	paving on sub-base; including excavation	m^2	76.90	-	91.30
	Cobblestone paving				
6.1.66	50 mm - 75 mm diameter	m^2	43.20	-	53.20
6.1.67	cobblestones on sub-base; including excavation	m^2	50.40	-	65.90
	Car Parking alternatives				
	Surface level parking; including lighting and drainage				
6.1.68	tarmacadam on sub-base	car	800	-	1100
6.1.69	concrete interlocking blocks	car	900	-	1200
6.1.70	"Grasscrete" precast concrete units filled with top soil and grass seed	car	490	-	670
6.1.71	at ground level with deck or building over	car	3925	-	4750
	Garages etc				
6.1.72	single car park	nr	515	-	845
6.1.73	single; traditional construction; in a block	nr	1680	-	2400
6.1.74	single; traditional construction; pitched roof	nr	3845	-	4900
6.1.75	double; traditional construction; pitched roof	nr	5250	-	6725
	Multi-storey parking; including lighting and drainage on roof of two storey shopping centre; including				
6.1.76	ramping and strengthening structure	car	3500	-	5320
6.1.77	split level/parking ramp	car	4625	-	5450
6.1.78	multi-storey flat slab	car	5600	-	6725
6.1.79	multi-storey warped slab	car	6175	-	7500
	Extra for				
6.1.80	feature cladding and pitched roof	car	750	-	1275
	Underground parking; including lighting and drainage				
6.1.81	partially underground; natural ventilation; no sprinklers	car	8000	-	11000
6.1.82	completely underground; mechanical ventilation and sprinklers	car	11000	-	14000
6.1.83	completely underground; mechanical ventilation; sprinklers and landscaped roof	car	13000	-	18000

Item nr.	SPECIFICATIONS	Unit	ALL AREAS £ range £

6.1   **SITE WORK - cont'd**

surface area (unless otherwise described)

Roads and barriers
Tarmacadam or reinforced concrete roads, including all earthworks, drainage, pavements, lighting, signs, fencing and safety barriers (where necessary); average cut 1.50 m

6.1.84	two lane road 7.30 m wide-rural location	m	1242	-	1421
6.1.85	two lane road 7.30 m wide-urban location	m	1400	-	1681
6.1.86	two lane road 10.00 m wide-rural location	m	1345	-	1544
6.1.87	two lane road 10.00 m wide-urban location	m	1544	-	1681

Road crossings
NOTE: Costs include road markings, beacons, lights, signs, advance danger signs etc.

6.1.88	Zebra crossing	nr	3225	-	3775
6.1.89	Pelican crossing	nr	13176	-	14000

Footbridges
Footbridge of either precast concrete or steel construction 4.00 m wide, 6.00 m high including deck, access stairs and ramp, parapets etc.

6.1.90	15.00 m - 20.00 m span to two lane road	nr	131044	-	145628
6.1.91	30.00 m span to four lane dual carriageway	nr	145628	-	174726

Roadbridges
Roadbridges including all excavation, reinforcement, formwork, concrete, bearings, expansion joints, deck water proofing and finishings, parapets etc.
RC bridge with precast beams

6.1.92	10.00 m span	deck area m^2	769.00
6.1.93	15.00 m span	deck area m^2	727.00
	RC bridge with prefabricated steel beams		
6.1.94	20.00 m span	deck area m^2	762.00
6.1.95	30.00 m span	deck area m^2	714.00

Underpass
Provision of underpasses to new roads, constructed as part of a road building programme
Precast concrete pedestrian underpass

6.1.96	3.00 m wide x 2.50 m high	m	2800	-	3294
	Precast concrete vehicle underpass				
6.1.97	7.00 m wide x 5.00 m high	m	7824	-	9800
6.1.98	14.00 m wide x 5.00 m high	m	19936		
	Bridge type structure vehicle underpass				
6.1.99	7.00 m wide x 5.00 m high	m	13863	-	17088
6.1.100	14.00 m wide x 5.00 m high	m	33902		

Roundabouts

6.1.101	Roundabout on existing dual carriageway; including perimeter road, drainage and lighting, signs and disruption while under construction	nr	254814	-	375187

Guard rails and parking bollards etc.

6.1.102	Open metal post and rail fencing 1.00 m high	m	94.00	-	109.00
6.1.103	Galvanised steel post and rail fencing 2.00 m high	m	105.00	-	137.00
6.1.104	Steel guard rails and vehicle barriers	m	34.00	-	50.00
	Parking bollards				
6.1.105	precast concrete	nr	75.00	-	89.00
6.1.106	steel	nr	122.00	-	161.00
6.1.107	cast iron	nr	143.00	-	196.00
6.1.108	Vehicle control barrier; manual pole	nr	659.00	-	707.00
6.1.109	Galvanised steel cycle stand	nr	28.00	-	36.00
6.1.110	Galvanised steel flag staff	nr	741.00	-	940.00

Item nr.	SPECIFICATIONS	Unit	ALL AREAS £ range £		
6.1	**SITE WORK - cont'd**				
	surface area (unless otherwise described)				
	Street Furniture				
	Reflectorised traffic signs 0.25 m² area				
6.1.111	on steel post	nr	67.00	-	122.00
	Internally illuminated traffic signs				
6.1.112	dependent on area	nr	145.00	-	196.00
	Externally illuminated traffic signs				
6.1.113	dependent on area	nr	357.00	-	940.00
	Lighting to pedestrian areas and estates				
6.1.114	roads on 4.00 m - 6.00 m columns with up to 70 W lamps	nr	161.00	-	237.00
	Lighting to main roads				
6.1.115	10.00 m -12.00 m columns with 250 W lamps	nr	371.00	-	453.00
6.1.116	12.00 m -15.00 m columns with 400 W high pressure sodium lighting	nr	474.00	-	570.00
6.1.117	Benches - hardwood and precast concrete	nr	139.00	-	189.00
	Litter bins				
6.1.118	precast concrete	nr	139.00	-	161.00
6.1.119	hardwood slatted	nr	56.00	-	75.00
6.1.120	cast iron	nr	238.00		
6.1.121	large aluminium	nr	419.00		
6.1.122	Bus stops	nr	253.00		
6.1.123	Bus stops including basic shelter	nr	583.00		
6.1.124	Pillar box	nr	210.00		
6.1.125	Telephone box	nr	2306.00		
	Playground equipment				
	Modern swings with flat rubber safety seats:				
6.1.126	four seats; two bays	nr	937.00		
6.1.127	Stainless steel slide, 3.40 m long	nr	1036.00		
6.1.128	Climbing frame - igloo type 3.20 m x 3.75 m on plan x 2.00 m high	nr	1077.00		
6.1.129	Seesaw comprising timber plank on sealed ball bearings 3960 mm x 230 mm x 70 mm thick	nr	748.00		
6.1.130	Wicksteed "Tumbleguard" type safety surfacing around play equipment	m²	63.00		
6.1.131	Bark particles type safety surfacing 150 mm thick on hardcore bed	m²	8.40		
	Fencing and screen walls, ancillary buildings etc				
	Chain link fencing; plastic coated				
6.1.132	1.20 m high	m	11.70	-	14.10
6.1.133	1.80 m high	m	16.80	-	18.90
	Timber fencing				
6.1.134	1.20 m high chestnut pale facing	m	13.10	-	15.40
6.1.135	1.80 m high close-boarded fencing	m	33.60	-	41.90
	Screen walls; one brick thick; including foundations etc.				
6.1.136	1.80 m high facing brick screen wall	m	168.00	-	210.00
6.1.137	1.80 m high coloured masonry block boundary wall	m	189.00	-	237.00
6.1.138	Squash courts, independent building, including shower	nr	50956	-	59637
	Demolish existing buildings				
6.1.139	of brick construction	m³	3.50	-	6.30

Item nr.	SPECIFICATIONS	Unit	ALL AREAS £ range £

6.20   **EXTERNAL SERVICES**

gross internal area (unless otherwise described)

Service runs
All laid in trenches including excavation
Water main

6.2.1	75 mm uPVC main in 225 mm diameter ductile iron pipe as duct	m	35.00
	Electric main		
6.2.2	600/1000 volt cables. Two core 25 mm diameter cable including 100 mm diameter clayware duct	m	23.00
	Gas main		
6.2.3	150 mm diameter ductile or cast iron gas pipe	m	35.00
	Telephone		
6.2.4	British Telecom installation in 100 mm diameter uPVC duct	m	14.10
6.2.5	External lighting (per m² of lighted area)	m²	1.80 - 2.70

Connection areas
The privatisation of telephone, water, gas, and electricity has complicated the assessment of service connection charges. Typically, service connection charges will include the actual cost of the direct connection plus an assessment of distribution costs from the main. The latter cost is difficult to estimate as it depends on the type of scheme and the distance from the mains. In addition, service charges are complicated by discounts that may be offered. For instance, the electricity boards will charge less for housing connections if the house is all electric. However, typical charges for an estate of 200 houses might be as follows

6.2.6	Water	house	384.00 - 782.00
	Electric		
6.2.7	all electric	house	196.00
6.2.8	gas/electric	house	384.00
	Extra cost of		
6.2.9	sub-station	nr	9814 - 14549
6.2.10	Gas	house	384.00 - 494.00
	Extra cost of		
6.2.11	governing station	nr	9814
6.2.12	Telephone	house	126.00
6.2.13	Sewerage	house	295.00 - 384.00

Item nr.	SPECIFICATIONS	Unit	ALL AREAS £ range £
6.3	**DRAINAGE**		
	gross internal area (unless otherwise described)		
	comprising:		
	Overall £/m² allowances		
	Comparative pipework		
	Comparative manholes		
	Overall £/m² allowances		
6.3.1	Site drainage (per m² of paved area)	m²	5.00 - 13.00
6.3.2	Building drainage (per m² of gross floor area)	m²	5.00 - 11.30
6.3.3	Drainage work beyond the boundary of the site and final connection	nr	1245 - 7549
	Drains; hand excavation, grade bottom, earthwork support, laying and jointing pipe, backfill and compact, disposal of surplus soil; land drain, clay field drain, pipes, nominal size		0.75m £
6.3.4	75 mm diameter	m	18.90
6.3.5	100 mm diameter	m	20.20
6.3.6	150 mm diameter	m	21.30
	Land drain, vitrified clay perforated sub-soil pipes, nominal size		
6.3.7	100 mm diameter	m	21.30
6.3.8	150 mm diameter	m	25.30
6.3.9	225 mm diameter	m	30.20
	Machine excavation, grade bottom, earthwork support, laying and jointing pipes and accessories, backfill and compact, disposal of surplus soil (excluding beds, benchings and coverings)		
	Vitrified clay pipes and fittings, socketted, cement and sand joints, nominal size		1.00m £
6.3.10	100 mm diameter	m	15.40
6.3.11	150 mm diameter	m	17.50
6.3.12	225 mm diameter	m	26.60
6.3.13	300 mm diameter	m	40.50
6.3.14	450 mm diameter	m	74.10
	Vitrified clay pipes and fittings, "Hepseal" socketted with push fit flexible joints, nominal size		
6.3.15	100 mm diameter	m	17.50
6.3.16	150 mm diameter	m	21.30
6.3.17	225 mm diameter	m	32.90
6.3.18	300 mm diameter	m	50.40
6.3.19	450 mm diameter	m	102.30
	Class M tested concrete centrifugally spun pipes and fittings, flexible joints, nominal size		
6.3.20	300 mm diameter	m	31.60
6.3.21	450 mm diameter	m	43.20
6.3.22	600 mm diameter	m	56.30
6.3.23	900 mm diameter	m	-
6.3.24	1200 mm diameter	m	-
	Cast iron "Timesaver" drain pipes and fittings, mechanical coupling joints, nominal size		
6.3.25	75 mm diameter	m	36.40
6.3.26	100 mm diameter	m	39.10
6.3.27	150 mm diameter	m	59.00
	uPVC pipes and fittings, lip seal coupling joints, nominal size		
6.3.28	100 mm diameter	m	12.60
6.3.29	160 mm diameter	m	16.10

AVERAGE DEPTH

1.00 m £	1.25 m £	1.50 m £	1.75 m £	2.00 m £	
25.00	32.90	47.40	56.30	64.50	6.3.4
26.60	33.60	49.10	57.60	65.90	6.3.5
28.10	35.00	50.40	59.00	68.60	6.3.6
28.10	35.00	50.40	59.00	68.60	6.3.7
30.90	37.70	54.60	61.80	70.00	6.3.8
35.00	44.60	59.00	68.60	75.50	6.3.9

AVERAGE DEPTH OF DRAIN

1.50 m £	2.00 m £	2.50 m £	3.00 m £	3.50 m £	
18.90	22.60	30.20	35.00	47.40	6.3.10
21.30	26.80	32.90	37.70	50.40	6.3.11
30.20	35.00	41.90	47.70	50.40	6.3.12
45.60	49.10	54.60	60.40	64.50	6.3.13
78.20	82.40	92.30	96.80	102.30	6.3.14
21.30	26.80	32.90	37.70	50.40	6.3.15
25.40	28.80	35.00	40.50	54.60	6.3.16
36.40	40.50	47.40	53.20	74.10	6.3.17
53.90	59.00	65.90	70.00	74.10	6.3.18
106.40	110.50	119.10	124.90	130.40	6.3.19
35.00	40.50	46.00	51.80	56.30	6.3.20
50.40	53.20	61.80	67.30	71.40	6.3.21
63.10	67.30	75.50	82.40	87.80	6.3.22
107.70	113.20	124.90	131.80	138.60	6.3.23
-	173.60	185.30	194.90	201.80	6.3.24
40.50	45.30	51.80	56.30	68.60	6.3.25
42.50	46.00	54.60	59.00	71.40	6.3.26
64.50	67.30	74.10	79.60	92.00	6.3.27
16.50	21.30	28.10	32.30	44.60	6.3.28
21.30	25.00	32.30	36.40	50.40	6.3.29

Item nr.	SPECIFICATIONS	Unit	
			1.00 m
6.3	**DRAINAGE - cont'd**		£
	gross internal area (unless otherwise described)		
	uPVC "Ultra-Rib" ribbed pipes and fittings, sealed ring push fit joints, nominal size		
6.3.30	150 mm diameter	m	14.10
6.3.31	225 mm diameter	m	21.60
6.3.32	300 mm diameter	m	30.20

			100 mm thick
			£
	Pipe beds, benching and coverings granular filling, pipe size		
6.3.33	100 mm diameter	m	1.47
6.3.34	150 mm diameter	m	1.62
6.3.35	225 mm diameter	m	1.88
6.3.36	300 mm diameter	m	2.15
6.3.37	450 mm diameter	m	2.68
6.3.38	600 mm diameter	m	2.92
	In situ concrete 10.00 N/mm^2 - 40 mm aggregate (1:3:6), pipe size		
6.3.39	100 mm diameter	m	2.96
6.3.40	150 mm diameter	m	2.96
6.3.41	225 mm diameter	m	3.49
6.3.42	300 mm diameter	m	4.15
6.3.43	450 mm diameter	m	5.34
6.3.44	600 mm diameter	m	5.89
6.3.45	900 mm diameter	m	7.08
6.3.46	1200 mm diameter	m	9.46
	In situ concrete 20.00 N/mm^2 - 20 mm aggregate (1:2:4), pipe size		
6.3.47	100 mm diameter	m	3.02
6.3.48	150 mm diameter	m	3.02
6.3.49	225 mm diameter	m	3.62
6.3.50	300 mm diameter	m	4.24
6.3.51	450 mm diameter	m	5.46
6.3.52	600 mm diameter	m	6.05
6.3.53	900 mm diameter	m	7.26
6.3.54	1200 mm diameter	m	9.69
	Brick Manholes		
	Excavate pit in firm ground, partial backfill, partial disposal, earthwork support, compact base of pit, plain in situ concrete 20.00 N/mm^2 - 20 mm aggregate (1:2:4) base, formwork, one brick wall of engineering bricks PC £175.00/1000 in cement mortar (1:3) finished fair face, vitrified clay channels, plain insitu concrete 25.00 N/mm^2 - 20 mm aggregate (1:1:5:3) benchings, reinforced insitu concrete 20.00 N/mm^2 - 20 mm aggregate (1:2:4) cover and reducing slabs, fabric reinforcement, formwork step irons, cast iron cover and frame, depth from cover to invert		600mm x450mm
			£
6.3.55	0.75 m	nr	240.00
6.3.56	1.00 m	nr	294.00
6.3.57	1.25 m	nr	353.00
6.3.58	1.50 m	nr	406.00
6.3.59	1.75 m	nr	463.00
	with reducing slab and brick shaft internal size 600 mm x 450 mm; depth from cover to invert		
6.3.60	2.00 m	nr	-
6.3.61	2.50 m	nr	-
6.3.62	3.00 m	nr	-
6.3.63	3.50 m	nr	-
6.3.64	4.00 m	nr	-

AVERAGE DEPTH OF DRAIN					Item nr
1.50 m	2.00 m	2.50 m	3.00 m	3.50 m	
£	£	£	£	£	
17.50	21.30	28.80	34.30	46.70	6.3.30
25.40	30.20	36.40	41.90	44.60	6.3.31
35.00	37.70	44.60	50.40	54.60	6.3.32

BED	BED AND BENCHING		BED AND COVERING		
150 mm thick	100 mm thick	150 mm thick	100 mm thick	150 mm thick	
£	£	£	£	£	
2.15	2.92	3.21	4.24	6.27	6.3.33
2.40	3.03	3.51	5.19	7.07	6.3.34
2.68	3.93	4.67	7.07	9.11	6.3.35
2.92	4.49	5.81	8.48	10.83	6.3.36
3.87	6.81	8.13	12.09	15.24	6.3.37
4.56	8.85	10.16	15.55	18.36	6.3.38
4.15	5.53	6.19	7.75	11.61	6.3.39
4.74	6.19	6.84	9.03	12.90	6.3.40
5.34	7.43	8.65	12.90	16.77	6.3.41
5.89	8.65	11.12	15.47	20.00	6.3.42
7.69	13.01	15.47	21.92	27.75	6.3.43
8.88	16.70	19.76	28.38	33.55	6.3.44
11.23	27.18	31.55	43.22	54.83	6.3.45
13.57	40.19	44.50	59.35	77.41	6.3.46
4.24	5.67	6.33	7.92	11.87	6.3.47
4.86	6.33	7.00	9.24	13.20	6.3.48
5.46	7.60	8.87	13.20	17.21	6.3.49
6.05	8.87	11.39	15.84	20.45	6.3.50
7.88	13.31	15.85	22.44	28.38	6.3.51
9.09	17.10	20.25	29.30	34.33	6.3.52
11.50	27.85	32.31	44.21	56.10	6.3.53
13.93	41.16	45.55	60.72	79.20	6.3.54

INTERNAL SIZE OF MANHOLE

750mm x 450mm	900mm x 600mm	900mm x 900mm	900mm x 1500mm	1200mm x 1800mm	
£	£	£	£	£	
262.00	323.00	373.00	500.00	627.00	6.3.55
321.00	391.00	453.00	600.00	748.00	6.3.56
383.00	464.00	537.00	704.00	873.00	6.3.57
443.00	534.00	618.00	803.00	992.00	6.3.58
502.00	604.00	697.00	905.00	1115.00	6.3.59
-	-	771.00	983.00	1194.00	6.3.60
-	-	924.00	1161.00	1401.00	6.3.61
-	-	1042.00	1283.00	1532.00	6.3.62
-	-	1153.00	1404.00	1658.00	6.3.63
-	-	1267.00	1522.00	1783.00	6.3.64

Item nr.	SPECIFICATIONS	Unit

6.3   **DRAINAGE - cont'd**

gross internal area (unless otherwise described)

Concrete manholes
Excavate pit in firm ground, disposal, earthwork support, compact base of pit, plain insitu concrete 20.00 N/mm^2 - 20 mm aggregate (1:2:4) base, formwork, reinforced precast concrete chamber and shaft rings, taper pieces and cover slabs bedded jointed and pointed in cement:mortar (1:3), weak mix concrete filling to working space, vitrified clay channels, plain insitu concrete 25.00 N/mm^2 - 20 mm aggregate (1:1:5:3) benchings, step irons, cast iron cover and frame; depth from cover to invert

6.3.65	0.75 m	nr
6.3.66	1.00 m	nr
6.3.67	1.25 m	nr
6.3.68	1.50 m	nr
6.3.69	1.75 m	nr

with taper piece and shaft 675 mm diameter; depth from cover to invert

6.3.70	2.00 m	nr
6.3.71	2.50 m	nr
6.3.72	3.00 m	nr
6.3.73	3.50 m	nr
6.3.74	4.00 m	nr

| INTERNAL DIAMETER OF MANHOLE | | | Item nr |
1350 mm £	1500 mm £	1800 mm £	
406.00	480.00	630.00	6.3.65
457.00	535.00	697.00	6.3.66
508.00	593.00	770.00	6.3.67
560.00	649.00	839.00	6.3.68
609.00	704.00	906.00	6.3.69
747.00	883.00	1060.00	6.3.70
852.00	965.00	1206.00	6.3.71
946.00	1068.00	1340.00	6.3.72
1034.00	1167.00	1467.00	6.3.73
1120.00	1267.00	1594.00	6.3.74

Cost Limits and Allowances

Information given under this heading is based upon the cost targets currently in force for buildings financed out of public funds, i.e., hospitals, schools, universities and public authority housing. The information enables the cost limit for a scheme to be calculated and is not intended to be a substitute for estimates prepared from drawings and specifications.

The cost limits are generally set as target costs based upon the user accommodation. However ad-hoc additions can be agreed with the relevant Authority in exceptional circumstances.

The documents setting out cost targets are almost invariably complex and cover a range of differing circumstances. They should be studied carefully before being applied to any scheme; this study should preferably be undertaken in consultation with a Chartered Quantity Surveyor.

The cost limits for Public Authority housing generally known as the "Housing Cost Yardstick" have been replaced by a system of new procedures. The cost criteria prepared by the Department of the Environment that have superseded the Housing Cost Yardstick are intended as indicators and not cost limits.

HOSPITAL BUILDINGS

Cost Allowances for all health buildings are now set at a MIPS Variation of Price (VOP) index level of 295 with a firm price (FP) differential allowance of 5.1% increase on the VOP level, that is, an FP index level of 310. The effective date for these increased allowances was 1 April 1998.

Both the Cost Allowances (DCAGs) and the Equipment Cost Allowance Guides (ECAGs) are now included in version 1.0 of the Health Capital Investment (HCI) document, issued in March 1997. This supersedes previous publications including version 13 of the Concise 4D/DCAG database. In the HCI, the costs of ECAGs are revised to a June 1997 Equipment Price Index level of 673.

"Quarterly Briefing" is now the official document for the notification of all new/revised DCAGs and ECAGs. Users should check Briefings issued from and including volume 7 no. 1 to ensure that all revisions to the HCI have been identified.

Further advice can be obtained from:

NHS Estates
Department of Health
1 Trevelyan Square
Boar Lane
Leeds
LS1 6AE
Tel: 0113 254 7000

UNIVERSITY BUILDINGS

The Universities Funding Council and the Polytechnics & Colleges Funding Council merged in April 1993 to form the Higher Education Funding Council for England. Procedures for appraising funding requirements for University buildings have been under review for a number of years and due to public spending constraints the Government have encouraged the use of Private Finance Initiatives for proposed estates projects. For guidance on techniques to be used by higher education institutions when appraising proposals that involve the development, ownership, leasing and occupation of land and buildings contact:

Higher Education Funding Council for England
Northavon House
Coldharbour Lane
Bristol
BS16 1QD
Tel: 0117 931 7317

Information regarding Scotland and Wales can be obtained from:

Scottish Higher Education Funding Council
Donaldson House
97 Haymarket Terrace
Edinburgh
EH12 5HD
Tel: 0131 313 6500

Higher Education Funding Council for Wales
Lambourne House
Cardiff Business Park
Llanishen
Cardiff
CF4 5GL
Tel: 01222 761861

EDUCATIONAL BUILDINGS (Procedures and Cost Guidance)

In January 1986 the then Department of Education and Science introduced new procedures for the approval of educational building projects.

In its Administrative Memorandum 1/86 and subsequent letter AB13/12/028, dated 12 November 1991, the Department currently requires detailed individual approval only for projects costing £2 million and over. Minor works i.e., costing less than £200,000, require no approval except where the authority requires such or where statutory notices are involved. Projects of £200,000, up to £2 million require approval which will be given automatically upon the submission of particulars of the scheme and performance data relating to it.

Capital works and repair projects supported by grant from the Department for Education will continue to require individual approval.

EDUCATIONAL BUILDINGS

The Department for Education and Employment publishes information on costs and performance data for school building projects.

Building Guide Costs

The Building Guide Costs are intended to provide reasonable and achievable target costs for use in the cost planning of new schools and extensions. The values relate to median values between middle and lower quartile costs in LEA projects.

The Building Guide Costs relate to Q1 1999 national average price levels. The values *exclude* the cost of:

- 'Abnormal' substructure costs (i.e. the proportion of the total substructure costs over £57/m^2 at Q1 1999 prices).
- External works.
- Furniture, fittings and equipment, whether built-in or loose.
- Fees and VAT.

If used as the basis for project cost planning, the values should be adjusted to take account of tender date, location and contract size factors. Other factors affecting costs will include design, specification and site conditions. The guide values for primary and secondary extensions are intended to relate to projects providing an average mix of accommodation types. Actual costs may therefore be higher in schemes providing disproportionately more specialist accommodation.

The Building Guide Costs may be adjusted to reflect tender price movements by reference to DETR's PUBSEC index. It is suggested that adjustments for location and contract size may be made by reference to factors published by the RICS's Building Cost Information Service.

The table below provides indicative unit costs for four common types of project. The Department intends to use these values for reference when scrutinising cost standards in grant-aided school projects.

Building Guide Costs per m^2 at Q1 1999 prices
(Relating to DETR PUBSEC indicative index 115, Q1 1999)
(NOTE: DETR PUBSEC indicative index 1995 = 100)

New primary school	£774/m^2
Primary extension	£738/m^2
New secondary school	£692/m^2
Secondary extension	£680/m^2

HOUSING ASSOCIATION SCHEMES

Grant rates 1999/2000 and other current literature is available from The Housing Corporation, 149 Tottenham Court Road, London, W1P 0BN. Tel: 0171 393 2000. For the benefit of readers, the TCI system instigated by Housing Corporation Circular HC 33/91 has been reproduced here in full and amended to accord with the cost information in F2 - 29/98 and Guidance Notes effective from 1 April 1999.

Advises associations of:

(i)   the Total Cost Indicators, and grant rates effective from 1 April 1999.

(ii)   the grant rates applicable to 1999/2000 approvals for mixed and publicly funded schemes for rent and housing for sale schemes approved under the Housing Act 1988 and funded by the Housing Corporation or by local authorities.

The Association Investment Profile system, and the associated Guidance **(last updated in September 1989),** has now been withdrawn and replaced by a new, simpler system entitled Performance Assessment and Investment Summary (PAIS). This brings together the various assessments of associations made by the Corporation in the following areas, to inform its decisions on making allocation to associations:

♦   Development Programme Delivery
♦   Development Function
♦   Scheme Audit
♦   Control and Conduct
♦   Landlord
♦   Financial Control
♦   Financial Health

The further reduction in grant rates for **1995/96** led the Corporation to develop improved tools for satisfying itself that associations developing for rent or sale using mixed funding will be in a position to raise the necessary private finance. The Corporation has a duty to safeguard the public investment in associations and the interests of the existing occupiers of their dwellings. As part of the Financial Health element of the PAIS, the Corporation will therefore appraise associations' financial position against typical private lender tests of gearing and interest cover.

The Corporation's objective in carrying out these tests is to satisfy itself before making mixed funded allocations that associations will in due course be able to obtain the necessary private finance. If an association has difficulty at present in satisfying the Corporation tests it will discuss with it its ability, over an agreed timescale, to satisfy typical private lender tests. It will not be debarred from receiving allocations; if it can show to the Corporation's satisfaction that it will be able to secure the necessary private finance when it is required, its bids for ADP resources will be considered.

Conversely, satisfying the tests will not carry an automatic entitlement to an allocation.

From 1 April 1995, special needs schemes receiving approval for Special Needs Management Allowance (SNMA) will no longer necessarily receive a grant rate of 100%. The grant rate will be determined on a scheme by scheme basis at 100% or such lower level as is embodied in the association's bid for funding.

Enquiries about the contents of this Circular to Regional offices of the Corporation.

Annex to Circular HC 27/93

PERFORMANCE ASSESSMENT AND INVESTMENT SUMMARY (PAIS)

Introduction

(i) The Performance Assessment and Investment Summary (PAIS) is designed to assist accountable investment decisions by the Corporation by ensuring that all relevant aspects of an association's performance are taken into account. The PAIS therefore fulfils the same function as, and supersedes, the previous system of Association Investment Profiles.

(ii) A PAIS will be produced annually for each association seeking development funding from the corporation. (Associations seeking only TIS or Miscellaneous Works allocations will not normally have a PAIS). Each association will receive a single PAIS from the Corporation, produced by the lead Regional Director for the association.

Contents of the PAIS

(iii) The PAIS brings together the Corporation's most recent assessments of associations under the following general headings.

- Development Programme Delivery
- Development Function
- Scheme Audit
- Control and Conduct (embracing control and propriety, accountability, agency services, and equal opportunities).
- Landlord (embracing access to housing; housing management and maintenance)
- Financial Control
- Financial Health

(iv) The sources for the above are:

- Performance audit reports
- Scheme audit reports
- Programme Delivery assessments (see paragraph (viii) below)
- Annual accounts review
- Quarterly financial returns.

Associations will previously have been informed of any areas of concern in all of these areas; the process of producing the PAIS does not involve the Corporation in making any fresh judgements of the association's performance.

(v) **It is essential that associations provide both audited annual accounts and quarterly financial returns to the published timetables.**

(vi) As well as recording the assessments previously made, the PAIS also includes a brief narrative summarising the performance of the association and setting out the implications, as seen by the Corporation, for future ADP-funded development by the association. This narrative will take into account the association response to any Corporation concerns expressed in the earlier assessments. If any new assessment which substantively alters the position is made by the Corporation between the issue of a PAIS and allocation decisions being made, the Corporation will issue an updated PAIS.

(vii) The format and content of the PAIS as initially used in the current year will be further developed by the Corporation in the light of experience and feedback, and to take account of changes in the Corporation's regulatory arrangements. Comments on the PAIS issued this year will therefore be welcome, and should be sent to the lead Regional Director for the association.

Programme Delivery Assessment

(viii)   The PDA summarises the association's performance on the ADP in the following areas:

- ◆   Cash Spend Performance
- ◆   Allocation performance for each programme heading
- ◆   Cost Control/Development Finance (embracing cost movement between allocation and scheme approval; cost overruns post-approval; prompt payment of debts to the Corporation; prompt submission of HAG recovery forms to the Corporation).

(ix)   Programme Delivery Assessments (PDA) will in future be produced during the first quarter of each financial year, covering the association's performance during the previous year.

(x)   A separate PDA will be sent to the association by each Corporation Region in which it had a Cash Planning Target (CPT) in the relevant year.

TOTAL COST INDICATORS 1999/2000 GUIDANCE NOTES

1.   Introduction

1.1   These guidance notes are designed to explain the use of Total Cost Indicators (TCI) and grant rates in the Social Housing Grant (SHG) funding framework. They are intended to help registered social landlords (RSLs) complete scheme submissions. The notes are effective from 1 April 1999.

1.2   Enquiries about the contents of this guidance should be directed to the regional offices of the Housing Corporation.

2.   Main changes from the 1998/99 TCI

2.1   The main change from the 1998/99 Total Cost Indicators is that a number of local authority areas have changed TCI cost groups, reflecting latest evidence of relative costs.

3.   Explanation of TCI

3.1   A key objective of the funding system is to achieve value for money in return for grant, and to ensure the correct level of grant is paid. TCI form the basis of this system, and are divided into unit type and cost group area categories.

3.2   TCI apply equally to units funded with SHG by the Housing Corporation, or those sponsored by a local authority.

3.3   TCI represents the basis for a cost evaluation of SHG funded units. TCI are also used to calculate the maximum level of grant or other public subsidy payable. Further details on this inter-relationship between TCI and grant levels are given in the separate grant rate guidance notes on page 839.

3.4   Key and supplementary multipliers are applied to the base TCI figures to allow for scheme variations as outlined in the multiplier tables on pages 823 to 829. Thus, there is a relationship between the base norm cost of a unit and its unit type.

4.   Types of accommodation

4.1   Different types of accommodation other than self contained housing for general needs are classified as follows:

4.2   Accommodation for older people

(i)   Category 1 - self-contained accommodation for the more active older person, which may include an element of support and/or additional communal facilities;

(ii)   Category 2 - self-contained accommodation for the less active older person, which includes an element of support and the full range of communal facilities;

The term "sheltered" is used generally to describe Category 1 and Category 2 schemes;

(iii)   Frail older people - supported extra care accommodation, which may be either shared or self-contained, for the frail older person. Includes the full range of communal facilities, plus additional special features, including wheelchair user environments and supportive management.

4.3   Shared accommodation

Accommodation predominantly for single persons, which includes a degree of sharing between tenants of some facilities (e.g. kitchens, bathrooms, living room) and may include an element of support and/or additional communal facilities.

4.4   Supported housing

Accommodation, which may be either shared or self-contained, designed to meet the needs of particular user groups for intensive housing management (see the Housing Corporation's Guide to Supported Housing). Such accommodation may also include additional communal facilities.

4.5   Accommodation for wheelchair users

Accommodation, which may be either shared or self-contained, designed for independent living by people with physical disabilities and wheelchair users. Where such accommodation is incorporated within schemes containing communal facilities, these facilities should be wheelchair accessible.

4.6   Communal facilities

Ancillary communal accommodation, the range of which comprises:

(i)   Common room - consisting of common room/s of adequate size to accommodate tenants and occasional visitors, chair store and kitchenette for tea-making;

(ii)   Associated communal facilities - consisting of warden's office, laundry room and guest room.

5.   Treatment of combined supported housing and general needs schemes

5.1   Arrangements exist which allow the combination of supported housing and general needs units within a single scheme. Further guidance with regards to supported housing schemes is set out on page 824.

6.   Temporary housing

6.1   Temporary Social Housing (TSH) Grant and Temporary Market Rent Housing (TMRH) Grant are terms used to describe SHG paid to RSLs to cover the cost of bringing properties into temporary use.

6.2   TSH and TMRH are procedurally the same. In practice, there has been little difference between rent levels on each programme. For 1999/2000 therefore there will be a single temporary housing programme, referred to in this guidance as TSH.

6.3   Properties are eligible for TSH Grant if they are available for use by the RSL for a period of time covered by a lease or licence for not less than two years and not more than 29 years.

6.4   A capital grant contribution will be available towards initial acquisition costs or periodic lease charges up to a grant maximum. The maxima are based upon the Housing Corporation's own assessment of what constitutes a reasonable contribution to the capitalised lease value. This is calculated using capitalised lease premium factors.

6.2   The *TSH multipliers and capitalised lease premium factor tables for 1999/2000* are included in this guidance on pages 829 and 830.

7.   The composition of TCI

7.1   TCI comprise the following elements:

Acquisition

(i)   Purchase price of land/property.

Works

(i)   Main works contract costs (including where applicable adjustments for additional claims and fluctuations, but excluding any costs defined as on-costs below) (see note below);

(ii)   major site development works (where applicable). These include piling, soil stabilisation, road/sewer construction, major demolition;

(iii)   major pre-works (rehabilitation) where applicable;

(iv)   statutory agreements, associated bonds and party wall agreements (including all fees and charges directly attributable to such works) where applicable;

(v)   additional costs associated with complying with archaeological works and party wall agreement awards (including all fees, charges and claims attributable to such works) where applicable;

(vi)   home loss and associated costs. This applies to new build only;

(vii)   VAT on the above, where applicable.

On-Costs

(i)   Legal fees, disbursements and expenses;

(ii)   stamp duty;

(iii)   net gains/losses via interest charges on development period loans;

(iv)   building society or other valuation and administration fees;

(v)   fees for building control and planning permission;

(vi)   fees and charges associated with compliance with European Community directives, and the Housing Corporation's requirements relating to energy rating of dwellings;

(vii)   in-house or external consultants' fees, disbursements and expenses (where the development contract is a design and build contract) (see note below);

(viii)   insurance premiums including building warranty and defects/liability insurance (except contract insurance included in works costs);

(ix)   contract performance bond premiums;

(x)   borrowing administration charges (including associated legal and valuation fees);

(xi)   an appropriate proportion of the RSL's development and administration costs (formerly Acquisition and Development allowances), excluding Co-operative Promotional Allowance (CPA) and Special Projects Promotion Allowances (SPPA) and including an appropriate proportion of any abortive scheme costs;

(xii)   furniture, loose fittings and furnishings;

(xiii)   home loss and disturbance payments for rehabilitation;

On-Costs - cont'd

(xiv)   preliminary minor site development works (new build), pre-works (rehabilitation), and minor works (off-the-shelf) and minor works and repairs in connection with existing satisfactory purchases;

(xv)   marketing costs - for sale schemes only;

(xvi)   post completion interest - for sale schemes only;

(xvii)   legal, administrative and related fees and costs associated with negotiating and arranging leases - for TSH only;

(xviii)   VAT on the above, where applicable.

Note: Where the development contract is design and build, the on-costs are deemed to include the builder's design fee element of the contract sum. Therefore the amount included by the builder for design fees should be deducted from the works cost element submitted by the RSL to the Housing Corporation.

Similarly, other non-works costs that may be included by the builder such as fees for building and planning permission, building warranty and defects/liability insurance, contract performance bond and energy rating of dwellings should also be deducted from the works cost element submitted by the RSL to the Housing Corporation.

The Housing Corporation will subsequently check compliance through its compliance audit framework.

8.   Explanation of on-costs

8.1   TCI are inclusive of on-costs contained in the relevant on-cost table. The on-costs vary according to TCI cost group and the general purpose of the scheme. TCI levels are set with the assumption that the RSL's development and administrative costs will be contained within the percentages in the relevant on-cost table.

8.2   In order to allow a proper comparison between the total eligible costs and the relevant TCI it is necessary to add the percentage on-cost (from the relevant table) to the estimated eligible costs of acquisition and works.

8.3   Major repairs schemes and adaptation schemes are not measured against TCI. However, on-costs (from the relevant table) should be added to such schemes. Supplementary on-costs may not be used in any circumstances in connection with major repairs or adaptation schemes.

9.   Selection of on-costs

9.1   One key on-cost will apply per scheme. To this should be added any appropriate supplementary on-cost.

9.2   Supplementary on-costs may be used when the accommodation is designed to meet the relevant standards set out in the Housing Corporation publication Scheme Development Standards (latest version August 1998).

9.3   The appropriate key or supplementary on-cost is determined by the predominant dwelling type in a scheme. Predominance is established, where necessary, by the largest number of persons in total.

9.4   Where two key on-costs or two supplementary on-costs are equally applicable (e.g. supported housing and shared), the higher should be used.

KEY ON-COSTS 1999/2000 BY COST GROUP

Note: only one of the following to be used.

Key on-costs			A %	B %	C %	D %	E %
a)	**New Build**						
	(i)	acquisition and works	12	13	13	14	15
	(ii)	off-the-shelf	7	7	7	7	7
	(iii)	works only	16	16	16	16	16
b)	**Rehabilitation**						
	(i)	acquisition and works					
		- vacant	12	13	13	14	14
		- tenanted	15	15	16	18	18
	(ii)	existing satisfactory	9	9	9	9	9
	(iii)	purchase and repair	7	7	7	7	7
	(iv)	works only					
		- vacant	21	21	21	21	21
		- tenanted	26	26	26	26	26
	(v)	re-improvements	21	21	21	21	21
	(vi)	TSH					
		- unimproved vacant	21	21	21	21	21
		- improved vacant	9	9	9	9	9
c)	**Major repairs and miscellaneous works**		25	25	25	25	25
d)	**Adaptation works**		13	13	13	13	13

SUPPLEMENTARY ON-COSTS 1999/2000

	Supplementary on-costs (all cost groups)	Purchase & Repair and Acquisition & Works %	Works only and reimprovements %	Off-the-Shelf existing satisfactory %
a)	Sheltered with common room or communal facilities	+2	+3	+1
b)	Frail older persons	+4	+5	+3
c)	Supported housing:			
	I) supported housing	+4	+5	+3
	ii) with common room or communal facilities	+5	+7	+4
d)	Shared	+5	+7	+5
e)	Standard house types	-1	-2	0
f)	Housing for Sale	+8	+11	+5
g)	TSH:			
	I) shared unimproved +7			
	ii) shared improved +5			

10. Tranches

10.1 For units developed under the Housing Act 1988, a set percentage of approved grant can be paid once a unit reaches certain key development stages. These grant payments are known as tranches.

10.2 The key stages are:

(i) exchange of purchase contracts (ACQ);

(ii) start on site of main contract works (SOS); this is deemed to be the date when the contractor took possession of the site/property in accordance with the signed main building contract;

(iii) practical completion of the scheme (PC).

10.3 Where a *public subsidy* is given by way of discounted land, (acquisition public subsidy), the whole subsidy is deducted from the first tranche; any excess balance should be deducted from the second tranche. This is to ensure that grant is not paid in advance of need. In other circumstances any other public subsidy will be deducted from each tranche on a pro-rata basis.

10.4 In the case of *land inclusive packages* the first and second tranches are paid together at start on site stage.

10.5 Tranche details for Special Project Promotion Allowances (SPPA) and Co-op Promotion Allowances (CPA), together with further guidance relating to tranches got management contracting arrangements, can be found in the Capital Funding System Procedure Guide.

10.6 The grant on outstanding mortgages for reimprovement schemes will be paid in accordance with the tranche percentage for the scheme.

10.7 All tranche payments may be paid directly to RSLs rather than via solicitors.

GRANT PAYMENTS FOR TRANCHES 1999/2000

Tranche percentages

Housing for Rent	Scheme	Cost Groups	Acquisition & Works			Works Only & Reimprovements		Off-Shelf/ Existing Satisfactory	Purchase & Repair	
			(I)	(ii)	(iii)	(ii)	(iii)	(I)	(I)	(ii)
Mixed Funded	New Build	ALL	40%	40%	20%	65%	35%	100%	80%	20%
	Rehab.	ALL	50%	30%	20%	60%	40%	100%		
100% SHG	New Build	A, B & C	30%	35%	35%	50%	50%	100%		
		D & E	20%	35%	45%	45%	55%	100%		
	Rehab.	A, B & C	50%	20%	30%	40%	60%	100%	80%	20%
		D & E	45%	20%	35%	35%	65%	100%	80%	20%
TSH	Un-improved					65%	35%			
	Improved							100%		
Housing for Sale										
Mixed Funded	New Build & Rehab.	ALL	50%	45%	5%	95%	5%	100%	95%	5%

11. The use of the TCI base table

11.1 The unit size in square metres shown in the TCI *base table 1999/2000: self-contained accommodation* (on page 822) relates to the total floor area of the unit. The probable occupancy figure in the tables is only a guideline figure. The number of occupants is derived from the total number of bedspaces provided.

11.2 The TCI for a unit where total floor area exceeds 120 m^2 will be the cost of a unit of 115 - 120 m^2 plus for each additional 5 m^2 or part thereof, the difference between the cost of a 110 - 115 m^2 unit, and the cost of a 115 - 120 m^2 unit.

11.3 In calculating the appropriate TCI floor area band the relevant floor area should be rounded to nearest whole number.

For self-contained accommodation

11.4 Self-contained units provide each household, defined as a tenancy, with all their basic facilities behind their own lockable front door.

11.5 For self-contained units the base TCI is determined by its total floor area and the cost group in which it is located. The dwelling floor area is determined by the area of each unit for the private use of a single household. Communal areas or any facilities shared by two or more households should be excluded.

11.6 The total floor area of self-contained accommodation is measured to the finished internal faces of the main containing walls on each floor of the accommodation and includes the space, on plan, taken up by private staircases, partitions, internal walls (but not "party" or similar walls), chimney breasts, flues and heating appliances. It includes the area of tenants' internal and/or external essential storage space. It excludes:

For self-contained accommodation - cont'd

    (i)   any space where the height to the ceiling is less than 1.50 m (e.g. areas in rooms with sloping ceilings, external dustbin enclosures);

    (ii)   any porch, covered way; etc., open to the air;

    (iii)   all balconies (private, escape and access) and decks;

    (iv)   non-habitable basements, attics or sheds;

    (v)   external storage space in excess of 2.50 m^2;

    (vi)   all space for purposes other than housing (e.g. garages, commercial premises etc.).

11.7   The TCI for Frail older persons dwellings should always be calculated as *self-contained* units even if they have some characteristics which are more typical of shared accommodation.

For shared accommodation

11.8   Shared accommodation is defined as one household (i.e. one tenancy or licence) which shares facilities (i.e. bathroom, kitchen) with other households. Each household sharing such accommodation may comprise more than one person. The base TCI for shared accommodation should be calculated separately to any self-contained accommodation in the scheme. The base TCI for shared accommodation is calculated on a per bedspace basis and may include any staff with a residential tenancy for shared accommodation. Staff sleep over accommodation which is not subject to a tenancy is not regarded as a bedspace for TCI purposes. The relevant base TCI cost for the cost group from the *TCI base table 1999/2000: shared accommodation* on page 822 is used.

For TSH shared accommodation

11.9   The relevant floor area, for TCI and capitalised lease premium calculation purposes only, should be taken as the overall building gross floor area measured to the finished internal faces of the main containing walls all as otherwise described for self-contained units above, divided by the number of people sharing. This calculation will result in the correct band size per person sharing which will then be used to select the base figure from the TCI base table: self-contained on page 822. This figure should then be multiplied by the number of people sharing prior to applying the relevant TSH key and supplementary multipliers or capitalised lease premium factor.

TCI BASE TABLE 1999/2000: SELF CONTAINED ACCOMMODATION

Total unit costs		All self-contained accommodation (including all frail older persons and TSH) £ per unit Cost Group				
Unit Floor Area (m²)	Probable occupancy (persons)	A	B	C	D	E
Up to 25	1	51,400	43,000	38,300	35,300	32,900

Exceeding/not exceeding

25/30	1	56,500	47,100	41,700	38,100	35,400
30/35	1 and 2	61,600	51,200	45,100	40,900	37,800
35/40	1 and 2	66,700	55,300	48,400	43,700	40,300
40/45	2	71,800	59,400	51,800	46,500	42,800
45/50	2	76,900	63,500	55,100	49,300	45,200
50/55	2 and 3	82,000	67,500	58,500	52,100	47,700
55/60	2 and 3	87,100	71,600	61,900	54,900	50,200
60/65	3 and 4	92,200	75,700	65,200	57,700	52,700
65/70	3 and 4	97,300	79,800	68,600	60,500	55,100
70/75	3, 4 and 5	102,500	83,900	71,900	63,300	57,600
75/80	3, 4 and 5	107,000	87,500	74,900	65,700	59,700
80/85	4, 5 and 6	111,600	91,200	77,900	68,200	61,900
85/90	4, 5 and 6	116,100	94,800	80,900	70,600	64,000
90/95	5 and 6	120,700	98,400	83,800	73,100	66,200
95/100	5 and 6	125,300	102,000	86,800	75,500	68,300
100/105	6 and 7	129,800	105,600	89,800	78,000	70,500
105/110	6 and 7	134,400	109,300	92,700	80,400	72,600
110/115	6, 7 and 8	138,900	112,900	95,700	82,900	74,800
115/120	6, 7 and 8	143,500	116,500	98,700	85,300	76,900

TCI BASE TABLE 1999/2000: SHARED ACCOMMODATION

	All shared accommodation (except TSH) £ per person sharing Cost Group				
Total costs per person	A	B	C	D	E
Each person bedspace	60,600	49,500	42,400	37,100	33,700

12. Selection of key multipliers

12.1   Only one key multiplier can be used per unit.

12.2   *New build acquisition and works* is the basic key multiplier, hence its neutral value.

12.3   The *off-the-shelf* multiplier is used where new dwellings to a standard suitable for social housing letting are purchased, following inspection, from contractors/developers or their agents. The cost of any minor works required should be set against the on-cost allowance.

12.4   The *existing satisfactory* multiplier is used where existing dwellings of a standard and in a condition suitable for social housing letting are purchased, following inspection, from the second-hand property market. The cost of any minor works required should be set against the on-cost allowance.

12.5   The *purchase and repair* multiplier is used where existing dwellings are purchased, following inspection, from the property market which necessitate a degree of repair to bring them to a standard and condition suitable for social housing but not full rehabilitation. Purchase and repair classification will apply where the estimated repair/improvement costs of each dwelling exceed £1,500 but are less than £10,000.

12.6   The *works only* multiplier is used for accommodation which involves the development of land or property already in the RSL's ownership and for which no acquisition costs (other than legal charges) apply.

12. Selection of key multipliers - cont'd

12.7 The *reimprovement* multiplier is used for dwellings which have already received some form of public/grant subsidy and are now being rehabilitated. Reimprovement schemes are generally expected to be submitted no less than 15 years after a rehabilitation or 30 years after construction. It should be noted that the outstanding mortgage of the original works can be considered an eligible cost and will attract the grant rate applicable to the new scheme as a whole. The reimprovement key multiplier is now linked to that of the Rehabilitation works only (vacant) multiplier rather than the Rehabilitation works only (tenanted) multiplier in order to reflect the average cost of provision.

12.8 The *TSH improved and unimproved vacant* multiplier is used for accommodation with a lease of between two and 29 years.

KEY MULTIPLIERS 1999/2000 BY COST GROUP
Note: only one of the following to be used.

Scheme Type		TCI calc. form line No.	A	B	Cost group C	D	E
a)	New build						
(i)	acquisition and works	0010	1.00	1.00	1.00	1.00	1.00
(ii)	off-the-shelf	0020	0.96	0.95	0.95	0.94	0.93
(iii)	works only	0090	0.65	0.68	0.75	0.83	0.87
b)	Rehabilitation						
(i)	acquisition and works						
	- vacant	0100	1.23	1.13	1.07	1.03	1.01
	- tenanted	0105	1.16	1.06	1.01	0.97	0.96
(ii)	existing satisfactory	0120	0.96	0.95	0.95	0.94	0.93
(iii)	purchase and repair	0110	0.95	0.93	0.93	0.92	0.91
(iv)	works only						
	- vacant	0125	0.61	0.57	0.57	0.61	0.63
	- tenanted	0130	0.64	0.59	0.60	0.63	0.66
(v)	Re-improvements	0135	0.61	0.57	0.57	0.61	0.63
(vi)	TSH						
	- vacant improved	0030	1.23	1.13	1.07	1.03	1.01
	- vacant unimproved	0035	1.23	1.13	1.07	1.03	1.01

13.   Selection of supplementary multipliers

13.1   *The table on page 826 is used for acquisition and works, off-the-shelf, existing satisfactory and purchase and repair schemes. For other scheme types use the table on page 827. None of these supplementary multipliers are applicable to TSH schemes.*

13.2   Supplementary multipliers can be applied to new build and rehabilitation units when the accommodation is designed to meet the relevant standards set out in the Corporation publication Scheme Development Standards.

13.3   More than one supplementary multiplier can be used per unit. However certain combinations of multipliers are invalid. Multipliers for sheltered, frail older people, supported housing and extended families cannot be combined. The matrix on page 828 gives a comprehensive list of valid combinations of multipliers.

13.4   The main reason for combinations of multipliers being invalid is that the combination of those multipliers would lead to a duplication of the financial provision for the facilities accounted for in the multipliers. e.g. category 2 includes allowance for new lifts or single storey. This means that in these circumstances the other relevant multiplier does not apply i.e. a new lift or single storey multiplier cannot be used with a category 2 multiplier.

13.5   The *supported housing* multiplier and on-costs will only apply to schemes approved within the funding framework introduced in 1995. A scheme which is developed within this framework must be eligible to receive SHMG whether or not SHMG is actually being claimed for the scheme. Applications for approval of capital only supported housing schemes which utilise the supported housing multiplier must be accompanied by form TS1 (revenue budget). This multiplier should only be used where it is the RSL's plan to use the accommodation to provide supported housing in the long term.

13.6   Supported housing schemes with shared facilities cannot be combined with either of the three common room multipliers in *part (h)* of the supplementary multiplier table.

13.7   The supported housing multiplier cannot be used for staff units.

13.8   The *extended families* multiplier is used when a self-contained dwelling is to cater for eight or more persons and additional or duplicate facilities i.e. kitchen and/or sanitary fittings/equipment are provided. The additional space requirement is accounted for in the size band selection.

13.9   The appropriate shared supplementary multiplier is determined by the total number of bedspace provided within all of the households sharing facilities in the scheme. Where a cluster (i.e. more than one) of shared accommodation is provided the appropriate shared supplementary multiplier is determined by the total number of bedspaces contained within the households comprising each independent and self sufficient shared accommodation arrangement. The *TCI base table: shared accommodation* on page 822 is deemed to include all communal and ancillary facilities.

13.10   The shared multiplier does not apply to either sheltered or frail older people schemes.

13.11   The *served by new lifts* multiplier is used when new vertical passenger lift provision is incorporated for access to dwelling entrances and communal accommodation. The multiplier does not apply to dwellings with entrances at ground floor level unless, exceptionally, the scheme includes essential communal accommodation provided at a level other than at ground floor level.

13.12   The *wheelchair with individual carport* multiplier should be used only with individual self-contained dwellings designed in accordance with the relevant standards set out in the Housing Corporation publication Scheme Development Standards. Where non-individual self-contained wheelchair user dwellings are provided e.g. on some category 2 schemes, or where a waiver for non-compliance with the carport provisions has been obtained from the regional office, the wheelchair without individual carport multiplier should be used.

13.13   The *wheelchair* multiplier does not allow for any fixed additional equipment for people with disabilities; these needs should be met via the adaptations funding framework.

13.14   The *standard house types* multiplier is used for new build when the design of the dwelling internal shell is derived, without significant amendment, from generic house plan designs or pattern books produced by contractors, developers, architects, surveyors, RSLs or other similar organisations or persons, resulting in a significant reduction in the detailed design input commissioned by the client RSL. In assessing whether application of the multiplier is appropriate the Housing Corporation will have regard to:
        (i)   the extent to which detailed design is to be specifically commissioned by the RSL; and
        (ii)   the scope which exists for reduction in design fees due to repetition of design.

13. **Selection of supplementary multipliers** - cont'd

13.15 The *parent with children refuges* multiplier applies to shared accommodation specifically designed to meet the needs of parents with children, including vulnerable women with babies and women and children at risk of domestic violence. The TCI is calculated on a per bedspace basis with children counted as full bedspaces. The provision of additional bunk-bedspace should be disregarded for TCI calculation purposes.

13.16 The *housing for sale* multiplier is used for all sale schemes. It cannot be used with the supported housing or shared multipliers.

13.17 The *rehabilitation to pre-1919 properties* multiplier is used where the scope of the refurbishment or conversion work is carried out on a property or properties originally constructed prior to 1919. It cannot be used in connection with existing satisfactory or purchase and repair multipliers.

13.18 The *no VAT rehabilitation* multiplier is used when the scope of the refurbishment or conversion work is such that the relevant local Customs and Excise office determines that VAT is not chargeable on the works.

13.19 The *rural housing* multiplier is used for schemes identified by rural investment codes R, G and F. Rural areas mainly comprise those with 1,000 or less inhabitants and a minimum of 60% of the rural programme is targeted to relieve housing need in these settlements. Exceptionally, the limit may be extended to 3,000 inhabitants on a case by case basis by the relevant regional office of the Housing Corporation. (See the Housing Corporation's Guide to the Allocations Process, for details of population settlements, the Housing Corporation's Rural Settlements Gazetteer, last published in 1998). In addition the rural housing multiplier may be applied to any scheme within a formerly designated National Park.

13.20 The TSH supplementary multiplier is used for all schemes with a lease length of between two and 29 years requiring works, (see table on page 829) and it can only be used with the TSH shared supplementary multiplier. It does not apply to improved TSH schemes.

13.21 *Note:* Where a RSL is in any doubt concerning the appropriateness of the application of any supplementary multiplier, it is advised to seek advice from the relevant regional office of the Housing Corporation. RSLs should also ensure that relevant information relating to the appropriateness of the application of supplementary multipliers is maintained on file for compliance audit purposes.

SUPPLEMENTARY MULTIPLIERS FOR ACQUISITION AND WORKS, OFF-THE-SHELF, EXISTING SATISFACTORY AND PURCHASE AND REPAIR SCHEMES ONLY 1999/2000

SCHEME TYPE		TCI calc. form line no.	COST GROUP				
			A	B	C	D	E
a)	Sheltered:						
	(i) category 1	0140	1.01	1.01	1.01	1.01	1.01
	(ii) category 2 (includes new lifts/single storey)	0170	1.26	1.27	1.29	1.31	1.32
b)	Frail older person (use alone only)	0180	1.35	1.37	1.39	1.42	1.44
c)	Supported housing	0186	1.09	1.09	1.10	1.10	1.11
d)	Extended general families	0195	1.13	1.13	1.15	1.17	1.18
e)	Shared (not used with Frail older person) Bedspaces per scheme/cluster						
	i) 2 to 3	0200	1.00	1.00	1.00	1.00	1.00
	ii) 4 to 6	0210	0.90	0.90	0.90	0.90	0.90
	iii) 7 to 10	0220	0.81	0.81	0.81	0.81	0.81
	iv) 11 and over	0235	0.76	0.76	0.76	0.76	0.76
f)	Served by new lifts (not used with Frail older person and Sheltered category 2)	0245	1.08	1.08	1.09	1.10	1.10
g)	Single Storey (New build only not used with Frail older person and Sheltered category 2 or Wheelchair with carport)	0095	1.19	1.18	1.16	1.13	1.12
h)	Common room etc. (Sheltered category 1 and Self-contained supported housing only)						
	i) common room only	0250	1.08	1.08	1.08	1.09	1.09
	ii) associated communal facilities only	0260	1.06	1.06	1.06	1.07	1.07
	iii) common room and communal facilities	0270	1.14	1.14	1.15	1.16	1.16
i)	Standard house types (not used with off-the-shelf and purchase and repair)	0300	0.99	0.99	0.99	0.99	0.99
j)	Rehabilitation to pre-1919 properties (not used with existing satisfactory and purchase and repair)	0310	1.08	1.07	1.07	1.08	1.08
k)	No VAT rehabilitation	0320	0.92	0.92	0.92	0.91	0.91
l)	Wheelchair (except Single storey and where included as above)						
	i) with individual carport (not used with Frail older person or Single storey)	0380	1.30	1.30	1.27	1.24	1.22
	ii) without individual carport (not used with Frail older person) (Note: provision (ii) requires a waiver from the regional office)	0385	1.08	1.08	1.09	1.10	1.10
m)	Parent with children refuges (Shared general needs and Shared supported housing only)	0420	0.48	0.48	0.48	0.48	0.48
n)	Housing for sale	5100	1.05	1.05	1.05	1.04	1.04
o)	Rural housing	0430	-	1.10	1.11	1.12	1.13

SUPPLEMENTARY MULTIPLIERS FOR WORKS ONLY AND REIMPROVEMENT SCHEMES 1999/2000

	SCHEME TYPE	TCI calc. form line no.	A	B	C	D	E
a)	Sheltered i) category 1	0140	1.01	1.01	1.01	1.01	1.01
	ii) category 2 (includes new lifts/ single storey)	0170	1.40	1.39	1.38	1.38	1.37
b)	Frail older person (use alone only)	0180	1.54	1.53	1.52	1.51	1.50
c)	Supported housing	0186	1.14	1.14	1.13	1.13	1.12
d)	Extended general families	0195	1.19	1.20	1.20	1.20	1.21
e)	Shared (not used with Frail older person) Bedspaces per scheme/cluster						
	i) 2 to 3	0200	1.00	1.00	1.00	1.00	1.00
	ii) 4 to 6	0210	0.85	0.85	0.87	0.88	0.88
	iii) 7 to 10	0220	0.71	0.72	0.75	0.77	0.78
	iv) 11 and over	0235	0.63	0.65	0.68	0.71	0.72
f)	Served by new lifts (not used with Frail older person and Sheltered category 2)	0245	1.12	1.12	1.12	1.12	1.12
g)	Single storey (New build only not used with Frail older person and Sheltered category 2 or Wheelchair with carport)	0095	1.07	1.07	1.07	1.07	1.07
h)	Common room etc. (Sheltered category 1 and Self-contained supported housing only) i) common room only	0250	1.07	1.07	1.07	1.07	1.07
	ii) associated communal facilities only	0260	1.08	1.08	1.08	1.08	1.08
	iii) common room and communal facilities	0270	1.16	1.16	1.16	1.15	1.15
i)	Standard house types	0300	0.98	0.98	0.99	0.99	0.99
j)	Rehabilitation to pre-1919 properties	0310	1.13	1.13	1.13	1.13	1.13
k)	No VAT rehabilitation	0320	0.86	0.86	0.86	0.86	0.86
l)	Wheelchair (except Single storey and where included as above) i) with individual carport (not used with Frail older person or Single Storey)	0380	1.15	1.16	1.16	1.16	1.16
	ii) without individual carport (not used with Frail older person) (Note: provision (ii) requires a waiver from the regional office)	0385	1.12	1.12	1.12	1.12	1.12
m)	Parent with children refuges (Shared general needs and Shared supported housing only)	0420	0.20	0.24	0.31	0.37	0.40
n)	Housing for sale	5100	1.08	1.07	1.06	1.05	1.05
o)	Rural housing	0430	-	1.15	1.15	1.15	1.15

VALID COMBINATION OF SUPPLEMENTARY MULTIPLIERS 1999/2000

	CAT1 0140	CAT2 0170	FE 0180	SN 0186	ExFm 0195	SH23 0200	SH46 0210	SH710 0220	SH11+ 0235	LIFT 0245	SS 0095	CR 0250	FAC 0260	CR&FC 0270	SHT 0300	1919 0310	VAT 0320	WC+C 0380	WC 0385	PWCR 0420	HFS 5100	RH 0430
CAT1 0140	■									•	•	•	•	•	•	•	•	•	•		•	•
CAT2 0170		■													•	•	•	•	•		•	•
FE 0180			■												•	•	•				•	•
SN 0186				■	•	•	•	•	•	•	•	•	•	•	•	•	•	•	•	•		•
ExFm 0195				•	■					•	•					•					•	•
SH23 0200				•		■				•	•				•	•	•	•	•	•		•
SH46 0210				•			■			•	•				•	•	•	•	•			•
SH710 0220				•				■		•	•				•	•	•	•	•			•
SH11+ 0235				•					■	•	•				•	•	•	•	•			•
LIFT 0245	•			•	•	•	•	•	•	■		•	•	•	•	•	•	•	•	•	•	•
SS 0095				•	•	•	•	•	•		■	•	•	•		•	•		•		•	•
CR 0250	•			•						•	•	■			•	•	•	•	•		•	•
FAC 0260				•						•	•		■		•	•	•	•	•		•	•
CR&FC 0270	•			•						•	•			■	•	•	•	•	•		•	•
SHT 0300	•	•	•	•		•	•	•	•	•	•	•	•	•	■		•	•	•	•	•	•
1919 0310	•	•	•	•	•	•	•	•	•	•	•	•	•	•		■	•	•	•	•	•	•
VAT 0320	•	•	•	•	•	•	•	•	•	•	•	•	•	•	•	•	■	•	•	•	•	•
WC+C 0380	•	•		•		•	•	•	•	•	•	•	•	•	•	•	•	■		•	•	•
WC 0385	•	•		•		•	•	•	•	•	•	•	•	•	•	•	•		■	•	•	•
PWCR 0420				•		•	•	•	•	•		•			•	•		•	•	■		•
HFS 5100	•	•	•		•					•	•	•	•	•	•	•	•	•	•		■	
RH 0430	•	•	•	•	•	•	•	•	•	•	•	•	•	•	•	•	•	•	•	•		■

Key:　•　indicates a valid combination

CAT1	0140	Category 1	LIFT	0245	Served by new lifts	VAT	0320	No VAT rehabilitation	
CAT2	0170	Category 2	SS	0095	Single storey	WC+C	0380	Wheel chair and individual carport	
FE	0180	Frail older person	CR	0250	Common room				
SN	0186	Supported housing	FAC	0260	Common room associated communal facilities only	WC	0385	Wheelchair without individual carport	
ExFm	0195	Extended families							
SH23	0200	Shared 2-3 bedspace per unit	CR&FC	0270	Common room and communal facilities	PWCR	0420	Parent with children refuges	
SH46	0210	Shared 4-6 bedspace per unit				HFS	5100	Housing for sale	
SH710	0220	Shared 7-10 bedspace per unit	SHT	0300	Standard house types	RH	0430	Rural housing	
SH11+	0235	Shared 11+ bedspace per unit	1919	0310	Rehab pre-1919 properties				

It is valid to combine each supplementary multiplier singularly with each key multiplier with the following exceptions:

◆　the Housing for Sale multiplier cannot be combined with the Rehabilitation reimprovement key multiplier;
◆　the Single storey multiplier can only be combined with the New build acquisition and works, New build off-the-shelf and New build works only key multipliers;
◆　the Standard house type multiplier cannot be combined with the New build off-the-shelf, Rehabilitation existing satisfactory or Purchase and repair key multipliers;
◆　the Rehabilitation pre-1919 multiplier cannot be combined with the Existing satisfactory or Purchase and repair key multipliers.

TSH is not included in this matrix. Refer to guidance on page 825.

SUPPLEMENTARY MULTIPLIERS (INCLUSIVE OF ON-COSTS) FOR TEMPORARY HOUSING (TSH) 1999/2000

| | | TCI calc. form line no. | Cost group | | | | |
			A	B	C	D	E
TSH		4000					
term:	29 years		0.53	0.51	0.53	0.57	0.59
	28 years		0.53	0.51	0.52	0.56	0.58
	27 years		0.52	0.50	0.52	0.55	0.58
	26 years		0.51	0.49	0.51	0.55	0.57
	25 years		0.51	0.49	0.50	0.54	0.56
	24 years		0.49	0.47	0.49	0.52	0.55
	23 years		0.48	0.46	0.48	0.51	0.53
	22 years		0.46	0.45	0.46	0.49	0.51
	21 years		0.45	0.43	0.45	0.48	0.50
	20 years		0.44	0.42	0.44	0.47	0.48
	19 years		0.42	0.41	0.42	0.45	0.47
	18 years		0.41	0.40	0.41	0.44	0.46
	17 years		0.40	0.38	0.40	0.43	0.44
	16 years		0.39	0.37	0.39	0.41	0.43
	15 years		0.38	0.36	0.38	0.40	0.42
	14 years		0.33	0.32	0.33	0.35	0.36
	13 years		0.29	0.28	0.29	0.30	0.32
	12 years		0.25	0.24	0.25	0.27	0.28
	11 years		0.22	0.21	0.22	0.23	0.24
	10 years		0.19	0.18	0.19	0.20	0.21
	9 years		0.19	0.18	0.19	0.20	0.21
	8 years		0.18	0.18	0.18	0.19	0.20
	7 years		0.18	0.17	0.18	0.19	0.20
	6 years		0.18	0.17	0.18	0.19	0.20
	5 years		0.15	0.15	0.15	0.16	0.17
	4 years		0.13	0.12	0.13	0.14	0.14
	3 years		0.10	0.10	0.10	0.11	0.11
	2 years		0.08	0.08	0.08	0.09	0.09
TSH (shared)		4001					
term:	2 - 29 years		1	1	1	1	1

Keep your figures up to date, free of charge
Now available on the web at www.efnspon.com

This section, and most of the other information in this Price Book, is brought up to date every three months with the Price Book Updates, until the next annual edition.

The Updates are available free to all Price Book purchasers.

To ensure you receive your free copies, either complete the reply card from the centre of the book and return it to us or register via the website www.efnspon.com

The updates will also be available to download from the website.

CAPITALISED LEASE PREMIUM FACTORS FOR TEMPORARY HOUSING (TSH) 1999/2000

		TCI calc. form line no.	Cost group A	B	C	D	E
TSH		n/a					
term:	29 years		0.20	0.20	0.19	0.18	0.17
	28 years		0.19	0.20	0.19	0.17	0.17
	27 years		0.19	0.19	0.18	0.17	0.16
	26 years		0.18	0.19	0.18	0.16	0.16
	25 years		0.18	0.19	0.18	0.16	0.16
	24 years		0.17	0.18	0.17	0.16	0.15
	23 years		0.17	0.17	0.17	0.15	0.15
	22 years		0.16	0.17	0.16	0.15	0.14
	21 years		0.16	0.16	0.16	0.14	0.14
	20 years		0.15	0.16	0.15	0.14	0.13
	19 years		0.15	0.15	0.15	0.14	0.13
	18 years		0.15	0.15	0.14	0.13	0.13
	17 years		0.14	0.14	0.14	0.13	0.12
	16 years		0.14	0.14	0.14	0.12	0.12
	15 years		0.13	0.14	0.13	0.12	0.11
	14 years		0.13	0.13	0.13	0.12	0.11
	13 years		0.12	0.13	0.12	0.11	0.11
	12 years		0.12	0.12	0.12	0.11	0.10
	11 years		0.12	0.12	0.11	0.10	0.10
	10 years		0.11	0.11	0.11	0.10	0.10
	9 years		0.11	0.11	0.11	0.10	0.09
	8 years		0.10	0.10	0.10	0.09	0.09
	7 years		0.10	0.10	0.10	0.09	0.08
	6 years		0.09	0.10	0.09	0.08	0.08
	5 years		0.07	0.08	0.07	0.07	0.06
	4 years		0.06	0.06	0.06	0.05	0.05
	3 years		0.05	0.05	0.05	0.04	0.04
	2 years		0.04	0.04	0.04	0.03	0.03

14.   Calculation of maximum grant contribution to lease costs

14.1   The above factors are used to calculate maximum grant contributions for lease premiums outside the normal TCI framework. Whilst the factors are applied to the appropriate figures in the TCI base table and the relevant TSH key multiplier to determine the maximum contribution, any grant paid is additional to that paid in respect of works costs, which is subject to separate value for money assessment using the TCI multipliers set out on page 829. The grant payment will be calculated according to the actual cost of the lease premium.

14.2   The above factors should be used only in conjunction with the *TCI base table for 1999/2000: self-contained accommodation* (see table on page 822) and the relevant TSH key multiplier. The resultant value reflects the maximum grant contribution towards any capitalised lease premium payable to acquire the lease. No other factors or supplementary multipliers apply. The on-costs associated with setting up the lease are included within the TCI element of eligible costs. The different principles underlying the calculation of TCI for self-contained accommodation and for shared accommodation as outlined on page 821 apply equally to the calculation of capitalised lease premiums.

TCI COST GROUP TABLES

TCI shall apply to schemes in cost groups as follows:

GROUP A
Comprises:

The following inner London boroughs:

Brent	Camden
City of London	Hackney
Hammersmith and Fulham	Islington
Kensington and Chelsea	Lambeth
Southwark	Tower Hamlets
Wandsworth	Westminster

The following outer London boroughs:

Barnet	Ealing
Haringey	Harrow
Hillingdon	Hounslow
Kingston upon Thames	Merton
Richmond upon Thames	

The following unitary authority:

Windsor and Maidenhead

The following local authorities in the counties of:

Buckinghamshire
South Buckinghamshire

Cornwall and Isles of Scilly
Isles of Scilly

Hertfordshire
Three Rivers

Surrey
Guildford

GROUP B
Comprises:

The following inner London boroughs:
Greenwich   Lewisham

The following outer London boroughs:
Barking and Dagenham   Bexley
Bromley   Croydon
Enfield   Newham
Redbridge   Sutton
Waltham Forest

The following unitary authorities:
Bracknell Forest   Reading
Slough   Wokingham

The following local authorities in the counties of:

Buckinghamshire
Chiltern   Wycombe

Cambridgeshire
Cambridge

Essex
Epping Forest   Harlow

Hampshire
Basingstoke and Deane   East Hampshire
Hart   Rushmoor
Winchester

Hertfordshire
Broxbourne   Dacorum
East Hertfordshire   Hertsmere
St. Albans   Watford
Welwyn Hatfield

Kent
Sevenoaks   Tonbridge and Malling

Oxfordshire
Oxford

Surrey
Elmbridge   Epsom and Ewell
Mole Valley   Reigate and Banstead
Runnymede   Spelthorne
Surrey Heath   Tandridge
Waverley   Woking

West Sussex
Crawley   Horsham
Mid Sussex

GROUP C
Comprises:

The following outer London borough:
Havering

The following unitary authorities:

Bath and North East Somerset	Bournemouth
Brighton and Hove	Bristol
Luton	Milton Keynes
Plymouth	Poole
Portsmouth	South Gloucestershire
Southampton	Southend-on-Sea
Swindon	The Meadway Towns
Thurrock	West Berkshire
York	

The following local authorities in the counties of:

Bedfordshire

Mid Bedfordshire	North Bedfordshire
South Bedfordshire	

Buckinghamshire
Aylesbury Vale

Cambridgeshire
South Cambridgeshire

Cheshire
Macclesfield

Devon
South Hams

Dorset

Christchurch	East Dorset
North Dorset	Purbeck
West Dorset	Weymouth and Portland

East Sussex

Eastbourne	Hastings
Lewes	Wealdon

Essex

Basildon	Braintree
Brentwood	Castle Point
Chelmsford	Colchester
Maldon	Rochford
Uttlesford	

Gloucestershire

Cheltenham	Cotswold

Greater Manchester

Manchester	Stockport
Trafford	

Hampshire

Eastleigh	Fareham
Gosport	Havant
New Forest	Test Valley

GROUP C - cont'd

Hertfordshire
North Hertfordshire   Stevenage

Kent
Ashford   Canterbury
Dartford   Dover
Gravesham   Maidstone
Swale   Thanet
Tunbridge Wells

Lancashire
West Lancashire

North Yorkshire
Harrogate

Oxfordshire
Cherwell   South Oxfordshire
Vale of White Horse   West Oxfordshire

Warwickshire
Stratford-on-Avon   Warwick

West Midlands
Birmingham   Solihull

West Sussex
Adur   Arun
Chichester   Worthing

Wiltshire
Kennet   North Wiltshire
Salisbury

Worcester
Bromsgrove   Wyre Forest

GROUP D
Comprises:

The following unitary authorities:

Blackburn	Blackpool
Darlington	East Riding
Halton	Hereford
Isle of Wight	Kingston-upon-Hull
Leicester	Middlesbrough
North East Lincolnshire	North West Somerset
Nottingham City	Peterborough
Rutland	Stoke-on-Trent
The Wrekin	Torbay
Warrington	

The following local authorities in the counties of:

Cambridgeshire

East Cambridgeshire	Huntingdonshire

Cheshire

Chester	Congleton
Crewe and Nantwich	Ellesmere Port and Neston
Vale Royal	

Cornwall and Isles of Scilly

Carrick	Kerrier
Penwith	

Cumbria

Allerdale	Barrow-in-Furness
Carlisle	Copeland
Eden	South Lakeland

Derbyshire

Chesterfield	Derbyshire Dales
High Peak	North East Derbyshire

Devon

East Devon	Exeter
Mid Devon	North Devon
Teignbridge	Torridge
West Devon	

Durham

Durham

East Sussex

Rother

Essex

Tendring

Gloucestershire

Forest of Dean	Gloucester
Stroud	Tewkesbury

Greater Manchester

Bolton	Bury
Oldham	Rochdale
Salford	Tameside
Wigan	

GROUP D - cont'd

Kent
Shepway

Lancashire
Burnley
Fylde
Lancaster
Preston
Rossendale
Wyre

Chorley
Hyndburn
Pendle
Ribble Valley
South Ribble

Leicestershire
Blaby
Harborough
Melton
Oadby and Wigston

Charnwood
Hinckley and Bosworth
North West Leicestershire

Lincolnshire
Lincoln

Merseyside
Knowsley
Sefton
Wirral

Liverpool
St. Helens

Norfolk
Broadland
Norwich

King's Lynn and West Norfolk

North Yorkshire
Craven
Richmondshire
Scarborough

Hambleton
Ryedale
Selby

Northamptonshire
Corby
East Northamptonshire
Northampton
Wellingborough

Daventry
Kettering
South Northamptonshire

Northumberland
Alnwick
Castle Morpeth

Berwick-upon-Tweed
Tynedale

Nottinghamshire
Broxtowe
Rushcliffe

Gedling

Shropshire
Bridgnorth
Shrewsbury and Atcham

Oswestry
South Shropshire

Somerset
Mendip
Taunton Deane

South Somerset
West Somerset

South Yorkshire
Doncaster

Sheffield

GROUP D - cont'd

Staffordshire

Cannock Chase	Lichfield
South Staffordshire	Stafford
Staffordshire Moorlands	Tamworth

Suffolk

Babergh	Forest Heath
Ipswich	Mid Suffolk
St Edmundsbury	Suffolk Coastal

Tyne and Wear

Gateshead	Newcastle upon Tyne
North Tyneside	South Tyneside
Sunderland	

Warwickshire

North Warwickshire	Nuneaton and Bedworth
Rugby	

West Midlands

Coventry	Dudley
Sandwell	Walsall
Wolverhampton	

West Yorkshire

Bradford	Calderdale
Kirklees	Leeds

Wiltshire

West Wiltshire

Worcestershire

Malvern Hills	Redditch
Worcester City	Wychavon

GROUP E
Comprises:

The following unitary authorities:

City of Derby   Hartlepool
North Lincolnshire   Recar and Cleveland
Stockton-on-Tees

The following local authorities in the counties of:

Cambridgeshire
Fenland

Cornwall and Isles of Scilly
Caradon   North Cornwall
Restormel

Derbyshire
Amber Valley   Bolsover
Erewash   South Derbyshire

Durham
Chester-le-Street   Derwentside
Easington   Sedgefield
Teesdale   Wear Valley

Lincolnshire
Boston   East Lindsey
North Kesteven   South Holland
South Kesteven   West Lindsey

Norfolk
Breckland   Great Yarmouth
North Norfolk   South Norfolk

Northumberland
Blyth Valley   Wansbeck

Nottinghamshire
Ashfield   Bassetlaw
Mansfield   Newark and Sherwood

Shropshire
North Shropshire

Somerset
Sedgemoor

South Yorkshire
Barnsley   Rotherham

Staffordshire
East Staffordshire   Newcastle-under-Lyme

Suffolk
Waveney

West Yorkshire
Wakefield

GRANT RATES 1999/2000 GUIDANCE NOTES

1.   Introduction

1.1   These guidance notes are designed to explain the use of grant rates in the Social Housing Grant (SHG) funding framework, and help registered social landlords (RSLs) complete scheme submissions. The notes are effective from 1 April 1999; they are issued together with separate Total Cost Indicator (TCI) guidance notes.

1.2   Enquiries about the contents of this guidance should be directed to regional offices of the Housing Corporation.

2.   Explanation of grant rates

2.1   A key objective of the funding system is to achieve value for money in return for grant, and to ensure the correct level of grant is paid. Grant rates are an essential part of this system; they are divided into cost group area categories and unit types.

2.2   Grant rates apply equally to units funded with SHG by the Housing Corporation and to those sponsored by a local authority.

2.3   Grant rates represent the maximum proportion of scheme costs which will be funded by any form of public subsidy including SHG. (The definition of public subsidy in this context is contained in appendix 6 of the Capital Funding System Procedure Guide). Where there are contributions of public subsidy to a scheme from sources other than SHG, the maximum amount of SHG payable is reduced pound for pound.

2.4   The grant percentages published in this booklet represent the maxima which may be paid. Grant paid to RSLs will be based upon the lower of the amount allocated in response to bids or the amount produced by the calculations set out in this part of the guidance notes.

3.   Treatment of combined supported housing and general needs schemes

3.1   The Housing Corporation has arrangements which allow the submission of schemes containing a combination of supported housing and general needs units within a single scheme.

3.2   Consequently such schemes may have two grant rates, one for the supported homes and one for the other homes.

3.3   The calculation of the grant rate for capital funded supported housing schemes follows the procedures set out in the Capital Funding System Procedure Guide.

4.   Cost group areas

4.1   The local authority area in which a scheme is located defines the cost group for the scheme. A list of the local authority areas in each cost group is included in the TCI guidance notes. Different grant rates apply in each cost group area.

5.   Unit type

5.1   Because of the different capital and revenue costs of different dwelling types, separate grant rates are published for a range of units. The TCI multipliers which are applied to a unit (see separate TCI guidance notes) define the dwelling type for grant rate purposes.

6.   The grant rate tables

6.1   Grant rates for schemes for rent - Appendix 1
Set out the grant rates which apply to schemes for rent by TCI cost group area.

6.3   Grant rates for schemes for sale - Appendices 2 and 3
Set out the grant rates which apply to schemes for sale; together with the Low Cost Home Ownership (LCHO) factors which are applied for housing for sale schemes to the appropriate grant rates in the table *Grant rates for schemes for rent* (Appendix 1). The value limits and discount amounts applicable to home ownership schemes, including Homebuy, are included here.

Sets out the grant rates which apply to Do-It-Yourself Shared Ownership; together with the Low Cost Home Ownership factors which, in the case of other housing for sale schemes, are applied to the appropriate grant rates in appendix 1.

7.   Using the grant rate tables - Schemes for rent

7.1   To use the tables (Appendix 1) to identify the appropriate grant rate, the cost group and gross TCI multiplier must be identified.

7.2   The Total Cost Indicator Guidance Notes list the TCI cost groups into which local authority areas fall. Those notes also list the current TCI multipliers and an explanation of their use.

7.3   For housing for rent units, the gross multiplier and maximum grant rate is calculated for each unit type on Form SFN1, which is also used to derive the aggregate maximum grant rate for the scheme on a weighted basis according to the mix of units.

7.4   To identify the grant rate for units for rent:

i)   *find the TCI gross multiplier* (rounded to two decimal places) in one of the ranges established by the "Lowest" and "Highest" columns at the left of the table

ii)   *determine the appropriate grant column* by referring to the column headings and the key at the foot of the table

iii)   *read off the grant rate* from the appropriate column for the particular unit type.

iv)   where appropriate *apply any necessary Standard Percentage Adjustment* calculation to the grant percentage taken from the table, using the formula set out on form SFN1.

7.5   "Standard" grant rates for rented projects are shown in bold. These have been calculated as follows:

i)   the standard rate is the rate for the unit type at the top of the column in the absence of any other design or need characteristics which, by attracting additional key or supplementary multipliers, would produce an adjusted TCI and a different gross multiplier. For example, a category 1 acquisition and works unit in TCI cost group area A with no additional characteristics has a standard grant rate at a gross multiplier of 1.01, reflecting the fact that category 1 dwellings attract a supplementary multiplier of 1.01 which is applied to the basic new build TCI.

ii)   the standard rate for shared housing is calculated by applying to the basic TCI the adjustment for acquisition and works schemes with between 4 and 6 bedspaces. Schemes with higher or lower numbers of bedspaces attract different supplementary multipliers leading to grant rates above or below the standard.

7.6   Grant rates are shown for a wide range of gross multipliers, but it is possible that a scheme may attract a multiplier outside these ranges. In such cases, the grant rate appropriate to the nearest published range should be used.

8.   Using the grant rate tables - Schemes for sale

8.1   For all shared ownership schemes, the first stage is to use the table for schemes for rent (appendix 1) in exactly the same way as described above for schemes for rent. Then turn to the *LCHO factors* (appendix 2) and apply the appropriate factor to the result from tables in appendix 1 to calculate the grant appropriate to the scheme.

8.3   *Homebuy value limits* and *Voluntary Purchase Grant and Right to Acquire discount amounts* are on page 847.

9.   Standard percentage adjustments (SPAs)

9.1   Standard Percentage Adjustments (SPAs) can be set by the Housing Corporation to reflect particular high or low cost locations within a single TCI cost group area. These adjustments are intended to make the TCI more sensitive to local circumstances and will be fixed in a range between 80 - 120% of TCI. SPAs have the effective of:

i)   *amending the norm cost level used in the assessment of schemes.* For example, in a location for which an SPA is set at 105%, only schemes with costs greater than 105% of TCI will be treated as over TCI cases for scheme appraisal purposes. If an SPA is set in a location at 85% of TCI, all schemes with costs of more than 85% of TCI will be regarded as over TCI.

ii)   *modifying the grant rate for schemes approved in these areas*, so that the cost of operating the acknowledged high or low cost areas is only partly translated into loan requirements and thereby rents.

9.2   The SPA grant adjustment calculation (shown on Form SFN1) only partially compensates for the effects of operating in areas with high or low norm costs. In evaluating their development options RSLs will need to consider the potential for achieving lower rents on schemes produced at norm cost in low cost areas within TCI areas and conversely, the disadvantages in terms of rent levels of working in particularly high cost areas.

10.   Grant calculation and cost over-runs

All schemes

10.1   Projects above TCI for rent or sale will be subject to value for money assessment. Schemes will not be approved at more than 130% of TCI.

Schemes for rent

10.2   For schemes for rent the maximum grant percentage is fixed at grant confirmation stage. Maximum grant entitlement calculated at this stage is estimated eligible cost x grant rate. The costs are reviewed at practical completion, and grant eligibility recalculated as eligible outturn cost x the original grant rate. For RSLs following the scheme contract funding route grant will not be paid on an outturn cost greater than 110% of the estimate at grant confirmation or 130% of TCI (excluding any SPA), whichever is the lower. RSLs following the programme contract funding route will calculate grant eligibility on cost over-runs as above, but these will be funded from their grant pot or from their own resources, rather than by allocation of additional Housing Corporation resources.

Schemes for sale

10.3   For housing for sale schemes maximum grant eligibility is calculated at grant confirmation as:

Estimated eligible cost x grant rate (modified by any SPA) x LCHO factor = grant in £

10.4   The grant is fixed at grant confirmation; it is not recalculated at practical completion.

GRANT RATE TABLES   **"STANDARD" GRANT RATES SHOWN IN BOLD**

UNIT TYPE KEY:

GEN, SH* NB S/C	New build housing for general needs or non-framework supported housing, self contained.
GEN, CAT½#, SH* RH S/C	Rehabilitation housing for general needs or CAT½# elderly or for non-framework supported housing, self contained.
CAT 1 NB S/C	New build Category 1 housing for the elderly, self contained.
CAT 2# NB S/C	New build Category 2# housing for the elderly, self contained.
GEN, SH* NB SHD	New build housing for general needs or non-framework supported housing, shared.
GEN, SH* RH SHD	Rehabilitation housing for general needs or non-framework supported housing, shared.
EXT FAM NB S/C	New build housing for extended families, self contained.
EXT FAM RH S/C	Rehabilitation housing for extended families, self contained.

*   To be used for appropriate supported housing units if not under the supported housing framework.

\#   All self-contained units meeting wheelchair design requirements or units for frail elderly, but which are not under the supported housing framework, use CAT2 (NB or RH) grant rates.

GRANT RATES FOR SCHEMES FOR RENT: TCI COST GROUP A
APPENDIX 1

GROSS MULTIPLIER		GEN SH* NB S/C	GEN, CAT ½# SH* RH S/C	CAT 1 NB S/C	CAT 2# NB S/C	GEN, SH* NB SHD	GEN, SH* RH SHD	EXT FAM NB S/C	EXT FAM RH S/C
LOW	HIGH	G010	G020	G030	G040	G050	G060	G070	G080
1.96	2.00	82.8	92.6	91.8	96.7	81.3	90.6	87.0	94.9
1.91	1.95	82.1	92.1	91.3	96.3	80.5	90.0	86.4	94.5
1.86	1.90	81.3	91.5	90.8	96.0	79.7	89.4	85.8	94.0
1.81	1.85	80.5	90.9	90.3	95.6	78.9	88.8	85.1	93.5
1.76	1.80	79.7	90.3	89.7	95.2	78.0	88.1	84.4	93.0
1.71	1.75	78.8	89.7	89.1	94.8	77.1	87.4	83.7	92.4
1.66	1.70	77.9	89.0	88.5	94.3	76.1	86.7	82.9	91.8
1.61	1.65	76.9	88.3	87.8	93.8	75.1	85.9	82.1	91.2
1.56	1.60	75.8	87.5	87.1	93.3	73.9	85.0	81.2	90.5
1.51	1.55	74.7	86.7	86.4	92.8	72.8	84.1	80.2	89.8
1.46	1.50	73.5	85.8	85.6	92.2	71.5	83.2	79.2	89.0
1.41	1.45	72.3	84.9	84.7	91.6	70.2	82.1	78.1	88.2
1.36	1.40	70.9	83.9	83.8	90.9	68.7	81.0	77.0	87.3
1.31	1.35	69.4	82.8	82.8	90.2	67.1	79.8	75.7	86.3
1.26	1.30	67.8	81.6	81.8	89.4	65.5	78.6	74.4	85.3
1.21	1.25	66.1	80.4	80.6	88.5	63.6	77.2	72.9	84.2
1.18	1.20	64.6	79.3	79.6	87.8	62.1	76.0	71.7	83.2
1.15	1.17	63.4	78.4	78.8	87.2	60.8	75.0	70.7	82.5
1.12	1.14	62.2	77.5	78.0	86.6	59.5	74.0	69.6	81.7
1.09	1.11	60.9	76.5	77.1	86.0	58.1	73.0	68.5	80.8
1.06	1.08	59.5	75.5	76.2	85.3	56.7	71.9	67.4	79.9
1.03	1.05	58.0	74.4	75.2	84.6	55.1	70.7	66.1	79.0
1.00	1.02	56.5	73.3	74.2	83.8	53.5	69.4	64.8	78.0
0.97	0.99	54.8	72.1	73.1	83.0	51.8	68.1	63.4	76.9
0.94	0.96	53.1	70.8	71.9	82.2	49.9	66.7	61.9	75.8
0.91	0.93	51.2	69.5	70.6	81.3	47.9	65.2	60.4	74.6
0.88	0.90	49.2	68.0	69.3	80.3	45.8	63.6	58.7	73.3
0.85	0.87	47.1	66.4	67.9	79.2	43.6	61.9	56.9	71.9
0.82	0.84	44.8	64.8	66.3	78.1	41.2	60.0	54.9	70.4
0.79	0.81	42.3	63.0	64.7	76.9	38.6	58.1	52.9	68.8
0.76	0.78	39.7	61.0	62.9	75.6	35.8	55.9	50.6	67.1
0.73	0.75	36.8	58.9	61.0	74.2	32.7	53.6	48.2	65.3
0.70	0.72	33.7	56.6	58.9	72.7	29.4	51.1	45.6	63.3
0.67	0.69	30.3	54.1	56.6	71.0	25.9	48.4	42.7	61.1
0.64	0.66	26.6	51.4	54.1	69.2	21.9	45.4	39.6	58.7
0.61	0.63	22.5	48.4	51.4	67.2	17.6	42.1	36.1	56.1
0.58	0.60	18.0	45.2	48.4	65.0	12.9	38.5	32.3	53.2
0.55	0.57	13.0	41.5	45.1	62.6	7.7	34.5	28.1	50.0
0.52	0.54	7.5	37.5	41.4	59.9	1.8	30.0	23.5	46.4
0.49	0.51	1.3	32.9	37.2	56.9	1.0	25.0	18.2	42.4
0.46	0.48	1.0	27.8	32.5	53.4	1.0	19.4	12.3	37.8
0.43	0.45	1.0	21.9	27.2	49.5	1.0	13.0	5.6	32.7
0.40	0.42	1.0	15.2	21.0	45.0	1.0	5.6	1.0	26.8
0.37	0.39	1.0	7.4	13.9	39.8	1.0	1.0	1.0	19.9
0.34	0.36	1.0	1.0	5.5	33.7	1.0	1.0	1.0	11.9
0.00	0.33	1.0	1.0	1.0	26.5	1.0	1.0	1.0	2.3

* To be used for appropriate special needs units if not under the special needs framework.

\# All self-contained units meeting wheelchair design requirements or units for frail elderly, but which are not under the special needs framework, use CAT2 (NB or RH) grant rates.

GRANT RATES FOR SCHEMES FOR RENT, TCI COST GROUP B
APPENDIX 1

GROSS MULTIPLIER		GEN SH*	GEN, CAT ½# SH* RH	CAT1	CAT2#	GEN, SH* NB	GEN, SH* RH	EXT FAM NB	EXT FAM RH
		NB S/C	S/C	NB S/C	NB S/C	SHD	SHD	S/C	S/C
LOW	HIGH	G010	G020	G030	G040	G050	G060	G070	G080
1.96	2.00	76.5	87.9	88.0	94.0	76.5	87.4	81.5	90.8
1.91	1.95	75.6	87.3	87.4	93.6	75.6	86.8	80.7	90.2
1.86	1.90	74.6	86.6	86.8	93.1	74.7	86.1	79.9	89.6
1.81	1.85	73.6	85.8	86.1	92.7	73.7	85.3	79.1	88.9
1.76	1.80	72.6	85.1	85.4	92.2	72.7	84.5	78.2	88.3
1.71	1.75	71.5	84.2	84.7	91.6	71.6	83.7	77.3	87.5
1.66	1.70	70.3	83.4	83.9	91.0	70.4	82.8	76.3	86.8
1.61	1.65	69.1	82.4	83.1	90.4	69.2	81.9	75.2	85.9
1.56	1.60	67.8	81.5	82.2	89.8	67.9	80.9	74.1	85.1
1.51	1.55	66.4	80.4	81.3	89.1	66.5	79.8	72.9	84.1
1.46	1.50	64.9	79.3	80.3	88.4	65.0	78.7	71.6	83.2
1.41	1.45	63.3	78.1	79.2	87.6	63.4	77.4	70.2	82.1
1.36	1.40	61.5	76.8	78.1	86.8	61.6	76.1	68.8	**81.0**
1.31	1.35	59.7	75.5	76.9	85.9	59.8	74.7	67.2	79.7
1.26	1.30	57.7	74.0	75.5	**84.9**	57.8	73.2	65.5	78.4
1.21	1.25	55.5	**72.4**	74.1	83.8	55.6	71.6	63.6	77.0
1.18	1.20	53.7	71.0	72.9	82.9	53.8	70.2	62.1	75.8
1.15	1.17	52.2	69.9	71.9	82.2	52.3	69.1	60.8	74.8
1.12	1.14	50.6	68.7	70.9	81.5	50.7	67.9	**59.5**	73.8
1.09	1.11	49.0	67.5	69.8	80.7	49.1	**66.6**	58.1	72.7
1.06	1.08	47.2	66.2	68.6	79.8	47.4	**65.3**	56.6	71.5
1.03	1.05	45.4	64.8	67.4	78.9	45.5	63.9	55.0	70.3
1.00	1.02	**43.4**	63.4	**66.1**	78.0	43.6	62.4	53.3	69.1
0.97	0.99	41.4	61.9	64.7	77.0	41.5	60.9	51.6	67.7
0.94	0.96	39.2	60.2	63.3	75.9	39.3	59.2	49.7	66.2
0.91	0.93	36.8	58.5	61.7	74.8	37.0	57.4	47.7	64.7
0.88	0.90	34.3	56.6	60.1	73.5	**34.5**	55.5	45.6	63.0
0.85	0.87	31.7	54.6	58.3	72.2	31.8	53.5	43.3	61.3
0.82	0.84	28.8	52.5	56.4	70.8	29.0	51.3	40.8	59.4
0.79	0.81	25.7	50.2	54.4	69.3	25.9	49.0	38.2	57.4
0.76	0.78	22.4	47.7	52.1	67.7	22.6	46.5	35.4	55.2
0.73	0.75	18.8	45.1	49.8	66.0	19.0	43.8	32.3	52.8
0.70	0.72	14.8	42.2	47.2	64.1	15.1	40.8	29.0	50.2
0.67	0.69	10.6	39.0	44.3	62.0	10.8	37.6	25.3	47.4
0.64	0.66	5.9	35.5	41.3	59.7	6.2	34.0	21.4	44.3
0.61	0.63	1.0	31.7	37.9	57.3	1.1	30.2	17.0	41.0
0.58	0.60	1.0	27.6	34.1	54.5	1.0	25.9	12.2	37.3
0.55	0.57	1.0	22.9	30.0	51.5	1.0	21.2	6.9	33.2
0.52	0.54	1.0	17.7	25.4	48.1	1.0	15.9	1.0	28.6
0.49	0.51	1.0	12.0	20.2	44.3	1.0	10.0	1.0	23.4
0.46	0.48	1.0	5.4	14.4	40.0	1.0	3.4	1.0	17.6
0.43	0.45	1.0	1.0	7.8	35.2	1.0	1.0	1.0	11.0
0.40	0.42	1.0	1.0	1.0	29.6	1.0	1.0	1.0	3.5
0.37	0.39	1.0	1.0	1.0	23.1	1.0	1.0	1.0	1.0
0.34	0.36	1.0	1.0	1.0	15.5	1.0	1.0	1.0	1.0
0.00	0.33	1.0	1.0	1.0	6.4	1.0	1.0	1.0	1.0

* To be used for appropriate special needs units if not under the special needs framework.

\# All self-contained units meeting wheelchair design requirements or units for frail elderly, but which are not under the special needs framework, use CAT2 (NB or RH) grant rates.

GRANT RATES FOR SCHEMES FOR RENT: TCI COST GROUP C

APPENDIX 1

GROSS MULTIPLIER		GEN SH* NB S/C G010	GEN, CAT ½# SH* RH S/C G020	CAT1 NB S/C G030	CAT2# NB S/C G040	GEN, SH NB SHD G050	GEN, SH* RH SHD G060	EXT FAM NB S/C G070	EXT FAM RH S/C G080
LOW	HIGH								
1.96	2.00	74.4	87.0	85.9	92.6	76.1	87.7	78.5	88.9
1.91	1.95	73.4	86.3	85.2	92.1	75.1	87.0	77.6	88.2
1.86	1.90	72.4	85.5	84.5	91.6	74.2	86.2	76.7	87.5
1.81	1.85	71.3	84.7	83.8	91.0	73.1	85.5	75.7	86.8
1.76	1.80	70.2	83.9	83.0	90.4	72.1	84.6	74.7	86.0
1.71	1.75	69.0	83.0	82.2	89.8	70.9	83.8	73.7	85.2
1.66	1.70	67.7	82.1	81.3	89.2	69.7	82.9	72.5	84.3
1.61	1.65	66.3	81.1	80.4	88.5	68.4	81.9	71.3	83.4
1.56	1.60	64.9	80.0	79.4	87.7	67.0	80.8	70.0	82.4
1.51	1.55	63.4	78.9	78.3	87.0	65.6	79.7	68.7	81.3
1.46	1.50	61.7	77.6	77.2	86.1	64.0	78.6	67.2	80.2
1.41	1.45	60.0	76.4	76.0	85.2	62.3	77.3	65.7	79.0
1.36	1.40	58.1	75.0	74.7	84.3	60.6	75.9	64.0	77.7
1.31	1.35	56.1	73.5	73.3	83.2	58.6	74.5	62.2	**76.3**
1.26	1.30	53.9	71.9	71.8	**82.1**	56.5	72.9	60.3	74.8
1.21	1.25	51.6	70.1	70.2	80.9	54.3	71.2	58.2	73.2
1.18	1.20	49.5	68.6	68.8	79.9	52.4	69.8	56.4	71.8
1.15	1.17	47.9	67.4	67.6	79.1	50.8	68.6	**54.9**	70.7
1.12	1.14	46.2	**66.2**	66.5	78.2	49.2	67.4	53.4	69.5
1.09	1.11	44.4	64.9	65.2	77.3	47.5	66.1	51.8	68.3
1.06	1.08	42.5	63.5	63.9	76.3	45.7	64.7	50.1	67.0
1.03	1.05	40.5	62.0	62.5	75.3	43.8	**63.3**	48.3	65.6
1.00	1.02	**38.4**	60.4	**61.1**	74.2	41.8	61.7	46.5	64.2
0.97	0.99	36.2	58.7	59.5	73.1	39.6	60.1	44.5	62.6
0.94	0.96	33.8	57.0	57.9	71.8	37.3	58.4	42.3	61.0
0.91	0.93	31.2	55.1	56.1	70.5	34.9	56.6	40.0	59.2
0.88	0.90	28.5	53.1	54.2	69.1	**32.3**	54.6	37.6	57.3
0.85	0.87	25.6	50.9	52.2	67.6	29.5	52.5	35.0	55.3
0.82	0.84	22.5	48.6	50.1	66.0	26.5	50.2	32.2	53.2
0.79	0.81	19.1	46.1	47.7	64.3	23.3	47.8	29.2	50.9
0.76	0.78	15.5	43.4	45.2	62.5	19.8	45.2	26.0	48.4
0.73	0.75	11.5	40.5	42.5	60.5	16.1	42.4	22.5	45.7
0.70	0.72	7.3	37.4	39.6	58.3	12.0	39.3	18.7	42.7
0.67	0.69	2.6	34.0	36.4	55.9	7.6	36.0	14.6	39.5
0.64	0.66	1.0	30.2	32.9	53.3	2.8	32.3	10.1	36.0
0.61	0.63	1.0	26.1	29.0	50.5	1.0	28.3	5.1	32.2
0.58	0.60	1.0	21.6	24.8	47.4	1.0	23.9	1.0	28.0
0.55	0.57	1.0	16.5	20.1	43.9	1.0	19.0	1.0	23.3
0.52	0.54	1.0	10.9	14.9	40.0	1.0	13.5	1.0	18.1
0.49	0.51	1.0	4.7	9.0	35.7	1.0	7.4	1.0	12.3
0.46	0.48	1.0	1.0	2.4	30.8	1.0	1.0	1.0	5.7
0.43	0.45	1.0	1.0	1.0	25.2	1.0	1.0	1.0	1.0
0.40	0.42	1.0	1.0	1.0	18.8	1.0	1.0	1.0	1.0
0.37	0.39	1.0	1.0	1.0	11.4	1.0	1.0	1.0	1.0
0.34	0.36	1.0	1.0	1.0	2.6	1.0	1.0	1.0	1.0
0.00	0.33	1.0	1.0	1.0	1.0	1.0	1.0	1.0	1.0

* To be used for appropriate special needs units if not under the special needs framework.

\# All self-contained units meeting wheelchair design requirements or units for frail elderly, but which are not under the special needs framework, use CAT2 (NB or RH) grant rates.

GRANT RATES FOR SCHEMES FOR RENT: TCI COST GROUP D
APPENDIX 1

GROSS MULTIPLIER		GEN SH* NB S/C	GEN, CAT ½# SH* RH S/C	CAT1 NB S/C	CAT 2# NB S/C	GEN, SH* NB SHD	GEN, SH* RH SHD	EXT FAM NB S/C	EXT FAM RH S/C
LOW	HIGH	G010	G020	G030	G040	G050	G060	G070	G080
1.96	2.00	74.9	88.1	82.3	90.0	76.2	88.9	76.2	87.6
1.91	1.95	73.9	87.4	81.5	89.5	75.2	88.2	75.2	86.9
1.86	1.90	72.8	86.6	80.7	88.8	74.2	87.5	74.2	86.1
1.81	1.85	71.7	85.8	79.8	88.2	73.2	86.7	73.1	85.3
1.76	1.80	70.6	85.0	78.9	87.5	72.0	85.8	72.0	84.4
1.71	1.75	69.3	84.1	77.9	86.7	70.8	85.0	70.8	83.5
1.66	1.70	68.0	83.1	76.8	85.9	69.6	84.0	69.6	82.5
1.61	1.65	66.6	82.1	75.7	85.1	68.2	83.0	68.2	81.5
1.56	1.60	65.2	81.0	74.5	84.2	66.8	82.0	66.8	80.3
1.51	1.55	63.6	79.8	73.3	83.3	65.3	80.8	65.3	79.2
1.46	1.50	61.9	78.6	71.9	82.3	63.7	79.6	63.7	77.9
1.41	1.45	60.1	77.3	70.5	81.2	62.0	78.4	62.0	76.6
1.36	1.40	58.2	75.8	68.9	80.0	60.1	77.0	60.1	75.1
1.31	1.35	56.1	74.3	67.2	78.8	58.1	75.5	58.1	73.6
1.26	1.30	53.9	72.7	65.4	77.4	56.0	73.9	55.9	71.9
1.21	1.25	51.5	70.9	63.5	76.0	53.6	72.2	53.6	70.1
1.18	1.20	49.4	69.4	61.8	74.7	51.6	70.7	51.6	68.5
1.15	1.17	47.8	68.1	60.5	73.7	50.0	69.5	50.0	67.3
1.12	1.14	46.0	66.9	59.1	72.7	48.3	68.2	48.3	66.0
1.09	1.11	44.2	65.5	57.6	71.6	46.6	66.9	46.6	64.6
1.06	1.08	42.2	64.1	56.1	70.4	44.7	65.5	44.7	63.1
1.03	1.05	40.2	62.6	54.4	69.2	42.7	64.1	42.7	61.6
1.00	1.02	38.0	60.9	52.7	67.9	40.6	62.5	40.6	60.0
0.97	0.99	35.7	59.2	50.8	66.5	38.4	60.8	38.4	58.2
0.94	0.96	33.2	57.4	48.8	65.0	36.0	59.1	36.0	56.4
0.91	0.93	30.6	55.5	46.7	63.4	33.5	57.2	33.5	54.4
0.88	0.90	27.8	53.4	44.5	61.7	30.8	55.2	30.8	52.3
0.85	0.87	24.8	51.2	42.1	59.9	27.9	53.1	27.9	50.1
0.82	0.84	21.6	48.9	39.5	58.0	24.8	50.8	24.8	47.7
0.79	0.81	18.2	46.3	36.7	55.9	21.5	48.3	21.5	45.1
0.76	0.78	14.5	43.6	33.7	53.7	17.9	45.6	17.9	42.3
0.73	0.75	10.4	40.6	30.5	51.3	14.0	42.7	14.0	39.3
0.70	0.72	6.1	37.4	27.0	48.6	9.8	39.6	9.8	36.0
0.67	0.69	1.3	33.9	23.1	45.8	5.2	36.2	5.2	32.4
0.64	0.66	1.0	30.0	19.0	42.6	1.0	32.5	1.0	28.5
0.61	0.63	1.0	25.8	14.4	39.2	1.0	28.4	1.0	24.2
0.58	0.60	1.0	21.2	9.3	35.4	1.0	23.9	1.0	19.5
0.55	0.57	1.0	16.1	3.7	31.2	1.0	18.9	1.0	14.3
0.52	0.54	1.0	10.3	1.0	26.5	1.0	13.3	1.0	8.4
0.49	0.51	1.0	3.9	1.0	21.3	1.0	7.1	1.0	1.9
0.46	0.48	1.0	1.0	1.0	15.4	1.0	1.0	1.0	1.0
0.43	0.45	1.0	1.0	1.0	8.6	1.0	1.0	1.0	1.0
0.40	0.42	1.0	1.0	1.0	1.0	1.0	1.0	1.0	1.0
0.37	0.39	1.0	1.0	1.0	1.0	1.0	1.0	1.0	1.0
0.34	0.36	1.0	1.0	1.0	1.0	1.0	1.0	1.0	1.0
0.00	0.33	1.0	1.0	1.0	1.0	1.0	1.0	1.0	1.0

* To be used for appropriate special needs units if not under the special needs framework.

\# All self-contained units meeting wheelchair design requirements or units for frail elderly, but which are not under the special needs framework, use CAT2 (NB or RH) grant rates.

GRANT RATES FOR SCHEMES FOR RENT: TCI COST GROUP E
APPENDIX 1

GROSS MULTIPLIER		GEN SH*	GEN, CAT ½# SH* RH	CAT1	CAT2#	GEN, SH* NB	GEN, SH* RH	EXT FAM NB	EXT FAM RH
		NB S/C	S/C	NB S/C	NB S/C	SHD	SHD	S/C	S/C
LOW	HIGH	G010	G020	G030	G040	G050	G060	G070	G080
1.96	2.00	72.3	89.5	79.9	88.5	74.6	91.0	72.7	87.8
1.91	1.95	71.3	88.7	79.0	87.8	73.6	90.3	71.6	87.1
1.86	1.90	70.1	88.0	78.1	87.1	72.5	89.6	70.5	86.3
1.81	1.85	68.9	87.2	77.1	86.4	71.4	88.9	69.3	85.4
1.76	1.80	67.7	86.3	76.1	85.6	70.2	88.1	68.1	84.5
1.71	1.75	66.3	85.5	75.0	84.8	69.0	87.2	66.8	83.6
1.66	1.70	64.9	84.5	73.9	84.0	67.6	86.3	65.4	82.6
1.61	1.65	63.4	83.5	72.6	83.0	66.2	85.4	63.9	81.5
1.56	1.60	61.8	82.4	71.3	82.1	64.7	84.4	62.3	80.4
1.51	1.55	60.1	81.3	69.9	81.0	63.1	83.3	60.6	79.2
1.46	1.50	58.3	80.1	68.5	79.9	61.4	82.1	58.8	77.9
1.41	1.45	56.4	78.8	66.9	78.7	59.5	80.9	56.9	76.5
1.36	1.40	54.3	77.4	65.2	77.5	57.6	79.6	54.8	75.0
1.31	1.35	52.0	75.9	63.3	76.1	55.5	78.2	52.6	73.5
1.26	1.30	49.6	74.3	61.4	74.6	53.2	76.7	50.2	71.7
1.21	1.25	47.0	72.5	59.2	73.0	50.7	75.0	47.6	69.9
1.18	1.20	44.8	71.0	57.4	71.7	48.6	73.6	45.4	68.3
1.15	1.17	43.0	69.8	55.9	70.6	46.9	72.5	43.6	67.0
1.12	1.14	41.1	68.6	54.4	69.4	45.1	71.3	41.8	65.7
1.09	1.11	39.1	67.2	52.8	68.2	43.2	70.0	39.8	64.3
1.06	1.08	37.0	65.8	51.1	66.9	41.3	68.7	37.7	62.8
1.03	1.05	34.8	64.4	49.2	65.6	39.2	67.3	35.5	61.2
1.00	1.02	32.4	62.8	47.3	64.1	36.9	65.8	33.2	59.6
0.97	0.99	29.9	61.1	45.3	62.6	34.6	64.2	30.7	57.8
0.94	0.96	27.3	59.3	43.1	61.0	32.1	62.5	28.1	55.9
0.91	0.93	24.4	57.4	40.8	59.3	29.4	60.8	25.2	53.9
0.88	0.90	21.4	55.4	38.3	57.4	26.5	58.8	22.3	51.8
0.85	0.87	18.2	53.3	35.7	55.5	23.5	56.8	19.0	49.5
0.82	0.84	14.7	50.9	32.8	53.3	20.2	54.6	15.6	47.0
0.79	0.81	10.9	48.4	29.8	51.1	16.7	52.3	11.9	44.4
0.76	0.78	6.9	45.7	26.5	48.6	12.8	49.7	7.9	41.5
0.73	0.75	2.6	42.8	22.9	45.9	8.7	47.0	3.6	38.4
0.70	0.72	1.0	39.7	19.1	43.1	4.3	44.0	1.0	35.1
0.67	0.69	1.0	36.2	14.9	39.9	1.0	40.7	1.0	31.4
0.64	0.66	1.0	32.5	10.3	36.5	1.0	37.2	1.0	27.4
0.61	0.63	1.0	28.3	5.2	32.7	1.0	33.2	1.0	23.1
0.58	0.60	1.0	23.8	1.0	28.6	1.0	29.0	1.0	18.2
0.55	0.57	1.0	18.7	1.0	24.0	1.0	24.2	1.0	12.9
0.52	0.54	1.0	13.1	1.0	18.9	1.0	18.9	1.0	6.9
0.49	0.51	1.0	6.8	1.0	13.1	1.0	13.0	1.0	1.0
0.46	0.48	1.0	1.0	1.0	6.6	1.0	6.2	1.0	1.0
0.43	0.45	1.0	1.0	1.0	1.0	1.0	1.0	1.0	1.0
0.40	0.42	1.0	1.0	1.0	1.0	1.0	1.0	1.0	1.0
0.37	0.39	1.0	1.0	1.0	1.0	1.0	1.0	1.0	1.0
0.34	0.36	1.0	1.0	1.0	1.0	1.0	1.0	1.0	1.0
0.00	0.33	1.0	1.0	1.0	1.0	1.0	1.0	1.0	1.0

*   To be used for appropriate special needs units if not under the special needs framework.

\#   All self-contained units meeting wheelchair design requirements or units for frail elderly, but which are not under the special needs framework, use CAT2 (NB or RH) grant rates.

HOUSING FOR SALE GRANT RATES
APPENDIX 2

LOW COST HOME OWNERSHIP (LCHO) FACTORS

Sale programme	Priority Investment Areas	Other Areas
Shared ownership	58 %	50 %
Shared ownership for the elderly	68 %	60 %
Shared ownership for the elderly	33 %	

HOUSING FOR SALE GRANT RATES
APPENDIX 3

1. HOMEBUY VALUE LIMITS

TCI COST GROUP

	A	B	C	D	E
- Homes with up to and including two bedrooms	105,900	85,300	73,500	64,500	58,400
- Homes with more than two bedrooms	128,200	102,800	87,800	76,200	68,600

Note: TIS and DIYSO programmes are to be replaced with the new scheme called "Homebuy". Further details of this new scheme will be published separately.

2. VOLUNTARY PURCHASE GRANT (VPG) AND RIGHT TO ACQUIRE (RTA) DISCOUNT AMOUNTS

TCI COST GROUP

	A	B	C	D	E
- VPG and RTA discount amounts (£)	16,000	13,500	11,000	10,000	9,000

Note: The RTA discount amounts, and the local authorities they apply to, are set by Statutory Instrument (1997 No 626, The Housing (Right to Acquire Discount) Order), and may be varied by subsequent orders. The current intention is that RTA discount levels should continue to reflect those for VPG. Any discrepancies should be reported to the Housing Corporation.

The Housing Corporation registers, promotes, funds and supervises non-profit making housing associations. Its mission is to support social housing in England by working with housing associations and others to provide good homes for those in housing need.

In England, there are some 2,300 registered housing associations, providing half a million homes for rent for people in housing need. They also provide homes for sale through low cost home ownership. The Corporation is also responsible for helping tenants interested in Tenants' Choice, and for the approval and revocation of new landlords in relation to this scheme.

THE HOUSING CORPORATION'S OFFICES

HEADQUARTERS
149 Tottenham Court Road,
London
W1P 0BN
Tel: (0171) 393 2000

REGIONAL OFFICES

LONDON
Waverley House,
7-12 Noel Street,
London
W1V 4BA
Tel: (0171) 434 0026
Working in Greater London

SOUTH EAST
Leon House,
High Street,
Croydon,
Surrey
CR9 1UH
Tel: (0181) 253 1400
Working in Berkshire, Buckinghamshire, East Sussex, Hampshire, Isle of Wight, Kent, Oxfordshire, Surrey, and West Sussex

SOUTH WEST
Beaufort House,
51 New North Road,
Exeter
EX4 4EP
Tel: (01392) 51052
Working in Bath and North East Someset, Bristol, Cornwall & Isles of Scilly, Devon, Dorset, Gloucestershire, North West Somerset , South Gloucestershire and Wiltshire

EAST
Attenborough House,
109/111 Charles Street,
Leicester
LE1 1QF
Comprising:
♦   East Midlands
Working in Derbyshire, Leicestershire, Lincolnshire, Northamptonshire and Nottinghamshire
♦   Eastern
Working in Bedfordshire, Cambridgeshire, Essex, Hertfordshire, Norfolk and Suffolk

WEST MIDLANDS
Norwich Union House,
Waterloo Road,
Wolverhampton
WV1 4BP
Tel: (01902) 24654
Working in Hereford and Worcester, Shropshire, Staffordshire, Warwickshire and West Midlands

NORTH EASTERN
St Paul's House,
23 Park Square South,
Leeds
LS1 2ND
Tel: (0113) 233 7100
Comprising:
♦   Yorkshire and Humberside
Working in East Riding, Kingston-upon-Hull,
North East Lincolnshire, North Lincolnshire, North Yorkshire, South Yorkshire, West Yorkshire, York
♦   North East
Working in Darlington, Durham, Harlepool, Middlesbrough, Northumberland, Redcar and Cleveland, Stockton-on-Tees, Tyne and Wear

NORTH WEST
Elisabeth House,
16 St. Peter's Square,
Manchester
M2 3DF
Tel: (0161) 242 2000
Working in Cheshire (except Ellesmere Port, Neston, Halton and Warrington), Cumbria, Greater Manchester, Lancashire (except West Lancashire)

MERSEYSIDE
6th Floor,
Corn Exchange Building,
Fenwick Street,
Liverpool
L2 7RD
Tel: (0151) 236 0406
Working in Merseyside Ellesmere Port and Neston, Halton, Warrington, West Lancashire

Property Insurance

The problem of adequately covering by insurance the loss and damage caused to buildings by fire and other perils has been highlighted in recent years by the increasing rate of inflation.

There are a number of schemes available to the building owner wishing to insure his property against the usual risk. Traditionally the insured value must be sufficient to cover the actual cost of reinstating the building. This means that in addition to assessing the current value an estimate has also to be made of the increases likely to occur during the period of the policy and of rebuilding which, for a moderate size building, could amount to a total of three years. Obviously such an estimate is difficult to make with any degree of accuracy, if it is too low the insured may be penalized under the terms of the policy and if too high will result in the payment of unnecessary premiums.

There are variations on the traditional method of insuring which aim to reduce the effects of over estimating and details of these are available from the appropriate offices. For the convenience of readers who may wish to make use of the information contained in this publication in calculating insurance cover required the following may be of interest.

1 PRESENT COST

The current rebuilding costs may be ascertained in a number of ways:

(a)   where the actual building cost is known this may be updated by reference to tender prices (page 672);
(b)   by reference to average published prices per square metre of floor area (page 683). In this case it is important to understand clearly the method of measurement used to calculate the total floor area on which the rates have been based;
(c)   by professional valuation;
(d)   by comparison with the known cost of another similar building.

Whichever of these methods is adopted regard must be paid to any special conditions that may apply, i.e., a confined site, complexity of design, or any demolition and site clearance that may be required.

2 ALLOWANCE FOR INFLATION

The "Present Cost" when established will usually, under the conditions of the policy, be the rebuilding cost on the first day of the policy period. To this must be added a sum to cover future increases. For this purpose, using the historical indices on pages 671 - 673, as a base and taking account of the likely change in building costs and tender climate the following annual average indices are predicted for the future.

	Cost Index	Tender Index
1988	293	309
1989	314	340
1990	337	309
1991	355	262
1992	365	243
1993	372	235
1994	382	252
1995	401	265
1996	411	267
1997	421	283
1998	439	313
1999	456	333
2000	478	349
2001	497	362

3 FEES

To the total of 1 and 2 above must be added an allowance for fees.

4 VALUE ADDED TAX (V.A.T.)

To the total of 1 to 3 above must be added Value Added Tax. Historically, relief may have been given to total reconstruction following fire damage etc. Since the 1989 Finance Act, such work, except for self-contained dwellings and other residential buildings and certain non-business charity buildings, has attracted V.A.T. and the limit of insurance cover should be raised to follow this.

5 EXAMPLE

An assessment for insurance cover is required in the fourth quarter of 1999 for a property which cost £200,000 when completed in 1976.

Present Cost
Known cost at mid 1976   £   200,000.00

Predicted tender index fourth quarter 1999 = 339
Tender index fourth quarter 1976 = 100
Increase in tender index = 239%
applied to known cost =   £   478,000.00

Present cost (excluding any allowance for demolition)   £   678,000.00

Allowance for inflation
Present cost at day one of policy   £   678,000.00
Allow for changes in tender levels during 12 month currency of policy

Predicted tender index fourth quarter 2000 = 356
Predicted tender index fourth quarter 1999 = 339
Increase in tender index = 5.00%
applied to present cost = say   £   34,000.00

Anticipated cost at expiry of policy   £   712,000.00

Assuming that total damage is suffered on the last day of the currency of the policy and that planning and documentation would require a period of twelve months before re-building could commence, then a further similar allowance must be made.

Predicted tender index fourth quarter 2001 = 370
Predicted tender index fourth quarter 2000 = 356
Increase in tender index = 3.93%
applied to cost at expiry of policy = say   £   28,000.00

Anticipated cost at tender date   £   740,000.00

Assuming that reconstruction would take one year, allowance must be made for the increases in costs which would directly or indirectly be met under a building contract.

Predicted cost index fourth quarter 2002 = 527
Predicted cost index fourth quarter 2001 = 506
Increase in cost index = 4.15%
This is the total increase at the end of the one year period.
The amount applicable to the contract would be about half,   say   £   15,000.00

Estimated cost of reinstatement   £   755,000.00

SUMMARY OF EXAMPLE

Estimated cost of reinstatement	£	755,000.00
Add professional fees at, say 16%	£	120,000.00
	s/t £	875,000.00
Add for V.A.T., currently at 17½% say	£	155,000.00
Total insurance cover required	**£**	**1,030,000.00**

Profiled Sheet Roofing and Cladding

A Guide to Good Practice

National Federation of Roofing Contractors

Edited by Nick Selves, J. Shanahan and Colin Sproul

This new edition of the NFRC's handbook, is intended as an accessible and practical guide to the application, design and installation of profiled sheeting for roof and wall cladding. It distills the knowledge of many of the leading experts in this area of construction with hands-on site experience.

Profiled Sheet Roofing and Cladding sets out principles whereby all necessary components can be successfully integrated to provide an external envelope meeting all the required performance standards. The special requirements of insulated structures are also considered. It contains up-to-date advice and information on the exceptional performance and developments which have occurred since the earlier second edition was published in 1991.

Contents: Chapter 1. Common Requirements for Light Weight Profiled Cladding. **Chapter 2**. Profiled Metal Roof and Wall Cladding. **Chapter 3**. Built-up Metal Roofing Systems **Chapter 4**. Composite Panels. **Chapter 5**. Fibre-Cement Sheeting. **Chapter 6**. Rooflights. **Chapter 7**. Fasteners and Fixings. **Chapter 8**. Sealants and Profile Fillers. **Chapter 9**. Rainwater Goods. **Chapter 10**. Construction, Safety and Maintenance.

May 1999: 297x210: 128pp
51 line drawings
Pb: 0-419-23940-5: £29.99

To Order: Tel: +44 (0) 8700 768853, or +44 (0) 1264 343071
Fax: +44 (0) 1264 343005, or **Post:** E & FN Spon Customer Services, ITPS Andover, Hants, SP10 5BE, UK

All orders must be pre-paid and will be sent free in the UK. Europe please add: £2.95 for the first book, thereafter £1.25 per book. ROW please add: Airmail £6.50 for the first book, thereafter £2.50 per book. Please add £12.50 delivery charge for items over £100.00.

PART V

Tables and Memoranda

This part of the book contains the following sections:

Green Building Handbook: Volume 2

A guide to building products and their impact on the environment

Edited by Tom Woolley, Queens University of Belfast, UK and Sam Kimmins, Ethical Consumer Research Association, UK

From reviews of the Green Building Handbook: 'The Publisher is to be congratulated on this book' - **Building**

This new handbook provides a detailed reference for environmentally concerned purchasers of building products, and complements the first Green Building Handbook. Following the format of the original, this book discusses current issues in green building before moving on to consider eight building component types: Fencing Products, Flat Roofing Membranes, Glazing Products, Electrical Wiring, Adhesives, Straw Bale Building, Interior Decoration and Indoor Air Quality and Ventilation. Invaluable for the specifier, this companion handbook will be useful to all those interested in finding greener ways of designing and making buildings.

Contents: Part One. 1.Introduction: a discursive essay highlighting important trends in green building and explaining the rationale and methodology behind the handbook. **Part Two**. How to use the handbook. Key to product table headings. 2. Fencing products. 3. Flat roofing membranes. 4. Glazing products. 5. Electrical wiring. 6. Adhesives. 7. Straw bale building. 8. Interior decoration. 9. Indoor air quality and ventilation. Further reading. Useful information on relevant organizations. Index.

December 1999: 297x210: 152pp
Illus drawings and b+w photographs
Pb: 0-419-25380-7: £29.95

To Order: Tel: +44 (0) 8700 768853, or +44 (0) 1264 343071
Fax: +44 (0) 1264 343005, or Post: E & FN Spon Customer
Services, ITPS Andover, Hants, SP10 5BE, UK

All orders must be pre-paid and will be sent free in the UK. Europe please add: £2.95 for the first book, thereafter £1.25 per book. ROW please add: Airmail £6.50 for the first book, thereafter £2.50 per book. Please add £12.50 delivery charge for items over £100.00.

Tables and Memoranda

CONVERSION TABLES

	Unit	Conversion factors			

Length

Millimetre	mm	1 in	= 25.4 mm	1 mm	= 0.0394 in
Centimetre	cm	1 in	= 2.54 cm	1 cm	= 0.3937 in
Metre	m	1 ft	= 0.3048 m	1 m	= 3.2808 ft
		1 yd	= 0.9144 m		= 1.0936 yd
Kilometre	km	1 mile	= 1.6093 km	1km	= 0.6214 mile

Note: 1 cm = 10 mm 1 ft = 12 in
    1 m = 1 000 mm 1 yd = 3 ft
    1 km = 1 000 m 1 mile = 1 760 yd

Area

Square Millimetre	mm^2	$1\ in^2$	$= 645.2\ mm^2$	$1\ mm^2$	$= 0.0016\ in^2$
Square Centimetre	cm^2	$1\ in^2$	$= 6.4516\ cm^2$	$1\ cm^2$	$= 1.1550\ in^2$
Square Metre	m^2	$1\ ft^2$	$= 0.0929\ m^2$	1 m	$= 10.764\ ft^2$
		$1\ yd^2$	$= 0.8361\ m^2$	$1\ m^2$	$= 1.1960\ yd^2$
Square Kilometre	km^2	$1\ mile^2$	$= 2.590\ km^2$	$1\ km^2$	$= 0.3861\ mile^2$

Note: $1\ cm^2 = 100\ mm^2$ $1\ ft^2 = 144\ in^2$
    $1\ m^2 = 10\ 000\ cm^2$ $1\ yd^2 = 9\ ft^2$
    $1\ km^2 = 100$ hectares $1\ acre = 4\ 840\ yd^2$
       $1\ mile^2 = 640$ acres

Volume

Cubic Centimetre	cm^3	$1\ cm^3$	$= 0.0610\ in^3$	$1\ in^3$	$= 16.387\ cm^3$
Cubic Decimetre	dm^3	$1\ dm^3$	$= 0.0353\ ft^3$	$1\ ft^3$	$= 28.329\ dm^3$
Cubic Metre	m^3	$1\ m^3$	$= 35.3147\ ft^3$	$1\ ft^3$	$= 0.0283\ m^3$
		$1\ m^3$	$= 1.3080\ yd^3$	$1\ yd^3$	$= 0.7646\ m^3$
Litre	l	1 l	= 1.76 pint	1 pint	= 0.5683 l
			= 2.113 US pt		= 0.4733 US l

Note: $1\ dm^3 = 1\ 000\ cm^3$ $1\ ft^3 = 1\ 728\ in^3$ 1 pint = 20 fl oz
    $1\ m^3 = 1\ 000\ dm^3$ $1\ yd^3 = 27\ ft^3$ 1 gal = 8 pints
    1 l = $1\ dm^3$

Neither the Centimetre nor Decimetre are SI units, and as such their use, particularly that of the Decimetre, is not widespread outside educational circles.

Mass

Milligram	mg	1 mg	= 0.0154 grain	1 grain	= 64.935 mg
Gram	g	1 g	= 0.0353 oz	1 oz	= 28.35 g
Kilogram	kg	1 kg	= 2.2046 lb	1 lb	= 0.4536 kg
Tonne	t	1 t	= 0.9842 ton	1 ton	= 1.016 t

Note: 1 g = 1000 mg 1 oz = 437.5 grains 1 cwt = 112 lb
    1 kg = 1000 g 1 lb = 16 oz 1 ton = 20 cwt
    1 t = 1000 kg 1 stone = 14 lb

CONVERSION TABLES

	Unit	Conversion factors		

Force

Newton	N	1 lbf	= 4.448 N	1 kgf	= 9.807 N
Kilonewton	kN	1 lbf	= 0.004448 kN	1 ton f	= 9.964 kN
Meganewton	MN	100 tonf	= 0.9964 MN		

Pressure and stress

Kilonewton per		$1\ lbf/in^2$	$= 6.895\ kN/m^2$
square metre	kN/m^2	1 bar	$= 100\ kN/m^2$
Meganewton per		$1\ tonf/ft^2$	$= 107.3\ kN/m^2 = 0.1073\ MN/m^2$
square metre	MN/m^2	$1\ kgf/cm^2$	$= 98.07\ kN/m^2$
		$1\ lbf/ft^2$	$= 0.04788\ kN/m^2$

Coefficient of consolidation (Cv) or swelling

Square metre per year	$m^2/year$	$1\ cm^2/s$	$= 3\ 154\ m^2/year$
		$1\ ft^2/year$	$= 0.0929\ m^2/year$

Coefficient of permeability

Metre per second	m/s	1 cm/s	= 0.01 m/s
Metre per year	m/year	1 ft/year	= 0.3048 m/year
			$= 0.9651 \times (10)^8 m/s$

Temperature

Degree Celsius °C $°C = \dfrac{5}{9} \times (°F - 32)$ $°F = \dfrac{(9 \times °C)}{5} + 32$

FORMULAE

Two dimensional figures

Figure	Area
Square	$(side)^2$
Rectangle	Length x breadth
Triangle	½ (base x height) or $\sqrt{(s(s-a)(s-b)(s-c))}$ where a, b and c are the lengths of the three sides, and s = $\dfrac{a+b+c}{2}$ or $a^2 = b^2 + c^2 - (2b\ c cosA)$ where A is the angle opposite side a
Hexagon	$2.6 \times (side)^2$
Octagon	$4.83 \times (side)^2$
Trapezoid	height x ½ (base + top)
Circle	$3.142 \times radius^2$ or $0.7854 \times diameter^2$ (circumference = 2 x 3.142 x radius or 3.142 x diameter)
Sector of a circle	½ x length of arc x radius
Segment of a circle	area of sector - area of triangle

FORMULAE

Two dimensional figures

Figure	Area
Ellipse	3.142 x AB (where A = ½ x height and B = ½ x length)
Bellmouth	$\frac{3}{14}$ x radius^2.

Three dimensional figures

Figure	Volume	Surface Area
Prism	Area of base x height	circumference of base x height
Cube	(side)^3	6 x (side)^2
Cylinder	3.142 x radius^2 x height	2 x 3.142 x radius x (height - radius)
Sphere	$\frac{4}{3}$ x 3.142 x radius^3	4 x 3.142 x radius^2
Segment of a sphere	$\frac{(3.142 \times h) \times (3 \times r^2 + h^2)}{6}$	2 x 3.142 x r x h
Pyramid	⅓ of area of base x height	½ x circumference of base x slant height
Cone	⅓ x 3.142 x radius^2 x h	3.142 x radius x slant height
Frustrum of a pyramid	⅓ x height [A + B + √(AB)] where A is the area of the large end and B is the area of the small end	½ x mean circumference x slant height
Frustrum of a cone	(⅓ x 3.142 x height (R^2 + r^2 + R x r)) where R is the radius of the large end and r is the radius of the small end	3.142 x slant height x (R + r)

Other formulae

Formula	Description
Pythagoras' theorum	$A^2 = B^2 + C^2$ where A is the hypotenuse of a right-angled triangle and B and C are the two adjacent sides
Simpson's Rule	Volume = $\frac{x}{3}$ [(y$_1$ + y$_n$) + 2(y$_3$ + y$_5$) + 4(y$_2$ + y$_4$)]

The volume to be measured must be represented by an odd number of cross-sections (y$_1$ -y$_n$) taken at fixed intervals (x), the sum of the areas at even numbered intermediate cross-sections (y$_2$, y$_4$, etc.) is multiplied by 4 and the sum of the areas at odd numbered intermediate cross-sections (y$_3$, y$_5$, etc.) is multiplied by 2, and the end cross-sections (y$_1$ and y$_n$) taken once only. The resulting *weighted average* of these areas is multiplied by ⅓ of the distance between the cross-sections (x) to give the total volume.

FORMULAE

Other formulae

Formula	Description
Trapezoidal Rule	(0.16 x [Total length of trench] x [area of first section x 4 times area of middle section + area of last section])

Note: Both Simpson's Rule and Trapezoidal Rule are useful in accurately calculating the volume of an irregular trench, or similar longitudinal earthworks movement, e.g. road construction.

DESIGN LOADINGS FOR BUILDINGS

Note: Refer to BS 6399: Part 1: 1996 Code of Practice for Dead and Imposed Loads for minimum loading examples.

Definitions

Dead load: The load due to the weight of all walls, permanent partitions, floors, roofs and finishes, including services and all other permanent construction.

Imposed load: The load assumed to be produced by the intended occupancy or use, including the weight of moveable partitions, distributed, concentrated, impact, inertia and snow loads, but excluding wind loads.

Distributed load: The uniformly distributed static loads per square metre of plan area which provide for the effects of normal use. Where no values are given for concentrated load it may be assumed that the tabulated distributed load is adequate for design purposes.

Note: The general recommendations are not applicable to certain atypical usages particularly where mechanical stacking, plant or machinery are to be installed and in these cases the designer should determine the loads from a knowledge of the equipment and processes likely to be employed.

The additional imposed load to provide for partitions, where their positions are not shown on the plans, on beams and floors, where these are capable of effective lateral distributional of the load, is a uniformly distributed load per square metre of not less than one-third of the weight per metre run by the partitions but not less than 1 kN/m².

Floor area usage	Distributed load kN/m²	Concentrated load kN/300 mm²
Industrial occupancy class (workshops, factories)		
Foundries	20.0	-
Cold storage	5.0 for each metre of storage height with a minimum of 15.0	9.0
Paper storage, for printing plants	4.0 for each metre of storage height	9.0
Storage, other than types listed separately	2.4 for each metre of storage height	7.0
Type storage and other areas in printing plants	12.5	9.0
Boiler rooms, motor rooms, fan rooms and the like, including the weight of machinery	7.5	4.5

DESIGN LOADINGS FOR BUILDINGS

Floor area usage	Distributed load kN/m²	Concentrated load kN/300 mm²
Industrial occupancy class (workshops, factories) - cont'd		
Factories, workshops and similar buildings	5.0	4.5
Corridors, hallways, foot bridges, etc. subject to loads greater than for crowds, such as wheeled vehicles, trolleys and the like	5.0	4.5
Corridors, hallways, stairs, landings, footbridges, etc.	4.0	4.5
Machinery halls, circulation spaces therein	4.0	4.5
Laboratories (including equipment), kitchens, laundries	3.0	4.5
Workrooms, light without storage	2.5	1.8
Toilet rooms	2.0	-
Cat walks	-	1.0 at 1 m centres
Institutional and educational occupancy class (prisons, hospitals, schools, colleges)		
Dense mobile stacking (books) on mobile trolleys	4.8 for each metre of stack height but with a minimum of 9.6	7.0
Stack rooms (books)	2.4 for each metre of stack height but with a minimum of 6.5	7.0
Stationery stores	4.0 for each metre of storage height	9.0
Boiler rooms, motor rooms, fan rooms and the like, including the weight of machinery	7.5	4.5
Corridors, hallways, etc. subject to loads greater than from crowds, such as wheeled vehicles, trolleys and the like	5.0	4.5
Drill rooms and drill halls	5.0	9.0
Assembly areas without fixed seating, stages gymnasia	5.0	3.6
Bars	5.0	-
Projection rooms	5.0	-

DESIGN LOADINGS FOR BUILDINGS

Floor area usage	Distributed load kN/m²	Concentrated load kN/300 mm²
Institutional and educational occupancy class (prisons, hospitals, schools, colleges) - cont'd		
Corridors, hallways, aisles, stairs, landings, foot-bridges, etc.	4.0	4.5
Reading rooms with book storage, e.g. libraries	4.0	4.5
Assembly areas with fixed seating	4.0	-
Laboratories (including equipment), kitchens, laundries	3.0	4.5
Corridors, hallways, aisles, landings, stairs, etc. not subject to crowd loading	3.0	2.7
Classrooms, chapels	3.0	2.7
Reading rooms without book storage	2.5	4.5
Areas for equipment	2.0	1.8
X-ray rooms, operating rooms, utility rooms	2.0	4.5
Dining rooms, lounges, billiard rooms	2.0	2.7
Dressing rooms, hospital bedrooms and wards	2.0	1.8
Toilet rooms	2.0	-
Bedrooms, dormitories	1.5	1.8
Balconies	same as rooms to which they give access but with a minimum of 4.0	1.5 per metre run concentrated at the outer edge
Fly galleries	4.5 kN per metre run distributed uniformly over the width	-
Cat walks	-	1.0 at 1 m centres
Offices occupancy class (offices, banks)		
Stationery stores	4.0 for each metre of storage height	9.0
Boiler rooms, motor rooms, fan rooms and the like, including the weight of machinery	7.5	4.5

DESIGN LOADINGS FOR BUILDINGS

Floor area usage	Distributed load kN/m^2	Concentrated load kN/300 mm^2
Offices occupancy class (offices, banks) - cont'd		
Corridors, hallways, etc. subject to loads greater than from crowds, such as wheeled vehicles, trolleys and the like	5.0	4.5
File rooms, filing and storage space	5.0	4.5
Corridors, hallways, stairs, landings, footbridges, etc.	4.0	4.5
Offices with fixed computers or similar equipment	3.5	4.5
Laboratories (including equipment), kitchens, laundries	3.0	-
Banking halls	3.0	4.5
Offices for general use	2.5	2.7
Toilet rooms	2.0	-
Balconies	Same as rooms to which they give access but with a minimum of 4.0	1.5 per metre run concentrated at the outer edge
Cat walks	-	1.0 at 1 m centre
Public assembly occupancy class (halls, auditoria, restaurants, museums, libraries, non-residential clubs, theatres, broadcasting studios, grandstands)		
Dense mobile stacking (books) on mobile trucks	4.8 for each metre of stack height but with a minimum of 9.6	7.0
Stack rooms (books)	2.4 for each metre of stack height but with a minimum of 6.5	7.0
Boiler rooms, motor rooms fan rooms and the like, including the weight of machinery	7.5	4.5
Stages	7.5	4.5
Corridors, hallways, etc. subject to loads greater than from crowds, such as wheeled vehicles, trolleys and the like. Corridors, stairs, and passage ways in grandstands	5.0	4.5
Drill rooms and drill halls	5.0	9.0
Assembly areas without fixed seating dance halls, gymnasia, grancstands	5.0	3.6
Projection rooms, bars	5.0	-

DESIGN LOADINGS FOR BUILDINGS

Floor area usage	Distributed load kN/m²	Concentrated load kN/300 mm²
Public assembly occupancy class (halls, auditoria, restaurants, museums, libraries, non-residential clubs, theatres, broadcasting studios, grandstands) - cont'd		
Museum floors and art galleries for exhibition purposes	4.0	4.5
Corridors, hallways, stairs, landings, footbridges, etc.	4.0	4.5
Reading rooms with book storage, e.g. libraries	4.0	4.5
Assembly areas with fixed seating	4.0	-
Kitchens, laundries	3.0	4.5
Chapels, churches	3.0	2.7
Reading rooms without book storage	2.5	4.5
Grids	2.5	-
Areas for equipment	2.0	1.8
Dining rooms, lounges, billiard rooms	2.0	2.7
Dressing rooms	2.0	1.8
Toilet rooms	2.0	-
Balconies	Same as rooms to which they give access but with a minimun of 4.0	1.5 per metre run concentrated at the outer edge
Fly galleries	4.5 kN per metre run distributed uniformly over the width	
Cat walks	-	1.0 at 1 m centres
Residential occupancy class		
Self contained dwelling units and communal areas in blocks of flats not more than three storeys in height and with not more than four self-contained dwelling units per floor accessible from one staircase		
All usages	1.5	1.4
Boarding houses, lodging houses, guest houses, hostels, residential clubs and communal areas in blocks of flats other than type 1		
Boiler rooms, motor rooms, fan rooms and the like including the weight of machinery	7.5	4.5

DESIGN LOADINGS FOR BUILDINGS

Floor area usage	Distributed load kN/m²	Concentrated load kN/300 mm²
Residential occupancy class - cont'd		
Boarding houses, lodging houses, guest houses, hostels, residential clubs and communal areas in blocks of flats other than type 1 - cont'd		
Communal kitchens, laundries	3.0	4.5
Corridors, hallways, stairs, landings, footbridges etc.	3.0	4.5
Dining rooms, lounges, billiard rooms	2.0	2.7
Toilet rooms	2.0	-
Bedrooms, dormitories	1.5	1.8
Balconies	Same as rooms to which they give access but with a minimum of 3.0	1.5 per metre run concentrated at the outer edge
Cat walks	-	1.0 at 1 m centres
Hotels and Motels		
Boiler rooms, motor rooms, fan rooms and the like, including the weight of machinery	7.5	4.5
Assembly areas without fixed seating, dance halls	5.0	3.6
Bars	5.0	-
Assembly areas with fixed seating	4.0	-
Corridors, hallways, stairs, landings, footbridges, etc.	4.0	4.5
Kitchens, laundries	3.0	4.5
Dining rooms, lounges, billiard rooms	2.0	2.7
Bedrooms	2.0	1.8
Toilet rooms	2.0	-
Balconies	Same as rooms to which they give access but with a minimum of 4.0	1.5 per metre run concentrated at the outer edge
Cat Walks	-	1.0 at 1 m centres
Retail occupancy class (shops, departmental stores, supermarkets)		
Cold storage	5.0 for each metre of storage height with a minimum of 15.0	9.0
Stationery stores	4.0 for each metre of storage height	9.0

DESIGN LOADINGS FOR BUILDINGS

Floor area usage	Distributed load kN/m²	Concentrated load kN/300 mm²
Retail occupancy class (shops, departmental stores, supermarkets) - cont'd		
Storage, other than types separately	2.4 for each metre of storage height	7.0
Boiler rooms, motor rooms, fan rooms and the like, including the weight of machinery	7.5	4.5
Corridors, hallways, etc. subject to loads greaterthan from crowds, such as wheeled vehicles, trolleys and the like	5.0	4.5
Corridors, hallways, stairs, landings, footbridges, etc.	4.0	4.5
Shop floors for the display and sale of merchandise	4.0	3.6
Kitchens, laundries	3.0	4.5
Toilet rooms	2.0	-
Balconies	Same as rooms to which they give access but with a minimum of 4.0	1.5 per metre run concentrated at the outer edge
Cat walks	-	1.0 at 1 m centres
Storage occupancy class (warehouses)		
Cold storage	5.0 for each metre of storage height with a minimum of 15.0	9.0
Dense mobile stacking (books) on mobile trucks	4.8 for each metre of storage height with a minimum of 15.0	7.0
Paper storage, for printing plants	4.0 for each metre of storage height	9.0
Stationery stores	4.0 for each metre of storage height	9.0
Storage, other than types listed separately, warehouses	2.4 for each metre of storage height	7.0
Motor rooms, fan rooms and the like, including the weight of machinery	7.5	4.5
Corridors, hallways, foot-bridges, etc. subject to loads greater than for crowds, such as wheeled vehicles, trolleys and the like	5.0	4.5
Cat walks	-	1.0 at 1 m centres

DESIGN LOADINGS FOR BUILDINGS

Floor area usage	Distributed load kN/m²	Concentrated load kN/300 mm²
Vehicular occupancy class (garages, car parks, vehicle access ramps)		
Motor rooms, fan rooms and the like, including the weight of machinery	7.5	4.5
Driveways and vehicle ramps, other than in garages for theparking only of passenger vehicles and light vans not exceeding 2500 kg gross mass	5.0	9.0
Repair workshops for all types of vehicles, parking for vehicles exceeding 2500 kg gross mass including driveways and ramps	5.0	9.0
Footpaths, terraces and plazas leading from ground level with no obstruction to vehicular traffic, pavement lights	5.0	9.0
Corridors, hallways, stairs, landings, footbridges, etc. subject to crowd loading	4.0	4.5
Footpaths, terraces and plazas leading from ground level but restricted to pedestrian traffic only	4.0	4.5
Car parking only, for passenger vehicles and light vans not exceeding 2500 kg gross mass including garages, driveways and ramps	2.5	9.0
Cat walks	-	1.0 at 1 m centres

PLANNING PARAMETERS

Definitions

*   For precise definitions consult the Code of Measuring Practice published by the Royal Institution of Chartered Surveyors and the Incorporated Society of valuers and Auctioneers.

General definitions

Plot ratio *
Ratio of GEA to site area where the site area is expressed as one.

Gross external area (GEA) *
Gross area on each floor including the external walls of all spaces except open balconies and fire escapes, upper levels of atria and areas less than 1.5 m (5ft) such as under roof slopes, open covered ways or minor canopies, open vehicle parking areas, terraces and party walls beyond the centre line. Measured over structural elements and services space such as partitions and plant rooms. Roof level plant rooms may be excluded from the planning area

Site area *
Total area of the site within the site title boundaries measured on the horizontal plane.

PLANNING PARAMETERS

General Definitions - cont'd

Gross site area *
The site area, plus any area of adjoining roads enclosed by extending the side boundaries of the site up to the centre of the road, or to 6 m (20 ft) out from the frontage, whatever is the less.

Gross internal floor area (GIFA) *
Gross area measured on the same basis as GEA, but excluding external wall thickness.

Net internal floor area (NIFA) *
Net usable area measured to the internal finish of the external walls excluding all auxiliary and ancillary spaces such as WC's and lobbies, ducts, lift, tank and plant space etc, staircases, lift wells and major access circulation, fire escape corridors and lobbies, major switchroom space and areas used by external authorities, internal structural walls and columns, car parking and areas with less than 1.5 m headroom, such as under roof slopes, corridors used in common with other occupiers or of a permanent essential nature such as fire corridors, smoke lobbies, space occupied by permanent air-conditioning, heating or cooling apparatus and surface mounted ducting causing space to be unusable.

Cubic content *
The GEA multiplied by the vertical height from the lowest basement floor or average ground to the average height of the roof.

Internal cube
The GIFA of each floor multiplied by its storey height.

Ceiling height *
The height between the floor surface and the underside of the ceiling.

Building frontage *
The measurement along the front of the building from the outside of the external walls or the centre line of party walls.

External wall area
The wall area of all the enclosed spaces fulfilling the functional requirements of the buildings measured on the outer face of the external walls and overall windows and doors etc.

Wall to floor ratio
The factor produced by dividing the external wall area by the GIFA.

Window to external wall ratio
The factor produced by dividing the external windows and door area by the external wall area.

Circulation (C)
Circulation and ancillary area measured on plan on each floor for staircases, lift lobbies, lift wells, lavatories, cleaners' cupboards usually represented as the allowances for circulation and ancillary space as a percentage of NIFA.

Plant area
Plant rooms and vertical duct space.

Retail definitions

Sales area *
NIFA usable for retailing excluding store rooms unless formed by non-structural partitions.

Storage area *
NIFA not forming part of the sales area and usable only for storage.

Shop frontage *
Overall external frontage to shop premises including entrance and return shop frontage, but excluding recesses, doorways and the like of other accommodation.

Overall frontage *
Overall measurement in a straight line across the front of the building and any return frontage, from the outside of external walls and / or the entire line or party walls.

PLANNING PARAMETERS

Retail definitions - cont'd

Shop width *
Internal measurement between inside faces of external walls at shop front or other points of reference.

Shop depth *
Overall measurement from back of pavement or forecourt to back of sales area measured over any non-structural partitions.

Built depth *
Overall external ground level measurement from front to rear walls of building.

Zone A
Front zone of 6 m in standard retail units 6 m x 24 m.

Housing definitions

Number of persons housed
The total number for whom actual bed spaces are provided in the dwellings as designed.

Average number of persons per dwelling
The total number of persons housed divided by the total number of dwellings.

Density
The total number of persons housed divided by the site in hectares or acres.
The total number of units divided by the site area in hectares or acres.

Functional units

As a "rule of thumb" guide to establish a cost per functional unit, or as a check on economy of design in terms of floor area, the following indicative functional unit areas have been derived from historical data. For indicative unit costs see "Building Prices per Functional Units" (Part IV - Approximate Estimating) on page 677.

Car parking	- surface	20 - 22 m²/car
	- multi storey	23 - 27 m²/car
	- basement	28 - 37 m²/car
Concert Halls		8 m²/seat
Halls of residence	- college/polytechnic	25 - 35 m²/bedroom
	- university	30 - 50 m²/bedroom
Hospitals	- district general	65 - 85 m²/bed
	- teaching	120 + m²/bed
	- private	75 - 100 m²/bed
Hotels	- budget	28 - 35 m²/bedroom
	- luxury city centre	70 - 130 m²/bedroom
Housing		**Gross internal floor area**
Private developer:	1 Bedroom Flat	45 - 50 m²
	2 Bedroom Flat	55 - 65 m²
	2 Bedroom House	55 - 65 m²
	3 Bedroom House	70 - 90 m²
	4 Bedroom House	90 - 100 m²
Offices	- high density open plan	20 m²/person
	- low density cellular	15 m²/person

PLANNING PARAMETERS

Functional units - cont'd

Schools	- nursery	3 - 5 m^2/child
	- secondary	6 - 10 m^2/child
	- boarding	10 -12 m^2/child
Theatres	- small, local	3 m^2/seat to
	- large, prestige	7 m^2/seat

Typical planning parameters

The following are indicative planning design and functional criteria derived from historical data for a number of major building types.

Gross internal floor areas (GIFA)

Offices

Feasibility assessment of GIFA for:

| Curtain wall office | GEA x 0.97 |
| Solid wall office | GEA x 0.95 |

These measures apply except for thick stone façades - take measurements on site.

Typical dimensions measured on plan between the internal finishes of the external walls for:

Speculative offices	13.75 m
Open plan offices	15.25 m
Open plan / cellular offices	18.3 m

Retail

Typical gross internal floor areas:

Food courts, comprising	232 to 372 m^2
Kiosks	37 m^2
Services - per seat	1.1 to 1.5 m^2
Seating area in mall - per seat	1.2 to 1.7 m^2
Retail Kiosks	56 to 75 m^2
Small specialist shops	465 to 930 m^2
Electrical goods	930 to 1 395 m^2
DIY	930 to 4 645 m^2
Furniture / carpets	1858 to 5 575 m^2
Toys	3715 to 4 645 m^2
Superstores	3715 to 5 575 m^2
Department stores within shopping centres	5575 to 27 870 m^2
Specialist shopping centres	5574 to 9 290 m^2

Leisure

Standard sizes:

Large sports halls	Medium sports halls	Small sports halls
36.5 x 32 x 9.1 m	29 x 26 x 7.6 - 9.1 m	29.5 x 16.5 x 6.7 - 7.6 m
32 x 26 x 7.6 - 9.1 m	32 x 23 x 7.6 - 9.1 m	26 x 16.5 x 6.7 - 7.6 m
	32 x 17 x 6.7 - 7.6 m	22.5 x 16.5 x 6.7 - 7.6 m

| Community halls |
| 17.2 x 15.6 x 6.7 m |
| 17 x 8.5 x 6.7 m |

PLANNING PARAMETERS

Leisure - cont'd

Court sizes:

badminton	13.4 x 6.1 m	volleyball	18 x 9 m
basketball	26+2 x 14+1 m	tug of war	35 (min) x 5 m (min)
handball	30 - 40 x 17 - 20 m	bowls	4.5 x 32 m (min) per rink
hockey	36 - 44 x 18 - 22 m	cricket nets	3.05 (min) x 33.5 m per net
women's lacrosse	27 - 36 x 15 - 21m	snooker	3.7 x 1.9 m table size
men's lacrosse	46 - 48 x 18 - 24m	ice hockey	56.61 x 26 - 30.5 m
netball	30.50 x 15.25 m	racquets	18.288 x 9.144 m
tennis	23.77 x 10.97 m	squash	9.754 x 6.4 x 5.64 m

Typical swimming pool dimensions:

Olympic standard	50 m x 21 m (8 lanes) water depth 1.8 m (constant)
ASA, national and county	25 or 33.3 m long with width multiple of 2.1 m wide
championship standard	lanes minimum water depth 900 mm
	1 m springboard needs minimum 3 m water depth
Learner pool	width 7.0 - 7.5 m
	depth 600 - 900 mm
Toddlers pool	450 mm depth
Leisure pool	informal shape: will sometimes encompass 25 m in one direction to accommodate
	roping-off for swimming lanes; water area from 400 - 750 m^2
Splash pool	minimum depth 1.05 m
Changing cubicles	minimum dimensions: 914 x 1057 mm

Note: For 25 m pool developments the ratio of water area to gross floor area may average 1:3. For free form leisure pool developments, a typical ratio is 1:5.5.

Multiplex space planning data:

Ideal number of screens	10 (minimum six)
Average area per screen	325 m^2
Typical dimensions:	71 x 45 m (10 screens)
	66 x 43 m (8 screens)
	plus 20 m^2 food area

Housing

Typical densities	**Persons per hectare**	**Units per hectare**
Urban	200	90
Suburban	150	55
Rural	110	35

Typical gross internal floor areas for housing associations / local authorities schemes:

	(m^2)
Bungalows	
one-bed	48
two-bed	55 - 65
Houses	
one-bed	44
two-bed	62 - 80
three-bed	75 - 95
four-bed	111 - 145
Flats	
bedsitters	23
one-bed	35 - 63
two-bed	55 - 80
three-bed	75 - 100

PLANNING PARAMETERS

Housing - cont'd

Gross internal floor areas for private developments are much more variable and may be smaller or larger than the indicative areas shown above, depending on the target market. Standards for private housing are set out in the NHBC's Registered House Builders Handbook. There are no floor space minima, but heating , kitchen layout, kitchens and linen storage, WC provisions, and the number of electrical socket outlets are included.

Average housing room sizes - net internal floor areas:

	Living room (m²)	Kitchen (m²)	Bathroom (m²	Main bedroom (m²)	Average bedroom size (m²)
Bungalows					
one-bed	15.0	6.0	3.5	11.0	-
two-bed	17.0	9.0	3.5	12.5	10.0
Houses					
one-bed	14.5	6.5	3.5	11.0	-
two-bed	17.5	9.5	4.5	10.0	9.0
three-bed	17.5	13.5	7.0	13.0	10.5
four-bed	22.5	12.5	8.0	17.5	12.5
Flats					
bedsitters	18.0	-	3.0	-	-
one-bed	13.5	7.5	4.5	10.0	-
two-bed	17.0	10.0	5.5	13.5	11.5
three-bed	23.0	3.5	5.5	14.0	14.0

Storage accommodation for housing

NHBC requirements are that in every dwelling, enclosed domestic storage accommodation shall be provided as follows:

Area of dwelling (m²)	Minimum volume of storage (m³)
less than 60	1.3
60 - 80	1.7
over 80	2.3

Hotels

Typical gross internal floor areas per bedroom: m²

Five star, city centre hotel	60+
Four star, city centre / provincial centre hotel	45 to 55
Three star, city / provincial hotel	40 to 45
Three / two star, provincial hotel	33 to 40
Three / two star bedroom extension	26 to 30

Indicative space standards (unit):

Suites including bedroom, living room bathroom and hall (nr)	55 to 65
Double bedrooms including bathroom and lobby (nr)	
large	30 to 35
average	25 to 30
small	20 to 25
disabled	3 to 5 m² extra
Restaurant (seat)	
first class	1.85
speciality/grill	1.80

PLANNING PARAMETERS

Hotels - cont'd

Indicative space standards (unit) - cont'd:	m²
Coffee shop (seat)	1.80
Bar (customer standing)	0.40 to 0.45
Food preparation/main kitchen/storage	40% to 50% of restaurant and bar areas
Banquet (seat)	1.40
Catering to banquets	10 % to 25 % of banquet area
Function/meeting rooms (person)	1.50
Staff areas (person)	0.40 to 0.60
Staff restaurant and kitchen (seat)	0.70 to 0.90
Service rooms (floor)	30 to 50
General storage and housekeeping	1.5 to 2% of bedroom and circulation areas
Front hall, entrance areas, lounge	2 to 3% average (up to 5%) of total hotel area
Administrative areas	Allowances based on number of accounts staff. Additional area if self accounting 15 to 25 per cent for bedroom floors depending on number of storeys, layout and operating principles, 20 to 25 per cent for public areas
Plant rooms and ducts	4 to 5 % of total hotel area for non-air-conditioned areas, 7 to 8% for air conditioned areas

Typical internal bedroom dimensions:

Bedroom including bathroom	
five star	8.0 m x 4.0 m
four star	7.5 m x 3.75 m
three/two star	7.0 m x 3.5 m
Typical corridor width	1.4 m to 1.6 m

Circulation (C)

Figures represent net area which is gross area less space to be set aside for staircases, lift lobbies, lift wells, lavatories, cleaners' cupboards, service risers, plant space, etc.

Typical NIFA to GIFA areas:	Percentage of GIFA
Offices	
2 to 4 storey	82 - 87
5 to 9 storey	76 - 82
10 to 14 storey	72 - 76
15 to 19 storey	68 - 72
20 + storeys	65 - 68
Adjustments	
for fancoil air-conditioned offices	deduct 2 - 3
for VAV air-conditioned offices	deduct 6 - 7

PLANNING PARAMETERS

Circulation - cont'd	**Percentage of GIFA**

Flats

Staircase access	85
Enclosed balcony	83
Internal corridor and lobby	80

Typical sales to gross internal areas

Retail

Superstores	45 - 55
Department stores	50 - 60
Retail warehouses	75 - 85

Wall and Window to floor ratios

Typical ratios based on historic data:

Legend:	(1) W/F	- External wall to gross floor area (GIFA) ratio
	(2) W/W	- External window to external wall ratio
	(3) IW/F	- Internal wall to gross floor area (GIFA) ratio

Building types	(1) W/F	(2) W/W	(3) IW/F
Industrial			
warehouse	0.45	0.04	-
factory	0.60	0.14	-
nursery	0.70	0.14	-
Offices			
open	0.80	0.35	0.30
cellular	0.80	0.35	1.10

Plant area	**Percentage of GIFA**

Industrial	3 - 5

Offices	4 - 11

	Percentage of treated floor area

Leisure

all air, low velocity	4.0 - 6.0
induction	2.0 - 3.0
fan coil	1.5 - 2.5
VAV	3.0 - 4.5
versatemp	1.5 - 2.0
boiler plant	0.8 - 1.8
(excluding hws cylinders)	
oil tank room	1.0 - 2.0
refrigeration plant	1.0 - 2.0
(excluding cooling towers)	
supply and extract ventilation	3.0 - 5.0
electrical (excluding input substation or standby generation)	0.5 - 1.5
lift rooms	0.2 - 0.5
toilet ventilation	0.3 - 1.0

PLANNING PARAMETERS

Other key dimensions

Structural grid and cladding rail spacing for industrial buildings

Typical economic dimensions	**m**
spans	18
column spacing	6 - 7.5
purlin spacing	1.8

Wall to core for offices

Typical dimensions measured on plan between the internal finish of external wall to finish of core	7.3

Floor to floor heights

Typical dimensions, measured on section

Industrial

top of ground slab to top of first floor slab	3.9 - 4.5
top of first floor slab to underside of beams / eaves	3.4 - 3.7

Minimum dimensions; floor finish to floor finish

Offices

speculative centrally heated	3.3
speculative air-conditioned	3.8
trading floors air-conditioned	4.7

Hotels

bedrooms	2.7 - 3
public areas	3.5 - 3.6

Floor to underside of structure heights

Industrial
Minimum internal clear height

minimum cost stacking warehouse/light industrial	5 - 5.5
minimum height for storage racking	7.5
turret trucks used for stacking	9
automatic warehouse with stacker cranes	15 - 30

Clearance for structural members, sprinklers and lighting in addition to the above

Retail
Clear height from floor to underside of beams / eaves:

shop sales area	3.3 - 3.8
shop non-sales area	3.2 - 3.6
retail warehouse	4.75 - 5.5

Leisure
Specified by each sport's governing body

badminton/tennis to county standard	7.6
badminton/tennis/ trampolining to international standard	9.1
pool hall from pool surround	8.4 - 8.9

PLANNING PARAMETERS

Other key dimensions - cont'd	**m**

Floor to underside of structure heights

Industrial floor to eaves height
Typical dimensions measured on section:

low bay warehouse	6
high bay warehouse	9 - 18

Floor to ceiling height

Typical dimensions measured on section:
Industrial

top of ground slab to underside of first floor slab	3.7 - 4.3
top of first floor finish to ceiling finish	2.75 - 3

Minimum dimensions measured on section from floor finish to ceiling finish:
Offices

Speculative offices	2.6
Trading floors	3

Leisure

Multiple cinemas	6
Fitness/dance studios	5 - 6
Snooker room	3
Projectile room	3
Changing rooms	3.5

Houses

Ground floor	2.1 - 2.55
First floor	2.35 - 2.55
Flats	2.25 - 2.65
Bungalows	2.4

Hotels

Bedrooms	2.5
Lounges	2.7
Meeting rooms	2.8
Restaurant / coffee shop / bar	3
Function rooms	4 - 4.8

Raised floor areas	**mm**
Minimum clear void for:	
Speculative offices	100 - 200
Trading floors	300

Note: one floor box per 9 m^2

Suspended ceilings	**mm**
Minimum clear voids (beneath beams)	
Mechanically ventilated offices	300
Fan coil air-conditioned offices	450
VAV air-conditioned offices	550
Trading floors	760

PLANNING PARAMETERS

Typical floor loadings

For more precise floor loadings according to usage refer to section on *DESIGN LOADINGS FOR BUILDINGS* earlier in this section.

Typical loadings (based on minimum uniformly distributed loads plus 25% for partition loads) are:

	KN/m^2
Industrial	24 - 37
Offices	5 - 7
Retail warehouse / storage	24 - 29
Shop sales areas	6
Shop storage	12
Public assembly areas	6
Residential dwelling units	2 - 2.5
Residential corridor areas	4
Hotel bedrooms	3
Hotel corridor areas	4
Plant rooms	9
Car parks and access ramps	3 - 4

Fire protection and means of escape

BS 5588: Fire Precautions in the Design and Construction of Building: includes details of:
     angle between escape routes
     disposition of fire resisting construction
     permitted travel distances

The Building Regulations fire safety approved document B 1992 provides advice on interpretation of the Building Regulations and is still the relevant controlling legislation for fire regulations, although the Loss Prevention Council have recently produced an advisory note, the *Code of Practice for the Construction of Buildings* which argues for a higher performance than the mandatory regulations.

Some minimum periods of fire resistance in minutes for elements of a structure are reproduced hereafter, based on Appendix A Table A2 of the Building Regulations fire safety approved document B, but refer to the relevant documentation to ensure that the information is current.

PLANNING PARAMETERS

Building group   **Minimum fire resistance in minutes**

	Basement storey		Ground and Upper storey			
	<10m deep	>10m deep	<5m high	>20m high	<30m high	>30m high
Industrial						
not sprinklered	120	90	60	90	120	not allowed
sprinklered	90	60	30*	60	60	120#
Offices						
not sprinklered	90	60	30*	60	90	not allowed
sprinklered	60	60	30*	30*	60	120#
Shop, commercial and leisure						
not sprinklered	90	60	60	60	90	not allowed
sprinklered	60	60	30*	60	60	120#
Residential dwelling houses						
	-	30*	30*	60	-	-

   *   Increase to a minimum of 60 minutes for compartment walls separating buildings
   #   Reduce to 90 minutes for elements not forming part of the structural frame

Section 20
Applies to buildings in the Greater London area - refer to *London Building Acts (Amendment) Act 1939: Section 20, Code of Practice*. Major cost considerations include 2 hour fire resistance to reinforced concrete columns, possible requirement for sprinkler installation in offices and / or basement car parks, automatic controls and smoke detection in certain ventilation trucking systems, 4 hour fire resistance to fire fighting lift/stair/lobby enclosures and requirements for ventilated lobbies with a minimum floor area of 5.5 m² to fire fighting staircases.

Sprinkler installations

Sprinkler installations should be considered where any of the following are likely to occur:

◆   rapid fire spread likely, for example warehouses with combustible goods/packaging
◆   large uncompartmented areas
◆   high financial or consequential loss arising from fire damage

Refer to BS 5306: Part 2: 1990 for specification of sprinkler systems and associated Technical Bulletins from the Fire Officers Committee.

Sanitary provisions

For the provisions of sanitary appliances refer to BS 6465: Part 1: 1994, which suggests the following minimum requirements (refer to the relevant documentation to ensure information is correct).

Factories (table 5)	Males	Females
WC's	1 per 25 persons or part thereof	1 per 25 persons or part thereof
Urinals	As required	Not applicable
Baths or showers	As required	As required

	Male and Female
Wash basins	1 per 20 persons; for clean processes 1 per 10 persons; for dirty processes 1 per 5 persons; for injurious processes

PLANNING PARAMETERS

Sanitary provisions - cont'd

Housing (table 1)	2 - 4 person	5 person	6 person and over

One level, eg. bungalows and flats

	2 - 4 person	5 person	6 person and over
WC's	1	1	2
Bath	1	1	1
Wash basin *	1	1	1
Sink and drainer	1	1	1

On two or more levels, eg. houses and maisonettes

	2 - 4 person	5 person	6 person and over
WC's	1	2	2
Bath	1	1	1
Wash basin *	1	1	1
Sink and drainer	1	1	1

* in addition, allow one extra wash basin in every separate WC compartment which does not adjoin a bathroom.

Tables 2 and 3 deal with sanitary provisions for elderly people

Office building and shops (table 4)	Number per male and per female staff
WC's (no urinals) and wash hand basins	1 for 1 to 15 persons 2 for 16 to 30 persons 3 for 31 to 50 persons 4 for 51 to 75 persons 5 for 76 to 100 persons add 1 for every additional 25 persons or part thereof
Cleaners' sink	At least 1 per floor

For WC's (urinals provided), urinals, incinerators, etc. refer to BS 6465: Part 1: 1984. One unisex type WC and one smaller compartment for each sex on each floor where male and female toilets are provided - refer to BS 5810: 1979 and Building Regulations 1985 Schedule 2 (shortly to be replaced by part M).

PLANNING PARAMETERS

Sanitary provisions - cont'd

Swimming pools (table 11)

	For spectators		For bathers	
	Males	Females	Males	Females
WC's	1 for 1 - 200 persons 2 for 201 - 500 persons 3 for 501 - 1000 persons Over 1000 persons, 3 plus 1 for every additional 500 persons or part thereof	1 for 1 - 100 persons 2 for 101 - 250 persons 3 for 251 - 500 persons Over 500 persons, 3 plus 1 for every additional 400 persons or part thereof	1 per 20 changing places	1 per 10 changing places
Urinals	1 per 50 persons	n/a	1 per 20 changing places	n/a
Wash basins	1 per 60 persons	1 per 60 persons	1 per 15 changing places	1 per 15 changing places
Showers	n/a	n/a	1 per 8 changing places	1 per 8 changing places

Refer also to BS 6465: Part 1: 1994 for sanitary provisions for schools, leisure, hotels and restaurants, etc.

Minimum cooling and ventilation requirements

General offices	40 W/m^2
Trading floors	60 W/m^2
Fresh air supply	
offices/dance halls	8 - 12 litres/person/second
bars	12 - 18 litres/person/second

Recommended design values for internal environmental temperatures and empirical values for air infiltration and natural ventilation allowances

	Temperature $^{\circ}$C (winter	Air infiltration rate (changes per hour)	Ventilation allowance (W/m^3 degrees C)
Warehouses			
working and packing spaces	16	0.5	0.17
storage space	13	0.25	0.08
Industrial			
production	16	0.5	0.17
offices	20	1.0	0.33
Offices	20	1.0	0.33
Shops			
small	18	1.0	0.33
large	18	0.5	0.17
department store	18	0.25	0.08
fitting rooms	21	1.5	0.50
store rooms	15	0.5	0.17

PLANNING PARAMETERS

Recommended design values for internal environmental temperatures and empirical values for air infiltration and natural ventilation allowances - cont'd

	Temperature °C (winter	Air infiltration rate (changes per hour)	Ventilation allowance (W/m³ degrees C)
Housing			
living rooms	21	1.0	0.33
bedrooms	18	0.5	0.17
bed sitting rooms	21	1.0	0.33
bathrooms	22	2.0	0.67
lavatory, cloakrooms	18	1.5	0.50
entrance halls,			
staircases, corridors	16	1.5	0.50
Hotels			
bedrooms (standard)	22	1.0	0.33
bedrooms (luxury)	24	1.0	0.33
public rooms	21	1.0	0.33
corridors	18	1.5	0.50
foyers	18	1.5	0.50

Typical design temperatures and mechanical ventilation allowances for leisure buildings

	Air temperature °C	Mechanical airchange rates (changes per hour)
Leisure buildings		
ice rink	below 25(heating temperature in winter:-8)	6
sports hall	16 - 21	3
squash courts	16 - 21	3
bowls halls	16 - 21	3
activity rooms	16 - 21	3
function room/bar	21 $\pm$ 2	2 - 4
fitness / dance studio	16 - 21	3 - 6
snooker room	16 - 21	3 - 6
projectile room	16 - 21	3 - 6
changing rooms	22	10
swimming pools	28	4 - 6
bar and cafe areas	23	2 - 4
administration areas	21	2 - 4

	Pool water temperature °C	
Swimming pools		
main pool	27	Ventilation rates must be related to the
splash pool	27	control of condensation. The criteria is
learners pool	28 - 30	the water area and the recommended basis
diving pool	27	is 20 litres/per m² of water surface,
leisure pool	29	plus a margin (say 20 per cent) to allow
jacuzzi pool	35	for the effect of wet surrounds.

PLANNING PARAMETERS

Typical lighting levels

Lighting levels for a number of common building types are given below. For more precise minimum requirements refer to the IES Code.

	Lux
Industrial building - production/assembly areas	100 - 1000(varies)
Offices	500
Conventional shops with counters or	
wall displays and self-service shops	500
Supermarkets	500
Covered shopping precincts and arcades	
main circulation paces	100 - 200
lift, stairs, escalators	150
staff rooms	150
external covered walkways	30
Sports buildings	
multi use sports halls	500
squash courts	500
dance / fitness studio	300
snooker room	500 on table
projectile room	300 generally
	1000 on target
Homes	
living rooms	
general	50
casual reading	150
bedrooms	
general	50
bedhead	150
studios	
desk and prolonged reading	300
kitchens	
working areas	300
bathrooms	100
halls and landings	150
stairs	100
Hotels	
internal corridors	200
guest room sleep area; stair wells	300
guest room activity area; housekeeping areas	500
meeting / banquet facilities	800

Electrical socket outlets (NHBC)	**Desirable provision**	**Minimum provision**
Homes		
working area of kitchen	4	4
dining area	2	1
living area	5	3
first or only double bedroom	3	2
other double bedrooms	2	2
single bedrooms	2	2
hall and landing	1	1
store/workshop/garage	1	-
single study bedrooms	2	2
single bed sitting rooms		
in family dwellings	3	3
single bed sitting rooms in self		
contained bed sitting room dwellings	5	5

PLANNING PARAMETERS

Lifts
Performance standard to be not less than BS 5655: Lifts and service Lifts.

Industrial
Typical goods lift - 1000 kg

Offices
Dependant on number of storeys and planning layout, usually based on:

	Number of lifts
< 4 storeys	1
> = 4 storeys and < 10 000m² GIA	2
> = 4 storeys and > 10 000m² GIA	3

Hotels
Dependant on number of bedrooms, number of storeys and planning layout.
Typical examples

120 bed hotel on 3 floors	two 6 - 8 person lifts and service lift
200 bed hotel on 10 floors	four 13 person lifts and fireman's lift and service lift

Car park

Typical car space requirements	One car space per
Industrial 45 - 55m² GIA	
Offices	
medium tech	28 - 37 m² GIFA
high tech	19 - 25 m² GIFA
Retail	
superstores	8 - 10 m² GIFA
shopping centres/out of town retailing	18 - 23 m² GIFA
furniture/DIY stores	20 - 30 m² GIFA
Leisure	
swimming pools	
patrons	10 m² pool area
staff	2 nr staff
leisure centres	
patrons	10 m² activity area
Residential	1 - 2 dwellings (depending on garage space, standard of dwelling, etc)

Goods and reception and service vehicles

Typical goods reception bay suitable for two 15 m articulated lorries with 1.5 m clearance either side. Loading bays must be level and have a clear height of 4.73 m. Approach routes should have a clear minimum height of 5.03 m. Minimum articulated lorry turning circle 13 m.

Typical design load for service yard 20 KN/m².

PLANNING PARAMETERS

Recommended sizes of various sports facilities

Archery (Clout)	7.3 m firing area Range 109.728 (Women), 146.304 (Men) 182.88 (Normal range)
Baseball	Overall 60 m x 70 m
Basketball	14 m x 26 m
Camogie	91 - 110 m x 54 - 68 m
Discus and Hammer	Safety cage 2.74 m square Landing area 45 arc (65° safety) 70 m radius
Football, American	Pitch 109.80 m x 48.80 m overall 118.94 m x 57.94 m
Football, Association	NPFA rules Senior pitches 96 - 100 m x 60 - 64 m Junior pitches 90 m x 46 - 55 m International 100 - 110 m x 64 - 75 m
Football, Australian Rules	Overall 135 - 185 m x 110 - 155 m
Football, Canadian	Overall 145.74 m x 59.47 m
Football, Gaelic	128 - 146.40 m x 76.80 - 91.50 m
Football, Rugby League	111 - 122 m x 68 m
Football, Rugby Union	144 m max x 69 m
Handball	91 - 110 m x 55 - 65 m
Hockey	91.50 m x 54.90 m
Hurling	137 m x 82 m
Javelin	Runway 36.50 m x 4.27 m Landing area 80 - 95 m long, 48 m wide
Jump, High	Running area 38.80 m x 19 m Landing area 5 m x 4 m
Jump, Long	Runway 45 m x 1.22 m Landing area 9 m x 2.75 m
Jump, Triple	Runway 45 m x 1.22 m Landing area 7.30 m x 2.75 m
Korfball	90 m x 40 m
Lacrosse	(Mens) 100 m x 55 m (Womens) 110 m x 73 m
Netball	15.25 m x 30.48 m
Pole Vault	Runway 45 m x 1.22 m Landing area 5 m x 5 m
Polo	275 m x 183 m
Rounders	Overall 19 m x 17 m

Recommended sizes of various sports facilities - cont'd

400m Running Track	115.61 m bend length x 2
	84.39 m straight length x 2
	Overall 176.91 m long x 92.52 m wide
Shot Putt	Base 2.135 m diameter
	Landing area 65° arc, 25 m radius from base
Shinty	128 - 183 m x 64 - 91.50 m
Tennis	Court 23.77 m x 10.97 m
	Overall minimum 36.27 m x 18.29 m
Tug-of-war	46 m x 5 m

SOUND INSULATION

Sound reduction requirements as Building Regulations (E1/2/3)

The Building Regulations on airborne and impact sound (E1/2/3) state simply that both airborne and impact sound must be reasonably reduced in floors and walls. No minimum reduction is given but the following tables give example sound reductions for various types of constructions.

Sound reductions of typical walls	Average sound reduction (dB)
13 mm Fibreboard	20
16 mm Plasterboard	25
6 mm Float glass	30
16 mm Plasterboard, plastered both sides	35
75 mm Plastered concrete blockwork (100 mm)	44
110 mm half brick wall, half brick thick, plastered both sides	43
240 mm Brick wall one brick thick, plastered both sides	48
Timber stud partitioning with plastered metal lathing both sides	35
Cupboards used as partitions	30
Cavity block wall, plastered both sides	42
75 mm Breeze block cavity wall, plastered both sides	50
100 mm Breeze block cavity wall, plastered both sides iincluding 50 mm air-gap and plasterboard suspended ceiling	55
As above with 150 mm Breeze blocks	65
19 mm T & G boarding on timber joists including plasterboard ceiling and plaster skim coat	32
As above including metal lash and plaster ceiling	37
As above with solid sound proofing material between joists approx 98 kg per sq metre	55
As above with floating floor of T & G boarding on batten and soundproofing quilt	75

SOUND INSULATION

Impact noise is particularly difficult to reduce satisfactorily. The following are the most efficient methods of reducing such sound.

1)   Carpet on underlay of rubber or felt;
2)   Pugging between joists (e.g. Slag Wool); and
3)   A good suspended ceiling system.

Sound requirements

Housing

NHBC requirements are that any partition between a compartment containing a WC and a living-room or bedroom shell have an average sound insulation index of not less than 35 dB over the frequency range of 100 - 3150 Hz when tested in accordance with BS2750.

Hotels

Bedroom to bedroom or bedroom to corridor 48dB

THERMAL INSULATION

Thermal properties of various building elements

Thickness (mm)	Material	(m^2k/W) R	(W/m^2K) U - Value
n/a	Internal and external surface resistance	0.18	-
	Air-gap cavity	0.18	-
103	Brick skin	0.12	-
	Dense concrete block		
100	ARC conbloc	0.09	11.11
140	ARC conbloc	0.13	7.69
190	ARC conbloc	0.18	5.56
	Lightweight aggregate block		
100	Celcon standard	0.59	1.69
125	Celcon standard	0.74	1.35
150	Celcon standard	0.88	1.14
200	Celcon standard	1.18	0.85
	Lightweight aggregate thermal block		
125	Celcon solar	1.14	0.88
150	Celcon solar	1.36	0.74
200	Celcon solar	1.82	0.55
	Insulating board		
25	Dritherm	0.69	1.45
50	Dritherm	1.39	0.72
75	Dritherm	2.08	0.48
13	Lightweight plaster "Carlite"	0.07	14.29
13	Dense plaster "Thistle"	0.02	50.00
	Plasterboard		
9.5	British gypsum	0.06	16.67
12.7	British gypsum	0.08	12.50
40	Screed	0.10	10.00
150	Reinforced concrete	0.12	8.33
100	Dow roofmate insulation	3.57	0.28

THERMAL INSULATION

Resistance to the passage of heat

Provisions meeting the requirement set out in the Building Regulations (L2/3):

		Minimum U - Value
a)	**Dwellings**	
	Roof	0.35
	Exposed wall	0.60
	Exposed floor	0.60
b)	**Residential, Offices, Shops and Assembly Buildings**	
	Roof	0.06
	Exposed wall	0.60
	Exposed floor	0.60
c)	**Industrial, Storage and Other Buildings**	
	Roof	0.70
	Exposed wall	0.70
	Exposed floor	0.70

TYPICAL CONSTRUCTIONS MEETING THERMAL REQUIREMENTS

External wall, masonry construction:

Concrete blockwork	**U - Value**
200 mm lightweight concrete block, 25 mm air-gap, 10 mm plasterboard	0.68
200 mm lightweight concrete block, 20 mm EPS slab, 10 mm plasterboard	0.54
200 mm lightweight concrete block, 25 mm air-gap, 25 mm EPS slab, 10 mm plasterboard	0.46

Brick/Cavity/Brick

105 mm brickwork, 50 mm UF foam, 105 mm brickwork, 3 mm lightweight plaster	0.55

Brick/Cavity/Block

105 mm brickwork, 50 mm cavity, 125 mm Thermalite block, 3 mm lightweight plaster	0.59
105 mm brickwork, 50 mm cavity, 130 mm Thermalite block, 3 mm lightweight plaster	0.57
105 mm brickwork, 50 mm cavity, 130 mm Thermalite block, 3 mm dense plaster	0.59
105 mm brickwork, 50 mm cavity, 100 mm Thermalite block, foilbacked plasterboard	0.55
105 mm brickwork, 50 mm cavity, 115 mm Thermalite block, 9.5 mm plasterboard	0.58
105 mm brickwork, 50 mm cavity, 115 mm Thermalite block, foilbacked plasterboard	0.52
105 mm brickwork, 50 mm cavity, 125 mm Theramlite block, 9.5 mm plasterboard	0.55
105 mm brickwork, 50 mm cavity, 100 mm Thermalite block, 25 mm insulating plasterboard	0.53
105 mm brickwork, 50 mm cavity, 125 mm Thermalite block, 25 mm insulating plasterboard	0.47
105 mm brickwork, 25 mm cavity, 25 mm insulation, 100 mm Thermalite block, lightweight plaster	0.47

THERMAL INSULATION

TYPICAL CONSTRUCTIONS MEETING THERMAL REQUIREMENTS - cont'd

Brick/Cavity/Block - cont'd	U-Value
105 mm brickwork, 25 mm cavity, 25 mm insulation, 115 mm Thermalite block, lightweight plaster	0.44
Render, 100 mm "Shield" block, 50 mm cavity, 100 mm Thermalite block, lightweight plaster	0.50
Render, 100 mm "Shield" block, 50 mm cavity, 115 mm Thermalite block, lightweight plaster	0.47
Render, 100 mm "Shield" block, 50 mm cavity, 125 mm Thermalite block, lightweight plaster	0.45

Tile hanging

10 mm tile on battens and felt, 150 mm Thermalite block, lightweight plaster	0.57
25 mm insulating plasterboard	0.46
10 mm tile on battens and felt, 190 mm Thermalite block, lightweight plaster	0.47
25 mm insulating plasterboard	0.40
10 mm tile on battens and felt, 200 mm Thermalite block, lightweight plaster	0.45
25 mm insulated plasterboard	0.38
10 mm tile on battens, breather paper, 25 mm air-gap, 50 mm glass fibre quilts, 10 mm plasterboard	0.56
10 mm tile on battens, breather paper, 25 mm air-gap, 75 mm glass fibre quilts. 10 mm plasterboard	0.41
10 mm tile on battens, breather paper, 25 mm air-gap, 100 mm glass fibre quilts, 10 mm plasterboard	0.33

Pitched roofs

Slate or concrete tiles, felt, airspace, Rockwool flexible slabs laid between rafters, plasterboard

Slab	40 mm thick	0.62
	50 mm thick	0.52
	60 mm thick	0.45
	75 mm thick	0.38
	100 mm thick	0.29

Concrete tiles, sarking felt, rollbatts between joists, plasterboard

Insulation	100 mm thick	0.31
	120 mm thick	0.26
	140 mm thick	0.23
	160 mm thick	0.21

THERMAL INSULATION

TYPICAL CONSTRUCTIONS MEETING THERMAL REQUIREMENTS - cont'd

Pitched roofs - cont'd   **U-Value**

Steel frame Rockwool insulation sandwiched between steel exterior
profiled sheeting and interior sheet lining

Insulation	60 mm thick	0.53
	80 mm thick	0.41
	100 mm thick	0.34

Steel frame, steel profiled sheeting, Rockwool insulation over purlins
and plasterboard lining

Insulation	60 mm thick	0.51
	80 mm thick	0.38
	100 mm thick	0.32
	120 mm thick	0.27
	140 mm thick	0.24
	160 mm thick	0.21

Flat roofs

Asphalt, Rockwool roof slabs, 25 mm timber boarding, timber joists
and 9.5 mm plasterboard

Insulation	30 mm thick	0.68
	40 mm thick	0.57
	50 mm thick	0.49
	60 mm thick	0.44
	70 mm thick	0.39
	80 mm thick	0.35
	90 mm thick	0.32
	100 mm thick	0.29

Asphalt, Rockwool roof slabs on 150 mm dense concrete deck and
screed with 16 mm plaster finish

Insulation	40 mm thick	0.68
	50 mm thick	0.57
	60 mm thick	0.49
	70 mm thick	0.43
	80 mm thick	0.39
	90 mm thick	0.35
	100 mm thick	0.32

Asphalt, Rockwool roof slabs on 150 mm dense concrete deck and
screed with suspended plasterboard ceiling

Insulation	40 mm thick	0.60
	50 mm thick	0.52
	60 mm thick	0.45
	70 mm thick	0.40
	80 mm thick	0.36
	90 mm thick	0.33
	100 mm thick	0.30

THERMAL INSULATION

TYPICAL CONSTRUCTIONS MEETING THERMAL REQUIREMENTS

Flat roofs - cont'd	U-Value

Steel frame, asphalt on insulation slabs on troughed steel decking

Insulation	50 mm thick	0.59
	60 mm thick	0.51
	70 mm thick	0.45
	80 mm thick	0.39
	90 mm thick	0.35
	100 mm thick	0.33

Steel frame, asphalt on insulation slabs on troughed steel decking
including suspended plasterboard ceiling

Insulation	40 mm thick	0.67
	50 mm thick	0.57
	60 mm thick	0.49
	70 mm thick	0.43
	80 mm thick	0.38
	90 mm thick	0.34
	100 mm thick	0.32

WEIGHTS OF VARIOUS MATERIALS

Material		kg/m³	Material		kg/m³
Aggregates					
Ashes		610	Lime:	Chalk (lump)	704
Cement	(Portland)	1600		Ground	961
Chalk		2406		Quick	880
Chippings	(stone)	1762	Sand:	Dry	1707
Clinker	(furnace)	800		Wet	1831
	(concrete)	1441	Water		1000
Ballast or stone		2241	Shale/Whinstone		2637
Pumice		640	Broken stone		1709
Gravel		1790	Pitch		1152
Metals					
Aluminium		2559	Lead		11260
Brass		8129	Tin		7448
Bronze		8113	Zinc		7464
Gunmetal		8475			
Iron:	Cast	7207			
	Wrought	7687			
Stone and brickwork					
Blockwork:			Brickwork:		
	Aerated	650		Common Fletton	1822
	Dense concrete	1800		Glazed brick	2080
	Lightweight concrete	1200		Staffordshire Blue	2162
	Pumice concrete	1080		Red Engineering	2240
				Concrete	1841

Material	kg/m³	Material	kg/m³

Stone and brickwork - cont'd

Stone:

Artificial	2242	Granite	2642
Bath	2242	Marble	2742
Blue Pennant	2682	Portland	2170
Cragleith	2322	Slate	2882
Darley Dale	2370	York	2402
Forest of Dean	2386	Terra-cotta	2116

Wood

Blockboard	500 - 700	Jarrah	816
Cork Bark	80	Maple	752
Hardboard:		Mahogany:	
Standard	940 - 1000	Honduras	576
Tempered	940 - 1060	Spanish	1057
Wood chipboard:		Oak:	
Type I	650 - 750	English	848
Type II	680 - 800	American	720
Type III	650 - 800	Austrian & Turkish	704
Type II/III	680 - 800	Pine:	
Laminboard	500 - 700	Pitchpine	800
Timber:		Red Deal	576
Ash	800	Yellow Deal	528
Baltic spruce	480	Spruce	496
Beech	816	Sycamore	530
Birch	720	Teak:	
Box	961	African	961
Cedar	480	Indian	656
Chestnut	640	Moulmein	736
Ebony	1217	Walnut:	
Elm	624	English	496
Greenheart	961	Black	720

MEMORANDA FOR EACH TRADE

EXCAVATION AND EARTHWORK

Transport capacities

Type of vehicle	Capacity of vehicle m³ (solid)
Standard wheelbarrow	0.08
2 ton truck (2.03 t)	1.15
3 ton truck (3.05 t)	1.72
4 ton truck (4.06 t)	2.22
5 ton truck (5.08 t)	2.68
6 ton truck (6.10 t)	3.44
2 cubic yard dumper (1.53 m³)	1.15
3 cubic yard dumper (2.29 m³)	1.72
6 cubic yard dumper (4.59 m³)	3.44
10 cubic yard dumper (7.65 m³)	5.73

MEMORANDA FOR EACH TRADE

EXCAVATION AND EARTHWORK - cont'd

Planking and strutting

Maximum depth of excavation in various soils without the use of earthwork support

Ground conditions	Metres (m)
Compact soil	3.65
Drained loam	1.85
Dry sand	0.30
Gravelly earth	0.60
Ordinary earth	0.90
Stiff clay	3.00

It is important to note that the above table should only be used as a guide. Each case must be taken on its merits and, as the limited distances given above are approached, careful watch must be kept for the slightest signs of caving in.

Baulkage of soils after excavation

Soil type	Approximate bulk of 1m³ after excavation
Vegetable soil and loam	25 - 30%
Soft clay	30 - 40%
Stiff clay	10 - 15%
Gravel	20 - 25%
Sand	40 - 50%
Chalk	40 - 50%
Rock, weathered	30 - 40%
Rock, unweathered	50 - 60%

CONCRETE WORK

Approximate average weights of materials

Materials	Percentage of voids (%)	Weight per m³ (kg)
Sand	39	1660
Gravel 10 - 20 mm	45	1440
Gravel 35 - 75 mm	42	1555
Crushed stone	50	1330
Crushed granite		
(over 15 mm)	50	1345
(n.e. 15 mm)	47	1440
"All-in" ballast	32	1800

MEMORANDA FOR EACH TRADE

CONCRETE WORK - cont'd

Common mixes for various types of work per m³

Recommended mix	Class of work suitable for:	Cement (kg)	Sand (kg)	Coarse Aggregate (kg)	No. of 50 kg bags of of cement per m³ of combined aggregate
1:3:6	Roughest type of mass concrete such as footings, road haunchings 300 mm thick	208	905	1509	4.00
1:2.5:5	Mass concrete of better class than 1:3:6 such as bases for machinery, walls below ground, etc.	249	881	1474	5.00
1:2:4	Most ordinary uses of concrete such as mass walls above ground, road slabs etc. and general reinforced concrete work	304	889	1431	6.00
1:1.5:3	Watertight floors, pavements and walls, tanks, pits, steps, paths, surface of two course roads, reinforced concrete where extra strength is required	371	801	1336	7.50
1:1:2	Work of thin section such as fence posts and small precast work	511	720	1206	10.50

Bar reinforcement

Cross-sectional area and mass

Nominal sizes (m)	Cross-sectional area (mm²)	Mass per metre run (kg)
6*	28.3	0.222
8	50.3	0.395
10	78.5	0.616
12	113.1	0.888
16	201.1	1.579
20	314.2	2.466
25	490.9	3.854
32	804.2	6.313
40	1256.6	9.864
50*	1963.5	15.413

*   Where a bar larger than 40 mm is to be used the recommended size is 50 mm. Where a bar smaller than 8 mm is to be used the recommended size is 6 mm.

MEMORANDA FOR EACH TRADE

CONCRETE WORK - cont'd

Fabric reinforcement

Preferred range of designated fabric types and stock sheet sizes

Fabric reference	Longitudinal wires			Cross wires			
	Nominal wire size (mm)	Pitch (mm)	Area (mm²/m)	Nominal wire size (mm)	Pitch (mm)	Area (mm²/m)	Mass (kg/m²)
Square mesh							
A393	10	200	393	10	200	393	6.16
A252	8	200	252	8	200	252	3.95
A193	7	200	193	7	200	193	3.02
A142	6	200	142	6	200	142	2.22
A98	5	200	98	5	200	98	1.54
Structural mesh							
B1131	12	100	1131	8	200	252	10.90
B785	10	100	785	8	200	252	8.14
B503	8	100	503	8	200	252	5.93
B385	7	100	385	7	200	193	4.53
B283	6	100	283	7	200	193	3.73
B196	5	100	196	7	200	193	3.05
Long mesh							
C785	10	100	785	6	400	70.8	6.72
C636	9	100	636	6	400	70.8	5.55
C503	8	100	503	5	400	49.0	4.34
C385	7	100	385	5	400	49.0	3.41
C283	6	100	283	5	400	49.0	2.61
Wrapping mesh							
D98	5	200	98	5	200	98	1.54
D49	2.5	100	49	2.5	100	49	0.77

Stock sheet size   4.8 m x 2.4 m, Area 11.52 m²

Average weight kg/m³ of steelwork reinforcement in concrete for various building elements

Substructure	kg/m³ concrete		
Pile caps	110 - 150	Plate slab	150 - 220
Tie beams	130 - 170	Cant slab	145 - 210
Ground beams	230 - 330	Ribbed floors	130 - 200
Bases	125 - 180	Topping to block floor	30 - 40
Footings	100 - 150	Columns	210 - 310
Retaining walls	150 - 210	Beams	250 - 350
Raft	60 - 70	Stairs	130 - 170
Slabs - one way	120 - 200	Walls - normal	40 - 100
Slabs - two way	110 - 220	Walls - wind	70 - 125

Note: For exposed elements add the following % :

Walls 50%, Beams 100%, Columns 15%

MEMORANDA FOR EACH TRADE

BRICKWORK AND BLOCKWORK

Number of bricks required for various types of work per m² of walling

Description	Brick size	
	215 x 102.5 x 50 mm	**215 x 102.5 x 65 mm**
Half brick thick		
Stretcher bond	74	59
English bond	108	86
English garden wall bond	90	72
Flemish bond	96	79
Flemish garden wall bond	83	66
One brick thick and cavity wall of two half brick skins		
Stretcher bond	148	119

Quantities of bricks and mortar required per m² of walling

	Unit	No of bricks required	Mortar required (cubic metres)		
			No frogs	Single frogs	Double frogs
Standard bricks					
Brick size 215 x 102.5 x 50 mm					
half brick wall (103 mm)	m²	72	0.022	0.027	0.032
2 x half brick cavity wall (270 mm)	m²	144	0.044	0.054	0.064
one brick wall (215 mm)	m²	144	0.052	0.064	0.076
one and a half brick wall (322 mm)	m²	216	0.073	0.091	0.108
Mass brickwork	m³	576	0.347	0.413	0.480
Brick size 215 x 102.5 x 65 mm					
half brick wall (103 mm)	m²	58	0.019	0.022	0.026
2 x half brick cavity wall (270 mm)	m²	116	0.038	0.045	0.055
one brick wall (215 mm)	m²	116	0.046	0.055	0.064
one and a half brick wall (322 mm)	m²	174	0.063	0.074	0.088
Mass brickwork	m³	464	0.307	0.360	0.413
Metric modular bricks			**Perforated**		
Brick size 200 x 100 x 75 mm					
90 mm thick	m²	67	0.016	0.019	
190 mm thick	m²	133	0.042	0.048	
290 mm thick	m²	200	0.068	0.078	
Brick size 200 x 100 x 100 mm					
90 mm thick	m²	50	0.013	0.016	
190 mm thick	m²	100	0.036	0.041	
290 mm thick	m²	150	0.059	0.067	
Brick size 300 x 100 x 75 mm					
90 mm thick	m²	33	-	0.015	
Brick size 300 x 100 x 100 mm					
90 mm thick	m²	44	0.015	0.018	

Note: Assuming 10 mm thick joints.

MEMORANDA FOR EACH TRADE

BRICKWORK AND BLOCKWORK - cont'd

Mortar required per m^2 blockwork (9.88 blocks/m^2)

Wall thickness	75	90	100	125	140	190	215
Mortar m^3/m^2	0.005	0.006	0.007	0.008	0.009	0.013	0.014

Standard available block sizes

Block	Length x height		
	Co-ordinating size	Work size	Thicknesses (work size)
A	400 x 100	390 x 90	(75, 90, 100,
	400 x 200	440 x 190	(140 & 190 mm
	450 x 225	440 x 215	(75, 90, 100
			(140, 190, & 215 mm
B	400 x 100	390 x 90	(75, 90, 100
	400 x 200	390 x 190	(140 & 190 mm
	450 x 200	440 x 190	(
	450 x 225	440 x 215	(75, 90, 100
	450 x 300	440 x 290	(140, 190, & 215 mm
	600 x 200	590 x 190	(
	600 x 225	590 x 215	(
C	400 x 200	390 x 190	(
	450 x 200	440 x 190	(
	450 x 225	440 x 215	(60 & 75 mm
	450 x 300	440 x 290	(
	600 x 200	590 x 190	(
	600 x 225	590 x 215	(

ROOFING

Total roof loadings for various types of tiles/slates

	Slate/Tile	Roof load (slope) kg/m^2 Roofing underlay and battens	Total dead load kg/m^2
Asbestos cement slate (600 x 300)	21.50	3.14	24.64
Clay tile interlocking	67.00	5.50	72.50
plain	43.50	2.87	46.37
Concrete tile interlocking	47.20	2.69	49.89
plain	78.20	5.50	83.70
Natural slate (18" x 10")	35.40	3.40	38.80

		Roof load (plan) kg/m^2	
Asbestos cement slate (600 x 300)	28.45	76.50	104.95
Clay tile interlocking	53.54	76.50	130.04
plain	83.71	76.50	60.21
Concrete tile interlocking	57.60	76.50	134.10
plain	96.64	76.50	173.14
Natural slate (18" x 10")	44.80	76.50	121.30

MEMORANDA FOR EACH TRADE

ROOFING - cont'd

Tiling data

Product		Lap (mm)	Gauge of battens	No. slates per m²	Battens (m/m²)	Weight as laid (kg/m²)
CEMENT SLATES						
Eternit slates	600 x 300 mm	100	250	13.4	4.00	19.50
(Duracem)		90	255	13.1	3.92	19.20
		80	260	12.9	3.85	19.00
		70	265	12.7	3.77	18.60
	600 x 350 mm	100	250	11.5	4.00	19.50
		90	255	11.2	3.92	19.20
	500 x 250 mm	100	200	20.0	5.00	20.00
		90	205	19.5	4.88	19.50
		80	210	19.1	4.76	19.00
		70	215	18.6	4.65	18.60
	400 x 200 mm	90	155	32.3	6.45	20.80
		80	160	31.3	6.25	20.20
		70	165	30.3	6.06	19.60
CONCRETE TILES/SLATES						
Redland Roofing						
Stonewold slate	430 x 380 mm	75	355	8.2	2.82	51.20
Double Roman tile	418 x 330 mm	75	355	8.2	2.91	45.50
Grovebury pantile	418 x 332 mm	75	343	9.7	2.91	47.90
Norfolk pantile	381 x 227 mm	75	306	16.3	3.26	44.01
		100	281	17.8	3.56	48.06
Renown inter-locking						
tile	418 x 330 mm	75	343	9.7	2.91	46.40
"49" tile	381 x 227 mm	75	306	16.3	3.26	44.80
		100	281	17.8	3.56	48.95
Plain, vertical tiling	265 x 165 mm	35	115	52.7	8.70	62.20
Marley Roofing						
Bold roll tile	420 x 330 mm	75	344	9.7	2.90	47.00
		100	-	10.5	3.20	51.00
Modern roof tile	420 x 330 mm	75	338	10.2	3.00	54.00
		100	-	11.0	3.20	58.00
Ludlow major	420 x 330 mm	75	338	10.2	3.00	45.00
		100	-	11.0	3.20	49.00
Ludlow plus	387 x 229 mm	75	305	16.1	3.30	47.00
		100	-	17.5	3.60	51.00
Mendip tile	420 x 330 mm	75	338	10.2	3.00	47.00
		100	-	11.0	3.20	51.00
Wessex	413 x 330 mm	75	338	10.2	3.00	54.00
		100	-	11.0	3.20	58.00
Plain tile	267 x 165 mm	65	100	60.0	10.00	76.00
		75	95	64.0	10.50	81.00
		85	90	68.0	11.30	86.00
Plain vertical	267 x 165 mm	35	110	53.0	8.70	67.00
tiles (feature)		34	115	56.0	9.10	71.00
CLAY TILES						
Redland Roofing						
Old English pantile	342 x 241 mm	75	267	18.5	3.76	47.00
Bold roll Roman						
tiles	342 x 266 mm	75	267	17.8	3.76	50.00

MEMORANDA FOR EACH TRADE

ROOFING - cont'd

Slate nails, quantity per kilogram

	Type			
Length	Plain wire	Galvanised wire	Copper nail	Zinc nail
28.5 mm	325	305	325	415
34.4 mm	286	256	254	292
50.8 mm	242	224	194	200

Metal sheet coverings

Thicknesses and weights of sheet metal coverings

Lead to BS 1178

BS Code No	3	4	5	6	7	8
Colour Code	Green	Blue	Red	Black	White	Orange
Thickness (mm)	1.25	1.80	2.24	2.50	3.15	3.55
kg/m^2	14.18	20.41	25.40	28.36	35.72	40.26

Copper to BS 2870

Thickness (mm)		0.60	0.70

Bay width			
Roll (mm)		500	650
Seam (mm)		525	600

Standard width to form bay		600	750

Normal length of sheet		1.80	1.80

Density kg/m^2

Zinc to BS 849

Zinc Gauge (Nr)	9	10	11	12	13	14	15	16
Thickness (mm)	0.43	0.48	0.56	0.64	0.71	0.79	0.91	1.04
Density kg/m^2	3.1	3.2	3.8	4.3	4.8	5.3	6.2	7.0

Aluminium to BS 4868

Thickness (mm)	0.5	0.6	0.7	0.8	0.9	1.0	1.2
Density kg/m^2	12.8	15.4	17.9	20.5	23.0	25.6	30.7

MEMORANDA FOR EACH TRADE

ROOFING - cont'd

Type of felt	Nominal mass per unit area (kg/10m)	Nominal mass per unit area of fibre base (g/m²)	Nominal length of roll (m)
Class 1			
1B fine granule surfaced bitumen	14 18 25	220 330 470	10 or 20 10 or 20 10
1E mineral surfaced bitumen	38	470	10
1F reinforced bitumen	15	160 (fibre) 110 (hessian)	15
1F reinforced bitumen, aluminium faced	13	160 (fibre) 110 (hessian)	15
Class 2			
2B fine granule surfaced bitumen asbestos	18	500	10 or 20
2E mineral surfaced bitumen asbestos	38	600	10
Class 3			
3B fine granule surfaced bitumen glass fibre	18	60	20
3E mineral surfaced bitumen glass fibre	28	60	10
3E venting base layer bitumen glass fibre	32	60*	10
3H venting base layer bitumen glass fibre	17	60*	20

* Excluding effect of perforations

MEMORANDA FOR EACH TRADE

WOODWORK

Conversion tables (for timber only)

Inches	Millimetres	Feet	Metres
1	25	1	0.300
2	50	2	0.600
3	75	3	0.900
4	100	4	1.200
5	125	5	1.500
6	150	6	1.800
7	175	7	2.100
8	200	8	2.400
9	225	9	2.700
10	250	10	3.000
11	275	11	3.300
12	300	12	3.600
13	325	13	3.900
14	350	14	4.200
15	375	15	4.500
16	400	16	4.800
17	425	17	5.100
18	450	18	5.400
19	475	19	5.700
20	500	20	6.000
21	525	21	6.300
22	550	22	6.600
23	575	23	6.900
24	600	24	7.200

Planed softwood

The finished end section size of planed timber is usually 3/16" less than the original size from which it is produced. This however varies slightly depending upon availability of material and origin of the species used.

Standards (timber) to cubic metres and cubic metres to standards (timber)

Cubic metres	Cubic metres standards	Standards
4.672	1	0.214
9.344	2	0.428
14.017	3	0.642
18.689	4	0.856
23.361	5	1.070
28.033	6	1.284
32.706	7	1.498
37.378	8	1.712
42.050	9	1.926
46.722	10	2.140
93.445	20	4.281
140.167	30	6.421
186.890	40	8.561
233.612	50	10.702
280.335	60	12.842
327.057	70	14.982
373.779	80	17.122
420.502	90	19.263
467.224	100	21.403

MEMORANDA FOR EACH TRADE

WOODWORK - cont'd

Standards (timber) to cubic metres and cubic metres to standards (timber)

1 cu metre = 35.3148 cu ft = 0.21403 std

1 cu ft = 0.028317 cu metres

1 std = 4.67227 cu metres

Basic sizes of sawn softwood available (cross sectional areas)

Thickness (mm)	Width (mm)								
	75	100	125	150	175	200	225	250	300
16	X	X	X	X					
19	X	X	X	X					
22	X	X	X	X					
25	X	X	X	X	X	X	X	X	X
32	X	X	X	X	X	X	X	X	X
36	X	X	X	X					
38	X	X	X	X	X	X	X		
44	X	X	X	X	X	X	X	X	X
47*	X	X	X	X	X	X	X	X	X
50	X	X	X	X	X	X	X	X	X
63	X	X	X	X	X	X	X		
75		X	X	X	X	X	X	X	X
100		X		X		X		X	X
150				X		X			X
200						X			
250								X	
300									X

* This range of widths for 47 mm thickness will usually be found to be available in construction quality only.

Note: The smaller sizes below 100 mm thick and 250 mm width are normally but not exclusively of European origin. Sizes beyond this are usually of North and South American origin.

MEMORANDA FOR EACH TRADE

WOODWORK - cont'd

Basic lengths of sawn softwood available (metres)

1.80	2.10	3.00	4.20	5.10	6.00	7.20
	2.40	3.30	4.50	5.40	6.30	
	2.70	3.60	4.80	5.70	6.60	
		3.90			6.90	

Note: Lengths of 6.00 m and over will generally only be available from North American species and may have to be recut from larger sizes.

Reductions from basic size to finished size by planing of two opposed faces

Reductions from basic sizes for timber

Purpose		15 - 35 mm	36 - 100 mm	101 - 150 mm	over 150 mm
a)	constructional timber	3 mm	3 mm	5 mm	6 mm
b)	Matching interlocking boards	4 mm	4 mm	6 mm	6 mm
c)	Wood trim not specified in BS 584	5 mm	7 mm	7 mm	9 mm
d)	Joinery and cabinet work	7 mm	9 mm	11 mm	13 mm

Note: The reduction of width or depth is overall the extreme size and is exclusive of any reduction of the face by the machining of a tongue or lap joints.

Maximum spans for various roof trusses

Maximum permissible spans for rafters for Fink trussed rafters

Basic size (mm)	Actual size (mm)	Pitch (degrees)								
		15 (m)	17.5 (m)	20 (m)	22.5 (m)	25 (m)	27.5 (m)	30 (m)	32.5 (m)	35 (m)
38 x 75	35 x 72	6.03	6.16	6.29	6.41	6.51	6.60	6.70	6.80	6.90
38 x 100	35 x 97	7.48	7.67	7.83	7.97	8.10	8.22	8.34	8.47	8.61
38 x 125	35 x 120	8.80	9.00	9.20	9.37	9.54	9.68	9.82	9.98	10.16
44 x 75	41 x 72	6.45	6.59	6.71	6.83	6.93	7.03	7.14	7.24	7.35
44 x 100	41 x 97	8.05	8.23	8.40	8.55	8.68	8.81	8.93	9.09	9.22
44 x 125	41 x 120	9.38	9.60	9.81	9.99	10.15	10.31	10.45	10.64	10.81
50 x 75	47 x 72	6.87	7.01	7.13	7.25	7.35	7.45	7.53	7.67	7.78
50 x 100	47 x 97	8.62	8.80	8.97	9.12	9.25	9.38	9.50	9.66	9.80
50 x 125	47 x 120	10.01	10.24	10.44	10.62	10.77	10.94	11.00	11.00	11.00

MEMORANDA FOR EACH TRADE

WOODWORK- cont'd

Sizes of internal and external doorsets

Description	Internal		External	
	Size (mm)	Permissible deviation	Size (mm)	Permissible deviation
Co-ordinating dimension: height of door leaf height sets	2100		2100	
Co-ordinating dimension: height of ceiling height set	2300 2350 2400 2700 3000		2300 2350 2400 2700 3000	
Co-ordinating dimension: width of all door sets	600 S 700 S		900 S 1000 S	
S = Single leaf set	800 S&D		1200 D	
D = Double leaf set	900 S&D 1000 S&D 1200 D 1500 D 1800 D 2100 D		1500 D 1800 D 2100 D	
Work size: height of door leaf height set	2090	± 2.0	2095	± 2.0
Work size: height of ceiling height set	2285) 2335) 2385) 2685) 2985)	± 2.0	2295) 2345) 2395) 2695) 2995)	± 2.0
Work size: width of all door sets	590 S) 690 S) 790 S&D)		895 S) 995 S) 1195 D)	± 2.0
S = Single leaf set	890 S&D)		1495 D)	
D = Double leaf set	990 S&D) 1190 D) 1490 D) 1790 D) 2090 D)	± 2.0	1795 D) 2095 D)	
Width of door leaf in single leaf sets	526 F) 626 F)		806 F&P) 906 F&P)	± 1.5
F = Flush leaf P = Panel leaf	726 F&P) 826 F&P) 926 F&P)	± 1.5		

MEMORANDA FOR EACH TRADE

WOODWORK - cont'd

Description	Internal		External	
	Size (mm)	Permissible deviation	Size (mm)	Permissible deviation
Width of door leaf in double leaf sets F = Flush leaf P = Panel leaf	362 F 412 F 426 F 562 F&P 712 F&P 826 F&P 1012 F&P	)))) $\pm$ 1.5)))	552 F&P) 702 F&P) 852 F&P) 1002 F&P)	$\pm$ 1.5
Door leaf height for all door sets	2040	$\pm$ 1.5	1994	$\pm$ 1.5

STRUCTURAL STEELWORK

Tables showing the mass and surface area per metre run for various steel members

Size (mm)	Mass (kg/m)	Surface area per m run (m^2)
Universal beams		
914 x 419	388	3.404
	343	3.382
914 x 305	289	2.988
	253	2.967
	224	2.948
	201	2.932
838 x 292	226	2.791
	194	2.767
	176	2.754
762 x 267	197	2.530
	173	2.512
	147	2.493
686 x 254	170	2.333
	152	2.320
	140	2.310
	125	2.298
610 x 305	238	2.421
	179	2.381
	149	2.361
610 x 229	140	2.088
	125	2.075
	113	2.064
	101	2.053
533 x 210	122	1.872
	109	1.860
	101	1.853
	92	1.844
	82	1.833

MEMORANDA FOR EACH TRADE

STRUCTURAL STEELWORK - cont'd

Tables showing the mass and surface area per metre run for various steel members - cont'd

Size (mm)	Mass (kg/m)	Surface area per m run (m²)
Universal beams - cont'd		
457 x 191	98	1.650
	89	1.641
	82	1.633
	74	1.625
	67	1.617
457 x 152	82	1.493
	74	1.484
	67	1.474
	60	1.487
	52	1.476
406 x 178	74	1.493
	67	1.484
	60	1.476
	54	1.468
406 x 140	46	1.332
	39	1.320
356 x 171	67	1.371
	57	1.358
	51	1.351
	45	1.343
356 x 127	39	1.169
	33	1.160
305 x 165	54	1.245
	46	1.235
	40	1.227
305 x 127	48	1.079
	42	1.069
	37	1.062
305 x 102	33	1.006
	28	0.997
	25	0.988
254 x 146	43	1.069
	37	1.060
	31	1.050
254 x 102	28	0.900
	25	0.893
	22	0.887
203 x 133	30	0.912
	25	0.904

MEMORANDA FOR EACH TRADE

STRUCTURAL STEELWORK - cont'd

Tables showing the mass and surface area per metre run for various steel members - cont'd

Size (mm)	Mass (kg/m)	Surface area per m run (m²)
Universal columns		
356 x 406	634	2.525
	551	2.475
	467	2.425
	393	2.379
	340	2.346
	287	2.312
	235	2.279
356 x 368	202	2.187
	177	2.170
	153	2.154
	129	2.137
305 x 305	283	1.938
	240	1.905
	198	1.872
	158	1.839
	137	1.822
	118	1.806
	97	1.789
254 x 254	167	1.576
	132	1.543
	107	1.519
	89	1.502
	73	1.485
203 x 203	86	1.236
	71	1.218
	60	1.204
	52	1.194
	46	1.187
152 x 152	37	0.912
	30	0.900
	23	0.889
Joists		
254 x 203	81.85	1.193
254 x 114	37.20	0.882
203 x 152	52.09	0.911
152 x 127	37.20	0.722
127 x 114	29.76	0.620
127 x 114	26.79	0.635
114 x 114	26.79	0.600
102 x 102	23.07	0.528

MEMORANDA FOR EACH TRADE

STRUCTURAL STEELWORK - cont'd

Tables showing the mass and surface area per metre run for various steel members - cont'd

Size (mm)	Mass (kg/m)	Surface area per m run (m²)	
Joists - cont'd			
89 x 89	19.35	0.460	
76 x 76	12.65	0.403	

Circular hollow sections - outside dia (mm)	**Mass**	**Surface area per m run (m²)**	**Thickness (mm)**
21.3	1.43	0.067	3.20
26.9	1.87	0.085	3.20
33.7	1.99	0.106	2.60
	2.41	0.106	3.20
	2.93	0.106	4.00
42.4	2.55	0.133	2.60
	3.09	0.133	3.20
	3.79	0.133	4.00
48.3	3.56	0.152	3.20
	4.37	0.152	4.00
	5.34	0.152	5.00
60.3	4.51	0.189	3.20
	5.55	0.189	4.00
	6.82	0.189	5.00
76.1	5.75	0.239	3.20
	7.11	0.239	4.00
	8.77	0.239	5.00
88.9	6.76	0.279	3.20
	8.38	0.279	4.00
	10.30	0.279	5.00
114.3	9.83	0.359	3.60
	13.50	0.359	5.00
	16.80	0.359	6.30
139.7	16.60	0.439	5.00
	20.70	0.439	6.30
	26.00	0.439	8.00
	32.00	0.439	10.00
168.3	20.10	0.529	5.00
	25.20	0.529	6.30
	31.60	0.529	8.00
	39.00	0.529	10.00

MEMORANDA FOR EACH TRADE

STRUCTURAL STEELWORK - cont'd

Tables showing the mass and surface area per metre run for various steel members - cont'd

Size (mm)	Mass (kg/m)	Surface area per m run (m²)	Thickness (mm)
Circular hollow sections **- outside diameter (mm) - cont'd**			
193.7	23.30	0.609	5.00
	29.10	0.609	6.30
	36.60	0.609	8.00
	45.30	0.609	10.00
	55.90	0.609	12.50
	70.10	0.609	16.00
219.1	33.10	0.688	6.30
	41.60	0.688	8.00
	51.60	0.688	10.00
	63.70	0.688	12.50
	80.10	0.688	16.00
	98.20	0.688	20.00
273.0	41.40	0.858	6.30
	52.30	0.858	8.00
	64.90	0.858	10.00
	80.30	0.858	12.50
	101.00	0.858	16.00
	125.00	0.858	20.00
	153.00	0.858	25.00
323.9	62.30	1.020	8.00
	77.40	1.020	10.00
	96.00	1.020	12.50
	121.00	1.020	16.00
	150.00	1.020	20.00
	184.00	1.020	25.00
406.4	97.80	1.280	10.00
	121.00	1.280	12.50
	154.00	1.280	16.00
	191.00	1.280	20.00
	235.00	1.280	25.00
	295.00	1.280	32.00
457.0	110.00	1.440	10.00
	137.00	1.440	12.50
	174.00	1.440	16.00
	216.00	1.440	20.00
	266.00	1.440	25.00
	335.00	1.440	32.00
	411.00	1.440	40.00

MEMORANDA FOR EACH TRADE

STRUCTURAL STEELWORK - cont'd

Tables showing the mass and surface area per metre run for various steel members - cont'd

Size (mm)	Mass (kg/m)	Surface area per m run (m²)	Thickness (mm)
Square hollow sections			
20 x 20	1.12	0.076	2.00
	1.35	0.074	2.50
30 x 30	2.14	0.114	2.50
	2.51	0.113	3.00
40 x 40	2.92	0.155	2.50
	3.45	0.154	3.00
	4.46	0.151	4.00
50 x 50	4.66	0.193	3.20
	5.72	0.191	4.00
	6.97	0.189	5.00
60 x 60	5.67	0.233	3.20
	6.97	0.231	4.00
	8.54	0.229	5.00
70 x 70	7.46	0.272	3.60
	10.10	0.269	5.00
80 x 80	8.59	0.312	3.60
	11.70	0.309	5.00
	14.40	0.306	6.30
90 x 90	9.72	0.352	3.60
	13.30	0.349	5.00
	16.40	0.346	6.30
100 x 100	12.00	0.391	4.00
	14.80	0.389	5.00
	18.40	0.386	6.30
	22.90	0.383	8.00
	27.90	0.379	10.00
120 x 120	18.00	0.469	5.00
	22.30	0.466	6.30
	27.90	0.463	8.00
	34.20	0.459	10.00
150 x 150	22.70	0.589	5.00
	28.30	0.586	6.30
	35.40	0.583	8.00
	43.60	0.579	10.00
	53.40	0.573	12.50
	66.40	0.566	16.00

MEMORANDA FOR EACH TRADE

STRUCTURAL STEELWORK - cont'd

Tables showing the mass and surface area per metre run for various steel members - cont'd

Size (mm)	Mass (kg/m)	Surface area per m run (m²)	Thickness (mm)
Square hollow sections - cont'd			
180 x 180	34.20	0.706	6.30
	43.00	0.703	8.00
	53.00	0.699	10.00
	65.20	0.693	12.50
	81.40	0.686	16.00
200 x 200	38.20	0.786	6.30
	48.00	0.783	8.00
	59.30	0.779	10.00
	73.00	0.773	12.50
	91.50	0.766	16.00
250 x 250	48.10	0.986	6.30
	60.50	0.983	8.00
	75.00	0.979	10.00
	92.60	0.973	12.50
	117.00	0.966	16.00
300 x 300	90.70	1.180	10.00
	112.00	1.170	12.50
	142.00	1.170	16.00
350 x 350	106.00	1.380	10.00
	132.00	1.370	12.50
	167.00	1.370	16.00
400 x 400	122.00	1.580	10.00
	152.00	1.570	12.50
Rectangular hollow sections			
50 x 30	2.92	0.155	2.50
	3.66	0.153	3.20
60 x 40	4.66	0.193	3.20
	5.72	0.191	4.00
80 x 40	5.67	0.232	3.20
	6.97	0.231	4.00
90 x 50	7.46	0.272	3.60
	10.10	0.269	5.00
100 x 50	6.75	0.294	3.00
	7.18	0.293	3.20
	8.86	0.291	4.00
100 x 60	8.59	0.312	3.60
	11.70	0.309	5.00
	14.40	0.306	6.30

MEMORANDA FOR EACH TRADE

STRUCTURAL STEELWORK - cont'd

Tables showing the mass and surface area per metre run for various steel members - cont'd

Size (mm)	Mass (kg/m)	Surface area per m run (m²)	Thickness (mm)
Rectangular hollow sections - cont'd			
120 x 60	9.72	0.352	3.60
	13.30	0.349	5.00
	16.40	0.346	6.30
120 x 80	14.80	0.389	5.00
	18.40	0.386	6.30
	22.90	0.383	8.00
	27.90	0.379	10.00
150 x 100	18.70	0.489	5.00
	23.30	0.486	6.30
	29.10	0.483	8.00
	35.70	0.479	10.00
160 x 80	18.00	0.469	5.00
	22.30	0.466	6.30
	27.90	0.463	8.00
	34.20	0.459	10.00
200 x 100	22.70	0.589	5.00
	28.30	0.586	6.30
	35.40	0.583	8.00
	43.60	0.579	10.00
250 x 150	38.20	0.786	6.30
	48.00	0.783	8.00
	59.30	0.779	10.00
	73.00	0.773	12.50
	91.50	0.766	16.00
300 x 200	48.10	0.986	6.30
	60.50	0.983	8.00
	75.00	0.979	10.00
	92.60	0.973	12.50
	117.00	0.966	16.00
400 x 200	90.70	1.180	10.00
	112.00	1.170	12.50
	142.00	1.170	16.00
450 x 250	106.00	1.380	10.00
	132.00	1.370	12.50
	167.00	1.370	16.00

MEMORANDA FOR EACH TRADE

STRUCTURAL STEELWORK - cont'd

Tables showing the mass and surface area per metre run for various steel members - cont'd

Size (mm)		Mass (kg/m)	Surface area per m run (m²)
Channels			
432 x 102		65.54	1.217
381 x 102		55.10	1.118
305 x 102		46.18	0.966
305 x 89		41.69	0.920
254 x 89		35.74	0.820
254 x 76		28.29	0.774
229 x 89		32.76	0.770
229 x 76		26.06	0.725
203 x 89		29.78	0.720
203 x 76		23.82	0.675
178 x 89		26.81	0.671
178 x 76		20.84	0.625
152 x 89		23.84	0.621
152 x 76		17.88	0.575
127 x 64		14.90	0.476
Angles - sum of leg lengths	**Thickness (mm)**		
50	3	1.11	0.10
	4	1.45	0.10
	5	1.77	0.10
80	4	2.42	0.16
	5	2.97	0.16
	6	3.52	0.16
90	4	2.74	0.18
	5	3.38	0.18
	6	4.00	0.18
100	5	3.77	0.20
	6	4.47	0.20
	8	5.82	0.20
115	5	4.35	0.23
	6	5.16	0.23
	8	6.75	0.23

MEMORANDA FOR EACH TRADE

STRUCTURAL STEELWORK - cont'd

Tables showing the mass and surface area per metre run for various steel members - cont'd

Angles - sum of leg lengths - cont'd	Thickness (mm)	Mass (kg/m)	Surface area per m run (m²)
120	5	4.57	0.24
	6	5.42	0.24
	8	7.09	0.24
	10	8.69	0.24
125	6	5.65	0.25
	8	7.39	0.25
200	8	12.20	0.40
	10	15.00	0.40
	12	17.80	0.40
	15	21.90	0.40
225	10	17.00	0.45
	12	20.20	0.45
	15	24.80	0.45
240	8	14.70	0.48
	10	18.20	0.48
	12	21.60	0.48
	15	26.60	0.48
300	10	23.00	0.60
	12	27.30	0.60
	15	33.80	0.60
	18	40.10	0.60
350	12	32.00	0.70
	15	39.60	0.70
	18	47.10	0.70
400	16	48.50	0.80
	18	54.20	0.80
	20	59.90	0.80
	24	71.10	0.80

MEMORANDA FOR EACH TRADE

PLUMBING AND MECHANICAL INSTALLATIONS

Dimensions and weights of tubes

Outside diameter (mm)	Internal dia (mm)	Weight per m (kg)	Internal dia (mm)	Weight per m (kg)	Internal dia (mm)	Weight per m (kg)
Copper to EN 1057:1996						
	Table X			Table Y		Table Z
6	4.80	0.0911	4.40	0.1170	5.00	0.0774
8	6.80	0.1246	6.40	0.1617	7.00	0.1054
10	8.80	0.1580	8.40	0.2064	9.00	0.1334
12	10.80	0.1914	10.40	0.2511	11.00	0.1612
15	13.60	0.2796	13.00	0.3923	14.00	0.2031
18	16.40	0.3852	16.00	0.4760	16.80	0.2918
22	20.22	0.5308	19.62	0.6974	20.82	0.3589
28	26.22	0.6814	25.62	0.8985	26.82	0.4594
35	32.63	1.1334	32.03	1.4085	33.63	0.6701
42	39.63	1.3675	39.03	1.6996	40.43	0.9216
54	51.63	1.7691	50.03	2.9052	52.23	1.3343
76.1	73.22	3.1287	72.22	4.1437	73.82	2.5131
108	105.12	4.4666	103.12	7.3745	105.72	3.5834
133	130.38	5.5151	-	-	130.38	5.5151
159	155.38	8.7795	-	-	156.38	6.6056

MEMORANDA FOR EACH TRADE

PLUMBING AND MECHANICAL INSTALLATIONS - cont'd

Dimensions and weights of tubes - cont'd

Nominal size (mm)	Outside diameter max (mm)	min (mm)	Wall thickness (mm)	Weight (kg/m)	Weight screwed and socketted (kg/m)
Steel pipes to BS 1387					
Light gauge					
6	10.1	9.7	1.80	0.361	0.364
8	13.6	13.2	1.80	0.517	0.521
10	17.1	16.7	1.80	0.674	0.680
15	21.4	21.0	2.00	0.952	0.961
20	26.9	26.4	2.35	1.410	1.420
25	33.8	33.2	2.65	2.010	2.030
32	42.5	41.9	2.65	2.580	2.610
40	48.4	47.8	2.90	3.250	3.290
50	60.2	59.6	2.90	4.110	4.180
65	76.0	75.2	3.25	5.800	5.920
80	88.7	87.9	3.25	6.810	6.980
100	113.9	113.0	3.65	9.890	10.200
Medium gauge					
6	10.4	9.8	2.00	0.407	0.410
8	13.9	13.3	2.35	0.650	0.654
10	17.4	16.8	2.35	0.852	0.858
15	21.7	21.1	2.65	1.220	1.230
20	27.2	26.6	2.65	1.580	1.590
25	34.2	33.4	3.25	2.440	2.460
32	42.9	42.1	3.25	3.140	3.170
40	48.8	48.0	3.25	3.610	3.650
50	60.8	59.8	3.65	5.100	5.170
65	76.6	75.4	3.65	6.510	6.630
80	89.5	88.1	4.05	8.470	8.640

MEMORANDA FOR EACH TRADE

PLUMBING AND MECHANICAL INSTALLATIONS - cont'd

Nominal size (mm)	Outside diameter max (mm)	min (mm)	Wall thickness (mm)	Weight (kg/m)	Weight screwed and socketted (kg/m)
Medium gauge - cont'd					
100	114.9	113.3	4.50	12.100	12.400
125	140.6	138.7	4.85	16.200	16.700
150	166.1	164.1	4.85	19.200	19.800
Heavy gauge					
6	10.4	9.8	2.65	0.493	0.496
8	13.9	13.3	2.90	0.769	0.773
10	17.4	16.8	2.90	1.020	1.030
15	21.7	21.1	3.25	1.450	1.460
20	27.2	26.6	3.25	1.900	1.910
25	34.2	33.4	4.05	2.970	2.990
32	42.9	42.1	4.05	3.840	3.870
40	48.8	48.0	4.05	4.430	4.470
50	60.8	59.8	4.50	6.170	6.240
65	76.6	75.4	4.50	7.900	8.020
80	89.5	88.1	4.85	10.100	10.300
100	114.9	113.3	5.40	14.400	14.700
125	140.6	138.7	5.40	17.800	18.300
150	166.1	164.1	5.40	21.200	21.800
Stainless steel pipes to BS 4127					
8	8.045	7.940	0.60	0.1120	
10	10.045	9.940	0.60	0.1419	
12	12.045	11.940	0.60	0.1718	
15	15.045	14.940	0.60	0.2174	
18	18.045	17.940	0.70	0.3046	
22	22.055	21.950	0.70	0.3748	
28	28.055	27.950	0.80	0.5469	
35	35.070	34.965	1.00	0.8342	

MEMORANDA FOR EACH TRADE

PLUMBING AND MECHANICAL INSTALLATIONS - cont'd

Maximum distances between pipe supports

Pipe material	BS nominal pipe size		Pipes fitted vertically support distances in metres	Pipes fitted horizontally onto low gradients support distances in metres
	inch	mm		
Copper	0.50	15.0	1.90	1.3
	0.75	22.0	2.50	1.9
	1.00	28.0	2.50	1.9
	1.25	35.0	2.80	2.5
	1.50	42.0	2.80	2.5
	2.00	54.0	3.90	2.5
	2.50	67.0	3.90	2.8
	3.00	76.1	3.90	2.8
	4.00	108.0	3.90	2.8
	5.00	133.0	3.90	2.8
	6.00	159.0	3.90	2.8
muPVC	1.25	32.0	1.20	0.5
	1.50	40.0	1.20	0.5
	2.00	50.0	1.20	0.6
Polypropylene	1.25	32.0	1.20	0.5
	1.50	40.0	1.20	0.5
uPVC	-	82.4	1.20	0.5
	-	110.0	1.80	0.9
	-	160.0	1.80	1.2

Litres of water storage required per person in various types of building

Type of building	Storage per person (litres)
Houses and flats	90
Hostels	90
Hotels	135
Nurse's home and medical quarters	115
Offices with canteens	45
Offices without canteens	35
Restaurants, per meal served	7
Boarding school	90
Day schools	30

MEMORANDA FOR EACH TRADE

PLUMBING AND MECHANICAL INSTALLATIONS - cont'd

Cold water plumbing - thickness of insulation required against frost

Bore of tube	Pipework within buildings declared thermal conductivity (W/m degrees C)		
	Up to 0.040	0.041 to 0.055	0.056 to 0.070
(mm)	Minimum thickness of insulation (mm)		
15	32	50	75
20	32	50	75
25	32	50	75
32	32	50	75
40	32	50	75
50	25	32	50
65	25	32	50
80	25	32	50
100	19	25	38

Cisterns

Capacities and dimensions of galvanised mild steel cisterns from BS 417

Capacity (litres)	BS type	Dimensions (mm) length	width	depth
18	SCM 45	457	305	305
36	SCM 70	610	305	371
54	SCM 90	610	406	371
68	SCM 110	610	432	432
86	SCM 135	610	457	482
114	SCM 180	686	508	508
159	SCM 230	736	559	559
191	SCM 270	762	584	610
227	SCM 320	914	610	584
264	SCM 360	914	660	610
327	SCM 450/1	1220	610	610
336	SCM 450/2	965	686	686
423	SCM 570	965	762	787
491	SCM 680	1090	864	736
709	SCM 910	1170	889	889

Capacities of cold water polypropylene storage cisterns from BS 4213

Capacity (litres)	BS type	Maximum height (mm)
18	PC 4	310
36	PC 8	380
68	PC 15	430
91	PC 20	510
114	PC 25	530
182	PC 40	610
227	PC 50	660
273	PC 60	660
318	PC 70	660
455	PC 100	760

MEMORANDA FOR EACH TRADE

HEATING AND HOT WATER INSTALLATIONS

Storage capacity and recommended power of hot water storage boilers

Type of building	Storage at 65°C (litres per person)	Boiler power to 65°C (kW per person)
Flats and dwellings		
(a) Low rent properties	25	0.5
(b) Medium rent properties	30	0.7
(c) High rent properties	45	1.2
Nurses homes	45	0.9
Hostels	30	0.7
Hotels		
(a) Top quality - upmarket	45	1.2
(b) Average quality - low market	35	0.9
Colleges and schools		
(a) Live-in accommodation	25	0.7
(b) Public comprehensive	5	0.1
Factories	5	0.1
Hospitals		
(a) General	30	1.5
(b) Infectious	45	1.5
(c) Infirmaries	25	0.6
(d) Infirmaries (inc. laundry facilities)	30	0.9
(e) Maternity	30	2.1
(f) Mental	25	0.7
Offices	5	0.1
Sports pavilions	35	0.3

Thickness of thermal insulation for heating installations

Size of tube (mm)	Up to 0.025	0.026 to 0.040	0.041 to 0.055	0.056 to 0.070
		Declared thermal conductivity		

Minimum thickness of insulation

LTHW Systems

15	25	25	38	38
20	25	32	38	38
25	25	38	38	38
32	32	38	38	50
40	32	38	38	50
50	38	38	50	50
65	38	50	50	50
80	38	50	50	50

MEMORANDA FOR EACH TRADE

HEATING AND HOT WATER INSTALLATIONS - cont'd

	Minimum thickness of insulation			
Size of tube (mm)	Up to 0.025	0.026 to 0.040	0.041 to 0.055	0.056 to 0.070

LTHW Systems - cont'd

100	38	50	50	63
125	38	50	50	63
150	50	50	63	63
200	50	50	63	63
250	50	63	63	63
300	50	63	63	63
Flat surfaces	50	63	63	63

MTHW Systems and condensate

	Declared thermal conductivity			
15	25	38	38	38
20	32	38	38	50
25	38	38	38	50
32	38	50	50	50
40	38	50	50	50
50	38	50	50	50
65	38	50	50	50
80	50	50	50	63
100	50	63	63	63
125	50	63	63	63
150	50	63	63	63
200	50	63	63	63
250	50	63	63	75
300	63	63	63	75
Flat surfaces	63	63	63	75

HTHW Systems and steam

15	38	50	50	50
20	38	50	50	50
25	38	50	50	50
32	50	50	50	63
40	50	50	50	63
50	50	50	75	75
65	50	63	75	75
80	50	63	75	75
100	63	63	75	100
125	63	63	100	100
150	63	63	100	100
200	63	63	100	100
250	63	75	100	100
300	63	75	100	100
Flat surfaces	63	75	100	100

MEMORANDA FOR EACH TRADE

HEATING AND HOT WATER INSTALLATIONS - cont'd

Capacities and dimensions of copper indirect cylinders (coil type) from BS 1566

Capacity (litres)	BS Type	External diameter (mm)	External height over dome (mm)
96	0	300	1600
72	1	350	900
96	2	400	900
114	3	400	1050
84	4	450	675
95	5	450	750
106	6	450	825
117	7	450	900
140	8	450	1050
162	9	450	1200
206	9 E	450	1500
190	10	500	1200
245	11	500	1500
280	12	600	1200
360	13	600	1500
440	14	600	1800

Capacity	BS Type	Internal diameter (mm)	Height (mm)
109	BSG 1M	457	762
136	BSG 2M	457	914
159	BSG 3M	457	1067
227	BSG 4M	508	1270
273	BSG 5M	508	1473
364	BSG 6M	610	1372
455	BSG 7M	610	1753
123	BSG 8M	457	838

Energy costs (July 1999)

GAS SUPPLIES

With the deregulation process now complete all consumers can purchase their gas from a variety of independent suppliers. The market is currently divided into two main sectors, Domestic and Commercial.

Domestic

This sector refers to individual supply points which do not consume more than 73,250 kw/hrs (2,500 therms) per annum, or approximately £1,100 per annum at British Gas Tariffs. In this sector suppliers must supply at their published tariff rates, although there are exceptions to this for bulk purchasing schemes. By contracting with an independent supplier savings of up to 25%can be achieved over British Gas Tariffs. Care should be exercised when selecting a supplier, look beyond the savings as some supply contracts contain onerous clauses. A typical "all-in" supply rate would be 1.20 p/kw hr for a domestic property.

Commercial

This sector refers to all other gas supplies. There are in excess of 50 companies licensed to supply gas in this sector. The market can be quite volatile suffering dramatic fluctuations in the supply rate, although during the past 12 months the price has remained fairly constant.

MEMORANDA FOR EACH TRADE

Energy costs (July 1999) - cont'd

ELECTRICITY SUPPLIES

Over 100 KVA Supplies

For supplies in this sector of the market there are many options to choose from regarding the charging structure. A typical contract for a supply site with an annual expenditure of £50,000 could obtain an "all-in" rate in the region of 4.10 p/kw hr.

Under 100 KVA Supplies (Non Domestic)

This sector of the market completed its deregulation process earlier this year. Consumers can purchase their electricity from any authorised supplier generally a Regional Electricity Company (REC) or Generator, although there are other companies in the market place. Your host REC must supply at his published tariffs. Other supplies generally offer a discount off the hosts tariff.

Discounts achieved vary from region to region depending on the competitiveness of the host REC's tariff. Typical discounts vary from 9% in the SWEB region to 22% in the southern regions.

Domestic Tariff Supplies

The domestic market has now just completed the deregulation process. Generally the principle is the same as the 'Under the 100 KVA' market except that the typical discounts are lower. A typical discount being 12% off the host REC tariff.

Generally

For users who are able to group purchase their fuels (eg. schools, health trusts, local authorities, housing associations) further, sometimes significant, savings can be achieved. Advice on how to go about this or energy purchasing in general can be obtained from the editor's, Davis Langdon & Everest's, Cambridge office who have considerable experience in both purchasing energy and the establishment of bulk purchasing schemes.

MEMORANDA FOR EACH TRADE

VENTILATION AND AIR-CONDITIONING

Typical fresh air supply factors in typical situations

Building type	Litres of fresh air per second per person	Litres of fresh air per second per m² floor area
General offices	5 - 8	1.30
Board rooms	18 - 25	6.00
Private offices	5 - 12	1.20 - 2.00
Dept. stores	5 - 8	3.00
Factories	20 - 30	0.80
Garages	-	8.00
Bars	12 - 18	-
Dance halls	8 - 12	-
Hotel rooms	8 - 12	1.70
Schools	14	-
Assembly halls	14	-
Drawing offices	16	-

Note: As a global figure for fresh air allow per 1000 m² 1.20 m³/second.

Typical air-changes per hour in typical situations

Building type	Air changes per hour
Residences	1 - 2
Churches	1 - 2
Storage buildings	1 - 2
Libraries	3 - 4
Book stacks	1 - 2
Banks	5 - 6
Offices	4 - 6
Assembly halls	5 - 10
Laboratories	4 - 6
Internal bathrooms	5 - 6
Laboratories - internal	6 - 8
Restaurants/cafes	10 - 15
Canteens	8 - 12
Small kitchens	20 - 40
Large kitchens	10 - 20
Boiler houses	15 - 30

MEMORANDA FOR EACH TRADE

GLAZING

Float and polished plate glass

Nominal thickness (mm)	Tolerance on thickness (mm)	Approximate weight (kg/m²)	Normal maximum size (mm)
3	+ 0.2	7.50	2140 x 1220
4	+ 0.2	10.00	2760 x 1220
5	+ 0.2	12.50	3180 x 2100
6	+ 0.2	15.00	4600 x 3180
10	+ 0.3	25.00)	
12	+ 0.3	30.00)	6000 x 3300
15	+ 0.5	37.50	3050 x 3000
19	+ 1.0	47.50)	
25	+ 1.0	63.50)	3000 x 2900

Clear sheet glass

2 *	+ 0.2	5.00	1920 x 1220
3	+ 0.3	7.50	2130 x 1320
4	+ 0.3	10.00	2760 x 1220
5 *	+ 0.3	12.50)	
6 *	+ 0.3	15.00)	2130 x 2400

Cast glass

3	+ 0.4		
	- 0.2	6.00)	
4	+ 0.5	7.50)	2140 x 1280
5	+ 0.5	9.50	2140 x 1320
6	+ 0.5	11.50)	
10	+ 0.8	21.50)	3700 x 1280

Wired glass

(Cast wired glass)

6	+ 0.3	-)	
	- 0.7	)	3700 x 1840
7	+ 0.7	-)	

(Polished wire glass)

6	+ 1.0	-	330 x 1830

*   The 5 mm and 6 mm thickness are known as *thick drawn sheet*. Although 2 mm sheet glass is available it is not recommended for general glazing purposes.

MEMORANDA FOR EACH TRADE

DRAINAGE

Width required for trenches for various diameters of pipes

Pipe diameter (mm)	Trench n.e. 1.5 m deep	Trench over 1.5 m deep
n.e. 100 mm	450 mm	600 mm
100 - 150 mm	500 mm	650 mm
150 - 225 mm	600 mm	750 mm
225 - 300 mm	650 mm	800 mm
300 - 400 mm	750 mm	900 mm
400 - 450 mm	900 mm	1050 mm
450 - 600 mm	1100 mm	1300 mm

Weights and dimensions of typically sized uPVC pipes

Nominal size	Mean outside diameter (mm) min	max	Wall thickness	Weight kg per metre
Standard pipes				
82.40	82.40	82.70	3.20	1.20
110.00	110.00	110.40	3.20	1.60
160.00	160.00	160.60	4.10	3.00
200.00	200.00	200.60	4.90	4.60
250.00	250.00	250.70	6.10	7.20

Perforated pipes

Heavy grade as above

Thin wall

82.40	82.40	82.70	1.70	-
110.00	110.00	110.40	2.20	-
160.00	160.00	160.60	3.20	-

Vitrified clay pipes

Product	Nominal diameter (mm)	Effective pipe length (mm)	Limits of bore load per metre length min	max	Crushing strength (kN/m)	Weight kg/pipe (/m)
Supersleve	100	1600	96	105	35.00	15.63 (9.77)
Hepsleve	150	1600	146	158	22.00 (normal)	36.50 (22.81)
Hepseal	150	1500	146	158	22.00	37.04 (24.69)
	225	1750	221	235	28.00	95.24 (54.42)
	300	2500	295	313	34.00	196.08 (78.43)
	400	2500	394	414	44.00	357.14 (142.86)

MEMORANDA FOR EACH TRADE

DRAINAGE - cont'd

Vitrified clay pipes - cont'd

Product	Nominal diameter	Effective pipe length	Limits of bore load per metre length		Crushing strength	Weight kg/pipe (/m)
			min	max		
	(mm)	(mm)			(kN/m)	
Hepseal - cont'd	450	2500	444	464	44.00	500.00 (200.00)
	500	2500	494	514	48.00	555.56 (222.22)
	600	3000	591	615	70.00	847.46 (282.47)
	700	3000	689	719	81.00	1111.11 (370.37)
	800	3000	788	822	86.00	1351.35 (450.35)
	1000	3000	985	1027	120.00	2000.00 (666.67)
Hepline	100	1250	95	107	22.00	15.15 (12.12)
	150	1500	145	160	22.00	32.79 (21.86)
	225	1850	219	239	28.00	74.07 (40.04)
	300	1850	292	317	34.00	105.26 (56.90)
Hepduct (Conduit)	90	1500	-	-	28.00	12.05 (8.03)
	100	1600	-	-	28.00	14.29 (8.93)
	125	1250	-	-	22.00	21.28 (17.02)
	150	1250	-	-	22.00	28.57 (22.86)
	225	1850	-	-	28.00	64.52 (34.88)
	300	1850	-	-	34.00	111.11 (60.06)

USEFUL ADDRESSES FOR FURTHER INFORMATION

**ACOUSTICAL INVESTIGATION & RESEARCH
ORGANISATION LTD (AIRO)**
Duxon's Turn
Maylands Avenue
Hemel Hempstead
Hertfordshire
HP2 4SB
Tel: 01442 247 146
Fax: 01442 256 749

**ALUMINIUM ROLLED PRODUCTS
MANUFACTURERS ASSOCIATION**
Broadway House
Calthorpe Road
Five Ways
Birmingham
West Midlands
B15 1TN
Tel: 0121 456 1103
Fax: 0121 456 2274

ALUMINIUM FEDERATION LTD (ALFED)
Broadway House
Calthorpe Road
Five Ways
Birmingham
West Midlands
B15 1TN
Tel: 0121 456 1103
Fax: 0121 456 2274

ALUMINIUM FINISHING ASSOCIATION
Broadway House
Calthorpe Road
Five Ways
Birmingham
West Midlands
B15 1TN
Tel: 0121 456 1103
Fax: 0121 456 2274

AMERICAN HARDWOOD EXPORT COUNCIL (AHEC)
10 Throgmorton Avenue
London
EC2N 2DL
Tel: 0171 588 8811
Fax: 0171 588 8855

APA - THE ENGINEERED WOOD ASSOCIATION
The Business Exchange
Hinton Road
Bournemouth
BH1 2EF
Tel: 01202 201 007
Fax: 01202 201 008

ANCIENT MONUMENTS SOCIETY (AMS)
Saint Ann's Vestry Hall
2 Church Entry
London
EC4V 5HB
Tel: 0171 236 3934
Fax: 0171 329 3677

ARCHITECTS AND SURVEYORS INSTITUTE (ASI)
Saint Mary House
15 Saint Mary Street
Chippenham
Wiltshire
SN15 3WD
Tel: 01249 444 505
Fax: 01249 443 602

**ARCHITECTURAL ADVISORY SERVICE CENTRE
(POWDER/ANODIC METAL FINISHES)**
Spendale House
The Runway
South Ruislip
Middlesex
HA4 6SJ
Tel: 0181 842 3111
Fax: 0181 845 9798

ARCHITECTURAL ASSOCIATION (AA)
34 - 36 Bedford Square
London
WC1B 3ES
Tel: 0171 887 4000
Fax: 0171 414 0782

ARCHITECTURAL CLADDING ASSOCIATION (ACA)
60 Charles Street
Leicester
Leicestershire
LE1 1FB
Tel: 0116 253 6161
Fax: 0116 251 4568

ASBESTOS INFORMATION CENTRE (AIC)
PO Box 69
Widnes
Cheshire
WA8 9GW
Tel: 0151 420 5866
Fax: 0151 420 5853

**ASBESTOS REMOVAL CONTRACTORS' ASSOCIATION
(ARCA)**
Friars House
6 Parkway
Chelmsford
Essex
CM2 0NF
Tel: 01245 259 744
Fax: 01245 490 722

USEFUL ADDRESSES FOR FURTHER INFORMATION

ASSOCIATION OF INTERIOR SPECIALISTS
Jago House
692 Warwick Road
Solihull
West Midlands
B91 3DX
Tel: 0121 705 9270
Fax: 0121 711 2892

BOX CULVERT ASSOCIATION (BCA)
60 Charles Street
Leicester
Leicestershire
LE1 1FB
Tel: 0116 253 6161
Fax: 0116 251 4568

BRITISH ADHESIVES & SEALANTS ASSOCIATION (BASA)
33 Fellowes Way
Stevenage
Hertfordshire
SG2 8BW
Tel: 01438 358 514
Fax:

BRITISH AGGREGATE CONSTRUCTION MATERIALS INDUSTRIES LTD (BACMI)
156 Buckingham Palace Road
London
SW1W 9TR
Tel: 0171 730 8194
Fax: 0171 730 4355

BRITISH APPROVALS FOR FIRE EQUIPMENT (BAFE)
Neville House
55 Eden Street
Kingston upon Thames
Surrey
KT1 1BW
Tel: 0181 541 1950
Fax: 0181 547 1564

BRITISH APPROVALS SERVICE FOR CABLES (BASEC)
Silbury Court
360 Silbury Boulevard
Milton Keynes
Buckinghamshire
MK9 2AF
Tel: 01908 691 121
Fax: 01908 692 722

BRITISH ARCHITECTURAL LIBRARY (BAL)
Royal Institute of British Architects
66 Portland Place
London
W1N 4AD
Tel: 0171 580 5533
Fax: 0171 631 1802

BRITISH ASSOCIATION OF LANDSCAPE INDUSTRIES (BALI)
9 Henry Street
Keighley
West Yorkshire
BD21 3DR
Tel: 01535 606 139
Fax: 01535 610 269

BRITISH BATHROOM COUNCIL
Federation House
Station Road
Stoke-on-Trent
Staffordshire
ST4 2RT
Tel: 01782 747 123
Fax: 01782 747 161

BRITISH BOARD OF AGREMENT (BBA)
PO Box 195
Bucknalls Lane
Garston
Watford
Hertfordshire
WD2 7NG
Tel: 01923 665 300
Fax: 01923 665 301

BRITISH CABLE MAKERS CONFEDERATION (BCMC)
Cable House
56 Palace Road
East Molesey
Surrey
KT8 9DW
Tel: 0181 941 4079
Fax: 0181 783 0104

BRITISH CARPET MANUFACTURERS ASSOCIATION LTD (BCMA)
PO Box 1155
Kidderminster
Worcestershire
DY10 2ZH
Tel: 01562 747 351
Fax: 01562 747 359

BRITISH CEMENT ASSOCIATION (BCA), CENTRE FOR CONCRETE INFORMATION
Century House
Telford Avenue
Crowthorne
Berkshire
RG45 6YS
Tel: 01344 762 676
Fax: 01344 761 214

USEFUL ADDRESSES FOR FURTHER INFORMATION

BRITISH CERAMIC CONFEDERATION (BCC)
Federation House
Station Road
Stoke-on-Trent
Staffordshire
ST4 2SA
Tel: 01782 744 631
Fax: 01782 744 102

BRITISH CERAMIC RESEARCH LTD
Queens Road
Penkhull
Stoke-on-Trent
Staffordshire
ST4 7LQ
Tel: 01782 845 431
Fax: 01782 412 331

BRITISH CERAMIC TILE COUNCIL
Federation House
Station Road
Stoke-on-Trent
Staffordshire
ST4 2RT
Tel: 01782 747 147
Fax: 01782 747 161

**BRITISH COMBUSTION EQUIPMENT
MANUFACTURERS ASSOCIATION (BCEMA)**
The Fernery
Market Place
Midhurst
West Sussex
GU29 9DP
Tel: 01730 812 782
Fax: 01730 813 366

**BRITISH CONCRETE MASONRY ASSOCIATION
(BCMA)**
Grove Crescent House
18 Grove Place
Bedford
MK40 3JJ
Tel: 01234 353 745
Fax: 01234 353 745

**BRITISH CONSTRUCTIONAL STEELWORK
ASSOCIATION LTD**
4 Whitehall Court
Westminster
London
SW1A 2ES
Tel: 0171 839 8566
Fax: 0171 976 1634

**BRITISH CONTRACT FURNISHING ASSOCIATION
(BCFA)**
Suite 214
The Business Design Centre
52 Upper Street
Islington Green
London
N1 0QH
Tel: 0171 226 6641
Fax: 0171 288 6190

BRITISH DECORATORS ASSOCIATION (BDA)
32 Coton Road
Nuneaton
Warwickshire
CV11 5TW
Tel: 01203 353 776
Fax: 01203 354 513

**BRITISH ELECTRICAL SYSTEMS ASSOCIATION
(BESA)**
Granville Chambers
2 Radford Street
Stone
Staffordshire
ST15 8DA
Tel: 01785 812 426
Fax: 01785 818 157

**BRITISH ELECTROTECHNICAL APPROVALS BOARD
(BEAB)**
1 Station View
Guildford
Surrey
GU1 4JY
Tel: 01483 455 466
Fax: 01483 455 477

**BRITISH FIRE PROTECTION SYSTEMS
ASSOCIATION LTD (BFPSA)**
Neville House
55 Eden Street
Kingston-upon-Thames
Surrey
KT1 1BW
Tel: 0181 549 5855
Fax: 0181 547 1564

BRITISH FLAT ROOFING COUNCIL (BFRC)
177 Bagnall Road
Basford
Nottingham
Nottinghamshire
NG6 8SJ
Tel: 0115 942 4200
Fax: 0115 942 4488

USEFUL ADDRESSES FOR FURTHER INFORMATION

**BRITISH FURNITURE MANUFACTURERS
FEDERATION LTD (BFM Ltd)**
30 Harcourt Street
London
W1H 2AA
Tel: 0171 724 0851
Fax: 0171 706 1924

BRITISH GLASS
Northumberland Road
Sheffield
South Yorkshire
S10 2UA
Tel: 0114 268 6201
Fax: 0114 268 1073

**BRITISH INDEPENDENT PLASTIC EXTRUDERS
ASSOCIATION**
89 Cornwall Street
Birmingham
West Midlands
B3 3BY
Tel: 0121 236 1866
Fax: 0121 200 1389

**BRITISH INSTITUTE OF ARCHITECTURAL
TECHNOLOGISTS (BIAT)**
397 City Road
London
EC1V 1NE
Tel: 0171 278 2206
Fax: 0171 837 3194

**BRITISH LAMINATED PLASTICS FABRICATORS
ASSOCIATION**
c/o British Plastics Federation
6 Bath Place
Rivington Street
London
EC2A 3JE
Tel: 0171 457 5025
Fax: 0171 457 5038

**BRITISH LIBRARY BIBLIOGRAPHIC SERVICE AND
DOCUMENT SUPPLY CENTRE**
Boston Spa
Wetherby
West Yorkshire
LS23 7BQ
Tel: 01937 546 585
Fax: 01937 546 586

**BRITISH LIBRARY ENVIRONMENTAL INFORMATION
SERVICE**
25 Southampton Buildings
Chancery Lane
London
WC2A 1AW
Tel: 0171 012 7955
Fax: 0171 412 7954

**BRITISH LIBRARY, SCIENCE REFERENCE AND
INFORMATION SERVICE**
25 Southampton Buildings
Chancery Lane
London
WC2A 1AW
Tel: 0171 323 7494
Fax: 0171 323 7495

BRITISH NON-FERROUS METALS FEDERATION
10 Greenfield Crescent
Edgbaston
Birmingham
West Midlands
B15 3AU
Tel: 0121 456 3322
Fax: 0121 456 1394

BRITISH PLASTICS FEDERATION (BPF)
Plastics & Rubber Advisory Service
6 Bath Place
Rivington Street
London
EC2A 3JE
Tel: 0171 457 5000
Fax: 0171 457 5038

BRITISH PRECAST CONCRETE FEDERATION LTD
60 Charles Street
Leicester
Leicestershire
LE1 1FB
Tel: 0116 253 6161
Fax: 0116 251 4568

BRITISH PROPERTY FEDERATION (BPF)
35 Catherine Place
London
SW1E 6DY
Tel: 0171 828 0111
Fax: 0171 834 3442

**BRITISH RESILIENT FLOORING MANUFACTURERS
ASSOCIATION**
4 Queen Square
Brighton
East Sussex
BN1 3FD
Tel: 01273 727 906
Fax: 01273 206 217

**BRITISH RUBBER MANUFACTURERS'
ASSOCIATION LTD (BRMA)**
90 Tottenham Court Road
London
W1P 0BR
Tel: 0171 580 2794
Fax: 0171 631 5471

USEFUL ADDRESSES FOR FURTHER INFORMATION

BRITISH STANDARDS INSTITUTION (BSI)
389 Chiswick High Road
London
W4 4AL
Tel: 0181 996 9000
Fax: 0181 996 7400

BRITISH STEEL PLC
Swinden Technology Centre
Moorgate
Rotherham
South Yorkshire
S60 3AR
Tel: 01709 820 166
Fax: 01709 825 337

BRITISH WATER
1 Queen Anne's Gate
London
SW1H 9BT
Tel: 0171 957 4554
Fax: 0171 957 4565

BRITISH WELDED STEEL TUBE ASSOCIATION
2 Hudmans Close
Twyning
Tewkesbury
Gloucestershire
GL20 6DY
Tel: 01684 850 046
Fax: 01684 850 046

BRITISH WOOD PRESERVING & DAMP PROOFING ASSOCIATION (BWPDA)
Building No 6
The Office Village
4 Romford Road
Stratford
London
E15 4EA
Tel: 0181 519 2588
Fax: 0181 519 3444

BRITISH WOODWORKING FEDERATION
56 - 64 Leonard Steet
London
EC2A 4JX
Tel: 0171 608 5050
Fax: 0171 608 5051

BUILDING CENTRE
The Building Centre
26 Store Street
London
WC1E 7BT
Tel: 0171 692 4000
Fax: 0171 580 9641

BUILDING COST INFORMATION SERVICE LTD (BCIS)
Royal Institution of Chartered Surveyors
12 Great George Street
Parliament Square
London
SW1P 3AD
Tel: 0171 695 1507
Fax: 0171 695 1501

BUILDING EMPLOYERS CONFEDERATION (BEC)
82 New Cavendish Street
London
W1M 8AD
Tel: 0171 580 5588
Fax: 0171 631 3872

BUILDING MAINTENANCE INFORMATION (BMI)
Royal Institution of Chartered Surveyors
12 Great George Street
Parliament Square
London
SW1P 3AD
Tel: 0171 695 1516
Fax: 0171 695 1501

BUILDING RESEARCH ESTABLISHMENT (BRE)
Bucknalls Lane
Garston
Watford
Hertfordshire
WD2 7JR
Tel: 01923 664 000
Fax: 01923 664 010

BUILDING RESEARCH ESTABLISHMENT: SCOTLAND (BRE)
Kelvin Road
East Kilbride
Glasgow
G75 0RZ
Tel: 013552 339 41
Fax: 013552 418 95

BUILDING SERVICES RESEARCH AND INFORMATION ASSOCIATION
The Centre for Construction Ecology
Old Bracknell Lane West
Bracknell
Berkshire
RG12 7AH
Tel: 01344 426 511
Fax: 01344 487 575

BUILT ENVIRONMMENT RESEARCH GROUP
c/o Disabled Living Foundation
380 - 384 Harrow Road
London
W9 2HU
Tel: 0171 289 6111
Fax: 0171 273 4340

USEFUL ADDRESSES FOR FURTHER INFORMATION

CATERING EQUIPMENT MANUFACTURERS ASSOCIATION
Carlyle House
235/237 Vauxhall Bridge Road
London
SW1V 1EJ
Tel: 0171 233 7724
Fax: 0171 828 0667

CAVITY FOAM BUREAU
PO Box 79
Oldbury
Warley
West Midlands
B69 4PW
Tel: 0121 544 4949
Fax: 0121 544 3569

CHARTERED INSTITURE OF ARBITRATORS (CIArb)
24 Angel Gate
City Road
London
EC1V 2RS
Tel: 0171 837 4483
Fax: 0171 837 4185

CHARTERED INSTITUTE OF BUILDING (CIOB)
Englemere
Kings Ride
Ascot
Berkshire
SL5 8BJ
Tel: 01344 630 700
Fax: 01344 630 888

CHARTERED INSTITUTION OF BUILDING SERVICE ENGINEERS (CIBSE)
Delta House
222 Balham High Road
London
SW12 9BS
Tel: 0181 675 5211
Fax: 0181 675 5449

CLAY PIPE DEVELOPMENT ASSOCIATION (CPDA)
Copsham House
53 Broad Street
Chesham
Buckinghamshire
HP5 3EA
Tel: 01494 791 456
Fax: 01494 792 378

CLAY ROOF TILE COUNCIL
Federation House
Station Road
Stoke-on-Trent
Staffordshire
ST4 2SA
Tel: 01782 744 631
Fax: 01782 744 102

COLD ROLLED SECTIONS ASSOCIATION (CRSA)
Centre City Tower
7 Hill Street
Birmingham
West Midlands
B5 4UU
Tel: 0121 697 6000
Fax: 0121 697 6113

COMMONWEALTH ASSOCIATION OF ARCHITECTS (CAA)
66 Portland Place
London
W1N 4AD
Tel: 0171 636 8276
Fax: 0171 255 1541

CONCRETE ADVISORY SERVICE
37 Cowbridge Road
Pontyclun
Cardiff
South Wales
CF2 9EB
Tel: 01433 237 210
Fax: 01433 237 271

CONCRETE BRIDGE DEVELOPMENT GROUP
Century House
Telford Avenue
Old Wokingham Road
Crowthorne
Berkshire
RG45 6YS
Tel: 01344 725 727
Fax: 01344 727 204

CONCRETE LINTEL ASSOCIATION
60 Charles Street
Leicester
Leicestershire
LE1 1FB
Tel: 0116 253 6161
Fax: 0116 251 4568

CONCRETE PIPE ASSOCIATION (CPA)
60 Charles Street
Leicester
Leicestershire
LE1 1FB
Tel: 0116 253 6161
Fax: 0116 251 4568

CONCRETE REPAIR ASSOCIATION (CRA)
Association House
235 Ash Road
Aldershot
Hampshire
GU12 4DD
Tel: 01252 321 302
Fax: 01252 333 901

USEFUL ADDRESSES FOR FURTHER INFORMATION

CONCRETE SOCIETY
3 Eatongate
Windsor Road
Slough
Berkshire
SL1 2JA
Tel: 01753 693 313
Fax: 01753 692 333

CONFEDERATION OF BRITISH INDUSTRY (CBI)
Centre Point
103 New Oxford Street
London
WC1A 1DU
Tel: 0171 395 8020
Fax: 0171 240 0988

CONSTRUCT - CONCRETE STRUCTURES GROUP LTD
Century House
Telford Avenue
Crowthorne
Berkshire
RG11 6YS
Tel: 01344 725 744
Fax: 01344 761 214

CONSTRUCTION EMPLOYERS FEDERATION LTD (CEF)
143 Malone Road
Belfast
BT9 6SU
Tel: 01232 661 711
Fax: 01237 666 323

CONSTRUCTION INDUSTRY RESEARCH & INFORMATION ASSOCIATION (CIRIA)
6 Storey's Gate
Westminster
London
SW1P 3AU
Tel: 0171 222 8891
Fax: 0171 222 1708

CONSTRUCTION PLANT-HIRE ASSOCIATION (CPA)
28 Eccleston Street
London
SW1W 9PY
Tel: 0171 730 7117
Fax: 0171 730 7110

CONTRACT FLOORING ASSOCIATION (CFA)
4c Saint Mary's Place
The Lace Market
Nottingham
Nottinghamshire
NG1 1PH
Tel: 0115 941 1126
Fax: 0115 941 2238

CONTRACTORS MECHANICAL PLANT ENGINEERS (CMPE)
20 Knave Wood Road
Kemsing
Sevenoaks
Kent
TN15 6RH
Tel: 01959 522 628
Fax: 01959 522 068

COPPER DEVELOPMENT ASSOCIATION
Verulam Industrial Estate
224 Londons Road
Saint Albans
Hertfordshire
AL1 1AQ
Tel: 01727 731 200
Fax: 01727 731 216

COUNCIL FOR ALUMINIUM IN BUILDING (CAB)
191 Cirencester Road
Charlton Kings
Cheltenham
Gloucestershire
GL53 8DF
Tel: 01242 578 278
Fax: 01242 578 283

DRY STONE WALLING ASSOCIATION OF GREAT BRITAIN
c/o YFC Centre
National Agricultural Centre
Stoneleigh Park
Kenilworth
Warwickshire
CV8 2LG
Tel: 0121 378 0493
Fax: 0121 378 0493

DUCTILE IRON PIPE ASSOCIATION
The McLaren Building
35 Dale End
Birmingham
B4 7LN
Tel: 0121 200 2100
Fax: 0121 200 1306

ELECTRICAL CONTRACTORS ASSOCIATION (ECA)
ESCA House
34 Palace Court
Bayswater
London
W2 4HY
Tel: 0171 313 4800
Fax: 0171 221 7344

USEFUL ADDRESSES FOR FURTHER INFORMATION

ELECTRICAL CONTRACTORS ASSOCIATION OF SCOTLAND (ECA)
Bush House
Bush Estate
Midlothian
Scotland
EH26 0SB
Tel: 0131 445 5577
Fax: 0131 445 5548

ELECTRICAL INSTALLATION EQUIPMENT MANUFACTURERS ASSOCIATION LTD (EIEMA)
Westminster Tower
3 Albert Embankment
London
SE1 7SL
Tel: 0171 793 3013
Fax: 0171 735 4158

ELECTRICITY ASSOCIATION
30 Millbank
London
SW1P 4RD
Tel: 0171 963 5817
Fax: 0171 963 5957

ENERGY SYSTEMS TRADE ASSOCIATION LTD (ESTA)
Palace Chambers
41 London Road
Stroud
Gloucestershire
GL5 2AJ
Tel: 01453 767 373
Fax: 01453 767 376

EUROPEAN LIQUID ROOFING ASSOCIATION (ELRA)
Fields House
Gower Road
Haywards Heath
West Sussex
RH16 4PL
Tel: 01444 417 458
Fax: 01444 415 616

FABRIC CARE RESEARCH ASSOCIATION
Forest House Laboratories
Knaresborough Road
Harrogate
North Yorkshire
HG2 7LZ
Tel: 01423 885 977
Fax: 01423 880 045

FACULTY OF BUILDING
Central Office
35 Hayworth Road
Sandiacre
Nottingham
Nottinghamshire
NG10 5LL
Tel: 0115 949 0641
Fax: 0115 949 1664

FEDERATION OF MANUFACTURERS OF CONSTRUCTION EQUIPMENT & CRANES
Ambassador House
Brigstock Road
Thornton Heath
Surrey
CR7 7JG
Tel: 0181 665 5727
Fax: 0181 665 6447

FEDERATION OF MASTER BUILDERS
Gordon Fisher House
14 - 15 Great James Street
London
WC1N 3DP
Tel: 0171 242 7583
Fax: 0171 404 0296

FEDERATION OF PILING SPECIALISTS
Forum Court
83 Coppers Cope Road
Beckenham
Kent
BR3 1NR
Tel: 0181 663 0947
Fax: 0181 663 0949

FEDERATION OF PLASTERING & DRYWALL CONTRACTORS
18 Mansfield Street
London
W1M 9FG
Tel: 0171 580 5404
Fax: 0171 636 5984

FEDERATION OF THE ELECTRONICS INDUSTRY (FEI)
Russell Square House
10 - 12 Russell Square
London
WC1B 5EE
Tel: 0171 331 2000
Fax: 0171 331 2040

FENCING CONTRACTORS ASSOCIATION
Warren Road
Trellech
Monmouthshire
NP5 4PQ
Tel: 07000 560 722
Fax: 01600 860 614

USEFUL ADDRESSES FOR FURTHER INFORMATION

FIBRE CEMENT MANUFACTURERS ASSOCIATION LTD (FCMA)
3 Church Road
Northumberland
NE64 3RH
Tel: 01434 601 393
Fax: 01434 608 874

FINNISH PLYWOOD INTERNATIONAL
PO Box 99
Welwyn Garden City
Hertfordshire
AL6 0HS
Tel: 01438 798 746
Fax: 01438 798 305

FLAT GLASS MANUFACTURERS ASSOCIATION
Prescot Road
St Helens
Merseyside
WA10 3TT
Tel: 01744 288 82
Fax: 01744 692 660

FLAT ROOFING ALLIANCE
Fields House
Gower Road
Haywards Heath
West Sussex
RH16 4PL
Tel: 01444 440 027
Fax: 01444 415 616

FURNITURE INDUSTRY RESEARCH ASSOCIATION (FIRA)
Maxwell Road
Stevenage
Hertfordshire
SG1 2EW
Tel: 01438 313 433
Fax: 01438 727 607

GLASS & GLAZING FEDERATION (GGF)
44 - 48 Borough High Street
London
SE1 1XB
Tel: 0171 403 7177
Fax: 0171 357 7458

HEATING & VENTILATING CONTRACTORS' ASSOCIATION
ESCA House
34 Palace Court
Bayswater
London
W2 4JG
Tel: 0171 229 2488
Fax: 0171 727 9268

HOUSING CORPORATION HEADQUARTERS
149 Tottenham Court Road
London
W1P 0BN
Tel: 0171 393 2000
Fax: 0171 393 2111

INSTITUTE OF ACOUSTICS
77A Saint Peter' Street
Saint Albans
Hertfordshire
AL1 3BN
Tel: 01727 848 195
Fax: 01727 850 553

INSTITUTE OF ASPHALT TECHNOLOGY
Office 5
Trident House
Clare Road
Stanwell
Middlesex
TW19 7QU
Tel: 01784 423 444
Fax: 01784 423 888

INSTITUTE OF MAINTENANCE AND BUILDING MANAGEMENT
Keets House
30 East Steet
Farnham
Surrey
GU9 7SW
Tel: 01252 710 994
Fax: 01252 737 741

INSTITUTE OF MATERIALS
1 Carlton House Terrace
London
SW1Y 5DB
Tel: 0171 839 4071
Fax: 0171 839 2078

INSTITUTE OF PLUMBING
64 Station Lane
Hornchurch
Essex
RM12 6NB
Tel: 01708 472 791
Fax: 01708 448 987

INSTITUTE OF SHEET METAL ENGINEERING
Exeter House
48 Holloway Head
Birmingham
West Midlands
B1 1NQ
Tel: 0121 622 2860
Fax: 0121 666 6316

USEFUL ADDRESSES FOR FURTHER INFORMATION

INSTITUTE OF WASTES MANAGEMENT
9 Saxon Court
Saint Peter's Gardens
Northampton
Northamptonshire
NN1 1SX
Tel: 01604 204 26
Fax: 01604 213 39

INSTITUTE OF WOOD SCIENCE
Stocking Lane
Hughenden Valley
High Wycombe
Buckinghamshire
HP14 4NU
Tel: 01494 565 374
Fax: 01494 565 395

INSTITUTION OF BRITISH ENGINEERS
The Royal Liver Building
6 Hampton Place
Brighton
East Sussex
BN1 3DD
Tel: 01273 734 274

INSTITUTION OF CIVIL ENGINEERS (ICE)
1 - 7 Great George Street
London
SW1P 3AA
Tel: 0171 222 7722
Fax: 0171 222 7500

**INSTITUTION OF INCORPORATED ENGINEERS IN
ELECTRONIC, ELECTRICAL AND MECHANIC**
Savoy Hill House
Savoy Hill
London
WC2R 0BS
Tel: 0171 836 3357
Fax: 0171 497 9006

INSTITUTION OF STRUCTURAL ENGINEERS (ISE)
11 Upper Belgrave Street
London
SW1X 8BH
Tel: 0171 235 4535
Fax: 0171 235 4294

**INTERPAVE (THE PRECAST CONCRETE PAVING &
KERB ASSOCIATION)**
60 Charles Street
Leicester
Leicestershire
LE1 1FB
Tel: 0116 253 6161
Fax: 0116 251 4568

JOINT CONTRACTS TRIBUNAL
66 Portland Place
London
W1N 4AD
Tel: 0171 580 5533
Fax: 0171 255 1541

KITCHEN SPECIALISTS ASSOCIATION
PO Box 311
Worcester
Worcestershire
WR1 1DR
Tel: 01905 619 922
Fax: 01905 726 469

LIGHTING ASSOCIATION LTD
Stafford Park 7
Telford
Shropshire
TF3 3BQ
Tel: 01952 290 905
Fax: 01952 290 906

MASTIC ASPHALT COUNCIL LTD
8 North Street
Ashford
Kent
TN24 8JN
Tel: 01233 634 411
Fax: 01233 634 466

**METAL CLADDING & ROOFING MANUFACTURERS
ASSOCIATION**
18 Mere Farm Road
Noctorum
Birkenhead
Merseyside
L43 9TT
Tel: 0151 652 3846
Fax: 0151 653 4080

NATIONAL HOUSE-BUILDING COUNCIL (NHBC)
Technical Department
Buildmark House
Chiltern Avenue
Amersham
Buckinghamshire
HP6 5AP
Tel: 01494 434 477
Fax: 01494 728 521

**NATIONAL HOUSING AND TOWN PLANNING
COUNCIL**
14 - 18 Old Street
London
EC1V 9AB
Tel: 0171 251 2363
Fax: 0171 608 2830

USEFUL ADDRESSES FOR FURTHER INFORMATION

PIPELINE INDUSTRIES GUILD
14 - 15 Belgrave Square
London
SW1X 8PS
Tel: 0171 235 7938
Fax: 0171 235 0074

PLASTIC PIPE MANUFACTURERS SOCIETY
89 Cornwall Street
Birmingham
West Midlands
B3 3BY
Tel: 0121 236 1866
Fax: 0121 200 1389

PRECAST FLOORING FEDERATION
60 Charles Street
Leicester
Leicestershire
LE1 1FB
Tel: 0116 253 6161
Fax: 0116 251 4568

PRESTRESSED CONCRETE ASSOCIATION
60 Charles Street
Leicester
Leicestershire
LE1 1FB
Tel: 0116 253 6161
Fax: 0116 251 4568

READY-MIXED CONCRETE BUREAU
Century House
Telford Avenue
Crowthorne
Berkshire
RG45 6YS
Tel: 01344 725 732
Fax: 01344 761 214

REINFORCED CONCRETE COUNCIL
Century House
Telford Avenue
Crowthorne
Berkshire
RG45 6YS
Tel: 01344 725 733
Fax: 01344 761 214

ROYAL INSTITUTE OF BRITISH ARCHITECTS (RIBA)
66 Portland Place
London
W1N 4AD
Tel: 0171 580 5533
Fax: 0171 255 1541

ROYAL INSTITUTION OF CHARTERED SURVEYORS (RICS)
12 Great George Street
London
SW1P 3AD
Tel: 0171 222 7000
Fax: 0171 334 3800

RURAL DESIGN AND BUILDING ASSOCIATION
Harper Adams
Newport
Shropshire
TF10 8NB
Tel: 01952 814 555
Fax: 01952 814 777

RURAL DEVELOPMENT COMMISSION
Headquarters
141 Castle Street
Salisbury
Wiltshire
SP1 3TP
Tel: 01722 336 255
Fax: 01722 332 769

SCOTTISH BUILDING CONTRACT COMMITTEE
c/o MacRoberts Solicitors
27 Melville Street
Edinburgh
Scotland
EH3 7JF
Tel: 0131 226 2552
Fax: 0131 226 2501

SCOTTISH BUILDING EMPLOYERS FEDERATION
Carron Grange
Carron Grange Avenue
Stenhousemuir
Scotland
FK5 3BQ
Tel: 01324 555 550
Fax: 01324 555 551

SCOTTISH HOMES
Thistle House
91 Haymarket Terrace
Edinburgh
Scotland
EH12 5HE
Tel: 0131 313 0044
Fax: 0131 313 2680

SINGLE PLY ROOFING ASSOCIATION
177 Bagnall Road
Basford
Nottingham
NG6 8SJ
Tel: 0115 942 4200
Fax: 0115 942 4488

USEFUL ADDRESSES FOR FURTHER INFORMATION

SMOKE VENTILATION ASSOCIATION
Henley Road
Memmenham
Marlow
Buckinghamshire
SL7 2ER
Tel: 01491 578 674
Fax: 01491 575 024

SOCIETY OF GLASS TECHNOLOGY
20 Hallamgate Road
Broom Hill
Sheffield
South Yorkshire
S10 5BT
Tel: 0114 266 3168
Fax: 0114 266 5252

SPECIALIST ENGINEERING CONTRACTORS' GROUP
ESCA House
34 Palace Court
Bayswater
London
W2 4JG
Tel: 0171 243 4919
Fax: 0171 727 9268

THE SPRAYED CONCRETE ASSOCIATION
Association House
235 Ash Road
Aldershot
Hampshire
GU12 4DD
Tel: 01252 321 302
Fax: 01252 333 901

STAINLESS STEEL ADVISORY CENTRE
PO Box 161
Shepcote Lane
Sheffield
South Yorkshire
S9 1TR
Tel: 0114 244 0060
Fax: 0114 244 8280

THE STEEL CONSTRUCTION INSTITUTE
Silwood Park
Ascot
Berkshire
SL5 7QN
Tel: 01344 623 345
Fax: 01344 622 944

SUSPENDED ACCESS EQUIPMENT MANUFACTURERS ASSOCIATION
18 Mansfield Street
London
W1M 9FG
Tel: 0171 580 5404
Fax: 0171 636 5984

SWIMMING POOL & ALLIED TRADES ASSOCIATION
Spata House
Junction Road
Andover
Hampshire
SP10 3QT
Tel: 01264 356 210
Fax: 01264 332 628

TAR INDUSTRIES SERVICES
BCRA Scientific & Technical Services
Mill Lane
Wingerworth
Chesterfield
Derbyshire
S42 6NG
Tel: 01246 209 654
Fax: 01246 272 247

TIMBER AND BRICK INFORMATION COUNCIL
Gable House
40 High Street
Rickmansworth
Hertfordshire
WD3 1ES
Tel: 01923 778 136
Fax: 01923 720 724

TIMBER RESEARCH & DEVELOPMENT ASSOCIATION (TRADA)
Stocking Lane
Hughenden Valley
High Wycombe
Buckinghamshire
HP14 4ND
Tel: 01494 563 091
Fax: 01494 565 487

TIMBER TRADE FEDERATION
4th Floor
Clareville House
26-27 Oxenden Street
London
SW1Y 4EL
Tel: 0171 839 1891
Fax: 0171 930 0094

TOWN & COUNTRY PLANNING ASSOCIATION (TCPA)
17 Carlton House Terrace
London
SW1Y 5AS
Tel: 0171 930 8903
Fax: 0171 930 3280

TREE COUNCIL
51 Catherine Place
London
SW1E 6DY
Tel: 0171 828 9928
Fax: 0171 828 9060

USEFUL ADDRESSES FOR FURTHER INFORMATION

TWI (FORMERLY THE WELDING INSTITUTE)
Abington Hall
Abington
Cambridge
Cambridgeshire
CB1 6AL
Tel: 01223 891 162
Fax: 01223 892 588

VERMICULITE INFORMATION SERVICE
c/o Mandoval Coatings Ltd
Douglas Drive
Cattleshall Lane
Godalming
Surrey
GU7 1JX
Tel: 01483 425 326
Fax: 01483 426 881

WALLCOVERING MANUFACTURERS ASSOCIATION
James House
Bridge Street
Leatherhead
Surrey
KT22 7EP
Tel: 01372 360 660
Fax: 01372 376 069

WASTE MANAGEMENT INFORMATION BUREAU
AEA Technology Environment
F6 Culham
Abingdon
Oxfordshire
OX14 3DB
Tel: 01235 463 162
Fax: 01235 463 004

WATER RESEARCH CENTRE
PO Box 16
Henley Road
Medmenham
Marlow
Buckinghamshire
SL7 2HD
Tel: 01491 571 531
Fax: 01491 579 094

WATER SERVICES ASSOCIATION
1 Queen Anne's Gate
London
SW1H 9BT
Tel: 0171 957 4567
Fax: 0171 957 4666

WATERHEATER MANUFACTURERS ASSOCIATION
Milverton Lodge
Hanson Road
Victoria Park
Manchester
M14 5BZ
Tel: 0161 224 4009
Fax: 0161 257 2166

WIMLAS LTD
Saint Peter's House
6 - 8 High Street
Iver
Buckinghamshire
SL0 9NG
Tel: 01753 737 744
Fax: 01753 792 321

WOOD PANEL INDUSTRIES FEDERATION
28 Market Place
Grantham
Lincolnshire
NG31 6LR
Tel: 01476 563 707
Fax: 01476 579 314

WOOD WOOL SLAB MANUFACTURERS ASSOCIATION
26 Store Street
London
WC1E 7BT
Tel: 0171 323 3770
Fax: 0171 323 0307

ZINC DEVELOPMENT ASSOCIATION
42 Weymouth Street
London
W1N 3LQ
Tel: 0171 499 6636
Fax: 0171 493 1555

NATURAL SINES

Deg-rees	0' 0°.0	6' 0.1	12' 0.2	18' 0.3	24' 0.4	30' 0.5	36' 0.6	42' 0.7	48' 0.8	54' 0.9	Mean Differences 1 2 3 4
0	0.0000	0.0017	0.0035	0.0052	0.0070	0.0087	0.0105	0.0122	0.0140	0.0157	3 6 9 12
1	0.0175	0.0192	0.0209	0.0227	0.0244	0.0262	0.0279	0.0297	0.0314	0.0332	3 6 9 12
2	0.0349	0.0366	0.0384	0.0401	0.0419	0.0436	0.0454	0.0471	0.0488	0.0506	3 6 9 12
3	0.0523	0.0541	0.0558	0.0576	0.0593	0.0610	0.0628	0.0645	0.0663	0.0680	3 6 9 12
4	0.0698	0.0715	0.0732	0.0750	0.0767	0.0785	0.0802	0.0819	0.0837	0.0854	3 6 9 12
5	0.0872	0.0889	0.0906	0.0924	0.0941	0.0958	0.0976	0.0993	0.1011	0.1028	3 6 9 12
6	0.1045	0.1063	0.1080	0.1097	0.1115	0.1132	0.1149	0.1167	0.1184	0.1201	3 6 9 12
7	0.1219	0.1236	0.1253	0.1271	0.1288	0.1305	0.1323	0.1340	0.1357	0.1374	3 6 9 12
8	0.1392	0.1409	0.1426	0.1444	0.1461	0.1478	0.1495	0.1513	0.1530	0.1547	3 6 9 12
9	0.1564	0.1582	0.1599	0.1616	0.1633	0.1650	0.1668	0.1685	0.1702	0.1719	3 6 9 12
10	0.1736	0.1754	0.1771	0.1788	0.1805	0.1822	0.1840	0.1857	0.1874	0.1891	3 6 9 12
11	0.1908	0.1925	0.1942	0.1959	0.1977	0.1994	0.2011	0.2028	0.2045	0.2062	3 6 9 11
12	0.2079	0.2096	0.2113	0.2130	0.2147	0.2164	0.2181	0.2198	0.2215	0.2233	3 6 9 11
13	0.2250	0.2267	0.2284	0.2300	0.2317	0.2334	0.2351	0.2368	0.2385	0.2402	3 6 8 11
14	0.2419	0.2436	0.2453	0.2470	0.2487	0.2504	0.2521	0.2538	0.2554	0.2571	3 6 8 11
15	0.2588	0.2605	0.2622	0.2639	0.2656	0.2672	0.2689	0.2706	0.2723	0.2740	3 6 8 11
16	0.2756	0.2773	0.2790	0.2807	0.2823	0.2840	0.2857	0.2874	0.2890	0.2907	3 6 8 11
17	0.2924	0.2940	0.2957	0.2974	0.2990	0.3007	0.3024	0.3040	0.3057	0.3074	3 6 8 11
18	0.3090	0.3107	0.3123	0.3140	0.3156	0.3173	0.3190	0.3206	0.3223	0.3239	3 6 8 11
19	0.3256	0.3272	0.3289	0.3305	0.3322	0.3338	0.3355	0.3371	0.3387	0.3404	3 5 8 11
20	0.3420	0.3437	0.3453	0.3469	0.3486	0.3502	0.3518	0.3535	0.3551	0.3567	3 5 8 11
21	0.3584	0.3600	0.3616	0.3633	0.3649	0.3665	0.3681	0.3697	0.3714	0.3730	3 5 8 11
22	0.3746	0.3762	0.3778	0.3795	0.3811	0.3827	0.3843	0.3859	0.3875	0.3891	3 5 8 11
23	0.3907	0.3923	0.3939	0.3955	0.3971	0.3987	0.4003	0.4019	0.4035	0.4051	3 5 8 11
24	0.4067	0.4083	0.4099	0.4115	0.4131	0.4147	0.4163	0.4179	0.4195	0.4210	3 5 8 11
25	0.4226	0.4242	0.4258	0.4274	0.4289	0.4305	0.4321	0.4337	0.4352	0.4368	3 5 8 11
26	0.4384	0.4399	0.4415	0.4431	0.4446	0.4462	0.4478	0.4493	0.4509	0.4524	3 5 8 10
27	0.4540	0.4555	0.4571	0.4586	0.4602	0.4617	0.4633	0.4648	0.4664	0.4679	3 5 8 10
28	0.4695	0.4710	0.4726	0.4741	0.4756	0.4772	0.4787	0.4802	0.4818	0.4833	3 5 8 10
29	0.4848	0.4863	0.4879	0.4894	0.4909	0.4924	0.4939	0.4955	0.4970	0.4985	3 5 8 10
30	0.5000	0.5015	0.5030	0.5045	0.5060	0.5075	0.5090	0.5105	0.5120	0.5135	3 5 8 10
31	0.5150	0.5165	0.5180	0.5195	0.5210	0.5225	0.5240	0.5255	0.5270	0.5284	2 5 7 10
32	0.5299	0.5314	0.5329	0.5344	0.5358	0.5373	0.5388	0.5402	0.5417	0.5432	2 5 7 10
33	0.5446	0.5461	0.5476	0.5490	0.5505	0.5519	0.5534	0.5548	0.5563	0.5577	2 5 7 10
34	0.5592	0.5606	0.5621	0.5635	0.5650	0.5664	0.5678	0.5693	0.5707	0.5721	2 5 7 10
35	0.5736	0.5750	0.5764	0.5779	0.5793	0.5807	0.5821	0.5835	0.5850	0.5864	2 5 7 10
36	0.5878	0.5892	0.5906	0.5920	0.5934	0.5948	0.5962	0.5976	0.5990	0.6004	2 5 7 9
37	0.6018	0.6032	0.6046	0.6060	0.6074	0.6088	0.6101	0.6115	0.6129	0.6143	2 5 7 9
38	0.6157	0.6170	0.6184	0.6198	0.6211	0.6225	0.6239	0.6252	0.6266	0.6280	2 5 7 9
39	0.6293	0.6307	0.5320	0.6334	0.6347	0.6361	0.6374	0.6388	0.6401	0.6414	2 4 7 9
40	0.6428	0.6441	0.6455	0.6468	0.6481	0.6494	0.6508	0.6521	0.6534	0.6547	2 4 7 9
41	0.6561	0.6574	0.6587	0.6600	0.6613	0.6626	0.6639	0.6652	0.6665	0.6678	2 4 7 9
42	0.6691	0.6704	0.6717	0.6730	0.6743	0.6756	0.6769	0.6782	0.6794	0.6807	2 4 6 9
43	0.6820	0.6833	0.6845	0.6858	0.6871	0.6884	0.6896	0.6909	0.6921	0.6934	2 4 6 8
44	0.6947	0.6959	0.6972	0.6984	0.6997	0.7009	0.7022	0.7034	0.7046	0.7059	2 4 6 8

NATURAL SINES

Deg-rees	0' 0°.0	6' 0.1	12' 0.2	18' 0.3	24' 0.4	30' 0.5	36' 0.6	42' 0.7	48' 0.8	54' 0.9	Mean Differences 1 2 3 4
45	0.7071	0.7083	0.7096	0.7108	0.7120	0.7133	0.7145	0.7157	0.7169	0.7181	2 4 6 8
46	0.7193	0.7206	0.7218	0.7230	0.7242	0.7254	0.7266	0.7278	0.7290	0.7302	2 4 6 8
47	0.7314	0.7325	0.7337	0.7349	0.7361	0.7373	0.7385	0.7396	0.7408	0.7420	2 4 6 8
48	0.7431	0.7443	0.7455	0.7466	0.7478	0.7490	0.7501	0.7513	0.7524	0.7536	2 4 6 8
49	0.7547	0.7559	0.7570	0.7581	0.7593	0.7604	0.7615	0.7627	0.7638	0.7649	2 4 6 8
50	0.7660	0.7672	0.7683	0.7694	0.7705	0.7716	0.7727	0.7738	0.7749	0.7760	2 4 6 7
51	0.7771	0.7782	0.7793	0.7804	0.7815	0.7826	0.7837	0.7848	0.7859	0.7869	2 4 5 7
52	0.7880	0.7891	0.7902	0.7912	0.7923	0.7934	0.7944	0.7955	0.7965	0.7976	2 4 5 7
53	0.7986	0.7997	0.8007	0.8018	0.8028	0.8039	0.8049	0.8059	0.8070	0.8080	2 3 5 7
54	0.8090	0.8100	0.8111	0.8121	0.8131	0.8141	0.8151	0.8161	0.8171	0.8181	2 3 5 7
55	0.8192	0.8202	0.8211	0.8221	0.8231	0.8241	0.8251	0.8261	0.8271	0.8281	2 3 5 7
56	0.8290	0.8300	0.8310	0.8320	0.8329	0.8339	0.8348	0.8358	0.8368	0.8377	2 3 5 6
57	0.8387	0.8396	0.8406	0.8415	0.8425	0.8434	0.8443	0.8453	0.8462	0.8471	2 3 5 6
58	0.8480	0.8490	0.8499	0.8508	0.8517	0.8526	0.8536	0.8545	0.8554	0.8563	2 3 5 6
59	0.8572	0.8581	0.8590	0.8599	0.8607	0.8616	0.8625	0.8634	0.8643	0.8652	1 3 4 6
60	0.8660	0.8669	0.8678	0.8686	0.8695	0.8704	0.8712	0.8721	0.8729	0.8738	1 3 4 6
61	0.8746	0.8755	0.8763	0.8771	0.8780	0.8788	0.8796	0.8805	0.8813	0.8821	1 3 4 6
62	0.8829	0.8838	0.8846	0.8854	0.8862	0.8870	0.8878	0.8886	0.8894	0.8902	1 3 4 5
63	0.8910	0.8918	0.8926	0.8934	0.8942	0.8949	0.8957	0.8965	0.8973	0.8980	1 3 4 5
64	0.8988	0.8996	0.9003	0.9011	0.9018	0.9026	0.9033	0.9041	0.9048	0.9056	1 3 4 5
65	0.9063	0.9070	0.9078	0.9085	0.9092	0.9100	0.9107	0.9114	0.9121	0.9128	1 2 4 5
66	0.9135	0.9143	0.9150	0.9157	0.9164	0.9171	0.9178	0.9184	0.9191	0.9198	1 2 3 5
67	0.9205	0.9212	0.9219	0.9225	0.9232	0.9239	0.9245	0.9252	0.9259	0.9265	1 2 3 4
68	0.9272	0.9278	0.9285	0.9291	0.9298	0.9304	0.9311	0.9317	0.9323	0.9330	1 2 3 4
69	0.9336	0.9342	0.9348	0.9354	0.9361	0.9367	0.9373	0.9379	0.9385	0.9391	1 2 3 4
70	0.9397	0.9403	0.9409	0.9415	0.9421	0.9426	0.9432	0.9438	0.9444	0.9449	1 2 3 4
71	0.9455	0.9461	0.9466	0.9472	0.9478	0.9483	0.9489	0.9494	0.9500	0.9505	1 2 3 4
72	0.9511	0.9516	0.9521	0.9527	0.9532	0.9537	0.9542	0.9548	0.9553	0.9558	1 2 3 3
73	0.9563	0.9568	0.9573	0.9578	0.9583	0.9588	0.9593	0.9598	0.9603	0.9608	1 2 2 3
74	0.9613	0.9617	0.9622	0.9627	0.9632	0.9636	0.9641	0.9646	0.9650	0.9655	1 2 2 3
75	0.9659	0.9664	0.9668	0.9673	0.9677	0.9681	0.9686	0.9690	0.9694	0.9699	1 1 2 3
76	0.9703	0.9707	0.9711	0.9715	0.9720	0.9724	0.9728	0.9732	0.9736	0.9740	1 1 2 3
77	0.9744	0.9748	0.9751	0.9755	0.9759	0.9763	0.9767	0.9770	0.9774	0.9778	1 1 2 3
78	0.9781	0.9785	0.9789	0.9792	0.9796	0.9799	0.9803	0.9806	0.9810	0.9813	1 1 2 2
79	0.9816	0.9820	0.9823	0.9826	0.9829	0.9833	0.9836	0.9839	0.9842	0.9845	1 1 2 2
80	0.9848	0.9851	0.9854	0.9857	0.9860	0.9863	0.9866	0.9869	0.9871	0.9874	0 1 1 2
81	0.9877	0.9880	0.9882	0.9885	0.9888	0.9890	0.9893	0.9895	0.9898	0.9900	0 1 1 2
82	0.9903	0.9905	0.9907	0.9910	0.9912	0.9914	0.9917	0.9919	0.9921	0.9923	0 1 1 2
83	0.9925	0.9928	0.9930	0.9932	0.9934	0.9936	0.9938	0.9940	0.9942	0.9943	0 1 1 1
84	0.9945	0.9947	0.9949	0.9951	0.9952	0.9954	0.9956	0.9957	0.9959	0.9960	0 1 1 1
85	0.9962	0.9963	0.9965	0.9966	0.9968	0.9969	0.9971	0.9972	0.9973	0.9974	0 0 1 1
86	0.9976	0.9977	0.9978	0.9979	0.9980	0.9981	0.9982	0.9983	0.9984	0.9985	0 0 1 1
87	0.9986	0.9987	0.9988	0.9989	0.9990	0.9990	0.9991	0.9992	0.9993	0.9993	0 0 0 1
88	0.9994	0.9995	0.9995	0.9996	0.9996	0.9997	0.9997	0.9997	0.9998	0.9998	0 0 0 0
89	0.9998	0.9999	0.9999	0.9999	0.9999	1.0000	1.0000	1.0000	1.0000	1.0000	0 0 0 0
90	1.0000										

NATURAL COSINES

Deg-rees	0' 0°.0	6' 0.1	12' 0.2	18' 0.3	24' 0.4	30' 0.5	36' 0.6	42' 0.7	48' 0.8	54' 0.9	Mean Differences 1 2 3 4
0	1.0000	1.0000	1.0000	1.0000	1.0000	1.0000	0.9999	0.9999	0.9999	0.9999	0 0 0 0
1	0.9998	0.9998	0.9998	0.9997	0.9997	0.9997	0.9996	0.9996	0.9995	0.9995	0 0 0 0
2	0.9994	0.9993	0.9993	0.9992	0.9991	0.9990	0.9990	0.9989	0.9988	0.9987	0 0 0 1
3	0.9986	0.9985	0.9984	0.9983	0.9982	0.9981	0.9980	0.9979	0.9978	0.9977	0 0 1 1
4	0.9976	0.9974	0.9973	0.9972	0.9971	0.9969	0.9968	0.9966	0.9965	0.9963	0 0 1 1
5	0.9962	0.9960	0.9959	0.9957	0.9956	0.9954	0.9952	0.9951	0.9949	0.9947	0 1 1 1
6	0.9945	0.9943	0.9942	0.9940	0.9938	0.9936	0.9934	0.9932	0.9930	0.9928	0 1 1 1
7	0.9925	0.9923	0.9921	0.9919	0.9917	0.9914	0.9912	0.9910	0.9907	0.9905	0 1 1 2
8	0.9903	0.9900	0.9898	0.9895	0.9893	0.9890	0.9888	0.9885	0.9882	0.9880	0 1 1 2
9	0.9877	0.9874	0.9871	0.9869	0.9866	0.9863	0.9860	0.9857	0.9854	0.9851	0 1 1 2
10	0.9848	0.9845	0.9842	0.9839	0.9836	0.9833	0.9829	0.9826	0.9823	0.9820	1 1 2 2
11	0.9816	0.9813	0.9810	0.9806	0.9803	0.9799	0.9796	0.9792	0.9789	0.9785	1 1 2 2
12	0.9781	0.9778	0.9774	0.9770	0.9767	0.9763	0.9759	0.9755	0.9751	0.9748	1 1 2 3
13	0.9744	0.9740	0.9736	0.9732	0.9728	0.9724	0.9720	0.9715	0.9711	0.9707	1 1 2 3
14	0.9703	0.9699	0.9694	0.9690	0.9686	0.9681	0.9677	0.9673	0.9668	0.9664	1 1 2 3
15	0.9659	0.9655	0.9650	0.9646	0.9641	0.9636	0.9632	0.9627	0.9622	0.9617	1 2 2 3
16	0.9613	0.9608	0.9603	0.9598	0.9593	0.9588	0.9583	0.9578	0.9573	0.9568	1 2 2 3
17	0.9563	0.9558	0.9553	0.9548	0.9542	0.9537	0.9532	0.9527	0.9521	0.9516	1 2 3 3
18	0.9511	0.9505	0.9500	0.9494	0.9489	0.9483	0.9478	0.9472	0.9466	0.9461	1 2 3 4
19	0.9455	0.9449	0.9444	0.9438	0.9432	0.9426	0.9421	0.9415	0.9409	0.9403	1 2 3 4
20	0.9397	0.9391	0.9385	0.9379	0.9373	0.9367	0.9361	0.9354	0.9348	0.9342	1 2 3 4
21	0.9336	0.9330	0.9323	0.9317	0.9311	0.9304	0.9298	0.9291	0.9285	0.9278	1 2 3 4
22	0.9272	0.9265	0.9259	0.9252	0.9245	0.9239	0.9232	0.9225	0.9219	0.9212	1 2 3 4
23	0.9205	0.9198	0.9191	0.9184	0.9178	0.9171	0.9164	0.9157	0.9150	0.9143	1 2 3 5
24	0.9135	0.9128	0.9121	0.9114	0.9107	0.9100	0.9092	0.9085	0.9078	0.9070	1 2 4 5
25	0.9063	0.9056	0.9048	0.9041	0.9033	0.9026	0.9018	0.9011	0.9003	0.8996	1 3 4 5
26	0.8988	0.8980	0.8973	0.8965	0.8957	0.8949	0.8942	0.8934	0.8926	0.8918	1 3 4 5
27	0.8910	0.8902	0.8894	0.8886	0.8878	0.8870	0.8862	0.8854	0.8846	0.8838	1 3 4 5
28	0.8829	0.8821	0.8813	0.8805	0.8796	0.8788	0.8780	0.8771	0.8763	0.8755	1 3 4 6
29	0.8746	0.8738	0.8729	0.8721	0.8712	0.8704	0.8695	0.8686	0.8678	0.8669	1 3 4 6
30	0.8660	0.8652	0.8643	0.8634	0.8625	0.8616	0.8607	0.8599	0.8590	0.8581	1 3 4 6
31	0.8572	0.8563	0.8554	0.8545	0.8536	0.8526	0.8517	0.8508	0.8499	0.8490	2 3 5 6
32	0.8480	0.8471	0.8462	0.8453	0.8443	0.8434	0.8425	0.8415	0.8406	0.8396	2 3 5 6
33	0.8387	0.8377	0.8368	0.8358	0.8348	0.8339	0.8329	0.8320	0.8310	0.8300	2 3 5 6
34	0.8290	0.8281	0.8271	0.8261	0.8251	0.8241	0.8231	0.8221	0.8211	0.8202	2 3 5 7
35	0.8192	0.8181	0.8171	0.8161	0.8151	0.8141	0.8131	0.8121	0.8111	0.8100	2 3 5 7
36	0.8090	0.8080	0.8070	0.8059	0.8049	0.8039	0.8028	0.8018	0.8007	0.7997	2 3 5 7
37	0.7986	0.7976	0.7965	0.7955	0.7944	0.7934	0.7923	0.7912	0.7902	0.7891	2 4 5 7
38	0.7880	0.7869	0.7859	0.7848	0.7837	0.7826	0.7815	0.7804	0.7793	0.7782	2 4 5 7
39	0.7771	0.7760	0.7749	0.7738	0.7727	0.7716	0.7705	0.7694	0.7683	0.7672	2 4 6 7
40	0.7660	0.7649	0.7638	0.7627	0.7615	0.7604	0.7593	0.7581	0.7570	0.7559	2 4 6 8
41	0.7547	0.7536	0.7524	0.7513	0.7501	0.7490	0.7478	0.7466	0.7455	0.7443	2 4 6 8
42	0.7431	0.7420	0.7408	0.7396	0.7385	0.7373	0.7361	0.7349	0.7337	0.7325	2 4 6 8
43	0.7314	0.7302	0.7290	0.7278	0.7266	0.7254	0.7242	0.7230	0.7218	0.7206	2 4 6 8
44	0.7193	0.7181	0.7169	0.7157	0.7145	0.7133	0.7120	0.7108	0.7096	0.7083	2 4 6 8

NATURAL COSINES

Deg-rees	0' 0°.0	6' 0.1	12' 0.2	18' 0.3	24' 0.4	30' 0.5	36' 0.6	42' 0.7	48' 0.8	54' 0.9	Mean Differences 1 2 3 4
45	0.7071	0.7059	0.7046	0.7034	0.7022	0.7009	0.6997	0.6984	0.6972	0.6959	2 4 6 8
46	0.6947	0.6934	0.6921	0.6909	0.6896	0.6884	0.6871	0.6858	0.6845	0.6833	2 4 6 8
47	0.6820	0.6807	0.6794	0.6782	0.6769	0.6756	0.6743	0.6730	0.6717	0.6704	2 4 6 9
48	0.6691	0.6678	0.6665	0.6652	0.6639	0.6626	0.6613	0.6600	0.6587	0.6574	2 4 7 9
49	0.6561	0.6547	0.6534	0.6521	0.6508	0.6494	0.6481	0.6468	0.6455	0.6441	2 4 7 9
50	0.6428	0.6414	0.6401	0.6388	0.6374	0.6361	0.6347	0.6334	0.6320	0.6307	2 4 7 9
51	0.6293	0.6280	0.6266	0.6252	0.6239	0.6225	0.6211	0.6198	0.6184	0.6170	2 5 7 9
52	0.6157	0.6143	0.6129	0.6115	0.6101	0.6088	0.6074	0.6060	0.6046	0.6032	2 5 7 9
53	0.6018	0.6004	0.5990	0.5976	0.5962	0.5948	0.5934	0.5920	0.5906	0.5892	2 5 7 9
54	0.5878	0.5864	0.5850	0.5835	0.5821	0.5807	0.5793	0.5779	0.5764	0.5750	2 5 7 9
55	0.5736	0.5721	0.5707	0.5693	0.5678	0.5664	0.5650	0.5635	0.5621	0.5606	2 5 7 10
56	0.5592	0.5577	0.5563	0.5548	0.5534	0.5519	0.5505	0.5490	0.5476	0.5461	2 5 7 10
57	0.5446	0.5432	0.5417	0.5402	0.5388	0.5373	0.5358	0.5344	0.5329	0.5314	2 5 7 10
58	0.5299	0.5284	0.5270	0.5255	0.5240	0.5225	0.5210	0.5195	0.5180	0.5165	2 5 7 10
59	0.5150	0.5135	0.5120	0.5105	0.5090	0.5075	0.5060	0.5045	0.5030	0.5015	3 5 8 10
60	0.5000	0.4985	0.4970	0.4955	0.4939	0.4924	0.4909	0.4894	0.4879	0.4863	3 5 8 10
61	0.4848	0.4833	0.4818	0.4802	0.4787	0.4772	0.4756	0.4741	0.4726	0.4710	3 5 8 10
62	0.4695	0.4679	0.4664	0.4648	0.4633	0.4617	0.4602	0.4586	0.4571	0.4555	3 5 8 10
63	0.4540	0.4524	0.4509	0.4493	0.4478	0.4462	0.4446	0.4431	0.4415	0.4399	3 5 8 10
64	0.4384	0.4368	0.4352	0.4337	0.4321	0.4305	0.4289	0.4274	0.4258	0.4242	3 5 8 11
65	0.4226	0.4210	0.4195	0.4179	0.4163	0.4147	0.4131	0.4115	0.4099	0.4083	3 5 8 11
66	0.4067	0.4051	0.4035	0.4019	0.4003	0.3987	0.3971	0.3955	0.3939	0.3923	3 5 8 11
67	0.3907	0.3891	0.3875	0.3859	0.3843	0.3827	0.3811	0.3795	0.3778	0.3762	3 5 8 11
68	0.3746	0.3730	0.3714	0.3697	0.3681	0.3665	0.3649	0.3633	0.3616	0.3600	3 5 8 11
69	0.3584	0.3567	0.3551	0.3535	0.3518	0.3502	0.3486	0.3469	0.3453	0.3437	3 5 8 11
70	0.3420	0.3404	0.3387	0.3371	0.3355	0.3338	0.3322	0.3305	0.3289	0.3272	3 5 8 11
71	0.3256	0.3239	0.3223	0.3206	0.3190	0.3173	0.3156	0.3140	0.3123	0.3107	3 6 8 11
72	0.3090	0.3074	0.3057	0.3040	0.3024	0.3007	0.2990	0.2974	0.2957	0.2940	3 6 8 11
73	0.2924	0.2907	0.2890	0.2874	0.2857	0.2840	0.2823	0.2807	0.2790	0.2773	3 6 8 11
74	0.2756	0.2740	0.2723	0.2706	0.2689	0.2672	0.2656	0.2639	0.2622	0.2605	3 6 8 11
75	0.2588	0.2571	0.2554	0.2538	0.2521	0.2504	0.2487	0.2470	0.2453	0.2436	3 6 8 11
76	0.2419	0.2402	0.2385	0.2368	0.2351	0.2334	0.2317	0.2300	0.2284	0.2267	3 6 8 11
77	0.2250	0.2233	0.2215	0.2198	0.2181	0.2164	0.2147	0.2130	0.2113	0.2096	3 6 9 11
78	0.2079	0.2062	0.2045	0.2028	0.2011	0.1994	0.1977	0.1959	0.1942	0.1925	3 6 9 11
79	0.1908	0.1891	0.1874	0.1857	0.1840	0.1822	0.1805	0.1788	0.1771	0.1754	3 6 9 11
80	0.1736	0.1719	0.1702	0.1685	0.1668	0.1650	0.1633	0.1616	0.1599	0.1582	3 6 9 12
81	0.1564	0.1547	0.1530	0.1513	0.1495	0.1478	0.1461	0.1444	0.1426	0.1409	3 6 9 12
82	0.1392	0.1374	0.1357	0.1340	0.1323	0.1305	0.1288	0.1271	0.1253	0.1236	3 6 9 12
83	0.1219	0.1201	0.1184	0.1167	0.1149	0.1132	0.1115	0.1097	0.1080	0.1063	3 6 9 12
84	0.1045	0.1028	0.1011	0.0993	0.0976	0.0958	0.0941	0.0924	0.0906	0.0889	3 6 9 12
85	0.0872	0.0854	0.0837	0.0819	0.0802	0.0785	0.0767	0.0750	0.0732	0.0715	3 6 9 12
86	0.0698	0.0680	0.0663	0.0645	0.0628	0.0610	0.0593	0.0576	0.0558	0.0541	3 6 9 12
87	0.0523	0.0506	0.0488	0.0471	0.0454	0.0436	0.0419	0.0401	0.0384	0.0366	3 6 9 12
88	0.0349	0.0332	0.0314	0.0297	0.0279	0.0262	0.0244	0.0227	0.0209	0.0192	3 6 9 12
89	0.0175	0.0157	0.0140	0.0122	0.0105	0.0087	0.0070	0.0052	0.0035	0.0017	3 6 9 12
90	0.0000										

NATURAL TANGENTS

Deg-rees	0' 0°.0	6' 0.1	12' 0.2	18' 0.3	24' 0.4	30' 0.5	36' 0.6	42' 0.7	48' 0.8	54' 0.9	Mean Differences 1 2 3 4
0	0.0000	0.0017	0.0035	0.0052	0.0070	0.0087	0.0105	0.0122	0.0140	0.0157	3 6 9 12
1	0.0175	0.0192	0.0209	0.0227	0.0244	0.0262	0.0279	0.0297	0.0314	0.0332	3 6 9 12
2	0.0349	0.0367	0.0384	0.0402	0.0419	0.0437	0.0454	0.0472	0.0489	0.0507	3 6 9 12
3	0.0524	0.0542	0.0559	0.0577	0.0594	0.0612	0.0629	0.0647	0.0664	0.0682	3 6 9 12
4	0.0699	0.0717	0.0734	0.0752	0.0769	0.0787	0.0805	0.0822	0.0840	0.0857	3 6 9 12
5	0.0875	0.0892	0.0910	0.0928	0.0945	0.0963	0.0981	0.0998	0.1016	0.1033	3 6 9 12
6	0.1051	0.1069	0.1086	0.1104	0.1122	0.1139	0.1157	0.1175	0.1192	0.1210	3 6 9 12
7	0.1228	0.1246	0.1263	0.1281	0.1299	0.1317	0.1334	0.1352	0.1370	0.1388	3 6 9 12
8	0.1405	0.1423	0.1441	0.1459	0.1477	0.1495	0.1512	0.1530	0.1548	0.1566	3 6 9 12
9	0.1584	0.1602	0.1620	0.1638	0.1655	0.1673	0.1691	0.1709	0.1727	0.1745	3 6 9 12
10	0.1763	0.1781	0.1799	0.1817	0.1835	0.1853	0.1871	0.1890	0.1908	0.1926	3 6 9 12
11	0.1944	0.1962	0.1980	0.1998	0.2016	0.2035	0.2053	0.2071	0.2089	0.2107	3 6 9 12
12	0.2126	0.2144	0.2162	0.2180	0.2199	0.2217	0.2235	0.2254	0.2272	0.2290	3 6 9 12
13	0.2309	0.2327	0.2345	0.2364	0.2382	0.2401	0.2419	0.2438	0.2456	0.2475	3 6 9 12
14	0.2493	0.2512	0.2530	0.2549	0.2568	0.2586	0.2605	0.2623	0.2642	0.2661	3 6 9 12
15	0.2679	0.2698	0.2717	0.2736	0.2754	0.2773	0.2792	0.2811	0.2830	0.2849	3 6 9 13
16	0.2867	0.2886	0.2905	0.2924	0.2943	0.2962	0.2981	0.3000	0.3019	0.3038	3 6 9 13
17	0.3057	0.3076	0.3096	0.3115	0.3134	0.3153	0.3172	0.3191	0.3211	0.3230	3 6 10 13
18	0.3249	0.3269	0.3288	0.3307	0.3327	0.3346	0.3365	0.3385	0.3404	0.3424	3 6 10 13
19	0.3443	0.3463	0.3482	0.3502	0.3522	0.3541	0.3561	0.3581	0.3600	0.3620	3 7 10 13
20	0.3640	0.3659	0.3679	0.3699	0.3719	0.3739	0.3759	0.3779	0.3799	0.3819	3 7 10 13
21	0.3839	0.3859	0.3879	0.3899	0.3919	0.3939	0.3959	0.3979	0.4000	0.4020	3 7 10 13
22	0.4040	0.4061	0.4081	0.4101	0.4122	0.4142	0.4163	0.4183	0.4204	0.4224	3 7 10 14
23	0.4245	0.4265	0.4286	0.4307	0.4327	0.4348	0.4369	0.4390	0.4411	0.4431	3 7 10 14
24	0.4452	0.4473	0.4494	0.4515	0.4536	0.4557	0.4578	0.4599	0.4621	0.4642	4 7 11 14
25	0.4663	0.4684	0.4706	0.4727	0.4748	0.4770	0.4791	0.4813	0.4834	0.4856	4 7 11 14
26	0.4877	0.4899	0.4921	0.4942	0.4964	0.4986	0.5008	0.5029	0.5051	0.5073	4 7 11 15
27	0.5095	0.5117	0.5139	0.5161	0.5184	0.5206	0.5228	0.5250	0.5272	0.5295	4 7 11 15
28	0.5317	0.5340	0.5362	0.5384	0.5407	0.5430	0.5452	0.5475	0.5498	0.5520	4 8 11 15
29	0.5543	0.5566	0.5589	0.5612	0.5635	0.5658	0.5681	0.5704	0.5727	0.5750	4 8 12 15
30	0.5774	0.5797	0.5820	0.5844	0.5867	0.5890	0.5914	0.5938	0.5961	0.5985	4 8 12 16
31	0.6009	0.6032	0.6056	0.6080	0.6104	0.6128	0.6152	0.6176	0.6200	0.6224	4 8 12 16
32	0.6249	0.6273	0.6297	0.6322	0.6346	0.6371	0.6395	0.6420	0.6445	0.6469	4 8 12 16
33	0.6494	0.6519	0.6544	0.6569	0.6594	0.6619	0.6644	0.6669	0.6694	0.6720	4 8 13 17
34	0.6745	0.6771	0.6796	0.6822	0.6847	0.6873	0.6899	0.6924	0.6950	0.6976	4 9 13 17
35	0.7002	0.7028	0.7054	0.7080	0.7107	0.7133	0.7159	0.7186	0.7212	0.7239	4 9 13 18
36	0.7265	0.7292	0.7319	0.7346	0.7373	0.7400	0.7427	0.7454	0.7481	0.7508	5 9 14 18
37	0.7536	0.7563	0.7590	0.7618	0.7646	0.7673	0.7701	0.7729	0.7757	0.7785	5 9 14 18
38	0.7813	0.7841	0.7869	0.7898	0.7926	0.7954	0.7983	0.8012	0.8040	0.8069	5 9 14 19
39	0.8098	0.8127	0.8156	0.8185	0.8214	0.8243	0.8273	0.8302	0.8332	0.8361	5 10 15 20
40	0.8391	0.8421	0.8451	0.8481	0.8511	0.8541	0.8571	0.8601	0.8632	0.8662	5 10 15 20
41	0.8693	0.8724	0.8754	0.8785	0.8816	0.8847	0.8878	0.8910	0.8941	0.8972	5 10 16 21
42	0.9004	0.9036	0.9067	0.9099	0.9131	0.9163	0.9195	0.9228	0.9260	0.9293	5 11 16 21
43	0.9325	0.9358	0.9391	0.9424	0.9457	0.9490	0.9523	0.9556	0.9590	0.9623	6 11 17 22
44	0.9657	0.9691	0.9725	0.9759	0.9793	0.9827	0.9861	0.9896	0.9930	0.9965	6 11 17 23

NATURAL TANGENTS

Deg-rees	0' 0°.0	6' 0.1	12' 0.2	18' 0.3	24' 0.4	30' 0.5	36' 0.6	42' 0.7	48' 0.8	54' 0.9	Mean Differences 1 2 3 4
45	1.0000	1.0035	1.0070	1.0105	1.0141	1.0176	1.0212	1.0247	1.0283	1.0319	6 12 18 24
46	1.0355	1.0392	1.0428	1.0464	1.0501	1.0538	1.0575	1.0612	1.0649	1.0686	6 12 18 25
47	1.0724	1.0761	1.0799	1.0837	1.0875	1.0913	1.0951	1.0990	1.1028	1.1067	6 13 19 25
48	1.1106	1.1145	1.1184	1.1224	1.1263	1.1303	1.1343	1.1383	1.1423	1.1463	7 13 20 27
49	1.1504	1.1544	1.1585	1.1626	1.1667	1.1708	1.1750	1.1792	1.1833	1.1875	7 14 21 28
50	1.1918	1.1960	1.2002	1.2045	1.2088	1.2131	1.2174	1.2218	1.2261	1.2305	7 14 22 29
51	1.2349	1.2393	1.2437	1.2482	1.2527	1.2572	1.2617	1.2662	1.2708	1.2753	8 15 23 30
52	1.2799	1.2846	1.2892	1.2938	1.2985	1.3032	1.3079	1.3127	1.3175	1.3222	8 16 24 31
53	1.3270	1.3319	1.3367	1.3416	1.3465	1.3514	1.3564	1.3613	1.3663	1.3713	8 16 25 33
54	1.3764	1.3814	1.3865	1.3916	1.3968	1.4019	1.4071	1.4124	1.4176	1.4229	9 17 26 34
55	1.4281	1.4335	1.4388	1.4442	1.4496	1.4550	1.4605	1.4659	1.4715	1.4770	9 18 27 36
56	1.4826	1.4882	1.4938	1.4994	1.5051	1.5108	1.5166	1.5224	1.5282	1.5340	10 19 29 38
57	1.5399	1.5458	1.5517	1.5577	1.5637	1.5697	1.5757	1.5818	1.5880	1.5941	10 20 30 40
58	1.6003	1.6066	1.6128	1.6191	1.6255	1.6319	1.6383	1.6447	1.6512	1.6577	11 21 32 43
59	1.6643	1.6709	1.6775	1.6842	1.6909	1.6977	1.7045	1.7113	1.7182	1.7251	11 23 34 45
60	1.7321	1.7391	1.7461	1.7532	1.7603	1.7675	1.7747	1.7820	1.7893	1.7966	12 24 36 48
61	1.8040	1.8115	1.8190	1.8265	1.8341	1.8418	1.8495	1.8572	1.8650	1.8728	13 26 38 51
62	1.8807	1.8887	1.8967	1.9047	1.9128	1.9210	1.9292	1.9375	1.9458	1.9542	14 27 41 55
63	1.9626	1.9711	1.9797	1.9883	1.9970	2.0057	2.0145	2.0233	2.0323	2.0413	15 29 44 58
64	2.0503	2.0594	2.0686	2.0778	2.0872	2.0965	2.1060	2.1155	2.1251	2.1348	16 31 47 63
65	2.1445	2.1543	2.1642	2.1742	2.1842	2.1943	2.2045	2.2148	2.2251	2.2355	17 34 51 68
66	2.2460	2.2566	2.2673	2.2781	2.2889	2.2998	2.3109	2.3220	2.3332	2.3445	18 37 55 73
67	2.3559	2.3673	2.3789	2.3906	2.4023	2.4142	2.4262	2.4383	2.4504	2.4627	20 40 60 79
68	2.4751	2.4876	2.5002	2.5129	2.5257	2.5386	2.5517	2.5649	2.5782	2.5916	22 43 65 87
69	2.6051	2.6187	2.6325	2.6464	2.6605	2.6746	2.6889	2.7034	2.7179	2.7326	24 47 71 95
70	2.7475	2.7625	2.7776	2.7929	2.8083	2.8239	2.8397	2.8556	2.8716	2.8878	26 52 78 104
71	2.9042	2.9208	2.9375	2.9544	2.9714	2.9887	3.0061	3.0237	3.0415	3.0595	29 58 87 116
72	3.0777	3.0961	3.1146	3.1334	3.1524	3.1716	3.1910	3.2106	3.2305	3.2506	32 64 96 129
73	3.2709	3.2914	3.3122	3.3332	3.3544	3.3759	3.3977	3.4197	3.4420	3.4646	36 72 108 144
74	3.4874	3.5105	3.5339	3.5576	3.5816	3.6059	3.6305	3.6554	3.6806	3.7062	41 81 122 163
75	3.7321	3.7583	3.7848	3.8118	3.8391	3.8667	3.8947	3.9232	3.9520	3.9812	46 93 139 186
76	4.0108	4.0408	4.0713	4.1022	4.1335	4.1653	4.1976	4.2303	4.2635	4.2972	53 107 160 213
77	4.3315	4.3662	4.4015	4.4373	4.4737	4.5107	4.5483	4.5864	4.6252	4.6646	
78	4.7046	4.7453	4.7867	4.8288	4.8716	4.9152	4.9594	5.0045	5.0504	5.0970	Mean
79	5.1446	5.1929	5.2422	5.2924	5.3435	5.3955	5.4486	5.5026	5.5578	5.6140	
80	5.6713	5.7297	5.7894	5.8502	5.9124	5.9758	6.0405	6.1066	6.1742	6.2432	differences
81	6.3138	6.3859	6.4596	6.5350	6.6122	6.6912	6.7720	6.8548	6.9395	7.0264	
82	7.1154	7.2066	7.3002	7.3962	7.4947	7.5958	7.6996	7.8062	7.9158	8.0285	
83	8.1443	8.2636	8.3863	8.5126	8.6427	8.7769	8.9152	9.0579	9.2052	9.3572	cease to be
84	9.5144	9.6768	9.8448	10.0187	10.1988	10.3854	10.5789	10.7797	10.9882	11.2048	
85	11.4301	11.6645	11.9087	12.1632	12.4288	12.7062	12.9962	13.2996	13.6174	13.9507	sufficiently
86	14.3007	14.6685	15.0557	15.4638	15.8945	16.3499	16.8319	17.3432	17.8863	18.4645	
87	19.0811	19.7403	20.4465	21.2049	22.0217	22.9038	23.8593	24.8978	26.0307	27.2715	
88	28.6363	30.1446	31.8205	33.6935	35.8006	38.1885	40.9174	44.0661	47.7395	52.0807	accurate
89	57.2900	63.6567	71.6151	81.8470	95.4895	114.5887	143.237	190.984	286.478	572.957	
90	0.0000										

Multilingual Dictionary of Architecture and Building Terms

Edited by Chris Grech, Whitby & Bird Partners, UK

'...four easy-reference dictionaries for the price of one.' **Building -**

*concentrates on terms used regularly by the whole construction team
*compact layout makes it easy to use
*this project has been developed with the support of Bovis Construction

With an increasingly mobile workforce internationally, the need for good communication becomes greater. This new dictionary lists over 2000 key terms used in building design and construction in English, French, German, Spanish and Italian. The emphasis is on terms used most regularly in the design office and day-to-day running of a building job on site.

April 1998 246x189: 482 pages
Hb: 0-419-19920-9: £55.00

To Order: **Tel:** +44 (0) 8700 768853, or +44 (0) 1264 343071
Fax: +44 (0) 1264 343005, or **Post:** E & FN Spon Customer Services, ITPS Andover, Hants, SP10 5BE, UK

All orders must be pre-paid and will be sent free in the UK. Europe please add: £2.95 for the first book, thereafter £1.25 per book. ROW please add: Airmail £6.50 for the first book, thereafter £2.50 per book. Please add £12.50 delivery charge for items over £100.00.

Index

References in brackets after page numbers refer to SMM7 and the Common Arrangement of Work sections.

A PRELIMINARIES/GENERAL/CONDITIONS, 97, 396
Access
    and inspection chambers, 380 (R12), 654 (R12)
    covers and frames, 382 (R12), 655 (R12)
    flooring, 256 (K41), 766
"Accoflex" vinyl tile flooring, 301 (M50), 574 (M50)
Acrylic polymer flooring 760
Addresses for further information, 925
Afrormosia,
    268 (L20), 543 (L20)
Agba, basic price, 196 (G20)
Air conditioning systems, 784
Air bricks, 180 (F30), 473 (F30)
Albi products, 310 (M60), 584 (M60)
Alterations, 397 (C20)
Alternative material prices
    blocks, 169 (F10)
    facing bricks, 158 (F10)
    insulation, 326 (P10)
    sheet linings and casings, 240 (K10)
    slate or tile roofing, 219 (H60)
    tile slab and block finishings, 296 (M40)
    timber, 196 (G20)
Altro
    "Altroflow 3000" epoxy grout, 288 (M12)
    "Mondopave" tile flooring, 302 (M50), 576 (M50)
    safety flooring, 301 (M50), 574 (M50), 764
Aluminium
    covering, 229 (H72), 506 (H72)
    eaves trim, 234 (J21), 238 (J41), 511 (J21), 515 (J41)
    flashings, 229 (H72), 506 (H72)
    grates and covers, 376 (R12), 650 (R12)
    gutters, 356 (R10), 633 (R10)
    "Kal-Zip" cladding, 213 (H31)
    paint, 312, (M60), 588, (M60)
    patio doors, 271 (L20), 546 (L20)
    pipes, rainwater, 355 (R10), 632 (R10)
    polyester powder coated flashings, 230 (H72), 506 (H72)
    roof decking, 239 (J43), 714
    windows, 744
American White Ash
    260 (L10), 269, 274 (L20), 333 (P20), 535 (L10), 545, 549 (L20), 609 (P20)
    basic price, 196 (G20)
Anchor slots, 149 (E42), 447 (E42)
Anchors, 182 (F30), 218 (H51), 475 (F30)
Andersons roofing, 236 (J41), 513 (J41)

Angles, 185 (G10)
    galvanised steel, 335 (P20), 611 (P20)
    mild steel, 185 (G10), 335 (P20), 611 (P20)
    stainless steel, 335 (P20), 611 (P20)
"Anticon", sarking membrane, 225 (H60), 501 (H60)
Antivlam board, 247 (K11), 523 (K11)
APPROXIMATE ESTIMATES, 691
"Aquaseal" timber treatments, 196 (G20)
ARC "Conbloc", 171 (F10), 465 (F10)
Arch frames, steel, 295 (M30), 569 (M30)
Arches, brick, 155 (F10), 160 (F10), 163 (F10), 166 (F10), 451 (F10), 454 (F10), 458 (F10)
    461 (F10)
ARCHITECTS' FEES, 4
Architraves
    hardwood, 331 (P20), 333 (P20), 607 (P20), 609 (P20)
    softwood, 329 (P20), 605 (P20)
"Arlon" tile flooring, 301 (M50), 575 (M50)
"Armstrong" vinyl sheet flooring, 301 (M50), 574 (M50)
"Artex", 305 (M60), 580 (M60), 768
Asbestos-free
    accessories, "Eternit", 225 (H61), 502 (H61)
    cladding, "Eternit", 211 (H30), 494 (H30)
    corrugated sheets, "Eternit", 211 (H30), 494 (H30)
    slates, "Eternit", 225 (H61), 502 (H61)
Asphalt
    acid-resisting, 287 (M11), 562 (M11)
    damp-proofing, 233 (J20), 510 (J20)
    flooring, 287 (M11), 562 (M11)
    roofing, 234 (J21), 511 (J21), 726
    tanking, 233 (J20), 510 (J20)
"Astra-Glaze" blocks, 173 (F10), 467 (F10)
Atrium, 704
Attendance upon electrician, 340 (P31), 616 (P31)

Balloon gratings, 355 (R10), 632 (R10)
Balustrades
    metal, 280 (L30), 555 (L30), 732
    stainless steel, 280 (L30)
    timber, 276 (L30), 551 (L30)
Bar reinforcement, 121 (D40), 124 (D50), 141 (E30), 429 (D50), 439 (E30)
Basements
    approximate estimates, 700

Index to Advertisers

Keep your figures up to date, free of charge

Now available on the web at www.efnspon.com

This section, and most of the other information in this Price Book, is brought up to date every three months with the Price Book Updates, until the next annual edition.

The Updates are available free to all Price Book purchasers.

To ensure you receive your free copies, either complete the reply card from the centre of the book and return it to us or register via the website www.efnspon.com

The updates will also be available to download from the website.